THE OXFORD HANDBOOK

GLOBAL MODERNISMS

THE OXFORD HANDBOOK OF

GLOBAL MODERNISMS

Edited by

MARK WOLLAEGER

WITH

MATT EATOUGH

OXFORD
UNIVERSITY PRESS

OXFORD
UNIVERSITY PRESS

Oxford University Press is a department of the University of Oxford.
It furthers the University's objective of excellence in research, scholarship,
and education by publishing worldwide.

Oxford   New York
Auckland   Cape Town   Dar es Salaam   Hong Kong   Karachi
Kuala Lumpur   Madrid   Melbourne   Mexico City   Nairobi
New Delhi   Shanghai   Taipei   Toronto

With offices in
Argentina   Austria   Brazil   Chile   Czech Republic   France   Greece
Guatemala   Hungary   Italy   Japan   Poland   Portugal   Singapore
South Korea   Switzerland   Thailand   Turkey   Ukraine   Vietnam

Oxford is a registered trade mark of Oxford University Press
in the UK and certain other countries.

Published in the United States of America by
Oxford University Press
198 Madison Avenue, New York, NY 10016

Library of Congress Cataloging-in-Publication Data
The Oxford handbook of global modernisms / edited by Mark Wollaeger; with Matt Eatough.
p.   cm.
Includes index.
ISBN 978-0-19-533890-4 (hardcover); 978-0-19-932470-5 (paperback)
1. Modernism (Literature) I.
Wollaeger, Mark A., 1957– II. Eatough, Matt.
PN56.M54O94 2012
809'.9112—dc23   2012008781

Printed in the United States of America
on acid-free paper

Contents

....

Acknowledgments   ix

Introduction   3
Mark Wollaeger

PART I: OPENING PLACES, OPENING METHODS

1. The Balkans Uncovered: Toward *Historie Croisée* of Modernism   25
   Sanja Bahun

2. Caribbean Modernism: Plantation to Planetary   48
   Mary Lou Emery

PART II: TEMPORALITY

3. Berber Poetry and the Issue of Derivation: Alternate Symbolist
   Trajectories   81
   Edwige Tamalet Talbayev

4. The Temporalities of Modernity in Spanish American *Modernismo*:
   Darío's Bourgeois King   109
   Gerard Aching

5. Nation Time: Richard Wright, *Black Power*, and Photographic
   Modernism   129
   Sara Blair

6. Chinese Modernism, Mimetic Desire, and European Time   149
   Eric Hayot

PART III: WHOSE MODERNISM?

7. The Will to Allegory and the Origin of Chinese Modernism:
   Rereading Lu Xun's *Ah Q—The Real Story*   173
   Xudong Zhang

8. Neither Mirror nor Mimic: Transnational Reading and Indian
   Narratives in English   205
   Jessica Berman

9. Modernism and African Literature   228
   Neil Lazarus

PART IV: FORMS AND MODES

10. "Petro-Magic Realism": Ben Okri's Inflationary Modernism   249
    Sarah L. Lincoln

11. Little Magazine, World Form   267
    Eric Bulson

12. Poetry, Modernity, and Globalization   288
    Jahan Ramazani

PART V: COMPARATIVE AVANT-GARDES

13. Futurist Geographies: Uneven Modernities and the Struggle for
    Aesthetic Autonomy: Paris, Italy, Russia, 1909–1914   313
    Harsha Ram

14. Modernity's Labors in Latin America: The Cultural Work of Cuba's
    Avant-Gardes   341
    Vicky Unruh

15. Queer Internationalism and Modern Vietnamese Aesthetics   367
    Ben Tran

PART VI: FORMS OF SOCIALITY

16. Cosmopolitanism and Modernism   387
    Janet Lyon

17. Jean Rhys: Left Bank Modernist as Postcolonial Intellectual   413
    Peter Kalliney

18. The Urban Literary Café and the Geography of Hebrew
    and Yiddish Modernism in Europe   433
    Shachar Pinsker

PART VII: LOCATING THE TRANSNATIONAL

19. The Circulation of Interwar Anglophone and Hispanic
    Modernisms   461
    Gayle Rogers

20. Scandinavian Modernism: Stories of the Transnational
    and the Discontinuous   478
    Anna Westerståhl Stenport

21. World Modernisms, World Literature, and Comparativity   499
    Susan Stanford Friedman

PART VIII: TRANSLATION ZONES: CULTURE, LANGUAGE, MEDIA

22. Modernism Disfigured: Turkish Literature and the "Other West"   529
    Nergis Ertürk

23. Modernism's Translations   551
    Rebecca Beasley

24. Japanese Modernism and "Cine-Text": Fragments and Flows at
    Empire's Edge in Kitagawa Fuyuhiko and Yokomitsu Riichi   571
    William O. Gardner

PART IX: FILM AS VERNACULAR MODERNISM

25. Tracking Cinema on a Global Scale   601
    Miriam Bratu Hansen

26. Visions of Modernity in Colonial India: Cinema,
    Women, and the City   627
    Manishita Dass

27. Vernacular Modernism and South African Cinema: Capitalism,
    Crime, and Styles of Desire   646
    Rosalind C. Morris

                        PART X: AFTERWORD

28. Modernist Studies and Inter-Imperiality in the Longue Durée   669
    Laura Doyle

    Notes on Contributors   697

    Index   703

Acknowledgments

....

Collaboration among many people, across many continents and disciplines, made this volume possible. First and deepest thanks go to my editors at Oxford University Press: to Shannon McLachlan, who responded with enthusiasm to my query, "why not a handbook on *global* modernism?" She has offered exemplary support in this and other projects over the years, and I have tremendous respect for her insight and professionalism. And many thanks as well to Brendan O'Neill, a first responder of the first order. My assistant editor, Matt Eatough, was invaluable to the long process of shaping this volume: his keen eye for argument was appreciated by many contributors. I am also grateful to the many friends and colleagues who steered me toward possible contributors as I began to piece this project together. Kevin Dettmar, Jed Esty, Gayle Rogers, and Paul Saint-Amour were good enough to read and comment on my introduction and to listen to my ideas, complaints, and questions over drinks on many happy occasions. Much of the intellectual energy found in this volume was generated out of the Tenth Annual Conference of the Modernist Studies Association, or MSAX, which drew a large crowd of scholars to Nashville to exchange papers under the rubric of Modernism and Global Media. That conference would not have come together without the labors of my co-organizer, Paul Young, and our conference assistants, Derrick Spires and Amanda Hagood. At the last stages of production, Elizabeth Barnett, more than up to proof, stepped in to provide expert help with the final grooming of the copyedited manuscript; may her infant daughter dream of Turkish modernism and other permutations of modernism across the globe. An extract from Richard Aldington's letter to T. S. Eliot (held at Houghton Library, Harvard University) is reproduced here by kind permission of Richard Aldington's Estate c/o Rosica Colin Limited, London. An earlier version of Jahan Ramazani's "Poetry, Modernity, Globalization" was published in his *A Transnational Poetics* (Chicago: University of Chicago Press, 2009) and is reprinted with kind permission of the University of Chicago Press.

THE OXFORD HANDBOOK OF

GLOBAL MODERNISMS

INTRODUCTION

MARK WOLLAEGER

THE recent global turn in modernist studies has generated a good deal of discussion, much of it in the form of exciting new comparative work, but much as well in the form of cautionary theorizing and anxious questioning. The challenge of defining modernism has been difficult enough when confined to Anglo-American and European traditions, but what counts as modernism when one starts looking for examples from across the globe? What kind of agendas might be encoded in the comparisons required by a global perspective? How does the effort to think modernism globally affect received time lines for the beginning and end of modernism? Is "global" even the right word, or is "transnational," "planetary," or some other term more appropriate? This handbook addresses such questions, sometimes directly in the form of theoretical reflection, but more often in chapters grounded in a particular place, problem, or disciplinary perspective.

The volume has been compiled in the belief that this is a good time to bring together not only scholars dedicated to working beyond the national paradigm but also experts working from within diverse national and linguistic traditions. What does the concept of modernism mean to scholars working in Latin American studies, Caribbean studies, Asian studies, and Spanish American studies, and for those working on the Balkans, African literatures, on Turkish, Scandinavian, Russian, and Indian literatures? Is it productive to discuss under the rubric of modernism literary movements that assigned themselves (or later were assigned) different names, be they *modernismo, futurisme, modanizumu, moderna, vanguardismo, chủ nghĩa hiện đại*, or *avant-garde*? And how does our understanding of the concept change if we think about film, the most significant and well-traveled art form developed in the twentieth century?[1]

Our collective goal here has been to open a comparative space within Anglophone scholarship for discussion of a wide range of foreign language productions.

Thus while the majority of contributors work in departments of English, contributions come as well from departments or programs in comparative literature, romance studies, Japanese, cinema and media studies, Asian studies, anthropology, Hebrew literature and culture, French, Scandinavian studies, Latin American literary and cultural studies, world cinema, Slavic and comparative literatures, and Chinese. Contributors were asked to introduce literary territory likely to be unfamiliar to the majority of readers while also exploring new critical and theoretical concerns in their fields. Each writer negotiates these potentially competing aims in different ways, but all have been responsive to the suggestion that they seize on opportunities to provide comparative perspectives, whether by identifying charged nodal points in which diverse traditions converge or by throwing out lines of connection to well-known figures on the received maps of modernism that this volume aims to revise.

The Oxford Handbook of Global Modernisms does not aim for "complete coverage" of the globe by scribbling over imagined white spaces on the map. The task would be enormously difficult (how could I have forgotten Liechtenstein!) though not necessarily, in theory, impossible. More important, although the notion of the wrongly uncharted contributes to the shape of the collection—hence the inclusion of essays on the Balkans, Vietnam, and South African film, and the absence of contributions devoted exclusively to France, Germany, the United Kingdom, or the United States—a global conception of modernism requires more than the geographical addition of previously ignored or marginalized traditions. On one hand, the historical reality of nations and their institutions still requires analytic attention: the concept of the transnational presupposes the crossing of national borders, and premature nation-blindness fails to acknowledge that too many national traditions have hitherto been left out of the discussion. On the other hand, the transnational turn taking place across the humanities has directed attention to cultural phenomena that otherwise get short shrift within the stubbornly national organization of the modern university,[2] for instance what might be called resident-alien modernisms: Yiddish, Hebrew, or Gadže.[3] Accordingly, although individual essays within the volume's ten clusters may concentrate on a single locale, they do so with an eye on that location's relation to an encompassing "large-scale vision" or "world literary space."[4]

The first cluster, "Opening Places, Opening Methods," underscores how attention to particular places motivates new forms of large-scale vision. In the first essay, Sanja Bahun argues that Balkan literature challenges "the assumption that the definition of modernism requires a developmentalist model of historical progression, from tradition (the period of "other" aesthetic movements) to modernity . . . (the realm of modernism)"; rather, the compound and multidirectional nature of historical processes, as exemplified in the Balkans, calls out for a "flexible conceptual template . . . that is *constantly redefined by the very object of its inquiry*," a method that might be found, she suggests, in *histoire croisée*, or crossed history.[5] Mary Lou Emery also moves from historical particularity to theoretical and methodological generality, in this instance by arguing that Caribbean modernism offers an emerging vision of "the planetary"—a model of relatedness she adapts from Édouard Glissant and Gayatri Spivak. Taking Claude McKay's *Banjo* and Jean Rhys' *Voyage in the Dark* as her chief examples, but touching as well on Kamau Brathwaite and Wilson Harris, Emery shows how the plantation's place in global capitalism reveals links between Caribbean modernism and "modernity's foundational exchange of commodified human be- ings." For Emery, the word global aligns too closely with globalization; the planetary, in contrast, names "a necessarily elusive concept [that] opens imaginative spaces and temporalities from which literature may emerge apart, yet also from, the violent mar- ket forces of globalization." Both essays in this opening section, like many that follow, shuttle dialectically between local complexity and large-scale visions.

In part a legacy of postcolonial studies, this dialectic is fundamental: if transna- tional analysis is to produce what this volume is calling a global perspective, that perspective must be mobile and continuously provisional. (For me, "planetary" conjures the distraction of the interplanetary, whereas "global" suggests horizons that shift with the curve of the earth and the position of the observer.[6]) For a global perspective to be something more than "the view from nowhere" that has been at- tributed to an older understanding of cosmopolitanism, it must be willing to engage in a double movement of acknowledgment and decentering: an acknowledgment of one's own position and an effort to think beyond it. Hannah Arendt, articulating the ethical and political dimensions of a similar dynamic, has described it as an "enlarged way of thinking" that "needs the presence of others 'in whose place' it must think."[7] Enlarged thinking insists on an inescapable web of relations, one in which the communal nature of the self finds analogues on the global scale in the circulation of texts and the interpenetration of communities.[8]

Janet Lyon's contribution to the "Forms of Sociality" section explores enlarged thinking by providing a genealogy of cosmopolitanism. Lyon argues that modernist modes of cosmopolitanism serve "to invoke intercultural forms of exchange that *could* be or *might* be or *shouldn't* be, over and against (or in keeping with) the text's account of 'what is.'" Cosmopolitanism thus conjures unrealized possibilities for community that are dialectically engaged by the residual realism of modernism, or "the conditional sense of worldly engagement" that permeates modernist imaginings of sociality. In the same cluster, Peter Kalliney explores intersections between mod- ernism and postcolonial discourse through the figure of Jean Rhys, who began as a Left Bank experimentalist and, after long neglect, was reincarnated as a postcolonial intellectual. The hinge between Rhys' two identities, Kalliney suggests, has to do with related forms of dissidence, or what Gilles Deleuze and Felix Guattari would consider forms of minorness: "If artists of the Left Bank could offer a hint of life on the other side of respectability, colonial and postcolonial writers were expected to give a glimpse of life on the other side of the imperial divide."[9] Shachar Pinsker's focus on the Euro- pean café as a decentered set of migratory, ephemeral sites for Hebrew and Yiddish modernism rounds out the section's exploration of the ways in which new forms of sociality—usually modes of belonging at a distance—emerge in response to decolo- nization, globalization, diaspora, and the cultural diminution of the nation-state.

Other clusters also organize essays into broad rubrics that highlight analytic affinities and transnational comparisons. Part V, "Comparative Avant-Gardes," con- tains essays on modern Vietnamese aesthetics (Ben Tran), experimental literature in Cuba (Vicky Unruh), and comparative analysis of futurism in Paris, Italy, and Russia (Harsha Ram); the "Temporality" cluster, taking up debates about developmental versus differential models of temporality, features essays on the transformation of French symbolist aesthetics in Berber poetry (Edwige Tamalet Talbayev), Rubén Darío and Spanish American *modernismo* (Gerard Aching), Richard Wright's photographs of the Gold Coast (Sara Blair), and the role of mimetic desire in the formulation of Chinese modernism (Eric Hayot). The contingency of these clusters reflects the exploratory nature of the collective project. A reshuffling and recrossing of contributions could produce a coherent yet diverse group of essays on race (e.g., Rosalind Morris, Peter Kalliney, Janet Lyon); another might yield a cluster on spatial models (Susan Stanford Friedman, Shachar Pinsker, Mary Lou Emery); while yet others present new accounts of the relation between postcoloniality and modernism (Kalliney, Blair, Talbayev, Neil Lazarus). The many dialogues among essays suggest the desirability of a hypertext organization: multiple links from essay to essay would underscore implicit and explicit points of contact among them, and the reader interested in following, say, a French thread, might weave her way from Talbayev's discussion of the transformation of Mallarmé's symbolist aesthetic in North Africa to Ben Tran's examination of André Gide in Vietnam to Anna Stenport's commentary on Gide and Proust in Scandinavian literature and on to the dozen or so essays to touch on Baudelaire. Tracing French symbolism would yield a related but not identical network of connections. As we await the brave new world of simultaneous hypertext publication, the index will have to suffice.

The volume's emphasis on decentered comparison also means that the focus does not fall on familiar figures who, for a long time, dominated modernist studies. But neither are such figures absent from the scene. T. S. Eliot, for instance, figures in his role as an influential editor in Rebecca Beasley's discussion of the translation of Russian literature into English (in the "Translation Zones" cluster) and in Gayle Rogers' essay on the circulation of interwar Anglophone and Hispanic modernisms (in "Locating the Transnational"). Ezra Pound too crops up in many places, as do monumental figures in the Anglo-European canon such as Kafka, Conrad, Brecht, Mann, Joyce, Khlebnikov, Faulkner, and Woolf. But rather than devote an entire chapter to any of them, each "monument" is typically seen on the horizon, from a perspective that knows them, acknowledging their influence without remaining in their shadow. And just as Eliot and company become provisionally peripheral, so lesser known figures (in the North American curriculum) become provisionally central: the Algerian Berber poet Jean El Mouhoub Amrouche in Edwige Talbeyev's essay, and the Turkish writer Yahya Kemal Beyatlı in Nergis Ertürk's essay.

The sense of reorientation, or possibly disorientation, produced by what Dipesh Chakrabarty has called the provincializing of Europe, should not be construed as a simple rejection of center-periphery perspectives. Rather than dissolve through the agency of relativization or disappear through the stigmatizing of models of cultural diffusion, concepts of center and periphery still operate in many of the essays, though not in the rigidly binary way that characterized some older ways of thinking about world literature.[10] World-systems theory provides a materialist account for why the terms "core," "periphery," and "semi-periphery" should still matter: they map the unequal distribution of economic power across the globe; Harsha Ram puts them to good use in his comparative analysis of futurism: "If modernism's initial orientation was generally centripetal, a gravitation toward metropolitan modernity as embodied by the core nations and cities of Europe, then international futurism pursued a secondary movement that might be seen as a *return to the periphery.*" Center-periphery models, moreover, are not just materialist methods: continuing interest in center and periphery as tropes has as much to do with cultural processes and strategic defamiliarization. Careful analysis of cross-cultural influences requires attention to the historical experience of "being at the core or on the periphery" that shapes the reception of concepts and texts as they travel, and compensatory attention to authors, texts, and concepts that have previously eluded received categories of understanding (most of which derive from a Eurocentric core) aims to open up the potential for new hierarchies of value by promoting a fresh vision of the cultural field.[11]

The implied hypertextual chatter among essays here derives in part from design; in part it is inevitable. On one hand, I encouraged collaboration among contributors by posting all drafts to a password-protected website and organizing the writers into reading groups designed to draw out implicit dialogues among essays. In an ideal world, all essays would have undergone radical revision in response to my homework assignment; I am pleased that a good number of contributors incorporated cross-references to one another, and many substantially altered key points in revision. I also enlisted Laura Doyle to write an Afterword, and in "Modernist Studies and Inter-Imperiality in the Longue Durée," she teases out additional common threads among the contributions while in effect suggesting another grouping, a quite large one, "Inter-Imperiality," in which she highlights "the legacies of centuries of inter-imperial cultural accretion" that inflect modernism. On the other hand, the interchange among essays was inevitable insofar as the contributors do seem to be addressing a common critical field, that thing we have been calling, for some time now, "modernism."

That this would be so was not a foregone conclusion. A good deal of the vitality of modernist studies over the last decade or so has derived from various efforts to destabilize what is meant by "modernism," and the emergence of what is now commonly called the new modernist studies bears on the kind of definitional complications exacerbated by the global turn in criticism. These complications include the issues of temporal delimitation (*when* was modernism?), the geographies of modernism (*where* was modernism?), modernism's conceptual contours (*what* was modernism?), and its motivations (the historical, cultural, and individual *whys* of modernism).

FROM OLD MODERNISM TO NEW

The impetus for the new modernist studies drew on diverse sources but was largely motivated by critics' desire to revitalize a field that had fallen into disfavor.[12] In the American academy, modernism as a field of study and historical period (roughly 1890–1945) was firmly entrenched by 1960, when Harry Levin, in a nostalgic and celebratory account of Stephen Dedalus as prototype of the modernist artist, published "What Was Modernism?" The formal complexity and pervasive irony of modernist texts was also well suited to the New Criticism, which had proved useful as a classroom technique during the postwar boom in university enrollment. Yet the fortunes of modernism differed from place to place and depended as well on its institutional context. By 1960, the great majority of British writers had turned against what was perceived as the politically irresponsible aesthetic experimentalism and cultural elitism of 1920s, but this was less true for writers and artists in the United States and in many postcolonial nations, where modernist forms were often turned to political ends.[13] Although British and American academic criticism lagged behind poets and novelists, the critical tide eventually turned against modernism (though undergraduate courses in the field continued).

The initial critical construction of Anglo-American modernism as a realm of giants—the men of 1914—rendered the relatively new field ripe for criticism of its apparently masculinist, elitist, and authoritarian bearings. Taking up such a critique, postmodern literary criticism contributed to a devaluation of modernism in the literary marketplace while also laying the ground for its renewal. Emphasizing process and play, postmodernism in literary studies carried forward the anti-monumentalism of postmodern architecture, but it also morphed into a form of multicultural critique that found a perfect target in the early canon of modernism, taking the notoriously illiberal politics of Ezra Pound, Wyndham Lewis, W. B. Yeats, and T. S. Eliot as representative of the whole. Postmodernism shook up that canon, opening it to new voices, and subsequent studies of modernism have become much more attentive to a wider range of authors and texts. At the same time, postmodern critics' tendency to equate formal experimentation with a retreat from history also fostered distrust of formalism and the correlative doctrine of aesthetic autonomy (a suspicion later reinforced by Pierre Bourdieu's influential sociological account of the "taste" for modernism as a form of class distinction).[14] By the 1980s, the study of modernism had become relatively suspect, especially on political grounds.

Of course some *writers*, as opposed to the field, were less suspect than others. Joyce tended to get a pass for several reasons. Deconstruction found his textual play congenial, as did the linguistic turn in psychoanalysis; this was unsurprising, insofar as both Jacques Derrida and Jacques Lacan were profoundly influenced by Joyce. Joyce also benefited posthumously from his abject status as a lower-middle-class Irishman: it could only redound to his credit that Pound and Eliot were horrified by his shabby shoes. Moreover, Joyce's resistance to colonial oppression while writing exclusively about Ireland from a position of exile made him, as Colin MacCabe (1988) was the first to declare, "the very prototype of the postcolonial artist" (12). Beginning in the 1970s, Virginia Woolf also thrived. Prior to the rise of feminism, female writers did not receive a great deal of attention in a male-dominated academy, and Woolf was explicitly excluded from the early modernist canon by at least one influential champion of modernism, Hugh Kenner.[15] Because of the efforts of leading feminist critics such as Carolyn Heilbrun, however, Woolf reentered discussions of modernism and ultimately earned the status she currently enjoys as a major figure.[16]

The new modernist studies emerged in part as an effort to restore the value of modernism by rejecting the opprobrium cast on it by the rise of literary critical postmodernism, and there is a great deal of evidence to suggest that the effort was successful, from the establishing in 1994 of a journal devoted to the field, *Modernism/modernity*, to the founding in 1999 of an organization, the Modernist Studies Association, whose membership has steadily grown. The feminist revision of the canon has continued, with writers such as Mina Loy, Rebecca West, and Willa Cather coming back into play (though not yet, it seems, Dorothy Richardson), as have other phases of expansion: ethnic studies focused attention on writers such as Henry Roth and Richard Wright, race (completely ignored in the earliest discussions of modernism) has become a significant concern, and transnational studies have rediscovered early twentieth-century border-crossers (or, as the Anglo-Saxon called them, *mearcstapas*), such as Rabindranath Tagore and Mulk Raj Anand.[17] Most recently, attention has turned to the place of new media such as film and radio in the emergence of modernism, in part because of the general cultural turn that has taken place across the humanities and social sciences,[18] but also because the highly mediated nature of symbolic systems and social existence in the early twenty-first century, brought into sharp focus by the rise of media studies and information theory, has prompted interest in genealogies of art as mediation.[19]

Part IX, "Film as Vernacular Modernism" takes up one aspect of the new interest in media by testing and extending Miriam Hansen's concept of Hollywood cinema as vernacular modernism. Hansen's contribution aims to lay the ground for a transnational history of film by looking at examples of Chinese and Japanese films of the 1930s; Manishita Dass shows how ambivalence about India's new urban spaces—"at once the site of India's colonial subjection and the embodiment of modernity's emancipatory promise"—was projected onto the figure of the woman in Hindi films of the 1920s and 1930s; and Rosalind Morris explores South African appropriations of film noir, or "the vernacularization of noir stylishness in South Africa," through the figure of the *tsotsi*, "not merely a gangster. . . . an icon of masculinity . . . of youthful insouciance . . . of autonomy that is yet in need of recognition." The notion that Hollywood cinema should count as a form of modernism—a claim that has not gone unchallenged—provides an index of how much the field has changed in recent decades.

Yet periods of rapid change inevitably generate new questions without necessarily settling old ones. Douglas Mao and Rebecca Walkowitz have summed up the transformation of modernist studies under the rubric of an "expansion" taking place along three axes—temporal, spatial, and vertical (737)—and the term "expansion," regardless of vector, conjures questions about modernism's global turn that have been debated under the rubric of imperialism. As Laura Doyle and Laura Winkiel observe in their introduction to *Geomodernisms*, a pioneering collection of global approaches to modernism, "the globalization of criticism, like that of trade, inevitably sends forth the specter of appropriation"; and yet, they continue, "if we step back from cross-cultural conversations about 'modernism' under the assumption that 'the Western,' English language economy defines and holds the conversation *utterly* in its grip, we collude in another way in an ideology of dominance" (6). Sharing the belief that "there is no pure path to be taken," the present collection aims to unfold the value of these conversations, essay by essay. Or to put the case in more positive terms, the contributions here, which extend and reflect on the three-way expansion mapped by Mao and Walkowitz, demonstrate the value of impurity.[20]

Cultural Expansion: Modern or Modernist?

Although the first two modes of expansions are most obviously implicated in the global turn—the "when" and "where" of modernism cannot be separated from the "what"—so too is verticality, the notion that modernism should not be restricted to high culture. As a result of vertical expansion, in Mao and Walkowitz's summary, "once quite sharp boundaries between high art and popular forms of culture have been reconsidered . . . canons have been reconfigured . . . works by members of marginalized and social groups have been encountered with fresh eyes and ears . . . scholarly inquiry has increasingly extended to matters of production, dissemination, and reception" ("The New Modernist Studies" 737-38). Vertical expansion—another expression of the cultural turn—characterizes many of the essays in this volume, from the film cluster to Eric Bulson's essay on little magazines as a "world form." Bulson's essay raises, if only in passing, the main challenge to definitions of modernism posed by the cultural turn when he refers to a little magazine published in Ghana as "modern but not necessarily modernist." The relationship between "modern" and "modernist" is clearly fundamental to the field, but as modernist studies takes on the methodological force of decentering modernism, of refusing, that is, to circle around the same limited set of canonical texts, criticism has not really confronted the full implications of asserting a distinction between the two.

In his 1987 lecture "When Was Modernism?" Raymond Williams embraced the distinction between modern and modernist for purposes that were at once analytic and political. Criticizing the narrowness and elitism of the modernist canon as it was constructed in the 1950s and 1960s, Williams does not object to modernist artifacts per se, as Georg Lukács did from a Marxist perspective in "The Ideology of Modernism" (1957). Rather, he criticizes the process of canon formation that made certain works—the "high" modernist ones—stand in for the era's whole.[21] Thus he argues not so much against modernism as for a recovery of "the modern" from the ideologically constrained category of "the modernist." On one hand, then, the new modernism's characteristic move, exemplified in the subtitle of Michael North's *Reading 1922*—"a return to the scene of the modern"—can be seen as fulfilling

Williams' desire for a more culturally inclusive mode of analysis. On the other hand, if the notion that modernism defined itself against the perceived threat of contamination by mass culture needed revision (primarily to acknowledge complex forms of interchange between high and low),[22] the inevitable swing of the pendulum away from excessively selective definitions of modernism presents its own analytic challenges.

In particular, the cultural turn, while enormously fruitful, has also had the effect—or, depending on the critic, the unintended consequence—of erasing the distinction between modern and modernist. The majority of contributors to this volume share the belief that in a time of rapid change along the lines mapped by Mao and Walkowitz, it makes sense to hold on to the distinction, not in order to preserve, as was once the case, an honorific status for modernism, but rather to continue the process of defining a field of inquiry that is sufficiently shared to make rigorous analytic discussions possible. In literary historical terms, the concept of modernism clearly has traveled the globe, transmitted through widely disseminated texts and transformed through multiform acts of translation and cultural consumption.[23] Yet the sea changes effected through the agency of reception as a mode of production—repurposings, creolizations, indigenizations and the like—do not obscure what Wittgenstein called the family resemblances that make multiple modernisms recognizable as members of a class.

For some critics, the cultural turn, along with the rapid multiplication of geographical and temporal coordinates, nevertheless seems to be making "modernist" dispensable. But if modernism is simply, as some have argued, the expressive dimension of modernity,[24] and if modernity itself is defined very broadly, the utility of the term "modernist," as opposed to "modern," begins to fade. At the 2010 meeting of the Modern Language Association, this issue came to the fore during a session (sponsored by the Modernist Studies Association) designed to explore what it means to "do" modernism when the field is changing so rapidly. During the question-and-answer session, the panelists were asked whether modernist studies could do without some long-standing points of reference, such as modernism as a crisis of representation, as anti-realist or experimental, and whether there is any value in identifying particular aesthetic forms or techniques as intrinsically modernist, such as collage, montage, interior monologue, or the day-in-the-life novel. The questions were meant as a provocation to what seemed an unstated ideal of unboxedness, a conception of modernism liberated from definitional corners and dead-ends. There was insufficient time, of course, to thoroughly debate such questions, but despite some cautious intimations from the audience that, in the words of E. M. Forster, "We must exclude someone from our gathering, or we shall be left with nothing" (37), some panelists engaged in a bravado refusal of limits, one professed no longer to care about distinctions between modern and modernist, and the session concluded inconclusively.

If continued attention to the distinction promotes analytic rigor, the question of how best to rethink, explore, and challenge the boundaries between modern and modernist remains. Reluctance to attach any formal criteria to a definition of modernism no doubt derives in part from a residual notion that questions of form may threaten to reinstate a limited canon of difficult works, but attention to form clearly does not *entail* limitation of any kind, even if, in times past, attention to form tended to correlate with a high valuation of particular *kinds* of form. The "Forms and Modes" cluster speaks to such issues. It begins with Sarah Lincoln's discussion of magic realism as a modernist mode that emerges in South America and Nigeria from similar material conditions, in particular the kind of hyperinflation associated with oil-based economies. Bulson's analysis of little magazines as a form that mediates between global and local also appears in this section, along with Jahan Ramazani's exploration of creolizations of modernism in Caribbean poetry. Ramazani discusses, among other things, "the modernist concept of poetry as a personal verbal rite" and bricolage as a modernist form. Essays in other clusters also address matters of form without making purely formalist claims. Vicky Unruh retains an emphasis on experimentalism in Cuban literature, Harsha Ram shows how what has often been understood as key formal feature of literary modernism—literariness—emerges from a specific set of historical pressures, and Anna Stenport's hugely informative essay on Scandinavian modernism observes that Eyvind Johnson, "credited with introducing the stream of consciousness technique to Swedish literature," drew on the formal innovations of Gide, Proust, Joyce, and Faulkner.

What is needed, then, is not a static definition that attempts to specify the *sine qua non* of modernism, but something more like, as I suggested earlier, Wittgenstein's family resemblance, a polythetic form of classification in which the aim is to specify a set of criteria, subsets of which are enough to constitute a sense of decentered resemblance. While some criteria undoubtedly will be formal—fragmentation as a marker of modernism is not likely to go away anytime soon—others will be more conceptual or historical, such as Perry Anderson's compelling claim that modernism is catalyzed by "the imagined proximity of revolution." Equally important will be the need to remain sufficiently attentive to the definition of interdependent terms to ensure that what Hayot calls the "intercontamination of terms"—which is, after all, fundamental to the differential logic of definition—ends up working toward the production of new knowledge. Nor should key terms, such as experimentalism, be allowed to remain excessively narrow.[25] As Hayot's salutary injunction to rethink modernism from "*from the ground up*" suggests, we need to proceed as if we do not already know what modernism is in order to develop a truer account—even as (always the kicker) logic requires some idea of what we are looking for before we can start. Relying solely on received criteria will not work, but that doesn't mean that all the older criteria were wrongheaded. If, for instance, formal criteria are entirely ruled out, the definitional challenge is simply displaced, without being simplified, onto the problem of modernity: are there alternative modernities, or only, as Fredric Jameson has argued, a singular modernity?

The Oxford Handbook of Global Modernisms does not aim for finality in such matters. Rather, it throws into relief what is at stake in various unresolved questions. Taking up the question of alternative modernities, for instance, Neil Lazarus, writing on African literature, offers a persuasive clarification of Jameson's argument in *A Singular Modernity* in order to counter the arguments for the pluralization of modernity that have been championed most influentially by Dilip Parameshwar Gaonkar:

> Jameson understands modernity as representing something like the time-space sensorium corresponding to capitalist *modernization*. In this sense, it is, like the capitalist world system itself, a singular phenomenon. But far from implying that modernity therefore assumes the same form everywhere, as Jameson has sometimes mistakenly been taken to suggest, this formulation in fact implies that it is everywhere irreducibly specific. Modernity might be understood as the way in which capitalist social relations are "lived"—different in every given instance for the simple reason that no two social instances are the same. Jameson emphasizes both the *singularity* of modernity as a social form and its "*simultaneity*."

Attempts to pluralize modernity, in this argument, fail to take into account the concept of uneven development: "singularity here does not obviate internal heterogeneity and . . . simultaneity does not preclude unevenness or marked difference." Or, in Jameson's words, "modernism must . . . be seen as uniquely corresponding to an uneven moment of social development, or to what Ernst Bloch called the 'simultaneity of the nonsimultaneous' . . . the coexistence of realities from radically different moments of history—handicrafts alongside the great cartels, peasant fields with the Krupp factories or the Ford plant in the distance" (*Postmodernism* 307). The desire to postulate alternative modernities presupposes an "original" modernity formed in Europe that must be subjected to Eurocentric critique, but as Harry Harootunian has observed, the notion of a European origin inevitably entails the notion that modernity elsewhere is both "belated" and "derivative," "a series of 'copies' and lesser inflections."[26] Rather than accept the logic of original and copy, Jameson's account of a singular modernity, as elaborated by Lazarus and Harootunian, aims to acknowledge difference and heterogeneity without instituting the hierarchical relations that follow from the positing of an origin.[27] As Lazarus, citing Harootunian, writes: "the specific modes of appearance of modernity in different times and places—St. Petersburg in the 1870s, say, Dublin in 1904, Cairo in the 1950s, a village on a bend in the Nile in the Sudan in the 1960s—ought to be thought about not as 'alternative' but as 'coeval . . . modernities or, better yet, peripheral modernities . . . in which all societies shared a common reference provided by global capital and its requirements.'"

Following a similar line of thought, Sarah Lincoln argues that what constitutes modernity for Jameson is "above all the impulse to make sense of—to document and to order or aestheticize—the disruptions, dislocations, and disjunctures brought about by modernization itself. Neither material transformation nor innovative aesthetics, 'modernity' signifies instead the attempt to reconcile the two, to bring together 'modernization' and 'modernism' under a common conceptual and affective umbrella." Some may object to any model that implies a form of economic determinism. But if such elaborations of Jamesonian thinking insist on global capitalism as a common frame of reference, they also leave room for the reciprocal influence of culture and economics. Again, Lincoln and Lazarus don't end debates about modernity—or about matters of form. Indeed, they clearly diverge on the second issue. Lincoln cites "the disruptions, dislocations, and disjunctures brought about by modernization itself"; older, formalist accounts of modernism often used similar terms to describe its aesthetic qualities. Does shifting the concept of disruption from the domain of the aesthetic to the material constitute a correction, an overcorrection, or a displacement? For Lazarus, modernism clearly does not entail a particular set of formal qualities; rather, any cultural production that attempts to grapple with the realities of modernization might qualify as modernist.

Here I would want to intervene in order to delimit the potentially huge historical expanse of modernization by citing Laura Doyle, who, acknowledging that the "inter-imperial positionality" she understands as fundamental to modernism has "very likely shaped texts for millennia," nevertheless argues that in the late nineteenth and early twentieth centuries, modernists operate "more self-consciously from this position" owing to, among other things, "new global forms of rapid communication, finance, and travel," and "the high numbers of uprooted persons created by the escalating invasions, wars, anti-colonial resistance, and pogroms."[28] Like Doyle, most of the contributors to this volume presuppose something like what Mao and Walkowitz refer to as a "core period of about 1890 to 1945" (738), even as they are willing to identify other instances of modernism coming either earlier or (more often) later. Thus the *annus mirabilis* of French modernism, 1857, gets renewed attention from contributions that return to reworkings of *Les fleurs du mal* and *Madame Bovary*; a famous year in Anglo-American modernism, 1922, gets new entries (Lu Xun's *Ah Q–The Real Story* was serialized in Beijing and the Turkish Republic was founded); Jahan Ramazani writes about Christopher Okigbo's "Heavensgate" (1962); and Sarah Lincoln analyzes Ben Okri's *Stars of the New Curfew* (1988). It is the persistence of conceptual affinities and various formal preoccupations that makes the identification of instances of modernism outside the temporal core both possible and increasingly uncontroversial.

Yet the comparisons that both enable and derive from the recognition of similarity (and, one is obliged to say, from difference) present a range of theoretical challenges. It seems clear, for that reason, that national literature departments interested in global approaches need to emulate programs in comparative literature, which have long devoted attention to the challenges of comparison.

COMPARISON AND APPROPRIATION

In her contribution on comparativity, Susan Stanford Friedman argues that studies of modernism on "a planetary scale" require "a more sophisticated discourse of comparison" in order to avoid homogenizing the local in the name of a universal modernism. True to this aim, the global analyses conducted here aim to develop more accurate accounts of cultural productions in particular locations by understanding them as part of more inclusive systems of exchange, circulation, and multidirectional flows. Global comparisons of this sort can turn certain assumptions upside down. Peter Kalliney, commenting on Jean Rhys, notes that "the association between elite literature and dissidence was a staple of modernist ethnographies," but that linkage, so familiar to modernist studies, is utterly severed in Turkey, where, as Bahun observes, cultural and political conservatives found great utility in modernism's "invocation of suppressed cultural and linguistic models." Ertürk follows up: "to attend to the connection between literary modernism and conservatism in Turkey is . . . to turn from the assimilative search for reflective mimicry of European modernism to the complex and contradictory dialogues that constitute such formations to begin with." Nevertheless, efforts to reduce the distortion produced by exclusively Eurocentric categories of analysis do not easily exorcize, to return to Doyle and Winkiel's phrase, the specter of appropriation.

In a special issue of *New Literary History* on comparison, R. Radhakrishnan articulates the fundamental concern: "comparisons are never neutral: they are inevitably tendentious, didactic, competitive, and prescriptive. Behind the seeming generosity of comparison, there always lurks the aggression of a thesis." And yet, he continues, "if comparative studies are to result in the production of new and destabilizing knowledges, then apples and oranges do need to be compared, audaciously and precariously" (454). Radhakrishnan resists facile suspicion of comparison by emphasizing the "double consciousness" necessary to effective comparison: "on the one hand, act as though the comparison is being made in an ideal world and at the same time deconstruct such an idealist ethic in the name of lived reality and its constitutive imbalances" (459). This handbook accepts comparison as both necessary and valuable, but it also tries to respond to anxious fears about comparison's covertly Eurocentric project by promoting this sort of double consciousness; it aims as well to counter concerns about the potential homogenizing effects of critical discourse by sharpening the terms of comparison.

One cluster—"Whose Modernism?"—gathers essays that directly confront the collection's paradoxical goal of being comparative and precomparative at once. Xudong Zhang's "The Will to Allegory and the Origin of Chinese Modernism" undertakes a rereading of *Ah Q—The Real Story*, a novella extremely well known in China and "firmly established [for the Chinese reader] on the very top of the totem pole of national allegory" as a specifically Chinese form of modernism, even though it would be difficult to extract from it "evidence of textbook features of modernism, including the usual suspects of metaphoric depth, formal disruption and distortion, aesthetic intensity." What makes *Ah Q* modernist for Zhang is the way its concern with the Confucian doctrine of the rectification of names—the notion (to simplify) that proper naming is fundamental to social harmony—ends up replicating a form of modernism as linguistic rebellion by turning European modernism inside out: "The most ruthless modernist aesthetics can be found not in the usual domain of stylistic choices or technical innovations, but rather in an extra-aesthetic decision, namely the rejection of the temptation to associate or identify, safely and comfortably, with an extraneous but prevailing system of names and words, form and narrative—namely, the discursive and institutional framework of modernism as a purely literary and aesthetic norm." Lu Xun's modernism, far from being absorbed into a European model by aping it, is specifically Chinese in the way that it refuses modernism through a modernist form of refusal. Zhang himself mirrors what he sees in Lu Xun in his rigorous use of European theory, from Walter Benjamin to Fredric Jameson, to isolate what is least European in *Ah Q*. Zhang's essay can also be seen as an implicit response to Eric Hayot's injunction that "to think seriously about Chinese modernism means negotiating the very conceptual framework through which the history of literature emerges, as though from the history of a void, into the possibilities of thought." Zhang's essay is one kind of dialectical attempt to do so.

Also in the "Whose Modernism?" section, Jessica Berman's essay on the fiction of Mulk Raj Anand takes up the challenge of negotiating the undeniable fact of European influence on Indian fiction and the need to understand these novels on their own terms. Complicating the supposed binary between modernist and indigenous, Berman points out, as did Salman Rushdie before her, that "modernism seems already to inhabit the early twentieth-century Indian novel in English as it comes of age, rather than belatedly appearing . . . in the post-independence period." Instead of seeing Indian modernism as a "secondary formation" in relation to the imperial metropolis, Berman grasps them as interrelated, coeval productions: "Indian narratives in English of the late-colonial period reveal strikingly innovative approaches to the twin problems of subjectivity and political engagement that at the same time also interact with the European literary tradition and challenge our preconceived notions about what modernism can be and do." Berman's essay shows not only how Anand appropriated particular modernist techniques toward specifically Indian ends but also how that process of cultural appropriation reveals European modernism to have been more politically engaged than some versions of postmodern critique would have us believe.

"Whose Modernism?" concludes with Neil Lazarus's essay on African literature, but the fundamental concerns of this cluster circulate throughout the volume. Gerard Aching explores the poet's death in Rubén Darío's most famous short story, "El rey burgués" (The Bourgeois King), in order to take on "the most frequently mentioned critique of the *modernistas* in Spanish American literary history," namely, debates about "excessive" imitation of European models. Nergis Ertürk explains how "the problem presented by the idea of 'Turkish modernism' is not merely that of the recovery of an excluded object": "it involves the very possibility of addressing the absence of an 'authentic' Turkish modernism within national-critical discourse itself"; and in "Japanese Modernism and the 'Cine-Text,'" William Gardner's analysis of Kitagawa Fuyuhiko shows why one of his most famous poems, "Rush Hour"—"At the ticket gate a finger was clipped off with the ticket"—cannot be reduced to an imitation of Pound's "In a Station of the Metro." Indeed, Gardner doesn't even make the comparison—an index, perhaps, of how far criticism of Japanese modernism has come since (only a decade ago) Western critics could casually deem it "a failure" in comparison with European originals[29]—but I suspect those who teach imagism may well do so in the future.

Finally, readers will find that while critical distance from the text varies a good deal in this collection, many contributions engage in close reading. This is by design. Franco Moretti has called for distant reading, a self-consciously polemical inversion of close reading, as the key to studying world literature because "it allows you to focus on units that are much smaller or much larger than the text: devices, themes, tropes—or genres and systems" ("Conjectures on World Literature" 57). Gleefully welcoming the disappearance of the text, Moretti makes a good case for distant reading as the only way to carry out his particular project, a mapping of world literature that uses world-systems theory to uncover laws of evolution governing the development of genres and modes across the globe. This mapping relies on new critical synthesis of existing scholarship in English on a wide range of foreign language productions. But critical pushback has thrown into relief the magnitude of the losses entailed by this approach. One is loss of attention to the historical roles played by specific languages within globalization, in particular what Jonathan Arac has called "the unavowed imperialism of English" within Moretti's "monolingual master scheme" (44). Distant reading ignores the kind of long-term consequences of linguistic change that Ben Tran discusses in Vietnam—in this instance specifically *written* language—where the French government's promotion of romanized Vietnamese script displaced the character-based writing systems of classical Chinese and the ideographs of demotic Vietnamese script, or, to turn to a more well-known example, Ngũgĩ wa Thiong'o's return to Gĩkũyũ from English, which he considered a means of decolonizing the mind (see Lazarus). Granted, this handbook is written in English and discusses many works in translation, but contributors often pay attention to linguistic complications that resist easy translation, and in doing so press distant reading back to a middle distance that permits a truer account of the object. I think here of one of the writers whose relative absence from this collection pains me the most—Joseph Conrad, whose Marlow thinks he sees "ornamental balls" on stakes along the border of Kurtz's compound until his binoculars reveal the ornaments to be human heads. Modernist perspectivism has its limits.

A second loss entailed by resolutely distant reading has to do with the value of aesthetic particularity. Although Moretti associates close reading with the American academy and a highly limited canon of close readable texts, Haun Saussy, in a two-pronged argument against purely thematic readings ("the constant pedagogical temptation in world literature") and for close attention to form, has observed that "formalist reading is a great dissolver of canons": "If all works of literature share a set of characteristics which it is the business of literary theory to explore, then any work, read with enough attention, is as good as any other." (14, 17). Not everyone will accept Saussy's claim that literariness is the proper focus of comparative literary theory, but the *disciplinary* force of his argument—that is, his willingness to say what he thinks that specifically literary analysis ought to be doing—speaks to another of Arac's worries about Moretti's sociological approach: "what can the future hold for a mode of critical performance that is losing its home base? Must it learn the arts of diaspora?" (45).

The Oxford Handbook of Global Modernisms aims to stimulate new ways of thinking about such questions, typically by grounding them in specific comparative relationships, and often by posing new questions in response. Consensus has neither been sought nor found, but in closing I think the contributors would agree on at least two things. First, in the words of José Martí, "to know diverse literatures is the best way to liberate oneself from the tyranny of any of them."[30] Second, if modernist studies is to remain coherent as it expands through comparison, continuing efforts of recursive definition must accompany its expansion. Bringing together a wide range of perspectives, this collection aims to deepen our understanding of modernism by self-consciously unraveling the edges of the field.

NOTES

1. Literature provides the main focus of this handbook, but four of the twenty-seven essays focus on film and one analyzes photography.

2. Key early contributions to the transnational turn include pioneering work on the economics of globalization by David Harvey, as well as more culturally oriented work, such as Appadurai, *Modernity at Large* (1996); Moretti, *Modern Epic* (1996) and *Atlas of the European Novel* (1998); and Robbins, *Feeling Global* (1999). Recent overviews include Jay, *Global Matters* (2010) and the excellent collection edited by Connell and Marsh, *Literature and Globalization* (2011).

3. This list is not meant to be exhaustive. Conceivably, formations such as Chicano/a or *Gastarbeiter* (guest worker) modernisms might fall into this category. For Yiddish and Hebrew modernisms, see, in addition to Shachar Pinsker's essay in this volume, Schachter, *Diasporic Modernisms*. For the relevance of the construction of the Gypsy to modernism, see Lyon, "Gadže Modernism."

4. The phrase "large-scale vision" is associated with the world-systems theory of Immanuel Wallerstein; see Palumbo-Liu, Robbins, Tanoukhi, eds., *Immanuel Wallerstein* (9–10). "World literary space" comes from Casanova (1–6). Although this volume does not collectively endorse any particular system—for constructive critiques of Casanova's important though controversial book, see Ram, Bulson, and Friedman—many essays implicitly share the sense in the editors' introduction to *Immanuel Wallerstein* (10–12) that the best approaches to global analysis aspire to a systematic conceptualization that preserves the value of contingency.

5. To date there is no widely accepted English translation. For the concept of *histoire croisée*, see Werner and Zimmerman, who note that, like other relational approaches, the method is attentive to a "multiplicity of possible viewpoints and the divergences resulting from languages, terminologies, categorizations and conceptualizations, traditions and disciplinary usages" but places particular emphasis on "what, in a self-reflexive process, can be generative of meaning" (31–32). They also invoke related approaches in the social sciences that have been called "shared history," "connected history," and "entangled history," though mainly in order to define what distinguishes their own approach.

6. For a good account of the importance of "placedness" to the kind of comparative analysis practiced in this volume, see Doyle and Winkiel's introduction to *Geomodernisms*, 1–4.

7. Arendt, "The Crisis in Culture," quoted by Benhabib, *Situating the Self*, 9. See also Benhabib, *The Reluctant Modernism of Hannah Arendt*, 185–93.

8. I am indebted to Berman, *Cosmopolitan Communities*, 13–15, for alerting me to Arendt's relevance here. See also Cuddy-Keane on the reversal of perspectives within global modernism, especially 547–48.

9. For the concept of minor literature and its relation to modernism, see Deleuze and Guattari, *Kafka*.

10. For reflections on the concept of world literature that inform my thinking here, see Damrosch (1–36).

11. I draw here on Marjanen's thoughts on *histoire croisée*; the quoted phrase is from page 244.

12. See Mao and Walkowitz, *Bad Modernisms*, 1–8.

13. On the British postwar rejection of modernism, see Sinfield (182–202). On postcolonial reworkings of modernism, see Gikandi, who argues that "it was primarily . . . in the language and structure of modernism that a postcolonial perspective came to be articulated and imagined in literary form" (420), and Ramazani's more politically pointed claim: "To insist, in the name of anti-Eurocentricity, that Euromodernism be seen as an imperial antagonist is to condescend to imaginative writers who have wielded modernism in cultural decolonization and, ironically, to impose as universal a Eurocentric standard: the antimodernism of postwar American and British poetry" (448).

14. See Bourdieu, *Distinction*, especially the first chapter (published in French in 1979 and translated into English in 1984). For modernism and autonomy, see Ram's contribution and Goldstone.

15. In *The Pound Era*, he refers to Woolf only glancingly in order to mock her cultural pretensions and the quality of her mind (443, 553); in *A Sinking Island*, he devotes more attention to showing that she is not a modernist but "a classic English novelist of manners" (175), and not a very good one. Granted, Kenner, for all his excellence as a reader of other modernists, had a blind spot on matters of gender as large as the Atlantic, but his disregard for Woolf typifies the gender bias exemplified in the canon in the early 1970s.

16. But see Silver for the way later culture wars in the humanities shaped the versions of Woolf that were allowed to circulate in the university and in popular letters.

17. The bibliography here is potentially massive, so let me just point to Sollors, *Ethnic Modernism*, and note that 1994 saw the publication of three major publications on race and modernism; North, *The Dialect of Modernism*; Doyle, *Bordering on the Body*; and the first issue of *Modernism/modernity*.

18. Discussions of the cultural turn begin in the early 1990s but typically trace the development to earlier moments. See, for instance, Lentricchia and McLaughlin on the new essays in the second edition of their *Critical Terms for Literary Study*: "they reflect the cultural turn in literary study, long ago predicted in the work of Kenneth Burke, for which literary works are cultural practices that relate in complex ways to other cultural practices" (ix). Jameson's *The Cultural Turn* was published in 1998 but includes essays published as early as 1983.

19. See, for instance, Wollaeger, *Modernism, Media, and Propaganda*, and Goble, *Beautiful Circuits*.

20. For related collections contributing to the global turn, see Brooker and Thacker, *Geographies of Modernism*, and Eysteinsson and Liska, vol. 2, which includes "case studies" on Brazilian, Australian, Catalonian, French, and Spanish-American modernisms, as well as a fourteen-part section entitled "Borders of Modernism in the Nordic World" that ranges over additional locales.

21. Although Williams' critique here dovetails with the postmodern multicultural critique, he is explicitly concerned to reject any understanding of the postmodern as

coming after modernity and therefore existing outside of history, when in fact, for Williams, we still swim in the currents of modernity, however "late" those currents might be in relation to the waves of history still tumbling forward from the Enlightenment.

22. The classic work on modernism as a defensive response to the encroachment of mass culture is Huyssen's *After the Great Divide*. For its mutant middlebrow cousin, more invested in condemnation than analysis, see Carey, *Intellectuals and the Masses*.

23. Like *histoire croisée*, Mieke Bal's theory of traveling concepts emphasizes self-reflexive definitions in the context of intercultural analysis and therefore has promise as a methodological tool for modernist studies. See Bal's "Introduction: Travelling Concepts and Cultural Analysis," in *Travelling Concepts*, ed. Goggin, 7–25.

24. See, for instance, Friedman, "Periodizing Modernism," 432–35.

25. See Berman's contribution, which develops R. K. Narayan's (non-formalist) observation that "we are all experimentalists." See also Miller, *Accented America*, who argues that too narrow a definition of experimentalism has failed to register the kind of experiments with idiom that he sees as fundamental to a broader grasp of American modernism (esp. 24–7).

26. Harootunian, *History's Disquiet*, 62–63, quoted in Lazarus, "Modernism and African Literature," 233. The Lazarus quotation at the end of this paragraph also cites these pages from *History's Disquiet*.

27. Compare the brief critique in the introduction to *Immanuel Wallerstein*, ed. Palumbo-Liu, Robbins, and Tanoukhi: the concept of alternative modernities "properly rejects the stigma of cultural inferiority imposed by developmentalism, but also disguises the severe political, social, and economic hierarchies that continue to structure the world" (9).

28. And Janet Lyon's essay on cosmopolitanism in this volume: "Late nineteenth- and twentieth-century incarnations of cosmopolitanism share with modernism many of the same conditions of possibility, including accelerated globalization and burgeoning world market systems, imperial crises and the falling dominoes of decolonization, and new networks of mass media and mass transportation, all of which, in various combinations, contributed to expanded zones and concentrated experiences of intercultural contact."

29. For a brief history of the critical reception of *modanizumu* in the West, see William Tyler's introduction to *Modanizumu*, esp. 6–14.

30. "Conocer diversas literaturas es el medio mejor de libertarse de la tiranía de algunas de ellas." My translation.

WORKS CITED

Anderson, Perry. "Modernity and Revolution." *New Left Review* I/144 (1984): 96–113.

Arac, Jonathan. "Anglo-Globalism?" *New Left Review* 16 (2002): 35–45.

Benhabib, Seyla. *The Reluctant Modernism of Hannah Arendt*. London: Sage, 1996.

———. *Situating the Self: Gender, Community and Postmodernism in Contemporary Ethics*. New York: Routledge, 1992.

Berman, Jessica. *Modernist Fiction, Cosmopolitanism, and the Politics of Community*. Cambridge: Cambridge University Press, 2001.

Brooker, Peter, and Andrew Thacker, eds. *Geographies of Modernism: Literature, Cultures, Spaces*. New York: Routledge, 2005.

Carey, John. *Intellectuals and the Masses: Pride and Prejudice among the Literary, 1880–1939*. London: Faber and Faber, 1992.

Casanova, Pascale. *The World Republic of Letters.* Trans. M. B. DeBoise. Cambridge: Harvard University Press, 2004.

Connell, Liam, and Nicky Marsh, eds. *Literature and Globalization: A Reader.* New York: Routledge, 2011.

Cuddy-Keane, Melba. "Modernism, Geopolitics, Globalization." *Modernism/modernity* 10.3 (2003): 539–88.

Damrosch, David. *What Is World Literature?* Princeton: Princeton University Press, 2003.

Deleuze, Gilles, and Félix Guattari. *Kafka: Toward a Minor Literature.* Trans. Dana Polan. Minneapolis: University of Minnesota Press, 1984.

Doyle, Laura. *Bordering on the Body: The Racial Matrix of Modern Fiction and Culture.* New York: Oxford University Press, 1994.

Doyle, Laura, and Laura Winkiel, eds. *Geomodernisms: Race, Modernism, Modernity.* Bloomington: Indiana University Press, 2005.

Eysteinsson, Astradur, and Vivian Liska. *Modernism.* 2 vols. Philadelphia: John Benjamins, 2007.

Forster, E. M. *A Passage to India.* 1924. New York: Harcourt Brace, 1953.

Friedman, Susan Stanford. "Periodizing Modernism: Postcolonial Modernities and the Space/Time Borders of Modernist Studies." *Modernism and Transnationalisms.* Spec issue of *Modernism/modernity* 13.3 (2006):425–43.

Gaonkar, Dilip Parameshwar, ed. *Alternative Modernities.* Durham: Duke University Press, 2001.

Gikandi, Simon. "Preface: Modernism in the World." *Modernism and Transnationalisms.* Spec issue of *Modernism/modernity* 13.3 (2006): 419–24.

Goble, Mark. *Beautiful Circuits: Modernism and the Mediated Life.* New York: Columbia University Press, 2010.

Goggin, Joyce, and Sonja Neef. *Travelling Concepts I: Text, Subjectivity, Hybridity.* Amsterdam: ASCA Press, 2001.

Goldstone, Andrew. *Fictions of Autonomy: Modernism from Wilde to de Man.* Forthcoming from Oxford University Press.

Harootunian, Harry. *History's Disquiet: Modernity, Cultural Practice, and the Question of Everyday Life.* New York: Columbia University Press, 2000.

Huyssen, Andreas. *After the Great Divide: Modernism, Mass Culture, Postmodernism.* Bloomington: Indiana University Press, 1986.

Jameson, Fredric. *A Singular Modernity.* London: Verso, 2002.

———. *The Cultural Turn: Selected Writings on the Postmodern.* London: Verso, 1998.

———. *Postmodernism.* Durham: Duke University Press, 1991.

Jay, Paul. *Global Matters: The Transnational Turn in Literary Studies.* Ithaca: Cornell University Press, 2010.

Lentricchia, Frank, and Thomas McLaughlin, eds. *Critical Terms for Literary Study.* 2nd edition. Chicago: University Chicago Press, 1995.

Levin, Harry. "What Was Modernism?" *The Massachusetts Review* 1. 4 (1960): 119–31.

Lukács, Georg. "The Ideology of Modernism." *The Meaning of Contemporary Realism.* Trans. John and Necke Mander. London: Merlin, 1963.

Lyon, Janet. "Gadže Modernism." Doyle and Winkiel 187–205.

MacCabe, Colin. "Broken English." *Futures for English.* Ed. Colin MacCabe. Oxford: Manchester University Press, 1988: 3–14.

Mao, Doug, and Rebecca L. Walkowitz, eds. *Bad Modernisms.* Durham: Duke University Press, 2006.

———. "The New Modernist Studies." *PMLA* 123.3 (2008): 737–48.

Marjanen, Jani. "Undermining Methodological Nationalism: Histoire Croisée of Concepts as Transnational History." *Transnational Political Spaces: Agents—Structures—Encounters.* Ed. Mathias Albert, Gesa Bluhm, Jan Helmig, Andreas Leutzsch, and Jochen Walter. New York: Campus, 2009. 239–63.

Miller, Joshua L. *Accented America: The Cultural Politics of Multilingual Modernism.* Oxford: Oxford University Press, 2011.

Moretti, Franco. *Atlas of the European Novel, 1800–1900.* London: Verso, 1998.

———. "Conjectures on World Literature." *New Left Review* I (2000): 55–67.

———. *Modern Epic: The World-system from Goethe to García Márquez.* Trans. Quintin Hoare. London: Verso, 1996.

North, Michael. *The Dialect of Modernism: Race, Language, and Twentieth-Century Literature.* New York: Oxford University Press, 1994.

———. *Reading 1922: A Return to the Scene of the Modern.* New York: Oxford University Press, 1999.

Palumbo-Liu, David, Bruce Robbins, and Nirvana Tanoukhi, eds. *Immanuel Wallerstein and the Problem of the World: System, Scale, Culture.* Durham: Duke University Press 2011.

Radhakrishnan, R. "Why Compare?" *New Literary History* 40.3 (2009): 453–71.

Ramazani, Jahan. "Modernist Bricolage, Postcolonial Hybridity." *Modernism and Transnationalisms.* Spec issue of *Modernism/modernity* 13.3 (2006): 445–63.

Robbins, Bruce. *Feeling Global: Internationalism in Distress.* New York: New York University Press, 1999.

Saussy, Haun. "Exquisite Cadavers Stitched from Fresh Nightmares." *Comparative Literature in an Age of Globalization.* Ed. Haun Saussy. Baltimore: Johns Hopkins University Press, 2006. 3–42.

Schachter, Allison. *Diasporic Modernisms: Hebrew and Yiddish Literature in the Twentieth Century.* New York: Oxford University Press, 2011.

Silver, Brenda R. *Virginia Woolf: Icon.* Chicago: University of Chicago Press, 1999.

Sinfield, Alan. *Literature, Politics, and Culture in Postwar Britain.* Berkeley: University of California Press, 1989.

Sollors, Werner. *Ethnic Modernism.* Cambridge: Harvard University Press, 2008.

Spivak, Gayatri. *Death of a Discipline.* New York: Columbia University Press, 2003.

Tyler, William, ed. *Modanizumu: Modernist Fiction from Japan, 1913–1938.* Honolulu: University of Hawaii Press, 2008.

Werner, Michael, and Bénédicte Zimmerman. "Beyond Comparison: *Histoire Croisée* and the Challenge of Reflexivity." *History and Theory* 45.1 (February 2006): 30–50.

Williams, Raymond. "When Was Modernism?" *New Left Review* I/175 (1989): 48–52.

Wollaeger, Mark. *Modernism, Media, and Propaganda: British Narrative from 1900 to 1945.* Princeton: Princeton University Press, 2006.

PART I

OPENING PLACES, OPENING METHODS

CHAPTER 1

THE BALKANS UNCOVERED: TOWARD *HISTORIE CROISÉE* OF MODERNISM

SANJA BAHUN

There—on Šar Mountain, on the Urals—stands
THE NAKED MAN BARBARO-GENIUS . . .
Break, bound chains! Fall, suburbs of big and plague-ridden
West European cities! Shatter, window panes of gilded courts,
High towers of National Stockmarkets and Banks! . . .
Close your doors West—North—Central Europe—
The Barbarians are coming!
Close them close them but
we shall still enter.

—Ljubomir Micić, *The Zenitist Manifesto* (1921)

And now what shall become of us without any barbarians?
Those people were some kind of solution.

—Constantine Cavafy, "Waiting for the Barbarians" (1904)

MODERNISTS AND BARBARIANS;
OR, WHAT THE BALKANS?

Voicing an avant-garde response to the closing conundrum of Constantine Cavafy's (1863–1933) poem "Waiting for the Barbarians," Ljubomir Micić (1895–1971) prophesized in 1921 that "the rotten fruits of European pseudo-culture and civilized progress" (idolaters of "European Venus" and "coffeehouse decadents" alike) would be destroyed by an aggressive aesthetic entity, regional in its outlook, cosmopolitan in its effects. Wild-eyed, racist, and sexist (as Balkan people are still sometimes pictured today), the "barabaro-genius," Micić argues, will provide Western culture with all that it yearns for and fears from this imagined other: violence, danger, sex, and (thus) global artistic renewal ("Zenitism").[1] These pronouncements come from a specific locale, contemporaneously described as a real-imagined place where the "national hobby" is "assassinating kings and having revolutions" (Christie 105). Micić proudly takes on the shroud of this Western orientalism and turns it *upside down*, or "*tumbe*" (*tr* and *hbs*; also the title of a Zenitist manifesto): he makes Western European culture the object of inquiry and the patient in need of cure, exulting in the same sense of historical inevitability which the West customarily ascribes to Balkan histories.

To be sure, the figure of *barbaro-genius*, and indeed of the Balkans itself, as playfully celebrated by Micić, serves to remind us that concepts such as Europe or the West are equally contestable tropes conveying historically and contextually variegated meanings (Stråth 14; Mishkova 239). But Micić is also in earnest: for him, the Balkan poet *may* rejuvenate stagnant Western culture. So, what if he is not entirely wrong? A remarkable stream of diverse modernist and avant-garde expressions (of which Micić's manifesto poetry is but a particle) issued from the Balkans in the first decades of the twentieth century. Integrally related to the well-documented sites of modernist activity (Paris, London, New York, Berlin, Moscow) and yet chronically living out the paradoxes of linguistic and cultural isolation, Balkan modernisms boast rich aesthetic production—varied in intentions, diverse in the forms, shapes, and modes of execution, and of unequal degrees of impact on regional and international literature and arts. In this chapter, I aim to introduce this multicolored production and, by indicating some heuristic problems, to offer a perspective on the methodological implications of investigating under-documented modernist sites. One specific property of the modernist locale under discussion, namely, its indeterminate geographical and conceptual mapping, is quintessential for this twin purpose, and thus I would like to open this inquiry by delineating the space-construct of the Balkans.

The Balkans has been, and remains, both an (ambiguous) mental map and an (uncertain) geographical entity. While the many ethnicities of the Balkans have been there for centuries, the name—and, together with it, the concept of the Balkans as a politically volatile cluster of nations—came into being only at the end of the nineteenth century. In the 1880s, the term, initially applied to the mountain range that dominates the peninsula, came to supplant the previously used phrase "Turkey-in-Europe," which, for a long time, had disquietingly signaled the inter-penetration of Europe and Asia. Even though based on a geographical fallacy (the range in question is irregular and it does not cover the assumed territory), the term "Balkans" gained currency. For the liberation struggles in the region had already set up a success-pattern: Greece declared independence from the Ottoman Empire in 1829, followed by Serbia (1867), Montenegro, Bosnia, Wallachia, and Moldova (1875), and the Turkish defeat in the Russo-Turkish war (1877–1878) announced the end of Ottoman rule in the region. The 1878 Congress of Berlin politically autho-rized the new states, and the Albanian rebellion (1911), and the formation of the Balkan League (1912) compounded the Turkish defeat in the First Balkan War (1912–1913), thereby fueling the hope of independence among Slavs in the neigh-boring Habsburg Empire. Unfortunately, these military campaigns handicapped the nascent economies of Balkan states: productivity was low, the markets were unstable, and modernization was, more often than not, symbolic (Berend and Ránki in Sandqvist 49). The relative growth of these economies in 1890–1914 was, however, supported by substantial foreign investment, since European countries were actively involved in the internal affairs of the new Balkan states. Europe defined borders, appointed kings and civil authorities, and offered models of legal and educational systems, which has led Artemis Leontis to argue that modern Balkan nations endured a "colonization of the mind" (68).

Such allegations are grave, but they are frequently accurate. Early twentieth-century cultural exchanges in the region—so important for Balkan modernist trends—were manifestly based on the struggle for political dominance: Germany supported education and arts in the Austro-Hungarian dominions and Bulgaria; Italy invested in Catholic seminaries in Albania; France competed against Russia in Romania and Serbia; and the British, Germans, and French all viewed Greece as a strategic locale for cultural encroachment. But Europe also gave the Balkan peo-ples ideological weapons—in the shape of modern nationalisms (Mazower 16). The synthesis of nationalist themes and modernist techniques in Balkan litera-tures testifies to the accentuated relation between state-nationalism and artistic experimentation in the context of "delayed" modernisms (Armstrong 45). Yet Bal-kan modernist aesthetic production also relies on what Anthony D. Smith has termed *pre-national* "ethno-symbolic heritage"—a cluster of *ethnies*, myths, famil-ial and regional memories, values and symbols which are customarily thought to have been questioned by modernism (79). As these developments indicate, the Balkan peoples and their artists forged their cultural identity in relation to mul-tiple sets of affiliations. Their regional cultural identification was shaped by a mixture of empathy and enmity. Extra-regionally, they defined their cultural iden-tity in relation—and sometimes in opposition—to Western Europe and Russia. This complex positionality made the exploration of identity—personal, national, migratory, split, and interactive—the single most important concern of Balkan modernists.

But what was Europe's reaction to this new-old neighbor? The Balkan states imported legislative, economic, and educational frameworks that Western Europe had adopted a while ago, the model whose supremacy the West hoped to see confirmed in this fringe area. Precisely because it is an emblem of Europe's endeavors to prove its political and cultural mold successful, and because it so obstinately defied that model on a number of momentous historical occasions, the Balkans has been a fulcrum for Europe's anxieties, desires, and self-imaging ever since (Bjelić 3). The region, however, turned into a host for Enlightenment projections exactly at the time when those became suspect in the rest of Europe, and the "failures" to "enlighten" the Balkans poignantly reminded Europe of its own difficulties in maintaining the model. The ambivalence of feelings that attended this discovery was reflected in a rapid change of the European image of the Balkans from 1850 to 1930: from a site of "primordial unity" and evidence for European cultural ascendency (the extended realm of the pagan and ancient Greeks), through a romantic locus of Byzantine-Oriental excess, to a constant source of European and global instability. Yet the region has also presented a conundrum for Western orientalizing vision because of its proximity and the consequent potential for this outsider's "irrational acts" to have real-life repercussions on Western European politics, a potential famously manifested when an impressionable Balkan student triggered World War I. (That Gavrilo Princip, the youngster in question, was a member of the same radical group *Mlada Bosna* [*Young Bosnia*] as Dimitrije Mitrinović, a vocal avant-garde poet and affiliate of Wassily Kandinsky, should perhaps come as no surprise.) Now and then, the Balkans has boisterously asserted its historical presence, and it is this emphatic historicity, together with the markedly heterogenic outlook of the area, that make Edward Said's terms only partly adequate when applied to the region (see Skopetea; Todorova). For all these reasons, the conceptual optics through which the West views the Balkans—and through which the Balkan peoples have sometimes viewed themselves—is remarkably disorganized: the region has been seen as at once homogenous (as an image or a trope) and heterogeneous (as a space of perennial battle of antithetical identities and insurmountable differences); both part of Europe and not part of Europe; a bridge between the East and the West and the impossibility of such a bridge; finally, a paradigmatic borderline-space, and, as such, perhaps only tangentially a real place. Thence comes the region's prodigious potential for semantic investment.

However discursively positioned, though, the Balkans has invariably functioned as both a site and an epitome of crises, political and cultural, real and imagined. And it is not accidental that this cumulative representation of the Balkans as a failed utopia and a crisis-bound cluster was consolidated in the epoch of modernism. Before moving forward, I should like to propose that the simultaneity of two distinct series of phenomena—the rise of the Balkans (as a site of primordial and modern crisis in the geopolitical sphere and collective imaginary) and the rise of modernism (understood as a response to a climate of crisis as well as an epiphanic search for "unmediated unity" or "merging with the other" [Taylor 471])—be treated as more than a coincidence. These differently scaled phenomena, whose crossed history delineates the compound field of my enquiry, are not only concurrent but also inextricably connected.

Not surprisingly, then, the Balkans swiftly resumed centrality in the representational interests of Anglophone, German, French and Russian modernists. But there were problems in embracing this "next door neighbor" as a *contributor* to the modernist project in its own right, and the Western modernists' interest in the artistic production of the region was, at its best, relative to personal circumstances. Virginia Woolf, an ardent reader of the ancient Greeks and twice an inquisitive visitor to Greece (1906 and 1932), felt that modern Greece offered a somewhat substandard version of ancient glory, and she never showed any interest in exploring modern Greek literature. In her spirited defense of Balkan identity, *Black Lamb and Grey Falcon: A Journey through Yugoslavia*, Rebecca West relegated regional cultural achievements to a mythic past and devalued the contemporary cultural potential of, specifically, Muslim Balkan peoples (yet see MacKay 44–70). Guillaume Apollinaire enthusiastically praised the acumen of Albanian Faik bey Konitza, but failed to recognize in him a major conduit for modernism in the region. More explicitly, Hans Richter denounced Micić's zenitism as reactionary, and although the French surrealists collaborated with the Belgrade Surrealist Circle from 1922–1932, Breton never mentioned Yugoslav surrealists in his later lectures.[2]

The slight discomfort which the Western modernists felt (and sometimes expressed) at the idea of embracing the modernist aesthetic production of their "next door" other is not without relevance for the examination of Balkan modernisms, since modernist practices in the Balkans were indebted to such contradictory relays of historical and cultural meanings. Yet it is my intention here, as per Micić's advice, to turn the matters "*tumbe*": to insert the heteroglossia of the Balkan modernist margin into scholarly discourse so as to enable not only the discursive acquisition of a new modernist space, but also a reconfiguration of the definitional scope of modernism. As Chana Kronfeld recently proposed, such accounts of "marginal modernisms" may help us "construct the major through the minor" and diversify our picture of canonical modernism (5); or, as I have argued elsewhere, they may assist our reevaluation of the "obliqued" relations between modernist "centers" and "margins" (Bahun-Radunović). Most importantly, however, they may improve our methodology.

THE MODERNIST BALKANS: RECORDED AND UNRECORDED

Already hampered by the linguistic, cultural, and political divisions of this vibrant geo-cultural space, the introduction of Balkan modernisms into international scholarship is additionally complicated by the lack of historical record and by politically sponsored misrecognition/misappropriation of modernist aesthetics in the region. As a result of these and other empirical contingencies, the regional and international record of Balkan modernisms is remarkably uneven: little (or nothing) is known about Albanian and Bulgarian literary modernisms; Turkish literary modernism is a relatively new subject of inquiry, but the study of Romanian modernism has been "transnational" for a while; until recently, the Yugoslav variants of modernist avant-garde have been rarely recognized outside the former Yugoslavia, but Greek modernism has traditionally scored well in the international arena, thanks mostly to a scholarly diaspora keen on translating and critically assessing the work of modern Greek writers. And while the Balkans is increasingly being recognized as a lively modernist space, international scholars have thus far focused on visual arts and architecture, offering limited discussion of modernist tendencies in literature (for this reason, I will concentrate on literary modernisms here).

The unbalanced record of Balkan modernisms is exemplary of a whole series of problems that face modernist studies today; yet the real challenge of exploring Balkan modernist activities lies elsewhere. To discuss Balkan modernisms means to address an extraordinarily diverse corpus of texts and artifacts in different languages, a corpus which is, after all, as fruitfully provisional as the concept of the Balkans itself. As a contiguity-based group of (linguistic and cultural) differentials, Balkan modernisms are worthy of both individual and joint discussion, and there are compelling reasons to pursue both paths. To use the term "the Balkans" also carries a risk: consequential to interregional conflicts and the introjection of stereotyped imagery, the cultures involved sometimes shun the affiliation, claiming that their heritages should be "debalkanized." Yet the geocognitive liminality of the Balkans makes the region a terrain "rich with theoretical possibility" (Fleming 1223), and thus these procedural conundrums take on heuristic value. Thanks to an object of study which implies a multitude of distinct cultural entities and empirical-cultural "intercrossings," a researcher concerned with Balkan modernisms is forced constantly to "cross scales, categories, and viewpoints" (Werner and Zimmermann 30) and to reflect on the grounding terms and definitions in the field of modernist studies. This pursuit is close to the methodological framework of *histoire croisée* ("crossed history"), an approach to relational studies which has recently gained currency in the social and human sciences (see Werner and Zimmerman). Reliant on the *histoire croisée* apparatus, the following overview juxtaposes the modernist spaces of Albania, Bulgaria, Greece, Romania, Turkey, and former Yugoslavia in a non-homogenizing and diachronic fashion. It invites scholars to think out the markedly heterogeneous and polyglot cultural space of the Balkans as an artistic crucible that is most productively understood in the juxtaposition of its respective "minor cultures."

Albania

Albanian modernism is virtually unknown outside Albania, and indigenous scholars themselves have started recovering their modernist heritage only recently. This occlusion, a by-product of the lengthy rule of an autarkic Communist regime and social realist aesthetics, sharply contrasts the marked transnationalism and dynamic exploratory spirit of Albanian literature in the first decades of the twentieth century. Coalesced around periodicals *Përpjekja Shqiptare* (*The Albanian Endeavour*), *Ilyria*, and *Bota e Re* (*New World*), Albanian writers such as Ernest Koliqi (1903–1975), Migjeni (Millosh Gjergj Nikolla, 1911–1938), Lasgush Poradeci (Llazar Gusho, 1899–1987), and Sterjo Spasse (1914–1989) explored modernist aesthetics to different degrees and with different aims.[3] A minority in Albanian letters, they developed their aesthetic strategies in opposition (or relation) to the two dominant discursive trends of Albanian literature, Romantic nationalism and social realism. Their activities were conditioned by the consolidation of the Standard Albanian language (1908), the formation of the Albanian Independent State (1912), and cross-cultural routes of transmission. Albanian proto-modernism is marked by two intellectual figures, Faik bey Konitza (1875–1942) and Fan S. Noli (1882–1965), whose lobbying and scholarly and literary activities in Albania, Western Europe, and the United States championed the creative individual's task to bring about a new "Albanian consciousness." Noli's seamless interweaving of his political work and his cultural and translation activities, which included his promotion of Freud's thought in the region, made him the most visible proponent of the ideology of individual creativity as a central force in the national life.[4] In the Albanian cultural imaginary of the period, this ideology frequently intertwined with the organic state theory, and this particular conjunction informed Konitza's writings. Such development was characteristic of Balkan modernisms in general and also dominated Western European modernism at the time (see P. Lewis 1–8). Guillaume Apollinaire, for one, was an enthusiastic supporter of Konitza's cultural project and an admirer, in particular, of the latter's writings on language, such as his "Essai sur les langues naturelles et les langues artificielles" ("On Natural and Artificial Languages," 1904) (Starova 127–147, 231). Konitza's Cratylist espousal of "natural" languages in this essay, written in French, poignantly announces the preeminent concern of Balkan modernists: the ethno-historical exigencies of language. The pangs of linguistic belonging are also audible in Konitza's unfinished, satiric soliloquy-novel, *Dr. Gjëlpëra zbulon rrënjët e dramës së Mamurrasit: Përrallë* (*Dr. Needle Unearths the Origins of Mamurrasi Tragedy: A Fairy Tale*, 1924).

The language question also animates the creative output of one of the most significant Albanian modernist writers, Millosh Gjergj Nikolla (Migjeni). The disastrous economic, educational, and legislative state in which Albania found itself in the interwar period constitutes the backdrop of Migjeni's opus, consisting of twenty-four prose sketches published in periodicals during his short lifetime, and the 1936 collection of verse *Vargjet e lira* (*Free Verse*, 1936, trans. to English 2001). Albanian Marxist scholars swiftly appropriated Migjeni as a prototype social realist writer; yet, as Arshi Pipa emphasized, "there is nothing in [Migjeni's] writings to invite that inference" (13). The new generation of researchers is more likely to recognize in Migjeni's seditious text precisely those aspects that defy the official literary record: the emotive clusters of suffering and Nietzschean rebellion, cross-generic experimentation, elision of the lyric subject, and the avant-gardist reworking of religious metaphors. One awaits, in particular, critical reassessment of Migjeni's idiosyncratic use of Albanian, a rebellion in language born out of heteroglotic inflection. A Serb in Albania, educated in Montenegro and Greece, Migjeni decided to write in his "second" language, Albanian, and to use the dialect of Gheg (rather than the standard language dialect of Tosk). Migjeni's poetic idiom, which Pipa astutely compared to Italo Svevo's Italian, is thus an exotopic marker of one's "foreignness" in language—a position praised by, among others, Gertrude Stein.

In the Balkans, the creation of a language of resistance is frequently a function of such interregional transits and multiethnic mixtures: the diasporic writer Ernest Koliqi fused the aesthetic strategies of European symbolism and the indigenous forms of Albanian folk verse in *Gjurmat e stinve* (*The Traces of the Seasons*, 1933) into an expression he described as "moderated modernism" (Shehri, English translation forthcoming); and Lasgush Poradeci, an Aromanian-Albanian poet, revolutionized Albanian literature with his linguistically innovative collections of verse, *Vallja e yjve* (*The Dance of the Stars*, 1933) and *Ylli i zemrës* (*The Star of the Heart*, 1937). Rife with mystic-pantheistic images, archaisms, neologisms, and surprising juxtapositions of substantives (Elsie, *History* 1: 444), Poradeci's remarkable poetry was at odds with the cultural politics of communist Albania, and he remained a literary "outsider" for almost fifty years. Belated recognition was also the fate of an early novel by Macedonian-Albanian writer Sterjo Spasse, entitled *Nga jeta në jetë—Pse!?* (*From Life to Life—Why!?*, 1935). Schopenhauerean in inspiration, pessimistic in tone, inter-generic in form, *Why!?*, like many other "buried" modernist texts, presented a conundrum to Albanian Marxist critics. It is only recently that these texts have returned to the Albanian public, the audience that now resentfully realizes that the most vibrant part of its national literature has been occluded.[5] When these works will become widely available in international translations remains an open question.

Bulgaria

After the Berlin Congress and the establishment of an autonomous province of Bulgaria in 1878, the state of Bulgaria was ushered into a swift and semi-successful urbanization and vigorous European cultural exchange, the paradoxes of which affected the cultural production of its inhabitants in the years to follow. At first, Bulgarian writers and artists fervently engaged with European philosophy and aesthetics (in particular, Bergson, Kierkegaard, Nietzsche, Schopenhauer, and Solovyev), but this enthusiasm was soon tempered by the untoward result of the Balkan Wars (1912–1913). Russia and the Western countries were seen as instrumental to Bulgarian territorial losses, and an anti-Western climate developed, even as international exchanges continued. These intercessions found their expression in Bulgarian modernist literature and arts in the particularly emphatic working through of urban (stereotypically seen as Westernized) and rural (seen as indigenous) cultural identities (Nankov). A revisiting of this modernist juncture also informs current scholarly "retrieval" of Bulgarian modernism, performed in the context of the country's recent joining of the EU and a renewed need to define the country's (pro-Western or anti-Western) identity.

Bulgarian modernism evolved in clusters, in literary, artistic, and scholarly groups associated with distinct café-locales and periodicals such as *Misal* (*Thought*), *Zlatorog* (*Golden Horn*), *Nov put* (*New Way*), *Hyperion*, *Vezni* (*Libra*), and *Lebed-Crescendo* (*Swan-Crescendo*) and located both in large cities (the capital Sofia) and semi-rural towns (Stara Zagora, Yambol). Bulgarian modernism has been customarily described through the critical distinction of two modernist "waves," the first identified with the symbolist aesthetics and individualism of the turn-of-the-century (as opposed to the communalist nationalism of Bulgarian Romanticism), and the other recognized as a mature development of Bulgarian modernist expression. The first-wave Bulgarian modernists coalesced around the periodical *Thought*, dominated by the figures of the individualist philosopher Krustyo Krustev (1866–1919) and the writer, artist, and critic Pencho Slaveykov (1866–1912), both enthusiastic propagators of Nietzsche's philosophy. Krustev's and Slaveykov's ideas found artistic expression in the introspective neo-romantic poetry of Peyo Yavorov (Peyo Kracholov, 1878–1914), Petko Todorov (1879–1916), and Mara Belcheva (1868–1937), but the two thinkers also inaugurated what was to become the self-fashioning trope of Bulgarian modernism: the figure of modernist polyhistor. The tendency to engage in cross-disciplinary and scholarly practice would become an explicit artistic politics in the second wave of Bulgarian modernism in the early 1920s; the latter fashioned itself as both an heir and an opponent to the "first modernist wave."

The second-wave symbolists reinjected mystery into the body of ideals. Todor Trayanov (1882–1945), Emanuil Popdimitrov (1888–1943), Nikolai Lilyev (1885–1960), Nikolai Rainov (1889–1954), and others avidly engaged Eastern philosophy, theosophy, and the occult, but also explored the country's rich folklore and culture of indigenous pagan sects like the Bogomils (Manning and Smal-Stocki 134–35). Perhaps the best representative of this synthetic symbolism is the writer and painter Nikolai Rainov, whose collections of poetry/poetic prose *Bogomilski Legendi* (*The Bogomil Legends*, 1912) and *Salnchevi prikazki* (*The Tales of the Sun*, 1918) (selection, trans. to English 2006) also activate various avant-garde techniques. Rainov, like many other Bulgarian symbolists, frequently interacted with the seemingly (and, sometimes, vocally) opposed "avant-gardists": Atanas Dalchev (1904–1978), Nikolai Marangozov (Nikolai Canev Neikov, also known as Nikolai Iantar, 1900–1967), Geo Milev (1895–1925, trans. to English 1990), Chavdar Mutafov (1889–1954), and many others. For a great number of these writers and artists, expressionism was the artistic mode of choice, but the bent toward liberal eclecticism actually dominated the group aesthetics. Regardless of their manifesto-pronouncements, the artists insouciantly crossed movement boundaries, synthesizing in their work avant-garde strategies that would have looked irreconcilable in other contexts: Mutafov blended expressionist themes and futurist aesthetic strategies into a unique brand of literary and artistic cubo-expressionism; both the surrealist Marangozov and the objectivist Dalchev flirted with neo-symbolism (via Paul Valéry); finally, Milev seems to have been ready to subscribe to any form of avant-garde expression as long as it was "radical." One may detect such relaxed attitudes toward the politics and practice of modernist association throughout the Balkans, usually with good effects. This artistic inter-positionality was informed by Balkan modernists' liminal-transitory location in the symbolic system, but also fostered by the dynamics of historical compression. It is this "historical compression" in the Balkans, however, that also relegated Bulgarian modernism to oblivion: with the notable exception of Milev, all authors that are now being consolidated into a Bulgarian modernist corpus went unnoticed (or denounced) for decades because of Communist cultural politics. Compression fosters compression: the eventual publication of Nikolai Rainov's collected writings in 1989 coincided with the appearance of the first samizdat anthology of Bulgarian postmodernism (Krasztev 342). This publishing coincidence can be bitterly lamented or regarded as a curiosity. Far more useful than any of these options, I suggest, is to treat such temporal conflations in fringe modernisms as a call to reassess our perception of literary history.

Greece

In comparison to other Balkan modernisms, Greek modernist literature was fortunate: widely available in translation in all major languages, it is also the subject of many excellent studies in English. Overviews of Greek modernism can start from geography (what comprised "modern Greece" before and after the Greco-Turkish war of 1918–1922), economy (industrialization, demographic shifts), politics (nationalist or cosmopolitan Greece), and cultural politics (the contradictory relay of images of "Greece" between Western Europe and Greece);[6] or one can start from language (the simultaneous use of two distinct languages, the *katharevusa* [the purified] and the *dimotiki* [the demotic]). The last seems to be the best point of departure, Dimitris Tziovas suggests, as it was in and out of the conflict between the purists (the elite using the artificial register of *katharevusa*) and the populists (the multi-strata using the vernacular) in the period 1880–1930 that Greek modernism was born (Tziovas, *Nationalism* 124–25). The demoticists agreed with the purists (and their Albanian neighbors) that the nation was to be built in and through language, but they argued that the use of the *katharevusa*, intended to integrate the modern Greek nation, failed at every step. To demonstrate the primacy of the vernacular for the nation-building project, however, they had to prove its ability to become a literary idiom: symbolic capital was gained through vigorous publishing of contemporary authors (Jusdanis 77), many of whom were educated in the West or who maintained migrant lifestyles. Thus the project of forging a Greek *national* content became the incentive for the exploration of *transnational* artistic strategies. These would find an eclectic, mystical articulation in Angelos Sikelianos's (1884–1951) "Delphic" poetry and performance (trans. to English 1980) and Nikos Kazantzakis's (1883–1957) writings—the proto-existentialist play *Komodia: Tragodia monoprachti* (*Comedy: A Tragedy in One Act*, 1909, trans.

to English 1982), the epic *Odissia* (*The Odyssey: A Modern Sequel*, 1925–1938, trans. to English 1958), and the novel *Teleftaios Peirasmos* (*The Last Temptation of Christ*, 1950–1951, trans. to English 1961).

This compelling campaign notwithstanding, it would take a long time before the demotic became the official language in 1976. Thus the early twentieth-century "demoticists" had to turn to para-institutional spaces for the advance of the "demotic public sphere"—literary cafés, salons, and art societies, where they fervently discussed Constantine Cavafy's free iambic verse, Nietzsche, futurism, and surrealism (Jusdanis 151–53). The "modernist spirit" was, however, fortified externally through a series of turbulent political events that started with the Balkan Wars and ended with the Greco-Turkish war and the so-called Asia Minor catastrophe in 1922 (the Turkish army's defeat of the Greeks in Asia Minor and the concomitant exchange of population). The last event—one rarely mentioned in the various accounts of the modernist *annus mirabilis*—was perceived in Greece as a "national trauma of apocalyptic proportions" (Jusdanis 78): it engendered the emotive amalgam of nation loss, nation promotion, and rebellion, which, recomposed into a reconciliatory structure of feeling termed "*Ellinikotita*" ("Greekness"), was to dominate Greek modernism in the 1930s.[7] The latter was announced by several differently scaled events: George Theotokas's (1906–1966) essay *Elefthero pnevma* (*Free Spirit*, 1929); the sudden proliferation of periodicals dedicated to new literature and art (e.g., *Nea Grammata* [*The New Letters*], *Trito Mati* [*The Third Eye*], and others); and the public emergence of "new poets." New poets included George Seferis (1900–1971), whose collections of verse *Strophe* (meaning both *A Strophe* and *Turning Point*, 1931) and *Mythistorema* (*Mythistory*, 1935, trans. to English 1995) introduced a specifically Greek modernist idiom, through a vernacular, intimate voice, intertwining mythology and history; Andreas Embirikos (1901–1975), whose surrealist prose poems in *Ypsikaminos* (*Blast-Furnace*, 1935) shocked the literary establishment and who, together with Nikos Gatsos (1911–1990; see *Amorgos* [1943]), assured the longevity of surrealist revolution in Greek letters; Odysseus Elytis (Odysseas Alepoudelis, 1911–1996), whose collections *Prosanatolismoi* (*Orientations*, 1939) and *Helios o protos* (*Sun The First*, 1943) show the development of surrealist poetics into a sensuous national discourse (trans. to English 2004); and finally, Yannis Ritsos (1909–1990), whose first three collections of verse, *Trakter* (*Tractor*, 1934), *Pyramides* (*Pyramids*, 1935) and *Epitafios* (*Epitaph*, 1936), ushered Greek literature into a socialist-futurist avant-garde (trans. to English 1989).

Modernism's durability in Greek space was confirmed not only in the later poetry of Ritsos, Elytis, and Seferis (the latter two winning the Nobel Prize in Literature in 1979 and 1963, respectively), but also in that of postwar writers who forged their poetic voice both in continuation of and contradistinction to the generation of the 1930s. Actively engaged with the turbulent politico-historical space of Greece in the 1950s and 1960s, Greek/diasporic writers such as Miltos Sachtouris (1919–), Hector Kaknavatos (1920–), and Nanos Valaoritis (1921–) reinvigorated Greek poetry with a new, synthetic expression based on neo-surrealism (trans. to English 2000). And they forced on literary historians the question that is relevant throughout the region: how to categorize, demarcate, and "close" the tidal history of modernism in the Balkans?

Romania

The last decade has seen a steady flow of scholarly publications on Romanian modernism (Răileanu, Impey, Mansbach, Sandqvist). These and other accounts document vigorous modernist activity in the capital Bucharest, but also in towns such as Iași, Botoșani, and Craiova from 1880–1940—activities publicized in the periodicals *Simbolul* (*The Symbol*), *Contimporanul* (*The Contemporary*), *Chemarea* (*Call*), *unu* (*one*), *75HP*, and others. Scholars emphasize Romanian contributions to the development of the avant-garde, attributing the vibrancy of Romanian cultural production to a cluster of historical and cultural paradoxes besetting the country in the early twentieth century. Like other Balkan nation-states, turn-of-the-century Romania was a site of historical contradictions: a place of foreign investments and peasants' uprisings, of ox-drawn carts and electric trams, where modernization and the rushed introduction of Western liberalism were tempered by a weak economy, xenophobia, and the *poporanists'* (populists') efforts to awaken the "Romanian spirit." While these paradoxes persisted well into the 1920s and 1930s, the enlargement of Romanian territory and economic growth after World War I thoroughly reconfigured the cultural sphere: Bucharest became the Balkan center of publishing, education, and the arts. Yet the most distinctive characteristic of the Romanian cultural space of the first half of the twentieth century was its heteroglossia. In 1918, ethnic non-Romanians (Hungarians, Jews, Germans, Bulgarians, Turks, and others) comprised 30 percent of the country's population, and we are well advised to seek the roots of a Romanian avant-garde in this polyvocality (Sandqvist 102). This claim may be extended to Balkan modernisms in general: it is the heteroglotic everyday experience in a multi-ethnically striated culture that made Balkan modernists particularly attentive to language—to layering of discourse, semantic slipperiness, political-linguistic abuse, and, also, the subversive potential of innovative structuring.

In tune with European currents, Romanian modernists' engagement with the exigencies of language first took the form of a hunt for a primal word/symbol. The symbolists' activities were galvanized by an eccentric cultural transmitter, the poet Alexandru Macedonski (1854–1920), whose first collection of verse, *Prima verba* (*First Words*, 1880), announced the advent of modernism in Romanian letters. The Romanian proto-avant-garde is usually dated contemporaneously and associated with the writings of Ion Luca Caragiale (1852–1912) and Urmuz (Demetru Dem. Demetrescu Buzău, 1883–1923). Later, both writers were much admired by Eugene Ionesco (1909–1994), and for understandable reasons: Caragiale's string-stories like "Temă și variațiuni" ("A Theme and Variations," 1892) and one-act plays such as *Căldură Mare* (*Great Heat*, 1901) are replete with logical somersaults, syllogisms, and other devices that "question and expose the socially-, culturally- and linguistically-established status quo" (Varga 133); and Urmuz's prose ("Ismail și Turnavitu" ["Ismail and Turnavitu"], *Pâlnia și Stamate (Roman în patru părți)* [*The Funnel and*

Stamate (Novel in Four Parts)], and other texts dated 1907–1922, trans. to English 1985) is a surrealist motley of undecided objects and incongruous systems of thought, reminiscent of Franz Kafka's contemporaneous writing. While "imported" avant-gardes such as futurism and expressionism also found a fertile ground in Romania,[8] scholars have frequently warned that the relationship between symbolist and avant-garde orientations in Romania was one of continuity rather than antithesis. The periodical *Simbolul*, founded in 1912 by two Dadaists-to-be, Marcel Janco (Marcel Iancu, 1895–1984) and Tristan Tzara (Samuel Rosenstock, 1896–1963), and the future constructivist Ion Vinea (Ion Eugen Iovanaki, 1895–1964), is a manifest testimony to this rapport. Tzara's poetry in Romanian (1912–1915, trans. to English 1976) is symbolist; and it is illuminating that Tzara did not perceive his poetics as in any way discontinuous with his "Dadaist" activities, either in Bucharest and Iași (1913–1915), or in Zurich and Paris (post-1915).

In the interwar period, Bucharest became the focal point of international avant-garde activities (Sandqvist 216 *et passim*), a loose aesthetic umbrella which was provided by the indigenous variant of constructivism nurtured by the Contimporanul group (1922–1932, led by Vinea and Iancu) and the Integral group (1925–1928, led by the painter M. H. Maxy). The Integral group's ambition to amalgamate all avant-garde movements in a constructivist mold finds an apt expression in the constructivist-surrealist poetry of Ilarie Voronca (Eduard Marcus, 1903–1946), and in the collections *Ulise* (*Ulysses*, 1928) and *Plante și animale* (*Plants and Animals*, 1929) (selection, trans. to English 2006). Surrealism was alternatively espoused and rejected throughout the 1920s and 1930s, but when a programmatic group assembled in 1940, it was established on firm sociopolitical grounds: Gherasim Luca (1913–1994) and Dolfi Trost's (1916–1966) vigorous message-manifesto *Dialectique de la dialectique* (*Dialectic of Dialectic*, 1945) warned international surrealists of the dangers of complacency and advocated focusing on the revolutionary materiality of object-dynamics (such as erotic love). This stance is well exemplified in Luca's poetic prose in *Un lup văzut printr-o lupă* (*A Wolf Seen through a Magnifying Glass*, 1945) and *Inventatorul iubirii* (*The Inventor of Love*, 1945, trans. to English 2009) and Gellu Naum's (1915–2001) verse collections *Libertatea de a dormi pe o frunte* (*Liberty to Sleep on a Forehead*, 1937) and *Culoarul somnului* (*Sleep Passage*, 1944) (selection, trans. to English 2007). Finally, a whole plethora of Romanian writers autonomously integrated various avant-garde tendencies. One of the nonaligned was the young Eugene Ionesco, who used the World War II years to draft his first play, *Englezește fără profesor* (*English Without a Teacher*, ca. 1943). The author and the play, soon to be adapted into French as *La Cantatrice Chauve* (*The Bald Soprano*), became an (e)migrant testimony to the effervescence of Romanian modernism.

Turkey

To talk about Turkish modernism implies engaging with an even greater number of incomparables, contradictions, and hermeneutic bridges than in the case of other Balkan modernisms. (See also Ertürk's contribution to this volume.) For Turkish modernism bifurcates as an object of study. It involves a discussion of at least three distinct historical periods: that of the beginning of the twentieth century and those of the 1950s and 1970s–1980s; an appraisal of disparate developments of different arts (fine arts and literature); and an examination of the specific conceptual framing of the terms "modern" and "modernist" in Turkish historic-political and cultural context. Precisely because of these hermeneutic complexities, however, Turkish modernism is likely to become the most compelling subject matter for modernist scholars.

To be "modernist" in Turkey has always been both an aesthetic and a political decision, involving a painfully contradictory evaluation of one's engagement not only with Western cultural models but also with one's own (dis)inherited culture. In the period that scholars associate with the rise of the U.S.-European modernist idiom, Turkey incrementally transformed from a multiethnic empire into a secular nation-state. Geographically and symbolically posed among its former dominions, Turkey also had to define itself in contradistinction to the empire. The Republic of Turkey in 1923 thus engaged in perhaps the most consistent rejection of past models that modernism ever knew. In less than fifteen years, from 1923 to 1936, the state replaced all Ottoman social, political, and cultural institutions with "Western" models; most sensationally perhaps, it replaced the Arabo-Persian alphabet with Latin phonetic orthography (1928) and "purified" the official language by simplifying the convoluted syntax of Ottoman Turkish and purging borrowings (see G. Lewis). These revolutionary changes were intended to create a national consciousness based on the virtues of ethnic homogeneity, territorial unity, and rational modernity. They gathered a substantial amount of enthusiasm, particularly among artists and architects, who seized the opportunity to use contemporary artistic techniques to represent and build the nation-in-becoming. Yet, implemented by an authoritarian bureaucratic apparatus, the rapid move from a culturally and politically self-sufficient empire into a West-modeled/dependent state also introduced a sense of loss, belatedness, and marginality. In the case of literature, this cluster of emotions attached itself to functional changes in the medium of expression (language)— the dynamics finely theorized by the writer and critic Ahmet Hamdi Tanpınar (1901–1962)—and it encouraged an aesthetic realignment, which, albeit logical in local terms, is hardly compatible with the Western paradigm of modernism.

The most distinctive feature of Turkish modernism is the asynchronous development of its poetry and prose.[9] Both symbolism and avant-gardism were articulated relatively early in Turkish poetry, finding a particularly compelling expression in Ahmet Haşim's (1885–1933) symbolist verse in *Göl Saatleri* (*Hours of the Lake*, 1921); *Piyâle* (*The Wine Cup*, 1926) (selection, trans. to English 2004); Nâzim Hikmet's (1902–1963) engaged futurist poetry in *835 Satir* (*835 Lines*, 1929); and *Jokand ile Si-Ya-U* (*Mona Lisa and Si-Ya-U*, 1929) (selection, trans. to English 1994). The modernist/avant-garde trends in poetry continued after World War II, most prominently in the poetically diversified production of *Ikinci Yeni* (*The Second New*), featuring the works of Ece Ayhan Çağlar (1933–2002), İlhan Berk (1918–) (trans. to English 2006), Özdemir İnce (1936–), and others (see Halman). By contrast,

modernist strategies became visible in Turkish prose only in the early 1950s, in
Tanpınar's novels such as *Huzur* (*A Mind at Peace*, 1949, trans. to English 2008) and
Saatleri ayarlama enstitüsü (*The Clock-Setting Institute*, 1954; pub. 1962, trans. to
English 2002); and, more emphatically, in the 1970s, in Oğuz Atay's (1934–1977) syn-
tactically adventurous novel *Tutunamayanlar* (*The Disconnected*, 1970–1972), Adalet
Ağaoğlu's (1929–) feminist interventions in prose (e.g., *Ölmeye Yatmak* [*Lying Down
To Die*, 1973]), and similar texts.

The uneven development of Turkish literary modernism may be a consequence
of the different epistemological, cultural, and political functions of poetry and prose
in the Turkish semiosphere, as suggested by Parla (38), or of the practical vicissitudes of the 1920s (interaction between avant-garde arts and poetry was easier
because their encounters were routinely staged in periodicals such as *Servet-i Fünun*
[*Wealth of Knowledge*], *Resimli Ay* [*Monthly Illustrated*], and *Varlik* [*Existence*]).
Whatever the case, generalization is unadvisable. For these concerns also inform
the main "paradox" of Turkish literary modernism, a phenomenon which expressly
defies Western perceptions of modernism: while modern(ist) reformers who had
created the new Republic frequently rushed to adopt literary models that, in the
Western context, "preceded" modernism (mimetic realist narration and romantic
nationalism), the "conservatives," or the silent opponents to the Republic's manifold
reforms, often found their invocation of suppressed cultural and linguistic models
consonant with modernist tendencies. Thus the conservative Ismayil Hakki
Baltacıoğlu's (1889–1978) attempt to "rescue" Turkish Islamic script paradoxically
seeks support in the project's affiliation with surrealist-cubist aesthetics (*Türklerde
Yazi Sanati* [*Turkish Script Arts*, 1958]; Ertürk, "Surrealism and Turkish Script Arts";
and her contribution to this volume); and Tanpınar's novels, replete with recognizably modernist themes (alienation, father-son struggle, split identity), are entrenched
in a linguistic nostalgia that directs itself toward the late Ottoman cultural past. But
the scholarly division of Turkish modern literature into multiethnic/traditional
modernism and national/modern *realism* is also challenged by writers like Nâzim
Hikmet, whose poetry, swinging between futurist aesthetics and realist didacticism,
both champions and criticizes modernity-as-project (Aguiar 119–20). Rather than
signaling inconsistencies, these affiliative and heuristic difficulties indicate that the
examination of Balkan modernisms also entails a perturbation of Western models
of historical progress—both traditional and contemporary ones.

Yugoslavia

Observed in retrospect, the case of Yugoslav modernism is vexing. While in the
light of pre-1918 and post-1991 historical events, it may be justifiable to distinguish
between a few different literatures and art histories in the region, the phenomenon/
mode of "Yugoslav" modernism is inextricably linked to the now nonexistent country that "lived" between these dates. As Miško Šuvaković points out, even the earliest manifestations of modernist currents in South Slav lands (the Serb Stanislav
Vinaver's [1891–1955] futurist volume *telegrafski soneti* [*Telegraph Sonnets*, 1911], the

Bosnian Dimitrije Mitrinović's [1887–1953] essay "Estetičke kontemplacije" ["Aesthetic Contemplations," 1913], the Slovene Anton Podbevšek's [1898–1981] collection of futurist verse *Žolta pisma* [*Yellow Letters*, 1915], and the Croat Miroslav Krleža's [1893–1981] expressionist play *Kraljevo* [1915]) were developed and distributed in a multiethnic context and were, to a significant extent, galvanized by the project of a unified country (12). Hence, it is only possible to discuss Yugoslav modernisms and avant-gardes in reference to one cultural space, that of Yugoslavia, whose real historical characteristics compellingly reflect the modernist avant-garde modes themselves: flux, conflict, and continuous redefinition (3).

In the three major languages of former Yugoslavia ("Bosnian/Croatian/Serbian," Macedonian, and Slovenian), "modernism" has been frequently and problematically denoted with the term *Moderna* (feminine form of the adjective "modern," a general referent to modernity as well as an aesthetic referent to the Viennese Secession). The *Moderna* is a definitional casualty of the accelerated pace of artistic response to modernization in Yugoslav lands: it sometimes indiscriminately refers to *modern* literature (neo-romantic, symbolist, and realist responses to modernization, spanning 1890–1916 or 1890–1940) and to *modernist* literature—a variegated aesthetics developed in interaction with European modernist and avant-garde trends from the 1910s onward, facilitated by cultural transmitters such as Mitrinović and Rastko Petrović (1898–1949). But the semi-misnomer *Moderna* is also a necessity, for it captures the aesthetic flexibility and the relaxed, anti-systemic attitude toward self-classification that are characteristic of a "small nation's" articulation of modernism: Yugoslav authors such as Ivo Andrić (1892–1975) or Miloš Crnjanski (1893–1977) could write in a modernist vein (Andrić's poetic prose *Ex Ponto* [1918]; Crnjanski's collection of verse *Lirika Itake* [*Lyrics of Ithaca*, 1918] and *Seobe I* [*Migrations I*, 1929, trans. to English 1994]), then shift to a realist mode, then sporadically revert to modernist expression—without worrying too much about being inconsistent or disingenuous.

Like other Balkan modernists, Yugoslav writers indicated their permanent or temporary affiliation by associating with periodicals—*Putevi* (*Ways*), *Svedočanstva* (*Testimonies*), *Nadrealizam sada i ovde* (*Surrealism Here and Now*) (Belgrade); *Vijavica* (*Snowstorm*), *Plamen* (*Flame*) (Zagreb); *Svetokret* (*World-turn*), *Ljubljanski zvon* (*Ljubljana Bell*) (Ljubljana), and others. Tellingly, modernist activities in Yugoslavia reflected three axes of external cultural domination: German, French, and Russian. An indigenous variant of expressionism found its best representatives in Crnjanski (poetry) and Krleža (poetry, early plays, and the novel *Povratak Filipa Latinovicza* [*The Return of Philip Latinovicz*, 1932; trans. to English 1959]), while surrealism manifested itself in the national and international activities of the Belgrade Surrealist Circle (1922–1932), surprisingly coterminous with the early development of the movement in Paris (see Bahun-Radunović). Slightly less prominent but equally vocal was the fluctuating group of Dadaists, pro-Dadaists, and anti-Dadaists who coalesced around matinee happenings and little magazines such as *Dada Jazz*, *Dada Tank*, *Dada Jok* in Belgrade and Zagreb, and the Slovene *Tank!* group. Futurism and constructivism found particularly fertile ground in Slovenia, where Podbevšek published the first Yugoslav collection of visual poetry, *Človek z bombami* (*The Man with Bombs*, 1925), and Srečko Kosovel (1904–1926) wrote the constructivist poems of *Integrali* (*Integrals*, 1925–1926; pub. 1967, selection trans to English 2008). Finally, Micić's *zenitism* emerged as a boisterously regional response to expressionism and cubism. As one of the most reputable indigenous avant-gardes of East-Central Europe, the movement and its periodical *Zenit* (*Zenith*, published first in Zagreb, then in Belgrade, 1922–1926) succeeded in "[converting] a presumed Balkan cultural deficiency into a Barbarian virtue" (Levinger 267; see Benson and Forgács 284–300, 345–56, 505–28).

As a result of political realignment and distancing from the Soviet cultural model in 1948–1952, the artistic taste of Yugoslavia was subsequently dictated by modernist trends.[10] This course of events allowed prewar modernists and new authors such as Vasko Popa (1922–1991), Vladan Desnica (1905–1967), Slobodan Novak (1924–), Ranko Marinković (1913–2001), and Slavko Janevski (1920–2000) to pursue high modernist aesthetics in poetry, prose, and drama. Interestingly, the fact that "moderate modernism" became an important part of official culture made it vulnerable to questioning: some contemporary scholars argue that the ideological neutrality of postwar Yugoslav modernism belied epigonism, and they contrast "state-sponsored modernism" to the more adventurous Yugoslav neo-avant-garde (Šuvaković 11–12). While such strict division of the aesthetic sphere is always problematic, these assessments remind us that modernism, for all its insolence, can become inert, co-optable, even corruptible.

Balkan Modernisms and Methodological Apertures

Rather than generating a summary model, which would unnecessarily homogenize the modernist space of the Balkans, let us assemble a random list of Balkan modernists' "positions," as inferable from the snapshots of Balkan literary modernisms in the previous section. On a general level, these positions confirm Franz Kafka's designation of the literary production of small peoples as aesthetically less constrained, but vigorously intersected by local history/politics (150–51). For these reasons, the relational configuration of Balkan modernisms is dynamic and contradictory. Balkan modernists engaged in an activist-progressive model of modernism; but they also pursued (perhaps even more so) a national-organicist-regressive model of modernism. The exposure to heteroglossia made them linguistically adventurous while attentive to the historical vicissitudes of discourse; it also made them parochially defensive. Their artistic strategies were informed by a simultaneous embracing and rejection of modernity; a sense of belatedness (even when their activities were contemporaneous to those in "modernist centers"); a belief in cosmopolitanism as a formal rather than contentual choice; and a comfortable eclecticism. They imported Western modernist/avant-garde models with disregard for original definitional demarcations; they exported indigenous models with disregard for their own national-cultural specificity. The list could go on—yet the extraordinary potential of examining the modernist production of the Balkans lies not only in what we may *discover* about this under-discussed hub of modernist practices, but also in what we may *learn* about our own methodology. So, what do we *learn* from my *histoire croisée* snapshots?

One of the acknowledged problems in describing modernist practices outside of the European-North American canon is the persistence of Western terminology: a play can be expressionist or surrealist; a poem can be symbolist or constructivist; a text can use stream of consciousness or not; and so on. Identifying these trends and perspectives is crucial for the introduction of a new modernist space in expert discourse. But, if understood seriously, the fringe variants are also bound to alter our perception and evaluation of Western modernist trends. For instance, symbolism, which is frequently understood as an inchoate form of, or even antithesis to, modernism, was the most pervasive and enduring *modernist* aesthetic form in the Balkans: it productively interacted with the poetics of the radical avant-garde as well as with the indigenous means of expression, and, for many Balkan modernists, symbolism became synonymous with modernism. Rather than bemoaning definitional quagmires or accusing the Balkan modernists of tardiness (or non-modernism!), we should use those variant-practices to reflect back on our understanding of symbolism itself. The same goes for the Bürgerian treatment of modernism and the avant-garde as separate categories—a research strategy which shows itself as singularly restrictive in the case of Balkan modernisms.[11] At the same time, it is evident that all identifications generated and confirmed in the discourse on canonical modernisms (through terms such as symbolism, futurism, expressionism, avant-gardism, and so on) are dislimning for the newly introduced space. If we argue, on the grounds of the preceding overview, that various types of modernist aesthetics comfortably converged and nonhierarchically interacted in Balkan modernisms (and that there is nothing wrong with such eclecticism), we are effectively invited to reconfigure the concept of an aesthetic-function group itself. Consider: should we discuss the Bulgarian author Chavdar Mutafov's poetics as futurist, expressionist, cubo-expressionist, or we should create an entirely new designating framework for his practice—without the burdensome accretion of dashes?

To probe such constraints is a shared task in new modernist studies. But the study of Balkan modernisms, I submit, may be particularly useful for the reconfiguration of frameworks of inquiry. One of the most profound challenges posed to modernist studies by the case of Balkan modernisms is the imperative to rethink the assumption that the definition of modernism requires a developmentalist model of historical progression, from tradition (the period of "other" aesthetic movements) to modernity, whenever and however that modernity may occur (the realm of modernism).[12] The simultaneous occurrence of bidirectional processes, alteration, intermittence, inertia, or regressive movement, the compound nature of historical processes, as disclosed in the "anti-modernist strategies" of Balkan modernisms (Tziovas, *Greek* 2), all have to be taken into account if we wish to assess global modernisms; or, indeed, if we wish to refine our understanding of canonical modernism.[13] To approach this issue without imposing various models of "alternative modernity" exterior to the subject of study, we need to adopt a procedure based on a more flexible conceptual template, one that is *constantly redefined by the very object of its enquiry*. To this end, I suggest the inclusion of the reflexive and dynamic methodological framework of *histoire croisée* in our "tool kit" for the discussion of global modernisms. Such a move would not only support our recalculation of geo-temporal boundaries of modernism and evaluation of such paradoxically framed practices as Micić's "modernist barbarianism," but would also enable us to pursue a continuous and responsible revision of the principles and methods guiding our own research activity.

NOTES

1. The name "barbaro-genius," Esther Levinger surmised, referred to the Slavs in general and to the people of the Balkans in particular (260).
2. There were, of course, cases of genuine interest in indigenous modernist production. Lawrence Durrell, for instance, frequented Greek "modernist" cafés in the late 1930s and wrote enthusiastically to T. S. Eliot about George Seferis's poetry (Durrell 357).
3. See anthologies of Albanian poetry in English 1993 and 2008 and Robert Elsie's website, *Albanian Literature in Translation*. The following merits a mention: while Elsie's scholarly work is pioneering, his translational style has been sometimes criticized as rigid and particularly ill-suited to the rendition of experimental texts.
4. For an account of Fan S. Noli's political, religious, cultural-literary activities in English, see Prifti 5–17, 113–17.
5. For a comprehensive overview of Albanian modernism, see Asllani (forthcoming).
6. The nineteenth-century Greeks based their national cultural politics not on classical antiquity, which was seen as "alien and incomprehensible fiction," but on the continuity of the Orthodox Church (Tsoukalas 35–40). The link to antiquity was forged only with the help of German and English scholars; later, however, this "rediscovered" antiquity profoundly influenced modernist poets such as Sikelianos and Seferis.
7. The hellenocentric context of Greek modernism has been reassessed in Jusdanis, Leontis, Vayenas, and Pourgouris.
8. *The First Manifesto of Futurism* was published in the Romanian newspaper *Democrația* on the same day (February 20, 1909) as in the French *Le Figaro* (Sandqvist 236–43).
9. For varying views on this issue, see G. Lewis, Holbrook 30–31, and Parla ft. 5, 38.
10. On "realists" versus "modernists" debates in Yugoslavia from 1949–1952, see Peković 90–135.
11. For a similarly negative assessment of the relevance of Peter Bürger's theory beyond Franco-German cultural space, see Ram in this volume. For Bürger's influential model, see Bürger.
12. Grounded in Neil Smith's theory of uneven geographical development, this unwittingly restrictive model has been proposed by, among others, Fredric Jameson (141–42). For an overview of the criticism of this model, see Ram in this volume.
13. For a similar argument with regard to Scandinavian modernism, see Stenport in this volume.

WORKS CITED

Aguiar, Marian. "Nâzim Hikmet's Modernism of Development." *Journal of Modern Literature* 30.4 (2007): 105–21.

Armstrong, Tim. *Modernism: A Cultural History.* Cambridge: Polity Press, 2005.

Asllani, Persida. "Modernists in Early Twentieth Century Albania." *Balkan Modernisms: Approaches and Sources.* Ed. Sanja Bahun. Forthcoming.

Bahun-Radunović, Sanja. "The Value of the Oblique (Notes on Relational Funhouses, Historical Occlusions, and Serbian Surrealism)." Bahun-Radunović and Pourgouris 129–53.

Bahun-Radunović, Sanja, Marinas, and Pourgouris, eds. *The Avant-garde and the Margin: New Territories of Modernism.* Newcastle: Cambridge Scholars Publishing, 2006.

Beldiman, Alexandru, Magda Cârneci, and Mihai Oroveanu, eds. and curs. *Bucureşti anii 1920–1940: între avangardă şi modernism/Bucharest in the 1920s–1940: Between Avant-Garde and Modernism.* Bucharest: Editura Simetria and Uniunea Arhitecţilor din România, 1994.

Benson, Timothy, ed. *Central European Avant-gardes: Exchange and Transformation, 1910–1930.* Cambridge: MIT Press, 2002.

Benson, Timothy, and Éva Forgács, eds. *Between Worlds: A Sourcebook of Central European Avant-gardes, 1910–1930.* Cambridge: MIT Press, 2002.

Berend, Iván, and György Ránki. *The European Periphery and Industrialization, 1780–1914.* Cambridge: Cambridge University Press, 1982.

Berk, İlhan. *A Leaf About To Fall: Selected Poems.* Trans. George Messo. Great Wilbraham: Salt Publishing, 2006.

Bjelić, Dušan I., and Obrad Savić, eds. *Balkan as Metaphor: Between Globalization and Fragmentation.* Cambridge: MIT Press, 2002.

Bürger, Peter. *Theory of the Avant-garde.* Trans. Michael Shaw. 1974. Minneapolis: University of Minnesota Press, 1984.

Bynum, David E., ed. and trans. *A Bulgarian Literary Reader.* The Hague: Mouton, 1968.

Christie, Agatha. *The Secret of Chimneys.* New York: Dell, 1975.

Crnjanski, Miloš (transliterated as Milos Tsernianski). *Migrations.* Trans. Michael Henry Heim. London: Harvill, 1994.

Durrell, Lawrence. "Letters to T. S. Eliot." *Twentieth Century Literature* 33.3 (1987): 348–58.

Elsie, Robert, ed. and trans. *An Elusive Eagle Soars: Anthology of Albanian Modern Poetry.* Boston: Forest Books, 1993.

———. *History of Albanian Literature.* 2 vols. Boulder: Social Science Monographs; New York: Columbia University Press, 1995.

Elsie, Robert, and Janice Mathie-Heck, eds. and trans. *Lightning from the Depths: An Anthology of Albanian Poetry.* Evanston: Northwestern University Press, 2008.

Elytis, Odysseus. *The Collected Poems of Odysseus Elytis.* 2nd rev. ed. Trans. Jeffrey Carson and Nikos Sarris. Baltimore: Johns Hopkins University Press, 2004.

Ertürk, Nergis. "Surrealism and Turkish Script Arts." *Modernism/modernity* 17.1 (2010): 47–60.

Firan, Carmen, Paul Doru Mugur, and Edward Foster, eds. and trans. *Born in Utopia: An Anthology of Modern and Contemporary Romanian Poetry.* Jersey City: Talisman House Publishers, 2006.

Fleming, Kathryn. "Orientalism, the Balkans, and Balkan Historiography." *American Historical Review* 105.4 (2000): 1218–1233.

Halman, Talat Sait. *Living Poets of Turkey*. Istanbul: Dost Publications, 1989.

Harteis, Richard, and William Meredith. *Window on the Black Sea: Bulgarian Poetry in Translation*. Pittsburgh: Carnegie Mellon University Press, 1992.

Hikmet, Nâzim. *Poems of Nazim Hikmet*. Ed. Randy Blasing and Mutlu Konuk Blasing. Trans. Mutlu Konuk. New York: Persea Books, 1994.

Holbrook, Victoria Rowe. *The Unreadable Shores of Love: Turkish Modernity and Mystic Romance*. Austin: University of Texas Press, 1994.

Impey, Michael. "Before and After Tzara: Romanian Contributions to Dada." *The Eastern Dada Orbit: Russia, Georgia, Ukraine, Central Europe, and Japan*. Ed. Gerald Janecek and Toshiharu Omuka. New York: G. K. Hall, 1998. 126–36.

Jameson, Fredric. *A Singular Modernity: Essay on the Ontology of the Present*. New York: Verso, 2002.

Jusdanis, Gregory. *Belated Modernity and Aesthetic Culture*. Minneapolis: University of Minnesota Press, 1991.

Kafka, Franz. *The Diaries, 1910–1923*. Ed. Max Brod. New York: Schocken Books, 1976.

Kazantzakis, Nikos. *The Last Temptation of Christ*. Trans. Peter A. Bien. New York: Simon Schuster, 1960.

———. *The Odyssey: A Modern Sequel*. Trans. Kimon Friar. New York: Simon Schuster, 1958.

———. *Two Plays: Sodom and Gomorrah and Comedy, A Tragedy in One Act*. Trans. Kimon Friar and Peter Bien. Minneapolis: Nostos Books, 1982.

Keely, Edmund, and Philip Sherrard, eds. and trans. *Voices of Modern Greece: Selected Poems by C. V. Cavafy, Angelos Sikelianos, George Seferis, Odysseus Elytis, Nikos Gatsos*. Princeton: Princeton University Press, 1981.

Kosovel, Srečko. *The Golden Boat: Selected Poems of Srečko Kosovel*. Trans. David Brooks and Bert Pribac. Great Wilbraham: Salt Publishing, 2008.

Krasztev, Péter. "From Modernization to Modernist Literature." *History of the Literary Cultures of East-Central Europe: Junctures and Disjunctures in the 19th and 20th Centuries*. Ed. Marcel Cornis-Pope and John Neubauer. Philadelphia: John Benjamins, 2006. 332–47.

Krleža, Miroslav. *The Return of Philip Latinovicz*. Trans. Zora G. Dopolo. London: Lincolns-Prager, 1959.

Kronfeld, Chana. *On the Margins of Modernism*. Berkeley: University of California Press, 1995.

Leontis, Artemis. *Topographies of Hellenism: Mapping the Homeland*. Ithaca: Cornell University Press, 1995.

Levinger, Esther. "Ljubomir Micić and the Zenithist Utopia." Benson 260–78.

Lewis, Geoffrey. *The Turkish Language Reform: A Catastrophic Success*. Oxford: Oxford University Press, 1999.

Lewis, Pericles. *Modernism, Nationalism, and the Novel*. Cambridge: Cambridge University Press, 2000.

Luca, Gherasim. *Inventor of Love*. Trans. Julian and Laura Semilian. Boston: Black Widow Press, 2009.

MacKay, Marina. *Modernism and World War II*. Cambridge: Cambridge University Press, 2007.

Mansbach, Steven A. *Modern Art in Eastern Europe: From the Baltic to the Balkans, ca. 1890–1939*. Cambridge: Cambridge University Press, 1999.

Mazower, Mark. *The Balkans*. London: Weidenfeld & Nicolson, 2000.

Micić, Ljubomir. "Zenitizam kao balkanski totalizator novoga života i nove umetnosti." ["Zenitism as a Balkan integrator of life and new art"]. *Zenit* 21 (February 1923): n.p.

Micić, Ljubomir, Ivan Goll, and Boško Tokin. "The Zenitist Manifesto." *Zenit* 1 (1921). (English translation available in *Between Worlds*, Benson and Forgács, eds.: 284–91.)

Migjeni [Millosh Gjergj Nikolla]. *Free Verse.* Trans. Robert Elsie. Peja: Dukagjini, 2001.

Milev, Geo. *The Road to Freedom: Poems and Prose Poems.* Grantham: Forest Books, 1990.

Miller, Tyrus. "Incomplete Modernities: Historicizing Yugoslavian Avant-Gardes." Rev. of *Impossible Histories: Historical Avant-gardes, Neo-avant-gardes, and Post-avant-gardes in Yugoslavia, 1918–1991*, ed. Dubravka Djurić and Miško Šuvaković and *Modernism in Serbia: The Elusive Margins of Belgrade Architecture, 1919–1941*, by Ljiljana Blagojević. *Modernism/modernity* 12:4 (2005): 713–22.

Moser, Charles A. *A History of Bulgarian Literature.* The Hague: Mouton, 1972.

Nankov, Nikita. *V ogledalnata staia: Sedem obraza na bulgarskiia literaturen selograd [In the Hall of Mirrors: Seven Images of Bulgarian Literary Hicktown].* Sofia: Izdatelstvo Sonm, 2001.

Naum, Gellu. *Vasco da Gama şi alte poheme/Vasco da Gama and Other Pohems (sic!).* Trans. Alistair Ian Blyth. Bucharest: Humanitas, 2007.

Nemet-Nejat, Murat, ed. and trans. *EDA: An Anthology of Contemporary Turkish Poetry.* Jersey City: Talisman House, 2004.

Pană, Saşa, ed. *Antologia literaturii române de avangardă [Anthology of Romanian Avant-garde Literature].* Bucharest: Editura pentru literatură, 1967.

Parla, Jale. "The Wounded Tongue: Turkey's Language Reform and the Canonicity of the Novel." *PMLA* 123.1 (January 2008): 27–40.

Peković, Ratko. *Ni rat ni mir: Panorama književnih polemika 1945–1965 [Neither War Nor Peace: A Panorama of Literary Debates 1945–1965].* Belgrade: Filip Višnjić, 1986.

Pipa, Arshi. *Contemporary Albanian Literature.* Boulder: East European Monographs; New York: Columbia University Press, 1991.

Prifti, Peter. *Unfinished Portrait of a Country.* Boulder: Eastern European Monographs; New York: Columbia University Press, 2005.

Pop, Ion. *Avangarda în literatura română [The Avant-garde in Romanian Literature].* Bucharest: Minerva, 1990.

Pourgouris, Marinos. "Topographies of Greek Modernism." Bahun-Radunović and Pourgouris 88–112.

Răileanu, Petre, ed. *L'avant-garde roumaine [Romanian Avant-garde].* Bucharest: Fondation Culturelle Roumaine, 1995.

Rainov, Nikolai. "White Tents." Trans. Zoya Marincheva. *Washington Square Review* 18 (Summer 2006): 66–68.

———. "The Wind." Trans. Zoya Marincheva. *Washington Square Review* 18 (Summer 2006): 63–65.

———. "Woman of Marble." Trans. Zoya Marincheva. *Washington Square Review* 18 (Summer 2006): 69–73.

Ritsos, Yannis. *Selected Poems, 1938–1988.* Brockport: BOA Editions, 1989.

Russeva, Violeta. *Aspekti na modernostta v bulgarskata literatura prez 20-te godini [Aspects of Modernism in Bulgarian Literature of the 1920s].* Veliko Turnovo: Alfa, 1993.

Sandqvist, Tom. *DADA East: The Romanians of Cabaret Voltaire.* Cambridge: MIT Press, 2006.

Seferis, George. *Collected Poems.* Princeton: Princeton University Press, 1995.

Shehri, Dhurata. "Ernest Koliqi and the 'Epiphany' of Modernity." *Balkan Modernisms: Approaches and Sources.* Forthcoming.

———. "*Koliqi mes malit dhe detit [Koliqi between Mountain and Sea].* Tirana: Onufri, 2006.

Sikelianos, Angelos. *Selected Poems*. London: Allen & Unwin, 1980.

Skopetea, Ellie. *I Dysi tis Anatolis: Eikones apo to telos tis Othomanikis Autokratorias [The Orient's West: Last Images of the Ottoman Empire]*. Athens: Gnosi, 1992.

Smith, Anthony D. "Nationalism and Modernity." Benson 68–80.

Smith, Neil. *Uneven Development: Nature, Capital, and the Production of Space*. 1974. 3rd ed. Athens: University of Georgia Press, 2008.

Starova, Luan. *Faïk Konitza et Guillaume Apollinaire: Une amitié européenne [Faïk Konitza and Guillaume Apollinaire: A European Friendship]*. Paris: L'Esprit des Péninsules, 1998.

Stråth, Bo. "Introduction: Europe as a Discourse." *Europe and the Other and Europe as the Other*. Ed. Bo Stråth. Brussels: PIE Lang, 2000. 13–44.

Šuvaković, Miško. "Impossible Histories." *Impossible Histories: Historical Avant-gardes, Neo-avant-gardes, and Post-avant-gardes in Yugoslavia, 1918–1991*. Ed. Dubravka Djurić and Miško Šuvaković. Cambridge: MIT Press, 2003.

Tanpınar, Ahmet Hamdi. *The Time Regulation Institute*. Trans. Ender Gürol. Madison: Turko-Tatar Press, 2002.

Taylor, Charles. *Sources of the Self: The Making of the Modern Identity*. Cambridge: Harvard University Press, 1992.

Todorova, Maria. *Imagining the Balkans*. Oxford: Oxford University Press, 1997.

Tsoukalas, Constantin. "The Irony of Symbolic Reciprocities—The Greek Meaning of 'Europe' as a Historical Inversion of the European Meaning of 'Greece.'" *The Meaning of Europe: Variety and Contention within and among Nations*. Ed. Mikael af Malmborg and Bo Stråth. Oxford: Berg, 2002. 27–50.

Tzara, Tristan. *Primele Poeme. First Poems*. Trans. Michael Impey and Brian Swann. New York: New Rivers, 1976.

Tziovas, Dimitris, ed. *Greek Modernism and Beyond: Essays in Honor of Peter Bien*. Lanham: Rowman & Littlefield, 1997.

Tziovas, Dimitris. *The Nationism of the Demoticists and Its Impact on Their Literary Theory (1888–1930)*. Amsterdam: Adolf M. Hakkert, 1986.

Valaoritis, Nanos, and Thanasis Maskaleris, eds. and trans. *Twentieth-Century Greek Poetry*. Jersey City: Talisman House, 2000.

Varga, Adriana. "Periphery to Center and Back: Exploring Dada and the Absurd in the Context of Romanian Literary Traditions." Bahun-Radunović and Pourgouris 129–53.

Vayenas, Nasos. "Hellenocentrism and the Literary Generation of the Thirties." Tziovas 43–48.

Werner, Michael, and Bénédicte Zimmermann. "Beyond Comparison: *Histoire Croisée* and the Challenge of Reflexivity." *History and Theory* 45 (February 2006): 30–50.

Urmuz [Demetru Dem. Demetrescu Buzău]. *Pagini bizarre/Weird Pages*. Trans. Stavros Deligiorgis. Bucharest: Cartea Românească, 1985.

CHAPTER 2

....

CARIBBEAN MODERNISM: PLANTATION TO PLANETARY

....

MARY LOU EMERY

THE recent emphasis on space in modernist studies takes us back to time, or rather, to newly modern times. In the new critical practices of "geo-" and "polycentric" modernisms, regions of the globe not previously considered sites of modernist activity, or even under modernity's influence, come forward as parts of a dynamically interconnected field, expanding modernism's spatial reach and decentering its sites of artistic creativity.[1] Inevitably, new and modern times emerge. If these times seem uncanny in their doubling of an older modernism's "new," it is not only because we have experienced the excitement of making it new before. It is, more significantly, because they appear as the previously suppressed and now released "Other" to that older modernism. They emerge as the local history of a region (China, the Sudan) newly charted on modernism's enlarged map; or as an eclipsed past (the Middle Passage, the Haitian Revolution) brought forward newly significant, even central, to our concepts of modernity and modernism; or as a familiar history (the English Civil War) read differently so that, for example, we question the privileged play of freedom in modernist style.[2] However, stretching our sense of modernism's place and time, we are doing more than acknowledging alternate locations of modernist production or extended periods of modernist activity. With this newly spatialized model of modernism, new notions of time itself—as sedimented and cumulative, for example—become possible and necessary. As a result, our sense of the "global" is transforming—from an awareness of the worldwide interconnections of information, commerce, and culture, vastly accelerated in the past century, to what critics from Caribbean, comparative, postcolonial, American, and now modernist studies are calling the "planetary."

The concept of the planetary appears frequently in appeals for newer models of modernism, often with different meanings and implications.[3] I do not attempt in this chapter to fully trace its history in literary studies, but rather to value the possibilities certain versions of the concept suggest. Neither equivalent to the global nor opposed to it, the planetary registers possibilities of multiple spatial and temporal dimensions beyond the rational ordering of the global. And for reasons I will discuss later, the concept should, necessarily, remain difficult to define. For now, it's important to note that the planetary view as I invoke it here refers not to a vast scale that produces distant, abstracted knowledge, but to a weblike interrelatedness that might be associated with the "conjunctural" approach described in this volume by Susan Stanford Friedman. The planetary, however, exceeds the conjunctural approach in its attention to the earth itself. Through alternate temporalities and evoking an ecological imagination, the planetary vision becomes especially compelling in the context of the Caribbean. It is from critics, poets, and novelists of the Caribbean that this concept first emerged in literary studies, and in their writings, we find dynamic transitions from global to planetary readings of modernity and modernism.

In the work of Caribbean writers and critics, transitions from a rationally ordered model of the global to the more elusive, still-evolving planetary model pivot on four interrelated visions of a *contramodernity*: in foundational scenes of the Middle Passage, the Amerindian presence, the Haitian Revolution, and what the Martinican theorist and novelist Édouard Glissant has called the matrix of the plantation. Homi Bhabha's concept of contramodernity, "contingent to modernity, discontinuous or in contention with it," helps us to make a crucial distinction in assessing the emergent models of modernism and their potential for this planetary vision: we can revise modernism as global by merely adding new and different modernities to a picture already drawn, or we can reimagine the larger picture by locating the constitutive alterity simultaneously within and outside of modernity, a project that recognizes the previously unassimilated as necessarily so (6). Caribbean writers have contributed to the latter project by recognizing in these foundational scenes of contramodernity the ongoing presence of a circum-Atlantic past—a past in which particular interactions among land, sea, and human beings are crucial to the formation of modernity yet continually suppressed in modernity's received history.

Countering the rationalist logic of received histories, Caribbean writers work also with a *contramodern poetics of the past*, as in Glissant's trope of *marronage*, the revolutionary flight and improvisational resistance of escaped slaves. Developed further by Simon Gikandi, *marronage* offers a model for new modernisms and a framework for reading Caribbean literatures as modernist. Additionally crucial to the transition from global to planetary is the figure of "limbo gateways" in the poetry of Kamau Brathwaite (Barbados) and the essays of Wilson Harris (Guyana)—a method of reading, differently, the broken parts of cultures and their improvisational reconnections through creolized arts. Glissant's model of "Relation" offers another version of this broken past, reconnected and extended worldwide. Finally, in Glissant's analysis of what he terms the "cry of the plantation," we find the particularly Caribbean terrain—geographical, temporal, cultural, and ecological—that grounds a planetary vision, evolving from, but also countering the global.

Exploring these foundational scenes and poetics as envisioned by Caribbean writers, I hope to demonstrate in this chapter the development and significance of Caribbean modernism. A larger, related argument, however, concerns the significance of the plantation to the emerging concept of the planetary in modernist studies. As a point of departure for rethinking the Caribbean in these terms, I read Claude McKay's *Banjo* and Jean Rhys' *Voyage in the Dark* as transforming the plantation mythologies of slave economies by extending the "cry of the plantation" worldwide, remapping space and reimagining time in ways that approach the larger scale of alterity evoked by the planetary.

Even as the emerging field of Caribbean modernist studies opens new narratives of the past and new models for time and space, the place name "Caribbean" troubles our notions of geographical location. A region of mostly islands, it also includes the rims of two continents and echoes the name of the sea that surrounds and connects them to other islands and continental landmasses. Its topography ranges from dense rain forests to island beaches; mountains, rivers and waterfalls to savannahs and swamps. Taking one of its names from indigenous peoples, for over five hundred years, this "small place"[4] has been shaped and reshaped by incursions of Europeans and the mostly forced or coerced migrations of peoples from West Africa, India, China, and the Middle East who, in their encounters with one another, have created uniquely creolized languages and cultures. The Caribbean is also a place from which these newly created peoples have migrated in their own diaspora, so that the Caribbean occupies, among other places, Toronto, London, New York City, and Miami. Perhaps nowhere more than in "the Caribbean" does the study of place open the past and overturn previous assumptions of geography, history, and identity. This is particularly true for our constructions of modernity and global modernisms.

For the Caribbean, long perceived as "elsewhere" to *modernity* and marginal to *modernism*, the two terms are inextricably linked. What we have called modernity, whether dated from seventeenth-century Anglo-Saxon appeals to liberty or from eighteenth-century European notions of Enlightenment, depended economically, politically, and discursively on the slave trade and colonization of the Americas. The concepts of freedom, reason, and the rights of man required their constitutive opposites, systematically located in the apparently ungoverned savagery of the "New World." There, against all odds—or because of them—creolized forms of language, music, and the visual and dramatic arts emerged from multiple traditions in inequitable and frequently violent encounters of numerous world cultures; yet, these cultural innovations appeared as negligible or exotic, cast on the margins of European high culture. In recovering the contramodernity of the Caribbean, paradigms of the circum-Atlantic suggest new readings of Caribbean literature as modernisms.

CARIBBEAN MODERNISM: PLANTATION TO PLANETARY

These modernisms emanate from a region, the sea surrounding it, and the transformative passages to and from virtually all parts of the world. We can read Caribbean modernism as constitutive of a previously defined modernism and also counter to it: simultaneously interconnected with alternate modernisms, for instance, of Rabindranath Tagore and the Bengali Renaissance, Latin American surrealism, the Mexican muralists, William Faulkner, Jean Toomer, and the southern United States, the Harlem Renaissance, and the Francophone cultural and political movement of Négritude.[5] Its globalism is foundational, inherent in the creation, since the sixteenth century, of creolized cultures and their art forms that continually "make it new" while contributing to the modernities and modernisms of other places, such as England, France, and the United States. To recognize the inherent globalism of these creolized arts means also to acknowledge the global forces of European conquest, the slave trade, and empire building from which they emerged. These are aspects of modernity only recently explored in Western literary studies from any but a Eurocentric perspective. European philosophies of aesthetics have typically dismissed creolized arts as imitations at best, while European histories have found the historical contributions to modernity of enslaved and colonized peoples to be "unthinkable."

FOUNDATIONAL SCENES

As intellectuals from the Caribbean have stressed, an "unthinkable modernity," forged in the obsessively suppressed past of the black and circum-Atlantic, generated spatial and temporal dynamics only barely discerned through empire's overwhelmingly privileged nationalist geographies, vectoral movements, and linear histories.[6] Insisting that we recognize those suppressed spatio/temporal dynamics, they have repeatedly emphasized the centrality of the Middle Passage, the Amerindian presence, the Haitian Revolution, and, as I will discuss in a subsequent section, the plantation, to a modernity that consistently denies their significance. Many of these writers also resist realism in historical and literary narratives. They have created instead far-flung yet rooted modernisms in response to modernity as already formulated and to the contramodernity their writings illuminate.

Citing writers from the Caribbean, including Édouard Glissant and Kamau Brathwaite, Ian Baucom argues that the foundational scenes of this contramodernity are those of the Middle Passage—the slave trade, slave ship, and the haunting image of the drowning slave, cast overboard for the sake of an insurance payment.[7] In Baucom's analysis, the formal contracts between eighteenth-century insurance companies and slave ship owners signal a cycle of finance capital that activated a "long twentieth century," extending from the eighteenth century and continuing into the present. Understanding history in this way brings the current sense of globalization as shaped through financial markets and trade into immediate relation with imperial forces and fortunes of earlier centuries. This meaning of the term globalization accords with Gayatri Spivak's distinction between the "global" and the "planetary." Recognizing that globalization has a long history in ancient world systems, she identifies the "financialization of the globe" as a characteristically modern and imperialist feature. In distinction (but not in opposition) to the global, she proposes "planetarity." A necessarily elusive concept, the planetary opens imaginative spaces and temporalities from which literature may emerge apart, yet also from, the violent market forces of globalization, gesturing beyond their terms and conditions for being.[8]

Such literatures invoke alternate times, including the sense of time described by Baucom as accumulative rather than linear, and circulatory rather than progressive. In his analysis, the Middle Passage spaces of the ship and the sea become sedimented with time's multiple layers.[9] Those past modern times are still here, now, as writers ranging from Jean Rhys to Simone Schwartz-Bart and Erna Brodber; Claude McKay to Aimé Césaire and Wilson Harris; George Lamming to Michelle Cliff and Fred D'Aguiar insist.[10] Often expressed through experimental and hybridized poetics, their modern times oscillate, spiral, circulate, and repeat; they appear as layered sediments, light years, palimpsests, and holographs; and they emanate from land and seascapes imprinted with signs of the past: rock paintings, tides, cosmograms, riverbeds, bottle trees, waterfalls, and the bush gone to ruin.

Their contramodern temporalities bring forward other equally foundational scenes—those from the encounter between conquistadores and Amerindians and those from the Haitian Revolution—as crucial to the shaping of modernities and generative of modernisms. These scenes also haunt the present, layering the "long twentieth century" with other spaces and alternate concepts of time and self. Wilson Harris, Pauline Melville, and the painter Aubrey Williams—all from Guyana—have emphasized the significance of Amerindian cultures as formative of modernity's landscapes and what Harris deems the potential for "the open capacity of the person." This capacity for a fulfillment of historically broken heritages contrasts to the "sovereign individual" of European modernity and narrative realism ("Tradition" 143). In Harris's experimental fiction, native encounters with Europeans, and often images depicting those encounters, appear as myths of European history undone by native arts, such as *zemi* carvings and bone flutes, emblems of space and time formed differently. The Amerindian presence appears also in work by writers from islands where the native people were supposedly exterminated, but where, in some instances, they still live, and where their cultures still have an impact.[11] Harris argues that the indigenous presence offers glimpses—through the "monument[s] of consolidation" that realist narratives present—of other times, spaces, and ways of being ("Tradition" 142). Recognizing the near erasure yet ongoing impact of indigenous cultures in the Americas yields for Harris alternate temporalities and subjectivities, otherwise invisible within the modernity they help create. The landscape itself inscribes the Amerindian presence in the pictographs of the Guyanese *timehri*, for example, and thus signals multitemporalities in the same space, the ground, so to speak, for the simultaneously catastrophic and creative encounters among peoples that have shaped the Caribbean.[12]

That these peoples actively contributed to modernity while at the same time becoming its objects is a point made by a number of Caribbean intellectuals in their analysis of the Haitian Revolution.[13] As they have argued, the Haitian revolutionaries fought for liberty, equality, and fraternity, according to ideals absorbed through French colonial culture joined with West African notions of freedom.[14] More specifically and paradoxically, they fought for freedom from what was arguably the first modern system of labor, plantation slavery (see James; Scott; Mintz; Benítez-Rojo). Their successful revolt extended Enlightenment notions of liberty to include the very slaves claimed as rightful property by their revolutionary counterparts in France and North America. J. Michael Dash has pointed to the early years of the Revolution, before Napoleon's opposition turned it into a nationalist war, as generating a radically new and universal subject of modernity—transnational, transracially "black," and free.[15] This more truly universal subject, however, remained an object of property in the Anglo-European imagination and in its world economy until the mid-nineteenth century and later, making the Haitian Revolution an unthinkable event or, at best, a distant and absurd imitation of the real thing.

The Barbadian novelist and essayist George Lamming has insisted on recognizing this unthinkable moment, depicting it in the portrait of an instrument of labor, a plow, transformed into a speaking subject. For Lamming, this is also a portrait of Caliban turned revolutionary, "re-ordering history," and demanding "some new sense of language":

> Some new sight as well as some new sense of language is required to bear witness to the miracle of the plough which now talks. For as those hands in unison move forward, the plough achieves a somersault which reverses its traditional posture. Its head goes into the ground, and the prongs, throat-near, stand erect in the air, ten points of steel announcing danger. (121)

We can interpret the new language prompted by Caliban's reversal as a global modernism, a truly revolutionary response to the modernity that conscripted him (to borrow David Scott's phrase) as a commodity in a global market of finance capital and an object fought over by several European powers.[16] Transnational, transcultural, and transracial, this new language erupted in the contradictory encounter of global forces of modernity, those that made human beings into objects of property and those that promised emancipation. It continued to develop through the dynamic interaction of creolized cultures and languages of the Caribbean with the other modernities and modernisms of Europe and North America. It is now beginning to find a place as one among a number of global modernisms—and while we may view the bigger picture of these modernisms in relation to one another as spatially figured, this new modernist project calls upon us also to recognize the alternate temporalities and transitions to a planetary vision made possible through their interconnections.

LIMBO GATEWAYS

To actually "think" modernity in these terms, Caribbean writers and critics have worked less through the logic of historical analysis and more through a poetics of the past by formulating specifically Caribbean tropes for "re-ordering history." One of the major tropes in this poetics is that of "limbo." A staple of carnival and night-club acts, the limbo dance may seem, as it does to Walcott in "What the Twilight Says," a sign of the degradation of Caribbean cultures under neocolonialism. However, in the late 1960s, the poetics of Kamau Brathwaite's epic trilogy, *The Arrivants*, transformed the limbo into a sign of the Middle Passage and the creative survival of African cultures in the Americas. Taken up by other writers, especially Wilson Harris, the trope has expanded to suggest a gateway among diverse cultures into a "protean space," a history ruptured by "interior time," and "a new kind of drama, novel, and poem." Harris's essay, "History, Fable, and Myth in the Caribbean and the Guianas," appeared in 1970, one year after the publication of *Islands*, the third long poem of Brathwaite's trilogy, and quotes the following lines:

> drum stick knock
> and the darkness is over me
> knees spread wide
> and the water is hiding me
> *limbo*
> *limbo like me* (157)

In Brathwaite's poem, the limbo dance becomes a means of survival in the cramped spaces of the slave ship, a ritual invocation of the African gods, and a trickster strategy, related to the spider fables of Anancy. Harris extends the trope to signify a trans-Caribbean link among European, African, and Amerindian cultures and, through association with Haitian vodun, a bridge across Anglophone and Francophone cultures of the Caribbean. Instead of superstition in their elements of folk cultures, Harris finds "arts of the imagination" (156) and gateways to a buried philosophy of history. Punning on "limbo" with the absent presence signified by "phantom limb" allows Harris to associate the limbo with spiritual traditions of many cultures in the reassembly of "dismembered slave and god," including the Egyptian Osiris, resurrected Christ, "many-armed deity of India," legends of the ancient Caribes, and Haitian vodun rites of possession (158). An interiorized drama of trance and memory exteriorized in the kinetic sculpture of dance, the Haitian vodun ritual brings the "life from within" and the "life from without" into communion and, thus, "has indeed a close bearing on the language of fiction, on the language of art" (161–62). These languages of fiction and art appear close to modernism in their emphasis on interiority and form, but much more is at stake than simply a new aesthetic, even though it requires an innovative, even transgressive style.

This limbo imagination is crucial, Harris argues, to the rewriting of history, for it disrupts the uniformity of historical narrative and opens its *"habitual boundaries of prejudice"* to the renaissance potential of cross-cultural communities (164). The vehicle for imagining this new space and time is literary language, and Harris's writing, in critical essays and fiction, performs as "limbo gateway," drawing especially on the arts of Amerindia to catalyze his radical and often lyrical ruptures from realism. In *Tumatumari*, for example, an experimental novel published in 1968, Harris responded indirectly to the events leading to Guyana's recent independence through a reflection on and narrative performance of the rewriting of history. The dominant tropes for this revisionary process are those of Amerindian culture, including a Mayan ceremonial well, or *cenote*; the Olmec heads of Mexico; the Guyanese legend of Chief Kaie; and the "sleeping," painted rocks, or *tumatumari*, of the title. Harris interweaves these figures with allusions to classical Greek, medieval, and renaissance arts of memory, and Afro-Caribbean traditions of spirit possession. The interplay of such diverse elements defamiliarizes and reconfigures them through a dynamic, culturally syncretic prose.

When the novel's protagonist, Prudence, dreams of carving on the rock lid of a well a date found in papers written by her father, the Chair of History, her pen slips. Transposed, the numbers create a "rock of association—primitive gateway" through which she inadvertently links her family history with "the earliest exploring steps . . . taken by the Mediterranean world" (88). This "primitive gateway" reconnects Prudence to the conquered peoples of Amerindian, African, and Asian descent haunting her own psyche and lineage, but suppressed by her father's familial and nationalist histories. The connection, made through the gateway of the *tumatumari*, indicates a suppressed ancestral link across cultures and times. It depends on a slip not only of the pen, but also of the categories separating races, ethnicities, genders, nations, and historical periods. By animating the "sleeping rocks," Prudence's slip also erases the lines opposing the extra-human and human worlds, a crucial element, as I shall discuss later, of a planetary vision.[17]

In Harris's Prudence, we see the necessity of "re-ordering history" and remapping space for the generation of Caribbean writers that includes Harris, James, Lamming, Sam Selvon, and others. Their "new sense of language," along with the writing of Alejo Carpentier, Paule Marshall, Zee Edgell, Merle Hodge, and Michelle Cliff inspired Simon Gikandi to write the first study of Caribbean modernism, published in 1992, and titled *Writing in Limbo: Modernism and Caribbean Literature*.[18]

Gikandi argues that writers from the Caribbean worked in a limbo space fraught with anxieties concerning colonial cultural authority, including the conflicted intersections of colonialism and modernism. However, the poetics made possible through creolization allowed writers such as Aimé Césaire to oppose colonial histories by appropriating modernist styles of surrealism to spark a newly visionary cross-cultural imagination. Citing the anthropologist Richard Price, the Haitian writer René Depestre, and the African American critic Houston Baker, Gikandi explores the possibilities of *marronage*, the rebellious flight of enslaved natives and Africans, as a metaphor for Caribbean modernism. In his analysis this modernism escapes Western colonial culture by appropriating its skills and knowledge and improvising beyond them.

An enabling colonial anxiety remains paramount in Gikandi's analysis of Caribbean modernism, and it leads him to dismiss Anglo-American "high modernism," deeming it an insignificant context for Caribbean writers. Though this judgment further obscures the suppressed contributions of Caribbean writers to what has been called Anglo-American or European modernism, it does allow Gikandi to suspend the conventional determinants of period and style in order to propose a modernism that responds instead to conditions of colonial exile, problems of language in a colonial context, contradictions in forming new nations, and the colonialist repression of Caribbean perspectives on global historical events. This dislocation of modernism and redefinition of modernity has opened the way for new configurations of modernisms generally and, more specifically, for further considerations of Caribbean modernism. Subsequent critical studies have explored, for example, the relation between Caribbean nationalism and modernism, transatlantic modernist poetics, canon formations of Caribbean literatures, the intersections of colonial, postcolonial, and Caribbean literatures, and the emphasis on visuality in a transatlantic Caribbean modernism.[19] Also following *Writing in Limbo*, Gikandi's more recent work has examined modernist cultures from an alternate and crucially important direction, recognizing the contributions of Africa and its diaspora to the arts of modernism and constructions of modernity.[20]

CRIES OF THE PLANTATION

As a figure for remapping space, reimagining the past, and rewriting history in accordance with alternate notions of time, Harris's "limbo gateways" bear close resemblance to the "poetics of Relation" advanced by Édouard Glissant. And it is not surprising that recent proposals for new models of alternative, geo-, or global modernisms and modernities refer to Glissant's work. His "poetics of Relation" has inspired, among others, Charles Pollard's *New World Modernisms*, Susan Stanford Friedman's "Periodizing Modernism," and Ian Baucom's remarkable analysis of modernity's time in *Specters of the Atlantic: Finance Capital, Slavery, and the Philosophy of History*. Glissant reads Caribbean cultures in a global perspective as a weblike relational dynamic based on three interrelated geographical and historical movements. One trajectory moves outward from an imperial "Center" toward a peripheral horizon, while another reverses it in the journeys from the periphery to the Center undertaken by colonial émigrés. And in a third dynamic, "the arrowlike projection becomes curved . . . makes every periphery into a center; furthermore, it abolishes the very notion of center and periphery" (29). In Glissant's analysis, these "entanglements of a worldwide relation" emerge in Francophone literatures of the late nineteenth to early twentieth centuries, entangled with the cultures they broke into, and effecting a Relation of uncertainty and errancy, in which all cultures are shaped by one another but not in equitable or mutual relationships, rather as an "open totality."[21] The circulation of literary writing thus moves beyond the cultural expressions of distinct peoples and conjectures "the evolution of the planet Earth" (32). This planetary vision of openness allows Glissant to insist that these dynamics operate for all other literatures, each time from a different perspective, each time opening into "the fluctuating complexity of the world" (32).

While this vision is suggestive for new models of modernism, for Glissant the planetary is rooted in something very particular—the plantation. In accord with arguments put forward by other scholars of the Caribbean such as C. L. R. James, Sidney Mintz, Philip Curtin, and David Scott, the plantation becomes, in Glissant's writing, a foundational matrix of modernity. Its legacies remain in places of destitution and poverty across the Americas. However, in these extensions of the plantation, its role as laboratory of modernity and catalyst for modernist arts has continued in what Glissant calls "the cry of the Plantation, transfigured into the speech of the world" (73).[22]

Referring not to the plantation system but to Glissant's notion of Relation, Susan Stanford Friedman has proposed a planetary model for our mapping of modernism ("Periodizing" 430).[23] If we retain, however, Glissant's crucial link to the plantation and keep in mind that versions of the plantation system have appeared worldwide—including in Hawaii and the Pacific islands, India, and Africa—we might find grounds for a polycentric and multitemporal planetary modernism in these multiple, alternate locations. Philip Curtin's comparative world history of the "plantation complex," published in 1990, the same year as Glissant's *Poetics of Relation*, suggests the basis for such an extension of Glissant's relational connection between planet and plantation. Wai Chee Dimock cites Curtin in her proposal for extending the spatial and temporal reach of American literary studies to something approximating the planetary. The history of slavery documented in Curtin's work becomes evidence for the much broader context ("five continents and some thirteen hundred years") needed in order to understand slavery in the United States (see Dimock, "Introduction" 7). Implicit, however, in Dimock's turn to Curtin's study in an essay concerned with the planetary perspective is the foundational importance of the plantation to modernity and to modernism. For Glissant, its importance stems from the dynamic contradiction between the apparent marginality of the plantation and its actual place in the global economy.

Arguing that the plantation was, in its appearance, a closed and pyramidically hierarchical structure, Glissant points to its actual dependence on the politics and markets of the external world and to the constant mixings and crossings that broke through its hierarchical and enclosing borders.[24] In this intensely contradictory environment, literature emerged as an act of survival among those enslaved, initially as an oral culture born paradoxically of an imposed silence. This literature of tales, proverbs, and songs worked "to say without saying" through detours or

discontinuities that he compares to acts of *marronage*. As in Simon Gikandi's evocation of *marronage* as a metaphor for Caribbean modernism, this revolutionary
escape has come to represent for many critics and writers of the Caribbean a resistant and creative aesthetic strategy. As a trope it underscores for Glissant the importance of movement in the process of creolization. Rather than a static "Creole"
identity, creolization proceeds rapidly but with interruptions and qualities that, in
his description, resemble those typically attributed to modernism:

> Thus, Caribbean literatures, whether in English, Spanish, or French, tended to
> introduce obscurities and breaks—like so many detours—into the material they
> dealt with; putting into practice, like the Plantation tales, processes of intensifica-
> tion, breathlessness, digression, and immersion of individual psychology within
> the drama of a common destiny. The symbolism of situations prevailed over the
> refinement of realisms, by encompassing, transcending, and shedding light upon
> it. (71)

Glissant continues this description of a modernism born of the plantation by identifying its "driving force and hidden design" as the "derangement of memory" (71).
By this, he means a memory and a sense of time not tied to the calendar but emerging
from the marginalized "void" of the plantation where multiracial and multilin-
guistic connections break through the apparent clarity and linearity of Western
thought.

Transfigured through creolization, these forms of expression burst out in musical form through spirituals, the blues, calypso, salsa, reggae, and jazz, affecting cultures worldwide. Even after the plantation's decline, these cries echo in the arts and
literatures of the Caribbean, beginning in the modernist movements of, for example,
the Harlem Renaissance, Négritude, and *modernismo* and continuing into what we
might call postcolonial modernisms of the African and Caribbean diasporas.

In the Anglophone Caribbean, movements on behalf of labor and for colonial independence in the 1920s and 1930s catalyzed new arts, literary journals,
and art schools that were simultaneously rooted in specific islands, yet also
energized by transatlantic modernist movements to which émigrés from those
specific Caribbean locations made important contributions. Sculptors Edna
Manley and Ronald Moody from Jamaica; editor, playwright, and poet Una
Marson, also from Jamaica; novelist, playwright, and cultural critic C. L. R.
James, from Trinidad; novelist and short story writer Jean Rhys from Dominica
(for more on Rhys, see contributions to this volume by Kalliney [chapter 17] and
Lyon [chapter 16]); and poet, journalist, and novelist Claude McKay from
Jamaica all contributed to a transatlantic Caribbean modernism that made an
important, if often unacknowledged, impact in England, the United States, and
Europe (see Emery, *Modernism, the Visual, and Caribbean Literature*). Leading
figures of Négritude, for example, credited Claude McKay's novel *Banjo* (1929)
with inspiring their politics and aesthetics, while McKay became a noted poet
and novelist in the Harlem Renaissance and a socialist journalist in England.
Jean Rhys' novel *Voyage in the Dark* (1934) also received credit as "our first novel
of Negritude" (Ramchand 3), and, as I will argue, extended the plantation's cry

to join with a tradition in the European visual arts to record the entangled if silenced voices of women enslaved in the colonies and cast onto the urban streets of England and Europe.

Plantation Melodies and *Cries of London*

Read together, *Banjo* and *Voyage in the Dark* expand modernism into what Glissant calls an "open totality" of uncertain, mutually shaping Relation. They bring inflections of black and creole speech, song, and dance to the innovations of modernist prose, and they embed scenes of Africa, the American South, Harlem, and the Caribbean within narratives centered in France and England. Creating new models for aesthetics and for rethinking "race," these two novels transform nostalgic "plantation melodies" into webs of Relation, linking migrant workers across the Americas and Europe and also across the centuries of what we have called modernity.[25] Both novels evoke a palimpsest of times and mutable spaces of land and sea, gesturing toward a larger vision of the planetary even as they portray the contradictory violence and creativity of global exchange.

Throughout *Banjo*, subtitled *A Story without a Plot*, jazz and the blues punctuate the narratives with their bawdy lyrics and strong rhythms. Bursts of musical energy shape the prose, animate the characters, and move them from one café, brothel, or bar to another. The loose couplings of the picaresque narrative echo the improvisational qualities of the music played and the lives lived by the characters—drifters and often unemployed dockworkers from Africa and its diaspora, temporarily landed on the beaches of Marseilles. This "story without a plot" does not, however, wander randomly on a surface of improvised present moments but, focusing on the banjo, continually opens onto layered depths of the past, bringing to the narrative troubling and contradictory cultural associations.

When the main character, named for the banjo he carries with him, declares, "I never part with this, buddy. It is moh than a gal, moh than a pal; it's mahself" (6), he identifies with the musical instrument associated variously with Africa, minstrelsy, blues, jazz, and nostalgic scenes of the U.S. plantation. When another character nicknamed Goosey insists that a banjo is "the instrument of slavery," that it means bondage, Dixie, and "the land of cotton and massa and missus and black mammy," Banjo rejects what he calls that "time past stuff" in favor of "lively tunes," "saxophone-jazzing," and "them 'blues'" (90–91). Their argument reveals the conflicting meanings of the banjo in the 1920s: an icon of plantation nostalgia beginning to signify also an original black creativity in the blues and jazz. Moreover, between the mid-nineteenth century, when plantation stereotypes of blackface minstrelsy reached their highest popularity, and the early twentieth century, when banjos held large sections of their own in the jazz orchestras of New Orleans and Harlem, the banjo appeared in another and unexpected place— in the hands of young upper-class white women (see figure 2.1). Interpreted as

Figure 2.1 : Frances Benjamin Johnston, "Miss Apperson" c. 1895 platinum print, Library of Congress, Prints and Photographs Division, Washington, DC

emblems of transgressive bohemian independence and eroticism, this coupling of the banjo with women complicated its already conflicted racial meanings (Burns). Even the shape of the instrument could suggest gendered and sexual associations, ranging from masculine and phallic to voluptuously feminine (see figure 2.2 on facing page).

All the while, the banjo retained and transformed its origins in Africa, sur- facing across the Atlantic throughout the Caribbean as well as the southern and the eastern United States—some of the many places represented in McKay's novel by the migrant workers playing music in the Café African in Marseilles.[26] This café becomes the scene of an ecstatic ensemble performance as Banjo and his friends play repeatedly the song, "Shake That Thing." We could read the banjo in this scene as a "limbo gateway" for a new black masculine agency that displaces the plantation nostalgia of blackface minstrelsy in favor of the cry of blues and jazz

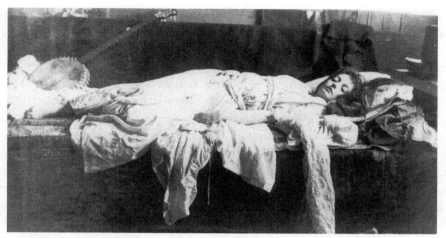

Figure 2.2 : Thomas Eakins, 1885, "Blanche Gilroy in Classical Costume Reclining with Banjo"

orchestras of Harlem, transported across the Atlantic again, this time to modernist, cosmopolitan Europe. It is a momentous transformation, especially when we consider the history and marketing of the song Banjo plays.

Just three years before McKay made this song emblematic of a new black international jazz, a 1926 cover for the sheet music to "Shake That Thing" revealed a lingering commercial reliance on associations with black minstrelsy. The cover credits the African American composer and banjo player "Papa" Charlie Jackson by name only, giving over the rest of the page to two images. The main image depicts a looming blackface minstrel, dancing in tuxedo and top hat and waving his cane; in the other hand, he dangles a tiny marionette reproducing his likeness but with a few differences—a white beard, a cast on its leg, and crutches.[27] Alongside this doubled figure appears a second image: a framed photograph of an apparently all-white band that supplants the actual composer, who does not appear at all, and his signature six-string banjo.[28] Whatever else is happening in this complex image, the reproduction of the minstrel, manipulating in his own hands a crippled version of himself in the figure of the puppet, self-reflexively comments on an image that defiantly repeats itself with renewed and, perhaps, disabling power.

In vivid contrast to these racist marketing strategies, Banjo's playing of "Shake That Thing" at the Café African brings the banjo's African origins and Middle Passage crossings into view, along with its immediate global "magic" among the enthusiastic audience of black men from all over the African diaspora. In this "great event," Banjo transforms persistent plantation stereotypes into what Glissant calls the "speech of the world." But this scene and others like it alternate with misogynist outbursts and violence against women that shape the narrative almost as much as the music, indicating that at least one feature of blackface minstrelsy has not disappeared—the portrayal of black women as grotesque and comic.[29]

Women often appear as grotesque, if not comic, in *Banjo* and are frequently targets of verbal and physical violence. In one scene, a sailor slaps a prostitute, knocks her down, and kicks her. The men's responses range from disgust toward the woman (perceived as "a demi-crone," "loathsome white worm," and "obscene bird" [93]) to appreciation of the "tout" who knocks her down ("Got to treat 'em rough, all right") and murderous anger ("I woulda choked her to death with these black hands of mine" [100]). This violence follows on another transcendent scene of music making, one that comes the "nearest that Banjo, quite unconscious of it, ever came to an aesthetic realization of his orchestra" (97).[30] Noting that Banjo presides at the center of all these performances, continually equated with the "dominating" banjo he plays, we might turn to the instrument itself and the temporal layering of contradictory cultural associations it carries in our reading of the misogynist violence that punctuates these scenes. The charged sexual and gendered associations with young upper-class white women could help to explain the violent rejection of the feminine. But also the ambiguous circuiting in the song's lyrics of sexual references to "jelly roll" and "that thing," and the feminizing, infantilizing, and crippling of black men in stereotypes of plantation nostalgia may all add to the troubling cultural baggage burdening Banjo's instrument and through which he must assert the freedom of his music and vagabond life. In *Banjo*, women seem to pay the price for the victory won in transforming "the instrument of slavery" into "saxophone jazzing" and "them 'blues'."

When it is time to leave Marseilles, Banjo casually abandons a woman who has cared for him, claiming, "A woman is a conjunction. Gawd fixed her different from us in moh ways than one. And theah's things we can git away with all the time and she just kain't" (326). As much or more than his music, Banjo's mobility matters. An exclusively masculine freedom, it remains precarious, requiring repeated and often violent rejections of the feminine and of actual women—a freedom that, as Banjo recognizes, a woman cannot "git away with."

As if to prove Banjo right, Jean Rhys creates in *Voyage in the Dark* the character of a young woman from the Caribbean, drifting about England in 1914, who definitely does not get away with anything. In Rhys' Caribbean modernism, however, multiple voices of migrant laboring women from across the globe and the centuries converge in the portrayal of Anna Morgan, creating a counterpart to the migrant workers in *Banjo* and their conflicted global music. An underpaid performer with a traveling music hall company, Anna has been disinherited by her family, seduced and abandoned by an older wealthy Englishman, and increasingly isolated from any community such as the one Banjo experiences. Drafted into an amateurish form of prostitution, she comes into contact with some visiting American men, an encounter that sparks memories of minstrel songs, including "Waiting for the Robert E. Lee" and the Stephen Foster song "Camptown Racecourse." Among a number of songs that surface in Anna's consciousness, these explicitly evoke plantation nostalgia, reflecting on her split colonial subjectivity and sexual exploitation. In the final section of the novel, the narrative portrays Anna's fevered consciousness as she suffers the effects of an illegal abortion; here, scenes and voices from her past in the West Indies erupt alongside those from her present in England, including carnival costumes and masks and the song "Brown Girl in a Ring." Wallis Tinnie has claimed that through this song, Anna imaginatively asserts a disallowed black voice and embraces her "multiple selves" (279). These include an ancestral connection with an eighteen-year-old house slave, Maillotte Boyd, whose name Anna recalls from an old slave list at her mother's estate in Dominica. Through Tinnie's reading we can see how *Voyage in the Dark* opens the plantation myths countered in *Banjo* to further transformations. These register in the changes from minstrel masks that perpetuate plantation stereotypes to carnival masks that reverse and undermine them, and from Foster's plantation melodies to an African American ring song—a resounding "derangement of memory" and "cry of the plantation," in Glissant's terms, that reaches even farther when we consider the presence of a series of images called the "Cries of London."

These images decorate the rooms Anna temporarily inhabits, including the bedroom of a flat where she lies hemorrhaging from the abortion. Images of street hawkers, "Cries" first appeared in Paris in 1500, becoming established as a genre by 1550, and eventually characterizing the street peddlers of Nuremberg, Vienna, London, Boston, Philadelphia, and New York. As Sean Sheshgreen has demonstrated, the "Cries of London" portrayed urban street peddlers in styles and from perspectives that varied widely through the centuries—variously dignifying, ridiculing, naturalizing, and romanticizing sellers of everything from strawberries, brooms, and chairs to milk and sheet music. The London Cries reached the height of popularity in the Victorian period but persisted as popular images into the twentieth century. They pictured local scenes and characters, but from cities all over the world and, when sold as broadsheets, were often accompanied by maps so that Samuel Pepys claimed they offered a discovery "of the whole world, and the most observable things therein" (27). Even as they developed into ensembles of prints and illustrated books, they continued to portray a global commerce of the street emblematized in both the commodities and the sellers. For example, one Cry (figure 2.3) portrays an "exotic Turkish vendor of medicinal rhubarb from Tibet" (15), and another depicts the flirtation between a milkmaid and a man of African descent as they lean toward one another, just about to kiss in a doorway (figure 2.4).

Often portraying liminal figures standing in doorways or on thresholds, Cries pictured the commerce made possible by global trade routes as carried on in major world cities by the very outcasts of that modernity. The name given to the genre, capitalized as "Cries," refers to the vendors, or their likenesses, but their distinctive shouts, rendered visually, are thus silenced. As Sheshgreen notes, the actual cries were likely to sound vulgar and transgressive in life, "even threatening, socially and politically" (2).

Figure 2.3 : William Marshall Craig, Cries, "Rhubarb!" 1804

Figure 2.4 : Thomas Rowlandson, Cries, "Milk," 1820

Rhys' novel clearly refers to the transgressive quality of the street sellers' shouts and brings the actual hawkers into modernist London when, early in the novel, Anna hears a street cry, or "song":

> Somebody went past in the street, singing. Bawling:
>   Bread, bread, bread,
>   Standard bread,
>   A little bit er Standard bread,
>   Pom, pom,'
>   over and over again.
>   I thought, 'a song! Mad as a hatter that song is. It's the tune that's so awful; it's like blows.' But the words went over and over again in my head and I began to breathe in time to them. (25)

Perceived as a "mad," "bawling" song, the bread seller's cry threatens not only the respectability of the street but also Anna's physical and mental state, striking her "like blows." We might read its blows as battling with her memories of other street peddlers, market women in Dominica selling fish cakes: "The black women . . . call out, 'Salt fishcakes, all sweet an' charmin', all sweet an' charmin'" (7). Confronting her own racialized nostalgia, entering her mind, and giving measure to her breath, the London cry has, in a sense, possessed Anna.

It is not surprising then that the images, "Cries of London," should later appear, as if these outcast voices of the streets had moved inside to become not only part of Anna's interiority but also part of the interior furnishings of the flat she occupies. Though it is not clear which versions of the London Cries decorate these rooms, likely candidates would include Francis Wheatley's scenes of sentimentalized feminine vendors who cast a romantic glow on streets haunted by more grim and somber figures. Wheatley's prints, first published in 1795 and republished as an illustrated book in 1924, would have been familiar to many readers when *Voyage in the Dark* appeared ten years later (Roberts).

In one of them, we see the portrayal of a hard-laboring strawberry seller, with her enormous basket, the strawberries she sells, and her silent cry (figure 2.5). But most prominent in this and other images is the attractive young woman herself, as if she, too, were a commodity displayed for sale. Moreover, the large basket on the strawberry seller's head visually echoes stereotyped images of Afro-Caribbean market women (figure 2.6), suggesting an impossibly composite figure much like Anna, neither and both English/West Indian, white/black.[31] Anna's allusions to *The Cries* indicate that she recognizes her "place" in these London rooming houses, already staged for her occupation as another liminal and silenced woman. The nostalgia associated with the images casts a critical light on Anna's own memories of West Indian market women. However, they also signal a paradox of representation and a model for the final section of the novel in which silenced "cries" of the plantation and of London join one another, soundlessly recorded.

In these passages, surrounded by the "Cries of London" and delirious with fever, Anna hears "The Brown Girl in a Ring," recalls dizzying carnival scenes in which she

Figure 2.5 : Francis Wheatley, "Strawberrys Scarlet Strawberrys," Cries of London, 1795, reprinted 1924

Figure 2.6 : Market Woman, Studio Portrait Postcard, 1910

joins black dancers wearing white or pink masks, and dreams of riding a horse on a road by the sea to her mother's estate.[32] The carnival dream reverses her implied position in the "Camptown Racecourse" lyrics—now she is the rider rather than the horse—turns around the dynamics of minstrelsy, and brings the land and seascape of the Caribbean into the space of a London flat. Her carnival memories reply also to Banjo's song, "Shake That Thing," when she dances to the music of the chak chak, "the thing like seeds being shaken," no longer alluding to an individual sexual performance, but the "rhythm of the seeds of seed," or as Tinnie argues, of racial mixing.[33] Discovering her family's plantation in ruins, Anna fears falling and "[clings] desperately" to the horse but also we could argue, to the multiple selves emerging in her own silent cry. Rhys turns Banjo's metaphor ("a woman is a conjunction") into a paradoxical conjunction of discrepant times, places, and voices, racial and cultural identities. She reveals, through this modernist montage, the suppressed web of Relation engendered by the plantation while exposing as fallen the nostalgic myth of the plantation home. Though Anna cannot "git away with" anything as an immigrant woman from the West Indies, in Rhys' Caribbean modernism, these emergent multiple voices resound, even if silently, conjoining in their cacophony that of the West Indian peddler of fish cakes, the "brown girl in a ring," the house slave, Maillotte Boyd, and the outcast street sellers of England, Europe, and their empires.

THE PLANETARY CARIBBEAN

At the risk of belaboring a metaphor, we might read these plantation cries and their transformations in *Banjo* and *Voyage in the Dark* as heralding the birth of an inherently global Caribbean modernism, but a modernism also moving in the direction of the planetary vision evoked by Glissant. Not only do they portray the global connections of migrant workers and their "cries," but they also give us a glimpse of a larger terrain, emanating from the plantation, on which we might locate a planetary modernism. This terrain spans the full reach of black Atlantic contramodernity, the transatlantic arts springing from its foundational scenes, and their alternate notions of space and time. McKay's portrayal of Marseilles reveals the French port as a "protean space" of the African diaspora, and the performative banjo punctuates the incidental wanderings of the narrative with a point of contact for multiple, entangled past times and their tense associations of race, gender, and sexuality. Rhys' portrayal of England makes visible the suppressed colonial system and its slave past; her explicit rendering of the past as "side by side with the present, not behind it" creates what Harris might call an "inner time" of multiple yet silenced voices of laboring women across the empire, from the colonial plantation to modernist London and across four centuries of Europe's modernity.[34] In both novels, the characters' migrancy—a product of global exchange yet also dependent on the sea and its fluid boundaries with the earth as well as its connections to other places and times—remaps the cities they inhabit as sites of human history interrelated with the extra-human past. For a number of critics, this alterity beyond the human distinguishes the concept of the planetary from that of the global.

In the opening pages of this chapter, I described the concept of the planetary as necessarily elusive. The extended alterity of the planet requires that knowledge of it partially escape us. For Gayatri Spivak, this extended alterity allows a greater scale of heterogeneity than is possible in the rationalized system of exchange that comprises the global. The greater scale exceeds human control and encompasses more than we can fully imagine for "[t]he planet is in the species of alterity, belonging to another system; . . . we inhabit it on loan" (*Death of a Discipline* 72). Its alterity is "underived from us" (73). Moreover, as a way of thinking and feeling, the planetary does not consolidate the self: "If we planet-think, planet-feel, our 'other'—everything in the unbounded universe—cannot be the self-consolidating other, an other that is a neat and commensurate opposite of the self" ("World Systems and the Creole" 108).[35] Spivak's gesture toward a nonoppositional self-universe planetary relation recalls the language of Glissant when he writes of "the evolution of the planet Earth" (32), and also that of Wilson Harris who recognizes "our being on an earth that moves as we move upon it" ("Epilogue" 263). Elaborating on the concept of planetarity, Wai Chee Dimock has stressed the importance of the planet as "an unknown quantum," a horizon impossible to define and hospitable to that impossibility." From the perspective of the planetary, we read literature within a greater scale of heterogeneity than the rational ordering of globalization allows, not denying the global yet displacing it in favor of "phenomena as yet emerging, not quite in sight" ("Planet and America" 5).[36] In *Banjo* and *Voyage in the Dark*, we catch a glimpse of such phenomena in their portrayals of interconnected and mutually embedded cities, plantations, islands, oceans, and continents and their deeply stratified temporalities. We can begin to read them as offering what recent critics of Caribbean literature, following Glissant, have called an "aesthetics of the earth."

Marking an increasingly important branch of Caribbean studies, the editors of a collection of essays on *Caribbean Literature and the Environment* define an aesthetics of the earth as departing from romanticized landscapes and colonial notions of the "primitive," intruding into and disrupting the global market forces of tourism, and, as in Wilson Harris's writing, catalyzing an "ecological imagination that ranges from the deep history of geology to the frenetic energy of quantum physics" (DeLoughrey, Gosson, and Handley, eds., 26).[37] This earth, including the plantations historically located on it, extends into and becomes entangled with the sea in what M. Allawaert calls a watery "plantation zone" (341).[38] In *Roots and Routes: Negotiating Caribbean and Pacific Island Literatures*, Elizabeth DeLoughrey has recently urged us to see beyond the European myth of the isolated island and to recognize the archipelagoes in which islands interconnect with one another, the ocean, and other landmasses. She shifts our attention to the ocean itself and a "transoceanic imaginary" as model for reenvisioning geographical space-time. Recognizing the "alterity of the ocean" allows her to connect literatures of the Caribbean with those of the Pacific islands and, though she does not employ the term "modernism," the Caribbean writers to whom she most frequently refers are those, such as Glissant, Harris, and Cliff, who reject realism in fiction and those, such as Walcott and Brathwaite, who have created a new, diversely creolized, Caribbean poetics.

As I have suggested, we can see the beginnings of this planetary alterity in the contramodernist Relational disorderings of identity, place, and time in *Banjo* and *Voyage in the Dark*. Their versions of the plantation's cry displace the global by transfiguring Caribbean icons of the exchange of commodified human beings into gateways for new webs of historical and geographical relations. They become precedents for Caribbean narratives that extend such transfigurations, evoking the land, sea, and cosmos as coextensive with one another, with the Caribbean person, and the eclipsed past of the circum-Atlantic. We can read such planetary visions in the powerful metamorphoses of river-into-mother-into-*jablesse* in Jamaica Kincaid's *At the Bottom of the River*; or in the African diasporic voices from "the other side" unknowingly tape recorded by a character resembling Zora Neale Hurston in Erna Brodber's *Louisiana*; or in the hologrammatical Malcolm X who "waits his time" in the nineteenth-century Parker House Hotel, watching the "Ethiopian Delineator Extraordinaire" jump "Jim Crow" in Michelle Cliff's *Free Enterprise*. We might find their precedents in the uncanny déja vu of Jean Rhys' "prequel" to *Jane Eyre* in *Wide Sargasso Sea*; or the surrealist explosions of Aimé Césaire's *Cahier d'un Retour aux Pays Natal*. When Harris portrays in *The Four Banks of the River of Space* the petroglyphs of the Americas as scripts performed in the patterns of the constellations, and when David Dabydeen's poetic figure, "Turner," refers simultaneously to the painter and to the lost yet imaginatively recovered subjectivities of those drowning in the Middle Passage in Turner's painting, they create glimpses of the planetary. Portraying the plantation's global forces of exchange, including modernity's foundational exchange of commodified human beings, these innovative narratives offer also a necessarily elusive planetary vision for our new models of modernism.[39]

NOTES

1. In "Periodizing Modernism," Friedman (2006) calls for a "full spatialization of modernism" and in response to Fredric Jameson's "Always historicize!" urges us to "Always spatialize!" (426). The move to spatialization is necessary in her argument to dislodge the conventional periodization of modernism and allow her to theorize "the geohistory of twentieth-century modernism" (439).

2. For an argument concerning the eclipsed past of the Haitian Revolution as generative of an alternate modernity and Caribbean modernism, see Emery, "Taking the Detour, Finding the Rebels: Crossroads of Caribbean and Modernist Studies," in *Disciplining Modernism*, ed. Caughie. For the last example, see Doyle, "Liberty, Race, and Larsen in Atlantic Modernity," *Geomodernisms*, 51–76, and her recent book *Freedom's Empire*.

3. Most theorists and critics who employ the term "planetary" do so in order to recognize an increasing awareness of interconnections—political, economic, and cultural—that span the planet, and many use the term interchangeably with "global." Yet the implications for how we study literature may vary from the "distant reading" promoted by Moretti, to one that includes a close and distant view in models inspired by fractal geometry (Dimock, "Genre as World System") or Google Earth (Heise). Friedman proposes a planetary modernism as an expansive and creative epistemological project that, in the most recent version of her argument, extends to include the planet but avoids any discussion of political/economic forces and institutions ("Planetarity: Musing Modernist Studies"). Spivak (*Death of a Discipline* and "World Systems and the Creole"), Gilroy (*Postcolonial Melancholia*), and Dimock ("Planet and America") employ the term more precisely by distinguishing it from the global, while Spivak and Dimock have insisted on its meaning as necessarily elusive.

4. I am quoting the title to Jamaica Kincaid's parody of a Caribbean guidebook, *A Small Place*.

5. See, for example, Emery's analysis of the circuiting of elite and popular, English and Bengali poetry in poems by the Jamaican writer and editor Una Marson (*Modernism, the Visual, and Caribbean Literature* 116–24). For helpful models of cross-empire influences on anticolonial nationalism and modernism, see Boehmer. As is already well known, Claude McKay, the Jamaican writer who was also central to the Harlem Renaissance, helped to spark the Négritude movement among African intellectuals living in Paris in the 1930s with his novel *Banjo*.

6. For the concept of "unthinkable modernity," see Michel-Rolph Trouillot, *Silencing the Past*. While he uses the term to refer to the Haitian Revolution and surrounding events, I expand it here to include other suppressed, yet continually haunting, events of the circum-Atlantic.

7. Baucom, *Spectres of the Atlantic*. This practice became known to the public through the court case that followed on the murder in 1781 of 131 enslaved Africans by the captain and crew of the slave ship *Zong*. Considering them too ill to survive the journey, the captain and crew threw the slaves overboard, planning to sue the insurance company for the loss. In the past fifteen years, scholars, writers, and artists of the Caribbean have returned to this event, seeing it as emblematic of the suppressed past of modernity.

8. For example, Dimock (2003) has written of "planetary time," and reads the circulations of texts through time and across the globe as indicative of this wider, deeper context.

9. See also Gilroy, especially in *The Black Atlantic*, and before him, numerous essays and studies by the Trinidadian intellectual, C. L. R. James. More recently, critical studies by Edwards and Stephens have further developed a black Atlantic perspective on modernity. See Nielsen for a recent assessment of these contributions and those of others, such as W. E. B. DuBois.

10. They occupy what Bhabha has termed the "time-gap" of Western modernity through which a contramodernity and, we might argue, a contramodernism emerges, alternate to yet constitutive of Europe's modern times.

11. These include writings by, among others, Jean Rhys (from Dominica), Derek Walcott (St. Lucia), Kamau Brathwaite (Barbados), Jamaica Kincaid (Antigua), and Michelle Cliff (Jamaica). Yet references to Amerindian cultures, such as the Taino, Arawak, and Carib, do not appear in these writers' works to the same degree or with the same valence. Walcott, for instance, tends to incorporate such references as signs of an ancient past rather than a significant present, and Brathwaite added the significance of

indigenous peoples to his theories of creolization after much discussion with Harris and Williams during the period of the Caribbean Artists Movement (1960s/1970s). Using Glissant's term, "Indianization," DeLoughrey has written about recent interest in Amerindian cultures in the Caribbean and distinguishes between a shallow and fashionable interest in "Indians" and one that radically revises colonial narratives (*Roots and Routes* 234–40). Hulme provides crucial background to any reading of the Amerindian presence in the Caribbean.

12. For an introduction to Harris's writing, see *Selected Essays of Wilson Harris*, introduction by Andrew Bundy. Harris has also written numerous novels, including the first to be published and probably his best known, *Palace of the Peacock*.

13. See, for instance, C. L. R. James, *The Black Jacobins*; George Lamming, *The Pleasures of Exile*, especially the chapter "Caliban Orders History"; Michel-Rolph Trouillot, *Silencing the Past*; J. Michael Dash, "The Theater of the Haitian Revolution/The Haitian Revolution as Theater"; and David Scott, *Conscripts of Modernity*. Buck-Morss has also made this argument in "Hegel and Haiti."

14. Here, I am suggesting that the arguments by Trouillot—that the revolutionaries were influenced by their West African inheritance rather than ideas acquired from the French—and Scott—that they were swept into the overwhelming forces of Western modernity—are not mutually exclusive.

15. He adds that revolutionary Haiti was named in the language of the indigenous Taino, ruled by an emperor in the European manner of their enemy Napoleon, and populated by newly declared black citizens and by the Polish who fought with them against the French.

16. In *Writing in Limbo*, Gikandi connects Caliban's "new sense of language" with modernism and states that it and the reversal of his "traditional posture" exemplifies Caribbean modernism (65). Yet he dissociates this Caribbean modernism from what he considers "the high modernist aesthetic of Anglo-American writers such as Ezra Pound, T. S. Eliot, and James Joyce" (5).

17. In essays contributed to *Caribbean Literature and the Environment*, both Wilson Harris and the foremost critic of his work, Hena Maes-Jelinek, chose *Tumatumari* as an example of this theme in Harris's work.

18. Although Gikandi's book was the first to address a number of authors, studies published before 1992 included discussions of intersections between modernism and Caribbean literature in the work of individual authors. These include, among others, Arnold, Cooper, Drake, and Emery, *Jean Rhys at World's End*.

19. See, for instance, Rosenberg, Donnel, Bongie, Puri, Pollard, Ramazani, Torres-Saillant, and Emery (2007).

20. See Gikandi, "Picasso, Africa, and the Schemata of Difference" and "Africa and the Epiphany of Modernism." See also Lazarus, "Modernism and African Literature," chapter 9 in this volume.

21. Glissant describes the term "Relation" as referring to a totality (but one that "proceeds from no absolute") and distinguishes it from a word, such as the English "relationship," which implies the question: "relation between what and what?" (27). It is crucial to recognize the dynamic quality of this totality and the permutations of violence and inequality operating within it. While the notion of Relation allows us to move beyond nationalisms, it does not erase cultural difference; rather, it helps us to imagine how cultural difference comes into play.

22. Glissant is not the first among Caribbean writers to view the plantation as location for experiments in modernity. In an appendix to the 1963 edition of *The Black Jacobins*,

C. L. R. James described the sugar plantation as a modern system of largely mechanized and highly regularized means of agricultural production, noting its importation of cloth and food through which to reproduce the slave's labor, its exportation of the products of their labor, the proximity of the slaves to one another, "far closer than any proletariat of the time" (392) and, simultaneously, to the colonial European culture of the plantation owners. They lived, he claimed, "in its essence a modern life" (392). A number of writers, including anthropologist Sidney Mintz, writer and critic Antonio Benítez-Rojo, anthropologist David Scott and, recently, historian Linda Colley, have repeated this emphasis on the modernity of the plantation system, while Benítez-Rojo and Glissant have followed James in suggesting its implications for literature and the arts. Of these, Glissant has become most influential in the new modernist studies for his model of Relation.

23. Friedman's essay in this volume again promotes the "planetary scale" for modernism and asserts that, as modernist studies becomes a branch of "new world literatures," it requires a comparatist approach to literatures in many languages worldwide. As a multilingual region, with an extensive diaspora and worldwide historical "Relation" through the "plantation complex," the Caribbean offers a productive focus for such a comparatist approach. Indeed, it has long required a transnational perspective and has generated influential models of the black Atlantic and circum-Atlantic; models for diasporic studies and studies of the construction of "race," identity, and hybridity (or creolization); and provides, as in Kalliney's essay in this collection, examples of the historical and discursive intersections of modernism with postcolonial literatures.

24. In his contribution to this volume, Ramazani argues for the importance of the creolization and hybridization of transnational poetry as "among the engines of modern and contemporary poetic development and innovation." The examples he gives and the readings he performs pay attention to both conflicts and harmonies in the mixings of forms, styles, and themes and recognize the intricacies in modernism's interlinking of distant geographical sites. Though he does not mention the plantation, his transnational poetics and references to Glissant's poetics of Relation implicitly evoke the plantation as foundational matrix for many of these creolized poems.

25. McKay and Rhys appear repeatedly in recent essays on modernist geographies (see, for example, Nielsen, Snaith, Rosenberg, and Lyon), and it is easy to see why. If we define modernism as a period, their work fits the conventional parameters of 1890–1939; moreover, their migrant lives brought them from the Caribbean to the metropolitan centers of the United States, England, and Europe and into contact with influential writers and groups long considered modernist. Lyon's chapter in this volume opens with a discussion of Rhys' 1928 novel *Quartet* as representative of a modernist negative critique of cosmopolitanism. In addition to the factors Lyon considers, we might view Rhys' Caribbean background and the colonial (or emergent postcolonial) perspective in all of her writing as basis for her insight into what Lyon calls "the dark side of the city of light" (19).

26. The Senegalese *xalam*, the West African *molo*, and the *nkoni* of the Manding creolized through the Atlantic crossing of the slave ships and settlement of the Americas into the *banja* (or *bonja*) of eighteenth-century Jamaica, the *banza* of Martinique, *bangil* of Barbados, *banshaw* of St. Kitts, *bagnio* of South Carolina, and *banjou* of Philadelphia. See Michael D. Harris, 146; Mazow, "Banjo Cultures" 2–3, and "From Sonic to Social" 96–99.

27. http://www.riverwalkjazz.org/jazznotes/chasin_the_blues (accessed February 12 2011).

28. The band is identified online ("Gift Music Book & Collectibles": (http://www.tias.com/1401/PictPage/1922563279.html [accessed February 14, 2011]) as Bernie Schultz and his Crescent Orchestra, from Davenport, Iowa, active between 1923 and 1928. The puppet figure is described as "a TINY old coon dancer with white beard, a cast on his leg, and crutches beneath him who did a little too much shakin' that thing. . . ." A subsequent disclaimer ("we do not condone or encourage any racial or ethnic stereotyping or prejudice") rings transparently false in this very recent reproduction of the racist stereotypes of plantation mythology.

29. Lott (159–68) has analyzed minstrel cross-dressing, or "acting the wench," as a way to assert white working-class masculine identity in the mid-nineteenth century. He cites frequent, if coded, references to black male genitalia in minstrel songs as indications of both cross-racial homosexual desire and reassertions of male sexual power, fortified in the portrayal of black women as grotesque and comic "wenches." In Lott's analysis, the contradictory desires performed through minstrelsy have to do with white working-class "structures of feeling" in the mid-nineteenth century and not with those of African American or African diasporic people. But in presenting the banjo through both Goosey's perspective and Banjo's, McKay gestures toward the process of cultural translation from racist icon to creative gateway for the new "lively tunes" of blues and jazz.

30. As Edwards has pointed out, jazz and Banjo's dream of an orchestra provide models for this male vagabond community. By implication they also provide models for McKay's "story without a plot," in which Edwards finds more than one meaning, including the indication that music is the only ground on which to stand. Yet the collective misogynist violence that frames these musical scenes suggests that their standing, at least as plot for masculine identity, remains extremely precarious.

31. I am grateful to Leah Rosenberg for reminding me of this connection with images of Caribbean market women.

32. In addition to the published version of Part IV, an original and longer version exists, which Rhys altered at the request of her publisher (Brown). In both versions, the masks, dancing, music, and journey on horse to the estate appear. Unless noted otherwise, page numbers refer to the published version.

33. Though the concertina man appears in both versions, these particular lines are present only in the original version (Brown 53).

34. In a letter to a friend, written in 1934, Rhys explained what she called "[t]he big idea" in her writing of *Voyage*: "Something to do with time being an illusion I think. I mean that the past exists—side by side with the present, not behind it; that what was—is." Later, in 1963, Rhys wrote to her editor about trying to convey in the original ending a sense of "time and place abolished, past and present the same." Quoted in Brown, 41 and 43.

35. Spivak makes this important point in a dialogue with Dimock concerning the epic as a genre that crosses time and space. She urges Dimock to forgo the seemingly arbitrary metaphor of fractal geometry as a model for a planetary scale that can include the close and the distant, and to take up instead "creolity" as a way of envisioning the planetary. Spivak refers briefly here to Glissant's notion of Relation, but does not mention that he grounds that notion in the plantation. She does make a crucial distinction, however, between planetarity and the idea of taking care of the planet, being its custodian, though that is not an idea she dismisses. Planetarity, however, "cannot authorize itself over against a self-consolidating other" ("World Systems and the Creole" 108). In *Postcolonial Melancholia*, Gilroy follows Spivak in distinguishing the planetary from the global. He, however, emphasizes the possibilities for a planetary humanism and an activism in which urgent issues of human rights and the environment intersect (75).

36. By following the emphasis of Spivak, Dimock, and Harris on the planet's alterity in excess of human control and representation, my use of the concept "planetary" differs from that of Ramazani, whose contribution to this volume identifies what he calls the "planetary poem" as one that views the earth from an "extraterritorial perspective," as in Seamus Heaney's portrayal of the astronaut's view of the globe as an "O." It differs also, though in a different way, from Lyon's use of the term in her discussion in this volume of a "planetary cosmopolitanism" derived from Kant and emerging in certain historical situations as "unannounced and unaestheticized," "portable and episodic."

37. For earlier criticism focusing on the entanglements of landscape and Caribbean subjectivity, especially in the work of Rhys and Harris, see Highfield, "The Dreaming Quipucamayoq: Myth and Landscape in Wilson Harris' *The Dark Jester*" and "Mapping Amazonia: 'Relief Data Unreliable.'" See also Johnson, "Mapping the Sea Change: Postcolonialism, Modernism and Landscape in Jean Rhys' *Voyage in the Dark*"; "Translations of Gender, Pain and Space: Wilson Harris's *The Carnival Trilogy*"; and "From Muse to Majesty: Landscape, Rape and Agency in the Early Novels of Wilson Harris."

For a recent version of the development of discourses of globalization and environmentalism, see Heise, who mentions Spivak's and Dimock's concepts of the planetary in an endnote in which she is somewhat dismissive of their contributions. Her promotion of an "eco-cosmopolitanism," however, which she defines as "an attempt to envision individuals and groups as part of planetary 'imagined communities' of both human and nonhuman kinds" (61), comes close to the planetary vision that they espouse. But unlike their approaches, hers does not stress a necessary elusiveness to the concept; rather, she works carefully to define and demonstrate it as preferable to previous discourses concerning globalization and the environment.

38. In her analysis of William Bartram's *Travels . . .* and William Blake's illustrations for John Stedman's *Narrative of a Five Years Expedition against the Revolted Negroes of Surinam*, Allawaert also turns to Glissant in her emphasis on the plantation and to the trope of *marronage* as one that makes of the Maroons "ecological actors."

39. I would like to thank Kerry Johnson, Leah Rosenberg, and Peter Kalliney for their helpful comments on an early version of this essay.

WORKS CITED

Allawaert, M. "Swamp Sublime: Ecologies of Resistance in the American Plantation Zone." *PMLA* 123.3 (2008): 340–57.

Arnold, James A. *Modernism and Negritude: The Poetry and Poetics of Aimé Césaire.* Cambridge: Harvard University Press, 1981.

Baucom, Ian. *Specters of the Atlantic: Finance Capital, Slavery, and the Philosophy of History.* Durham: Duke University Press, 2005.

Benítez-Rojo, Antonio. *The Repeating Island: The Caribbean and the Postmodern Perspective.* Durham: Duke University Press, 1996.

Bhabha, Homi K. *The Location of Culture.* London: Routledge, 1994.

Boehmer, Elleke. *Colonial and Postcolonial Literature: Migrant Metaphors.* New York: Oxford University Press, 2005.

———. *Empire, the National, and the Postcolonial, 1890–1920: Resistance in Interaction.* New York: Oxford University Press, 2002.

Bongie, Chris. *Islands and Exiles: The Creole Identities of Post/colonial Literature*. Stanford: Stanford University Press, 1998.

Brooker, Peter, and Andrew Thacker. *The Geographies of Modernism: Literatures, Cultures, Spaces*. New York: Routledge, 2005.

Brown, Nancy Hemond. "Jean Rhys and Voyage in the Dark." *London Magazine* April–May 1985: 40–59.

Buck-Morss, Susan. "Hegel and Haiti." *Critical Inquiry* 26.4 (2000): 821–65.

Burns, Sarah. "Whiteface: Art, Women, and the Banjo in Late Nineteenth-Century America." Mazow 71–94.

Cooper, Wayne F. *Claude McKay: Rebel Sojourner in the Harlem Renaissance*. Baton Rouge: Louisiana State University Press, 1987.

Dash, J. Michael. "The Theater of the Haitian Revolution/The Haitian Revolution as Theater." *Small Axe* 9.2 (2005): 16–23.

DeLoughrey, Elizabeth. *Roots and Routes: Navigating Caribbean and Pacific Island Literatures*. Honolulu: University of Hawaii Press, 2007.

DeLoughrey, Elizabeth, Renée K. Gosson, and George B. Handley, eds. *Caribbean Literature and the Environment: Between Nature and Culture*. Charlottesville: University of Virginia Press, 2005.

Dimock, Wai Chee. "Genre as World System: Epic and Novel on Four Continents." *Narrative* 14.1 (2006): 85–101.

———. "Introduction: Planet and America, Set and Subset." *Shades of the Planet: American Literature as World Literature*. Ed. Dimock and Lawrence Buell. Princeton: Princeton University Press, 2007.

———. "Planetary Time and Global Translation: 'Context' in Literary Studies." *Common Knowledge* 9.3 (2003): 488–507.

Donnell, Alison. *Twentieth-Century Caribbean Literature: Critical Moments in Anglophone Literary History*. London: Routledge, 2006.

Doyle, Laura. *Freedom's Empire: Race and the Rise of the Novel in Atlantic Modernity, 1640–1940*. Durham: Duke University Press, 2008.

Doyle, Laura, and Laura Winkiel, eds. *Geomodernisms: Race, Modernism, Modernity*. Bloomington: Indiana University Press, 2005.

Drake, Sandra. *Wilson Harris and the Modern Tradition: A New Architecture of the World*. New York: Greenwood Press, 1986.

Edwards, Brent Hayes. *The Practice of Diaspora: Literature, Translation, and the Rise of Black Internationalism*. Cambridge: Harvard University Press, 2003.

Emery, Mary Lou. *Jean Rhys at "World's End": Novels of Colonial and Sexual Exile*. Austin: University of Texas Press, 1990.

———. *Modernism, the Visual, and Caribbean Literature*. Cambridge: Cambridge University Press, 2007.

———. "Taking the Detour, Finding the Rebels: Crossroads of Caribbean and Modernist Studies." *Disciplining Modernism*. Ed. Pamela Caughie. Basingstoke: Palgrave Macmillan, 2009.

Friedman, Susan Stanford. "Periodizing Modernism: Postcolonial Modernities and the Space/Time Borders of Modernist Studies." *Modernism/modernity* 13.3 (2006): 425–43.

———. "Planetarity: Musing Modernist Studies." *Modernism/modernity* 17.3 (2010): 471–99.

Gikandi, Simon. "Africa and the Epiphany of Modernism." Doyle and Winkiel 31–50.

———. "Picasso, Africa, and the Schemata of Difference." *Modernism/modernity* 10.3 (2003): 455–80.

———. *Writing in Limbo: Modernism and Caribbean Literature*. Ithaca: Cornell University Press, 1992.

Gilroy, Paul. *The Black Atlantic: Modernity and Double Consciousness*. Cambridge: Harvard University Press, 1993.

———. *Postcolonial Melancholia*. New York: Columbia University Press, 2005.

Glissant, Édouard. *Poetics of Relation*. Ann Arbor: University of Michigan Press, 1997.

Harris, Michael D. "From *The Banjo Lesson* to *The Piano Lesson*: Reclaiming the Song." Mazow 145–60.

Harris, Wilson. "Epilogue: Theatre of the Arts." DeLoughrey, Gosson, and Handley 261–68.

———. "History, Fable, Myth in the Caribbean and Guianas." *Selected Essays of Wilson Harris: The Unfinished Genesis of the Imagination*. Ed. Andrew Bundy. New York: Routledge, 1999: 152–66.

———. *Palace of the Peacock*. London: Faber and Faber, 1960.

———. "Tradition and the West Indian Novel." Bundy 140–51.

———. *Tumatumari*. London: Faber and Faber, 1968.

Heise, Ursula K. *Sense of Place and Sense of Planet: The Environmental Imagination of the Global*. Oxford: Oxford University Press, 2008.

Highfield, Jonathan. "The Dreaming Quipucamayoq: Myth and Landscape in Wilson Harris' *The Dark Jester*." *Atlantic Studies*, 1.2 (2004): 196–209.

———. "Mapping Amazonia: 'Relief Data Unreliable'." *Passages: A Journal of Transnational and Transcultural Studies*. 2.2 (2000): 123–58.

Hulme, Peter. *Colonial Encounters: Europe and the Native Caribbean, 1492–1797*. New York: Methuen, 1986.

James, C. L. R. *The Black Jacobins: Toussaint L'Ouverture and the San Domingo Revolution*. Rev. Ed. New York: Vintage Books, 1963.

Johnson, Kerry. "From Muse to Majesty: Landscape, Rape and Agency in the Early Novels of Wilson Harris." *World Literature Written in English*. 35.2 (1996): 71–89.

———. "Mapping the Sea Change: Postcolonialism, Modernism and Landscape in Jean Rhys' Voyage in the Dark." *Journal of Caribbean Literatures*, 3.3 (2003): 47–62.

———. "Translations of Gender, Pain and Space: Wilson Harris's *The Carnival Trilogy*." *Modern Fiction Studies*, 44.1 (1998): 123–43.

Lamming, George. *The Pleasures of Exile*. Ann Arbor: University of Michigan Press, 1960.

Lott, Eric. *Love and Theft: Blackface Minstrelsy and the American Working Class*. New York: Oxford University Press, 1993.

Mazow, Leo G. "Banjo Cultures." Mazow 1–48.

———. "From Sonic to Social: Noise, Quiet, and Nineteenth-Century American Imagery." Mazow 95–114.

———, ed. *Picturing the Banjo*. University Park: Pennsylvania State University Press, 2005.

Mintz, Sidney. *Sweetness and Power: The Place of Sugar in Modern History*. New York: Viking, 1985.

Nielsen, Aldon. "The Future of an Allusion: The Color of Modernity." Doyle and Winkiel 17–30.

Pollard, Charles. *New World Modernisms: T. S. Eliot, Derek Walcott, and Kamau Brathwaite*. Charlottesville: University of Virginia Press, 2004.

Puri, Shalini. *The Caribbean Postcolonial: Social Equality, Post-Nationalism, and Cultural Hybridity*. New York: Palgrave Macmillan, 2004.

Ramazani, Jahan. *The Hybrid Muse: Postcolonial Poetry in English*. Chicago: University of Chicago Press, 2001.

Ramchand, Kenneth. "An Introduction to This Novel." *The Lonely Londoners.* By Sam
     Selvon. Essex: Longman Group, 1987.
Rhys, Jean. "Original Ending to *Voyage in the Dark.*" Brown 45–59.
———. *Voyage in the Dark.* 1934. NewYork: W. W. Norton, 1982.
Roberts, W. *The Cries of London.* London: The Connoisseur, 1924.
Rosenberg, Leah. "Caribbean Models for Modernism in the Work of Claude McKay and
     Jean Rhys. *Modernism/modernity* 11.2 (2004): 219–38.
———. *Nationalism and the Formation of Caribbean Literature.* New York: Palgrave
     Macmillan, 2007.
Scott, David. *Conscripts of Modernity: The Tragedy of Colonial Enlightenment.* Durham:
     Duke University Press, 2004.
Sheshgreen, Sean. *Images of the Outcast: The Urban Poor in the Cries of London.* New
     Brunswick: Rutgers University Press, 2002.
Snaith, Anna. "'A Savage from the Cannibal Islands': Jean Rhys and London." Brooker and
     Thacker 76–85.
Spivak, Gayatri Chakravorty. *Death of a Discipline.* New York: Columbia University Press,
     2003.
———. "World Systems and the Creole." *Narrative* 14.6 (2006): 102–12.
Stephens, Michelle. *Black Empire: The Masculine Global Imaginary of Caribbean
     Intellectuals in the United States, 1914–1962.* Durham: Duke University Press, 2005.
Tinnie, Wallis. *Miscegenation Discourse in Faulkner, Rhys, and Toomer: Literary Texts and
     Legal Subtexts.* Diss. The University of Iowa, 1997.
Torres-Saillant, Silvio. *Caribbean Poetics: Toward an Aesthetic of West Indian Literature.*
     Cambridge: Cambridge University Press, 1997.
Trouillot, Michel-Rolphe. *Silencing the Past: Power and the Production of History.* Boston:
     Beacon Press, 1995.
Walcott, Derek. "What the Twilight Says." *What the Twilight Says: Essays.* New York: Farrar,
     Straus, and Giroux, 1998: 3–35.

PART II

TEMPORALITY

CHAPTER 3

....

BERBER POETRY AND THE ISSUE OF DERIVATION: ALTERNATE SYMBOLIST TRAJECTORIES

....

EDWIGE TAMALET TALBAYEV

WHILE global interaction between various areas of the world has played an active part in the development of civilizations for millennia, the recent predominance of globalization as a critical framework has triggered a transnational turn in literary and cultural studies, accompanied by an increased interest in dynamics of circulation, cultural translation, and diaspora on the global level. These efforts have highlighted the imbrications of modernist aesthetic and global dynamics of power (political, economic, and literary) in the colonial and postcolonial worlds.[1] This evolution has led to the growing integration of various disciplines (postcolonial studies, anthropology, and diaspora studies, to name a few) into new fields of study that have moved beyond the frame of the nation to consider the geo-cultural dynamics of modernity on the regional or planetary level, thereby reinstating issues of comparison and commensurability at the heart of their investigations.[2] By testing the boundaries of a modernist global literary system resting on a rigid binary center-periphery model, recent new paradigms in modernist studies propose an alternative mapping of literary conjunctions that emphasizes the planetary dynamics of interaction, coercion, and mutually constitutive influences intricately connecting the European center and the many territories lying on its peripheries. Attempting to exhume plural, disjunctive genealogies of modernism, such efforts undermine diffusionist models of global cultural production in order to restore visibility to silenced, rival non-Western forms of literacy (or, in certain cases, orality), whose itineraries have been historically excluded by dominant literary circuits that made cultural recognition by the center the prerequisite to consecration on the global level (see Eric Hayot's contribution to this volume).

The reclaiming of repressed sites of modernist production requires a spatial revision of global literary models in which Europe and the United States are configured as the exclusive sites of artistic agency, and recent efforts along these lines have put on the map forms of modernist production hailing from spaces formerly considered to lie outside the purview of modernity. Yet such a project entails more than mere geographic adjustments. Inasmuch as Eurocentric linear narratives of history and modernity have underpinned the global charting of modernism, rigorous attention to alternative conceptions of time has become equally necessary. Scholars of Caribbean studies have greatly contributed to the reconsideration of time as a sedimented and multilayered concept, especially through compelling reinterpretations of familiar narratives of history in which silenced genealogies and vernacular counter-memories are reclaimed as generative of a global modernity born of crisscrossings and interactions between Europe and its colonies.[3] Their focus on concomitant, antinomic memories bring to the fore the disjunctive nature of time in formerly colonized spaces, where the European intrusion has been predicated on a logic of assimilation through the imposition of all-inclusive Western epistemic models. These conversations provide invaluable inroads into issues of cultural identity in formerly colonized areas throughout the world.

Building on this project, this chapter explores the poetry and political writings of Algerian Berber Jean El Mouhoub Amrouche as alternative delineations of time in a colonial context—temporal models that disengage a local, fractal form of modernity from a historicist Eurocentric narrative of global development. Amrouche's writing addresses issues of cultural derivation and identity politics in an anticolonial, nationalist moment, and thus makes a compelling contribution to the ongoing conversation. With this aim in mind, I intend to engage Amrouche's complex consideration of the status of indigenous cultures in global discussions of modernity, as well as his vision of time within the framework of the nation-state, both of which challenge ingrained critical models. I will show how Amrouche attempted to create a literature of memory purportedly free from the taint of French historicism in his introduction to the *Chants Berbères de Kabylie* (*Berber Chants* [sung poetry] *from Kabylia*) and in a 1941 essay, "Saint Stéphane Mallarmé." Amrouche's conflation of Mallarmé's symbolist poetic aesthetics and "traditional" Berber oral poetry, I argue, highlights the ubiquity of certain strands of modernist practice independently from geographical, cultural, or historical considerations and therefore sheds new light on the issue of cultural derivation in a global colonial context. Amrouche's idiosyncratic engagement with Mallarmé disrupts the totalizing logic of global literary periodizations based on a center-periphery model, as does his understanding of the heterogeneity of time within a given historical moment. His reinterpretation of time in colonial space brings a present of coexistence into focus and prefigures his commitment to an independent Algerian nation that would rest on egalitarian multiculturalism. Ultimately, my aim is to throw into relief the ways in which an understanding of Amrouche's complex poetic negotiations between European and vernacular forms of modernity can help criticism continue to think its way beyond enduring Eurocentric practices.

AMROUCHE, MALLARMÉ, AND THE REINTRODUCTION OF VERNACULAR CULTURE

The impact of Amrouche's interventions stems from his unique subject position within colonial society. The son of Berbers who converted to Christianity in their youth, Jean El Mouhoub Amrouche carries the mark of profound cultural ambivalence. Educated in the French tradition, both in Tunisia and in Paris, the Algerian-born young man epitomizes the ambiguous position of indigenous intellectuals within world systems of cultural production and dissemination founded on the primacy of the metropolitan centers. In 1913, his family was awarded French citizenship, and, after a year in Algerian Kabylia, Amrouche began his education in French colonial schools. Throughout his student years, which took him to the prestigious *Ecole Normale Supérieure de Saint-Cloud* in France, he became familiar with the canon of European literature, and it is as a perceptive critic of French *Belles Lettres* that he set out on a literary career in the Tunisian protectorate—both as a teacher in Tunisian schools and an active contributor to several North African literary journals (Le Baut, *Mythes* 9–17). From his extensive engagement with the ideals professed in French schools emerged Amrouche's awareness of a discrepancy between the ideal image of a humanist France and the harsh realities of French colonial rule in North Africa.[4] Identifying both as Jean, thus claiming a Catholic faith which he embraced as a constant source of inspiration, and as El Mouhoub, in homage to the ancestral Berber culture he came to regard as essential to his identity and poetic transfiguration, Amrouche occupies an unusual space within colonial society, which inspires an exile's sensitivity in his early poetry. Alienated from the colonized Muslim majority because of his Christianity and French education and yet distanced from French national culture by the colonial formation of his racial difference, Amrouche expressed identity in differential terms (neither Arab/Muslim nor French), a dynamic which ultimately conflates Berber origins with an idyllic unitary self that the experience of colonialism and diglossia is supposed to have torn asunder. Amrouche's first collection of poems, suggestively entitled *Cendres* (*Ashes*), reverberates with this post-lapsarian gloominess. Published in 1934 in the colonial margin of Tunis, the volume emphasizes the poet's ontological exile from his original community as well as the betrayal experienced in the midst of his European colleagues. Guilt over having forsaken God and ancestral Berber culture for the allure of colonial modernity pervades the poems. Within this logic, only a symbolic return to the land of childhood through poetry could bring about the much-longed-for (if imaginary) reconciliation with abandoned origins.

However, it is on the evocation of inescapable estrangement (inescapable because the utopia of a stable, homogeneous identity is necessarily doomed to failure) that the volume ends. Only with the next collection of poems, *Etoile Secrète* (*Secret Star*, 1937), did the poet recover some spiritual quietude. Here, Amrouche's quest for a mythical, univocal identity reconfigured poetic creation as a palliative to the haunting feeling of exile that emerged in the wake of French colonialism. His poems attempt to conciliate a French-inspired modern mind-set with the idealized "traditional" (i.e., in oppositional terms, "premodern") intuition inherent in the poet's ancestral culture, a radical dichotomy in itself oblivious to the necessary hybridity lying at the heart of any culture. Amrouche was in fact one of the first to explore the effects of colonial domination on the colonized psyche, an investigation which he undertook as a personal, even ontological enterprise and which would eventuate in his opposition to the colonial power in the early days of the Algerian war.[5] For if poetry acts as a remedy against the psychological schism brought about by a colonial education on the subjective level, it also facilitates Amrouche's engagement with the issue on a broader level. As Albert Memmi and Frantz Fanon have emphasized, the psychological trauma of colonialism did not only affect the subject; it also shaped cultural dynamics at the social level. Amrouche's shift from the consideration of his personal conflict to that of the predicament of Algeria has led many critics to construe his poetic writing as the first step in a quest for subjective identity and authorial recognition that would culminate in his ultimate engagement in favor of Algerian nationalism and independence.[6] In this respect, his identification with and subsequent distantiation from the tutelary figure of Stéphane Mallarmé, a poetic patricide of sorts, takes on added significance.

Meaghan Morris has defined modernity as "a known history, something that has *already happened elsewhere* and which is to be reproduced, mechanically or otherwise, with a local content" (quoted in Chakrabarty 39; emphasis in original). Interpretations of the modern have invariably put to the fore the derivative nature of non-Western progress. Either through the concept of cultural mimicry or that of economic development, Eurocentrism has been configured as a necessary category—if only as the dominant theoretical model to contest. The relation to the exotic locale is thus conceived exclusively in terms of mimicry of a European-born model, which alone can guarantee inclusion into linear time. Modernity has construed itself as part of the Enlightenment process, which, in its pedagogic project, aimed to obliterate the subject's "bondage of being-in-nature" (Cheah, "Given Culture" 295). Such was the rationale behind the inducement to colonial mimicry: through geographic expansion would come worldwide historical (and technical) progress.[7] Yet modernization paradoxically took place at the cost of freedom and autonomy—at home, that of the classes whose labor produced the wealth supporting modernization; in the colonies, that of all natives, given that the universal narrative of modernity absorbed all third world national contexts into the same

Eurocentric framework, a configuration in which the colonized has been refused agency.

Amrouche's literary and critical production, I argue, needs to be considered in the light of its dismissal of teleological history as the colonized subject's sole entry-way into modernity. Through his exaltation of traditional Berber sung poetry and through his strategic (if problematic) recuperation of the mythical figure of Berber king Jugurtha as the epitome of the North African character, Amrouche attempts to create a literature of memory, one supposedly exempt from any corrupting relation to French historicist perceptions. This literature would incorporate the immemorial time of Berber tradition as a foundation for identity and an alternative, nonderiva-tive mode of engagement with history in which the colonial subject, or at least, here, the poet, would be endowed with (relative) agency. The genealogy of this project can be traced through two key texts: Amrouche's little-known article "Saint Stéphane Mallarmé," published in 1941 in the literary supplement to a Tunisian newspaper, *La Tunisie Française Littéraire*; and his introduction to the *Chants Berbères de Kabylie* (*Berber Chants* [sung poetry] *from Kabylia*).

Amrouche's 1939 edition of the *Chants* partakes of the effort to preserve imper-iled forms of cultural creation at odds with the internal logic of cultural modernity.[8] The Berber tribes of North Africa (*Imazighen*, in their own words) constitute the bedrock of native populations that predate the Arab conquest of North Africa in the wake of Mohammed's death. Berbers were part of the ancient Roman Empire (Au-gustine himself was a Berber from present-day Algeria) and had therefore mostly converted to Christianity prior to their Arabization and Islamization in the seventh century. European representations of Berber cultures drew from this mythical golden age of a Christian, Latin North Africa to repudiate the significance of the Arab conquest of the land and provide in its place an *a posteriori* justification of French colonialism in the region. French Algerian author Gabriel Audisio thus depicted the successive experiences of colonization as well as its ensuing hybridity as historical constants in the area (Audisio 55). The argument was taken further by Latinist political groups in Algeria that made the reaffirmation of a Latin Christian civilization in Algeria their platform. These groups correspondingly supported the fascist conquest in Ethiopia after 1935 in the utopian hope of a modern-day *pax romana* in North Africa. In the realm of colonial literature, the *Algérianiste* move-ment, which emerged in Algiers at the turn of the century, idealized the Berbers as the true noble savages in the Maghrebi landscape whose simpler, more primitive way of life was an ideal to which the new "race" of French Algerian subjects should aspire. (They called it *rebarbarisation*, or rejuvenation from corrupted metropolitan life, which is to be understood as a response to the national self-doubt plaguing France in the wake of its 1870 defeat in the Franco-Prussian War.) In addition, Ori-entalist anthropology emphasized elements of kinship between the Berbers and various Indo-European peoples: the Scythians (Zhiri), the Vandal hordes (Anselin), or even the Basques (Michel). These anthropologists predicated the supposed supe-riority of Berbers over their Semite counterparts (the Arabs) on both biological and cultural terms.

Native intellectuals at the turn of the century, such as Said Cid Kaoui or Amar
Ou Said Boulifa, diverged from colonial ethnographic representations of their culture by producing linguistic and literary manuals of Berber culture organized from
a native perspective. These efforts were deemed by metropolitan ethnographers to
be "too simple, primitive, unrefined, repetitive, and subservient to Arabo-Islamic
models" (quoted in Chaker 15).[9] Nevertheless, they spearheaded the first significant
attempt to commit oral Berber culture to writing. Their project constituted a
response to the disappearance of the traditional bard community brought about by
political and socioeconomic changes in late-nineteenth-century Berber Algeria. In
this respect, it aimed to restore the transmission of culture through means other
than declining orality, and one could say with Salem Chaker that it is to Boulifa's
strategic use of writing in his *Recueil de Poésie*, albeit as a nontraditional, colonial-
imposed form of expression, that we owe the preservation of the works by Si
Mohand, the great Berber poet (15). Amrouche's Berber magnum opus extended
these early efforts to carve out a space for Berber culture in the backdrop of colonial
culture.

Amrouche's work consists precisely in disengaging the *chants* of Berber collective memory from their appropriation by the diffusionist logic of colonial history. A
recent effort reminiscent of Amrouche's project, Dipesh Chakrabarty's *Provincializing Europe*, similarly aims to pluralize historical narratives and disengage them
from historicist, exclusive perspectives.[10] Discussing the inadequacy of the European divide between public and private as a standard for measuring modernity in
India, Chakrabarty explains that Indian "narratives of the self and community . . .
often themselves bespeak an *antihistorical* consciousness, that is, they entail subject
positions and configurations of *memory* that challenge and undermine the subject
that speaks in the name of history" (37; my emphasis). Amrouche would appreciate
Chakrabarty's claim that "'History' is precisely the site where the struggle goes on to
appropriate, on behalf of the modern, . . . these other collocations of memory" (37).
In his Berber *Chants*, Amrouche re-situates his poetic persona in the culture of his
ancestors and so turns the *chants* into a self-referential *lieu de mémoire* in which he
can construct a unified identity and gain a voice.[11] This fragmentation of the condition of modernity into various components of the modern, without consideration
of geography or sequentiality, theoretically dislodges privileged European practices
of history and social theory to the benefit of alternative conceptions springing from
an area traditionally construed as marginal. As we will see, however, the productive-
ness of Amrouche's conceptions on the theoretical level does not carry over into
praxis in the context of nationalism and nation-formation. Amrouche thus reconfigures colonial history not as a universal, linear historical process, but rather, to
borrow Harry Harootunian's formulation, as a "politics of time capable of locating
practice immanently within a modernity that housed the temporalization of new
cultural forms developing everywhere" (32).

In this way, I argue, Amrouche strives to put vernacular Berber, as well as Algerian literature generally, on a par with French symbolism. Amrouche's dealings with
both modernism and colonial modernity must be considered in the ambiguity and

complexity of his position as a colonial artist, since his introduction to modernism was overdetermined by the rhetoric of his colonial education. Going a long way toward complicating recent questionings of the ideological implications of dominant periodizations of modernism, Amrouche discounts any consideration of typicality or Eurocentrism to focus on modernism as the spirit of the age of modernity. But if Amrouche's identification of Mallarmé's symbolism with "traditional" Berber oral poetry puts to the fore common modernist practices across cultural contexts, I do not mean to suggest that his poetry follows a strict line of symbolist poetics inaugurated by Mallarmé or that it simply extends, through an exact rendering of his aesthetic, the genealogy of canonical symbolism through time and space. In fact, Amrouche is not really concerned with Mallarmé's central position in the canon of symbolism, although his repressed envy for what he construes as the poet's hermeticism surfaces in many instances. Rather, it is the modernity to which Mallarmé's aesthetics lays exclusive claim that Amrouche proposes to appropriate. By elaborating an *ars poetica* reverberating with both canonical French modernism and Berber forms of expression, Amrouche obliterates the primacy of the center/margin paradigm of diffusionist cultural development and attempts to rid "traditional" forms of expression of primitivist recuperations and objectification.

His strategic juxtaposition with French symbolist aesthetics is thus performed in an effort to instrumentalize the similarity between Kabyle and European cultures for the benefit of counter-hegemonic views of cultural politics in a colonial context. Reintroducing incommensurability at the core of all cultures involved in the interaction specific to colonialism in Algeria, Amrouche disengages characteristics usually associated with modernism from a homogenous, diffusionist perspective and redefines vernacular colonial cultures as intrinsic "contact zones."[12] This process is endowed with political relevance, as Amrouche's vision of egalitarian multiculturalism in independent Algeria is predicated on the reintroduction of alterity and coevality at the core of the process of nation-formation.

RECONSTRUCTING BERBER MEMORY: THE STAKES OF CONCOMITANT TEMPORALITIES

The existence of diverse temporalities within concomitant nationalisms on the global stage calls into question homogeneous understandings of time in a historicist perspective. Anticipating recent assertions of a distinction between modernization and modernity, Amrouche's *Chants Berbères de Kabylie* aims to establish coevality between cultures by enunciating a multiple, shared present of synchronicity as the only acceptable form of temporal reference within which to situate oneself, regardless of a society's position in the modernization time line.[13]

For French historian Pierre Nora, the advent of official historiography with the onset of modernity in Western societies breached the subject's immediate experience of tradition for the benefit of an objective, official retrospective reconstruction of the past.[14] This instrumentalization of memory is often linked to the emergence of the nation-state as an imaginary construct that requires the foundation of a new national tradition and the eradication of alternative memories, individual and collective. Through the appropriation of select traces in the past, the collective memory of the nation-state projects a teleological narrative into the past, thereby legitimizing the national construct as authentic and potentially linked to mythical, sacred time. This historiographic evolution of European societies intersects with the unfolding of the inclusive process of modernity that it facilitates. Although Nora's argument mostly considers the context of metropolitan France, his analysis can be extended to a variety of locales in which communities that had established themselves around a continuous, eternal present of tradition were violently propelled into a modern historical time, where they inevitably found themselves marginalized as primitive and backward, i.e., "not yet" able to take history into their own hands. The constant revision of the discourse of history must therefore be understood from a historicist perspective of progress and development over time.

Benedict Anderson has convincingly argued that the emergence of an imaginary national community coincided with the shift to Walter Benjamin's "homogeneous, empty time" of History (Anderson 24–26). In this process, the subjective apprehension of time undergoes "homogenization" (Reinhart Koselleck's term) as time is construed as a supposedly objective, synchronized phenomenon throughout the nation. But Anderson's position requires some revision, for even in the distinctive, limited context of the nation, the idea of a unique temporality in which all phenomena would take place cannot account for the discrepancies pertinent to colonial spaces. Homi Bhabha suggests that the enunciative performance of the sign of modernity is marked by the specificities of the geographical and social contexts of its repetition:

> [W]hat *seems* the 'same' within cultures is negotiated in the [(post)colonial] time-lag of the 'sign'. . . . Because that lag is indeed the very structure of difference and splitting within the discourse of modernity . . . then each repetition of the sign of modernity is different, specific to its historical and cultural conditions of enunciation. (364; emphasis in original).

He posits modernity as "the historical construction of a specific position of historical enunciation and address" (Bhabha 360). Quoting Paul Gilroy, Mary-Louise Pratt calls for an "ethnohistorical reading of [the aspirations of] Western modernity [as a whole]" that would deconstruct the seemingly universal value of homogeneous, totalizing narratives of European modernity (Gilroy 8; quoted [partly] in Pratt "Modernity and Periphery" 28). To that end, Pratt marks out a sharp distinction between modernization and modernity, which in the Latin American context of her analysis are incommensurable.[15]

A similar distinction informs Amrouche's project in *Chants Berbères de Kabylie*. For the sense of dismay permeating the collection of poems *Cendres*, which he wrote from a position of historical and cultural exclusion, Amrouche substitutes in the *Chants Berbères de Kabylie* the hope of a renewed subject-position inscribed in history, albeit in a non-Eurocentric form. The *chants* were painstakingly collected by Amrouche mostly from his sister Taos and his mother Fadhma, the two demiurgic figures at the origin of the project. For it is through the voice of the eternal Mother that Berber culture is transmitted and communion with one's ancestral past achieved. (Taos subsequently recorded the songs from the volume in Kabyle.) The book consists of a translation of the original texts into French, which aims to provide as faithful a transcription as possible so as not to obscure the inherent musicality of the original sung text. To Amrouche, "only the original words transfigured by the music truly constitute [these *chants*]" (*AM* 68).[16]

The volume is divided into several sections, each echoing the social circumstance to which each song is pertinent: songs of exile, songs of love, satirical songs, songs of early childhood (*berceau*), songs of labor, dancing songs, songs of meditation, songs of pilgrimage. The *chants* become the accompaniment of the life from which they spring and whose daily spirituality they aim to transfigure. Inspiration comes from the mundane: a wishful return to "the spirit of childhood," understood as traditional life and the original language, is performed through poetic expression, which supposedly establishes union with one's deepest identity. This dynamic is particularly visible in the songs of exile. Only through the power of the word can the poet be imaginatively reconciled with his lost origins:

> Peace and greetings, o my country!
> My eyes have roamed worlds
> My sight is a spring storm
> In the tumult of thawing snow
> Mother, O my beloved Mother
> Ah! Exile is a long calvary. (Songs of Exile 17)[17]

Through poetic creation, Amrouche expresses his "memory of the original Language" (Amrouche, "Note" 165).[18] For the poet, "poetry . . . directly sparks the resurrection of the Mother-Form in one's metaphysical memory . . . [it is] a spiritual process prolonged through language" (166–67).[19] The verbal texture of the poem reinstates the purportedly intrinsic bond tying the voice to the spiritual order of the tribe. Each individual is connected to the group and, beyond, to the cosmic life of which it harmoniously partakes. The overlapping of the subject and his world is marked by numerous allegories that assign to the subject, in a process reminiscent of Baudelaire's correspondences, a direct correlative in another realm of cosmic life; the two elements are simply different incarnations of the original Idea they have come to represent: "With the Falcon, I flew in harmony / I was enraptured with freedom" (Satirical Songs 2).[20] This generative connection to immutable ideas carries with it a disruption of European conceptions of time and belonging.

To the authority of linear chronology, Amrouche opposes the disruptive power of a Berber alternative time line, an internal temporality which, through the mediation of the poetic voice, blends into the cosmic time of tradition: "Those poets . . . sang in unison with the world; they sang their present and they did not know that they were singing at the same time a past and a future that did not belong to them." (*AM* 63).[21] It would be easy to misconstrue Amrouche's opposition to calendar time as a mere inversion of the temporal dichotomy he means to displace. But, as I will show below, rather than invoke a conventional notion of the "premodern," Amrouche insists on the persistence of the "non-modern."[22]

The correspondence between the instant of the present of enunciation and correlated moments in both the past and the future is certainly reminiscent of Anderson's simultaneous time, and it is undeniable that Amrouche resorts to the mythical temporality of a utopian Berber Golden Age, which, through its claim to irrationality, defines itself quite blatantly in opposition to Eurocentric modernity: "Civilization too often estranges man from his nature; it dissipates a certain mental and affective disposition, that of the man who remains close to the land and who feels, as a natural and self-evident principle, that he and his life are not detached from cosmic life" (*AM* 62).[23] Amrouche gives another name to the Berber persona reciting the *chants*: "homme-enfant" (child-man), in reference to its innocence and purportedly unmediated inscription in a state of nature. Detached from any influence that would come from outside the voice of tradition, the child-man embodies Koselleck's concept of an internal time of phenomena, which Amrouche pitches against the abstract calendrical time necessary for a national community to imagine itself:

> [The child-man] does not tick off days and hours as a clock would, but rather feels that he follows his own interior time . . . and this interior flux is tightly connected to all other times . . . the time-span of the universe is . . . the sum of all these particular times. The singing of the world . . . is made up of the associated voices of these innumerable times (*AM* 64).[24]

Rife with Bergsonian echoes, this notion of "interior time" is conflated with an "interior poetry, which aims for silence, but a silence rife with a thousand toneless voices, the voices of the futures which come to completion in the live being that we are, at the very instant when we feel our unique and predestined nature in the chain of beings" (*AM* 67).[25]

In "Some Thoughts on Comparability and the Space-Time Problem," Harootunian argues that a consideration of internal temporalities cannot escape a logic of hierarchization and derivation. Drawing from Koselleck's analysis of the post-Enlightenment temporal order, Harootunian's argument lays bare the existence of an "internal time" of phenomena which would follow diverse simultaneous temporalities within the same space, thus exposing the deceitful attempts of the nation-state to present time as a unique, universally shared continuum. Insofar as the existence of an "internal time" of phenomena sanctions the predominance of the comparative method, this insight, for Harootunian, lies at the root of social sciences' approach to events (and cultures) in history. The problem, however, is that once this structure of time is extended to a global colonial world, it allows for the conception of simultaneous histories only within a Eurocentric model of development in which differing historical paces in different regions of the world are subjected to an historical ordering grounded in notions of completion and, therefore, adequacy. As Nora points out, "history can only conceive the relative" (9), which implies, outside the context of relational theories such as Glissant's, the existence of a unique standard used as a universal norm against which other histories are weighed, stripped of their absolute character, and reconfigured within a hierarchy of cultures. By upholding chronological difference predicated on a linear axis as the absolute standard, the development of comparative methodologies relegated non-Western cultures to a position of belatedness, on both the temporal and cultural levels.

Here, however, is Amrouche's key intervention: he appropriates this logic of internal temporality and, through his elaboration of concomitant temporalities within the colonial time frame, negates its hierarchical undercurrent. For the eternal present of tradition that he presents is not to be mistaken for the objectifying present of the Orientalist gaze, the *"présent sans mémoire et sans avenir"* [memoryless and futureless present] of colonial temporality. ("Le Combat Algérien," [The Algerian Struggle] *AM* 55). Amrouche's present embraces various concomitant temporalities in the same space while eschewing the historicist characterization of any component of this differential moment in terms of "anachronis[m]" (Chakrabarty 12). This present, indeed, subsumes the Messianic time of myth and, through its deep rooting in the past, opens a path to the future. It is a present of inclusion in a wider historical context. It supplies the poet with (relative) agency within his ancestral culture and therefore breaks the dynamics of exclusion and objectification imposed by the colonial order. In addition, it fosters an immediate sense of brotherhood as the first step toward political praxis: "This position of man within the Cosmos and face-to-face with himself may be called *presence to oneself and to the world*. He who is present in this way feels that he is the brother of rocks, of plants, of animals and stars; the brother of men, but through a brotherhood distinct from the diffuse sentiment stirred in him by an abstract concept." (*AM* 64–65).[26] In this context, the poetic persona is thus given a voice as part of a community with which he will be able to participate, some fifteen years later, in the political debates saturating the public sphere on the eve of the war of independence.

This fervent sense of community, supposedly missing from subjective experiences of modern life, is associated with a strong cosmic, even religious, sentiment. The "singing of the world" designates the voice of tradition manifesting itself to the younger generations, and, as the lines surrounding this passage in the text show, the collective memory which Amrouche constructs as an alternative rests on a spiritual conception of life.[27] This spirituality is expressed through the submission to a superior will which guides its progression toward the "orient" of its fate (Amrouche's term, here to be taken in the sense of "orientation," purpose). Amrouche thus draws a distinction between modern abstract categories and personal experience. The subject lies at the root of this configuration, as time becomes an experience not just of one individual but of his whole community through him: "Through him all times unfold. Time does not exist independently from him; on the contrary, it is through him that it is created. Once time comes to an end, he will come out of it and move into the Contemplation of the Face of God. Then, living divine Life, he will know true

liberty." (*AM* 66).[28] I will gloss over the implications of the obvious mystical resonance of this passage for now to concentrate instead on this notion of mediation.

For if the subject is central to the unfolding of universal time, the absorption
into this alternative, circular temporality of tradition does not go smoothly. The
issue of agency is at the very least problematic and would deserve to be examined in
more detail than I am permitted here. Suffice it to say for our purposes that the
freedom hinted at in the text can be achieved only in death, a pessimism that
Amrouche has also expressed elsewhere and that makes one wonder whether he
himself did not grow aware of the ineffectualness of his conception of a nostalgic,
idealized Berber culture purged of individual subjective agency as the touchstone of
anticolonial praxis.

Despite his delineation of a space of internal temporality coeval with historical
time, Amrouche's work bears the mark of his hybrid, elite status (he has French
citizenship) and fails to embrace the dynamics of subaltern insurgency. Absolute
secession from France was not originally the solution advocated by Amrouche, who
was rather partial to the historically dominant argument in favor of federalization.
Amrouche at first conceived of his mission as that of a representative of the Algerian
people to the French government and was hoping to serve as a mediator between
his two cultures.[29] Therefore, his identification with irrational, nonsecular cultural
forms in no way assimilates him to what Guha has described as "subaltern peasants," whose inscription in time necessarily obeys non-European, nonlinear dynamics.
Amrouche's position in colonial temporality is much more ambiguous. His idealized vision of Berber culture *re-creates* his past in a self-oriented process of mimicry; since Berber culture does not constitute an immediate site of inscription, it
must be imitated in an imaginative vision which, as is the case for all mimicry, can
only reproduce its original incompletely. Amrouche therefore remains as indelibly
alienated from his ancestral past as he feels that he is from the future: "I am a cultural hybrid. Cultural hybrids are monsters, very interesting monsters but monsters
with no future. I consider that I have been condemned by History" ("Notre Algérie,"
[Our Algeria] *AM* 134).[30] His "monstrosity" in the face of a tradition to which
he does not belong anymore resembles what Radhakrishnan has termed, echoing
Derrida, a "prosthesis of origin" (Radhakrishnan, "Derivative Discourses" 793). His
position is first and foremost a liminal one, that of an intellectual much indebted to
the categories of European political thought. His very interest in his ancestral culture is mediated through European protocols of encounter and the project behind
the volume resembles the anthological efforts carried out by Europeans in North
Africa in the interest of preserving an oral folkloric culture threatening to disappear
under the influence of global modernity.

It is thus not surprising that beneath the nativist facade of Amrouche's depiction
of Berber culture, the repressed residue of a primitivist approach to his own culture
should surface in (among other places) his milestone essay "L'Eternel Jugurtha:
Propositions sur le Génie Africain" (The Eternal Jugurtha: Propositions on African
Genius, 1946). The essay constitutes a Berber-inspired, imaginative depiction of the
North African character. The account purports to be a rationalization of the features

pertaining to the poet's culture and own subjectivity and, as such, promises relative identification with the object of study on the part of Amrouche. Yet, surreptitiously, the analysis shifts toward a more critical perspective. The discussion first evokes Jugurtha's fiery passion, which surfaces in his commitment to revolt as a mode of inscription into the world. Jugurtha is first and foremost resilient to the waves of conquest that marked the history of the Maghreb. His ability to deceive, his exaltation of freedom, and his instrumentalization of foreign cultures for the benefit of his rebellion are the object of much praise; Jugurtha truly seems a worthy inspiration for current-day nationalism. Yet in contrast with this uplifting vision, Amrouch, then emphasizes Jugurtha's incapacity to incarnate a European-inspired political subject who "engages with the world not only in terms of an object of aesthetic contemplation or . . . an endless source of ephemeral pleasure and pain" (Amrouche, *Jugurtha* 111).[31] The immediacy of Berber culture's relation to the world, which Amrouche greatly commended in the introduction to the *Chants,* is here reconfigured in terms of a lack. Jugurtha is enjoined to adopt a more rational, scientific disposition and to move away from an overly religious and mythical worldview—in a word, to become modern by developing a spirit of initiative and by promoting intensive modernization as a prerequisite to political modernity and emancipation.

Although Jugurtha's vernacular praxis of insurgency is the logical extension on the political level of the cultural argument elaborated in the introduction to the *Chants*, Amrouche seems to discount it here as a fruitful alternative to the embracing of Eurocentric modernity. In "L'Eternel Jugurtha," European modernity becomes an indispensable preliminary to nationalist revolt. His primitivist perception of Berber cultures as being steeped in a previous stage of development stands in blatant contradiction with his purported plea for a return to tradition. It thus appears that his aspiration to an inscription into tradition was no more than the expression of a desire of belonging, which the exclusive dynamics of European modernity had frustrated.

It is therefore important here to qualify Amrouche's radical questioning of Eurocentric essentialist perceptions as well as his positionality with regard to modernity. The construal of Berber culture as "traditional" throughout his whole production is enacted only in contrast to the traumatic imposition of colonial modernity, as is the case in many other colonial contexts. Construed on its own, as we will see, Berber culture reveals coincidentally both elements of Eurocentric modernity and "traditional" characteristics. As Peter J. Taylor has argued, "it is now impossible to write from outside the modern and therefore all critiques [of modernity] are themselves inherently modern" (2). The very anxiety expressed at the idea of the future demise of Berber folklore in the wake of modernization is in itself eminently modern, and, as much as Amrouche attempts to displace the modernity/tradition binary, his essentialist fetishization of Berber poetry imaginatively configured as free of any contact with Western civilization exposes him as being more complicit with modern conceptions of culture than he claims to be. The positing of modernization as the necessary preamble to political modernity in "L'Eternel Jugurtha" (i.e., the failure to preserve a distinction between modernization and modernity, as Mary-Louise Pratt

has advocated) evinces Amrouche's inherent complicity with colonial discursive formations and, therefore, his fundamental duplicity. Tradition is desirable only in the
guise of an imaginative construct, one superimposed on a solidified bedrock of
modern identity. Amrouche's construction of a timeless Kabyle character, which was
meant to endow him with agency and vocality, reveals its obvious limits: the ambiguity of his subjectivity resonating with the failure of his political commitment, he
appears as a divided subject caught in between the two poles of his identity.[32] In light
of "L'Eternel Jugurtha" and other late texts, the illusory character of his categoriza-
tion of Berber culture undoubtedly debilitates the political ramifications of his argument. The alternative presented to the modern inscription of subjects into history
relies on a delusion, which remains incommensurable with the material demands of
nationalist anticolonial praxis.

Amrouche's vision cannot eventuate in productive political nationalism—in
part owing to the antinomy of the subject-position from which he writes, but also
because the imagined, mythical Berber past that he calls upon is discrepant with the
purpose of the Arab Muslim majority. Deprived of materialization, his invocation
of an archaic past is confined to a marginal, ahistorical position in the midst of the
process of nation-formation that consecrated the inclusion of the Algerian nation
into history. Although resigned to the de facto necessity of the category of the nation in the fight for independence, his configuration of national politics retains the
same fragmentary, non-totalizing logic he opposed to Eurocentric categories in his
aesthetics. His transnational national ideal based on the coevality of cultures (Berber,
Arab, and European) and the inalienable right to expression and protection within
the frame of nation thus contravenes the modern narrative of nation-formation,
which necessarily requires the imaginative construction of a common historical tradition, particularly through the silencing of minority voices.

It is thus no surprise that Amrouche's death on the eve of the war of independence should have been interpreted as the utmost expression of the historical failure
of his project (Guibert). Despite his inscription in anticolonial struggle, the ambiguity
that plagued him to the end of his life had long since made his liminal position politically untenable. More convincing, however, is his discussion of Berber traditional
literature as an alternative to Eurocentric forms of modernism, to which I now return.

THE ISSUE OF DERIVATION IN GLOBAL
VISIONS OF MODERNITY

As I discussed earlier, my use of the term "symbolist" to characterize Amrouche's
poetic is not meant to conflate French and Berber aesthetic traditions. Berber oral
poetry may be best depicted as possessing plural, uneven symbolist characteristics

held in dialectical tension with concomitant non-Western characteristics, and it is in this sense and in this sense only that I use the term "symbolist" in reference to Amrouche's writing.[33] The relationship between these forms of symbolism raises a series of important questions: To what form of modernity does this aesthetic respond? How does that modernity relate to Western modernity? What is its position on the global map of the modern? How does the modernism which it engenders relate to European models?

In "Periodizing Modernism: Postcolonial Modernities and the Space/Time Borders of Modernist Studies," Susan Stanford Friedman makes a convincing plea against absolute, Eurocentric conceptions of what does or does not constitute modernism. Adapting global relational theories to the cultural encounters forced by colonialism, Friedman questions the relevance of theories that would limit modernity and its cultural expression to one period and location. For Friedman, the emergence of postcolonial spaces brings about the concurrent emergence of indigenous forms of modernity, and she associates this engagement with modernity with the nationalist experience, understood as a central, formative occurrence in the accession of formerly colonized nations to the very phenomenology of modernity. Yet this claim, as we shall see, proves problematic in the case of Amrouche's poetry.

Drawing on theories of multiple modernities, Friedman emphasizes the permeability of the cultural and geopolitical boundaries isolating societies and describes the unprecedented (and sometimes violent) interactions brought about by colonial encounters as a fruitful reciprocal exchange between cultures that had been relatively isolated. Modernism in all its forms and locations thus bears the mark of this mutual indebtedness, be it under the guise of primitivism (e.g., in the Africanist leanings of Picasso's cubist period) or in the incorporation of Western modernist strands in local cultural production: "Traveling and intermixing cultures are not unidirectional, but multidirectional; not linear influences, but reciprocal ones; not passive assimilations, but actively transformative ones, based in a blending of adaptation and resistance." She then concludes, "All modernisms develop as a form of cultural translation or transplantation produced through intercultural encounters" (430).

It is the modalities of this concept of "transplantation" as well as its implications that I would like to interrogate here. Distancing her argument from diffusionism, Friedman turns to geographer J. M. Blaut's definition of the concept in *The Colonizer's Model of the World* to underscore the Eurocentric dynamics that presuppose modernity as a synonym for the Westernization of the Third World. This binary conception construes emergent postcolonial national literatures either as removed from modernism altogether, or, at best, as deriving from Euro-American models. Friedman rightly makes the articulation of the issue of sequentiality (and simultaneity) between European and postcolonial forms of modernism the touchstone of her argument by presenting a substitute concept, "indigenization," which she envisions as "a form of making *native* or *indigenous* something from elsewhere"; this process "presumes an affinity of some sort between the cultural practices from elsewhere and those in the indigenizing location" (430). Modernism in emergent literatures is not belated or derivative in relation to a "center" but proceeds from a *mutual* enrichment between the two cultures drawn together over time. "Polycentric modernities" (426), a concept derived from Gaonkar, which I here call vernacular in their individuality, are formed from the incorporation of nontypical cultural practices adopted from elsewhere. The adjunction of imported "modern" elements to "traditional" practices forms a discrete form of engagement with the general concept of modernity, one that, in keeping with Bhabha's concept of "time-lag," reflects the intrinsic sociohistorical circumstances of the locale. Modernism therefore represents what Friedman calls "the expressive dimension of modernity" (432). Inasmuch as modernist form for Friedman reflects engagement with the specific characteristics of a vernacular postcolonial modernity, modernism can only result from the incorporation of the new into the old. The mutually constitutive nature of this dynamic stands at the origin of both European and non-Western forms of modernism and seems to eschew the totalizing logic of global literary periodizations based on a center-periphery model. Yet Amrouche's juxtaposition of canonical symbolist aesthetics with what he presents as purely "traditional" Berber oral sung poetry in a colonial context complicates the issue in at least two ways. First, the way in which Amrouche combines his critique of canonical French modernism and his analysis of traditional Berber forms of expression suggests a lingering element of historicist sequentiality in Friedman's analysis. Second, it underscores the need to recognize the importance of the endogenous in relation to adapted or creolized elements of culture. Appreciating the full complexity of the fruitful intersection of supposedly distinct forms of cultural production is crucial to understanding the significance of Amrouche's reflections on the nature of poetic creation.

"Saint Stéphane Mallarmé," as its title suggests, is a (mostly) laudatory opinion piece on the aesthetics perfected by the French Symbolist poet. A fervent admirer of Baudelaire's treatment of the relationship between reality and an imagined world, Mallarmé develops the theory that poetic creation must do away with the impure form of everyday language(s) and must aspire to the condition of music—the sound he considered closest to the Supreme language, the "stamp of Truth Herself Incarnate." ("From 'Crisis in Poetry'" 124). Mallarmé associates the immateriality of language with the autotelic quality of the poetic text, whose intrinsic objective is to give voice to a "Spirit" exterior to the poet: "If the poem is to be pure, the poet's voice must be stilled and the initiative taken by the words themselves, which will be set in motion as they meet unequally in collision" (126). The true value of the poem, it would seem, rests in its obliteration of authorial intention; rhythm and structure spring from within as the Spirit becomes incarnated through poetic language. Music is therefore presented as an ideal medium for an expression free of the contaminating power of corrupted words. In Mallarmé's view, silence reigns supreme in the economy of the work of art; impersonal, predestined interactions preside over the emergence of suggestion as the privileged mode of representation. Amrouche reads Mallarmé's position as being eminently symptomatic of the modernist escape from the hustle of the empirical, modern world into an estranged world of pure value. In keeping with Friedman's strategy of "cultural parataxis," Amrouche's withdrawal into the spirituality of Berber reified tradition thus takes on new meaning when read in parallel with Mallarmé.[34]

"Saint Stéphane Mallarmé" presents a somewhat contradictory misreading of the poet. Amrouche immediately emphasizes the unorthodoxy of his reading by distancing himself from French criticism's hostile response to Mallarmé's arcane expression and poetic detachment. Amrouche introduces his personal fascination with Mallarmé as a provocation, and he positions himself as an outcast from French academia. Although he praises Mallarmé for the "despotism" of his writing, which for him reflects the poet's intentionality, it is Mallarmé's "purity" that seduces Amrouche, his absolute impassiveness in the face of the world.[35] Amrouche sees Mallarmé as a martyrlike figure at the service of a higher principle who despises both the fame and the solace that poetry can bring its author. Refusing the convenience of inspiration, Mallarmé, in Amrouche's eyes, does not succumb to the imperious call of his inner voice. In this respect, Mallarmé comes to embody an ideal, stable authorial position, one that Amrouche, who conceived of poetry as a means to find unity and harmony when suffering from the schism of colonial ambiguity, has so many times failed to attain. Mallarmé's writing persona assumes the form of a mere vehicle for pure *chant* (here, as in the *chants,* an invocation, a term closer in its connotations to the Latin *carmen* than to the more prosaic *cantus* from which the French word is etymologically derived). Through its autotelic aesthetic, Mallarmé's text reintroduces transcendence (both in the text and in its reader) in the shape of an inner metaphysical quality of its language: "He systematically elaborates a metaphysics of poetry, which he elevates to the level of divinity. He reveals in the language a specific virtue, which he assimilates to the divine Word" ("Saint Stéphane Mallarmé").[36]

Yet Amrouche does not *completely* value Mallarmé's aspiration to the expression of universal truth in a depersonalized manner. On the contrary, to Amrouche, Mallarmé's endeavor is akin to a demiurgic attempt to play God, a project which he envisions as aporic. The refusal of inspiration comes down to negating the power of poetic creation. Throughout Amrouche's contradictory and at times misinformed analysis of Mallarmé's dealings with poetic intentionality, he comes to deplore the excess of asceticism in Mallarmé's symbolism: "To abolish chance! Such a hubristic endeavor, a major and fatal temptation, which was to lead the poet to barenness" ("Saint Stéphane Mallarmé").[37] The temptation to play God is one from which Amrouche is preserved through his resort to Berber tradition as a source for inspiration: in the purported immemorial wisdom of his people, Amrouche gains a harmonious understanding of the workings of the universe, an insight of which purely modern subjectivities are, in his view, devoid.

Amrouche's introduction to the *Chants Berbères de Kabylie,* which delineates a poetic specific to Berber culture, hints obliquely at the similarities between symbolist aesthetics and "traditional" Berber poetry. Although no direct discussion of Mallarmé or any other canonical modernist is introduced, an implicit comparison with symbolist aesthetics underlies the whole argument. Amrouche confessed in a later interview to "[having] interpreted the *chants* through [his] . . . knowledge of

French poetry which [he] had acquired and, through this very knowledge of French poetry, a certain intuition of universal poetry."[38] Traditional Berber forms are said to *naturally* possess the purity of symbolist poetical language: "Nothing links these images together; there are no grounds for comparison. It may be that the language did not provide them with a very developed grammatical apparatus. It is not a language meant for intellectuals. But it constitutes a prime medium for poetry" (*AM* 63).[39] While these poets have made artificial opaqueness the hallmark of poetical language, Berber traditions offer a creativity that finds its origin in everyday life and its expression in the most popular forms of the language. The distinction between the beautiful and the useful is abolished as poetic creation is by nature intuitive, the expression of the poet's absolute communion with his environment:

> Without a doubt, they are exceptionally successful. The work of art only expresses the real nature of things and of everyday life through detachment. Here, on the contrary, the work immediately reflects reality . . . our *chants* are at the same time works of art and useful instruments. They fuse nature and art. (*AM* 66)[40]

For Amrouche, the "works of art" mentioned here are undoubtedly symbolist creations, but for their suspicious estrangement from the real world, the touchstone of the critique developed in "Saint Stéphane Mallarmé," Amrouche substitutes a poetic of social engagement and communication.

Amrouche refuses to restrict the power of Berber poetry to the primitive, to that of an anthropological object of study. This poetic experience, like a symbolist one, rests on its spiritual affect, its esoteric character. Echoing Jean Moréas' "Symbolist Manifesto," Amrouche describes Berber poetry in its disembodied, ascetic structure, its pure verbal logic.[41] Purified to the extreme, just as it is in symbolist aesthetics, the underlying verbal weft is weighed, the density of each word highlighted, while the resonance of the lines in the interspersed moments of silence provides the remaining words with intensity. Associative through complex associations of images ("symbols," in Amrouche's words), Berber poetry expresses through its minimalism the clarity of its vision, its insight into the dynamics presiding over the march of the world. The *chant* becomes the truest incarnation not of the generalized Spirit in Mallarmé's disincarnate vision but of the tribe's Spirit. As such, the *chant* constitutes a vocal manifestation of its harmonious engagement with the world. Through the comparison with Berber poetics, commitment to the community is affixed to Mallarmé's symbolist aesthetic: "Thus, one can say that our *chants* are simply *what they are* and do not *pretend* to be what they are not and that, because of that, they are deeply rooted in human nature" (*AM* 66; emphasis in original).[42] This reference to human nature is significant; through its use, one can fathom how deeply the humanist ideals duplicitously advocated by French colonial discursive formations have left their mark on Amrouche's mind-set. Thus, while his text moves beyond purely aesthetic considerations, his argument attempts to inflect what he sees as European symbolist detachment with a moral concern for the world. Amrouche's political musings about the future of independent

Algeria, we recall, revolved around the same notion of a universal propensity to humanism, here redefined as a genuine ethics that formerly colonized people need to embrace in order to achieve political justice and balance in their soon-to-be-formed nation.

Liberating Berber cultures from primitivist perceptions, Amrouche reappropriates the traditional cultures of North Africa and displaces creative agency from the West to its peripheries (albeit with the notable limits evoked earlier). By conflating canonical symbolist aesthetics and traditional Berber inspiration, Amrouche does much to challenge the traditional/modern dichotomy and to disrupt the exoticist definitions of Berber culture dominant in contemporaneous Eurocentric taxonomies. Amrouche's juxtaposition of French high culture and Berber folklore emphasizes the similarities existing between the two traditions and elevates Kabyle culture to the status of a legitimate alternative to the spiritual experience underlying symbolism. Through this effort, Amrouche therefore prompts a revision of Friedman's concept of indigenization, which rests on the hypothesis that all forms of modernity partake in an adaptation of foreign concepts into more local, malleable forms.

In Friedman's eyes, all modernities, and, in a related fashion, all modernisms, emerged from such creolization. But Amrouche's treatment of the intersection between Berber culture and European symbolism highlight additional considerations. First, contrary to Friedman's anticipation, Amrouche's elaboration of a vernacular engagement with symbolism occurs at the height of the colonial period (the *chants* were published in 1939), not after a successful nationalist experience has been achieved through independence.[43] Although Friedman acknowledges a possible inscription of modernity in colonial emancipatory efforts predating independence, her paradigm tends to fall prey to the same logic of sequentiality that informs historicism, as it is only through the adoption of the Western-inspired political form of the nation-state upon independence that colonial spaces can access modernity. Amrouche's production re-situates modernism in the interstitial space of early (and sometimes failed) anticolonial activism. Second, Amrouche underscores *common* features to two distinct, and supposedly isolated, strands of poetic creation. Although the ancestral "purity" of "traditional" Kabyle culture is undeniably the object of unmitigated conflation on the part of Amrouche, the symbolist characteristics of its poetry are first and foremost presented as endogenous, not as adapted. He presents the similarities as an accident, a phenomenon that no global dynamics of cultures and histories could have infallibly caused. In the light of my previous comments regarding Amrouche's own liminal position with regard to the modern/traditional binary, it may be wise to question his presentation of Kabyle culture as being perfectly preserved from any contact with European modernity; unquestionably, there is more creolization at stake here than he claims to see—at least in the modalities of his own hybrid vision. But his analysis of Kabyle culture still carries with it important corollaries, not least in its revelation of Amrouche's ambivalent (and characteristically modernist) engagement with the issue of culture and tradition. More significant than the question of creolization is the reconfiguration of the relational dynamics of the modern and the traditional that Amrouche's modernist-inspired vision imposes on our contemporary considerations of modernism and, beyond, of the modernity that emerges through this dichotomy.

THE ISSUE OF CULTURAL TRANSLATION

Whether the result of creolization or not, the presence of independent symbolist traits in Berber poetry successfully challenges the supremacy of European aesthetic models. Amrouche's Berber-specific form of poetic engagement with modernity aims to produce poetry on a par with Euro-American symbolism. But if Amrouche's project represents (to return to Friedman's formulation) the "expressive dimension of modernity," what he responds to is a specifically vernacular form of modernity rooted in Berber culture. The characteristics of this modernity are developed further in political writings that address the problem of translating Eurocentric modernity into local instantiations. How, he asks, can one negotiate a space in the globalized economy of colonialism in which the local can be mapped out on a par with the de facto universal model?

Through his critique of modernist detachment in Mallarmé's aesthetic, which he associates with an unethical social position that duplicates colonial practices of exclusion, Amrouche aims to disrupt the segregationist ideology of colonial modernity. In *Culture and Imperialism*, Edward Said emphasizes the shift from early-twentieth-century literature, nurtured by triumphalist geography, to a literature where artistic constriction reinvents spatiality as a purely formal attribute. He argues that the focus of modernist literature during the early twentieth century shifted from the reality it purported to represent toward the mode of representation, thus distancing itself from a world perceived as inescapably slipping away (189–90). It is such a shift toward further detachment from political and social reality that Amrouche condemns, a shift he associates with a lack of ethical (especially anticolonial) engagement. His theorization of the gap separating theoretical humanism in French thought and its supposed applications in a colonial context is central to his vision of aesthetics and poetic creation. If he condemns the unconscionable use of humanistic philosophy by colonial France, he nevertheless does not obliterate the intrinsic worth of the concept itself. Like other contemporaneous francophone colonial intellectuals, Amrouche seems reluctant to forsake the cultural paradigm that so influenced his own intellectual and poetic identity. Therefore, rather than discounting French humanist modernity altogether, he prefers to question its universalism and to suggest a vernacular revision of the concept from a "traditional" Berber perspective in order to make it more appropriate to his struggle against the inequity at work in colonial Algeria and to the country's need for social and political change. His adjunction of the ethical dimension of Berber spirituality, one connected to the non-modern time of ancestral history, aims to revise humanism into a more adapted instrument of political emancipation, one seeking, in Radhakrishnan's words, "to find the other within the hegemonic moment of representation in the name of a multilateral and universal alterity" (791).

It is on this renewed concept of humanism and respect for cultural and religious plurality that Jean El Mouhoub Amrouche bases his idea of an untainted form of modernity, which independent Algeria, beyond the war of independence, should aim to embrace while adapting it to its vernacular specificities. Despite the failure of his political project and the problematic subject-position informing his writing (not least in his choice of a European humanist model as the backbone of his vision of Berber vernacular modernity), the most fruitful aspect of Amrouche's work lies in his treatment of the issue of the local "translation" of Eurocentric modernity, that is, in his outlook on the modalities of the interaction between a local that presents itself as a universal (the West) and a local which cannot afford to (the rest of the world).[44]

Harootunian presents a quite pessimistic prospect when he argues that the only alternative to a diffusionist logic of culture lies in the exacerbation of "anticolonial nationalism as evidence of difference resting on the claims of authentic cultural resources that have managed to remain free from contamination," a dynamics that "matches perfectly a view that has privileged the stolidity of an enduring and apparently unchanging spatialscape where time is rooted in a primordial and infinite repetitiveness" (36). Regardless of Harootunian's critique of the term "alternative modernity," in his perspective local embodiments of modernity are inescapably anchored in a Western-led developmental prospect. In fact, Harootunian ascribes an alternative character only to countries that have undergone late economic modernization—late with respect to linear time. In his view, the only possible foundation of an alternative modernity thus necessarily lies in the positing of an imaginative non-modern authenticity of which local culture can avail itself and which gives it legitimacy on the global level. This legitimacy, however, rests on an illusion (that of cultural isolation) and ultimately duplicates the colonial dynamics of temporal inequality. We have seen the limits of Amrouche's use of a mythical authentic tribal culture as a starting point for nationalism. Although the imaginative construction of a national past is indispensable in the context of nation-formation, the legitimization of local culture in a Eurocentric geopolitical paradigm is coeval with its accession to the temporality of linear history, that is, when the local culture is elevated to the status of national culture in the moment of independence.[45]

Yet Amrouche offers an alternative solution less vulnerable to recuperation into the diffusionism of colonial modernity. His comparative reading of French symbolism and Berber oral poetry emphasizes the presence of common features of cultural modernity in different spaces that emerge independently of economic modernization. If Berber culture can evince elements of a premodern mindscape through its conception of time and still retain endogenous modern features (as does Indian modernity for Chakrabarty), its hybridity precludes any historicist reading of its past. Therefore, the linear representation of time as a teleological process whose ending stage is necessarily exemplified by Western modernity is an irrelevant theoretical construct in the specific context of the native cultures of Algeria. Berber cultures do not fit into a homogenous, continuous conception of history; they possess their own internal time. Even if this modernity provides an inadequate basis for the process of nation-formation, Amrouche, unlike Harootunian, does not understand vernacular modernity as suffering from a fundamental lack.

The purpose here is not to supplant Europe in Eurocentric perspectives, but rather to dismantle the practice of Eurocentrism. Although decentered notions of temporality pervade Amrouche's critical production, it is important to note that no consistent theory of alternative modernity is even hinted at in his work. On the contrary, Amrouche lays claim to the primacy historically granted to the categories of European political thought, albeit unsuccessfully. The preponderance of Eurocentric models remains undefeated, but the task of dismantling them must be undertaken even as its inherent limitations are embraced. Amrouche's contribution to this project lies in his elaboration of fluid critical models for the analysis of native productions and of their relation to global systems of modernity. In this respect, his approach advantageously reveals a site of resistance through which what Appadurai calls the "disjunctions" of global modernity can be investigated. Chakrabarty's concept of a "politics of despair" acknowledges the inevitability of European thought as the structural framework informing implementations of political modernity on the global level. Our analytical practices, according to Chakrabarty, must remain true to the material realities of our world: "The point is not to reject social science categories but to release into the space occupied by particular European histories . . . other normative and theoretical thought enshrined in other existing life practices and their archives" (20). Only through the relational reading of contemporaneous, non-totalizing cultural practices in the perspective of history—a mode of reading enacted, if imperfectly, by Amrouche—can we expect our theoretical paradigms to provide compelling alternatives to despair.[46]

NOTES

1. See most notably Booth and Rigby; Jameson "Modernism and Imperialism"; Gikandi.

2. Important efforts in this direction include Doyle and Winkiel (2005); Friedman "Paranoia, Pollution, and Sexuality" and "Periodizing Modernism"; Geist and Monléon; Kronfeld; Pollard; Cuddy-Keane.

3. See Emery's contribution to this volume for an in-depth discussion.

4. This theme will be developed extensively in Amrouche's political writings. See, for instance, "Une certaine image de la France" (A Certain Image of France), "Quelques raisons de la révolte algérienne" (A Few Causes of the Algerian Revolt), and "La France comme mythe et réalité" (France as Myth and Reality), all in *Jean Amrouche: L'Eternel Jugurtha (1906–1962)*, hereafter abbreviated as *AM*.

5. This effort prefigured the work of Amrouche's student in Tunis, Albert Memmi, and that of Martiniquan psychiatrist Frantz Fanon, who was no stranger to the psychological effects of the colonial situation in Algeria. Assigned to a hospital in the colony, he had firsthand experience of the mental disorders suffered as a result of colonialism. While his first book, *Black Skin, White Masks,* was anchored in the reality of the racial question in the Antilles, *A Dying Colonialism* and *The Wretched of the Earth* were written in the wake of his growing sympathies for the fate of the colonized in Algeria and his support for the nationalist movement. Of special interest is the chapter exclusively dedicated to the report of Fanon's observations on several case studies encountered between 1954 and 1959 in Algeria, all related to the afflictions caused by the atrocities of the independence war—torture in particular (in the English translation, "Colonial War and Mental Disorders" in *The Wretched of the Earth*).

6. See, for instance, Déjeux's chapter on Amrouche in *La Littérature Maghrébine de Langue Française*; also his "La Quête Inapaisée (The Unrequited Quest): Jean Amrouche et Patrice de la Tour du Pin" and Giuliana Toso-Rodinis's "Jean Amrouche et Giuseppe Ungaretti: une Identité Retrouvée (Identity Regained)?," both in *AM.*

7. Postcolonial theory has shed light on the shortcomings of the mimetic process between two cultures. Chakrabarty argues that "the mode of self-representation that the 'Indian' can adopt . . . is what Homi Bhabha has justly called 'mimetic.' Indian history, even in the most dedicated socialist or nationalist hands, remains a mimicry of a certain 'modern' subject of 'European' history and is bound to represent a sad figure of lack and failure." (40). Whether one understands mimicry in the sense developed here or rather in terms of a subversive imitation (as Bhabha himself suggests, quite differently from Chakrabarty's interpretation), the process of flawless imitation is in any case doomed to failure. Its result is always incomplete and eventuates in a condition of hybridity, whose very existence belies the essentialist turn of historicist theories of difference.

8. For the text of the introduction to the volume, I used "Introduction aux Chants Berbères de Kabylie," *AM* 62–68, hereafter "Amrouche *Chants*."

9. ". . . pauvre, primitive, fruste, répétitive, servile par rapport aux modèles arabo-islamiques . . ." Unless otherwise noted, all translations from the French are mine.

10. Chakrabarty, in an epilogue to the introduction to *Provincializing Europe*, emphasizes two main features of historicism: the object of historicist analysis needs to be "internally unified" and its "develop[ment takes place] over time" (23). While the development need not be sequential, historicism postulates an evolution from an early incomplete form to a unified whole that has reached the full development of its potential. This process "seeks to find the general in the particular," i.e., in a context of hegemony, to endow one particular memory with universal authority and normativity (23).

11. I use here Nora's concept of sites of memory, "where memory crystallizes and secretes itself . . ., certain sites where a sense of historical continuity persists" (7). Nora sees *lieux de mémoire* as symptoms of the displacement of the unmediated, intimate subjective experience of tradition by the advent of modern historiography and the related project of nation-formation (8).

12. One could even argue, to extend Pratt's paradigm, that his attempt to reconstruct his Berber identity in a nostalgic, primitivist fashion constitutes a case of "autoethnography," which, roughly speaking, she defines as "partly collaborating with and appropriating the idioms of the conqueror" (*Imperial Eyes* 9). In this respect, it is significant that the project of the *Chants* should have been carried out through the mediation of the French language.

13. Harootunian presents a similar vision of synchronicity, although one based on the primacy of capital: "received comparative approaches have consistently denied a relationship of coevality to precisely those societies targeted for study, misrecognizing a coexistent present we all inhabit by demanding a perspective located in a different temporal register from those societies and cultures we are seeking to understand, making them outside to our inside" (32–33).

14. In Nora's words, "Each historian was convinced that his task consisted in establishing a more positive, all-encompassing, and explicative memory" (8). By "collective memory," I refer to K. L. Klein's definition as "a set of recollections attributable to some overarching group mind that could recall past events in the (admittedly poorly understood) ways in which we believe that individuals recall past events." (Klein 135).

15. Drawing inspiration from Norbert Lechner's postulate, Pratt envisions modernization as "the unfolding of instrumental rationality" (through history) and modernity as "the unfolding of normative rationality leading toward autonomy and self-determination" (34).

16. "Seules les paroles originales, transfigurées par la musique, les constituent dans leur vérité."

17. "Paix et Salut, ô mon pays! / Mes yeux ont parcouru des mondes / Ma vue est un orage de printemps / Dans le tumulte des neiges fondants / Mère, ô ma mère bien aimée, / Ah! L'exil est un long calvaire!"

18. "Le souvenir du Langage originel."

19. "La poésie . . . suscite directement dans la mémoire métaphysique la résurrection de la Forme-Mère . . . [c'est] une opération spirituelle qui se prolonge dans le langage."

20. "Avec le faucon, je volais de conserve / J'étais ivre de liberté."

21. "Ces poètes . . . ont chanté à l'unisson du monde; ils ont chanté leur présent et ils ne savaient pas qu'ils chantaient en même temps un passé et un avenir étrangers."

22. The notion of the premodern informs many historicist critiques, notably Jameson's *A Singular Modernity*.

23. "La civilisation a trop souvent pour effet d'éloigner l'homme de lui-même, de dissiper un certain climat mental et affectif, celui de l'homme qui demeure proche de la terre et qui éprouve, avec la force d'une donnée première et évidente, le sentiment que lui-même et sa vie ne sont pas detachés de la vie cosmique."

24. "[L'homme-enfant] ne compte pas les jours et les heures comme une horloge, mais il se sent le facteur d'une durée intérieure . . . et ce flux intérieur est étroitement associé à toutes les autres durées . . . la durée de l'Univers ne serait autre chose que la composante de toutes les durées particulières. Le chant du monde . . . c'est le choeur de ces innombrables durées associées."

25. "Poésie intérieure qui tend au silence, mais un silence peuplé de mille voix sans timbre, les voix des devenirs qui s'achèvent dans l'être vivant que nous sommes, en l'instant précis où nous nous éprouvons comme un être unique et prédestiné dans la chaîne des êtres."

26. "cette position de l'homme dans le Cosmos et en face de lui-même . . . on peut appeler la *Présence à soi-même et au monde.* Celui qui est présent de cette manière, celui-là se sent le frère des pierres, des plantes, des animaux et des étoiles; le frère des hommes, mais d'une fraternité qui n'est pas le sentiment diffus que répercute en lui une formule abstraite."

27. The influence of religion on Amrouche's writing has been the object of much criticism, be it as Catholicism or as a native religious sensibility. See, for instance, Déjeux, "La Quête inapaisée [The Unrequited Quest]"; Le Baut, *Jean El Mouhoub Amrouche*.

28. "En lui les temps s'accomplissent. La durée n'existe pas indépendamment de lui, tout au contraire c'est en lui qu'elle se crée. Une fois révolue, il sortira du temps, pour entrer dans la Contemplation du Visage de Dieu. Alors, participant à la Vie Divine, il connaîtra la vraie liberté." Amrouche's vision of the subject is in no way coextensive with the category underlying Western post-Enlightenment philosophy; the subject is rather envisioned as a channel through which tradition is enacted in the material world, and his subjectivity is conceived only in terms of his expression of a communal identity. The issue of free will is excluded from this paradigm.

29. *Jean Amrouche: L'Eternel Jugurtha (1906–1962)* contains a few letters exchanged with General De Gaulle, the French president during the Algerian war (see page 138 in particular). For an enunciation of his role as a representative of the subalterns, see "Aux Algériens" (To Algerians) and "Quelques raisons de la révolte algérienne" (A Few Causes of the Algerian Revolt) in the same volume.

30. "Je suis un hybride culturel. Les hybrides culturels sont des monstres. Des monstres très intéressants, mais des monstres sans avenir. Je me considère donc comme condamné par l'Histoire."

31. ". . . s'intéresse à ce monde autrement que comme un objet de contemplation esthétique ou . . . une source inépuisable de voluptés et de douleurs éphémères."

32. In Radhakrishnan's words, Amrouche's failure can be construed as the inability to simultaneously adopt a "double strategy: redeem [one]self specifically from the mark of derivativeness by signifying on modernity and the West in a certain way, and engage [one] self in the multilateral demonstration that there is nothing that is not derivative" (790).

33. For a related meditation on cultural translations of symbolism, see Ram's contribution to this volume.

34. For Friedman, who echoes Pratt and Appadurai, on cultural parataxis, see her "Paranoia, Pollution, and Sexuality," 245–47, and her contribution to this volume.

35. Amrouche's reading of Mallarmé is as partial as it is at times misinformed. Recent key critiques of the poet have in fact downplayed his putatively disinterested persona to explore his engagement with various aspects of contemporary life. See, for instance, Ancet and Oster.

36. "Il compose systématiquement une métaphysique de la poésie, qu'il élève au rang de la divinité. Il découvre dans le langage une vertu spécifique qui s'assimile au Verbe divin."

37. "Abolir le hasard! Surhumaine entreprise et tentation majeure, tentation mortelle qui devait conduire le poëte à la stérilité"

38. ". . . je les ai interprétés à travers la connaissance . . . de la poésie française que j'avais pu acquérir et, à travers même cette connaissance de la poésie française, une certaine intuition de la poésie universelle" (Conference-debate on "Culture and Colonialism," Cercle Ouvert, Paris, 7 May 1957). Quoted in Déjeux, "Jean Amrouche ou l'Eternel Jugurtha," 103.

39. "Aucun lien logique entre ces images, aucun terme de comparaison. Sans doute la langue elle-même ne mettait-elle pas à leur disposition un appareil grammatical très développé. Ce n'est pas une langue faite pour les intellectuels. Mais elle est un instrument poétique de premier ordre."

40. "Sans aucun doute, [ces chants] sont une réussite exceptionnelle. L'oeuvre d'art n'exprime la nature profonde des choses et de la vie quotidienne qu'en se détachant d'elles. Ici au contraire l'oeuvre adhère immédiatement au réel.[. . .] nos chants sont en même temps des œuvres d'art et d'utiles instruments. En eux s'accomplit la fusion de la nature et de l'art."

41. Moréas defines symbolist aesthetics as the attempt to "clothe the Ideal in a perceptible form": "In this art, scenes from nature, human activities, and all other real world phenomena could not be described for their own sake; here, they are perceptible surfaces destined to represent their esoteric affinities with primordial Ideas" (Symbolist Manifesto).

42. "Aussi peut-on dire que nos chants se sont contentés d'*être* au lieu de chercher à *paraître*, et que, à cause de cela aussi, ils sont profondément enracinés dans l'humain."

43. Friedman, "Periodizing Modernism," links the development of (post)colonial modernity to the moment of nation-formation (427).

44. Chakrabarty associates the issues surrounding "capitalist modernity" with what he calls "a problem of translation" between cultures (17).

45. See Fanon's discussion of the problems specific to this concept of "national culture" in a postcolonial context (especially *The Wretched of the Earth*).

46. Two of the texts addressed in this chapter—"Saint Stéphane Mallarmé," *La Tunisie Française Littéraire* (21 mai 1941) and Armand Guibert, *Jean Amrouche (1906–1962) par un témoin de sa vie*—were procured from the *Fonds Roblès-Patrimoine Méditerranéen* archives at the Université Paul Valéry-Montpellier III, France. I wish to thank Guy Dugas and Florence Chaudoreille for facilitating my research at the *Fonds*.

WORKS CITED

Amrouche, Jean. *Cendres* [Ashes]. Paris: L'Harmattan, 1983.

———. *Chants Berbères de Kabylie* [Berber sung poetry of Kabylia]. 1939. Ed. Tassadit Yacine. Paris: L'Harmattan, 1988.

———. *Etoile Secrète* [Secret Star]. Tunis: Edition des Mirages, 1937.

———. "Introduction aux Chants Berbères de Kabylie." *Jean Amrouche: L'Eternel Jugurtha (1906–1962)*. Archives de la Ville de Marseille. Marseille: Palais de Beaux-Arts, 1985: 62–68.

———. "L'Eternel Jugurtha: Propositions sur le Génie Africain" [The Eternal Jugurtha: Propositions on the African Genius]. *Jean Amrouche: L'Eternel Jugurtha (1906–1962)*. Archives de la Ville de Marseille. Marseille: Palais de Beaux-Arts, 1985: 108–11.

———. "Note sur la Grâce de Ravissement en Poésie" [Note on the Grace of Ravishing in Poetry]. *Fontaine* 19–20 (Mars–Avril 1942): 161–67.

———. "Saint Stéphane Mallarmé." *La Tunisie Française Littéraire* 21 mai 1941.

Ancet, Jacques. "Le Chant sous les Mots" [The Song beneath the Words]. *Europe* 825–26 (Jan.–Fév. 1998): 33–48.

Anderson, Benedict. *Imagined Communities.* New York: Verso, 1991.

Anselin, Jules-René. "Rapport sur Bougie" [Report on Bougie]. *Bulletin de la Société d'Anthropologie de Paris* [Bulletin of the Anthropology Society of Paris] (1860): 155–68.

Appardujai, Arjun. *Modernity at Large: Cultural Dimensions of Globalization.* Minneapolis: University of Minnesota Press, 1996.

Archives de la Ville de Marseille. *Jean Amrouche: L'Eternel Jugurtha (1906–1962).* Marseille: Palais de Beaux-Arts, 1985.

Audisio, Gabriel. *Jeunesse de la Méditerranée.* Paris: Gallimard, 1935.

Bhabha, Homi. "'Race,' Time, and the Revision of Modernity." *Theories of Race and Racism. A Reader.* Ed. Les Back and John Solomos. London: Routledge, 2000.

Blaut, J. M. *The Colonizer's Model of the World: Geographical Diffusionism and Eurocentric History*. New York: Guilford Press, 1993.

Booth, Howard J., and Nigel Rigby, eds. *Modernism and Empire*. Manchester: Manchester University Press, 2000.

Chaker, Salem. "L'affirmation identitaire berbère à partir des 1900." *Revue de l'Occident Musulman* 44 (1987): 13–33.

Chakrabarty, Dipesh. *Provincializing Europe: Postcolonial Thought and Historical Difference*. Princeton: Princeton University Press, 2000.

Cheah, Pheng. "Given Culture: Rethinking Cosmopolitical Freedom in Transnationalism." *Cosmopolitics: Thinking and Feeling Beyond the Nation*. Ed. Pheng Cheah and Bruce Robbins. Minneapolis: University of Minnesota Press, 1998.

———. "Grounds of Comparison." *Grounds of Comparison: Around the World of Benedict Anderson*. Ed. Jonathan Culler and Pheng Cheah. London: Routlege, 2003.

Cuddy-Keane, Melba. "Modernism, Geopolitics, Globalization." *Modernism/modernity* 10.3 (2003): 539–58.

Déjeux, Jean. *La Littérature Maghrébine de Langue Française [Maghrebi Literature in French]*. Sherbrooke: Naaman, 1973.

Doyle, Laura, and Laura Winkiel, eds. *Geomodernisms: Race, Modernism, Modernity*. Bloomington: Indiana University Press, 2005.

Dunwoodie, Peter. *Writing French Algeria*. Oxford: Clarendon, 1998.

Fanon, Frantz. *Black Skin, White Masks*. Trans. Charles Lam Markmann. New York: Grove Weindenfeld, 1967.

———. *A Dying Colonialism*. Trans. Haakon Chevalier. New York: Grove Weindenfeld, 2003.

———. *The Wretched of the Earth*. Trans. Constance Farrington. New York: Grove Weindenfeld, 1963.

Friedman, Susan Stanford. "Paranoia, Pollution, and Sexuality: Affiliations between E. M. Forster's *A Passage to India* and Arundhati Roy's *The God of Small Things*." Doyle and Winkiel 245–61.

———. "Periodizing Modernism: Postcolonial Modernities and the Space/Time Borders of Modernist Studies." *Modernism/modernity* 13.3 (2006): 425–43.

Gaonkar, Dilip Parameshwar, ed. *Alternative Modernities*. Durham: Duke University Press, 2001.

Geist, Anthony L., and José B. Monleón, eds. *Modernism and Its Margins: Reinscribing Cultural Modernity from Spain and Latin America*. New York: Garland, 1999.

Gikandi, Simon. "Modernism in the World." *Modernism/modernity* 13:3 (2006): 419–24.

Gilroy, Paul. *The Black Atlantic: Modernity and Double Consciousness*. New York: Verso, 1993.

Guibert, Armand. *Jean Amrouche, 1906–1962, par un témoin de sa vie [Jean Amrouche by a witness of his life]*. Paris: G. Lachurie, 1985.

Harootunian, Harry. "Some Thoughts on Comparability and the Space-Time Problem." *boundary* 2 32.2 (2005): 23–52.

Jameson, Fredric. "Modernism and Imperialism." *Nationalism, Colonialism, and Literature*. Ed. Terry Eagleton, Fredric Jameson, Edward W. Said, and Seamus Deane. Minneapolis: University of Minnesota Press, 1990: 43–66.

———. *A Singular Modernity: Essay on the Ontology of the Present*. London: Verso, 2002.

Klein, Kerwin Lee. "On the Emergence of Memory in Historical Discourse." *Representations* 69 (2000): 127–50.

Koselleck, Reinhart. *Futures Past: On the Semantics of Historical Time*. Trans. Keith Tribe. Cambridge: MIT Press, 1985.

———. *The Practice of Conceptual History: Timing Histories, Spacing Concepts.* Trans. Todd Samuel Presner. Stanford: Stanford University Press, 2002.

Kronfeld, Chana. *On the Margins of Modernism: Decentering Literary Dynamics.* Berkeley: University of California Press, 1996.

Le Baut, Réjane. *Jean El Mouhoub Amrouche, Algerien universel: Biographie. [Jean El Mouhoub Amrouche, Universal Algerian: A Biography.]* Paris: Alteredit, 2003.

———. *Jean El-Mouhoub Amrouche (1906–1962): Mythes et Réalités* [Myths and Realities]. Blida: Editions du Tell, 2005.

Les Amis des Archives de la Ville de Marseille. *L'Eternel Jugurtha: Colloque Jean Amrouche.* Marseille: Edition du Quai, 1987.

Mallarmé, Stéphane. "From 'Crisis in Poetry.'" *Modernism: An Anthology of Sources and Documents.* Ed. Vassiliki Kolocotroni, Jane Goldman, and Olga Taxidou. Chicago: University of Chicago Press, 1998: 123–27.

Memmi, Albert. *The Colonizer and the Colonized.* Trans. Howard Greenfeld. New York: Orion, 1965.

Michel, M. "Sur la parenté des Egyptiens, des Berbères et des Basques" [On the kinship between Egyptians, Berbers, and Basques]. *Bulletin de la Société d'Anthropologie de Paris* 4 (1863): 365–67.

Moréas, Jean. "Manifeste du Symbolisme" [Symbolist Manifesto]. *Le Figaro* 18 Septembre 1886.

Morris, Meaghan. *Too Soon, Too Late: History in Popular Culture.* Bloomington: University of Indiana Press, 1998.

Nora, Pierre. "Between Memory and History: Les Lieux de Mémoire." *Representations* 26 (Spring 1989): 7–25.

Oster, Daniel. "Ce que je pourrais dire de Stéphane Mallarmé" [What I could say on Mallarmé]. *Mallarmé ou l'Oscurité Lumineuse [Mallarmé or luminous obscurity].* Ed. Bertrand Marchal and J.-M. Steinmetz. Paris: Hermann, 1999.

Pollard, Charles W. *New World Modernisms: T. S. Eliot, Derek Walcott, Kamau Brathwaite.* Charlottesville: University of Virginia Press, 2004.

Pratt, Mary-Louise. *Imperial Eyes: Travel Writing and Transculturation.* New York: Routledge, 2008.

———. "Modernity and Periphery: Towards a Global and Relational Analysis." *Beyond Dichotomies: Histories, Identities, Culture and the Challenge of Globalization.* Ed. Elizabeth Mudimbe-Boye. Albany: State University of New York Press, 2002: 21–48.

Radhakrishnan, R. "Derivative Discourses and the Problem of Signification." *The European Legacy* 7.6 (2002): 783–95.

Said, Edward. *Culture and Imperialism.* New York: Vintage, 1993.

Taylor, Peter J. *Modernities—A Geohistorical Interpretation.* Minneapolis: University of Minnesota Press, 1999.

Zhiri, Oumelbanine. *L'Afrique au Miroir de l'Europe. Fortunes de Jean Léon l'Africain à la Renaissance [Africa in the Mirror of Europe: Fortunes of Jean Leon the African in the Renaissance].* Geneva: Droz, 1991.

CHAPTER 4

THE TEMPORALITIES OF MODERNITY IN SPANISH AMERICAN *MODERNISMO*: DARÍO'S BOURGEOIS KING

GERARD ACHING

ONE of the purposes of this chapter is to investigate a mysterious death: namely, that of the poet at the end of Rubén Darío's famous short story, "El rey burgués" (The Bourgeois King). Published in Darío's *Azul. . . .* (Chile, 1888)—the twenty-one-year-old Nicaraguan-born poet's first book of lyrical and prose compositions and one that arguably has been regarded as the text that launched Spanish American *modernismo* (roughly 1880–1914)[1]—"El rey burgués" is usually interpreted as a tragic commentary on the waning social status of poets and romantic poetic discourse in Spanish America toward the close of the nineteenth century. From a broad perspective in Western letters, this satirical take on the antagonism between the *poète maudit* (which Darío appreciated but never claimed to be) and the modern metropolis is certainly germane; but this view does not exhaust the complex historical, socioeconomic, and epistemological elements that inform Darío's composition of the brief narrative. That the poet in the story should have frozen to death still clutching the handle of the music box that the monarch obliged him to keep turning for his livelihood readily lends itself to a Marxist reading of the declining social position and proletarianization that urban poets began to experience during the second half of the nineteenth century. But what are we to make of the enigmatic smile on the poet's face when the king and his courtesans discover his lifeless body?

Following the Marxist approach, the smile suggests that the poet's death culminated in a final but joyful deliverance from wage labor. I do not dispute this interpretation, but, by posing a fundamental question about the circumstances in which the poet died, I would like to supplement this reading with a more global context. Despite the fact that the discovery of the poet's body revealed no external signs of violence, I nonetheless want to ask who or what was responsible for his death. In this study, I examine "El rey burgués" for what the poet's death tells us about the *modernistas'* engagement with the modern.

At first glance, there appears to be little doubt that the bourgeois king should be held responsible for the poet's death: it was ultimately the monarch who confined the poet to the repetitive, mind-numbing labor of turning the handle of a music box in the royal garden regardless of the time of year. Eventually, the winter's cold penetrated the poet's body and soul and caused his brain to "petrify," all of which coincided, as the narrator puts it, with the oblivion into which the "grandes himnos" (great anthems) had fallen. (Darío 34). The poet in Darío's tale seems to succumb to what José Martí referred to in 1882 as the "decentralization of intelligence" that characterized modern life and to a concomitant nostalgia "for great deeds" among poets (("Prologue to Juan Antonio Pérez Bonalde's *Poem of Niagara*" 47). Yet it appears unjustified to blame the bourgeois king for anything more incriminating than his purported ignorance about what a poet and poetry were:

> —What's this? He asked.
> —A poet, sire.
> The king had swans in the pond, canaries, sparrows, *cenzontles* in the aviary; a poet was something new and strange. (31)[2]

The monarch's ignorance and the negligence to which it gave rise clearly proved fatal for the poet. But even if we were to concede that the bourgeois king's ignorance kills, in any attempt at assigning culpability it would still be crucial to assess if this neglect had been conscious or avoidable. Because the king possesses the trappings of a historically and geographically vague European monarch—his customs and the objects that he owns correspond to a premodern royal court as well as to eighteenth- and nineteenth-century Europe—it is improbable that he would not have known what poets and poetry were. What, then, could account for this failure to acknowledge the bard and his language?

Given the manner in which the poet had been presented to him, it is more likely that even though the bourgeois king was willing to add the poet to his collection of exquisite art objects and fauna, the monarch could not make sense of the poet's soliloquy (the only occasion when he speaks), in which the bard describes poetry, his bravura, and the exclusivity of poetic discourse. Not even after confining the poet to wage labor with a succinct "Pieza de música por pedazo de pan"

(A musical piece for a bit of bread) (33) does the king come to appreciate the sound (the constant "Tiriririn") of the music box and the labor involved in producing it. Hence, if the monarch were to be held accountable for the poet's demise in any way, this responsibility would not emerge from conscious knowledge but from a subtler contingency of forces that the conjunction of "bourgeois" and "king" generates. In his nuanced reading of "El rey burgués," Angel Rama notes the literary skill with which Darío conjures the gap between the possessor of objects (the king) and the objects that he possesses (Rama 98–99). The critic argues that the monarch's ignorance about the artistic value of his own belongings reveals a contradiction that juxtaposes the bourgeois king's nouveau riche consumerist ideology and the artistic refinement of the material environment in which he lived (99); Rama further suggests that this contradiction must have been common during the Hispano-American bourgeoisie's rapid rise to wealth in the last decades of the nineteenth century, thus making the bourgeois king representative of the emergence of a new, local literature and art consumer. The bourgeois king displays the duplicitous economic practices that his name suggests: he is an aristocrat and, like a proper capitalist, forces the poet to work for his living. Nevertheless, as a member of the leisure class who enjoys the "non-productive consumption of time" (Veblen 41), the monarch appears to be ignorant about how to exact use and exchange value from this labor source: he does not know to what use the poet should be put, requests counsel from his court, and accepts that of a street philosopher, who recommends leaving the poet outdoors.[3]

There is, as it were, a great deal to be said in this short story about the sites, articulation, and status of particular areas of knowledge. There are two such areas that I investigate in this chapter in order to describe and assess an articulation of modernity in Spanish American *modernismo*. The first of these is informational for readers unfamiliar with this field; it concerns epistemological/taxonomical debates about "excessive" imitation—the most frequently mentioned critique of the *modernistas* in Spanish American literary history—and approaches this field-defining debate by asking a deceptively simple question: how did Darío have access to what he knew about the latest in French literature, art, and culture? In the second section of the chapter, I examine the opposition between the bourgeois king and the poet around which the tale is structured as a statement about modernity. The definition of modernity to which I subscribe in this chapter derives from an analysis of this constitutive disjuncture between, on the one hand, a neocolonial economic liberalism that commodifies, rationalizes, and socializes objects in a particular way and, on the other, a discourse that laments the loss of a poetic knowledge of objects in the face of the poet's inexorable subordination to wage labor. Drawing from Étienne Balibar's reminder in *The Philosophy of Marx* (1995) that Marx's thesis of historical rationality is more complex than the relentless determinism that gets attributed to it, I interrogate the figures of the bourgeois king and poet and the antagonism between them as commentaries on the heterogeneous temporality of the region's modernity in the period when the *modernistas* wrote.

BEYOND IMITATION

As a field, Spanish American *modernismo* and its criticism remain isolated in modernist studies. In spite of the enormous quantity of verse, prose, and reportage that the *modernistas* wrote—every Spanish-speaking nation possesses its *modernista* literary canon—most of its figures, with the probable exception of José Martí (1853–1895) and Rubén Darío, are little known outside of Hispanic letters. The reasons for this isolation are complex and are not the principal business of this chapter, but some of them include the paucity of edited volumes of the *modernistas'* complete works until the 1960s and beyond; the long tradition of viewing literary criticism in the region as a set of institutions and practices whose primary concern was to determine and maintain national literary canons; the continuing dominance of English, French, and German literatures in modernist and comparative literary studies; and, the most challenging of all, the reductive commonplace within and outside the region that *modernista* literature merely imitated French literary and artistic currents, such as Symbolism and the Parnassian School. Yet describing the *modernistas* as compulsive imitators of metropolitan currents has done little to elucidate the complexity of their engagements with modern life.

Despite the fact that Paris, the perceived capital of the nineteenth century for most modernists, was as much a beacon of inspiration for Spanish American artists and intellectuals, the *modernistas* have rarely been considered interlocutors in the global exchange of ideas about late-nineteenth-century modernity and modernist literatures. Drawn from many parts of Spanish America, but especially concentrated in large cosmopolitan cities like Buenos Aires, Mexico City, Bogotá, Montevideo, Caracas, and Havana, they and their experiences of modernity are unfamiliar, unacknowledged, or presumed to be fundamentally distinct from their metropolitan counterparts. This last misconception derives from historical and cultural biases (both inside and outside the region) that associate economic, scientific, and social "advances" with modern "civilized" nations and concomitantly privilege the anguish, melancholy, and iconoclasm of literature by figures such as Baudelaire as autonomously and universally illustrative of the experience of modernity. Even though in the preface to the first German edition of *Capital* (1859) Marx likens metropolitan experience of the incompleteness of capitalist production to that of their Latin American counterparts, comparative work has yet to take up Marx's cue (Preface 296). Among the first generation of *modernistas*, Julián del Casal (Cuba, 1863–1893) and José Asunción Silva (Colombia, 1865–1896) stand out because of their adroit use of lyricism to articulate the deep melancholy that characterizes their respective engagements with penury and commerce, both of which were local phenomena with tangible connections to global capitalism.[4] In short, "modernity," defined by Marshall Berman in the early 1980s as "a mode of vital experience—experience of space and time, of the self and others, of life's possibilities and perils—that is shared by men and women all over the world today" (15) points to a specifically global occurrence that today still requires elaboration as a *relational* experience beyond notions of compulsive and relentless imitation.

If *modernista* literature and criticism continue to be located at the margins of the contemporary study of modernisms, the field has not fared better vis-à-vis the category of world literature and postcolonial literary criticism. World literature emerged as a late-twentieth-century publishing phenomenon in the West that brought due attention to contemporary, mostly narrative, nonmetropolitan literatures and their authors. Even though the *modernistas* wrote from the first nations in the western hemisphere (except for Cuba and Puerto Rico) to achieve political independence after the United States and Haiti, their turn-of-the-twentieth-century bids for an autonomous literary expression, mainly in lyrical poetry, precluded them from a publishing market that later welcomed and in part facilitated the Latin American literary boom that began in the 1960s. If generalizations may be applied to so broad a literary production, the *modernistas'* penchant for the use of a refined Spanish as lingua franca, their attention to debates on art for art's sake, their defense of artistic elitism in light of an incipient democratization of cultural institutions and practices, and their ambiguous relationship with the region's oligarchies and bourgeoisies made them undesirable subjects for a publishing market that has concentrated on narratives that directly and indirectly engage with decolonization.

Even though Spanish American *modernismo* was the first literary current to extend its influence from former colonies to the Spanish peninsula, this mostly elitist, nonmetropolitan literature presents particular challenges to postcolonial critical approaches to the issue of imitation.[5] Postcolonial theories have successfully elucidated early colonial and twentieth-century Latin American literatures and cultural practices—in other words, the period before and after *modernismo*—but *modernismo* itself remains insufficiently explored. If reading for and interrogating decolonizing struggles and strategies may be considered primary aims in postcolonial criticism, then what sense can be made of the *modernistas'* predilection for refined Spanish (i.e., the cultivation of a "standard" lingua franca that had also been the official language of the Spanish empire) and their appetite for European literatures and cultural referents? Fetishization certainly provides part of the answer. But the matter of how the *modernistas* promoted an autonomous literary expression by liberally drawing from western Europe's literary and cultural production is best understood not as a complex, ambivalent relationship with Europe alone; rather, this ambivalent relationship must be viewed in light of regional concerns about a U.S. territorial, economic, and cultural presence in the hemisphere beginning as early as the second half of the nineteenth century.

The challenge for postcolonial critical approaches, then, is how to theorize the *modernistas'* modes of engagement with European literatures as, among other factors, resistance to the appeal that the United States had for some of Spanish America's political and intellectual leadership. Iris M. Zavala, one of the first and few critics to conjoin *modernismo* and postcoloniality, underscores the significance of a common language, stating that the "linguistic code of a common symbolic geography produced modernism/modern as a social category" and that "the question of language at that point was political, cultural, and literary in its most material sense, since a defense of language by the Latin Americans, and specifically by the Caribbeans, was a choice of identity" (3). This uneasy, shifting, tripartite relation of cultural alliances and resistance (Spanish America–Europe–United States) informs the *modernistas'* defense of a Pan-Hispanism that often and paradoxically, from a postcolonial perspective, included Spain.

This tripartite relation contextualizes the urgency with which Martí, who, in response to U.S dominance and Latin American disunion at the First Pan-American Conference (1889–1890) and at the International Monetary Conference (1891) in Washington, developed his seminal essay, "Nuestra América" ("Our America," 1891), which addresses the pitfalls of "too much imitation" and the need for local knowledge to enhance self-government ("Our America" 294). The triangular relation also provides exact coordinates for José Enrique Rodó (Uruguay, 1871–1917), who, in his essay, *Ariel* (1900)—one of the earliest literary uses of Shakespeare's *Tempest* in the Americas to work through issues of political and cultural autonomy— warned against "imitación inconsulta" (ill-advised imitation) (Rodó, 79) and posited the United States as Caliban and Spanish America as Ariel, the heir to European classical and Christian civilization. Finally, the tripartite relation inspires Darío's "A Roosevelt" ("To Roosevelt," 1905), in which he describes the U.S. president as the "futuro invasor / de la América ingenua que tiene sangre indígena, / que aún reza a Jesucristo y aún habla en español" (*Cantos de vida y esperanza* 123; vv. 6–8).[6] The majority of the nations from which the *modernistas* wrote had achieved political independence by the 1830s. The challenge that these poets and writers faced, as these excerpts attest, was to contribute to the forging of discourses of national and regional culture in a period of hegemonic neocolonial incursions that originated mostly in Britain, France, and the United States.

Given the extensive debates about how to forge Spanish American national/ regional cultures at the time, it would be disingenuous to disavow the critical attention that had been paid to issues of imitation. However, rather than conceive of imitation as compulsive mimicry and the absence of originality, I would assert that the *modernistas'* awareness of the assimilability of literary and cultural forms and practices worthy of emulation or disdain provided them with uniquely situated approaches to culture based on the reading, translation, and assimilation of a wide spectrum of literary texts (poetry, narrative fiction, travel writing), columns, reviews, and news items from Europe, the United States, and Latin America. In other words, their cosmopolitan reading and writing habits afforded them the opportunity to appreciate how national and regional cultures could be grasped for their literariness as textual constructions. Harsha Ram, in his contribution to this volume, examines a similar eagerness on the part of the Russian futurists to identify literariness with what he calls an alternative universalism. In the *modernistas'* case, this literariness—the studied consideration of and open attitude toward the textuality of cultural representations—is precisely what allows us to broach the question of Darío's access to the latest French literature and art.

In the first of two letters that the Spanish critic, Juan Valera, wrote to Darío (October 22, 1888) reviewing *Azul . . .*, the critic admits that after initially refraining from opening Darío's book—since its title invoked for him the emptiness of Victor Hugo's "l'art c'est l'azur"[7]—he states that he was astonished to discover the poet's impressive but "originalidad muy extraña" (very strange originality) ("Carta-Prólogo" 10):

> Extraordinary was my surprise upon learning that you, according to well-informed persons who assure me of it, did not leave Nicaragua except to go to Chile, where you have been residing for no more than two years. How, without the influence of the environment, have you been able to assimilate all the elements of the French spirit, while maintaining the Spanish form that holds together and organizes these elements and transforming them into your own material? (11)[8]

Taking umbrage in Valera's biased description of Darío's immersion in French letters and culture on the other side of the Atlantic as a "galicismo mental" (mental Frenchness) (25), many commentators have missed the opportunity to interrogate the difficulty with which Valera attempted to communicate the poet's originality at the same time that he compliments him for the "perfection" (25) of his knowledge of the latest French literature, art, and fashion. For Valera, the book is so suffused with a cosmopolitan spirit and its stories so thoroughly appear to have been composed in France that the critic concludes that there is no writer in Spanish more French than Darío (12). Yet, after listing a number of French writers with whom he thought the poet to be "saturated," Valera also asserts that Darío "no imita a ninguno" (does not imitate any); rather, "You have stirred it all up: heated it in the distilling flask of your brain, and have drawn from it a peculiar quintessence" (12).[9] It should be said that this distillation was not the product of Darío's genius alone; it could be found in the works of the first generation of *modernistas* as well as in the translations of Baudelaire, Mallarmé, Verlaine, Catulle Mendès, and others that they disseminated in Spanish American journals and magazines that began sprouting in various Spanish American cities in the 1890s.[10] In short, this assimilation of contemporary European letters, thought, and fashions took place through a network of readership, commentary, translation, and creativity whereby the *modernistas* came to recognize one another as interlocutors in a cosmopolitan exchange of ideas about modern social life in capitals on both sides of the Atlantic.

Yet Valera also hints at an intriguing aspect of Darío's assimilation of French letters and artistic currents for which there is no simple explanation. The critic states that Darío is so in tune with fashions in Paris and displays such *chic* and distinction that he "se adelanta a la moda y pudiera modificarla e imponerla" (13).[11] How could the poet be said to have accomplished this feat from such a distance? Carlos Alonso, focusing on textual practices and the rhetoric of modernity in Spanish America during the nineteenth century, notes that the "obsessive readings of the latest books, the scrupulously documented travels to the metropolitan countries, the incisive, painstaking, and pained studies of local reality—they all served first to measure the distance still to be traveled to become modern, but they also helped to identify and master the most effective strategies for never leaving home" (vi). Darío, Casal, and other *modernistas* did not travel to Paris before they began composing a literature imbued with French cosmopolitanism; nor, as Alonso asserts, had these modern artistic pilgrimages been necessary in order to keep abreast of literary fashions there. As Octavio Paz puts it, the *modernistas* were not interested in becoming French but in being modern ("El caracol y la sirena" 12–13). In Darío's case, although his living conditions were precarious after he arrived in Valparaíso, Chile, at the age of nineteen, Pedro Balmaceda Toro—a poet and the Chilean president's son—befriended the Nicaraguan and provided him with access to his private collection of the latest European literature and magazines. Recalling his influences when he composed *Azul . . .*, Darío acknowledged his ability to be in tune with the latest in Paris, stating that he had become familiar with the Parnassians at about the time that the "Symbolist struggle" was just beginning in France and was still unknown abroad and especially so in "nuestra América" (*Historia de mis libros* 36). He thus credits himself with stimulating directions in the region's literature, which brings us closer to elucidating Valera's claim that the poet anticipated fashions in France without ever having been there.

Darío cultivated this sensibility for emerging literary and artistic currents and defined his role, as he stated in the prologue to *Prosas profanas*—his second book of poems—as that of informant and leader of the new literary currents in Spanish America. The year after his brief, first visit to Paris in 1893, he began to publish in Buenos Aires' *La Nación* a series of portraits (*semblanzas*) of nineteen unconventional, mostly French poets and writers that he admired or found fascinating. The series, which he collected and eventually published as *Los raros* (*The Odd Ones*) in 1896 includes figures such as Poe, Martí, Leconte de Lisle, Moréas, Ibsen, Nordau, Lautréamont, and Verlaine. The portraits conjure these figures through a journalistic combination of observations and critiques by their contemporaries, physical descriptions, attention to transgressive or quirky comportment, direct quotes from their works, foreign colloquial and erudite terms, and a plethora of references to past and modern literature and art that offers the knowledgeable reader an illusion of tangible immediacy and cliquish social prestige. According to Paz, Darío's "instinct" for anticipating the future relevance of some of these figures was astonishing; he was, for instance, the first to call attention to Lautréamont outside of France and, arguably, the first Spanish-language writer to allude to Sade (11–12). More recently, Julio Ortega has examined Darío's prescience, asserting that *Los raros* can be simultaneously considered an "archivo transitorio" (transitory archive) and a "genealogía del futuro" (genealogy of the future) that centers its creativity in a system of reading through which Darío identified novelty in past and coetaneous literary currents and constructed a future lineage on the force of a signifying present (2). *Los raros*, Ortega states, is a book whose plot is fundamentally about reading the new Atlantic literature (3), and it facilitates this reading by glossing, quoting, and translating (4) in ways, I would add, that Borges would take to an internationally recognized level of sophisticated reflection in the twentieth century.

As Valera initially observed and Paz later attested, Darío's originality lay in the innovations in meter that he introduced into Spanish-language poetry, the related freedom from academicism that he brought to verse, the bold cosmopolitan spirit that suffuses his texts, and the daring eroticism (for the times) of some of his works. These innovations transcend the notion of spontaneous or mindless imitation of metropolitan Europe. In fact, Fredric Jameson refers to Darío's introduction of the term *"modernismo"* into Spanish-language usage in 1888 as a "scandal" since it marked a more evident "break" with literary traditions than in other languages (100). Darío's and the *modernistas'* familiarity with the latest trends in literature, art, culture, and modern life in the Atlantic world's most influential capitals was the result of critical processes that included the regular reading, translation, modeling of texts on, as well as against, European influences—Casal, for example, praised literary decadentism while Gutiérrez Nájera deplored it—and the creation of original works, especially in poetry, literary journalism, and reportage. The elite transatlantic circuit of readers and writers that gave rise to *modernista* cultural claims of belonging to a modern world established the basis for a social imaginary of Spanish America's relation to the foremost capitalist nations of the Western world as a regional, class, and language-based identity that interpellated members according to the economic and/or intellectual means that they had at their disposal to travel and/or "transport" themselves, for instance, to an illusory Paris.

A Transatlantic Modernity

Countering relativist arguments for the cultural exceptionalism that the "ideologues of 'modernity'" proffer, Jameson reminds the reader in *A Singular Modernity* (2002) that the fundamental meaning of modernity is global capitalism. In his assessment of how such stances avoid this basic meaning, he asserts wryly:

> Everyone knows the formula by now: this means that there can be a modernity for everybody which is different from the standard or hegemonic Anglo-Saxon model. Whatever you dislike about the latter, including the subaltern position it leaves you in, can be effaced by the reassuring and 'cultural' notion that you can fashion your own modernity differently, so that there can be a Latin-American kind, or an Indian kind or an African kind, and so forth. (12)

Jameson's point about the limits of exceptionalism is well taken, for any attempt at cultural chauvinism is worthy of analysis and critique. In this section, I describe and examine an example of nineteenth-century transatlantic modernity that not only emerges through global capitalism but also acknowledges that experiences of modernity are indeed global. Following Jameson's lead and in concert with Neil Lazarus' assessment of his model in this volume, what I propose is not an "alternative" modernity but the opportunity to recognize that if it is at all possible to speak of global capitalism and its history, then it is crucial to bring to light the infrastructural, extra-European *circuits* of social and economic activities, transactions, and influences that helped to stimulate global capitalism in the first place. To imagine modernity in this way avoids problems of the one-sidedness in Eurocentric accounts of modernity because it assumes, as E. San Juan Jr. asserts, that global experiences of modernity occur "within a differentiated, not centralized, ontology of determinate and concrete social formations" (223–24). The evidence of transatlantic modernity that I describe below is graspable, then, not as stark oppositions between center and periphery, modern and premodern, Paris and Spanish America, but as circuits of texts, reading, translation, and literary composition that I refer to as an evaluative readership. The intelligibility of Darío's short story relies on the difference that knowledge or ignorance of the value of the art objects and cultural referents in the narrative makes for the subjectivities of the bourgeois king, the poet, and the worldly reader.

If the evaluative readership that I describe provides evidence of a transatlantic modernity, then the Spanish American bourgeoisie's desire to belong to Western civilization and participate in global capitalism as well as its sponsorship of the movement of texts and ideas across the Atlantic need to be accounted for not only as an infrastructural issue but also in relation to the nineteenth-century evolutionist idea of historical progress.[12] Martí's observation in "Our America" that Spanish Americans "were a whole fancy dress ball, in English trousers, a Parisian waistcoat, a North American overcoat, and a Spanish bullfighter's hat" (293) alludes to presumably overactive circuits of trade and consumption that present obstacles for autochthonous creativity. Yet he also underscores the historical uniqueness of nation-building in the Americas in temporal terms, claiming that "[n]ever before have such advanced and consolidated nations been created from such disparate factors in less historical time" (289–90).[13] Although Martí is aware that the speed of these advances has also been problematic, his statement nonetheless invites us to interrogate the temporal heterogeneity of late-nineteenth-century "historical progress" in the region. As I will show, the bourgeois king's hybridity invokes this heterogeneity.

The conflict between the bourgeois king and the poet and the latter's unavoidable subjection to wage labor are also indicative of "historical progress" in another crucial way. Asserting that even though it was practically impossible for the theorist "not to be an evolutionist in the nineteenth century" (91), Étienne Balibar argues that "the idea of progressive evolution in Marx is inseparable from a thesis on the rationality of history or, if one prefers, the intelligibility of its forms, tendencies and conjunctures" (92). In order to move beyond the vulgar determinism that has been ascribed to Marx's investigatory "schema of historical causality" (92), Balibar advocates analyzing the *development* of the contradiction in the social relations between capitalists and workers, which would in effect serve to describe the history of a society's social formations: the deepening opposition between "the relations of production and the development of productive forces" (94) in capitalism that leads to a growing conflict between an increasingly rationalized production and the super-exploitation of labor (the second level of development) and that ends with a class struggle that is not simply about the telos of transforming capitalism's mode of production; it is also about pressuring workers in order to exact surplus value and forcing capitalists to find other methods when proletarian resistance proves too strong (96). The analysis that follows examines the figures of the bourgeois king and the poet and their mutual antagonism for the "intelligibility of [their] forms, tendencies and conjunctures." In essence, the modernity to which I refer in this section of the chapter is spatial (transatlantic), temporally heterogeneous, and measurable according to the nature and outcome of the conflict between the bourgeois king and the poet.

The figure of the bourgeois king accurately captures some of the unevenness of global capitalism from the purview of late-nineteenth-century teleological discourses on socioeconomic development and progress. When Marx called attention to the incompleteness of capitalist development in Europe in his preface to the first German edition of *Capital*, he also critiqued the "inherited evils" that derived from "the passive survival of antiquated modes of production, with their inevitable train of social and political anachronisms." (296). The presence of these "anachronisms" in mid-nineteenth-century Europe provides a partial explanation for "the 'crises of Marxism' before Marxism as such existed" (Balibar 8): the unexpected failure of the revolutions of 1848, when Marx and others were convinced that a major crisis of capitalism was about to happen and did not; and the combined Franco-Prussian War of 1870 and the suppression of the Paris Commune the following year, when, to Marx's chagrin, it became evident that other crucial factors competed with class struggle as explanations for the idea of progress (9). A bourgeois king at the time when Marx and Engels penned *The Communist Manifesto* (1848) might have represented part of that enigmatic mix of classes in the "holy alliance" against the "spectre of Communism" to which Marx and Engels refer in the document's opening line (Marx and Engels 29); later in the century, however, the hybrid figure would more readily capture the "passive survival of antiquated modes of production" in modern times and their accompanying temporal disjunctures, which, it should be noted, Marx reads as being "social and political." European modernism itself emerged through such disjunctures or, as Perry Anderson puts it, "at the intersection between a semi-aristocratic ruling order, a semi-industrialized capitalist economy, and a semi-emergent, or semi-insurgent, labor movement" (326).

The bourgeois king's configuration is also intelligible on the other side of the Atlantic. During the first half of the nineteenth century, the figure might have been illustrative of an inner turmoil in national politics and imperial economic policies: the aristocracy and the bourgeoisie throughout the Atlantic world were perennially at odds over whether chattel slavery—one of colonialism's "inherited evils" and the forced labor regime that facilitated the modernization of global capitalism—was an obstacle to economic and moral progress. Nevertheless, whenever the bourgeoisie gains the upper hand, Marx and Engels wrote in their manifesto, it "has put an end to all feudal, patriarchal, idyllic relations" (32). Rama argues that by the final quarter of the nineteenth century, a period to which he refers as the "imperial" expansion of capitalism, one of the "secret" reasons why Marx's hopes for proletarian victory in the Paris Commune came to naught was the wealth and resilience that intensified incorporation of Latin America and its primary raw materials brought to Europe's bourgeoisies during the Belle Époque (23). Tulio Halperin Donghi documents how the whole political spectrum (oligarchies, the new bourgeoisie, the urban middle classes) embraced the establishment of a Latin American branch of the European bourgeoisie (228) and that a neocolonial order was firmly in place in Latin America by 1880 (280). By way of illustration, this historian reports that during the first Pan-American Conference (Washington, DC, 1889–1890), Roque Sáenz Peña, a member of the Argentine delegation, opposed the U.S. agenda of America for Americans with the idea of America for humanity, which, Halperin Donghi states, reflected the position of some Latin American countries to maintain its unbalanced trade with Europe and that of others to oppose U.S. hegemony (287). It is worth noting that several stories from Darío's *Azul* . . . would first be published in newspapers during this decade in Valparaíso, Chile, a city that had already begun to display the wealth that its copper exports to Europe generated by the time the poet arrived. In late-nineteenth-century Spanish America, the bourgeois king would thus reflect the diverse but conciliatory political spectrum to which Halperin Donghi refers, so that the figure's specificity would consist in this *active* survival and simultaneity of different modes of production within a hegemonic neocolonial order.

In Darío's tale, the bourgeois king is undoubtedly a member of a wealthy, urban, leisure class whose accumulated riches proceed from diverse areas of the globe. He dons fine, whimsical clothes and possesses a splendid palace with a large contingent of slaves, servants, and courtiers. He enjoys and supports painting, sculpture, and music; he fences, hunts for sport, takes lessons in rhetoric, ponders grammatical problems, and reads novels by the late-nineteenth-century French novelist Georges Ohnet for pleasure.[14] The narrative's fictive depiction of the bourgeois king's life of leisure is sociologically accurate. Writing in the 1890s, the American economist and social critic Thorstein Veblen asserted that leisure produces "'immaterial' goods," some of which included "quasi-scholarly or quasi-artistic accomplishments," such as the knowledge of dead languages, correct spelling, syntax, prosody, and the "latest proprieties" of dress, furniture, games, sports, fancy-bred animals, and other "branches of learning" (45). What is most illustrative of the bourgeois king's involvement in global capitalism, however, is his collection of a large number of rare and beautiful objects of art from Europe and the Orient—"por lujo y nada más" (for the sake of luxury and nothing more) ("El rey burgués" 30). The collection includes Chinese and Japanese porcelains, fans, and masks, marble sculptures in the Greek salon, and, in the "salon de los tiempos galantes" (merry times salon), paintings by the French, Rococo artists Jean-Antoine Watteau and Jean-Baptiste Siméon Chardin. According to the narrator, the bourgeois king could have enjoyed a salon "worthy of the taste of a Goncourt and of the millions of a Croesus" (30).[15]

The collection of luxury goods and international art, a frequent *modernista* trope that Silva, for example, skillfully develops in the opening pages of his novel *De sobremesa* (posthumously published in 1925), indicates that the bourgeois king is immersed in a realm of commodity fetishism whereby the objects he owns reveal, as the narrator states, his "Buen gusto" (Good taste) and "Refinamiento" (Refinement) (30)—qualities that emanate from his possessions and associate him with the likes of a Goncourt. Yet, as a collector, the monarch is also faced with "the Sisyphean task of divesting things of their commodity character by taking possession of them" (Benjamin, "Paris, the Capital of the Nineteenth Century" 39).[16] The irony of indulging in and, at the same time, attempting to undo commodity fetishism not only captures an experience of modernity in which men struggle against the proverbial melting of all that is solid into air; it is also a specific reminder that leisure "does not leave a material product" (Veblen 45). In other words, at the summit of his acquisitive power to collect objects from across the globe at whim, the collector produces immaterial values that he then wishes to reify through the acquisition and display of his collection. According to Walter Benjamin,

> Since the days of Louis Philippe, the bourgeoisie has endeavored to compensate itself for the fact that private life leaves no traces in the big city. It seeks such compensation within its four walls—as if it were striving, as a matter of honor, to prevent the traces, if not of its days on earth then at least of its possessions and requisites of daily life, from disappearing forever. ("The Paris of the Second Empire in Baudelaire" 77).[17]

The affective intensity that accompanies this knowledge of disappearing immaterial values is a nineteenth-century literary commonplace that the *modernistas* widely employed and which places them in the duplicitous position of being both inculcators of the modern and experts on melancholic, aristocratic and bourgeois decadentism in Spanish America. According to Halperin Donghi, the neocolonial order in the region was born old because it demonstrated clearly visible signs of a rapid exhaustion (280); similarly, Anderson claims that capitalist development in regions like Latin America (before the 1980s) is usually "far more rapid and dynamic, where it does occur, than in metropolitan zones, yet it is infinitely less stabilized or consolidated" (329). Even though it is certain that a related and developed transatlantic readership facilitated the *modernistas'* extensive cultivation of the trope of the art and luxury object collection, Halperin Donghi and Anderson also provide infrastructural reasons for appreciating the intensity with which the Spanish American bourgeoisie experienced (and the *modernistas* represented) the disappearance of immaterial values within the walled interiors of its urban communities.

When Benjamin avers that the best that the collector could do in his vain attempt to annul commodity fetishism was to bestow "connoisseur" rather than "use value" ("Paris" 39) on the objects in his possession, he points to the nineteenth-century critique of another deleterious effect of modern capitalism with which the *modernistas* were familiar: the division of labor and the forced specialization of knowledge it induces. (In *Ariel*, for example, Rodó assails utilitarianism and its purportedly nefarious consequences for the spiritual and intellectual integrity that privacy and leisure should provide Spanish Americans.) The bourgeois king illustrates that he is embedded in a world that he fosters yet from which he cannot extricate himself. Evocative of Martí's allusion to the "decentralization of intelligence," the monarch surrounds himself with courtesans, rhetoricians, riding and dance teachers, and a petty philosopher, all of whom provide him with discrete areas of knowledge that he calls upon at leisure; even though they make their appearance in the privacy of the bourgeois king's court, these characters only come to into being in the text through the division of intellectual and quasi-intellectual labor and reveal the increasing specialization of knowledge that leads to the monarch's reliance on chosen "specialists" to provide him with a connoisseur's knowledge of his world.

Even though the poet in Darío's story must also submit to the division of labor and the specialization of knowledge, he still claims to possess a comprehensive view of the world that the bourgeois king and his court fail or refuse to appreciate. When the king commands the poet to speak, the poet's attitude and complaints are reminiscent of Baudelaire's pointed remarks "To the Bourgeois" in "The Salon of 1846": "Some of you are 'learned'; others are the 'haves'. A glorious day will dawn when the learned will be 'haves', and the 'haves' will be learned. . . . Until such time as this supreme harmony is ours, it is just that the mere 'haves' should aspire to be learned; for knowledge is a form of enjoyment no less than ownership" (47). As if he were imparting the knowledge that Baudelaire deemed "just," the poet instructs the bourgeois king: "Sire, art is not to be found in frigid marble folds, nor in overworked paintings, nor in the excellent Mr. Ohnet! Sire! Art does not don trousers, nor speaks bourgeois, nor dots all the 'i's'" ("El rey burgués" 32).[18] The poet's declaration that the king's collection of precious and exotic art objects is not true art questions the king's social status and undermines his belief that by collecting these objects in the privacy of his salons he has the power to exempt them from circulation in the marketplace. As a further reminder of the contradiction that characterizes the bourgeois king's actions, the poet complains that if the shoemaker criticizes his verses and the pharmacology professor punctures his inspiration it is because the king authorizes these affronts (33). In response to these authorized challenges to the exclusivity of poetic discourse, the poet publicly discloses the monarch's attempts to disavow his role in bourgeois capitalism. The king reacts to the poet's revelation that the monarch may be counted among the "haves" but not the "learned" by confining the poet to winding a music box in his garden, thereby transforming him into another collected item.

In contrast to the bourgeois king's socioeconomic rationalization of his possessions, the poet's grandiloquent soliloquy lists a number of subject-object relations that the bard promotes as poetic knowledge of the world. The poet announces that he has abandoned the city's Bohemian decadence as a source of inspiration and renewed himself through Nature: "I have caressed Nature, and I have sought ideal warmth, the verse that resides in the star, at the far end of the sky, in the pearl, at the bottom of the ocean" (32).[19] In addition to this Symbolist insight and idealism, the poet claims to perceive vast panoramas that he appropriates for the future: "Sire, I have for some time sung the verb of the future. I have spread my wings before the hurricane, I was born at the moment of the aurora; I seek the chosen race that must await, with a hymn on its lips and a lyre in hand, the emergence of the great sun"

(32).[20] Ironically, this claim to envision the future—with its looming revolutions and the need for a poem that would greet a Messiah with a "triumphal arch, of stanzas made of steel, stanzas made of gold, stanzas of love" (32)[21]—constitutes a defense of the prophetic power of poetic discourse at a time when, faced with the division of intellectual and artistic labor and the rules of the market, the Hispano-American poet saw himself, as Rama puts it, "condemned to disappear" (50). Analogous to the bourgeois king's self-generated fiction that he could evade capitalist relations of production, the poet claims to possess a unified conception of the world on the basis of a poetic subjectivity that he locates outside of capitalism but which none-theless emerges with the subjectivation that characterized the rise of bourgeois lib-eralism in Spanish America at the time (13). The multiple subject positions that punctuate the poet's soliloquy belie his claim to possess an unfragmented subjectivity.

Although Rama's analysis of Darío's tale accurately describes how the poet is embedded in capitalism, it does not recognize the antagonism between the mon-arch and the poet as an evolving contradiction that the bard's death brings to a close. For the critic, the poet's subjection to wage labor and the repetitive production of specialized poetry (the music box's relentless "Tiriririn") represent the outcome of a process by which the Spanish American poet had been gradually losing the social status that the figure enjoyed at the beginning of the nineteenth century. No longer the civil poet, as Rama asserts, who simultaneously performed the roles of "politi-cian, ideologue, moralist, educator" (7), the poet, now stripped of the pedagogical and ideological functions that might have allowed him to transform the "haves" into the "learned" in the bourgeois king's court, is forced to abandon his poetic "totalizing vision" (44). Yet the poet's death represents a tragic local resolution to a contradiction in which he succumbs to the "super-exploitation" that Balibar iden-tifies with the capitalists' rationalization and socialization of production. Other stories from *Azul . . .* also denounce the pervasive exploitation that characterizes what Balibar calls the second level in the development of the contradiction between capitalists and workers: A poet in "El velo de la reina Mab" (Queen Mab's Veil) declares that he would compose something immortal were it not for his being over-whelmed by misery and hunger; and in "La canción del oro" (Gold's Song), the bard appears as a ragged, wandering beggar. In "El rey burgués," as in these other exam-ples from *Azul . . .*, there are no possibilities for "historical progress" toward the transformation of capitalism's relations of production beyond this second stage of the conflict between knowledge capitalists and workers.

The winter in Darío's story, which chills the poet's body and petrifies his mind, and the glacial air, which bites his flesh, lashes his face, and eventually leaves him dead like a frozen sparrow ("El rey burgués" 34), resonates with Benjamin's charac-terization of commodity culture in his study of Baudelaire's Paris. Referring to the Second Empire as a period of growing exploitation, Benjamin argues that the more conscious the person qua "labor power" is of his existence as a commodity and the more he proletarianizes himself, "the more he will be gripped by the *chilly breath of the commodity economy*, and the less he will feel like empathizing with commodities"

("Second Empire" 88–89; my emphasis). Even though, Benjamin asserts, the situation had not yet reached this point for the petty bourgeoisie to which Baudelaire belonged (89), Darío's poet, who must endure the court's response to the bourgeois king's query about what should be done with him, is openly subject to evaluation, objectification, and commodification. The poet's demise, in other words, illustrates the temporal heterogeneity of Spanish American "historical progress" and modernity: on the one hand, the threat of being "gripped by the chilly breath" of commodification is immanent in Benjamin's perception of the French petty bourgeoisie in the 1840s yet fully representable some forty years later in *Azul . . .*; on the other, it is also the case that a phenomenon such as Darío's radical transformation of the poet into a collectible thing could not have been theorized by Marx, as Balibar points out, but had to await Georg Lukács at the beginning of the twentieth century (69).

In "El rey burgués," the poet's death forecloses the continuing evolution of the contradiction between bourgeois capitalism and working-class proletarianization that informs nineteenth-century "historical progress" according to Marx. That the poet's demise alludes to the political weakness of urban, working-class struggles in the face of the wide political spectrum intent on creating local branches of the European bourgeoisie in late-nineteenth-century Spanish America is a thesis worth documenting. As such, the poet's death would signify the gradual disappearance of opportunities for working-class resistance, the absolute victory of the "haves," and the dissolution of a social antagonism upon which "historical progress" was based. But it should not be assumed that the poet is necessarily driven into oblivion as a powerless victim. As I indicated earlier, the poet's frozen corpse showed no external signs of violence, which brings to mind another hypothesis. According to Benjamin, it was understandable that under the strain of modernity individuals might become "exhausted and take refuge in death" ("Second Empire" 104). In "El pájaro azul" ("The Blue Bird"), another of Darío's stories from *Azul . . .*, the poet commits suicide rather than abandon poetry in order to enter his father's business. Arguing that Baudelaire penned his first notes on the theory of the modern in 1845 when "the idea of suicide became familiar to the working masses" (105), Benjamin asserts that "[m]odernity must stand under the sign of suicide, an act which seats a heroic will that makes no concessions to a mentality inimical toward this will. Such a suicide is not resignation but heroic passion. It is *the* achievement of modernity in the realm of passions" (104). Whether the poet succumbs to relentless capitalist exploitation or heroically takes his life because of it, how do we account for the smile that exceeds the tragic end that is common to both hypotheses? Bitterness may be considered a reasonable response to the super-exploitation that assailed the poet, but the pleasure that his rigor mortis simultaneously captures defies this expectation.

More dynamic an oxymoron than the "frozen unrest" in Baudelaire's features that Benjamin attributes to the poet's lack of "great knowledge and a comprehensive view of history" (100), the bitter smile of Darío's poet not only connotes a joyful delivery from a modern society that no longer requires his unspecialized knowledge of the world. The gesture also provides evidence of an agency unavoidably embedded in global capitalism even as its very ambiguity reminds us that the intelligibility of the poet's bitter smile emerges through a more decentered and temporally heterogeneous historical rationality than that posited in the deterministic teleological accounts so often employed to describe it. In short, the transcendent ambiguity of the poet's smile invokes the unevenness of "progress" and "development" as an experience of modernity that we might today consider universal.

NOTES

1. As in all such conventions to historicize literary movements, these years provide a rough estimate. A traditional strain within Spanish American literary history closely linked the movement's duration with Darío's biography: such was his influence in the Spanish-speaking world that his first book was said to mark the beginnings of *modernismo* and his death, in 1916, signaled its end. In choosing the years 1880 to 1914 to refer to *modernismo*, I follow Angel Rama's lead when he points out that the period 1870–1914 coincided with the Belle Époque, when western European nations intensified their incorporation of Latin America into global capitalism and the Spanish American bourgeoisies correspondingly rose to prominence in their respective nations (Rama 24). It should be noted that in Spanish American letters, *posmodernismo* or *vanguardia* are the names that are normally applied to the avant-garde artistic and literary activities and movements that followed. Also, Brazilian *modernismo* is distinguishable from Spanish American *modernismo* since the former was contemporaneous with the European avant-garde movements beginning in the interwar period. For more about the Brazilian movement, see Martins, Schwartz, and Unruh.

2. Darío, "El rey burgués"; all translations of the short story are mine.

3. I have not come across evidence that Darío specifically had the French king, Louis Philippe, the Duc d'Orléans (1773–1850), in mind. This monarch had been nicknamed the Citizen King because he ostensibly courted popular sovereignty—his exile in Massachusetts had also familiarized him with U.S. democracy—but in fact, he drew his support from and privileged the wealthy bourgeoisie during a reign (the July Monarchy, 1830–1848) in which working-class conditions deteriorated considerably. Baudelaire, who wrote about Louis Philippe, states in "The Salon of 1846": "Bourgeois—be you king, lawgiver or merchant—you have established collections, museums, galleries. Some of these, which sixteen years ago were accessible only to the monopolizers, have opened the door to the masses" (48).

4. In addition to Martí, Darío, Casal, and Silva, the first generation of Spanish American *modernistas* included Manuel Gutiérrez Nájera (Mexico, 1859–1895), Salvador Díaz Mirón (Mexico, 1853–1928), and Ricardo Jaimes Freyre (Bolivia, 1868–1933). The second generation, many of whom straddled *modernismo* and *posmodernismo*, included Leopoldo Lugones (Argentina, 1874–1938), Amado Nervo (Mexico, 1870–1919), José Juan Tablada (Mexico, 1871–1945), Enrique González Martínez (Mexico, 1871–1952), Julio Herrera y Reissig (Uruguay, 1875–1910), Delmira Agustini (Uruguay, 1886–1914), and José Santos Chocano (Peru, 1875–1934).

5. A traditional commonplace in Hispanic literary history posits a clearly delineated distinction between Spanish American and Spanish *modernistas* and the members of

Spain's Generation of 1898; what purportedly distinguished both groups was the idea that the former were cosmopolitan practitioners of art for art's sake while the latter were introspective and immersed in reflections on the meaning of Spanishness. Needless to say, the end of the Spanish American War in 1898, in which Spain lost its last overseas colonies to the United States, concretized a significant geopolitical and cultural transformation that had been taking place for Latin America through which Spanish political influence receded and the United States began extending its own via the territorial expansion that its "Manifest Destiny" justified. Even though there is consensus that Spanish American *modernistas* and Darío in particular influenced Spanish poetry (including before 1898), the differences in the aesthetic practices of *modernistas* and members of the Generation of 1898 are neither absolute nor reducible to cultural nationalisms.

    6. Future invader / of the innocent America that possesses indigenous blood, / that still prays to Jesus Christ and still speaks in Spanish. (my translation).

    7. Valera did not share Hugo's romantic enthusiasm for the limitless azure of the sky as a trope for the goal and limits of poetic creativity. Darío's engagement with this trope has been frequently attributed, first, to his reading of Hugo before the publication of *Azul* and, subsequently, to his interest in Mallarmé's use of the same trope.

    8. All translations from this text are mine.

    9. "Usted lo ha revuelto todo: lo ha puesto a cocer en el alambique de su cerebro, y ha sacado de ello una rara quintaesencia."

    10. These publications included the *Revista Azul* (1894–1896) and the *Revista Moderna* (1896–1911) in Mexico City; *La Habana Elegante* (1883–1896) and *El Fígaro* (1885–1899) in Havana; *Cosmópolis* (1894–1895) and *El Cojo Ilustrado* (1895–1907) in Caracas; and *La Revista de América* (1894), *La Biblioteca* (1896–1898), and *El Mercurio de América* (1898–1900) in Buenos Aires. It must also be remembered that French publications, such as *Le Mercure de France*, *Revue des Deux Mondes*, *Revue de Revues*, *La Plume*, and others, were aware of their Latin American reading republic and contributed actively to this transatlantic literary network in columns that were often penned by leading *modernistas* such as Darío, Lugones, and Pedro Emilio Coll. For more on the role of translation in the Spanish American journals, consult José Ismael Gutiérrez, "Traducción y renovación literaria en el modernismo hispanoamericano" *HISTAL* January 2004 at http://www.histal.umontreal.ca/espanol/documentos/traduccion_y_renovacion_literatura.htm (accessed July 23, 2008).

    11. "He is ahead of the fashion and could modify and impose it." It was compliments like this one that probably encouraged Darío to publish Valera's letters as the prologue to the second and subsequent editions of *Azul*.

    12. For most of the nineteenth century, the term that theorists employed to speak of social, economic, and moral progress was not "modernity" but "civilization." For a succinct analysis of the meaning of the latter since the eighteenth century, when its modern usage emerged, see Bruce Mazlish's *Civilization and Its Contents*.

    13. Roberto Schwartz also offers an illustration of this heterogeneity when he states, regarding Brazil, that "[t]he latifundia, little changed, saw the baroque, neoclassic, romantic, naturalist and modernist cultures pass by, cultures which in Europe reflected immense transformations in its social order" (27).

    14. The choice of Georges Ohnet (1848–1918)—a popular Parisian novelist and playwright especially in the 1880s—is not arbitrary. In *Le Maître des forges* (1882), Ohnet focuses on social tensions between an aristocracy in decline and a rising bourgeoisie. That the bourgeois king should read such novels is a metaliterary marker that alludes to the literature that Darío read in Chile.

15. Again, the selection of Watteau would not have been arbitrary on Darío's part since Edmond de Goncourt (1822–1896) and his brother Jules (1830–1870), members of a French aristocratic family who debated art and politics with Hugo, Baudelaire, Flaubert, and others and whose writings were widely read in the second half of the nineteenth century, published "Philosophie de Watteau" (1856) in which they compared the artist to Rubens.

16. Hereafter abbreviated as "Paris."

17. Hereafter abbreviated as "Second Empire."

18. "¡Señor, el arte no está en los fríos envoltorios de mármol, ni en los cuadros lamidos, ni en el excelente señor Ohnet! El arte no viste pantalones, ni habla en burgués, ni pone los puntos en todas las íes."

19. "He acariciado a la gran Naturaleza, y he buscado el calor ideal, el verso que está en el astro, en el fondo del cielo, y el que está en la perla, en lo profundo del océano."

20. "Señor, ha tiempo que yo canto el verbo del porvenir. He tendido mis alas al huracán, he nacido en el tiempo de la aurora; busco la raza escogida que debe esperar, con el himno en la boca y la lira en el mano, la salida del gran sol." Darío elaborates this language in "Salutación del optimista" ("Optimist's Salute"), a poem that he read in Spain shortly after the debacle of 1898 and in which he evoked a Pan-Hispanic race. It was published in his *Cantos de vida y esperanza* in 1905.

21. "Arco triunfal, de estrofas de acero, de estrofas de oro, de estrofas de amor."

WORKS CITED

Allen, Esther, ed. and trans. *José Martí: Selected Writings*. New York: Penguin Books, 2002.

Alonso, Carlos. *The Burden of Modernity: The Rhetoric of Cultural Discourse in Spanish America*. Oxford: Oxford University Press, 1998.

Anderson, Perry. "Modernity and Revolution." *Marxism and the Interpretation of Culture*. Ed. Cary Nelson and Lawrence Grossberg. Hampshire: MacMillan Education, 1988. 317–33.

Balibar, Étienne. *The Philosophy of Marx*. Trans. Chris Turner. London: Verso, 1995.

Baudelaire, Charles. "The Salon of 1846." *Charles Baudelaire: Selected Writings on Art and Literature*. Trans. P. E. Charvet. London: Penguin Books, 1972. 47–107.

Benjamin, Walter. "Paris, the Capital of the Nineteenth Century." Trans. Howard Eiland. Jennings 30–45.

———. "The Paris of the Second Empire in Baudelaire." Trans. Harry Zohn. Jennings 46–133.

Berman, Marshall. *All That Is Solid Melts Into Air*. New York: Simon Schuster, 1983.

Casal, Julián del. "Decadentismo y americanismo." *Prosas*. Vol 1. La Habana: Consejo Nacional de Cultura, 1963. 24–32.

Darío, Rubén. "Cantos de vida y esperanza." *Azul. . . . El salmo de la pluma. Cantos de vida y esperanza. Otros poemas*. México: Editorial Porrúa, 1969. 105–33.

———. "El rey burgués" *Azul . . ..* Mexico, D.F.: Espasa-Calpe Mexicana, 1991. 29–34.

———. *Historia de mis libros*. Managua: Editorial Nueva Nicaragua, 1988.

Halperin Donghi, Tulio. *Historia contemporánea de América Latina*. Madrid: Alianza Editorial, 2005.

Jameson, Fredric. *A Singular Modernity: Essay on the Ontology of the Present*. London: Verso, 2002.

Jennings, Michael W., ed. *The Writer of Modern Life: Essays on Charles Baudelaire*. Cambridge: Belknap Press, 2006.

Martí, José. "Our America." Allen 288–96.

———. "Prologue to Juan Antonio Pérez Bonalde's *Poem of Niagara*." Allen 43–51.

Martins, Wilson. *The Modernist Idea: A Critical Survey of Brazilian Writing in the Twentieth Century*. New York: New York University Press, 1970.

Marx, Karl, and Friedrich Engels. *The Marx-Engels Reader*. Ed. Robert C. Tucker. 2nd ed. New York: W. W. Norton and Company, 1983.

———. "The Communist Manifesto" *Manifesto: Three Classic Essays on How to Change the World*. Melbourne: Ocean Press, 2005. 27–67.

Mazlish, Bruce. *Civilization and Its Contents*. Stanford: Stanford University Press, 2004.

Nájera, Manuel Gutiérrez. "El arte y el materialismo." *Obras. Crítica literaria*. Vol 1. México: UNAM, 1959: 49–64.

Ortega, Julio. "Vuelta a Rubén Darío." *Revista de la Universidad de México. Nueva Época*. 50 (Abril 2008): n. pag. Web. 24 July 2008.

Paz, Octavio. "El caracol y la sirena (Rubén Darío)" *Cuadvivio*. Barcelona: Editorial Seix Barral, 1991. 7–44.

Rama, Angel. *Rubén Darío y el modernismo*. Caracas: Alfadil Ediciones, 1985.

Rodó, José Enrique. *Ariel*. Río Piedras, Puerto Rico: Editorial Edil, 1979.

San Juan, Jr., E, "Postcolonialism and the Problematic of Uneven Development" *Marxism, Modernity and Postcolonial Studies*. Ed. Crystal Bartolovich and Neil Lazarus. Cambridge: Cambridge University Press, 2002. 221–39.

Schwartz, Roberto. "Misplaced Ideas: Literature and Society in Late-Nineteenth-Century Brazil." *Misplaced Ideas: Essays on Brazilian Culture*. Ed. John Gledson. London: Verso, 1992. 19–32.

Unruh, Vicky. *Latin American Vanguards: The Art of Contentious Encounters*. Berkeley: University of California Press, 1994.

Valera, Juan. "Carta-Prólogo de Juan Valera." *Azul. . . . By Rubén Darío*. Mexico, D.F.: Espasa-Calpe Mexicana, 1991. 9–26.

Veblen, Thorstein. *The Theory of the Leisure Class*. New York: Prometheus Books, 1998.

Zavala, Iris M. *Colonialism and Culture: Hispanic Modernisms and the Social Imaginary*. Bloomington: Indiana University Press, 1992.

CHAPTER 5

NATION TIME: RICHARD WRIGHT, *BLACK POWER*, AND PHOTOGRAPHIC MODERNISM

SARA BLAIR

WHAT does it mean for an African American writer revisiting his own relations to the legacies of modernism to address the fraught subject of modernizing Africa? How might the resources of modernism underwrite a narrative of the African nation at the moment of its coming-into-being as such, an exploration of the "nature" of the colony on the verge of transformation into the postcolonial state? And what kind of narrative—fractured, self-interrupting, self-reflexive—can do justice to what is, in the mid-twentieth century, a world-historically new entity: the African colony form, imposed by imperial fiat and the violence of the Western state, in the process of reinventing itself as the proto-postcolonial, emergently independent nation?[1] At the epochal moment of political independence, the African colony is forcibly placed in a vexed relation to history and to narrative. Asserting its claims on modernity and the present, the colony on the verge of no longer being one bears the burdensome weight of the past, the power of its own currency as a token of the prehistory of the West. The space of decolonization exemplifies the crisis—perhaps the possibility—of a split temporality, a bifurcated being in time that evades, as it is beggared by, linear narrative. If modernism can be defined as a set of techniques for exploring felt dislocations in spatial experience and in temporality, it might well serve as a resource for a writer confronting the social form that seems to mark its ending as a cultural project.

Paradoxically, we may best be able to explore the problem of writing the postcolonial state by turning to a visual form: that of photography, with its own histories of formal experimentation and response to social crisis. To hazard a critical analogy, we might say that the relation of the emergently postcolonial state to history approximates the relation to history of the photograph, a quintessentially modern artifact with a distinctive ontology and historical effects. This formulation is indebted to Roland Barthes' plangent (and fundamentally modernist) argument in the storied volume *Camera Lucida* about the photograph as, in essence, "a superimposition . . . of reality and the past" (76). It is, for Barthes, the co-presence in the photographic image of the "Real" (the "*necessarily* real thing which has [at one time] been placed before the lens") and the "Live" (that which has had being, and has being again, in the present of photographic encounter) that defines its temporal being as irrevocably mixed (76). (Thus the invention of photography, Barthes claims, itself "divides the history of the world" [88].) With the photograph, the colony on the verge of independence shares a specific temporal duality: only in being sutured to a past that constitutes "mythic Time" does either enter into being, or circulation, in the now (93).

It is precisely this understanding of the temporal framework of modernity that Richard Wright intuits as he produces a founding work of emergently transnational critique, *Black Power: The Record of Reaction in a Land of Pathos*. Wright began working on the text in the summer of 1953, during a ten-week visit to Africa's Gold Coast to witness firsthand the activities of Kwame Nkrumah's Convention People's Party, then campaigning for independence from British rule (it was achieved in 1957, when Ghana became the first independent black African nation). Billed as a travelogue and published in 1954 on the eve of this transformation, *Black Power* was a paradigmatic text of uneven development by a literary figure who might himself be said to embody that state. Wright produced *Black Power* eight years into his exile from the United States in Paris, and some thirteen years after the influential Chicago sociologist Robert Park had remarked, on meeting Wright for the first time, "How in hell did you happen?"[2] The grandson of four former slaves and the son of a Mississippi sharecropper, a school-leaver who completed his first full year of education only at age twelve, Wright had risen to meteoric fame in the United States with the publication of his first novel, *Native Son*, in 1940—and had fallen just as spectacularly out of favor within a decade, in the wake of critical rejection, a public break with the cultures of the left, and troubled relations with other African American writers.[3] The first literary response on the American horizon to the new specter haunting Europe—that of a liberated, self-governing Africa—*Black Power* inaugurates a final phase in the career of a writer precariously perched in his reception and literary models on the divide between socially conscious conventions and modernist aesthetics, between "Negro" writer and transnational artist, between native son and citizen of a rapidly reordinating global culture.[4]

In every sense, then, *Black Power* is an exemplary text of the self-reinvention of the black writer after modernism, confronting the eddying currents of modernity and its histories of forward motion and regression (or, to borrow Walter Benjamin's terms, civilization and barbarism). Not surprisingly, *Black Power* has led an uneven life of its own. It named the epochal Africanist identity movement of the 1960s—the two men credited with giving the term its political cachet, statesman Adam Clayton Powell and radical Stokely Carmichael, both appear to have read Wright's text—and helped create a transnational frame for liberation struggles; it is also structurally indebted to colonialist tropes of self-discovery and self-realization.[5] But perhaps the most important piece of evidence bespeaking Wright's own understanding of the fugitive temporality of the emergent postcolonial state, and of his own response to it—at once forward-looking and an Orphic look back at a past whose belonging to him is highly vexed—has historically been suppressed.

During the ten weeks in 1953 Wright spent living, traveling, and writing in Gold Coast, he shot over 1,500 photographs with his own professional-grade camera (an apparatus with which he was intimately familiar; its use had helped Wright generate the widely popular and critically acclaimed 1941 photo-text *12 Million Black Voices*) (see Fabre, *Unfinished Quest* 399). The making and use of photographs during his travels was of such a high order of priority that Wright went to great lengths—not only in port towns or larger villages and the capital, but in far more remote areas in the bush country—to obtain chemicals and supplies for developing and printing his negatives as he traveled. Only thirty-four of these images were ever published as part of Wright's text, and only then outside the United States (they appeared in the British edition of the text).[6] Elsewhere, I have written at length about Wright's deep and career-long engagements with photographic practice, including his experiments with photographic modernism in the context of New Deal–era cultural politics, and the logic of *Black Power* as a photo-text (Blair). In what follows, I want more specifically to consider Wright's uses of the photograph as an object with a radically mixed temporality. This temporal instability becomes a signal resource in his own attempt, as a transnational black intellectual in the wake of modernism, to create a narrative form equal to the history of the emergent African nation. Read in conjunction with its extensive image archive, and the responsiveness of that archive to legacies of photographic modernism, *Black Power* helps us map the afterlives of modernism more broadly in the face of mobile, far-flung, transcultural histories in the making.

If such key strategies as indirection, the proliferation of disparate signifying codes, and suppression of context are benchmarks of modernist expressivity, we can usefully understand the larger archive of *Black Power* as a kind of modernist artifact. Preserved as negatives and paper prints in the Special Collections of Yale's Beinecke Library, and partially mounted on the Beinecke's website in the form of digital images, Wright's extensive body of Gold Coast photographs have floated more or less free of his manuscript and published text. Only a series of lengthy descriptive captions—typed on slips of paper that have been preserved among Wright's papers or appended to images in his photographic archive—give the latter-day reader any indication as to the links between specific images, Wright's actual encounters with African institutions and practices, and his published narrative.

This structural disjunction is generative, and it calls attention to the remarkable range of Wright's images and his mixed understanding of his own imaging practices: in part documentary, predicated on the felt need to produce evidentiary images or illustrations of his narrated encounters; in part formalist, committed to exploring the visual logic and dynamics of "the newness and strangeness" of Africa (Wright, *Black Power* 144); in part expressionist, interested in the camera as an instrument for registering highly subjective responses to a charged social experience.[7] This demonstrated array of registers is testimony to the difficulty Wright experienced as he encountered "Africa" and its essential "blackness," with their fraught history as founding tropes for Anglo-American modernism (as Michael North has noted, mimicry of black expressive codes and racial masquerade were "strategies without which modernism could not have arisen" [v]). It is also, however, an index to the critical importance of photographic experimentation for Wright's project. In producing a manuscript he variously called "O, My People!," "Stranger in Africa," "Africa Turns Black" and—after the often-cited lines of Countee Cullen—"What is Africa to Me?," Wright turns to photographic modernism as a resource for negotiating his own psychic dislocation in the face of a radically uneven historicity.[8]

Even those readers familiar with the photographs chosen by Wright's British editors for inclusion in the UK edition of *Black Power* are likely to be surprised by the number and variety of images in his Gold Coast archive that bespeak his deep interest in the modernist legacies of the camera.[9] A sustained strategy of his photographic responses resolves the problem of what Wright called "approaching Africa" (*BP* 3) by adapting conventions associated with the influential projects of such photographers as Berenice Abbott and Paul Strand, with whose work he was long familiar.[10] In an image of fishing boats near the Takoradi harbor (figure 5.1), for example,

Figure 5.1 : Richard Wright, untitled, Gold Coast, 1953. Beinecke Library, Yale University

a markedly high angle and tight framing, in conjunction with the effects of near midday, near equatorial sunlight, evidence awareness of Strand's formal abstractionism. Here, as in Strand's iconic "Wall Street" (1915), Wright's emphasis on the formal properties of the photograph aims to balance sharp-focus realism and abstraction and their respective claims on documentation and expressive form.[11] Yet in Wright's photograph, this aim implicates the historically urgent problem of Africa and its modernity; it is encoded as a tension between motion and arrest, between richly textural natural forms (sunlit skin, the wood of the boats, the froth of churned water) and the apparent flatness and impenetrability of the sea, which appears no less depthless than the sheet of photographic paper on which the image is printed. Stasis and dynamic change; surface and depth; visibility and impenetrability: here, the definitive paradoxes of the photograph as a document, so central to Strand's founding modernist work, are put in service of the animating question of Wright's text: how to understand the "completely different order" of history that is decolonizing Africa (*BP* 42).

With different aims, Wright's photograph of two young girls in an urban marketplace, likely Accra or Kumasi, also invokes the history of photographic formalism (figure 5.2). The shot features a powerfully rhythmic composition and a luminous play of tonalities, of rounded and angular forms, of positive and negative spaces. Here, however, formal abstraction is not only a strategy of the observer's framing, or a property produced by the camera. It is also a documented feature of the expressive cultures of the Gold Coast: note the vivid, dynamic patterning of the dress fabric of

Figure 5.2 : Richard Wright, untitled, Gold Coast, 1953. Beinecke Library, Yale University

the girl in the foreground and the apparent play between forms, as the wall ornamentation mimes the shape of the wooden bowls perched on the girl's head. Even
the physical postures that unite the two subjects in a kind of mirroring suggest a
quality of abstraction organic to Gold Coast culture, if not to African bodies. Yet
Wright is well aware of the fraught role played within African American modernism
by claims for the "innate" capacity of Africa and Africans for abstraction, beginning
with Alain Locke's Harlem Renaissance–era arguments for the unwaveringly "rigid,
controlled, disciplined, abstract" character of "African art expressions" (254).[12] In
Wright's image, in the presence of distinguishable African subjects, the modality of
formal abstraction becomes a productively uncertain property; its assignment both
to these subjects and to the photographic observer suggests Wright's awareness of
the problem of an imaginary Africa whose "adher[ence]" to the past, in Barthes's
sense, displaces the lived experience and being-in-time of its inhabitants (Barthes
6). In such self-consciously static, formalist images as that of the young girls, Wright
has made the effect of photographic capture productively unstable. Against the
anticipated experience of a timeless, premodern organicism organic to "Africa," his
image counterposes a distinctly photographic arrest: a suspension of temporality
produced by the photograph, and conducing to a deeper apprehension of this
encountered world.

   Apprehension, in its dual senses, is a particularly apt term with respect to
Wright's narrative of encounter in *Black Power*. Read in conjunction with that narrative, his invocations of photographic formalism are legible as a mode for managing overwhelming alterity—"the unsettled feeling engendered" by "gazing upon a
world whose laws I did not know, upon faces whose reactions were riddles to me"
(*BP* 42). Throughout the text, Wright describes the difficulty of getting "my eyes . . .
accustomed" to the landscape (*BP* 43), of being "faced with the absolute otherness
and inaccessibility of this new world" (*BP* 44). Again and again, within his account,
he "t[akes] out my camera to photograph the scene" (*BP* 75) and thus to make trial
of his own presumptions (*BP* 68). Aligned with his mobile, fitful narrative, Wright's
photographic formalism hardly suggests a retreat from the epistemological and psychic difficulties of confronting emergently postcolonial Africa.[13] Rather, it highlights his own uncertain status as a self-conscious artist, member of the tribe, and
definitive outsider, who shifts among socially conscious, formalist, and nonobjec-
tive modes in response to a world-historical reality, "something new under the sun"
(*BP* 71). Only in the complex play between Wright's self-consciously formal images,
with their insistence on rhythmic patterning, textures, and geometric forms, and his
accounts of his fraught and even failed attempts to "see" Africa under conditions in
which "chances of a natural photograph were impossible" (*BP* 75), do the most powerful achievements of his text as a meditation on the emerging nation in its time
make themselves visible.

   This is the case with one of Wright's most strikingly formalist images, whose
invocation of the modernist photographic legacy resonates powerfully with his narrative. On the occasion of finally meeting with an Ashanti chief, one of the traditional tribal leaders whose traditionally vast social power was being "terminat[ed]"

by the coalescence of a Westernized state and its institutions (*BP* 249), Wright decisively positions himself on the side of development policies and the nation form,
arguing that "[a] central government is an absolute necessity if man is to live at all
rationally" (*BP* 250) rather than under the spell of "magical authority" (*BP* 251). Yet
the force of this encounter attaches equally to the fact of "a 'decent' man . . . being
driven out of power" and to the possibility of a national future as "dark" as the pre-
national past (*BP* 250). While such chiefs vainly "wan[t] a chance to turn the clock
back," their former subjects are "being strait-jacketed into the future," a no less troubling temporal orientation (*BP* 251). For the Gold Coast to adopt the historicity
of progress along with the form of the nation, it seems, is for its citizens-in-the-
making to be "plunged into . . . a future that smack[s] of Chicago or Detroit"—
synecdoches for the failed histories of the West (*BP* 251). How might a native son of
these very histories bring his gaze to bear on a past multiply removed and "gone," or
on "the native genius of the people" who are and are not his own? (*BP* 251).

Although this question is left dramatically unresolved—his account of the
meeting ends in a gesture of ventriloquism, with ellipses and a question mark—
Wright negotiates the meaning of the African past, and of his own stance in face of
it, photographically. Among the images published in the British edition of the text
is Wright's portrait of an Ashanti chief (figure 5.3). A remarkably tight shot taken at
ground level, the image foregrounds the traditional symbols of Ashanti power—
the ruler's baton, the ornately carved stool traditionally believed to contain the
souls of ancestors—and the visually striking objects of Gold Coast craft and expressive traditions. Wright's emphasis on patterning and visual structure is readily

Figure 5.3 : Richard Wright, untitled, Gold Coast, 1953. Beinecke Library, Yale University

familiar in the context of modernist visual legacies; it also recalls the work of African photographer Seydou Keïta, whose portrait images of emergently middle-class
Malians from 1950 to 1955 highlight the mutual mediation of African and Western
attire, poses, and forms for subjects defining themselves in the unstable territory of
the proto-postcolonial.[14] What is most striking in Wright's image, however (and
particularly by comparison with Keïta's work), is its conduct as a portrait that
negates the very possibility of face-to-face exchange, or any play of returned gazes
between the figure of African prehistoricity and the exilic observer burdened by
historical consciousness. In dialogue with his own narrative and with modernist
photographic practices, Wright's photographic formalism suggests a generative
uncertainty on his part about how to frame, how to respond to, signifiers of African
historicity as such.

Ultimately, the effect of Wright's formalism in this portrait, as in much of his
photo archive, is to stress the enormous gap between his experience as a Western
black man and that of the subjects he has come to observe. In the face of Africans
who are often thought to be "less adaptable than other races to change" and a decolonizing Africa whose historicity is virtually illegible, it is paradoxically Wright himself who becomes "completely immobilized" (BP 295, 151). The notable arrest of his
images—their static compositions, their emphasis on formal patterning—becomes
a mode of self-representation, a response to the burden and limits of what he calls
"the mystic influence of 'race'" (BP 73). The question posed by Cullen and invoked
by Wright as an epigraph to Black Power—"What is Africa to me?"—becomes the
urgent question of how, and even whether, "Africa" constitutes a history for him,
and further, how any history of black self-determination, necessarily predicated on
fraught trafficking in race and ideologies of progress, might be told. His structural,
generative uncertainty is summed up in the questions he poses himself early in the
text: "How much am I a part of this? . . . Why could I not feel [racial belonging]?"
(BP 63). The formalist abstraction of Wright's most powerful photographic images
is a tactic for negotiating these questions. Creating a caesura, a stoppage of time,
they aim not to take "Africa" out of time, in the Western mode of the primitive or
radical other. Rather, they allow Wright to dwell in his own vexed relationship with
its multiple, fractured, violent and contending histories—the layering of colonial
institutions over complex tribal, ethnic, and kinship practices; the facts of uneven
development shot through with traditions of revolution and resistance.

Describing his extraordinary sense of dislocation in the space of the market at
Accra, for example, Wright insists on his status as an outsider confronting a culture
that's not unknowable but powerfully resistant to his ongoing attempts "to look," "to
know," to create a temporal narrative frame that would locate tribal social logics and
"survivals," as well as colonial exploitation, in a pre-national past (BP 68, 73). (That
photographic practice is a favored strategy and analogue for this problem is made
evident in Wright's account of the attempt to buy a tin pan for making chemical
solutions in which to develop his films; his African interlocutors, contemptuous of
a man lowering himself for the purchase of such a humble domestic object, inquire
"if Massa cook chop in pan," or "make peepee" in it [BP 92].) A hallmark of Black

Power is Wright's sustained failure to recognize continuity between himself and his subjects, in the form of practices evolving toward recognizably modern social struc-tures or even of an experience of "*feel[ing]* . . . race" that would bridge linguistic, cultural and temporal divides (*BP* 241). In its place, the narrative actively sustains a temporally disruptive, fracturing "sense of panic" (*BP* 44). Again and again, the text enacts a traumatophilic "burden of alertness" about the contexts in which lived experience and nation time, Western idioms of progress and African practices for preserving the past, collide (*BP* 44). In his photographic archives, Wright experi-ments with the possible uses of the photograph's temporal duality to explore those spaces—or in a notion embraced by African American photographer Bettye Saar, to "extend the frozen moment"—so as more fully to experience the ongoing life of what history marks as the vanished (and pre-national) past (Stewart). In other words, Wright's insistence via photographic formalism on what Barthes calls the "*intense immobility*" of the photograph enables him to explore more fully the prob-lem of placing Gold Coast Africa in a historical narrative of modernity, of framing its colonial past as the grounds or condition of being for its regeneration in the Western form of the state (Barthes 49).

Such formalism is only one photographic mode through which Wright hazards expressive possibilities for telling this story. Throughout the text and his photo archive alike, he is intensely interested in what he calls, at the very outset of *Black Power*, the power of "frontal vision" (*BP* 38). Associated with his epiphanic arrival—as Wright sets foot on Gold Coast soil, he notes: "I saw Africa for the first time with frontal vision: black life was everywhere" (*BP* 38)—that phrase resonates deeply with Wright's mixed motives and genres. By the early 1950s, the convention of fron-tality had a dense photographic history of its own, of which Wright was well aware. Much of the storied work of New Deal–era imaging that was a critical model for Wright's photographic forays was predicated on the direct gaze of represented sub-jects—so much so that an unflinching frontality became a benchmark or guarantee of the objectivity and truthfulness of the photographic image, as exemplified by Walker Evans's portraits of tenant farmers in Hale County, Alabama (figure 5.4).[15] Yet whatever the social status of the frontal subject, Barthes asserts, the returned and frontal gaze is the very feature of the photograph in which its temporal duality, its superimposition of being in history and distance in time from us, is most pow-erfully activated. Thus *Camera Lucida* opens with Barthes' charged, wounded rec-ognition, as he gazes at a photographic portrait of Napoleon's brother, that "I am looking at eyes that looked at the Emperor" (3).

The power of fallen empires aside, Wright consistently stages his experience of proto-postcolonial social space as a contest of frontal visions, according his photo-graphic subjects the power not only of a look back, but of a look that collapses as it heightens the temporal gap between then and now, between "Africa" and the West, between the transnational ethnographic gaze and the returned look of the subject of its power. His portraits of African subjects—that is, his portraits self-consciously conceived as such—thoughtfully explore this contest of temporalities, as they sug-gest the disenchantment of Western codes of the nation's progressive self-realization

Figure 5.4 : Walker Evans, Floyd Burroughs, Hale County, Alabama, 1936.
Library of Congress, FSA/OWI

as political entity. An exemplary instance of this work is Wright's image of a woman and her child in the market at Accra (figure 5.5). Here, the frontal gaze that initially appears for the reader of *Black Power* to function as an instrument of ethnographic observation, in service of a predictable narrative of African modernization, is leveled coolly back at Wright (and, by implication, at the reader). Both mother and child clasp their hands with a monitory effect; the mother, comb lying in her lap, has apparently ceased to braid her hair in response to the intrusion of the camera. Wright's text describes this encounter as a successful one, in the sense that his efforts to frame his informants as usable subjects in the business of creating a transnational modernity for long-colonized peoples are in effect legitimated. But the supplemental photograph tells a more complicated story. Guarded, dignified, fully present, the mother and child defy inclusion in the framework of progressive encounter; they defy Wright's initial confidence in his power to create a *temporizing* narrative, one readily appropriate to the experience and historicity of decolonization. Unlike a James Town youth who pleads with Wright to make a gift of his camera, saying, "I'll send you money for it, I swear, sar" (*BP* 110), and unlike the "magnificent" woman in the fishing village of Labadi who demands, "Penny, massa," in exchange for permission to take her portrait but lunges triumphantly into her mud hut before Wright can even cock his camera (*BP* 163), these figures in the market demand neither face time nor payment. In effect, they defy the temporal hegemony of the modernizing, temporizing gaze (I came, I saw, I preserved the experience as past), staking a claim to full presence in the moment of the encounter, and beyond it, in the narrative Wright's account will enter.

Figure 5.5 : Richard Wright, untitled, Gold Coast, 1953. Beinecke Library, Yale University

Consistently, Wright's photographic record serves to underscore the fragility and limits of his own attempts to encompass decolonizing Africa via the frontal look, with its presumed claims on cultural knowability and on the power of modern Western institutions to decolonizing Africa enlightenment and the fruits of industrial capitalism's historicity. Tellingly, the photographic subjects who turn out most frequently to stage the failure of Wright's historicizing gaze and his temporizing are women. Indeed, "frontal vision" as both a technology for seeing Africa and an effect of that experience is sutured from the outset to the iconography of mother Africa, in the figure of "a woman wearing a brightly colored length of cloth which held a baby strapped to her back" (*BP* 38). Yet such figures, appearing throughout Wright's text and his archive, are hardly the eroticized Venus Hottentots, or even the Europeanized Madonnas, so deeply embedded in the Western iconographic tradition. Whatever mystery these women embody suggests their power to resist the temporizing gaze of the transnational black intellectual, seeking to represent the fraught present-tense moment of his encounter with the decolonizing life-world in all its layered temporality (figure 5.6).

As a result of one such encounter, Wright describes himself as "suddenly . . . self-conscious" about his own presumptions (*BP* 163). Increasingly, the narrative of *Black Power* records not just failures of knowing or contact but a process of "question[ing] myself, *my* assumptions" about the value for the Ashanti (and soon to be Ghanaian) people of those most cherished institutions—industrialization,

Figure 5.6 : Richard Wright, untitled, Gold Coast, 1953. Beinecke Library, Yale University

state education, literacy—whereby the nation reproduces its power and its legitimating narratives (*BP* 163). As the repressed images for the text show, Wright establishes a pattern, or at least a rhythm, of disruption of his own authority and practice
via his photographic record; he thereby undermines his own agency to offer instrumental and temporizing judgments. Dwelling in the freighted present of encounter
with those who level the frontal look back, Wright entertains the felt inadequacy of
Western modernity and its signal institutions to do justice to Africa's living history.
Finally, he openly admits, it is on the basis of a failure of alternative imagination of
historical being, rather than an untroubled investment in Western progressivism or
valuations of historicity, that he makes his stand: "if not that [the embrace of Western modernity for Africa], then what? I didn't know" (*BP* 164).

A particular image in Wright's archive, one predicated on photo-modernist
conventions and the history of frontality, can be said to literalize his understanding
of the Western notion of historicity as modernity's blind spot (figure 5.7). Wright's
portrait of a tribal elder, whose left eye appears glaucous, opaque, clouded by cata-
ract or some other dysfunction, clearly recalls the iconic portrait by Paul Strand,
"Blind Woman" (1916), and the many meditations on photography's powers that it
inspired (figure 5.8). Walker Evans would later note that it was Strand's inclusion of
the crudely lettered sign—"BLIND"—that opened to him, and later documentary
photographers, a sense of urgency and possibility with respect to photography's distinctive representational logic—that is, its powers of iconography versus those of
the symbol, the instantaneous and split being-in-time of the image as opposed to
the temporality of the word (Rathbone 13). Among contemporaries whose work

Figure 5.7 : Richard Wright, untitled, Gold Coast, 1953. Beinecke Library, Yale University

Figure 5.8 : Paul Strand, Blind Woman, 1916

Wright knew, the émigré photographer Lisette Model was equally engaged by this play of phenomenologies and temporalities, and specifically in the context of exploring photography's power to respond to experiences of fraught, riven, and incommensurable temporal frames.[16]

Wright's archive and broader involvement with photographic practice show that he was aware of these concerns as they emerged and developed during the postwar decades (see Blair, 69–73). In the context of his attempts to account narratively for the coming-into-being of the African state, his production of the elder's portrait is more than merely mimetic. It serves, however gesturally, as a meditation on the contest of historicities that decolonizing Africa and his own narrative will inevitably become. Unlike Strand and Model's subjects, Wright's is hardly a beggar, and he is not, it would seem, fully blind; to borrow from the anguished idiom of Ralph Ellison's invisible man as he confronts the Cyclopean glass eyeball of Brother Jack, it is unclear in Wright's portrait "which eye is really the blind one" (478). Bifurcating Africa's look back at the historicizing witness, framing the figure of the tribal past as a subject of blindness and insight, the image turns itself back on the gaze of its maker and viewers. Located in the history of images to which it responds, it can be seen to resonate with uncertainty: whose vision of the future, of futurity or history itself, is most organic? Most alert to historical complexities? Most compelling? In order for Wright—himself a figure of sameness and difference, of nationalism and of transnationality—to make sense of what he experiences and sees, what is required is an accounting, a figuring, capable of arresting time and forestalling the adhesion of temporal duration to Western historical logics.

The force of that insight, however latent it may be within the text of *Black Power*, helps account for the singularly and famously anticlimactic quality of its conclusion. In the final section of the text, Wright describes his visits to Christianborg, Cape Coast, and Elmina castles, the "great slave headquarters" in which traders imprisoned and sold their captives for embarkation on the Middle Passage, and offers his infamous open letter to Nkrumah about Africa's future (*BP* 383). Many readers have concluded, perhaps rightly, that Wright's politics as educed here are insufficient to the realities of decolonization. Of interest in any case is what I take to be the deliberately flattening effect of the narrative, positioned at what should rightly be the thundering climax of Wright's story, his "record of reactions" to the most intense historical "pathos." Again and again, in face of this material history, Wright seeks to create something of the effect of the photograph—the sense of a past both "Real" and "Live," auratic in its insistence on the literal, indexical survival, the haunting physical impress, of experience within the present. Thus he muses that "the same iron bolts which secured the doors to keep the slaves imprisoned" in the dungeons at Christianborg Castle are "the ones that my fingers now touched" (*BP* 382). Thus Wright positions himself, within the "awe-inspiring" Elmina Castle (*BP* 383; the largest and most prosperous slave headquarters of the Gold Coast slave trade) in the former observation room of Ashanti chiefs. They stood—as Wright now stands, camera in hand—in the "tiny enclosure" of the auction room to watch "their captives being bid for by Europeans" through "slits in the wall" (*BP* 383). Although Wright confesses that "my mind refused to function" in this space, his camera is at work, seeking to create an image with "a sheen that outshines" the "horrible tales of what went on within these walls" by registering both the violence of history and the effects of contending historicities (*BP* 383; figure 5.9).

It is with this telling image, belonging to yet suppressed from the conclusion of the published text of *Black Power,* that I want to conclude. Here, as throughout his narrative, Wright positions himself as a figure behind the camera; he also becomes an occupant of that ages-old imaging device, the *camera obscura* (from the Latin, "dark

Figure 5.9 : Richard Wright, untitled, Gold Coast. Beinecke Library, Yale University

chamber"), a pre-photographic technology for producing highly realistic, per-spectively accurate representations.[17] The oddly disjunctive, snapshotlike quality of the text—which fails, or refuses, to gather itself toward a conventional conclusion or even what we might call a resolved perspective—serves to heighten this thrust of his self-representation. Even as Wright calls for the militarization of African life as the only viable mode of modernization and entry into the historicity of the nation-state, his own narrative as such aims to dwell in the temporally unstable oscillation between the past of experience and the present of encounter, lived historicity and "the hunger [of the] *Weltanschauung*," spiritual time and nation time (*BP* 387). It is, fi-nally, the mixed temporality of the photograph, with all its indexical charge, the persistence within it of a historical past palpably real yet irrecoverable, visible yet illu-sory, to which Wright's own narrative aspires. Read in light of this aspiration, *Black Power* can become part of a rich history of response by black intellectuals to the prob-lem of history's narrative, which turns out also to be the problem of the legacies of modernism: that of finding suitable forms in which to address it.

NOTES

1. Questions of temporality have played an increasing role in shaping postcolonial theory as well as studies of anticolonial movements. Atwell, *Rewriting Modernity* 8, points to a salutary shift in the historiography of South Africa, "from an emphasis on how to write about sameness and difference, to writing about temporality, which is to say, writing about one's place in history or one's place in the present and future." Korang, *Writing Ghana,* considers the work of writers who develop the concept of the "African Nation" within the horizon of colonial rule, and thereby respond to modernity in ways that anticipate and address late-twentieth and twenty-first century contexts. Wenzel, *Bulletproof,* offers a longer history of decolonization with an emphasis on the unrealized aspirations of earlier anticolonialism, so as to rethink failures of resistance in terms of their charged afterlives and fugitive temporalities, as a dialectic between retrospection and anticipation, memory and prophecy. Such readings frequently gesture toward the influential work of Osborne, *Politics of Time*, who argues for the force with which "time [in Western modernity] becomes a historical force in its own right," and historical consciousness becomes identified with temporal experience—an effect of "the irreducible doubling of the concept of modernity as something that has happened, yet continues to happen" (13). To date, there has been little if any emphasis on photographic history or practice as a resource for exploring these concerns with temporality; Pinney and Peterson, *Photography's Other Histories,* include work on the changing contract between colonialist photographers and indigenous subjects, and on imaging practices in postcolonial Nigeria, Kenya, and India. For related discussion of the experience of temporality as a critical component of modernism's "new," and the introduction of new notions of time itself in the wake of scholarship on global modernities, see Emery's contribution to this volume, "Caribbean Modernism: Plantation to Planetary"; Lazarus's contribution, "Modernism and African Literature," offers a pointed survey of the issue of competing time scales as they enter into the attempt to frame various modernities and modernisms as coeval, pluralist, or differential.

2. Rowley, *Life and Times*, 250.

3. *Native Son* sold 250,000 hardcover copies in the first three weeks after its publication. In his infamous 1963 essay "Black Boys and Native Sons," literary lion Irving Howe proclaimed that "The day *Native Son* appeared, American culture was changed forever." Wright's career has long been read, in the received accounts, as a story of meteoric success and precipitate fall from same, both in the quality of his work and in his larger reception.

4. Wright's last decade of writing was dedicated to a body of work usually subsumed under the rubric of travel writing; arguably, however, its social, political and expressive interests exceed the conventions of that genre. After *Black Power*, he published *The Color Curtain* (1956), an account of his travel in Indonesia for the 1955 Bandung Conference, the first global meeting of postcolonial and postindependent states, which brought together representatives of The People's Republic of China and the Democratic Republic of North Vietnam with those of other Asian and African nations; *Pagan Spain* (1957); *White Man, Listen!* (1957), three of whose four lecture/essays, based on Wright's readings and travel, concern the role of Westernized elites who are in the forefront of nationalist movements in Asia, Africa, and the West Indies; and his observations on French West Africa, written c. 1959 and unpublished at the time of Wright's death. Considered readings of this body of work are given in Smith.

5. Powell used the term during a baccalaureate address at Howard University on May 29, 1966; it was first used as a political slogan by Carmichael during a Student Nonviolent Coordinating Committee rally on June 16, 1966, after the shooting of civil rights activist James Meredith.

Critical responses to Wright's account of emergently postcolonial Africa have long been (and continue to be) decidedly mixed. On one hand, there is a venerable tradition of sharp critique, embodied by such figures as Appiah, "Long Way Home," who describes Wright's reading of Gold Coast Africa as a "paranoid hermeneutic," resulting from Wright's rejection of any logic of racial identification (181); Chiwengo, "Gazing through the Screen," who argues that Wright replicates a colonialist logic by historicizing not his encounter with emergently postcolonial Africa but rather "the rise to manhood of the African American" (27); Leopold Senghor, the Senegalese poet, leading figure in the Négritude movement, and postindependence president, who argued that Wright misread the broader movement for African independence as antiracist or reverse racism rather than as a legitimate attempt to counter the social and psychic alienation of Africans and peoples of African descent (cited in Fabre, *World of Richard Wright* 209–11); and West, "Black Radicalism" (51–56), who claims that Wright's work more broadly is defined by "individualistic revolt" (not to mention misogyny) rather than an affinity for "black collective insurgency," and that Wright "devalued" black power and African postcolonial movements as mere "props for the petty bourgeoisie," thus undermining his status as a theorist or exponent of radical black nationalism. On the other hand, scholars who grapple with broader histories of response to modernity, diaspora, and racialization tend to read Wright more sympathetically; these prominently include Gilroy, *Black Atlantic*, who argues for Wright's productive discomfort with his structural role as a multiply marginal figure (see especially 151); Pratt, *Imperial Eyes*, who argues that Wright "directly set himself to work parodying and reworking the inherited tropology" of colonialist travel narrative, and thereby achieved a richly "ambivalent complexity" of stance and expression (222); and Gaines, "Revisiting Richard Wright in Ghana," who argues for the power of Wright's work as a revisionist and dialectical reading of black diaspora, one that is particularly valuable in that it "offers an explicit critique of the diaspora-homeland binary" (75). For additional readings of *Black Power* in relevant critical, social, and literary contexts, see Shankar, Reilly, and particularly Lowe, who argues that Wright's late travelogues "pionee[r] a new, hybrid kind of literary/scientific work" in dialogue with cultural anthropology and self-conscious about photographic resources (128).

6. Fabre, *Unfinished Quest*, 404, notes that the U.S. publisher, Harper's "for some reason omitted" the photographs Wright carefully chose and captioned. The Sunday *New York Times Book Review* piece on *Black Power* was not only denunciatory—reviewer Michael Clark, equally appalled by Wright's representation of Christian missionary practices under colonialism and his insistence on the necessity of black leadership and institutions, notes that "One wonders to what extent Mr. Wright has projected into the Gold Coast situation his own hidden or sublimated desires for racial revenge" (3)—it altered Wright's captions. Several hundred of Wright's Gold Coast images have been made available digitally on the Beinecke Library's website; these can be found at http://beinecke.library.yale.edu/dl_crosscollex/ (February 17, 2011).

7. Hereafter, *Black Power* will be cited parenthetically as *BP*.

8. For the full range of Wright's proposed titles, see Fabre, *Unfinished Quest*, 399, 401, 404.

9. The selection, placement, and treatment of images in the British edition of *Black Power*, it should be noted, essentially narrow their range of reference by assimilating them to socially conscious imaging and photo-textual conventions of the prewar era, just as the shortened titled of the volume suppresses Wright's insistence on self-representation as a critical element of his account. See the British edition of the text, Wright, *Black Power* (Dennis Dobson).

10. Wright presumably first encountered the work of Berenice Abbott—whose photographs shaped a formalist aesthetic that sutured documentary to fine art photographic production—during his service on the WPA joint Federal Arts/Federal Writers Project guidebooks *New York Panorama* (1938) and *The WPA Guide to New York City* (1939), which included images from Abbott's WPA-sponsored project *Changing New York* and for which Wright served as Harlem "chief" and representative. In 1942, Wright had been invited to speak at a symposium at a left-leaning downtown gallery called ACA (American Contemporary Artists) in conjunction with an exhibition of the work of Abbott, Strand, and Lisette Model; he had at this point also reviewed the work of Helen Levitt. For a more detailed reading of Wright's engagements with midcentury and postwar photographic practice, see Blair, 64–73.

11. On the influence of Strand's early, astonishingly original body of photographic work as a model for this balance, see Brown. A digital reproduction of Strand's "Wall Street" can be found at Masters of Photography, "Paul Strand: Photographs," http://www.masters-of-photography.com/S/strand/strand_wall_street_full.html (February 17, 2011).

12. On the broader context of black modernist investment in abstraction, see Helbling.

13. Here it is useful to note Robinson's insistence, in his introduction to Wright's *White Man, Listen!*, on the lability of Wright's intellectual stances, and his argument that Wright's "conceptual restlessness needs to be emphasized: in some moments Wright resorts to methodological individualism, his interest in existentialism coming to the fore or becoming more muted, providing license for explanations centered on psychoanalytic forces; at others, Wright weaves his way dialectically through the contest for priority between cultural and materialist approaches, nominating religion and reason as sometimes liberating and sometimes oppressive" (xx).

14. Keïta, a self-taught photographer, conducted his career in his hometown of Bamako, then in the French Sudan, where he made a considerable body of portrait

images from 1950 to 1955. Paradoxically, the declaration of Malian independence from colonial rule in 1960 put an end to Keïta's career, given his decision under duress to become an approved state photographer. It is highly unlikely that Wright knew Keïta's work directly, given its essentially private circulation during the 1950s, but the historical adjacency of their projects, and their shared interest in recording and responding to fugitive historicities, are suggestive. A helpful account of Keïta's career and of the troubled afterlives of his images in the postcolonial (that is to say, commercial and Western) context is given by Rips, "Who Owns Seydou Keïta?" Representative images that provide a useful context for Wright's photographic work can be found online at Fifty One: Fine Art Photography, http://www.gallery51.com/index.php?navigatieid=9&;fotograafid=16 (February 17, 2011).

15. Lalvani, notes that "rigid frontality" of the kind associated with FSA fieldwork has a long history predating photographic portraiture, where it conventionally signifies "the bluntness and 'naturalness' of a culturally unsophisticated class"; the fully frontal gaze, he argues, "should be read in contrast to the cultivated asymmetries of aristocratic pose, for pose is a function of leisure while frontality confirms the complete lack of it" (66).

16. See Model's "Blind Man, Paris" (1937) online at http://photo.box.sk/history.php3?id=13 (February 17, 2011).

17. Jonathan Crary, *Techniques of the Observer*, evidences the critical importance of the camera obscura in the development not only of modern imaging technologies, but as "the most widely used model" in modern philosophy and science "for explaining human vision, and for representing the relation of a perceiver and the position of a knowing subject to an external world" (25). As a conceptual model, Crary argues, the camera obscura was thus critical in defining (and limiting) relations between subjects and the observed world, not least by disembodying vision, supplanting "the observer's physical and sensory experience . . . by the relations between a mechanical apparatus and a pre-given world of objective truth" (39–40).

WORKS CITED

Appiah, Kwame Anthony. "A Long Way from Home: Wright in the Gold Coast." *Richard Wright*. Ed. Harold Bloom. New York: Chelsea House, 1987. 173–90.

Blair, Sara. *Harlem Crossroads: Black Power and the Photograph in the Twentieth Century*. Princeton: Princeton University Press, 2007.

Brown, Milton W. *Paul Strand: Essays on His Life and Work*. Ed. Maren Stange. New York: Aperture, 1991.

Chiwengo, Ngwarsungu. "Gazing through the Screen: Richard Wright's Africa." Ed. Virginia Whatley Smith 20–44.

Clark, Michael. "A Struggle for the Black Man Alone?" Rev. of *Black Power*, by Richard Wright. *New York Times Book Review*, September 26, 1954: 3.

Crary, Jonathan. *Techniques of the Observer: On Vision and Modernity in the Nineteenth Century*. Cambridge: MIT Press, 1992.

Ellison, Ralph. *Invisible Man*. New York: Random House, 1995.

Fabre, Michel. *The Unfinished Quest of Richard Wright*. Trans. Isabel Barzun. New York: William Morrow, 1973.

———. *The World of Richard Wright*. Jackson: University of Mississippi Press, 1985.

Gaines, Kevin K. "Revisiting Richard Wright in Ghana: Black Radicalism and the Dialectics of Diaspora." *Social Text* 19.2 (2001): 75–101.

Gilroy, Paul. *The Black Atlantic: Modernity and Double Consciousness.* Cambridge: Harvard University Press, 1996.

Helblung, Mark. "African Art: Albert C. Barnes and Alain Locke," *Phylon* 43.1 (1982): 57–67.

Howe, Irving. "Black Boys and Native Sons." *Dissent* 10 (Autumn 1963): 353–68.

Korang, Kwaku Larbi. *Writing Ghana, Imagining Africa: Nation and African Modernity.* Rochester: University of Rochester Press, 2009.

Lalvani, Suren. *Photography, Vision and the Production of Modern Bodies.* Albany: State University of New York Press, 1996.

Locke, Alain C. "The Legacy of the Ancestral Arts." *The New Negro: Voices of the Harlem Renaissance.* Ed. Alain Locke. 1925. New York: Simon & Schuster, 1992. 254–69.

Lowe, John. "Richard Wright as Traveler/Ethnographer: The Conundrums of Pagan Spain." Smith 121–43.

North, Michael. *The Dialect of Modernism: Race, Language, and Twentieth-Century Literature.* Oxford: Oxford University Press, 1994.

Pinney, Christopher, and Nicolas Peterson, eds. *Photography's Other Histories.* Durham: Duke University Press, 2003.

Pratt, Mary Louise. *Imperial Eyes: Travel Writing and Transculturation.* New York: Routledge, 1992.

Rathbone, Belinda. *Walker Evans: A Biography.* New York: Houghton Mifflin Company, 1995.

Reilly, John M. "Richard Wright and the Art of Non-Fiction: Stepping Out on the State of the World." *Callaloo* 9.3 (Summer 1986): 507–20.

Rips, Michael. "Who Owns Seydou Keïta?" *New York Times*, January 22, 2006, sec. 2: 32.

Robinson, Cedric. Introduction. *White Man, Listen!* By Richard Wright. New York: Harper-Collins, 1995. xiii–xxv.

Shankar, S. "Richard Wright's Black Power: Colonial Politics and the Travel Narrative." Smith 3–19.

Smith, Virginia Whatley, ed. *Richard Wright's Travel Writings: New Reflections.* Jackson: University Press of Mississippi, 2001.

Stewart, James Christen. *Betye Saar: Extending the Frozen Moment.* Berkeley: University of California Press, 2005.

Wenzel, Jennifer. *Bulletproof: Afterlives of Anticolonial Prophecy in South Africa and Beyond.* Chicago: University of Chicago Press, 2009.

West, Cornell. "Black Radicalism and the Marxist Tradition." *Monthly Review* 40 (September 1988): 51–6.

Wright, Richard. *Black Power: A Record of Reactions in a Land of Pathos.* 1954. New York: HarperCollins, 1995.

CHAPTER 6

CHINESE MODERNISM, MIMETIC DESIRE, AND EUROPEAN TIME

ERIC HAYOT

Where there is an historically specific modernity, there will
be an historically specific cultural response, despite outward
and seemingly "outmoded" formal appearances.

—Gregory Lee[1]

WHO owns "modernism"? And who owns "Asia"? Or rather, to put it in terms more appropriate to our contemporary discourse: what are the terms of their intertwined and mutual *belonging*?

The phrase is conventionally written "Asian modernism," or, perhaps even more conventionally, "Chinese modernism" or "Japanese modernism," the adjective delimiting the scope of reference to a national tradition of the type that subtends the field's normative imaginaries. The national framework establishes, in advance of the approach to the aesthetic work, a dialectic of inside and outside. So scholarship on national modernisms tends to arrange its objects in an oscillation between origin and difference, stability and alteration: what in this text or this tradition emerges *sui generis* from the "natural" culture of the nation; and what in it intervenes from the exterior of that plenitude? Or, to focus on the specific case before us: what in Chinese modernism belongs to "modernism," and what in it is "Chinese"?

Insofar as it addresses that question, scholarship on Chinese modernism differs little from scholarship on any "local" modernism, so long as we understand that the generic modernism to which these local modernisms refer has for some time now been the modernism of a select few national or urban locations in Europe and North America, and of aesthetic attitudes, and objects that express those attitudes, produced between the middle of the nineteenth century and the middle of the twentieth century. Scholarship on all "local" modernisms will tend, as a result of this framework, to move first toward the production of generic identity (there is such a thing as modernism in a Chinese or Japanese context) before generating a sequence of local differences (and this modernism is not the same as modernism in general in ways X, Y, and Z). The belonging of modernism outside Europe thus proceeds along the axis of resemblance; the non-European claim to modernism relies on the production of difference inside a field of general similarity.

This chapter thematizes four issues whose consideration ought to precede any discussion of how any such local modernism is thought, especially insofar as the notion of the local (or the national) operates within a larger field whose "other" pole is the global.[2] Each of these themes forms part of the philosophical ground of the notions of modernism, of history, and of the relation between the local and the "global"—the ground, that is, that makes the consideration of something like Chinese modernism possible, and the ground that makes the concept such a difficult, uncomfortable, and, in its current formation, ultimately untenable one, as we shall see.

MODERNISM AND THE (WESTERN) HISTORY OF THE MODERN

As one of the few terms commonly used to divide up and parse the history of the aesthetic, "modernism" shares with "Romanticism" the unusual characteristic of denoting both an attitude and a period. In English and American literature, few other fields have this capacity: it makes no sense to talk about whether Aemilia Lanyer "belongs" to the "early modern" period, or whether Jonathan Edwards is a "colonial American" author, whereas much ink has been spilled on the "modernist or not?" status of a number of authors who, though they were contemporaries of the most canonical of modernists, somehow seem not to fit in the club. Willa Cather? Katherine Mansfield? Jean Toomer? Tellingly, the first three examples that spring to mind all emerge from outside the ferment of London circa 1914, directing us toward the intensely geographic logic of the modernist core (more on this in a moment). This disconnection between temporality and the aesthetic produces a certain useful flexibility—modernism can appear in both "high" (attitude) and "late" (period) varieties, for instance—but the disconnect between period and attitude is clearly not so strong as to allow any person exhibiting the right attitude to be labeled by the term.[3] As much we might like to think of a "crisis of representation" in the allegorical excesses of Dante, the rules of the game do not permit us to call him a modernist.[4]

How temporally flexible is modernism, either as a concept or as a scholarly field? In recent years, the opening of Anglo-American scholarship on modernism has produced significant changes in the field's boundaries and limits, changes that have largely addressed the early side of the historical equation. In 1995, Peter Nicholls opened one of the first and most influential Pan-European surveys of modernism, *Modernisms: A Literary Guide*, with the disclaimer that "the beginnings of modernism . . . are largely indeterminate," a problem he resolves by reconstituting "a pre-history of the various modernisms without which their own exemplary work can hardly be understood" (1). Nicholls includes in this prehistory not only the French Symbolist poets (Baudelaire, Rimbaud, Mallarmé), but also Karl Marx, Herman Melville, and Fyodor Dostoyevsky.

Whatever might have felt controversial to Nicholls about the decision to open with "pre-history" has faded in recent years. Two more recent surveys of the field open with extensive discussions of Baudelaire, without any mention at all of his being "pre-historical." Pericles Lewis began the first full chapter of his 2007 *Cambridge Introduction to Modernism* with Baudelaire and Flaubert, writing that they "were among the first authors to register the crisis of representation that would lead to the development of literary modernists in the twentieth century" (37). And Peter Gay started his *Modernism: the Lure of Heresy* (2008), as did Lewis, with the "absolutely indispensable" Baudelaire, before moving on, as did Lewis in *his* first chapter, to that other "founder" of modernism, Wilde (34).

The force of this consensus about modernism's status as an attitude (or complex of attitudes), set of affiliations, and forms of influence on the history of modernism as a concept can be measured if we remember that the term "modernism's" first explicitly *aesthetic* use came in 1888 from the Nicaraguan poet Rubén Darío. Darío used the term *modernismo* in a review of the work of the poet Ricardo Contreras. In that same year, he published *Azul . . .*, a collection of poems and stories widely considered to have launched *modernismo* as a Spanish-language literary movement.[5] But Darío's work remains widely unknown outside the Spanish-speaking world, and his importance in the history of what I have been calling "modernism in general" is so minimal that he appears only once in Lewis's *Cambridge Introduction to Modernism*, twice in Nicholls's *Modernism: A Literary Guide,* and not a single time in the 563 pages of Gay's *Modernism: The Lure of Heresy.*[6] (The appearance of an entire chapter devoted to Darío and the situation of *modernismo* in this volume is a sign of our changing scholarly future, one that appears against the paradoxical backdrop, as Gerard Aching notes, of the historical isolation of Spanish American modernism from modernist studies.)

So the "founders" of modernism—Baudelaire, Wilde, Dostoyevsky—never called themselves modernists. And the first person to do so, Darío, barely registers in the major recent surveys of the movement. These facts indicate the degree to which the geographic or temporal coherence of modernism's belonging—its belonging to the places where it belongs and the belonging of those who are understood as part of it—develops its periodizing impulse secondarily to its attitudinal one. Here we might begin to suspect that the forms of analysis that allow Darío to be ignored, or that require the inclusion of Baudelaire, have to do as much with the economic and cultural prestige of northern Europe over the last two centuries as they do with any hard and fast rules about what should count as modernist and what should not. But this is no revelation: it is now possible to reframe the history of all modern literature as an effect of that prestige, allowing it to become, essentially, a history of the kinds of recognition that emerge from Paris.[7]

Should anyone doubt the depth of the problem created for something like "global modernisms" by this history of prestige, consider the degree to which the very terms for "modern" and "modernist" appear in Asia initially as *transcriptions* rather than as translations: *modeng* in 1930s China, *modanizumu* in Japan.[8] Each of these is the effect of an attempt to transcribe without alteration the sound-space of the idea of the modern, its prestige as a signifier divorced from the usual secondary labor of semantic translation, its foreign sound serving to give the term some of the same novel kick it had when it first appeared in England or the United States. (That is, the word "modern," whose first application to the realm of the aesthetic in English the *Oxford English Dictionary* has appearing as late as 1820, felt new to Americans and the English as well; it is not only the belated non-Europeans who get impressed by the novelty of the modern as such.) But the fact that the terms began this way (before succumbing, in Chinese, to the pleasures of translation, and becoming *xiandai*) shows that for Chinese and Japanese artists, the notion of a Western origin was embedded in the concept of the modern or the modernist from its first apprehension.[9] This creates a number of complications for the project of global modernism, since the actual history of the development of disparate modernisms in Asia (and in many other parts of the world) includes, from its inaugural moments, a conception of periodization and originality whose geographic fulcrum is Europe.

And so a first theme: *the mise-en-abyme of history*. If we want to think of modernism globally, we must face the fact that any attempt to get past the Eurocentric story about what modernism is and does must encounter, first, the history of that Eurocentric story as it has been incorporated into national systems of literature (including European ones) and into the world literary system as a whole. To see that what has been recognized as "modern" or "modernism" in China is at least partially an effect of European modernism; or to look in Chinese aesthetic history for evidence of the attitudes that have been associated with those European modernists is essentially to bring to bear on a "global" situation a conception of modernism whose most basic meanings—both attitudinal and temporal—have already been established and owe everything to the understood history of Western aesthetics. To speak about global modernism in China requires recognizing that the actual history of the modern and the modernist has in advance accepted—and, what is more, been built on—a relation to modernism that includes within itself a substantive theory of the "global" and its relation to Europe. There is no point external to the system of European modernism from which we might rethink the history of the term.

GLOBALITY AND THE GEOGRAPHY OF MIMETIC DESIRE

The past decade or so has seen a number of attempts to expand the historical and geographic range of the frameworks of modernism, extending the term beyond its traditional sites (France, Germany, Great Britain, and the United States) and moments of origin (1857, 1910, 1914, 1922) into such places as Latin America, Africa, southern and eastern Europe, the Middle East, and Asia.[10] Marjorie Perloff's keynote address at the 2007 conference of the Modernist Studies Association, which devoted much of its time to the work of Brazilian poet Haroldo de Campos (1929–2003), offered one prominent validation of a modernism that extends beyond the geographic and temporal boundaries that have defined it since the 1960s.[11]

From the Chinese perspective—but really from the perspective of any member of the cultural periphery, whether that periphery lies in the French provinces, in the American West, in Hungary, or in East Asia—such theories of a temporally and geographically expanded modernism must account for the history of what Rey Chow has called "a mimetic desire, responsive and oriented toward the West's imposition of itself on the Rest" (83). By "mimetic desire," Chow means the desire to imitate a powerful other in order to gain recognition from that other as an equal. In the case of our literary history, this means, as Chow remarks throughout *The Protestant Ethnic and the Spirit of Capitalism*, adopting the particular aesthetic *styles* associated with cultural prestige, *and in a manner appropriate to the global balance of cultural power,* so that such adoptions always come from a peripheral subject in relation to the core. The project of such a mimesis—whether one engages it from the "inside," as a Chinese artist asserting the legitimacy of Chinese literature in the global field, or from the "outside," as a scholar writing the history of Chinese aesthetics—has almost inevitably been to insist on Chinese comparability with the West on the basis of its having some version of what the West has. This has been true not only in the literary fields, but also across culture more broadly; hence the histories of the assertions of the existence of a coeval tradition of Chinese (or Japanese, or Indian) "modernism," "philosophy," or "literary criticism," as though Chinese writing or thought could only be respected in terms that recognized its equivalence to the West's most prominent cultural forms.[12]

Consider in this context the "Nobel Complex," identified by Julia Lovell as a signal feature of Chinese intellectual life in the 1980s and 1990s. In those years, hundreds of articles in academic and literary journals and occasional "waves of media hype" addressed the question of why no Chinese writer had yet to win a Nobel Prize in literature (3). As Lovell notes, these anxieties expressed a more general tension about the Chinese relation to modernity in any number of fields, including athletic and military prowess, scientific ability, and economic might.[13] But literature had a special place in that pantheon of developmental anxiety. Lovell attributes that place to the nature of modernity itself, arguing that the modern separation of the aesthetic from the realms of politics or the social—the idea of aesthetic autonomy embodied in the common understanding of the work of Immanuel Kant—allows the work of art to bear a unique burden in the relation between culture, modernity, and modernization. In the modernizing culture, the aesthetic becomes the lone field of achievement capable of bearing some "pure" version of the traditional culture (i.e., "real" Chineseness), since its theoretical autonomy (its separation from the technological or the political) allows it to remain relatively untouched by foreign influences. Success in the aesthetic arena thus demonstrates the contemporary legitimacy of a culture in ways that excellence in areas already dominated by the West (military technology, for instance) cannot, since the very terms and objects of those nonaesthetic successes—industrial factories, communication technology, or battleships—will necessarily be seen as having "foreign" origins.[14] International recognition in the form of the Nobel Prize thus seemed likely to prove the legitimacy not only of Chinese modernization, Lovell argues, but of Chinese tradition as well, even as the anxious expressions of desire for the Nobel indicated the "real-world imbalances and inequalities that belie the universalistic promise of national and world literatures" (18).[15]

It is not the case, of course, that China has no "philosophy," no "literary criticism," or no "aesthetic" until the West recognizes it there; the mimetic production of these categories in the Chinese context aims to fill a lack that does not "belong" to China proper. I emphasize that it is the lack that does not belong to China, not the category that might be thought of as lacking. Such a lack belongs, rather, to the international context in which one's perception of self operates necessarily through reference to the eyes of an other, in which one produces the grounds for a legitimating recognition by translating oneself into the other's language. As Naoki Sakai has put it, "our desire to know what we have supposedly known in our own language . . . arrives by way of our desire for the figure of a foreign language"; that is, the desire to determine what "we" know proceeds always in relation to the desire to translate that knowledge into terms that will matter elsewhere. The coin of recognition and merit is most valuable when minted in foreign currencies (59). The implied genitive of phrases like "Japanese philosophy" or "Chinese modernism" marks simultaneously a claim of possession (China, too, has modernism) and the fact of being possessed by a desire for recognition.

Here, then, the second theme of this chapter: the ways in which the question of global modernism is caught up from the beginning in a network that orients its belonging around a *geography of mimetic desire*. We may notice the ways in which that desire flows, illustrate its topographies, observe its tributaries, swamps, and deltas, or register its relation to the other landscapes of power and desire over which it layers itself and with which it interacts. Any attempt to think modernism globally, to seek out or recognize those forms of the aesthetic that attempt to be responsible to modernism as an attitude and a period, will have to cope with the fact of this mimetic drive, the degree to which it replicates both the developmental logic that guides the history of the term "modernism," and the ways in which that logic organizes in advance of the apprehension of any local modernism the very substance of the distinction between locality, universality, and globality that subtends it.

GLOBAL THINKING AND THE
INTERCONTAMINATION OF TERMS

To speak of global modernisms, then, is from the start to establish a particular kind of framework for thinking the history of aesthetics. Finding modernism elsewhere than in Europe or the United States means, among other things, bestowing a certain form of cultural recognition on countries outside the cultural cores. Such a recognition may well undermine the centrality of those cores, since at its best, the globalizing impulse aims to denaturalize centrisms of all types; and it may well open up the field of literary history to a new kind of story about the history of modernism itself (one where it has, for instance, multiple points of origin, rather than just a mid-nineteenth-century French one). At the same time, the politics of literary recognition suggest that the impulse to recognize the prestige of modernism elsewhere will participate in the very system it attempts to dismantle, by fueling a sense that a particularly northern European modernism names one important and universal aspect of the aesthetics of modernity, and by reinforcing a sense of literary history as largely a process of the interaction between "local" nations and universal modalities.[16]

As should be clear from the Nobel example, these issues have as much to do with modernization as they do with modernism, with the result that the temporal logics proper to the former tend to bleed over into thinking about the history of the latter. The developmental logic of modernization—the sense that modernization as a historical event forces the planet into a single, monocultural history defined by the universal appeal (and power) of technological innovation, the division of labor and the free flow of capital, producing a historical "line" along which each country's progress can be measured—constitutes a major shaping force in both common-sense and philosophical theories of world history, which have tended, since the rise of Europe in the eighteenth and nineteenth centuries, to normalize a vision of historical progress on the European or North American model. (But see Dipesh Chakrabarty: "in the awakening of this sense of anachronism [in which the other is 'behind' us] lies the beginning of modern historical consciousness" [238]; from this perspective, there may be no truly *modern* history that does not internalize the progressivist ideal, which is why we may need a non-modern or genuinely post-modern historical consciousness to write a different story history of modernism.) When such a model carries over to the aesthetic, it tends to imagine literary or artistic innovation spiraling out from centers of high-level innovation and development—Paris or London, on the model of Silicon Valley—to the peripheries, which follow in the wake of the aesthetic vanguard. In such a scheme, the passage of modernism from Europe to the globe can become merely another history of capitalist development, one that can justify a lack of serious interest in "other" modernisms on the grounds that they are belated, secondary, or imitative.

This can be true even when the critic in question seeks to defend local literature against the presumptive universality of European models. The classic example of such an approach in the Chinese context comes from Stephen Owen's review of the work of the Chinese poet Bei Dao, first published in *The New Republic* in 1990, and now widely recognized as a controversial point of embarkation for thinking the relation between contemporary Chinese literature and the categories of the world, the global, and the universal.[17]

The problem with the world literary economy, Owen remarks, is that poets who do not write in its preferred languages will inevitably alter their writing to adapt to its standards. This creates bad literature, since the "pressure for an increasing fungibility of words" will cause poets who wish to be read to write a kind of experiential Esperanto made up of "universal images" and easily digestible ethnographic details (28). The pressures of such a situation, Owen writes, constitute "the quintessence of cultural hegemony, when an essentially local tradition (Anglo-European) is widely taken for granted as universal" (29). The invisibility of the hegemonic pressure exerted by world literary markets will cause Chinese literature to acquire aesthetic value (i.e., to be recognized as "good" abroad, and then at home) only insofar as it matches the topical and formal expectations created by the European and American traditions. Or, as Andrew F. Jones puts it, extending Owen's argument a bit further: "world literature, more often than not, has served as a site for the (almost invariably unequal) exchange, appropriation, and accumulation of (financial *and* cultural) capital between the West and its others" (173).

Underlying Owen's critique of the hegemonic force of Western cultural and economic power is a particular concern with the deadening effects it has on the literary output of poets in the People's Republic of China, who, in the 1980s, came heavily under the influence of the Anglo-European modernists of the first half of the twentieth century. "Chinese poetry of this century has committed to grow by means of the engagement with modernist Western poetry," he writes, but "in any cross-cultural exchange that goes in only one direction, the culture that receives influence will always find itself in the secondary position" (30).[18] Though Owen recognizes that such modernism is new "in the context of the intense conservatism of Chinese literature," he nonetheless finds only occasional things to admire in Bei Dao's poetry, writing that though it "achieves moments of beauty," it "does not have a history, nor is it capable of leaving a trace that might constitute a history," largely because it has come unmoored from the tradition that is proper to it—the *Chinese* tradition (and its classicism and history)—in order to become translatable and familiar to a Western audience long accustomed to modernism (32). Chinese modernism, or pseudo-modernism, is thus not "alive" in a real sense; it offers, rather, the dead or deadening spirit of imitation, disconnected from its native soil, in which the mimetic desire of the Chinese poet mirrors back to the imaginary Anglo-European audience a kind of poetry that will allow that audience to register the fact of ethnic or cultural difference within a familiar form. For this reason, such poetry will—at least from a formal perspective—"always appear slightly 'behind the times'" (30).[19]

The phrase "behind the times" indicates how closely a sense of literary development can align with the history of economic or technological development that dominates the contemporary world picture. This makes visible the temporal burden of mimetic desire: the desire to speak in the other's language in order to be recognized by the other imposes a historical lag between the other's behavior and one's own. To be caught up in mimetic desire requires one invariably to be "behind the times," since the person or culture one imitates defines "the times" and thus establishes a stranglehold on the idea of the historical present itself (or, slightly differently, the status of the present *as* the present is determined more or less by the person who others imitate). Given that she can never precede Anglo-European authors inside the history of global modernisms, the Chinese poet who writes a "version" of modernism can never catch up to Baudelaire, Virginia Woolf, or William Carlos Williams; she can only work toward a poetic form that might allow her one day to be the one imitated.

The problem of "the times" is especially intense when it comes to modernism, whose Poundian rallying cry, "Make It New," seemed—especially when read out of context—to demand a level of innovation that required thinking of art as a perpetual revolution. The rapid-fire sequence of modernist movements (Symbolism, imagism, Fauvism, Futurism, Vorticism, cubism, surrealism, dada), its declarations and manifestoes, its love-hate relationship with technology and mass culture, its emphasis on estrangement and defamiliarization, the value it placed on experimentation, its hostility to the familiar or the commonsensical: all these speak to the high value the modernists placed, quite self-consciously, on the idea of the innovation, and the degree to which their programs tended to stand in for "liberation from the burdens of the past," as Peter Gay writes (46). In this respect, modernism as a general cultural phenomenon borrowed its logics from both the political demands for revolutionary culture borne of the inequities of capitalist industrialization, as well as from the capitalist logics of change and accumulation, which effected the massive cultural shift from sumptuary laws to the fashion system.[20]

To think of contemporary Chinese poets as "behind the times," then, is at least partially to think of them in modern(ist) terms, to imagine literary development as the history of innovators rather than of imitators, even as we see how closely the prestige of certain forms of innovation cleaves to sites of economic and/or technological power. Thus, the mimetic desire "oriented toward the West's imposition of itself on the Rest," as Chow defines it, has to do as much with the problem of historical progress, the relation between national and universal culture (or culture perceived as national as opposed to culture perceived as universal), as it does with the desire for recognition. When Owen wants the Chinese poets to write poetry that is truly "Chinese" (as opposed to "literature that began in the Chinese language" [31]), he wants them to remain true to what was originally or truly Chinese in their culture, namely the classical tradition as it appears prior to large-scale contact with the West. And when he argues that their poetry is merely a "version" of Anglo-American or French modernism, he follows a logic of innovation in which the "version" of something cannot take precedence over its original—which, though we occasionally refer to an "original version," is not a "version" of anything at all, but the *sui generis* production of a culture or a mind that *does not imitate but invents*.

"Blind imitation of foreign models is unlikely to bring foreign recognition," W. J. F. Jenner advised Chinese writers in an essay published the same year as Owen's review (Jones 185). "Blind imitation" is, at least within the culture of modernism, a redundancy, since imitation from a certain historical perspective is always a form of blindness, a limitation or handicap whose undervaluation of novelty bespeaks a failure not only of perception but of judgment. The imposition of this framework on the history of Chinese modernisms extends across the literature of the twentieth century. Here is Sung-sheng Yvonne Chang, writing on the use of the device of stream of consciousness in the work of the Taiwanese authors of the 1950s and 1960s: "if one looks at the often-cited works by Taiwan's Modernists that contain stream-of-consciousness passages . . . it is evident that their authors *merely mimicked* the devices that had already been standardized and normalized in Western literature. Although these writers appropriated the techniques with considerable competence, and the outcome usually served the artistic purposes of individual works well, such an appropriation showed no sign of the *essential modernist spirit of experimentation and innovation*" (63–64; my emphases). To imitate a modernist is to fail the test of modernism.[21] What possibilities for "Chinese modernism" in such a framework?

Not many. And whatever small light glimmers from the end of that philosophical tunnel dims further in light of the cultural history of invention: for at least two centuries, one of the key features of Chinese historiography and anthropology (as written both inside and outside China) has been the claim that the Chinese, while excellent mimics, cannot truly innovate. At their most serious such claims belong to the critique of Chinese economic and historical stagnation that dates back to the late eighteenth century (and includes Adam Smith, Hegel, and Marx).[22] We find a slightly more naked version of them in the claim of American missionary Arthur Smith, made in the late nineteenth century, that though the Chinese might successfully adopt Western technology (including military technology), they will not be able to imitate the high qualities of the Western character: "British character and conscience have been more than a thousand years in attaining their present development, and they cannot be suddenly taken up by the Chinese for their own, and set in operation, like a Krupp gun from Essen, mounted and ready to be discharged" (329).[23] And we find them again in a book published in 2003 by the University of

Pennsylvania Press, in which William Hannas asserts that "without the incentive alphabetic writing provides to think analytically and abstractly, users of Chinese-based character scripts [i.e., people in China, Japan, and the Koreas] are at a handicap vis-à-vis the West in their capacity to generate new ideas and create entirely new technologies" (284; the word "entirely" is a very funny hedge). Though capable of imitating the structures of technological modernity (and thus catching up to the West), Asians (at least the ones who do not become bilingual) remain unable to come up with anything genuinely new.[24]

No use of the term "new" in the contemporary global context can escape the geographic shadow cast by the history of modernization and its effects on large-scale perceptions of the temporality of history. What this history shows is that "Chinese" is one of the terms through which the notion of innovation comes to mean what it means. Hence, a third theme: the *intercontamination of terms*. The key terms of this argument—modern, modernity, modernization, imitation, novelty, innovation, history, progress, temporality, the aesthetic, the literary, the national, geography, the Chinese, the European—belong to a single system, and none of them can be thought without the others, or the forms of belonging that relate them. It is not a question of applying one of the terms, taken from outside of the system, to its inside; it is a question of recognizing the ways in which the meaning and value of each of these terms operates in a continuous negotiation with the others in the system. The history of criticism of these subjects has not adequately parsed this structure. It has groped among its pieces and made declarations. To think seriously about Chinese modernism means negotiating the very conceptual framework through which the history of literature emerges, as though from the history of a void, into the possibilities of thought.

AFTER EUROPEAN TIME

Alexandre Kojève, rewriting Hegel, wrote that the desire for recognition by an other was the fundamental feature of a history peopled by properly human beings (1–31, 37–40).[25] There is nothing wrong with that desire, even or especially when it crosses national boundaries. The world might be a better place if more people were willing to acknowledge their desire for the other's recognition, which is the beginning of social life, in a less murderous form. The problem is not that we yearn to think ourselves with reference to the other's recognition, but rather that inequities in the relative distribution of that recognition, themselves factors of military and economic power, have unbalanced the field of scholarly advance and intellectual play. So you get questions about whether there can be Chinese modernism, or an African "nation," while in the European or U.S. context the internal divergences and difficulties of categories like "modernism" or "nation" fail to raise the possibility of geographic or cultural incompatibility. What about England and Englishness, for instance, made English modernism inadequate to its best dreams of itself? Where is the suggestion that modernism itself (wherever it arises) is the product of a "desire to know what we have supposedly known in our own language," arriving "by way of our desire for the figure of a foreign language"?

These questions open onto a fourth and final theme: the *reversibility of desire*. As many readers will know, one of the signal features of the history of Anglo-European modernism was its unceasing and intense relation to China and Chinese literature, which was in turn but a subset of modernism's more general interest in East Asia, Africa, and the Orient, all of which provided modernist artists and writers with formal innovations in literature and art, powerful rhetorical figures, new geographic imaginaries, grounds for revolutionary changes in theories of translation, and fresh models of language and reference. The scholarship on these changes, much of it done under the influence of postcolonial theory (especially when directed toward Europe) and critical race studies (for the Americanists), has been part of the far larger project to revise the entire conceptual framework that has governed commonsense notions of European historical originality.[26] (In recent years, that work has extended to culture, history, and political economy, as crucial new work on world-systems has forced major reevaluations of the stories told about the "rise of Europe" and the concepts of modernity. A review of that literature would take us far afield of the immediate concerns here, though given the relations between modernity, modernization, and modernism, work on the economic and social history of the concept of modernity will have important ramifications for something like modernism as well.[27])

Chief among the figures whose work has been completely reevaluated as at least a partial effect of the history of China—in a move that reversed decades of criticism that simply dismissed his work's Chinese content (even in the translations!) as decoration, chaff, or disguise—is the American poet Ezra Pound, whose 1914 book of translations from the Chinese, *Cathay*, prompted T. S. Eliot to claim that Pound was the "inventor of Chinese poetry for our time." (I note in passing the word "inventor" and remark the interesting relationship it develops between origin and originality.) Over the course of a lifetime's continuous engagement with China, Pound learned the language, translated Confucian texts and poems, included cribs on Chinese characters in his Cantos, and maintained an active correspondence with a number of Chinese friends, all of which have been extensively documented and theorized in the past ten years or so in such works as Robert Kern's *Orientalism, Modernism, and the American Poem*, Steven G. Yao's *Translation and the Languages of Modernism*, Mary Patterson Cheadle's *Ezra Pound's Confucian Translations*, Josephine Park's *Apparitions of Asia*, and four different books by Zhaoming Qian: *Orientalism and Modernism* (1995), *The Modernist Response to Chinese Art* (2003), *Ezra Pound and China* (2003; a collection of essays), and *Ezra Pound's Chinese Friends* (2008).[28]

But Pound is only the most obvious example of the powerful influence of China on the history of Anglo-European modernism; Qian has documented the interest shared by William Carlos Williams and Marianne Moore in Chinese visual art, and Patricia Laurence has explored the extensive intellectual and interpersonal contacts that Virginia Woolf had with Chinese writers in *Lily Briscoe's Chinese Eyes*. In German studies, the relation between Bertolt Brecht and East Asia has been the subject of a number of books and essays dating already from the late 1970s, while Franz Kafka's relation to China has been written about by Rolf Goebel (*Constructing China: Kafka's Orientalist Discourse*); and Walter Benjamin's frequent but frequently unnoticed references to China get some much-needed attention in Christopher Bush's *Ideographic Modernism*.[29] On the French side, the anarchist Octave Mirbeau's *Le Jardin des supplices*, which is entirely set in China, takes its place alongside the fan poems of Paul Claudel, the work of Paul Valéry, and the novels and poetry of Victor Segalen, in an archive of the European experience of Chineseness whose recent uncovering may contribute "to the current qualitative shift in our understanding of modernism as the culture of *transnational* modernity," as Timothy Billings and Christopher Bush wrote in the introduction to their new translation of Segalen's *Stèles* (27; my emphasis).[30]

Anyone who reads over these scholarly works, which outline the deep debt owed by the Anglo-European modernists to the languages, histories, cultures, and literatures of East Asia, will be tempted to turn the tables of innovation-critique. Among other things, it is worth remembering that even Pound's mantra, "Make It New," which has become a fixture of barefoot doctor definitions of modernism, was taken from an entry he found in Morrison's multivolume dictionary of Chinese. The entry describes an inscription on a basin believed to have belonged to Tang, the founder of the Shang dynasty (c. 1500–1045 BCE), and led Pound to produce, in Canto 53, the following:

> Tching prayed on the mountain and
>   wrote MAKE IT NEW   新
> on his bath tub   日
>   Day by day make it new
> cut underbrush,   日
> pile the logs   新
> keep it growing. (264–65)

As Louis Menand has noted, "the 'It' in 'Make It New' is the Old—what is valuable in the culture of the past," meaning that Pound's own revision of 新日日新 is also an example of the process he describes, a making new of a bathtub inscription which later scholarship suggests had nothing to do with making things new at all.[31] Whatever "innovation" emerges from the statement might best be true to the spirit and historical origins of the phrase in thinking of innovation not as novelty but as *renewal*, the development of a relation to the past that brings it back to life in the present, that activates the history and tradition of thought within the contemporary, and opens up space for a transformation that is also a *return*.

These reminders of Anglo-European modernism's profound debt to the history and thought of China, and the degree to which that debt has historically been ignored, dismissed, or conceived as a veneer over the driving force of genuine originality has prompted Gregory B. Lee to remark, with no small spirit of irony, that the East's imitations of the West are "taken as an indication of a lack of originality and authenticity," while the notion that "the West should recuperate the East is glossed as the inventive creativity of high modernist genius" (79). In the face of recent scholarship, the continued holding of such a position can no longer subtend the mask of intellectual seriousness (though it may well remain a symptom of ignorance).

If we can say, then, that Europeans too are subject to forms of mimetic desire, and recognize that the "normal" procedure whereby the imitated establishes the presentness of the present is itself merely an effect of the distribution of cultural capital and power—if we can recognize, that is, that what is wrong with the contemporary discourse on modernism is not its recourse to analyses focused on mimetic desire, but rather its under-recognition of mimetic desire (national or otherwise) as the "global" condition of *all* modernism, which has tended to enforce a developmental consensus borrowed from histories of political economy across the entire human experience, including the experience of the aesthetic—then it may be possible to begin to theorize global modernism, following Gregory Lee, as a set of "historically specific cultural responses" that have foregrounded with a particular intensity the desire that Sakai identifies "to know what we have supposedly known in our language . . . by way of our desire for the figure of a foreign language."[32] Under such a condition, it would not be simply a matter of extending the "boon" of modernism to the planet's belated others, or a question of cultural sensitivity that would declare all modernisms equal in value, but rather of rethinking the concept of modernism *from the ground up*. Such a rethinking, which would allow us truly to recognize modernism as a "central phenomenon in cultural history" (Lewis xxvi)—*global* cultural history—would require seriously reevaluating the temporal and geographic assumptions that undergird the term "modernism" as we use it today, and which make any consideration of global modernism, not to mention global modernisms, such a fraught and tautological activity. The crucial turn in such a process would be the abandonment, in *the study* of modernism and of the highly charged modernist notions of originality, innovation, and historical time, which form the core of its philosophical presumptions and which are as much an effect of modernism as a literary movement as they are of the history of the theorization of modernity in the West. (This is why it is not only modernist scholarship, but all literary scholarship, that tends to think in terms of founders of movements, of origins and followers, in ways that make negative mimetic desire—a desire doomed to "blind" or "mere" mimicry—an inevitable feature of histories of the aesthetic.) What would it mean for us to imagine the "origin" of modernism otherwise? How might we think of the "founders" of the field in terms that do not privilege being temporally "first"? What would modernist studies look like, if it could imagine the formative importance to the very concept of modernism of work being produced today, tomorrow, or a hundred years from now?

To include China among the global modernisms, to discover a global modernism at all, requires abandoning the temporal logic that has until now structured the field (and which has served as a screen for its geographic centrisms).

Whether modernism as a concept can survive such a breach, or rather, what kind of modernism will emerge from that breaching, is one of the questions that remains before us.

NOTES

1. Lee, *Troubadours, Trumpeters, and Troubled Makers*, 127.

2. It may well be, in fact, that the local and the global do not have a polar relation, as we often assume they do. We do not have good language to describe the ways in which two terms related to one another in a system might escape the pressure of the geometric line, whether that line produces a binary, a continuum, or a dialectic. What would it be like to imagine two terms as though they were on the same "side," without being balanced by a third term that would restore to such an imaginary system the forceful logic of the double? Here we might—if we wish to insist on the systemic metaphor, and thus retain spatiality as a metric—posit the idea of a system organized as a multidimensional hypercloud, with the word "cloud" allowing us to imagine a system ungoverned by stable boundaries (and indeed in which the ideas of boundaries would or could be considered elements of the system), and the prefix "hyper-" estranging us from the too-familiar three-dimensionality of clouds as we know them. In such a system, the relation between two points would not necessarily divide a field of play or meaning into two parts; nor would it necessarily force a consideration of those points as the *endpoints* of a system.

3. On high modernism, see Lewis, *The Cambridge Companion to Modernism*, 120–25, and Nicholls, *Modernisms*, 251–78; on late modernism, see Miller, *Late Modernism*.

4. But consider: in the first major book of criticism on modernist poetry in English, *A Survey of Modernist Poetry* (1927), Laura Riding Jackson and Robert Graves remark that Gerard Manley Hopkins' editor, Dr. Robert Bridges, "postponed publication of [Hopkins's] poems for thirty years, *thus making Hopkins even more of a modernist poet*" (44; my emphasis). Here, Riding and Graves imagine that a delay in distribution rather than production produces a substantive effect on the modernism of the work; thus we get a sense that part of what creates "modernism" is the literary and cultural context in which the work of art appears.

5. The term "modernism" was also widely used in early twentieth-century debates over trends in the Catholic Church. Of the earliest twenty or thirty books owned by the Penn State libraries whose titles include the word "modernism," only one—Laura Riding Jackson and Robert Graves's 1927 survey of modernist poetry—has to do with the authors and period we now think of when we say "modernism"; the rest are on the Spanish-language *modernistas* and the Catholic debates.

6. The difference between modernism and *modernismo* has been the subject of some debate. Stavans writes in his introduction to Darío's selected writings in English that "the term Modernism—in spite of the way Paz, or better, his translators, and others use it—should not be confused with its Spanish version, *Modernismo* . . . the meaning of the words in the two languages is diametrically different, identifying trends that belong to radically divergent cultural landscapes" (xxxi). Despite this clear insistence on the difference between the terms, the fact that Stavans refers to *modernismo* as a "Spanish version" of modernism suggests that the difference he asserts is not the one he believes in. Stavans goes on to say that modernism refers only to English-language work written largely

between 1914 and the 1950s; this relatively conservative position, which dominated the critical consensus from the 1960s through the 1990s, is part of what sustains the difference between *modernismo* and modernism, since the temporal break it establishes allows one to justify the asserted difference in attitude between the terms. For more on *modernismo,* see Aching's contribution to this volume.

7. See Casanova, *The World Republic of Letters,* and Ram's chapter in this volume, which rather neatly sums up the situation: "Casanova's premise ignores the vast, centuries-old and still vibrant cosmopolitan literacies of South and East Asia or the Islamic world, as well as the more recent socialist internationalism of the Second world, whose interconnections point to alternative cultural trajectories that have frequently bypassed the West."

8. I owe my thoughts on the relation between transcription and translation to Haun Saussy's "Translation and Transcription: Media Creoles and the Invention of the *Delufeng*."

9. In Japanese, my colleague Jon Abel tells me, the katakana モダニズム (*modani-zumu*) remains widely in use, though the kanji formulation 現代主义 (*gendaishugi*, the same characters as the Chinese *xiandaizhuyi*) has also been used to refer to modernism, especially to movements of the late nineteenth and early twentieth centuries.

10. In many ways, these attempts are modeled on the history of the feminist criticism's attempt to expand the house of modernism to include female authors, who preceded them by a half decade or so. Three landmarks are Scott, *The Gender of Modernism* (1990); Clark, *Sentimental Modernism* (1991); and Felski, *The Gender of Modernity* (1995). These books offered large-scale frameworks for thinking through the troubled relation between women and modernism (or, in Felski, modernism's historical frame, modernity), responded to a much wider variety of critical work on partially canonical female modernists, such as H. D. and Virginia Woolf, and attempted to bring other, more marginalized female writers (Cather, Mansfield, and even Stein) into the modernist fold.

11. The impetus for thinking about global modernisms derives from the general movement across the humanities and social sciences known as the "transnational turn," which in the United States academy has taken up much of the energy formerly organized around the word "multiculturalism." The movement between 1994's *Comparative Literature in the Age of Multiculturalism,* edited by Charles Bernheimer, and 2004's *Comparative Literature in the Age of Globalization,* edited by Haun Saussy, emblematizes this trend. On the relation between the Bernheimer report and the use of "multiculturalism" in an international frame—in an essay that anticipates, accordingly, some of the differences between the two reports—see Michelle Yeh's "International Theory and the Transnational Critic: China in the Age of Multiculturalism."

12. For a recent discussion of the history of debates over whether China "has" allegory, see Zhang Longxi's *Allegoresis.*

13. These sites of potential national pride have long been topics of discussion in the work of Chinese intellectuals, a problem C. T. Hsia famously diagnosed as an "obsession with China" and which remains, as Louise Edwards has remarked, part of Chinese intellectual history and scholarship into the present. Perry Link's introduction to a special issue of *Modern China* on Hsia's influential take offers up a useful summary of the positions available in 1993 to Chinese intellectuals dealing with Hsia's legacy.

14. As Lovell notes, China is not alone in having this anxious relation to modernity; citing Gregory Jusdanis, she notes a similar structure in Greece (16).

15. The model of international recognition here—which China is by no means the first or the only nation to adopt—thus reinforces the system of nation-states, both as a *system* (which arranges its members in a hierarchy), and as a system of *nation-states* (which become the epistemological and historical fields through which cultural change is

addressed and measured). An attempt to be inclusive from the outside, to recognize in China the prestigious literariness that goes by the name "modernism," plays into this network of associations and reinforces the structure whereby recognition from the cultural center validates the accomplishments of the periphery. Resistance to that form of recognition (e.g., "China should have its own Chinese-style literature") will tend to take the form of an unpalatable nationalism whose values are no less driven by a relation to the core, since they have simply taken the structure of mimetic desire, and reversed it. All of this became more complicated when the 2000 Nobel Prize in literature was awarded to the expatriate writer Gao Xingjian; see Lovell's fifth chapter.

16. My objections here are not to the politics of a nationalist, post-Westphalian world system, but rather to the unconscious adoption of the basic structure of that system as an organizing metric for literary study. Though of course the nation-state system will have effects on cultural fields—the entire discipline of comparative literature, never mind fiction or poetry, can be seen to grow out of the forms of apprehension of national culture driven by the rise of the modern nation-state (see Saussy, "Exquisite Cadavers")—that does not mean that the history of literature is identical with the history of national literatures (whether or not these are conceived as competing, on the model of nation-states, for territory and prestige).

17. As Andrew F. Jones has noted, Owen's essay has largely been read in the context of the Orientalism of East Asian Studies, mainly because those were the terms foregrounded by the responses to him of Michelle Yeh ("The Anxiety of Difference") and Rey Chow (*Writing Diaspora*) in the years immediately after the review's publication. On Owen, see chapter 4 of Gregory Lee's *Troubadours, Trumpeters, Troubled Makers*; Yunte Huang's *Transpacific Displacement*, 165–68; and David Damrosch, *What Is World Literature?*, 19–24.

18. Of the several critics who have discussed this review, David Damrosch alone focuses on the word "modernism" in it. Damrosch goes on to discover a number of explicitly modernist echoes in Bei Dao's translated work, including a line rendered by Donald Finkel as "I don't believe what the thunder says," a clear nod to Eliot's "Waste Land" (Damrosch 23).

19. That there might be something wrong with such a perspective—that it is odd for the Western sinologist to encourage the Chinese to go back to their tradition and not be tempted to copy the West—is the subject of Rey Chow's critique. Chow's argument that this "melancholic" position belongs to a more general strain of thought in American Sinology can be supported by this example, from an essay by W. J. F. Jenner, written in the form of advice to Chinese authors: "please don't write for us, but write for your primary readers, leaving us to choose . . . what may be accessible to us ignorant Anglophones. And don't worry in the least about what we think. . . . Take whatever you like from abroad, but only what you need for your own purposes. Blind imitation of foreign models is unlikely to bring foreign recognition" (cited in Jones, 185). Since not paying attention to what Anglophones think would, following a reading of this chapter, require paying attention to what the Anglophones think (given Jenner's liberal use of the second-person plural), the project seems likely to have a hard time getting off the ground.

20. In fact, the fashion system provides us with the cultural ground that allows us to understand what a phrase like "behind the times" means. On the historical and temporal conditions of that shift, see Appadurai, chapter 4.

21. The problem here revolves around the role of the Anglo-European standard as a legitimating force. Consider Leo Ou-fan Lee on Dai Houying's novel, *Ren, a ren!*: "What Dai claims to be experiments in 'stream-of-consciousness' are nothing but straightforward interior monologues or emphatic descriptions of the character's thinking. . . . *Against any*

Western standard, this novel can hardly be called modernist" (66). As Lee goes on to note, Dai's novel is nonetheless highly innovative in the context of PRC literature of its time. As for other PRC writers, Lee writes: "If one uses a high standard (that of 'high modernism'), it becomes immediately clear that the young Chinese pioneers are all beginners . . . ": but why, despite the pleasures of the pun on "high," should high modernism itself be the high standard, unless Anglo-European modernism has become the universal measure of literary quality? One sees here again the *force* of a *particular* modernism as a measure of literary development, and more generally the ways in which a theory of *global* literary development will disadvantage local literary production, even, or perhaps especially, when the local work addresses itself to a local context that is already "behind the times."

22. On Hegel, see Saussy, *The Problem of a Chinese Aesthetic*; on Marx, see the first appendix to Perry Anderson, *Lineages of the Absolutist State*; on Smith, see Frank, *ReOrient*, Arrighi, *Adam Smith in Beijing*, and the introduction to Hayot, *The Hypothetical Mandarin*.

23. The contrast Smith draws between military might and character replicates, with a slight twist, the relation Lovell describes between modernization and the autonomy of the aesthetic; in both cases the form of culture is held in reserve against the possibility of too-successful imitation in other fields, and the bar of equality thereby held just that much further out of reach of the developing nation.

24. Also: "authoritarianism, concrete thinking, borrowing, and excessive attachment to the past . . . are abetted by the use of character-based writing" (287). This is not the place to address Hannas at length, but his claims are at their weakest when they fail to recognize that his argument depends on evidence of the economic situation of the past two centuries, and that for most of the period in which humans have written Chinese civilization was well ahead of the alphabetic world by most technological and scientific measures.

25. On Kojève, see Pirotte, who writes that for Kojève, "Desire for desire, in its very structure, expresses itself only as *desire for the desire of an Other* who one seeks to recognize, and whose recognition one seeks" (84).

26. Modernism was, it is fair to say, a little late to this field. Gayatri Spivak's influential rereading of Jane Austen, "Three Women's Texts and a Critique of Imperialism," was controversial when it appeared in 1985, but the intersection between postcolonial theory and nineteenth-century Britain had become a crucial part of nineteenth-century studies in English by the beginning of the next decade; modernism's relation to postcolonial theory took longer to develop.

27. The most important of these new world histories of modernity and the so-called rise of Europe are those by R. Bin Wong, *China Transformed*, Andre Gunder Frank and Kenneth Pomeranz, *The Great Divergence*, and Arrighi, *Adam Smith in Beijing*.

28. Just as importantly, a new critical edition of Ernest Fenollosa's essay on the Chinese written character, which under Pound's hand became one of the signal manifestos of modernist poetry, has just been reissued under the editorial guidance of Haun Saussy, Jonathan Stalling, and Lucas Klein. On Pound and China, see also Yunte Huang's *Transpacific Displacement*, which covers Amy Lowell's Chinese translations in more depth and with more generosity than most; Ming Xie's *Ezra Pound and the Appropriation of Chinese Poetry*; Daniel Katz, *American Modernism's Expatriate Scene*; and Guiyou Huang's *Whitmanism, Imagism, and Modernism in China and America*. For a critical overview of the history of scholarship on Pound and China, see the first chapter of Hayot, *Chinese Dreams*. On Pound's influence on the Chinese Misty Poets, see Chen, *Occidentalism*.

29. For a review of Laurence, see Lin. On Brecht, see Tatlow, *The Mask of Evil*.

30. On Mirbeau, see Apter; on Claudel, see Bush, "Reading and Difference"; on Segalen, see Billings' and Bush's introduction to *Stèles*; on prewar France and China, see

Hsieh. On postwar French interest in China, see Hughes, Ha, and for discussions of Georges Bataille, see Brook, Bourgon, and Blue, *Death by a Thousand Cuts*, and Hayot, *The Hypothetical Mandarin*.

31. Saussy cites Edward L. Shaughnessy's *Sources of Western Zhou History*, which notes that Guo Muoro "has shown that the text [that includes the phrase 新日日新] is probably nothing more than a composite of ancestor dedications on Shang dynasty bronze vessels," and "suggests that the words transcribed as *ri xin* 日新 (daily renew) must originally have read *ri xin* 日辛, in which *xin* is one of the ten 'heavenly stems' (*tiangan* 天干) routinely used in the temple names of Shang ancestors" (Saussy, *Great Walls* 183).

32. On this subject Rubén Darío, writing to Miguel de Unamuno in 1899, explains why his work is not exactly written in Spanish: "I think ideographically, which is why work is not 'pure,'" a sentence whose use of the word "ideographically" points us, once again, to modernism's Orient (Stavans xxv).

WORKS CITED

Anderson, Benedict. *Imagined Communities: Reflections on the Origin and Spread of Nationalism*. London: Verso, 2003.

Anderson, Perry. *Lineages of the Absolutist State*. New York: Verso, 1974.

Appadurai, Arjun. *Modernity at Large: Cultural Dimensions of Globalization*. Minneapolis: University of Minnesota Press, 1996.

Apter, Emily. "The Garden of Scopic Perversion from Monet to Mirbeau." *October* 47 (Winter 1988): 91–115.

Arrighi, Giovanni. *Adam Smith in Beijing: Lineages of the Twenty-first Century*. New York: Verso, 2007.

Bernheimer, Charles, ed. *Comparative Literature in the Age of Multiculturalism*. Baltimore: Johns Hopkins University Press, 1994.

Billings, Timothy, and Christopher Bush. Introduction. *Stèles*. By Victor Segalen. Middletown: Wesleyan University Press, 2007. 1–45.

Brook, Timothy, Jérôme Bourgon, and Gregory Blue. *Death by a Thousand Cuts*. Cambridge: Harvard University Press, 2008.

Bush, Christopher. *Ideographic Modernism: China, Writing, Media*. New York: Oxford University Press, 2010.

———."Reading and Difference: Image, Allegory, and the Invention of Chinese." *Sinographies: Writing China*. Ed. Eric Hayot, Haun Saussy, and Steven G. Yao. Minneapolis: University of Minnesota Press, 2007. 34–63.

Chakrabarty, Dipesh. *Provincializing Europe: Postcolonial Thought and Historical Difference*. Princeton: Princeton University Press, 2000.

Chang, Sung-sheng Yvonne. *Modernism and the Nativist Resistance: Contemporary Chinese Fiction from Taiwan*. Durham: Duke University Press, 1993.

Cheadle, Mary Patterson. *Ezra Pound's Confucian Translations*. Ann Arbor: University of Michigan Press, 1997.

Chen, Xiaomei. *Occidentalism: A Theory of Counter-discourse in Post-Mao China*. New York: Oxford University Press, 1995.

Chow, Rey. *The Protestant Ethnic and the Spirit of Capitalism*. New York: Columbia University Press, 2002.

———. *Writing Diaspora: Tactics of Intervention in Contemporary Cultural Studies.* Bloomington: Indiana University Press, 1993.

Clark, Suzanne. *Sentimental Modernism: Women Writers and the Revolution of the Word.* Bloomington: Indiana University Press, 1991.

Damrosch, David. *What Is World Literature?* Princeton: Princeton University Press, 2003.

Edwards, Louise. "The 'Problem of China' and Chinese Exceptionalism." *Journal of Contemporary History* 43.1 (2008): 155–64.

Felski, Rita. *The Gender of Modernity.* Cambridge: Harvard University Press, 1995.

Fenollosa, Ernest, and Ezra Pound. *The Chinese Written Character as a Medium for Poetry.* Ed. Haun Saussy, Jonathan Stalling, and Lucas Klein. New York: Fordham University Press, 2008.

Frank, Andre Gunder. *ReOrient: Global Economy in the Asian Age.* Berkeley: University of California Press, 1998.

Gay, Peter. *Modernism, the Lure of Heresy: From Baudelaire to Beckett and Beyond.* New York: W.W. Norton, 2008.

Goebel, Rolf. *Constructing China: Kafka's Orientalist Discourse.* Rochester: Camden House Press, 1997.

Ha, Marie-Paule. *Figuring the East: Segalen, Malraux, Duras, and Barthes.* Albany: State University of New York Press, 2000.

Hayot, Eric. *Chinese Dreams: Pound, Brecht, Tel quel.* Ann Arbor: University of Michigan Press, 2004.

———. *The Hypothetical Mandarin: Sympathy, Modernity, and Chinese Pain.* New York: Oxford University Press, 2009.

Hsieh, Yvonne. *From Occupation to Revolution: China through the Eyes of Loti, Claudel, Segalen, and Malraux (1895–1933).* Birmingham: Summa Publications, 1996.

Huang, Guiyou. *Whitmanism, Imagism, and Modernism in China and America.* Selingsgrove: Susquehanna University Press, 1997.

Hughes, Alex. *France/China: Intercultural Imaginings.* London: Legenda Research Monographs, 2007.

Jackson, Laura Riding, and Robert Graves. *A Survey of Modernist Poetry and a Pamphlet against Anthologies.* Ed. Charles Mundye and Patrick McGuiness. Manchester: Carcanet, 2002.

Jones, Andrew F. "Chinese Literature in the 'World' Literary Economy." *Modern Chinese Literature* 8.1–2 (1994): 171–90.

Katz, Daniel. *American Modernism's Expatriate Scene: The Labour of Translation.* Edinburgh: Edinburgh University Press, 2007.

Kern, Robert. *Orientalism, Modernism, and the American Poem.* Cambridge: Cambridge University Press, 1996.

Kojève, Alexandre. *Introduction to the Reading of Hegel: Lectures on the Phenomenology of Spirit Assembled by Raymond Queneau.* Ed. Allan Bloom. Trans. James H. Nichols Jr. New York: Basic Books, 1969.

Laurence, Patricia. *Lily Briscoe's Chinese Eyes: Bloomsbury, Modernism, and China.* Columbia: Univeristy of South Carolina Press, 2003.

Lee, Gregory. *Troubadours, Trumpeters, and Troubled Makers.* London: Hurst and Co., 1996.

Lee, Leo Ou-fan. "Beyond Realism: Thoughts on Modernist Experiments in Contemporary Chinese Writing." *Worlds Apart: Recent Chinese Writing and Its Audiences.* Ed. Howard Goldblatt. London: M. E. Sharpe, 1990.

Lewis, Pericles. *The Cambridge Introduction to Modernism.* Cambridge: Cambridge University Press, 2007.

Lin, Lidan. "The Hybrid Matrix of Modernism: Bloomsbury and the (Chinese) Crescent Moon Group." *Modernism/modernity* 12.4 (2005): 705–11.

Link, Perry. "Ideology and Theory in the Study of Modern Chinese Literature: An Introduction." *Modern China* 19.1 (January 1993): 4–12.

Menand, Louis. "The Pound Error." *The New Yorker.* June 9, 2008: 123–27.

Miller, Tyrus. *Late Modernism: Politics, Fiction, and the Arts between the World Wars.* Berkeley: University of California Press, 1999.

Nicholls, Peter. *Modernisms: A Literary Guide.* Berkeley: University of California Press, 1995.

Owen, Stephen. "What Is World Poetry?" *The New Republic.* 19 Nov.1990: 28–32.

Park, Josephine. *Apparitions of Asia: Modernist Form and Asian American Poetics.* New York: Oxford University Press, 2008.

Pirotte, Dominique. *Alexandre Kojève: Un système anthropologique.* Paris: Presses Universitaires de France, 2005.

Pomeranz, Kenneth. *The Great Divergence: China, Europe, and the Making of the Modern World Economy.* Princeton: Princeton University Press, 2000.

Pound, Ezra. *The Cantos of Ezra Pound.* New York: New Directions, 1993.

Qian, Zhaoming, ed. *Ezra Pound and China.* Ann Arbor: University of Michigan Press, 2003.

———, ed. *Ezra Pound's Chinese Friends: Stories in Letters.* New York: Oxford University Press, 2008.

———. *The Modernist Response to Chinese Art: Pound, Moore, Stevens.* Charlottesville: University of Virginia Press, 2003.

———. *Orientalism and Modernism: The Legacy of China in Pound and Williams.* Durham: Duke University Press, 1995.

Sakai, Naoki. *Translation and Subjectivity: On "Japan" and Cultural Nationalism.* Minneapolis: University of Minnesota Press, 1997.

Saussy, Haun, ed. *Comparative Literature in the Age of Globalization.* Baltimore: Johns Hopkins University Press, 2006.

———. "Exquisite Cadavers Stitched from Fresh Nightmares: Of Memes, Hives, and Selfish Genes." Ed. Saussy 3–42.

———. *Great Walls of Discourse, and Other Adventures in Cultural China.* Cambridge: Harvard East Asia Press, 2001.

———. *The Problem of a Chinese Aesthetic.* Stanford: Stanford University Press, 1995.

———. "Translation and Transcription: Media Creoles and the Invention of the Delufeng." Cambridge University, Cambridge. 3 May 2008. Address.

Scott, Bonnie Kime. *The Gender of Modernism: A Critical Anthology.* Bloomington: Indiana University Press, 1990.

Spivak, Gayatri Chakravorty. "Three Women's Texts and a Critique of Imperialism." *Critical Inquiry* 12.1 (1985): 243–61.

Stavans, Ilan. Introduction. *Rubén Darío: Selected Writings.* New York: Penguin, 2005.

Tatlow, Anthony. *Brechts chinesische Gedichte.* Frankfurt am Main: Suhrkamp, 1973.

———. *Brechts Ost Asien.* Berlin: Pathas, 1998.

———. *The Mask of Evil: Brecht's Response to the Poetry, Theatre and Thought of China and Japan.* Bern: Peter Lang, 1977.

Wong, R. Bin. *China Transformed: Historical Change and the Limits of European Experience.* Ithaca: Cornell University Press, 1997.

Xie, Ming. *Ezra Pound and the Appropriation of Chinese Poetry: Cathay, Translation, and Imagism.* New York: Garland, 1999.

Yao, Steven G. *Translation and the Languages of Modernism: Gender, Politics, Language.*
      London: Palgrave, 2002.

Yeh, Michelle. "International Theory and the Transnational Critic: China in the Age of
      Multiculturalism." *Modern Chinese Literary and Cultural Studies in the Age of Theory:
      Reimagining a Field.* Ed. Rey Chow. Durham: Duke University Press, 2000. 251–80.

Zhang Longxi. *Allegoresis: Reading Canonical Literature East and West.* Ithaca: Cornell
      University Press, 2005.

PART III

WHOSE
MODERNISM?

THE WILL TO ALLEGORY AND THE ORIGIN OF CHINESE MODERNISM: REREADING LU XUN'S *AH Q—THE REAL STORY*

XUDONG ZHANG

To read *Ah Q—The Real Story* (1921–1922)—the most elaborate fictional work by the foremost modern Chinese writer, published in the heyday of the Chinese Vernacular Revolution—in modernist terms challenges both the mainstream reading of this text and the conventional assumptions of modernism as an aesthetic and theoretical framework. Within Lu Xun studies, one might meet with only mild resistance to the claim that *Diary of a Madman* (1918) or the prose poetry collected in *Wild Grass* (1925) are modernist works of art. It would be an entirely different—and far more contested—matter if one were to rank *Ah Q* among high modernist monuments such as *The Waste Land* (1922), *The Castle* (1926), or *The Sound and the Fury* (1929).

Serialized in nine installments in *Chenbao fukan* (The Literary Supplement of the *Morning Post*) in Beijing (then Beiping) between December 1921 and February 1922, *Ah Q* first appeared under Lu Xun's pseudonym Ba Ren, derived from the proverbial phrase "xiali baren," or "something catering to the unrefined taste of the commoners." A superficial glance at the work, about the length of a novella, may lead one to believe that it is a lighthearted, generic collage of social satire, a parody of the traditional "chapter-novel" (*zhanghui ti xiaoshuo*), and the literary feuilleton of the new mass media. It would be taxing, indeed, to try to compile evidence of textbook features of modernism, including the usual suspects of metaphoric depth, formal disruption and distortion, and aesthetic intensity or, for that matter, to see it in the light of the modern European novel, with its familiar narrative deliberativeness, character development, social-moral analysis, and psychological drama. Compared to some of Lu Xun's own stories, *Ah Q* does not stand out for its technical innovation, for which Lu Xun is praised by fellow modern Chinese writers and critics of his generation.[1]

At the same time, it is nevertheless unthinkable for anyone to deny that of all the major works of the New Literature (*xinwenxue*) produced since the May Fourth Movement (also known as the New Culture Movement) (1919), *Ah Q* alone has reached, within the Chinese context, the height of monumentality, autonomy, originality, as well as the kind of "all-encompassing, all-explanatory" status pursued and dreamed about by high modernism.[2] No other works in modern Chinese literary history even come close to *Ah Q*'s literary and political intensity and popularity, which seem to have crystallized into a monad, a pure thought-image capable of confronting History—both in the ahistorical sense as tradition, culture, and morality and in the historicist sense as process, scheme, and the new as the next—by means of its allegorical complexity and simplicity in one. In modern China and beyond, *Ah Q*'s reception history has firmly established the novella at the very top of the totem pole of national allegory. No other work is like *Ah Q* in its invention of a name that, like a specter, sticks to, embarrasses, sobers, and haunts a country, a people, and a culture as a whole. To that extent, "Ah Q" is the proper name for the most intense, interior, and even neurotic self-consciousness of modern China.

This preunderstanding, historically important and politically relevant, cannot be allowed to reduce the present rereading of *Ah Q* to mere intellectual-historical material for a critique of "national character," even if such critique was undoubtedly one of the central missions of the New Culture discourse. My interest here is to show that the significance of this work lies not so much in its moral or intellectual exposition or argument, however profound or ambiguous, but rather in the formal and formal-political playfulness, even autonomy, in which the social implications of Chinese modernism reside. Even if one were to continue to use *Ah Q* as a textbook for a critique of national character, its formal-allegorical structure offers more on the enumeration of the "realistic" behavioral traits of Ah Q as a person or a type. If those traits or features can be compared to the individual entries of a dictionary (e.g., of critique of Chinese national character), then our present critical or theoretical challenge is to analyze the invisible ways in which this dictionary is conceived, designed, and structured—as a system of names, naming, and the symbolic capacity or authority to name, to identify, to define—rather than to luxuriate in the figurative and representational vividness or immediate social referents of individual semantic items.

It is important to realize that in *Ah Q*, it is through the will to allegory that the leitmotif of modern China, namely the demise of tradition and the struggle toward modernity, is given shape in a radically modernist formal-aesthetic space, namely language as a socially symbolic system of names, naming, identity, differentiation, and alienation. More specifically, the modernist design of *Ah Q*, in this light, lies in its unique formal and narrative engineering of an allegorical subversion and reconstruction of the basic categories of Confucian cultural-imperial order, such as name (*ming*), words or speech (*yan*), action (*xing*), and biography/history (*zhuan*). This allegorical procedure operates so rigorously and thoroughly that the story ultimately becomes a characterless story of the (im)possibilities and (in)capacities of China as the Name that names and as a desire for self-identity and self-identification; it becomes a plotless narrative that turns a collective crisis of meaning and existence into the truth-content of the New Literature as a modern literature. It is in this strong and literal sense that I seek to define Lu Xun's allegorical mode of writing in general, and *Ah Q* in particular, as the origin of modern Chinese literature.[3]

Ah Q and/as Chinese Modernism

From this perspective, a useful concept of modernism cannot continue to rely on the mainstream and largely unchallenged assumptions of post-Mao Chinese intellectual and critical discourse, which had loosely borrowed or "translated" from an imagined domain of formal autonomy and value-neutrality of "Western Modernism," the basic building blocks if not aesthetic arsenal for a postrevolutionary Chinese modernism: imagism, metaphoric depth, stylistic intensity and formal innovation, suspension and distortion of narration, stream of consciousness, metafiction, and so forth. Nor should modernism as a theoretical and historical notion allow itself to be subsumed into the "Scholarly Turn" in 1990s' China and become a more or less sentimental footnote to disciplinary research in history, economy, society, and political institutions, often as an implicit comparative modernization study.[4] The pitfalls in post-Mao China of fetishizing modernism as a symbolic and aesthetic fast track into the global market—a means of integration—invariably results in an unproductive and uninteresting reading of Chinese modernist movements as either a pale, derivative, and underdeveloped echo of Euro-American high modernism; or, alternately, as a literary-aesthetic valorization of the experiences and impressions of the enclaves of semicolonial modernity exemplified by the so-called everyday sphere of prerevolutionary Shanghai. A more affirmative concept of Chinese modernism must come from recognizing both the aesthetic and the political internalization of the historical situations and conditions of possibility in modern China, which find their allegorical expressions in the coming into being of a moral as well as a cultural subject, that is, the subject constituted by Chinese modernism as a language.

An analytic disposition of such modernist subjectivity will necessarily include the intellectual understanding and moral acceptance of modernity embodied by modern science and technology; the capitalist notion of competition and the "social evolution" implicitly or explicitly based on it; individual freedom; and political democracy. The enumeration of such socioeconomic and politico-institutional necessities can be found in mainstream Chinese Enlightenment discourse since the May Fourth Movement, which to this day still undergirds cultural, political, and aesthetic discourse in modern China. Recognizing this historical understanding, however, does not mean that one should allow it to obscure a countermovement that is more intimately involved in the construction of Chinese modernism: namely, the subjective and passionate attempt to resist and interiorize such external and objective conditions through formal and aesthetic labor in order to turn the decidedly "premodern" into the allegorical raw material for a convincing and privileged form of non-Western modernism.

For this purpose, three synchronic steps can be teased out from within the phenomenological space of such resistance and interiorization. First, there is the intense agony, often at a highly personal or personalized level, over the collective failure—social, political, and cultural—of an ailing imperial China vis-à-vis the modern West, an agony culminating in a rationalized cultural self-critique of China as a civilization. Second comes a modernist-metaphysical suspension of Chinese history as a temporal process of continuum, progression, and destiny. This suspension is carried out by the modernist will to supersede the old with a utopian new, and by an iconoclastic will to launch a wholesale critique of tradition, whose suspension and destruction gives rise to a new historical subject in action. The effect of this dual attack on history resembles that of Nietzsche's "positive forgetting," which, by overcoming the burden and abuse of the past, blasts away the barriers and obstacles to a self-realizing "now." As Nietzsche puts it: "With the term 'ahistorical' I designate the art and power to be able to *forget* and to enclose oneself in a limited *horizon*; I term 'suprahistorical' those powers that divert one's gaze from what is in the process of becoming to what lends existence the character of something eternal and stable in meaning" (163).[5]

The New Culture as a modernist intervention, then, desires to destabilize and supersede a limited horizon, an "eternal and stable" system of meaning that is tradition by an artistic and political power of forgetting and self-enclosure, that is, by inventing a utopian horizon of time as a new culture, new humanity. The metaphysical *Weltanschauung* thus achieved—as implied by Lu Xun's Madman's vision of the two Chinese characters "Eat People" leaping from between the lines of Chinese history books—is not so much a psychological-moral judgment on the past as the projection of the modern Self, its objectification into the new symbolic order that is the new language as such. Compared to this kind of negative, allegorical modernism (of resistance and subjectification), the positive and positivistic modernism derived from the socioeconomic enclaves of semicolonial metropolises proves to be secondary and feeble. In other words, rather than locating the inherent energy and formal innovativeness of non-Western modernism in the aesthetic-technical gratification of the individual chasing and identifying with the forever new, whose rhythm and pace were set elsewhere, its distinctiveness can more often be derived from the allegorical, phenomenological reconstruction of the collective experience of defeat at home. Thus, the third and last step in the making of the inner space of non-Western modernism is a poetics of cultural-moral breakdown, a poetics that grasps the impossibility of meaning and value creation: in short, a nihilistic aesthetics aiming at the creation of a new humanity out of a ruthless, indeed total revolt against culture as an all-encompassing system of naming and meaning-giving.

As with all works of severe originality, *Ah Q—The Real Story* does not lend itself easily to the scholarly effort to crack its generic code. Loosely speaking, however, it may appear to be a humorous mixture of a miniature chapter-novel from early vernacular Chinese fiction, on the one hand, and the satirical, even the chivalrous, branches of the modern European novel on the other (Ah Q, although a modernist product, may find a kindred spirit in Don Quixote). Considering that the work was first serialized in the newspaper, its formal design is all the more striking: every installment must be independently and immediately effective vis-à-vis its implied reader while being an integral part of the allegorical and cultural-critical whole. If *Ah Q* is a characterless, plotless narrative (as I will argue below), then its effectiveness must go beyond formal arrangement in the technical sense but come from an allegorical appeal supported by a larger if implicit framework of interpretation, an appeal in sync with a deeper moral and historical milieu.

The newspaper serialization of *Ah Q* not only points to its explicit correspondence with "public opinion," and thus to a kind of built-in performativity of its literary articulation; it also reveals a national-theatrical space in which the "story" unfolds. This theatrical space explains the spatial-temporal identity of the staging of the allegorical figure, which is in every sense "called forth" by the anticipation of the audience. Rather than a player on the stage of village opera in southern China (a character vividly and nostalgically depicted by Lu Xun in his other works), Ah Q is here a tragic hero placed at the center of a natural-historical amphitheater, with the imagined nation—chorus and audience in one—forming the background. And yet Ah Q is not a conventional tragic character, whose destruction by his inner conflict produces fear and sympathy that complete the process of catharsis. Rather, the tragic element of *Ah Q* comes with the novella's comical, satirical, and sometimes utterly farcical portrayal of a character that turns out to be a ghost, a specter, and a malfunctioning sign trapped within a failing system of order, hierarchy, honor, and shame. Such a narrative design is not so much an aesthetic counterbalance to tragedy as a moral-political and allegorical reminder that the novella dramatizes a cultural trial whose defendant—that fellow without family, writable name, birthplace, or any action worthy of a realist novel—is China itself (as both history and culture) dying a farcical, that is, at least a self-conscious, death. This staged trial, with the audience as the designated jury, defines the relationship between the reader and the text, a relationship that is at the center of the allegorical enterprise of *Ah Q*.

This explains why *Ah Q*'s formal shapelessness and minimalism (vis-à-vis the formal requirements of the realist novel) actually contribute to not only its transmitability and lucidity, but also its allegorical intensity. The "story" of Ah Q flies out of the natural-historical theater/court as a slew of interconnected or isolated anecdotes, gossips, accusations, records, testimonies, diagnoses, and announcements, all of which circulate in the predetermined socio-allegorical space, and all of which are received, confirmed, and consumed in the same way political jokes and rumors circulate in a police state, thus erecting a distorted, farcical, and yet devastatingly accurate mirror in front of the absence of a "public sphere." Beneath the level of storytelling, language deliberately loses its representational or expressive dramaticality but single-mindedly concentrates on an allegorical mimesis that collects, documents, imitates, and—openly or secretly—enjoys. As a result, there is no narrative or moral surprise in *Ah Q*. Everything that "happens" happens in the fashion of repetition and predetermination, as Ah Q has no memory or capacity to reflect on his behavior, but only fulfills his—or should one say "its"?—structural function as a sign within structure of semiotic differentiation.

Here, one seems to confront a classic example of the so-called hermeneutic circle: one does not understand the whole unless one understands the parts, and vice versa. The transmitability and lucidity of those anecdotes and rumors about Ah Q cannot be comprehended without a preunderstanding of *Ah Q*'s allegorical totality, and vice versa. In the actual history of its reception both inside and outside China, however, the well-known "stories" of Ah Q work and exist as a distraction. Every educated Chinese person, it can be said without exaggeration, knows something about Ah Q: his being banned from adopting or identifying with Master Zhao's family name; his confrontation with the "Fake Foreign Devil" and his exclusion from the "revolution"; his aborted love affair with Amah Wu and his crude fantasies about women, coupled with his moral contempt for women; his repeated physical defeat and public humiliation at the hands of the fellow villagers he regards as his inferiors; his overcoming of trauma by means of "moral victory" or a psychological trick on himself; his daydreams about revolt and redistribution of wealth and power (including his wish to take over the nice Ningbo-style bed owned by the Budding Talent's wife); and, last but not least, his execution as a common thief and his laughable efforts at pleasing the spectators before his death. Owing to their vividness and familiarity, these well-known incidents and characteristics threaten to short-circuit any sustained critical rereading of *Ah Q* and foreclose any attempt at fully grasping its formal intricacies and allegorical poignancy. A critical process of estrangement or defamiliarization is therefore required to read it allegorically, beginning with the insistence that Ah Q is not a person, a character, a figure, or an image. Quite the contrary, Ah Q is a sign and a concept produced by an allegorical understanding of China as a cultural-historical totality. The productive question to be asked is not "Who is Ah Q?" but rather "What is Ah Q?"—or, more precisely, "To what semiotic- and value-system does Ah Q belong? How is Ah Q produced by this system? How does *Ah Q*, while following the directories of the system, reveal its irreversible and systematic paralysis, unraveling, chaos, and collapse?"

To maintain that Ah Q is in this sense a sign is to follow its traces as clues leading to the inner workings of the semiotic system. Ah Q's function as a narratological and epistemological proxy reminds one of the allegorical agents and devices Walter Benjamin examines in Baudelaire's poetry of alienation in the phantasmagoria of the modern city. Instead of locating this allegorical proxy/sensor in figures of capitalist mass production and commodity fetishism such as the flâneur and the prostitute, as in Benjamin's reading of Baudelaire, one can see the same allegorical will at work in Lu Xun but within the decidedly "premodern," indeed, prehistorical, world of language: the symbolic order of the Chinese cultural system of naming, hierarchy, rite, and order, and in particular its moral internalization and individuation as conduct of behavior, self-identity, and, ultimately, the concept of the human. Just as the allegorical figures of capitalist alienation or reification are structurally determined by the system of capitalist production, social division of labor, and abstraction, which find their psychological or aesthetic projections and symptoms in the behavior of the flâneur, the prostitute, the gambler, and the Blanqui-type of bohemian revolutionaries[6]—the allegorical figures of cultural-imperial paralysis and ennui are structurally determined by the system of nominalisms that is every bit as reified and totalizing as its modern capitalist counterpart. Ah Q is the *lumpenproletariat* of this nominalistic system. To regard Ah Q as a sign is to make visible the system that dictates its activity or function and constitutes its "unconscious." This critical perspective then allows us to identify Ah Q not only as a product of the system, but also as its structural surplus and waste—a rogue signifier and a wandering ghost that can neither be contained nor eliminated by the system itself. As it strives for its own identity and proper location, it destroys the very system that creates it, like a virus turning on the cells or programs in which it resides—in this case, a virus planted in the eco-cultural system of the Wei Village (a microcosm of China as such) by the rebel programmer that is the author of *Ah Q*. The real story of Ah Q is, in the fullest sense of the word, a phenomenology of the spirit/ghost of China as a system of meaning and value in its self-inflicted meltdown and dispersal. The intensity of this self-destruction gives rise to a peculiar modernist tension and totality that defines Chinese modernism at its origin.

In light of this critical interest, one cannot overemphasize the importance of the first chapter of the "Real Story," or its introduction, without which it would be critically pointless to follow the happenings and events to follow. Here the present reading differs sharply from the conventional realist or "critique-of-national-character" approach. The latter, by understanding Ah Q as a "typical character under typical circumstances" (see Engels 30–40), dwells on a character analysis that attributes character flaws to traditional society, class oppression, the limits of half-measured bourgeois revolutions, and the backwardness of Chinese peasantry. What follows this realist or "critique-of-national-character" approach is that the abuse of Ah Q at the hands of his fellow Wei Village dwellers, and eventually his death, stand not only as critique but also as a humanist catharsis that anticipates a real social revolution to be led by the proletariat.[7] All this, to be sure, draws legitimacy and interpretative power from the social and ideological conflicts of modern China. What is missing in this reading, however, is an account of the introductory chapter's formal design, which makes it clear that the central difficulty in—hence the narrative challenge to—writing the "story" is not concrete or representational but rather allegorical-rhetorical, namely, laying bare the impossibility of telling such a story along conventional lines.

AH Q AS ROGUE SIGN AND THE CONFUCIAN SYSTEM OF NAMING (RECTIFICATION)

Let's begin by rendering the title, *Ah Q Zheng Zhuan*, word for word, as "the straight-forward/official biography of Ah Q." The fictional worthiness of the story, therefore, relies on the credible probability of a fictitious biography. Lu Xun, however, begins the "story" not by establishing the probability of a biography, but by throwing it into irredeemable awkwardness, to the extent that the subject of this self-claimed bio-graphical project becomes so uncertain and obscure that no story can be meaning-fully told at all.

The opening paragraph of *Ah Q—The Real Story* offers a mock reference to the motto of classical Chinese historiography documented in *Zuozhuan* (third or fourth century BC), "*Forgeth words of immortalitie / For generations yet to be*" (101). Ironi-cally, this stands only as a reminder, to the narrator and the reader alike, of the embarrassing illegitimacy of the biographical endeavor: Ah Q's accidental becoming of the subject of a biographical-historical project indicates precisely the violation of the classical standard and thus constitutes the suspension of the Confucian symbolic order of meaning and value. As China plunged into a de facto semi-colony of West-ern powers by the end of the nineteenth century, emperors, princes, generals, and ministers disappeared from the center stage of history, leaving behind a political and cultural void yet to be filled by the emergent Chinese counterpart to modern Europe's middle class. The mass majority of the Chinese population, namely the peasantry, before being molded by genuinely transformative forces of modernity (such as the Chinese revolution) into a creative agency of history, could only passively reproduce the genetic codes of imperial order, and thus existed as a cultural fossil or sacrifice to a moribund tradition. The "voicelessness" of the peasantry was painfully felt by the isolated and besieged Enlightenment elite of which Lu Xun was a member. The ahis-torical, politico-ontological legitimacy governing the traditional concept of Chinese historiography (of which biography, or *zhuan*, is a basic mode) rests on three "im-mortal establishments" of the virtuous man: to establish virtue (*li de*); to establish action or merits (military or civil, *li xing*); and to establish words (and by extension, writings, *li yan*). Even though—from the viewpoint of Confucian morality—virtue and deeds are more important than words, when it comes to the writing of history, the third immortality (the becoming writing) turns out to be the real obsession of the Confucian scholar-officialdom: "to establish words" is the only means by which virtue and deeds can possibly go down into "history" and become immortal.

The transhistorical privilege of writing vis-à-vis spatio-temporal specificities of events and actions turns the external sphere and internal order of writing into an ultimate source of symbolic power and moral authority. The properly Confucian concept of historiography/biography, therefore, requires the convergence of im-mortal words and immortal people (as virtue and merits in one), from the general framework of meaning and value down to every single word bearing a critical judg-ment. The wordy, ironical, self-mocking discussion of the Confucian principle being subverted by the subject of history/biography, the name of namelessness called Ah Q, goes like this:

> [I]f you're going to get your words to last all that long, they have got to be about someone worth remembering all that long in the first place. Then the man gets remembered because of the words, and the words because of the man. And then after a while people gradually lose track of which one's remembered because of which. Knowing all of this, why did I finally settle on the likes of Ah Q for a biography? Guess the devil made me do it. (101)

In this regard, the cultural and moral legitimacy of writing a biography or "real story" of Ah Q is completely nebulous and obscure. Indeed, the difficulty of placing Ah Q in the existing moral and symbolic order constitutes the central formal challenge to the writing of *Ah Q*. In fact, it is the historiographical question of how to bring Ah Q into and make sense in the world of words—how to establish this image-thought in the value system of China—that leads to the most basic literary-critical question concerning this text: What is Ah Q? Is "he" "noble-minded" (*junzi*) or a "little people" (*xiaoren*)? Is he good or evil? Is he human or a ghost? Does he stand for the normative or the exception, being or nothingness? These questions necessarily move the reader away from the conventional questions about *Ah Q* and point to a post-humanist, post-historicist reading. The impossibility of meaning in the formal sense corresponds to the impossibility of "establishing Man" (*li ren*) in the value-system that characterized the young Lu Xun's commitment to reinventing a new national culture.[8]

Thus the narrative motivation of *Ah Q* comes not from the dynamic momentum of events or character-making, or from purely formal-stylistic design, but from the philosophical distinction between name (*ming*, as the Name that names, the system of naming or the moral-symbolic order as such) and words (*yan*, or speech as socially significant action)—or, more precisely, from the perceived discrepancy and contradiction between the two. This is, to be sure, the first concrete challenge of the storytelling deliberately played up by the narrator: "The question of a title (*ming*). What kind of biography was it to be? As Confucius once said, '*Be the title just so / Then the words refuse to flow*'" (101). This famous quotation from the Confucian *Analects* is rendered in a great variety of ways in the scholarly community. For the purpose of the present analysis, it is useful to introduce the immediate context from which it is taken:

> Adept Lu said: "If the Lord of Wei wanted you to govern his country, what would you put first in importance?"
> "The rectification of names," replied the Master. "Without a doubt."
> "That's crazy!" countered Lu. "What does rectification have to do with anything?"
> "You are such an uncivil slob," said the Master. "When the noble-minded cannot understand something, they remain silent.
> "Listen. If names are not rectified, speech does not follow from reality. If speech does not follow from reality, endeavors never come to fruition. If endeavors never come to fruition, then Ritual and music cannot flourish. If Ritual

and music cannot flourish, punishments do not fit the crime. If punishments do
not fit the crime, people cannot put their hands and feet anywhere without fear of
losing them.

"Naming enables the noble-minded to speak, and speech enables the
noble-minded to act. Therefore, the noble-minded are anything but careless in
speech." (Confucius 139–40)

It is clear that the difficulty of "rectification of names" encountered by the narrator
of *Ah Q* is not a technical one, but is rather of historical substance and pertains to
the imperial moral-cultural system whose disintegration gives rise to the allegorical
form of the story. There is little wonder why the "real story of Ah Q" cannot set up
its name or title in the first place: "Narrative biography, autobiography, private biography, public biography, supplementary biography, family biography, biographical
sketch. Trouble is—not one of them fits" (*Ah Q—The Real Story* 102). All of these
available forms or genres are embedded in the Confucian-imperial order's system of
naming. As the order crumbles to the ground, the "real" story of Ah Q can only be
a ghostly invention evoking the void, not the reality, of its socio-ontological being.
In other words, Ah Q, as a concept and a sign, points to the dysfunction and absence
of the moral-symbolic system that determines the meaning of its words and action,
now rendered a non-meaning, a non-sense.

Japanese scholar Maruo Tuneki discusses an ambiguity in the last sentences of
the full discussion of rectification excerpted above: "Why did I finally settle on the
likes of Ah Q for a biography? Guess the devil made me do it." Maruo compares the
differences between the classic Japanese translations of Lu Xun by Takeuchi Yoshimi,
on one hand, and those by Matueda Shigeo and Wada Takeshi on the other. Takeuchi's translation is close to the present English version, which highlights the "bedev-
iled" or "possessed" nature. But Matueda's and Wada's version, which Maruo
considers a more literal rendition, reads: "as if the ghost of Ah Q still dwells in my
mind" (Maruo 99–100). If we regard the basic formal organization of *Ah Q* as a
phenomenology of absence, then it is first of all a phenomenology of the specter.
Through the "speech" or "action" of Ah Q (or the words of *Ah Q*), the ruin of the
moral-cultural order of imperial China, not the rectification, is brought into full
play as an allegorical drama of forgetting, haunting, and mourning. In its reduced
form, this drama of lamentation is often regarded in modern Chinese literary historiography as a humanist or realist critique of the peasantry and the *lumpenproletariat* before the arrival of the vanguard party of the working people, the communists.
While this highly political reading has served its historical purpose in combining a
cultural revolution with a social one, in the postsocialist era, a new politics and
aesthetics of unpacking *Ah Q* must strive to measure its full energy and innovativeness, which come from the text's own topology, determined by the moral-symbolic
breakdown, and with its own cultural-political agenda, motivated by the will to
overcome the void left by the collapse of Confucian China.

The modernist allegory of China as a phenomenology of crumbling and dispersal takes shape through the frenzied but aimless activities of Ah Q as ghost—
through its roaming around; its self-negating search for an identity; its rejection by

the very moral-symbolic system it strives to join; and, finally, by its feebleness and homelessness. Lu Xun's fragmentary, cartoonish portrayals of Ah Q do not partake in a realist density of "content"; nor do they seek a symbolic unity that can elevate itself to a kind of existential truth of the human condition. Rather, these subplots and anecdotes resist any strong narrative and descriptive development, as if to keep the formal-aesthetic edifice to the bare-bone minimum; at the same time, following an ethics and poetics of allegorical writing elaborated in the foreword of Lu Xun's collection of prose poems, *Wild Grass* (*Yecao* 3–6), they wish and long for a "swift perishing" (*suxiu*) of aesthetic form per se. Thus, the seemingly underdeveloped, caricatural storytelling of *Ah Q* corresponds to a duality of the allegorical will in Lu Xun: on one hand, to make the invisible visible, the vanishing permanent, and to endow the silent and wordless with "speech" and action; on the other hand, to guard against the excesses and reification of form, which tend to perpetuate the hierarchy between the modern and the premodern, presence and nothingness, center and periphery, the West and China. As the allegorist struggles to capture the dispersal of the Chinese moral-symbolic order formalistically and aesthetically, deliberate shapelessness and provisionality effect a suspension of form, system, and totality. This radical aestheticization—in the sense that appearance is understood to be content—is also a radical cultural politics of time: it bears the quintessential modernist birthmark of wanting to suspend the past, by means of poetic condensation, and turn it into an ahistoric (and politically charged) moment, a metaphysical concept or thought-image, while simultaneously re-historicizing (and de-formalizing) the moment as ephemeral and transitional, that is, as a moment *in history* (cf. Nietzsche 156–57). It is through this politics of writing that a politics of time makes itself available to a sustained cultural radicalism, which ultimately finds its sociopolitical articulation in Mao's theory of permanent revolution: by making revolution constant and perpetual, time and form are brought into a new relationship conducive to the making of a new cultural and political Subject of History. And it is through this politics of time that Lu Xun—precisely by his intertwinement with the old and the ghostly—becomes one of the most trusted guides for those who pursue the eternal new.

What is "real" in *Ah Q*, therefore, is the allegoricalization of the sur- and the un-real, of the impossibility, that is, of any meaningful words flowing from reality before names can be rectified by extra-linguistic and extra-cultural forces of history. A radical nihilism, which animates a playful nominalism, constitutes the inner perspective of this narrative without a character, without an event, and without a socio-historical horizon in sight. Sheer negativity as a constructive principle allows the impossibility of naming and the ghost of Ah Q to work themselves into a farcical frenzy. The more fragmented, non-sensible, and narratively superficial the storytelling is, the more firmly it establishes itself, albeit only in the more abstract and intense domain of modernism, as the story of a dogged search for identity and approval and its merciless rejection and disastrous failure. A fantastic, farcical, and completely self-destructive ritual of "rectification of names" forms the only reality about Ah Q in the real story about him—as anti-reality. To this extent, *Ah Q* must be read as a phantom play of the real and a real play of the phantom. To the full extent of both dimensions, the story is about a misguided, hopeless struggle for identity, recognition, and self-realization—a struggle enacted by the systematic waste and programmatic flaw that is Ah Q, a familiar village vagabond and all-time superfluous man. As a textbook example of Jameson's notion of national allegory, Ah Q does not merely symbolize China; it *is* China.

As the meta-fiction of a crumbling imperial China drawn into the vortex of modernity, *Ah Q* stages the impossibility of names and naming and turns a structural, nominalistic dilemma and stalemate into a full-fledged farce about the social meaninglessness of words and action. Contrary to the conventional reading of *Ah Q*, which focuses on the question "What's wrong with Ah Q?," rereading it as a modernist masterpiece of allegory reorients the question toward a normative-systematic analysis of the logical, programmatic error exposed and allegorized by the normal and technically precise operation of Ah Q as a sign, a loyal, dutiful semiotic cog within the system. The spectral nature of Ah Q, often disguised by its allegorical specificities, determines the premeditated narrative futility of fitting to the protagonist an identifiable family name, a writable given name, and a traceable birthplace, an impossibility which corresponds to the structural misplacement of the story in the existing order of virtue (*de*), merits (*xing*), and words (*yan*, here as biography, historiography, and storytelling). The telling of the untold and untellable story of Ah Q sets itself up as an allegorical game in representing or giving shape to a hollowed out historical-cultural substance and a social-moral chaos. But the moral or cultural-critical intensity can be reached only through the allegorical parody of China in symbolic disarray, hence sacrificing Ah Q's ability to self-explain, self-justify, and self-assert, no matter what it does or says. This sacrifice constitutes not merely a loss of identity, but, more fundamentally, of sovereignty—sovereignty not only in the political-philosophical sense but, more precisely, in the cultural-political sense as a self-sustained power of naming and interpreting, the ultimate guarantor of meaning and value. The comical, farcical nature of Ah Q as a thought-image derives logically from this loss of moral-symbolic sovereignty, which determines *a priori* that every act, every move, every passing thought of Ah Q is bound to be ridiculous and laughable, because China per se, not knowing where to turn and not able to make sense regardless of what it says or does, has lost its moral and symbolic certainty.

If this is a "national allegory" in the strong, literal sense, then its effectiveness is achieved only through a ruthless modernist aesthetics under the disguise of some pre-realist form of storytelling. Calling *Ah Q* a tragedy misses the point: its modernist fervor does not harbor any ambiguity or contradiction, emotionally or morally, and shows no mercy or sympathy for any of the characters (there are none, really) as they embrace their own destruction. The only dramatic tension is a structural and semiotic one within the system of names, a tension between structure and sign as they turn against and devour each other, which leads to the collapse of the symbolic order; and this order, of course, is the not-so-hidden source of both pleasure and pain in the literary community of modern China. The most ruthless modernist aesthetics can be found not in the usual domain of stylistic choices or technical innovations, but rather in an extra-aesthetic decision, namely the rejection of the temptation to associate or identify, safely and comfortably, with an extraneous but prevailing system of names and words, form and narrative—namely, the discursive and institutional framework of modernism as a purely literary and aesthetic norm. In other words, the perspective by which Ah Q is scrutinized and portrayed allegorically is not from outside but from within; not from a "higher," condescending point of view (be that of "critique of national character," theory of evolution, or Marxist notion of mode of production), but from a consciousness that identifies Ah Q as one's own fate, indeed as the eternal return of the sameness of the collective Self. The story about "rectification of the names," which determines the impossibility of words being grounded in or following from the real, turns out to be an internal work of detection performed by and on the system itself, in which Ah Q, as an allegorical agent, actively helps the investigative process.

The interest of this rereading of *Ah Q* for comparative modernism is twofold. On the one hand, the formal intensity and complex operations of consciousness (as self-consciousness) prove to be attainable and applicable in precapitalist modes of production as a cultural critique, where the reification of the names in the imperial order constitutes a phenomenological and historical space similar to that found in the state-form of commodity capitalism, with the rectification of names operating more or less as a substitute for advanced capitalism in formal-aesthetic production. On the other hand, and equally poignantly, the allegorical radicalism of non-Western modernism, in its critical and subversive energy vis-à-vis tradition, can and did resist the aesthetic and moral ontology of Western modernism by staying within the space of the crumbling and vanishing in order to achieve aesthetic and political intensity in the form of "quick perishing." Although the loss of moral-symbolic certainty and sovereignty produced, as is widely observed,[9] a profound melancholy for the destruction of the cultural "home" in modern China, in Lu Xun that loss did not lead to a metaphysical discourse of what Lukács called "transcendental homelessness," nor did Chinese modernism in general, in its intimate encounter with the ossification of tradition, give rise to a philosophical discourse on reification.

For the purpose of the present reading of *Ah Q*, I would like to argue that Ah Q, a wandering ghost and a rogue sign within the system of names, is limited to a formal space that allegorically represents a historical moment of tension, cultural self-destruction, and chaos, whose aesthetic purposefulness serves the larger political (and cultural-political) goal of regarding this moment as transitional, transient, and provisional, that is, as a negative utopia. By refusing to normalize and perpetuate the state of the scattered, fragmentary, and homeless, the allegorical form of formlessness—the stated strategy of "quick perishing"—blocks the discursive and stylistic reification of Chinese modernism from moving toward its own metaphysical-formal consolidation as the Chinese copy of an institutionalized Euro-American high modernism. It betrays a penchant for the early Chinese modernists to constrain—willfully or not—the shattered real within an imagined totality of allegory. The radical will to allegory is, therefore, also a will to overcoming, to wrestling with the now in order to secure a historical horizon within the particular political intensity of language. The deliberately preliminary, tentative, uncertain, and open structure of the narrative and language of *Ah Q* suggests a conscious abandonment of the international currency of aesthetic privilege and institutional prestige in exchange for the present danger of critique, resistance, radicalism, and revolution in both literary-cultural and social domains. In terms of this politics of language and politics of form, *Ah Q* not only marks the culmination of Lu Xun's fiction writing, but also anticipates and prefigures his late essays (*zawen*), in which a self-conscious and political concept of writing takes shape.

The Two Halves of *Ah Q*: From Proscription to the Desire for Identity

In this section I examine the narratology of *Ah Q*, which unfolds in two halves to form structural counterpoints with almost musical precision, and at the same time creates a formal and anecdotal effect of development—of character, of history, and as moral. The title *Ah Q—The Real Story* gives the reader a fictitious guarantee that the narrator is here to offer a story about a certain character. The meta-fictional problem of finding a genre or format that honors the Confucian standard of immortalities of virtue, merits, and words, though of grave importance in (de)legitimating the work in the literal sense, effectively drives the story forward allegorically by necessitating a tireless search for the symbolic location of Ah Q, an act of rectification which proves to be impossible. As this purely formal or structural "plot" moves forward, the reader realizes that the narrator is unable to ascertain the family name, given name, birthplace, offspring, or posterity of the protagonist. As a matter of fact, throughout the "real story of Ah Q," there is simply no story to tell, only disconnected anecdotes and incidents. To speak the unspeakable thus characterizes the poetics of storytelling in *Ah Q*, whose narrative production is the production of absence, meaninglessness, and nothingness. Yet the production of nonsense and void constitutes the work of *Ah Q* proper in all its allegorical richness.

The first and introductory chapter makes up the entire first half. A preamble dwelling on the impossibility of a story or biography (*zhuan*) in the properly Confucian sense is followed by a numbered list of problems of the proposed "real story." Animated by the narrative voice's now mocking, now serious search for Ah Q's identity, the first narrative event of the "real story" begins with Ah Q's comical striving for a respectable family name. Upon the news arriving in the village that Old Master Zhao's son passed the Budding Talent exam, a slightly drunk Ah Q "danced for joy" and "told everyone what a great honor this was to him personally because he belonged to the same clan as Old Master Zhao" (103):

> As a matter of fact, the way Ah Q had it worked out, he even came out three
> notches above the *Budding Talent* in the clan's generational pecking order! The
> people who were standing around when Ah Q announced this actually began to
> treat him with more respect too. (103)

The problem, of course, is that this self-serving identification does not sit well with
the Zhao clan, which has an obviously higher perch in the Confucian social and
cultural order. The first of a slew of dramatic scenes in *Ah Q* goes as follows:

> Who could have foreseen that the very next day the local sheriff would order
> Ah Q to hightail it on out to the Zhaos' place? As soon as Old Master Zhao
> clapped eyes on Ah Q, the old fellow's face flushed scarlet. "Ah Q, you miserable
> bastard," he bellowed, "did you say you're a clansman of mine?"
> Ah Q didn't let out a peep. The more the old man looked at him, the madder
> he got. He bore in a few steps closer: "How dare you talk such rubbish? How
> could *I* possibly have a clansman like *you*?"
> Still not a peep. Just as Ah Q was about to beat a hasty retreat, Old Master
> Zhao bolted forward and slapped him across the face. "How could *you* be named
> Zhao? How could you even *deserve* to be named Zhao?" (103–04)

Ah Q's family name is not only unknown, but it also cannot exist because it is excluded from the structure of class, caste, kinships, and genealogies. The exclusion,
moreover, is not an accident but an institutional and symbolic certainty rendered
legible by Ah Q's wanton and unrectifiable desire to have a name and an identity. It is
only logical, then, that socially sanctifying words, speeches, and actions do not follow.

Ah Q does not have a definite given name, either: he is called only "Ah Q," and
nobody knows what the "Q" stands for; hence the narrator's decision to use the
roman letter to "name" the unnameable. If the absence of a family name suggests Ah
Q's obscurity in terms of group identity, the uncertainty of his given name indicates
a lack of individuation—not belonging to a group does not necessarily turn Ah Q
into a so-called atomic universal individual. In China, the written form of the name
(family or given) is the only way to ascertain its meaning, which resides in the chosen Chinese characters. Using a roman letter to designate Ah Q thus introduces a
decisive new historical epoch in which Chinese civilization as a system of names
and naming not only must coexist with other systems of names and naming as competing frames of reference, but also must risk the danger of being named. Morally
and symbolically, being named in this way means being defined by and thus subject
to another language as the universal language of power, history, meaning, and value.
Chinese names and morality, in comparison, are reduced to a mere vocabulary li-
able to renaming. Politically or cultural-politically, to call the protagonist "Ah Q" is
no different from calling China "China" and not the "Middle Kingdom" (*Zhongguo*),
represented and symbolized by the two Chinese characters, Zhong (middle) and
Guo (country). How Japanese media and textbooks refer to China—either by the
more "respectful" form "*Chokokku*" (using Kanji characters) or the "disrespectful"
form "Shina," (technically equal to Western nations' "China")—remains to this day
a politically and psychologically sensitive issue.[10] Ah Quei or Ah Q stands for the
same kind of de-Sinification, but one adopted by the Chinese themselves as a matter

of necessity, a necessity here allegorized as a dilemma of storytelling: it is impossible to tell the story of Ah Q in a properly Chinese way, as the character cannot be registered or named in an intact Chinese moral-symbolic order. Ah Q becomes nameable or representable only by means of a different system of naming, one which renders the properly Confucian notion of biography unfitting and worthless. As the narrator confesses, the preconditions for the writing of this story are no other than the loss of autonomy and traditional norms, thus the first chapter's self-mocking guilt in anticipation of "violating the hallowed principles of historiography" (106).

Finally, nobody knows where Ah Q comes from. Even if Ah Q has always been around, he is seen as an outcast by the locals who form the close-knit community of Wei Village, a microcosm of China. Nobody, including Ah Q himself, knows where his ancestors came from, which renders Ah Q a cultural-geographical orphan whose origin belongs not to any particular region or locale, but to China as a cultural-moral abstraction. On a more concrete level, Ah Q's daily behavior suggests a typical *lumpenproletariat* living on the margins of society. A temporary laborer for hire, Ah Q does not have a regular job; living inside the Land-and-Grain Temple as a perennial sojourner, Ah Q does not have a regular residence. He travels back and forth between town and country, either seeking revolution or fleeing from punishment. Blurring the lines between fantasy and reality, the world of men and the world of ghost, obedience, and rebellion, Ah Q exists in a limbo of possibilities and dead ends. In spatial as well as cultural terms, Ah Q's existence is that of a homeless ghost, a haunting specter whose search for a home and an identity simply makes explicit the fact that the old order has long since crumbled, leaving behind the rubble of identity and a void of meaning. As a die-hard son of the system of names that is China, Ah Q's name cannot be found on the books. And any attempt to locate him or make sense of his existence will necessarily turn into an allegorical representation of the unraveling, chaos, and nonsense of the moral-symbolic order.

The marginal and alienated position of Ah Q within the system of names also carries a utopian element within its uncertainty and fantasies, from which the "thoughts" of Ah Q sometimes flare up to mingle with that of the prototypical modern Chinese intellectual. Both are "madmen" to be found living precariously on the margins of Chinese villages and towns; both seem to be eternal dream chasers indulging in the blueprints and daydreams of radical change but lacking the means to bring them into reality; both stand on the opposite side of village gossip, common sense, and tradition; and, in their role as the abnormal par excellence, both define and even reinforce the normal that constitutes the unconscious of the abnormal as a language—the language of the Other, the majority, the normal that excludes and punishes. Both Ah Q and the prototypical modern Chinese intellectual share an on-again, off-again sensation of intoxication, of flying above the ground, away from their familiar environment, in disregard or defiance of material and social necessity:

> Although his intention in going out was to "scare up something to eat," yet when he saw the familiar wineshop, the familiar steamed breadrolls, strange to tell, he walked right on by. Not only did he fail to stop, but what's more, he didn't even

want the bread or wine. That's not what he was really looking for. Then, exactly what was it that he *was* looking for? Even Ah Q himself couldn't have told you.
(137)

There can be nothing more misleading and self-indulgent than the discourse in modern Chinese literary critical and intellectual history that regards Lu Xun's *Ah Q—The Real Story* as a sympathetic critique of the lamentable backwardness of Chinese peasantry. For modern Chinese intellectuals who seek to restore the moral-symbolic autonomy and sovereignty of China, Ah Q is not a "typical character in the typical environment" to be objectified, but, rather, a specter haunting the system as a symptom of its historical situation and inner crisis. They all descend from Ah Q, have his genes and blood, and meet him in their dreams over and over again. On the only night when Ah Q's dark, small, dirt-floored room in the temple is illuminated by candlelight, we read the following scene, pregnant with allegorical richness:

> Alone in his little room at last, luxuriating, Ah Q lit the candle and lay down. He was indescribably happy. . . . The flames shimmered and danced as if it were New Year's Eve, and Ah Q's thoughts began to do some high stepping too. "Throw in with the troublemakers? Yeah, that would be fun. I can see it now. A bunch of those Revolution Party guys'll come by the temple here, all decked out in white armor and white helmets, wearin' sabers too! They'll come marchin' right in and shout: 'Let's go, Ah Q, come with us!' And I'll go with them too! Steel maces, bombs, foreign rifles, spears, knives—they'll have it all. Then those cocksuckin' villagers will find out how pitiful they really are. I can see 'em kneeling' on the ground and beggin' me to spare 'em. Fat chance!" (152)

The propensity to revolt, the quick imagination about a sweeping revolutionary rearrangement of social order, and above all the fantastic images spawned by inner concentration or the withdrawal into inwardness, make this scene strangely and startlingly fitting for an oil painting portrait of the modern Chinese intellectual. At the threshold of modernity and revolution, before the new modes of production and class antagonism emerge, the flickering image of the modern Chinese intellectual can readily recognize itself in the wandering specter of a fallen empire of names. The birth of Ah Q—the sign, the specter, the thought-image—marks a moment of ambiguity and paradox. On the one hand, there is the need to overcome the tautological hollowness of culture by exteriorizing it through satire and allegory. On the other hand, one must interiorize an external trauma—the trauma resulting from the encounter with the Modern in the image of the West as the alien—through narrative and representation. The politics of naming the unnamable in *Ah Q—The Real Story*, while recognizing an existential reality of namelessness and homelessness, keeps a cautious distance from the formal-aesthetic institutions and properties of the modern as the new universal symbolic order.

The other half of the story, unfolding like a musical counterpoint, provides a running account of Ah Q's odd behavior and a series of bizarre incidents that eventually leads to his execution. This "plot line," however, must be viewed with regard to its structural and allegorical relationship to the first half of the story, the meta-fictional, allegorical "rectification" of the Name of Ah Q. Insofar as the name cannot be rectified, the narration of those events drives home the failure of the whole system of meaning, value, and order on which the Confucian empire rests. As the insanity of the word exposes the chaos of a world, Ah Q emerges as a specter triggering and showing the "quick perishing" from within and hence functions as the (de)constructive principle of the allegorical phenomenology of the Real.

Beginning from the third paragraph, the seemingly formless slew of anecdotes about Ah Q—above all those gossips and incidents dramatizing the impossibility of his identity—methodically contributes to a rigorous, though hidden, allegorical configuration of Ah Q as an abstract sign struggling selflessly but hopelessly for its belonging to the system that rejects and excludes it. Structurally and conceptually, if the first half of the story constitutes the series of "You Are Not Allowed" or "You Don't Deserve"—Ah Q is not allowed to have the family name Zhao, to fall in love, to make revolution, etc.—then the second half, to be examined in this section, can be regarded as a series of "I Want": Ah Q wants an identity, respect, women (hence posterity), revolt, and, ultimately, life. If the incidents and anecdotes in the first series invariably end with Ah Q's being dealt a sudden, violent (but highly predictable) blow—being struck by a large bamboo pole or chased by a vicious dog—then the desires and efforts collected in the second series offer a structural analysis and presentation of Ah Q as a sign of the deeper unconscious of a crumbling cultural-moral norm/order that continues to manipulate its nameless ghost. The persistence and aimlessness of this abandoned ghost convey the dark force and unrelenting self-centeredness of the life-denying inner constitution of the Confucian order, but only in a farcical way, as the last and definitive evidence of its irreversible dispersal.

The "events" of these two series are thus intertwined with each other, structurally and conceptually, along a seeming line of narrative development. Ah Q, in his request for identity and respect, must prove his position within the system of naming; thus, the fantastic sense of belonging to the Zhao clan must come with a claimed pecking order within the family genealogy three generations prior to the Budding Talent (103). What this means, moreover, is that Ah Q, in recognizing and overcoming his loss of identity, must also be striving, wittingly or not, to rectify, restore, and repair the system of names more strenuously than are its socially sanctioned guardians—namely, the gentry-literati class—who do not seem to be nearly as concerned about the cultural crisis and moral chaos of China. They will, of course, never accept Ah Q's wishful yet unwarranted class identification, or his cultural striving. This is not so much Ah Q doing the bidding of the ruling class, but something more profoundly symbiotic with his search for identity and sense of belonging, attainable only in a stable and respected system of names and naming in the first place. Ah Q must rectify the name of China before his own name can be rectified; he must prove the validity of the system before his own worth can be proven. Nothing said or done by Ah Q will make any sense until China can make sense to the world and to itself.

Ah Q's search for meaning and self-identity makes explicit both the impossibility of meaning and identity in the self-contained Chinese system and the impossibility of any alternative as long as that system clings to its universal claim and demands unconditional loyalty from its subjects. The farcical effort at restoring and rectifying the symbolic order by an outcast is not only the formal principle of allegorical organization in *Ah Q*, but also the historical substance of the "moral victory" ("winning psychological victories" in Lyell's translation), the signature psychological mechanism by which Ah Q operates. The twist is that this substance is structured linguistically rather than psychologically. It lies in the self-compatibility and self-referentiality of a private language that rectifies the disorder rather than the order of the names but has no validity or traction beyond itself in the public world of heterogeneity and otherness.

The celebrated documentation of Ah Q's behavior in Chapters 2 and 3, "A Brief Account of His Victories" and "A Brief Account of His Victories (cont.)," begins with Ah Q's ridiculous sense of pride and superiority:

> Since he thought so well of *himself*, Ah Q considered the other villagers simply beneath his notice. He went so far with this that he even looked down his nose at the village's two *Young Literati*. He didn't realize, of course, that up there in the rarefied world of scholar-officialdom *those whom one doeth Young Literati name* can darn well get to be those *whom one must Budding Talents proclaim*—if you don't keep an eye on them. That's why Old Master Qian and Old Master Zhao were so all-fired respected in the village: they were daddies to those two *Young Literati*—and rich to boot. Ah Q, however, was less than impressed. "My son gonna be a lot richer." (108)

Ah Q's self-positioning through self-naming as a "father" whose imagined son would be "a lot richer" than the representatives of the scholar-officialdom in the village suggests nothing "psychological," a misunderstanding that informs mainstream critical discourse on "moral victory" as a metaphor for China's wounded pride, an overcompensation for its *ressentiment* before the Western Powers. Ah Q's self-proclaimed membership, even superiority, within the Confucian order of names must be read literally, that is, allegorically, as a self-justifying righteousness resulting from his determined desire to rectify the names, whose maintenance has long been neglected by the corrupt and clueless gentry-literati class, which does not seem to deserve its prestige and power. It is in this sense that I argue that Ah Q, as a rogue sign in the symbolic order of names, also marks the latter's futile, doomed effort at self-correction and self-restoration. In other words, the "victory" in question, though truly a virtual and fantastic one, is driven not by the vengeful desire to win, to overpower the physical or emotional adversary, but rather by the desire to set the word/world straight according to the moral and symbolic self-understanding, dignity, and autonomy of China, a desire now farcically carried around and wantonly executed by its disowned ghost, Ah Q. As an instance of Ah Q's private language, "moral victory" actually works: it repairs the linguistic chain and erases the glitches within his consciousness, making him content and his life bearable once again, though only for a moment and only within his own universe, which is as logical as it is capricious, arbitrary, chaotic, and insane. The currency and effectiveness of such "moral victory" stop at the boundary of Otherness, to be rejected by everyone else—the Zhaos and the Qians, Bearded Wang, Little D, Amah Wu, the

Fake Foreign Devil, and the "Revolutionaries" and their court. It is a misnomer to call this imagined, subjective overcoming of the broken chain of signification "psychological," because the innermost social anxiety and energy it registers is structural, linguistic, and allegorical.

Just as Ah Q must pinpoint his place in the genealogy of the Zhao clan before he can establish his identity, he must restore the entire Confucian order to gain his humanity. Besides the irony that this grave cultural-political task now falls on the shoulders of a semi-drunk, homeless, nameless, and childless outcast, the allegorical intensity of the story lies in the fact that every single wishful, self-indulgent, mud-headed, and ludicrous act of Ah Q turns out to be strictly logical and clear in purpose, not to mention selfless and persistent. The series of trial-and-error attempts to restore and rectify the system of names unfolds as a line of binary oppositions governing the norms of Confucian culture and society: high and low; respectable and disrespectable; rich and poor; strong and weak; official and nonofficial; town and country; male and female; true and false; human and inhuman.

Ah Q's touchy sense of self-respect and self-importance entails in its vainglory and wantonness a strong tendency to endorse and reaffirm the Confucian hierarchy. Homeless and penniless, he looks down not only on his fellow day laborers, such as Bearded Wang and Little D, but also on those of higher social stature, including scholars fit for government office. The reason can only be that he identifies not with actual and yet accidental representatives of this system, but with the system as such, as a totality from top down. After being soundly beaten by Bearded Wang, Ah Q feels more "surprised" than humiliated, as his defeat is not taken personally or physically, but is attributed, remarkably, to something systematic and symbolic: the abolishment of the civil service examinations (1905), which can be viewed as the symbolic and institutional ending of the Confucian scholar-official tradition of the past millennia. The passage goes like this:

> "His fists need never be swung, for the gentlemen useth his tongue," quoted Ah
> Q, head cocked to one side. . . . It would appear, however, that Bearded Wang was
> no gentleman, for ignoring this classical lore, he slammed Ah Q's head against the
> wall five times in succession. . . . In Ah Q's memory, this could probably be
> reckoned as the first real disgrace of an entire lifetime, for Bearded Wang—flawed
> by a beard growing rampant all over his face—had always been the object of Ah Q's
> taunts, and had certainly never before made light of Ah Q, much less dared to lay
> hands on him. Thus the event that had just transpired was something totally
> unexpected. Could it possibly be true, as people were saying in town, that the
> emperor had put an end to the civil service examinations and did not need *Budding
> Talents* anymore? Could it be that the Zhao family's prestige had consequently
> declined and that people now felt free to look down on Ah Q as a result? (118)

In this light, the moral courage in the absurdity of Ah Q's "moral victory" comes, literally, from the (unauthorized, thus illegitimate) internalization of the imperial social and cultural order, which is rendered hollow and invalid precisely by the futility and illegitimacy of such identification. Here, the desire for the normal (and normative) becomes the allegorical representation of the abnormal, and the abnormal (and illegitimate) presents itself allegorically as the norm (or social and moral chaos). This dialectical standstill of history and culture not only consumes itself but subsumes anything new, and promises to negate even radical social revolution by its unfathomable nihilistic intensity.

In Chapter 8, "Request to Revolt Denied" (*Buxu geming*, literally, "Revolution Not Permitted"), one finds a cynical change of names that prove to be not social, cultural, and political, but only nominal—a non-change of the same system of naming that continues to name the new rather than being renamed by the new:

> The word from town was that although the Revolutionary Party had indeed taken over, it hadn't made any changes to speak of. His honor the country magistrate was still the same man, though they called him something else now. Old Master *Selectman* had also acquired some sort of new label (the Wei Village couldn't keep track of all these new revolutionary titles). And the same old lieutenant was in charge of the soldiers, too. (154–55)

What can be inferred from this continuation of the system of names and naming, which renders the "words" and "deeds" of history empty, differs from the mainstream critical theme of the "betrayal" of peasantry by the bourgeois revolution or reform. It focuses instead on the "grammar" of history that tricks the "words" of social change out of their intended meaning, a ruse of the system of which Ah Q is actively, though unwittingly, a part. Once again, Ah Q as a rogue sign in a semiotic system going astray becomes the allegorical-narrative *actant* that makes visible what is invisible: the "normalcy" of chaos, the cultural-moral norm of hollowness, and the playful figuration of China in irreversible self-dissolution.

Throughout the story, Ah Q is often semi-intoxicated, forgetful, and full of glee. Nonetheless, when it comes to reading, perceiving, and deciphering the signs and emblems of the hierarchical system of names and naming, he never loses his natural-born sensitivity and sharpness, which is in dramatic contrast to his animalistic reaction to sudden, violent physical punishment. In Chapter 4, "Tragedy of Love," Ah Q shows once again his innate acumen as a connoisseur of official, symbolic abuse, this time in response to the punishment following his crude propositioning of Amah Wu ("Sleep with me! Sleep with me!"):

> The heavy pole clove the air again. Ah Q grabbed the top of his head with both hands. *WHACK!* The blow landed on his knuckles and hurt more than a little. As he burst through the kitchen door, he seemed to feel yet another hard blow land on his back.
>
> "Turtle's egg!" the *Budding Talent* cursed from behind.
>
> Ah Q ran to the hulling shed as fast as his legs would carry him. He stood there alone. Pain lingered in his fingers, and the expression "turtle's egg" in his mind, for that was one locution that the countryfolk of Wei Village never used. Only rich people who rubbed noses with officials said fancy things like that, and thus it made a deep impression on Ah Q and gave him quite a fright to boot. (127)

Most frightening to Ah Q is the symbolic power of what sounded to him like an exclusively upper-class phrase, "turtle's egg," which stands beyond the pole falling on his back as the Name that punishes. This mechanical (non)production of experience, knowledge, and even wisdom by trauma is not meant to evoke moral indignation, to be sure, but to highlight one more time the intimate relationship between Ah Q and the symbolic order that creates him. This might be the reason the final chapter, about Ah Q's death, is titled "The Grand Reunion" (*datuanyuan*), a phrase for "grand finale" in traditional Chinese stories, which suggests a happy, harmonious coming-together of long-separated family members who finally can live a happy, normal life together forever after. The title thus hints at a final homecoming of Ah Q as a rogue sign destined to be recycled by the system. When his short-lived career as a self-styled rebel ends after the "revolution" with his capture and trial as a common thief, Ah Q, though dazed and in fear, proves his worth as true product of the system:

> Every mother's son of them looked mean and ugly. What was more, they nailed Ah Q with dirty looks. At this juncture, it occurred to Ah Q that there must be something more to the bald old geezer than met the eye. Ah Q's knees instantly loosened of their own accord and he sank to a keeling position.
>
> "Stand! Stand while addressing this court! No kneeling!" barked the long-gowned types virtually in unison.
>
> Ah Q appeared to understand, but didn't seem able to stay on his feet. As if of its own accord, his body collapsed into a squat and then, capitalizing on the momentum already built up, continued right on down into a full-fledged kneel.
>
> "A born slave!" observed the long-gowned types with contempt, but they didn't try to get him to stand up again either. (163–65)

"A born slave": despite the fact that this title is given to him contemptuously by the postrevolutionary and not the imperial court, it is in fact the first (and last) *official* recognition Ah Q receives from the system of names and naming.

The narrator of *Ah Q—The Real Story* reminds us that "Ah Q's thinking was, as a matter of fact, thoroughly in accord with the sagacious morality of our classical tradition" (124). That one finds this observation in "The Love Tragedy" chapter does not mean that it is limited to Ah Q's thoughts on women or male-female relationship, even though in this area he is particularly fervent about observing and reinforcing the "sagacious morality of our classical tradition" by attributing all personal miseries and dynastic troubles to women as a source of bad luck. Even Ah Q's "unbridled" lust for women, once formed as language, takes the shape of Confucian teachings such as "*Of three things which do unfilial be / The worst is to lack posteritie*" (124). Ah Q may indeed harbor less orthodox views, such as "any nun is bound to be secretly shacked up with a monk"; or, "if a woman is out walking on the street, she's certainly trying to seduce a man or two"; or, "if a man and woman are talking to each other, they're sure to be arranging a tryst" (125). But those function only as a pretext for his one-man crusade of rectification, during which he "often employed his dirtylookism to punish such miscreants" and "rigorously observed *the great barrier that should be 'twixt the he and the she*" (125).

What is at stake for Ah Q, ultimately, is no less than the greatest question of all, namely the Confucian final distinction of human and nonhuman. The "moral uprightness" Ah Q carries along with his often clownish behavior always demands that this distinction be observed to the fullest degree and in the most discriminating fashion. Instead of being defensively or narcissistically "moral" and "upright," Ah Q proves to be a judgmental, aggressive censor in the village, going about the community to practice his self-righteous politics of excluding dissent. In fact, exclusion and homogenization form the flip side of Ah Q's misguided search for identity and belonging, as the latter requires the rigorous restoration of the moral-symbolic order as an ontological politics of being—the rectification of the name and definition/qualification of humanity. The boatman from the next village, Sevenpounder, after falling into the hands of the revolutionaries in the city, "had been so transformed [i.e., having his queue, or ponytail—a bodily sign of being a subject of the Manchu Emperor—cut off] that he no longer looked even human" (155). Fake Foreign Devil "has lost all claim to humanity" (119) for not only cutting off his queue but also attaching a fake one; his wife, "willin' to sleep with a husband that's got no queue," "can't be any damn good" (152). In Ah Q's China, in the absence of modern class and national and historical antagonisms—aristocracy versus bourgeoisie, or bourgeoisie versus proletariat; the nation versus perceived external threats; the new, the eternal, iconoclastic present versus the petrified, timeless past, etc.—the distinction between the human and nonhuman is not only the ultimate cultural-political distinction: it is also the self-identity and self-assertion of an insular, homogeneous cultural universalism that disregards, obscures, suppresses, depoliticizes, and erases substantive contradictions and conflicts in the social domain.

AH Q'S DEATH: MODERNIST FORGETTING AND THE DESIRE FOR RECOGNITION

The desire called Ah Q, therefore, is the desire to be(come) human, and yet the concept of humanity in this context is overdetermined by the system of names and naming that both constitutes and dissolves (and are constituted and dissolved by) Ah Q as structural *différance*. Ah Q is as thoroughly a cultural phenomenon as he/it is a natural or natural-historical one. He is structured by his cultural norm to the same extent that his existence is a state of nature—a naturalized culture or culturalized nature, brought into seamless totality and autonomy by the monopoly of meaning and its internal decay.

Ah Q's blind loyalty to the culture that mercilessly takes his life reminds the reader of Kong Yiji, the ruined would-be scholar who holds on to the imagined dignity of the gentry-literati;[11] his/its semi-craziness is reminiscent of the Madman, with Ah Q's confusion and intoxication forming an interesting contrast to the Madman's acute self-consciousness, which borders on clinical paranoia. One may wonder if it is this kind of unreserved cultural loyalty and sacrifice that prompted the young Lu Xun to search for "a few noble-minded individuals" (*yi er shi*) and for "a

nation of real human beings" (*renguo*) (see Lu Xun, "Wenhua pianzhi lun" (on deviation of culture), 1: 56–7). Lu Xun's imagining of a new, modern China is conditioned
negatively by this kind of over-culturalization, or semioticization, as a corruption of
nature. As the polar opposite of the Nietzschean *Ubermensch*, Ah Q nonetheless
stands for a mode of being that exists beyond shame and guilt, and beyond good and
evil. Unlike the Nietzschean notion of Nature, however, which is conversant with the
Darwinian or Social-Darwinian idea that "life finds a way," Ah Q carries the natural/
cultural force of what can be called anti-life, with culture as the sole purpose and
highest achievement of humanity: not culture as creativity and affirmation of life,
but culture as the moralization and symbolization of life, its over-codification in the
system of names—as both meaning and meaninglessness, as chaos.

Like Kong Yiji, Ah Q is healthy and optimistic. Ah Q sleeps a lot in the story.
He needs sleep, which separates not so much the day and night as one instant from
the next. Ah Q lives in the perennial present, happy and blissfully forgetful, react-
ing only to the immediate physical and symbolic environment. Never before in
Chinese literature has a thoroughly cultural and moral creature also been thoroughly animalistic, and yet in its state of nature, driven and determined purely by
the system of names. The suspension of memory (including memory of pain, injustice, humiliation, and trauma) proves to be necessary for such an impossibly paradoxical being, as amnesia and oblivion nourish a will to happiness in Ah Q that
comes from the self-identity of the system of names to which he belongs. Every
time reality forces Ah Q to the brink of having to recognize and wrestle with danger
and otherness—that is, to the outer limits of the natural womb of culture and
morality—his will to happiness, in the form of "moral victory," animalistic forgetting, or harmless, childlike sleep, brings him back to the comfort zone of the
self-identity and self-autonomy of meaning, value, and order that has long ceased
to exist in any meaningful way.

This natural-historical or natural-cultural state of being also characterizes Ah
Q's forgetfulness. The binary of memory and forgetting—they always appear hand-
in-hand in Lu Xun's writings—occupies the central spot in Lu Xun's modernist poetics. Whereas the most intimate and elaborate writings on memory and forgetting
can be found in Lu Xun's prose poems and essays, one can also find sustained philosophical and narrative operations about the issue in his stories, such as "Mourning
the Dead" (*Shangshi*).[12] For Lu Xun, memory is conditioned by forgetting; it sur-
vives forgetting, surging from underneath it unexpectedly and irrepressibly as the
unforgettable, haunting and shattering, like a utopian dream or dystopian nightmare, the cozy, oblivious order of the status quo. Moreover, forgetting in particular
plays a radical, nihilistic role in obliterating the deadening pile-up of violent events
that constitute the hardened shell of reality. By means of its equalizing power of
negation, memory thus opens a way toward the unknown, toward a potentially
explosive and productive future. One suspects that for Lu Xun, forgetting, in the
fullest modernist sense, is a positive, constructive principle; it rejects the historicist
continuum and meaningless chain of events, and offers true guidance for a new life.
Forgetting, in other words, always means an amoral decision to forget, to move

forward no matter what, against and beyond the ethics and morality of remembering and regretting, but with the heavy weight of forgetting existing as the unfathomable depth of memory or, rather, as the dead bodies of memory, which contain within their corpses the only hope for redemption.[13]

At a superficial level, Ah Q's forgetting is a parody of the modernist will to forget that brings a radical rupture to history and thus suspends the onslaught of the past. Ah Q's forgetfulness, rather than a redemptive trait, simply marks a constitutive flaw, an incapacity for learning, reflecting, watching out for trouble, or avoiding the same mistakes over and over again; it condemns Ah Q to an eternal "all of a sudden" or "for the first time." The prison-house of the now, as the tight, breathless embrace of the timeless past, prefigures Ah Q's death as the ultimate defeat and humiliation of the allegorical hero joining an endless cycle of repetition. In this light, Ah Q's is the radical opposite of modernist forgetting: it is a historicist forgetting constantly and passively awaiting the eternal next moment, next insult, next blow, and the next disaster. Whereas modernist forgetting, like modernist time, is constructive and revolutionary in nature, forging, condensing, and fusing the past, the present, and the future into a tension-charged constellation of an epoch, a monad from which it derives the energy to smash the petrified continuum of history, historicist time is simply there, like Walter Benjamin's "empty homogenous time," yielding nothing other than more time, thus lending itself objectively to the allegorist's contemplation of non-change, which nonetheless has its own ghostly indulgence, ecstasy, and abandon ("Theses"). Ah Q the specter is like a test agent that makes visible the colors of non-change created by the chemical reactions of pseudo-changes in the glass tube of modern Chinese history, a history parodied by the subtitles of various chapters: "From Dynastic Revival to the Fading Days of Empire" (Chapter 6); "Revolution" (Chapter 7); "Request to Revolt Denied" (Chapter 8), all the way to "Grand Reunion" as an "end of history" within the imperial Time-Space that, dialectically, anticipates a true cultural revolution, one marking the beginning of history heralded by the arrival of a new humanity.

The formal deliberateness of *Ah Q* is nowhere demonstrated more forcefully than in its ending, the death of Ah Q. Throughout the story, Ah Q works tirelessly, not for himself in the mundane sense, but heroically for his identity, for his place within the system of names and naming. In an elevated (and ironical) Hegelian way, one can say that Ah Q's is a life-and-death struggle for recognition. Unlike Hegel's dialectic of Lord and Bondsman, where recognition is to be gained from the Other as the mortal enemy faced down in the arena of history (Hegel 111–19), the recognition Ah Q strives for is bestowed by and within one's own cultural norm and symbolic order, as self-identity and identification. This decidedly un-Hegelian struggle for recognition means Ah Q is by design other-driven, and honor- or prestige-motivated, rather than aimed at security and enjoyment (of others' labor). The peculiar Hegelian and Orientalist prejudice that non-Western subjectivity is—by virtue of its being non-European and non-bourgeois (i.e., atheist, non-profit seeking, and no rule of law)—decidedly premodern, turns out to be technically, that is, allegorically, useful for the purpose of a formal-structural analysis of the national allegory of the May

Fourth Era, whose explicit modernist politics uses the images of the modern West to create a metaphysical break from the Chinese past. The ending of the story brings all this to the fore in sharp focus. Ah Q dies a decidedly meaningless and senseless death, but what is important is not the death itself, but what death activates at the moment of its negation of life. The negativity of death breathes into Ah Q the ghost of a kind of life in the modern, individuated sense when he cries out—or at least attempts to—"Help" (*jiuming*, literally, "Save [my] life!").

The end of the story orchestrates Ah Q's death with much fanfare. The passages are conventionally seen as Ah Q's one last show, completing his miserable life as an unselfconscious clown and victim of an oppressive, inhumane, even antihuman society. Such readings necessarily focus on his ludicrous efforts to please the crowd of spectators and the court clerks, including his belabored effort to draw a better circle on his own death sentence—Ah Q does not know how to write—in lieu of a signature. To many, Ah Q's seeming hope to finally win respect by dying with style comes as the ironic climax of his life journey and hence functions as the effective end of the story. This would make sense in terms of conventional character buildup and dramatic closure, but the story is anything but conventional. The elaborate and excessive descriptions of the proceedings of Ah Q's execution only pave the way to a moment of truth when Ah Q, with modernist clarity, bluntness, and intensity, self-consciously faces his imminent death.

One must keep in mind that "Help! Save my life!" is not audibly uttered but exists only as the last thought-language, if not neural-electric shockwave, passing through Ah Q's mind and dwelling on the threshold of becoming language, even if only for a split second. This sudden allegorical intensity marks the belated awakening of Ah Q, but only as he plunges into a nothingness brought upon him by death. This coming-into-being of Ah Q, the May Fourth-style "beginning of Man," takes place and coincides with the dissolution and dispersal of Ah Q as a ghost of the system of names, as its perfect program error. The physical as well as symbolic destruction of Ah Q is described as follows: "But before Ah Q could get ["Help!"] out, everything went black before his eyes, there was a loud ringing in his ears, and he felt his entire being crumble like so much dust" (172). What is striking here is not so much Ah Q's imminent physical and structural dissolution but, once again, his ritualized decomposition into tiny, dustlike particles. Decades and many revolutions later, such a ritual would be performed once again, as the dispersal of the Subject of socialist humanism performed by the post-Mao Chinese avant-garde in its symbolic definition of yet another rupture of history.[14] In such moments, a Self comes into being through its instantaneous deconstruction, but the assemblage of this mind/body unity by its imminent and permanent destruction is also the only placeholder for any meaning, value, identity, and self-consciousness. Death here must be understood in an unapologetically Hobbesian sense as the sudden "violent death"—negating "culture" and "history" and "morality" as mere decadence—that is the ultimate emblem of the state of nature (Hobbes 74–78).

Facing this fusion of culture and history, which exists as the obliterating wildness of natural-history (*Naturgeschichte*) properly speaking (cf. Adorno),[15] Ah Q's final cry of "Help!" is as philosophically and politically poignant as the Madman's cry of "Save the Children!" at the end of *Diary of a Madman*. Both pinpoint a metaphysical rupture and a new beginning—the beginning of History and Man as the supreme ideology of Chinese Enlightenment. But unlike *Madman*'s utopian signal for help, which throws in its lot with an imagined future, Ah Q's last word focuses on and vanishes with the allegorical hero himself. As a silent "voice of the heart" (*xinsheng*) (to use one of the thought-images from Lu Xun's early essays), it begs the question of "Who can and will hear it?" as it threatens to disappear into the other end of the "gate of darkness,"[16] only to be captured by the allegorist as a deep, deafening roar vibrating under all the boisterous speeches and discourses of modern China.

And yet the real story of Ah Q does not stop here. To say Ah Q's sense of himself as a human being is belatedly activated by death is to say that forgetting is, at the end, overcome by memory triggered by Hobbesian fear. Ah Q, the child of Nature as fallen culture, completes his being in his own eternal return of the same, a Buddhist intuition he loudly shares with the large crowd of bystanders who have gathered to watch him die: "Twenty years from now . . ." (170); left unsaid but understood is the defiant assertion, commonly made by condemned criminals: "I will be back as a new man." The birth of Man as envisioned by the May Fourth ideal requires an intervention that breaks and disrupts this cycle, without which no true individuality can be distinguished from the nameless crowd that is an integral part of the natural-historical background. As Ah Q continues to try to please and impress, he is, unexpectedly, shocked and shaken by cheers from the gathered spectators, which sound like the "howls of so many wolves" (170). Of all the possible triggers for the modern individual's "self-consciousness," Lu Xun chooses the least sentimental—the least cultural or historical—namely, the fear of violent death, of one's physical destruction, which alone indicates the allegorical ruthlessness of the author.

The most intensely modernist moment of the story, its true dramatic turning point, is as follows:

> Within an instant, thoughts began to swirl around like a cyclone in his brain. He was taken back to a time four years earlier when he had encountered a hungry wolf at the foot of a mountain. It had stalked him with persistent tenacity, neither closing in nor dropping back by so much as half a step, patiently awaiting its chance to tear into his flesh. Ah Q had been terrified and it was only because he happened to be carrying a small hatchet at the time that he had mustered the courage to make it back to Wei Village. He had never forgotten that wolf's eyes—ferocious and timid at the same time and glowing like two fiendish flames that merged into one nebulous atmosphere, biting on and nibbling at his soul. (170, translation revised)

"Never forgotten" means, of course, "had completely forgotten," which only points to the real but latent content of memory, which, as a form of collective unconscious, and through forgetting, drives Ah Q's cheerful, selfless, misguided, and yet logical pursuit of a name, an identity, a sense of belonging and security within the hollowed, corrupt inner space of the system of naming that is China as a civilizational as well as a natural being. The "awakening" of Ah Q results from the regaining of lost memory and experience and leads to the recognition of dangerous enemies who seek his destruction. The "fiendish flames" of the wolves' gleaming eyes, turning into a misty background, mingle with the apathetic, predatory gaze of Ah Q's fellow villagers, who are responsible not so much for tearing the soul apart as for shaping and programming it in the first place. It is against this background of the natural-historical theater that Ah Q is talked about as a legend—ridiculed, suspected, kicked around, but "permanently recorded on the lips of the people" (*koubei*, which literally means "a monument of mouth," 115). The tortuous rationale for the cautious, guarded respect paid to Ah Q goes like this:

> Though it's true that Ah Q got slapped for claiming to be a clansman of Old Master Zhao, who's to say that there might not be some truth to it? On the off chance that there was, it would still be prudent to treat Ah Q with respect. Or perhaps it may have been related to the example of the Sacrificial Ox in the Confucian Temple. Although the ox is just as much a domestic animal as the pig or sheep, Confucian scholars would not dare commit the blasphemy of eating its meat once the spirit of Confucius had set his chopsticks to it during the sacrifice. (115)

Although Ah Q is denied the recognition and identity he so keenly seeks, his reputation actually always precedes him, separating him from the crowd and placing him under the dazzling limelight of allegorical contemplation—as a sacrificial lamb, a selfless clown, and a modern(ist) hero in one. Compared to his allegorical stature, others in the story are reduced to the faceless herds of the natural-historical swamp, whose rank in the world of allegory is infinitely lower.

Beginning with the name/words distinction or the "rectification of names," a parody of Confucian orthodoxy, and ending with spectators' "disappointment" at a dead man's failure to entertain the public, *Ah Q—The Real Story* builds upon the ironical tension and connection between the preface/introduction and the story proper pioneered by *Diary of a Madman*; it also prefigures the critical distance and reflexivity that unfolds more explicitly in his later stories, such as *New Year's Sacrifice*. The meticulous interweaving through circulation and cross-reference of gossip, reputation, public opinion, spectatorship, the wolves' howls and those gleaming eyes in the dark creates a densely allegorical yet prosaic story about the culture of cannibalism that emblematizes Chinese history in *Diary of a Madman*. It is this particular literary and political intensity that allows *Ah Q—The Real Story* to go beyond an Enlightenment critique of tradition and evolve into the metaphysical and discursive height of a radical and singular modernism.

The cultural-political and political-philosophical implications of such a modernist representation—the self-representation of an ossified culture as fallen nature—is this: in view of Ah Q's "moral" or "psychological victories," understood properly as the systematic self-identification and self-correction of an irreversibly crumbling cultural norm, a collective rectification of the names of a society must step out of the self-enclosed "private language" of self-naming and instead engage in open social and political struggle with the Other within the material history of economic production, class antagonism, and cultural renewal. When it comes to "recognition" as a philosophical issue, Hegel's seminal observation—the truth of the master is the truth of the slave—can only mean its opposite if this contradiction is not grasped in terms of socioeconomic and political substance: with respect to empathy, the truth of the slave is, in fact, the master.[17] Put differently, the new universal, in this case implicit even in Ah Q's longing for identity, respect, and a sense of belonging, can only stem from concrete processes of labor, production, and political struggle that give rise to a new definition of freedom and a new value system. In this light, *Ah Q—The Real Story* is not only a fable of Enlightenment critique and an indictment of tradition—crystallized in the "national soul" of slave mentality, hierarchy, and moral-symbolic excesses and decadence—but also, and in a more enduring way, an allegory of the systematic and symbolic disorder of China as a sovereign producer of meaning and value whose sovereignty was nevertheless increasingly devoid of economic and political substance. It is from the allegorical radicality of the "real story" of the nameless ghost of China, seeking in vain its return and reinvention, that the origin of Chinese modernism surges into being and acquires its formal-aesthetic as well as its political properties and intensities—as a radical, nihilistic phenomenology of decay, void, dispersal, and, dialectically, as renewal, rebirth, and hope.

NOTES

1. Mao Dun, for instance, observed in the 1920s that with every single story Lu Xun devised a new, stylistically and technically innovative style. Mao Dun also set the tone for realist readings of *Ah Q* by maintaining that the story is a "loyal portrayal of an aspect of the Xinhai Revolution, written according to an accurate impression left to him at that time" (36).

2. The May Fourth New Culture Movement, a term that often refers to the 1915–1921 period of cultural and political upheaval in China, takes its name from student protests in Beijing on May 4, 1919, against the perceived weakness of the Chinese government's response to the Treaty of Versailles.

3. The "New Literature" (*xinwenxue*) as an integral part of the May Fourth New Culture Movement is commonly seen as driven by: (1) a social-reformist agenda to break free from traditional values and morality, and to forge a new national character conducive to the modernization of China, which it shared with the larger May Fourth Movement; (2) a more specific linguistic-literary scheme to invent a new language by which to reach the people or the new citizenry, and which requires the practice of a new literature to concretize, popularize, and aestheticize it; and (3) an intellectual-artistic search for and invention of a new vision and a new spirit (individualism, interiority and self-consciousness, romanticism, modernism, etc.), which was to find in New Literature a suitable vehicle and form. While the social-intellectual concerns of New Literature put it squarely in the historical paradigm of romanticism and realism, such conventional literary-historical and literary-critical approaches seem ill-fit to address the radically modernistic stance the New Literature demonstrates vis-à-vis the past as a whole, which gives rise to its metaphysical picture of culture and self; and vis-à-vis its stylistic and aesthetic intensity and self-referentiality, which unfolds more along symbolist-allegorical lines as much as a representational-didactic

line. The present rereading of Lu Xun's *Ah Q—The Real Story* attempts to supplement and complement the existing body of Lu Xun scholarship that, by and large, continues to rely on realist and socio-reformist frames of analysis.

4. Most scholars of contemporary Chinese intellectual history agree that, in contrast to the kind of idealism, political passion, and utopian if hasty impulses of the 1980s, the Chinese 1990s, namely the decade following the Tiananmen Incident of 1989, witnessed a cautious turn to empirical research, positivistic argument, and revisionist historiography, all following professional, even careerist, lines and with a self-conscious retreat from the role of an "intellectual" to that of a "scholar." Even though most regard the divide between "idea" and "scholarship" as unnecessary and unfortunate, such division and dichotomy have come to define the turn between the Chinese 1980s and 1990s.

5. A similar negative-constructivist stance toward the past is deeply embedded in the utopian vision of Chinese New Culture, whose practice, from the anti-Confucian outcries of the Vernacular Revolution to the Maoist will to a "socialist new man" and "permanent revolution," seems to respond to the Nietzschean call: "only if you are architects of the future and are familiar with the present will you understand the oracular voice of the past. . . . By looking ahead, setting yourself a great goal, you will simultaneously subdue that over-exuberant analytical impulse that currently reduces the present to a wasteland and makes all tranquil growth and maturation almost impossible. . . . Create within yourselves an image to which the future should conform, and forget the false conviction that you are epigones. You have enough to ponder and invent by pondering that future life, but do not ask history to show you how and by what means" (130).

6. Cf. Benjamin, *Charles Baudelaire,* especially Part I, "Second Empire in Baudelaire."

7. For example, see Zhi Kejian, "Guanyu Ah Q de geming wenti" (regarding the question of Ah Q's revolution, 1979), in which the author maintains that "as a story representing the peasant question in revolution, *The Real Story of Ah Q* sums up the main lesson of the Xinhai Revolution, which is that for a real revolution to take place in China, there must be real revolutionaries. . . . The peasantry must fight to change the society and their own fate, for which they must change the economy of petty production that had lasted for several thousand years" (853).

8. See Lu Xun's early essays, "Wenhua pianzhi lun"(on deviation of culture, 1907) and "Moluo shili shuo" (on the power of Mara Poetry, 1907), 1: 44–115; and "Po e'sheng lun" (on refutation of the sound of evil), 8: 23–38.

9. For a compelling example, see Levenson, who holds that the demise of Confucian China as a cultural-civilizational empire must seek its redemption in the modern nation-state, and that in this transition Chinese culture may exist only at the level of "vocabulary," while the universal culture of (Western) modernity serves as "grammar."

10. "Shina" is not seen by the Chinese government or general population as a value-neutral place name but as a deliberate jargon that connotes disrespect and a sense of Chinese inferiority relative to Japan's successful modernization following the Meiji Restoration; it also evokes the century-long humiliation of China at the hands of Japanese imperialism, colonialism, and militarism.

11. Lu Xun's *Kong Yiji* is about a downtrodden man living in his fantasy world of being a scholar gentleman. The protagonist's loyalty to an ailing system (of civil service examination) bears family resemblance to Ah Q's obsession with the rectification of names.

12. Lu Xun's "Mourning the Dead" (*Diary of a Madman* 338–62) is about a young couple's failed experiment in free love in the immediate post-May Fourth period. The deceptively simple and even generic story begins and ends with lengthy discussions of forgetting, memory, and the struggle against solitude and the emptiness of existence.

13. "Mourning the Dead" ends thus: "But all these thoughts are even more vacuous than the new roads that appear and then disappear again into the darkness. All that I actually possess at the moment is this early spring night—and it is so long, so very, very long. . . . I must take the first step and make my way silently down that new road, hiding the truth within my heart's deepest wound and taking falsehood and forgetfulness as my guides" (*Diary of a Madman* 361–62).

14. For a textbook example, see Yu Hua, *1986*, which ends with the protagonist's body parts being sent to different labs, an anatomical dissection hailed by critics as a symbolic-ritualistic ending of the Enlightenment and the revolutionary Subject.

15. Benjamin's idea of natural history proves to be highly relevant in understanding Lu Xun modernist stance vis-à-vis tradition: "The word 'history' stands written on the countenance of nature in the characters of transience. The allegorical physiognomy of the nature-history, which is put on stage in the *Trauerspiel*, is present in reality in the form of the ruin. In the ruin history has physically merged into the setting. And in this guise history does not assume the form of the process of an eternal life so much as that of irresistible decay. Allegory thereby declares itself to be beyond beauty. Allegories are, in the realm of thoughts, what ruins are in the realm of things" (*Origin of German Tragic Drama* 177–78).

16. Cf. Lu Xun, "What Is Required of Us as Fathers Today" (jintian zenyang zuo fuqin [1919]), in which one reads: "Burdened as a man may be with the weight of tradition, he can yet prop open the gate of darkness with his shoulder to let the children through to the bright, wide-open spaces, to lead happy lives henceforward as rational human beings" (2: 71).

17. In *Phenomenology of Spirit*, Hegel observes that "the fear of the lord is indeed the beginning of wisdom," and yet the bondsman "through his service . . . rids himself of his attachment to natural existence in every single detail; and gets rid of it by working on it" (117). It can be inferred that without the mediation of work, indeed production in the Hegelian-Marxian sense, "recognition" can only be "one-sided and unequal," with the bondsman "taking the lord as the absolute" (116).

WORKS CITED

Adorno, T. W. "The Idea of Natural History." Trans. Bob Hullot-Kentor. *Telos* 60 (1984): 11–24.

Benjamin, Walter. *Charles Baudelaire: A Lyric Poet in the Era of High Capitalism*. Trans. Harry Zohn. London: Verso, 1973.

——. *Origin of German Tragic Drama*. Trans. John Osborne. London: Verso, 1977.

——. "Theses on the Philosophy of History." *Illuminations*. Ed. Hannah Arendt. Trans. Harry Zohn. New York: Schocken Books, 1968. 253–64.

Confucius. *The Analects*. Trans. David Hinton. Washington, DC: Counterpoint, 1998.

de Man, Paul. *Blindness and Insight*. Minneapolis: University of Minnesota Press. 1983.

Engels, Friedrich. "To Margaret Harkness in London, April 1888." *Marxist Literary Theory*. Ed. Terry Eagleton and Drew Milne. London: Blackwell Publishers, 1996. 39–41.

Hegel, G. W. F. *Phenomenology of Spirit*. Trans. A. V. Miller. Oxford: Oxford University Press, 1977.

Hobbes, Thomas. *Leviathan*. Ed. Edwin Curley. Cambridge: Hackett Publishing Company, 1994.

Jameson, Fredric. "Third World Literature in the Age of Multinational Capitalism." *Social Text* 15 (1986): 65–88.

Levenson, Joseph. *Confucian China and Its Modern Fate*. Berkeley: University of California Press, 1965.

Lu Xun. *Ah Q—The Real Story. Diary of a Madman*. Trans. William A. Lyell. Honolulu: University of Hawaii Press, 1990.

———. "Moluo shili shuo" [On the power of Mara Poetry (1907)]. *Lu Xun Quan Ji* [*Collected work of Lu Xun*]. Vol. 1. Beijing: Renmin wenxue chubanshe, 1980.

———. "Mourning the Dead." *Diary of a Madman*. Trans. William A. Lyell. Honolulu: University of Hawaii Press, 1990. 29–41.

———. "Po e'sheng lun" [On refutation of the sound of evil]. *Lu Xun Quan Ji*. Vol. 8.

———. "Wenhua pianzhi lun" [On deviation of culture]. *Lu Xun Quan ji*. Vol. 1.

———. "What Is Required of Us as Fathers Today" [jintian zenyang zuo fuqin (1919)]. *Lu Xun: Selected Works*. Vol. 2. Trans. Yang Xianyi and Gladys Yang. Beijing: Foreign Languages Press, 2003. 56–71.

———. *Wild Grass*. Trans. Yang Xianyi and Gladys Yang, Hong Kong: The Chinese University Press, 2003.

Lukács, Georg. *The Theory of the Novel*. Cambridge: MIT Press, 1987.

Mao Dun, "Du Nahan" [Reading 'Cheering from the Sidelines']. 1923. Originally published in *Xuedeng, Shishi xinbao wenxue fukan*. 16 October 1923. Cited from *Lu Xun yanjiu xueshu lunzhu ziliao huibian* [Collected scholarly works in Lu Xun studies]. Vol. 1. Beijing: Zhongguo wenlian chuban gongsi, 1985.

Maruo Tuneki. *Lu Xun, the entanglement between man and ghost: a study of Lu Xun's fiction*. Tokyo: Iwanami Publishers. Chinese translation by Qin Gong, Beijing: Renmin wenxue chubanshe, 1995.

Nietzsche, Friedrich. "The Utility and Liability of History for Life." *Unfashionable Observations*. Trans. Richard T. Gray. Stanford: Stanford University Press, 1998. 83–168.

Zhi Kejian. "Guanyu Ah Q de geming wenti." [Regarding the question of Ah Q's revolution]. 1979. *Lu Xun yanjiu xueshu lunzhu ziliao huibian*. Vol. 5, 1949–1983. Beijing: Zhongguo wenlian chuban gongsi, 1989.

CHAPTER 8

NEITHER MIRROR NOR MIMIC: TRANSNATIONAL READING AND INDIAN NARRATIVES IN ENGLISH

JESSICA BERMAN

AT the end of Mulk Raj Anand's celebrated novel *Untouchable*, Bakha, the poor sweeper boy who is its hero, encounters the problem of how to reconcile India's past and its future within contemporary politics. Having attended a speech by Gandhi on the plight of the untouchables, he feels thrilled, emboldened, and almost ready to move to Gandhi's ashram to resume his scavenging there: "Each word of the concluding passage seemed to him to echo as deep and intense a feeling of horror and indignation as his own at the distinction which the caste Hindus made between themselves and the Untouchables. The Mahatma seemed to have touched the most intimate corner of his soul" (149). Yet immediately, Bakha's euphoria is broken by criticism of Gandhi from an English-educated Indian and a poet who pass nearby.[1] Gandhi's perspective is old-fashioned and caught in the fourth century, one of them claims, whereas the "spirit of our age" (150) demands democracy and the machine. The machine, and the modern flush toilet in particular, might even liberate the untouchables from their drudgery and inferior status, as Gandhi cannot. Though he cannot fully understand the debate among these men, Bakha effects his own synthesis of these perspectives, so key to the political debates in late colonial India. "I shall go on doing as Gandhi says," he comments on the final page of the book, meaning that he will continue to perform his work assiduously, but he will also someday "find the poet and ask him about his machine" (157), thereby entering modernity and using its machinery to change his material status.

I evoke this famous scene at the end of one of the best-known novels of late colonial India not simply to paraphrase the arguments about modernity voiced by anticolonial movements in the thirties and forties. Rather, I want to highlight Bakha's synthesis, the culmination of this day-in-the-life novel, as deeply engaged with the question of modernity. What, he seems to ask, can a sweeper boy do, if he is neither willing to give up Gandhi's call to dignity and self-sufficiency (*swadeshi*), nor turn his back on the possibilities of a modern future? How can this novel, caught up in representing Bakha's often naïve yet ever-perceptive point of view, participate in the development of an independent literary tradition for India without rejecting either India's impending modernity or the challenges to narrative fiction that it presents?

In this light, the last episode of *Untouchable* can be seen to mark the complex terrain of Indian fiction in English in the late colonial period, and the place where, I will argue, modernism emerges. In a period of extraordinary growth in the number and variety of narratives being written in English, Indian writers such as the justly celebrated Anand and the sadly out of print Iqbalunissa Hussain forged modernist textual responses to the challenges of India's colonial status, its changing economy, and its modernizing roles for men, women, and their families, and used modernist narration to explore ethical and political perspectives on Indian life. Many of the writers of the period (including Anand, Hussain, Raja Rao, Aubrey Menen, Sudhin Ghose, and others) were educated on the continent and most were well versed in European narrative forms and movements. But the strength of their narrative innovation comes not out of re-creation of continental trends in India, but rather from their ability to use and transform the expectations of such narrative genres as the *Bildungsroman* in specific response to the demands of India in the thirties and forties. In such texts as Anand's *Untouchable*, his second novel, *Coolie*, and Hussain's *Purdah and Polygamy*, I will argue, we can see not only a complex version of modernism that responds to the specific demands of the Indian context, but also an imbrication of narrative experimentalism and political engagement which has much to teach us about modernism writ large.

Most critical discussion about modernism in late colonial India focuses on its lines of transmission from the continent. Along with the "borrowed" form of the English novel, the discussion goes, writers who traveled to Europe or were steeped in its literary traditions also borrowed the tools and attitudes of modernism to represent their Indian situation. Those tools may have been particularly appropriate for the colonial writer who already inhabited a forcibly fragmented, polyglot, and displaced world, and whose experiences were often split between metropolis and homeland. As Salman Rushdie has commented, we might say that within the colonial situation, these writers had modernism thrust upon them (12). Thus, modernism seems already to inhabit the early twentieth-century Indian novel in English as it comes of age, rather than appearing belatedly, as many have claimed, in the postindependence period. Further, as Elleke Boemer puts it, it is important to "recognize that aspects of colonized and colonial expatriate reality were distinctly, perhaps in some cases even definitively modernist. It is also to observe that modernism as a body of discursive

practices was not simply imposed on the Empire. We see in modernism signs of colonial writers critically engaging with the writing of the centre . . . and metropolitan
modernism, in turn, was deeply influenced by the new aesthetic perspectives which
Western expansion across the globe had laid bare" (125). Thus, to try to segregate
Indian modernism as a secondary formation, or to assign it a different time line, is to
denigrate its dialogue with European modernisms of the interwar period and to presume that lines of literary and cultural transmission moved only in one direction
from the metropolis to the colony, rather than from colony back to metropolis, from
colony to colony, or even from language to language within the same colony.

Yet reading the writers of late colonial India *only* in terms of their relationship
to continental modernisms can serve to reinforce the false assumption that modernism radiated from its centers in Paris and London and must always be judged by
reference to the attitudes, modes, and styles in evidence there. If instead we acknowledge with Boehmer, Rushdie, and others—such as Priya Joshi and Sangeeta Ray—
that the work of Indian writers of the 1930s and 1940s engages with matters of
hybridity, displacement, multilingualism, and historical disruption within Indian
contexts—even as it challenges the nature and status of European forms—then we
will not see it as simply mirroring or mimicking the metropolitan canon. When
writers seek new narrative techniques for representing the challenges of a rapidly
changing social world, exploring the problem of subjectivity and citizenship within
a colonial setting, or for working through adjustments in family life and the status
of women, it is not because modernism is forced upon them or that they speak back
to a version imported from afar, but rather that modernist modes arise in response
to social and historical developments in India and within the developing tradition
of Indian writing in English. Taken on their own terms, Indian narratives in English
of the late colonial period reveal strikingly innovative approaches to the twin problems of the development of subjectivity and political engagement that at the same
time also interact with the European literary tradition and challenge our preconceived notions about what modernism can be and do.

Mulk Raj Anand and the Politics of Indian Modernism

Mulk Raj Anand's formation as a writer emerges out of just such a complex combination of influences and interests. Born in Peshawar in 1905 to a family of civil servants, he distinguished himself as a teenager by his studiousness, his extensive
reading in Urdu, Persian, and English (especially the British Romantics), and his
interest in poetry. He began writing poetry at an early age as a disciple of the poet
Iqbal. In the heady period after 1918, Anand got swept up in the growing rebellion
in the Punjab. He was arrested and caned in Amritsar, where his family had been
living, for innocently breaking curfew during the Jallianwalla Bagh Massacre of

1919, one of the most bloody and infamous conflicts in the history of the Raj, in which soldiers opened fire on 10,000 civilians (Cowasjee 9).[2] He was again arrested in 1924 for political activism in Lahore. His father, a government functionary, became infuriated by Anand's involvement in politics and punished Anand's mother in retaliation. To stop this punishment, with money from his mother and his mentor, Iqbal, Anand traveled to London, where he studied philosophy at the University of London while also attending lectures by luminaries such as G. E. Moore and C. D. Broad. His connections within the London literary world brought him into the living rooms of Leonard and Virginia Woolf, and into contact with E. M. Forster, T. S. Eliot, and most of the figures of literary Bloomsbury, though he became increasingly uncomfortable in that milieu. He experienced the 1926 General Strike in London as a watershed event in which he recognized similarities between the British workers and the untouchables in India. As he put it, "not only were the British imperious and strong-minded in the colonies, but [they] also could suppress their own working people" (quoted in Fisher, 17).

But his long and illustrious career as a writer of fiction began in 1922.[3] In that year he first read Joyce, devouring both *A Portrait of the Artist* and *Ulysses* (which he found on a trip to Paris) and discovering in them a new vocation. In his collection of essays, *Conversations in Bloomsbury*, he describes his encounter with Joyce's *Portrait of the Artist as a Young Man*: "[I] recognized myself in the hero of *Portrait*," he says (7). In *Portrait*, Joyce presented not only Stephen Dedalus's inner world, compelling to Anand in its own right, but also, importantly, a version of what was taking place within Anand himself. Comparing Joyce to his mentor, the important Islamic poet Iqbal, and his poetic cycle, *Secrets of the Self*, Anand prefers to follow Joyce, claiming him as a kindred spirit and model, if not strictly a compatriot. He decides that "the portrait is a good model for me, if I want to stage the recovery of self . . . in a novel," and resolves to begin that novel almost immediately. Anand secretly determines to pattern himself after Joyce, taking specific instruction not merely from Joyce's mode of narration and his representation of self-development, but also from his focus on material life rather than a mystical or spiritual world and his use of sound to transmit extra-linguistic meaning in prose (7). From this moment, he begins his effort to forge a new English language tradition in fiction for India.

Untouchable, Anand's first novel (written between 1928 and 1932), grows out of Anand's dialogue with Joyce and his own efforts to create a narrative form that might represent everyday Indian life, especially among the poor, even while pushing toward its political transformation. Rather than look back to Indian folklore or traditional forms, Anand embraces the modernism he encounters in London and, like Bakha, his hero, attempts a synthesis between this modernism and the Gandhian principles of *swadeshi* (self-sufficiency) and *swaraj* (self-rule).[4] A story is often recounted about Anand's efforts to bridge these two positions and about Gandhi's direct influence on this novel, which Anand took with him in 1927, half written, from London to Gandhi's Sabarmati Ashram. The story goes that Gandhi himself edited the manuscript, cutting the excess from it, and insisting that its hero become less of "a Bloomsbury intellectual" (Mehrotra 175). In his description of the event, Anand claims that "I set down to re-write my novel because Mahatma had said that I use too many big English words. I told him that I was under influence of James Joyce. . . . Gandhi had said: you forget all big writers" ("Preface" xi). Though there is no extant manuscript, and Anand himself recounts the story several different ways in his late-life essays, the assumed trajectory of Anand's early career rests on this tale, guiding critics to comment on Anand's return to India as a "decisive shift," a return to authenticity, or what we might call an allegiance to Gandhian *swadeshi*, and an embrace of social realism ("Preface" 11).

Still, clearly, *Untouchable*, like much of the succeeding work, continues to speak to Joyce and the European fiction of the period, which Anand still read and admired. As Paul Saint-Amour has put it, "though the substrate of its first 120 pages is a documentary, 'day-in-the-life' realism, this unfussy surface is warped and ornamented by a boggling variety of other styles, modes, and lexicons, many of which owe recognizable debts to European narrative modes" (5). Bakha is in a distinctly Indian situation, abused by upper-class and British characters, suffering the indignity of being forced by caste to clean latrines for others, and the rejection, even when trying to rescue an injured boy, that his "polluted" status brings upon him. Yet, as many have remarked, Bakha's self-awareness forms the core of the novel, allowing us to look at the material circumstance of his restricted life as focalized through his perceptive though limited eyes and presented from time to time through interior monologue.[5] As Anand said of the work, he had wanted to show Bakha's "unique sensitiveness as against the people of the upper caste who thought that merely touching him is a degradation" (quoted in Fisher, 30).

In the published novel, Bakha could in no way be termed a "Bloomsbury intellectual"; indeed, he is most often described by critics as "naïve." Yet the novel's "one day in the life" structure must certainly be discussed in connection with *Mrs. Dalloway* and *Ulysses*, which we know Anand read and recommended to his friends, as well as in relation to Joyce's emphasis on material existence within the context of a focalized narrative. The novel's triumph is in the combination of the view of its untouchable hero (the complexity of his inner thoughts and emotions, which are often granted guiding power over the narration) and prose that "subtly picks up the dense corporeality and tactility of Bakha's existence" (Mehrotra 177). Like Bakha's synthesis of the perspectives overheard at the end of the novel, which combine Gandhian self-sufficiency with the potential for material relief from the modern machine, Anand's novel merges experimental techniques for presenting the subjectivity of its ordinary hero with the specific and nuanced representation of his particularly Indian, lived experience. Further, as the opening out beyond Bakha's everyday world at the end of the novel makes clear, *Untouchable* draws implications from the circumstances of its ordinary hero to the political situation of India and invites political response from the reader. Not only must we sort through the options presented by Gandhi and his critics at the end of the novel, but we must also recognize the political significance of our attention over the course of the novel to the inner life of an untouchable boy. If Anand sets out to "stage the recovery of self in a novel," he paints that self within the constraints of his material situation, which needs political and social transformation in order for any full recovery to occur.

In Anand's second novel, *Coolie*, the day-in-the-life structure of *Untouchable* is replaced with a more expansive narrative tracing of a character's life history and a deeper exploration of the possibilities of narrative as critique. In *Coolie* we see the young hero Munoo forced out of his home in a hill village and sent to find his way through a number of menial jobs in an extraordinary series of locations throughout India. While working as a servant for a bank official, in a pickle factory, in a cotton mill, or as a rickshaw boy, before his death at age fifteen from consumption, Munoo encounters the entire social fabric of India. He is befriended in unexpected places: among other servants, coolies, and cotton mill workers, but also in the house of the pickle factory owner and in the home of an emancipated Anglo-Indian woman.[6] His coming of age is seen always in the context of the economic hardships that dog him, and his almost picaresque series of adventures become a story of struggle and resiliency. Yet the brilliance of the novel is not in the specific details of the various trials that Munoo is made to face: rather, as in *Untouchable,* it lies in the novel's focus on Munoo's internal life and his struggle to respond to the varieties of discourse that surround him and the power hierarchies associated with them. The novel makes clear that the hero comes of age within a social and discursive sphere that can both raise expectations of self-development and thwart them at the same time.

Much as in *Untouchable*, Anand's style in *Coolie* highlights the limitations of its hero and his possible life trajectory, even as its ironic stance makes us understand its political consequence. The novel is focalized in much the same way as is Joyce's *Portrait*, with a third-person perspective limited to what Munoo can know and understand and which develops over the course of the novel as Munoo grows up. Munoo's lack of experience in the opening chapters, while not quite on the order of Stephen Dedalus's, is strikingly represented in a tone both limited in perspective and deeply ironic. For example, in an early scene that takes place in the house where his uncle leaves him to work as a servant, he is constantly reprimanded because he has no idea of the rules of proper servant conduct and no one bothers to tell him. We follow along with Munoo as he blunders over and over again and is punished. When the lady of the house turns on the gramophone, Munoo wanders in from the kitchen with dripping utensils in hand. "He felt emboldened. He wanted to hear the music, to see and touch the singing machine . . . 'how lucky I am,' he thought, 'that there is a wonder machine in the house where I have come to serve'" (29). Munoo's naïveté guides the narrative here, which can only hint at what he does not understand. He gets carried away by the music and begins to dance around on all fours like a monkey, but Munoo is completely unaware that he is literally fulfilling the expectation of the lady of the house, who has been calling him a monkey all along. A few pages later, the same dynamic of subservience is played out at the Bank of India between the householder and his boss, aptly named Mr. England, whom he has invited to tea. The household does its utmost to impress the Englishman, who recoils in disgust at their food and cannot wait to leave. By the end of the scene, however, it is he who has been called "monkey-faced" (55) by the highly educated Indian doctor who lives there. The ironic stance of the narrative is such that only we as readers are aware of the many levels operating here; for Munoo, our eyes and ears, the visit of the Englishman is all spectacle. This scene highlights the layering of irony in the novel, which, like the rest of Anand's work, is too often simplified by being called "social chronicle" (Mehrotra 177).

Like Joyce's *Portrait*, this complex novel makes use of the expectations of the *Bildungsroman* to acknowledge, appropriate, and critique social and political expectations. In other words, Anand plays on the expected coincidence between the hero and his epoch, which in most *Bildungsromane* grants the hero world historical significance, in order to highlight the limitations Munoo must face. As Bakhtin puts it, in the *Bildungsroman*,

> [the] hero emerges *along with the world* and he reflects the historical emergence
> of the world itself. He is no longer within an epoch, but on the border between
> two epochs, at the transition point from one to the other. This transition is
> accomplished in him and through him. (22)

In *Coolie*, Munoo is not only limited in the degree to which he can undergo the kind of individuation and self-development expected of the hero, but he is also dramatically restricted in his ability to matter to the political world. If *Coolie* shows us the difficulty of Munoo's coming of age, his constant reinscription into a subservient position, even as he gains insight into his self and status, it is in order to demonstrate how much that difficulty has to say about India's social hierarchies and colonial status. Anand twists the expectations of the *Bildungsroman* in order to critique its assumptions not only about self-development and heroism but also about the sources of epochal transition and the development of the nation.

Coolie also raises questions about the status of the "universal man" within the *Bildungsroman* tradition and his relationship to political citizenship, nationality, and human rights. Its emphasis on Munoo's poverty and his social exclusion serves to foreground the matter of who has access to subjecthood and civic citizenship in a more direct and far-reaching manner than Joyce's critique in *Portrait*. Anand's engagement with his late colonial Indian context enables him to highlight, in *Coolie*, the material conditions of everyday life for the very possibility of a hero's self-development, while also making clear the connections between the *Bildungsroman* and assumptions about universal liberal citizenship. Moretti describes the goal of the *Bildungsroman* as the idea of the final synthesis of self and normative world into the "free individual of liberalism," a universal model of subjectivity and political citizenship (16). This universal man becomes the world-historical individual, who aspires to the rights and responsibilities of civil life and whose development parallels the emergence of the nation-state. The *Bildungsroman* emerges alongside the development of enlightenment liberalism, coincides with and contributes to the development of modern versions of nationality, and its heroes can often be seen to stand as heroic emblems of their nations. Bakhtin puts it in a different way, writing of Goethe: "his creative imagination is also restricted and subordinated to the *necessity* of a given locality, the iron-clad logic of its historical and geographical existence" (37). The intrusion of the imperial or colonial situation into the tradition, however, serves to interrupt not only the *Bildungsroman* itself but also the model of the nation that is figured there. As Jed Esty puts it,

> Colonial modernity unsettles the discourse of national culture by breaking up its
> cherished continuities linking a people to its language, its territory, and its
> political history. It is not just the accelerating pace of economic and technological
> change that has this effect, nor even the values conflict between, for example,
> Britain's liberal heritage and the New Imperialism, but also—and more directly to
> the narratological point—it is that imperialism brings the bildungsroman and its
> humanist ideals into the zone of uneven development, breaking the Goethean
> bond between biographical and "national-historical time." (76)

Further, Joseph Slaughter makes clear that *Bildung* is often configured as the very process of "civicization" by which the subject becomes able to "express itself through the media of the nation-state and citizenship" (1409). The process can be dialogic. The *Bildungsroman* can serve as a place for critique of the political structure, as Slaughter makes clear: "the *Bildungsroman* has the dual capacity to articulate claims of inclusion in the rights regime and to criticize those norms and their inegalitarian implementation" (1411). But the assumption of a universalizable man, in whom human rights and citizenship inhere, and who has access to the very project of *Bildung*, is still presumed. For Munoo, perpetually caught in a category of people considered "coolies" and excluded from the possibility of civic citizenship both by virtue of his class and his colonial status, *Bildung* in the traditional sense seems impossible. The hero cannot even dream of development. Beginning from his character's inseparability from his class, inability to become the universalizable man, and exclusion from the very project of "civicization," Anand's *Coolie* thus accomplishes a wide-ranging critique of the *Bildungsroman* mode that extends Joyce's critique in *Portrait*.

But it is not simply the setting of *Coolie* or its hero's insertion into the disrupted civic sphere of late colonial India that accomplishes Anand's critique of the *Bildungsroman*. Just as Joyce's *Portrait of the Artist* employs linguistic play in order to mark the places where its hero might escape definition within the discourses of power surrounding him, so in *Coolie* language often threatens to exceed the boundaries of direct signification and, in so doing, signals the possible disruption of the social and political regimes that restrict Munoo. The matter of the uncontrollability of words and the impossibility of restricting their meaning even within the multiple power hierarchies surrounding them play a crucial role in Anand's alternative political logic. At the textual level language itself often escapes limitation to strict meaning-making and operates by other principles. This is what Derrick Attridge, echoing Derrida, has identified in the Joycean context as "the remainder, that aspect of language's functioning, which in spite of its necessity is often repressed from our consciousness," and that we can often identify in certain varieties of literary modernism (66). Sound often takes the place of semiotics as the focus of language use, with the result that another level of play complicates the social terrain our hero must traverse. As Attridge points out, there are many moments in *Portrait* where nonsense, or repetition, or rhythm and melody emerge (68). This is precisely what Anand responds to in pointing out the musicality of Joyce's language as an important element that connects them. As he puts it, "the sound of the words dictating sense" in Joyce's writing was like his "mother's mumbo-jumbo prayers" (*Conversations* 7). We know from Anand's autobiography that this was not a criticism, since he loved listening to his mother's Sikh prayers, which were in a language he did not understand. So, when the first three paragraphs of *Coolie* each begin with the repeated utterance of a version of its hero's name, "Munoo ohe Munooa oh Mundo" (7), turned into a musical mantra—much like the schoolboys' shouts of "stephaneforus" in *Portrait*—we know that we are being asked to attend to the "remainder," to the level of language use that escapes semiotics and the control of the user and that can confuse or resist conventional discursive authorities.[7]

These kinds of moments appear regularly throughout *Coolie*—as frequently as in *Portrait*—though in forms derived from Indian vernaculars and religious utterances rather than from Joyce's Irish context. Sometimes it is in the form of a cry of fear or surprise uttered by Munoo as he is accosted or derided; other times it is in the form of a string of abuse not meant to be interpreted literally: "ohe you seducer of your daughter!" (143); "you illegally begotten . . . you son of a pig" (154). Still other times it is the rhythmic repetition of syllables or sounds, which add extra dimension to the connotative power of speech. It becomes, however, directly political in the climactic scene when the union leader Sauda exhorts the factory workers to strike and the crowd calls back "Shabash! Shabash! Sauda Sahib!" (Bravo! Bravo! Sir sauda!) (260). Here the political importance of linguistic remainder emerges as the workers begin to take on force through their appropriation of a mode of meaning-making not within the purview of conventional systems of discursive power. This speech is in many ways the climax of the novel and one of its most moving moments, as we sense the potential for collective action among the disenfranchised crowds and see Munoo rise to real engagement. Despite the fact that the authorities successfully break up the strike by pitting Hindus against Muslims, it unites the workers—or, more broadly speaking, the coolies—as possessors of the remainder—of play, of the power of language outside the bounds of authority, and of layers of meaning not glimpsed by their British and Indian overlords.

The unusual quality of language in Anand's fiction has also been marked as crucial to the development of Indian writing in English and its representation of India's linguistic diversity. As Feroza Jussawalla points out, in the 1930s and 1940s the question of what kind of language might best be used to represent Indian experience in literature becomes a crucial subject of debate (*Family Quarrels*). Critics take R. K. Narayan to task, for example, for using English almost exclusively, especially when at times his English seems either stilted or impoverished (Jussawalla 70–75). Others defend the unusual syntax or vocabulary in Narayan's work as an effort at representing Tamil speech patterns within an English language narrative. As one critic puts it, "Narayan's novels are so satisfyingly Indian perhaps because they are so authentically South Indian . . . through skillful use of the English language he delineates people whose actions, behaviour, and responses are shaped by a language different from English" (Jussawalla 74).

Anand, however, in those moments of nonliteral meaning-making in which the remainder emerges, also takes a significant step toward the incorporation of local languages and habits of speech into English language writing. At times he attempts to translate Hindi and Punjabi phrases into English; at other moments what emerges is a representation of the sound of that language in English, without concern for its absolute intelligibility. As he puts it,

> I found, while writing spontaneously, that I was always translating dialogue from the original Punjabi into English. The way in which my mother said something in the dialect of Central Punjab could not have been expressed in any other way except in an almost literal translation, which might carry over the sound and sense of the original speech. (quoted in Jussawalla, 84)

At other times Anand will mix the two languages, putting snippets of English within a Hindi phrase or vice versa. He incorporates new coinages without apology, arguing in his essay "Pigeon-Indian: Some Notes on Indian Writing in English" that the real everyday use of a combined language, no matter whether it is transparent in meaning or not, ought to be represented in the fiction that emerges out of India.

Anand's resistance to verbal transparency and his synthesis of more than one language often engender critical responses that try to reinforce the values of mimetic realism and verisimilitude.[8] Yet it is inadequate to describe these quasi-Hindi, quasi-English moments in Anand purely in terms of verisimilitude. However important they may be to the development of a new vernacular in India, they are equally crucial as moments of disruption and play and mark the text in that sense as "modernist." Further, if the new "pigeon-English" of the Coolie or the Untouchable cannot be assimilated into either the standard English of Empire or the Hindi of a caste-conscious India, then it contains the possibility of resistance to both. This neither/nor language provides the moment of potential power for those shut out of conventional hierarchies, since it creates its own system of signification. Thus, this use of language—of style, if you will—carries heavy political and social weight here. It belies the truism that engaged writing lacks interest in stylistics and that political novels tend toward stripped down realism. It also expands the political dimension of our understanding of style in *Coolie*. What escapes control in Anand's novel is Munoo, the coolie, positioned as he is outside the rubric of the representative man, yet at the heart of the orphan nation. If we see Anand's *Coolie* as very definitely and dramatically an anticolonial novel because it musters the forces of a revised model of *Bildung* to the side of an orphaned laborer, and because it presents the many layers of discourse within a highly focalized novel as still leaving a remainder that might be the domain of the disenfranchised, then we might also read those elements as key to Anand's synthesis of modernist writing and the Indian political struggle.

MODERNISM AND THE ZENANA: IQBALUNNISA HUSSAIN'S *PURDAH AND POLYGAMY*

For women writing in India during this period, the terms and conditions of self-development are still more fraught, even as the problem of how to incorporate the hero into the community presents a more complicated matter of civic polity. Writers in the late colonial period like Iqbalunnisa Hussain, G. Ishvani, and Mumtaz Shah Nawaz also engage in complex ways with the conventions of narrative fiction and the *Bildungsroman*, and develop an intersecting critique of genre and gender roles that helps resist women's social and political disenfranchisement. By focusing on the complexity of life in the zenana (or women's sphere), these writings posit an inherent connection between the politics of the domestic sphere and the traditional figure of "mother India." By placing domestic servants and secluded women at the center of their narratives, women writers in late colonial India not only raise questions about narrative voice and authority and the representative status of the *Bildungsroman*'s hero, but also challenge the public/private, modern/traditional dichotomies that carry heavy political weight in the period. Their writings thereby also challenge the prevailing notion that the political contest for India is a struggle for control of public (not private) space. Narratives by Hussain, G. Ishvani, Shah Nawaz, and others suggest that women need not leave the zenana to raise public concerns, and that they often exhibit their modernity by way of their very participation in traditional sites and practices. Like Anand's *Coolie*, these narratives by Indian women of the period use formal innovation as a means toward engagement in the political struggle over the role of women in India's impending modernity, thus bringing formal innovation to bear on the exigencies of late colonial life.[9]

The major histories of Indian literature identify only a handful of women writers in this period, and those, like Sarojini Naidu—often called the Nightingale of India—are noted more for their politics than for their writings.[10] K. R. Srinivasa Iyengar's classic book on Indian writing in English treats all women novelists together in one chapter and remarks that "it is only after the second world war that women novelists of quality have begun enriching Indian fiction in English" (438). The writings of Iqbalunnisa Hussain, once referred to as "the Jane Austen of India," are out of print and unavailable (Reddy 1).[11] It is thus surprising to discover that many women participated in the development of Indian writing in English in the twentieth century, and that their narratives exhibit extraordinary range and candor about the situation of women in late colonial India.

These narratives by women also ask us to reconsider the role of women in Indian responses to modernity and to examine the various modes of political engagement that they evidence. As Gaytri Spivak, Sangeeta Ray, Antoinette Burton, and others have argued, ideas of nationality and culture in India during the period of colonialization and early independence often depict a feminized and domesticated nation brought under scrutiny within the masculine sphere of public discourse and reform.[12] Commentary by a wide range of public voices in the period characterize India as feminine, connected to the home and to an idealized past, while the role of public women was often sanctioned by their concern for domestic affairs. Much of the discourse surrounding the modernization of Indian domestic life in the first decades of the twentieth century contains the assumption that modernity is being foisted on Indian households from outside and must either be resisted as a force of imperialism or embraced as a means around it. Modernization becomes double edged, promising education, progress, and global connection, while often seen as Westernized, dangerously violent, and spiritually disruptive. The home in these critiques also becomes the space for resistance to modernity's discontents.

By contrast, in one of the most striking narratives of its period, Iqbalunnisa Hussain's 1944 *Purdah and Polygamy: Life in an Indian Muslim Household* (sadly, out of print), the domestic world takes center stage as the location not only of conflict over modernization, but also as one of its generative forces. The novel foregrounds the matter of space, and in particular domestic space, as the crucial matrix not only of female coming of age but also of India's impending modernity. If not quite "laborator[ies] for social experimentation," as were the private homes of British modernists such as Virginia Woolf, the domestic spaces for Hussain and other late colonial Indian women writers held the possibility of new arrangements of family life with profound social and political implications for late colonial India.[13] As in Virginia Woolf's work, shifting attention to the nuances of identity and power within this domestic sphere also meant expanding notions of narrative structure, and refocusing the conventions surrounding plot, action, and the development of subjectivity in the novel. In Hussain's *Purdah and Polygamy*, the matter of purdah, or of the female role in Indian households more generally, is no longer beyond reproach, nor is a modernized female identity within the home inconceivable, and the narrative that emerges reflects the complexity and nuance of the evolving private sphere. The novel refuses the absolute dichotomy of home and world even as it negotiates strategies of female development in and around the constant surveillance of the domestic compound, generating a complex modernist narrative that revolves around the coming of age of several women at once. It thereby resists the reinscription of the model of the nation as embodied in the traditional domestic woman and posits instead the possibility that a plural or communal model of female *Bildung* might emerge from the zenana.

To begin, *Purdah and Polygamy* seems most obviously to respond to the tradition of the English novel. Compared by one commentator to a novel by Jane Austen, the novel introduces us to the compound of a modernizing Muslim household that conveys much about its inhabitants, just as the description of Mansfield Park or Pemberley in Austen's novels introduces crucial information about characters and relationships. The house itself, "an imposing building, standing in the heart of a city" that "commanded respect and awe," holds clues to the family within: it was "peculiar . . . like its inhabitants" (1). Yet, by the third sentence we also learn "its high blind walls made a stranger take it for an unguarded jail, and literally it was so for its women folk." If the inhabitants are to be understood by reference to the physical structure of the compound, then by the third sentence of this novel we know that the place is not benign and that the women within are prisoners. The awe-inspiring view from the outside belies the constrained and supervised view from within, and the novel fluctuates regularly between the two.

The quick passage from one perspective to the other in this opening paragraph also highlights the novel's sophisticated use of irony, employed much as in Anand's *Coolie*, as a tool for critique. We might call this extended use of irony for the purpose of critique a mark of the novel's modernist impulses, extending as it does throughout the narrative into every level of the text. While on its surface, *Purdah and Polygamy* presents a dispassionate description of the family that inhabits this compound, through use of free indirect style to represent the characters' points of view, through allusion to outmoded, extreme, or ill-conceived habits of education and religious expression, or through occasional overt criticism by the narrator, the narrative constantly undermines the practices of this household. The comparison to Jane Austen is in some ways apt: Hussain, like Austen, presents her social commentary under what appears to be the realist surface of a novel of domestic life. The opening line of Chapter V, "It is a well known fact that man is superior to woman in every respect" (49), makes explicit reference to the opening line of *Pride and Prejudice*. Yet the narrator of Hussain's *Purdah and Polygamy* is bolder in her condemnation of the world of her characters, alluding to the "plight" of the women in this compound (1). The plot of the novel, as it unfolds, makes clear that these characters will not redeem themselves or overcome their limiting situation. Though we may come to feel sympathy for its heroine, Nazni, there is little in her to admire at the outset and still less by the end of the novel, when we learn that after her mother-in-law's death she will perpetuate the polygamous household system and the power structure that has formed her. The 1944 foreword to this novel points out that Hussain "deals with the ordinary, the familiar, not with the romantic and heroic," yet castigates her for the "fervour of a moral and social purpose which sometimes leads her to didactic outpourings" (1). But we can see in this novel an extraordinary attempt to narrate what the author of the foreword calls "social purpose" by way of an "unsparingly ironic" tone (De Souza and Pereira). Under the unflinching gaze of the narrator in this novel, both men and women of the compound are seen as deeply limited. Their way of life, along with its understanding of Islam, its insistence on purdah, and its unreflective espousal of polygamy, is placed under indictment, and the only possibility of an ethical or just situation must emerge through the ironic undermining of the unified narrative perspective and the multiplicity of points of view that develop by the end.

At the same time, *Purdah and Polygamy* shares with the work of other English language writers of the period, such as Anand, Narayan, and Rao, concern with the everyday lives of nonelite people and with their connection to the broad contexts of late colonial Indian politics. We are accustomed to remark of European modernism that it breaks conventions in its championing of the everyday and its interest in ordinary heroes. Modernist writing in late colonial India is perhaps even more direct in its connection of interest in the everyday to public politics. If for Rao the village of Kanthapura in his eponymous novel provides the setting for the emergence of Gandhian political virtues, and the ordinary women and men there become the vehicles for a powerful wave of public activism, for Hussain the domestic sphere might have potential to be the location for activism on behalf of women and for changes in the everyday private lives of Muslim families. The novel focuses around the power relationships within the zenana and the importance of such domestic affairs as marriage agreements, sleeping arrangements, kitchen chores, and child-care, making clear that these are serious and complex affairs that determine the lives of women. In placing women's daily conflicts in the kitchen and their efforts at em-powerment at the center of the novel, she invites an implicit juxtaposition with the many public struggles for education, economic self-sufficiency, and self-rule that surround the writing and publication of this novel.

Still, the narrator's modernist, ironic tone undermines any inclination to cast these women as potential models for Mother India or to mark the zenana as the center of nostalgia for traditional Indian life. The novel resists espousing traditional domesticity as a virtue to hang onto and the home as the bastion of resistance to modernity, in part because Hussain depicts the Muslim home in this novel as only barely affected by modernization. If, as Burton claims, in this period the kitchen becomes the site for a contest over modernization, in the kitchen of the compound in *Purdah and Polygamy* the contest has barely begun. The kitchen in this novel functions as the central place of surveillance, where wives must be present, visible, and subject to the controlling gaze of the mother-in-law. Despite the possibilities it holds for female-centered, communal awareness, the shared and central kitchen, as in the rest of the sequestered female quarters of the compound, remains throughout the majority of the book the place of most resistance to modernization or change.

Hussain's biography and political writings serve as intertexts here to expand and elucidate the critique of the practices of both purdah and polygamy in this novel. Hussain was herself raised in strict purdah, married at age fifteen and had several children before becoming the first female graduate of the Mahrani College in Mysore in 1930. She studied further in England and became deeply involved in the education of Muslim girls and women, founding an Urdu girl's middle school and a teacher's association for Muslim women when she returned. Although the record of her life has been mostly erased, we know that in 1935 she traveled to the International Women's Congress in Istanbul, spoke on education in London and in Mysore, and became a member of the All India Women's Congress, one of the most important national women's organizations of the late colonial period.[14]

Hussain published her lectures, along with other articles she wrote for newspa-pers like *The Deccan Times* and *The Eastern Times*, in a 1940 collection entitled *Changing India: A Muslim Woman Speaks*. That volume includes essays on the dif-ference between the principles of Islam and the practices of Mohammedanism, on the position of women in Islam, and the differences between Muslims and Hindus, as well as position pieces discussing the obstacles that purdah presents to social progress, the effect of early marriage on Indians, and the principle that "There is no

Polygamy in Islam." She reserves her harshest words for the overly ritualized practices of what she called Mohammedanism, which differs from Islam in that it does not adhere to scriptural tenets and "lays fixed religious dogmas and sets a rigid spiritual truth" (3). These dogmas form the basis of the practice of both rigid purdah and polygamy, for which she finds no support in the spiritual texts. As the writer of the foreword to *Changing India* puts it, "her main objective has been to release the women of India and particularly the women of the Indian Muslim world from the state of ignorance and quiescent resignation which false tradition has imposed on them" (iii). Thus, when the first chapter of *Purdah and Polygamy* raises the question of the family's religious practice and highlights their lack of concern for spiritual education, it is to alert us to the problems inherent in this kind of "Mohammedan" Muslim household and to the falsity that Hussain believes undergirds it.

Purdah and Polygamy also asks us to reexamine our assumptions about women's experience of coming of age in the early twentieth century and to revise our expectations of a female *Bildungsroman*. The novel participates in the development of a subgenre of coming-of-age narratives in which the heroine often travels no farther than to her husband's compound, her personal challenges may come from within the family unit rather than from without, and the matter of growing independence requires negotiation with the strict surveillance of enclosure.[15] Susan Fraiman argues, in *Unbecoming Women*, that the female novel of development in Britain often contains "counternarratives" that work against a unilinear, encompassing model of appropriate self-development for women, often including indecorous or "unbecoming" women who disrupt the assumptions of the *bildungsroman* (xi). Lorna Ellis argues that, for most heroines of British *Bildungsromane*, "learning to understand and work within the limits of society simultaneously forces the heroine to decrease her sphere of action and to 'grow down'" (18). The difference in *Purdah and Polygamy* is that the disruption of the indecorous woman and the danger of growing down instead of up become the subject of a deeper level of ironic critique that I would term modernist. The novel both depicts and works to undermine the status of the polygamous household it presents, revising the conventions of *Bildung* and, in particular, its focus on the self-development of an individual hero (even when that implies a devolution). If the traditional *Bildungsroman* takes a hero, separates him from his family, and subjects him to a series of trials and tribulations along his journey to maturity, *Purdah and Polygamy* places the struggle toward development within the home and behind the purdah screen, never shows its heroines by themselves, and ends with recognition of the intersubjectivity of female life within the zenana. In developing multiple points of view as the basis for female agency in a polygamous household, *Purdah and Polygamy* offers a modernist model of a plural female *Bildungsroman* that not only revises the expectations that have emerged from the Euro-focused canon, but also helps imagine possible new roles for women within modern India.

Within the novel *Purdah and Polygamy*, however, female development always takes place within the context and exigencies of the domestic realm. The problems of women's domestic spaces, their status, and their bodies are intricately interwoven and tied to the question of familial progress and modernization. It is clear that a successful wife is defined by a body that will submit to supervision, domestic service, and strict enclosure while retaining its strength and beauty. The matter of polygamy in this novel represents the family's quest for such a woman/body and stands as commentary about the futility of such a search, especially in the modern era, when matters of religion, commerce, and domestic economy are shifting.

After the death of the father in the household, his widow, Zuhra, moves quickly to marry off her son, Kabeer. A suitable wealthy girl is chosen, and Kabeer, who has not been consulted, becomes obsessed with her beauty: "He was worried about her physical beauty. The question of temperament never struck him" (31). His new wife Nazni is a beauty, who at times is described as "looking like Venus" (560), yet marriage has a clear bodily affect on her. As a new bride in her husband's home, she must restrain herself physically, making her presence in the home negligible: "She was not expected to open her eyes in her husband's house for five weeks and not to talk for about two months . . . . She was not expected to eat more than a morsel" (48). In fact, this physical self-abnegation becomes permanent as Nazni almost immediately becomes ill in pregnancy, retreats to her parents' house, gives birth, and is diagnosed with heart disease. The narrative makes clear that her illness is in part a physical response to her marriage and her enclosure in Kabeer's family compound: "[S]he felt better in her mother's house. As soon as she returned home her illness reappeared" (64). Her mother-in-law, who has counted on her new daughter to be present in the kitchen on a daily basis and to take on the cooking, is immediately full of disdain. Once Nazni has removed herself from the kitchen and the compound and shows her body to a male doctor, she considers Nazni an unsuitable wife and immediately plans Kabeer's second marriage.[16] Because Nazni's body is unruly in so many ways, she is cast off as Kabeer's primary wife.

Within the space of four pages, Kabeer marries a second wife, Munira, a lower caste girl whose family has conspired to hide her ugliness from her prospective mother-in-law. If Nazni is described as "small, thin and delicate," (64), Munira is "dark, with deep-pock marks, and her upper teeth projected prominently" (70). As Zuhra tells her, "you have neither beauty nor wealth . . . . Your only weapons are your strength and spirit" (73). From the moment she arrives she is constantly on the move, cleaning, cooking, and serving Kabeer and Zuhra, which ingratiates her to her mother-in-law, if not to her husband. Though she manages to seduce him once, carefully closing her lips over her protruding teeth as she smiles, he disdains her, referring to her as an "ape" and "the negress" (100–01). Zuhra rejoices in having a daughter-in-law who obeys her meekly and works "vigorously" (99), but Kabeer responds to her color, her looks, and her energy as animalistic and unbefitting of his wife. While it is clear that Munira fits the servile role of wife better than Nazni and that her body is better able to sustain the rigors of becoming a mother, her darkness and lack of beauty nonetheless mark her as unfit. Ironically, neither woman embodies what a "wife" is meant to be in this household. In fact, as the narrative makes clear, the expectations of women, to be both able housekeepers and frail tremulous creatures, vigorous and yet contained, companionable and yet willingly servile, are contradictory and impossible to fulfill. The commentary on polygamy in this novel results from Kabeer's endless quest to find the embodiment of a wife who doesn't exist. Thus, *Purdah and Polygamy* creates a more obvious and explicit counter-narrative to the *Bildungsroman* than those that, as Fraiman points out, are implicit in novels such as *Jane Eyre* and *Villette*.

The inner rooms of the compound and the kitchen become contested territory as a third wife, Mahgbool, is added to the polygamous household and rooms are shifted. The architecture of private life thus comes to play a role in the possibilities for development among the compound's inhabitants and its confrontation with the modern idea of private spaces. The supervision of behavior within the communal enclosed spaces becomes paramount since, as a sign of his escape from his mother's control, Kabeer moves out of the house and into his offices. Zuhra, his mother, changes her quarters so she can observe and control the compound with almost panopticon-like discipline, but, despite her constant watching and peeking through keyholes, she is unable to retain full control. The third wife, Mahgbool, is figured as the counterpoint to Munira since she is active and vigorous, but competent, learned, and worldly—that is, like a man rather than a servant—and as such cannot fulfill the role of ideal wife any more than can Munira.

> She was an institution in herself. Her mastery over the Urdu language had made her crazy after papers, magazines, romance and poetry . . . . She was a good organizer and an economical manager of the house . . . . Her father often said that she was as a son to him, his secretary and his right hand. She was active and hated to while away her time . . . . Everything she did was self-learnt. (189)

Unlike the other women in the household, Mahgbool benefits from the modern monetary economy and from Kabeer's willingness to sell off his patrimony for ready cash. The fact that she receives pocket money not only makes her able to purchase food rather than cook it in the kitchen (thus removing herself from identification with that space), but it also further defines her as modern, masculinized, and connected to the bourgeois economy that the household rejects for women. As Munira puts it, when hearing of Mahgbool's bank account, "How disgraceful! Then all the men know your name. It is only bad women's names come to the notice of men" (197). Mahgbool not only does not recoil at the idea of her name being known, she spends her money on the publication of a collection of her own poetry with her name attached, which she hopes will make the family fortune (242), thus underscoring both her usurpation of masculine roles and her connection to the modern economy. Mahgbool is further marked as an unsuitable wife when her body is scarred in a kitchen accident. Zuhra sees Kabeer sneak expensive medicines to her, recognizes Mahgbool as a body she cannot control through her vigilance, and uses her knowledge to reassert her authority over her son, her surveillance of the inner compound, and the reestablishment of codes of gendered conduct. By the time Mahgbool's wounds have healed, the potential of her modernity to smash the complacency of the zenana and disrupt the gendered roles of the entire household has been both revealed and contained, and she is ostracized almost into nonexistence.

The remaining chapters of the book succumb to a disorder of both plot and structure that mirrors the disorder of this household. But the signs of narrative "disorder"—interruption of order, acceleration of temporal progress, shifts in point of view, gaps in knowledge—which grow in the final chapters of this novel are also visible earlier in the narrative and demonstrate the challenge of this important text. The moments when, in earlier chapters, the reader is dropped suddenly, through free indirect style, into the minds and voice of a character, or when, between chapters, the narrative goes back in time and starts forward again from a different perspective, demonstrate experimental techniques meant to disrupt the calm surface of a mimetic narrative, just as the increasingly unregulated activities in the household belie the calm exterior of its enclosure walls. Between Chapter VIII and IX, for example, when Nazni's family first learns of Kabeer's second marriage, the perspective shifts: "Nazni's family thought about the remarriage very differently from Kabeer's people" (112). The narrative drops back in time, before the events that take place at the end of the previous chapter, and then moves forward again in Nazni's parents' household, as though the disynchronous perspectives demand a similarly disynchronous time frame. Nazni's brother embraces a modernized perspective on women's roles, defends Nazni's "rights" (116) and considers it a "blessing to make a woman independent and strong" (115), arguing that she should not be forced to return to the zenana. The novel employs this structural innovation in order to highlight the conflict between modernity with its language of civic identity and citizenship and a false attachment to the residual formation of polygamous Islam.

At several other points, *Purdah and Polygamy* jumps from one perspective to another, quickly elides time, or unapologetically presents gaps in knowledge or in causality. From the moments when Zuhra's perspective on marriage invades the narration ("Why do people bring daughters-in-law if not to have real and well-earned comfort?" [50]) to the scene of dispute over Nazni's trip to the cinema, where the narration skips abruptly back and forth from Kabeer's conversation with his mother to his discussion of this conversation with Nazni (62), to the elision of the years before the final episodes, the novel often departs dramatically from the realism evoked by its connection to Austen. These vagaries elicit an apology from the author of the forward, who attributes them to Hussain's lack of knowledge of the language (Foreward, 4). Yet, her *Changing India*, written several years before *Purdah and Polygamy*, exhibits an extraordinary fluency of expression in English, making it unlikely that the novel's disruptions are the result of her inabilities in the language. Rather, I would argue, they show us the reverse: Hussain's competence in English allows her to use word choice, narrative structure, emplotment, and experimentation with narrative perspective as vehicles for her critique of zenana life. If modernity creeps into the novel through the byways—through Nazni's mobility, through Maghbool's authorship and financial independence, through the changing architecture and use of the rooms in the compound, and through the final disruption of the calm surface of zenana life—then it also invades the style and structure of the novel, making it vastly different, in the end, from a Muslim remake of *Pride and Prejudice*.

At the same time, these disruptions of formal unity and use of multiple perspectives pair with the novel's trenchant critique of polygamy to undermine the dogma of the traditional *Bildungsroman* in a manner that connects it to the modernist critiques of Joyce, Woolf, and Anand, among others. If the opening of the novel makes clear that the heroines will be expected to experience their coming of age within the confines of the household, obviating the possibility of any outward journey of discovery, the rest of the novel works to disrupt expectations of singular self-development. The problem cuts both ways: the impossible demands of the polygamous household make it impossible for any single woman to rise to the status of ideal wife, therefore creating an expectation that a community will replace the individual as the female "heroine" of the novel. At the same time, the novel constantly undermines any attempt to recuperate the individual woman as the locus of self-knowledge or the synthesis of Islam with modernity; Maghbool's utter failure and abrupt departure from the household is a clear case in point. Rather, the novel seems to want to present another alternative, a communal female perspective that might arise from within the household, behind the purdah screen, but nevertheless escape from the strict "Mohammedanism" that Hussain so condemned. By multiplying perspectives and shifting among the women, *Purdah and Polygamy* raises the possibility that a changing order within the household, where the strict surveillance and male focus is replaced by female interaction and independence from men, might lead to development and empowerment for its women even within the domestic sphere. If, after the death of both Kabeer and his mother at the end of the novel, Nazni "inherits" the position as head of the zenana, she is seen as constrained and mediated by the other female voices around her in a way that her mother-in-law was not. Thus, the novel's ironic narrative stance, its multiplication of perspectives, its disruption of emplotment, and its ultimate disorder give rise to a modernist challenge to ideas of individual female development that has broad social and political implications for late colonial India and beyond.

R. K. Narayan once said "we are all experimentalists," implying that the process of developing the English novel in India forced every writer to hazard the possibility of a new literary language and new Indian-Anglo forms (quoted in Desai, iii). For Mulk Raj Anand and Iqbalunissa Hussain, as for others, the demands of responding to a modernizing India and to the political concerns facing it in the 1930s and 1940s meant pressure to bring that experimentalism to bear on problems of self-development, civic citizenship, and domesticity. Thus, modernist narrative, as these writers invent it, responds aesthetically to social structures, economies, interpersonal relations, and domestic obligations within late colonial India even as it aligns itself with political efforts to change these structures. If we begin to read these narratives as part of a vibrant and developing English-language modernist tradition in India, rather than the mirror or mimic of European texts, then we will begin to see their ability to manage the dichotomy between *swadeshi* and the machine, the exigencies of Indian social life, and the possibilities of modernity, even as they teach us about the range and extant power of modernism's political engagement.

NOTES

1. These characters at the end of the book are usually described as based on Nehru and the real-life poet Iqbal (who was one of Anand's early mentors).

2. This massacre would become a crucial springboard for the growth of the twentieth-century independence movement. In the context of this essay, it is interesting to recognize that it was the Irish leader of the Punjab, Sir Michael O'Dwyer, who likely ordered the action.

3. Anand, who died in 2004, was the author of, at best count: eighteen novels, three collections of short stories, several books of essays, including such seminal works as "Is There a Contemporary Indian Civilization?," and many collections of Indian fairy tales. He also wrote art history and literary criticism, gathered Indian recipes, and published assessments of the philosophies of Gandhi and Nehru. In general, though, treatments of his work in histories of Indian writing in English focus on the novels written between his return trip to India in 1932 and Independence. Because his work is influenced by his reading in socialism, which he began in London at the time of the General Strike, and by his effort to provide a detailed account of the lives of ordinary Indians, Anand is often referred to quite simply as a "social realist" with attendant remarks upon his "limitations," especially in his later works.

4. These two principles are the bedrock of Gandhi's policy from the 1920s on. *Swadeshi* more literally means "of one's own country" and was the basis of the boycotts on British cloth and emphasis on local production. *Swaraj* is a term that can be translated as "self-rule" but for Gandhi also meant focus on government from the bottom up. His book *Hind Swaraj* is usually translated as *Indian Home Rule* (see http://www.mkgandhi.org/swarajya/coverpage.htm).

5. See Saint-Amour on the connections between *Ulysses* and Anand's *Untouchable*, and on the importance of reading style in Anand's novel.

6. See Marcus's wonderful reading of this relationship in her recent *Hearts of Darkness*. Bluemel also discusses this character from a feminist perspective (79–88).

7. Here we might also think about the recurring chant of "esmiss esmoor" at the end of the trial chapter of Forster's *Passage to India* (225). At that point in the novel, the proper name "Mrs. Moore" gets transformed into a similar kind of nonliteral marker, which takes on a political meaning not contained in its ordinary use. We can code this as remainder, since for most of the people chanting in the streets "esmiss esmoor" is pure musicality and has no real connection to Mrs. Moore herself. And yet it does not serve quite the same function in Forster's novel as does remainder in Anand's since the use of the name of Mrs. Moore does clearly invoke the position she has taken in the chapters surrounding the trial. Of course, since the novel emerges mainly out of the perspective of its British characters, the use of this chant is also caught up with the orientalist sense of Indian "mystery" that surrounds the caves and other native elements. If the Malabar caves are a floating signifier that can be coded in many different ways depending on context and perspective, so can "esmiss esmoor." This gives it power primarily as the "other" of rational language use and not as a true alternative to it.

8. Jussawalla, whose book *Family Quarrels* focuses a chapter on this question, argues strongly for the appropriateness of Anand's revisions of English. Still, she feels the need to cite linguists who endorse the linguistic combinations in Anand's novels as accurate. Other critics simply note that, "although awkward," Anand's novels "are pioneering in their attempt to render into English the exuberant dialects of Northern India" (Mehrotra 179).

9. Despite the enormous recent increase in critical writing on Indian literature, little attention has been paid to women writers of imaginative literature in the period between 1900 and 1947. Joshi (*In Another Country*) and others have focused our attention on the nineteenth century, when several strong Indian woman poets began writing in English and other English women living in India were writing sophisticated novels about Indian life. Ray (*En-Gendering India*) spans the period in her important study of the representation of women in fiction, but she does not linger there. The historian Antoinette Burton (*Dwelling in the Archives*) focuses on the 1920s and 1930s, but the only fiction in this book, which makes strong claims for the value of literary texts as historical "evidence," was written in the 1960s looking back on the 1930s. In the period after independence, scholars of the postcolonial have marked a strong tradition of female-authored narrative from Kamala Markandaya's *Nectar in a Sieve* (1954) on, but rarely if ever connect it to an established tradition of Indian women fiction writers.

10. For example, in *A History of Indian Literature in English*, discussion of the origins of the novel in English gives prominent place to Krupabai Satthianadhan and a section is devoted to Naidu and Sorobji, but subsequent chapters on Tagore, Aurobindo, Gandhi, Nehru, the anthropologist Verrier Elwin, and the novelists of the 1930s (Mulk Raj Anand, R. K. Narayan, and Raja Rao) barely mention a woman author. Readers of this history are left to assume that women did not participate in the development of the Indian novel in English and that post-Independence women writers were the heirs of Anand, Narayan, and Rao. Susie Tharu and Ke Lalita's two-volume anthology of Indian women writers was a crucial corrective to this record—but even there, the early years of the twentieth century get short shrift.

11. Though Oxford University Press has reprinted a laudable number of women's texts in their Oxford India Paperbacks series, very few women writers from the first half of the twentieth century appear. Even the editors of the 2002 anthology *Women's Voices: Selections from Nineteenth and Early-Twentieth Century Writing in English*, working in Bombay, found it difficult to retrieve texts and resurrect biographies for the forty women included in the volume.

12. See Burton 10. See also Spivak, *A Critique of Postcolonial Reason* and *Other Asias*, as well as Ray.

13. The phrase is Victoria Rosner's (5).

14. De Souza has described her efforts to discover biographical details of the lives of women writers from the period in *Women's Voices.*

15. What is perhaps most striking in these Indian narratives of female development is the extent to which these heroines develop and transform their own life stories as well as the possibilities for narrating subjectivity within community. Critics of the British female *Bildungsroman,* such as Fraiman and Ellis, grapple with the perception that many British novels in this subgenre seem to doom their heroines to failure. Girls in female *Bildungsromane* often seem to lead static or retrogressive lives in the face of societal restrictions, though, as Ellis makes clear, they often "construct themselves as subjects by manipulating the signs of their objectification" (10). Those who come of age as members of minority populations or, as Esty has pointed out, in colonized situations, are often described in a sort of opposite trajectory, where development is not only stifled but reversed. The narratives examined here, however, collectively challenge these expectations by showing their heroines as self-reflective ethical subjects flirting with new paradigms, and often, if not always, revising the specific demands of Indian domestic households.

16. Zuhra "determined that Nazni should be punished for having . . . been treated by a surgeon" (65).

WORKS CITED

Anand, Mulk Raj. *Conversations in Bloomsbury.* 1981. Oxford: Oxford University Press, 1995. Oxford India Paperbacks.

———. *Coolie.* New York: Liberty Press, 1952.

———. "Pigeon-Indian: Some Notes on Indian-English Writing." *World Literature Written in English* 21.2 (1982): 325–36.

———. Preface. *Mulk Raj Anand: A Reader: Selections from His Fictional and Non-Fictional Works.* Ed. Ama Ram. New Delhi: Sahitya Akademi, 2005.

———. *Untouchable.* New York: Penguin, 1990.

Attridge, Derek. *Joyce Effects.* Cambridge: Cambridge University Press, 2000.

Bakhtin, Mikhail M. "The *Bildungsroman* and Its Significance in the History of Realism: Toward a Historical Typology of the Novel." *Speech Genres and Other Late Essays.* Trans. Vern W. McGee. Austin: University of Texas Press, 1986.

Bluemel, Kristen. *George Orwell and the Radical Eccentrics: Intermodernism in Literary London.* New York: Palgrave, 2004.

Boehmer, Elleke. *Colonial and Postcolonial Literature.* Oxford: Oxford University Press, 1995.

Burton, Antoinette. *Dwelling in the Archives: Women Writing House, Home, and History in Late Colonial India.* Oxford: Oxford University Press, 2003.

Cowasjee, Saros. *So Many Freedoms.* Oxford: Oxford University Press, 1977.

Desai, S. K. ed. *Experimentation with Language in Indian Writing in English Fiction.* Kolhapur: Shivaji University Press, 1974.

De Souza, Eunice, and Lindsay Pereira, eds. *Women's Voices: Selections from Nineteenth and Early-Twentieth Century Indian Writing in English.* Oxford: Oxford University Press, 2002.

Ellis, Lorna. *Appearing to Diminish.* Lewisburg: Bucknell University Press, 1999.

Esty, Jed. "Virginia Woolf's Colony and the Adolescence of Modernist Fiction." *Modernism and Colonialism.* Ed. Richard Begam and Michael Valdez Moses. Durham: Duke University Press, 2006.

Fisher, Marlene. *The Wisdom of the Heart: A Study of the Works of Mulk Raj Anand.* New Delhi: Sterling Publishers, 1985.

Forster, E. M. *A Passage to India.* New York: Harbrace, 1924.

Fraimain, Susan. *Unbecoming Women: British Women Writers and the Novel of Development.* New York: Columbia University Press, 1993.

Gandhi, Mohandas K. *Hind Swaraj or Indian Home-rule.* 1933. *Mamahta Gandhi: Interactive Multimedia.* Gandhain Institute & Gandi Research Foundation, n.d. Web. 21 March 2010.

Hussain, Iqbalunnisa. *Changing India: A Muslim Woman Speaks.* Bangalore: Hosali Press, 1940.

———. *Purdah and Polygamy.* Bangalore: Hosali Press, 1944.

Iyengar, K. R. Srinivasa. *Indian Writing in English.* 3rd ed. New Delhi: Sterling, 1983.

Joshi, Priya. *In Another Country: Colonialism, Culture, and the English Novel in India.* New York: Columbia University Press, 2002.

Jussawalla, Feroza. *Family Quarrels: Towards a Criticism of Indian Writing in English.* New York: Peter Lang, 1985.

Marcus, Jane. *Hearts of Darkness.* New Brunswick: Rutgers University Press, 2004.

Mehrotra, Arvind Krishna, ed. *A History of Indian Literature in English*. New York: Columbia University Press, 2003.

Moretti, Franco. *The Way of the World: The Bildungsroman in European Culture*. London: Verso, 2000.

Ray, Sangeeta. *En-gendering India: Woman and Nation in Colonial and Postcolonial Narratives*. Durham: Duke University Press, 2000.

Reddy, Sir Ramalinga. *Purdah and Polygamy*. Bangalore: Hosali Press, 1944.

Rosner, Victoria. *Modernism and the Architecture of Private Life*. New York: Columbia University Press, 2005.

Rushdie, Salman. *Imaginary Homelands*. London: Granta, 1991.

Saint-Amour, Paul. "From Ulysses to Untouchable: Mulk Raj Anand's Joycean Transmigrations." International James Joyce Symposium. Dublin, Ireland, June 2004. Paper.

Slaughter, Joseph. "The Bildungsroman and International Human Rights Law." *PMLA* 121.5 (2006): 1405–23.

Spivak, Gayatri Chakravorty. *A Critique of Postcolonial Reason*. Boston: Harvard University Press, 1999.

———. *Other Asias*. Malden: Blackwell, 2008.

Tharu, Susie, and Ke Lalita. *Women Writing in India: 600 B.C. to the Present*. 2 vols. New York: Feminist Press, 1993.

CHAPTER 9

MODERNISM AND AFRICAN LITERATURE

NEIL LAZARUS

"Decolonizing the mind": Ngũgĩ wa Thiong'o's famous slogan (1986) succinctly captures a central concern of African intellectuals (and progressive Africanist scholars) in the decades of the 1950s, 1960s, and 1970s—the years leading up to and immediately following political independence on the continent. The injunction to "unthink Eurocentrism," associated most strongly with the name of Edward W. Said,[1] and which came to constitute the essential gesture of postcolonial studies in the Anglophone academic world in the late 1980s and early 1990s, had already been sounded in the field of African literature some twenty years earlier, in the 1960s and 1970s. Among the tasks that were felt to be most pressing, at that time, was that of developing a corrective critique of the unambiguous Eurocentrism of much of the commentary on Africa and African culture that was finding its way into print as "African literature" began, for the first time, to command the attention of an academic readership in the West.

Among the most notorious of these Eurocentric commentaries was Charles Larson's *The Emergence of African Fiction*, which, published at the beginning of the 1970s, generously allowed that "there are already half-a-dozen African novelists whose works deserve serious consideration and who have attained a level of distinction comparable to that of the most talented writers now living in the West—with whose writing it seems inevitable ensuing African fiction will be compared" (277). Proposing that as African societies continued to "develop" or "modernize," so "emergent" African literature would tend to become increasingly "Western" (read: intricate, sophisticated, subtle) in its cardinal aspects, Larson's culturally supremacist argument was underpinned by a stark determinism. "Modernity" is "Western"; therefore, "modernization" must be understood in terms of the universalization of "the West." "[I]n a few short years," Larson wrote, African societies have moved from analphabetic to literate, from largely rural to increasingly urban, from communal to individual. And the fiction itself has mirrored these evolutions in its own patterns. Situational plots are being replaced by works which concentrate on character individuality. Description, and treatment of time and space are becoming more typically Western. Experimentation tends now toward Western techniques which replace the traditional conscious or subconscious incorporation of oral literary materials into the text. With some novels it is even difficult to tell whether or not the writer is an African. (279)

This kind of argument received the criticism it deserved almost immediately. In a celebrated essay published in 1975, for instance, Chinua Achebe denounced "a certain specious criticism which flourishes in African literature today and which derives from the same basic attitude and assumption as colonialism itself and so merits the name *colonialist*" (3). Achebe focused particularly, in his essay, on the propensity of Eurocentric critics (Larson was among those named directly) to contrast the presumed "universality" of "Western" literature with what they took to be the restricted "localism" of such African works as his own *Things Fall Apart*, *No Longer at Ease*, and *Arrow of God*. He drew attention to the extraordinary lack of reflexivity of these critics, to whom

> [i]t would never occur . . . to doubt the universality of their own literature. In the nature of things the work of a Western writer is automatically informed by universality. It is only others who must strain to achieve it. So and so's work is universal; he has truly arrived! As though universality were some distant bend in the road which you may take if you travel out far enough in the direction of Europe or America, if you put adequate distance between you and your home. I should like to see the word *universal* banned altogether from discussions of African literature until such a time as people cease to use it as a synonym for the narrow, self-serving parochialism of Europe, until their horizon extends to include all the world. (9)

Similarly pointed critiques of Larson were advanced by other African intellectuals, such as Omolara Ogundipe Leslie (in a book review), Chinweizu, Onwuchekwa Jemie, Ihechukwu Madubuike (esp. 87–146), and Ayi Kwei Armah, who, in a particularly biting riposte, proposed that the term "Larsony" be pressed into service to refer to any Western critics who subscribed to Larson's general precepts.

The common target of all these critiques was what Achebe called "latter-day colonialist critic[ism]." But between Achebe's and Leslie's critiques and those of Armah and Chinweizu, Jemie, and Madubuike, it is possible to discern a significant ideological difference, whose implications for the discussion of "modernism" and African literature are considerable. What is phrased, in Achebe and Leslie, as an assault on *Eurocentrism*, features, in the "Afrocentric" discourse favored by Armah and Chinweizu et al., as a blunt hostility to Europe (and "the West") as such. Best understood in these terms as a subset of "third-worldism," the Afrocentric position is marked by a civilizational essentialism (both of "Africa" and "the West") that is as unpalatable ideologically as that of the colonialist discourse it is intended to oppose, but that, for all its claims to radicalism, lacks the conceptual resources to damage.

I have written elsewhere of Chinweizu's general vision, which seems to me to offer an exact, if inverted, reflection of the Eurocentric vision, to which it therefore remains paradoxically bound; and also of the disastrous effects of the turn to Afrocentrism in Armah's fiction and sociological writings.[2] Here, however, where our concern is more narrowly with African *literature*, it will be more apt to focus on the fierce dispute that erupted between Chinweizu, Jemie, and Madubuike, on the one hand, and Wole Soyinka, on the other, in the mid-1970s, and which took the form of an argument about the thrust, tendency, and significance of modern(ist) African poetics.

The battle was first joined when Chinweizu published an essay, "Prodigals, Come Home!" in the Nigeria-based journal, *Okike*, in 1973. In this essay, he sought to distinguish between what he called "modern poetry in Africa" and "modern African poetry"—to celebrate the latter (which he defined as "poetry written today in styles informed by traditional African poetics") and to castigate and deplore the former (defined as "poetry written by Africans [but . . .] dominated by modern European sensibility" [219]). Central to Chinweizu's commentary was the work of Christopher Okigbo, whose short career tracked, according to the critic, from the "anemic modernity" and "tired syntactic jugglery" of his early (allegedly Western-modernist derived) work to the "triumphant juvenescence" of the work composed just before his untimely death in the Nigerian Civil War in 1967. For Chinweizu, Okigbo's last work succeeded in breaking free of the prison-house represented by "modernism," whose lexicon it abandoned "for a language of African particulars." In these last poems, Chinweizu writes, Okigbo

> accepts an African poetic landscape with its flora and fauna—a landscape of elephants, beggars, calabashes, serpents, pumpkins, baskets, towncriers, iron bells, slit drums, iron masks, hares, snakes, squirrels; a landscape that is no longer used as an exoticism for background effect, no longer used for exotic references sprinkled among anemic images, but a landscape which has been moved to the dramatic centre of his poetry; a landscape portrayed with native eyes to which aeroplanes naturally appear as iron birds; a landscape in which the animals behave as they might behave in African folk-lore, or animals presented through native African eyes. And "native" is not a pejorative! (221)

This advocacy of "traditionalism" is reiterated in *Toward the Decolonization of African Literature*, in which Chinweizu, now writing in collaboration with Jemie and Madubuike, pours scorn on the work of such poets as Soyinka, J. P. Clark, and the early Okigbo, who are condemned for their supposedly slavish mimicry of European modernist models. "[T]he euromodernists . . . have assiduously aped the practices of 20th century European modernist poetry," the three Nigerian critics write (*Toward the Decolonization of African Literature* 163); and they add insult to injury by insisting also that what has been produced by the "Euromodernists" is not even *good* derivative work: the imitators "are for the most part *ineffectual imitators*. . . . The only things these disciples appear to have learned from their models are their well-known faults. Prominent among the characteristics of Nigerian Euromodernist poetry are Hopkinsian syntactic jugglery, Poundian allusiveness and sprinkling of foreign phrases, and Eliotesque suppression of narrative and other logical linkages of the sort that creates obscurity in 'The Waste Land'" (173). Denouncing what, in these terms, they label "the Hopkins disease," Chinweizu et al. attempt to provide a tool kit for a modern African (i.e., Afrocentric) literary idiom, outlining, under rubrics such as "community, craft, and language," "commitment and the writer's social responsibilities" and "cultural continuity: the African writer and the African past," the forms, themes and techniques that writing of this kind should, in their view, embrace.

Soyinka's poetry is singled out for particular censure and ridicule in *Toward the Decolonization of African Literature*. It is held to be gratuitously complex, ideologically incoherent, poorly conceptualized, and trivial. Of Soyinka's poem, "Dawn," for instance, Chinweizu et al. write that "[n]ot only does it not make immediate sense . . . but it is not even easy or pleasurable to read. On the contrary, it is heavy, tongue-twisting, difficult to articulate, and it cannot keep the reader's attention" (168). One supposes that the three critics would have recognized in advance that a writer as prodigious and as exuberantly, irrepressibly, multifarious as Soyinka would be unlikely to suffer such criticism in silence. And he did not suffer it in silence. His counterblast, when it came, was devastating—and also, it has to be said, wickedly entertaining. Referring variously to "Messrs Chinweizu, Jemie and Madubuike," "Chinweizu and Co.," "our critics" and "the troika"[3], he excoriated what he called their "neo-Tarzanism," suggesting that their wooden Afrocentric pieties would play directly into the hands of racists and cultural supremacists in the West, all too willing to concede "tradition" to African people by way, precisely, of emphasizing their civilizational superiority over them. Where "the troika" had specified the "African poetic landscape with its flora and fauna"—including the "*natural*" representation of aeroplanes as iron birds—Soyinka responded that he was "not at all certain how this proves more acceptable than the traditional Hollywood image of the pop-eyed African in the jungle." *His* "African world," he wrote, by telling contrast, "is a little more intricate and embraces precision machinery, oil rigs, hydro-electricity, my typewriter, railway trains (not iron snakes!), machine guns, bronze sculpture, etc., plus an ontological relationship with the universe including the above listed pumpkins and iron bells" ("Neo-Tarzanism" 294).

Centrally at issue in this dispute is the relationship between modernism and *modernity*. Presenting modernity as "Western" and suggesting, accordingly, that it be understood in "civilizational" terms as part and parcel of the colonial project, Chinweizu et al. leave themselves with no alternative but to uphold some competing notion of an essential "African" way of life. Merely inverting the colonialist construction of the dialectic of modernity and tradition, "the troika" concede that trains and planes and automobiles are culturally "Western," insist on the interior adequacy of "traditional" "African" sociality, and—just like their Eurocentric opponents—fail to reckon with the obvious rejoinder that the idea of "tradition" is itself a product of the modernist imaginary, within which it is designed to serve as a perpetual conceptual foil to the idea of "the modern."

The particular value of Soyinka's critique of "the troika," in this context, is that it consistently refuses their essentialist premises, instead understanding "modernity" as a globally dispersed social logic over which no particular culture can claim ownership or monopoly. As Biodun Jeyifo has correctly pointed out, Soyinka's work

> decisively refute[s] what [Paulin] Hountondji has described as the "artificial choice" between "Westernization" or "Europeanization," the "teleology" decreed by so many African and foreign critics of modern African literature, especially those written in the European languages, and its reactional, Manichean product— a naïve, simplistic, romantic "Africanization," "Africanity," "Negritude," "authenticity" of many of the appellations by which it is promoted as cultural nationalism." (xxix)[4]

Readers acquainted with Soyinka's critique, earlier in his career, of *négritude*, will recall its elegant argument that inasmuch as *négritude*—or, by implication, Afrocentric thought at large—concedes to "Europe" or "the West" exactly what *Eurocentric* thought also and already claims for it, it will have lost the battle against colonial-style reason in advance. If, like Senghor, you allow that reason is "Western," your counterclaim that emotion is "African" will loom as mere consolatory compensation, and all your attempts to preach complementarity—as, for instance, in the appeal to New York, to let "black blood" "wash the rust" from its "steel joints," in Senghor's well-known poem from *Éthiopiques* (1956)—will only move those who already believe.[5] Soyinka's demolition of the case advanced by the "neo-Tarzanists" reiterates this argument, homing in also on the leaden reductionism—and, indeed, the sheer falsity— of the loaded opposition that they draw between the attenuated "individualism" that they take to characterize modern "Western" literary production *tout court* and the solidaristic "collectivism" that they seek to promote in its (again, *singular*) "African" counterpart. He responds waspishly that if even such existential prerequisites as private reflection, "individual experimentation," solitude, momentary withdrawal, the dedicated time and space in which to write, are going to be characterized as "Western," and repudiated as such, then "African" writers will be left only with the choice between being derivative writers and being bad ones.

CAPITALISM, MODERNITY, MODERNISM

In his work over the course of the past two decades, Fredric Jameson has elaborated a powerful revisionary conception of modernity that involves delinking it from the idea of "the West" and yoking it to that of the capitalist world system. Insisting that it can only be conceptualized adequately through reference to worldwide capitalism (*Singular Modernity* 13), Jameson understands modernity as representing something like the time-space sensorium corresponding to capitalist *modernization*. In this sense, it is, like the capitalist world system itself, a singular phenomenon. But far from implying that modernity therefore assumes the same form everywhere, as

Jameson has sometimes mistakenly been taken to suggest, this formulation in fact implies that it is everywhere irreducibly specific. Modernity might be understood as the way in which capitalist social relations are "lived"—different in every given instance for the simple reason that no two social instances are the same. Jameson emphasizes both the *singularity* of modernity as a social form and its *"simultaneity."* This latter concept he derives from Ernst Bloch's ostensibly oxymoronic formula, *Gleichzeitigkeit des Ungleichzeitigen* ("simultaneity of the nonsimultaneous").[6] Modernity is in these terms to be understood as governed *always*—that is to say, *definitionally*—by unevenness, the historically determinate "coexistence," in any given place and time, "of realities from radically different moments of history—handicrafts alongside the great cartels, peasant fields with the Krupp factories or the Ford plant in the distance" (Jameson, *Postmodernism* 307).

This formulation stands as a compelling repudiation of the various recent attempts to pluralize the concept of modernity through the evocation of "alternative," "divergent," "competing," or "retroactive" modernity/modernities.[7] Inasmuch as these invariably derive from an initial assumption as to the "Western" provenance of modernity—rather than situating it in the context of *capitalism as a world system*—they are both unnecessary and misguided. Of course, if one believes that modernity is a "Western" phenomenon, it is only possible to understand its global dispersal in terms of the "universalization" of "the West"—to be celebrated or, as in the avowedly anti-Eurocentric conception currently so influential in postcolonial studies, deplored as imperialistic.[8] To postulate "the existence of an 'original' formulated in Europe" is, as Harry Harootunian has argued, inevitably to suppose that the form of appearance of "modernity" elsewhere must be both "belated" and "derivative"—"a series of 'copies' and lesser inflections" (62–63). No wonder then that theorists who view modernity in these terms and yet are committed to the critique of Eurocentrism should want to argue for "alternative" modernities!

Against this postcolonialist line of thought, however, which attributes modernity to the gifts or the luck of the capitalist homelands, the account elaborated by Jameson (and Harootunian) emphasizes modernity's singularity and global simultaneity, while insisting that singularity here does not obviate internal heterogeneity and that simultaneity does not preclude unevenness or marked difference. In these terms, the specific modes of appearance of modernity in different times and places—St. Petersburg in the 1870s, say, Dublin in 1904, Cairo in the 1950s, a village on a bend in the Nile in the Sudan in the 1960s—ought to be thought about not as "alternative" but as "coeval . . . modernities or, better yet, peripheral modernities . . . in which all societies shared a common reference provided by global capital and its requirements" (Harootunian 62–63).

To allude to St. Petersburg, Dublin, Cairo, etc. is, of course, already to suggest an analytical movement from the politico-philosophical category of modernity to that of its literary correlate. (One might have achieved the same effect by providing a list of self-consciously fictionalized place-names: Middlemarch, Christminster, Yoknapatawpha County, Malgudi, Umuofia, Ilmorog, etc.) Jameson operates with a tripartite conceptualization—capitalist world system/modernity/modernism—in terms of which the latter is understood as the literature (more generally, culture) that registers and encodes the social logic of modernity. If, as he puts it, "modernization is something that happens to the base, and modernity the form the superstructure takes in reaction to that ambivalent development, then perhaps modernism characterizes the attempt to make something coherent out of their relationship" *(Postmodernism* 310). The logic of determination deployed here positions "modernity" as—to borrow the phrase that Nicholas Brown uses as the subtitle of his 2005 study, *Utopian Generations*—the "political horizon" of "modernism."

Of course, Theodor W. Adorno has already given us one reading of modernism as the form of (modern) culture that says "no" to modernity. Adorno casts modernism as an aesthetic formulation of resistance to the prevailing—indeed, the hegemonic—modes of capitalist modernization in late nineteenth- and early twentieth-century Europe. Hence, the "modernism" of, for example, Ibsen and Dostoevsky, Breton and Kafka, Karl Kraus and T. S. Eliot. Adorno pays considerable attention to both the *aesthetic* dimension implicated by his theory—that is to say, to the question of the singularity of culture, to what culture *is* and *means* and *represents* as a specific form of social practice—and to the category of "resistance." Provided we are prepared, for the sake of argument, to abstract provisionally from the precise determinants, contours, and coordinates of this "modernist" projection, the Adornian conception is relatively elastic. It can readily be extended backward in time—certainly as far as Romanticism, say—and also forward. But it can also, and notwithstanding Adorno's own deep-seated Eurocentrism, be extended geographically— or rather geopolitically— to incorporate writers such as Lu Xun and Lao She, Aimé Césaire and Miguel Asturias, Saadat Hasan Manto and Ismat Chughtai, Abdelrahman Munif and Ngũgĩ wa Thiong'o, in whose work the dissenting registration of capitalist modernization takes the historically unforgoable form of a critique of imperialism.

Certainly it is the case, as Brown has pointed out in his consideration of the relation between European modernist and independence-era African literatures, that both of these formations revolve around and are animated by the same world-historical process. "The mere fact that European imperialism names a key moment in the spread of capitalism as a global economic system already implies a certain baseline of universality," Brown writes, before cogently drawing the key implication that "there can be no question of merely applying the methodological norms developed for [the] one literature [European modernist] to the texts of the other [African]." Rather, what is required is to "reconstellate . . . modernism and African literature in such a way as to make them both comprehensible within a single framework within which neither will look the same. This framework will hinge neither on "literary history" nor abstract "universal history" but on each text's relation to history itself" (Brown 2–3).[9]

In its emphasis on imperialism as a specific moment in the history of *capitalist* development (one recalls of course the Leninist formula, "the highest stage of capitalism"), Brown's argument provides a corrective to the understanding of imperialism predominant in postcolonial studies, where "imperialism" is routinely severed from the concept of "capitalism." Even on the best postcolonialist accounts, such as Edward Said's in *Culture and Imperialism*, "imperialism" is typically cast as a *political* dispensation and referred to "the West," rather than to capitalism. Thus Said holds "imperialism" to implicate military conquest, alien governance, systematized top-down violence, social asymmetry, cultural and symbolic domination, Eurocentrism as a set of deeply patterned "structures of attitude and reference" (61); he makes very little of the fact that it also involves accumulation under conditions of monopoly, exploitation, class struggle, or the imposition of a (capitalist) mode of production.

For theoretical reasons alone, therefore, it seems important to fly in the face of the prevailing wind in postcolonial studies and insist that whatever else it might have and, indeed, *did* involve—all the way from the systematic annihilation of whole communities to the cultivation of aesthetic tastes and preferences—colonialism as an historical process involved the forced integration of hitherto uncapitalized societies, or societies in which the capitalist mode of production was not hegemonic, into a capitalist world system. Over the course of a couple of centuries in some territories, mere decades in others, generalized commodity production was imposed: production for exchange rather than use; monetization; private ownership; the development of specifically capitalist markets (involving "free wage labor," the buying and selling of labor power) and of ancillary systems and institutions designed to enable and facilitate the consolidation, extension, and reproduction of capitalist production and capitalist class relations. Along the way, existing social relations and modes of existence were undermined, destroyed, reconfigured; new social relations and modes of existence were brought into being. Peasantries were destroyed, along with subsistence economies, to be replaced by capitalized agriculture in one location, proletarianization in another, with more or less regulated waves of migratory labor in between.

Yet it is not only for theoretical reasons that it is necessary to insist on the centrality of capitalism to colonialism. It is also because this point is steadily figured (and often given explicit emphasis) across the full range of "postcolonial" literature—in poetry and drama as much as in fiction. What the social scientist Immanuel Wallerstein speaks of as "the commodification of everything" (1996) is registered equally succinctly, thus, by the Congolese novelist Sony Labou Tansi in *The Anti-people*: "The invasion of money into everyday life is something the Belgians left us as a mark of love" (28).

Indeed, the process through which peasant economies, both material and "moral" or symbolic, were undermined and disrupted—with capitalist class relations being superimposed over them, historic patterns of land-tenure and corresponding modes of community decimated, new forms of community, and of resistance, forged—this protracted, brutal, and violently disruptive process constitutes the very subject matter of a number of significant literary works. Ngũgĩ wa Thiong'o's panoramic novel, *Petals of Blood* (1977), for instance, centers on Ilmorog, which mutates over its course from a peasant village—"at its most expansive a haven, but subject still to the ravages of nature" (Sivanandan 15)—into the horror of "New Ilmorog," an industrial wasteland of factories and slums, leaving the bulk of its inhabitants ruined—dispossessed, impoverished, and demoralized. As Tamara Sivanandan observes, "[t]he juxtaposition of the village/city in the story is no mere provider of incidental background, but effectively maps a geography of imperialism, and is a metaphor for the contrast between the potential for autochthonous development—a realization of the dreams of independence that the common people struggled for—and its supersession by a native capitalism in cahoots with a global imperialism" (15). The same process also forms the backdrop of F. Sionil José's major fiction (most notably the "Rosales Saga," comprising *Dusk* [1998], *Tree* [1978], and *My Brother, My Executioner* [1979]; and *The Sampsons* [2000] comprising *The Pretenders* [1962] and *Mass* [1984]), which, considered as a whole, offers a Balzacian portrait of Filipino culture and society from the mid-nineteenth century to the end of the twentieth. One could also cite here such masterworks as Munif's *Cities of Salt* (1989 [1984]), Fuentes' *The Years with Laura Díaz* (2000 [1999]), and Lovelace's *Salt* (1996), which, as vastly different from one another in form, tone, and ideology as they are in location (an unnamed state in the Persian Gulf, Mexico, and Trinidad, respectively), are nevertheless all directed to the *longue durée* of a specifically capitalist imperialism.

To say that the forced introduction of capitalism in the historical contexts of colonialism spawned the development of new classes, and of new forms of class domination and struggle, is not, of course, to say that the social relations previously existing were simply overwritten or replaced. On the contrary, capitalism in these contexts was superimposed on the preexisting relations, strengthening or reinforcing them in some respects or some situations, weakening or ameliorating them in others. As Perry Anderson has argued, an appreciation of the "complex and differential temporality" of the capitalist mode of production, "in which episodes or eras were discontinuous from each other, and heterogeneous within themselves" is already observable in Marx's writings from the late 1840s onward (101).[10] In these writings there is an awareness of the fact that even within capitalist or capitalizing social formations, vast rural populations continued to provide the material ground for the persistence of earlier economic conditions, social relations, cultural practices, and psychic dispositions. This insight was then notably amplified in Trotsky's writings of the 1930s, in which, on the basis of his consideration, first of conditions in Russia in 1905, and subsequently of those in China in 1925–1927, he formulated a "Law of Uneven and Combined Development." In Russia, China, and other analogous contexts, Trotsky suggested, the imposition of generalized commodity production and capitalist class relations tends not to have the effect of supplanting (or is not allowed to supplant) preexisting modes and structures. Rather, capitalism is forcibly conjoined with these preexisting modes and structures. The outcome, he wrote, is a contradictory "amalgam of archaic with more contemporary forms"—an urban proletariat working in technologically advanced industries existing side by side with a rural population engaged in subsistence farming; modern plants built alongside "villages of wood and straw," and peasants "thrown into the factory cauldron snatched directly from the plow" (Trotsky 432).

Some of Jameson's writings—concerned centrally with the relations between capitalist modernity and literary form—begin to sketch in the relevance of this theory of combined and uneven development for the analysis of "postcolonial" modernism. While his essay on "Third-World Literature in the Era of Multi-national Capitalism" has regrettably received attention only because of its claims about "national allegory"—claims which, as I have argued elsewhere (Lazarus, "Fredric Jameson on 'Third-World Literature'" 2004), have been tendentiously misunderstood—Jameson's commentary in that essay on the "crisis of representa-tion" in non-metropolitan cultures that were, and remain, "locked in a life-and-death struggle with first-world cultural imperialism" ("Third-World Literature" 68), strikes me as decisive. It certainly enables him to offer remarkably suggestive readings of Lu Xun's "A Madman's Diary" (1978 [1918]) and Ousmane Sembene's *Xala* (1976 [1974]), the two texts that he chooses to focus on in his essay. (For a reading of Lu Xun that engages with Jameson, see Zhang in this volume.) His thought-provoking argument that the violence entailed in the imposition of capitalism in such societies made for the "generic discontinuities" of the litera-tures subsequently produced (83), receives elaboration also in "On Magic Realism in Film," another essay addressing "postcolonial" cultures—published, like the "Third-World Literature" essay, in 1986—in which Jameson proposes that magic realism be considered a "formal mode . . . constituently dependent on a type of historical raw material in which disjunction is structurally present," and in which the content

> betrays the overlap or the coexistence of precapitalist with nascent capitalist or technological features. In such a view . . . the organizing category of magic realist film . . . is one of modes of production, and in particular, of a mode of production still locked in conflict with traces of the older mode. . . . [T]he articulated superpo-sition of whole layers of the past within the present. . . is the formal precondition for the emergence of this new narrative style. ("On Magic Realism in Film" 311)[11]

In a footnote to the "Third-World Literature" essay, Jameson speculates further that this way of thinking about combined unevenness demands a new type of literary com-parativism: namely the "comparison, not of the individual texts, which are formally and culturally very different from each other, but of the concrete situations from which such texts spring and to which they constitute distinct responses". (86–87, fn. 5)[12]

Combined and Uneven Modernisms?

These considerations already take us quite far into the discussion of modernism in relation to African literature. If we understand modernism neither in terms of technique, abstractly conceived, nor—despite the provocations of Eurocentric discourse—through definitive reference to "Western" modernity, but in relation to a heterogeneous, locally inflected, but nevertheless *global* and *singular* modernity, we can begin to think about the meaning and significance—the particular resonances and identifications, cuts and thrusts, bearings and effects—of "modernist" practice in various different writers—Achebe and Armah, say, or Laing and Okri, Gordimer and Coetzee, Mda and Vladislavic, Vera and Hove, Mahfouz and Djebar.[13]

Perhaps the scholar who has done most to think through these issues in the African context is Simon Gikandi. Two points of emphasis in Gikandi's writing on "modernism" in relation to African literature are especially worth registering here. First, there is his clear-sighted awareness of the need to uncouple the question of modernism in Africa from colonialism and, more narrowly, from the suspicion that it inevitably entails colonial cultural domination. It might be argued that even if we were to follow Adorno in supposing that modernism's essential gesture has been to say "no" to modernity, we would have left unresolved the question of the relation of modernism to *colonialism*. For while colonialism is commonly taken as intrinsic to the sociohistorical project of *modernity, modernism* is not typically viewed—for all its vaunted "dissidence"—as featuring an *anticolonial* dimension. On the contrary, modernism is typically viewed as a Eurocentric projection, as itself latently if not explicitly colonialist in character, hence the antimodernist cultural nationalism of Chinweizu et al., for instance. Gikandi offers a splendid challenge to this received construction of modernism, however, arguing that in Africa at least, modernism and anticolonialism must be understood not as oppositional, but as mutually enabling and mutually entailing discourses:

> In the colonial African context . . . the relationship between modernism and modernity was complicated by their contemporaneousness, the fact that the two categories became central to African reflections on their identity and destiny at about the same time. More significantly, while European modernism self-consciously posited itself as a structure opposed to modernity and modernization, even when it was a consequence of these processes, colonial modernism, like nationalism itself, could not legitimize itself without some kind of self-willed affiliation with modernity. In arguing for the liberation of the African, nationalist intellectuals premised their claim on the fact that modernity could be achieved without the tutelage of colonialism, that indeed, the colonization of Africa stunted its modernity. ("The Short Century" 19)

Gikandi argues not only that "African modernism was produced in relation to mainstream European movements and ideas" and that "African intellectuals were important players in the European centers of modern art"—two truths very widely accepted nowadays—but, rather more consequentially, that "while their Western counterparts sought to use the ideology of modernism to undo nationalism, African artists adopted the same aesthetic ideology to imagine and will into being new nations. Nationalism has become a dirty word in some circles, but for the colonized it was a redemptive project that needed an aesthetic dimension in order to fulfill its mandate" (24–25).

A second, related insight in Gikandi's recent work on modernism in/and Africa—hinted at in the sentence just quoted—is that, both because of the radical unevenness of the social and cultural or ideological transformations wrought by colonialism, and because of their exogenous nature, the negotiation and interrogation of "modernity" by African intellectuals could only be achieved in the mediated and relatively displaced realm of aesthetics. As Gikandi writes,

> the colonial process presented an interpretative enigma: colonial culture had transformed many African societies through voluntary and enforced modernization, but as many observers of the African scene were quick to note, this process did not seem to penetrate too deeply into the fabric of local communities. Ostensibly, colonialism touched every aspect of social and political life on the continent, but its impact also seemed to be superficial because, in spite of the predominance and preponderance of colonial modernity, so-called traditional society seemed to function as if the colonial event was a mere interruption in the *longue durée* of African history. For the men and women who came to produce modern African literature, the subjects who were most affected by the colonial process, the simultaneous existence of a modern and traditional world could only be negotiated through works of the imagination. It is not accidental that the foundational texts of modern African literature in the European languages were concerned with the dialectic of modernity and tradition as it was played out on the continent under colonialism. ("African Literature and the Colonial Factor" 56–57)

"[T]he men and women who came to produce modern African literature" felt the need to challenge the institutionalized forms of "modernism," which reached *them*, in still colonial or just decolonizing African contexts, as part and parcel of the colonial enterprise—as "modernism" under the sway of a Eurocentric ideology of "the modern," and overdetermined in this respect by its minoritarianism (amounting *de facto* if not necessarily *de jure* to elitism), its appearance in European languages exclusively and its militantly partisan selectivity. African writers sought to cast *their* "modernism" instead as an articulatory form of practice, in this respect just like the nationalism that they themselves often lived and breathed, mediating between their wider communities and the colonial order beyond. This form of practice could only be symbolic. The resort to aesthetics involved no necessary "ideology of the aesthetic": instead, it registered their commitment to social self-determination, an historic project requiring, as a *sine qua non*, precisely what *intellectuals* alone are capable of furnishing—a vision with the symbolic capacity, as Basil Davidson has memorably put it, "to save or restore the sense and fact of community against all the pressures of the colonial system" (155).

We should note that what is being said here is not unique or specific to Africa. The fierce debates about "modernity" and "modernization" surrounding the revolution of 1911 in China and the great intellectual upsurge of 1919–1920, known as the May Fourth Movement, for instance, have much in common with the debates subsequently waged in Africa. And one could refer, just as easily, to analogous debates in Turkey, Iran, *Indochine*, the Indian subcontinent, and the Arab world. Let us close by considering, as one case in point, the discussion of modernism and modernity presented in the Arab poet Adonis's important commentary, *An Intro-duction to Arab Poetics* (1985).

Like Gikandi with respect to Africa, so too Adonis with respect to Arab society presents "the problematic of poetic modernity" as going "beyond poetry in the narrow sense. . . . [It] is indicative of a general cultural crisis, which is in some sense a crisis of identity" (76). Gikandi speaks of the "interpretative enigma" engendered by colonial modernity; Adonis too suggests that "modernity has tended to be a force which rejects, questions, and provokes without entering in any conscious, radical way into the structure of the Arab mind or into Arab life as a whole" (77). A problem in Africa is that in opposing themselves to the Eurocentric ideology of the modern, many African intellectuals were led, like the "neo-Tarzanists," to throw out the baby with the bathwater, modernity as such with "Euro-modernity," and to resort instead to an equally attenuated and alienated language of "tradition." So it has been in the Arab world, too, according to Adonis. Opposing themselves to those who unreflex-ively "imitate modern Western poetry," many Arab intellectuals advocated instead

> a revival of forms of expression developed in past ages to respond to present problems and experiences, which was also a resuscitation of old ways of feeling and thinking and methods of approach. [This] . . . helped to establish these forms as absolute inviolable principles, to be eternally perpetuated as the single true poetry. The result was that the Arab personality, as expressed through this poetry, appeared to be a bundle of self-delusion, and Arab time to stand outside time. (Adonis 79–80)

Suggesting that "at the level of practical politics and daily life, the *nahda* (renais-sance in Arab thought) was set in motion in a state of almost complete dependency on the West," Adonis draws out the implications of this contradiction in Arab social consciousness:

> In this way the period laid the foundations of a double dependency: a depen-dency on the past, to compensate for the lack of creative activity by remembering and reviving; and a dependency on the European-American West, to compensate for the failure to invent and innovate by intellectual and technical adaptation and borrowing. (Adonis 80)

One further similarity: what Biodun Jeyifo, following Paulin Hountondji, describes in terms of the "artificial choice" between "Westernization" and "cultural nation-alism" finds an echo in what Adonis says about the falsity of each of the antinomies through which the "clash of civilizations" has been waged in Arab culture in the colonial era—the Eurocentric idea of "modernity" on one hand, the reactive idea of an essential "tradition" on the other.

One difference between Adonis and Soyinka, at least, must be registered. Adonis writes that, ironically enough, he began to appreciate the "modernity" of Arabic poetry not through his encounter with Abu Nuwas or the Arabic poetic archive more generally, but through his encounter with Baudelaire and Mallarmé:

> I was one of those who were captivated by Western culture. Some of us, however, went beyond that stage, armed with a changed awareness and new concepts which

enabled us to reread our heritage with new eyes and to realize our own cultural independence. I must also admit that I did not discover this modernity in Arabic poetry from within the prevailing Arab cultural order and its systems of knowledge. It was reading Baudelaire which changed my understanding of Abu Nuwas and revealed his particular poetical quality and modernity, and Mallarmé's work which explained to me the mysteries of Abu Tammam's poetic language and the modern dimension in it. My reading of Rimbaud, Nerval and Breton led me to discover the poetry of the mystic writers in all its uniqueness and splendor, and the new French criticism gave me an indication of the newness of al-Jurjani's critical vision.

I find no paradox in declaring that it was recent Western modernity which led me to discover our own, older, modernity outside our "modern" politico-cultural system established on a Western model. (Adonis 80–81)

Adonis is closer here to a figure like the great Caribbean intellectual C. L. R. James than to such African writers as Soyinka, Ngũgĩ, Ama Ata Aidoo, or Cheikh Hamidou Kane, to whom, one ventures, the radical "modernity" of African culture has always seemed self-evident. As Soyinka puts it in concluding his essay on the "neo-Tarzanists," the "aesthetic matrix" of Yoruba culture

is the fount of my own creative inspiration; it influences my critical response to the creation of other cultures and validates selective eclecticism as the right of every productive being, scientist or artist. Sango is today's god of electricity, not of white-man magic-light. Ogun is today's god of precision technology, oil rigs and space rockets, not a benighted rustic cowering at the "iron bird." ("Neo-Tarzanism" 305)

Despite this, what Adonis says about the conditions of possibility of modernist writing *does* strike me as being "transferable" to the modernist African context. His formulation marks a useful point from which to consider the general question of "modernism" in literary production, above all in contexts of peripheral or semi-peripheral modernity—that is, in the shadow of imperialist hegemony:

I want to stress that modernity requires not only freedom of thought, but physical freedom as well. It is an explosion, a liberation of what has been suppressed. To think and write what is truly new means above all to think about what has never been thought about and write what has never been written: that huge, constant area of suppression—religious and cultural, individual and social, spiritual and physical. This implies that modernity is an immersion in history, a kind of writing which subjects this history to constant questioning, and a form of self-awareness that exposes writing itself to constant scrutiny within the framework of a continuous exercise to discover the powers of language and investigate the possibilities and limitations of experiment. (Adonis 100–01)

NOTES

1. See Said; Shohat and Stam.

2. On Chinweizu, see Lazarus, "The Fetish of 'the West' in Postcolonial Theory"; on Armah, see Lazarus, *Resistance in Postcolonial African Fiction*, and also Sole, "Criticism,

Activism and Rhetoric," and Wright, esp. 187–220. For telling critiques of Afrocentrism more widely, see Howe; Lemelle; and Gilroy.

3. The term "troika," especially, strikes home. Since they had accused him of a "sprinkling of foreign phrases," Soyinka's selection of this particular word, of Russian origin, and hence gesturing, in context, toward the bureaucratic mismanagement of the Soviet regime—toward "design by committee"—is both mischievous and rhetorically winning.

4. Jeyifo refers here to Paulin Hountondji's *African Philosophy: Myth and Reality* (1982).

5. See *Myth Literature and the African World* (1978), esp. 126–39, where Soyinka argues that *négritude* "not only accepted the dialectical structure of European ideological confrontations but borrowed from the very components of its racist syllogism" (127). See also the 1967 essay, "The Writer in a Modern African State," where Soyinka pours cold water on the "call . . . to bring about the salvation of the world by a marriage of abstractions." "This reconciliation of cultures," he writes, "this leaven of black contribution to the metallic loaf of European culture, is only another evasion of the inward eye" (19–20).

6. Bloch originally developed his concept of *Ungleichzeitigkeit* in *Erbschaft dieser Zeit* (1935). English translation, *Heritage of Our Times* (1991). See also Bloch, "Nonsynchronism and Dialectics," and the commentaries in Brennan, 47ff., and Durst, esp. 1–32.

7. The case for "alternative" modernities has been advanced most notably by Gaonkar, "On Alternative Modernities." See also his edited collection, *Alternative Modernities*. For a critique, see Lazarus and Varma, "Marxism and Postcolonial Studies."

8. This line of thought is represented in the work of Chakrabarty, Nandy, Mitchell, Scott, and Serequeberhan, among others.

9. In a subsequent passage, Brown notes that such a "reconstellation" would involve a deconstructive demystification of the very ideas of "Western" and "non-Western" literature: "The question," as he puts it, "would not be whether the most vital writing of the second half of the twentieth century was produced by Third World writers: it was. The question is rather what we mean by 'literature' and what we mean by 'West,' what agendas reside in those words and whether they have any meaning at all. . . . What we usually call 'non-Western' literature is rarely the expression . . . of some other culture, if by that we understand some other set of norms and rules that has developed along its own internal logic; rather, it must be thought of in terms of the positions that economically, ethnically, sexually, and geographically differentiated subjects occupy within the single culture of global capitalism that has more or less ruthlessly subsumed what was once a genuinely multicultural globe.

All of this should be obvious, even if our entire mainstream multicultural discourse is built around its explicit denial. But the recognition of what multiculturalism denies should not be taken to signify a celebration of, or acquiescence to, the power of some henceforth inescapable 'Western' tradition. Indeed, the capitalist monoculture dissimulated in multicultural discourse is not strictly speaking 'Western' at all" (Brown 6).

10. In this sense, the famous passages from the *Communist Manifesto* that seem to evoke a transformation that is as abrupt as it is total, are potentially misleading: "All fixed, fast-frozen relations, with their train of ancient prejudices and opinions are swept aside, all new-formed ones become antiquated before they can ossify. All that is solid melts into air," etc. (Marx and Engels 38). But just as readings of such passages in the *Manifesto* as being infused with enthusiasm for capitalism typically "forget" that the writings of Marx and Engels are notable also for recording and protesting the violence of expropriation, the systematized misery and servitude that the imposition of capitalist social relations visited on populations everywhere, so too it is necessary to insist that the authors were well aware

of the fact that the "capitalist revolution" was not a once-and-for-all event, but rather a sprawling, erratic, and bloody historical process.

11. Cf. also the argument in the concluding section of Jameson's book on postmodernism that modernism itself must be seen as "uniquely corresponding to an uneven moment of social development," in which there is a "peculiar overlap of future and past," such that "the resistance of archaic feudal structures to irresistible modernizing tendencies" is evident (*Postmodernism* 307, 309). Jameson illustrates this argument through reference to Kafka's *The Trial*, focusing on the juxtaposition in the novel of a thoroughly modernized economic order and an older, indeed archaic, legal bureaucracy and political order deriving from the Austro-Hungarian Empire.

12. He adds that comparative analysis of this kind "would necessarily include such features as the interrelationship of social classes, the role of intellectuals, the dynamics of language and writing, the configuration of traditional forms, the relationship to western influences, the development of urban experience and money, and so forth."

13. Cf. Sarah Lincoln's essay on Ben Okri in this volume, in which, also following Jameson's lead, she argues generally that "modernist literary form can be described historically—not by tracing a genealogy of influence, as is often the case, but by locating the shared material experience that underwrites formal resemblances." With respect to Okri's work in particular, Lincoln suggests that "[t]he encounter with 'modernity' as a perpetually receding horizon—the promise of modernization that never fully arrives—is expressed . . . through the singularly modernist mode of magical realism, one whose transnational character has less to do with traveling trends than with the profound ambivalences common to experience at the very edge of global modernity." See also Lincoln, "Expensive Shit," for wider discussion of this argument.

WORKS CITED

Achebe, Chinua. "Colonialist Criticism." *Morning Yet on Creation Day: Essays.* London: Heinemann, 1975: 3–18.

Adonis. *An Introduction to Arab Poetics.* 1985. Trans. Catherine Cobham. London: Saqi Books, 2003.

Anderson, Perry. "Modernity and Revolution." *New Left Review* I/144 (1984): 96–113.

Armah, Ayi Kwei. "Larsony, or Fiction as Criticism of Fiction." *New Classic* 4 (1977): 33–45.

Bloch, Ernst. *Heritage of Our Times.* (1935). Trans. Neville and Stephen Plaice. Berkeley: University of California Press, 1991.

———. "Nonsynchronism and Dialectics." *New German Critique* 11 (1977): 22–38.

Brennan, Timothy. *Wars of Position: The Cultural Politics of Left and Right.* New York: Columbia University Press, 2006.

Brown, Nicholas. *Utopian Generations: The Political Horizon of Twentieth-Century Literature.* Princeton: Princeton University Press, 2005.

Chinweizu. "Prodigals, Come Home!" 1973. *African Literature: An Anthology of Criticism and Theory.* Ed. Tejumola Olaniyan and Ato Quayson. Cambridge: Blackwell, 2007. 219–25.

———. *The West and the Rest of Us: White Predators, Black Slavers and the African Elite.* New York: Vintage, 1975.

Chinweizu, Onwuchekwa Jemie, and Ihechukwu Madubuike. *Toward the Decolonization of African Literature. Vol. 1: African Fiction and Poetry and Their Critics.* Washington, DC: Howard University Press, 1983.

Davidson, Basil. *Let Freedom Come: Africa in Modern History.* Boston: Little, Brown and Company, 1978.

Durst, David C. *Weimar Modernism: Philosophy, Politics, and Culture in Germany, 1918–1933.* Lanham: Lexington Books, 2004.

Fuentes, Carlos. *The Years with Laura Díaz.* 1999. Trans. Alfred Mac Adam. New York: Farrar, Straus Giroux, 2000.

Gaonkar, Dilip Parameshwar. "On Alternative Modernities." *Public Culture* 11.1 (1999): 1–18.

———. ed. *Alternative Modernities.* Durham: Duke University Press, 2001.

Gikandi, Simon. "African Literature and the Colonial Factor" (2004). *African Literature: An Anthology of Criticism and Theory.* Ed. Tejumola Olaniyan and Ato Quayson. Cambridge: Blackwell, 2007. 54–59.

———. "The Short Century: On Modernism and Nationalism." *New Formations* 51 (2004): 10–25.

Gilroy, Paul. *The Black Atlantic: Modernity and Double Consciousness.* Cambridge: Harvard University Press, 1993.

Harootunian, Harry. *History's Disquiet: Modernity, Cultural Practice, and the Question of Everyday Life.* New York: Columbia University Press, 2000.

Hountondji, Paulin. *African Philosophy: Myth and Reality.* London: Hutchinson, 1982.

Howe, Stephen. *Afrocentrism: Mythical Pasts and Imagined Homes.* London: Verso, 1998.

Jameson, Fredric. "On Magic Realism in Film." *Critical Inquiry* 12 (1986): 301–25.

———. *Postmodernism, or, The Cultural Logic of Late Capitalism.* 1991. Durham: Duke University Press, 1995.

———. *A Singular Modernity: Essay on the Ontology of the Present.* London and New York: Verso, 2002.

———. "Third-World Literature in the Era of Multinational Capitalism." *Social Text* 15 (1986): 65–88.

Jeyifo, Biodun. "Wole Soyinka and the Tropes of Disalienation." 1988. Introduction to *Wole Soyinka, Art, Dialogue and Outrage: Essays on Literature and Culture.* London: Methuen, 1993: ix–xxix.

Larson, Charles. *The Emergence of African Fiction.* Rev. ed. Bloomington: Indiana University Press, 1972.

Lazarus, Neil. "The Fetish of 'the West' in Postcolonial Theory." *Marxism, Modernity and Postcolonial Studies.* Ed. Crystal Bartolovich and Neil Lazarus. Cambridge: Cambridge University Press, 2002. 43–64.

———. "Fredric Jameson on 'Third-World Literature': A Qualified Defence." *Fredric Jameson: A Critical Reader.* Ed. Douglas Kellner and Sean Homer. Basingstoke: Palgrave, 2004. 42–61.

———. *Resistance in Postcolonial African Fiction.* New Haven: Yale University Press, 1990.

Lazarus, Neil, and Rashmi Varma. "Marxism and Postcolonial Studies." *The Critical Companion to Contemporary Marxism.* Ed. Jacques Bidet and Stathis Kouvelakis. Leiden: Academic Publishers, 2008. 309–31.

Lemelle, Sidney J. "The Politics of Cultural Existence: Pan-Africanism, Historical Materialism and Afrocentricity." *Imagining Home: Class, Culture and Nationalism in the African Diaspora.* Ed. Sidney J. Lemelle and Robin D. G. Kelley. London: Verso, 1994. 331–50.

Lenin, V. I. *Imperialism, the Highest Stage of Capitalism: A Popular Outline.* 1917. Peking: Foreign Languages Press, 1970.

Leslie, Omolara Ogundipe. Review of Charles Larson, *The Emergence of African Fiction.* *Okike: An African Journal of New Writing* 4 (1973): 81–89.

Lincoln, Sarah L. "Ben Okri's Inflationary Modernism." *The Oxford Handbook of Global Modernisms.* Ed. Mark Wollaeger. Oxford: Oxford University Press, 2012.

———. "Expensive Shit: Aesthetic Economies of Waste in Postcolonial Africa." Diss. Duke University, 2008.

Lovelace, Earl. *Salt.* London and Boston: Faber and Faber, 1996.

Lu Hsun [Lu Xun]. "A Madman's Diary." 1918. *Selected Stories of Lu Hsun.* Trans. Yang Hsien-yi and Gladys Yang. Peking: Foreign Languages Press, 1978: 7–18.

Marx, Karl, and Friedrich Engels. *Manifesto of the Communist Party.* 1848. Beijing: Foreign Languages Press, 1988.

Munif, Abdelrahman. *Cities of Salt* (1984). Trans. Peter Theroux. New York: Vintage, 1989.

Ngũgĩ wa Thiong'o. *Decolonising the Mind: The Politics of Language in African Literature.* London: James Currey, 1986.

———. *Petals of Blood.* London: Heinemann, 1977.

Said, Edward W. *Culture and Imperialism.* London: Chatto and Windus, 1993.

Sembene, Ousmane. *Xala.* 1974. Trans. Clive Wake. London: Heinemann, 1976.

Shohat, Ella, and Robert Stam. *Unthinking Eurocentrism: Multiculturalism and the Media.* London: Routledge, 1994.

Sionil José, F. *Dusk.* New York: Modern Library, 1998.

———. *My Brother, My Executioner.* 1973. Quezon City: New Day, 1979.

———. *The Sampsons.* New York: Modern Library, 2000. (Comprises *The Pretenders* [1962] and *Mass* [1984]).

———. *Tree.* Manila: Solidaridad, 1978.

Sivanandan, Tamara. "'Lies of Our Own Making': The Post-Colonial Nation-State in the Writings of Ngugi wa Thiong'o, V. S. Naipaul and Salman Rushdie." MA Thesis. University of Essex, 1993.

Sole, Kelwyn. "Criticism, Activism and Rhetoric (or: Armah and the White Pumpkin)." *Inspan* 1.1 (1978): 129–41.

Soyinka, Wole. *Myth, Literature and the African World.* 1976. Cambridge: Cambridge University Press, 1978.

———. "Neo-Tarzanism: The Poetics of Pseudo-Tradition." 1988. *Art, Dialogue and Outrage: Essays on Literature and Culture.* London: Methuen, 1993. 293–305.

———. "The Writer in a Modern African State" (1967). *Art, Dialogue and Outrage: Essays on Literature and Culture.* London: Methuen, 1993. 15–20.

Tansi, Sony Labou. *The Antipeople* (1983). Trans. J. A. Underwood. London and New York: Marion Boyars, 1988.

Trotsky, Leon. *History of the Russian Revolution [1932–33].* Vol. 1. Trans. Max Eastman. London: Sphere Books, 1967.

Wallerstein, Immanuel. *Historical Capitalism with Capitalist Civilization.* London: Verso, 1996.

Wright, Derek 1989. *Ayi Kwei Armah's Africa: The Sources of His Fiction.* London: Hans Zell, 1989.

PART IV

FORMS AND MODES

CHAPTER 10

"PETRO-MAGIC REALISM": BEN OKRI'S INFLATIONARY MODERNISM

SARAH L. LINCOLN

In this chapter, I argue for a reading of Nigerian magical realism, epitomized in Ben Okri's 1988 collection *Stars of the New Curfew*, in terms of the country's experience of oil boom and inflationary bust during the 1970s and 1980s. "Magic realism" was first described by German art critic Franz Roh, in the context of post-Expressionist painting in 1925.[1] Recalling how deeply this early account of magic-realist form, and the artwork it described, was informed by the devastating German inflation of 1922–1923, I suggest that modernist literary form can be described historically—not by tracing a genealogy of influence, as is often the case, but by locating the shared material experience that underwrites formal resemblances. In this case, the shared experience is of speculative mania: the typically modern process by which financial value comes detached from its material base and becomes dependent instead on public opinion, sentiment, and superficial perception. The encounter with "modernity" as a perpetually receding horizon—the promise of modernization that never fully arrives—is expressed in both contexts through the singularly modernist mode of magical realism, one whose transnational character has less to do with traveling trends than with the profound ambivalences common to experience at the very edge of global modernity.

Toward the end of *Postmodernism*, Fredric Jameson turns to a question he considers insufficiently addressed in debates about postmodernism: what is *modernity*, and where then does moderni*sm* fall in relation to this phenomenon? In his account, what constitutes modernity is above all the impulse to make sense of—to document *and* to order or aestheticize—the disruptions, dislocations, and disjunctures brought about by modernization itself. Neither material transformation nor innovative aesthetics, "modernity" signifies instead the attempt to reconcile the two, to bring together "modernization" and "modernism" under a common conceptual and affective umbrella; we might say, though Jameson does not, that it is, in a certain sense, a mode of *reading*, a materialist aesthetics (or indeed an aesthetic materialism).

It follows, then, that the modern has to do with the experience of looking at something from the inside, from such close proximity that it appears wondrous and strange, even as this proximity reveals the fissures and contradictions that may not be apparent from a further vantage.[2] Modernity is to be found in the self-regard of modern subjects, their attempt to make sense of their often confusing and alienating circumstances. For Jameson, the way "'modern' people feel about themselves," and their effort to "make something coherent" out of their often profoundly ambivalent encounter with modernization, and the promises and expectations it spawns, is what here represents the real "modernity" (*Postmodernism* 310).

In his short story collection, *Stars of the New Curfew* (1988), Nigerian novelist Ben Okri presses the limits of literary realism against what he sees as the "fantastic" ("Stars" 84) realities of a culture and economy predicated on oil. Identifying this oil closely with excrement and other wastes, Okri works through the paradoxical structure of value in an inflationary context: the more oil is extracted, the more wealth accrues, the more money there is, the less and less value pertains to interpersonal relations, to concepts like beauty, truth and the "authentic" (143), and to nature, certain regions, individual people, and indeed entire populations. Ultimately, in the volume's most chilling insight, these people are rendered genocidally disposable.

Through a reading of the collection, which was composed during the worst of the inflationary "bust" that followed the collapse of world oil prices in the early 1980s, I will indicate some of the ways in which the resulting material and psychic conditions manifested as a crisis of representation. Inflation in one sphere—monetized modern life—finds symptomatic expression in a second-order inflation, in the sphere of literary modernism. Focusing on two of the volume's stories, I suggest that we read Okri's magical realist vision as an attempt to bear witness to the oil economy's radical disruption of the bond holding signifier to signified, representation to reality, and the signs of value to its substance—what I will contend represents a pervasive "inflationary culture" at all levels of social and political life. Okri's modernist mode is also a formal mechanism by which the author looks to memorialize the wasted bodies, social relations, landscapes, and dreams cast off in its wake.

A TOUR OF NIGERIAN INFLATION

In Nigeria, the horizon of modernity was illuminated by oil, which had been discovered in commercially viable deposits by Shell in the late 1950s. The rapid rise in oil prices that followed the 1973 embargo and supply-cut orchestrated by the Organization of Oil-Producing Countries (OPEC), of which Nigeria was a recent member, meant an astonishing rise in national income from oil exports, a development heralded, as Andrew Apter observes, as a miraculous "blessing from Providence" (22). As the price of oil rose steadily through the decade, eventually peaking in 1980 at around 3,600 percent above its 1973 level, cash poured into the country. Nigeria's oil revenues increased during the 1970s by 2,200 percent (from £170 million [$467.5 million] in 1966–1967 to ₦7,650 million [$4,636 million] in 1977–1978 [Barber 431 n.1]),[3] positioning petroleum at the center of the country's economy and radically transforming its sociopolitical and physical landscape.

The oil boom effected profound changes in the psychic and imaginative lives of Nigerians, who were thrust into the newly monetized economy and polity, a development thematized by Okri in his stories. On one hand, the new wealth brought about by the influx of "petrodollars" stimulated a period of wild optimism, a speculative frenzy in which everything and anything seemed possible for the newly endowed nation-state. After four years of devastating civil war, and over a decade of postcolonial disillusionment, the world's "oil shock" was initially experienced in Nigeria as a miraculous windfall, an unexpected gift that presented an opportunity to completely reimagine—and indeed remake—the country as the very representative of African modernity.

The translation of oil money into spectacular buildings, infrastructural improvements and social services gave tangible form to the otherwise vertiginous unreality of figures like "$9.1 billion"—the country's income from petroleum exports during 1976 alone (Darnton IES44). The grandiose scale of the monuments, factories, and social programs implemented with these petrodollars reflected the sublime hyperbole of money counted in the billions, the skyscrapers sprouting overnight from the earth offering an objective correlative for the dizzying wealth that was apparently being conjured alchemically from thin air (or, rather, from the earth itself).

What Andrew Apter calls the "magic of Nigeria's nascent modernity" (8)—the popular vision of the state as a conjuror or alchemist, turning the "devil's excrement" of black oil into shiny naira bills and sparkling new clinics and hotels[4]—was thus at least initially experienced as a certain magical *reality*, as a social and physical landscape that was daily being transformed by the power of magical money. This spectacle of wealth and modernity, the set of visual images through which the oil boom and its marvelous effects were mediated, must be understood, however, as profoundly ideological—as both a fetishistic misrecognition of the social and ecological relations on which the wealth was founded, and a political project in which legitimacy and authority were entirely constituted on the basis of illusion and display, the *spectacle* of sovereignty without any reference to an underwriting content.

The buildings and bridges, roads and clinics served as the signs and substance of the state's sovereignty (increasingly based on its control of the petrodollar purse strings) through a spectacle of expenditure, a simulacral symbolic economy that deflected popular attention from its otherwise distinctly shaky legitimacy.[5] In his account of Venezuela's oil boom, Fernando Coronil identifies this feature of political life in oil states more generally as a kind of "petro-magic," a term that describes not only the state's turn to modes of interpellation-by-spectacle but also the investment of every aspect of life in such contexts with an unreal quality. The state not only "bought" legitimation through its new role as distributor of oil incomes, but also deployed a "magical performance" of authority that served to dazzle "through the marvels of power rather than convinc[e] through the power of reason" (Coronil 5). Coronil's work suggests that this reliance on political cosmology—the state as a "magnanimous sorcerer"—typifies oil-boom states more generally, and thus seems tied in specific ways to the particular qualities of this commodity: oil's "power to awaken fantasies enables state leaders to fashion political life into a dazzling spectacle of national progress through 'tricks of prestidigitation'" (Coronil 2). This vision of the oil economy's "petro-magical" effects is the thematic concern and, we might say, the chief protagonist of the titular "Stars of the New Curfew," to which we will now turn.

In this story, Okri takes us on a dizzying tour of a Nigerian society being transformed by the excess of petrodollars flooding the country during the 1970s oil boom. The protagonist is a salesman of quack medicines, small translucent bottles of "green liquid" that recall uneasily both the sewage-ridden "green" waters of the lagoon at the center of Lagos, and the other liquid commodity—petroleum—whose commodification, circulation, and frenzied consumption constitute the story's allegorical subtext. The phantasmagoric effects of the liquid commodities that circulate through the narrative are what interest Okri most profoundly. The narrative trajectory of "Stars of the New Curfew" implicitly links these phantasmagorical or "petro-magical" qualities of oil-commodity politics and culture to the brutal devaluation of human life.

At the story's opening, the protagonist exemplifies the logic of semblance and spectacle that governs all levels of social and political life in oil-boom Nigeria. He prides himself on his work as a theatrical salesman, performing dazzling routines, dances, songs and other "tricks" to attract potential customers and persuade them of the miraculous, transformative powers of what he cynically acknowledges to be "rather dubious locally-made medicines" (84). Where other salesmen play on customers' jingoistic pride or plant friends in the audience to testify to the drugs' efficacy, the unnamed protagonist abandons all pretence of rational forms of persuasion and relies (at least initially) exclusively on the power of spectacle itself: "I dressed like a clown. I set off fireworks. I developed the most sensational dances and songs to accompany my sales talks. I spent all my energy thinking up new tricks" (84). His major challenge is retaining the "shock" value of his performances in a rapidly modernizing urban culture where what George Simmel (330) identified as the "blasé" outlook predominates: people "get used" to his methods and are less easily persuaded as the initial impression wears off. But rather than adapting his product or conceiving new relations between producer and consumer, the salesman responds by increasing the affective impact, finding "new tricks" and increasingly shocking techniques to punctuate the nervous exhaustion of overstimulated Lagosians. Though the quality of his product, and his performance, remains stagnant, he uses quantitative inflation—more and more of the same—to obscure and mystify the reality of this qualitative lack.

The connection that Okri identifies and stylizes here between sensation, spectacle and inflationary devaluation illuminates some of the "petro-magical" features of social and political life during the era of oil-fueled modernization in Nigeria. The oil "boom," which stimulated such exaggerated hopes for the country's future as poster-child for African modernity, was experienced simultaneously—and more depressingly—as a period of monetary inflation. The flood of petrodollars that so radically transformed Nigeria's social, political, and cultural landscapes, made for a 300 percent increase in the money supply between 1970 and 1976, an average annual increase of 43 percent (Adamson). In a period when the average rate of economic growth was only around 9 percent, and when the onset of the "Dutch Disease"[6] led to the gradual and irreversible wasting of other productive industries, such as agriculture, the inflationary effects of this monetary increase created an ultimately devastating cycle, in which oil, the very source of prosperity, laid the structural foundations of the nation's economic destruction. Between 1972 and 1975, the annual rate of inflation climbed from 2.8 percent to 33.5 percent (Adamson 5), destabilizing the value of the new currency, the naira, which had increasingly come to serve as the denominator and determinant of all forms of value—social, subjective, and cultural, as well as economic—in "modern" Nigeria.

The "fantastic" and "unreal" quality of the oil boom, exacerbated by the immateriality of the commodity on which it depended—and in fact its invisibility, underground, in pipes, behind barbed wire or even offshore[7]—characterized Nigeria's anticipated modernity as what Walter Benjamin describes as a "dream-world": a world predicated symbolically upon the appearance of perpetual newness, the seductive dazzle of the surface, and the occlusion of histories and conditions of production. In this context, values and meanings derive exclusively from appearances and from the collective frenzy of mass desire, not from any substantial quality.

And here we arrive at the inflationary character of the petrodollar culture. In an earlier essay on the inflation that ravaged Germany in 1922–1923, Benjamin suggested that a similar "degeneration of things," the phantasmagorical displacement of things by their images, served as a cultural correlate of the currency devaluation-by-inflation that represented the era's dominant economic mode (Benjamin, "Imperial Panorama" 58–59). Inflation is a process by which the presumed nexus between signifier (monetary value) and signified (material commodity), representation and "reality," becomes strained or even broken altogether. In the case of the German mark during the 1920s, monetary value as a "representation of abstract equivalence (i.e., its price) ultimately lost virtually all (stable) reference to a material referent (i.e., a commodity), becoming something of a shadow without substance, form without content, or an appearance without a corresponding essence" (Durst 76; cf. also Widdig 239 n.14). As the value and meaning of money spirals further and further away from any material referent (whether gold or bread), the value and meaning of commodities and other objective features of everyday life comes to seem similarly fantastical. In the face of the imminent starvation confronting most Germans, for example, the "reality" of luxuries seems so fantastical as to defy even visual comprehension: Benjamin tells us that the "luxury goods swaggering before us now

parade such brazen solidity that all the mind's shafts break harmlessly on their surface" ("Imperial Panorama" 60). The air, he muses darkly, "is full of phantoms" (56).

Benjamin's observations about the perceptual unreality of everyday life during
an inflation anticipate the emergence of the artistic mode that would come, within
a few years, to be known as "magical realism." The term was first used by critic
Franz Roh in his 1925 volume *Nach Expressionismus: Magischer Realismus: Prob-
leme der neusten europäischen Malerei* (Post Expressionism: Magical Realism: Problems of the newest European painting) to describe the German Post-Expressionist
movement of the mid-1920s. The work of painters like Otto Dix, George Grosz,
Anton Räderscheidt, and Georg Schrimpf returned artistic attention to the banal
details of the external world, seeking a "new sobriety" after the excesses of war, inflation, and aesthetic Expressionism. Their interest in the defamiliarizing effects of
scrupulous realism—impossibly smooth surfaces, perspectival contrasts and strict,
even austere objectivity—emphasized the isolation and confusion of perceiving
subjects in postwar, post-inflationary German society. Linking Roh's "magical
realism" to the recent experience of the "worst monetary inflation in history," Irene
Guenther suggests that these painters were concerned above all with the challenges
of representing the generalized state of epistemological, existential, and social crisis
that characterized the economic emergency. Most importantly, in Guenther's view,
magical realism represented a response to radical disillusionment, to the promise of
modernity heralded and then withdrawn. Post-expressionist painting was, she
insists, an "art of controlled bitterness that festered as the hopes and idealism of 1918
were dashed by the early 1920s, and the dreams of a better society gave way to resignation and despair" (43). The inflationary crisis, with its hourly adjustments in
the value of the mark, made it impossible to plan for or even think about the future,
promoting a culture of cynicism and uncertainty that undermined the very basis of
political life. Like post–oil-boom Nigeria, it was simultaneously haunted by the
recent memory of the optimistic moment when the modernization and prosperity
of postwar German society seemed tangibly available.[8] More than simply a representation of semiotic crisis, therefore, magical realism can also be seen as an expression of the doubleness or *Unheimlichkeit* of modernity itself—the simultaneity of
modernity as expectation and disillusionment.

In Fredric Jameson's terms, the emphasis on perception and illusion that
Benjamin locates at the heart of inflationary culture, and which Roh associated
with the work of the Post-Expressionists, is simply an intensification of a more
general characteristic of this stage of capitalist development. "If [exchange value
and the notion of monetary equivalence] had once announced and provoked a
new interest in the properties of objects," Jameson writes in "Culture and Finance
Capital," "now, in this new stage, equivalence has as its result a withdrawal from
older notions of stable substances and their unifying identifications" (151). Phenomenal qualities and perceptual features, he suggests, have in this stage become
"semi-autonomous," leading cultural and psychic existences independent from
their objects. Elsewhere, in his influential account of magic realism, Jameson specifically associates this activation of sensuous qualities with the dematerialized

finance capitalism that characterizes the postmodern phase of accumulation, but more generally with moments of historical transition in which conflicting modes of production coexist within a shared physical and imaginative space. Magical realism itself, he insists, "depends on a content which betrays the overlap or the coexistence of precapitalist with nascent capitalist or technological features" (Jameson, "On Magic Realism in Film" 311): the very kind of transitional moment explored in Okri's stories.[9] In such contexts, Jameson argues, the "permutations of the gaze" are the only mode of perception available to the subject trying to make sense of experience, resulting in "perforated history, which includes gaps not immediately visible to us, so close is our gaze to its objects of perception" ("On Magic Realism in Film" 303).

This loss of perspective is the subject of "What the Tapster Saw," a surreal account of a palm-wine tapster who falls from a tree and spends a week in a hallucinatory coma, before reviving the morning of his scheduled funeral. While he hovers between life and death, the tapster wanders through a devastated "unchanging landscape," populated by "terrible inhabitants" and "monstrous shapes" and haunted by prophetic visions and memories of childhood and "ancient heroes" (Okri, "Tapster" 187, 189). Apart from the apparent materiality of fantastical figures like talking turtles or metamorphosing dogs, the tapster is haunted throughout his wanderings by fragmented bodies and sensory qualities detached from their referents. The wounded, bleeding trees that entrap and torture him, and his rape by a creature whose only characteristic is its stench of "rotting agapanthus," serve as vivid examples of a device that frequently appears in Okri's work, wherein sensory characteristics, like color or smell, and metaphorical figures, like these wounded trees, assume a life of their own and address the human subject directly.

Such reliance on literalization or demetaphorization has been identified as a characteristic feature of magical realism, a representational mode in which metaphors "take on a special sort of textual life, reappearing over and over again until the weight of their verbal reality more than equals that of their referential function" (Faris 170–71). At the same time, this stylistic innovation is more than literary virtuosity on Okri's part: in this story, it is clearly associated with the author's attempt to make sense of—and to represent his characters' attempt to make sense of—a radically changing historical context.

In "Stars of the New Curfew," which explicitly addresses the inflationary culture of petro-era Nigeria, the semi-autonomy of phenomena takes the form of signs that skew dramatically away from their referents. As his business grows, a medicine salesman decides to focus his attentions on captive audiences of bus passengers as they travel the streets of the baroque city, their precarious existence on its dangerous roads and enforced collectivity making them easy targets for cure-all commodities. His boss, a "man of our times" who "understood the spirit of city business" (90), develops increasingly "powerful" medicines that promise cures for a growing range of ailments and "three times the energy" of previous formulations; the salesman intensifies his sales pitches for the new drug accordingly, bombarding his fellow passengers with what can only be called exercises in hyperbole—or discursive inflation: "I said it could cure anything from headaches to elephantiasis, that they could either drink it, bathe with it, rub it on their skin, or sniff its essences in boiling water. I said it was good for children and old people, that it gave more power, more iron, than any existing drug" (104). Beyond the benefits to be enjoyed from the drug's chemical substance, the salesman presents the drug's *sensuous* qualities (its smell and other "essences") as themselves having salubrious material effects. Its perceived ability to act on the world in ways that exceed its material substance is what makes the new "Power Drug" such a powerful and profitable commodity, heralded by the boss as the "ultimate money-making machine" (97)—a metaphor that itself tends toward a certain demetaphorized literalism: a counterfeit economy with inflationary consequences.[10]

The trade in deadly quack medicine and other "occult economies" in this story helps Okri explore the question of magical money and its relationship to representation. This particular commodity—a mysterious liquid with unknowable properties —establishes an intermediary step between legitimate, commodity-based wealth production and the "magical money" that was associated with witchcraft and corruption. If, as Karin Barber has shown, legitimate wealth creation was seen to depend on the intermediary commodity (Marx's M—C—M') and thus on a certain productive economy based on (someone's) labor, then "magical money" was feared and despised precisely for its fantastical elision of materiality through the "breeding" of monetary wealth from itself (a popular view that corresponds to Marx's M—M').[11] The overnight wealth that catapulted many Nigerians into the upper classes was widely regarded with suspicion by those less fortunate: such fortunes were seen, accurately, as riches acquired without labor, without a real foundation in the physical labor regarded by Yoruba tradition as the only legitimate basis of personal wealth (Barber 434–35).

The "Power Drug" is a commodity, to be sure, but its source is unclear and its effects dangerously unpredictable, qualities given substantial form in its liquid state and semi-opaque color (a color that additionally, we should note at this point, invokes the naira banknotes flowing around the country). This commodity, like its allegorical correlate, cannot be known or valued based on its appearance alone— only from what the salesman says about it and in a context of collective speculative mania.[12] Even what Marx might call its "use value" is questionable, and perhaps even negative: the medicines cause more health problems than they cure, even as petroleum contaminates and corrupts those it appears to enrich.

The protagonist's uneasy awareness of the dark side of "magical money" is revealed in his chronic nightmares, in which everything is put up for auction and given a price, from the stars to the man himself. Crowds of bloated rich men from every nation throng the nightmarish market, their "indifferent eyes" and "acutely wise and callous" expressions filling him with fear as he finds himself an object of the calculating mentality that now defines modern monetarized life (93–94; cf. Simmel 327). The man's nightmare describes a cultural landscape in which the value of human life itself becomes subject to the vagaries of the speculative market. Just as "the people who bought [the stars] paid either with huge sums of money, a

special part of the human anatomy, or the decapitated heads of newly-dead children" (93), the bids offered for the man on the auction block range wildly from "a
miserable price" to "a thousand naira for my head"; "ten cows"; "the heads of three
children"; "the thighs of a famous wrestler" (94). One army general even offers,
portentously, a "machine for making money—a machine secretly approved by the
nation's cabal of power" (94). Sold to an unknown bidder, the man finds himself
branded by the monetary form to which he has been reduced—"As they led me
from the constellation to a familiar world the sunlight would cut through the holes
in the zinc ceiling and would burn a copper coin in the middle of my forehead"
(95)—marking him as one more commodity in a vast and teeming marketplace.
The dreams are so vivid that they begin to invade his waking life, such that "on a
given day I couldn't tell whether I was in real life or in one of my dreams" (95). The
commodification and inflationary devaluation of human life that so terrified him
in his sleep are of course the basis of his everyday business, a commerce in which
the physical health, economic security, and sanity of customers are daily sacrificed
to the profit-motive.

Okri reminds us repeatedly that, underlying this entire economic and psychic
complex, flows the liquid commodity on which all depends. In one daytime dream,
the man "felt [him]self falling into a void" into "a still, green sea" (101). The stench
of excrement rising from the actual green lagoon that his bus passes as he drifts into
unconsciousness reinforces the association between the oil economy, commodification, waste, and the degradation played out in his dreams. After his final sales
pitch on behalf of "Power-Drug," his fellow passengers and their driver are so intoxicated by his inflated rhetoric, and the effects of the drug itself, that they transform
into a frenzied mob falling over themselves to pay for the wondrous product. The
bus driver, high on an overdose of "Power," steers the vehicle in a mad race against
another bus and crashes in the very area of the lagoon where night soil is regularly
dumped (an ironic allegory, we understand, of the eventual fate awaiting the ship of
state at the hands of its intoxicated leaders). The vertiginous experience of the
crash—"For a moment I saw nothing but sky. Then I saw the city tumbling, turning,
upside down" (108)—materializes the disorienting quality of everyday life in the
inflationary economy for the protagonist and his customers. After the crash, the
man's eyes are "opened to the madness I had been living with all those years" (96),
and he escapes Lagos for his hometown of "W." But instead of the expected premodern refuge, he finds to his surprise that W has also been radically transformed
by its abundance of oil wells. Here fantasy, falsehood, and performance define interpersonal relations as thoroughly as they do political life; spectacle and style now
substitute entirely for rational discourse or material action. Political contests
between the town's two strongmen take the form of exaggerated potlatches, with
air-conditioned banknotes distributed from a Rolls-Royce and silver coins cast like
rain from a hovering helicopter on the desperate crowds below. In "a moment of
hallucinated illumination," the man identifies this scene with the inflationary
economy it serves to conceal: "the miracle we had come to witness, which seemed
to comprise the other side of ritual drums and dread, was that of the multiplying

currency. We had come to be fed by the giant magicians of money, masters of our age" (136). What Okri describes here is the phantasmagorical form that mediates the economic and political realms in oil-boom Nigeria, the way in which "petro-magic" and its simulacral logics effectively describe both the creation of wealth and the spectacle of power.

For Walter Benjamin, the concept of "phantasmagoria" helps explain the relationship between commodities and the way they are experienced and understood culturally, and it offers a useful trope for understanding the oil-commodity-culture of Okri's Nigeria as well. In the *Arcades Project*, Benjamin identifies the phantasmagoria as the "expressive form taken by the products of a 19th-century commodity culture" and, simultaneously, as a central conceptual element in his critical methodology (Cohen 89–90).[13] In Benjamin's view, the structure of the commodity itself gives rise to a mode of experience in which surface appearance, and its aesthetic, affective power, conceals and substitutes for intellectual understanding, for material and historical substance. In his moment of vision, as Okri's narrator watches even educated, "rational" modern subjects (like himself) caught up in the frenzy of desire for "miracles" during the political spectacle in W, he recognizes a similar effect in the inflationary frenzies of the oil boom. In "petro-magical" Nigeria, illusion is rendered as, in itself, reality, not its representation—and this conflation of illusion and/as reality is in fact an object of desire for the inflationary subjects represented here.

The concept of "phantasmagoria" allows Benjamin and Okri to press Marx's thoughts about ideology beyond the rationalist limitations of the earlier thinker's approach. If Marx's analogy of the *camera obscura* (in which "reality" appears inverted) suggests a simple binary of real/false, light/dark, in which the critic's work entails the simple telling of things "as they are," then the phantasmagoria analogy to which Benjamin turns offers by contrast a more philosophically and politically complex approach to the problem of "false consciousness." Where the audience for the *camera obscura* is simply duped by a false representation, as Margaret Cohen describes, the "observer of the phantasmagoria is both participant and dupe, caught up in the pleasurable frisson of its machinations even while knowing them to be fraudulent" (228).[14] The visual spectacles of commodity culture are pleasurable, even if they are understood as illusions, and the critical examination of ideology demands, therefore, that such "irrational" realities be taken into account.

This argument has two facets: in the first place, we must recognize what Okri and his narrator clearly identify (albeit retrospectively) as the ideological function of this new "petro-magical" reality in constituting a certain mode of state sovereignty; and, second, less voluntaristically, we can understand such phantasmagorias as fundamental formal expressions of the nature of the commodity on which the economy is organized—qualities that come to characterize all levels of social experience, not just political performance. The rhetoric and semiotics of petro-modernity depend on a mystificatory emphasis on radical newness, a break from history based on "clean" money elevated from the grimy world of labor and production, and thus a "magical" transcendence of materiality and historicity.

In Okri's account, however, the phantasmagorical inflation of political value in this context leads inevitably to a radical devaluation that leaves the political itself emptied of content, predicated on a series of illusions and performances that are ultimately revealed to be bankrupt. Though the people gather excitedly to participate in the ritual spectacles and give themselves over to the promised "miracles" of magical wealth, the narrator finds himself unable, in the face of so much symbolic and monetary excess, to feel appropriately impressed: "It went on like that, one spectacle on top of another, leaving us perplexed by the mindless excess and drained of any possibility of wonder" (139). The phantasmagoric organization of political life, this suggests, has been evacuated of the affective quality necessary for genuine political embodiment, turning the political body into a serial assemblage of devalued individual actors who are becoming increasingly extraneous to the health of the whole. Later that night, after the mad scramble for money, the narrator walks the streets of the town and notices how its abject spaces have been constituted by the banknotes over which the people had fought. His description not only registers a clearly counterfeit logic of value, but also hints at an underlying logic of genocide:

> Everywhere we went that night we saw that the naira notes had fallen over the graves of the dead, over the market stalls, on the huts of the poor, on stationary cars, on heaps of garbage. It was only when I began to pick up the notes on my way to the hotel that I realized we had all been the victims of a cruel prank. When I turned the notes, wet in my hands, the ink began to run. Then I saw that one side of the currencies was authentic, but the other side washed away and became blank. We had been fighting for joke currencies. (140)

This disjuncture between signifier and signified—between banknotes and the value for which they stand—is the very basis of inflationary devaluation. But as the man recognizes with horror when he understands that the brutal conflict of the day before has been waged over worthless simulacra, the phantasmagorical organization of political life has some direly material consequences, ones that his unconscious earlier represented quite accurately in the charred bodies of children "piled on the backs of trucks" (92).

If money, according to Simmel, is "the most terrible destroyer of all form," tending to hollow out all intrinsic value and destroy fixed substances, then the soul of the modern monetary subject, in an inflationary context, becomes similarly debased. As Durst remarks, "Without an underlying foundation of intrinsic meaning, the soul of the modern subject resembles something akin to a collage whose hollow background is pasted over by arbitrarily related fragments" (Durst 80). During an inflation, when these general tendencies of monetary culture confront the individual most immediately, this existential fragility tips over into ontological collapse.

Writing in the aftermath of World War II, Elias Canetti recognized the sense in which, under particular historical circumstances, the logical culmination of rampant inflation—"a witches sabbath of devaluation" in which people come to feel as worthless as their money—may be genocide (Canetti 186). Canetti suggests, in "Inflation and the Crowd," that the feeling of ontological devaluation experienced by Germans during the 1920s inflation was displaced onto the Jews, who were associated, as moneylenders and speculators, with the crisis itself. The treatment of the Jews, he argues, "repeated the process of inflation with great precision." From first being "attacked as enemies," they were "more and more depreciated," until finally "they were treated literally as vermin, to be destroyed with impunity by the million" (188).

Although the genocidal inflation-by-proxy described by Canetti is never predicted explicitly in Okri's story, it haunts the narrative subconscious just as it haunts the narrator's. The association Okri wants to draw between inflationary economies and genocidal politics, a theme introduced in the Lagos section of the story, is more carefully developed through the events in W. After the semi-comical excesses of the potlatch competition and the citizens' desperate struggles to win the silver coins, things take a more sinister turn when murderous "thugs" representing various "cults" begin a violent rampage through the streets of the city. The day reaches an apocalyptic climax in a devastating flood that pours through W late that night.

The deluge, which symbolically references the unstable liquid basis of the Nigerian economy, reinforces the man's new understanding of the inflationary economy's inevitable devaluation of human life: "We were the garbage carried away on waves of mud" (140). The floodwaters sweep through the streets but fail to transform the deep structure of material life in the town, simply "transferring the garbage from one area to another" (129) as "mounds of rubbish, knee-high, formed around me" (130). The ominous "cults," whose rituals closely resemble those of more modern political spectacles in W, serve as an expression of the occult economies that are seen to underwrite material and therefore political power in Nigeria.[15]

The liquid commodity on which these economies are ultimately understood to depend in the story is in fact blood, which the cults are said to need in order to prepare elixirs for their leader (128). This shift in symbolic emphasis between the first and subsequent sections of the story corresponds with a formal distinction, as when the climactic flood (an event that itself corresponds to the bus crash that ends the Lagos section) transforms the narrative's dominant color scheme from the green that has been associated with oil, excrement and money, to blood red. The moon turns red and the man's soaked shirt is "dyed red by the rain" (130). In some parts of town it is even rumored to have rained blood (as well as lobsters).

But even this, the liquid basis of life itself, becomes a phantasmagoria in the political logic of oil-boom Nigeria. Often a symbol of relationality, genealogy, and belonging, blood here becomes a surrogate for cynical relations of exchange and exploitation.[16] The morning after the devastating flood and political rioting, the man's friend tells him that "if I wanted to survive in the country, or anywhere in the world, the secret was to join the strongest side and 'pour your blood into the basin'" (133–34). On his return to Lagos, his boss offers to reinstate his sales job at a higher salary, asking "if I was ready to take my measure as a full-blooded national . . . a man, an African" (141–42). It is neither the abstract bonds of citizenship nor the material bonds of blood kinship that now constitute the Nigerian "nation," but the shared culture of inflationary excess, the willingness to sacrifice other people's "blood" in order to get ahead.

The recognition of the oil economy's phantasmagoric power to turn excrement into wealth,[17] and in turn to transform human life into excrement, is not specific to Nigeria. Citing Coronil's study of Venezuela's oil boom, Michael Watts recalls one minister's feeling that the "natural bounty of oil had, in the magical and mysterious process of being transformed into money, become a putrid and toxic waste. . . . Oil had vastly increased the national appetite and the capacity to consume, yet ingesting petroleum only served to contaminate everything."[18] The illusion of "magical money" derived cleanly and effortlessly from the national soil is revealed as a mystification: a phantasmagorical trick that occludes the real waste product cast off by this wealth production. The siphoning of petroleum from beneath Nigeria's earth, and the circulatory economy of appearance and fraud that operated above, left "mounds of garbage" and piles of excrement in its wake—in the form of devalued, disposable human bodies and devastated ecological landscapes. By the time Okri published *Stars of the New Curfew*, the struggles by residents of the Niger Delta for political and ecological justice had not yet achieved the visibility that would come with the arrest and execution of Ken Saro-Wiwa in 1995; but he had witnessed firsthand the social and ecological impact of oil drilling in the region around his hometown of Warri, near Port Harcourt in the Niger Delta, a scene he describes proleptically in "What the Tapster Saw" (see Wenzel).

The aftermath of the oil boom saw the generalization of the period's excremental logics. By the mid-1980s, structural adjustment policies, foreign debt, military coups, and a growing ecological crisis had intensified the political and economic alienation of a majority of Nigerians, for whom the oil boom was seen to have brought nothing but misery and degradation. The decaying infrastructures of Lagos and other urban centers, and the half-completed development projects that dotted the country, provided stark daily reminders of the hollowness at the core of the petroleum economy; they served as ironic material monuments to the failures of petro-modernity and the country's rude awakening from its dream of itself as an icon of African modernism and a full participant in global modernity. The infamous Ajaokuta Steel Complex, never completed and continuing to drain state monies, stands "as a pathetic monument to oil, to oil politics and to oil money" (Watts, "Oil as Money" 430).

If the 1970s (Okri's formative teenage years) were defined in Nigeria by the dream of modernist development, then the late 1980s, when Okri was writing *Stars of the New Curfew*, represent the far side of that modernist dream-deferred, a period in which the nightmare of "de-modernization" had become fully realized (Ferguson 255). Anticipated in Okri's texts, the "pathetic monuments" and crumbling ruins that define Nigeria's contemporary landscape give physical form to this painful contradiction: the brutal reality of failure and defeat that remains haunted by the crumbling hopes of the past.

MAGICAL REALISM AND MODERNIST TIME

In his investigation of urban life on the Zambian copperbelt, James Ferguson identifies such contradictory simultaneity as characteristic of "post-modern" experience—life, that is, at the far end of modernity. He suggests that just such a "cynical skepticism has replaced an earnest faith when it comes to the idea of a modernizing, progressing Zambia"—a skepticism that is, nevertheless, ironically inflected by the memory of what might have been, the future anterior that was never fully realized.[19] This double-vision constitutes, we might say, the "magical/reality" of postcolonial Nigeria and Zambia alike, where the confidence and optimism of the earlier moment are, as Ferguson argues, "both absent and, in its very absence, somehow present. . . . Like a dream, the idea of moving proudly into the ranks of the first class was both vividly remembered and manifestly unreal" (14).

This "untimeliness" or *Ungleichzeitigkeit* of postmodernist postcolonial disillusionment recalls Jameson's interest in historical contexts in which "whole layers of the past" and elements of the future survive within the present ("On Magic Realism in Film" 311), and thereby returns us to the question of magical realism as a literary mode. More than simply a representation of semiotic crisis, therefore, magical realism can also be seen as an expression of the doubleness or *Unheimlichkeit* of modernity itself—the simultaneity of modernity as expectation and disillusionment.[20] In a review of Okri's work, critic Biodun Jeyifo suggests that this paradox underlies the narrative experimentation and stylistic innovation that characterize later generations of African writers. Realist representation is itself called into question, Jeyifo argues, by the confusing and often tragic transformation of material reality in postcolonial, postmodern Africa: "the work of fiction can no longer complacently proffer a fictional 'reality' axiomatically at variance with the socio-historical reality of alienation, degradation, chaos and instability for the vast majority of its living generations" (Jeyifo, cited in Quayson 156). In a similar vein, Ferguson points to the epistemological challenges of conducting ethnographic research in postmodernist Zambia, where subjects themselves are unable to make sense of their circumstances, let alone explain these understandings to an outsider: "when I tried to get an insider's view of their social world," he recalls, "what I found resembled less a stable, systemic order of knowledge than a tangle of confusion, chaos, and fear" (19). In the postcolonial context, with which magical realism is now so closely associated, the question of representation, narrative, and even realism itself thus assumes political as well as economic and existential significance. The realization of the dream of postcolonial independence, of human dignity and economic self-determination promised by the anticolonial movements, has in almost every instance come to seem a reality that is infinitely deferred, a dream whose instantiation has been radically called into question by the brute materiality of everyday life in the postcolony.

Once again, this identifies postcolonial Africa—particularly countries like Nigeria, where economic prosperity and cultural productivity once seemed eminently attainable—as a kind of "magical" reality, one that calls into question the very possibility of representation itself. For Guenther, the early "magical realists," artists such as De Chirico and his Post-Expressionist heirs, presented a "pictorial vision of man's alienation and disorientation" (38). While landscapes and city scenes were frequent subjects for post-expressionist painters, Guenther insists that their primary theme is in fact "the alienated individual placed in a modern world he could neither fathom nor control" (43) and the challenges of making sense of and representing a reality that had come to seem meaningless or even orchestrated by dark spirits and witchcraft.[21] The return to representation after the fulgurations of Expressionism represented an effort to make artistic sense of the ways in which these crises demanded "new way[s] of seeing and rendering the everyday," and the sense, induced by the inflation, that the superficial reality and tangibility of everyday objects—their "objectivity"—could no longer be taken for granted (Guenther 36).

The fascination with surface, perspective, juxtaposition, and temporality that defines post-expressionist "magical realism" and its postcolonial heirs can therefore be seen as a stylistic engagement with the problematic qualities of signification in a post-inflationary era. If the inflation radically disrupted ordinary Germans' faith in the stability of the signifying bond, it also precipitated a general crisis of value that affected all modes of signification. Though cognate crises have long been thought to underlie modernism more generally, the specific link between inflationary culture and magical realism suggests that this mode serves as a centrally significant stylistic attempt to represent the uncertainty of signification in a context of monetarized (post-)modernity. Emerging out of situations that are characterized by an "awareness of the ineluctable lack in communication," magical realist texts endeavor to "increase the likelihood of complete signification through magical means, to make the text—a decidedly unreal construct—become real through a deceptive seeming" (Simpkins 148). "Magic" serves, in Scott Simpkins' view, as a representational supplement: a tool for addressing the shortcomings of language as a mode of signification and a kind of insurance to boost the "credit-worthiness" of the text. Believability and referentiality are matters, in these works, consciously of *effect* rather than of essence. Manipulated by the artist, they are functions of point-of-view and perception.

The experience of postcolonial modernity as a "real" memory experienced as a "manifestly unreal" reality returns us to Okri, whose works are consistently concerned with the problem of exploring the expanse stretching between the real and the ideal. For Okri, magical realism functions as a mode by which to account for the excesses, expectations, losses, and disillusionments that characterize petro-magic-reality, and to memorialize, at the level of form, the broken bodies and spirits of ordinary Nigerians, the devastated natural landscapes and ravaged cultures that continue to haunt its people.

NOTES

1. I borrow the term in my title, "Petro-Magic Realism," from Wenzel.

2. For an intriguing consideration of postcolonial modernism in terms of this perceptual "proximity," see Baucom.

3. The Nigerian naira (₦) was introduced in 1973 to replace the British pound as the national currency. Barber's figures are in pounds sterling and then naira; the contemporaneous U.S. dollar equivalent is given in parentheses.

4. "We are drowning in the devil's excrement." Juan Pablo Perez Alfonso, founder of OPEC, in 1976 (cited in Watts, "Oil as Money" 406).

5. See Achille Mbembe, "The Aesthetics of Vulgarity."

6. The term, originally referring to damage to Dutch manufacturing by North Sea gas development, was coined by the World Bank to describe how booms fueled by natural resource exploitation produce overvalued currencies that discourage other export sectors and overwhelm domestic producers who must compete with cheap imports.

7. Barber (435–36) notes that very few Nigerians participated in the actual labor of extracting and distributing the country's oil, another reason its profits were "not seen to be produced by work."

8. For a helpful account of the "time horizon" of inflation, see Widdig 84.

9. As Wenzel notes, "What the Tapster Saw" details the "superimposition of a petroleum economy over a palm economy in the Niger Delta" (449), while "Stars of the New Curfew" is explicitly concerned with the social and ethical effects of the new petro-economy.

10. See Apter, 42–44, for a discussion of a 1970s' Nigerian advertisement for Saxon Photocopiers that plays on a similar demetaphorized metaphor: "Anyone in your office can make money," the ad proclaims, "simply by pressing two buttons."

11. See Barber, esp. 434–38.

12. In a reminder of OPEC's artificial scarcity, which initiated the boom in the 1970s, the salesman notes with satisfaction that "we brought in surprisingly excellent profits on the days when we were bold enough to auction our drugs to the highest bidders" (91).

13. In the 1939 essay "Paris, Capital of the Nineteenth Century," Benjamin identifies phantasmagoria as the defining feature of modernity itself: "The world dominated by its phantasmagorias—this, to make use of Baudelaire's term, is 'modernity'" (Benjamin, "Paris" 26).

14. Cohen continues: "While the *camera obscura* does not attempt to fool its audience into mistaking its two-dimensional inversions of reality for the outside world, the phantasmagoria endows its creations with a spectral reality of their own" (94).

15. See Comaroff & Comaroff, "Occult Economies."

16. Cf. Apter's complementary insight (14, 50, 249–55) that during the boom's optimistic early phase, oil was also figured as a kind of life-giving blood circulating around the national body politic.

17. "[Oil] is a filthy, foul-smelling liquid that squirts obligingly up into the air and falls back to earth as a rustling shower of money" (Kapuściński 34).

18. Watts, "Oil as Money" 407. Watts cites from Coronil, 233.

19. Ferguson 14. Ferguson associates Zambia's economic decline—the failure of its modernist dream—with an inflationary devaluation in purchasing power (7). Though Ferguson does not make much of this point, it does suggest the centrality of the inflationary experience to the experience of modernity as a magical/reality, a promise or expectation conjoined with its realist dissolution.

20. See Neil Lazarus's essay, "Modernism and African Literature," in this volume.

21. For one interesting account of this association, see Widdig 204–09.

WORKS CITED

Adamson, Yahya K. "Structural Disequilibrium and Inflation in Nigeria: A Theoretical and Empirical Analysis" April 1989: 1–17. Unpublished manuscript. Web. 1 November 2011. http://netdrive.montclair.edu/~lebelp/CERAFRM007Adamson1989.pdf

Apter, Andrew. *The Pan-African Nation: Oil and the Spectacle of Culture in Nigeria*. Chicago: University of Chicago Press, 2005.

Barber, Karin. "Popular Reactions to the Petro-Naira." *The Journal of Modern African Studies* 20.3 (1982): 431–450.

Baucom, Ian. "Township Modernism." *Geo-Modernisms: Race, Modernism, Modernity*. Ed. Laura Doyle and Laura Winkiel. Bloomington: University of Indiana Press, 2005.

Bayart, Jean-Francois. *The State in Africa: The Politics of the Belly*. Trans. Mary Harper, Christopher and Elizabeth Harrison. New York: Longman, 1993.

Benjamin, Walter. "Convolut G: Exhibitions, Advertising, Grandville." *The Arcades Project*. Trans. Howard Eiland and Kevin McLaughlin. Cambridge: Belknap Press, 2003.

———. "Imperial Panorama: A Tour of German Inflation." *One-Way Street and Other Writings*. Trans. Edmund Jephcott and Kingsley Shorter. London: Verso, 1992.

———. "Paris, Capital of the Nineteenth Century (1939)." *The Arcades Project*. Trans. Howard Eiland and Kevin McLaughlin. Cambridge: Belknap Press, 2003.

Canetti, Elias. "Inflation and the Crowd." *Crowds and Power*. Trans. Carol Stewart. New York: Farrar, Straus Giroux, 1984.

Cohen, Margaret. "Walter Benjamin's Phantasmagoria." *New German Critique* 48 (1989): 87–107.

Comaroff, Jean, and John L. Comaroff. "Millennial Capitalism: First Thoughts on a Second Coming." *Public Culture* 12.2 (2000): 291–343.

———. "Occult Economies and the Violence of Abstraction: Notes from the South African Postcolony." *American Ethnologist* 26.2 (1999): 279–301.

Coronil, Fernando. *The Magical State: Nature, Money, and Modernity in Venezuela*. Chicago: University of Chicago Press, 1997.

Darnton, John. "Oil Riches Unleash a Major Boom in Nigeria." *New York Times* January 30, 1977: IES44. Print.

Derrida, Jacques. *Given Time: I. Counterfeit Money*. Trans. Peggy Kamuf. Chicago: University of Chicago Press, 1994.

———. *Of Grammatology*. Trans. Gayatri Chakravorty Spivak. Baltimore: Johns Hopkins University Press, 1998.

Durst, David C. *Weimar Modernism: Philosophy, Politics and Culture in Germany, 1918–1933*. Oxford: Lexington Books, 2004.

Faris, Wendy. *Ordinary Enchantments: Magical Realism and the Remystification of Narrative*. Nashville: Vanderbilt University Press, 2004.

Ferguson, James. *Expectations of Modernity: Myths and Meanings of Urban Life on the Zambian Copperbelt*. Berkeley: University of California Press, 1999.

Geschiere, Peter. *The Modernity of Witchcraft: Politics and the Occult in Postcolonial Africa*. Charlottesville: University of Virginia Press, 1997.

Goux, Jean-Joseph. *Symbolic Economies: After Marx and Freud*. Trans. Jennifer Curtiss
      Gage. Ithaca: Cornell University Press, 1990.
Guenther, Irene. "Magical Realism in the Weimar Republic." *Magical Realism: Theory,
      History, Community*. Ed. Lois Parkinson Zamora and Wendy B. Faris. Durham: Duke
      University Press, 1995.
Jameson, Fredric. "Culture and Finance Capital." *The Cultural Turn: Selected Writings on
      the Postmodern 1983–1998*. London: Verso, 1998: 136–61.
———. "On Magic Realism in Film." *Critical Inquiry* 12 (1983): 301–25.
———. *Postmodernism; or, The Cultural Logic of Late Capitalism*. Durham: Duke University
      Press, 1992.
Jeyifo, Biodun. "The Voice of a Lost Generation: The Novels of Ben Okri." *The Guardian
      (Lagos)*, 12 July 1986.
Kapuściński, Ryszard. *Shah of Shahs*. Trans. William R. Brand and Katarzyna Mroczkowska-
      Brand. San Diego: Harcourt Brace, 1985.
Marx, Karl. *Capital*, Vol. 1. 1887. Trans. Samuel Moore and Edward Aveling. New York:
      International Publishers, 1967. 76–77.
Mbembe, Achille. "The Aesthetics of Vulgarity." *On the Postcolony*. Berkeley: University of
      California Press, 2001.
———. "Life, Sovereignty and Terror in the Fiction of Amos Tutuola." *Research in African
      Literatures* 34.4 (2003): 1–26.
———. "Necropolitics." Trans. Libby Meintjies. *Public Culture* 15.1 (2003): 11–40.
Okri, Ben. "Stars of the New Curfew." *Stars of the New Curfew*. New York: Viking. 1988.
———. "What the Tapster Saw." *Stars of the New Curfew*. New York: Viking, 1988.
Quayson, Ato. "Esoteric Webwork as Nervous System: Reading the Fantastic in Ben Okri's
      Writing." *Essays on African Writing: 2, Contemporary Literature*. Ed. Abdulrazak
      Gurnah. Oxford: Heinemann, 1995.
Rotman, Brian. *Signifying Nothing: The Semiotics of Zero*. London: Macmillan, 1987.
Saro-Wiwa, Ken. *Genocide in Nigeria: The Ogoni Tragedy*. Port Harcourt: Saros Inter-
      national Publishers, 1992.
Shell, Marc. *The Economy of Literature*. Baltimore: Johns Hopkins University Press, 1994.
———. *Money, Language, and Thought: Literary and Philosophical Economies from the
      Medieval to the Modern Era*. Baltimore: Johns Hopkins University Press, 1994.
Simmel, Georg. "The Metropolis and Mental Life." *On Individuality and Social Forms:
      Selected Writings*. Ed. Donald N. Levine. Chicago: University of Chicago Press, 1971.
Simpkins, Scott. "Sources of Magical Realism." *Magical Realism: Theory, History Community*.
      Ed. Lois Parkinson Zamora and Wendy B. Faris. Durham: Duke University Press, 1995.
Watts, Michael J. "Oil as Money: The Devil's Excrement and the Spectacle of Black Gold."
      Money, Power and Space. Ed. Stuart Corbridge, Nigel Thrift, and Ron Martin.
      Cambridge: Blackwell, 1994.
———. "Petro-Violence: Community, Extraction, and Political Ecology of a Mythic
      Commodity." *Violent Environments*. Ed. Nancy Lee Peluso and Michael Watts. Ithaca:
      Cornell University Press, 2001.
Wenzel, Jennifer. "Petro-magic-realism: Toward a Political Ecology of Nigerian Literature."
      Postcolonial Studies 9.4 (2006): 449–64.
West, Harry G., and Todd Sanders, eds. *Transparency and Conspiracy: Ethnographies of
      Suspicion in the New World Order*. Durham: Duke University Press, 2003.
Widdig, Bernd. *Culture and Inflation in Weimar Germany*. Berkeley: University of California
      Press, 2001.

CHAPTER 11

LITTLE MAGAZINE, WORLD FORM

ERIC BULSON

The history of contemporary letters has, to a very manifest
extent, been written in such magazines.

—Ezra Pound, 1930[1]

The history of literary movements is more often written
in some long forgotten dead little magazines.

—Lewis Nkosi, 1964[2]

LITTLE magazines made literary history in the twentieth century. On that point
Lewis Nkosi and Ezra Pound would agree. But if you begin to ask for more specific
details, whose history, what literature, which magazines, these two would necessarily part ways. When writing a brief history of "the small magazine," as he called
it, Pound had in mind a European high modernism made in the pages of *The Egoist*,
The Little Review, and *The Dial* in the 1910s and into the 1920s. Nkosi, who made
this observation in a review of *Okyeame*, a little magazine published in Ghana in the
1960s, was referring more generally to modern African literature after 1950. Same
medium, different time and place: modern but not necessarily modernist. And in
both cases, the little magazine functioned as a world form, a place in which writers,
readers, critics, and translators could imagine themselves belonging to a global
community that consisted of, but was not cordoned off by, national boundaries.

And yet, you begin to wonder, if that is really all there is to the story of the little
magazine: European modernists inventing the medium in the first half of the

twentieth century to house their artistic experiments, and non-Western, often postcolonial, writers adapting it in the second half of the century to accommodate independent national literatures. This particular spin on the little magazine's transmission ends up making European modernism responsible on some level for the birth of modern literature in places like Africa and the West Indies—which is to radically oversimplify and misrepresent the issue. The form of the little magazine, which we identify with the birth of modernism, was already in place in non-Western countries around the globe, including Japan and Argentina. It does not only belong to the West, even if it was the vehicle that carried so many modernist texts in and between England, the United States, and Europe. When the little magazine comes to Africa in the 1950s, its owes as much to the legacy of Anglo-American and European avant-garde magazines as it does to the pamphlet culture of India and an expansive network of Lusophone and Francophone newspapers and periodicals that ballooned in the 1940s. The African little magazine, then, is a strange amalgam of print media, something that could emerge only under postwar conditions when independent nations were being borne out of the wreckage of collapsed empires and modernist magazine culture that was already a thing of the past.

The little magazine, as I will argue in this chapter, doesn't just make history: it *is* history. Which is to say, it is a medium shaped by the material conditions of its time and place, including everything from print technologies and prudish censors to postal rates and paper costs. It takes on different shapes and actively responds to the particular audience, literary tradition, and print culture out of which it emerges. When it comes to the little magazine, one size does not fit all. And as I'll explain in what follows, the sheer variety of structural differences in little magazines indicates just how malleable the form could be as it moved, and how the arrangement of everything from the contents and the cover design to the presence or absence of book reviews, correspondence, distribution lists, and editorial blurbs reflects the complicated process by which this medium negotiated local literary production and the emergence of a global literary field in modernism's aftermath.

THE DECENTERED UNIVERSE OF LITTLE MAGAZINES

If the little magazine is part of a global literary history in the twentieth century, why haven't we been able to see it? As a quick answer, we might blame it all on scale. There are too many magazines to account for, somewhere in the tens of thousands, maybe even more.[3] Despite the herculean efforts of patient bibliographers and archivists, no one knows for sure just how many of them popped up and dropped out over the past century. The impossibility of collecting this kind of empirical data has a lot to do with the size of the print runs and the fragility of the materials: little magazines, to put it another way, were not built to last. But there's also the question of specialization. These magazines, no matter how worldly they may have been, are often appropriated for particular national histories. And once little magazines are circumscribed by nations and twenty-five-year time lines, they usually stop having a lot in common with one another, and the transnational circuits of exchange, on which so many magazines depended for their existence, are lost in the process.

There is also the related problem of translation. The category of the "little magazine" cannot be applied universally. This medium appears under a variety of different names, many of them firmly entrenched in the traditions of a nation-based print culture: *rivista, revista, revue, periódico, zhurnal, zeitschriften, dōjin zasshi*. The Italian Futurists, for example, didn't have a "little magazine," but they did have *Noi*, a *rivista* (literary translated into English as "review"). And the same could be said for Japan: there was no "little magazine" but there was *Mavo*, a *dōjin zasshi*, or "coterie magazine," intended for a small circle of like-minded writers and readers interested in contemporary Japanese literature. Little magazines have appeared all over the world, but the conditions of their production have varied widely. The modernization of print technologies made it easier for writers around the globe to take over the means of literary production. In some cases, the little magazine was an alternative to the specialized scholarly periodical or the mass-produced newspaper. In other cases, it was intended to supplement a lack in the general art and culture magazines on the market. Whatever the formal differences, titles, readerships, or size (some little magazines were simply bigger than others), they all shared one thing in common: an interest in the present. The little magazine, whatever its provenance and itinerary, was always a medium intended for the publication of contemporary literature and criticism, and it was this obsession with the "NOW" of literary production and consumption, in fact, which made so many little magazines futuristic, in the general sense of the term, forward-looking, eager to map out new directions of an experimental literary culture.

When we talk about the globality of modernism, there is a tendency to privilege the medium of the book. In her widely influential *République mondiale des lettres*, in fact, Pascale Casanova anchors her theory of literary globalization in the publication of books in the literary capitals of Paris and London throughout the twentieth century. The little magazine is removed from sight, tucked away into the occasional footnote to identify the original publication of this or that modernist masterwork. According to Casanova, an open and democratic world literature is one of those beautiful fictions, a utopian dream that ignores the capitalist exploitation of minor literatures from so many postcolonial nations around the world (Ireland, Trinidad, Africa, and India among them). In this center-periphery model of the world literary system, writers from the postcolonial periphery achieve international literary recognition only by moving through Paris, the literary capital of the world (in her theory), if not the universe.

Although critics have roundly attacked Casanova for having a myopic "Francophilic" view of world literature, her work has been very useful in laying out some ways that the global book business depends on Western-based editors, critics, and translators, who have the power to confer "prestige," or symbolic capital, on writers eager to reach an international audience. Bearing in mind Casanova's theory of world literature, we can begin thinking about how the little magazine provides an alternative model of the global literary field, one that is not confined to the movement of minor literatures through Western-based capitals. In fact, the little magazine is such a valuable subject for the analysis of world literature precisely because it does not belong to a single nation, continent, or hemisphere. It helped generate a world literary system that was semi-autonomous: connected to the book publishing conglomerates, and yet not driven by the unequal power relations of a Western literary marketplace. There was, strictly speaking, no center to the world of little magazines, precisely because the system was not dependent on the movement of authors from one nation-based magazine to another, from the periphery to the center.

A decentered literary universe: that, in effect, is what the little magazine created in the twentieth century. Writers and critics still had their eye on Western models, but literary production and reception were not dependent, finally, on Western capitals or their editors, critics, translators, and readers. In fact, the proliferation of independent little magazines in some of the more isolated regions of the world is evidence enough of their ability to exist in spite of a capitalist system that would exclude or exploit them. And that's what makes Africa such a compelling case study in the history of the little magazine, one that I will return to in greater detail later on. Suffice it to say for now that in the 1950s, the little magazine comes into being in Nigeria at the same time that the London-based publishing houses, such as Heinemann, Longman, Oxford University Press, and Cambridge University Press, are beginning their scramble for Anglophone African literature. The huge success of Amos Tutuola's *Palm-Wine Drinkard*, published by Faber and Faber in 1952 (when T. S. Eliot was editor), helped put Africa on the map for many Western publishers and readers. The so-called African novel was the most popular genre for export, but there was very little chance for drama and poetry to make the leap. And that's where the little magazine comes in. It functioned as an alternative to the global book business and was engineered to bring Nigerian, and more generally African literature, to an African audience within and outside of the continent. For this reason, it doesn't make much sense to talk about the African little magazine only in terms of specific national or regional affiliations. The urgency for its existence was being determined by what was happening thousands of miles away, far beyond the continent.

There has always been a myth surrounding the little magazine's mobility. Like the book, it is cast as a medium that magically transcends national boundaries, uniting global readerships along the way. The illusion of the magazine's cosmopolitanism, I suspect, derives from some confusion between the realities of the magazine and the globetrotting writers it published. Little magazines were always faced with material challenges: postal costs, customs, shipping timetables, printing and distributions networks, and newsstands and booksellers who did not pay up. And with few exceptions, little magazines were a modest affair confined to a particular region and nation. Even the Dadaists, with their extensive networks in dozens of cities across Eastern, Western, and Central Europe, Asia, and Latin America, were very much based in specific urban centers, each one a hub for a different title.[4] In the case of "expat" magazines, such as *Broom*, whose editorial offices moved from Rome to Berlin to Paris between 1921 and 1924 (always with a home base in New York City), the situation was a little more complicated. The original decision to produce an avant-garde magazine in Europe and distribute it in the United States was prompted by Harold Loeb's impractical desire for cheaper paper. Before long, Loeb discovered that transatlantic distribution costs far exceeded the money he intended to save: in addition, large shipments of individual issues were regularly lost, damaged, or delayed along the way. As cosmopolitan as *Broom* may have been, it could not get away from the material challenges that come with international travel: every move from one city and country to another required figuring out where to find local printers, how to accommodate increased international postal rates and unreliable transatlantic timetables, and how to collect payments from bookstores.

Magazine mobility is one of the many myths that continue to circulate in discussions of modernism. But no magazine was big enough to take on the world. Not even *Ulysses* could enjoy world publication when it was serialized in *The Little Review*. Issues were coming out to a very limited audience (barely 1,000), most of them subscribers living in the United States. The *Little Review* did team up with *The Egoist* for a brief *Ulysses* "simulcast," but it was a disaster from beginning to end. Printers in England, who could be brought up on obscenity charges, kept asking for cuts, or, on numerous occasions, they simply refused to set the type. In the end, *The Little Review* managed to print thirteen and a half episodes with a few confiscations along the way; *The Egoist* had sections from five of them, and you can only imagine what British readers were to make of a novel like *Ulysses* appearing in fragments with significant time delays in between. *The Waste Land* had a little more success when it was published with a one-month delay in *The Criterion* and *The Dial* and reached more than 10,000 readers. The dual publication was, in part, influenced by a complex negotiation that Eliot had arranged, but it is worth making a simple point. Two magazines were needed to access a British and American public. While it was certainly conceivable that either magazine could make the transatlantic journey, they had a better chance of reaching a wider audience by limiting themselves to a single nation with an established subscription list and a reliable domestic postal route.

Indeed, there are many myths surrounding the little magazine's mobility, but this is not to say that they didn't move. Throughout the century, versions of this medium popped up on five continents. It was not a particular magazine moving across international boundaries so much as it was the form of the magazine itself. Writers, editors, critics, and translators were quick to realize that the magazine was an effective way of consolidating literary energies both at home and abroad. Some magazines were more international than others, but all had the potential to tap into an ever-expanding network. When Goethe first began thinking about *weltliteratur* in 1827, this mediated form of an international exchange was something that he had in mind: not a global book business or an all-inclusive canon of literatures, but an international conversation about contemporary literature mediated by *zeitschriften*. At the time, the dream of transcending national boundaries with periodicals was hampered by very real material difficulties (postal and paper costs among them). It was hard enough communicating across the Rhine let alone the post-Napoleonic boundaries of Europe, which is why *weltliteratur* never got far beyond Goethe's cursory observations.

Which leaves us with the question: how did the magazine make modernism global? The answer, I think, can be found in the form. Formal questions rarely come up in discussions of the little magazine. Critics instead have focused a lot of attention on the magazine's materiality (the space of the page, the arrangement of the cover design, the layout of poems and plays), and it is an approach that has yielded valuable information about how magazines mediate between popular and elite cultures (see Bornstein; Morrison). But I also have in mind the narratological valence of the term: form as referring to the structure and design of the magazine in its full runs, with beginnings and endings, editors that act like narrators, contributors that take on the role of characters, contents that read like chronologies, and a variety of other formatting devices that organize the information readers consume and digest between the covers.

A formal approach to the magazine has its benefits. For one thing, it provides a way to build on the kind of material analysis that focuses more exclusively on a single national culture or literary history. Form, in other words, encourages the kind of comparative work that helps us understand how the magazine belongs to a transnational system, one in which it is as much a product of a specific culture as it is of a global one that developed with such ferocity throughout the twentieth century. As much as we need to know about the particular national contexts out of which so many magazines emerged, it is just as crucial to examine the networks that they worked within and against, sometimes moving writers and texts across national borders, other times importing them for a foreign audience in translation. Form, in the end, will provide a perspective on the history of modern and modernist literature that is truly global in scale.

Before any comparative formal analysis is even possible, we need to expand the time line and enlarge the geography. It is a step that requires adjusting a narrative about the rise and fall of little magazines that has been in place for almost a century: born on or around 1910 during Ford Madox Ford's brief reign at *The English Review* (1908–1909) or the founding of Harriet Monroe's *Poetry* (1912), Harriet Shaw Weaver's *The Egoist* (1914), and Margaret Anderson's *The Little Review* (1914), reaching middle age in the 1920s with *The Dial*, *The Criterion*, *the transatlantic review*, and *transition*, and taking its last gasp in the late 1930s with the closing of *The Criterion* and the *N.R.F.* Accurate to a degree, this tale is, finally, partial, incomplete, and misleading. What do you do with *Shirakaba* in Japan (1910), *Ma* in Hungary (1916), *Kallol* (1923) and *Kabita* (1930) in India, *Martín Fierro* (1924–1927) in Argentina, *La Revue Indigène* (1927) in Haiti, *Voorslag* (1926) in South Africa, *The Beacon* (1931) in Trinidad, *Tropiques* (1941) in Martinique, *Kyk-over-al* (1945) in Guyana, *Bim* (1942) in Barbados, *Focus* (1943) in Jamaica, *Black Orpheus* (1957) in Nigeria, *Transition* (1961) in Uganda, and *Okyeame* (1961) in Ghana?

Here we have more than a dozen little magazines outside the usual transatlantic or trans-European orbit, and this is only a tiny fraction of the titles and places they were published. They appeared during the rise and, in some cases, after the fall of the Western little magazine, but with the exception of *Ma*, none of them were plugged into this network. In most cases, they flew under the radar, some of them becoming part of an emerging flood of Francophone and Anglophone magazines crossing and recrossing the Atlantic, others remaining stubbornly anchored in their town, province, or nation (voluntarily and involuntarily). And perhaps that's why they have been so easily excluded from view. They have nothing explicitly to do with the production or reception of European modernism (Western, Eastern, or Central), belonging instead to the pile of those "long forgotten dead little magazines" identified by Nkosi in the mid-1960s.

The non-Western little magazines challenge the most basic assumptions we've been making all along about the history and geography of this medium, of which the brief account provided in Malcolm Bradbury and James McFarlane's introductory book on modernism is representative: "It was largely through such magazines that the evolving works of modernism achieved their transmission, sought out their audiences, as *Ulysses* did through the American *Little Review*. And, gradually, it was the self-consciously small paper, in an era of large publishing ventures, that began to take over not only the localized work of particular movements but the larger tasks of cultural transmission" (Bradbury and McFarlane 203). Indeed, this is the narrative that most of us are familiar with: the little magazine struggling against the big bad book business and bringing out works that would have otherwise gone unpublished.

With non-Western magazines, the historical, political, and social conditions of the field could be quite different, and they often involved an enemy that was identified explicitly with a foreign empire (before and after independence). "Cultural transmission" across national borders, then, was less urgent, especially in the early stages, than a mode of cultural production at home. And this is a distinction worth emphasizing: transmission would eventually happen along diasporic networks connecting the West Indies, Africa, South Asia, the United States, and Europe, but the little magazine was mobilized to generate regional identities as well, many of them realized through exchanges. Eventually, the little magazine was recognized as a cosmopolitan technology precisely because it created circuits for communication without denationalizing or deregionalizing the specificity of the writers and the works that traveled through them. Pound, Joyce, Eliot, Lewis, and so many others proved that magazines could effectively generate a cosmopolitan community, but in the second half of the century, it was this same medium that was being adapted to create a modern literature whose cosmopolitanism was expressed through its regional, national, and transregional, transnational attachments.[5]

Little magazines in the West Indies and Africa, especially, fostered the kinds of literary and critical affiliations that would end up reinforcing their status as both national *and* cosmopolitan. It was an association that editors and reviewers attributed to the rise of a global book business firmly planted in London, New York, and Paris. One reviewer in *Black Orpheus* 15 (May 1964) argued that magazines like *Bim* (Barbados) and *Présence Africaine* (Dakar) were "reservoirs for Afro-Caribbean literature" precisely because they published "a great deal of indigenous writing that might otherwise never be printed in English, French, and American journals which demand a kind of compromise from their overseas contributors in order to make their material suitable for their own readers." For Arthur Seymour, editor at *Kyk-Over-Al* (Trinidad, 1945–1961) the "third-world magazine," as he called it, was a repository for the "values of the past" with the power to guide African and West Indian writing in the future (Seymour 3). And for an anonymous reviewer at *Bim*, little magazines were an antidote to the exclusion of "metropolitan publishing houses," and they allowed for the preservation of a "national linguistic expression" that would otherwise have been lost (Rodriguez 121–28; Lindfors, "African Little Magazines"; Morris, 3–9). Indeed, the little magazine's impact on global literary production often came from its isolation. And these various testimonies articulate the strange paradox that the formation of national languages and literatures within this medium actually required occupying a position on the margins of the system. The marginality of the little magazine not only leads to the formation of more local, national literatures but also ends up reinforcing a global literary system in which the little magazine moves in and between continents without ever having to pass through a metropolitan center along the way.

Black Orpheus, or, the Rise of the Little Magazine in Africa

The little magazine, as I mentioned, didn't die out after World War II: it moved. And the African continent was one of the places that benefited enormously from its arrival. As was true during its modernist "prehistory," the little magazine both catered to a preexisting public and helped to create a new one. And yet, in Africa, this issue of readership and distribution gets complicated immediately. Transport and communication technologies were lagging behind those connecting the Western metropoles like London, Paris, and New York, which made the most basic movement of people, print, and paper from region to region difficult, costly, and time-consuming. Indeed, there was an infrastructure that British, French, and Belgian empires helped to create, but with the independence of dozens of African countries in the 1950s and 1960s, movement by land, sea, and air became even more difficult, unreliable, and expensive. In the early years of *Transition*, which was based in Kampala, Uganda, there were plans to publish a West African edition with more space for criticism and the potential to reach a wider non-African public. Once Rajat Neogy and Christopher Okigbo realized how expensive such a collaborative venture would be, they were forced to drop it (Okigbo).

The rise of the little magazine in Africa is intimately linked with two related changes in the geopolitical and world-economic order in the mid-twentieth century: decolonization and the formation of the global book business.[6] The withdrawal of Western empires from African nations in the 1950s and 1960s coincided with the entrenchment of commercial conglomerates, which were eager to establish their interests in newly independent nations, and the book business was no exception.[7] British publishers, in particular, realized the potential of an untapped Anglophone market and soon began consolidating their interests. This commercial literary exchange between imperial metropoles and their former colonies was also working in the other direction: Anglophone African and West Indian writers were getting published by these same British firms and becoming part of a postcolonial novel craze that is still with us today (Low 15–33).

Amos Tutuola's *Palm-Wine Drinkard* was one of the first modern African novels to reach a wider Western audience. It was comprised entirely of Yoruba folktales woven together around the figure of the trickster (in this case one who loves palm-wine) and written in what Tutuola described self-consciously as "wrong English." When Faber and Faber published the novel, they included an image of an original manuscript page in Tutuola's own hand with a few editorial corrections in order to authenticate their latest discovery. Eileen Julien has called this novel and so many others produced in the 1950s and 1960s "extroverted" (685). It is a term that identifies those novels produced in one place (in this case Nigeria) for consumption abroad (in this case England). And there is a very real cost to this kind of exported, or extroverted, literary production. Extroversion is dependent on exclusion. Writers like Tutuola were being published abroad, but their books very often could not be afforded or, in some cases, even found, in their native countries.

This is where the little magazine comes in. While foreign publishers were extroverting African literature, the little magazine was, you might say, "introverting" it by bringing together, issue-by-issue, modern Anglophone texts for an African readership. In what follows, I will focus specifically on two of the most successful examples of this introversion: *Black Orpheus*, which published twenty-two issues in Lagos, Nigeria, between 1957 and 1967, and *Transition*, which published thirty-two issues between 1961 and 1968.[8] When *Black Orpheus* first started in 1957, Nigeria already had a lively and established print culture in place.[9] In addition to the many foreign-controlled newspapers, there were literary magazines, leaflets, periodicals, and scholarly journals printed and distributed by the University of Ibadan. With the exception of the popular general culture magazine, *Nigeria Magazine*, which regularly included a literary supplement, most of them were amateurish ventures intended for a small audience comprised mostly of students and faculty (Lindfors, "Popular Literature for an African Elite"). With its matte cover, woodcut images in bold colors, and thick paper, *Black Orpheus* stood out. Between the covers, readers would find the contents laid out on the page with generous margins, free from advertisements or letters from readers (and/or the editor). *Black Orpheus* was professional in quality, but it would never be confused with a popular magazine, and before long, issues were being picked up by Nigerian universities and used as anthologies for the classroom.

Unlike so many of its Western precursors, *Black Orpheus* was a little magazine intended for a general readership; it was not predisposed to experimental writing; it was not an enemy of the mainstream commercial literary marketplace (because there was none). There were no wealthy patrons (such as John Quinn or Harriet Shaw Weaver) to support production, so *Black Orpheus* relied on funding it received from a government-sponsored agency (Ministry of Education), something else that a Western little magazine would/could never do. The circulation numbers were on the "high" end of the spectrum (around 3,500 at its peak), and that was because it did not have to compete with other commercial or noncommercial publications for contemporary Anglophone literature. Instead of catering to the fit and few, the readership for *Black Orpheus* was still very much in the making, and the editors were more preoccupied with finding a general audience than offending them.

From its inception, *Black Orpheus* wanted to do for Anglophone literature what *Présence Africaine* had done for Francophone literature a decade earlier: provide a space for African writers to publish their work and establish a network of contacts that would put them in dialogue with writers and readers from the West Indies, United States, Europe, as well as East, West, and, when possible, South Africa. And the impact of *Présence Africaine* on the overall scope, scale, and direction of *Black Orpheus* cannot be overemphasized. *Présence Africaine* set the standard for African magazines during this period. It was an ambitious venture devoted to Francophone art, politics, and culture with a base of operations in Dakar and Paris. Not only did it help consolidate the philosophical and aesthetic principles behind the négritude movement, it was also an active ideological force behind anticolonial movements worldwide. *Présence Africaine* was as much a magazine as it was an institution with connections to the leading Francophone and French writers and intellectuals of the time (included among them Léopold Senghor, Aimé Césaire, André Breton, and Jean-Paul Sartre). And it was part of a subversive tradition of Francophone periodicals published in Paris, Senegal, and New York that were, as Brent Edwards explains, "a threat above all because of the transnational and anti-imperialist linkages and alliances they practiced" (Edwards 9).

From the beginning, founding editor Ulli Beier believed that *Black Orpheus* could mediate between Francophone literature and an Anglophone reading public. In his one and only editorial statement (*Black Orpheus* 1), Beier laments the fact that "it is still possible for a Nigerian child to leave a secondary school with a thorough knowledge of English literature, but without even having heard of such great black writers as Léopold Sédar Senghor or Aimée Césaire." Indeed, *Black Orpheus* lived up to its promise of making the Francophone world accessible to a wider non-French speaking audience, and its association with writers and editors from *Présence Africaine* provided the cultural prestige that it needed to get started. The title itself is a direct translation of *Orphée noir*, the title for an essay written by Jean-Paul Sartre appended to the wildly popular *Anthologie de la nouvelle poésie nègre et malgache* (1948) edited by Senghor. The Francophone and Anglophone writers were part of a shared colonial history, but if the case of *Black Orpheus* is any indication, there were often marked ideological differences. *Black Orpheus*, though sympathetic to the négritude movement, eventually distanced itself, focusing more explicitly on literature. Contemporary political and social critiques were avoided, and there was an almost stubborn attempt to keep Anglophone writers free from the stain of politics.

Reading *Black Orpheus* for its form requires taking a panoramic view of its entire print run with an eye toward structural additions and omissions.[10] As much as the content changed with every issue, the format remained largely the same: a matte cover with a woodcut image, the magazine title in block print on the masthead, printing and publication information with names of the editorial board, table of contents, an assortment of prose, poetry, and fiction in no particular order, followed by a note on the contributors. One of the more significant formal changes occurs in the fourth issue when a distribution list appears with the addresses of bookstores that carry *Black Orpheus*: Nigeria, Ghana, Sierra Leone, Kenya, Germany, Switzerland, Italy, Holland, Denmark, and Sweden (England, United States, France, and Belgium are added the following issue). The presentation of this information is strange if you consider that it would already be available to the reader with a copy in hand, presumably one picked up by an outlet carrying the magazine. Whatever was behind the decision, the distribution list disappeared an issue later, never to be seen again.

The disappearing distribution list raises an interesting question about the real and imagined globality of little magazines in general, all of them forced to deal with the question of advertising their range and, in doing so, defining their audience. Being global in such concrete terms does have its benefits: for one thing, it provides clear geographical parameters making the world of the magazine imaginable and showing readers that they are connected to a community of others in Ghana, Germany, and Sweden, who are leafing through the same material at the same time. But global concreteness can also work the other way: it makes the magazine seem more provincial precisely by drawing attention to gaps in and between places where it should be going. Where on the list is Uganda, Zimbabwe, or South Africa? How about Barbados, Trinidad, or Jamaica? The Pan-African and West Indian trajectories, which would become so critical to the success of *Black Orpheus* in the Anglophone world, are conspicuously absent. Global distribution, then, may make more of an impact when it remains abstracted, maybe even fictional. Instead of being circumscribed by definite locations, the effect of a global magazine culture can be generated by their absence, by the possibility that a little magazine printed in Nigeria could end up making its way to Sri Lanka or São Paolo.

So far, I've brought up some of the issues around the real and imagined distribution of *Black Orpheus* and the way this information can increase or decrease the perception of its worldliness. But it is critical to mention that the magazine didn't only travel the official distribution routes set up by the Ministry of Education or (from issue 13 onward) Longman. It was part of a pass-along readership and could move undetected in multiple directions across national and international boundaries. Andrew Salkey, for one, claims that he came across individual copies in the United States, Jamaica, England, France, and Germany (Beier). But as much as these sightings confirm *Black Orpheus*'s reach, they are also a reminder that numbers are always approximate and the range of influence can never be assessed with absolute certainty. If copies of *Black Orpheus* are circulating as far afield as Jamaica and Germany, it is possible that they could end up anywhere. When meeting a reader from South Africa, Beier inquired how much copies were being sold for on the newstands. "I don't know," the man replied, "I usually buy a stolen copy" (Beier).

Although the distribution list was dropped, *Black Orpheus* developed other formal strategies for signifying its affiliation with an international literary and critical scene. A section for book reviews began appearing with issue 3 and remained in place for the entire run. In the beginning, Beier did a majority of the reviewing himself, often under the *nom de plume* Sangodare Akanji, but with every issue new names popped up, many of them of African writers and intellectuals on their way to becoming part of an organic intelligentsia. It would seem logical, of course, to have book reviews in a literary magazine, but in this case, the situation is not so clear-cut. Since so many African novels were being exported and published abroad, the book review was often put there in place of the book itself. The review, for that reason, was not so much concerned with consumption as it was with the less lucrative pursuit of local critical evaluation. This displaced critical practice, one that involved the recognition of books written by African writers and published in England, was part of a symbolic strategy for national and regional reclamation. Africa may have been "losing" so many of its writers to foreign publishers, but magazines like *Black Orpheus* were helping to reappropriate them, making these same books share review space with locally produced plays, poetry, and anthologies, many of them printed by Mbari publications, a publishing house run by Beier for the sole purpose of bringing writers such as Christopher Okigbo, Wole Soyinka, Gabriel Okara, and J. P. Clark to an African audience.

In addition to the "foreign" books by African writers, it was just as common in *Black Orpheus* to see reviews of the latest Anglophone little magazines coming out of the West Indies, South Asia, and around Africa. In this case, the affiliation was motivated less by a symbolic reappropriation of African writers than it was by the desire for solidarity. There is often a paternalistic tone in these reviews, one meant as much to encourage other ventures, some of them already in print for ten years, as it is to recognize *Black Orpheus*'s triumphs. Something else is going on as well. The review of other magazines was a way of establishing a shared postcolonial print culture, one in which the connections between regional literatures only reaffirmed their indigenous, local affiliations. When assessing the importance of *Bim* (Barbados) and *Okyeame* (Ghana), one reviewer in *Black Orpheus* 14 put it this way: "The function of periodicals in nurturing the new literatures in Africa and the Caribbean cannot be overstated. They represent necessary documentary proof of fashion and growth. Their function is not so much to preserve as to link. Often they stand at the very beginning of the development of local literature, setting up standards and providing a literary market for buyer and seller—the indigenous reading public and the artist."

There is an awareness in this synopsis that different media perform different functions in the literary field. In this case, the reviewer contrasts the archival function of the anthology with the ephemerality of the little magazine; the relatively rapid production time of the magazine gives it a spontaneity that other literary media lack. The monthly or bimonthly turnover of literary production, sometimes at the expense of quantity over quality, has a way of encouraging "links," as this reviewer put it, between Africa and the Caribbean because it involves a mode of literary production in the present, one that is becoming possible because little magazines are creating the conditions for an international literary standard. Literature produced in Africa and the Caribbean, then, will not only be judged according to a national or regional literary marketplace or tradition. Rather, it will have to stand up in quality against what is coming out in other postcolonial countries with which it shares a common literary-historical trajectory.

Reviews were one place for this international critical standard to be applied, but it was even more forcefully introduced within the longer essays that began to appear under a separate heading in issue 9 (June 1961). "Criticism" is one of the more complicated generic categories in *Black Orpheus*. Before it began appearing, there were scholarly journals devoted to traditional, and especially oral, African literature, but there was no available critical tradition in Nigeria for modern Anglophone literature.[11] But the wider availability of a more substantial body of fiction and poetry in five years (engendered largely by *Black Orpheus*) made it necessary to establish criteria upon which it could be evaluated and judged both as African literature and as world literature. A majority of the critical essays that appeared in *Black Orpheus* are devoted to Francophone writers and texts, but they are interwoven with more general surveys of African literature, traditional visual art and poetry (Yoruba, Hausa, and Igbo), and the self-consciously modern Anglophone arrivals (Achebe, Clark, Soyinka, D. O. Fagunwa).[12]

This separate category for "criticism" reflects a concrete change in the African literary field, one that involved critics from African countries worried about a European takeover and the imposition of foreign standards. The question of who speaks for African writers was hotly contested in the following decades, in newspapers, literary journals, and big magazines alike, but what interests me here is the role that a little magazine like *Black Orpheus* played in the process. It had European and African critics writing side by side about everything from West Indian novels to Haitian poetry to South African short stories. There were no clearly defined critical practices in place or ready-made concepts to draw from, and though Western comparisons were there to be found, some critics chose to emphasize regional contexts instead.

Elsewhere in England, Germany, and France, where African works were being published, the question of critical standards was especially vexed. Some African writers wanted to be judged as equals with their Western counterparts, others argued for their cultural, historical, and linguistic singularity. One article about Wole Soyinka's trip to a drama conference in Edinburgh captures the complexity of the situation. "He was insistent," writes Scottish actress Una MacClean, "that drama from Africa deserved to be judged by universal standards of criticism and that the enduring value of any African drama must depend upon the adequacy of its representation of universal human experiences" (MacClean 46). For Soyinka and so

many others, there was always the danger of being exoticized and treated as something marginal to Europe's history and literary tradition. "Universal standards,"
then, was his way of emphasizing the links that existed between them, a subtle reminder to his foreign audience of a shared history that went well beyond the borders
of a single country or continent.[13] The critics writing in *Black Orpheus* realized that
the field of English literature was opening up to accommodate new human experiences from its former colonies, and it was an association that would take some getting used to. But leafing through the pages of this little magazine, you discover that
criticism was less about anchoring African literature in a European past and tradition than it was in imagining what such an affiliation would look like in a literary
historical future that included both.

Transition, or, the Formation of a Global Readership

Black Orpheus earned its reputation as "the doyen of African literary magazines."
But even Beier recognized that his magazine had lived long enough to experience
middle age. Worried that *Black Orpheus* was losing its edge and with a civil war in
Nigeria on the horizon, Beier retired from his post in 1968. During an interview that
same year, he explained that *Black Orpheus* was a propaganda magazine meant to
fill a need in what had been a barren literary field. In a decade, the Anglophone literary scene had changed significantly both within Africa and around the world. It
was time, he thought, to encourage the local production of low-cost poetry magazines, or, if possible, to reinvent his own magazine by changing the title to *Orpheus*.
That would be a way to distance the magazine from its original associations with an
ideological program established by *Présence Africaine* and, in doing so, reach out to
an even wider audience, one in which Anglophone African writers could be published alongside their English-speaking counterparts (Beier). After Beier's departure, Abiola Irele and J. P. Clark took over the editorship, keeping the original title
and bringing out issues sporadically until 1976. The black internationalism that was
so carefully orchestrated by Beier and his team of editors gave way to a more parochial focus on Nigeria and Ghana, which was compounded by a collapse of the
distribution structure that made *Black Orpheus* available only to readers in Lagos.[14]

All was not lost, however. On the other side of Africa, in Kampala, Uganda,
another little magazine, which overlapped with *Black Orpheus* for four years, was in
full swing. It was called *Transition*, and under the editorship of Rajat Neogy, it continued laying the foundations for a network of little magazines that would connect
Africa with readers, writers, and critics around the world. "Both authors and editors, as well as the reader," Neogy wrote in one editorial, "must feel gratified when,
to cite one example, a Nigerian writer in the United States has an article published
in a magazine in Uganda which is replied and discussed by correspondents in London, Nairobi, Kampala, Ibadan, Cape Town, and Edinburgh" (Neogy, "Editorial
Note" 3). In the seven-year run (1961–1968) of its first phase with Neogy, *Transition*
became a truly international little magazine with a print-run that eventually
exceeded 12,000.[15] Considering that East African literature at the time was lagging

far behind Nigeria, that there was very little institutional funding to support it, and that a majority of the audience was hard-pressed for cash, the circulation of *Transition*, which equaled *The Dial* in its heyday, was no small achievement. When *Transition* received ecstatic praise from the *New York Times*, the *Observer* (London), the *Oslo Dagbladet*, the *Globe and Mail* (Toronto), and *Die Zeit* (Hamburg) for achieving such success on a "shoestring budget," Paul Theroux was quick to remind readers that "in a country like *Uganda* where 90% of the population is barefoot, even shoestrings are hard to come by" (Theroux 41).

Black Orpheus paved the way for another little magazine in Africa by providing a crew of writers and readers trained in its pages and a design for what the medium might look like. But *Transition* was very much a creation of its own, more avant-garde than its predecessor, and prepared to rouse, shock, and alienate. It immediately distinguished itself from other print media by claiming, in its inaugural issue, "to provide an intelligent and creative backdrop to the East African scene, to give perspective and dimension to affairs that a weekly or daily press would either sensationalise or ignore." Topics were not introduced in one issue and then forgotten; they were meant to develop organically over time, and the editor, for that reason, functioned much like an "obstetrician" (Neogy's phrase). After Obiajunwa Wali's "The Dead End of African Literature?" appeared (*Transition* 10), in which he argued that African writers should reject the foreign languages imposed on them by colonialism and write in their native tongues, letters poured in for two years. As a courtesy, space was always made for the debate to unfold, and it was assumed that readers would be able to keep track of its attenuated twists and turns.

Transition also found a way to make the reality of a global readership more tangible by introducing a "Letters to the Editor" section, one of the formal features that *Black Orpheus* lacked. The letters included in this section ran the gamut from appreciation and bewilderment to disdain and outrage. It was the space in the magazine that allowed readers to communicate not just with the authors of the articles and the editor but with one another. Each letter was preceded by a title and concluded with a name and address where they could be contacted directly. As polite as Neogy was with his correspondents (even correcting their grammatical and spelling mistakes when necessary), he was not afraid to pit them against one another or turn their discomfort to the magazine's advantage. Such was the case after Paul Theroux's fierce critique of the white expatriate community in East Africa, with the sardonic title, "Tarzan Is an Expatriate" (*Transition* 32). Letters of complaint arrived for over a year, and Neogy decided to republish them together with the original article and offer it as a gift to new subscribers.

Though letters to magazines are often treated as a curiosity, one of the guilty pleasures readers indulge in before getting to the real content, this was not true of *Transition*. These letters were critical to the goals of the magazine because they allowed for the kind of dialogue that could not happen anywhere else. Positioned in the opening pages, they acted as an entryway into the discussion, and helped to establish continuity from one issue to another. In the first few issues, this section took up a page or two, and often included letters of appreciation from countries far and wide. Later on as the magazine gathered momentum, it was just as common for the letters to run a full four or five pages, some of them long enough to function as stand-alone essays or editorials. Abiola Irele believes that the conversational aspect gave *Transition* its force because it "helped reduce African problems to some kind of unified intellectual order" (Irele, "Review of *Transition*" 444). The lead articles in each issue were not treated as the final word; they were printed in order to be "analysed, commented upon, queried—turned inside out, as it were—and sometimes more closely scrutinized" in the letters that followed in subsequent issues, sometimes with half a dozen arguments alive at once (Irele, "Review of *Transition*" 444). Neogy was very tactical about the kinds of letters he would print, but in his capacity as an editor, he actively engineered a space where ideas could be debated; and he did it in such a way that the barriers between critics and readers were lowered. Everyone was free to have an opinion, but only if they were ready for debate. In a lengthy editorial on the subject, Neogy put it this way: "Unless writers and readers sense this atmosphere of 'aggressive non-prejudice' they will not be tempted to be provocative or even just plain naughty, and the kind of humour that accompanies such exaggerations of sensibilities will be markedly missing. More important, what might creep into the magazine's columns is a tone of genteelness, sinister and syrupy, where everyone is quietly patting everyone else on the back" (Neogy, "Do Magazines Culture?" 31).

By making the letters to the editor such a prominent feature, *Transition* created an expansive community of readers who could engage in a conversation about current literary and cultural events without a significant time lag. Time was indeed passing between issues, usually two or three months, but the back and forth provided an urgency to what was being published between the covers. *Transition*, then, functioned as a cultural medium in a very literal way, bringing Uganda, East Africa, and Africa to a wider audience, making domestic issues involving African literature and politics a topic for discussion, and demonstrating, finally, that the little magazine can cater to local and global readerships all at once without ever losing sight of its particular time and place. Is it a surprise, then, to find that in the mass of letters from poets, politicians, academics, and students, one arrived from Lionel Trilling in 1965 telling Neogy that "no magazine I can remember reading—except maybe the *Dial* of my youth—has ever told me so much about matters I did not know about" (Trilling 6). As Trilling himself noticed, *Transition* and *The Dial* did have a lot in common. Though produced under radically different conditions, they created a space in which modern literature could happen. The medium harnessed critical and cultural energies and delivered the message to a public that might otherwise miss out on "matters" worth knowing.

The globality of *Transition* was managed in other ways as well. Evidence of its international circulation was scattered throughout the pages from the different prices on the cover, to the advertisements for oil, steel, and foreign car manufacturers, to the addresses of the correspondents. One subscription flier that popped up frequently in *Transition* contained an image of an unidentified bookstand with magazines arranged neatly on the shelves. Because of the angle from which the photograph was taken, only one title can be read with any certainty. Copies of *Transition* are tucked away on a back shelf, in the middle of the rack, and seem larger than the others. And that, of course, is the point. This little magazine stands out in a sea of print, and for the reader who misses the signs, the caption at the top is there to provide direction: "What kind of magazine do you read?" What I find so striking about this image is its generic, placeless quality. This bookstand could be anywhere in the world, and that, in the end, is what makes it advertise the globality of *Transition* in a way that no distribution list ever could. This advertisement makes readers wonder if they're cultured enough for the magazine, and vice versa, but it also produces another effect. It asks readers *where* they are in the world, and has them consider whether or not their own magazines are connecting them to the literary network beyond the bookstand.

All of these paratextual details suggested one thing: mobility. The world was moving through these pages, and the magazine was moving through the world. *Transition* did not exist in an autonomous literary or cultural sphere free from mass consumption, capital, and geopolitics. It was itself an object of global production and consumption—an example of a postcolonial culture trying to establish itself within a much larger world system. The title of Neogy's magazine couldn't have been better chosen. It gestures backward toward Eugene Jolas' *transition*, one of the most successful little magazines published in France in the 1920s, while at the same time acknowledging the difference, which is immediately discernible in the capital "T." *Transition* was a magazine meant to register the shocks that were being felt across Africa at a decisive moment in its history: empires collapsing, nations rising, traditions dying, cultures being born. Unlike *Black Orpheus*, it engaged head-on with contemporary social and political issues (love, violence, war, democracy, socialism, drugs, racism), and was unafraid to challenge hypocrisy in all of its forms, especially when it was being advertised as independence or freedom. It was politics, in fact, that put an end to Neogy's editorship. His status as the disinterested editor was severely shaken when it was discovered that *Transition* was receiving financial support from the Fairfield Foundation (*Transition* 5), which was subsidized by the Congress for Cultural Freedom, an organization funded by the CIA.[16] Even after Neogy pleaded his ignorance of this connection, the magazine never fully recovered its reputation.

But a second, more fatal, blow came when Milton Obote's government arrested Neogy under an Emergency Powers Act for sedition.[17] One article by Abu Mayanja in *Transition* 32 and a letter to the editor by Steve Lino in *Transition* 34, both of them critical of Obote's proposals to a Ugandan constitution, were cited as evidence of the magazine's anti-Ugandan stance, and they were both used to justify Neogy's arrest. After an inconclusive trial in which he was acquitted and then rearrested, Neogy spent four months in solitary confinement before being abruptly released (Lapcek-Neogy 245). *Transition* was revived two and a half years later in Accra, Ghana, one of the few democratic governments in Africa where the magazine could be published with relative freedom. Its first editorial replied to the events that transpired in Uganda, and argued that the arrest of its editor and closing of its offices was a sign that "a magazine such as *Transition* has obviously no useful function in that society" (Anonymous [1971] 5).

    Transition was not alone. Every little magazine has had to deal with the politics of print in some form or another. *The Little Review* had its prudish censors just as *Transition* had its political tyrants. But the general lesson has more to do with the form of the magazine. *Transition*, as I discussed earlier, prided itself on a democratic mode of communication that encouraged dialogue between everyone involved. This particular form was necessary precisely because there was no other medium in existence that was capable of generating a global readership of this sort. And it was this opening up of Africa to the world that gave the magazine its force, making it a forum for intense political and literary discussion as well as a target for political leaders within Africa afraid of opposition. *Transition* might not have been welcome any longer in Uganda, but as Neogy explained in an open letter to readers, it didn't matter: "*Transition's* home is also all Africa. And it was at home in the world out-side" (Neogy, "Letter to the Editor" 6).

THE DIGITAL AFTERLIFE OF THE LITTLE MAGAZINE

At a time when people are beginning to lament (or applaud) the possible death of the "book," the little magazine is alive and well, still appearing in print, with no signs of imminent extinction. Scholars will continue to track down the old little maga-zines in archives, on microfilm, and through private collections, but the more recent rise of the "digittle" magazine is making it possible to access digital reproductions of entire runs on the Web.[18] The wider accessibility of West Indian, African, European, and Asian little magazines allows scholars to access information that would, in all likelihood, have belonged only to the specialist working within a particular national literary tradition.

    Indeed, it is imperative to continue the archival work that allows for the search and rescue of so many lost magazines and a more nuanced understanding of this me-dium in specific national histories. But if we want to figure out how the magazine worked on a global scale, then we need to establish the kinds of transnational connec-tions that bring magazines from so many parts of the world into conversation with one another. A comparative approach will, of course, enlarge the scope of material that can be worked on. But equally important, it will force us to revisit, and in many cases revise, some of the critical assumptions that we've been making about what a little magazine is, how it works, and where it travels (and does not). *Black Orpheus* and *Transition* demonstrate, above all, that the magazine was one of modernism's enduring legacies: not so much for its publication of specific authors or texts, but as a medium with the power to create a real and imagined community of writers, critics, and readers working to produce a modern literature always in flux. The histories and geographies of magazines like *Black Orpheus* and *Transition* are a strong reminder that behind the route of every magazine is a transnational history of modernity waiting to be uncovered, a space in which the global ambitions of writers and critics became a reality, if only for a moment, before the form moved in other directions.

NOTES

1. See Pound 702.
2. See Nkosi 28.
3. Any comprehensive list would require scouring library collections around the globe, but there are two collections alone, one in India the other in the United States, that indicate the enormous amount of effort that would be required for such an endeavor. The Kolkata Little Magazine Library alone has a research center with 22,000 little magazines from pre- and postcolonial India. The Little Magazine collection at the University of Wisconsin, Madison, lists 7,000 titles from the United States, England, Canada, Australia, and New Zealand.
4. For an extensive list of Dada magazines published in Western and Central Europe, see Meyer.
5. See Janet Lyon's discussion of alternative cosmopolitanisms in this volume.
6. For a valuable overview of the global book business, see Schriffin.
7. For a discussion of the complex associations between Africa and modernism see Neil Lazarus in this volume.
8. For a valuable archival account of these two magazines, see Benson.
9. The *Daily Times* had a readership of around 100,000, and the weekly *Sunday Times* around 127,000, both of them exceeding the average circulation for a West African newspaper by five times. See *Report on the Press in West Africa* (1960).
10. Critics who have tracked the development of *Black Orpheus* (22 issues in 10 years, collecting 224 writers from 26 African nations), notice the marked shift in content over the years: there are, at first, frequent translations of Francophone poets such as Léopold Senghor, Aimé Césaire, Leon Damas that later open up to West Indian and African American writers before arriving at a more consistent run of Anglophone contributions from all over the continent.
11. For an informative account about Nigerian magazines before *Black Orpheus*, see Lindfors, "Popular Literature for an African Elite."
12. *In Black Orpheus* 19, a sample of each of them can be found: "Naive Nigerian Painting" by Ulli Beier; "Two African Playwrights" (Soyinka and J. P. Clark) by Marin Esslin; "Senghor Without a Propeller" by Janheinz Jahn; and "South African Literature" by Lewis Nkosi.
13. Lazarus points out in this handbook that Chinua Achebe would put a different spin on the term "universal," seeing it instead as a code word for "Western," "Modern," or "European."
14. For a discussion of this about-face (and a valuable overview of the first ten years), see Lindfors, "Black Orpheus."

15. For *Transition*, 1,200 copies of issue 1 were printed; 800 copies of issue 2 followed. An advertisement in issue 33 (October/November 1967) boasted a readership of 36,000. I have been unable to confirm whether this is true.

16. For a full discussion of these events, see Benson, 160–89.

17. Ali Mazrui's controversial piece, "Nkrumah: The Leninist Czar," published in *Transition* 26, convinced some that the magazine was publishing propaganda for the United States government.

18. Full runs of *Transition*, for instance, can be found on JSTOR. Italian magazines can be seen through the *Catologo Informatico Riviste Culturali Europee* (C.I.R.C.E.) (http://circe.lett.unitn.it/main_page.html). The largest collection of Anglo-American magazines is in the process of being compiled by the Modernist Magazines Project, which is a collaboration between Brown University and the University of Tulsa (http://www.cts.dmu.ac.uk/exist/mod_mag/magazine_index.htm). Links to various West Indian magazines can be accessed through the Digital Library of the Caribbean, based in the University of Florida (http://www.uflib.ufl.edu/ufdc/?m=hitcollect&;n=dloc); with a subscription, Alexander Street gives you access to *Black Orpheus* (http://asp6new.alexanderstreet.com/blfi/blfi.index.map.aspx).

WORKS CITED

Beier, Ulli. "Black Orpheus" [discussion of the aims of the magazine]. *A conversation with Andrew Salkey and Gerald Moore*. London. London Transcription Service, 1966. Schomburg Center for Research in Black Culture. SC-audio C-27, no.2, side 2.

Benson, Peter. *Black Orpheus, Transition, and Modern Cultural Awakening in Africa*. Los Angeles: University of California Press, 1986.

Bornstein, George. *Material Modernism: The Politics of the Page*. Cambridge: Cambridge University Press, 2001.

Bradbury, Malcolm, and James McFarlane, eds. *Modernism: A Guide to European Literature, 1890–1930*. London, New York: Penguin, 1978.

Casanova, Pascale. *La République mondiale des lettres*. Paris: Seuil, 1999.

"Editorial." *Transition* 38 (June/July 1971): 5.

Edwards, Brent Hayes. *The Practice of Diaspora: Literature, Translation, and the Rise of Black Internationalism*. Cambridge: Harvard University Press, 2003.

Irele, Abiola. "Review of Black Orpheus." *The Journal of Modern African Studies* 3.1 (1965): 151–54.

———. "The Criticism of Modern African Literature." *Perspectives on African Literature*. Ed. Christopher Heywood. London: Heinemann, 1971.

———. "Review of *Transition* (Issues 1–32)." *Journal of Modern African Studies* 5.3 (November 1967): 442–47.

Julien, Eileen. "The Extroverted African Novel." *The Novel: History, Geography, and Culture*. Vol. 1. Ed. Franco Moretti. Princeton: Princeton University Press, 2006. 667–702.

Lapcek-Neogy, Barbara. "A Matter of Transition." *Transition* 75/76 (1997): 244–48.

Lindfors, Bernth. "African Little Magazines." *Loaded Vehicles: Studies in African Literary Media*. Trenton: Africa World Press, 1996.

———. "Black Orpheus." *European-language Writing in Sub-Saharan Africa*. Vol. 2. Ed. Albert Gerard. Budapest: Akademiai Kiado, 1986. 668–79.

———. "Popular Literature for an African Elite." *Journal of Modern African Studies* 12.3 (1974): 471–86.

Low, Gail. "The Natural Artist: Publishing Amos Tutuola's Palm-Wine Drinkard in Post-War Britain." *Research in African Literatures.* 37.4 (2006): 15–33.

MacClean, Una. "Soyinka's International Drama." *Black Orpheus* 15 (1964): 46.

Meyer, Raimund, et al. *Dada Global.* Zurich: Limmat Verlag, 1994.

Morris, Mervyn. "Little Magazines in the Caribbean." *Bim* 17.68 (1984): 3–9.

Morrison, Mark. *The Public Face of Modernism: Little Magazines, Audiences, and Reception 1905–20.* Madison: University of Wisconsin Press, 2000.

Neogy, Rajat. "Do Magazines Culture?" *Transition* 24 (1966): 30–32.

———. "Editorial Note." *Transition* 12 (1964): 3.

———. "Letter to the Editor." *Transition* 38 (1971): 6.

Nkosi, Lewis. "On Okyeame." *Transition* 12 (1964): 28.

Okigbo, Christopher. *Interviewed by Dennis Duerden.* London, Transcription Service. London. August, 1963. Schomburg Center for Research in Black Culture (Moving Image and Recorded Sound). Sc-Audio C-3 [Side 1, No. 1].

Pound, Ezra. "Small Magazines." *The English Journal* 19.9 (1930): 689–704.

Report on the Press in West Africa: Prepared for the International Seminar on 'Press and Progress in West Africa.' Ibadan: The University of Ibadan, 1960.

Rodriguez, Emilio. "An Overview of the Caribbean Literary Magazine: Its Liberating Function." *Bim* 17.66–67 (June 1983): 121–28.

Schriffin, Andre. *The Business of Books: How International Conglomerates Took Over the Book Business and Changed the Way We Read.* New York: Verso, 2001.

Seymour, Arthur. "Literature in the Making—The Contribution of Kyk-over-al." *Kyk-over-al* 33–34 (1986): 3–7.

Theroux, Paul. *Transition* 37 (1968): 41.

Trilling, Lionel. "Letter to the Editor." *Transition* 18 (1965): 6.

CHAPTER 12

....

POETRY, MODERNITY, AND GLOBALIZATION

....

JAHAN RAMAZANI

THE narrator of Derek Walcott's "The Schooner 'Flight,'" a sailor nicknamed Shabine in West Indian patois because of his light black skin, memorably declares his cross-regional allegiances and inheritances:

> I'm just a red nigger who love the sea,
> I had a sound colonial education,
> I have Dutch, nigger, and English in me,
> and either I'm nobody, or I'm a nation. (346)

Shabine would be a "nobody," if to be somebody one had to belong to a single cultural or ethnic group, if a literary voice were recognizable only when it could be slotted into a national category, or if the nineteenth-century British historian James Anthony Froude were right to say of the culturally and racially mixed Caribbean, "no people there in the true sense of the word" (347). But in Walcott's twist on a moniker adopted by wily Odysseus, as by Emily Dickinson and Sylvia Plath, and so suggestive of the cipher of the poetic "I," this supposed "nobody" is teeming with bodies—the bodies genetically deposited in his fictive body by Dutch, African, and English ancestors, the bodies of various national and ethnic literatures incorporated in this literary character (Homer, book 9; Emily Dickinson, "I'm Nobody, Who Are You?" [#288], 206–07; Plath, "Tulips" 160–62). This nobody contains multitudes. If a "nation," he is so as an irreducibly plural aggregate, not in the sense of a people united by common descent and language living in the same territory, as in the Dutch or English nation, or even—in extended usage—the Pan-African nation. A character of cross-cultural as well as cross-racial heterogeneity, he announces his plural attachments, to the Caribbean Sea and to a British education imposed from overseas; his odyssey, set in the Caribbean basin, is told in Standard English iambic pentameter in alternating rhyme, inflected by vernacular triple speech rhythms and West Indian verb forms ("who love the sea"). The difference between the racist slur used for his African inheritances, though proudly transvalued, and the Standard English terms for his European inheritances marks the painful discrepancies of power between the cultural spheres soldered in his diction, grammar, and body. Learning that he fits the identitarian preconceptions of neither white settlers nor black nationalists, Shabine remarks, "I had no nation now but the imagination" (Walcott, "Schooner" 350). Playing on the embeddedness of the word "nation" in "imagination," Walcott, like many other modern and contemporary poets, conceives the poetic imagination as transnational, a nation-crossing force that exceeds the limits of the territorial and juridical norm.[1]

Walcott's Shabine is hardly the first or last such "compound" figure in twentieth-century poems written in English, to recall T. S. Eliot's adjective for the "compound familiar ghost" whose spectral address not incidentally compounds elements at once English and American, Italian (terza rima), and Irish (over half a dozen echoes of Yeats) (Eliot, "Little Gidding," *Four Quartets* 53). In Mina Loy's semi-autobiographical "Anglo-Mongrels and the Rose," the narrator witnesses the comically awkward sexual union of a Hungarian Jewish father and a Protestant English mother that will eventually issue in her "mongrel" birth—and the birth of her "mongrel" poem (109–72). The school composition anticipated in Langston Hughes's "Theme for English B" will interfuse African American student and European American instructor across inequities of power; it will likely be as cross-cultural as the student's bilabially entwined list of favorite "records—Bessie, bop, or Bach" (410). "*Am I a slave or a slave-owner? / Am I a Londinio or a Nubian?*" asks the self-dramatizing "composite" character Zuleika—the Afro-Roman, black British protagonist of Bernardine Evaristo's *The Emperor's Babe* (201). The very name Marilyn Chin—"Marilyn" a star-struck, immigrant Chinese American father's transliteration of "Mei Ling"—becomes a trope for trans-hemispherically splayed identity in "How I Got that Name," a Pacific Rim poem plaited out of Chinese, Euromodernist, confessional, and black feminist strands (16–18). These and a host of other cross-cultural figures personify the variegated transnational poetries of the twentieth century and beyond, from the modernism of W. B. Yeats, T. S. Eliot, Ezra Pound, Mina Loy, and W. H. Auden, and Harlem Renaissance of Claude McKay, Jean Toomer, and Langston Hughes, to post–World War II North American poets Elizabeth Bishop and Sylvia Plath, British and Irish poets Seamus Heaney, Tony Harrison, and Paul Muldoon, contemporary "ethnic American" poets Dionisio D. Martínez and Li-Young Lee, "black British" poets Linton Kwesi Johnson and Bernardine Evaristo, and postcolonial African, Caribbean, and South Asian poets Wole Soyinka, Lorna Goodison, and Agha Shahid Ali. Although creolization, hybridization, and the like are often regarded as exotic or multicultural sideshows to literary histories of formal advancement or the growth of discrete national poetries, these cross-cultural dynamics are arguably among the engines of modern and contemporary poetic development and innovation.

Poetry may seem an improbable genre to consider within transnational contexts. The global mobility of other cultural forms, such as digital media and
cinema, is more immediately visible, and the bulk of the commentary on literary
cosmopolitanism has been on prose fiction, one scholar theorizing cosmopolitan
fellow-feeling as the "narrative imagination" (Nussbaum 85–112).[2] Poetry is more
often seen as local, regional, or "stubbornly national," in T. S. Eliot's phrase, "the
most provincial of the arts," in W. H. Auden's (Eliot, "The Social Function of
Poetry" 8; Auden, "Writing" 23). In another critic's summation, it is understood as
"the expression and preservation of local attachment," "the vehicle of particular
attachments, to mother, home, and native place" (Livingston 151, 150). While prose
fiction's interdiscursive heterogeneity and intercultural porosity are frequently
rehearsed, lyric poetry especially is seen as a genre of culturally and psychologically inward turns and returns, formally embodied in canonical attributes such as
brevity, self-reflexivity, sonic density, repetition, affectivity, and subtlety.

Mikhail Bakhtin famously distinguished between the "centripetal," "singular,"
"unitary, monologically sealed-off" qualities of poetry and the dialogic and double-
voiced, heteroglot and centrifugal structure of the novel (272–73). To subvert his
distinctions on the basis of counterexamples is easily done; even Bakhtin conceded
that his classifications blurred, especially in the twentieth century, when he saw
poetry as being radically prosaicized (Eskin 84–86). The intercultural congress
within postcolonial and ethnic minority poetries and the anti-Romanticism of
modernist and Language poetries obviously challenge Bakhtin's definitions of poetry as unitary, subjective, and monologic. But perhaps more productive than dissolving these theoretical antitheses altogether would be an effort to examine how
transnational poems such as Walcott's "The Schooner 'Flight'" twist together the
polarities. These are poems of heteroglossia, perhaps, but internalized (e.g., the
intersection of standard and dialectal discourses in Shabine's self-reflections), of
psycho-cultural inwardness, but shot through with cross-cultural heterogeneity
(Shabine as self-obsessed poet and Caribbean collectivity). They display Bakhtin's
centripetal vortex of intentionality (the poet's self-recasting as Shabine), but torqued
by the centrifugal counterforce of cosmopolitan experience, allusion, and travel.
The paradigm of a continuum between transnational poetry's centripetal and centrifugal, internalized and double-voiced tendencies, avoids the Scylla of strictly
post-structuralist models, in which the poem as discursive collage is evacuated of
subjectivity, and the Charybdis of overly intentional models, in which the poem as
personal utterance is reduced to authorial speech act. Although many transnational
poems are "lyric" in being compressed, self-aware, and sonically rich, they also
evince Bakhtin's dialogism, heteroglossia, and hybridization—a term that Bakhtin
uses for the literary mixture of "utterances, styles, languages, belief systems" (358).
From Eliot and Sterling Brown to Brathwaite, Muldoon, and Grace Nichols,
cross-cultural poems cannot be reduced to Bakhtin's putative lyric homogeneity:
instead, they switch codes between dialect and standard, cross between the oral and
the literary, and interanimate foreign and indigenous genres; they span distances
among far-flung locales, frame discourses within one another, and indigenize borrowed forms to serve antithetical ends. Because poetic compression demands that

discrepant idioms and soundscapes, tropes and subgenres be forced together with
intensity, poetry—pressured and fractured by this convergence—can be seen as a
luminous discursive site for examining at close hand how global modernity's
cross-cultural vectors sometimes fuse, sometimes jangle, sometimes vertiginously
counterpoint one another. Bringing poetry into critical conversations about globalization can thus help focus attention on the complexly creolized discursive, social,
and geographic texture of transnational experience as it is formally and imaginatively embodied.

A lyric that partly confirms poetry's grounding in "mother, home, and native
place" is Christopher Okigbo's invocation of a local river goddess of eastern Nigeria
in his sequence "Heavensgate" (published in 1962, revised in 1964):

> Before you, mother Idoto
>   naked I stand;
> before your watery presence,
>   a prodigal
>
> leaning on an oilbean,
> lost in your legend. (3)

This poem enacts a longed-for communion with the ancestral goddess of the village
stream, near where Okigbo grew up, in Ojoto, part of the Biafra for which he died
fighting in the Nigerian Civil War in 1967. Its devices for bringing together goddess
and supplicant, leaning on her totemic West African oilbean, include an imagery of
watery reflection, the "I-Thou" formation of second-person lyric address, the sym-
metry between the first two and last two stanzas, and the mirroring figure of epana-
lepsis in the line "watchman for the watchword," more subtly in the alliterations of
"leaning on an oilbean, / lost in your legend." The resources of poetry enseam the
speaker and his toponymically and botanically localized world. The poem could be
seen as acting out a role Okigbo was to have taken up in life as the inheritor of his
grandfather's priestly responsibilities to Idoto's shrine.

Yet, ironically, the poet's mythologization of his return to indigenous roots is
routed through the detours of Euromodernist syncretism and free verse, the Christian story of the prodigal son and—in the last two lines—the language of the psalms:[3]

> Under your power wait I
>   on barefoot,
> watchman for the watchword
>   at *Heavensgate*;
>
> out of the depths my cry:
> give ear and hearken . . . (3)

With its deep formal and allusive memory, lyric both locates and dislocates
the speaker. Even as he elects a native return, he superimposes the language of

monotheistic prayer on Igbo polytheism, redeploys Latinate syntactic inversions, and Africanizes the modernist concept of poetry as a personal verbal rite. A priestly offering to a local goddess, the sequence is also, according to Okigbo's introductory comments, an Orphic exploration of the poetic creativity that results, implicitly, in the very poem we read (xi). If the speaker is at one and the same time the prodigal son, a psalmist, an Orphic poet, and an Igbo supplicant, the goddess he invokes, later appearing in the guises of lioness and watermaid, is an Igbo river deity, earth mother, muse, maternal culture, Eurydice, the Madonna, and the beloved. Okigbo holds in a rich poetic solution his Igbo, Christian, classical, and high modernist sources. Whereas Walcott's Shabine emphasizes the jarring discordances between the unlike spheres compacted in his being, this speaker melds a trans-hemispheric range of local and distant references in his poetry's musical resonances, alliterations, and fluid syntax, in accordance with Okigbo's avowed sense that there was no contradiction between his European, African, and other inheritances (Whitelaw 55). Still, for all these differences, poetry functions for both Walcott and Okigbo, as for a host of other writers, as a language that can mediate seemingly irresolvable contradictions between the local and global, native and foreign, suspending the sometimes exclusivist truth claims of the discrepant religious and cultural systems it puts into play, systems forced together by colonialism and modernity.

If modernity is "inherently globalising" (Giddens 63, 177), then despite the persistence of mononational critical paradigms, twentieth- and twenty-first-century poetry's participation in the processes threading across geographic and political boundaries should be axiomatic. An Igbo Catholic, or Catholic Igbo, with a classical education and African upbringing who read manuscripts in Nigeria for Cambridge University Press, Okigbo lived a life and built a body of work on various global and ex-colonial crisscrossings; so too, in different ways, have transnational poets from Pound to Walcott, Loy to Chin. Under modernity, to summarize baldly, global space and time have contracted; ever more people have traveled and migrated; technology and communication systems circulated ideas, images, and voices across distant locales; empires have transferred armies, religions, goods, canons, and artifacts; militaries have unleashed destruction worldwide; and capitalism has "glocalized" products and services across national borders. Globalization—understood here as having a long prehistory in empire and trade but having been dramatically sped up by modernity (Giddens 63–64), especially in the twentieth century—is the large and amorphous term that lumps together these and other distinct but entangled processes, different aspects of which are highlighted by different models.

Often globalization is represented as the one-way homogenization and Westernization of the world, a model that accentuates the persisting asymmetries of economic and political power, in the wake of formal decolonization. Indeed, in defiance of the erasure of their cultural worlds, poets such as Kamau Brathwaite, Lenrie Peters, and Agha Shahid Ali champion poetry as a tool of resistance to the ravages of (neo)colonialism and modernity. Already in Okot p'Bitek's 1966 book-length poem *Song of Lawino*, an Acoli village woman named Lawino, anticipating anti-globalization discourse, rails against the displacement of rural African practices by

Western technologies, foods, dances, religions, and beauty ideals. She protests to her Mercedes-driving, whiteness-adoring, Africa-denying husband:

> Listen, Ocol, my old friend,
> The ways of your ancestors
> Are good,
> Their customs are solid
> And not hollow. . . .
> I do not understand
> The ways of foreigners
> But I do not despise their customs.
> Why should you despise yours? (41)

But Ocol is a lost cause, having thoroughly internalized imperial attitudes toward African rural culture as primitive and backward. He and others like him, reports Lawino, dress

> As if they are in the white man's country.
> At the height of the hot season
> The progressive and civilized ones
> Put on blanket suits
> And woollen socks from Europe,
> Long under-pants
> And woolen vests,
> White shirts;
> They wear dark glasses
> And neck-ties from Europe.
> Their waterlogged suits
> Drip like the tears
> Of the *kituba* tree
> After a heavy storm. (45)

Lawino's comparison of the sweat-dripping suits to "the *kituba* tree / After a heavy storm" wryly indigenizes her husband's tragic infatuation with everything Western. A resolute defender of African cultures against Western assimilation, Okot records in loving ethnographic detail the songs and dances, medicinal and religious practices of the rural Acoli.

Even so, the form, structure, and language of his long poem complicate the notion of poetry as local or national resistance to a hegemonic modernity, since *Song of Lawino*, though hardly woolen-suited, combines the long Western dramatic monologue in free verse with the repetitions and oral urgency of Acoli songs, its diction intertwines Acoli words and semi-translated proverbs with a robustly Africanized English, and its anti-Western localism is informed, ironically, by Okot's Western anthropological training at Oxford (Ramazani, *Hybrid Muse* 141–78).

The poem's literary transnationalism dialogically interanimates the monodirectional thrust of Western homogenization on the one hand and, on the other, of nativist assertion. In language, form, and subject matter, such poems articulate and imaginatively remake the contending forces of globalization and localization, alien influx and indigenizing resistance. In a later long poem that grapples with economic globalization, *Omeros*, Walcott places in a volcanic hell the "traitors," or local government officials, who "saw the land as views / for hotels," and so abetted the tourist industry's despoliation of his natal Saint Lucia (289). Yet Walcott also acknowledges his book's complicity in the tourist exploitation of his island, its picturesque poverty, and its violent history; the poet is like his character Philoctete, who "smiles for the tourists" at the opening of the book, and for extra money, "shows them a scar," emblematic of the ancestral wounds of slavery (3, 4). The poem works both within and against the globalizing circuits that simultaneously stamp touristic sameness on the poet's cherished island locality and yet help give rise to the unique synthesis of Walcott's cross-cultural epic. Like other transnational poems crisscrossing unequal and discrepant worlds, it carves out what Homi Bhabha calls an "interstitial" or "third space," born of the imaginative "negotiation of incommensurable differences" (218).

As the complex texture of these poems reveals, the homogenizing model of globalization is inadequate for the analysis of specifically poetic transnationalism. Applied to poetry and other cultural forms, moreover, it risks replicating methodologically the totalization it is meant to critique. Poetry indicates the oversimplification in believing, as Andreas Huyssen writes, that "the local opposes the global as authentic cultural tradition, whereas the global functions as . . . a force of alienation, domination and dissolution," "that only local culture or culture *as* local is good, authentic and resistant, whereas global cultural forms must be condemned as manifestations of cultural imperialism" (9, 13). To the extent that this non-dialogic paradigm represents "each national culture" as what Fredric Jameson calls "a seamless web of habits and habitual practices which form a totality or a system," threatened by a "singular modernity," it can be of little help in analyzing the dynamic crosscurrents and exchanges in long-memoried poetic forms, genres, and vocabularies, whether across even or uneven terrain (Jameson, "Notes on Globalization" 63; *A Singular Modernity*). The nuances of cultural influx and efflux are lost when non-Western poetry and other forms are assumed to be irreparably "destroyed" (Jameson, "Notes" 63) or diluted by Western influences: in one of the few critical works on poetry and globalization, Stephen Owen bemoans modernism's degradation of an authentically "local" and "national" Chinese poetry into a homogenized "world poetry" ("World Poetry"; see also his "Stepping"). Similarly, the authors of *Toward the Decolonization of African Literature* complain that the influence of modernism on poets such as Okigbo is an imperial imposition that derails African orature into privatist and obscurantist writing (Chinweizu, Jemie, and Madubuike).

Yet a close look at transnational poetry reveals more complex patterns of assimilation and resistance. If criticism is to be alert to both globalization and to any particular poem as text, literally a woven thing, with sometimes contending and overlapping discourses, forms, techniques, and ideologies, it might look instead to dialogic or enmeshment models, attuned to the "growing *extensity, intensity*, and *velocity* of global interactions" and the "deepening enmeshment of the local and global" (Held et al. 2). Such models involve both homogenization and heterogenization, both standardization and resistant diversification. Stuart Hall highlights the coexistence of pressures of "homogenization and absorption" and "forms of local opposition and resistance" at "exactly the same moment" (34). A poem such as *Song of Lawino* exemplifies both local defiance and, in its formal and conceptual hybridity, a measure of accommodation with, and remaking of, the hegemonic impositions it resists. According to Arjun Appadurai, for whom the "central problem of today's global interactions is the tension between cultural homogenization and cultural heterogenization," to overemphasize homogenization is to fail to consider "that at least as rapidly as forces from various metropolises are brought into new societies they tend to become indigenized in one or another way: this is true of music and housing styles as much as it is true of science and terrorism, spectacles and constitutions" (32). Okigbo indigenizes Western poetic forms to pay homage to the Igbo river goddess dwelling near his home village, and Okot refashions Western ethnographic monologue to give literary voice to the rural Acoli. Such poets demonstrate what the anthropologist Ulf Hannerz calls Third World cultural entrepreneurs' "tampering and tinkering" with alien forms to create new ones responsive to their experience (124), akin to what Janet Abu-Lughod terms the "orientalization" of Western cultural influences (133). Inflected by postcolonial studies, this model of globalization sees culture not as simply transferring "in a unilinear way," in Revathi Krishnaswamy's summary, "because movement between cultural/geographical areas always involves selection, interpretation, translation, mutation, and adaptation—processes designated by terms such as *indigenization* and *vernacularization*— with the receiving culture bringing its own cultural resources to bear, in dialectical fashion, upon cultural imports" (11).[4] While globalization produces homogeneity, writes Kwame Anthony Appiah, it "is, equally, a threat to homogeneity," since people "are constantly inventing new forms of difference: new hairstyles, new slang, even, from time to time, new religions," and, we might add, new kinds of poetry (101, 103).[5] Without losing sight of the losses inflicted by a globalizing modernity, we can explore how poets, working in a genre with especially abundant formal and linguistic traces, have also transvalued and creolized these global forces to bring into expression their specific experiences of globalized locality and localized globality.

In contrast to the one-way, homogenizing model, poetry's transnational flows can be seen as moving in multiple directions, or in leaps and loops, or in what creolization theorist Édouard Glissant styles as detours and returns *(le retour et le détour)* (*Caribbean Discourse* 14–26; *Le Discours Antillais* 28–36).[6] To cite complementary examples I explore in detail elsewhere ("Modernist Bricolage"), Kamau Brathwaite describes West Indian writers as being given access for the first time to their local speech rhythms as *materia poetica*, ironically, through the detour of none other than T. S. Eliot's voice transmitted to Barbados by the British Council, the Caribbean writer becoming more "indigenous" by virtue of becoming at the same time more "modernist." In another trans-hemispheric detour, Ezra Pound discovers in haiku and other East Asian cultural forms possibilities for breaking through the impasse of European symbolism to an imagist poetics of the natural image, though perhaps predicated on a creatively naïve misreading of East Asian poetry as nonsymbolic (Xie 41, 69, 223; Chen; Hayot). Not that Brathwaite's northward- and Pound's eastward-detouring transnationalisms are the same: Brathwaite hears a recorded voice from the "frozen Nawth" by way of a propaganda arm of the British Empire, while Pound's arrogation of Asian minimalism may not be innocent of American expansionism (Brathwaite, "Calypso" 49; Park 23–56). Despite these geo-political discrepancies, both poets fashion a locally responsive poetics, paradoxically, by virtue of a bypass through the global. Nourished by poetry's cross-national and ever-mutating storehouse of forms, techniques, genres, and images, individual poems give expression to locality at the same time that they turn formally, linguistically, allusively in other directions. Perhaps the most vivid twentieth-century poetic testimony to East African experience, Okot's *Song of Lawino* mediates Acoli village life in part through the reterritorialization of Longfellow's American ethnographic *Song of Hiawatha* and the biblical *Song of Solomon* (Peterson 89; Lindfors 282–83). Even when poets hark back to local or national precedents, the imagistic, linguistic, and formal building blocks of their poetry, especially under conditions of a globalizing modernity, are shot through with transnational ingredients.

In efforts to theorize the cross-cultural on a global scale, orientalism—the concept that the East is discursively a subordinate and exoticist product of the West—has helped foreground an important part of the story of interactions between East and West, or global North and South (Said, *Orientalism*). Yet Edward Said's early paradigm for trans-hemispheric studies is sometimes deployed in ways that ironically limit the boundary-traversing power of poetry and harden rather than complicate identitarian boundaries. Criticism that reduces high modernist and later cross-regional "appropriations" to orientalist theft or primitivist exoticism may risk circumscribing instead of opening up possibilities for global and transnational analysis.[7] The conceptual framework of a closed, nonporous discursive system, determinative of Western interactions with the orient, is inadequate to the counter-discursive frictions within Western modernism, as suggested by poems by Yeats, Eliot, and Pound, in which "alien" cultural materials are sometimes assimilated incompletely and disjunctively, and so retain at least some capacity to interrogate and disrupt the cultural episteme of their host texts (Ramazani, "Modernist Bricolage"). As Dennis Porter writes, such "only partially silenced counter-hegemonic voices" and "counter-hegemonic energies" call into question a "monolithic" orientalism (153–54, 155). Nor is the orientalist model sufficient to what Said, later countering the limitations of his earlier paradigm, analyzed as the cross-national solidarities of the poetry of decolonization (Said, *Culture and Imperialism* 191–281). These solidarities are often South-South, but they also traverse the global divide, including alliances forged by such Northern hemispheric poets as Yeats, Allen Ginsberg, Tony Harrison, and Joy Harjo when they have threaded their experience through the literatures and cultures of the South.

Perhaps the most famous and controversial example of artistic appropriation across the North/South divide is Pablo Picasso's incorporation of African masks and forms in *Les Demoiselles d'Avignon* (1907), a work that notoriously echoes primitivist ideologies and may aesthetically reenact colonial importation. At the same time, the painting also disrupts binaries of Western high art and African folk art, of advanced one-point perspective and backward nonrepresentational handicraft, making possible new transcontinental forms without prior existence in either European or African aesthetics.[8] If one standard against which to gauge such transnational engagements across uneven global terrain is whether they reflect dominant ideologies, another perhaps more aesthetically calibrated measure is whether they afford fresh imaginative possibilities that generate new cultural work, either locally or globally. Poetry's still more intricate enmeshments—contrapuntal rhythms and layered landscapes, creolized idioms and vernacularized forms in a poem by Yeats or Toomer, Lorna Goodison or Agha Shahid Ali—belie not only criticism's no-escape discursive models but also less sophisticated if more popular cultural models of the world as divisible into irreconcilable units, as proposed by Samuel Huntington among others. Poetry's cross-cultural knotting, dramatized by Shabine's self-description as a multi-vectored, trans-hemispheric subject, or Okigbo's invocation as Igbo-classical-modernist supplicant, provides a vastly more nuanced and cross-hatched picture of intercultural borrowings, affinities, and flows than does Huntington's sinisterly dichotomizing and crudely cloisonné vision of the "great divisions among humankind" and "clash of civilizations." For global and transnational studies of poetry, we need, in short, dialogic alternatives to monologic models that represent the artifact as synecdoche for a national or local culture imperiled by global standardization, a monolithic orientalist epistemology deaf to alterities within and without, or a self-contained civilizational unit in perpetual conflict with others.

This is not to suggest that the nation will vanish from modern and contemporary poetry studies, any more than the flows of global capital will render the state obsolete in the analysis of world political history. To imagine and articulate identities at a national (e.g., Jamaican or Irish), subnational (e.g., Biafran or East Asian American), or cross-national regional scale (e.g., Pan-African or West Indian) is a powerful impetus of twentieth- and twenty-first-century poetry. Though mocking and questioning the sufficiency of the nation-state as telos of the decolonizing project, Louise Bennett uses poetry to champion Creole as the very tissue of Jamaican cultural identity. And though richly and self-consciously hybridized and cross-national in its origins and effects, Yeats's poetry also helps rename and remythologize a nation emerging from colonial rule. As Pascale Casanova states, many a writer's position can be understood as "a double one, twice defined," "inextricably national and international" (though her Eurocentric framework for world literature may concede too much to the national paradigm) (81). Brathwaite's poetics is centered in the Caribbean, Okot's in East Africa, Yeats's in Ireland, at the same time that these and other poets also participate through poetic, ideological, and other transnational circuits in global imaginaries. Even "world texts," as Simon Gikandi writes, though perhaps "exemplars of globalization," reflect "the persistence of the nation-state in the very literary works that were supposed to gesture toward a transcendental global culture" ("Globalization" 632). The effacement of newly articulated minoritarian and postcolonial identities under the all-flattening sign of globality would be particularly unfortunate—hence my emphasis on the muddy footprints of the *transnational* and the *translocal*.[9] As Edward Said's work indicates, poetry and decolonization can be seen as intimately interlinked (*Culture* 220–38). Despite Benedict Anderson's emphasis on narrative as forming the imagined community of the nation, he asserts that the "contemporaneous community" of the nation is evoked by language "above all in the form of poetry and songs," which provide the "echoed physical realization of the imagined community" (145). The irony is, however, that because poetry is such a long-memoried form, it is enmeshed—even when stridently nationalist in ideology—by a complexly cross-national weave in its rhythms and tropes, stanza patterns and generic adaptations. Under globalization, poetry extends its imaginative reach ever farther along a horizontal spatial axis, but unlike more evanescent and shallow-tentacled global media, it simultaneously activates the vertical, temporal axis of tropes, etymologies, and forms embedded in the nation-crossing language it reshapes. Because of the interconnecting cultural traces wound into the DNA of poetic forms and poetic language, poetry's cross-national molecular structure betrays the national imaginary on behalf of which it is sometimes made to speak.

Poetic genres such as epic, ghazal, and pastoral elegy, let alone stanza forms and rhetorical figures, have long been circulated and adapted transnationally, but modernity-fueled globalization has accelerated and intensified this process. Under modernity, writes Anthony Giddens in *The Consequences of Modernity*, the level of interactions across distant regions "is much higher than in any previous period, and the relations between local and distant social forms and events becomes correspondingly 'stretched.'" Elaborating his rich explanatory metaphor, he continues: "Globalization refers essentially to that stretching process, insofar as the modes of connection between different social contexts or regions become networked across the earth's surfaces as a whole," and "local happenings are shaped by events occurring many miles away and vice versa" (64). Globalization can thus be seen as perpetuating and multiplying the bipolar "spatial disjunction" of empire, since, as Jameson remarks, "It is Empire which stretches the roads out to infinity, beyond the bounds and borders of the national state," with globalization's webs spinning out and tightening these interconnections still further (Jameson, "Modernism" 51, 57).[10] In Jameson's words, "colonialism means that a significant structural segment of the economic system as a whole is now located elsewhere," a disjunctiveness that leaves its formal mark on literature's "cognitive mapping" ("Modernism" 50, 52).

Modernists, postcolonials, and other writers have put poetry's resources to work in figuring this incompletely graspable geo-spatial stretch. Indeed, in a suggestive coincidence, poetic uses of language are also often regarded as "a stretch": the elasticity of poetry—its figural and allusive traversals of space, its rhythmic and sonic coordinations of distances, its associative suspension of rational boundaries—is well suited to evoking global modernity's interlinking of widely separated sites, from Eliot's *Waste Land* and Hughes's "The Negro Speaks of Rivers" to Elizabeth

Bishop's "In the Waiting Room" and Dionisio D. Martínez's "Hysteria." Grabbed from a roof and turning the speaker's body (and the poem) into a switchboard, the electric wires in Les Murray's "The Powerline Incarnation" could be seen as both exemplifying and figuring the stretch of poetry. In the poem's onrushing, unpunctuated, geography-spanning lines, mountains connect with plains, Australian farms with towns, European classical music with American country tunes:

> I make a hit in towns
> I've never visited: smoke curls lightbulbs pop grey
> discs hitch and slow I plough the face of Mozart
> and Johnny Cash I bury and smooth their song. . . . (20)

Murray's border-crashing syntax and grammatical elisions evoke the place-enjambing potentialities of both poetry and modernity.

Poetry's translocal stretch is easily seen in Eliot's intermapping of the River Thames with sites in the Mediterranean and South Asia, Evaristo's of Londonium with parts of the global South later colonized by Great Britain, Seamus Heaney's of Ireland with Jutland, Goodison's of Jamaica with Ireland; but it is also discernible in poetry that may seem unambiguously local in its grounding. Printed during World War II in Jamaica, Louise Bennett's "South Parade Peddler" firmly situates its higgler by the use of Creole and a Kingston street name. But under modernity, even a "national poet" turns out, on closer inspection, also to be a transnational poet. In this instance, the global reach of modern warfare, as of the communication systems reporting it, distends the scope of even such autochthonous poetry. Puffing herself up by deploying a vocabulary of military aggression, this female petty trader cautions one passerby to spend money lest she "bus up like Graf Spee," a German battleship recently blown up by its captain in Montevideo, Uruguay; she punningly berates another spendthrift, "yuh / Dah suffer from hair raid!," and asks yet another, "Dem torpedo yuh teet, sah, or / Yuh female lick dem out?" (83–84). This is more than a question of topical references that are extrinsic or incidental to the poem. In the stretched fabric of Bennett's translocal puns, metaphors, and allusions, the poem formally embodies the interpenetration of Jamaican space, both imaginative and real, with the so-called theater of global war. So too, its conjoined ballad stanzas creolize a poetic structure from the British Isles with Jamaican diction, orthography, and rhythms, inverting the earlier penetration of Jamaican space by European colonialism. In the twentieth century, even localist poems evince the contracted space and time of transnational flows and imaginaries.

Although the editors of the generative collection *Geomodernisms* call for a "locational approach to modernism," these and other examples of modernity's literary stretch suggest that what may be needed is a co-locational or translocational approach to modernism, as also to postcolonialism, alert to how such art and literature interlace localities and nationalities with one another in a globally imagined space—Bennett's Kingston extending to Uruguay, Germany, and Scotland, as Walcott's Antilles stretch to the Greek archipelago as mediated by the British Isles (Doyle and

Winkiel 3).[11] Poets and singers of the African diaspora, from Claude McKay to Wole Soyinka and Grace Nichols, have creolized metropolitan Britain with African and Caribbean spaces and styles, remaking London, in the words of Lord Kitchener's buoyant calypso, as "the place for me" ("London Is the Place for Me"). Colonial interpenetration and postcolonial migration anticipate the ever more enmeshed localities of a global age. Highlighting what he calls "situatedness-in-displacement," Bruce Robbins states: "If our supposed distances are really localities, as we piously repeat, it is also true that there are distances *within* what we thought were *merely* localities" ("Comparative Cosmopolitanisms" 250). In Langston Hughes's exactly situated "Theme for English B" ("I cross St. Nicholas, / Eighth Avenue, Seventh, and I come to the Y, / the Harlem Branch Y"), a student studying at the predominantly white City College of the City University of New York (CCNY) pronominally and sonically intertwines himself with an apostrophized Harlem as if to insist, in a bebop-inspired riff, on their mirror relation—"hear you, hear me—we two—you, me, talk on this page" (409–10). As in Okigbo's invocation, poetry enables the speaker to rhyme himself with a toponymically localized environment. Even so, the ensuing line, complicating this micro-locational poetics, widens the geographic and cultural scope of the identity-shaping place to the larger city—"(I hear New York, too.) Me—who?"—and subsequent lines open out still further to thematize identity as both discretely located and thoroughly enmeshed, networked, cross-racialized. Insofar as his composition is mediated by a white teacher ("it will be / a part of you, instructor"), preexisting racialized power structures ("you're older—and white— / and somewhat more free"), and self-reflexive lyric conventions ("This is my theme for English B"), the speaker cannot define himself in the immediate locational present ("I'm what / I feel and see and hear") without detouring through these various pasts that simultaneously root him in Harlem and relocate him elsewhere. Stretched in scale between the microcosmic ("the Harlem branch Y") and the macrocosmic (New York, the United States, interpenetrating human races), this and other poems also extend from the now through the long-echoing histories encoded in the literary and oral conventions they remake. By virtue of its linguistic compression, poetry readily evinces the "time-space compression" of globalization (Harvey 260–307).

The reverse of verses such as Bennett's and Hughes's seemingly localist forms and topographies—Kingston, Harlem—planetary poems such as Auden's "Prologue at Sixty," Walcott's "The Fortunate Traveller," and Heaney's "Alphabets" peer down on the Earth from beyond its surface and figure the world as "O," or maybe "zero" (Auden, *Selected Poems* 286; Walcott, *Collected Poems* 458). "It is striking that one of the effects of the process of globalization," writes Mike Featherstone, "has been to make us aware that the world itself is a locality, a singular place" (92). In the ontogenetic poem "Alphabets," Seamus Heaney returns repeatedly to the trope of the globe as "O":

> As from his small window
> The astronaut sees all that he has sprung from,
> The risen, aqueous, singular, lucent O
> Like a magnified and buoyant ovum—(3)

Borrowing the astronaut's literally *cosmo*politan perspective, the poet—aided by the split consciousness of poetry as a densely metaphoric and defamiliarizing genre—views the world from afar as his finite and fragile home. In the tradition of lyric self-reflexivity, he traces himself back through the multiple languages—English, Latin, Irish—that are the origins, the ground, as it were, from which his poetry has sprung. The "O" of which he is born is the planet and a maternal ovum, yet it is also language, the fabricated "wooden O" of literary artifice, the apostrophic "O" of poetry, spoken as if in an echo of the roundness of a wonder-inspiring world.

Whereas the localist poem requires one kind of critical attention to tease out its cross-culturalism in borrowed verse forms, sea-traversing allusions, or subterranean influences that establish unexpected lines of cross-cultural relationality (Glissant's "poétique de la Relation" [*Caribbean Discourse* xii, 134–44; *Discours Antillais* 246–54]), the planetary poem, viewing the Earth from the extraterritorial perspective of Heaney's astronaut, Auden's orbiting dog, or Walcott's air traveler, requires another kind of critical pressure, to specify its local, regional, and national bearings. In between these poles are most of the poems I explore under the local-global-mediating rubric of a transnational and translocal poetics. "In this emphasis we avoid, at least," according to James Clifford, "the excessive localism of particularist cultural relativism, as well as the overly global vision of a capitalist or technocratic monoculture" (36). Even Heaney's brief imaginative glimpse of his planetary origins from a spaceship window quickly pivots to a recognition of his more immediate, if unhomely, origins—the family name inscribed on a gable, written with the plasterer's "trowel point, letter by strange letter" ("Alphabets" 3). To borrow Gayatri Spivak's distinction between the abstract geometry of the global and the lived history of the planetary, transnational poems are written from the perspective of "planetary subjects rather than global agents, planetary creatures rather than global entities" (73). Although Spivak limits her definition of globalization to a uniformly imposed system of exchange as distinct from the planetary (72), globalization, understood as "the widening, deepening and speeding up of world wide interconnectedness," both "real and perceived," is the necessary condition for the lived experience of the planetary (Held et al. 2).

The figure of the astronaut or air-borne traveler might suggest an older model of cosmopolitanism, a claim to universality and detachment from bonds that Robbins styles the "luxuriously free-floating view from above"; but more useful for understanding this and other such poems may be concepts of a "located and embodied" cosmopolitanism that aesthetically enacts multiple attachments rather than none (Robbins, "Actually Existing Cosmopolitanism" 1, 2–3).[12] As seen in our initial examples of the sometimes contending, sometimes melding, allegiances in poems by Walcott, Eliot, Loy, Hughes, Evaristo, and Chin, interstitial poetries— whether ethnic American, postcolonial, or black British, Harlem Renaissance or Euromodernist—articulate a verbal space that resembles a "cosmopolitan public sphere": limited and located, such translocal cosmopolitanisms intersect with national and subnational public spheres, but unlike ethnic and state nationalisms, foster transnational engagement, dialogic encounter, and civil contestation (see Delanty 5, 143, 145). Indonesian-born, Chinese American poet Li-Young Lee's

"Persimmons," for example, conjoins American confessionalism (painful personal memories of being slapped by a teacher) with a Chinese father's ars poetica of calligraphic precision, memory, and texture—a painterly emphasis that the poem transmutes into the son's feel for the sensuous texture of persimmons and of words: *"the feel of the wolftail on the silk, / the strength, the tense / precision in the wrist"* (19). Not that the poem effaces intercultural conflict or dominance. The American teacher's belligerently ignorant blindness toward her Chinese immigrant student, her slapping him for not being able to pronounce the difference between "persimmon" and "precision," produces the friction out of which the speaker retrospectively leverages a superior poetic mastery of English, developing poetic connections between words that he was once punished for conflating:

> Other words
> that got me into trouble were
> *fight* and *fright, wren* and *yarn.*
> Fight was what I did when I was frightened,
> fright was what I felt when I was fighting.
> Wrens are small, plain birds,
> yarn is what one knits with.
> Wrens are soft as yarn.
> My mother made birds out of yarn.
> I loved to watch her tie the stuff;
> a bird, a rabbit, a wee man. (19)

Even as it recalls violent intercultural collision, the poem explores, in its hybridizing mediation of Chinese and American stylistic elements, the possibilities of reconciliation at the aesthetic level that were unavailable in the schoolboy's lived experience. As Lee's poem indicates, transnational and intercultural poetry imaginatively reconfigures the relations among the ingredients drawn from disparate cultural worlds and fused within its verbal and formal space.

This poem's interweaving of English with Chinese—words both remembered and forgotten—might lead us to ask, why the delimitation of the field of study to poetry written primarily in English, since transnational poetries and influences surely are not bound by the covers of a single language's dictionary? After all, many such poems, whether by Pound and Eliot or Lee and Lorna Dee Cervantes, interlace English with other languages—German and Sanskrit, Chinese and Spanish—or reflect in their diction, syntax, and sound the pressure of other languages, as in Shahid Ali's Urdu-haunted, Okot's Acoli-shadowed, or Alberto Ríos's Spanish-inflected, English. From Pound to W. S. Merwin, Ali, and Lyn Hejinian, poets have been profoundly influenced by the languages and literatures they have translated into English. By limiting a study to English-language poetry, doesn't one risk following and perhaps even reinforcing what Spivak calls "the lines of the old imperialisms," including what she wryly terms "Anglophony" (9), or what Jonathan Arac calls "Anglo-Globalism"? (35–45).[13] The spread of English worldwide to its use by nearly a third of the world's population (though the mother tongue of a much smaller fraction) is indeed rooted in the might of the British Empire and has been perpetuated by the military and economic power of the United States (Fishman 434–46). Literary criticism on English and other imperial-language literatures must coexist with studies of writing in local and regional languages of the global South. Still, one way to complicate an imperial "Anglophony" from within criticism on English-language poetry is to explore the multiplicity of Englishes in which poetry is written, some of which, such as the Jamaican Creole of Claude McKay, Louise Bennett, and Linton Kwesi Johnson, was once seen as unworthy of poetry.[14] Another is to widen the geographic scope of Anglophone poetry studies, so that poems from the United States, Britain, and Ireland, instead of constituting the totality of the field, are read alongside poetries from English-speaking dominions, territories, and ex-colonies.

Still, a primary reason for drawing a somewhat artificial boundary around poems in English is that, simply put, in poetry, more than perhaps in any other literary genre, the specificities of language matter. Horace's use of the flexibilities of Latin syntax to create pictographic framing ("Quis multa gracilis te puer in rosa," Odes 1.5), Hafez's deployment of monorhyme, assonance, repeated long vowel sounds, and bunched stresses for the euphony of a Persian ghazal, and Baudelaire's rhythmic and sonic simulation of place ("tout n'est qu'ordre et beauté, / Luxe, calme et volupté") exemplify how poetry, especially in its lyric mode, cannot be adequately studied as poetry in translation in the same way that drama, epic, and the novel can be studied within their generic frameworks (Baudelaire, "L'Invitation au voyage" 42–43). The heuristic corollary of this observation is that poems are best taught in the original, and in an English department in a predominantly English-speaking country, the teacher devising a poetry syllabus cannot usually presume student competence in multiple languages. Moreover, although poetic influences continually cross linguistic lines, the language-specificity of poetry often grants the inheritances in a poet's working language(s) special weight. Usually, the language field out of which a poem is carved, and upon which it exerts the greatest pressure, is above all the language in which it is written. When Auden calls poetry "the most provincial of the arts" and claims that "in poetry . . . there cannot be an 'International Style,'" he highlights its language-specificity ("Due to the Curse of Babel"), not its geographic boundedness, as indicated by his own nation-spanning poems and career, his influence from England and the United States to Ireland, India, and the Caribbean ("Writing" 23). Finally, the spread of English and the rise of English-language literatures in Asia, Africa, the Caribbean, and the Pacific Rim are realities that need to be studied and are unlikely to be thwarted or slowed by English departments or scholars turning away from the study of Anglophone literatures. However diversified by region and nation, imaginative constructs in a shared language can be entered and animated across vast distances, and so the English language—once conceived as the stuff of English national identity—is a world language for poets, or at least a semi-global conduit through which poets encounter, advance, and redirect cross-cultural flows of tropes and words, ideas and images.

English-language poems, poets, and poetries of the twentieth and twenty-first centuries can no longer be seen, in Wai Chee Dimock's terms, as "the product of one nation and one nation alone, analyzable within its confines" (3). Straddling the Americas and the North Atlantic, the global North and South, East and West, this chapter is meant to suggest ways to remap the field transnationally and to sharpen the aesthetic alertness of transnational literary studies. This is not to suggest that all these poetries are transnational in the same way. They differ, for example, in how they configure the relations among their cross-cultural ingredients. What we might call disjunctive poetic transnationalisms, as we have seen in Walcott's "Schooner *Flight*," emphasize the intercultural discontinuities and conflicts between the materials they force together, while others—call them organic poetic transnationalisms—integrate these materials in works such as Okigbo's "Heavensgate" without playing up their unlikenesses.[15] They differ along lines of race. Some poetic transnationalisms, such as the black British and African Caribbean, are diasporic and thus emphasize a long, shared racial or ethnic history, whereas others radiate still more multinationally and multiethnically, drawing on formal and cultural materials with little or no shared cultural past. They differ geographically. The transnationalism of Eliot's "mind of Europe" is continentally bound, unlike his and later poets' imaginative traversals of distant intercontinental spaces. They differ in their global positionings. Transatlantic and other First World poetic transnationalisms—say, of Euro-American modernism or the avant-garde in the United States, the United Kingdom, Canada, Australia, and New Zealand—traverse less culturally and socially disjunctive spaces than inter-world poetic transnationalisms that cross divides between First and Third Worlds, ex-colonizer and ex-colonized. Distinctions between postcolonial and Euromodernist transnationalisms should be acknowledged. Still, while granting these lines of demarcation, we cannot be so fearful of blurring them that we retreat to understanding transnational poetries only within formal, national, or regional boundaries, and so we should continue to read poems within, across, and against these groupings. Poetic transnationalism needs to be explored from a variety of angles. But the ramifications for poetry of global migrations and diasporas, of cross-national influences and genres, of modernization and decolonization, of travels both real and imagined, will remain to be worked out, so long as poets ask what it means to be neither nobody nor a nation.

NOTES

1. I use the term "transnational" for poems and other cultural works that cross national borders, whether stylistically, topographically, intellectually, or otherwise; hence my emphasis on some exemplary clusters of transnational poetries. Some poems are more obviously "transnational" than others in this sense of the term—say, T. S. Eliot's more than William Carlos Williams's, or Christopher Okigbo's more than Okot p'Bitek's. I also apply the term to the hermeneutic lens through which the nation-traversing qualities of poetry

can be revealed and examined. In this second sense, a still wider array of different kinds of poetry, whether more locally or globally oriented, can be revealed as bearing transnational traces and filiations.

2. For two contrastive views on fiction and cosmopolitanism, see Walkowitz and Brennan. See also the narrative emphasis in two special issues published in the same year: "Anglophone Literature and Global Culture," *South Atlantic Quarterly* 100.3 (2001) and "Globalizing Literary Study," *PMLA* 116.1 (2001).

3. "Give ear to my words, O Lord. . . . Hearken unto the voice of my cry" (Psalm 5) and "Out of the depths have I cried unto thee, O Lord" (Psalm 130).

4. On the overlap and difference between the humanities-based (postcolonial) and social science-based (globalization) areas of study, see also Gikandi, "Globalization and the Claims of Postcoloniality."

5. See Appiah's description of how foreign television shows are absorbed within local cultural contexts that change their meanings (108–11), by contrast with Jameson's account of the global "Americanization or standardization of culture, the destruction of local differences," as instanced by the effects of exported American television programs ("Notes" 57–58, 70).

6. Dash translates these terms "diversion" and "reversion."

7. See, for example, Torgovnik, *Gone Primitive*, and Marx, *Idea of a Colony*, but also Perloff's critique of such approaches in her "Tolerance and Taboo."

8. For a thoughtful critique of Picasso's African appropriations, see Gikandi, "Picasso, Africa, and the Schemata of Difference."

9. My use of the term "translocal (not global or universal)" is indebted to Clifford (*Routes* 7).

10. Despite this convergence between Jameson and Giddens, it should be noted that Jameson sees his Marxist framework as incompatible with Giddens's sociology of globalization and attacks Giddens as an "ideologue of 'modernity'" (*A Singular Modernity* 11).

11. Among other recent essay collections seeking to open the "global horizons of modernism," see also *Geographies of Modernism*, and the special issue on "Modernism and Transnationalisms," Gikandi, ed. In influential essays, Friedman has been arguing for opening up modernism's period as well as spatial boundaries. On modernism and globalization, see also Melba Cuddy-Keane.

12. On hyphenated world citizenship, see Cohen, "Rooted Cosmopolitanism."

13. Yet while exhorting more immersion in the "languages of the global South" (languages, it should be noted, often also used in the global North), Spivak acknowledges that linguistic specificity often takes priority over the national: "The verbal text is jealous of its linguistic signature but impatient of national identity" (9).

14. See Buuck and Spahr's "Poetry and Other Englishes," and Ahmad's *Rotten English*.

15. Cf. M. M. Bakhtin's distinction between "intentional" and "organic" hybridity (258–62).

WORKS CITED

Abu-Lughod, Janet. "Going Beyond Global Babble." *Culture, Globalization and the World-System*. Ed. Anthony D. King. Minneapolis: University of Minnesota Press, 1997. 131–37.

Ahmad, Dohra, ed. *Rotten English: A Literary Anthology*. New York: Norton, 2007.

Anderson, Benedict. *Imagined Communities: Reflections on the Origin and Spread of Nationalism*. London: New Left, 1983.

Appadurai, Arjun. *Modernity at Large: Cultural Dimensions of Globalization*. Minneapolis: University of Minnesota Press, 1996.

Appiah, Kwame Anthony. *Cosmopolitanism: Ethics in a World of Strangers*. New York: Norton, 2006.

Arac, Jonathan. "Anglo-Globalism?" *New Left Review* 16 (2002): 35–45.

Auden, W. H. "Writing." *The Dyer's Hand and Other Essays*. New York: Vintage-Random House, 1968. 13–27.

———. "Prologue at Sixty." *Selected Poems: New Edition*. Ed. Edward Mendelson. New York: Vintage-Random House, 1979. 284–87.

Bakhtin, M. M. *The Dialogic Imagination: Four Essays*. Ed. Michael Holquist. Trans. Caryl Emerson and Michael Holquist. Austin: University of Texas Press, 1981.

Baudelaire, Charles. "L'Invitation au voyage." *Les Fleurs du Mal*. Paris: Librarie Larousse, 1959. 42–3.

Bennett, Louise. "South Parade Peddlar." *Selected Poems*. Ed. Mervyn Morris. Kingston: Sangster's Book Stores Ltd., 1983. 83–4.

Bhabha, Homi K. *The Location of Culture*. New York: Routledge, 1994.

Brathwaite, Edward [Kamau]. "Calypso." *The Arrivants*. New York: Oxford University Press, 1973. 48–50.

Brennan, Timothy. *At Home in the World: Cosmopolitanism Now*. Cambridge: Harvard University Press, 1997.

Buuck, David, and Juliana Spahr, eds. "Poetry and Other Englishes." *boundary* 2 33.2 (2006): 1–49.

Casanova, Pascale. "Literature as a World." *New Left Review* 31 (2005): 71–90.

Chen, Xiaomei. "Rediscovering Ezra Pound: A Postcolonial 'Misreading' of a Western Legacy." *Paideuma* 22.2–3 (1994): 81–105.

Chin, Marilyn. "How I Got That Name." *The Phoenix Gone, The Terrace Empty*. Minneapolis: Milkweed Editions, 1994. 16–18.

Chinweizu, Onwuchekwa Jemie, and Ihechukwu Madubuike. *Toward the Decolonization of African Literature*. Washington, DC: Howard University Press, 1983.

Clifford, James. *Routes: Travel and Translation in the Late Twentieth Century*. Cambridge: Harvard University Press, 1997.

Cohen, Mitchell. "Rooted Cosmopolitanism." *Toward a Global Civil Society*. Ed. Michael Walzer. Providence: Berghahn Books, 1995. 223–40.

Cuddy-Keane, Melba. "Modernism, Geopolitics, Globalization," *Modernism/modernity* 10.3 (2003): 539–58.

Delanty, Gerard. *Citizenship in a Global Age*. Buckingham: Open University Press, 2000.

Dickinson, Emily. "I'm Nobody, Who Are You?" (#288). *The Poems of Emily Dickinson*. Ed. Thomas H. Johnson. Cambridge: Belknap Press of Harvard University Press, 1963. 206–07.

Dimock, Wai Chee. *Through Other Continents: American Literature across Deep Time*. Princeton: Princeton University Press, 2006.

Doyle, Laura, and Laura Winkiel. "Introduction: The Global Horizons of Modernism." In *Geomodernisms: Race, Modernism, Modernity*. Ed. Doyle and Winkiel. Bloomington: Indiana University Press, 2005. 1–14.

Eliot, T. S. *Four Quartets*. London: Faber and Faber, 1959.

———. "The Social Function of Poetry." *On Poetry and Poets*. New York: Farrar, Straus Giroux, 1957. 3–16.

Eskin, Michael. "Bakhtin on Poetry." *Poetics Today* 21.2 (2000): 379–91.

Evaristo, Bernardine. *The Emperor's Babe*. London: Penguin, 2001.

Featherstone, Mike. *Undoing Culture: Globalization, Postmodernism and Identity*. London: Sage, 1995.

Fishman, Joshua A. "The New Linguistic Order." In *Globalization and the Challenges of a New Century*. Ed. Patrick O'Meara, Howard Mehlinger, and Matthew Krain. Bloomington: Indiana University Press, 2000. 435–42.

Friedman, Susan Stanford. "Definitional Excursions: The Meanings of Modern/Modernity/Modernism." *Modernism/modernity* 8.3 (2001): 493–514.

———. "Periodizing Modernism: Postcolonial Modernities and the Space/Time Borders of Modernist Studies." *Modernism/modernity* 13.3 (2006): 425–43.

———. "Modernism in a Transnational Landscape: Spatial Poetics, Postcolonialism, and Gender in Césaire's *Cahier/Notebook* and Cha's *Dictée*," *Paideuma* 32.1/2/3 (2003): 39–74.

Froude, James Anthony. *The English in the West Indies; or, The Bow of Ulysses*. New York: Charles Scribner's Sons, 1897.

Giddens, Anthony. *The Consequences of Modernity*. Cambridge: Polity, 1990.

Gikandi, Simon. "Globalization and the Claims of Postcoloniality." *South Atlantic Quarterly* 100.3 (2001): 627–58.

———. "Picasso, Africa, and the Schemata of Difference." *Modernism/modernity* 10.3 (2003): 455–80.

———. Ed. "Modernism and Transnationalisms." Spec. Issue of *Modernism/modernity* 13.3 (2006).

Glissant, Édouard. *Caribbean Discourse: Selected Essays*. Trans. J. Michael Dash. Charlottesville: University Press of Virginia, 1989.

———. *Le Discours Antillais*. Paris: Éditions du Seuil, 1981.

Hall, Stuart. "The Local and the Global: Globalization and Ethnicity." *Culture, Globalization and the World-System*. Ed. Anthony D. King. London: Macmillan, 1991. 19–39.

Hannerz, Ulf. "Scenarios for Peripheral Cultures." *Culture, Globalization and the World-System*. Ed. Anthony D. King. London: Macmillan, 1991. 107–28.

Harvey, David. *The Condition of Postmodernity*. Oxford: Blackwell, 1989.

Hayot, Eric. "Critical Dreams: Orientalism, Modernism, and the Meaning of Pound's China." *Twentieth Century Literature* 45.4 (1999): 511–33.

Heaney, Seamus. "Alphabets." *The Haw Lantern*. New York: Farrar, Straus Giroux, 1987. 1–3.

Held, David et al. *Global Transformations: Politics, Economics, and Culture*. Stanford: Stanford University Press, 1999.

Homer. *The Odyssey*. Trans. Robert Fagles. New York: Viking, 1996.

Hughes, Langston. "Theme for English B." *The Collected Poems of Langston Hughes*. Ed. Arnold Rampersad and David Roessel. New York: Knopf, 1997. 409–10.

Huntington, Samuel P. *The Clash of Civilizations and the Remaking of World Order*. New York: Simon & Schuster, 1996.

Huyssen, Andreas. "Geographies of Modernism in a Globalizing World." *Geographies of Modernism: Literatures, Cultures, Spaces*. Ed. Peter Brooker and Andrew Thacker. New York: Routledge, 2005. 6–18.

Jameson, Fredric. "Modernism and Imperialism." *Nationalism, Colonialism, and Literature*. Ed. Fredric Jameson et al. Minneapolis: University of Minnesota Press, 1990. 43–66.

———. "Notes on Globalization as a Philosophical Issue." *The Cultures of Globalization*. Ed. Jameson and Masao Miyoshi. Durham: Duke University Press, 1998. 54–77.

———. *A Singular Modernity*. New York: Verso, 2002.

Kitchener, Lord. "London Is the Place for Me." *London Is the Place for Me: Trinidadian Calypso in London, 1950–56*. Honest Jon's Records, 2002.

Krishnaswamy, Revathi. "Postcolonial and Globalization Studies: Connections, Conflicts, Complicities." *The Postcolonial and the Global*. Ed. Revathi Krishnaswamy and John C. Hawley. Minneapolis: University of Minnesota Press, 2008. 2–21.

Lee, Li-Young. "Persimmons." *Rose*. Brockport: Boa Editions LRD, 1986. 17–19.

Lindfors, Bernth. "An Interview with Okot p'Bitek." *World Literature Written in English* 16 (1977): 281–99.

Livingston, Robert Eric. "Glocal Knowledges: Agency and Place in Literary Studies." *PMLA* 116.1 (2001): 145–57.

Loy, Mina. "Anglo-Mongrels and the Rose." *The Lost Lunar Baedeker*. Ed. Roger L. Conover. Highlands: Jargon Society, 1982. 109–72.

Marx, Edward. *The Idea of a Colony: Cross-Culturalism in Modern Poetry*. Toronto: University of Toronto Press, 2004.

Murray, Les. "The Powerline Incarnation." *Learning Human: Selected Poems*. New York: Farrar, Straus Giroux, 2000. 20–21.

Nussbaum, Martha. *Cultivating Humanity*. Cambridge: Harvard University Press, 1997.

Okigbo, Christopher. *Labyrinths, with Path of Thunder*. London: Heinemann, 1971.

Okot p'Bitek. *"Song of Lawino" and "Song of Ocol."* Oxford: Heinemann, 1987.

Owen, Stephen. "Stepping Forward and Back: Issues and Possibilities for 'World' Poetry." *Modern Philology* 100 (2003): 532–48.

———. "World Poetry." *New Republic*. November 19, 1990. 28–32.

Park, Josephine Nock-Hee. *Apparitions of Asia: Modernist Form and Asian American Poetics*. New York: Oxford University Press, 2008.

Peterson, Kirsten. "Okot p'Bitek: Interview." *Kunapipi* 1.1 (1979): 89–93.

Perloff, Marjorie. "Tolerance and Taboo: Modernist Primitivisms and Postmodernist Pieties." *Prehistories of the Future: The Primitivist Project and the Culture of Modernism*. Ed. Elazar Barkan and Ronald Bush. Stanford: Stanford University Press, 1995. 339–54.

Plath, Sylvia. "Tulips." *The Collected Poems*. Ed. Ted Hughes. New York: Harper and Row, 1981. 160–62.

Porter, Dennis. "Orientalism and Its Problems." *Colonial Discourse and Post-Colonial Theory: A Reader*. Ed. Patrick Williams and Laura Chrisman. New York: Columbia University Press, 1994. 150–61.

Ramazani, Jahan. *The Hybrid Muse: Postcolonial Poetry in English*. Chicago: University of Chicago Press, 2001.

———. "Modernist Bricolage, Postcolonial Hybridity." *Modernism and Colonialism: British and Irish Literature, 1889–1939*. Ed. Richard Begam and Michael Valdez Moses. Durham: Duke University Press, 2007. 287–313.

Robbins, Bruce. "Comparative Cosmopolitanisms." *Cosmopolitics: Thinking and Feeling beyond the Nation*. Ed. Pheng Cheah and Robbins. Minneapolis: University of Minnesota Press, 1998. 246–64.

———. "Actually Existing Cosmopolitanism." *Cosmopolitics*. Ed. Cheah and Robbins. Minneapolis: University of Minnesota Press, 1998. 1–19.

Said, Edward W. *Culture and Imperialism*. New York: Random House, 1993.

———. *Orientalism*. New York: Vintage-Random House, 1978.

Spivak, Gayatri Chakravorty. *Death of a Discipline*. New York: Columbia University Press, 2003.

Torgovnik, Mariana. *Gone Primitive: Savage Intellects, Modern Lives.* Chicago: University of Chicago Press, 1990.

Walcott, Derek. *Collected Poems, 1948–1984.* New York: Farrar, Straus Giroux, 1986.

———. *Omeros.* New York: Farrar, Straus Giroux, 1990.

Walkowitz, Rebecca. *Cosmopolitan Style: Modernism Beyond the Nation.* New York: Columbia University Press, 2006.

Whitelaw, Marjory. "Interview with Christopher Okigbo." 1965/1970. *Critical Essays on Christopher Okigbo.* Ed. Uzoma Esonwanne. New York: G. K. Hall, 2000. 52–60.

Xie, Ming. *Ezra Pound and the Appropriation of Chinese Poetry.* New York: Garland, 1999.

PART V

COMPARATIVE AVANT-GARDES

FUTURIST GEOGRAPHIES: UNEVEN MODERNITIES AND THE STRUGGLE FOR AESTHETIC AUTONOMY: PARIS, ITALY, RUSSIA, 1909–1914

HARSHA RAM

FUTURISM is widely acknowledged as the earliest of the avant-garde literary movements to have swept through parts of Europe and Eurasia in the second decade of the twentieth century. The movement's opening volley was the characteristically belligerent "Fondation et Manifeste du futurisme" ("Founding and Manifesto of Futurism") published in French on February 20, 1909, by the Italian Filippo Tommaso Marinetti in the leading Paris newspaper *Figaro*, the "preferred journal for the artist declarations of the Belle Epoque."[1] The manifesto, perhaps the best known of Marinetti's works, reads as a hyperbolic litany of modernity's emancipatory as well as authoritarian and regressive effects, idiosyncratically fused as the inspiration for the futurist rebellion. It declared art to be linked indissolubly to aggression, glorified war as the "world's only hygiene," and celebrated "militarism, patriotism, the destructive gesture of the anarchists, beautiful Ideas that kill, and disdain for women."[2] Marinetti greeted the emergence of the masses, the "great crowds agitated by work, pleasure, and revolt," as the new protagonists of history whose discontent his vanguard coterie of young poets and artists would seek to unleash and direct well before this task would become the monopoly of the fascist state.

The "heroic" prewar years of Italian futurism coincided with a profound crisis in Italy's political institutions, a volatile period during which revolutionary anarchist as well as imperialist and proto-fascist tendencies found a shifting common ground in their subversive opposition to the liberal status quo. Eliding social struggle into a generalized celebration of war, Marinetti and his comrades left no doubt that theirs was a program of *national* renewal, a battle against the academy, the university, and the museum, perceived as cultural equivalents of Italy's political stagnation: "It is from Italy that we launch this manifesto of over-whelming, incendiary violence," declared Marinetti, "because we wish to deliver Italy from its gangrene of professors, archeologists, tour-guides (*cicérones*) and antiquarians."[3]

Militantly Italian yet lucidly addressing Paris as the center of cultural moder-nity and aesthetic modernism, the manifesto's chosen site and language of publica-tion, no less than its contents, betray some of the essential tensions of futurism as a whole. Promoting itself as the supreme expression of aesthetic modernity, futurism came into being in two regions—a belatedly unified Italy and the sprawl-ing if increasingly brittle tsarist *ancien régime*—whose relationship to the modern was tenuous at best. Italy's heyday was widely lamented as long past even as it heavily encumbered the present, while Russia's greatness was often proclaimed to be imminent. Most of the significant innovators of recent European poetry and painting, for instance, Baudelaire, Rimbaud, and Cézanne, had been French by birth or—in the case of the younger generation of Cendrars and Apollinaire—French by gravitation or adoption. In writing from Italy but addressing Paris as his primary interlocutor, Marinetti laid bare two of the more striking paradoxes of the futurist avant-garde: the *temporal* paradox of a radical modernity arising *within* "backwardness," and the *spatial* paradox of the core-status suddenly claimed by two of the key semiperipheral states of Europe.[4] This newly claimed centrality, however, would not generate any warm feelings between the Russians and the Ital-ians. Arising first in Italy, then, more diffusely, in Russia proper and subsequently in Russia's own imperial borderlands (Ukraine and Georgia), futurism was never a unitary phenomenon. Sharing more than a name but less than a unified poetics or ideology, futurism's regional manifestations, and the encounters between them, gave rise to sharply delineated national as well as factional differences. Few avant-garde movements were as transnational as futurism, yet few generated such shrill articulations of nationalist rivalry, local primacy, as well as utopian projections of alternative cultural universals. The futurist movements of Italy and the Russian empire tellingly illustrate how aesthetic modernism negotiated and tested the global literary system then coming into being, a system marked by centers of dominance and restless peripheries, and characterized by increasingly rapid cos-mopolitan cultural flows as well as the reaffirmation of cultural and geopolitical boundaries.

THE FUTURIST AVANT-GARDE AND THE TIME-SPACE OF MODERNITY

....

> Time and Space died yesterday. We already live in the absolute, because we have created eternal, omnipresent speed.
> —F. T. Marinetti, "Founding and Manifesto of Futurism"

The most vividly remembered aspect of the Italian futurists' polemic is their desire to break with the national past, which they rejected as the burden of a mummified tradition. Italian culture, they claimed, was lagging behind the reality of a new "dynamism of sensation," which had abolished time experienced as a cumulative succession of moments and space seen as the measurable distances that allowed for the arrangement of distinct objects within a defining environment.[5] Perspectivism was to painterly space what temporal sequence was to syntax and what historicism was to the dominant nineteenth-century models of European culture: the futurists denounced all three as interrelated prejudices made redundant by the new technologies of speed, communication, and warfare—the telegraph, the airplane, the machine gun, and the motor car (Marinetti, "Distruzione" 65–80; "Destruction" 95–106). Perhaps the greatest paradox of Italian futurist temporality was that it was ultimately not future-oriented at all: rather, it assumed an abstract, perpetually accelerating present whose ideal horizon was a simultaneity without history. While not unconvincing as an account of the effects of technological change and industrial production on the phenomenology of perception, Italian futurism's appeals to scientific innovation imply an oddly homogeneous and flattened view of modernity that stands in sharp contrast to the overwhelming material presence of Italy's past, the "numberless museums covering [Italy] like numberless graveyards" that were the perennial target of Marinetti's polemical ire (Marinetti, "Fondation" 12; "Founding" 22).

Nor should Marinetti's paeans to modernity be considered the final word of international futurism. The Russian futurists displayed a marked skepticism about the liberating potential of capitalist urbanization and industrial technology, and limited their dispute with history to the nineteenth century. They sought to measure and master time rather than to abolish it, and insisted on the radical contemporaneity of the remote past with the impending future. It might indeed be said that the most striking differences between Italian and Russian futurism were manifested precisely in their apprehension of time and space. While these discrepancies require careful exploration, they point equally to a shared awareness of the *uneven spatial diffusion* of modernity itself. Cognizant of Paris as the undisputed "capital of the nineteenth century," both the Italian and the Russian futurists strove to realize what I would call modernism's *second spatial turn*. If modernism's initial orientation was generally centripetal, a gravitation toward metropolitan modernity as embodied by the core nations and cities of Europe, then international futurism pursued a secondary movement that might be seen as a *return to the periphery*. The Italians and the Russians shared this centrifugal impulse, but came to ascribe very different meanings to center and periphery as geographical markers and cultural models. The futurists' noisy polemics with the past, and subsequently with one another, ask to be read as responses to the acutely felt discontinuities of time and space provoked by the increasingly rapid diffusion of modernity.

This question has at least two dimensions: the rhetoric and poetics of time-space *internal* to the avant-garde itself, and the normative metacritical vocabulary by which scholars of futurism have theorized or historicized the rupture the avant-garde claimed to represent, or the continuities it occluded. In his classic early study, *Teoria dell'arte d'avanguardia* (*Theory of the Avant-Garde*, 1962), Renato Poggioli began his "historical synthesis of the avant-garde" with its "prehistory" in "*Sturm und Drang* and the earliest romanticism, . . . passing on . . ., in a reconstruction both chronological and ideal, . . . [to] the French contribution, . . . the *Parnasse*, . . . decadence and symbolism." Poggioli then went on to invoke practically every major name and school of early twentieth-century European literature: in his account, the fin de siècle represented the "initial phase of the avant-garde experience," futurism the second, with dada and surrealism constituting "a third and more violent wave of avant-gardism." The fourth phase, "our own," is one "in which [being] avant-garde has become the second nature of all modern art" (*Teoria*, 252, 254, 256; *The Theory*, 226–30). Collapsing the avant-garde into vanguardism, Poggioli identified the latter as the fundamental assumption of all European literature once it had renounced the classicist imperative of imitating the ancients. Not only did Poggioli's reading conflate the avant-garde with modernism and even romanticism: it effectively identified its spirit as that of modernity itself, understood as an open-ended, indeterminate temporality that justified innovation for its own sake.[6] Poggioli's conclusions assumed the routinization of shock that is proper to our own time, but in a way that blunted the aesthetic and historical specificity of futurism's provocation.

Peter Bürger's *Theorie der Avantgarde* (*Theory of the Avant-Garde*, 1974) replaced Poggioli's narrative of broad continuities with one of dialectical negation. For Bürger the avant-garde emerged as a reaction to the increasing separation of art from life in bourgeois society. The principle of *l'art pour l'art* arose in turn-of-the-century Europe as the culmination of a century-long process by which art severed its links to society in order to constitute itself as an independent field. Formulated first by Kant and Schiller, the distinctness and increasingly fetishized autonomy of aesthetic experience became the actual content of poetry after Baudelaire, culminating in the great works of the European fin de siècle. The task of the avant-garde artistic movements of the early twentieth century—dada being Bürger's chief example—was to *invert* the premise of fin-de-siècle aestheticism by questioning the institutional basis of art's autonomy and restoring its relationship to social practice (Bürger, *Theorie*, 25, 28–29, 57–73; *Theory*, 22, 27, 42–43).

However sensitive to the significance of dialectical breaks in social history and aesthetic experience, Bürger's account remains normatively European in its reading of art's relationship to modernity, and can hardly be said to reflect shifts in the function and value ascribed to art outside the core nations of the West. In the Russian empire, for example, the autonomy of art never developed strong institutional or ideological foundations. The authority of Russian literature remained tied to its capacity for social critique and spiritual renewal. As a consequence, many of the Russian symbolists, the first in Russia to question the assumptions of nineteenth-century realism and pledge their abiding commitment to artistic technique, remained markedly religious and ultimately social in orientation. The Russian avant-garde, as a further consequence, could not simply invert the premises of symbolism, but arguably radicalized its totalizing impulses further in the direction of formal experimentation and revolutionary politics. Italian cultural history is equally resistant to Bürger's model. The precocious if discontinuous development of the Tuscan literary dialect and the exceptional brilliance of Italian art were not accompanied by the emergence of a centralized state until the unification of Italy during the 1860s. For this reason nineteenth-century Italy was far less preoccupied with the autonomy of literature than with its place in the struggle to establish and consolidate the nation-state and a national linguistic standard. Gabriele D'Annunzio, the most significant figure in Italian *decadentismo*, was likewise as much a political figure as an aesthete, intervening directly in the ongoing crises of the Italian liberal state in favor of military intervention to further Italy's irredentist and imperial goals. Marinetti's relationship to D'Annunzio was one of rivalry, however one-sided: D'Annunzio represented the most vivid Italian embodiment of the late symbolist culture within which Marinetti had himself debuted as a writer. Marinetti offered D'Annunzio, the "younger brother of the great French symbolists," "unlimited praise" for having "bewitched the minds of his age with his art," but equally faulted him for the "colossal misapprehension of believing that he was giving his literary works a political scope when he was only giving his life a literary scope." D'Annunzio's main error, in Marinetti's eyes, lay in believing that he could "overturn the world with a turn of phrase" and in "attribut[ing] to a book or a poem a direct impact on the crowds."[7] Marinetti in fact shared D'Annunzio's militant nationalism and his theatrical, self-aggrandizing voluntarism: he aspired only to realize what D'Annunzio and the symbolists had been unable, in his eyes, to accomplish. Marinetti's poetics of the "wireless imagination," based on "an analogical synthesis of the world embraced in a single glance and gathered as one whole in essential words," and the Russian futurist Khlebnikov's invention of a universal language based on the attribution of inherent meaning to consonantal sounds read as very different attempts to realize Baudelaire's vision of the world as a network of correspondences.[8] By shattering the famed "musicality" of symbolist verse while retaining and radicalizing symbolism's faith in the ontological power of poetic language, both Russian and Italian futurisms strove to fulfill their symbolist precursors' desire to reconcile art and national life. Neither the Italian nor the Russian experience corresponds to Bürger's account of literary history or the institutional role of art.

By contrast, Marjorie Perloff has opted for a synchronic approach, one that designates the years leading up to World War I as the "futurist moment," which produced a "short-lived but remarkable rapprochement between avant-garde aesthetic, radical politics, and popular culture" (xvii). Perloff's account has the merit of situating futurism alongside analogous developments in the European avant-garde, from cubist collage to Apollinaire's *calligrammes* to Ezra Pound and the English Vorticists. Perloff converts the temporal continuity assumed by Poggioli into a spatial one, a Pan-European vision of broadly simultaneous and comparable ruptures in artistic form. Yet if "the larger desire of the Futurists [was] to break down existing economic and political structures and to transcend nationalist barriers," then Perloff also notes the "particular mixture of radicalism and patriotism, of a worldly international outlook and a violently nationalist faith" that typified the avant-garde on the eve of World War I. The purpose of the pages to come is to explore more deeply "the tension between cosmopolitanism and a stubborn nationalism that gives the poetry and painting of the period its particular poignancy."[9]

The spatial or temporal continuities assumed in different ways by Poggioli and Perloff, and the Franco-German assumptions built into Bürger's model, are symptomatic of the larger interpretive challenges posed by futurism's relationship to modernism and modernity as normative periodizing categories. In 1923, the Bolshevik leader Leon Trotsky explained the curious fact that "futurism had obtained its most brilliant expression not in America and not in Germany, but in Italy and in Russia" as reflective of "a phenomenon which has been repeated in history more than once, namely that countries that were backward but which possessed a certain degree of spiritual culture reflected in their ideology the achievements of advanced countries more brilliantly and strongly."[10] This formulation has been theorized more recently in the work of Fredric Jameson and Perry Anderson as the condition of *incomplete* or *uneven modernity*: "What we call artistic or aesthetic 'modernism,'" argues Jameson, "essentially corresponds to a situation of incomplete modernization" that is "organized around two distinct temporalities: that of the new industrial big city and that of the peasant countryside." Modernism, in Jameson's account, would register aesthetically the shock of urban novelty against the persistence of "what can only anachronistically be called the pre-modern, or undervelopment."[11] While far more attentive to the discontinuities of global modernity, the neo-Marxist reading of modernism as a response to incomplete or uneven modernization remains wedded to the teleological and developmentalist assumptions of modernity itself, in which a still largely agrarian reality is negatively rendered as "backwardness." Moreover, it locates the origins of the modern essentially within Europe, whereby the gap between the European city and the rural hinterland—Milan and the Mezzogiorno, if you will—functions as a diminished substitute for modernity's larger geographies.

FUTURISM BETWEEN COSMOPOLITANISM AND NATIONALISM

> It is in the repressed spatial premises of the concept of modernity that its political logic is to be found.
>
> —Peter Osborne, *Politics of Time: Modernity and Avant-Garde*

An ambitiously global map of the modern literary world has been outlined recently by Pascale Casanova. Governed by "laws of rivalry, inequality, and specific struggles," a "world republic of letters" emerged, in Casanova's account, with the consolidation of the literary system in sixteenth-century France, whose specific configuration served, *mutatis mutandis*, as a model for the subsequent expansions and transformations by which a properly international literary order arose (Casanova 15). French was the first of the post-Latin European vernaculars to be refined, standardized and ratified by a range of legitimizing institutions, from the monarchical state to the French Academy to the literary salons that flourished under Louis XIV. This process of linguistic standardization was not related solely to the imperatives of political centralization, but equally to the accumulation of theoretical, aesthetic, and rhetorical resources through which the *literariness* of French was established. If the nation-state and linguistic nationalism were the essential prerequisites for the emergence of a modern literary system, then the cultural prestige and geographical diffusion of a language were vouchsafed by the capacity of its literature to distance itself from the narrow exigencies of politics. French became the language of European diplomacy, civility, and sensibility to the extent that it projected itself as a universal standard, free of the need to embody a national essence. By the nineteenth century, Paris had become the denationalized cosmopolitan center of an international literary system whose hierarchies were determined by the capacity of other emergent literatures to compete for legitimation by restaging the dialectic of national politics and aesthetic autonomy. The "world republic of letters" remains to this day an unequal geography of centers and peripheries, determined in its parts and as a whole by an ongoing struggle between centripetal forces oriented toward the cosmopolitan principle of autonomy and the centrifugal forces of cultural nationalism (Casanova 100, 126, 154–57). In its evident Gallocentrism, Casanova's theory can certainly be faulted for perpetuating the very logic it seeks to expose. Her narrative assumes a diffusionism by which both the aesthetic principle of "literariness" and the geographical base-unit of the nation-state are seen to have originated in Europe, specifically France, before spreading elsewhere. The cultural experience of peripheral or semiperipheral regions is thereby reduced to one of post-Herderian romantic nationalism arising in reaction to the imposition of European colonial languages or cultural norms. Casanova's premise ignores the vast, centuries-old, and still vibrant cosmopolitan literacies of South and East Asia or the Islamic world, as well as the more recent socialist internationalism of the Second world, whose interconnections point to alternative cultural trajectories that have frequently bypassed the West.

For all its limitations, Casanova's theory throws a very instructive light on the specific experience of the futurist avant-garde. The futurists displayed a hypertrophied awareness of the competitive and hierarchical nature of the international literary system, as well as its operative conventions. Their insistence on geographical categories and political delimitations such as nation and empire, east and west, reflects the traditional vocabulary by which the cultural peripheries of Europe had striven to distinguish themselves from one another as well as from the hegemony of Parisian artistic tastes. Yet in fusing an aggressive affirmation of national or regional identity with a radical poetics of the liberated linguistic sign, the Russian futurists in particular strove to *overcome* the opposition between politicized nationalism and a cosmopolitan literariness upon which the increasingly global literary order was based. Unlike past revolts against the cultural center, they strove not merely to synchronize the divergent temporalities of center and periphery but ultimately to refashion the spatial hierarchy that gave the center its authority. This rewriting of center-periphery relations was by no means consistent or entirely successful, and constitutes, as we shall see, a major difference of approach between the Italian and Russian futurists. It also serves to test the insights and limits of Casanova's center/periphery model, to which we might add the partial corrective of world-systems theory, according to which early twentieth-century Russia and Italy would be defined as *semiperipheral* nations that combined the economic patterns and institutional structures of both the core and the periphery. While still dependent to varying degrees on a global system dominated by core states, the semiperiphery is at the same time "fertile ground for social, organizational and technical innovation" and provides an "advantageous location for the establishment of new centers of power" (Chase-Dunn and Hall 79). The semiperipheral feature most relevant to avant-garde cultural production is an *upward mobility* that could be manifested in one of two ways: as the desire to ascend by means of competition to the dominant core, or as an anti-systemic challenge to the very logic that underlies the core's hegemony. Both tendencies were manifested within transnational futurism, and serve in part to distinguish the Italians from the Russians.

In either case, futurism calls into question the widespread assumption, common to Anglo-American as well as continental critics, that a purely *centripetal* impulse was in fact constitutive of aesthetic modernism as a whole. Raymond Williams, for example, identifies the historical avant-garde as the "expression of rapidly mobile émigrés" living in the "centers of metropolitan dominance" (Williams 37). The avant-garde's "deep mode . . . was precisely this mobility across frontiers: frontiers which were among the most obvious elements of the old order which had to be rejected, even when native folk sources were being included as elements or as inspiration of the new art. There was intense competition but also radical coexistence in the great imperial capitals of Paris, Vienna, Berlin, and Petersburg, and also, in more limited ways, in London" (Williams, "Introduction" 59). Williams' thesis certainly sheds light on the phenomenon of a Pablo Picasso or a Gertrude Stein, but requires considerable nuancing in the case of futurism. Pilgrimages to Paris were indeed almost obligatory for most protagonists of the "futurist moment," particularly in the visual arts. Yet a *centrifugal* impulse was no less constitutive of the futurist avant-garde. Futurist nationalism was an attempt either to repatriate or to redefine the cosmopolitan tropes of modernity as part of the semiperiphery's claim to creative agency.[12]

The biographical and artistic trajectories of some of futurism's key protagonists clarify this point. While it would be quite mistaken to equate Italian futurism with its self-appointed leader—the Florentine futurists Papini, Soffici, and Palazzeschi, for example, broke with "marinettismo" in the name of a more authentic futurism in 1915[13]—Marinetti's life journey is both extreme and exemplary. The poet was born in Alexandria, a major Levantine port that had seen a significant influx of Europeans since the building of the Suez Canal, which precipitated Egypt's surrender to French financial control and then to British military domination. Educated locally by French Jesuits and studying subsequently in Paris and Italy, Marinetti launched his literary career as a nominally bilingual writer shuttling between Milan and Paris whose chief works were composed almost exclusively in French until 1912. Acutely conscious of the provincialism of his ancestral land, Marinetti launched Italian futurism via the Parisian press and then propagated it throughout Italy, along with his newly gathered comrades, in a series of noisily confrontational "futurist evenings."[14] Renouncing the shared aesthetic pleasures of the salon for the headier "voluptuousness of being booed," Marinetti utilized the value of scandal as publicity in a precocious fusion of the arts and the mass media that would later be dubbed the culture industry ("La voluttà" 310–13).[15] Futurism's notoriety was further exacerbated with the bilingual publication of Marinetti's novel *Mafarka le futuriste* (1910), whose Italian translation led to several trials in Milan for "outrage to decency," even as its French edition enjoyed considerable success in Paris.[16] A novel rooted in the French orientalist tradition of *Salammbô* was projected onto the very different Italian context: the contrasts of tradition and reception between Italy and France were precisely what Marinetti was seeking to overcome, even as they were the welcome source of his immediate Italian notoriety.

Marinetti's embrace of Italy can thus be seen as a gradual and carefully constructed process of symbolic repatriation which accelerated rapidly with the birth of the movement he largely invented and strove to lead. Marinetti's futurist homecoming requires a modification of Raymond Williams's model of modernism's defining geography. A deterritorialized cosmopolitanism certainly characterized the Alexandria of the poet's childhood, albeit in ways enabled by a European colonialism which Marinetti would frequently invoke, explicitly or allegorically, in his works. It doubtless also typified Parisian cubism, for example, or dada in Zurich. Yet this *deterritorialization* was followed, in the case of both Italian and Russian futurism, by a *reterritorialized* sense of location that was often expressed in explicitly national terms. The "Italianness" of Italian futurism was not related to its use of the

Italian language, which at the outset was minimal, and still less to Italian mores or tradition, which the futurists would denounce vociferously as a hindrance to change. Rather, it involved aligning Italian literary and artistic practice with the enabling structures of modernity, understood as the latest technologies of transportation and warfare, and as the ensemble of competing political states within which Italy would be exhorted to assert its place. Theirs was a nationalism that, in Emilio Gentile's words, combined "an enthusiasm for modernity and a tragic sense of existence," the two elements being reconciled through "a particular vision of modernity conceived as an explosion of human and material energies, which had no precedents in human history and inaugurated a new era of life's expansion through struggle" (Gentile 107).

More heterogeneous and essentially leaderless, but by no means devoid of strong personalities, Russian futurism was never defined by a single protagonist, monolithic grouping, unified aesthetic ideology or even a name. Its most memorable literary representatives—Vladimir Maiakovskii, Velimir Khlebnikov, Aleksei Kruchënykh, and Benedikt Livshits—called themselves "Hylaeans," "cubofuturists," or even "futurians" (the Russian is *budetliane*, a Khlebnikovian Slavic neologism for which I would venture the alternative translation "will-be-ists"). Without doubt the most talented and celebrated of the Russian futurist groups, the Hylaeans achieved a certain visibility in early 1910 with the publication of their miscellany *Sadok sudei* (*A Trap for Judges*), though some of its participants, chiefly painters, had already been collaborating for several years. Marinetti's manifestos had been translated and his activities abundantly reported in Russia since 1909, although their diffusion and notoriety were as much a reflection of intense local interest in European cultural trends as the result of Marinetti's own propagandistic zeal (Michelis 191–97). The term "futurist" was first applied to a native Russian phenomenon in 1911, when it was appropriated by the Petersburg "ego-futurist" Igor Severianin—occasional rival to the Hylaeans and a poet-dandy of enormous if ultimately ephemeral popularity. Vadim Shershenevich, leader of another short-lived Moscow poets' group in alliance with the ego-futurists, was the chief propagator and translator of Marinetti's works in Russia. His *Futurizm bez maski* (*Futurism Unmasked*, 1913) hailed Marinetti for his celebration of speed and city life, but faulted his work for the "dominance of content over form," and its lapses into "journalism" and "demagogy," a frequent Russian criticism that would become the crux for the articulation of national differences (Shershenevich 49–50). During the years before World War I, "futurism" circulated in Russia as a loose signifier, broadly synonymous in the media and in the public eye with post-symbolist literary innovation, urban modernity, and public provocation. "Cubofuturism" arose in 1913. The term was advanced by Maiakovskii and the painter David Burliuk, Hylaea's organizational impresario: its coining was at once a concession to the times and a tactical manoeuvre designed to appropriate the terms of the debate and assert Hylaea's primacy over foreign as well as local competitors.[17]

A comparison between Marinetti's life trajectory and those of his Hylaean literary counterparts is instructive. The major poets of the Hylaean group were all provincial newcomers to Russia's metropolitan centers, for whom the multiethnic reality of the world's largest contiguous empire was culturally no less significant than their assimilation of the Russian and European literary canons. Aleksei Kruchenykh was born to a Ukrainian peasant family, while Maiakovskii spent his childhood in Georgia where his father, though of Russian noble ancestry, had worked as a forest ranger. The poet's youth, lived between Kutaisi, Georgia's second city, and Moscow, was devoted more to revolutionary agitation than to serious study. In retrospect, Maiakovskii would playfully derive his "futurism, atheism and internationalism" from an interlinguistic error made during the school entrance exam he nearly failed: the boy Maiakovskii mistook the Church Slavic word "oko," meaning "eye," for the Georgian word "oqa," an archaic measure of weight ("Ia sam"). The future poet thus instinctively rejected the official ecclesiastical and Russifying policies of the tsarist state for the regional Georgian milieu in which he was raised. While Maiakovskii drew far less than Marinetti, poetically speaking, from his "exotic" childhood, this episode highlights the poet's ability to rationalize his patchy education as evidence of a native Eurasian multiculturalism that functioned as a substitute for the European cosmopolitanism he acquired only through his later travels. Velimir Khlebnikov hailed from the Kalmyk steppe in the southern hinterland of Russia, and studied in Kazan, the former capital of the Volga Tatars: his own literary and intellectual horizons were crucially shaped, thematically and even epistemologically, by his geographical provenance. The poet's fantastical phonetic and numerological theories, which involved ascribing semantic or rhythmical consistencies to individual letters and numerical formulae, read as a quest for a deeper spatio-temporal logic to Russian-Eurasian and ultimately world history. Benedikt Livshits, an Odessan Jew, was the only member of the Hylaea group to possess the linguistic training and literary sensibility equal to the heritage of European modernism, from its French fin-de-siècle redactions to the latest innovations of the avant-garde in painting and in poetry. A connoisseur of Laforgue, Mallarmé, and Rimbaud, Livshits achieved a rarefied if ponderous fusion in his own verse of symbolist poetics and the analytical decomposition of form proper to cubism. Although his efforts approximated the poetry of Osip Mandel'shtam more closely than it did his fellow Hylaeans, Livshits was perhaps the sole Russian futurist capable of contesting Marinetti's terms of debate in a way that was cognizant of Russian specificity as well as of modernism's Parisian matrix. With the exception of Livshits, the Hylaean futurists were generally unable to match the cultural capital that Marinetti derived from his Francophone cosmopolitanism, a weakness they sought to turn to their advantage.[18] While the painters of the Russian avant-garde were better traveled and better informed than their literary counterparts, and could take for granted the greater capacity of the visual arts to cross linguistic and national boundaries, they too contributed significantly to the nativist turn that provided the cultural basis for the Eurasian nationalism of the Hylaea group.

The chronological priority of the Italians in the creation of futurism, as a term and as a coherent doctrine, is undeniable. But their precedence must be understood in the context of two very different means of constructing literary capital, based on the biographical and creative trajectories of its participants, and their respective practices of self-identification and self-promotion. While Marinetti's manifestos anticipated his actual creative practice instead of summarizing it, the Russian experience was precisely the reverse. The poet Khlebnikov was already composing his first lyric masterpieces in a notably post-symbolist idiom in 1908–1909, but the Hylaeans had no articulated program until December 1912, when they published their first manifesto, "Poshchëchina obshchestvennomy vkusu" ("A Slap in the Face of Public Taste").[19] Questions of primacy and influence with respect to futurism as a transnational phenomenon mattered greatly to the futurists themselves, who frequently distorted their own publication histories to prove their antecedence. These games of one-upmanship are in fact best understood as a reflection of the competitive and agonistic nature of futurism itself as a negotiation of time and place.[20]

Futurismo/Futurizm: Toward a Transnational Geography of the Futurist Avant-Garde

Filippo Marinetti's Italy was a territorial sign, hollow but continually expanding, to be refilled, through provocation, declamation, spectacle and incitement to war, with a modern but strikingly generic content. Marinetti's tireless propagation of futurism's literary ideals was synonymous in his eyes with national self-assertion. Even as he penned manifestos advocating revolutions in poetic form, Marinetti also wrote enthusiastic reportage from the frontlines of Italy's colonial campaign of 1911 in Libya, stridently advocated Italy's participation in the Great War during 1914–1915, and hailed the occupation, in Italy's name but against the will of the liberal Italian state, of the disputed (now Croatian) city of Fiume-Rijeka in 1919 by Gabriele D'Annunzio's band of legionnaires.[21] Significantly, the Italian futurists never agitated, aesthetically or politically, against France: indeed, Italy's status as France's ally provided the additional cultural gloss of "Latin" solidarity to her wartime role. Theirs was not a denunciation of the Parisian center as such, but an attempt at establishing an equal and ultimately dominant footing among Europe's leading nations, above all through Italy's military or discursive subjugation of regions more peripheral than herself.

Italy's modernization required her Europeanizing imperial mission abroad. Marinetti's own childhood in Egypt provided ample material in this regard and was often invoked allegorically in his work. His founding manifesto opens with a reference to the sumptuous oriental décor of his father's Milanese apartment, which functions simultaneously as a metaphor for the familial past and as a stylistic marker of fin de siècle languor, both playfully rejected as part of futurism's youthful embrace of the chaos of the modern street ("Fondation" 5; "Founding" 19). More complex still is Marinetti's novel *Mafarka le futuriste*, a parable of the birth of a winged futurist superman, set not in Italy but in a North African milieu that is anything but contemporary. Eliding entirely the immediate context of European colonialism as well as Western modernity, the novel opens with scenes of graphic sexual and racial violence that pit Arab rulers against their black African subjects. The sadism of the novel's opening pages allows for a grotesque recuperation of the primitive, the oriental, and the feminine as elements otherwise excluded from the Italian futurist vision, while its didactic conclusion argues for the subordination of the same elements to the higher goal of futurist creativity. Marinetti's racialized geography permits a celebration of the primitive as a crude, vital force as well as its necessary sublimation into the reproductive capacities of the male creative will, a self-fecundation that leads to the novel's improbable climax of male parthenogenesis, a father begetting a mechanical son.[22]

Russian futurism wrestled with similar questions of national and imperial identities but within the context of a large, restive multiethnic empire in which diverse communities had coexisted in varied histories of proximity, governed by an autocratic state that sought to impose its own identitarian forms, imperially charged but religiously and nationally inflected. Russia's territorial expansion was by no means uniform in its intents and effects: military conquest had been pursued concurrently with waves of migration, the large-scale relocation of Slavic peasant populations, and the selective cooptation of non-Russian élites from annexed lands into the administrative machinery of the state. In its final decades tsarism's legitimating ideologies were being eroded by peasant insurrection, worker unrest, restive subject populations with increasingly articulated nationalist demands, and intellectual ferment, both artistic and political. Russia's defeat by Japan in 1905 had revealed the weaknesses of autocracy as well as the rise of a rival Asiatic modernity. The military outcome fueled the abortive Russian revolution of 1905, which in turn sparked challenges to feudal-monarchical rule from Ottoman Turkey to Iran. Alternatives to the European, imperial path to modernity seemed discernible, and the multiple histories of the Russian-Eurasian landmass, of which Russian imperial domination was only one chapter, were open to reinterpretation.

Since Peter the Great, the perennial dilemma of Russian geography had been its threshold status between East and West, the absence of a definitive boundary between the Russian heartland and its colonized territories, in contrast to a sharp vertical divide separating the Europeanized élite and a disenfranchised Russian populace, the latter itself frequently perceived in Asiatic terms (Bassin 1–17). In Jane Ashton Sharp's words: "Shaped by centuries of human migration, Russian culture was defined by imaginary boundaries, a periphery that could be endlessly reconstituted to include or exclude" (37). Russia's writers and artists had been reexamining this dilemma in ways that were increasingly free of the rationalizations offered by the tsarist state. The nineteenth-century realist tradition had culminated in Tolstoi's late masterpiece *Haji Murat* (completed in 1904), a Rousseaustic denunciation of the delusions of imperial modernization in the Caucasus. The Russian symbolists had reacted to Asia's reawakening in apocalyptic terms, viewing the rise of the East as the harbinger of the Antichrist, or welcoming it by conflating its consequences with the goals of social revolution closer to home. Russian literary perceptions of the Yellow Peril myth generated a specific apprehension of time and space: on one hand, the Eastern threat would erase all known political boundaries, as the Mongols had done centuries before. On the other hand, this spatial open-endedness was counterbalanced by a millenarian vision of the end of history as such, in which Russia-Eurasia had a vital—destructive or regenerative—role to play.

The Russian avant-garde rejected the official representations of Russian nationality and imperial statehood, even as they also dismantled the xenophobic eschatology of the symbolists, rooted in anxieties of race and class. Aware of the energizing role of orientalism and primitivism in European modernist painting from Gauguin and Matisse to the cubists, the artists Mikhail Larionov and Natal'ia Goncharova argued for a syncretic aesthetic vision that would reconcile Russian peasant handicrafts, oriental decorative and ornamental styles, and the compositional properties of the Orthodox icon and the popular broadsheet. Yet while European modernism had sought to appropriate the structure and texture of exotic forms imported from overseas (Africa and Oceania), Russian modernism relied on the radical contiguity of existing local cultures *within* the Russian empire, or adjacent to it. This distinction is crucial, for it allowed the Russians to ascribe a cultural solidarity to the spatial continuity of the Eurasian landmass. Although Goncharova and Larionov were to break with the Hylaean futurists in 1913, they contributed significantly to the Eurasian primitivist turn that was arguably the main unifying premise of the Hylaean group, although Maiakovskii was little touched by it.

In his important memoirs of 1933, Benedikt Livshits derived the group's cultural orientation from the topography of the country estate of Chernianka where they first gathered. Located in steppeland along the Black Sea coast of southern Ukraine, it was a region known to the ancient Greeks as Hylaea:

> Restored to its sources, history creates itself anew. The wind from the Euxine Sea sweeps in like a blizzard, overturns Lübker's [classical Greek] mythology, unearths burial mounds covered over by the lethargic snow, throws up a swarm of Hesiodic phantoms, reshuffles them while they hang in the air, before resettling there, beyond the barely visible expanse, as a mytheme that gives wing to the will.
>
> Hylaea, ancient Hylaea, trodden by our feet, acquired the significance of a symbol, and was to become a banner. . . .
>
> In other, less ancient burial mounds, Vladimir [Burliuk], inspired to dedicate his summer months to archeological excavation, found Scythian bows and crowns and armed his own one-eyed archers with them for a fight to the death with the women of Paris, dismantled [by the cubists—H. R.] into their essential planes.
>
> Time, losing its boundaries, stratified in Chernianka in every direction.
>
> In one of these directions, it was still space that was only beginning to come to life.[23]

In these lines, Livshits envisions Russia-Eurasia as the barbarian other of the classical Greeks, coeval with antiquity, but also displacing it. Lacking the familiar

markers of European civilization, Eurasian history had to be interpreted archeologi-
cally for the material traces of lost nomadic cultures, and topographically by retrac-
ing the natural process of burial and unearthing by which time covers and then
upturns the past. The Hylaean futurists were seeking alternative models of time and
space by which to register the specificities of Eurasian history and cultural interaction. In the Eurasian steppe, time itself became space, without horizontal limits, but
vertically sedimented in meager but densely packed layers of human and natural
existence. This spatialization of Eurasian history allowed for the radical coexistence
of diverse epochs and aesthetic forms. If the Italian futurists sought to abolish time
and space by surrendering to the accelerating pace of modernity, then the Russian
futurists sought to make modernity itself heterochronous, composed of multiple
times, "atavistic strata and diluvian rhythms," acknowledged as coexisting in the
global present (Livshits, *Polutoraglazyi* 372; *The One* 92). While the Hylaeans also
urged "throwing Pushkin, Dostoevskii, Tolstoi and others off the Steamship of modernity," their quarrel was principally with the nineteenth-century literary canon
and not with history as such, which posed less of a burden to Russia than to Italy. If
"the Academy and Pushkin were less comprehensible than hieroglyphics," then a
new solidarity could be forged, in opposition to the *recent* past, between futurism
and the hieroglyph.[24]

The principal Russian futurist to realize the fusion of the modern and the archaic
was the poet Velimir Khlebnikov, who expounded a sweeping set of interconnected
theories of time-space which had a numerical as well as a linguistic and alphabetic
component. Khlebnikov's dialogue "Uchitel' i uchenik" ("Teacher and Pupil" 1912), the
first published formulation of his theory of time, outlines the poet's claimed discovery
of the underlying laws of history. The lines that follow, at least in Khlebnikov's later
estimation, contain nothing less than a prediction of the October Revolution of 1917:

> *PUPIL*: . . . I have sought the rules that dictate the destiny of nations. And I
> hereby assert . . . that 1383 years separate the fall of states and the loss of
> liberty. . . . I have found in general that time z separates such events where
> $z = (365+48y)x$, where y may have a negative or positive value . . . if $y = 2$,
> and $x = 3$, then $z = (365+48.2)3 = 1383$. The fall of states is divided by this
> period of time. . . . The Polovtsy conquered the Russian steppe in 1093, 1383
> years after the fall of Samnium in the year 290. And in the year 534 the
> kingdom of the Vandals was conquered; should we not expect the fall of a
> state in 1917?
>
> *TEACHER*: This is a real art. But how did you achieve it?
>
> *PUPIL*: The clear stars of the South awoke the Chaldean in me. On the day of
> Ivan Kupalo I found my fern—the law that governs the fall of states. I know
> about the mind of continents that is quite unlike the mind of islanders. The
> son of proud Asia cannot be reconciled with the peninsular reason of
> Europeans. ("Uchitel' i uchenik" 156; "Teacher and Student" 284).

Khlebnikov measured historical time by calibrating the dates that marked the
rise and fall of nations and empires. These ebbs and flows of power formed regular

spatio-temporal patterns, of which the ancient struggle between East and West was a crucial example. The perennial wars between the nomadic tribes of Eurasia and the sedentary urban cultures of Europe and the more recent expansion of the great European powers throughout Asia were all equally found to be the result of a temporal law of retributive justice, whereby former gains by one geographical region were counterbalanced by future losses, and vice versa. Khlebnikov's thinking assumed a positivist notion of history as a series of datable events, only to reinterpret these data as part of an East-West cycle that linked events remote in time into consistent spatial patterns of territorial gain and loss.

Within this model of time, East and West were not, theoretically speaking, absolute cultural polarities but changing spatial perspectives produced by the directional thrust of historical violence. In the actual polemics of the Hylaean group, however, this perspectival approach to culture generally lapsed into the binary logic of civilizational oppositions. The new science of time, as Khlebnikov himself claimed, was specifically "Asiatic," rooted in the topography of the Russian south. The most ambitious aspect of Hylaean futurism was precisely this quest for new epistemological universals, irreconcilable with the "peninsular reason of Europeans."

The Hylaeans' opposition to Europe allowed for a reconceptualizing of Eurasian space in terms that were markedly nationalist, but not chauvinistically Russian or overtly imperialist. Ascribing base geopolitical motivations to their opponents, the Hylaean futurists preferred to ground their arguments on the perceived cultural, aesthetic, or metaphysical commonalities that united Russia and Asia. A case in point is the leaflet-manifesto "We and the West," published in Russian, French, and Italian at the very beginning of 1914 by Benedikt Livshits, the composer Artur Lourié, and the painter Georgii Iakulov: "Ultimately, the art of the West is TERRITORIAL. The only country that to this day does not have a territorial art is RUSSIA. . . . All efforts made by the West in building a new aesthetic, because they are a priori and not a posteriori, are FATALLY CATASTROPHIC: a new aesthetic follows a new art and not the other way around" (138–39). In opposition to a Franco-Italian modernism driven by theoretical assumptions, territorial ambitions, and a "geometrical understanding of the world," Livshits would hail Russian art for its "secret proximity to material, our exclusive sensitivity (*chuvstvovanie*) to it, our inborn ability to metamorphose, abolishing all mediating links between the material and the creator." These capacities provided the "cosmic foundations" for a new art (Livshits, *Polutoraglazyi* 506; *The One* 208).

At its utopian limit, Russian futurism was characterized by a search for alternative universals that exceeded the narrow confines of Russian nationalism or imperialism, even as it remained deeply invested in the logic of territorial defensiveness and aesthetic rivalry that informed the global literary system, and which the futurist avant-garde reproduced to greater effect than perhaps any movement before it. More than any other Hylaean futurist, Velimir Khlebnikov encompassed all these possibilities. A case in point is Filippo Marinetti's visit to Russia at the beginning of 1914, an event that sparked a sharp delineation of national as well as subnational

divisions within the putatively international futurist movement. At the very end of
his life and in conditions of deteriorating health, Marinetti would dedicate a chapter
of his memoirs to his Russian travels: its title, "La nascita del Futurismo russo.
Milano Parigi Mosca Petrogrado" ("The birth of Russian Futurism. Milan Paris
Moscow Petrograd"), leaves no doubt as to Marinetti's understanding of the geographical trajectory of futurism.[25] These pages depict the last winter season of Russia's *belle époque* as the luxuriant growth of a torrid hothouse, an indoor tropical
fantasy shielded artificially from the frozen Russian wastes. Marinetti's recollections
amount to a self-aggrandizing and essentially worldly account of the poet's ability to
negotiate the hospitable curiosity, erotic possibilities, and openly voiced hostility he
encountered among Russia's sophisticated urban élites. For all its limitations, Marinetti's memoirs gleefully corroborate the range of responses he elicited from the
Russian press, the public, and above all from the representatives of Russia's lively,
factionalized modernist coteries.[26] Yet Marinetti never grasped, or indeed cared to
know, the precise articulations of poetic form and cultural nationalism that specified Russian futurism—in ways most vividly evidenced by Khlebnikov's work.[27] Perhaps the most curious document of this Italo-Russian encounter is the angry leaflet
authored and distributed by Khlebnikov and Livshits during Marinetti's first public
conference in St. Petersburg:

> Today certain natives as well as the Italian settlement on the Neva [a reference to the
> Stray Dog, the bohemian meeting place of Petersburg's modernist literati, located on
> the corner of Italian Street and Mikhailov Square—*H. R.*] are falling at the feet of
> Marinetti for personal reasons, betraying Russian art just as it takes its first step on the
> road to freedom and honour. They are making Asia bend its noble neck beneath
> Europe's yoke . . . .
>
> Foreigner, remember to what country you have come! ("Na priezd" 193).

As Giovanni Lista has astutely observed, this letter is directed primarily at
Marinetti's "native" Russian hosts, and at their beholdenness to the French
language and Parisian mediation.[28] The centrality of Paris and Russian obsequi-
ousness toward foreigners were at issue, no less than the hegemonic designs of the
Italians. Yet in dismissing the confrontation between "Pan-Russianism" and "Pan-
Italianism" as a matter that "did not touch on futurism itself," Lista simplifies the
issue considerably. Khlebnikov and Livshits denounced Marinetti's claim to lead
the international futurist movement as nothing less than the artistic equivalent of
territorial aggression. Europe's cultural ascendancy, pervasive in Russian high culture since the Western tilt effected by Peter the Great, was reinterpreted as a form
of colonial subjugation. Rooted in an established tradition of Russian anti-West-
ernizing polemic, the argument reflected the contradictions of Russia's semiperipheral status, above all the subjugation of the Russian peasantry by the
modernizing tsarist state, even as it obscured Russia's essentially colonial relationship to its own peripheries.[29] In an argument that has significant geopolitical currency even today, Russia's path to freedom was seen to lie in its liberation from
Western influence and in establishing an alternative Pan-Asian cultural axis. The
greatness of Russian futurism would be manifested in an initially defensive but

ultimately counter-hegemonic Eurasian vision, in sharp contrast to the aggressive Eurocentrism of the Italians.

Khlebnikov's geographical leanings and cultural sympathies were manifested in numerous interconnected ways. His poetic experiments with verbal roots and breathlessly inventive neologisms—sometimes offered to replace unwanted Latinisms such as *futurist* with *budetlianin*—relied profoundly on the intuition of a specifically Russian and Slavic linguistic continuum that was folk-romantic, philological as well as Pan-Slavic in inspiration. Khlebnikov's subsequent Pan-Asianism was considerably broader in scope, stretching to and beyond the limits of the Russian empire to project alliances between Asiatic states, with Russia as a key player. From his earliest declaration of Slavic solidarity when Austria-Hungary annexed Bosnia in 1908 to his call in 1913 to "counter the ring of European alliances" with a "friendship between Muslims, Chinese and Russians," to his final post-revolutionary manifestos, whose outline of a new universal language largely abstracted from its Slavic origins reads like a kind of Leninist Esperanto, Khlebnikov's thinking evolved in a utopian but profoundly historical tandem with ongoing events.[30]

AESTHETIC AUTONOMY AND THE SPATIALIZATION OF FORCE

Casanova's global literary map, we recall, is founded on a struggle between centripetal forces oriented toward the cosmopolitan principle of aesthetic autonomy and the centrifugal forces of cultural nationalism. Both the Russian and the Italian futurists strove to overcome this dichotomy, by questioning, in different ways, the Parisian monopoly over formal innovation. Marinetti proposed a universal poetics that assumed the defining impact of technology and mechanization on syntax, rhythm, and literary tropes. His verse relied significantly on sound-effect, chiefly onomatopoeia, whose impact on audiences when performed appears to have been electrifying, even as it invited frequent caricaturing by his opponents as the poetry of "boom-boom" and "rat-a-tat-tat." The escalation of acoustic intensity was accompanied by significant experiments with typographical layout: both aspects of Marinetti's poetics shared what John J. White has called an "iconic motivation," whereby the poetic sign acquires the properties of the object it denotes, according to a model that is partly mimetic but ultimately expressive rather than representationalist (26–27). We might conclude that the sole and ultimate referent of Marinetti's work was modernity rather than nationhood. While remaining ideologically nationalist, Marinetti's poetics pointedly did not rely on uniquely Italian literary forms or linguistic structures: its intended goal was in fact to synchronize Italy with the supranational rhythms of contemporary life.

The Russian response to Italian futurism was not limited to anti-Western rhetoric. The Hylaeans also offered a pointedly different vision of verbal play and of the literary autonomy of the word. This properly aesthetic divergence was highlighted in a 1913 declaration, authored by Khlebnikov and Kruchënykh, which accused Marinetti of "tendentiousness" in "celebrating modernity (*vospevali . . . sovremennost'*)" rather than allowing his message to "arise from his own art."[31] The linguist Roman Jakobson would subsequently synthesize these objections in a classic essay of Russian formalism, *Noveishaia russkaia poèziia* (*The Most Recent Russian Poetry*, 1919). By appealing to the need to "inform us of new facts in the physical and psychic world," Jakobson argued, Marinetti had subordinated form to content, resulting in a "reform in the field of reportage but not in the field of poetic language." The Russians, by contrast, had inaugurated the "self-made, self-validating word in which the laying bare of the material had itself become canonized (*samovitogo, samotsennogo slova kak kanonizovannogo obnazhënnogo materiala*)" (Jakobson 302–04).

The Russian "canonization" of formal play and linguistic autonomy or intransitivity was motivated in different ways by different futurists, which the formalist Jakobson could never bring himself to acknowledge. Aleksei Kruchënykh looked ahead to dada and the Freud-inspired surrealists in his embrace of randomness and error as sources of verbal experimentation, although critics have also pointed to the Russian, Ukrainian, and even Tatar phonetic specificity of his experimental transsense verse.[32] Khlebnikov's sense of play was still more profoundly circumscribed by his reverence for an archaic but protean Slavic linguistic heritage and by his scientific quest for the regularities of time and space. Ultimately, his abstract universalism was to trump his Slavic philologism. A Khlebnikov manifesto of 1919 denounced the multiplicity of world languages as a linguistic laissez-faire capitalism of "verbal markets," leading to competition, disunity, and war. In its place, Khlebnikov proposed a "new universal alphabet" based on the ascription of precise spatial relations of force as fixed meanings to individual letters, such as "*V*, which in all languages means the rotation of one point around another," or *S*, "a cluster of straight lines emanating from one point" ("Khudozhniki" 240–43: "Artists" 364–69). Marinetti's "words in freedom" had transformed language into lines of force, achieved acoustically through onomatopoeia and visually through the iconic use of typography. By contrast, Khlebnikov sought to domesticate the energies underlying spatial relations by affixing to them a written meaning that he saw as common to all humanity. The alliterative preponderance in poetry of consonants such as "*L*," a letter he regarded as denoting spatial breadth, the "*reduction* in force applied to each given point caused by the *expanding* field of its application," could actually neutralize the temporal cycles and spatial trajectories of political violence ("Nasha osnova" 250; "Our Fundamentals" 385; emphasis added). The abstract universalization of temporal and spatial units was Khlebnikov's contribution to a world without conflict.

The Russian futurists went considerably further than their Italian counterparts in undermining the principles that gave the European literary center its authority.

In this sense their Eurasian cultural nationalism was the ideological correlative to their desire to seize the monopoly over *literariness itself*, the principles of aesthetic freedom and radical formal abstraction, and the cultural capital associated with it, all defined, until recent times, by Paris and more recently and audaciously by the Italians. In doing so, they allied literariness to an alternative universalism, rooted initially in the multiethnic cosmopolitanism of late tsarist Russia and the geopolitical tensions that led to World War I, and then in the global implications of the Russian revolution. This was to be the essential gesture of the Russian avant-garde, from the futurism of Khlebnikov to the suprematism of Malevich. The properly Eurasian dimension of the avant-garde, however, cannot be restricted to the dominant Russian tradition taken in isolation. It is essential to take into consideration the cultural production of other nationalities of the Russian empire, above all the Ukrainians and the Georgians. The history of the Georgian avant-gardes of the prerevolutionary period, for example, shows the striking coexistence of decadent, symbolist, and futurist redactions of modernism in ways that confound the sequential model of literary history canonized in the West. Significantly, Georgian modernism displayed a marked anti-Russian tilt matched by a notable predilection for the French, resulting in an alternative trajectory leading from the Georgian capital Tbilisi to Paris, bypassing Moscow and St. Petersburg, and then back to Tbilisi.[33] This would suggest that Russian futurist Pan-Asianism was not always perceived favorably by the cultural élites of the most informed non-Russian peoples of the empire.

Italian futurism can be said to have established the parameters by which subsequent avant-garde movements could relate the temporal logic of modernity to the verbal properties of language, the cultural efficacy of negation, provocation and scandal, and the competitive spatial organization of the global literary system. For this very reason no unified or cohesive international movement could have accompanied futurism's emergence as a transnational phenomenon. This possibility was in any case soon to be undermined by larger events such as war and revolution, and by the irreconcilable political choices that the Italians and the Russians were ultimately to make, in favor of fascism and communism, respectively. Yet Marinetti's visit to Russia had exposed the discrepant visions of modernity—Europeanizing and urban, primitivist and anti-imperialist—that laid claim to the futurist mantle even before the outbreak of World War I. The mobility of modernist élites and the circulation and validation of texts and artwork passing through or emanating from the Parisian center can be readily explained according to the terms proposed by Raymond Williams or Pascale Casanova. Yet this same mobility coincided with the emergence of what I would call modernism's second spatial turn—the distinctly local initiatives, rival cosmopolitanisms, new supranational universalisms, and centrifugal impulses that questioned and even displaced the literary-artistic center. From Marinetti's Egypt to the steppes of southern Ukraine and the Caucasus, there were peripheries beyond peripheries, all intent on parrying the dictates of Paris, Milan, or Moscow.

NOTES

1. Puchner points out that the title of the manifesto as it appeared in Figaro was in fact "Le futurisme," and was altered in subsequent republications (72).

2. Marinetti, "Fondation" 11; "Founding" 22. This and all subsequent translations from other languages are mine; where published English translations are available, they will be indicated immediately after the original citation, but not necessarily quoted.

3. Marinetti, "Fondation" 12; "Founding" 22. Much has been written on the politics of early Italian futurism: see Lista, "Marinetti et le futurisme politique," the collection *Futurismo, cultura e politica*, and Berghaus, *Futurism and Politics: Between Anarchist Rebellion and Fascist Reaction*, the best account in English of the political ambiguities of early Italian futurism.

4. The concept of "semiperiphery" belongs to world-systems theory, in which it serves as a means of overcoming the rigid binarism of the core/periphery dichotomy and accounting for mobility as well as anti-systemic shifts in the global economic and political system. See Aynard, Arrighi, Terlouw, and Chase-Dunn and Hall.

5. Futurist notions of dynamism and simultaneity were most clearly articulated by the visual artists. See Boccioni, Carrà, Russolo, Balla, Severini, "La pittura futurista. Manifesto técnico" ("Futurist Painting: Technical Manifesto 1910").

6. For a *Begriffsgeschichte* of "modernity," see Jauss and Koselleck. For a discussion of the relationship between aesthetic modernism and political modernity, see Calinescu, Compagnon, and Wohl.

7. See Marinetti, "Les Dieux" 410, 401, 403; "Noi rinneghiamo" 302–06, especially 304. In a letter to Leon Trotsky published in Moscow on September 8, 1922, Gramsci noted that while "D'Annunzio never took an official position on futurism," the futurists themselves had been explicitly "anti-D'Annunzian," and this despite the fact that "during the war, the political programs of Marinetti and D'Annunzio were in accord in every way" (Gramsci, "Pis'mo t" 129). Also see "Marinetti rivoluzionario?" in which Gramsci hails the futurists as having been "revolutionaries in the field of culture" (22).

8. Marinetti, "Manifesto tecnico" 53. The question of futurism's relationship to symbolism was an ongoing concern of poets and critics alike: see, for example, the Russian critic Genrikh Tasteven, whose *Futurizm (na puti k novomu simvolizmu)* defined futurism as the radicalization of symbolist irrationalism and intuitionism. For a more recent but not dissimilar elaboration of the relationship of futurism to decadence and symbolism, see Rosa as well as Somigli.

9. Perloff, 6; xviii, xix. See also Hunkeler, who offers an excellent summary of Italian futurism's reception overseas and argues that examining the way in which "internationalist aspirations" within the artistic avant-garde "may be determined by nationalist motivations" might throw more light on the politics of futurism than its frequently denounced authoritarian tendencies (214–15). For a brief history of international futurism, particularly in its Italian, Russian, and Soviet forms, see Lawton.

10. Trotskii, *Literatura i revoliutsiia*, 103; *Literature and Revolution*, 126–27 (the published English translation of this passage contains a notable error, corrected above).

11. Jameson, *A Singular Modernity*, 141–42, 144. Cf. also Jameson, *Postmodernism*, 304–09, and Anderson: "European modernism in the first decades of this century thus flowered in the space between a still usable classical past, a still indeterminate technical present, and a still unpredictable political future. Or, put another way, it arose at the intersection between a semi-aristocratic ruling order, a semi-industrialized capitalist economy, and a semi-emergent, or insurgent, labour movement" (36).

Chakrabarty has criticized the notion of "uneven development" as a more sophisticated version of traditional historicism, with which it shares an assumption about an "underlying structural unity to historical process and time, that makes it possible to identify certain elements in the present as 'anachronistic'" (12ff). Osborne argues that "all such totalizations abstract from the concrete multiplicity of differential times co-existing in the global 'now' a single differential (however internally complex) through which to mark the time of the present" (28).

12. There is now a rich literature theorizing the phenomenon of "peripheral" modernism; cf. Deleuze and Guattari, Said, Schwarz, Kronfeld, Geist and Monleón, eds., Kapur, Ramos, and Friedman.

13. Insisting on a more dialectical relationship to tradition based on its absorption and supersession, the Florentines also dismissed Marinetti's "militarism and chauvinism" in favor of "combativity and patriotism." The latter did not prevent them from making their journal *Lacerba* a mouthpiece for the interventionist cause (Palazzeschi, Papini, and Soffici). See also Terza.

14. On the theatrical and performative aspects of Italian futurism, see Michael and Victoria Nes Kirby.

15. On Marinetti's publishing and propagandistic strategies, see Salaris, "Marketing Modernism." On Marinetti, the commodity, and the culture industry, see Adamson.

16. See Marinetti's recollections, "Processo di Mafarka il futurista," 586–88.

17. See Markov 117–19, and Livshits, *Polutoraglazyi strelets* 420–21, and *The One and a Half-Eyed Arche*r 138.

18. Mention should be made in this context of the non-Hylean futurist Ilya Zdanevich. Born in Tiflis (Tblisi), Georgia, to a Polish father, the descendant of exiled Polish aristocrats and a teacher of French, and a Georgian mother, Zdanevich had in common with the Hyleans a "peripheral" background and a primitivist orientation, but was far more sympathetic for a time to Italian futurism, and corresponded with Marinetti while a student in St. Petersburg. One suspects that he was emboldened by his greater cultural preparation to project himself more successfully onto the European stage: he emigrated to Paris in 1921.

19. Cf. Markov, 26–27: "One could agree with Burliuk and Kamensky that the beginning of Russian futurism dates from 1909. . . . Even if one accepts this early date, Italian futurism remains almost a year older, despite all the later efforts of the Russians to prove their seniority. . . . Kruchenykh and Mayakovsky dated futurism from 1912. . . . Livshits dated it from 1911."

20. Puchner has recently found it "difficult to determine where these squabbles were due to personal pride and where a more serious struggle about different futurisms was at work" (98). I will seek to show that substantial differences did exist, beyond the anxieties of influence arising from the importation of the manifesto as a genre, or the thematics of urban modernity.

21. Although Salaris has recently shown the occupation of Fiume to have been more than an exercise in protofascism or nationalist irredentism, the ideological heterogeneity of the protagonists of Fiume does not mitigate Marinetti's own specifically nationalist reading of the event. See Salaris, *Alla festa della Rivoluzione*.

22. Marinetti, *Mafarka le futuriste*, 19–47, 211–33; *Mafarka the Futurist*, 5–32; 185–206. On the sexual politics of the novel, see Spackman and Blum 55–78.

23. Livshits, *Polutoraglazyi strelets*, 321–22; *The One and a Half-Eyed Arche*r, 44–45. The latter English translation contains several errors corrected here.

24. Both quotes are from the manifesto "Poshchëchina obshchestvennomy vkusu," signed by D. Burliuk, A. Kruchënykh, V. Maiakovskii, and V. Khlebnikov, 41; "Slap in the Face of Public Taste" 51.

25. Marinetti, *La grande Milano*. In fact Marinetti hastened to establish the historic priority of Italian futurism, and its subsequent diffusion in Russia, even earlier, on the eve of his trip to Russia.

26. For Russian responses to Marinetti's visit and to Italian futurism as a whole, see Livshits' *Polutoraglazyi strelets*, Ch. 7, 470–507 (*The One and a Half-Eyed Archer*, 181–213); Markov 147–63; Michelis' precious collection of documents and analysis *Il futurismo italiano in Russia*; Lista, "Un siècle futuriste"; Khardjiev; and Aliakrinskaia.

27. Marinetti accused Khlebnikov, of whom he had received secondhand reports, of "archeological" tendencies and "savagery": see Khardjiev 222 and Mignot 240–48.

28. See Lista, "Un siècle futuriste," 46–47. Lista's analysis, while profoundly informed, minimizes the seriousness of Russian objections and does not do justice to the tensions between imperialist and anti-imperialist sentiment found in transnational futurism (cf. Lista 28). The role of Paris in mediating between Russian and Italian futurisms is clear: Marinetti was invited to Russia by Genrikh Tasteven, Russian delegate to the Société Universelle des Grandes Conférences, founded in Paris by Alexandre Mercereau in 1910. Marinetti's traveling companion A. Marasco recalls that several Russian futurists were prevented from intervening in Russian during Marinetti's conferences, French being the prevalent language of communication. See Marasco.

29. Etkind explores some of these contradictions in "Orientalism Reversed."

30. Khlebnikov, "Vozzvanie," "Zapadnyi drug," and "Khoduzhniki mira!" 172–74, 240–43. See also Arenzon. In February 1914, a day after circulating the anti-Marinetti flyer, Khlebnikov noted in a letter that he was convinced that "a duel between the Italo-German alliance and the Slavs" would take place sooner or later on the Dalmatian coast ("Nikolaiu Burliuku" 347). Khlebnikov's literary polemics were acutely sensitive to the geopolitics of the day.

31. Kruchënykh and Khlebnikov, "[Slovo kak takovoe]" 59; "[The Word as Such]" 55. The declaration, drafted in 1913, was only published in 1930, but recalls similar published criticisms made by Kruchënykh at the time: see his "Novye puti slova" 71. These opinions were not unique to the Hylaean futurists: Shershenevich expressed similar opinions in 1913, while Mikhail Larionov, Il'ia Zdanevich and others attacked Marinetti during his visit for not being sufficiently radical in his poetic innovations; see, for example, the article by art critic Iakov Tugendkhol'd, "Zapozdalyi futurism." The Italian Slavist De Michelis highlights these differences in poetics as the most significant aspect of the discord that arose between the Russian futurists and the Italians, differences that were partly obscured by the "folklore" surrounding Marinetti's voyage (*Il futurismo* 33). Cf. also Sola and Kovtoune.

32. On randomness as a poetic motivation, see Kruchënykh, "Novye puti slova." For the national linguistic codes implicit in Kruchënykh's trans-sense poetry, see Ake Nilsson.

33. I refer here to the Blue Horn group of Georgian modernists rather than to the local futurist movement that arose after the Bolshevik annexation of Georgia in 1921. The anti-Russian and pro-French sentiments of the Blue Horn group are amply evident in T'itsian T'abidze's manifesto of 1916 "Tsisperi Qants'ebit," while P'aolo Iashvili's manifesto "Pirveltkma," clearly reproduces Marinetti's nationalism and Francophile cosmopolitanism. Iashvili studied in Paris, and thus most obviously reproduces the spatial trajectory outlined above, while T'abidze in fact studied in Moscow. For a discussion of Georgian modernism, see Magarotto and my articles "Andrej Belyj and Georgia," and "The Sonnet and the Mukhambazi."

WORKS CITED

Adamson, Walter L. *Embattled Avant-gardes. Modernism's Resistance to Commodity Culture in Europe.* Berkeley: University of California Press, 2007.

Aliakrinskaia, N. P. "Marinetti v zerkale russkoi pressy." *Vestnik Moskvoskogo universiteta. Seriia 10 Zhurnalistika* (2003) 4: 77–89.

Anderson, Perry. "Marshall Berman: Modernity and Revolution." *A Zone of Engagement.* New York: Verso, 1992. 25–55.

Arenzon, E. "V. V. Khlebnikov. 'Zapadnyi drug,'" *Vestnik Obshchestva Velimira Khlebikova* 1 (1996): 29–36.

Arrighi, Giovanni. "Fascism to Democratic Socialism. Logic and Limits of a Transition." *Semiperipheral Development: The Politics of Southern Europe in the Twentieth Century.* Ed. Giovanni Arrighi. Beverly Hills: Sage Publications, 1985: 243–79.

Aynard, Maurice. "Nation-States and Interregional Disparities of Development." *Semiperipheral Development: The Politics of Southern Europe in the Twentieth Century.* Ed. Giovanni Arrighi. Beverly Hills: Sage Publications, 1985. 40–54.

Bassin, Mark. "Russia between Europe and Asia: The Ideological Construction of Geographical Space." *Slavic Review* 50.1 (1991): 1–17.

Berghaus, Günther. *Futurism and Politics: Between Anarchist Rebellion and Fascist Reaction, 1909–1914.* Oxford: Berghahn Books, 1996.

Blum, Cinzia Sartini. *The Other Modernism: F. T. Marinetti's Futurist Fiction of Power.* Berkeley: University of California Press, 1996.

Boccioni, Umberto, Carlo Carrà, Luigi Russolo, Giacomo Balla, and Gino Severini. "Futurist Painting: Technical Manifesto 1910." *Futurist Manifestos.* Ed. Umbro Apollonio. Boston: MFA Publications, 2001: 27–31.

———. "La pittura futurista. Manifesto tecnico." 1910. *I futuristi.* Ed. Francesco Francesco Grisi. Rome: Newton Compton, 1990: 46–54.

Bürger, Peter. *Theorie der Avant-garde.* Franfurt: Suhrkamp Verlag, 1974.

———. *Theory of the Avant-garde.* Trans. Michael Shaw. Minneapolis: University of Minnesota Press, 1984.

Burliuk, D., A. Kruchënykh, V. Maiakovskii, and V. Khlebnikov. "Poshchëchina obshchestvennomy vkusu." 1912. *Russkii futurizm. Teoriia. Praktika. Kritika. Vospominaniia.* Ed. V. N. Terëkhina and A. P. Zimenkov. Moscow: Nasledie, 2000.

———. "Slap in the Face of Public Taste." *Russian Futurism through its Manifestoes, 1912–1928.* Trans. and ed. Anna Lawton and Herbert Eagle. Ithaca: Cornell University Press, 1988. 51–52.

Calinescu, Matei. *Five Faces of Modernity.* Durham: Duke University Press, 1987.

Casanova, Pascale. *La République mondiale des lettres.* Paris: Seuil, 1999.

Chakrabarty, Dipesh. *Provincializing Europe: Postcolonial Thought and Historical Difference.* Princeton: Princeton University Press, 2000.

Chase-Dunn, Christopher, and Thomas Hall. *Rise and Demise: Comparing World Systems.* Boulder: Westview Press, 1997.

Compagnon, Antoine. *Les cinq paradoxes de la modernité.* Paris: Editions du Seuil, 1990.

de Felice, Renzo, ed. *Futurismo, cultura e politica.* Turin: Edizioni della Fondazione Giovanni Agnelli, 1988.

de Michelis, Cesare G. *Il futurismo italiano in Russia.* Bari: De Donato editore, 1973.

———. "Nouveaux documents marinettiens gardés dans les archives centrales de Moscou." *Présence de F. T. Marinetti: Actes du Colloque Internationale tenu à l'UNESCO.* Ed. Jean-Claude Marcadé. Lausanne: Editions l'Age d'Homme, 1982: 191–97.

Deleuze, Gilles, and Félix Guattari. *Kafka: pour une littérature mineure*. Paris: Editions de Minuit, 1975.

Etkind, Alexander. "Orientalism Reversed: Russian Literature in the Times of Empires." *Modern Intellectual History* 4.3 (2007): 617–28.

Friedman, Susan Stanford. "Periodizing Modernism: Postcolonial Modernities and the Space/Time Borders of Modernist Studies." *Modernism/modernity* 13.3 (2006): 493–514.

Geist, Anthony L., José B. Monleón, eds. *Modernism and Its Margins: Reinscribing Cultural Modernity from Spain and Latin America*. New York: Garland Publishing, 1999.

Gentile, Emilio. "Il futurismo e la politica. Dal nazionalismo modernista al fascismo (1909–1920)." *Futurismo, cultura e política*. Ed. Renzo de Felice. Turin: Edizioni della Fondazione Giovanni Agnelli, 1988.

Gramsci, Antonio. "Marinetti rivoluzionario?" 1921. *Socialismo e fascismo. L'Ordine Nuovo 1921–1921*. Turin: Giulio Einaudi, 1978.

———. "Pis'mo t. Gramshi ob ital'ianskom futurizme." *Literatura i revoliutsiia*. Ed. L. Trotskii. Moscow: Izdatel'stvo politicheskoi literatury, 1991.

Hunkeler, Thomas. "Cultural Hegemony and Avant-gardist Rivalry. The Ambivalent Reception of Futurism in France, England and Russia." *The Invention of Politics in the European Avant-garde (1906–1940)*. Ed. Sascha Bru and Gunther Martens. New York; Amsterdam: Rodopi, 2006: 203–15.

Iakulov, Georgii, Benedikt Livshits, and Artur Lourié. "My i Zapad, (Plakat No. 1)." January 1, 1914. *Manifesty i programmy Russkikh futuristov*. Ed. Vladimir Markov. Munich: Wilhelm Fink Verlag, 1967.

Iashvili, P'aolo. "Pirveltkma." 1916. *Kartuli lit'erat'uruli esse XX sauk'unis 20-iani ts'lebi*. Ed. Manana Khelaia. Tbilisi: Merani, 1986.

Jakobson, Roman. "Noveishaia russkaia poèziia. Nabrosok pervyi. Podstupy k Khlebnikovu." *Selected Writings*. Ed. Stephen Rudy and Martha Taylor. Vol. 5. The Hague: Mouton Publishers, 1975.

Jameson, Fredric. *A Singular Modernity: Essay on the Ontology of the Present*. New York: Verso, 2002.

———. *Postmodernism, or, the Cultural Logic of Late Capitalism*. Durham: Duke University Press, 1991.

Jauss, Hans Robert. "Literarische Tradition und gegenwärtiges Bewußtsein der Modernität." *Literaturgeschichte als Provokation*. Frankfurt: Suhrkamp Verlag, 1974.

Kapur, Geeta. *When Was Modernism: Essays on Contemporary Cultural Practice in India*. New Delhi: Tulika, 2000.

Khardjiev, Nicolas. "La tournée de Marinetti en Russie en 1914." *Présence de F. T. Marinetti: Actes du Colloque Internationale tenu à l'UNESCO*. Ed. Jean-Claude Marcadé. Lausanne: Editions l'Age d'Homme, 1982: 198–233.

Khlebnikov, V. "Artists of the World!" *Collected Works of Velimir Khlebnikov*. Trans. Paul Schmidt. Vol. 1. Cambridge: Harvard University Press, 1987. 364–69.

———. "Khudozhniki mira!" 1919. *Sobranie sochinenii v trekh tomakh*. Vol. 3. St. Petersburg: Akademicheskii proèkt, 2001.

———. "Nasha osnova." 1919. *Sobranie sochinenii v trekh tomakh*. Vol. 3. St. Petersburg: Akademicheskii proèkt, 2001.

———. "Nikolaiu Burliuku." *Sobranie sochinenii v trekh tomakh*. Vol. 3. St. Petersburg: Akademicheskii proèkt, 2001.

———. "Our Fundamentals." *Collected Works of Velimir Khlebnikov*. Trans. Paul Schmidt. Vol. 1. Cambridge, Mass.: Harvard University Press, 1987. 376–91.

———. "Teacher and Student. A Conversation (on words, cities, and nations)." *Collected Works of Velimir Khlebnikov*. Trans. Paul Schmidt. Vol. 1. Cambridge: Harvard University Press, 1987. 277–87.

————. "Uchitel' i uchenik. O slovakh, gorodakh i narodakh." 1912. *Sobranie sochinenii v trekh tomakh.* Vol. 3. St. Petersburg: Akademicheskii proèkt, 2001.

————. "Vozzvanie uchashchikhsia slavian." 1908. *Sobranie sochinenii v trekh tomakh,* Vo. 3. St. Petersburg: Akademicheskii proèkt, 2001.

————. "Zapadnyi drug." 1913. *Sobranie sochinenii v trekh tomakh.* Vol. 3. St. Petersburg: Akademicheskii proèkt, 2001.

Khlebnikov, Velimir, and Benedikt Livshits. "Na priezd Marinetti v Rossiiu." *Sobranie sochinenii v trekh tomakh,* Vol. 3. St. Petersburg: Akademicheskii proèkt, 2001. 193.

Kirby, Michael, and Victoria Nes Kirby. *Futurist Performance.* New York: PAJ Publications, 1986.

Koselleck, Reinhardt. "'Neuzeit': Remarks on the Semantics of the Modern Concepts of Movement." *Futures Past: On the Semantics of Historical Time.* Trans. Keith Tribe. Cambridge: MIT Press, 1979.

Kovtoune, Eugene. "Les 'mots en liberté de Marinetti et la 'transmentalité (zaoum) des futuristes russes." *Présence de F. T. Marinetti: Actes du Colloque Internationale tenu à l'UNESCO.* Ed. Jean-Claude Marcadé. Lausanne: Editions l'Age d'Homme, 1982. 234–38.

Kronfeld, Chana. *On the Margins of Modernism: Decentering Literary Dynamics.* Berkeley: University of California Press, 1996.

Kruchënykh, A. "Novye puti slova (iazyk budushchego smert' simvolizmu)." 1913. *Manifesty i programmy Russkikh futuristov.* Ed. Vladimir Markov. Munich: Wilhelm Fink Verlag, 1967. 64–73.

Kruchënykh, A., and V. Khlebnikov, "[Slovo kak takovoe]." *Manifesty i programmy Russkikh futuristov.* Ed. Vladimir Markov. Munich: Wilhelm Fink Verlag, 1967.

————. "[The Word as Such]." *Russian Futurism through Its Manifestoes, 1912–1928.* Trans. and ed. Anna Lawton and Herbert Eagle. Ithaca: Cornell University Press, 1988. 55–56.

Lawton, Anna. Introduction. *Russian Futurism through Its Manifestoes, 1912–1928.* Trans. and ed. Anna Lawton and Herbert Eagle. Ithaca: Cornell University Press, 1988: 1–48.

Lista, Giovanni. "Marinetti et le futurisme politique." *Futurisme: Manifestes Proclamations Documents.* Lausanne: Editions L'Age d'Homme, 1973. 11–28.

————. "Un siècle futuriste." *Futurisme. Manifestes Proclamations Documents.* Lausanne: Editions L'Age d'Homme, 1973. 15–79.

Livshits, Benedikt. *The One and a Half-Eyed Archer.* Trans. John E. Bowlt. Newtonville: Oriental Research Partners, 1977.

————. *Polutoraglazyi strelets: Stikhotvoreniia. Perevody. Vospominaniia.* Moscow: Sovetskii pisatel', 1989.

Magarotto, Luigi. "Storia e teoria dell'avanguardia georgiana (1915–1924)." *L'avanguardia a Tiflis. Quaderni del Seminario di Iranistica, Uralo-Altaistica e Caucasologia dell'Università degli Studi di Venezia.* Vol. 13. Ed. Luigi Magarotto, Marzio Marzaduri, Giovanna Pagani Cesa. Venice: University of Venice, 1982. 45–98.

Maiakovskii, Vladimir. "Ia sam" ("I myself"). *Polnoe sobranie sochinenii.* Vol. 1. Moscow: Gosudarstvennoe izdatel'stvo khudozhestvennoi literatury, 1956.

Marasco, A. "Marinetti en Russie." *Futurisme. Manifestes Proclamations Documents.* Lausanne: Editions L'Age d'Homme, 1973. 432–34.

Marinetti, F. T. "Destruction of Syntax—Imagination without Strings—Words-in-Freedom." *Futurist Manifestos.* Ed. Umbro Apollonio. Boston: MFA Publications, 2001. 95–106.

————. "Les Dieux s'en vont, D'Annunzio reste." 1908. *Scritti francesi.* Milan: Arnoldo Mondadori editore, 1983.

————. "Distruzione della sintassi. Immaginazione senza fili. Parole in libertà." *Teoria e invenzione futurista.* Ed. Luciano De Maria. Milan: Arnoldo Mondadori Editore, 1968: 65–80.

———. "Fondation et Manifeste du futurisme." *Enquête internationale sur le Vers libre et Manifeste du futurisme*. Milan: Éditions de "Poesia," 1909.

———. "Founding and Manifesto of Futurism." *Futurist Manifestos*. Ed. Umbro Apollonio. Boston: MFA Publications, 2001. 19–24.

———. *La grande Milano tradizionale e futurista: Una sensibilità italiana nata in Egitto*. Ed. Luciano de Maria. Milan: Arnoldo Mondadori Editore, 1969. 296–317.

———. *Mafarka le futuriste*. 1910. Paris: Christian Bourgois Éditeur, 1984.

———. *Mafarka the Futurist: An African Novel*. Trans. Steve Cox and Carol Diethe. Middlesex: Middlesex University Press, 1997.

———. "Manifesto tecnico della letteratura futurista." 1912. *Teoria e invenzione futurista*. Ed. Luciano De Maria. Milan: Arnoldo Mondadori Editore, 1968.

———. "Noi rinneghiamo i nostri meastri simbolisti ultimi amanti della luna." 1915. *Teoria e invenzione futurista*. Ed. Luciano De Maria. Milan: Arnoldo Mondadori Editore, 1968. 302–06.

———. "Processo di Mafarka il futurista." 1929. *Teoria e invenzione futurista*. Ed. Luciano De Maria. Milan: Arnoldo Mondadori Editore, 1968.

———. "La voluttà di esser fischiati." *Teoria e invenzione futurista*. Ed. Luciano De Maria. Milan: Arnoldo Mondadori Editore, 1968. 310–13.

Markov, Vladimir. *Russian Futurism: A History*. London: MacGibbon and Kee Limited, 1968.

Mignot, Yvan. "Marinetti et Khlebnikov." *Présence de F. T. Marinetti: Actes du Colloque Internationale tenu à l'UNESCO*. Ed. Jean-Claude Marcadé. Lausanne: Editions l'Age d'Homme, 1982.

Nilsson, Nils Ake. "Futurism, Primitivism and the Russian avant-garde." *Russian Literature* 8 (1980): 469–82.

Osborne, Peter. *The Politics of Time: Modernity and Avant-garde*. New York: Verso, 1995.

Palazzeschi, Aldo, Giovanni Papini, and Ardengo Soffici. "Futurismo e Marinettismo." *Lacerba* 7.14 (February 14, 1915).

Perloff, Marjorie. *The Futurist Moment: Avant-garde, Avant-guerre, and the Language of Rupture*. Chicago: University of Chicago Press, 1986.

Puchner, Martin. *Poetry of the Revolution: Marx, Manifestos and the Avant-gardes*. Princeton: Princeton University Press, 2006.

Poggioli, Renato. *Teoria dell'arte d'avanguardia*. Bologna: Il Mulino, 1962.

———. *The Theory of the Avant-garde*. Trans. Gerald Fitzgerald. Cambridge: Harvard University Press, 1968.

Ram, Harsha. "Andrej Belyj and Georgia: Georgian Modernism and the 'Peripheral' Reception of the Petersburg Text." *Russian Literature* 58.1–2 (July–August 2005): 243–76.

———. "The Sonnet and the Mukhambazi: Genre Wars on the Edges of the Russian Empire." *PMLA* 122.5 (2007): 1548–70.

Ramos, Julio. *Divergent Modernities: Culture and Politics in Nineteenth-Century Latin America*. Trans. John D. Blanco. Durham: Duke University Press, 2001.

Rosa, Alberto Asor. "Il futurismo nel dibattito intellettuale italiano dalle origini al 1920." *Futurismo, cultura e politica*. Turin: Edizioni della Fondazione Giovanni Agnelli, 1968. 49–66.

Said, Edward. *Culture and Imperialism*. New York: Vintage Books, 1994.

Salaris, Claudia. *Alla festa della Rivoluzione: Artisti e libertari con D'Annunzio a Fiume*. Bologna: Le edizioni del Mulino, 2008.

———. "Marketing Modernism: Marinetti as Publisher." *Modernism/modernity* 1.3 (1994): 109–27.

Schwarz, Roberto. *A Master on the Periphery of Capitalism: Machado de Assis*. Durham: Duke University Press, 2001.

Sharp, Jane. *Russian Modernism between East and West: Natal'ia Goncharova and the Moscow Avant-garde*. Cambridge: Cambridge University Press, 2006.

Shershenevich, Vadim. *Futurizm bez maski (kompiliativnaia introduktsiia)*. Moscow: Moskovskoe izdatel'stvo, 1913.

———. *Misplaced Ideas: Essays on Brazilian Culture*. London: Verso, 1992.

Sola, Agnes. "Un problèm de méthode: l'étude des rapports entre les futurismes russe et italien." *Présence de F. T. Marinetti: Actes du Colloque Internationale tenu à l'UNESCO*. Ed. Jean-Claude Marcadé. Lausanne: Editions l'Age d'Homme, 1982. 179–90.

Somigli, Luca. *Legitimizing the Artist. Manifesto Writing and European Modernism 1885–1915*. Toronto: University of Toronto Press, 2003.

Spackman, Barbara. *Fascist Virilities: Rhetoric, Ideology and Social Fantasy in Italy*. Minneapolis: University of Minnesota Press, 1996.

T'abidze, T'itsian. "Tsisperi Qants'ebit." 1916. *Sonet'ebi, rcheuli leksebi, esse*. Ed. Tamar Barbakadze. Tbilisi: Metsniereba, 1999. 82–113.

Tasteven, Genrikh. *Futurizm (na puti k novomu simvolizmu)*. Moscow: Iris, 1914.

Terlouw, C. P. "The Elusive Semiperiphery: A Critical Examination of the Concept Semiphery." *International Journal of Comparative Sociology* 1–2 (1993): 87–102.

Terza, Dante della. "F. T. Marinetti e i futuristi fiorentini: L'ipotesi politico-letteraria di *Lacerba*." *Italica* 61.2 (1984): 147–59.

Trotskii, L., ed. *Literatura i revoliutsiia*. Moscow: Izdatel'stvo politicheskoi literatury, 1991.

Trotsky, Leon. *Literature and Revolution*. Trans. Rose Strunsky. Ann Arbor: University of Michigan Press, 1960.

Tugendkhol'd, Iakov. "Zapozdalyi futurism." *Rech'* (February 1, 1914): 3–4.

White, John J. *Literary Futurism: Aspects of the first avant-garde*. Oxford: Clarendon Press, 1990.

Williams, Raymond. "Introduction: The Politics of the Avant-garde." *Visions and Blueprints: Avant-garde Culture and Radical Politics in Early Twentieth-Century Europe*. Ed. Edward Timms and Peter Collier. Manchester: Manchester University Press, 1988.

———. *The Politics of Modernism: Against the New Conformists*. London: Verso, 1989.

Wohl, Robert. "Heart of Darkness: Modernism and its Historians." *The Journal of Modern History* 74 (2002): 573–621.

CHAPTER 14

MODERNITY'S LABORS IN LATIN AMERICA: THE CULTURAL WORK OF CUBA'S AVANT-GARDES

VICKY UNRUH

A 1928 bildungsroman deploys telegraphic vanguard imagery, Afro-Cuban ritual, and naturalist descriptions in a portrait of Cuba's rural proletariat, displaced by U.S.-owned sugar mills, and links this group's creative rites with the cultural activity of Havana's intellectuals. A 1927 "Afro-Cuban Choreographic Mystery in One Act" by the same author stages a contest between the frenetic labors of a Hollywood businessman filming stereotypic fare about Cuban "natives" and a powerful Afro-Cuban initiation rite. A 1926 poem renders the Cuban *zafra* (sugar harvest) through eighteen cantos spanning condemnations of nineteenth-century slavery to racialist stereotypes of former slaves, nostalgic contrasts of colonial sugar planta-tions with mechanized U.S.-owned mills, and admonitions to *campesinos* to work harder. A 1931 poetic ode to a Cuban boxer in New York warns that his pugilistic labors on Broadway nourish the same predator that controls Cuba's cane fields. A 1929 best-selling melodramatic novel about the perils of a free-thinking new woman in 1920s Havana juxtaposes her tedious office work with the dynamic cultural activity of the male *tertulia*[1] she joins, a gathering of intellectuals debating Cuban and international art and politics. A 1935 lyric novel contrasts the creative activity of an upper-class Havana woman in the aristocratic *criollo*[2] mansion she inhabits with an encroaching modern work-world.

These dissimilar literary works—by Alejo Carpentier (1904–1980), Augstín Acosta (1886–1979), Nicolás Guillén (1902–1989), Ofelia Rodríguez Acosta (1902–1975), and Dulce María Loynaz (1902–1997)—constitute artifacts of Cuba's historical avant-gardes of the 1920s and 1930s. Beyond their differences of genre, style, form, and tone, their shared features exemplify the avant-garde moment of artistic modernism in Cuba and, by extension, in Latin America as a whole, a region whose modernity or modernism have been qualified as "divergent," "peripheral," "burdensome," "marginal," or "hybrid."[3] As artistic products of Latin America's vanguards, these Cuban works display a powerful awareness of the location, historical moment, and social or ontological position from which they are written, even as that position unfolds on unstable ground. In this sense, these works enact what Fernando Rosenberg (in the Latin American context) or Laura Doyle and Laura Winkiel (in the Anglo-American context) have called international modernism's self-aware "positionality" (Rosenberg 5, Doyle and Winkiel 3) or, in Doyle and Winkiel's terms, a "geocultural consciousness." In Latin America, this awareness plays out in self-conscious artistic and intellectual negotiations between local cultural or political projects and wide-reaching international, often neocolonial, entanglements.

These Cuban works, and their counterparts in Argentina, Peru, Mexico, Brazil, Chile, or other Latin American locales, also embody what I call—recasting Henry James's moniker for the nineteenth-century Russian novel—the "baggy monster" avant-garde text. I use this term not in reference to length (many Latin American vanguard works are quite short) but to highlight their unevenness or lack of containment that, while occasionally coalescing into stunning artistic successes, always manifests the "will to style" posited by José Ortega y Gasset in 1925 as the defining feature of the era's modern Western art (25).[4] Yet these texts rarely settle on a definitive style but instead rehearse a range of strategies to ground shifting perspectives. Some young experimental writers of the 1920s and 1930s produced more mature, acclaimed works in later decades, for example, Cuba's Carpentier, Guillén, and Loynaz.[5] But the vanguards in Latin America unfolded in an era of extraordinary social change paralleled by quests for new modes of engaging art with life, to echo Peter Bürger's rendering of Europe's historical avant-gardes. Thus, the variable subjectivity characterizing Latin American literary works of the period sends mixed signals about exactly whose stories they seek to tell. This is not surprising in an epoch marked by the changing demographics and social structures accompanying a massive influx of immigrants to some Latin American cities, internal migrations of rural populations, the growth of an urban middle class, women's entry to the workforce, and the politics of university reforms, labor movements, and first-wave feminism.

In this context, the shifting perspectives of Latin American avant-garde works encompass converging critical inquiries into uneven modernization undertaken by dissimilar texts, some more obviously experimental than others but all wrestling with the "modern." These divergent works often coalesce around a particular problem to expose contending views in an era of rapid change. For example, despite stylistic variations, the Cuban works I have mentioned here and to which I will later return, all display an intense preoccupation with modern work, register international forces impinging on changing work patterns in Cuba's early twentieth century, and take up shifting, sometimes contradictory positions toward such change. After Spanish rule ended in 1898, Cuba experienced the military presence of the United States and massive U.S. economic and political intervention until the founding of the independent Republic of Cuba in 1902, and Cuban avant-garde works explore losses and gains associated with this relationship, especially those accrued through modern work models and the possible connections between artistic or intellectual work and the changing toils of rural and urban laborers. As intimated in my opening examples, this focus on work also reveals a web of changing racial, gender, and class relationships specific to early republican Cuba. But the work theme in Cuba's avant-gardes also exhibits a strong international geocultural consciousness through unequivocal generational identifications with World War I and its aftermath.[6]

Cuba's World War I–era sugar boom—the "dance of millions"—witnessed the creation of *latifundia*, as owners of expanding U.S. mills displaced local *colonos* (small landowners) and subsistence farmers, imported Haitian and Jamaican migrants as cheaper labor, and generated a Cuban rural proletariat. The situation worsened with the postwar fall in sugar prices. In the 1920s and 1930s, more rural workers migrated to Havana, creating a disproportionately Afro-Cuban underclass whose situation deteriorated further after the 1929 economic collapse. In the mid-teens and 1920s, Cuba's new republican governments, with strong U.S. intervention, aimed to create a modern industrial base, expanding the civil-service bureaucracy, and increasing the ranks of blue-collar workers through substantial public works projects (Aguilar 46–51; Gott 125–29). Women entered the labor force in growing numbers as textile and tobacco workers, teachers, nurses, office clerks, journalists, and even minor bureaucrats (Stoner 38). The emergence of Cuba's artistic avant-gardes in the early 1920s coincided with the founding of the National Workers Confederation (CNOC) and the Cuban Communist Party, both in 1925, and the organization of National Women's Congresses in 1923 and 1925.

These changes brought new jobs and new ways of thinking about work, particularly for the *criollo* elite. Louis Pérez, who argues that "in the short space of ten years Cuba [particularly Havana] had catapulted into modernity" (145), has exhaustively documented the impact on the Cuban bourgeoisie of the U.S. market-based work ethic and ideas of the "self-made man," whereby hard work could enhance consumer purchasing power (143–46). Through projects in skills-education, production, and marketing, Protestant missionaries sought to reinforce this ethic throughout Cuba (Pérez 252). In the spirit of the landmark essay, *Ariel* (1900; *Ariel*)[7] by Uruguayan José Enrique Rodó, a generational pillow book for Latin America's intelligentsia, Cuban intellectuals registered deep ambivalence toward the U.S. market-driven work ethic. Some, like Rodó, whose essay imagined a hardworking, utilitarian, but creatively bereft U.S. Caliban contrasted to an ostensibly spiritual and intellectual Latin American Ariel, decried the emergence of a local "practical man" focused on the workaday world.[8] Others refashioned the utilitarian model in local terms. Cuba's first national playwright, José Antonio Ramos (1885–1946), for example, invested the middle-class Cuban hero of his *Tembladera* (1918), a foreman who rescues the sugar plantation he oversees from the grasp of the United States, with a dedication to hard work, implying that the best way to resist the U.S. presence was for Cubans to appropriate the market ethic for managing their own industries.

In this vein, the Cuban vanguards' literary inquiries into work parallel the striking fact that Havana's avant-garde Grupo Minorista (1923–1929), with whom most of the island's experimental writers had contact, explicitly defined themselves in their 1927 manifesto as "*trabajadores* intelectuales," or "intellectual *workers.*" In Latin America, such imagined ties between the labors of the "lettered city"—Angel Rama's critically canonized term for the region's hierarchical intellectual culture—and physical toil was not new in this epoch. But these links intensified with the artistic avant-gardes' conception of their projects as a form of action. I have argued elsewhere that a modern dynamic between manual labor and intellectual or artistic activity draws on the long-standing relationship of the word *culture* to productive labor, as in crop cultivation or animal husbandry.[9] Raymond Williams traced the arc of the word *culture* in Western thought from the care of animals to the care of the mind, from material culture to intellectual, spiritual, or artistic culture (87–90). In a parallel mapping of the word *work*—and I would argue the same for *trabajo* in Spanish—Williams observed that its meaning grew more complex with the modern era's exclusionary coinage to indicate regular paid labor. Still, he argued, the association of the word with any activity, effort, or achievement—paid or unpaid—persists (335). References to efforts of the mind as *intellectual work* also underscore the unshaken association of physical labor with the artistic or cultural kind.[10] Updates of Williams's disquisitions on *work* as a "key word" detail its contemporary permutations, as in such late twentieth-century neo-liberalist phrases as *deskilled work, welfare-to-work,* or *McJob* (Bennett 376). Williams himself emphasized this when, in the mid 1970s, he observed that when modern work became circumscribed to paid labor it excluded such activity as "a modern woman running a house and bringing up children," which, at that time, was not the same as "a woman who *works* (335; original emphasis). Such observations point to the geocultural consciousness that inhabits such key words themselves. Shifting representations of work in the Cuban vanguards of the 1920s and 1930s, then, embody the period's cultural dynamics between art and the changing workaday world.

Such contending subtexts of the word *work* play out as well, of course, in international modernism, which focuses self-reflectively on artistic work. Italian and Russian futurism, for example, celebrate the sheer physical force of modern labor, while other experiments critique modern work as alienating routine or the exploitation of the many by the few, as in Fritz Lang's film *Metropolis* (1927).[11] In Latin America, Roberto Arlt's avant-garde novels of the late 1920s, such as *El juguete rabioso* (1926; *Mad Toy*) and *Los siete locos* (1929; *The Seven Madmen*) critique work life in Buenos Aires during rapid immigrant influx, and Patrícia Galvão's 1933 novel, *Parque Industrial: Romance Proletârio* (*Industrial Park: A Proletarian Novel*) deploys vanguard syntax and collage in scathing condemnations of working conditions in the burgeoning São Paulo textile industry. Yet as I have argued elsewhere, in Latin America much modern literary activity that privileged artistic work also legitimized itself by paying compensatory homage to physical labor.[12] Aníbal González has demonstrated that the late nineteenth- and early twentieth-century aestheticist Spanish American *modernistas* compared their writing to a craftsman's painstaking labor (*La novela modernista hispanoamericana* 21).[13] Emulating Flaubert and the French Parnassians, the *modernistas*, González argues, "proclaimed . . . that writing (particularly in its 'artistic' form, that is, as literature) was hard work, an experience often approximating agony" (*Killer Books* 9). Thus Latin America's first modern literary writers of the late nineteenth and early twentieth centuries—the progenitors of the literary vanguards—in effect argued that intellectual activity was difficult material labor causing bodily pain. But they also privileged the intellectual location from which they wrote by implicitly moving to "dignify" physical work through analogies with labors of the mind.

THE WORK ETHIC OF HAVANA'S AVANT-GARDES

The writers of Havana's avant-gardes of the 1920s and 1930s inherited this dynamic between intellectual and physical labor from the journalist, intellectual, poet, novelist, and independence fighter José Martí (1853–1895), who executed metaphoric turns between intellectual and manual work. In prose and poetry, Martí defined the man of action as a worker and legitimized intellectuals as laborers rather than book learners. His landmark 1891 essay "Nuestra América" (Our America) for example, set forth a model of the Spanish American "natural man" who would reject "artificial" or "false" scholarship from foreign sources and acquire practical knowledge of his own context (88, 91). The lyric speaker in his "Versos sencillos" (*Simple Verses*) rejects the "pomp of the rhymester" and the "doctoral" hood and self-identifies with the poor laborers of the land (237). Similarly, Martí described tobacco workers as intellectuals working with their hands and, inverting the metaphor, compared thinking to "opening furrows" or "laying foundations" (*Obras escogidas* 2: 473).[14]

Cuba's avant-gardists claimed Martí as the cultural forefather of their own activism, and recent Cuban scholarship even locates the origins of the 1959 Revolution's strong work ethic in Martí's legacy.[15] But the Cuban vanguardists' attention to work and their self-representation as cultural workers manifest anxieties about rapidly changing work patterns and exemplify the self-conscious activism of the avant-gardes. I have long argued that Latin America's literary avant-gardes should be approached neither as a set of canonical texts nor through a checklist of technical strategies but as a performative cultural activity.[16] This activity, which, as Peter Bürger argues for the European avant-gardes, challenges the definition of the artwork as a finished product (56), draws on an available repertoire of *doings* around art, culture, or politics that coalesced in the quest for new styles, not only of writing but also of participation as artists in public life, akin to what Pierre Bourdieu termed the "art of living" to describe late nineteenth-century group-based European literary culture and its improvisational rehearsal of new intellectual personas (58). In addition to experimentation in journalistic forums or literary genres,[17] this repertoire included private or public group activities (*tertulias*, soirees, performances events, exhibitions); the creation of manifestoes; the publication of little magazines enacting cultural, artistic, or political positions; engagement in ethnographic, folkloric, or historical investigations in support of culturalist projects; or participation in political demonstrations and protests.[18]

Latin American vanguard groups of this epoch did partake in the audience-engaging capers associated with European futurists and Dada, and maintained a critical orientation toward public life. Interaction with European interwar avant-gardes and European and U.S. modernists was grounded in widely circulating literary journals and sojourns abroad by Latin American writer-artists and visits to Latin America of European and U.S. figures.[19] Although aesthetic positions ran the gamut from aspirations for "pure art" to interventions in local or world events, a majority of Latin American avant-garde groups were internationalist in their engagement with artistic innovations and their participation in a generational structure of feeling. But many were simultaneously immersed in local debates, for example, about how to define *mexicanidad* or *cubanía*, how to imagine a new Argentine *criollismo* in the face of immigration, or how to "Peruvianize Peru" by incorporating the indigenous into a national imaginary. Through these mediations of the international and the local, the Latin American avant-gardes showcased, as Rosenberg demonstrates through Brazilian and Argentine examples, site-specific dynamics of the geopolitics of modernization.[20] Key to these groups' enactment of a self-conscious positionality and manifesting the anxiety about U.S. intervention in Latin America embodied in *arielismo*, was the appeal to a comprehensive *Americanist* artistic politics, defined to encompass the Hispanophone and Lusophone portions of the Hemisphere, as in manifestoes issuing Americanist calls and in a hemispheric exchange of little magazines addressing cultural and political developments in multiple Latin American countries.[21]

With a periodic culturalist focus on the construction of *cubanía* in response to the massive U.S. presence under their new constitution's Platt amendment (1902–1934), Cuban vanguardists, too, negotiated the international with the local. But the Cuban avant-gardes of the period—encompassing the Grupo Minorista (1923–1929); the smaller circle from its ranks that published the magazine *Revista de Avance* (1927–1930); and unaffiliated writers with comparable cultural goals—stand out for an especially robust conception of intellectual activism and intense attention to the problematic of work. A heterogeneous ensemble of middle- to upper-middle-class artists and intellectuals, most born at the turn of the century, the Grupo Minorista, thirty-four of whose members signed a 1927 manifesto, took shape in 1923 through noontime meetings in the Havana law office of Emilio Roig de Leuchsenring (1889–1964). Roig directed the literary component of the popular illustrated monthly *Social*, which served as the group's primary outlet before the *Revista de Avance*. Sessions in his office were often followed by public lunches paying homage to local or visiting intellectuals, or (as Cairo points out) attacking works or writers canonized by Cuba's National Academy of Arts and Letters (37). Although *minorista* associates later took more defined ideological stands ranging from leadership roles in the Cuban Communist party to collaboration with the right-wing Batista regime, their common ground in the 1920s was support for broad-based artistic innovation and progressive political reform, as well as opposition to U.S. intervention in Cuba and to corruption and repression in the governments of Alfredo Zayas (1921–1925) and Gerardo Machado (1925–1933). The literary *minoristas* wrote poetry, essays, fiction, a group novel, and even a play. Members also published the first anthology of modern Cuban poetry in 1926, edited by Félix Lizaso and José Antonio Fernández de Castro; modernized the critical essay in multiple disciplines; helped organize the first Exposition of Modern Cuban Art in 1927; supported experiments in Cuban music; and—in the late 1920s and early 1930s—incorporated Afro-Cuban linguistic, folkloric, visual, musical, and ritual elements into their artistic work. Through *Social* and *Revista de Avance* they disseminated work by countless European, U.S., Latin American, and Cuban artists and writers. Several members, including Alejo Carpentier, were jailed by the Machado government as political subversives. *Minoristas* who later became stand-out figures in twentieth-century Cuban intellectual life include Carpentier, one of Latin America's most important twentieth-century novelists; Juan Marinello, a literary and political essayist who played signal cultural roles after the 1959 Revolution, including ambassador to UNESCO; Jorge Mañach, author of one of the first culturalist inquiries into *cubanía*; and Roig de Leuchsenring, who served from 1935 until 1964 as Havana's city historian.

In their 1927 manifesto, titled the "Declaración del Grupo Minorista," the *minoristas*' self-representation as intellectual *workers* underscores the vanguards' concerns about the relationship of cultural activity to modern labor in neocolonial Cuba. All the *minorista* signers had day jobs.[22] But the *minoristas* did not apply the term "intellectual work" to activity for which they were paid. With references to their "sabbatical lunches" (linked to the word *sábado* for Saturday), they in fact located their intellectual labors in the leisure sphere, even as they promoted its ties with the workaday world. Their moves from Roig's office, where their meetings began, to public locations for other events underscore this dynamic between their vocational and avocational work. Similarly their 1927 manifesto, with an eclectic reference to their first 1923 meeting as a gathering of "intellectuals, artists, journalists, lawyers," encompassed avocations and vocations in one sphere. And yet, when they explicitly defined themselves as "intellectual *workers*," their examples—literary artists, painters, musicians, sculptors—did not include wage-paying activity (7). The manifesto's description of the group's enterprises as lacking in rules, dues, fixed locations, or habitual practices underscores the improvisational nature of their group-work, in contrast to modern job routines.

Comparable vacillations in their self-conscious positioning as intellectuals in a modern work milieu—an alternating advance toward and retreat from the market ethic—play out in the group's short avant-garde novel *Fantoches* (Puppets), serialized in 1926 in twelve consecutive issues of *Social*. A different *minorista* author wrote each chapter, also illustrated by its own *minorista* artist. A collective rendition of the modern detective novel, *Fantoches* maximizes novelistic improvisation, as each chapter shifts the character positions from which events are perceived, relocates to a new setting in modern Cuba, and adds unanticipated plot twists and murders, all untangled in the last offering. Through its shifting Havana and (in one case) provincial locales, ranging from the Havana *hampa* (underworld) to a high society ball, the novel broadly satirizes modern Havana and corruption among civil service workers, politicians, the military, police, and judges. The actual *work* of crime-solving takes place in two privileged settings: the newsroom of a Havana daily and the lunchtime gathering of an intellectual group, named the *pequeñistas* (the "little-ists"), a parodic allusion to the *minoristas*, several of whom, with thinly veiled names, play meta-fictional roles in the novel.

Through analogies between these two settings, *Fantoches* critiques Cuba's rationalized neocolonial workplace, even as it locates inventive intellectual work in its heart: the modern city newspaper. Here the mind work of editors, reporters, and graphic artists consists of imagining alternative theories of a crime, an epistemological practice whose inventiveness the account underscores and whose collage-like creativity it showcases in the random visual assemblage for the story's graphic version. Once the journalists have invented a theory of the crime—the creative part of the task in a segment described as "wasting time"—the narrative then links the article's composition, "by obligation . . . more than conviction" (38), to the rationalized schedule of the newspaper's deadline and mechanical reproduction. The journalists' actual writing unfolds in the paradoxical "silence of redaction" linked "disharmoniously" to the "iron rain fiction of the linotypes," "impatient typing," "cutting phone calls," "hurried orders," and the "roaring Sonora rotary press, vomiting newspapers into the fatiguing repose of the newspaper dawn" (35, 37). Thus the workplace's mechanized cacophony disrupts—assembly-line style—the collaborative communication of creative intellectual work. The novel's subsequent account of the *pequeñistas*' raucous luncheon, where the attendees invent new crime theories, evokes the newsroom scene linking the workplace time-out with the creative assemblage of members' views and the creative work of *Fantoches* itself. The *pequeñistas*, a narrator observes, couldn't have invented a better theory had it "occurred to them to write a detective novel among them" (86).

In the same spirit as the *Fantoches* newsroom's inventive "time out" and the sabbatical lunches, then, the *minoristas* reserved the word *labor* for actions undertaken not in their day jobs but in their roles as unpaid cultural activists, a paradoxical separation of their *laboring* selves from their jobs and the lives of others. "Collectively, or individually, [the group's] true members *have labored* and *labor for* . . ." they declared in the 1927 manifesto, a sentence they completed with a list of causes. These included the promotion of new and vernacular art, the dissemination of new artistic

and intellectual currents in all disciplines, educational reform, greater citizen participation in government, collaboration with other Latin American nations, and improvements for Cuba's farmers, small landowners (*colonos*), and blue-collar workers.[23]
The *minoristas'* self-assigned social role, then, was to labor for artistic innovation
and also for the well-being of other workers. Their explanation for the group's name
exposed the tensions of such a combination. Their implicit "minority" position, they
explained, referred only to *artistic* judgments, but they were otherwise a "majority
group," the "voice, tribune, and index of the majority of the people" (7).

Considering this self-exalting claim to represent other Cubans, it is easy to
agree with Francine Masiello that *minorista* founders of the *Revista de Avance*,
which supported Afro-Cubanism as an anti-imperialist aesthetic allied with
international avant-garde primitivism, actually promoted "local *intellectual* interests
. . . at the expense of silent subalterns at home" (28; my emphasis). This conclusion
underscores contradictions in the intellectual worker model. And yet, the Cuban
avant-gardes' focus on work reveals a more complicated story, in which equating
cultural workers with laborers was not designed simply to legitimize the former.
Some *minorista* writing on changing Cuban work patterns, particularly those tied
to the U.S. sugar industry takeover, highlighted detrimental consequences for
workers. Rubén Martínez de Villena and Jorge Vivó's 1927 essay *Cuba, factoría
yanqui* (Cuba, Yankee Factory), regarded by Cairo as the pioneer of the Marxist
essay in Cuba (159), documented the growing U.S. ownership of the Cuban economy
and workers. In 1927, Roig de Leuchsenring published journalistic pieces on the
situation of Cuba's urban workers, including legislative proposals for improvements
(Cairo 160). *Minorista* Juan Antiga Escobar participated in the emergent Cuban
labor movement, advocating reforms to raise workers' living standards. Even as
they cast a critical eye on modern work's mechanization, market ethic, displacement of workers, disruption of community, and impact on local culture, then,
Cuban vanguardists lauded physical toil and identified selectively with contemporary laborers. Experimental Cuban literary works situated in the sphere of the
modern *zafra* (sugar-cane harvest) and the neocolonial dynamics underlying it
exemplify these shifting affiliations and the rehearsal of new literary forms or and
styles to express them.

"A Strong Smell of Sugarcane in the Air"

Artistic protests against the U.S. domination of the sugar industry and the parallel
exploration of Afro-Cuban culture as a corrective to U.S. influence are well-established
features of the Cuban cultural field of the 1920s and early 1930s.[24] These protests
emerged in painting, performance, poetry, and narrative. But such nonliterary work
as Ramiro Guerra y Sánchez's 1927 essays, *Azúcar y Población en las Antillas*

(Sugar and Population in the Antilles), and the anthropologist Fernando Ortiz's 1906 study of Havana's Afro-Cuban underworld, 1920s essays on Afro-Cuban folklore and language, and journal, *Archivos del Folklore Cubano*, launched in 1924 also shaped this cultural conversation. So, too, did interactions of Cuban writers with international avant-garde primitivism through such French and U.S. writers as Paul Morand and Langston Hughes. Joining the anti-Yankee charge and emergent interest in Afro-Cuban culture, experimental artistic works focused on the sugar world also illuminate nuances in the avant-gardes' engagement with the modern work ethic and exploration of the dynamic between cultural work and physical labor. These artistic portrayals map Cuba's rural sugar milieu as a World War I era internationalized space of local erasure, not only of the land, but also of the workers inhabiting it, a process seen as generating indolence, displacement, or loss of community. These texts idealize labor as a model for intellectual activity but vary in the agency ascribed to actual physical laborers. Like the *minoristas* who located their intellectual labors in the "time-outs" of the workplace, these experimental texts often relocate the dedicated worker outside the machinery of modern work itself, in the improvisational, the creative, or the ritualistic. In all these scenarios, the *zafra* (cane harvest) under U.S. dominance serves as an all-purpose metaphor for the modern market-ethic and its costs.

From the perspective of the *criollo* elite, Agustín Acosta's *La zafra: poema de combate* (The Sugar Harvest: A Combat Poem; 1926) uses the U.S. takeover of the sugar industry as a metonymy for Cuba's lost ideals from the independence revolt and calls on Cuba's workers to change. Although the eighteen-canto poem contains epic formulas—an invocation of the poetic muse, the claim to represent the experience of a people—and does not openly aspire to vanguard form, the mix of elitist and popular verse forms, uncommon at the time, and the modern sketches accompanying each canto by Acosta's brother, José M. Acosta, disrupt conventions. While drawn from the Hispanic repertoire, the verse forms fluctuate widely from canto to canto paralleling the poem's ideological segues. Thematically, the piece enacts the dance of advance and retreat with modernization typifying Latin America's avant-gardes.[25] Save for two brief mentions of Martí, there is little epic heroism here, and with backward glances at the nineteenth century, the poem constructs a deplorable present. The cantos lead from a modern-day plantation poised for the *zafra* to the cane-cut itself, to the transport of cane by oxcarts to U.S. processing mills, and then retrospectively to nineteenth-century cameos of plantation slavery under the Spaniards, the rising rebellion, and the post-independence "return of hope" (87). The poem then returns abruptly to cane processing in the modern U.S. mill, an ironic panegyric to processed sugars, a pedagogic lecture to rural Cuban workers, a portrait of blue-eyed Yankees with suspect souls, a snapshot of modern mill machinery, a depiction of the World War I era "dance of millions," and a closing welcome to Spanish peninsular immigrants willing to work. Randomly interspersed variants on a refrain—"There's a strong smell of sugarcane in the air . . .!" —whose sequential modifications—from a smell of sugar, to a "violent" smell of burning sugar, to the smell of "black honey" and then blood (34, 52, 61, 71)—build a menacing aura linking slave and independence rebellions with a potentially explosive present.

The poem's title reference to cane-cutting establishes a focus on work, reinforced by the poet's opening prose comments identifying the *zafra* as Cuba's "fountain of life," thus affirming the nation-building power of physical labor. But the poet's attitude toward such labors is paradoxical when it comes to his own: in return for the poem's insights, he explains, he expects "no state appointments as usher or custodian" (positions typically "reserved for poets") because he would be inept at such physical tasks (6). And yet, in the lyric prelude, the speaker claims sufficient physical power for his own "muscular verse" to revive the worker's "inert arm" (21–22). Tellingly, this synecdochic substitution for the full-bodied worker persists throughout this long poem; with the exception of the lauded cart-drawing oxen and the nineteenth-century slaves forced to labor by others, the contemporary harvest's actual, autonomous workers are invisible, idle, or in retreat. Thus the *zafra's* power lies in the work itself—"the steel, cutting the winnowed fruit, / casts its musical notes at the nascent sun" (38)—a celebratory scenario performed by oxen, cane, and iron machetes. The workers who actually wield blades appear only in retreat at day's end: "an exodus of skinny day workers, tired," who return to squalid homes that "laziness renders sterile / with the *horror of all independent labor*" (50; my emphasis).

Although the poetic speaker blames this supposed inertia of Cuba's destitute rural workers on U.S. invaders, he also appears to blame the workers themselves, particularly the descendants of slaves. Here his "geocultural consciousness" as a self-identified voice for all of Cuba contradicts the poem's declared progressive project, evident in analogies between contemporary oxen and nineteenth-century slaves, both emasculated, passive, and in bondage, but both praised—in contrast to Cuba's contemporary rural poor—for economic productivity. The canto "The Black Slaves" distances these earlier laborers with racist overtones: "semi-naked, sad, in their enslaved gentleness / oxen in the vigor of their virility / the poor blacks cultivate the promised-land / with the savage vision of their birth-nation" (60), a country that is implicitly not Cuban. References to the slaves' "illogical fetishism" reinforce the racist optic. Moreover, a description of the independence uprising as the joint enterprise of "rebel owners" and "docile blacks" further strips agency from those held up as model, if enslaved, hard workers, while also eliding the strong military role actually played by blacks and mulattos in Cuba's independence wars. In snapshots of slave life vacillating between ostensible condemnation and nostalgia, the speaker appears to conclude that, although slavery caused trauma to slaves, Cuban plantation life possessed the modern virtue of productivity and got the job done. By contrast, the *campesinos*, rarely seen at work in the poem, are eclipsed by the "iron brain" of mechanized productivity in the U.S.-run mill where "everything turns / everything works" under orders from a foreman compared to the pilot of an invading ship (96–97).

And yet, an aversion to hard work by the contemporary Cuban *campesinos*, whom the poem analogizes to its rendition of black slaves through their "spiritualist" superstitions and "larcenous *curanderos*" (native healers), is held equally responsible for low *Cuban* productivity. Thus the speaker claiming laborlike virtues for his own "muscular verse" distances himself from Cuba's workers, "those people" whose sordid life unfolds in a "place made sterile by indolence" (50). In the paternalist canto "Admonition," the speaker apostrophizes *colonos* and subsistence farmers with an explicit refusal of praise, blames them for relinquishing land to Yankees, and lays out a pedagogic program for self-improvement: to work hard and cultivate their own land, to clean themselves up and rebuild their homes, to educate themselves and their children, to abandon gambling and cockfights, to worship as good Christians, and, in sum, to "organize [their] lives" (109–14). Paradoxically, this program, framed as a nationalist response to U.S. intervention and in resistance to the rationalized work ethic displacing Cuba's rural workers, brings to mind the very skill-building projects launched by U.S. Protestant missionaries, as Pérez documents, to reinforce the modernization of Cuba on the model of the market ethic and the "self-made" man (252). Manifesting the poem's unstable "geocultural consciousness," the speaker laments that, with just a few extra hours of "stretching their arms," "these people" could once again prove that Cuba is "the richest land ever seen," an ironic reference to Columbus's words when setting eyes on the island. The speaker's closing welcome to contemporary *Spanish* immigrant laborers and his omission in turn of the Jamaicans and Haitians (who also came to Cuba during the World War I "dance of millions") confirm the poem's bias that some work-seekers—including Cuba's former colonizers—are preferable to others. Moreover, although the speaker calls Cuban workers his "brothers," his ultimate division of labor reinforces the divide between cultural workers of Latin America's "lettered city" and the physical labor of the unschooled: "you plow the land to offer me its fruit / and I [plow] my thoughts to give you the flower" (114).

Through a more sophisticated interplay of narrative focalization, Alejo Carpentier's *¡É-Yamba-Ó¡* (Lord, Praised be Thou), drafted in 1927 during his Havana imprisonment and published in 1933 during his Parisian exile, forges a stronger tie between the cultural work of the novel's learned narrator and the backbreaking physical toil and improvisational urban labors of its Afro-Cuban protagonist, Menegildo Cué.[26] A bildungsroman of Menegildo's short life, unfolding roughly between the first decade of the Cuban nation and 1930, the narration encompasses his birth, youth, and early work in the U.S. mill sphere; initiation into Afro-Cuban rituals; imprisonment in Havana for accidentally killing his lover's Haitian mate; post-release employment in multiple jobs in the Havana slums; initiation into an urban Afro-Cuban *ñáñigo* secret society; and ultimate death in the group's street battle with rivals. Although the novel periodically falls into primitivist stereotypes, as when it casts its Afro-Cuban subjects as indisposed toward the "arduous task of analyzing" (68) and their cultural forms as "elemental" (152), it portrays them as hard workers. Through focalization shifts, the text, in contrast to Acosta's poem, strives to locate them on even terrain with the ethnographic, participant-observer narrator. The work's stylistic instability manifests its quest to encompass multiple perspectives, and Carpentier himself later called the novel an "unavoidably hybrid product" (26). Thus it juxtaposes telegraphic chapter titles and imagery, shifting focalizers, vernacular character speech, Afro-Cuban lyrics and rituals, and collage-like descriptions with a residual naturalist air. This synthesis also registers Carpentier's interaction with the Parisian avant-gardes during his Afro-Cuban phase, initiated in the late 1920s.[27]

Although Acosta's poem and Carpentier's text both exhibit international modernism's sense of place, the novel's geocultural consciousness is more concrete and complex. The poem builds neat spatial oppositions between the brick, colonial Cuban plantation (with harmonious bells) and the modern, iron U.S. mill (with strident whistles) and counterposes the invading "iron ships" of U.S. modernization with an idealized lyrical beauty of a Cuban countryside that could be anywhere. Carpentier's narrative also portrays Cuba as invaded space, but its intricate juxtaposition of geocultural elements renders a more heterogeneous sugar world: the demographically and economically complex neocolonial workplace of the *zafra*, perceived through the narrator and through its international workers. The novel's opening chapters, titled "Landscape (a)" and "Landscape (b)," constitute self-conscious acts of geocultural emplacement. In a prologue to the definitive version, Carpentier called the first landscape a "vanguardist . . . vision of a sugar mill in the midst of the *zafra*" (27). Here, as the expanding "iron fungus" of the U.S. mill gradually absorbs ruined colonial plantations and Cuban terrain, the Yankee invasion, seen first through the eyes of Menegildo's father, Usebio, a former *colono* forced to sell his lands, unfolds as literal "conquests of space" (31). The parallel shrinkage of the hardworking Usebio's holdings reveals the expanding "great stain on the provincial map" (43). With Menegildo's displacement to the city, the Cués' home "disappears among the cane, surrendering to . . . [the] misery, mud, and isolation" of the economically devastating post-*zafra tiempo muerto* (idle time) (167–68).

But with the Cuban *zafra* portrayed as a heteroglossic international workplace—generated by the war in a Europe "over there" (36) and dependent on the war's shortages for its "dance of millions"—the cartographic takeover is also cultural and linguistic. Carpentier's *zafra* assembles "herds of laborers," American foremen, a French chemist, an Italian weigher, a Jewish peddler, "squadrons of Haitians in rags" and "Jamaicans . . . in discolored overalls," Galician immigrants, Polish salesmen, Asian horticulturalists, and Chinese wholesalers (33–34). Once the harvest begins, this hybrid mix unites in a modern work scenario, cogs in a globalized productivity machine, a cacophony of "leaping pistons," "greasy couplings of iron with iron," "bursts of whirling steel around axes," etc. (36). This work blurs boundaries between humans and machines, as "the men, unsexed, almost mechanical, climb ladders and cross platforms, attuned to the tiniest failures of the screw-jointed organisms that glisten and vibrate beneath winding sheets of steam" (37). In this rationalized workplace, where "all watches are synchronized when its sirens blow" and life is organized "according to its will," the mill "swallows interminable caravans of oxcarts, loaded with sufficient cane to sweeten an ocean," consumes the hundreds of workers delivered to it every six hours, and regurgitates them "extenuated, grease-stained, panting" (37).

As in Acosta's poem, the explicitly Cuban workers, in particular Usebio, contribute to the *zafra* as hired hands or cane haulers; but, as implied by their separate location in "Landscape (b)," they do so outside the productivity machine. Unlike the laziness attributed to laborers in Acosta's poem, however, here former *colonos* delivering cane to the mill think only of work: "repairing oxcarts, sharpening machetes, cleaning caldrons" (33). Moreover, the narrator portrays Usebio's decision to sell his land and purchase oxen as resourceful insofar as it allows a measure of independence. Such occupational ingenuity also characterizes the multiple tasks performable by the displaced cane-workers of Havana's underclass, where Menegildo lands. These would-be workers fall outside the modern workplace's synchronized machinery: "masons without jobs, political schemers without candidates, *son* musicians without a dance, newspaper salesmen, and itinerant confectioners," often forced to fall back on revenues from their "concubine's ironing" or "the invocation of a miracle" (142). Menegildo's temporary job performing as St. John the Baptist's executioner in an amusement park sideshow—an impromptu role he embraces with self-conscious gusto and dedication—epitomizes the improvisational urban creativity that sustains him and his cohort.

Yet, in *¡É-Yamba-Ó¡*, the Afro-Cuban community's most important labor is the ritual work of secret *ñáñigo* societies and their members' related musical and dance performances. As fraternal, clublike leisure activity comparable to the creative ventures of the *minoristas* (they, too, have their *tertulias* [115]), these endeavors fall outside workaday routines. The novel's glossary notes that, in Afro-Cuban usage, the word *trabajar* (to work) can refer to the preparation of objects or talismans for ritual ends. Portraying this activity as "work," moreover, mines the connections that, as I've noted, Williams signaled between culture and work and between material and "spiritual" culture. Ultimately, the *ñáñigo* society's ritualistic and attendant creative activity grounds Menegildo's identity in the modern city that casts him as an outsider. As an urban migrant, he finds community in these creative associations of ritual workers, implicitly analogized with the cultural workers of Havana's avant-gardes in their resistance to the neocolonialist market ethic. The narrator connects the dots—"The bongo, antidote to Wall Street!"—and adds that only Menegildo's people "conserve an Antillean character and tradition" (115). This Antillean reference reinforces the novel's internationalist geocultural positioning and contrasts with Acosta's nationalist poem. Although the novel does privilege its Cuban characters, it notes that Usebio's detachment from the mill allows him to feel superior to the Haitian and Jamaican migrant workers, a nationalist streak marked as a flaw through Menegildo's fatal rivalry with Haitians. By contrast, in the opening *zafra* scene, even as this hybrid assemblage fuels the neocolonial productivity machine, the gathering also generates creative power precisely because of its internationalism, as seen in the group's carnivalesque cornucopia of rich linguistic, gastronomic, musical, and recreational activity. Thus the opening *zafra* scenario anticipates the novel's ultimate focus, through Menegildo's city life, on the inventiveness of hybrid cultural work, not only intellectual but also popular and ritualistic, as a response to the dehumanizing market ethic embodied in the very neocolonialist, community-busting mill that convenes the multinational *zafra*.

Yet, Carpentier, too, privileged some creative work over others. In the spirit of the novel's nomination of the bongo as an antidote to Wall Street, he saw ritual, music, and dance as alternatives to U.S. mass entertainment, which was complicit for him with the market-based ethic of the new *zafra*.[28] Thus his avant-garde ballet script, *El milagro de Anaquillé* (The Miracle of Anaquillé, 1927), subtitled an "Afro-Cuban choreographic mystery in one Act," contrasts two styles of cultural work— U.S. filmmaking and Afro-Cuban ritual—in a scene with two *bohíos* (thatched huts) on opposite sides of the stage.[29] Employing stylized elements akin to futurist, Dadaist, and surrealist dramatic experiments, the ballet's action unfolds in two competing performances that engage Cuban *guajiros* (peasants) exhausted after a day's work: a film shoot on (Cuban) location by a Hollywood director (the Business Man) and the initiation of cane cutters into a *ñáñigo* society by its leader, the Iyamba. The *guajiros*, as an onstage audience, wear no makeup, in contrast to the performing Business Man and the Iyamba who wear oversized, stylized masks. As they relax, strum a guitar, and tap out the rhythm, the *guajiros* watch astonished while the Business Man, dressed like a U.S. tourist, enters with his two actors (a sailor and a flapper) and takes possession of the Iyamba's *bohío*. Backdrop images of a cane field, palms, and three large mill chimneys literalize the connection between the film shoot and the *zafra* market ethic.

In contrasting two models of cultural work, executed in ballet movements accompanied by corresponding tempos in Amadeo Roldán's musical score, the piece portrays the Business Man's directorial labors as frenetic, commercially motivated, and inauthentic. To prepare the film set he inflates a rubber skyscraper with a bicycle pump and plasters the Iyamba's *bohío* with ads for Wrigley's gum and the Church of the Rotarian Christ, an allusion to the Protestant missionary campaigns that, as I have noted, sought to reinforce the market ethic throughout Cuba. Against this backdrop, the Business Man films the sailor and flapper, dressed as a bullfighter and Spanish flamenco dancer, in a burlesque of a "Spanish dance." By contrast, the Iyamba, whose entry disrupts the Business Man's work-in-progress, enacts the cultural work of the ritual initiation with measured, solemn, and deliberate movements. Intrigued by the ritual, the Business Man dresses the sailor in a tiger skin and the flapper as a Hawaiian dancer and directs them to join the Afro-Cuban initiates for his film. In the resulting confrontation, each director deploys the weapons of his art: the Iyamba and an initiate performing the ritual's small devil conjure up fire under the Business Man's nose, while he destroys the Iyamba's altar with his tripod. The Iyamba's power—embodied in the cylindrical twins (*Jimaguas*) he summons— proves stronger; as they strangle the Business Man with the cord that connects them, the dancers freeze, the skyscraper deflates like a toy, and a "slow and lugubrious whistle of the siren rises from the sugar mill" (277).

Carpentier and Acosta's texts exemplify the *minorista* intelligentsia's self-assignment to represent Cuba's workers, as they sought on one hand to imbue their own cultural enterprises with the aura of strong physical labor and on the other hand to distance themselves, and Cuba's workers, from the market ethic embodied in the U.S. sugar industry. Whereas Acosta's lyric speaker undermines this position by preaching that very ethic to Afro-Cuban rural workers, Carpentier, in validating the cultural work of Afro-Cuban ritual, song, and dance, ostensibly narrows the gap between the intellectual elite and ordinary workers. He also teases out connections between the rural *zafra* and Cuba's urban work-world. But Carpentier, like other *minoristas*, engaged in Afro-Cubanist experiments more in pursuit of an imagined national or regional culturalist ideal than as a critical revelation of racial or social inequalities. Other experimental Cuban writers whose initial toehold in the *criollo* "lettered city" was less firm by reasons of class, race, or gender, offered more nuanced, critical portraits of Cuban modernity's own inequalities, particularly in urban settings.

Moving On Up in the City

Strikingly, the most successful Afro-Cuban poet of the *minorista* generation—Nicolás Guillén—did not seek his intellectual home among them. Guillén was mulatto and from more modest origins than many *minoristas*. He did sustain ties with José Antonio Fernández de Castro, a leading *minorista* who edited the Sunday literary supplement to the *Diario de la Marina*, where Guillén published his experimental collection *Motivos de son* (1930), which he dedicated to Fernández de Castro.[30] These experimental poems and those of *Sóngoro Cosongo* (1931) and *West Indies Ltd.* (1934) synthesized colloquialisms, stylized percussive elements, and intonations of popular Cuban speech with the acoustical effects, rhythms, and call-response conventions of such musical forms as the *son* associated with Afro-Cuban culture. Drawn from Guillén's familiarity with street activity, these poems often constituted performative speech acts from everyday life, including *piropos* (flirtatious calls by men to women), *pregones*, (street vendor cries), *adivinanzas* (riddles), or contentious encounters between Afro-Cubans revealing racial hierarchies among them.

Guillén scholars distinguish his project from contemporaneous Afro-Cubanism partly because of this greater attention to ordinary life and disinclination toward international vanguard primitivism.[31] Rather than deploying Afro-Cuban culture as an aestheticized response to foreign influence, Guillén focused on racism at home and abroad, including racial hierarchies within black Cuban culture and racism's attendant social inequities. His perspective was more consistently pan-Antillean, as in *West Indies, Ltd.*, where the neocolonialist control of the multiracial *zafra* transcends national borders in the Caribbean.[32] But Guillén shared the *minoristas'* attention to work and workers, and also claimed the power of physical labor for his art, as in the manifesto poem "Llegada" that announces the "arrival" of Afro-Antillean elements in Europeanized *criollo* life: "Our song / is like a muscle under the skin of the soul" (12). Numerous poems from his early collections give voice to laborers themselves, many of them working the city in improvisational modes: street vendors, organ grinders, drummers, singers, guitarists, dockworkers, or tourist-hustling maraca-players.

As in Carpentier's novel, Guillén's city dwellers execute creative cultural work, strengthening the poetic speaker's identification with their labors. But in contrast to Carpentier's dismissal of U.S. mass entertainment as threatening to Cuban culture, Guillén presented a more complex picture of social class. While sharing Carpentier's views on the ties of U.S. mass culture to neocolonialism, he acknowledged the social mobility it offered to those with little access to the city's class or race-based employment pipelines. Thus Guillén's "Pequeña oda a un negro boxeador cubano" ("Small Ode to a Black Cuban Boxer") portrays a Cuban boxer at work on Broadway. As detailed by Pérez, prize-fighting constituted one of several entertainment modes promoted by U.S. tourism in early twentieth-century Cuba (others include golf, horse-racing, modern amusement parks, and casino gambling), and in the late 1920s, the Cuban boxer Kid Chocolate (Eligio Sardiñas) achieved international fame (175–77).[33] In Guillén's poem, characterized by flexible versification and structure, the speaker addresses the boxer directly and, although noting his "weak Spanish" and even "feebler English" (15), is less paternalistic than either Acosta or Carpentier.[34] The speaker reminds the boxer of the ties between boxing and neocolonial exploitation, noting that the implicitly racist Broadway that cheers when he jumps like a "modern elastic monkey" is the same predator that "stretches its snout with its enormous humid tongue / to lick up gluttonously / all the blood of [Cuba's] canefields" (15). At the same time, the speaker admires the boxer's strength at work—"your explosive fists"—(15) and concedes that boxing gives him physical and psychological agency— "It's good, after all, / to find a punching bag" (15–16). Like the activity of intellectual workers, the poem also concludes that boxing accrues cultural currency, portraying the boxer's ability to "speak black for real" as a forceful rejoinder to European faddish yearnings for primitivism from Cuba and Harlem (16). Similarly, in Guillén's lyric world of this epoch modern tourism offers a measure of work autonomy to Havana's blacks, who play music for tourists or try to learn English to hustle tourist women.

Just as Guillén showcased the mobility modern work might offer Cuba's working-class blacks, so did Ofelia Rodríguez Acosta and Dulce María Loynaz explore its potential for women. Unlike Rodríguez Acosta, who was a working journalist with ties to the *minoristas*, Loynaz, born to an aristocratic family and whose father was a general in the independence wars, neither worked for a living nor attended vanguard gatherings. Her economic privilege provided home-schooling and European and U.S. tours, and she also earned a law degree from the University of Havana. Those *tertulias* she did attend were in her own home, as her family entertained such visiting cultural luminaries at Federico García Lorca and Juan Ramón Jiménez in the 1930s. The literary world eventually recognized Loynaz's poetic achievements with prestigious awards, but Loynaz's lyric novel *Jardín* (Garden), written between 1928 and 1935, is one of Cuba's most impressive avant-garde texts of its time.[35] Introduced by an author's prelude and framed by opening and closing scenes of the protagonist, Bárbara, looking out through the grillwork of her Havana mansion's window, the novel traces her self-guided education in the mansion's interior garden and its enclosed pavilion. Through interpretive reading, Bárbara recuperates her personal and family history in lost texts, letters, and photographs. Eventually, led by her soon-to-be husband, she is catapulted into the enticing modern city, teeming with "life" in contrast to the garden's familial ghosts. Here Bárbara traverses an internationalized modern world at a vertiginous pace (from New York, to Paris, London, Burgos, Buenos Aires, and Havana); assumes the role of a fashionable "new woman"; is drawn into "all the terror and all the voluptuousness" of the World War; rushes to the battlefront to bind wounds; suffers the "imperious haste to live" infecting her generation postwar; and leads a dizzying life that rushes by. When Bárbara returns to the mansion's garden, she dies from its collapsing debris, and we again see her staring out from the window's grillwork, as if for eternity. The novel's avant-garde features include its genre indeterminacy, blend of lyric prose with elliptical sentences, loose plot line, anti-mimetic treatment of time and space, and focus on representation.

The class-based privilege of leisurely intellectual pursuits grounds Bárbara's coming-of-age story, followed by her perspective-shattering immersion in modernity. Poised between this modern world and her garden sanctuary, the novel's geocultural consciousness is both supremely local—anchored in a Havana seaside mansion saturated with melancholy for a besieged *criollo* aristocracy—and eminently international, with Bárbara's globetrotting and identification of World War I as the defining event of her generation. Comparable to Carpentier's imagery of the U.S. mill consuming the Cuban landscape, *Jardín* portrays Havana's growth as a spatial takeover, framed through Bárbara's nature-based metaphors: "She sees the city grow . . . the huge chimneys erupt like shoots in a miraculous countryside, clusters of chimneys that darken the sky with their smoke" (106). Bárbara imagines the city "swelling like a wild fruit," her garden "devoured" by its stone and "crushed by its enormous cement gullet" (107).

Paradoxically, even as Bárbara's garden offers illusionary shelter from modernity's predatory incursion, her intellectual activity there (a "large open window") mobilizes her entry to the world. Comparable tensions drive the novel's shifting conceptions of work. The narrative casts Bárbara's interpretive activity as slow, deliberate, and laborious, like traditional hard work, but comparable to modern labor in its dynamism, for example in a metonymy between human reading and a sewing machine, with the "tireless joy of cylinders, axles, and rods . . . animated iron with living power, with human intelligence" (52). Bárbara, for whom the world of airplanes, telegraphs, and trans-Atlantics offers the freedom of new womanhood, is mesmerized by her all-seeing grasp of an entire world (North to South, from the Almendares to the Ganges)[36] transformed by modern work's mechanized power and its capacity to produce "sugar a minute away from the cane" (262) or to divert a river's course (263). In *Jardín*'s expressive system, this same power propels Bárbara's increased freedom. But the "virus of velocity" (277) and market ethic—"thousands of . . . urban Bárbaras put to producing numbers, to making retail clothing"—(105) threaten the leisure for intellectual work. With no time for curiosity, a liberated Bárbara finally attends a cultural *tertulia* only to find that she has nothing to say. For this daughter of Cuba's elite, the fallen world of new women "mannequins" generates nostalgia for the garden's deliberative cultural work. Registering modernity's loss of Benjaminian aura, she observes that people no longer refer to "an intelligent man or a *cultured* man, but rather to a man of advanced ideas" and that work is praised for the speed with which it was accomplished rather than for its quality (280; my emphasis). Calling to mind Williams's observations about the ties in the word *culture* between the care of the mind and the care of the land, or Martí's analogies between thinking and plowing, Bárbara's nostalgia for "cultured" people parallels yearnings for traditional laborers from someone who has never worked for a living: "She wanted to see men work and she saw them in the humble land from which people seemed to burst forth . . . amassed from the same earth clods that dissolve in their hands" (260). If *Jardín* concedes that the modern work-world offers greater mobility to women, class interests trump gender concerns in a novel that is kindred in structure of feeling to Carpentier's quest for premodern ritual authenticity as a hedge against the market ethic.

By contrast, in its account of an emergent middle-class woman making her daily living in Havana, Ofelia Rodríguez Acosta's best-selling 1929 novel *La vida manda* (Life Commands) embraces modern office work, for all its flaws, as the site of women's upward economic and cultural mobility. The author of short stories, seven novels, and a play, Rodríguez was not an official *minorista* member but shared their anti-Yankee politics and activist conception of cultural work; wrote on feminist, literary, and political matters for the *minorista* organ, *Social*; received *minorista* praise in the *Revista de Avance* for *La vida manda*; and in 1927 contributed a chapter for a second *minorista* experiment in collaborative novel writing. She, too, sought ties between intellectual and physical work. But her class-spanning concept of the "practical feminist" was more kindred in spirit to Guillén's exploration of the workaday city's potential for those outside the mainstream. This concept ascribed conceptual sophistication to women whose daily paid labors performed a real-life (rather than bookish) contestation of gender roles. These "practical feminists," she argued, included manual laborers, teachers, saleswomen, professionals, *and* intellectuals ("Feminismo teórico" 9), who by acting out women's social problems gained a conceptual understanding of their situation ("La intelectual feminista" 76).

Rodríguez Acosta embodied these ideas in Gertrudis, the protagonist of *La vida manda*, an emancipated woman who earns a paycheck in an office, engages in free love, participates in Havana's literary-cultural world, and encounters recurrent tragedy because modern Havana is unprepared for her. The novel's uneasy synthesis of naturalist convention, telegraphic vanguard lists, and melodrama manifest Rodríguez's confessed ambivalence about avant-garde stylistic tics. But her novel's juxtaposition of modern Havana's work-world with the cultural enterprises of literary activists locates it firmly within the avant-garde corpus. As a paid office worker who moonlights as a literary midwife, Gertrudis bridges these worlds. Even with the low salary, tedious tasks, and sexual harassments of office work, Gertrudis, with a "driving, ardent desire to move up," embraces the market ethic to become a "self-made" woman: she does her monotonous job well, saves money, and starts her own business on the side: editing, typing, proofreading, and working with printers and bookstores to disseminate the creative writing of men. Such work constituted a prototypical role for U.S., European, and Latin American women seeking access to modern literary culture. It provides

Gertrudis with economic independence and an entree to Havana's vibrant literary scene of the 1920s, depicted in four self-reflective artistic *tertulia*s where intellectuals and artists debate culture and politics. They also argue about Gertrudis's role as a new Cuban woman as viable material for a contemporary novel.

This meta-fictional move renders her both participant (Gertrudis, unlike Bárbara, does speak) and outsider in the group's cultural work, a shifting position echoed in the narrative's geocultural consciousness. On one hand, Gertrudis's wanderings through the city and the *tertulias'* references to local figures and political events anchor the novel in 1920s Havana. But an abrupt shift in one *tertulia* scene from a third-person narration focalized through Gertrudis to a first-person plural "we," gives body to the work's global self-awareness—the "century of aviation, the century that aims to reach Mars, the century of women, the century of surprises and disenchantments" (192). As in the other texts I have discussed here, Cuba and its characters are catapulted onto the world stage, in this instance through a strategic shift in voice: "There was talk of politics . . . of art, the country's new rival industry, where . . . conservative and avant-garde groups engaged in burning polemics; of science, where all worthy curiosities took flight; of sports, truly Cuba's latest novelty, and of feminism, the only appealing thing that the terrible, thousand times wicked European War of 1914, in its postscript of economic collapses, moral confusion, and artistic reversals has left us on the tray of History" (191). Speaking on this planetary stage but grounded in local strictures (the novel makes clear that sexism, not ambitions of the market ethic, bring down this "self-made" Cuban woman), Gertrudis also unmasks the class-based contradictions in the Cuban avant-gardes' analogies between cultural and physical work and their claim to speak for Cuba's workers. When an aspiring male writer observes that, even though intellectuals must support themselves in all manner of enterprises, at least he's never seen one working as a bricklayer, Gertrudis asks "What about your socialism?" He explains: "Don't worry. It's fine for a bricklayer to be a writer but not for a writer to be a bricklayer" (22).

AVANT-GARDE FISSURES IN THE LETTERED CITY

This heterogeneous sampling of Cuban avant-garde texts reveals a burning cultural conversation about the impact of neocolonial modernization on the country's shifting cultural and social relationships through work. The ambivalence toward the market-driven work ethic also brings to light the complex and shifting positionality from which stories about work were told and their geocultural mediations. Other vanguard thematic clusters—for example the polemical cultural politics of post-revolutionary Mexico, the role of immigration in Argentine identity discourse, the hierarchical dynamics between popular and literate language in Latin America—can showcase other, contemporaneous debates. One could contend that this approach reveals much about any epoch. But I would argue that the reason the avant-gardes took such widespread hold in Latin America lies precisely in what their "baggy monster" texts enact: the convergence of modernization-generated social change, a consequent lost consensus about whose stories literature should tell, and international avant-garde challenges to the strategies and purpose of art. We should remember that the avant-gardes regarded straightforward narration itself as complicit with the power imbalances implied in Cartesian subject-object relations. As a result, through incursions into other genres, Latin American vanguard fictions often manifest a will to be something other than a novel, a phenomenon that intensifies their heteroglossia. Although most Cuban vanguard texts ultimately privilege the intelligentsia's perspective, then, they also open the literary field to stories from outside the lettered city.

Based on the avant-gardes' stylistic renovation, critical convention holds that they paved the way for the "Boom" novel that put Latin America on the global literary-map in the 1960s. These novels did project Latin America's cultural specificity onto a plane of internationalist myth, for example when the Macondo story of *One Hundred Years of Solitude* (1967) evokes biblical or classical sagas. They also often registered the disastrous failures of state-sponsored modernization in Latin America. But most of these works, whose epistemologically totalizing impulse is perhaps most akin to Anglo-European high modernism, leave little doubt as to whose story—that of the male intelligentsia—predominates. Thus, as Jean Franco observes in reflections aptly titled *The Decline and Fall of the Lettered City*, even while exploring connections between literature and politics as sites of utopian imaginings, the Boom novels ran up against the limits of such fantasies because to transcend those limits "would have meant the collapse of their enterprise itself" (8). The openings to new stories and voices, then, that characterizes some of the avant-gardes' best intentions is actually more akin to Latin America's heterogeneous post-1968 (sometimes called post-Boom) literary field, characterized by such varied expressions as subaltern testimonial narratives, performance art, multi-lingual poetry, digital novels, *bolero*-novels, censorship-evading book-objects, hybrid film documentaries, and the lyrics of Brazilian *favela* funk and Cuban hip-hop. While we can't know what Cuba's avant-garde intelligentsia would make of all this, one suspects they might find its activist challenge to the lettered city's cultural work enticingly familiar yet unsettling beyond their sharpest imaginings.

NOTES

1. In Hispanic cultures, a *tertulia* is a regularly meeting social gathering for discussing art, culture, and politics.
2. In Spanish America, *criollo* traditionally refers to Europeans or persons of European descent born in the New World; this usage connotes colonialist hierarchies.
3. See Ramos, Sarlo, Alonso, Geist and Monleón, and Canclini.
4. Peter Bürger's designation of the avant-gardist artwork as non-organic (55–82) implies a deliberate challenge to the category of artwork itself that is not always true of

Latin American vanguard texts, although it is true of some. The "baggy monster" text I describe results from the self-conscious rehearsal (with various degrees of success) of a stylistic range with which to express changing experiences of the world.

5. Other major Latin American writers who cut their intellectual teeth in the early twentieth-century avant-gardes include Miguel Angel Asturias, César Vallejo, Pablo Neruda, and Jorge Luis Borges.

6. Cuba declared war on Germany April 7, 1917, one day after the U.S. declaration.

7. The majority of primary texts addressed here have no published English translations; for these I provide my own title translations in parentheses. For those with English translations, the parenthetical English title is italicized or placed in quotation marks, with publication date in the Works Cited. Unless otherwise indicated, all textual translations are my own.

8. Pérez draws on Jesús Castellanos's 1910 essay "Rodó y su Proteo" (Rodó and his Proteus) that decries the new Cuban "hombre práctico," as the counterpart of the U.S. self-made man (145).

9. See my "Gender, the Culture of Work, and the Work of Culture."

10. Williams notes the use of *work* to describe intellectual activity (170).

11. Early twentieth-century tensions between formalism and socialist realism, of course, also embody debates about the work of culture vs. the work of laborers as the appropriate subject matter of art. For a penetrating analysis of such socio-aesthetic tensions manifested in the dynamic between the national and the transnational in Italian and Russian futurism, see Harsha Ram's chapter in this volume.

12. See my "Gender, the Culture of Work, and the Work of Culture."

13. In Spanish America, the term *modernismo* refers exclusively to the late nineteenth- and early twentieth-century movement that, drawing on French Parnassians and symbolists, renovated lyric language (in prose and theater as well) with a focus on technical virtuosity; *modernismo*, strongly associated with Rubén Darío, constituted the first Spanish language literary movement initiated in Spanish America and picked up in Spain. In Brazil, *modernismo* is used to designate the movements corresponding to the *vanguardias* (interwar avant-gardes) in Spanish America. For an incisive account of Spanish American *modernismo*'s articulation of modernity in the context of international modernism, see Gerard Aching's chapter in this volume.

14. Enrique Mario Santí uses this quotation as a point of departure for "Thinking Through Martí."

15. See Molina Cintra and Rodríguez Lauzurique.

16. See my *Latin American Vanguards* (Introduction) and *Performing Women* (3–9).

17. Most Latin American vanguardists experimented with multiple genres.

18. I use the term *culturalist*, coined by Appadurai, as "identity politics mobilized at the level of the nation-state" (15) but expanded to include any exclusionary performance of communal power rooted in a particular version of ethnicity.

19. European sojourners contributing to Latin America's avant-gardes included Borges, Oliverio Girondo, and Victoria Ocampo (Argentina); Oswald de Andrade (Brazil); Vicente Huidobro (Chile); Carpentier (Cuba); Asturias (Guatemala); José Carlos Mariátegui (Peru). Key interwar visitors to Latin America included Marinetti, Ortega, Lorca, Juan Ramón Jiménez; Langston Hughes; Waldo Frank; Artaud, and André Breton. Ortega's influential journal, *Revista de Occidente* disseminated innovative currents in the region, as did, beginning in 1931, the Buenos Aires journal *Sur*, founded by Ocampo. For an intricate account of the interlocking modernist projects of Ortega, Frank, and Ocampo, see Gayle Rogers's chapter in this volume.

20. Thus the Buenos Aires Martin Fierro group (1924–1927), embraced international innovation, responding simultaneously to the immigration-based shifting class and ethnic

demographics with what Beatriz Sarlo terms "urban *criollismo*" (27). In Lima, diverse artists and intellectuals converged against the reformist dictatorship of Augusto B. Leguía (1919–1930) and followed José Carlos Mariátegui's avant-garde magazine *Amauta* (1926–1930) in seeking links between international aesthetic fashions and a cultural politics of *indigenismo* that could "Peruvianize Peru." In Brazil, São Paulo's *modernistas*, particularly through Oswald de Andrade, parodically recycled Parisian and Italian vanguard primitivism and ethnographic material on the region's indigenous groups to re-imagine an "anthropophagous" Brazilian culture. In post-revolutionary Mexican cultural politics of the 1920s and early 1930s, avant-garde groups polarized: the leftist *estridentistas* advocated an experimental aesthetics of *mexicanidad*, whereas the Contemporáneos group—even when focused on Mexico—pursued a more aestheticist and ostensibly internationalist line.

21. See Chapter 3 of my *Latin American Vanguards* on the network of little magazines in the region. For a rich account of the dynamic role of little magazines in global modernist networks, see Eric Bulson's chapter in this collection.

22. Cairo provides brief bios of each *minorista*.

23. They also vowed to labor *against* political dictatorships, Yankee imperialism, and "pseudodemocracy."

24. See, for example, Kutzinkski's *Sugar's Secrets* (Chapter 5) and Masiello.

25. Acosta, whose work has received scant critical attention outside Cuba, exhibited ambivalent aesthetic affiliations. For example, in her introduction to a 2004 facsimile edition of *La zafra*, García Ronda argues that Acosta's early poetry embodied Spanish American *modernismo* in the Rubén Darío style, and that even though Acosta explicitly rejected early aesthetic vanguardism in Cuba, *La zafra* is an innovative, self-conscious work, exhibiting "unconscious" avant-garde features that became more pronounced in Acosta's subsequent poetry (16–7, 20–21).

26. The version of *¡Ecué-Yamba-O!* published in Carpentier's *Obras completas* indicates in a concluding annotation that the first version was composed in the Havana Prison in August 1927 and that the "definitive version" was completed in Paris between January and August 1931, dating that confirms the importance of Carpentier's contact with the Parisian avant-gardes, in particular the surrealists, for this and other works (poems, plays, and short stories) of the Afro-Cuban phase of his literary corpus, all published in the 1930s. See González Echevarría (121–27) on Carpentier and surrealism.

27. On *¡Écue-Yamba-Ó!*, see González-Echevarría (63–86), Janney (33–68), and Pancrazio (Chapter 4). My own earlier analyses focus on the novel's discourse of an Americanist New World (*Latin American Vanguards* 136–37, 144–45, 155–57, 165).

28. See Borge on Latin American interwar writers' ambivalent reception of Hollywood film.

29. Written in 1927, *El milagro de Anaquillé* was published in *Revista Cubana* in 1937 but not staged in Cuba until after the 1959 Revolution. See Janney on its theatrical qualities (26–32), Rae on Carpentier's Parisian collaborations in its musical history, and my *Latin American Vanguards* (61–68) on its status as an avant-garde performance manifesto.

30. Fernández de Castro also introduced Guillén to Langston Hughes in 1930. See Kutzinski's "Fearful Asymmetries" and "Yo también soy América" on connections between these poets. See Podestá on the Harlem Renaissance and Latin America's Avant-Gardes.

31. See Ellis (58, 62).

32. Carpentier, too, later broadened his novelistic attention to the Caribbean as a whole, notably in *El reino de este mundo* (1949; *The Kingdom of This World*) and *El siglo de las luces* (1962; *Explosion in the Cathedral*).

33. An earlier version of this ode was titled "A Small Ode to Kid Chocolate."

34. Although a published translation of this poem appears in my Works Cited, I use my own translations here.

35. *Jardín* was not published until 1959. In 1992, Loynaz, recognized as one of Latin America's standout women poets, received Spain's Cervantes prize, one of the most prestigious in Spanish letters. For an excellent study of *Jardín* in English, see Rodríguez; her reading and Capote Cruz's thoughtful account of the work's innovative aesthetic affiliations are kindred in spirit to my own assessment of *Jardín* as a vanguard novel.

36. The Almendares River runs through Havana.

WORKS CITED

Acosta, Agustín. *La zafra*. Havana: Minerva, 1926.

Aguilar, Luis E. "Cuba, c. 1860–c.1930." *Cuba: A Short History*. Ed. Leslie Bethell. Cambridge: Cambridge University Press, 1993. 21–56.

Alonso, Carlos. *The Burden of Modernity: The Rhetoric of Cultural Discourse in Latin America*. New York: Oxford University Press, 1998.

Appadurai, Arjun. *Modernity at Large: Cultural Dimensions of Globalization*. Minneapolis: University of Minnesota Press, 1996.

Bennett, Tony, Lawrence Grossberg, and Meaghan Morris. *New Keywords: A Revised Vocabulary of Culture and Society*. Malden: Blackwell, 2005.

Borge, Jason. *Latin American Writers and the Rise of Hollywood Cinema*. New York: Routledge, 2008.

Bourdieu, Pierre. *The Rules of Art: Genesis and Structure of the Literary Field*. Trans. Susan Emanuel. Stanford: Stanford University Press, 1992.

Bürger, Peter. *Theory of the Avant-Garde*. Trans. Michael Shaw. Minneapolis: University of Minnesota Press, 1984.

Cairo, Ana. *El grupo minorista y su tiempo*. Havana: Ciencias Sociales, 1978.

Capote Cruz, Zaída. *Contra el silencio: otra lectura de la obra de Dulce María Loynaz*. Havana: Editorial Letras Cubanas, 2005.

Carpentier, Alejo. *Obras completas de Alejo Carpentier*. Vol. 1. Mexico City: Siglo Veintiuno, 1983.

"Declaración del Grupo Minorista." *Social* (June 1927): 7.

Doyle, Laura, and Laura Winkiel. "Introduction: The Global Horizons of Modernism." *Geomodernisms: Race, Modernism, Modernity*. Bloomington: Indiana University Press, 2005. 1–14.

Ellis, Keith. *Cuba's Nicolás Guillén: Poetry and Ideology*. Toronto: University of Toronto Press, 1983.

Franco, Jean. *The Decline and Fall of the Lettered City: Latin America in the Cold War*. Cambridge: Harvard University Press, 2002.

García Canclini, Néstor. *Hybrid Cultures: Strategies for Entering and Leaving Modernity*. Trans. Christopher Chiappari. Minneapolis: University of Minnesota Press, 2005.

García Ronda, Denia. "Agustín Acosta, el poeta de *La zafra*. Introduction to *La zafra: poema de combate*. Havana: Sociedad Económica Amigos del País, 2004. 7–32.

Geist, Anthony, and José Monleón. *Modernism and Its Margins: Reinscribing Cultural Modernity from Spain and Latin America*. New York: Routledge, 1999.

González, Aníbal. *Killer Books: Writing, Violence, and Ethics in Modern Spanish American Narrative*. Austin: University of Texas Press, 2001.

———. *La novela modernista hispanoamericana*. Madrid: Gredos, 1987.

González Echevarría, Roberto. *Alejo Carpentier: The Pilgrim at Home*. Rev. ed. Austin: University of Texas Press, 1990.

Gott, Richard. *Cuba: A New History*. New Haven & London: Yale University Press, 2004.

Guillén, Nicolás. "Small Ode to a Black Cuban Boxer." *Man-Making Words: Selected Poems of Nicolás Guillén*. 2nd ed. Trans. Roberto Márquez and David McMurray. Amherst: University of Massachusetts Press, 2003. 53–54.

———. *Sóngoro Cosongo y otros poemas*. Madrid: Alianza, 1980.

Janney, Frank. *Alejo Carpentier and His Early Works*. London: Tamesis, 1981.

Kutzinski, Vera. "Fearful Asymmetries: Langston Hughes, Nicolás Guillén, and Cuba Libre." *Diacritics* 34.3 (2006): 112–140.

———. *Sugar's Secrets: Race and the Erotics of Cuban Nationalism*. Charlottesville: University of Virginia Press, 1993.

———. "'Yo también soy América': Langston Hughes Translated." *American Literary History* 18.3 (Fall 2006): 550–78.

Loveria, Carlos et al. *Fantoches 1926: edición especial*. Havana: Capitán San Luis, 1993.

Loynaz, Dulce María. *Jardín*. Barcelona: Seix Barral, 1993.

Martí, José. "Nuestra América." In *Sus mejores páginas*. By Martí. Mexico City: Porrúa, 1972. 87–93.

———. *Obras escogidas en tres tomos*. 3 vols. Havana: Ciencias Sociales, 1992.

———. "Versos Sencillos." In *Sus mejores páginas. By Martí*. Mexico City: Porrúa, 1972. 235–40.

Masiello, Francine. "Rethinking Neocolonial Esthetics: Literature, Politics, and Intellectual Community in Cuba's Revista de Avance." *Latin American Research Review* 28.2 (1993): 3–31.

Molina Cintra, Matilde and Rosa Rodríguez Lauzurique. "Juventud y valores: ¿Crisis, desorientación, Cambio?" *Revista Temas* 15 (1998): 65–73.

Ortega y Gasset, José. *The Dehumanization of Art and Other Essays on Art*. Trans. Helene Weyl. Princeton: Princeton University Press, 1968.

Pancrazio, James. *The Logic of Fetishism: Alejo Carpentier and the Cuban Tradition*. Lewisburg: Bucknell University Press, 2004.

Pérez, Louis A. Jr. *On Becoming Cuban: Identity, Nationality and Culture*. 2nd ed. Chapel Hill: University of North Carolina Press, 2008.

Podestá, Guido. "An Ethnographic Reproach to the Theory of the Avant-Garde: Modernity and Modernism in Latin America and the Harlem Renaissance." *MLN* 106.2 (1991): 395–422.

Rae, Caroline. "In Havana and Paris: The Musical Activities of Alejo Carpentier." *Music & Letters* 89.3 (2008): 373–395.

Rama, Angel. *The Lettered City*. Trans. John Chasteen. Durham: Duke University Press, 1996.

Ramos, Julio. *Divergent Modernities: Culture and Politics in Nineteenth-Century Latin America*. Trans. John D. Blanco. Durham: Duke University Press, 2001.

Rodríguez, Ileana. *House/Garden/Nation: Space, Gender, and Ethnicity in Post-Colonial Latin American Literatures by Women*. Trans. Robert Carr with the author. Durham: Duke University Press, 1994.

Rodríguez Acosta, Ofelia. "Feminismo teórico y feminismo práctico." *Bohemia* 22.2 (January 12, 1930): 9.

———. "La intelectual feminista y la feminista no intelectual." *Revista de la Habana* 1.1 (1930): 75–79.

———. *La vida manda*. 2nd ed. Madrid: Biblioteca Rubén Darío, 1930.

Rosenberg, Fernando. *The Avant-Garde and Geopolitics in Latin America*. Pittsburgh: University of Pittsburgh Press, 2006.

Santí, Enrique Mario. "Thinking Through Martí." *Re-Reading José Martí (1853–1895): One Hundred Years Later*. Ed. Julio Rodríguez Luis. Albany: State University of New York Press, 1999. 67–83.

Sarlo, Beatriz. *Una modernidad periférica: Buenos Aires 1920 y 1930*. Buenos Aires: Nueva Visión, 1988.

Stoner, K. Lynn. *From the House to the Streets: The Cuban Woman's Movement for Legal Reform, 1898–1940*. Durham: Duke University Press, 1991.

Unruh, Vicky. "Gender, the Culture of Work, and the Work of Culture: Exemplary Tales from Cuba." *Brújula* 4.1 (2005): 9–32.

———. *Latin American Vanguards: The Art of Contentious Encounters*. Berkeley: University of California Press, 1994.

———. *Performing Women and Modern Literary Culture in Latin America*. Austin: University of Texas Press, 2006.

Williams, Raymond. *Keywords: A Vocabulary of Culture and Society*. New York: Oxford University Press, 1983.

SUGGESTED READING IN ENGLISH

García Canclini, Néstor. *Hybrid Cultures: Strategies for Entering and Leaving Modernity*. Trans. Christopher Chiappari. Minneapolis: University of Minnesota Press, 2005.

Geist, Anthony, and José Monleón. *Modernism and Its Margins: Reinscribing Cultural Modernity from Spain and Latin America*. New York: Routledge, 1999.

González Echevarría, Roberto. *Alejo Carpentier: The Pilgrim at Home*. Rev. ed. Austin: University of Texas Press, 1990.

Masiello, Francine. "Rethinking Neocolonial Esthetics: Literature, Politics, and Intellectual Community in Cuba's Revista de Avance." *Latin American Research Review* 28.2 (1993): 3–31.

Rosenberg, Fernando. *The Avant-Garde and Geopolitics in Latin America*. Pittsburgh: University of Pittsburgh Press, 2006.

Unruh, Vicky. *Latin American Vanguards: The Art of Contentious Encounters*. Berkeley: University of California Press, 1994.

CHAPTER 15

....

QUEER INTERNATIONALISM AND MODERN VIETNAMESE AESTHETICS

....

BEN TRAN

In 1928 Pierre Do-Dinh, a young Indochinese emigrant living in Paris, wrote to André Gide, asking for permission to translate *La Porte étroite* [*Strait Is the Gate*] into Vietnamese. To justify his request, the aspiring translator made the following observations about the literature of colonial Annam, which consisted of the three eastern regions of French Indochina that today make up the nation of Vietnam:

> As you know, Annam is a French colony. Of all the countries in the Far East, it is most influenced by French culture. It is not rare to hear people speak of Victor Hugo or of Lamartine with great seriousness and precision [. . .]. But contemporary literature, I would not go so far as to specify modern literature, is completely ignored.
>
> We are belated. Do our contemporary writers have little chance of success? Are we impermeable to modern thought? I do not believe so. I believe, to the contrary, that insofar as it [modern thought] is preoccupied with the mystery of interiority, which reverberates in the anxieties and darkness of our subconscious, it is even nearer to us. ("Pierre Do-dinh à André Gide" 93)[1]

For Do-Dinh, the contemporaneous formations of modern Vietnamese literature and French literature appear disjointed and asynchronous. It is Vietnam's presumed belatedness that compels him to contact Gide in hope of translating his work. Later in 1939 Do-Dinh compared modern Vietnamese literature's belatedness to Homais, the philistine pharmacist from Flaubert's *Madame Bovary*. When introducing Vietnamese literature to a Western audience, he writes, "That from the West which appeals to the Annamite is the philosophy of Monsieur Homais and all the inferior, pretentious forms of Western life" (Do-Dinh, "Les Conditions véritable d'un accord" 41). Do-Dinh's reference to Homais likens the cultural transmission between metropole and colony to that between city and province. In Flaubert's novel, ideas of art, fashion, love, and science flow from the urban center to the provincial outskirts, where they are received by unfit imitators like Homais. Thrown into sharp relief by the rigor of Flaubert's style, Homais, the pharmacist who cobbles together scientific information from unreliable journals and pamphlets, derives his ambitions as a reader and writer from dilettantish intellectualism. Convinced of Vietnam's cultural lag and the necessity for "modern thought," Do-Dinh completed and published his translation of Gide, who during the mid-1930s was emerging as one of the most influential contemporary French authors in colonial Vietnam.[2]

Do-Dinh's observations and speculations regarding Gide's significance in Vietnam raise a number of fundamental questions. How is the relevance of a modernist French writer of Gide's stature in Vietnam to be explained and characterized? Given the emergence of Vietnam's modern literature under French colonial rule, what are the literary forms and discourses that take shape as a consequence of modernity and modernism's cross-cultural transmission? Why did the contemporaneous formations of modern Vietnamese literature and French literature appear disjointed and asynchronous? Unlike Do-Dinh, the present discussion of Vietnam as a site of global modernism does not attempt to explain or correct the supposed shortsightedness of modern Vietnamese writers by taking French literature as the new, twentieth-century standard. Nor do I intend to appropriate modern Vietnamese literature to the paradigmatic category of European modernism. Colonial Vietnamese intellectuals' engagement with Gide exceeds Do-Dinh's prescribed belatedness. Indeed, Gide's significance for Vietnamese writers had more to do with the literary politics that stemmed from his idiosyncratic convergence of left-wing activism and sexual politics than his modernist forms, style, or narrative techniques.[3] Modern Vietnamese authors defined themselves in modern terms, yet critics do not understand this literature as "modernism" [chủ nghĩa hiện đại], but rather as either chủ nghĩa lãng mạn [romanticism] or chủ nghĩa tả chân [realism]. Vietnamese romanticism's concerns with subjective expression and Vietnamese realism's engagement with and representation of "the people" made the politicized aesthetics that Gide championed during the 1930s of deep and abiding interest. By looking at the connection that developed between André Gide and colonial Vietnam, I want to shift the coordinates of modern Vietnamese literature toward socialism and Marxism's internationalist tenets, the Art for Life's Sake versus the Art for Art's Sake debate, the emergence of a national literature, and the politics of sexuality.

Gide's influence on Vietnam was profoundly felt during the Nghệ thuật vị nghệ thuật [Art for Art's Sake] versus Nghệ thuật vị nhân sinh [Art for Life's Sake] debate, which, lasting from 1935 to 1939, was one of Vietnam's most significant literary exchanges during the interwar period. Readers of Anglo-European modernism will be familiar with how the debate played out on the continent.[4] In Vietnam, however, it turned out differently: both sides appropriated Gide's ideas of individual and national particularity, which, as will be discussed later, derive from his politics of homosexuality. The debate's interlocutors interrogated modern Vietnamese literature's purpose, as well as its content and form, while engaging with post–World War I literary discourses about the relationship between art and social reality, particularly their manifestations in Soviet cultural politics and the Comintern's shift toward the Popular Front strategy.[5]

Due to Vietnam's colonial relationship with France, Soviet cultural and aesthetic thought was first channeled through "French sensibilities and concerns" before reaching Annam (Hue-Tam Ho Tai 64). For Vietnamese intellectuals, Gide was the most significant mediator of Soviet cultural aesthetics' circuitous route through Paris. He proposed a literary system based on particularity as a viable means of reaching "internationalism," and it was this model that appealed to Vietnamese critics and writers. Gide's conception of an international literary system underscored a nation's self-constitution, sovereignty, and interdependence with other nations, rather than the transcendence of the particular that is central to models of modernism's transnational circulation, as well as paradigms of world literature.[6] Frantz Fanon has suggested the significance of national particularity in relationship to internationalism: "It is at the heart of national consciousness that international consciousness establishes itself and thrives" (180). Likewise, modern Vietnamese writers aimed to reach an international universality through national particularity.

By examining Vietnamese intellectuals' reception of Gide and his articulation of national particularity, I want to revisit the question of engagement and influence between European modernists and colonial writers. Scholars of modernism have examined particularity in its various iterations for three main purposes: to distinguish vernacular and "minor" modernisms from high modernism; to consider the dialogue between local specificity and cosmopolitan modernism; and to contextualize modernist texts within their varied local, socio-historical conditions of literary production.[7] Such studies have effectively argued for marginalized modernisms and their fraught, if not antagonistic, relationships with the canonized modernism of Western Europe and America. In contrast, I want to emphasize the political and aesthetic stakes of modern Vietnamese literature—its anticipation of a new reading public and its relationship to a national readership. In the same way that Fanon addressed his views on national and international consciousness directly to the Algerian people taking part in anti-colonial struggle, modern Vietnamese literature addressed an audience situated, temporally and geographically, within the immediate contexts of colonial modernity, rather than—as is often assumed when the scope of today's literary fields expand globally—a cosmopolitan, non-national reader.[8]

To be sure, as I discuss modern Vietnamese literature's national address and national particularity, I am not in agreement with nationalistic movements or nation-states that imperiously assert homogenous identities. Rather, I want to emphasize the historical contexts of nationalism after World War I: nationalism's dialectical relationship with communist internationalism, its conditions of anti-colonial struggle, and its transformation of cultural forms.[9] The cultural politics of

Vietnam's national literature was not an end in and of itself, but rather a means to integrate into an international community. Vietnamese thinkers followed the Comintern's attempts to unify revolutionary parties around the world—a vision that provided a dialectical model for synthesizing local politics within a globally defined situation. Beyond communism's critique of objective material conditions, the radical openness afforded by Gide's proposed interpellation of nonnormative sexuality, nonnormative particularity appealed to Vietnamese intellectuals, as they grappled with the inequalities and unevenness of colonial modernity.

Gide's Particularity

At the 1935 International Writers' Congress for the Defense of Culture, Gide argued for the particularity of the nation and of the individual.[10] Serving as co-chairman, Gide opened the meeting by rejecting fascism's suffocating grip on culture:

> There are, for people as for individuals, certain indices of particular refractions, and this is precisely the great interest of our cosmopolitan meeting: it allows us to understand the different aspects of these dangers, different ways of comprehending and confronting them. It is necessary to begin from this point: the culture that we aspire to defend is the sum of the particular cultures of each nation. This culture is our common good. It is common to all of us. It is international. (84)

Gide argued for the enunciation of the particularity of different cultures and individuals, rather than a subordination of the particularistic perspective, what Gide called *désindividualisation*, to the interest of the masses. In his "Défense de la culture" speech to the International Congress, Gide reiterated his rallying cry for the "triumph of the general in the particular, of the human in the individual" (86). Envisioned as a system premised on the "refractions" of different cultures as well as individuals, Gide's international model was intended to counteract fascism's agenda of national supremacy, imperial aggression, and aesthetic censorship. According to Gide, national and individual particularity would flourish, respectively, under a system of internationalism and communism. Particularity and social collectivity mutually define each other: "For my part, I claim to be strongly internationalist while remaining intensely French. In like manner, I am a fervent individualist, though I am in full agreement with the communist outlook, and am actually helped in my individualism by communism" (85). For Gide, the free development and articulation of the individual can only be realized by the free development and articulation of all.

Gide went on to suggest that human universality is mediated through the literary aesthetics of the particular. He invoked individualism and nationalism together as if the shared attribute of particularity canceled out their differences. To substantiate these claims, the French author declared, "What could be more *particularly* Spanish than Cervantes, what more English than Shakespeare, more

Russian than Gogol, more French than Rabelais or Voltaire—at the same time what could be more general and more profoundly human." These exemplary authors managed to reach a level of human universality by particularizing their own personal individuality and capturing the specificity of their respective national cultures ("Défense de la culture" 86). Here, the most forceful literary expression of individual particularity is seen as congruent with national identity, which, in turn, transcends to a level of universality. Gide's insistence on the specificity and sincerity of individual expression meant that he repudiated most of nineteenth-century French literature, which he deemed artificial, decadent, bourgeois, and, ultimately, devoid of social significance.

Calling for an engaged cultural aesthetics, Gide wanted the literary author to be in perfect union with the masses and fully committed to a new reading public: "The only remaining possibility is to write for the unknown reader of the future." Not only is the author to communicate with the new reader, but also to help this unknown, future reader "form and project himself." For literature to accomplish this communion—as was, supposedly, the case in the Soviet Union—the writer must effectively address and engage with the reading public, creating a new, more inclusive community. With the division between high and low, elite and popular cultures dissolved, literature would then take on new social meaning as it fosters a radically new society. The aesthetics of the particular gains the political power of emancipation as it disrupts and reconstitutes the established social body.

ART FOR VIETNAM'S SAKE

All of the issues taken up by Gide—the relevance of literary tradition, the social role of a contemporary author, and a new reading public—were of immediate concern for modern Vietnamese writers and intellectuals confronted with the uncertain future of colonial modernity and the ruptures of Vietnam's intellectual traditions. The French administration's educational and linguistic policies, particularly the promotion of *quốc ngữ* (romanized Vietnamese script)[11] and the French language, displaced the inveterate character-based writing systems of classical Chinese and *Nôm* (ideographic, demotic Vietnamese script) (see Osborne, DeFrancis).[12] By 1918, French opposition to the Chinese language manifested in official policies that rooted out the traditional civil service exam system based on the study of Confucian classics, a system that dates back to the eleventh century.[13] In the 1930s, the knowledge of those trained as mandarins became anachronistic, with the subsequent emergence of a new class of readers and writers for whom their fathers' texts were becoming obsolete. Vietnam's postwar generation began to embrace the romanized alphabet as a viable means toward modernization and to explore the potentialities of modern society—with both optimism and skepticism.

An explosion of *quốc ngữ* print culture during the late 1920s and 1930s, coupled with mass literacy movements, established *quốc ngữ* as Vietnam's primary written medium. A new generation of writers began publishing in the romanized alphabet, while an unprecedented reading public, which included nonelite classes and women, emerged. These were not only the agents and consumers of booming print capitalism, but of a national literature. Enforced by the French as a preventive measure against anticolonialism, *quốc ngữ* took on an antonymous significance, doubling back as the vehicle to negotiate and overcome French colonialism. This burgeoning development reverted *quốc ngữ* writing back to its etymological roots of "national script" or "national language."

Within this cultural and intellectual milieu, the participants of Vietnam's art-versus-life debate argued over the direction and purpose of modern Vietnamese literature, drawing Gide into the fray. Attentive to his call for individual and national particularity, they echoed Gide's reconceptualized literary aesthetics concerning the destabilization of established hierarchies of aesthetic subject and forms, the address to and transformation of the masses, and the formation of a new collective ethos through individual expression. Thiếu Sơn, Hoài Thanh, and Lưu Trọng Lư were the main proponents of the *duy tâm chủ nghĩa* [idealist] position, while Hải Triều was the most impassioned voice of the *duy vật chủ nghĩa* [materialist] camp.

One of the earliest critics to advocate for a Western-influenced literature, Thiếu Sơn initiated the art-versus-life debate when he published an article entitled "Hai quan niệm về văn học" [Two Literary Perspectives] and sided with Art for Art's Sake. Thiếu Sơn outlined Vietnamese literature's two paradigms: the first belonged to the previous generation of classical moralists who, still mired in Confucianism, doggedly viewed literature as a vehicle for didacticism and social obedience, while the second emphasized and celebrated authorial creativity and self-expression. He identified the former literary perspective as "Eastern" and the latter as "Western." Thiếu Sơn claimed that within the Confucian framework literature had the primary purpose of cultivating a compliant subject in Vietnamese society's hierarchical structures. If, Thiếu Sơn feared, such use of literature carried over to the 1930s, a period when nationalist and socialist political parties were gaining traction, then ideological paradigms would function as blinders for writers and readers. For Thiếu Sơn, social or political proselytization through literature subordinated aesthetic form to political considerations while continuing Confucianism's authoritative use of literature. The most effective way to break from the instrumental use of literature was to develop an aesthetics derived from creative imagination and personal expression.

Thiếu Sơn's proposed aesthetics challenge Confucianism's accepted ideological truths and frameworks to allow for an individual's liberation and self-realization. According to Thiếu Sơn, literature had the capacity to incite the sensibilities and conscience of ethically autonomous individuals, making way for a renewed social community and ultimately a renewed nation. Confucian heterodoxy had become outdated in a modernizing world, and a turn toward creative imagination and personal expression was necessary if Vietnamese literature was to "rise" to the level of other national literatures: "Given the rules of evolution, Vietnamese literature will develop like the literatures of other nations" ("Hai quan niệm về văn học" 109). Implicit in Thiếu Sơn's critique of Confucianism is an attack on French colonial cultural policies, which sought to stabilize Vietnamese society by buttressing its inveterate Confucian culture. The aesthetic experience then is independent of any ideological system, and art's social purpose and meaning are contingent upon this autonomy and its role in the formation of individual subjects for a "more beautiful, more dignified world" ("Nghệ thuật với đời người" 114).

In an immediate response, Hải Triều, one of the most ardent Marxist critics of the time, dismissed Thiếu Sơn's dichotomy of East and West. He refuted the claim that only Eastern literature was socially engaged and pragmatic. It was not a matter of East or West for Hải Triều; it was literature's engagement with social reality, an engagement epitomized by realist fiction. Hải Triều defined art as a product of social life and as a means for social reform. To make his point, Hải Triều provided a myriad of examples, including Dickens, Dostoevsky, Kuo Mo-jo, Maxim Gorky, the older Tolstoy, and Upton Sinclair. With a bellicose tone, Hải Triều accused Thiếu Sơn of identifying subjective expression as art's sole purpose and telos, while himself proclaiming the opposite: that art's natural trajectory worked toward social progress. He went so far as to announce the death of "impressionism, neoimpressionism, futurism, cubism, etc.," associating these movements with capitalism, which would, he predicted, come to an end in the twentieth century ("Nghệ thuật vị nghệ thuật hay nghệ thuật vị nhân sinh" 261).[14] Dismissive of avant-garde movements, Hải Triều advocated for an aesthetic movement grounded in realism—a more pragmatic medium for social critique and reform. If Vietnamese literature was to develop in a meaningful way, then it had to thematize objective, material conditions in order to awaken and mobilize the masses. Otherwise, Hải Triều warned, authorial self-expression would result in saccharine, effeminate romance or psychological novels.

Hải Triều's stand against Thiếu Sơn established the debate's polar extremes: art as a pure and transcendental exercise versus art as a social and political practice. However, Hải Triều's critique of Thiếu Sơn's aestheticism obscured the latter's wish to overthrow the hierarchies endemic to the Confucian literary paradigm. Thiếu Sơn was concerned with replacing the thesis-driven *văn có ích* [pragmatic literature] with the more prosaic *văn chơi* [literature of leisure] ("Hai quan niệm về văn học" 108). He wanted to democratize literature, to break down the barriers that separated the class of *quân tử* [scholarly gentry] from the *tiểu nhân* [commoners], who were all in service of the intellectual elites: "Because of that hierarchy, our past literature is a kind of cruel literature, a kind of privileged literature, with no pretensions of addressing the life, the situation, or the spirit of the common people" ("Văn học bình dân" 114). Thiếu Sơn's advocacy for an aesthetics based on self-realization was an attempt to liberate authors from ideological confines and differences so that they could engage with the masses and form a community premised upon a more universal conception of humanity, rather than political or intellectual allegiances. Both Thiếu Sơn and Hải Triều agreed on the need to address wider reading audiences, but they were at odds about the type of literature that would most effectively do so:

either a literature that emphasized individual expression and self-realization, or a literature that represented and addressed the social masses.

Literary critic Hoài Thanh, famous for his writings on the significance of individualism in modern Vietnamese literature, stepped in to reconcile the divide by arguing for the relationship between individualism and the social masses. He did so by excerpting Gide's "Défense de la culture" speech, delivered at the 1935 International Writers' Congress: "It is in being the most particular that each person most effectively serves a community" (cited in "Văn chương là văn chương" 33). Moreover, Hoài Thanh underscored and explained Gide's understanding of the compatibility between individualism and communism:

> Gide expresses his complete commitment to individualism. Individualism does not contradict communism, but rather individualism needs communism in order to reach complete fruition. The more an individual develops his character the more the collective benefits, Gide claims. The same is true for each national culture: the more each enunciates its distinctiveness, the more mankind benefits. ("Một bài diễn văn tối quan trọng về văn hóa" 84)

By introducing Gide into the debate, Hoài Thanh provided a reference point that was relevant to Thiếu Sơn's concerns for subjective expression as well as Hải Triều's demand for literature's political engagement.

For their main textual example, the interlocutors of Vietnam's art-versus-life debate focused on a popular 1935 collection of short stories, *Kép Tư Bền* [Tư Bền the Actor] by Nguyễn Công Hoan, a prolific writer of realist, and later socialist realist, short stories and novels. *Tư Bền the Actor* depicts a range of characters and social situations that reflect the rapid, often disorienting changes of modernity: educated or fashionable women who do not conform to familial expectations, the dual realities of the lower classes and urban elites, the estranged filial piety between the nouveau riche and their parents. Hoài Thanh attributed the success of *Tư Bền the Actor* to the "estranged style that Nguyễn Công Hoan meticulously worked into plots of nothing" ("Văn chương là văn chương" 25). He argued that *Tư Bền the Actor*'s aestheticized style, as a formal element, takes precedence over the stories' realistic content. Accordingly Nguyễn Công Hoan's privileging of style, rather than attending to the political urgencies of the time, produced eternal aesthetic qualities.

In a direct rebuttal to Hoài Thanh, Hải Triều proclaimed Nguyễn Công Hoan's collection of short stories to be one of the earliest manifestations of the Art for Life's Sake movement in Vietnam, praising the author as a writer not only of the people, but also of the "wretched" [khốn nạn] ("*Kép Tư Bền*" 268–69, 273). The critic favored the representation of characters toiling in the decrepit underside of urban, colonial life—from rickshaw pullers to petty thieves. According to Hải Triều, the stories provide an accurate cross-section of Vietnamese society, exposing the inequalities of everyday situations. Hải Triều considered the collection to be at the forefront of Vietnamese realism ("Nghệ thuật và sự sinh hoạt xã hội" 288). According to Hải Triều, aesthetic merit derives from Nguyễn Công Hoan's subject matter and content, that is, from his representation of the lower classes and thus his engagement with the reading public. Hải Triều explained the value and power of such art: "The sentiments of art do not derive from any one individual, but precisely from the synthesis of social sentiments. When an artist presents any sentiment onto a piece of paper or a stone . . . there is the intention for each person in society to see and to feel" ("Nghệ thuật và sự sinh hoạt xã hội" 305).[15] Influenced by Nikolai Bukharin's and Tolstoy's aesthetic ideas, Hải Triều viewed literature as an effective means to "socialize sentiments" or to "emotionally infect" readers ("Nghệ thuật và sự sinh hoạt xã hội" 304). According to Hải Triều, Nguyễn Công Hoan had created a literature in which content derived from and engaged with the social. Hải Triều also stressed that this type of realist literature was part of the Art for Life's Sake movement then gaining momentum worldwide, in part through its broad appeal to the masses ("*Kép Tư Bền*" 272–73).

Evident in his praise of *Tư Bền the Actor*, Hải Triều wanted literature to aspire to universal and equal representation. This ideological and aesthetic position was the seed of his future advocacy for socialist realism; however, his later views of literature were strikingly less inclusive and more orthodox—calling for literature to focus strictly on the working class. In his discussions of critical and socialist realism, Hải Triều specified the type of characters that should populate realist works:

> In discussions of social or popular literature there is only mention of beggars, orphans, rickshaw pullers, thieves, or prostitutes. There is no representation, no observation, no mention of the most important class, the class that is most exploited now, the class that will lay the foundation for a new society, namely, the working class. ("*Lầm Than*" 59)

In saying so, Hải Triều contradicts himself. The character types that Hải Triều dismisses in favor of the working class are precisely those that populate Nguyễn Công Hoan's *Tư Bền the Actor*—the very characters that he had lauded when arguing for realist literature as the appropriate medium for Art for Life's Sake.[16] Hải Triều initially praised *Tư Bền the Actor* for its representation of the "wretched"—not its representation of the working class.[17] In this respect, Hải Triều first qualified *Tư Bền the Actor* as a pioneering work of Art for Life's Sake for its democratic representation of social characters. Hải Triều's ordination of Nguyễn Công Hoan's *Tư Bền the Actor* as one of the inaugural moments of Vietnam's Art for Life's Sake movement precedes the stringent guidelines of socialist realism that would become dominant in the late 1930s and ultimately gain state sanction after the August Revolution of 1945. In his discussions of *Tư Bền the Actor*, Hải Triều's exaltation of the egalitarian and objective approach to social types had yet to submit to Vietnamese socialist realism's moralistic tendencies, which would come to denounce the vagrancy and trickeries, for instance, of prostitutes or thieves, no less regard them as heroic.

Hải Triều's initial interest in literature's democratic possibilities, as opposed to a magnified focus on the working class, is evident in one of the debate's slight, but consistent undercurrents: allusions to the law of equivalence in Flaubert's aesthetics. Hải Triều's reference to Flaubert is a decontextualized misreading that favors democratization of literary content over class politics. Unlike Do-Dinh's use of Homais to convey a sense of belatedness, Hải Triều cites Flaubert to argue that art and social life should constitute each other: "I believe in Form and Content . . . two entities that would not exist without the other" (cited in "Nghệ thuật và sự sinh hoạt xã hội" 292–93n).[18] Although the quote supports Hải Triều's claim that content and form are interdependent, the line's context, an ongoing correspondence with George Sand, suggests the opposite. Flaubert had declared to Sand his aesthetic credo to pursue beauty above all else.[19] With some similarities to Hải Triều, Sand encouraged Flaubert to "maintain [his] worship of form, but be more concerned with content" and to instill his readers with a sense of morality through ethically "good" literary characters (519). Hải Triều mistook Flaubert's aesthetics, suggesting that the author's focus on social content determined his literary form. On the contrary, Flaubert's *suprême impartialité*, to borrow Sand's term, sought to nullify the opposition between form and content through his writing style. Flaubert was indifferent to content, and thus stylized and aestheticized all content under a law of democracy and equivalence.[20]

When discussing *Tư Bền the Actor,* Hoài Thanh ascribed to Nguyễn Công Hoan Flaubert's ambitions to aestheticize everything and thus to write about nothing.[21] Hoài Thanh exalted Nguyễn Công Hoan's prioritization of an "estranged" style and its entwinement with "plots of nothing" ("Văn chương là văn chương" 25). Meanwhile, to punctuate his call for the pure aesthetic experience disconnected from any pragmatic function, Thiếu Sơn quoted Flaubert, emphasizing the author's principle of pure art: "Occasionally, I sense a spiritual state that transcends reality" (cited in "Nghệ thuật và đời người" 112). The quote corroborates Thiếu Sơn's opening argument that an author is omniscient yet transcendent in his work, not imparting personal ideologies or predilections.[22] In Flaubert, Thiếu Sơn found the epitome of an authorial, transcendent self-expression that provides the absolute sensation of an aesthetic experience, when art "skillfully allows for readers to see as if looking, to hear as if listening" ("Nghệ thuật và đời người" 112). For Thiếu Sơn and Hải Triều, Flaubert's allure was his *suprême impartialité*—his indifference to, respectively, ideological biases and content. The political impetus of equality translates into the literary democratization of subject matter, form, and readership.

THE CODED POLITICS OF HOMOSEXUALITY

Central to the art-versus-life debate, these egalitarian approaches to subject matter, as well as arguments for an author's personal writing style, hinged upon an unspoken queerness—both in Gide's political agenda and Nguyễn Công Hoan's collection of short stories. Gide's homosexuality was an open secret in Vietnam at the time, and the politics of particularity that made Gide relevant for these Vietnamese thinkers derived from the politics of this unspoken queerness. Consider, for example, writings on Gide by Hoài Thanh and the poet Lưu Trọng Lư. Hoài Thanh discusses Gide's homosexuality obliquely. He comments on Gide's "desire" [*lòng ham muốn*], while emphasizing the French author's physical attributes and tics to suggest a natural yet repressed, sexual energy. Gide is a person of "strength" [*khỏe mạnh*], "restless energy" [*bứt rứt khó chịu*], with the "inclinations to run and jump" [*ưa chạy nhảy*]; such a person is bound to feel hemmed in by confining "walls" [*bức tường*] ("Một bài diễn văn tối quan trọng về văn hóa" 89). Further employing coded language, Hoài Thanh claims that Gide committed to the communist party less out of political conviction than the desire to liberate himself from "his aristocratic inclinations, the inclinations that have since betrayed his natural self. His inclinations toward the people offer a new world, an infinite amount of resources still untouched by literature" ("Một bài diễn văn tối quan trọng về văn hóa" 91).

Lưu Trọng Lư also drifts into coded language about sexuality, while defending Gide's about-face and critical writings against the Soviet Union—found in Gide's *Retour de l'URSS* [Return from the USSR] and *Retouches au retour de l'URSS* [After-thoughts on the USSR]—in a 1939 essay, "Con đường riêng của trí-thức" [An Intellectual's Own Path]. The Vietnamese lyricist describes Gide's personal path as "alternative" and "discreet" [*một cách khác, lặng lẽ*] (433, 432). According to Lưu Trọng Lư, Gide is an intellectual who aimed for the realization of the "truth" [*sự thực*] and "potential from within" [*sức tiềm-tàng ở trong mình*]. Lưu Trọng Lư explains Gide's allegiance to communism more as a commitment to "humanity" [*lòng nhân đạo*] than as a narrowly ideological stance. In order to understand the efficacy of Gide's communism, Lưu Trọng Lư continues, "we must take off all the yokes: the yoke of the past, of the present, of prejudices, of rules, of ideologies, to have people return to their natural character" ("Con đường riêng của trí thức" 435).

Hoài Thanh and Lưu Trọng Lư's recognition of personal expression as political thought and action dovetails with Michael Lucey's observations on Gide's relationship to the Soviet Union: "Not that the expression of sexuality is the expression of some truth. Rather, it is the quality of interruption that marks Gide's writing of sexuality, often the interruption of an ideology that passes for truth, an interruption that refuses truths about sexuality, that offers perhaps unattainable politics of sexuality 'itself' as a possibly curious, radical openness" (216). Both Hoài Thanh and Lưu Trọng Lư sensed the sexual politics behind Gide's communist activism: the act of articulating, in Lưu Trọng Lư phrase, one's "natural character"—that is, one's sexuality—offered liberating political possibilities.

In "Nhân tình tôi" [My Love], a story from the collection *Tư Bền the Actor*, Nguyễn Công Hoan relates individual literary enunciation to the development of a national literature—specifically through the possibility of a homoerotic relationship between a reader and writer. Trần Văn Căn, the first-person narrator and protagonist of "My Love," is an aspiring writer who, educated in the Franco-Vietnamese system, writes in the romanized alphabet and has a particular interest in *quốc văn* [national literature]. Căn's dedication and interest in the national literature, developed within the realm of the romanized alphabet and print, starkly contrast with his father's career as a mandarin. As the protagonist attempts to contribute to a national litera-ture, he also seeks to fulfill his personal desires. Căn begins to write to female colum-nists, hoping to flirt with and possibly seduce one of them. Kim Chi, a newspaper columnist discussing gender equality, catches the protagonist's attention, and he begins to correspond with her by posing as a fellow woman columnist. He signs his articles "Minh Châu, Female Author." From their correspondence, Căn falls for Kim Chi. Soon he pens personal letters to her and eventually reveals his male identity. They begin to plan face-to-face meetings. But Kim Chi never appears at the prede-termined times and places. Still persistent in his efforts to meet Kim Chi, Căn then writes a romantic comedy for the stage and asks Kim Chi to play a leading role with him. The play is never realized, yet Kim Chi boldly writes a letter to invite Căn to visit her house while her family is away in the country. When Căn arrives, the house is dark, and Kim Chi is concealing her face.

Kim Chi speaks in furtive whispers, as if concealing something about herself. But Căn proudly declares that he has keen ears and can clearly understand the mumbling. Kim Chi says that she is hard of hearing, and so Căn offers to switch ears with her. Kim Chi, however, refuses a simple exchange and requests the ears as a gift. Căn complies and tells Kim Chi to go ahead and cut off his ears, which the protagonist deems as insignificant: "So you want me to 'sú-vơ-nia' my ears for you? I thought there would be something else since ears belong to the era of obedience" (Nguyễn 119). ("Sú-vơ-nia" is a transliteration of the French term *souvenir*, used here to mean "to give as a keepsake.") After trading flirtatious whispers and gestures, Kim Chi reveals herself to be a man. The unmasked Kim Chi raises a glimmering knife and says, "Here's a knife, please 'sú-vơ-nia' your ears for me" (Nguyễn 121). Hinting at castration, Kim Chi's line, the story's penultimate, takes literally Căn's suggestion that ears are no longer relevant, once their literary and epistolary correspondence has reached its culmination.

The sociocultural context of modern Vietnam's literary production also serves as the story's backdrop: the shift away from the literary figure of the mandarin, new social relations premised on individual sentiment and desire, and above all new gender roles and relations in modernizing Vietnam. The fluidity of sexual identity in the story is a result of print culture's revolutionary developments, namely the possibility of including women both as writers and readers. This is evident at an extra-diegetic level, through the narrator's male voice, and within the story's plot. Nguyễn Công Hoan initially published the story in *An Nam tạp chí* [Annam Journal] under the nom de plume "Hà Thành—nữ sĩ" [Hà Thành—female author]. The male narrator addresses an implied male audience through his vocative call, *các ngài* [your Excellencies]; however, the assumed homosocial relationship between nar-rator and reader is undermined by a plot that pivots around a female readership and concludes with a scene of homoeroticism. The story's protagonist encroaches upon the cultural sphere of, as it is called in the story, *nữ văn giới* [women's literature]. Căn tries to initiate a heterosexual relationship by forging a feminine writing per-sona and homosocial bond. Yet his attempts to veil male desire for a female object turn out to be the desire between two men.

The anxieties of the transition from the male literary world of mandarins to the inchoate realm of *nữ văn giới* plays out through the story's suggestive castration, when the two characters flirtatiously consider cutting off their ears. The lovers' first attempt to share with each other, to trade their sensual experiences, quickly turns into a suggestion of violent deformation. These men of modern letters, who must pose as female writers and readers to adapt to the evolving literary market, ultimately propose physical mutilation of each other. Although the men take on the role of female writers and imply female readers, their agency and legerdemain reflect a troubling historical paradox specific to modern Vietnam: a literary market orienting itself to women readers, yet still lacking female literary writers. Meanwhile, the perversely violent relationship also suggests the homosocial and homoerotic bonds implicit in the haunting revenant of Vietnam's literary tradition.

The story's aural theme also signals the material development of print culture, as well as the sphere of privacy provided by reading. Căn's aesthetic and personal interests depend upon the development of *quốc ngữ* newspapers as a public forum. The story juxtaposes the privacy of the written word against the public performance of theater, which proved to be ineffective during Căn's courtship of Kim Chi. When Kim Chi jokingly suggests that Căn cut off his ears as a gift for her, the protagonist dismisses the relevance of ears as anachronistic. Căn equates them with Confucian instruction and conformity, claiming the uselessness of ears. Unlike the aural channels of direct, face-to-face communication, the private world of print makes possible the characters' expression and pursuit of personal desire, and within print culture individual sentiments and relationships between readers and writers are as revealing as they are unexpected.[23] Căn's aims of fulfilling his personal desire are inextricably tied to his interests in *quốc văn*—or the national literature. The romanized alphabet, the medium for the national literature, and print culture, the forum for the national literature, are also the medium and forum employed by the protagonist. In Nguyễn Công Hoan's "My Love," as in Gide's notion of particularity, the enunciation and revelation of sexual desire through personal, literary expression allow for both individual and national particularity, while radically reconfiguring the community of readers.

CONCLUSION

André Gide's relevance to Vietnamese critics resides in the synthesis of his sexual politics, communist leaning, and the subsequent vision of a literature *engagé*. The unspoken queerness—the paradigm of sexual particularity—at the heart of Gide's politicized aesthetics not only reflected modern Vietnam's shifting sexual and gender roles, inextricably tied as they were to the practices of writing and reading and the material development of print, but it also served as the paradigm to address and examine the relationship between art and social reality. For the idealists, the politics of sexuality led to the articulation of individual desire that destabilized the established social order, while fostering new social relationships. For the materialists,

Gide's politicized aesthetics allowed for the literary representation and legitimization of social types previously unacknowledged. As a site of modernism, Vietnam was a contentious locale within the international circuit of Art for Life's Sake versus Art for Art's Sake. The debate, however, over literature's function and value was never about the autonomy of art, but how literature would affect, address, and shape the reading masses, specifically a national reading audience.

NOTES

1. All translations are mine, unless noted otherwise.

2. For a survey of Gide's presence in modern Vietnamese literature, see Lộc Phương Thủy.

3. This is not to say that Gide's homoerotic sensibilities did not inform his modernist techniques, such as stylistic indirection and fragmentation, but that Vietnamese writers were invested, primarily, in Gide's expressed literary politics and, secondarily, his literary practice.

4. Vietnam's art-versus-life debate, for instance, runs parallel with Bloch and Lukács's heated discussion over Expressionism. Both of these exchanges had the 1935 International Writers' Congress for the Defense of Culture as their backdrop. In both cases, it is realism, as a "coherent, infinitely mediated totality" (Bloch 22), that is set against the subjectivity of idealism. There are, of course, multiple deviations. For one, whereas the German case was a dispute between realism and modernism (see Bloch and Lukács), the Vietnamese debate was a division between realism and romanticism. As I am attempting to demonstrate in this essay, one of the most distinctive differences in the Vietnamese exchange was the influence of Gide's sexual politics.

5. See Brennan for a suggestive, intellectual history of how the Comintern's dissemination of Marxist ideas sought to level out the differences between Europe and its colonies, effectively altering the cultural politics and intellectual activism internationally, during the interwar period.

6. Pheng Cheah has discussed the nuances and differences among Goethe, Kant, and Marx's conceptualization of a "world literature." According to Cheah, Goethe perceives world literature as a process of translation and literary exchanges that move beyond national borders; Kant's *Third Critique* argues for the constitution of sociability through the communication, universally, of one's inmost self; and Marx understood world literature as an "epiphenomenon" of the global forces of capitalist production. What the three thinkers, however, hold in common—the belief in world literature's transcendence of local conditions—differs from Gide's international model premised on particularity. Cheah writes, "Like Kant and Goethe, Marx uses the word *world* to describe the transcendence of particular local and national barriers and limitations" (32; original emphasis). Also see Cheah's discussion of particularity and universality in "Universal Areas: Asian Studies in a World of Motion." Here, he insightfully argues that a "concrete universal is constitutively open to being affected by *other particulars* and, hence, by alterity and particularity in general. This radical openness to alterity and particularity is a type of finitude that cannot be transcended" (64; original emphasis).

7. See, for example, Baker, Gikandi, Kronfeld, Parry, Shih, Davis, and Jenkins.

8. In "Reading with One Eye, Speaking with One Tongue," Allan has argued for the necessary distinction between an addressed national audience and an assumed cosmopolitan readership: "For all of the important questions these various studies [of world literature] raise, they all tend to skirt the full potential of the non-national reader or, perhaps more precisely, the reader who is not addressed explicitly by a literary work. More important, however, this reader is at the heart of what gets termed world literature—that most delicate field within which reading and addressing never quite align" (3). Though pertaining to world literature, Allan's observations apply to the field of modernist studies as it expands its scope globally.

9. Lloyd has argued for a more nuanced understanding and contextualization of nationalistic movements as anticolonial struggles spurred by the common experience of domination, rather than, from our current "singular narrative of modernity," as the manipulation of the masses or a resurgence of atavistic, premodern political organization that is divisive and homogenizing.

10. With the tide of fascism rising in Germany and Italy, 230 delegates from 38 different countries gathered in Paris to reevaluate the purposes of cultural aesthetics and literature. Foreshadowing the formation of the Popular Front (which was officially proclaimed three weeks after the International Writers' Congress), the organizers of the congress invited writers of various leftist perspectives—communists and noncommunist leftists, radicals and moderates—from E. M. Forster to Bertolt Brecht to Louis Aragon. For English versions of Gide's speech, see Gide, "The Individual." For accounts of the conference, see Christina Stead, Shattuck, Hilden and Reiss, and Cowley.

11. *Quốc ngữ* was first employed as a mode of transcription by Catholic missionaries in the seventeenth century: *quốc ngữ* continued to be employed and diffused in the educational missions of the Catholic Church until it was implemented as an official written language by the French governing body (Milton 162–63).

12. For an account of Vietnam's multilayered linguistic history and how it was shaped by French colonization, see DeFrancis.

13. This decision capped off a series of policies that stemmed from French suspicion of the traditional exam system and of Chinese characters' incommensurability with the transmission of modern knowledge. In 1878, the French colonial government declared that as of 1882 *quốc ngữ* and French were to be the official written languages of Vietnam. In the years leading up to the First World War, French administrators had to suppress increasing anticolonial activities and the accompanying circulation of anti-French writings, most of which were composed in Chinese. Moreover, the revolutionary and modern ideas of European thinkers like Darwin, Diderot, Kant, Montesquieu, and Rousseau had been translated into Chinese. During World War I, these concerns were exacerbated by Germany's production of anti-French propaganda in Chinese and distribution of the material south of the Sino-Vietnamese border.

14. Hải Triều's insistence on realism anticipates Lukács's dismissal of avant-garde and modernist movements in his 1938 debate with Bloch on Expressionism. Lukács specifically attacked Expressionism's path toward Fascism, its irrational mythology and subjectivity, "abstract pacifism," "bourgeois qualities," and "escapist quality" (19). With Hải Triều's words as precedent, the attacks in Vietnam against "subjective" aesthetics persisted through the revolution against French colonialism, the two Indochinese Wars, and up until the 1986 *perestroika*, when the government opened the country to foreign capital investment. This literary history resulted from state-sponsored Marxist criticism and its attempts to legitimate a cultural history that justified communist insurgency while condemning bourgeois sensibilities.

15. Hải Triều's anti-individualism here is part of an attack on writers, particularly *Tự lực văn đoàn* [the Self-Strength Literary Group], which he labeled as *lãng mạn* [romanticist].

He claims that these works, unlike realism, were myopically focused on self-centered protagonists seeking amorous relationships.

16. For example, a prostitute tricks a rickshaw puller into helping her solicit customers by delaying payment in "Ngựa người, người ngựa" [Human Horse, Horse Human]. In "Thằng ăn cắp" [Thief], a beggar steals from a food vendor and is beaten by a street mob. A fatherless child remembers his father as his mother sleeps with another man in "Nỗi vui sướng của thằng bé khốn nạn" [The Comforts of a Wretched Child].

17. Literary realism in Vietnam burgeoned during the rise of the Popular Front in France and its loosened censorship policies. However, this does not completely explain the rapid emergence of Vietnamese realism. The significance of Vietnamese realism, I argue, originates from a democratic approach to subject matter that is in itself revolutionary, but often presupposed.

18. For the original letter, see Flaubert, "À George Sand," March 10, 1876.

19. See Flaubert, "À George Sand," December 31, 1875.

20. In a discussion of Flaubert's aesthetics, Rancière elucidates the "law of democracy, the law of universal equivalence" that underpins Hải Triều's and Thiếu Sơn's references to Flaubert. Rancière writes about Flaubert's aesthetics: "There is no border separating poetic matters from prosaic matters, no border between what belongs to the poetical realm of noble action and what belongs to the territory of prosaic life. This statement is not a personal conviction. It is the principle that constitutes literature as such. Flaubert underlines it as the principle of pure Art; pure Art has it that Art owes no dignity to its subject matters" ("Why Emma Bovary Had to Be Killed" 237).

21. Flaubert wrote to Louise Colet, "What seems beautiful to me, what I should like to write, is a book about nothing, a book dependent on nothing external, which would be held together by the internal strength of its style." See Flaubert, "À Louise Colet."

22. As Flaubert stated, "In my ideals of art, I believe that an author should not reveal any of this [convictions, anger, indignations], that an artist not appear in his work more than God in nature." See Flaubert, "À George Sand," December 31, 1875.

23. The fact that the short story is one of the primary literary genres at the crux of Vietnam's art-versus-life debate indicates print culture's significance in the formation of social relations and communities that previously had not existed. The short story's compact form and accessible prose made it the preferred literary genre for editors, authors, and readers of a burgeoning literary field that had been restructured and reoriented by print capitalism. Modern Vietnamese novels, most of which were published during the 1930s, first appeared serially as short fiction in magazines and journals. The specific cases of *Tư Bền the Actor* attest to the success of short fiction printed in journals and magazines. Before printing stories in book form under the title *Tư Bền the Actor*, the publishing house *Tân Dân* ran the stories individually in its journals *Tiểu thuyết thứ bảy* (Saturday Novel) and *Phổ thông bán nguyệt san* (Monthly Bulletin).

WORKS CITED

Allan, Michael. "Reading with One Eye, Speaking with One Tongue: On the Problem of Address in World Literature." *Comparative Literature Studies* 44 (2007): 1–19.

Baker, Houston. *Modernism and the Harlem Renaissance*. Chicago: University of Chicago Press, 1987.

Bloch, Ernst. "Discussing Expressionism." 1938. Trans. Rodney Livingstone. *Aesthetics and Politics*. Ed. Ronald Taylor. London: Verso, 2002. 16–27.

Brennan, Timothy. "Postcolonial Studies Between the European Wars." *Marxism, Modernity and Postcolonial Studies*. Ed. Crystal Bartolovich and Neil Lazarus. Cambridge: Cambridge University Press, 2002. 185–203.

Cheah, Pheng. "What Is a World? On World Literature as a World-Making Activity." *Dædulus* 137.3 (2008): 26–38.

———. "Universal Areas: Asian Studies in a World of Motion." *The Postcolonial and the Global*. Ed. Ravathi Khishnaswarmy and John C. Hawley. Minneapolis: University of Minnesota Press, 2008. 54–68.

Cowley, Malcolm. *The Dreams of the Golden Mountains*. New York: Penguin Books, 1992. 280–93.

Davis, Alex, and Lee M. Jenkins. Introduction. "Locating Modernisms: An Overview." *Locations of Literary Modernism*. Ed. Alex Davis and Jenkins. Cambridge: Cambridge University Press, 2000. 3–29.

DeFrancis, John. *Colonialism and Language Policy in Viet Nam*. The Hague: Mouton, 1977.

Do-Dinh, Pierre. "Les Conditions véritable d'un accord." *L'Homme de couleur*. Ed. S. E. le Cardinal Verdier. Paris: Librarie Plon, 1939. 34–48.

———. "Pierre Do-dinh à André Gide. 4 August 1928. Letter I of "Correspondance inédite avec André Gide." *Question colonial et écriture: actes du colloque organisé par le RIASEM à Nice*. Ed. Guy Degas. Poitiers: Torii, 1994. 93–94.

Fanon, Frantz. *The Wretched of the Earth*. 1963. Trans. Richard Philcox. New York: Grove Press, 2004.

Flaubert, Gustave. "À Louise Colet." 16 January 1852. *Correspondance*. Ed. Jean Bruneau. Vol. 2. Paris: Gallimard, 1973. 31.

———. "À George Sand." 31 December 1875. *Correspondance*. Ed. Jean Bruneau. Vol. 4. Paris: Gallimard, 1973. 999–1001.

———. "À George Sand." 10 March 1876. *Correspondance*. Ed. Jean Bruneau. Vol. 5. Paris: Gallimard, 1973. 25–27.

Gide, André. "Allocution d'ouverture." *Littérature engagée*. Ed. Yvonne Davet. Paris: Gallimard, 1950. 83–84.

———. "Défense de la culture." *Littérature engagée*. Ed. Yvonne Davet. Paris: Gallimard, 1950. 85–96.

———. "The Individual." *The Left Review* 1.11 (1935): 447–52.

Gikandi, Simon. *Writing in Limbo: Modernism and Caribbean Literature*. Ithaca: Cornell University Press, 1992.

Hải Triều. "*Kép Tư Bền*, Một tác phẩm thuộc về cái triều lưu 'Nghệ thuật vị dân sinh' ở nước ta" [*Tư Bền the Actor*, a Literary Work for 'Art for Life's Sake' in Our Country]. 1935. *Tòan Tập* [Collected Works]. Vol. 1. Hanoi: Văn học, 1996. 2 vols. 268–74.

———. "*Lầm Than*: Một tác phẩm đầu tiên của nên văn tả thực xã hội ở nước ta" [*Misery*: An Initial Work of Socialist Realism in Our Country]. 1938. *Về văn học nghệ thuật*. Hanoi: Văn Học, 1969. 57–61.

———. "Nghệ thuật vị nghệ thuật hay nghệ thuật vị nhân sinh" [Art for Art's Sake or Art for Life's Sake]. *Tòan Tập* [Collected Works]. 1935. Vol. 1. Hanoi: Văn học, 1996. 2 vols. 252–67.

———. "Nghệ thuật và sự sinh hoạt xã hội" [Art and Social Life]. T*òan Tập* [Collected Works]. 1935. Vol. 1. Hanoi: Văn học, 1996. 2 vols. 287–306.

Hilden, Patricia, and Timothy Reiss. "Discourse, Politics, and the Temptations of Enlightenment: Paris 1935." *Annals of Scholarship* 8.1 (1991): 61–78.

Hoài Thanh. "Một bài diễn văn tối quan trọng về văn hóa" [A Crucial Expression on
    Literature]. *Văn chương và hành động* [Literature and Action]. 1935. Hanoi: Hội nhà
    văn, 1999. 65–97.

———. "Văn chương là văn chương" [Literature Is Literature]. *Bình luận văn chương*. Ed.
    Nguyễn Ngọc Thiện and Từ Sơn. 1935. Hanoi: Giáo dục, 1998. 23–35.

Kelly, Gail Paradise. *French Colonial Education: Essays on Vietnam and West Africa*. Ed.
    David H. Kelly. New York: AMS Press, 2000.

Kronfeld, Chana. *On the Margins of Modernism: Decentering Literary Dynamics*. Berkeley:
    University of California Press, 1996.

Lloyd, David. "Nationalisms Against the State." *Gender and Colonialism*. Ed. Timothy
    P. Foley. Galway: Galway University Press, 1995. 256–81.

Lộc Phương Thủy. "André Gide ở Việt Nam: Một vài nhận xét bước đầu" [André Gide in
    Vietnam: Some Initial Observations]. *André Gide: Đời văn và tác phẩm*. Ed. Lộc
    Phương Thủy. Hanoi: Khao học xã hội, 2002. 77–108.

Lucey, Michael. *Gide's Bent*. New York: Oxford University Press, 1995.

Lukács, Georg. "Realism in the Balance." 1938. Trans. Rodney Livingstone. *Aesthetics and
    Politics*. Ed. Ronald Taylor. London: Verso, 2002. 29–59.

Lưu Trọng Lư. "Con đường riêng của trí thức" [An Intellectual's Own Path]. *André Gide:
    Đời văn và tác phẩm*. Ed. Lộc Phương Thủy. 1939. Hanoi: Khao học xã hội, 2002.
    429–40.

Nguyễn Công Hoan. "Nhân Tình Tôi." *Toàn tập*. Ed. Lê Minh. 1929. Vol. 1. Hanoi: Văn
    Học, 2003. 4 vols. 107–21.

Osborne, Milton. *The French Presence in Cochinchina and Cambodia: Rule and Response*.
    Ithaca: Cornell University Press, 1969.

Parry, Amie Elizabeth. *Interventions into Modernist Culture*. Durham: Duke University
    Press, 2007.

Rancière, Jacques. "Why Emma Bovary Had to Be Killed." *Critical Inquiry* 34.2 (2008):
    233–48.

Sand, George. Letter to Gustave Flaubert, 15 January 1876, *Gustave Flaubert-George Sand
    Correspondance*. Ed. Alphonse Jacobs. Paris: Flammarion, 1981. 519.

Shattuck, Roger. *The Innocent Eye*. New York: Farrar, Straus Giroux, 1984.

Shih, Shu-Mei. *The Lure of the Modern: Writing Modernism in Semicolonial China,
    1917–1937*. Berkeley: University of California Press, 2001.

Stead, Christina. "The Writers Take Sides," *The Left Review* 1.11 (1935): 453–62.

Tai, Hue-Tam Ho. "Literature for the People: From Soviet Policies to Vietnamese Polemics."
    Borrowings and Adaptations in Vietnamese Culture. Ed. Truong Buu Lam. Honolulu:
    Center for Asian and Pacific Studies, 1987. 63–83.

Thiếu Sơn. "Hai quan niệm về văn học" [Two Literary Perspectives]. *13 Năm tran luận văn
    học* [13 Years of Literary Debates]. Ed. Thanh Lãng. 1935. Vol. 1. Ho Chi Minh City: Hội
    nghiên cứu và giảng dạy văn học, 1995. 3 vols. 105–09.

———. "Nghệ thuật với đời người" [Art and Human Life]. *13 Năm tran luận văn học* [13
    Years of Literary Debates]. Ed. Thanh Lãng. 1935. Vol. 1. Ho Chi Minh City: Hội
    nghiên cứu và giảng dạy văn học, 1995. 3 vols. 109–14.

———. "Văn học bình dân" [Popular Literature]. *13 Năm tran luận văn học* [13 Years of
    Literary Debates]. Ed. Thanh Lãng. 1935. Vol. 1. Ho Chi Minh City: Hội nghiên cứu và
    giảng dạy văn học, 1995. 3 vols. 114–18.

PART VI

FORMS OF SOCIALITY

CHAPTER 16

COSMOPOLITANISM AND MODERNISM

JANET LYON

AT the outset of Jean Rhys' first novel, *Quartet*, a rootless English chorus girl reflects on her delightful but "haphazard" existence in Paris, where she lives in a Montmartre hotel with her Polish husband, a backstreet "*commissionaire*" of art (8, 17).[1] From its very first pages, the novel has all the markings of a modernist cosmopolitan narrative: the deracinated Marya and the "alien" Stephan drifting through Paris, foreign languages in the streets, and artists' studios and international cafés everywhere; even Marya's shabby little hotel is called the Hôtel de l'Univers. But the novel tells an unexpectedly brutal story about Marya's increasing isolation, sexual entrapment, and spiritual persecution in the world's most cosmopolitan city. *Quartet* is, in fact, a perfectly anti-cosmopolitan novel, though not in the conventional sense. Where most of the anti-cosmopolitan critiques over the past two centuries have argued from positions of nationalism, or nativism, or anti-imperialism, or sexual or racial conservatism, each in their way seeing cosmopolitanism as a corrosive force, Rhys' novel faults cosmopolitanism for failing to materialize. What should be the setting for cosmopolitan world-making—rootlessness in Paris—turns out to support the worst kinds of parochialisms and the most conservative forms of personal coercion. *Quartet* dramatizes the failure of cosmopolitan promises, even as those promises remain unarticulated and only obliquely suggested within the pages of the novel. In its critique of a cosmopolitan sense of belonging that should, but does not, happen, *Quartet* resembles many other modernist works which invoke cosmopolitanism as a set of fragile and evasive normative ideals.

Readers of this volume are undoubtedly aware of the role that the concept of cosmopolitanism plays in a range of discussions involving globalization, transnationalism, indigenization, localism, parochialism, nationalism, universalism, and, of course, modernism. In the past two decades, new scholarship on cosmopolitanism has appeared in multiple disciplines, including anthropology, philosophy, political science, sociology, and literary studies, to name only the most prominent fields; and this new work has informed and invigorated modernist studies, particularly as the field has sought to address an ever broader range of global cultural production. Late nineteenth- and twentieth-century incarnations of cosmopolitanism share with modernism many of the same conditions of possibility, including accelerated globalization and burgeoning world market systems, imperial crises and the falling dominoes of decolonization, and new networks of mass media and mass transportation, all of which, in various combinations, contributed to expanded zones and concentrated experiences of intercultural contact. Indeed the coextensive concerns of modernism and cosmopolitanism are such that one might suppose modernism always to be informed by the cosmopolitan, even if, as in the example of *Quartet*, it rarely conveys a viable picture of cosmopolitanism.

In what follows, I will lay out in a general way some of the main features of cosmopolitanism, and some of the discussions generated by its perceived promises and failures. This will take me in several directions, both historically and theoretically, but my particular interest lies in the way that ideas about and expectations for cosmopolitanism are transmitted through global modernist literary culture. My ultimate aim here is not one of epistemological closure: I am not seeking to define or even to descry a particular form of cosmopolitanism suited to one or another theory of modernism, global or otherwise. Rather, I am guided by more pragmatic questions of genealogy: that is, what kind of cultural work is done by the idea of cosmopolitanism as it appears in the literature, art, and aesthetic theories of modernism? How do the questions posed in the cosmopolitanism debates of the past few centuries inflect, or determine, or belie the putative worldliness of modernism? What are we to make, for example, of the "virtual cosmopolitanism" described by Partha Mitter in his account of the exchange between painters from Berlin and Calcutta in the 1920s? Or the loaded expectations for interracial cosmopolitanism in novels like *Autobiography of an Ex-Colored Man* or *Infants of the Spring*? Or the disastrous undercutting of the political stakes of cosmopolitanism in Christopher Isherwood's *Goodbye to Berlin*, or Kazuo Ishiguro's screenplay about Shanghai in the 1930s, *The White Countess*? How should we read Georg Simmel's prewar cosmopolitan sociology in the light of the crises of postwar nationalism (to say nothing of anti-Semitism) across Europe? And what role does cosmopolitanism play in the complicated emergence of decolonizing literatures in the early twentieth century in countries like Ireland and Venezuela and India? These heuristic questions about forms of belonging (and unbelonging) will help to direct me through the congested territory of cosmopolitanism.

COSMOPOLITANISMS, OLD AND NEW

To begin with, the term is notoriously overdetermined. "Cosmopolitanism" may designate an individual's attitude or a set of practices in the world: a cultivated stance of detachment from one's culture of origin, for example, or, more positively, a stance of active interest in, engagement with, and belonging to "parts of the world other than one's nation" (Robbins, "Comparative Cosmopolitanisms," 250), or a practice of unconditional receptivity to cultural others; or an active repudiation of parochialism, or a rejection of the restrictive bonds of the *patrias*. These stances of detachment and antiparochialism may be connected to principles of universal fellow-feeling; such were the putative foundations of Stoic and early Christian cosmopolitanism, particularly as it was elaborated by the likes of Cicero and Marcus Aurelius. But they may also reflect a less altruistic or more instrumentalist agenda, one of personal political detachment in the service of personal gain or individualist nonconformity: Diogenes, the first to proclaim himself a "citizen of the world," seems largely to have meant that he personally rejected the constricting claims of local conventions and political allegiances.[2]

"Cosmopolitan" may also describe the products or spaces of contact among cultures or cultural representatives, which would be characterized by mutual, palpable, interactive, frictional forms of change where such contact has occurred. This use of the term carries a strong geographical inflection: metropoles, maritime communities, colonial and decolonized regions, international cities, universities, bohemian quarters, migratory crossroads, trade routes, and other zones of sustained intercultural contact are typically adduced as the sites where "actually existing" cosmopolitanism may be found. Discussions of this kind of cosmopolitanism frequently address the "where" and the "what" of cosmopolitanism, as it were—the situated negotiations of cultural differences in mixed communities, for example, or the local effects of globalizing economies, or the adaptive shifts in aesthetics and values accompanying sustained intercultural exposure.

Often enough, these discussions of cosmopolitan conditions are grounded in another more foundational understanding of the concept. This third category of cosmopolitanism is normative in scope. It designates a planetary philosophical or political project based in the recognition of humanity as a universal community, a project that aims to hold governments and institutions to nonnegotiable standards for economic equality, social justice, and the "right to have rights," in Hannah Arendt's phrase.

As the range of these uses suggests, the concept is malleable, speculative, subject to revision and cooptation, and vulnerable to all kinds of criticism for its explicit universalism or its implicit moralism, or for the threat it poses to "defensive" nationalism, inherited traditions, and other forms of cultural solidarity that could serve as bulwarks against global expansionism, or for its foundational faith in rationalism and progress, or for its record of elitism, its historical orientation to the global north, its uncritical presumptions about mobility, its potential for complicity with capitalism and imperialism, and so forth. According to one representative critical position, for example, the detached "view from nowhere" claimed by nineteenth-century antiparochial cosmopolites was actually "a view from somewhere and from sometime, namely from the European Enlightenment of the eighteenth century"; on this view, cosmopolitanism is nothing more than "a higher form of parochialism," a false universalism mistaking itself for a picture of the world (Van der Veer 47).

Defenders of cosmopolitanism, meanwhile, point to the role that the concept historically has played in the propagation of intellectual and religious freedom, in the protection or acceptance of marginalized or persecuted populations (particularly "rootless"—that is to say, nonnational—Jews, homosexuals, and women), and in international efforts to stem the brutal effects of radical nationalism and imperialism. In recent decades, many of these defenses have been couched as modifications of the term, as evidenced in the latest round of pitched discussions about cosmopolitanism.[3] As has been the case with so many other putative universalisms (including universalism itself), these recent lexical qualifications are aimed chiefly at toning down the universal and foregrounding the local, or at undoing hierarchies of center and periphery. Thus "cosmopolitanism" has been modified by such terms as rooted, situated, discrepant, vernacular, critical, postcolonial, agonistic, and limited. Some of these modifications involve complicated schematic revisions. Walter Mignolo, for instance, distinguishes between cosmopolitanism and "global designs," and then between "cosmopolitan projects" and "critical cosmopolitanism"—the last of which he champions for the fact that it "comprises projects located in the exteriority [of modernity] and issuing forth from the colonial difference" (159). With proliferating qualifications like these, some proponents of a normative cosmopolitan ideal worry that the concept has been watered down to a pleasant tonic of cultural celebration, or that it may be facing extinction altogether. But it may in fact be the case that the sheer energy spent on finding ways to reframe cosmopolitanism references a widespread attempt to "add more theory" (in Kant's words) to a putatively workable theory that hasn't yet worked out in practice" ("On the Old Saw" 42). In other words, the concept of cosmopolitanism, however warty or incomplete, may be indispensable to global thinking.

Kant discusses his commitment to the "duty" of theory in "On the Old Saw, 'That may be right in theory but it won't work in practice,'" an occasional essay in which he revisits the subject of cosmopolitanism (as he does in other more famous short pieces, including "Perpetual Peace" and "Idea for a Universal History with a Cosmopolitan Purpose"). The view expressed in "On the Old Saw" that human nature nowhere appears "less lovable than in the relations of whole nations to each other" is crucial to the urgency with which Kant links principles of justice to world citizenship and international law ("On the Old Saw" 80). It also points to his persistent pessimism about the selfishness and aggression that inhere in human nature and which must therefore be harnessed, through law, into a "cosmopolitan condition" of mutual assistance and security.[4] Indeed, in the third and final article of "Perpetual Peace," which holds that "The Law of World Citizenship Shall Be Limited to Conditions of Universal Hospitality," Kant elevates the duty of protecting the stranger's right to hospitality from a religious ethos into a responsibility of nations, which must be enforced by international law ("Perpetual Peace" 47). This business of international law, Kant acknowledges, is tricky, even "wild and fanciful" ("Universal History" 47)—who, after all, is going to formulate it or enforce it? But his commitment to a cosmopolitan model stems from his faith in theory: so long as the theory of cosmopolitanism "proceeds from the principle of justice," its potential results are more important than the doxa that says it will never work ("On the Old Saw" 81).

Derrida also repudiates this doxa of common sense in one of his own meditations on cosmopolitanism, in which he casts cosmopolitanism as at once impossible and utterly necessary. Derrida is thinking in particular of the need for cosmopolitan cities of refuge—cities where the stateless will and must be welcomed unconditionally—in a world where statelessness is, for millions of people, the condition of what Agamben has made familiar to us as *homo sacer*: bare life without political status. And indeed, a version of this concern runs through much of the new thinking about the paradoxes of cosmopolitanism: on the one hand, cosmopolitan theory offers a justification of the unconditional hospitality that a city of refuge signifies; on the other hand, cosmopolitan hospitality must be "controlled by the law and the state police" (Derrida 22). Another way to put this conundrum is to say that the freedom and equality promised by Kantian cosmopolitan theory are in practice tethered to the dubious regulatory mechanisms of bureaucratic modernity.[5]

Philosophical forms of cosmopolitanism deriving from Kant (sometimes called "old" cosmopolitanism) usually depend upon two things: a universalist assumption of a constitutive human quality—be it reason, or a natural sociability shared by humanity, or the human capacity for a consecrated spirit—and an implicit (indeed, originary) scenario of divided loyalties between local attachments and global ideals, in which the global inevitably wins out. And while there are many contemporary thinkers who embrace both of these components and aim to work through the theoretical and practical challenges they present—most notably and most powerfully, Martha Nussbaum (e.g., "Patriotism and Cosmopolitanism")—there are at least as many who wish to distance themselves from this cosmopolitanism's normative universalism (e.g., its unfailing belief in the common denominator of a particular kind of reason), or from its diminishment of local/national cultures, or who worry—seriously—about the feasibility of institutional implementations of cosmopolitan ideals.

A recent exchange between Seyla Benhabib and Bonnie Honig may illustrate these stakes. In *Another Cosmopolitanism*, Benhabib calls cosmopolitanism "a philosophical project of mediations" and identifies her own Habermasian cosmopolitanism as a normative philosophy based in "a universalist moral standpoint" that is upheld through communicative ethics and entails a moral obligation to justify one's actions through reason "in a moral conversation which potentially includes all of *humanity*" (19; 18).[6] But the very idea of this "conversation" requires that it be displaced and abstracted into a system of institutional channels that in the end may have very little to do with the actual fate of individuals on the earth. According to Honig, this system cannot really be trusted, given the "sedimentations of power and discretion that accrete in such institutional contexts" (117). The problem, for Honig, is not so much Benhabib's recourse to a moral standpoint—after all, most people who are looking to revise cosmopolitanism do so because they have some investment in questions of right and wrong. Rather, the problem is Benhabib's implicit faith in the juridical administration of cosmopolitan ideals. Honig's corrective concept, which she calls "agonistic cosmopolitics," includes but also "reaches beyond" institutional safeguards and imagines improvised, on-the-ground interventions into contemporary human rights crises, such as the designation of cities of refuge and the development of "underground railroads devoted to the remainders of the state system" (117–18). Believe in the old cosmopolitanism, Honig suggests, but cover your bets with the new.

Honig's agonistic cosmopolitics counts as one of the "new" cosmopolitanisms which, generally speaking, aim to rescue a program of ethical commitment to global others from the taint it acquired through its association with nineteenth- and twentieth-century Euro-U.S. expansionism. Other species of the new cosmopolitanism insist on a perspective that is precisely not Euro-U.S., such as Mignolo's critical cosmopolitanism mentioned above, or, famously, James Clifford's "discrepant cosmopolitanisms," formulated as a kind of theoretical retraction of his own earlier condemnation of cosmopolitanism. Moving away from a conventional understanding of the term "cosmopolitan" as a narrow descriptor of a class of people who have "the security and privilege to move about in relatively unconstrained ways," Clifford's newer version focuses on populations whose global movements are more likely the result of the "displacement and transplantation" undertaken by all kinds of people under all kinds of conditions, and as a result of "specific, often violent, histories of economic, political, and cultural interactions" (108; 107; 108).[7]

As we shall see, Clifford's neologism and others like it have been taken up by modernist critics who find in such terms a way to begin accounting for global modernisms flourishing beyond the temporal and spatial boundaries of the (one might say provincial) Anglo-European model. But before pursuing these more recent critical developments, and perhaps by way of providing some historical contextualization, I want to mention an aspect of nineteenth-century European thinking about worldliness that bears directly on twentieth-century fantasies of cosmopolitanism: that is, the question of racial identity and the perceived threat of deracination that haunts many developmental accounts of "civilization."[8]

The Threat and the Promise: Race and Nation

With the early development of sociological inquiry and the concomitant rise of the so-called race sciences in the first third of the nineteenth century, questions about the mixing of populations dovetailed with concerns about cosmopolitanism's effects on national cultures. Auguste Comte, often called the father of sociology, believed that human progress depended upon the "progressive condensation of our species" (282), by which he meant the intensification of populations in geographical zones. Comte's goals for humanity were normative and positivist in the extreme: he advocated for a new class of social scientist (i.e., the sociologist), whose job it would be to review all of the sciences and "reduce their respective principles to the smallest number of general principles" (79); these principles could then be used to understand, predict, and ultimately control human nature through a kind of homogenization of shared moral principles.[9] The forms of integration and concentration taking place in "the great centers of population," he argued, would facilitate this control and thereby create a "new means not only of progress but of order, by neutralizing physical inequalities and affording a growing ascendancy to those intellectual and moral forces that are suppressed among a scanty population" (283). The desired end of *Cours de Philosophie Positive* [1830–1842] is a kind of monoculture arising not from a global technoculture or international capitalism (as Marx would have it), but rather from the ministrations of a "general mind" (73) and the gradual restriction of "individual divergences" (283), leading finally to a model of moral conformity that harmonizes the greater good.[10] On this reading, the human species will progress by way of the effacement of racial/local/individual traits; concentration and commingling in cities (of the kind characterizing cosmopolitan culture in general) will lead to a civilization flourishing through standardization and order; and for Comte, there is no progress without order.

But it is precisely the fear of such human standardization that motivates at least some of the race theory produced in the generation following Comte. Most famously—or infamously—Arthur de Gobineau's "Essay on the Inequality of the Human Races" [1853–1855] bemoans the fall of pure civilizations, which occurs when "the primordial race-unit is so broken up and swamped by the influx of foreign elements, that its effective qualities have no longer a sufficient freedom of action" (59). Gobineau isn't just talking about the fatal "crossing of blood" (62) in his melancholic narrative of human decline, although his main premise is that there are distinct human races that are ontologically unequal and hierarchical, and therefore subject to destruction through dilution. He's also talking about the permeability of national cultures: those nations with the most "vitality" (61) are also the least permeable and therefore the least cosmopolitan. To take one of Gobineau's more striking examples: he argues that the "Hindu race" has retained its integrity in spite of the long British occupation because India "keeps its soul erect and its thoughts apart" from the English. The English, by contrast, because they are too malleable, "are themselves influenced in many ways by the local civilization, and cannot succeed in stamping their ideas" on their Indian subjects (68).[11] But eventually all civilizations will fall, in Gobineau's scenario; they will do so because of the constitutional weaknesses produced by the cosmopolitan instinct: "when the majority of citizens have mixed blood flowing in their veins, they erect into a universal and absolute truth what is only true for themselves, and feel it to be their duty to assert that all men are equal" (70). This belief in equality will lead to the final, pathetic "age of unity" (172) characterized by "mediocrity in all fields," where "[n]ations, or rather human herds . . . will thenceforth live benumbed in their nullity, like the buffalo grazing in the stagnant waters of the Pontine marshes" (173). Enervated human buffalo on the one side, Comtean homogeneity and "perfection" on the other: these are the imagined extremes of intercultural mixing in the age of modernity.

By the turn into the twentieth century, the challenges posed by cosmopolitanism to national cultures take on especial urgency in those countries where colonialism or other forms of capitalist expansionism have threatened to efface local aesthetics and undercut inherited traditions to the point where cosmopolitan assimilation (whether economic, social, religious, or aesthetic) is all but assured. This would be an "imperializing cosmopolitanism" (29), as Pheng Cheah calls it, against which "decolonizing nationalism" (28) pits itself. Cheah's detailed discussion of the fluctuating relations between different forms of nationalism and cosmopolitanism in Asia (including their mutually supportive roles in certain instantiations of socialism) is also relevant to many of the cultures of decolonization in the early twentieth century.[12] The increasingly testy critique by Irish nationalists of the literary revival of 1890–1922 (deemed by some to be a product of Anglo-Irish opportunism), for example, entailed a form of anti-cosmopolitanism operating alongside an ethnocentric particularism focused on religion and language as signs of national essence. Similarly, certain strands of the nationalist movement in Scotland viewed cosmopolitanism and British rule as coextensive entities. But within these and many other decolonizing movements, cosmopolitanism provided a liberatory set of ideals, if not practices, for those national subjects whom nationalism itself deemed deviant or unworthy of inclusion in the body politic.

A particularly compelling case in point is elaborated in Camilla Fojas's study of South American *fin de siécle* cosmopolitanisms, which offers a superb account of the entangled freedoms and constraints in what she calls "cosmopolitanism from the margins" (5). Although the concept of cosmopolitanism was, for many Latin Americans, merely a cipher for European decadence and self-regard, some self-described cosmopolitan writers and poets, mostly congregating in cities like Caracas and Buenos Aires, saw their own work as part of an experimental arena in which new national identities could take shape. Especially for queer *modernistas* trying to write their way out of the trifecta of invasive U.S. imperialism, decayed Spanish colonialism, and heteronormative nativism, cosmopolitanism offered a way of living in and through modern culture while remaining somewhat apart from its disciplinary structures. But, as Fojas shows, cosmopolitanism always performed

vastly different kinds of work for different demographics. To take one of her examples: the editors of *Cosmópolis: Revista Universal* brought out their journal in 1894
with the aim of creating a modern Venezuelan literature that would be in conversation not only with Venezuelan intellectuals, and not only with a Pan-American
readership, but also implicitly with European cosmopolitan cultures in cities like
Paris and Madrid. "We think that Venezuela needs periodicals of this kind," wrote
one editor, "in order to show other countries that we have a youth that writes with
ideas, trends, steeped in all types of literature, and with the full knowledge of all the
recent developments in the arts and sciences" (105). But the cosmopolitan-national-
ist aims of the journal were troubled in several respects. In the first place, most
cosmopolitan efforts were viewed with suspicion by nativists who associated it with
European dandyism (and therefore an imported effeminate homosexuality), and in
spite of the *Cosmópolis* collective's deliberate discursive performance of a machismo
nationalism, it was nevertheless stigmatized by the habitual critical conflation of
cosmopolitanism and decadent femininity.[13] The irony here is that in its efforts to
conform to the implicitly homophobic and sexist expectations of the new Venezuelan nationalism, *Cosmópolis* practiced seemingly uncosmopolitan forms of homo-
phobia and misogyny. And at the same time (to deepen the irony and broaden the
circle), the very idea of a Latin American cosmopolitanism was treated with "contemptuous racism" by some artistic players in Europe: Paul Bourget, for one, viewed
non-European cosmopolitanism as "invalid and inorganic" (16) and very nearly an
oxymoron; the only "true" cosmopolitan, according to Bourget, was the pure
Frenchman. Nevertheless, as Fojas shows, the cosmopolitan cities of Latin America,
and especially Buenos Aires, became something like cities of refuge for certain
modernistas. There homosexual communities could form, women could act as their
own agents, and the free exchange of new ideas and experimental aesthetics could
flourish beyond the suffocating parochial constraints of traditional, conservative
values.

By casting parochialism in the role of conservative gatekeeper, I don't mean to
suggest that the vernacular values and inherited traditions typically associated with
parochialism are immanently reactionary or categorically oppressive; indeed it is
worth remembering in this regard that the synonymous words "parochialism" and
"provincialism" were always terms used by centers of power (particularly British) to
denote peripheries of diminished value and subordinate status. Thus the "parochial"
is the parish located far from the institutional seat of religious power; "provincial" is
the university that isn't Oxbridge; the colonies on the fringes are the "provinces."
Nevertheless, the parochialism against which cosmopolitanism is often set entails in
some cases a deadly form of coercion. Ifeome Kiddoe Nwankwo has demonstrated
recently the degree to which parochialism was seamlessly articulated to all sorts of
racialist agendas in the Americas. Nwankwo argues that in the nineteenth and
twentieth centuries, many writers of African descent deliberately identified themselves as citizens of the black world, a world accessible mainly through a literary
cosmopolitan vision of connectedness across continents and national boundaries.
From the perspective of this global blackness, the institutional power of U.S. slavery

depended particularly upon an enforced parochialism that endeavored to make the very idea of a black cosmopolitan world unthinkable to both blacks and whites. Charles L. Briggs, approaching race and cosmopolitanism from a different angle, points out that such an ideological parochialism may be wielded as a "purified" (90) vernacular—one that, because it contains no trace of its own historical complexity, may be opposed to a similarly purified or falsely simplified model of cosmopolitanism. He argues that W. E. B. Du Bois' lifelong cosmopolitan project was based in an understanding of racism as a kind of enforced provincialism that fostered "group imprisonment within a group," so that "the wider aspects of national life and human existence" were all but invisible to members of that racial group (91). To foster cosmopolitanism, on this reading, is to disrupt the centripetal forces of racism. And yet, to judge from James Weldon Johnson's powerful account of those forces in his anonymous novel, *The Autobiography of an Ex-Colored Man* (1912), cosmopolitanism is irrelevant to (or impotent in the face of) the racism that literally constitutes white America. Johnson's protagonist may float through Europe learning languages and cultivating international tastes, but when he returns home, it buys him nothing in the face of America's inhuman race violence. After watching a black man burned alive by a mob, the protagonist gives up on the idea of implementing a life of black cosmopolitanism in the United States and instead buries himself in a life of passing. If cosmopolitanism is understood as "a drive to define oneself in relation to the world beyond one's own" (Nwankwo 162) it must be said that the "world beyond" may, for many, become part of an infinitely receding horizon.

Impossible Cosmopolitanism

"Literature," writes Sheldon Pollock in an essay on cosmopolitanism, "constitutes an especially sensitive gauge of sentiments of belonging"; unlike other forms of production and circulation, "the practices of literary culture . . . are practices of attachment" that "actualize modes of cosmopolitan and vernacular belonging" (118–19).[14] It seems important to add that it is precisely this power that also endows literary texts with the capacity to render with force the absence or failure of attachment, the sense of unbelonging, the disjunction between expectations for attachment on one hand and conditions of alienation on the other. Thus the parable of Johnson's novel brings us closer to the fragility of cosmopolitan community as it is imagined in, or conveyed through, a variety of modernist works. I said earlier that while modernist expressive culture rarely conveys a picture of achieved cosmopolitanism, it is almost always *about* cosmopolitanism—which is not to suggest that, in modernism's barely rendered world of early twentieth-century globalization and imperial crises, depictions of cosmopolitanism do not exist: of course they do, and with varying degrees of irony, self-reflexiveness, disdain, and cautionary qualifications.[15] But what seems to me more significant than the overt staging of cosmopolitanism is the role that cosmopolitan fragility plays in the conditional sense of worldly engagement that permeates modernism (see, e.g., Berman; Lutz; Berman; Nava; Walkowitz). At the beginning of this essay, I suggested that it is possible to read cosmopolitanism as a normative ideal against which modernist aesthetics operate. Note that I am not claiming that "cosmopolitanism" equals "the good" in this formula, which would only serve to set up a litmus test according to which modernist works quite arbitrarily succeed or fail in some implied moral duty. Besides, plenty of modernists had reason to dislike or distrust received notions of cosmopolitanism. Rather, I mean that because of literature's ability to "actualize" different registers of belonging, received notions of cosmopolitanism become implicit objects of normative critique in many instances of literary modernism, and this critique acts to dislodge cosmopolitanism from its status as a universalism and to resettle it in the realm of the particular. The mode of cosmopolitanism varies from text to text, author to author, place to place, and certainly from decade to decade; but in the relationship I am describing, it serves to invoke intercultural forms of exchange that *could* be or *might* be or *shouldn't* be, over and against (or in keeping with) the text's account of "what is." Another way to put this is to say that a good deal of modernism—including that of the *modernistas*, and of James Weldon Johnson and Wallace Thurman, and of Mary Butts and Georg Simmel, and others to whom I will turn in a moment—may be understood as versions of what we are now calling "new" cosmopolitanism.

As I have suggested, *Quartet* offers an excellent example of the kind of negative critique described above. A version of interwar Parisian cosmopolitanism forms a backdrop for the lives depicted in the novel, focalized as they are through Marya Zelli's minimalist consciousness, which points insistently to the distributions of power that make "cosmopolitanism" a sovereign province of some, and impossible for others. The novel's plot is very nearly naturalist in its determinism: Marya's husband Stephan is arrested and imprisoned for fencing stolen art; the penniless Marya is taken in like a "homeless cat" (61) by an English art entrepreneur, Heidler, who, with his wife's cooperation, seduces her; Marya hears the "wheels of society clanking" during a crucial epiphany that "life is cruel and horrible to unprotected people" (51); the Heidlers tire of her and cast her out; she becomes addicted to Pernod and veronal; Stephan, shattered by his imprisonment, is released and deported from Paris; and on his way out of town he assaults Marya—perhaps fatally—when she tells him of her affair with Heidler. The end.

The naturalism underpinning Marya's downward spiral features the dark side of the City of Light. Bright boulevards and glittering crowds are contrasted to queues of silent women waiting to visit in the prison's "dark, dank corridor like the open mouth of a monster" (55). But it is through Marya's modernist focalization that the contrasts of Paris sharpen into critique: waiting with the women in the prison queue, she thinks about cosmopolitan Paris's "little arrangements, prisons and drains and things, tucked away where nobody can see" (55), all funneling away the city's dross, of which she and Stephan have become part. The novel's cityscape is peopled with immigrants from Hungary, refugees from Russia, expatriates from

England, tourists from America, people "of every nationality under the sun" (67), recalling to us Camilla Fojas's observation that big cities at this time had become "symbolic paradigms of radical inclusion, acceptance, and the coexistence and integration of difference" (14); but Marya's view of the city's transients penetrates to their individual ethnic vulnerabilities: as Stephan scrambles for the means by which to leave town, for example, he recalls a Jew he knows who might help him. "People abuse Jews," he says, "but sometimes they help you when nobody else will." "Yes," agrees Marya, "I think so, too. They often understand better than other people" (137). Jews certainly understand the conditions of alterity that subtend the performance of cosmopolitanism in the city. Paris may be a city of refuge in name, but woe to the rootless who come without money or filiation. Even the church offers no asylum to Marya: in a wicked parody of the traditional law of asylum, Marya visits St. Julien le Pauvre with Heidler one day, only to intuit, after viewing the impassive statue of "le pauvre," that the church and all the saints are on Heidler's side. "God's quite a pal of yours," she observes to Heidler. "Yes," he answers (96).

Paris throngs with postwar Bolsheviks and "internationals who invariably g[et] into trouble sooner or later," as the *patronne* of the Hotel L'univers muses (32). A newspaper gamely proclaims that *"Le mélange des races est à la base de l'évolution humaine vers le type parfait"* (33)—a dead-on Comtean prediction, but one with which the *patronne*'s husband, who has seen his share of internationals, wearily disagrees. The "mélange des races" in Paris is more like a scramble for survival, and Rhys stages that scramble against a warped cosmopolitanism ruled by the relentlessly British Heidlers. In this world, cosmopolitanism is just another name for a kind of social-sexual imperialism; intercultural contact is restricted to the art markets controlled by Heidler, and is structured by ludicrously transplanted "British" values. Thus the competing fictions of cosmopolitanism—the predatory version practiced within the English community in Paris, and the ideal, sanctuarial version that haunts the edges of Marya's consciousness—propel the novel through a negative dialectic that winnows Marya's existence down to bare life.

A similar, though inverted, tension structures Christopher Isherwood's *Goodbye to Berlin*, the series of novelistic memoirs published together in 1939, which chronicles "Christopher Isherwood's" life in cosmopolitan Berlin in the months leading up to the fall of the Weimar Republic. The text's narrative device aims for objective detachment; the narrator asserts that he is nothing more than a camera aperture mechanically registering his daily life. What eventually emerges from the overlapping snapshot-chapters is a detached self-portrait of an English tutor whose nationality (British) and class (shabby-genteel) secure his entry into working-class and wealthy homes, into the company of Nazis and Jews, into cabarets and beer halls, and into pastoral outings and gay bars. Isherwood scrupulously details his encounters with cultural others, but whatever cosmopolitanism enables his mobility is surely one of convenience, insofar as the narrative studiously avoids any subjective (or subjunctive) account of the political catastrophe that swirls around Berlin. The funeral of Hermann Müller is just an "elegant funeral" (46) down in the street (and not the symbolic beginning of the Third Reich); the Nazi riots and disappearing Jews are barely inflected elements in a dispassionate composition. To call this a cosmopolitanism of convenience is not to censure the novelistic enterprise, however: the narrative tension between Christopher's apparent political agnosticism on one hand and the wreckage of history piling up around him like Benjamin's angel on the other creates, in the end, a ghostly portrait of what Berlin of 1931 is not: it is no longer a city of refuge, it is no longer a homosexual haven, it is no longer the glorious capital of international culture that it was before and immediately after the war. Its capacity for planetary cosmopolitanism shrinks with every page, until finally, in the last brief chapter, the political emerges (explicitly for once) as the inevitable infrastructure upon which all else is strung. Patriotism now subsumes all culture, and the newspapers contain nothing but "new rules, new punishments, and lists of people who have been 'kept in'" (203).[16]

The strain between revanchist, ethnic nationalism and cultural cosmopolitanism in the decades after the war, and especially in the 1930s, is written in the Pan-European history of the rise of totalitarianism. Before the war, the avant-gardist Herwarth Walden saluted Berlin as a city where "the Germans speak French, the Russians German, the Japanese a broken German, and the Italians English" (quoted in Mendes-Flohr 30). Berliner Georg Simmel's influential cosmopolitan theories of sociality depended upon the radically anti-positivist proposal that a society is "a structure which consists of *beings who stand inside and outside of it at the same time*" (14–15), which is to say that there is no such thing as a pure insider (or outsider) for Simmel. Rather, the social is by definition a Venn diagram of intersections, entailing a profound heterogeneity organized along the lines of mutual recognition and the social formations engendered, however transiently, thereby. Nationalism may be said to play a part in the formation of some social groups, but in the context of Simmel's prewar idea of the socius *as process*, nationalism is no more significant than, say, occupation or education or aesthetic preference, and none of those are as important as time and place. Simmel's own classrooms at the University of Berlin exemplified his understanding of the social as infinitely malleable and heterogeneous: at his encouragement (and, ultimately, at his peril), they were filled with women and immigrants or refugees from the east.[17] In 1915, Freud himself narrated the cosmopolitan assumptions of the prewar years in Europe: "Relying on [a] unity among the civilized peoples [of Europe], countless men and women have exchanged their native home for a foreign one, and made their existence dependent on the intercommunications between friendly nations. Moreover, anyone who was not by stress of circumstance confined to one spot could create for himself out of all the advantages and attractions of these civilized countries a new and wider fatherland, in which he could move about without hindrance or suspicion."[18]

But after the war, with the rise of irredentist nationalism, this vision of a Pan-European community—which Freud admits was always an "illusion" (Mendes-Flohr 25)—becomes increasingly untenable. Giorgio Agamben's description of a "lasting crisis following the devastation of Europe's geopolitical order [in the First World War]" centers on the fact that what had once been a "hidden difference (*scarto*) between birth and nation" (129) is now overt, palpable, and figured literally in the postwar tidal wave of displaced and stateless refugees. In Agamben's argument, those immigrants and refugees belie the fiction of any purported identity between nativity and nationality, the latter of which can evidently be revoked or repudiated or restored with the stroke of a pen. This revelation puts into crisis, and simultaneously intensifies, that form of nationalism defined by originary appeals to "blood and soil." Moreover, for Agamben (and for Arendt before him), this "hidden difference between birth and nation" always threatens to reveal the fact that the "natural" rights ascribed to "man" since the French Revolution are in fact arbitrary designations assigned by sovereign nation-states to citizens; "man" is nothing more than "the immediately vanishing ground (who must never come to light as such) of the citizen" (128). Thus the geopolitical upheavals of the 1920s and 1930s in Europe and Asia, which cut cleanly through the links between birth and national identity, produced not only millions of refugees and stateless persons, but also a rash of laws discriminating between the "authentic life" of the citizen whose nativity and nationality could be said to be coterminous, on one hand, and the "life lacking every political value" of the noncitizen on the other (132). I would argue that in this context, the stakes of cosmopolitanism intensify exponentially.

Cosmopolitanism's fragility and the perils of postwar statelessness feature centrally in Kazuo Ishiguro's screenplay, *The White Countess*, where the retrospective restaging of the precariousness of the refuge city cannily takes its cue from modernism's attempts to imagine a new cosmopolitanism. Between the wars, Shanghai, a treaty port, was the only city of refuge in the world. Since entry could be gained without papers, it became an emergency destination for tens of thousands of stateless White Russians (whose citizenship had been cancelled) and tens of thousands of Jewish refugees (whose citizenship was always in doubt). Home to the huge extraterritorial International Settlement (comprised of British, Americans, Danes, Italians, New Zealanders, and others) and the separate but similarly extraterritorial French Concession, Shanghai was the site of what Marie-Claire Bérgère has called the golden age of the Chinese bourgeoisie, powered by a modern industrial business class and funded by the tariffs and traffic of the city's international shipping lanes. It was also a staging ground for the Chinese civil war begun in Shanghai in 1927 with Chiang Kai-shek's anti-communist purges—a war that was interrupted in 1937 by the commencement of the Second Sino-Japanese War, when Japan invaded Shanghai and bombed the city for ten days in August. In the decade leading up to the invasion, as Leo Ou-fan Lee has shown, there arose the "Shanghai Modern," a distinctly modern and yet legibly traditional set of aesthetics pervading the print cultures, literary cultures, and the energetic cabaret culture of the city.

The White Countess, set in 1936, wears the mantle of the Shanghai modern, but it is at bottom a meditation on cosmopolitanism—on its ephemerality, its artifice, its dependence upon detached sociability, and above all, its constitutive, if sometimes covert, relation to political flux. Ishiguro is well known for his interest in the forms and the work of cosmopolitanism, and especially for his fictional explorations of the tensions between cosmopolitanism and national particularism (in *An Artist of the Floating World*, for example); indeed, in *Cosmopolitan Style*, Rebecca Walkowitz

argues at length that Ishiguro's novels comprise part of a "revival of modernist cosmopolitanism" (31). *The White Countess* stages several iterations of cosmopolitanism as it tells the story of a former U.S. diplomat (Mr. Jackson) who, having lost
his family and his sight to terrorist bombings in the ongoing Kuomintang/commu-
nist struggle, retreats into the world of the Shanghai modern by opening what he
calls "the bar of my dreams," where he meticulously controls all the elements for
cosmopolitan sociability. Befriended by a mysterious Japanese businessman,
Mr. Matsuda, Jackson rolls out his plans, hiring as his hostess a White Russian refugee, a countess who now scrapes out a living as a taxi dancer and lives with other
White Russians in Shanghai's Jewish ghetto. She has "all the allure, the tragedy, the
weariness" for the part of hostess, Jackson tells Matsuda; she is "perfect" because
"history has no place for her kind anymore." When the nightclub (called The White
Countess) opens a year later, it is a cosmopolitan success, with its clientele seemingly comprising all races, nationalities and sexualities; but Jackson is dissatisfied
with what he calls the "pretty confection"; he wants political tension (though no
violence, which would "destroy a perfectly blended mood in seconds"), so Matsuda
arranges to bring in the "right number" of communists, Kuomintang soldiers,
Japanese sailors and businessmen, thereby perfecting the club's insulated mood,
which draws from yet exists beyond the politics of the streets. But of course, this
cosmopolitan world disappears in a fireball when the Japanese invade on August 13.
More than that: Matsuda turns out to be a menacing imperial nationalist who has
helped to plan the invasion. The film ends as boatloads of fleeing refugees teeter out
to sea, in search of the next port of refuge.

The White Countess sets up the nightclub as a kind of narrative prism through
which the cosmopolitan desires of Matsuda and Jackson are refracted. Together
those sets of desire "follow a narrative and conjure a world" (258) to use Anthony
Appiah's phrase for what he sees as the imaginative action that binds people into
cosmopolitan relations. The irony here is that while their intercultural friendship is
genuine and their appreciation of compounded cultures is palpable, each abuses the
ethics of cosmopolitanism in his own way. Matsuda the patriot tinkers with the
nightclub like a science project, mixing the nuances of international tension in a
kind of experimental counterpoint to his own uncomplicated imperial aspirations.
For his part, Jackson uses cosmopolitanism's "perfectly blended mood" both as an
antidote to his own personal tragedy, and as a formal, aesthetic rejoinder to the escalating hostilities in the city—hostilities that the film carefully chronicles in newspaper headlines that the blind Jackson cannot and does not wish to read. But, as
Ishiguro suggests, the fact is that cosmopolitanism is always more than a style or a
mood—or what Heidegger termed *Stimmung*. No matter how aesthetically rich or
ethnologically complex, the cosmopolitan *Stimmung*, by virtue of its internationalism, is grounded in particular political relations, and politics will out.

   In Jackson and Matsuda's careful staging of cosmopolitanism, nationalism is
neither challenged nor espoused—it is merely contained, as a kinetic element in a
composition. In fact, their nightclub is akin to a salon, where, in a controlled space,
the hostess, the guests, the entertainment and the atmosphere all coalesce, for the

moment, into a miniature canvas upon which intersubjectivity and sociability are rendered. And as with the salon, The White Countess's cosmopolitanism operates as a kind of sanctuary—a conditional zone of what Michel de Certeau might call "local authority," that is, an "area of free play on a checkerboard that analyzes and classifies identity" (106). Indeed, Jackson and Matsuda refer to The White Countess as a canvas upon which they paint their respective visions. And it is this instrumental malleability—the ease with which cosmopolitanism may be used for personal or political ends—that seems to be at the heart of Ishiguro's meditation. Because of cosmopolitanism's purchase on and association with a philosophical universalism, efforts to formalize cosmopolitanism may be "blind" to all kinds of inconsistencies and contradictions in the realm of the particular. Conversely, because of cosmopolitanism's discursive dependence upon the individualized trope of aesthetic, expansive experience (in literature and other forms of expressive culture), efforts at constituting or reproducing "the cosmopolitan" as a compensation for or exemption from brute political exigencies may be blind to the actual demands of political justice or its absence. That is, *Stimmung* as a "perfectly blended" aesthetic mood isn't necessarily commensurate with the historical dimension of *Stimmung* as a collective (imperfectly blended) political affect. The tragic Countess Sofia may be a perfect hostess for the nightclub because her "kind" is historically obsolete, but the fact is that "out there" in the squalid ghetto, where she and her Jewish and Chinese neighbors adjust to and take care of each other, she is part of a more planetary form of cosmopolitanism, one that is unannounced and unaestheticized. This urgent form of cosmopolitanism is portable and episodic; and in the closing shots of the refugees' fragile boats at sea, Ishiguro suggests that it exists as a latent, and perhaps distinctly modernist, counterdiscourse of filiation in the interwar world of *homo sacer*.

MODERNISM AND THE COSMOPOLITAN SITUATION

According to the art historian Partha Mitter, the interwar circulation of aesthetic modernist discourse through and between colonial cities and metropoles created what he calls a "virtual cosmopolis." In *The Triumph of Modernism: India's artists and the avant-garde, 1922–1947*, Mitter traces the rise of the various artistic strands comprising Indian modernism, beginning with the 1922 Bauhaus exhibit in Calcutta and the subsequent 1924 Bengali art show in Berlin. As the cosmopolitan center for the Bengali intelligentsia, Calcutta was part of this virtual cosmopolis—that is, the global "hybrid city of the imagination" where "the interactions between global and local were played out in the urban space of colonial culture, hosted by the intelligentsia who acted as a surrogate for the nation" (*Triumph* 11). Mitter argues that in virtual cosmopolitanism, this imaginary amalgam of art and ideas emanating from and circulating (largely via print culture) through most major world cities—including Shanghai, Beirut, São Paulo, and Bombay—rendered artistic modernism into a remarkably flexible discourse which as a matter of course led to "different questions and different aims" ("Reflections" 29) in each of its local settings. One needn't have traveled from any of these locations to become part of cosmopolitan culture; "native[s] of the peripheries" could be "intellectually engaged with the knowledge system of the metropolis" in ways that did not in the least resemble mere "simple colonial power relations" ("Reflections" 38, 39). What's more, Mitter suggests, this virtual transmission of modernism cut it loose from all but the most general geographical origins, so that modernism offered itself as a deracinated, capacious discourse, available for all kinds of uses, including explicitly Indian uses within Indian artistic circles. The Bengali avant-garde cultivation of modernist primitivism, for example, issued in art that was at once visually experimental, implicitly critical of nationalist historicism, and explicitly opposed to nineteenth-century British academic models of "gross materialism" ("Reflections" 36). Even *within* the discourse of international modernism, Indian experiments with particular schools, such as Cubism (most famously by Gaganendranath Tagore, the Nobel poet Rabindranath Tagore's nephew), reframed it as an exploratory medium for Indian "mystery" rather than as an analytic method ("Triumph" 23).[19]

For his part, in these same years, Rabindranath Tagore elaborated a philosophical cosmopolitanism that was tied to global art on one end and Indian civilization on the other.[20] Tagore is considered by many to be a model of old-school cosmopolitanism, particularly for his emphasis on reason and for his fervent antinationalism, among other things. But in fact, as Saranindranath Tagore has recently argued, Tagore's "reason" is not the detached, impartial exercise associated with Enlightenment rationalism; rather, it is directed by a hermeneutic engagement with the world and its various traditions. This is a hermeneutics that depends upon an interpretive standpoint which "make[s] it possible for one tradition to converse with another," thereby widening each tradition through the "importing [of] elements into it from another" (1077). As Tagore himself wrote, "Whatever we understand and enjoy in human products instantly becomes ours, wherever they might have their origins."[21]

This cosmopolitan vision of art (in the broadest sense) as universally appreciable—given the right measure of understanding and enjoyment—is curiously incomplete. Human products from anywhere may be appreciated by "us," but can an "us" from *anywhere* fulfill the role of appreciator? Obviously this question can potentially be informed by the strategic assumptions of nineteenth-century colonial regimes propped up in no small part by the racialist evolutionary narratives exemplified by Gobineau (the answer would be a resounding "no"), but it also points in another direction, toward a foundational modernist critique of those assumptions, perhaps best exemplified by Wilhelm Worringer's remarkable dissertation in art history, *Abstraction and Empathy* [1908]. In his conclusion to this book about non-Western art, Worringer argues that Europeans must radically alter their heretofore

404 FORMS OF SOCIALITY

unexamined universalist positions as appraisers and appreciators of art if they are "to pass beyond a narrowly European outlook" (135) on world art. In essence, Worringer exposes in the discipline of art history and in western European culture more generally a deeply parochial, unreflexive stance, which takes local (European) aesthetic values (themselves relatively new and quite fungible) for universal laws of art. Only by striving to encounter non-European art on its own terms—an impossible exercise in cosmopolitan detachment, Worringer knows, but nevertheless a necessary ideal—can Europeans come to a crucial hermeneutical understanding of the nearly untranslatable role of *style* (as opposed to form or content) in all modes of art, including those sculptures and masks with which they have filled colonial museums like the Trocadéro, where Worringer's thesis begins.[22]

Versions of Worringer's cosmopolitan problematic appear with frequency in modernism's various treatments of national versus global belonging, since the discourses of modernism offer milieux in which cosmopolitanism modifies national identity and vice versa. "The Dead," for example, has generated a long and tangled critical debate about Joyce's cosmopolitanism, which is often couched in a zero-sum relation to nationalism. On the one side, it is said that the story displays Joyce's rejection of Irish popular nationalism (which, in the story, amounts to a form of parochialism) and points the way toward his embrace of a cosmopolitan existence elsewhere—cosmopolitanism being the condition of possibility for his modernism; on the other side, it has been argued that the story in fact aligns modernism with cultural nationalism, both of which act as buffers against the atomizing forces of modernity, including, in this formulation, cosmopolitanism (see Robbins, "The Newspapers Were Right"). And indeed one could easily argue for a third kind of related reading that addresses the story's sustained focus on hospitality—which, as we have seen, is both a linchpin of Kant's planetary cosmopolitanism and is, according to Derrida, "culture itself" (16). The story is structured around the nouns and verbs of hospitality: entering, leave-taking, singing, conversing, with articles of food and drink fastidiously catalogued as though they were the objective correlatives of the story's frequent invocations of hospitality. This is not just any hospitality, of course; it's "Irish hospitality," and because it is explicitly tied to national character, its putative ambit is extra-national (since "Irish hospitality" makes no sense except in an implicitly comparativist context). But the story's major breach of this hospitality occurs when Miss Ivors, the nationalist, leaves abruptly before dinner, after accusing Gabriel of being a "West Briton" and hearing him reply that he is "sick of his own country" (189). If there is a fleeting "imagined community" in the story, it takes ironic shape in the dinner conversations about the singers of Europe and the irrationality of the Catholic Church. That is, it is sustained neither by Miss Ivors' constricted claims to authentic particularism, nor by Gabriel's weak conception of worldliness, but rather by an "Irish hospitality" which, if it ever existed, is fast becoming an instrumental fiction in the decolonizing visions of both Gabriel and Molly Ivors.

The English modernist Mary Butts explores the interface between cosmopolitanism and nationalism in a way that is nearly opposite to Joyce in "The Dead." Her stories, written mostly in Paris in those decades of displacement, the late 1920s and 1930s, elaborate subtle but abiding distinctions between nationalism and what might be thought of as an aestheticized patriotism; time and again, this latter quality helps to maintain equilibrium within the small (often homosexual) groups that gather together in cosmopolitan settings. In the story "Scylla and Charybdis" (the very title of which marks this precarious equilibrium), a female narrator reports the bohemian lives of her "own family group" (36) of four gay male friends in Paris—three Englishmen and one Russian refugee. The homeless Russian is impetuous and manipulative, but the group supports him and adores him, agreeing that "penniless russian boys are to be forgiven much" (33). When another Englishman, Crane, joins them in Paris on his way home from his work as an imperial administrator in the Middle East, the group's equilibrium unravels almost immediately. It is not just a question of numbers: Crane possesses an aura of Britishness that conflicts harshly with the aestheticized sociability of the English Parisians. He is no brute—in fact, he is in good measure a sensitive and self-reflexive man—but his sense of national character is tied inextricably to an imperial form of paternalistic masculinity, and that is a trait that can never be mixed into the group's cosmopolitan sociability.

Similarly, in "In Bloomsbury," the story for which Butts is probably best known, competing performances of Englishness and cosmopolitanism drive the plot: on the one side, a set of indulged postwar siblings imagine that they are cosmopolitans because they go back and forth to Paris and languidly talk in the lexicon of art; on the other side, their heretofore unknown cousins, South African colonials, imagine they can easily repatriate to England after murdering their black half brother. Both of these versions of worldliness are patently false: neither imperial domination nor Parisian dilettantism count as cosmopolitanism. And both versions of Englishness are just as suspect, since both depend upon unexamined assumptions of British entitlement that have nothing to do with vernacular English identity. And that identity, the story also suggests, is crucially rooted in history—specifically in England before the war (an "occurrence" that is "politely ignored" [39] by the siblings), and more generally, one may surmise from the body of Butts's work, in an imagined premodern England.

It is of course a truism that much British modernism grounds its critique of modernity in an implied, fantastic antediluvian England, and this grounding helps to support a nostalgic conservatism that cancels out the political core of liberal democracy. From this perspective, Butts, with her narrative reliance on an almost ghostly English historical essence, is even more conservative than most. But her work is instructive for the distinctions she makes between nationalism and a more ethereal patriotic *feeling*—an affect or mood, or, to return to Heidegger's term, *Stimmung*—and for the way she triangulates these with cosmopolitanism, which, in her hands, helps to sharpen the distinction. This configuration is perhaps most dramatically rendered in "From Altar to Chimney Piece," a story about an Englishman named Vincent, who lives most of the time in Paris, having been badly traumatized in the Great War and worrying that he will never regain a sense of wholeness. Paris's ancient balms are now leeching away into the frenetic postwar Americanization of

the city. England itself offers little succor for Vincent; for "like many men of profound patriotism, he liked less and less the way England was going" (238). Vincent
falls in love with an American ingénue who, he comes to realize, has been corrupted
by an evil cabal of experimentalists headquartered at (of all places) a thinly veiled
version of Gertrude Stein's salon. As this plot point suggests, the story verges on the
histrionic, but what is genuinely interesting is the narrative layering of the relations
among national character, patriotism, and history. Vincent's patriotism—his sense
of "Englishness" as an affective aesthetic of intelligent service and humility—contrasts sharply with the "unprincipled" young Americans who are taking over Paris,
leading the narrator to imagine that "in America, it would seem that a cheap and
strident idealism often takes the place of true discipline, the love of country or of
mankind" (247). American national identity, in other words, is so affectively superficial as to be devoid of the capacity either for patriotism or for genuine cosmopolitan feeling.

The bigger crime here is that, like the English siblings of "In Bloomsbury," the
Americans in Paris—and presumably American national character itself—lack a
sense of history; this vacuum makes cosmopolitan thinking impossible. Americans
speak "as though nothing had ever happened before they happened," and they write
"as though man had never put pen to paper before" ("Altar" 247). The story's insistence on the importance of historical consciousness within cosmopolitanism (putting
aside Butts's solemnly conservative view of "history") returns us to some central
questions about cosmo-modernism—questions that will, I hope, help to reframe cosmopolitanism as a textual heuristic device for making sense of twentieth-century
modernity.

First, what is the value—and for that matter the feasibility—of a detached cosmopolitan "view from nowhere" as it becomes the trope for a fulfilled or failed normative ideal of mutuality in modernist works? The answer to this will of course vary
widely, from the humanitarian heroism of Tagore's character Nikhil, who believes
(with echoes of Comte and in contrast to his nationalist nemesis) that "man's history
has to be built by the united effort of all the races in the world," to the cluelessness
of Ford Madox Ford's American character John Dowell, who carries wampum in his
pocket as he plods between European leisure spaces in a deluded domestic trance,
to the worldly writer in Langston Hughes's "Luani of the Jungle," who becomes a
victim of his own cosmopolitan passion, to Felix Volkbein, *Nightwood*'s lonely, rootless "wandering Jew," whose historical consciousness dwells in the fantasy of ancestral nobility, but whose fate is tied to an offstage regime of blood and soil.[23]

Second, how does the aesthetic stance of cosmopolitanism bear up under the
interwar pressures of nationalism and imperialism? What can we learn about its
contingency from an artist like Josephine Baker, for example, whose successful
public persona in Europe in the late 1920s and 1930s depended upon the entwinement of these three things—that is, the putative pluralism of cosmopolitan appreciation, the nationalist myth of French racial tolerance, and European imperialist
assumptions about the isomorphism of colonial others (which made it apparently
unremarkable for Baker to be at once Polynesian, Algerian, West African, and

African American)?[24] Or, to pose the question more philosophically, how does the cosmopolitan aesthetic help to mediate modernity's paradoxical claims to be at once unprecedented and at the same time breaking with a preexisting fabric (national, racial, historical)—how does it, that is, participate in what Fredric Jameson, following Sartre, calls the "situation" of modernity, the narrative structure that holds together modernity's "contradictory features of belonging and innovation" (57)? Aesthetic cosmopolitanism may be (and I believe it is) a key element in this representational sleight-of-hand, allowing modernism at once to make it new and to make it not entirely new. If this is so, then how well does cosmopolitanism work as a descriptor of the cultural products arising from James Clifford's "discrepant cosmopolitanisms"? There is no reason to believe that the frictional forces at work between cultures in a global economy would reproduce modern "newness" as a desideratum wherever those forces may be found—in India, Algeria, Papeete, or Nova Scotia.

Finally, is it possible for the explicit aims of planetary cosmopolitanism to persist within the self-reflexive irony—not to say cynicism—of modernist style? What *is* so funny about peace, love, and understanding, and how can they survive the wrecking ball of modernism, except in the breach? Moreover, what can a cosmopolitan refraction of historical consciousness—in Butts, Woolf, Cavafy, or Du Bois, for example—teach us about the limits of what Robbins calls "temporal cosmopolitanism"? ("The Newspapers Were Right" 109–112). That is, if any cosmopolitanism worthy of the name must have an anchor in materialist (and especially colonial) history, how long or short must the anchor-line be? Too long, and historical trauma becomes the bedrock of aesthetic valuation; too short, and the past sins of colonialism may be forgotten for the price of a new market. C. P. Cavafy's famously cynical question at the end of "Waiting for the Barbarians" (1904) nicely concentrates the dilemma through the long lens of history, setting it in antiquity but inflecting it with the assurances of modernity: "And now what shall become of us without any barbarians?"(19). One answer is: "we" shall become nationalists; another is: we will be cosmopolitans. A third, coming neither from metropole nor periphery but from the camps of the stateless, is under translation.

NOTES

1. Originally published in the UK as *Postures* (1928), and in the United States in 1929 as *Quartet*. Many thanks to the Penn State graduate students in my 2005 seminar, "Cosmo-modernism," and especially Amy Clukey, Liz Kuhn, and Shawna Ross for their unstinting participation in many of the questions addressed here.

2. Like its Greek precursor, Roman Stoic cosmopolitanism develops in a context of expanding and contracting empires, ever-shifting geographical boundaries, and competing claims for political belonging. Early Christianity transforms this model of competing ties into one that opposes local life (i.e., on our earthly polis) to a heaven-and-earthly sphere of

God's faithful. See Fine and Cohen, 137–39; Nussbaum, "Kant and Cosmopolitanism," 27–57. Theorist and Victorian scholar Amanda Anderson offers a very specific account of cosmopolitan "detachment," which, far from being a "view from nowhere" is, she argues, "self-consciously informed by a postconventional and ongoing interrogation of cultural norms and systems of power" (30). Anderson lists three key components of nineteenth-century cosmopolitanism: "reflective distance from one's original or primary cultural affiliations, a broad understanding of other cultures and customs, and a belief in universal humanity" (63).

3. These surges of interest in cosmopolitan theory recur almost unfailingly during historical moments of rapid global change, when the reach of modernity outstrips its assimilative mechanisms.

4. Kant, "Idea for a Universal History with a Cosmopolitan Purpose" [1784], "Seventh Proposition," 49 (hereafter cited parenthetically as "Universal History"). "Cosmopolitan condition" is the name Kant gives to the necessary and ongoing negotiation of a tension, intrinsic to man, between the desire for unrestricted freedom and the need for security through cooperation.

5. Kleingeld points out that Kant's is only one of several models for cosmopolitanism in circulation at the time; see 505–24.

6. For an excellent account of the strengths and shortcomings of the Habermasean cosmopolitan project, see Cheah, 45–79.

7. Robbins discusses the implications of Clifford's about-face in "Comparative Cosmopolitanisms," 253–62. Brennan offers a bracing critique of not only Clifford's but virtually all formulations of cosmopolitanism, whether new or old. In essence, he argues that the very concept marks an uneven playing field, which, *a priori*, awards hermeneutic power to the formulator.

8. See, for example, Hegel and Stirner; see also Marx's scathing critique of Stirner's developmental narrative, esp. 143–208.

9. In his ongoing critique of Comte, Adorno points out that the scientific ideals of "rational transparency" and "strictly observable facts" proposed by Comte for use in the development of a "science of society" couldn't really work, given that human subjects are (obviously) the creatures doing the observing (9–10; see also lectures 1–4).

10. The laudable "influence of civilization," Marx writes, will "subordinate the satisfaction of the personal instincts to the habitual exercise of the social faculties, [and] subject, at the same time, all our passions to rules imposed by an ever-strengthening intelligences, with the view of identifying the individual more and more with the species" (280–81). Thence modernism's discontents.

11. Gobineau continues with an interesting prophecy (the year is 1851): "The Hindu race has become a stranger to the race that governs it today, and its civilization does not obey the law that gives the battle to the strong. . . . A moment will come . . . when India will again live publicly, as she already does privately, under her own laws" (68).

12. Cheah argues that, prior to the nation's "annexation of the territorial state"—the nation, still more or less existing as an imagined conglomerate, as Ireland between 1916 and 1922, for example, or Italy before 1860, or Germany before 1808—"nationalism is not antithetical to cosmopolitanism" (25).

13. See Fojas's comparative discussion of the contemporaneous journals *Ariel* and *Cosmópolis*, and their diverse treatments not only of the genderized affect of cosmopolitanism, but also of nationalism and cosmopolitanism, 104–30. See also Bulson in this volume for an elaboration of the tension, inherent in modernist little magazines, between local conditions of production and putative global audiences.

14. Though Pollock is concerned mainly with the comparative uses of cosmopolitanism and vernacularism in the second millennium in South Asia and western Europe, he closes with a compelling discussion of Gramsci's attempts to come to terms with the (national) vernacular/(universal) cosmopolitan problematic, following it ultimately to the recognition that "the new must be made precisely through attachment to the past, and . . . that only such attachment enables one to grasp what can and must be changed" (46). This is a proposal to which I will return presently.

15. In the high modern Anglo-American canon, examples would include *The Good Soldier* (and especially that instrument of capitalism, Leonora Ashburnham), Katherine Mansfield's "*Je ne parle pas français*" (the predatory Raoul Duquette), *The Ambassadors* (Strether, enlightened), *Ulysses* (Bloom, innocent), and *Pilgrimage*, which, Kusch argues, displays the entrenched imperialism (i.e., the mendacity) of British modern cosmopolitanism—though of course I would wish to qualify that claim.

16. In *Christopher and His Kind* [1976], Isherwood fills in many of the narrative aporias of *Goodbye to Berlin*.

17. Simmel wasn't appointed professor until a few years before his death, thanks in part to the institutional anti-cosmopolitanism reflected in this official letter opposing his promotion: "His academic audience sits together. The ladies constitute what is, even for Berlin, a strong contingent. The remaining are students from the oriental world who have become residents, and those who stream in from eastern countries are extremely well represented. His entire manner corresponds with their tastes and leads in their direction." Quoted in Leck, 37.

18. Quoted in Mendes-Flohr, 24. Mendes-Flohr offers a compelling discussion of the imbrications of Jewish *bildung* and modern cosmopolitanism in Berlin before World War I.

19. For a homologous consideration of "imported" Euromodernisms (particularly in the form of poetry) and postcolonial Caribbean writers, see Ramazani 449: "In redeploying modernism . . . [postcolonial poets] have reshaped it through indigenous genres and vocabularies, have recentered it in non-Western landscapes and mythologies, and have often inverted its racial and cultural politics." See also Kalliney, in this volume.

20. Tagore's close associations with Yeats and Kandinsky, for example, are well known.

21. Quoted in S. Tagore, 1078. R. Tagore's emphasis on enjoyment within this elaboration of a situated cosmopolitanism—appreciating other cultures while remaining connected and in some sense beholden to the inherited bonds of one's own—is akin to what Appiah, in his last two books, has called "rooted cosmopolitanism." According to Robbins, Appiah's is a precarious kind of cosmopolitanism, because in its efforts to reconcile patriotism and cosmopolitanism it leaves out any game plan for reckoning with the worst excesses of the nation. That is, Robbins perceives in Appiah's "partial" cosmopolitanism (Appiah's phrase) an implicit communitarian hierarchy of attachments that works from the local (in the form of received tradition) to the national (in the form of a more abstract "imagined community") to the global. On Robbins's reading, this unexamined or unaccounted feature appears in many of the "new" cosmopolitanisms, rooted or otherwise: such an *a priori* ordering of allegiances renders them ill-equipped to do the work of normative, planetary cosmopolitanism. See Robbins, "Cosmopolitanism: New and Newer," passim.

22. For style as the linchpin of cosmopolitan modernism, see Walkowitz.

23. *The Home and the World*, 165–66; Ford, *The Good Soldier*; Hughes, "Luani of the Jungles" [1928]; Barnes, *Nightwood* [1936].

24. See Lyon, 29–47, for a discussion of Baker's cosmopolitanism.

WORKS CITED

Adorno, Theodor W. *Introduction to Sociology.* Ed. Christoph Gödde. Trans. Edmund
    Jephcott. Stanford: Stanford University Press, 2000.
Agamben, Giorgio. *Homo Sacer: Sovereign Power and Bare Life.* Trans. Daniel Heller-Roaz-
    en. Stanford: Stanford University Press, 1998.
Anderson, Amanda. *The Powers of Distance: Cosmopolitanism and the Cultivation of
    Detachment.* Princeton: Princeton University Press, 2001.
Appiah, Anthony. *The Ethics of Identity.* Princeton: Princeton University Press, 2005.
Barnes, Djuna. *Nightwood.* 1936. New York: New Directions, 2006.
Benhabib, Seyla. *Another Cosmopolitanism.* With Jeremy Waldron, Bonnie Honig, and Will
    Kymlicka. Ed. Rober Post. The Berkeley Tanner Lectures. New York: Oxford Univer-
    sity Press, 2005.
Bérgère, Marie-Claire. *The Golden Age of the Chinese Bourgeoisie, 1911–1937.* Trans. Janet
    Lloyd. Cambridge: Cambridge University Press, 1989.
Berman, Jessica. *Modernist Fiction, Cosmopolitanism, and the Politics of Community.*
    Cambridge: Cambridge University Press, 2001.
Brennan, Timothy. *At Home in the World: Cosmopolitanism Now.* Cambridge: Harvard
    University Press, 1997.
Briggs, Charles L. "Genealogies of Race and Culture and the Failure of Vernacular Cosmo-
    politanisms: Rereading Franz Boas and W. E. B. Du Bois." *Public Culture* 12.1 (2005):
    75–100.
Butts, Mary. "From Altar to Chimney-piece." *From Altar to Chimney-piece: Selected Stories.*
    Kingston: McPherson, 1992. 234–65.
———. "In Bloomsbury." *From Altar to Chimney-piece: Selected Stories.* Kingston:
    McPherson, 1992. 39–57.
———. "Scylla and Charybdis." *Several Occasions.* London: Wishart, 1932: 31–54.
Cavafy, C. P. "Waiting for the Barbarians." *C. P. Cavafy: Collected Poems.* Revised ed. Trans.
    Edmund Keeley and Philip Sherrard. Ed. George Savidis. Princeton: Princeton Univer-
    sity Press, 1992. 18–19.
Cheah, Pheng. *Inhuman Conditions: On Cosmopolitanism and Human Rights.* Cambridge:
    Harvard University Press, 2006.
Clifford, James. "Traveling Cultures." *Cultural Studies.* Ed. Lawrence Grossberg, Cary
    Nelson, and Paula Treichler. New York: Routledge, 1992. 96–113.
Comte, Auguste. *Course in Positive Philosophy [Cours de Philosophie Positive, 1830–42].*
    Auguste Comte and Positivism: The Essential Writings. Ed. Lenzer. New York: Harper,
    1975. 71–297.
de Certeau, Michel. *The Practice of Everyday Life.* Trans. Steven Rendall. Berkeley: Univer-
    sity of California Press, 1984.
Derrida, Jacques. *On Cosmopolitanism and Forgiveness (Thinking in Action).* Trans. Mark
    Dooley and Michael Hughes. London: Routledge, 2001.
Fojas, Camilla. *Cosmopolitanism in the Americas.* West Lafayette: Purdue University Press,
    2005.
Ford, Ford Madox. *The Good Soldier: A Tale of Passion.* 1915. New York: Oxford University
    Press, 2008.
Gobineau, Arthur Joseph, Comte de. "Essay on the Inequality of the Human Races."
    1853–1855. *Selected Political Writings.* Ed. Michael Biddiss. New York: Harper and Row,
    1970. 50–176.

Hegel, G. W. F. *Lectures on the Philosophy of World History*. Trans. H. B. Nisbet. Cambridge: Cambridge University Press, 1975.

Honig, Bonnie. "Another Cosmopolitanism? Law and Politics in the New Europe." *Seyla Benhabib: Another Cosmopolitanism*. Ed. Robert Post. The Berkeley Tanner Lectures. Oxford: Oxford University Press, 2005. 102–27.

Hughes, Langston. "Luani of the Jungles." 1928. *Short Stories*. Ed. Akiba Sullivan Harper. New York: Hill and Wang, 1996. 25–31.

Isherwood, Christopher. *Christopher and His Kind*. Minneapolis: University of Minnesota Press, 2001.

———. *Goodbye to Berlin. The Berlin Stories*. New York: New Directions, 1963.

Ishiguro, Kazuo. Screenplay, *The White Countess*. Dir. James Ivory. Prod. Ismail Merchant. Perf. Ralph Fiennes, Hiroyuki Sanada, Natasha Richardson, Vanessa Redgrave. Sony Pictures Classics, 2005.

Jameson, Fredric. *A Singular Modernity: Essay on the Ontology of the Present*. London: Verso, 2002.

Joyce, James. "The Dead." *Dubliners*. New York: Penguin, 1981. 175–223.

Kant, Immanuel. "Idea for a Universal History with a Cosmopolitan Purpose." *Kant: Political Writings (Cambridge Texts in the History of Political Thought)*. 2nd ed. Ed. H. S. Reiss. Trans. H. B. Nisbet. Cambridge: Cambridge University Press, 1991, 41–53.

———. "On the Old Saw, 'That May Be Right in Theory, But It Won't Work in Practice.'" Trans. E. B. Ashton. Philadelphia: University Pennsylvania Press, 1974.

———. "Perpetual Peace: A Philosophical Sketch." 1795. H. S. Reiss 93–130.

Kleingeld, Pauline. "Six Varieties of Cosmopolitanism in Late Eighteenth-Century Germany." *Journal of the History of Ideas* 60 (1999): 505–24.

Kusch, Celena E. "Disorienting Modernism: National Boundaries and the Cosmopolis." *Journal of Modern Literature* 30.4 (2007): 39–60.

Lasch, Christopher. *The Revolt of the Elites and the Betrayal of Democracy*. New York: Norton, 1995.

Leck, Ralph. *Georg Simmel and Avant-garde Sociology: The Birth of Modernity, 1880–1920*. Humanity Books. Amherst: Prometheus Books, 2000.

Lee, Leo Ou-fan. *Shanghai Modern: The Flowering of a New Urban Culture in China, 1930–1945*. Cambridge: Harvard University Press, 1999.

Lutz, Tom. *Cosmopolitan Vistas: American Regionalism and Literary Value*. Ithaca: Cornell University Press, 2004.

Lyon, Janet. "Josephine Baker's Hot House: Staging the Avant-garde." *Modernism, Inc.* Ed. Michael Thurston and Jani Scandura. New York: New York University Press, 2001. 29–47.

Marx, Karl, and Frederich Engels. *The German Ideology*. 1845. Amherst: Prometheus Books, 1998.

Mendes-Flohr, Paul. "The Berlin Jew as Cosmopolitan." *Berlin Metropolis: Jews and the New Culture, 1890–1918*. Ed. Emily D. Bilski. Berkeley: University California Press; New York: Jewish Museum, 2000, 14–31.

Mercer, Kobena, ed. *Cosmopolitan Modernisms*. Cambridge: Institute of International Visual Arts; MIT Press, 2005.

Mignolo, Walter D. "The Many Faces of Cosmo-polis: Border Thinking and Critical Cosmopolitanism." *Cosmopolitanism*. Ed. Carol A. Breckenridge, Sheldon Pollock, Homi K. Bhabha, and Dipesh Chakrabarty. Public Culture Books. Durham: Duke University Press, 2002. 157–87.

Mitter, Partha. *The Triumph of Modernism: India's Artists and the Avant-garde, 1922–1947*. London: Reaktion Books, 2007.

Mitter, Partha, and Koben Mercer. "Reflections on Modern Art and National Identity in Colonial India: An Interview." *Cosmopolitan Modernisms*. Ed. Kobena Mercer. Cambridge: Institute of International Visual Arts and MIT Press, 2005. 24–49.

Nava, Mica. "Cosmopolitan Modernity: Everyday Imaginaries and the Register of Difference." *Theory, Culture & Society*. 19.1–2 (2002): 81–99.

Nussbaum, Martha. "Kant and Cosmopolitanism." *Perpetual Peace: Essays on Kant's Cosmopolitan Ideal*. Ed. James Bohman and Matthias Lutz-Bachmann. Cambridge: MIT Press, 1997. 25–57.

———. "Patriotism and Cosmopolitanism." *For Love of Country: Debating the Limits of Patriotism, Martha Nussbaum with Respondents*. Ed. Joshua Cohen. Boston: Beacon, 1996, 3–17.

Nwankwo, Ifeome Kiddoe. *Black Cosmopolitanism: Racial Consciousness and Transnational Identity in the Nineteenth-Century Americas*. Philadelphia: University of Pennsylvania Press, 2005.

Pollock, Sheldon. "Cosmopolitan and Vernacular in History." *Cosmopolitanism*. Ed. Carol A. Breckenridge, Sheldon Pollock, Homi K. Bhabha, and Dipesh Chakrabarty. Durham: Duke University Press, 2002. 15–53.

Ramazani, Jahan. "Modernist Bricolage, Postcolonial Hybridity." *Modernism/modernity* 13 (2006): 445–64.

Robbins, Bruce. "Comparative Cosmopolitanisms." *Cosmopolitics: Thinking and Feeling Beyond the Nation*. Ed. Pheng Cheah, Bruce Robbins. Minneapolis: University of Minnesota Press, 1998. 246–64. Cultural Politics 14.

———. "Cosmopolitanism: New and Newer." *boundary* 2 34.3 (2007): 47–60.

———. "The Newspapers Were Right: Cosmopolitanism, Forgetting, and 'The Dead.'" *Interventions* 5.1 (2003): 101–12.

Rhys, Jean. *Quartet*. New York: Carroll and Graf, 1990.

Simmel, Georg. "How Is Society Possible?" 1908. Trans. Kurt H. Wolff. *Georg Simmel: On Individuality and Social Forms*. Ed. Donald N. Levine. Chicago: University of Chicago Press, 1971. 6–22.

Stirner, Max. *The Ego and His Own: The Case of the Individual Against Authority*. 1844. Trans. Steven T. Byington. Ed. James J. Martin. Mineola: Dover, 2005. Dover Books on Western Philosophy.

Tagore, Rabindrananth. *The Home and the World*. London: Penguin, 2005.

Tagore, Saranindranath. "Tagore's Conception of Cosmopolitanism: A Reconstruction." *University of Toronto Quarterly* 77 (2008): 1070–84.

Van der Veer, Peter. "Colonial Cosmopolitanism." *Conceiving Cosmopolitanism: Theory, Context, and Practice*. Ed. Steven Vertovec and Robin Cohen. Oxford: Oxford University Press, 2002. 165–79.

Walkowitz, Rebecca L. *Cosmopolitan Style: Modernism Beyond the Nation*. New York: Columbia University Press, 2005.

Worringer, Wilhelm. *Abstraction and Empathy [Abstraktion und Einfühlung]*. Trans. Michael Bullock. New York: International Universities Press, 1953.

CHAPTER 17

JEAN RHYS: LEFT BANK MODERNIST AS POSTCOLONIAL INTELLECTUAL

PETER KALLINEY

In the early 1960s, when Jean Rhys was trying to launch a comeback after decades of silence, she published "The Day They Burned the Books" in *London Magazine*. It is narrated by a white woman from the Caribbean. The story looks back on a childhood friendship with a light-skinned "colored" boy who has an English father and a mulatto mother. The boy's profligate father has little standing among the island's white community. Aside from marrying outside his race, "[h]e was not a planter or a doctor or a lawyer or a banker. He didn't keep a store. He wasn't a schoolmaster or a government official. He wasn't—that was the point—a gentleman" (*Tigers* 40). On top of that, he beats his wife and drinks. His one redeeming feature is his impressive library, from which his son, Eddie, and the narrator like to borrow books. Eddie's strange family and voracious reading have led him to some iconoclastic conclusions about "home," meaning England. While all the other white (or nearly white) children wax about the glories of London, the fog, the strawberries and cream, and the daffodils, Eddie would sit quietly. Of course, none of them had ever been to London, or eaten strawberries, or seen daffodils. On one occasion, Eddie blurts out that he doesn't like strawberries and doesn't care for daffodils either. His audience is shocked into silence, but the narrator secretly admires him, claiming "I for one was tired of learning and reciting poems in praise of daffodils, and my relations with the few 'real'

English boys and girls I had met were awkward. . . . Heads I win, tails you lose—that was the English" (42).

Most of the action in the story happens after Eddie's father dies. The young boy, probably about age twelve, puts a claim on the library, calling it "[m]y room" filled with "my books" (43). Shortly afterward, his mother, who had every reason to dislike the boy's father, pillages the library. The "good-looking" books—that is, those in hard-cover—are piled up for sale. The "unimportant books," the paperbacks and damaged volumes, are stacked for incineration. Eddie protests loudly, but his mother laughs at him. He grabs a book and runs, the narrator does the same, and they both escape. He makes off with a copy of Rudyard Kipling's *Kim*, missing the first nineteen pages, and she flees with a Guy de Maupassant novel, *Fort Comme La Mort*.

"The Day They Burned the Books" explores several issues prevalent in Rhys' later work. Her deep suspicion of the English comes through clearly. In this par-ticular story, her white narrator hides her feelings from others. She allows her not-quite-white friend to articulate their shared feelings of resentment against the English, seeming to create a special bond between them. Rhys' own criticisms of imperialism often took this oblique form: She might protest against metropolitan snobbery, but she rarely affirmed the need for political or cultural self-determination in the West Indies—especially where the rights of nonwhite people were con-cerned. Her hatred did not develop into full-blown anti-imperialism in any clear sense.

Significantly, the story's depiction of cross-racial collaboration occurs when race does not seem to be the main issue—it is a shared love of books and distrust of the English that allows the children to temporarily put aside racial differences. The two books that survive neatly encapsulate these running concerns about race and the value of high culture: *Kim* is a book about racial masquerade, while *Fort Comme La Mort* tells the story of a bohemian artist. The library itself, as a bone of contention between mother and son, has a multivalent function in mediating the children's understanding of racial difference. It is an inheritance from the boy's white, English father, and therefore despised by his mother, but it is also the thing that seems to teach Eddie how to properly hate English culture and all it stands for in the colonies. If their shared love of books might appear to outsiders as an investment in metropol-itan culture—all the books arrive from a London dealer on the transatlantic steamer—their mutual love of books also becomes a private code through which they can voice their suspicion of English arrogance.

The fragility of their alliance comes out into the open after they have escaped from Eddie's tyrannical mother. The narrator worries that his mother will get her in trouble with her own parents but then realizes that it won't matter all that much. "Why not?," Eddie prods her, "Because she's . . . because she isn't white" (45–46)? Eddie and the narrator both know the answer to that evasive rhetorical question. "You can go to the devil," Eddie snarls, insisting that his mother is much prettier than the narrator's; she passively concurs. This final twist implies that love—and hatred—of books was not restricted to one racial group, also suggesting that agreement about the value of books would not lead directly to racial reconciliation. Racial tension is something that can be downplayed or mitigated in the context of high culture, but out in the open, such tensions do not dissolve so easily.

One of the most interesting features of this story is the passivity of the white narrator, who envies and longs to emulate her mixed-race friend, both for his library and for his unorthodox anti-English sentiments. In the 1960s, when Rhys was trying to rebuild her career, this general observation would approximate her professional position. In the 1920s and 1930s, Rhys was a member of the Parisian bohemian scene. She published a collection of short stories and several novels, securing critical approbation but fairly modest sales. After World War II, she disappeared from the publishing world. In the intervening years, West Indian writing had become something of a phenomenon. In fact, many readers were calling black writers from Africa and the Caribbean a new breed of modernists. As one *Times Literary Supplement* reviewer put it, audiences reared on the linguistic experiments of James Joyce and Ezra Pound "have graduated to Mr. Amos Tutuola who seems unaware that rules exist." Metropolitan writers, who by the 1950s seemed to be turning toward social realism and away from more audacious experiments in syntax and narrative, no longer fit the bill. Instead, sophisticated readers were increasingly drawn to colonial writers who are comfortable deviating from conventional linguistic and narrative patterns. The popularity and visibility of West Indian writing in the 1950s, the article continues, was a direct consequence of modernist writing: "The emergence of a school of self-assured West Indian writers can thus be related to the composition of *The Waste Land*." Aspiring colonial writers, such as George Lamming, V. S. Naipaul, and Derek Walcott, have rushed to fill a niche left by the experimental modernists, most of them now dead or past their productive years.[1]

In the 1960s, Rhys thus found herself in an unusual position. She was an original Left Bank modernist in the mold of Joyce and Pound and T. S. Eliot, yet her accomplishments had been largely forgotten. In theory, at least, she was one of the experimental writers who laid the groundwork for the postwar boom of West Indian writing. She was Caribbean, a fact that might help breathe new life into her career, yet she was also white and a woman, whereas nearly all the writers of the Windrush Generation, as they came to be known, were men and not white. By the time she published *Wide Sargasso Sea* in 1966, Rhys would look enviously at the accomplishments of other West Indian writers, much as the narrator of "The Day They Burned the Books" looks enviously at her friend. In a curious reversal, Rhys' long and unusual career suggests that the record of interwar modernism was subtly but decisively shaped by the advent of colonial and postcolonial writing. There is little doubt that writers from the colonial world learned extensively from modernism, but Rhys' case further demonstrates that the record of modernism is partly a product of its reinvention by colonial and postcolonial writers.

Rhys' depictions of dissidence and racial difference suggest that interwar modernist styles could be productively adapted to the postwar literary and political climate. Comparisons of her earlier and later texts show the unexpected continuities, and underlying tensions, between interwar British modernism and postwar writing from colonial and postcolonial sources. In her writing from the 1920s and

1930s, Rhys closely identifies blackness with other forms of dissidence characteristic of bohemian modernism. Rhys sometimes fantasized about being black in order to convey her dissatisfaction with bourgeois metropolitan culture. Like many of her white colleagues, her protest implied a blend of aesthetic, political, and social nonconformity. In her later writing, however, her cross-racial fantasies were a reaction to a slightly different cultural and political environment: not only were British colonies gaining independence, but West Indian writers had become something of a hot commodity in the metropolitan literary world. White writers, by comparison, were fairly unremarkable creatures. After Rhys' reincarnation as a postcolonial intellectual, she would envy black people not for their righteous poverty and disenfranchisement, as she did in her younger days, but instead for their newfound political dominance in the Caribbean and their literary accomplishments in England.

LEFT BANK DAYS

Before taking a closer look at Rhys' published fiction, I would like to spend a few pages discussing some of the unusual features of her biography—not as a way to establish authorial intent, but in order to show how her identity as a credentialed modernist was connected to her postwar rediscovery. Particularly durable was the close association between dissidence and creative work. As any number of memoirs and accounts of the interwar Left Bank suggest, aesthetic masterpieces seemed to flourish principally in the rich soil of bohemia. If anything, the bond between dissidence and creative genius was tightened in the postwar period, especially with the advent of colonial and postcolonial writing. By the 1960s, Rhys' former bohemianism, now fairly passé, was greatly enhanced by her expertise in the colonial world. "The Day They Burned the Books" hints at this transition with its final sentences. The narrator, having escaped with Maupassant's novel about a sexually dissident artist, recalls disappointment with her plunder because the book "seemed dull" (47); much more exciting were Eddie's unexpected broadsides against English smugness. If artists of the Left Bank could offer a hint of life on the other side of respectability, colonial and postcolonial writers were expected to give a glimpse of life on the other side of the imperial divide. Rhys was particularly unusual in that she could do both. As her earliest critics noted, her unique gifts as a prose stylist were not incidental to, but utterly dependent on, her ability to see the world from the perspective of the dissident or outsider.

Rhys' life and early work conform to nearly all the prevailing stereotypes about Paris' Left Bank. She lived an unconventional life by most standards: she was poor, itinerant, a heavy drinker, and sexually liberated. Prurient interest in her sexual activities would resurface often in retrospective accounts of those years; she suffered an illegal abortion, lost a child in infancy, may have worked as a prostitute, and left her lone daughter in the charge of her ex-husband while she went to England to look for a publisher (himself only recently out of jail for trafficking in stolen goods). Between 1927 and 1939, she published one collection of stories and four novels, many of which draw on autobiographical materials. So similar are the novels that critics have assembled a composite "Rhys woman" out of their protagonists, often depicted as a down-and-out, aging, single woman flitting between London and Paris, overwhelmed by emotional problems and the consequences of failed sexual relationships.[2]

Rhys first emerged as a recognized participant-observer of bohemian life with the publication of *The Left Bank: Sketches and Studies of Present-Day Bohemian Paris* (1927). Rhys' collection tapped into a well-established tradition of representing the life of the gifted artist as notoriously unconventional. Ford Madox Ford, Rhys' patron and lover, introduces the volume, making a case for reading Rhys as the ideal ethnographer of Parisian bohemia: "Setting aside for a moment the matter of her very remarkable technical gifts, I should like to call attention to her profound knowledge of the life of the Left Bank—of many Left Banks of the world. For something mournful—and certainly hard-up!—attaches to almost all uses of the word *left*" (23). What she shows us is the Latin Quarter's seedy underbelly, stocked with cranks, petty criminals, prostitutes, disreputable cafes, radical students, and, of course, struggling artists—even by the late 1920s, well-worn snapshots of the Left Bank.[3] Ford closely associates her profound technical gifts, chiefly her stark, spare prose, with her ability to render convincingly the haunts of the resident artist community. In fact, her work represents the bohemian communities present in all the world's great cities. Beyond her technical abilities and her firsthand knowledge of the Left Bank, Ford claims that Rhys can evoke the atmosphere of bohemian Paris because she hails from "the Antilles, with a terrifying insight and a terrific—an almost lurid!—passion for stating the case of the underdog" (24). Although it would be decades before most readers made the explicit link between Rhys' participation in modernism, her ability to convincingly represent the underdog/minority figure, and her birth in the West Indies, Ford sets up this chain of causality from the very beginning of her career.

The fact that this observation remained buried for so long says as much about Ford's perspicacity as it does about the changing demands and interests of readers and scholars. Rhys's status as a dissident helped give her access to the scenes of modernist production in Paris, but it was not until her subsequent reclamation as a postcolonial writer that her status as a colonial had any special value in the metropolitan world of culture.[4] Her rediscovery confirmed legends about dissident modernism and helped reestablish Rhys as a figure with intimate knowledge of Joyce's Left Bank and the colonial world—two different stores of knowledge upon which she could draw to enhance her reputation as an artist in the postwar years. As her particular case illustrates, the emergence of postcolonial writing and the postwar history of modernism were related developments. The association between elite literature and dissidence was a staple of modernist ethnographies, as Ford's comments suggest, and it would become a prominent feature of postcolonial writing. But Rhys' rediscovery, coming during a period when metropolitan readers were turning to colonial writers for fresh literary ideas, shows that the emergence of postcolonial writing could also have a direct impact on the way scholars would write the history of interwar modernism itself.[5]

Although Rhys' biography may stand out for its sheer variety and noteworthy salaciousness, her case also serves as an exemplary instance of the close relationship between the marketing of unconventional literary personalities and the history of interwar modernism. As several recent studies have demonstrated, the myth of the self-standing work of modernist genius—a narrative that experimental writers themselves sometimes circulated—is dependent upon stamping particular texts with unique authorial credentials. In *Modernism and the Culture of Celebrity*, for example, Aaron Jaffe argues that the authorial imprimatur became an important feature of modernist literary production, a process carefully managed by artists and designed to confer distinction on individual texts through associations with an inimitable, often remote, genius. As Jaffe contends, recognizing the authorial signature as the primary sign of distinction grants a select group of artists the ability "to fix 'masterpieces' in emerging economies of cultural prestige," but this transaction also tends to efface "a matrix of secondary literary labors," such as the work of editing, promoting, reviewing, and teaching—activities that promote the myth of modernist inaccessibility by translating or explaining the significance of exceptionally difficult works for larger audiences (3). Modernist writers—and crucially, their agents, patrons, and publishers—were very aware that their desire to be recognized as unique geniuses could be dependent upon carefully managing the circulation of both their names and texts.[6]

According to Jaffe's model, Rhys's modernist career might be slotted into the "matrix of secondary literary labors," classified among the helpful contributions by modernism's lesser personalities. Not only did her work in *The Left Bank* lend an aura of mystique and inaccessibility to the artistic milieu of interwar Paris, but her other novels are often regarded as "minor masterpieces" against which the impressive bulk of the true heavyweights could be measured. Although such an account promises to explain the relative position of Rhys in a narrowly defined field of modernist culture (closer in stature to Ford or Djuna Barnes than to Joyce, say), it does not fully consider her entire career or her relations with other colonial and postcolonial artists. After the publication of *Wide Sargasso Sea*, Deutsch reissued most of her early fiction, thereby reconnecting the elderly Rhys with interwar modernism. But because of the subject matter of her later fiction and her posthumous biographies, Rhys also became more recognizable as a postcolonial writer just as her identity as a modernist became available once again. In Rhys's case, at least, modernism's bibliographic archive has changed substantially on the basis of its connection to late colonial writing in the 1950s. If figures such as Joyce or Pound profited from the labors of Rhys and others like her, Rhys herself benefited both from her associations with interwar modernists and from the work of other West Indian writers of the 1950s.

A Literary Reincarnation

During her revival, the titillating details of Rhys' life were frequently used by her handlers to enhance her status as a writer of unique gifts, revealing that the connection between symbolic capital and dissidence had not diminished with the advent of commonwealth writing, as it was then known. Rhys owed her rediscovery to an actress and enthusiastic fan, Selma Vaz Dias, who wanted to adapt *Good Morning, Midnight* for radio production. After years of trying to locate Rhys or her executor, as Vaz Dias recalled in "Quest for a Missing Author," she finally took out an advertisement in *New Statesman*, appealing for information. Amazingly, Rhys saw the ad and responded to it herself. Other key figures in Rhys' revival—John Lehmann, Francis Wyndham, and Diana Athill—had been involved in promoting several Windrush Generation writers in the 1950s. When *Wide Sargasso Sea* was finally published, Rhys' bizarre life became a useful marketing ploy. One review of Carole Angier's book on Rhys, for example, is accompanied by a caricature of her subject sitting unsteadily on an empty bottle of booze (*Sunday Times,* December 16, 1990). Without a hint of irony, Athill writes that Rhys' "inability to cope with life's practicalities went beyond anything I ever saw in anyone generally taken to be sane" (*Stet* 153). This, of course, comes from a "celebrity editor" who brags about being able to handle, and get the best out of, difficult literary personalities.

As Sarah Brouillette discusses in *Postcolonial Writers in the Global Literary Marketplace*, biographical details frequently serve as a template through which to read and evaluate postcolonial writers. The emergence of postcolonial writing as a distinct niche of the global culture industry means that postcolonial artists can no longer pretend, as their modernist predecessors sometimes did, that authorship could be divorced from the exigencies of commerce. If the Jean Rhys of the 1930s might appear blissfully unaware of herself as a commercial entity, the Jean Rhys of the 1960s is the product of a carefully designed marketing strategy. Postcolonial writers in particular are routinely pigeonholed by the publishing industry as representatives of and spokespeople for a marginalized corner of the globe from which they hail—whether they embrace such a role or not. The implied or explicit anti-imperial politics of many postcolonial writers only enhances this association of dissent with experimental writing. Whereas modernist artists reinforced the formal inaccessibility of their texts by sequestering themselves in bohemia, postcolonial intellectuals appear to metropolitan readers as an equally rare species because they come from, and serve as conduits to, far-flung regions of the world.

Describing the post-*Sargasso* Rhys as something of an industry, rather than an individual author, is another way of saying that we can usefully understand her reincarnation as a negotiation of intellectual property rights. As Paul Saint-Amour suggests, seeing authorial work as a form of intellectual property through copyright became an increasingly important feature of the culture industry in the late nineteenth and early twentieth centuries. The fact that Jean Rhys existed only as an author, not as a private person, neatly captures the sense of her literary identity as a site of cultural and commercial traffic (after her rediscovery, for example, most friends still knew her as Mrs. Hamer, the name she took from her third husband). As Angier tells the story, it was Ford who changed the writer's name from Ella Lenglet to Jean Rhys; Jean was the first name of her estranged husband, and Rhys was a variant of her father's surname (138). Because modern copyright relies on the notion of a unique aesthetic style (artists can copyright expression, but not content), writers with signature rhetorical devices have been able to benefit most from the protection offered by copyright law. Rhys' patently distinct, hard-boiled, style was particularly well suited to this sort of legal protection. In this light, the penchant for formal experimentation among interwar modernists can also be read as a sign of their awareness of their work as property, both commercial and cultural. For Rhys, and for many of her fellow Left Bank modernists, claims of aesthetic originality could be supplemented by a reputation for eccentricity.

Over the long haul of Rhys' career, we can see how these foundational elements of modernist culture—the related tropes of the bohemian author-dissident, of original genius, of formal experimentation—came to impact the emergence of postcolonial writing in English. This link between modernism and postwar global writing in English has both aesthetic and material significance, and it is this continuity in the materialist sphere that has been overlooked most by scholars of twentieth-century literature. Not only have colonial and postcolonial writers borrowed, reworked, and responded to modernist artistic models, but they also have labored under and circulated within market conditions established largely before World War II. As Saint-Amour argues, it is commonplace to read *Wide Sargasso Sea*'s rewriting of *Jane Eyre* as a postcolonial appropriation of the metropole's intellectual property, a kind of literary revenge upon the old colonial order. But Rhys's case also demonstrates how such symbolic plunder of metropolitan cultural capital was enabled by exercising intellectual property rights that were instrumental in defining modernist literary production. If anything, metropolitan literary institutions expanded in the postwar period by actively seeking to incorporate writers from the decolonizing world. In Rhys's unusual case, we can also observe how the emergence of postcolonial writing directly impacted the bibliographic record of interwar modernism. Not only did postwar writers from the colonial world style themselves the aesthetic descendants of Anglo-American modernism, but their emergence also helped redefine the parameters of twentieth-century literary history. With this in mind, I think it becomes feasible to characterize the postwar era less as a radical departure from modernism and more as a period when modernist culture was absorbing, at times aggressively so, diverse intellectuals who shared aesthetic interests with their metropolitan colleagues.

CROSSING THE COLOR LINE

Despite the aesthetic and institutional continuities straddling World War II, there are important differences between interwar modernism and late colonial/early postcolonial writing in English. These differences are especially apparent when we consider the relationship between experimental writing and depictions of racial difference. Broadly speaking, most scholars of modernism concur with Michael North's survey of the period: white modernists, such as Pound, Eliot, and Gertrude Stein (and, famously, Picasso in the plastic arts), selectively adopted black vernacular forms both to experiment technically and to disaffiliate themselves from mainstream culture. North and others have characterized these tactical representations of ethnic difference as racist: liberties taken by white artists that tend to reinforce, rather than dismantle, conventional racial hierarchies. By contrast, some scholars have prescribed postcolonial writing as the antidote to North Atlantic modernism, especially where depictions of racial difference are concerned.

Although these broad characterizations serve as a useful starting point for comparisons between interwar modernism and postwar colonial and postcolonial writing, there are some surprising areas of continuity in depictions of ethnic difference across these two generations of writers. In Rhys' case, there are marked differences between the early and late Rhys, or the modernist and postcolonial writer: the early Rhys seems to use race much like her fellow modernists, while the late Rhys seems more consistent with other postcolonial writers who contest racial hierarchies and British imperialism. But the continuity, as I will suggest, becomes most apparent when we examine how both the early and late Rhys use racial difference to depict the affect of vulnerability or disaffection—the underdog/minority figure identified by Ford as so crucial to Rhys' representations of Left Bank modernism. In the early Rhys, white characters affiliate themselves with blackness in order to give voice to feelings of alienation. But Rhys's reincarnation as a postcolonial writer happened after nonwhite intellectuals from the colonial world had emerged as some of the leading voices in experimental literature. Rhys's later depictions of racial difference appear less as the self-confident experiments of a white intellectual and more as a writer emulating and competing against her fellow West Indians—most of whom were not white, as she was. There is more than a touch of envy and vulnerability in those later texts. As both white and a colonial, she felt alienated from her white and black colleagues alike.

In her early work, Rhys depicts white protagonists fantasizing about being black to highlight the forms of sexual oppression and violence to which women are subjected. *Voyage in the Dark*, for example, tells the largely autobiographical story of a white woman from Dominica who comes to England. As a child, she remembers wishing she were black instead of white. "I wanted to be black, I always wanted to be black," Anna recalls, because "[b]eing black is warm and gay, being white is cold and sad" (31). These few phrases rely on common modernist fantasies: she thinks that Dominica's poor blacks lead more colorful lives, that they aren't weighed down by the cares of the world like the white bourgeoisie, and that they aren't suffocated by conventional morality. But even the young Anna shows an awareness of the island's racial antagonisms that complicate any simple desire to repudiate her whiteness. Anna's closest connection with the local black population is through Francine, the family's cook. With Francine, who is only a bit older than Anna, the young protagonist remembers being happy, away from the clutches of her English stepmother.

Anna senses, however, that the attachment may not be reciprocal: "But I knew that of course she [Francine] disliked me too because I was white; and that I would never be able to explain to her that I hated being white. Being white and getting like Hester [Anna's stepmother], and all the things you get—old and sad and everything" (72). Her wish to be black is a relatively safe emotional choice, capturing her sense of alienation from her family and doing nothing to redress political inequities endemic to Dominica. She knows she cannot renounce her whiteness any more than Francine can disavow her blackness. In fact, Anna's temporary desire to be black depends on the systemic disenfranchisement of nonwhite ethnic groups in the colonial Caribbean. Anna's cross-racial fantasies, as she knows well, are affective strategies that resonate precisely because the material realities of racial difference are so entrenched in local politics.

For the narrator's hated English stepmother, however, Anna's wish to be black is perhaps more than the simple fantasy of a disaffected child. As Hester, who moved back to England after the death of Anna's father, complains in an exchange with her stepdaughter, "I tried to teach you talk like a lady and behave like a lady and not like a nigger and of course you couldn't do it. Impossible to get you away from the servants. The awful sing-song voice you had! Exactly like a nigger you talked—and still do." Worse, Hester implies that Anna's mother had black ancestry—entirely possible for a fourth-generation Creole. Despite Anna's fantasies about being black, she vehemently denies Hester's accusation: "'You're trying to make out that my mother was coloured,' I said. 'You always did try to make that out. And she wasn't'" (65). Anna has it both ways. She imagines herself as black, and even emulates the songs and speech of her black servants in order to free herself from conventional codes of behavior, but she is comfortable falling back on established racial hierarchies when her own status is threatened by suggestions of racial mixing in the family.

The novel concludes with a scene of delirious hallucination, of a Dominican carnival procession, while the narrator hemorrhages from a botched illegal abortion. At first, the dream follows Anna as she sits at the window of her family house, voyeuristically watching black Dominicans, all masked, dancing and singing with frenzied abandon. But as the passage progresses, the young spectator suddenly becomes a participant by joining the procession. In an extended reading of this scene, Mary Lou Emery likens the Caribbean carnival to its European counterpart (influentially studied by Bakhtin), with a crucial twist: black West Indians wear white masks, and their festivities mimic and exaggerate white forms of behavior, thereby momentarily escaping and critiquing imperial racial hierarchies. As Emery puts it, Anna's sudden immersion in the life of the carnival marks an important shift in her consciousness: "Anna's moment of understanding the blacks' point of view transforms her from a distant and frightened observer to a giddy participant" (78). Elaine Savory, in another detailed reading of the carnival scene, argues West Indian carnival celebrations, "informed with African traditions after Emancipation, became a briefly licensed space for challenging authority, providing relief of tension as well as an encouragement to cultural and political resistance" (106–07). Combined with Rhys' ethnographies of the Left Bank and her reputation as a bohemian nonconformist, *Voyage in the Dark* suggests that cross-racial fantasies could disturb the smooth functioning of metropolitan heterosexual relations. The novel's racial politics do not, however, do anything to undermine the novel's association with modernist aesthetics, which Ford so characteristically associates with the underdog/minority figure.

Whether we read this scene and others like it as racist or as anti-imperialist, the early Rhys uses cross-racial fantasies to mark herself as an outsider and to criticize prevailing codes of metropolitan bourgeois conduct. Emery gives a convincing account of the scene as a moment when Anna's naïve fascination with racial otherness is transformed into a genuine critique of gender and racial inequities, both associated with British imperial culture; others, such as Brathwaite and Gayatri Spivak, have accused Rhys of condescending racial attitudes in her work. But the disagreement about how to understand *Voyage in the Dark*'s cross-racial fantasies is underwritten by the text's striking conjunction of modernist dissidence and racial difference. Anna's ambivalent affiliation with blackness—she embraces it when it allows her to voice feelings of alienation, but is less enthusiastic when it is thrust upon her by her stepmother—becomes a crucial narrative strategy for emphasizing Anna's position as an outsider. In this respect, the novel's treatment of race, regardless of whether we read it as an apology for or criticism of imperialism, adds another dimension to the novel's rendition of modernist urban anomie, psychic fragmentation, and inner turmoil. Although the narrator's understandings of racial difference have significant political implications, they also operate here in an affective economy consistent with high modernist depictions of alienation and disaffection long associated with Eliot, Joyce, and Pound.

WHITENESS AND VULNERABILITY

Published over three decades after *Voyage in the Dark*, *Wide Sargasso Sea* poses slightly different questions about race, gender, and imperialism than Rhys' early work. There are some clear similarities with *Voyage in the Dark*, especially in the novel's use of a young narrator who travels from the West Indies to England, only to be disappointed by her relations with men. Beyond that, differences abound. *Wide Sargasso Sea*'s more nuanced depictions of cross-racial affiliations have as much to do with metropolitan literary culture circa the early 1960s as they do with the British imperial project of the previous century. In particular, the novel hesitantly responds to the unusual position in which the elder Rhys found herself—a white colonial writer, forgotten but once active in interwar modernism, who now would be compared both to her white modernist colleagues and also to fellow West Indians, none of whom were white. As *Wide Sargasso Sea* shows, an affiliation with blackness was no longer a viable way for Rhys to maintain her distance from

bourgeois conventionality. Instead, the novel exhibits anxieties about the displacement of white intellectuals from the ranks of the literati by young, innovative black
writers from the colonial world.

Unlike *Voyage in the Dark*, where an older protagonist claims to know that the
cross-racial attachments of her youth were not mutual, *Wide Sargasso Sea* depicts
moments of genuine, reciprocal affection across the color line. *Wide Sargasso Sea*'s
main character and sometimes narrator Antoinette forms a close friendship with a
black girl, Tia; her true love, whom she forsakes for an unfortunate marriage to a
white Englishman, is her mixed-race cousin, Sandi. Yet these portrayals of cross-
racial affection only highlight the sheer impossibility of maintaining such bonds in
the political climate of 1830s Jamaica. Emancipation of slaves in British colonies,
begun in 1834 and completed in 1838, did little to ameliorate racial and political inequities in the West Indies, as the Morant Bay rebellion of 1865 suggests. There were
no efforts to redistribute land, for instance, and slave owners, rather than slaves
themselves, were offered monetary compensation by the British government. Predictably, this did little to mollify former slave owners (and even less to satisfy former
slaves), and many small planters struggled to adapt to the post-Emancipation
economy.

As Spivak and several other readers of the novel have noted, *Wide Sargasso
Sea*'s sympathies reside primarily with the West Indian whites who fell on hard
times in the wake of abolition. Through Antoinette, the daughter of an impoverished plantation family, the novel unambiguously casts Jamaica's relatively poor,
insecure whites in the underdog/minority role present in Rhys' earlier work. Their
oppressors, to state the case reductively, are wealthier whites who exclude small
planters from polite society and aggrieved former slaves seeking some form of
revenge. Being black, the text suggests, is not to be wealthy or powerful, but it is
associated with a populist politics that Rhys supposes to be in the ascendant at
that moment. Poor whites, sold down the river by their rich brethren, serve in the
novel as a sort of buffer between the real imperialists and newly emancipated
slaves, sometimes absorbing the retributive violence of the latter group. The historical situation of the 1830s was in certain respects similar to the nationalist liberation movements of the 1950s and early 1960s, coinciding with the writing of
Wide Sargasso Sea: with British imperialism on the wane and the short-lived West
Indian Federation set to assume political control, it seemed white dominance in
the region was being challenged, successfully, from below. The elderly Rhys was
both aware of and indignant about the changing political climate in the West Indies: she complained bitterly that "the Dreads" were "taking over" Dominica and
the rest of the islands, destroying the Caribbean of her youth (Plante 42). For
Rhys, twentieth-century black nationalism in the Caribbean could be likened to
the post-Emancipation uprisings of former slaves. These signs of racial antagonism and populist politics made the elderly Rhys less comfortable casting West
Indian blacks in the role of oppressed outsiders.

The opening lines of the novel illustrate the predicament of the small planters
ruined by a combination of Emancipation and intense social pressure from other

whites: "They say when trouble comes close ranks, and so the white people did. But we were not in their ranks" (17). From the novel's very first words, Antoinette locates herself as part of a marginal constituency, precariously teetering between the resentful black masses and the island's haughty, wealthier whites, especially those recently arrived from England as administrators. The untimely death of Antoinette's father leaves the family poor and vulnerable, especially to attacks from former slaves; were it not for the cunning of the family's loyal servants, they would not have survived at all. The key scene in the novel's first section depicts a group of angry, largely anonymous black Dominicans burning down the family's home. As Antoinette flees, she sees Tia and runs toward her, fantasizing that she will leave her family and live with her black playmate: "We had eaten the same food, slept side by side, bathed in the same river. As I ran, I thought, I will live with Tia and I will be like her." Tia, however, has other ideas: before Antoinette reaches her, Tia apparently throws a rock, hitting Antoinette squarely on the forehead. The scene ends, in Antoinette's words, with the two girls staring "at each other, blood on my face, tears on hers. It was as if I saw myself. Like in a looking-glass" (45).

This confrontation is engrossing because it simultaneously opens up and forecloses possibilities of cross-racial identification. Race here operates as a structure of difference that tears this burgeoning friendship apart. Tia, stirred by the anger of the mob, seems to reject Antoinette's advances, casting her lot with her own family and fellow former slaves against Antoinette and her family. Despite their affection for one another, they are both imprisoned by the materiality of racial oppression and the history of racial exploitation in the West Indies. Their mirrored selves are rendered affectively similar but politically incompatible by the exigencies in which they make decisions. Moreover, the act of exclusion originates here with Tia, not Antoinette: Tia may be an ambivalent participant, but she does take action. "The Day They Burned the Books" enacts a similar transfer, shifting determination and agency to her black characters, leaving her young white protagonists passive spectators. Antoinette's whiteness and poverty merge to become a sign of vulnerability: cut off from wealthier white society as well as the social networks among emancipated blacks, Antoinette becomes in Tia's words a "white nigger," too poor to maintain the veneer of gentility and comfort long associated with whiteness in the Caribbean (24). Unlike *Voyage in the Dark*, in which the narrator cannot easily shake off the privilege associated with her race, *Wide Sargasso Sea* depicts material insecurity, social isolation, and political marginalization as the hardships unique to post-Emancipation whites.

Beyond speaking to the predicament of a ruined white planter class—and in this respect, *Wide Sargasso Sea* is not so different from U.S. postbellum writers such as William Faulkner—the novel also responds to the unusual position in which Rhys, the intellectual, found herself in the 1960s. Once a participant-observer of the interwar Left Bank, and a respected author in her own right, the elder Rhys owed much of her revival to the successes of people like Lamming, Naipaul, and Walcott, when the market for Commonwealth literature, as it was then known, first opened in Britain. Stories about her interwar activities were used to her advantage, of course, but her earlier work was reissued only after the dramatic launch of *Wide Sargasso Sea*. In that novel, her depictions of racial difference hint at her discomfort with the inevitable comparison to black writers from the Caribbean, many of whom had come to prominence during her disappearance. Rhys herself expressed an admiration for the poetry of Walcott, and she must have been aware of Naipaul's work through the Deutsch connection (Athill had published several of Naipaul's novels before working with Rhys). It is also likely that Wyndham, Phyllis Shand Allfrey (another white Dominican writer), and others would have kept her informed, at least in broad outlines, of developments in the literary industry, especially those that might positively impact her own career. Most important, Rhys' slightly different portrayal of racial politics suggests a different perspective than her work of the interwar period. In the 1930s, blackness functioned in her work as an unambiguous site of oppression, and her white protagonists repeatedly fantasize about it in order to emphasize their disaffiliation with other whites. In *Wide Sargasso Sea*, however, Rhys is far less willing to cast blacks in the role of oppressed minority, instead reserving that role for a very select group of whites ruined by the end of slavery. The ability and desire to connect whiteness with the affect of vulnerability became newly available at precisely this juncture—and even then, predominantly in the narrow milieu of literary culture, where it seemed, if only for a brief period, that literary innovation rested in the hands of writers from the colonial world.

Rhys' ambivalent identification with her fellow West Indian writers is even more evident in one of her most successful pieces of short fiction, "Let Them Call It Jazz." The story features a mixed-race narrator who speaks a modified West Indian argot, using characteristic verb tenses and phrases such as "[t]oo besides" and "dam' fouti liar" (*Tigers* 57, 59). This more extensive experiment in Caribbean vernacular is a sharp departure from Rhys' novels, which use dialect sparingly, and then only when directly quoting black characters. The narrator, Selina Davis, is a postwar emigrant from an unnamed Caribbean island. Like Eddie from "The Day They Burned the Books," Selina has a white father and a mixed-race mother; in London, her skin tone, hair, and accent mark her out as a recent arrival. The first sentence of the novel places her as a resident of London's Notting Hill district, an area well known for its large West Indian population (and the scene of an infamous "race riot" in 1958). Selina is an unemployed seamstress who drifts from one untenable situation to the next before ending up in the psychiatric ward of Holloway prison, as Rhys herself did. Unlike Rhys, who attacked a neighbor during a drunken quarrel, Selina is a victim of racial discrimination: white neighbors, complaining that the neighborhood is "respectable," provoke the young narrator into a rash act of violence, for which she comes before the courts.

A feckless drunkard, Selina's lone comfort is singing and dancing to tunes that come to her after a few drinks—again, much like Rhys, who often wrote with bottle in hand, though she claimed to edit her work sober. "Sometimes," Selina thinks to herself during her brief stretch in prison, "'I'm here because I wanted to sing' and I have to laugh" (63). The story's turning point happens during her confinement, where Selina overhears a fellow inmate singing the "Holloway Song," a tune underlining the

427

courage and pluck of the convicts. The song, she thinks, has a remarkable life of its own: "it don't fall down and die in the courtyard; seems to me it could jump the gates of the jail easy and travel far, and nobody could stop it" (64). After her release, Selina returns frequently to the number she first heard in prison, humming it to herself and developing the melody into a full-blown song. While whistling the tune at a party, a man approaches her and asks her to sing it again. Selina complies, and the man plays the jingle on an old piano, "jazzing it up." Selina doesn't care for his version, "but everybody else say the way he do it is first class." Weeks later, after completely forgetting the incident, Selina receives a letter in the mail from the man at the party, telling her he had sold the song, "and as I was quite a help he encloses five pounds with thanks." Reading the letter makes Selina want to cry, "For after all, that song was all I had. I don't belong nowhere really, and I haven't money to buy my way to belonging. I don't want to either. . . . Now I've let them play it wrong, and it will go from me like all the other songs—like everything. Nothing left for me at all" (66–67).

Many critics rightly situate this story in the context of West Indian migration to England during the 1950s and early 1960s. Like much of her other work, Rhys takes experiences from her own life—her own stay in Holloway—and works them into fictional shape. In fact, Rhys was so concerned that people would think the story unadorned autobiography that she departed from her usual practice of having the piece typed by a professional; instead, she sent the manuscript, written in longhand, to the trusted Wyndham, who then typed it out and passed it on to *London Magazine* (Angier 485). At first reading, Rhys' pointed use of minstrelsy might seem troubling to contemporary readers, who could plausibly object to this form of racial masquerade, in which an elderly white woman adopts the persona of a poor black immigrant to give voice to her own feelings of alienation and paranoia. This reading undoubtedly has merit, but in the context of Rhys' career, it is quite remarkable that this is virtually the only instance in which her protagonist and narrator is black or visibly mixed race. "Let Them Call It Jazz" offers something quite different than her earlier representations of cross-racial fantasies, in which white characters long to (but cannot) escape the social conventions of white society. Significantly, she locates this black character in postwar London, where nonwhite characters can still function as alienated, downtrodden outsiders. In the Caribbean, as we see with *Wide Sargasso Sea*, Rhys seems far less willing to grant black characters the considerable power of being part of a marginalized constituency.

More importantly, Rhys here explicitly identifies herself with other London-based artists and writers of the Windrush Generation. The bits of the story in which Selina has her creative work stolen are not nearly as autobiographical as the other sections—the story's denouement is Rhys projecting the fate of the artist into a story about her experience in prison. Although several critics have made productive efforts to compare Rhys' fiction to that of other Caribbean writers of the postwar era (most notably Emery, Raiskin, and Savory), no scholars have commented on the ambivalent awareness of black West Indian writing displayed in these fictional transactions. "Let Them Call It Jazz" shows an alertness, for example, to Rhys' status as both an artist and a producer of intellectual property—and this awareness comes in the form of an artist whose work is expropriated by the metropolitan culture industry with only the smallest acknowledgment. This story reveals a volatile combination of jealousy, emulation, and straightforward identification in its treatment of West Indian artists. There is a good deal of jealousy, to the degree that creativity is the special attribute of the black artist; there is explicit emulation, in the sense that Rhys' language approximates the forms of linguistic innovation practiced by several of her fellow West Indian writers of the period; and there is also a sense of more straightforward identification with black writers, conveyed by the way in which the marginal colonial artist has her creative gifts absorbed (and even perverted) by a rapacious metropolitan culture industry.

If we can claim that the disappointments of Selina represent in some way Rhys' own fears, the story can be read not only as an example of Rhys' ability to put herself in someone else's position—that of a black West Indian artist—but also as an instance of Rhys casting her lot with other colonial writers against metropolitan culture. By thus affiliating herself with fellow Caribbean artists, "Let Them Call It Jazz" explores the vexed relations between an emergent postcolonial West Indian literary voice and its metropolitan audiences. On one hand, the story wholeheartedly endorses the idea that black colonial writers now equal, or surpass, the technical and imaginative skills of their white colleagues in the culture industry. What's more, both black artists and white audiences know this to be the case. On the other hand, the narrative implies that colonial writers should be wary in their dealings with such a world. Rhys' story thus offers a slightly different perspective than *Wide Sargasso Sea* on the relations between colonial artists and the British publishing world. Like the novel, "Let Them Call It Jazz" certainly looks enviously at the accomplishments of nonwhite colonial writers, yet it also articulates a sense of frustration and suspicion that make it more identifiable as a postcolonial text—or at least puts it in the camp of postcolonial texts that affirm the need to carry on the work of decolonization in the cultural sphere. Even here, though, it is worth recalling how this nascent version of postcolonialism is dependent on understandings of intellectual property, which were themselves incubated and developed in the milieu of interwar modernism. Like several members of the Windrush Generation, Rhys begins to explore in her later work feelings of antagonism toward metropolitan literary culture. In this respect, the story is very consistent with the early stirrings of postcolonialism as the theoretical elaboration of anticolonial movements.[7]

Conclusion

As I have been arguing, tracing the long arc of Rhys' career shows the unexpected continuities and the equally unexpected differences between interwar modernism and the emergence of a postcolonial literary tradition. That depictions of racial difference should serve as a representational forum for considerations of dissidence may come as no surprise, but the fact that whiteness could, in the latter stages of

Rhys' life, economically capture her feelings of alienation does seem remarkable. If the Rhys of the 1930s could offer cross-racial fantasies as a protest against white bourgeois respectability, the Rhys of the 1960s figures her white, West Indian subjects as victims, stranded between black populism on the one side and elitist metropolitans on the other. Similarly, when she decided to depict an artist in "Let Them Call It Jazz"—and it is worth emphasizing that Rhys very rarely depicted characters who are artists, and nowhere else does she put a protagonist in that role—she felt compelled to make this figure a black woman in postwar London. To be sure, there is much about her response that is particular and idiosyncratic, yet there is also much in it that reflects more general conditions of the metropolitan literary marketplace during the period in question. The strain of racial masquerade, or cross-racial identification, is much more apparent in her work from the 1960s than it is in her earlier fiction. This strain is informed by the decolonization movements of the postwar moment, but it is powerfully reinforced by her vexed relations with other Caribbean writers and a literary establishment that had forgotten her long ago. The conventional wisdom that the flagging fortunes of experimental writing could be revived by an infusion of colonial talent helps explain why whiteness—which, in Rhys' earlier work, is secure as a marker of privilege—could become a site of dispossession and marginality; and, similarly, why a black artist in postwar London could function as both a victim of cultural expropriation and as a site of vital creativity. This change of strategy has its political dimensions, but it also responds to the delicately shifting racial contours of the postwar literary landscape.

This subtle change in the racial composition of metropolitan literary culture, however, happened within a context of strong continuities that tended to reinforce and expand the scope of interwar modernist principles, especially those prizing aesthetic innovation. Although new literary talent began pouring in from the distant corners of a disintegrating British Empire, those figures found an audience disposed to appreciate both technical novelty and expressions of disaffection. The dissidence of modernist bohemia converted easily into the seeming dissidence of anticolonial intellectuals; incorporation of regional dialect, practiced by many postcolonial writers, could be seamlessly integrated into traditions of modernist experimentation. To thus conclude that Anglo-American modernism influenced the trajectory of postcolonial writing in English is true but very incomplete: I also want to suggest that this relationship was more (if not wholly) reciprocal because of the fact that postcolonial intellectuals, by continuing to deploy and develop interwar techniques, also helped secure legitimacy for modernist culture in the postwar climate. In recent years, scholars have become more sensitive to the formal and thematic similarities between Anglo-American modernism and postcolonial literature. It is now acceptable, for example, to compare the poetry of Walcott or Kamau Brathwaite with Eliot, or the prose of Lamming or Wilson Harris with Joyce. Despite this development, there is still much work to be done on the institutional relations between modernism and postcolonial writing. In this chapter, I have tried to use the strange case of Jean Rhys to examine the durability of the author-dissident figure. In so doing, I hope to have demonstrated the degree to which modernism and postcolonialism depend upon one another for self-definition, and even the extent to which such definitions include large regions of contiguity and overlap. Without smoothing out the discontinuities between them, political or otherwise—my discussion of racial conflict shows striking differences in the understandings attached to whiteness—my objective in this chapter has been to place both movements in the same literary-historical narrative. They ought to share this story not simply because one follows the other in some sort of natural progression, but because postcolonial literature was instrumental in reaffirming and redefining the status of experimentation in literature. The strong scholarly tendency to equate modernism with dissidence and formal experimentation owes more than we realize to the emergence of postcolonial writing in the latter half of the century.[8]

NOTES

1. See Peter Kalliney.

2. See Thomas Staley, the first full-length critical study of Rhys, Louis James, and Francis Wyndham's introduction to *Wide Sargasso Sea*.

3. Even by the early 1900s, the images of the bohemian artist were cliché. The Oxford English Dictionary suggests that "bohemian" was used to describe the connection between urban living, unconventionality, and artists as early as the 1840s. By the time Arthur Ransome wrote his memoirs in 1908, he was already referring to London bohemia with a knowing irony. As Michael Murphy notes, by the 1910s, bohemian enclaves were appearing in popular guidebooks and in glossy magazines such as *Vanity Fair*. See also Peter Brooker, Hugh David, and Mary Gluck.

4. The question of how to position Rhys is particularly vexed in the criticism. Early treatments of her work by Anglo-American scholars typically described her as a sort of modernist literary refugee, placeless, not properly belonging to the Caribbean, England, or Europe. This sense of displacement contributed to feminist treatments of her work (see Veronica Gregg and Nancy Harrison, for example). Her identity as a Caribbean writer was not firmly established until well into the 1970s; it was not uncommon to still refer to the Rhys of the 1960s as "the best living *English* novelist," as Al Alvarez did when reviewing *Wide Sargasso Sea* (my emphasis; as my introductory gloss on "The Day They Burned the Books" implies, Rhys despised England and reacted angrily when anyone referred to her as English). Not surprisingly, it was Caribbean intellectuals who first debated her status as a West Indian novelist, though her status was far from secure in their eyes. While Wally Look Lai and Kenneth Ramchand were comfortable placing her work in the West Indian canon, Kamau Brathwaite, in *Contadictory Omens*, strongly rejected her inclusion on the basis of her whiteness. He later softened his stance, calling *Wide Sargasso Sea* a "great Caribbean novel," but used it as an opportunity to reject the rubric "postcolonial" ("A Post-Cautionary Tale" 69). Since 1990 or so, nearly everyone agrees that the West Indian background is important for her work (Teresa O'Connor and Judith Raiskin were among the first U.S. scholars to explore this aspect of her work). Mary Lou Emery, Elaine Savory, and Helen Carr provide useful overviews of Rhys scholarship. For my part, I think the term postcolonial can be usefully applied to Rhys' later work because the depictions of race in her later work are deeply informed by the politics of decolonization.

5. For example, see Shari Benstock's extremely influential *Women of the Left Bank*.

6. See also Lawrence Rainey and Loren Glass.

7. Almost intuitively, Rhys depicts an environment in which white vultures prey upon nearly defenseless black colonial subjects. Brief as it may be, "Let Them Call It Jazz" has much in common with Lamming's *The Pleasures of Exile* (1960), in which the successful West Indian novelist of the 1950s turns his anger against the metropolitan "culture vultures" for the first time.

8. I would like to thank Mary Lou Emery and the Social Theory group at the University of Kentucky for their feedback on earlier drafts of this chapter. Sean Latham, Thomas Staley, and the staff at the McFarlin Library at the University of Tulsa were very helpful with my archival research on Rhys.

WORKS CITED

Alvarez, A. "The Best Living English Novelist." *New York Times Book Review*. 17 March 1974: 6–7.

Angier, Carole. *Jean Rhys*. London: Deutsch, 1990.

Athill, Diana. *Stet: An Editor's Life*. London: Granta, 2001.

Benstock, Shari. *Women of the Left Bank: Paris, 1900–1940*. Austin: University of Texas Press, 1986.

Brathwaite, Kamau. *Contradictory Omens: Cultural Diversity and Integration in the Caribbean*. Mona: Savacou, 1974.

———. "A Post-Cautionary Tale of the Helen of Our Wars." *Wasafiri* 22 (1995): 69–70.

Bronte, Charlotte. *Jane Eyre*. 1847. Ed. Richard J. Dunn. 3rd ed. New York: Norton, 2001.

Brooker, Peter. *Bohemia in London: The Social Scene of Early Modernism*. Basingstoke: Palgrave Macmillan, 2004.

Brouillette, Sarah. *Postcolonial Writers in the Global Literary Marketplace*. Basingstoke: Palgrave Macmillan, 2007.

Carr, Helen. "Jean Rhys: West Indian Intellectual." *West Indian Intellectuals in Britain*. Ed. Bill Schwarz. Manchester: Manchester University Press, 2003. 93–113.

David, Hugh. *The Fitzrovians: A Portrait of Bohemian Society 1900–1955*. London: Michael Joseph, 1988.

Emery, Mary Lou. *Jean Rhys at "World's End": Novels of Colonial and Sexual Exile*. Austin: University of Texas Press, 1990.

Glass, Loren. *Authors Inc.: Literary Celebrity in the Modern United States, 1880–1980*. New York: New York University Press, 2004.

Gluck, Mary. "Theorizing the Cultural Roots of the Bohemian Artist." *Modernism/modernity* 7 (2000): 351–78.

Gregg, Veronica Marie. "Jean Rhys and Modernism: A Different Voice." *The Jean Rhys Review* 1 (1987): 30–46.

Harrison, Nancy. *Jean Rhys and the Novel as Women's Text*. Chapel Hill: University of North Carolina Press, 1988.

Jaffe, Aaron. *Modernism and the Culture of Celebrity*. Cambridge: Cambridge University Press, 2005.

James, Louis. *Jean Rhys*. London: Longman, 1979.

Kalliney, Peter. "Metropolitan Modernism and Its West Indian Interlocutors: 1950s London and the Emergence of Postcolonial Literature." *PMLA* 122 (2007): 89–104.

Lamming, George. *The Pleasures of Exile*. 1960. London: Allison and Busby, 1984.

Look Lai, Wally. "The Road to Thornfield Hall: An Analysis of *Wide Sargasso Sea*." *New Beacon Reviews* 1 (1968): 38–52.

Murphy, Michael. "'One Hundred Percent Bohemia': Pop Decadence and the Aestheticization of Commodity in the Rise of Slicks." In *Marketing Modernisms: Self-Promotion, Canonization, and Rereading*. Ed. Kevin J. H. Dettmar and Stephen Watt. Ann Arbor: University of Michigan Press, 1996. 61–89.

O'Connor, Teresa. *Jean Rhys: The West Indian Novels*. New York: New York University Press, 1986.

Plante, David. *Difficult Women: A Memoir of Three*. London: Gollancz, 1983.

Raiskin, Judith L. *Snow on the Cane Fields: Women's Writing and Creole Subjectivity*. Minneapolis: University of Minnesota Press, 1996.

Ramchand, Kenneth. *The West Indian Novel and Its Background*. London: Heinemann, 1970.

Rhys, Jean. *The Complete Novels*. Introduction Diana Athill. New York: Norton, 1985.

———. *The Left Bank: Stories and Sketches of Present-Day Bohemian Paris*. Introduction. Ford Madox Ford. London: Cape, 1927.

———. *Tigers Are Better-Looking*. London: André Deutsch, 1968.

———. *Voyage in the Dark*. 1934. New York: Norton, 1982.

———. *Wide Sargasso Sea*. 1966. New York: Norton, 1982.

Saint-Amour, Paul. *The Copywrights: Intellectual Property and the Literary Imagination*. Ithaca: Cornell University Press, 2003.

Savory, Elaine. *Jean Rhys*. Cambridge: Cambridge University Press, 1998.

Spivak, Gayatri Chakravorty. "Three Women's Texts and a Critique of Imperialism." *Critical Inquiry* 12 (1985): 243–61.

Staley, Thomas. *Jean Rhys: A Critical Study*. Austin: University of Texas Press, 1979.

CHAPTER 18

THE URBAN LITERARY CAFÉ AND THE GEOGRAPHY OF HEBREW AND YIDDISH MODERNISM IN EUROPE

SHACHAR PINSKER

It is almost impossible to sketch a neat map or linear chronology of Hebrew and Yiddish modernism. The creation of modernist Hebrew and Yiddish literature in the early decades of the twentieth century was by and large a result of, and a response to, the encounter of East European Jewish society with urban modernity. Hebrew and Yiddish modernist literatures developed, to use Chana Kronfeld's influential term, on "the margins of modernism," and were written in distinctly minor languages, without the continuous tradition of belletristic writing that characterize most European national literatures. It is clear, though, that any attempt to understand the multilayered phenomena of modernist literature in Jewish languages must reckon with the transition of Hebrew and Yiddish modernist writers from the world of the East European shtetl to the world of the city. Moving to the city was an overwhelming experience for modernist Jewish authors and a major preoccupation in their fiction and poetry. Several cities and urban centers in Eastern, Central, and Western Europe (as well as in America and in Palestine) incubated Hebrew and Yiddish modernism in various guises: as literary centers and enclaves, as sites for contact and interaction with other literatures, and as settings for the shifting modernist literary representations of urban life (see Pinsker).

Unlike more established national literatures, Hebrew or Yiddish did not have a "literary center" but only peripheries and enclaves. Such enclaves existed in European cities like Odessa, Warsaw, Kiev, Vilnius (Vilna), and Moscow, and also in small frontier cities like Homel, Lvov/Lemberg, Łódź, and Krakow. Furthermore, these enclaves could be found both at the centers and the margins of these metropolitan areas, in the immigrant neighborhoods of cities like Vienna, Berlin, Paris, and London. One of the problems with charting these locations and studying their role in the development of Hebrew and Yiddish modernism is precisely their ephemeral, transitory nature, as well as the fact that they were not traditional homes of national culture, but sites of migration in which writers and artists were refugees and "resident aliens."

One of the best and most productive ways to grasp the problem of location in Hebrew and Yiddish modernism is through the prism of the urban European café. Cafés help chart the geography and spatial history of European modernism writ large, and they illuminate key aspects of modernity and modernism in general. They are particularly important to understanding Hebrew and Yiddish modernism. The urban café played a decisive role in each and every city in which modernist Hebrew and Yiddish literature was created: in Eastern European cities such as Odessa, Warsaw, and Kiev, and in Central European cities such Lvov/Lemberg, Berlin, and Vienna. The urban European café was also "imported" and re-reated in the new centers of Jewish culture, New York City and Tel Aviv.[1] Cafés were not only the setting in which modernist literature was created but also the object of a great deal of modernist literary representation in which the urban Jewish predicament was written in radically new ways. And yet these quintessentially modern spaces were far from being "Jewish spaces" in any simple way.

The café, I will argue, should be understood as a kind of "thirdspace," a concept that emerges from work on the "production of space" and "lived environment" by cultural geographers such as Henri Lefebvre and Edward Soja.[2] Thirdspace is important to a study of the café in modernism/modernity, especially to my exploration of Jewish modernism. First, it provides an epistemological starting point for developing a mobile methodology that is spatially, culturally, and historically aware. Second, the literary café is a thirdspace in which the theoretical, the historical, and textual meet and constantly intersect without an attempt to demarcate them. And third, it functions as a geographical metaphor: the modernist literary café is a thirdspace located at the thresholds and the slippery border-zone between the "public" and the "private," the "inside" and the "outside," the "real" and "imagined," the "immigrant" and the "native," the "elitist," artistic avant-garde and "mass" consumption. As we shall see, the café has been also a thirdspace that mediates between Jews and non-Jews. The café can be and has been a site of the enunciation of identity, lived experience, and contested meanings.

In later sections I will provide detailed discussions of the cultural and literary significance of particular cafés and three specific cities in which Hebrew and Yiddish interacted with other transnational modernisms: Odessa, Vienna, and Berlin. Before turning to café culture in these cities, however, it will be helpful first to pull back to sketch in the historical specificity of Hebrew and Yiddish literature and to place Hebrew and Yiddish modernism in relation to mainstream European modernism.

"MODERN JEWISH REVOLUTION" AND THE TRAJECTORY OF MODERNISM

Although Hebrew literature can lay some claim to the religious literary tradition that goes back to the Hebrew Bible and other ancient and medieval sacred texts, belletristic literature, in the modern European sense, is a relatively new phenomenon. It was mainly the product of the *Haskalah* movement (the Jewish Enlightenment), which emanated from Moses Mendelssohn and his circle in Berlin in the late eighteenth century and gained some momentum throughout Eastern and Central Europe in the nineteenth century. The proponents of the *Haskalah* were a small and elitist group of Jewish writers who wanted to promote rationality, secular education, the integration of Jewish society into modern Europe, and vernacular literature. Since Hebrew had not been used as a daily vernacular for many centuries, the literature created in this language faced all kinds of anomalies unknown to European literatures with more continuous literary traditions. Perhaps most acute was the need to develop a flexible and supple literary language, an issue that Hebrew writers dealt with throughout the nineteenth and early twentieth centuries.[3]

Yiddish literature reverses the relationship between vernacular and literary languages that is found in Hebrew. For centuries, Yiddish—a diasporic Jewish language that was defined by its chief historian, Max Weinreich, as a "fusion language" with Germanic, Slavic, and Semitic elements—was almost exclusively used as the daily, mundane vernacular of Ashkenazi Jews scattered all over Eastern Europe and the Pale of Settlement.[4] Yiddish was considered by most proponents of *Haskalah* as the lowly "jargon" of simple Jews and thus not fitting for "serious" belletristic literature. The very creation of belletristic literature in Yiddish in the nineteenth century was imbued with a folkish rhetoric, clearly connected with the Russian notion of Народничество ("Narodnichestvo," or populism). Yiddish literature was initially promoted as a literature for the masses, especially "suited" for women and the uneducated poor. It was only by the end of the nineteenth century that Yiddish literary institutions (including journals and book publishers) were formed, and a new "tradition"—complete with its "classic writers"—was invented and declared (see Frieden).

There was accordingly a "time lag" between major European literatures and Yiddish and Hebrew, and writing akin to romantic and realist fiction and poetry were created in these two literatures only in the last decades of the nineteenth century. This situation changed dramatically, however, at the turn of the twentieth century, when Jewish society in Europe underwent dramatic and far-reaching change—what Benjamin Harshav calls the "modern Jewish revolution." In the late nineteenth and early twentieth centuries, approximately two million Jews left the Pale of Settlement, fleeing poverty, pogroms, civil wars, and revolutions. This migration was accompanied by the abrupt erosion of traditional Jewish institutions, the rise of new ideologies, and an intense process of urbanization. As Harshav notes, there are many parallels between this Jewish historical and cultural revolution and the trajectory of literary and artistic modernism: "Modernism *impressed* all of Jewish culture and literature and, vice versa, many who were active in general modernism were Jews. Joining general culture was especially convenient when the whole previous tradition (not shared by Jews) was overthrown" (*Language in Time of Revolution* 67).

In light of recent studies of modernism and its complex relations with the literary traditions of the past, Harshav's sweeping assumption that the "whole previous tradition was overthrown" is questionable.[5] And yet, his emphasis on the parallels between radical changes in modern Jewish culture, language and literature and the rise of modernism helps explain the fact that the first modernist stage of Hebrew and Yiddish literature, however "belated" in relation to some other modernisms, occurred as early as 1900. When viewed from the global perspective of this volume, we can see that Hebrew and Yiddish modernism grappled with aesthetic and ideological issues not so different from those of Greek, Turkish, or even Asian modernisms. Apart from the question of language (vernacular vs. poetic language) and literary tradition, a significant part of "the modern Jewish revolution" in the late nineteenth and early twentieth centuries was an intense political fermentation. This period saw the simultaneous emergence of Jewish nationalism, Zionism, and socialism, all accompanied by massive transnational Jewish migration.

In some cases, tensions arose between these ideological movements and modernist poetics. Many Hebrew writers (such as Hayim Nahman Bialik, who was dubbed "the national poet") were compelled to provide the Zionist revival movement with romantic and "prophetic" poetry, as well as with "realist," mimetic representations of contemporary Jewish life, at the same time that they were experimenting with contemporary symbolist, impressionist and decadent poetic modes (see Bar Josef). In the interwar period, various modernist poetic groups and individual writers (loosely affiliated with expressionism, futurism, acmeism, and imaginism) became aligned with—and could be harnessed to—contradictory political and ideological means: from nationalist ideologies of renaissance and nation-building (notably in the context of Zionism, but also in the Jewish Territorialism in Europe that was tied to the ideology of Yiddishism) to radical Socialism, Communism, and everything in between.

The complexity of modernist literature in Jewish languages is further revealed in the substantial overlap in authorship and readership between Yiddish and Hebrew. In fact, many writers in this period were not only bilingual but multilingual, writing in three languages. At the same time, however, ideological confrontations between Yiddish and Hebrew compelled many writers to become active primarily in one literature and not the other. In hindsight, it is quite clear that Hebrew and Yiddish literatures were not, as some critics of the period proclaimed, "one unified literature in two languages," and yet it is impossible to trace and understand Yiddish and Hebrew modernism without examining them in relation to one another.[6]

Modernism in Jewish languages cannot be said to produce "poetic movements" in any conventional sense, but rather provisional constellations of writers, often with similar or intersecting poetic tendencies. Some writers and groups (especially in the interwar period) propagated manifestoes outlining their various poetic creeds. In most cases, however, the only "rule" was experimentation, accompanied by an acute sense of breaking with the past and an intense self-consciousness about the linguistic texture of a literature in a state of radical flux. These modernisms constituted a set of cross-cutting streams with a distinct Jewish accent even as they were also part of the larger currents of European and transnational modernism.[7] In order to begin tracing the tense but productive relation between Hebrew and Yiddish modernism and European cities, let me turn back now to the role of literary café. By grounding my discussion in this institution, I hope to counter the critical tendency to allegorize particular histories of displacement and diaspora into what Raymond Williams once called "a universal myth" of migration and transience (*The Politics of Modernism* 34).

MODERNISM AND THE THIRDSPACE OF THE LITERARY CAFÉ

Though the field of modernist studies lacks a good comparative study of cafés, individual sites—especially what is known as the "literary café" (*Literarische kaffeehäus* in German, *Literaturnoe kafe* in Russian)—have not of course gone unnoticed in criticism. Such cafés played a crucial role in literary and artistic modernism in the late nineteenth and early twentieth centuries in many major European cities.[8] Countless bohemians and avant-garde writers and artists sat, worked, and often put their unconventionality or eccentricity on display in these places, and many readers of this volume are probably acquainted to some degree with the importance of places such as Café Griensteidl and Central in Vienna, the Café-des-Westens and the Romanisches Café in Berlin, and the numerous cafés of the Left Bank and Montparnasse in Paris. Equally significant, however, are less famous cafés in cities in Rome, Zurich, Lisbon, Prague, St. Petersburg, Budapest, Odessa, Warsaw, and elsewhere.[9] The pivotal and complex role of the café can be better grasped by looking at the reflections of many modernist writers and thinkers on the café, as well as at more theoretical writings by Jürgen Habermas, Oskar Negt, Alexander Kluge, and George Steiner.[10]

Any study of the café in modernism must reckon with Jürgen Habermas's influential concept of the modern public sphere, for which the coffeehouses of London in the eighteenth century provide his exemplary case. As valuable as his account is, it has required some reassessment on historical grounds (See Eley; Ellis; and Cowan). For Habermas, the coffeehouse was a key example of how bourgeois culture necessitated the creation of new institutions, and the café emerges as a space somehow detached from the economic field of transactions and freed from the constraints of religious dogma, a place where reason and not social rank matters (see Norberg). Yet Habermas tends to idealize the coffeehouse as a space of "nonhierarchical deliberation," a view not entirely supported by historical research. What's more, even though the period between 1850 and 1939 was a golden age of café culture across almost all of Europe, for Habermas the coffeehouse as a space of the public sphere reached its heyday in the London of the eighteenth century and fell into a state of "decline" during the nineteenth century, when it was "invaded" by private interests (141–80).

In their study *Öffentlichkeit und Erfahrung* ("The Public Sphere and Experience," 1972), Oskar Negt and Alexander Kluge provide a useful corrective by arguing that the late nineteenth century saw not so much a decline but a further transformation of public culture, which was reconstituted in the context of new stages of economic, technical, and political organization. In the transformed public sphere of the late nineteenth and early twentieth century, Negt and Kluge claim, spatial and social experiences were mediated through what they call "public spheres of production." As Miriam Hansen has claimed in her introduction to their work, Negt and Kluge continue to use Harbermas's term *Öffentlichkeit* ("public sphere"), but in a new dialectical way that points to the tensions between space and the social relations that produce space, similar to the dialectical tensions between what Raymond Williams has called culture as "a way of life" and a "structure of feeling" ("Forward" ix).[11]

This dialectics of *Öffentlichkeit* in Negt and Kluge opens up new insights into the space and the culture of the urban café, especially the so-called literary café of late nineteenth- and early twentieth-century modernism. These dialectical tensions were documented in the writings of Hebrew and Yiddish immigrant modernists who frequented these institutions both by necessity and choice, as well as by modernists writing in Russian and German (most of them Jewish or of Jewish origins). In his essay *Berliner Chronik* ("Berlin Chronicle" 1932), Walter Benjamin uses various Berlin cafés (Victoria Café, Café-des-Westens, Romanisches Café and Café Princess) as a chief "guide" around which he creatively arranges his "lived experience" of Berlin, not as a linear history but as the "space of his life . . . on a map" (12). Articulating what he calls a "physiognomy" or "physiology" of Berlin cafés of the 1910s and 1920s, Benjamin attempts to divide Berlin cafés into "professional" and "recreational" establishments, but he quickly notes that the classification is superficial inasmuch as the two categories coincide and collapse upon each other ("Berlin Chronicle" 46). Benjamin thus demonstrates that the "lived experience" of the "literary café" in Berlin suggests that it is a liminal space marked by a subversion of distinctions between private and public, professional and recreational, bourgeois and bohemian, literary and consumer culture.

Related perspectives can be found in writings on the Viennese cafés. Especially important is Alfred Polgar's sardonic feuilleton *Theorie des Café Central* ("Theory of Café Central" 1926), in which he uses the famous Viennese *literarische kaffehäus* to sketch another "physiology" of the café:

> The Café Central is indeed a coffeehouse unlike any other coffeehouse. It is instead a worldview and one, to be sure, whose innermost essence is not to observe the world at all. . . . So much is experientially certain, that there is nobody in the Café Central who isn't a piece of the Central: that is to say, on whose ego-spectrum the Central color, a mixture of ash-gray and ultra-seasick-green, doesn't appear. . . . The Café Central lies on the Viennese latitude at the meridian of loneliness. Its inhabitants are, for the most part, people whose hatred of their fellow human beings is as fierce as their longing for people, who want to be alone but need companionship for it. . . . There are writers, for example, who are unable to carry out their literary chores anywhere but at the Café Central. Only there, only at the tables of idleness, is the worktable laid for them, only there, enveloped by the air of indolence, will their inertia become fecundity. (149)

Here again the literary café emerges as a public-private space with distinctively contradictory features: on one hand, a place of leisure and sociability, a literary market and information source exempt from the pressure to consume; on the other, a place of consumption and of noncommitment, of time-killing and gossip, a refuge for drop-outs and failures who can find their place only in the café (see Carr). Melekh Ravitch, a Yiddish modernist poet from Galicia and habitué of cafés in Lvov/Lemberg, Vienna, Warsaw, and Montreal, turns to an avian metaphor to get at the tension between the singular and the collective in Café Abatzya, an institution not far from the local Yiddish theater in the frontier city of Lvov/Lemberg: "Like pigeons, who can only live in company, and who immediately begin pecking at one another as soon as they come across a grain of food—this is the conduct of the regulars in Café Abatzya: the artists, the actors, and also we, the writers" (*Dos mayse-bukh fun mayn lebn* 115–16). The entire Yiddish and Hebrew artistic and literary community assembles in Café Abatzya—to peck at each other.

These accounts of the tensions and contradictions within the literary café describe what I am calling, following Soja, a thirdspace. Soja argues that the nature of human existence is made known to us through what he calls the "trialectics of being": spatiality (or the production of space), historicality (or time), and sociality (or being-in-the-world). Building on Henry Lefebvre and Homi Bhabha,[12] Soja attempts to problematize the distinction between real and imagined space by challenging the dichotomy of thinking of space as either real (i.e., physical or material) or imagined (i.e., mental, abstract or ideational). What Soja calls "thirdspace"—a "purposefully tentative and flexible term that attempts to capture what is actually a constantly shifting and changing milieu of ideas, events, appearances and meanings"—offers a new of way of thinking about "the inherent spatiality of human life: place, location, locality, landscape, environment, home, city, region, territory, and geography" ("Thirdspace: Toward a New Consciousness of Space and Spatiality" 49–50). Bearing in mind the notion of space as an active presence in human existence, let us turn now to Odessa, Vienna, and Berlin.

ODESSA: URBAN AMBIVALENCE AND THE NEW JEWISH WOMAN

Cafés in urban centers all over Europe were especially attractive spaces for Jews for both social and economic reasons. In the eighteenth century, coffee was a new commodity that Jews had not yet been prohibited from trading, and they were quick to take it up (see Liberles). When coffeehouses were founded in Europe—some of them by Sephardic Jews who brought the commodity and the institution of the café from the Middle East—Jews embraced them as well (Cowan 25). As Jews were not always welcomed in clubs and pubs where alcohol was the central beverage being served, the café emerged as an attractive alternative, first as a site for informal business and commodity exchange, and later as a site of political, cultural, and literary exchange. In many European cities, Jews were enthusiastic participants, and sometimes initiators, of café culture (see Wobick). Amid the upheaval and migrations at the turn of the twentieth century, the European urban café became a particularly alluring space for Jewish writers. Often a substitute home or community for émigrés, exiles, and refugees, the café was also where writers encountered modernism and modernity in the most intense way.

Let us begin in Eastern Europe in the thoroughly modern Russian city of Odessa. Odessa, established in 1794 by the Empress Catherine the Great, was in the nineteenth century a new frontier city. With handsome streets laid out by Italian and French architects, a harbor sending shiploads of grain to every Mediterranean port, and a unique ethnic mélange of Russians, Ukrainians, Jews, Greeks, Moldavians, Turks, Bulgarians, Armenians, French, and Italians, Odessa was the capital of Russia's "wild south" on the shores of the Black Sea. It also had a large Jewish presence. On the eve of World War I, Jews numbered 165,000, a third of the city's population. Even more important was the fact that nineteenth-century Odessa was perceived as a center of newfound Jewish freedom within the Russian Empire. This freedom was represented in a highly ambivalent way in the popular imagination. If to live in Odessa was to live *vi got in odes*—"like God in Odessa," according to a Yiddish proverb—the city was simultaneously imagined as the place where "the fires of hell burn for seven miles around it" (see Zipperstein 1). Odessa was accordingly envisioned in two very different ways. On one hand, it was understood as a center of modern Jewish culture and literature, complete with its "classic writers" and the circle known as "the Odessa sages." On the other hand, it was seen as a criminal underworld by writers such as Isaac Babel, who immortalized the fictional Jewish gangster Benya Krik in his *Odessa Tales*, and as a commercial center known for the stockmarket depicted by the Yiddish humorist Sholem Aleichem (Sholem Rabinovitz). The representation of Odessa's cafés in Jewish and Russian modernism, and the ways in which they were experienced, reflect a comparable ambivalence and complexity.

In this center of Jewish literature and culture, local institutions like Café Fanconi and Café Robina were well recognized as sites of consumption, leisure, and commodity spectacle, but also as the institutions regularly frequented by Russian and Jewish writers, journalists, and intellectuals. The Jewish-Russian writer and journalist Vladimiar Jabotinsky (who later became the leader of the Zionist Revisionist party) described the atmosphere of Odessa's two most famous institutions, Café Fanconi and Café Robina, located in the city's center, in his autobiographical novel *Pyatero* ("The Five" 1925): "noisy as the sea at a massif, filled to overflowing with seated customers, surrounded by those waiting to get in, one could see the trading terraces of [the cafés]" (58). Modernist literary engagement with Odessa and its cafés in the post–World War I era is found in the works of many Russian language writers (many of them Jewish), including Isaac Babel, Yuri Olesha, Valentin Kataev, Evgeni Petrov, Ilya Ilf, Eduard Bagritzki, and Vladimir Jabotinsky. For Babel in particular, Odessa loomed large in his literary imagination (see Sicher; Stanton). Café Fanconi was to him a locus of the unique and elusive Jewish-Odessan humor. Referring to a famous Odessa newspaper, he writes: "In every issue of *Divertissement* there are also jokes about Odessa Jews, about Cafe Fanconi, about brokers taking dance classes and Jewesses riding trams" (81). Babel's Benya Krik visits Café Fanconi on a regular basis (914, 922, 934).

Café Fanconi and Robina were sometimes described as "literary cafés" because they attracted many writers, journalists, and publishers, who used to meet and write in and about the café, but their appeal was not limited to writers. In a 1913 guide to the city, the writer and journalist Grigory Moskvich wrote that the dream of the "essential Odessan" was to "transform himself into an impeccable British gentleman or blue-blooded Viennese aristocrat." Then, "immaculately dressed, with an expensive cigar in his teeth," this Odessan would make an appearance by "getting into a carriage or sitting down in one of the better cafés on the boulevard or in the park." For people in the middle class, especially those who aspired to upward mobility, being a part of the café world meant being on the inside. One of the newspaper *Odesskaia pochta*'s regular columnists wrote: "Every Odessan, regardless of social position, considers it necessary to go to the Robina or Fanconi at least once in their lives . . . to live in Odessa and not go to the Robina is like being in Rome and not seeing the Pope" (quoted in Sylvester 817).

And yet if the Jewish immigrant writers and intellectuals who arrived in the city of Odessa from small provincial towns were highly curious about cafés like the Fanconi, some resisted its charms, especially the older writers who were educated on the ideals of the *Haskalah*. Indeed, the café scene was uncomfortable to the premodernist generation of Hebrew and Yiddish writers and intellectuals—for instance, Sholem Yankev Abramovitz (Mendele Moycher Sforim), the Zionist leader and essayist Ahad-Ha'am, the poet Haim Nahman Bialik, and the historian Simon Dubnov—who formed a closed circle that became known as "the Sages of Odessa" (see Miron). According to the writings of these "sages" and those who knew them, they enjoyed the freedom that Odessa gave them, but they were quite repelled by the mixture of business and pleasure, literature, and commodity spectacle found in cafés like Fanconi (figure 18.1). In a short essay called "City of Life" (1896), Elhonan Levinsky, a member of "the sages of Odessa" circle, reflects in

Figure 18.1 : Café Fanconi, Odessa, circa 1910

Hebrew on the cultural space in Jewish Odessa. He tells how he passes with sadness a building on Lanjeron Street, a bustling café that only a few years earlier had been a library. After a few years of absence, Levinsky asks the owner why, in a city full of "men of enlightenment and readers of books," the library couldn't attract more readers. The proprietor answers that Odessa Jews enjoy "boisterous activity, rich food, and harsh coffees," but not books. The Jews of Odessa, Levinsky writes, are the first to pay good money for "the sheer pleasure of having dirty water tossed in their faces" (see Zipperstein 27). The sages of Odessa thus met behind closed doors in the "literary salons" that took place in the private houses of Abramovitz and Dubnov (see Bairach).

Sholem Aleichem, who came to Odessa from Kiev in 1891 and lived in the city for a few years, vividly captures the contradictions of the café life. In his epistolary novel *The Letters of Menakhem-Mendl and Sheyne-Sheyndl* (1892–1913), Sholem Aleichem makes masterful comic use of the thirdspace of Café Fanconi. Menakhem Mendl, who arrives in Odessa from his tiny fictional shtetl Kasrilevka, is bewitched by the stockmarket of Odessa, where he believes he has made a large amount of money quickly and without much effort. Menakhem is equally allured by Café Fanconi, where business is done over a cup of coffee or tea. As he writes to his provincial wife, Sheyne, whom he left behind in the shtetl:

> If only you understood, my dearest, how business is done on a man's word alone, you would know all there is to know about Odessa. A nod is as good as a signature. I walk down Greek Street, drop into a cafe, sit at a table, order tea or coffee, and wait for the brokers to come by. There's no need for a contract or written agreement. Each broker carries a pad in which he writes, say, that I've bought two "shorts." I hand over the cash and that's it—it's a pleasure how easy it is! (*The Letters of Menakhem-Mendl and Sheyne-Sheyndl* 8)

After a few days, Menakhem Mendl boasts that he is so successful in Odessa that all the dealers already know him in Café Fanconi:

> By now they know me in every brokerage. I take my seat in Fanconi's with all the dealers, pull up a chair at a marble table, and ask for a dish of iced cream. That's our Odessa custom: you sit yourself down and a waiter in a frock coat asks you to ask for iced cream. Well, you can't be a piker—and when you're finished, you're asked to ask for more. If you don't, you're out a table and in the street. That's no place for dealing, especially when there's an officer on the corner looking for loiterers. Not that our Jews don't hang out there anyway. They tease him with their wisecracks and scatter to see what he'll do. Just let him nab one! He latches on to him like a gemstone and it's off to the cooler with one more Jew. (10–11)

It is hard to mistake the target of Sholem Aleichem's biting humor. The fact that the provincial Menakhem Mendl quickly loses all his money in the Odessa stockmarket (as Sholem Aleichem himself did in Kiev) goes almost without saying. But Menakhem's experience captures the essence of the urban café as a metonym for the contradictions of urban modernity. Sure, the café gives you an access to a marble-top table and to the business that can be done by a mere nod; a waiter in frock coat will serve you, but if you lack the money to order a few servings of the famed ice cream, you're out in the street, where you're in danger of being picked up by an anti-Semitic officer ready to roust any Jew who might interfere with the commodity spectacle of the café.

Eliezer Shteinman, a modernist Hebrew writer who lived in Warsaw and Odessa during much of the first two decades of the twentieth century, gets at the status of gender hierarchies in urban cafés in his novel *Esther Chajes* (1922), which features the "New Jewish Woman."[13] The novel devotes much narrative space to Café Fanconi in its depiction of Esther, a young Jewish woman who follows her older sister from their small town to Odessa. In the big city, she meets the young Russian Adolf Grigorovitz, "a native Odessan and the loyal, loving son of the city" (79). Adolf takes Esther and her sister Hanna for a walk in the boulevards of Odessa, and in no time they arrive in Café Fanconi. Seen through the eyes of the poor immigrant Esther, from whom the author keeps an ironic distance, the café, as the city itself, is a complex space of appearances and mirrors: "When the doormen opened the doors of the café, it seemed to Esther for a moment that the doors of new life had opened." Esther recognizes that "All the smiles, politeness and gentility were, of course, a matter of transaction, and yet the sham was not too jarring to her heart," for "in the café the deceit was elevated here to the level of truth." Unused to café life, for Esther "the mundane is transformed and elevated into a holy-day" (81). The café highlights the considerable currency of bourgeois appearance in Odessa. Fashionable clothing, traveling in a carriage, shopping at an expensive boutique, and going out to a chic café were part and parcel of the city's "respectable" lifestyle. And yet, as Esther notices, the café was also a place of social transactions: "Surely there was some order here, but the hierarchies were fluid. Each person here was a guest but also owner. Everything was different" (81). As a woman in Odessa, Esther learns that in the mirror-house of the café, the social order can be, to some degree, suspended, though it is unlikely to be completely upended.

The second part of the novel, when the two sisters, Hanna and Esther, wander through the streets of Odessa, suggests how the fluidity of social order in the café may enable, at least on the imaginary level, an indeterminacy of gender identities and hierarchies. The sisters, having become wary of the men they know, imagine themselves to be "Cavalier" and "Dame": "Let's walk around Deribasovskaia Boulevard without any men; leave them alone. Later we'll walk to Café Fanconi and catch a table. I will smoke a cigarette . . . and invite 'the dame of my heart,' feed her with pastry and chocolate . . . just like a man" (133). So, female flâneurs, they make their way to Café Fanconi, drink hot chocolate, and read the newspapers, which are full of sensational stories about all kinds of strange events and adventures in Odessa. But when they leave the café, the potential narrative energy of their imaginative release is immediately rebound when they meet a man, a medical student, who invites them to his "regular table" in the more fashionable and "exclusive" Café Robina (139). On one hand, Shteinman seems to articulate a critique—very common in the journalistic and literary writings of Odessa in this period—of the "ladies' chatter" that ridicules their attempts to appear "cultured." On the other hand, the femininity and the provincial Jewishness of Esther and her sister, which the narrator never lets the protagonists or the readers forget, also act as a double-edged sword. If the café is chiefly a masculine bourgeois domain to which urban men can chivalrously invite their "ladies," it also enables the two sisters to enact a performance of gender that exposes its social conventions. The thirdspace of Café Fanconi is a site in which the identity of the "New Jewish Woman" is enacted and examined: her social, personal and gender identity, her passions and desires, which are both real and imaginary, public and private at the same time.

VIENNA: INSIDE AND OUTSIDE THE "JEWISH SPACE" OF THE CAFÉ

Vienna highlights the tangled relationship between café culture, modernism and Jewishness. Unlike frontier cities such as Odessa or Lvov/Lemberg, Vienna was, at the turn of the twentieth century, one of the most important centers of modernism in literature, philosophy, art and architecture. In the years before and during World War I, an extraordinary group of Hebrew and Yiddish writers and thinkers emigrated from Eastern Europe to Vienna, the capital of the Habsburg Empire. The list includes Gershon Shofman, David Fogel, Avraham Ben-Yitzhak (Dr. Sonne), Zvi Disendrook, Ya'akov Horovitz, Melekh Ravitch, Melekh Chmelnicki, Meir Wiener, and many others. Most of them settled in Vienna's second district Leopoldstadt. This area, also known as *Mazzesinsel* ("Matzo Island"), had the highest proportion of Jews in Vienna, particularly newcomers from Eastern Europe (see Beckermann and Hermann). With its many synagogues, Jewish shops, markets, and crowded apartment buildings, the area looked and felt like an East European Jewish enclave, but the presence of many cafés made it impossible to forget that this was very much part of Vienna. The Viennese *kaffeehaus* proved to be the place that brought these immigrant writers together and opened new paths for them. Indeed, Vienna fostered close collaboration between Hebrew and Yiddish writers in a time when these two literatures were gradually separating from each other.[14] These writers were attracted both to cafés in recognizably "Jewish areas" of the city, like Leopoldstadt and Josephstadt, and to well-known "literary cafés" that tended to be in the old center of the city.

Scholars agree that cafés played a pivotal role in Viennese modernism. Harold Segal goes as far as to argue that "the modernist movement . . . arose in the fin-de-siècle within the context of the coffeehouse" (4). It is also impossible to ignore the huge presence of acculturated Jews in the renowned Viennese "literary cafés." Their presence was so pronounced that a common proverb claimed that "the Jew belongs in the coffeehouse" (Beller 22). Apparently, the coffeehouse was seen by many Viennese—for better or for worse—as "a Jewish space" (Beller 40–41). As we have seen, the attraction of Jews to cafés was far from unique to Vienna, but it is impossible to ignore the fact that many of the *stammgäste*, or habitués, in the Viennese *Kaffeehäuser* were Jews. Indeed, a legion of modernist Viennese writers, including Arthur Schnitzler, Karl Kraus Peter Altenberg, Richard Beer-Hofmann, Felix Salten, Hugo von Hofmannsthal, Stefan Zweig, Joseph Roth and Robert Musil, all Jewish or of Jewish origins and all firmly recognized as part of the history of Austrian and "German-language" modernism, were café habitués who worked in and wrote much about these beguiling spaces.

The "Jewishness" of the Viennese cafés received equivocal attention from both Jews and non-Jews. Alfred Torberg's retrospective account in *Die Tante Jolesch* ("Aunt Jolesch") accords great importance to the destroyed world of fin-de-siècle Vienna cafés by suggesting a hidden connection with the traditional Jewish "house of study." Vienna's café culture, he contends, "has taken on something from Tante Jolesch," who he sees as "the missing link between the Talmudic tradition of the ghetto and emancipated café culture: she was, as it were, the female ancestor of all those people who found in the coffeehouse the catalyst and central focus of their existence, and she was their primal mother whether or not they realized it, whether or not they wanted it to be so" (136). The journalist and founder of modern political Zionism, Theodor Herzl, associated the "Jewishness" of the café with a world destined—according to his analysis—to be destroyed. When Herzl wanted to portray the dire situation of Viennese Jews, he made Dr. Friedrich Loewenberg, a quintessential "coffeehouse Jew," a main protagonist in his Zionist utopian novel *Altneuland* (1902). The opening scene strikes a note of sadness and foreboding by situating Loewenburg, "[s]unk in deep melancholy," in a fin-de-siècle fictional Viennese *kaffeehaus*, where he appears with "bureaucratic punctuality" and is served by a "sickly, pale waiter" (3).

More attuned to the promise of sociality sealed off from bureaucratic existence in café culture, Joseph Roth, the modernist Jewish-Austrian writer, offers a very different portrait of the "coffeehouse Jew" during the interwar period, in his novella *Zipper und Sein Vater* ("Zipper and his Father" 1928):

> After Alfred began working in the Finance Ministry, his visits to the cafés became a passion rather than habit. . . . [H]e had found it difficult to spend an evening alone, he was now possessed by a real horror of solitude. Not that he wished to be part of a community. He just wanted to sit in a coffeehouse, nowhere else but his coffeehouse. . . . Only on entering this coffeehouse was Arnold free of his day. Here began his freedom, for although the revolving doors never ceased moving, Arnold could be certain that inside this coffeehouse he would never encounter anyone who reminded him of his work or indeed any work whatsoever. (Roth, *Werke*, vol. 1, 572–76)

Acculturated Jews like Roth, Arthur Schnitzler, and Stefan Zweig (who evoked the world of the Viennese café in his *Die Welt von gestern* [*The World of Yesterday*] from 1942), all well-known figures in modernism, were habitués of the cafés and wrote about Viennese café culture. But less familiar Hebrew and Yiddish writers who had immigrated from the Russian Pale of Settlement and Galicia were equally allured by the Viennese café. As for the fictional Arnold Zipper, for them it was a place to find a real and imaginary "community," a thirdspace in which they could meet, write, and be what Roth has called "effective spectators."

Although the war years were challenging for the Jewish immigrant writers in Vienna, in the years before World War I Arkaden Café, located opposite the Votive Church near the University of Vienna, emerged as an important thirdspace for East European Jews in the city.[15] Many Yiddish and Hebrew writers portray Arkaden Café as the meeting place of "students, writers, journalists, publishers, artists and bohemians from Austria and from all around the world," but they especially emphasized that it was a place in which Jewish immigrants from Galicia, Poland and Russia felt at home.[16] Meir Henish noted that Hebrew and Yiddish newspapers were available, which was a huge attraction that set it apart from the Café Central or Herrenhof. The Yiddish poet Melech Chmelnitzky even wrote a sonnet about the Votive Church as he looked at it from Arkaden (*Ruh un imru* 31). World War I, however, temporarily ended the pleasures of café life.

Some Jewish habitués served in the Habsburg army; others found themselves "behind enemy lines." During the fighting, the Hebrew and Yiddish cultural centers in Eastern Europe (and the nascent center in Palestine) were nearly defunct. The modernist Hebrew writer Gershon Shofman wrote a story, *Ba-matzor u'va-matzok* ("In Siege and Distress," 1922), set in Vienna during and after the war, in which the Viennese *kaffeehaus* is the space where a group of East European Jewish writers, artists, and intellectuals can look for some sense of social belonging. It is also of course where they try to assimilate into the local and international bohemian and intellectual life. The advent of the war, however, shakes the relatively calm capital of the empire and reveals the same café as a space that can be especially dangerous for émigrés and exiles from Eastern Europe:

> Never had there been as much smoke in the café as in these new, onerous days.
> People sucked on their cigarettes with all their might as if they intended to hide in
> their own smoke. But the police agents with the bristle mustaches peered through
> the windows with their sharp, crushing eyes, cutting through the clouds. (101)

Here the thirdspace of the café reveals a sinister face. With its elusive promise of
social engagement and sense of belonging, the café actually comes to prevent real
human connection and communication. Thick cigarette smoke masks people's
faces, at once linking people and alienating them within a shared miasma. Nor does
the café provide protection against policemen searching for army defectors. The
young protagonists quickly realize that the urban space of Vienna comprises many
locations that interfuse the private and the public, and that the desired "outside" can
actually become a series of closed and restricting spaces (the café, the army prison,
the soup kitchen, the sanatorium). Under the pressure of war, they learn, the
"inside," the closed space in which they try to create a protective, homey environment, is itself permeated by the "outside." Thus, two contradictory desires intersect
in the café: the desire for the outside, for Viennese, Central European society, and
the desire for an intimate, protective place. The conflicted yearning is so strong that
a poet in the story is indifferent to the prospects of sitting in an army prison, and a
painter gives himself to the police and ends up in a sanatorium (125–26).

Vienna of the 1910s and 1920s proved to be a fertile ground for Jewish modernism, in part because of its coffeehouses. Although Shofman's fiction does not
indicate that the collapse of the Habsburg Empire at the end of the Great War made
much difference to the world of the Jewish émigré writers in Vienna, history tells us
that the Hebrew and Yiddish modernist enclave became very active in the years
following the war. Shofman and Zvi Disendrook edited and published a short-lived
but highly important journal titled *Gevulot* ("Borders" 1918–1920) and later *Peret*
(1922–1924) that published innovative modernist works. This activity in Hebrew
publishing coincided with the peak of Yiddish publishing with the journal *Kritik*
and the publishing house Kval (Ravitch 363–69). Many Hebrew and Yiddish writers
and modernist figures working in German and other languages first encountered
one another in *Kaffeehäuser*. Shofman met Peter Altenberg in Café Central during
the war and ended up translating Altenberg's short stories into Hebrew.[17] This close
relationship left a strong impact on Shofman's modernist style, which became even
more inclined to the Viennese *kleinkunst* or cabaret. Elias Canetti met Avraham
Ben-Yitzhak ("Dr. Sonne") in Café Museum (designed by Alfred Loos) and admired
the modernist Hebrew poet. Canneti recorded the connections between Dr. Sonne
and figures like Musil, Hofmannsthal, Beer-Hofmann, Broch, and Joyce. The
Hebrew and Yiddish writers David Fogel and Meir Wiener were also acquainted
with Viennese modernists of the postwar period, and these connections are clearly
demonstrated in their poetry and prose fiction.[18]

All this rich literary and cultural activity occurred both in spite of and because
of the marginality of Hebrew and Yiddish in Vienna, a marginality that was not only
linguistic but also spatial. Hebrew and Yiddish writers lived and worked on the
visible and invisible borderlines between Vienna's cultural centers of modernism

and the geographically bounded sections of the city. Even in the 1920s and early 1930s when Meir Wiener, David Fogel, Avraham Ben-Yitzhak, and other Hebrew and Yiddish writers spent much time with intellectual friends in central locations like Café Herrenhof and Café Museum, Leopoldstadt—with its own cafés—remained their tentative and provisional "home," the base from which the writers and their fictional protagonists explore the city. This enclave of Hebrew and Yiddish modernism produced many literary representations of the cityscape and its cafés. Perhaps the most fascinating is David Fogel's Hebrew novel *Chaye Nisu'im* ("Married Life," 1929–1930).

Married Life is recognized today as the urban Hebrew modernist novel par-excellence. Its protagonist, Rudolf Gurdweill, is the ultimate Jewish flâneur, a man who wanders the streets and boulevards of Vienna. Gurdweill and his friends spend much time in Café Herrenhof, which displaced Café Central in the 1920s and early 1930s as "the most popular coffeehouse among Vienna's cultural elite" and became the favorite place of Hermann Broch, Robert Musil, Alfred Polgar and Joseph Roth (Segal 27). In *Married Life*, Café Herrenhof (figure 18.2) appears as a metonymy of Vienna: a substitute for a "real" home, a space that interfuses the public and the private, the inside and the outside, the culture of bohemia and the bourgeoisie. The café brings the city inside, but it also shields its regulars from the "crowd" and the "masses." One of the many times Gurdweill and his friends meet at the Herrenhof, a woman asks the group: "How long can you people go on sitting in cafés? Don't you ever get tired of it?" To which Gurdweill's friend Ulrich responds:

> Sitting in cafés is a barrier against the enforced activity which makes our lives miserable. . . . People like us always have the mistaken feeling that they are wasting time, missing something irretrievable. . . . As if a man had a set amount of things to get done in a set amount of time. . . . The harmful influence of our materialistic generation, a generation of physical labor and advanced tech-nology. . . . But the minute you enter a café, you're on a holiday—the yoke is lifted from your shoulders, snapped in half. (181–82)

Fogel's narrator idealizes the café less than Ulrich does, and if camaraderie is presented as a key element of Viennese *Kaffeehäuser*, the other side of the coin is the acrimony that is borne of the too-close, at times alienating, experience of the social space of the café. Like the pigeons pecking at each other in Ravitch's Café Abatzya, the patrons of Fogel's *Kaffeehäuser* demonstrate an ambivalence toward the café that captures much of the quality of urban experience in *Married Life*.

In spite of the centrality of Café Herrenhof, it is significant that some key narrative events in *Married* Life unfold in small local cafés in Leopoldstadt and in Josefstadt. Much of the irony and the power of the novel stems from Gurdweill's status as an immigrant East European Jew who lives not in Vienna but in Leopold-stadt, where he frequents a small café. It is in this café in fact, with its "ragged, threadbare velvet sofas around the walls and . . . dark, dirty, marble tables," that Gurdweill meets for the first time the "Viennese baroness" Thea Von-Tackow, who is, ironically, a "stranger" in the local (Jewish) café (21). This charged encounter sets in motion the entire plot of the novel. But much of the irony and the power of this

Figure 18.2 : Café Herrenhof, Vienna

scene, and the novel in general, stems from this position of Gurdweill as an immigrant East European Jew who lives in Leopoldstadt. Gurdweill is simultaneously an insider and an outsider, a *Stammgast* and a "stranger" in the café and in Vienna. The same is true of Fogel and other Hebrew and Yiddish modernist writers who lived in Vienna during the most productive period of their lives.

BERLIN: ROMANISCHES CAFÉ AND THE FLOWERING OF HEBREW AND YIDDISH MODERNISM

In Berlin, European café culture reached an unprecedented intensity and point of climax. Hebrew and Yiddish modernism had come into full flower in the interwar period all over Europe, as well as in America and Palestine, and Berlin became one of the primary beneficiaries of this rise in modernist production. During the Weimar period, the "new metropolis" of Berlin was the site of a massive influx of displaced East European writers, artists, and intellectuals.[19] Several coffeehouses, especially the Romanisches Café (figure 18.3), emerged as important places for the development of Hebrew and Yiddish modernism in Berlin.[20] Though attached

Figure 18.3 : Romanisches Café, Berlin

emotionally and imaginatively to the urban centers of Eastern Europe, émigré Hebrew and Yiddish writers nevertheless engaged with the contemporary modernist discourse and preoccupations of Weimar Berlin. They addressed issues of body, gender, and sexuality, surface (*oberfläche*), and visuality, that were inextricably linked not only to modernist "high culture"—the literature, art, and architecture of Expressionism and *Neue Sachlichkeit* (New Objectivity)—but also to new forms of "mass culture" in Berlin of this period: among other things, photography, cinema, fashion, and advertising.

In the first decade of the twentieth century, Café Monopol on Freidrichstrasse (by the Scheunenviertel), was a favorite meeting place for German writers and young theater artists, including Max Reinhardt and his theatrical group. It was during meetings and rehearsals within the space of the café that Reinhardt developed his ideas and an agenda for a new theater. Around the same time, the Hebraists of Berlin had a *stammtisch*, or regular gathering, at Café Monopol. Aharon Hermoni and Itamar Ben-Avi (Eliezer Ben-Yehuda's son) write that by 1908 even the waiter knew some Hebrew in order to accommodate their table, which included Shay Ish Hurwitz, Reuven Breinin, Horodetzky, and other Zionist activists and Hebrew writers (Ben-Avi 146–56; Hermoni 145–58). Hebrew journals like *Ha-olam* and *He-'atid* were edited on the black marble tops of this plush, oriental-style café (Berkovitz 209–10; Hermoni 151). The Hebraists in Café Monopol were far from isolated. Side by side with the Hebrew table were many "German tables," which included Reinhardt's theater circle, critics such as Alfred Kerr, and other literary-political figures, such as Erich Mühsam, Gustav Landauer, and Sammy Gronemann. A "Yiddish table" adjoined the "Hebrew table" and enjoyed visits by luminaries such as Sholem Asch, whose play *El nekamoth* ("God of Revenge") was performed by Reinhardt's theater, and Sholem Aleichem. Interaction between these groups in the café was inevitable and abundant (Berkovitz 210; Nash 172).

Several other Berlin cafés (Café Josty, Café Victoria, Café Bauer) were important for expressionist art and literature. Exhibitions, public reading, cabarets, and editorial activities of expressionist journals like *Der Sturm* and *Die Aktion* took place in cafés. The most important of these cafés was the small and rather homely Café des Westens on the Kurfürstendamm. By 1910 it was quickly becoming not only the chief gathering place for expressionist circles, but also a magnetic pole for modernists from all over Europe. The café became famous for the extravagant fashions and eccentric behavior of its "regulars," as well as for its artistic and literary activity. Else Lasker-Schüler was the queen of Café des Westens and portrayed it in her semiautobiographical novel *Mein Herz* (1912).[21] Hebrew and Yiddish writers were also attracted to the Café des Westens during the 1910s. Berdichevsky, Shay Hurtivz, David Shimonovitz, and other Hebrew, Yiddish, and German writers and intellectuals headed by Moritz Heimann used to meet every Thursday evening for "literary table" at the Monopol and then at Café des Westens.[22] The future Nobel Prize winner Shmuel Yosef Agnon, who arrived in Berlin in 1912, became acquainted with numerous German Jewish writers and intellectuals in the cafés.

Sometime around 1916, the Café des Westens "closed for remodeling" and banished the writers and bohemians in order to reopen as a more "respected" bourgeois establishment. From 1917 and throughout the Weimar period, the huge and shabby Romanisches Café became the new headquarters for the expressionists and the *Neue Sachlichkeit* movement, and in fact for all writers, artists, intellectuals, and bohemians—German and non-German alike. The Romanisches Café performed many of the functions of the Café des Westens, and also inherited the dubious name "Café Megalomania." The list of well-known figures of German modernism who frequented the café is huge. They described it as a second home for writers during the day; a place where heated debates were conducted far into the night; and a place where literary and artistic activities were carried on at all times. The Romanisches Café was indicative of Weimar culture in many ways. Far from being the exclusive domain of a small group of German expressionists, it was rather a place in which "insiders" and "outsiders," locals and strangers, bohemians and the bourgeoisie, politics and art, avant-garde and mass culture all coexisted in an elusive mixture that produced a great deal of both confusion and stimulation (see Schebera).

Accounts of the intense and notable presence of Hebrew and Yiddish writers and artists who flocked to the Romanisches Café after World War I were ubiquitous. However much these accounts conflict—some create the impression that Romanisches Café was a quasi-utopian Pan-Jewish urban space; others considered it a place of cultural exhaustion and betrayal—it is clear that café encounters between Yiddish and Hebrew writers and major figures of Berlin modernism left strong marks on their literary and intellectual development. Nahum Goldman wrote that "each [Jewish] group had its own table; there were the 'Yiddishists,' 'Zionists,' 'Bundists' and so on, all arguing among themselves from table to table," and the Yiddish poet Avrom Nokhem Stencl described the café, buzzing "like a beehive," as the "parliament" of "a kind of Jewish colony" in the west of Berlin populated by Jews fleeing the Russian Revolution and "the pogroms in Ukrainian shtetls" (Goldmann 21; Stencl 25). Lev Bergelson wrote that his father, the Yiddish modernist writer Dovid Bergelson, used to "spend many evenings in the Romanisches Café . . . Sitting around the marble tables, people would drink coffee, smoke and chat, but they would also read and write poems, create script for new films, and play chess" ("Memories of My Father" 79–88). Yet the highly visible presence of East European Jewish writers in the Romanisches Café also attracted strong criticism from people outside Germany. According to Melekh Ravitch, a habitué of cafés in other cities, "in the smoky atmosphere of the Romanisches Café, some of the best creators of Yiddish culture are hanging around, pretending to create a Yiddish culture. But those who are sitting in the Romanisches Café and looking at us from afar . . . are simply deserters" (quoted in Bechtel, 116).

Israel Rubin wrote that at "the tables of the Yiddish writers in the Romanisches Café all possible topics have already been exhausted. . . . Everyone has been denigrated and slandered. . . . All literary and social dialogues and prognoses have been outlined" ("Bay di tishlekh fun romanishn kafe," *Literarishe bleter*, January 17, 1930). These conflicting accounts of the Romanisches Café as at once "The Café of Pity," a new Jerusalem or Yavne, and a place of Kibetz Goluyos ("the ingathering of the exiles") testify to the tensions inherent in the thirdspace of the Berlin café and in more Berlin more generally.

The literary and artistic representations of the café paint a similarly divided picture. In his extravagant style, Uri Zvi Greenberg writes that he and Else Lasker-Schüler "drank together dark coffee in the Romanisches Café, and until midnight this bitter drink was dripping in our hearts, and sipping through even deeper to the 'inner existence,' around the heart and beyond it like dark blood" (*Kol ktavav*, vol. 1, 127). In the revolutionary expressionist *poemas* that Greenberg published in Berlin and in Palestine, the Romanisches Café operates as a trope of urban modernity: "We really loved the smoky hours in the cafés. Opera. Frock coat. Perfumed heads and dance halls. Opium. Ballet. . . . Boulevards and brothels. Hot electron . . . and the noise, the noise of the cities!" (66) The Romanisches Café appears in a less favorable modernist light in the guise of the fictional "Crocodile" in Lev Bergelson's story "For 12,000 Dollar He Fast 40 Days" (1926), in which the café-restaurant becomes a house of mirrors in which it is hard to tell what is "real" and what merely a mirage of glittering surfaces.[23] Likewise, the narrator of Sh.Y. Agnon's Hebrew novel *Ad Hena* ("To This Day" 1952) describes a number of grotesque scenes in Berlin cafés that are based on the Café des Westens and the Romanishces.[24]

I will conclude with one of the most interesting texts devoted to the Romanisches Café, a cycle of poems, "Sonnets from the Coffeehouse" (1922), by the Hebrew and Yiddish writer Ya'acov Shteinberg. The cycle was clearly inspired by the endless hours Shteinberg spent in the Romanisches Café during his "residence" there. Shteinberg saw the Romanisches as both a kind of "imaginary Jewish space" and a place "full of decadence, smoke and the syncopated rhythm of the metropolis" (Keshet 138). The cycle of sonnets creates a tightly knit narrative that occurs solely in the café, which become an object of observation and introspection. Each of the sonnets tells a short and concentrated "story" about characters and a specific event or situation in the café: e.g., the waiter, a couple indulging in "a desire that has been revealed," a "queen" or "prostitute" sitting alone, or abandoned newspapers rolling after the café's closing. The large but enclosed space of the café, with its ever-changing vistas and moods, contains everything because it can be full or empty, bright and dark, airy and smoky, friendly and hostile, familiar and anonymous. These different aspects of the café serve as an extended metonym for the urban experience of Berlin. The café is both a place of "happiness and chatter," and a space to which people can flock in order to avoid the "deep sadness" that lurks everywhere. This duality is beautifully captured in the metaphor of the "newspapers that are rolled up like idle hieroglyphic scrolls," as well as in the Hebrew expression *beit-moed*: a place where people congregate, and a space that houses the dead.

Shteinberg's sonnets epitomize the ways in which Hebrew and Yiddish writers represented the complex physiognomy and topography of the Romanisches Café, which in turn captures their encounter with the urban space of Berlin. Their experience of the thirdspace of the café as a "hieroglyphic" spatial image of Berlin emphasizes both their participation and their marginality in the modernist culture of Berlin, the commodity spectacle of "surface" and its potential for artistic creativity, the energy of the metropolis and its deep sense of despair.

NOTes

1. For accounts of Tel Aviv that trace its importation of Jewish culture, see Mann; Azaryahu, 106–23. On the cafés of Tel Aviv, see Carmiel.

2. See, for example, Lefebvre, *The Production of Space*.

3. For a good discussion of the development of literary Hebrew, see Alter.

4. The Pale of Settlement was a region of the Russian empire, along its western border, in which permanent residence of Jews was allowed. See Weinreich, *History of the Yiddish Language*.

5. For a good summary of the reassessment of the relation of modernism to literary traditions in recent studies of modernism, see Fernald.

6. See Bal Makhshoves's (Yisroel Elyashev) famous 1918 essay "Two Languages—One Literature." For a good discussion of the complexity of bilingual Jewish literature, see Miron.

7. Kronfeld, *On the Margins of Modernism*; see also Finkin.

8. Bradbury and McFarlane, for instance, touch on literary cafés in their classic chapter "Cities of Modernism."

9. Apart from studies of the role that these cafés played in the context of "national" modernism, and a number of "coffee-table books," the only comparative study of the "literary café" that I am aware of is Michael Rössner's *Literarische Kaffehäuser*. An important departure from this tendency is Edward Timms' mapping of several circles of Viennese modernism through various cafés in the city in *Karl Kraus, Apocalyptic Satirist*. Another recent study that makes an insightful use of cafés and teashops in English (but

also in German and Czech) modernism is McCracken's *Masculinities, Modernist Fiction and Urban Public Sphere.*

10. Steiner writes: "Europe is made of coffee houses, of cafés. . . . Draw the coffee-house map and you have one of the essential markers of 'the idea of Europe'" (17).

11. Williams discusses "ways of life" and "structures of feeling" in *Culture and Society, 1780–1950.* See the discussion of Williams, Negt, and Kluge in McCracken.

12. For Bhabha, the thirdspace involves a simultaneous coming and going in a borderland between different modes of action. To do so will require inventing creative ways to cross perceived and real "borders." The thirdspace is a place of invention and transformational encounters, a dynamic in-between space that is imbued with the traces, relays, ambivalence, ambiguities, and contradictions, with the feelings and practices of both sites, to fashion something different, unexpected (Bhabha, "The Third Space").

13. The term "New Jewish Woman" emerged in the turn of the twentieth century and referred to the acculturated Jewish woman in Eastern, Central, and Western Europe. See Hyman; Pinsker.

14. These ideological differences became strong after the 1908 Yiddish Language Conference, convened in Czernowitz. See Goldsmith.

15. The *Arkaden* is not as well known today as *Greinsteidel* or *Central*, but it was patronized by Wittgenstein and members of the philosophical Vienna Circle, as well as many students and musicians. See Janik and Veigl 188–89.

16. See, for example, Ravitch, *Dos mayse-bukh*, vol. 2, 209–11; Charney, *Di velt iz kaylekhdik*, 160–65; Weichart, *Zikhroynes*, vol. 1, 229–48.

17. Peter Altenberg, *Ktavim nivcharim.*

18. See Canetti, *The Play of the Eye*, 132–62; Hever 107.

19. On Berlin in context of Hebrew literature and culture, see Shavit. On Berlin in the context of Yiddish literature, see Bechtel; Valencia; Estraikh.

20. For an overview of Berlin cafés and their role in modernist literature and culture, see Allen; Rath.

21. See Allen 67–73; Bauschinger.

22. See Ben-Gurion 64–72.

23. The story was first published in the Yiddish newspaper "The Forward" (New York, 1926). For English translation, by Joachim Neuregschel, see David Bergleson, *The Shadows of Berlin.*

24. The novel was recently translated into English by Hillel Halkin as *To This Day.*

WORKS CITED

Agnon, S. Y. "Ad Hena." *Kol Sipurav shel S.Y. Agnon,* vol. 7. Tel Aviv and Jerusalem: Schocken, 1952. 5–170.

———. The Letters of Menakhem-Mendl and Sheyne-Sheyndl. Trans. Hillel Halkin. New Haven: Yale University Press, 2002.

———. *To This Day.* Trans. Hillel Halkin. New Milford: Tobby Press, 2008.

Aleichem, Sholem. *Ale verk fun Sholem-Aleichem.* Vol. 2. New York: Sholem-Aleichhem folksfond oysgabe, 1920.

Allen, Roy F. *Literary Life in German Expressionism and the Berlin Circles.* Ann Arbor: UMI Research Press, 1983.

Altenberg, Peter. *Ktavim nivcharim*. Trans. Gershon Shofman. New York: Shybel, 1921.

Alter, Robert. *The Invention of Hebrew Prose: Modern Fiction and the Language of Realism.* Seattle: University of Washington Press, 1991.

Azaryahu, Maoz. *Tel Aviv: Mythography of a City*. Syracuse: Syracuse University Press, 2007.

Babel, Issac. *The Complete Works of Isaac Babel*. Ed. Nathalie Babel. Trans. Peter Constantine. New York: W. W. Norton, 2001.

Bairach, Lea. *From Space to Symbol: The Memories of "Hebrew Odessa," 1881–1914*. [Heb.] MA Thesis, Tel Aviv University, 1991.

Bar Yosef, *Hamutal Ma'gaim shel dekadens*. Be'er Sheva': Hotsa'at ha-Sefarim shel Universitat Ben-Guryon Ba-Negev, 1997.

Bauschinger, Sigrid. "The Berlin Moderns: Else Lasker-Schüler and Café Culture." *Berlin Metropolis: Jews and the New Culture, 1890–1918*. Ed. Emily Bilski. Berkeley: University of California Press, 1999. 58–101.

Bechtel, Delphine. "Babylon or Jerusalem: Berlin as Center of Jewish Modernism in the 1920s." *Insiders and Outsiders: Jewish and Gentile Culture in Germany and Austria*. Ed. Dagmar C. G. Lorenz and Gabriele Weinberger. Detroit: Wayne State University Press, 1994. 116–23.

Beckermann, Ruth, and Teifer Hermann. *Die Mazzesinsel Juden in der Wiener Leopoldstadt 1918–1938*. Wien: Locker, 1984.

Beller, Steven. *Vienna and the Jews, 1867–1938: A Cultural History*. Cambridge: Cambridge University Press, 1989.

Ben-Avi, Itamar. *'Im shachar atzma'utenu*. Tel-Aviv: Magen, 1961.

Ben-Gurion, Immanuel. *Reshut ha-yachid*. Tel-Aviv: Reshafim, 1980.

Benjamin, Walter. *Berliner Chronik*. Frankfurt am Main: Suhrkamp Verlag, 1972.

———. "A Berlin Chronicle." *Selected Writings, Volume II*. Ed. Michael W. Jennings, Howard Eiland, and Gary Smith. Cambridge: Harvard University Press, 1999. 595–637.

Bergleson, David. *The Shadows of Berlin*. Trans. Joachim Neuregschel. San Francisco: City Lights, 2005.

Bergelson, Lev. "Memories of My Father: The Early Years (1918–1934)." *David Bergelson: From Modernism to Socialist Realism*. Ed. Joseph Sherman and Gennady Estraikh. London: Legenda, 2007. 79–88.

Berkovitz Y. D. *Ha-rishonim ki-vnei adam*. Tel Aviv: Dvir, 1959.

Bhabha, Homi. "The Third Space." *Identity, Community, Culture, Difference*. Ed. J. Rutherford. London: Lawrence and Wishart, 1991. 207–21.

Bradbury, Malcolm, and James McFarlane. *Modernism: A Guide to European Literature 1890–1930*. New York: Penguin, 1991.

Canetti, Elias. *The Play of the Eye*. New York: Farrar, Straus and Giroux, 1999.

Carmiel, Batya. *Bate ha-kafe shel Tel-Aviv, 1920–1980*. Tel-Aviv: Erets-Israel Museum, 2007.

Carr, Gilbert. "Time and Space in the Café Griensteidl." *The Viennese Café as an Urban Site of Cultural Exchange*. Ed. Simon Shaw-Miller and Tag Gronberg. Oxford: Berghahn Books, forthcoming.

Cowan, Brian W. *The Social Life of Coffee: The Emergence of the British Coffeehouse*. New Haven: Yale University Press, 2005.

Eley, Geoff. "Nations, Publics, and Political Cultures: Placing Habermas in the Nineteenth Century." *Habermas and the Public Sphere*. Ed. Craig Calhoun. Cambridge: MIT Press, 1992.

Ellis, Markam. *The Coffee House: A Cultural History*. London: Weidenfeld and Nicolson, 2004.

Estraikh, Gennady. "Vilna on the Spree: Yiddish in Weimar Berlin." *Aschkenaz* 16.1 (2006): 103–27.

Fernald, Anne. "Modernism and Tradition." *Modernism*. Ed. Astradur Eysteinsson and Vivian Liska. Amsterdam: John Benjamins, 2007. 157–71.

Finkin, Jordan. "Constellating Hebrew and Yiddish Avant-Gardes: The Example of Markish and Shlonsky." *Journal of Modern Jewish Studies* 8.1 (2009): 1–22.

Fogel, David. *Chaye Nisuim*. Tel-Aviv: Mitzpe, 1929–1930.

———. *Married Life*. Trans. Dalya Bilu. New York: Grove Press, 1989.

Frieden, Ken. *Classic Yiddish Fiction: Abramovitsh, Sholem Aleichem, and Peretz*. New York: SUNY Press, 1995.

Goldmann, Nahum. *The Jewish Paradox*. New York: Fred Jordan Books, 1978.

Goldsmith, Emanuel S. *Modern Yiddish Culture: The Story of the Yiddish Language Movement*. New York: Fordham University Press, 2000.

Greenberg, Uri Zvi. *Kol-Ktavav*. Jeruslaem: Mossad Bialik, 2004.

Habermas, Jurgen. *Strukturwandel der Öffentlichkeit: Untersuchungen zu einer Kategorie der bürgerlichen Gesellschaft*. Neuwied: Hermann Luchterhand, 1962.

———. *The Structural Transformation of the Public Sphere*. Cambridge: MIT Press, 1989.

Hansen, Miriam. "Foreword." Negt and Kluge ix–xlii.

Harshav, Benjamin. *The Meaning of Yiddish*. Berkeley: University of California Press, 1990.

———. *Language in a Time of Revolution*. Berkeley: University of California Press, 1993.

Hermoni, Aharon. *Be-ikvot ha-bilu'im*. Jerusalem: Reuven Mass, 1951.

Herzl, Theodor. *Altneuland*. Leipzig: H. Seemann Nachfolger, 1902.

———. *Old-New Land*. Trans. Lotta Levensohn. 2nd ed. New York: Bloch, 1960.

Hyman, Paula E. *Gender and Assimilation in Modern Jewish History: The Roles and Representation of Women*. Seattle: University of Washington Press, 1995.

Jabotinsky, Vladimir. *The Five: A Novel of Jewish Life in Turn-of-the-Century Odessa*. Trans. Michael R. Katz. Ithaca: Cornell University Press, 2005.

Janik, Allan and Veigl, Hans. *Wittgenstein in Vienna: A Biographical Excursion Through the City and Its History*. Wien: Springer, 1998.

Keshet, Yeshurun. *Maskiyot*. Tel Aviv: Dvir, 1953.

Kronfeld, Chana. *On the Margins of Modernism: Decentering Literary Dynamics*. Berkeley: University of California Press, 1996.

Lefebvre, Henri. *The Production of Space*. Oxford: Blackwell, 1991.

Liberles, Robert. "Les Juifs, le café et le négoce du café au XVIIIe siècle." [Jews, Coffee and Coffee Trade in the 18th Century] *Les Cahiers du Judaïsme* 26 (2009): 4–14.

Makhshoves, Bal (Yisroel Elyashev). "Two Languages—One Literature." *Geklibene verk*. New York: Tsiḳo bikher farlag, 1953. 112–23.

Mann, Barbara. *A Place in History: Modernism, Tel Aviv, and the Creation of Jewish Urban Space*. Stanford: Stanford University Press, 2006.

McCracken, Scott. *Masculinities, Modernist Fiction and Urban Public Sphere*. Manchester: Manchester University Press, 2007.

Miron, Dan. *Bodedim be-mo'adam*. Tel Aviv: 'Am'oved, 748, 1987.

———. "The Odessa Sages." *Homage to Odessa*. Ed. Rachel Arbel. Tel Aviv: Beth Hatefutzot, Nahum Goldman Museum of the Jewish Diaspora, 2002. 62–81.

———. "From Continuity to Contiguity: Thoughts on the Theory of Jewish Literature." *Jewish Literatures and Cultures: Context and Intertext*. Ed. Yaron Eliav and Anita Norich. Providence: Brown Judaic Studies, 2008. 9–36.

Nash, Stanley. *In Search of Hebraism: Shai Hurwitz and His Polemics in the Hebrew Press*. Leiden: Brill, 1980.

Negt, Oskar, and Kluge, Alexander. *Public Sphere and Experience: Towards an Analysis of the Bourgeois and Proletarian Public Sphere.* Trans. Peter Labanyi, Jamie Owen Daniel, and Assenka Oksiloff. 1972. Minneapolis: University of Minnesota Press, 1993.

Norberg, Jakob. "No Coffee." *Fronesis* 24 (2007): 214–25.

Pinsker, Shachar. *Literary Passports: The Making of Hebrew Modernist Fiction in Europe.* Stanford: Stanford University Press, 2010.

Polgar, Alfred. "Theorie des Café Central." *Das Wiener Kaffeehaus.* Ed. Kurt-Jürgen Heering. Frankfurt: Insel Verlag, 1991. 149–54.

Rath, Alfred. "Berliner Caféhäuser (1890–1933)." *Literarische Kaffehäuser.* Ed. Michael Rössner. Wien: Böhlau, 1999. 108–25.

Ravitch, Melech. *Dos mayse-bukh fun mayn lebn.* Vol. 2. Buenos Aires: The Central Committee, 1962–1964.

Rössner, Michael. *Literarische Kaffehäuser.* Wien: Böhlau, 1999.

Roth, Joseph. *Zipper und Sein Vater in Werke.* Ed. Hermann Kesten. Cologne: Kiepenheuer & Witsch, 1956.

Rubin, Israel. "Bay di tishlekh fun romanishn kafe." *Literarishe bleter.* 3 (1930): 53–54.

Schebera, Jürgen. *Damals Im Romanischen Café: Künstler Und Ihre Lokale Im Berlin Der Zwanziger Jahre.* Frankfurt: Büchergilde Gutenberg, 1988.

Segal, Harold B. *The Vienna Coffeehouse Wits 1890–1938.* West Lafayette: Purdue University Press, 1993.

Shavit, Zohar. "On the Hebrew Cultural Center in Berlin in the Twenties: Hebrew Culture in Europe—The Last Attempt." *Gutenberg-Jahrbuch* 68 (1993): 371–80.

Shofman, Gershon. "*Ba-matzor u'va-matzok,*" *Ha-tekufa.* Vol. 16 (1922), 101–09. Reprinted in *Kol-Kitvei,* vol. 2. Tel Aviv: Dvir, 1960, 125–37.

Shteinberg, Ya'acov. "Sonnetot mi-beit ha-kafe." *Kol-Kitvei Ya'acov Shteinberg.* Tel-Aviv: Dvir, 1964, 67–9.

Shteinman, Eliezer. *Esther Chjes.* Warsaw: Shtybel, 1922.

Sicher, Efraim. *Jews in Russian Literature after the October Revolution.* Cambridge: Cambridge University Press, 1995.

Soja, Edward. *Thirdspace: Journeys to Los Angeles and Other Real-and-Imagined Places.* Oxford: Blackwell, 1996.

——. "Thirdspace: Toward a New Consciousness of Space and Spatiality." *Communicating in the Third Space.* Ed. Karin Ikas and Gerhard Wagner. London: Routledge, 2008. 49–61.

Stanton, Rebecca. "Identity Crisis: The Literary Cult and Culture of Odessa in the Early Twentieth Century." *Symposium* 57 (2003): 117–26.

Steiner, George. *The Idea of Europe.* Tilburg: Nexus Institute, 2004.

Stencl, Avrom Nokhem, ed. *Loshn un lebn* 10–11 (1968).

Sylvester, Roshanna P. "Making an Appearance: Urban 'Types' and the Creation of Respectability in Odessa's Popular Press." *Slavic Review* 59.4 (2000): 802–24.

Timms, Edward. *Karl Kraus, Apocalyptic Satirist: Culture and Catastrophe in Habsburg Vienna.* New Haven: Yale University Press, 1986.

Torberg, Friedrich. *Die Tante Jolesch oder Der Untergang des Abendlandes in Anekdoten.* München: Langen-Müller, 1975.

Ury, Scott. "'Juste un café?' Le rôle des cafés juifs à Varsovie au tournant du XXe siècle." ["Just Coffee?" The Influence of Jewish Cafés in Warsaw at the Beginning of the 20th Century] *Les Cahiers du Judaïsme* 26 (2009): 26–30.

Valencia, Heather. "Yiddish Writers in Berlin 1920–1936." *The German Jewish Dilemma; From the Enlightenment to the Shoah.* Ed. Edward Timms and Andrea Hammel. Lewiston, NY: Edwin Mellen Press, 1999. 193–207.

Weinreich, Max. *History of the Yiddish Language.* 1973. New Haven: Yale University Press, 2008.

Williams, Raymond. *Culture and Society, 1780–1950.* New York: Columbia University Press, 1983.

———. *The Politics of Modernism: Against the New Conformists.* Ed. Tony Pinkney. London: Verso, 1989.

Wobick, Sarah. "Interdits de café. L'influence de la révolution de Juillet sur la condition des Juifs de Hambourg." [Banned from Coffeehouses. The Influence of the July Revolution on the Life of Jews in Hamburg] *Les Cahiers du Judaïsme* 26 (2009): 14–23.

Zipperstein, Steven. *The Jews of Odessa: A Cultural History, 1794–1881.* Stanford: Stanford University Press, 1985.

———. "Remapping Odessa, Rewriting Cultural History." *Jewish Social Studies* 2.2 (1996): 21–36.

PART VII

LOCATING THE
TRANSNATIONAL

....

THE CIRCULATION OF INTERWAR ANGLOPHONE AND HISPANIC MODERNISMS

....

GAYLE ROGERS

IN the wake of the cataclysmic destruction of the Great War, many writers and thinkers across Europe were convinced that, as Tim Armstrong writes, "moral, cultural, even biological degeneration [was] intrinsic to modernity" (1). For some, the German historian Oswald Spengler's influential *Decline of the West* (1918–1922) not only confirmed the imminent death of Western civilization and exposed the notion of "Europe" to be an "empty sound" (1: 16 n.1), but also provided a schematic vocabulary for interpreting the postwar wasteland as the mangled body of the historical Western "organism."[1] Against Spengler's fatalism, however, modernists in diverse locales undertook the project of reviving and reuniting Europe culturally, whether in T. S. Eliot's and Ezra Pound's revisionary genealogies of European literature, James Joyce's ideal of a new Ireland within a reformed continental community, or Valery Larbaud's and Ernst Robert Curtius's critical efforts to inscribe contemporary French and German writing into a pre-national European civilization. At the same time, modernist artists beyond Europe's traditional geopolitical and metaphysical borders saw in this moment an opportunity to revitalize both Europe and their local milieux by arguing that the entire West might find new life in previously overlooked corners of the world.

This chapter treats three such projects—interlocking projects in radically different contexts—that connected to one another along the political, cultural, and gendered margins of European modernisms.[2] Outside the "trinity of France, England, [and] Germany" (*Revolt* 135), Spanish philosopher and essayist José Ortega y Gasset rewrote Spengler's metaphors, positing that the continent would be rejuvenated in its forgotten sideline by the energy of a "Vital Spain" bodied forth by an enlightened vanguard of cosmopolitan intelligentsia. The ideal of reinventing Europe in sites that seemed relatively untouched by the war's devastation appealed to many, and Ortega was optimistic in the immediate postwar years that interchanges and cooperation among internationalist periodicals that were detached from ideological or partisan agendas had the power, as Eliot wrote of his *Criterion*, Ortega's *Revista de Occidente* [*Review of the West*], and their continental partners, to restore the "healthy . . . circulation . . . [of] the intellectual blood of Europe" (182).[3] As Eliot's multivalent metaphor of "circulation" implies, these reviews, many editors believed, could reanimate a war-torn European community in a manner that neither bombastic avant-garde journals nor staid national reviews could. Forging a collaborative transnational space—a modern public sphere at once local and global—for rapidly transmitting fresh ideas, aesthetics, and cultural politics, these polylogic media associated modernist circles, such as the one Ortega assembled around his *Revista* in 1923, not only with their counterparts in Paris, London, and Berlin, but also with others in Europe's former American colonies. (For more on little magazines as a global form, see Bulson in this volume.) In fact, Ortega's wide-ranging and mutually influential dialogues with the American journalist and novelist Waldo Frank and the Argentine writer, publisher, and feminist Victoria Ocampo evince a shared conviction that Europe might be resuscitated best in Madrid, New York, and Buenos Aires. At the same time, these three figures imagined that their respective insular capitals might emerge from moribund states through symbiotic relationships with a reconfigured Europe. Yet, as they couched within their civilizational narratives scathing local critiques, they were also upbraided by their peers—branded as elitist importers of the "dead" European ideals that had excluded or suppressed native cultural productions.

I trace below the controversial efforts of these writers and their colleagues at journals such as Frank's *Seven Arts* and Ocampo's *Sur* [*South*] to refashion Spengler's Western organism for their own aims, which extended from the reform of the liberal-democratic subject to that of an entire civilization. With "organicist" metaphors, as Pheng Cheah has described such language,[4] Frank's, Ortega's, and Ocampo's common work responds to modern iterations of technicism, fatalism, nationalism, and decadent aesthetics in ways that offer several Hispanic routes into Euro-American modernisms and vice versa.[5] I show that Frank's personal journeys, the dissemination of his works and his notion of "our America," and the evolution of his tropes for Pan-American and European collective identity, provide paths for delineating the conjunctions of three intersecting modernist movements—based in journals on three continents—that form a vibrant triangle of connections among competing centers of cultural capital in the interwar era. Frank's, Ortega's, and Ocampo's influential dialogues with their more familiar Euro-American modernist contemporaries also help to reorient our map of interwar literature and aesthetics toward the global, "polycentric modernities and modernisms" that Susan Stanford Friedman has adumbrated (426). In particular, these writers recast in their innovative, transatlantic reviews Spain's relation to Europe and the New World's relation to the Old in order to create an open-ended realm for reciprocally influential experimentation and critique. By doing so, they left an archive that calls contemporary scholars to write literary histories of their modernisms across the national, linguistic, and formal boundaries that their works traversed.

"OUR AMERICA," THROUGH EUROPEAN EYES

Though a minor figure in contemporary English- and Spanish-language criticism, Waldo Frank was a prominent interwar figure "who circulated through three worlds—the European, the North-American, and the Hispanic," Arnold Chapman writes ("Waldo Frank in the Hispanic World" 626). Frank's eclectic influences and interests, which ranged from messianism, transcendentalism, and Marx to Spinoza, Spengler, and Gurdjieffian mysticism, found their first expression in the short-lived journal of Greenwich Village radicalism *Seven Arts* (1916–1917). Here, Frank collaborated with Van Wyck Brooks, Randolph Bourne, James Oppenheim, and others of the Lyrical Left to found an "organ" for native artists that would disseminate the newest and best "expression[s] of our American life" in what the group saw as the country's "renascent period" (Frank, Editorial 52).[6] *Seven Arts* advertised itself as a peer to American literary magazines such as *Poetry*, and its nativist tendencies always were paired with Frank's desire to circulate this innovative and regenerative American "spirit" in Europe. Indeed, the centerpiece of the first number (and the only article advertised on its cover) was the Frenchman Romain Rolland's "America and the Arts." Frank explains that

> [b]efore the War, [Rolland's] message of internationalism, his plea for a European
> spirit, his profound study of the fallacy of boundaries in thought and culture,
> were welcome . . . throughout [an] intellectual Europe . . . [that has now]
> disappeared. . . . [But if] the War is a destroyer, it is also a creator. The philoso-
> pher, the artist and the teacher may snap back to a primitive state, like elastic
> bands released from their strain[.] (Editorial 54–55)

Frank sees Rolland as a European frustrated by the "fallacy of boundaries in thought and culture" who looks to American art—seen by generations of Europeans as derivative—to "release" and guide Europe out of its period of self-destruction and into an era of re-creation.

Such transatlantic intellectual idealism is captured in Bourne's seminal piece of cultural criticism "Trans-National America" (1916), an implicit manifesto for the *Seven Arts* circle. Against reigning assimiliationist models, Bourne argues that while

Europe has fallen into internecine warfare, the United States, as a nation of European immigrants, finally might forge the "cultural wreckage" of a "transplanted Europe" into the model of a "cosmopolitan federation of national colonies, of foreign cultures" (271, 272, 276). "America," Bourne argues, "is coming to be, not a nationality but a transnationality": a counterbalance to Europe's retrogressive and "weary nationalism[s]" that will harmonize diverse cultures into a "dual spiritual citizenship" in order to "save this Western world of ours from suicide" (283, 272, 281, 278).[7] But the "plastic[, . . .] fluid and dynamic generation" that converged around *Seven Arts* was never able to offer a definitive answer to Bourne's question, "What shall we do with our America?" (283). In 1917, the review was forced to suspend production after only twelve issues, unable to secure financial backers because of its writers' unpopular opposition to America's entry into the Great War (the Wilson administration was suppressing dissident leftist voices at the time). The following year, Bourne died of influenza, and Frank, presumed by his peers to be the heir to Bourne's groundbreaking thought, began his quest to become a "cultural envoy" of a new America to Europe (*Our America* ix).

Like Bourne, Frank had studied in France before the war. While there, he established relations in Paris with the central figures of the paradigmatic European literary magazine, the *Nouvelle Revue Française* (*NRF*).[8] André Gide, Gaston Gallimard, and Jacques Copeau became Frank's informal patrons, securing him translation jobs and commissioning him to write his widely successful study *Our America* (1919), which he called a "book for France about my country . . . [written] also *for* my country . . . *to* my country" (xi; emphases in original). Maintaining this dual gaze in his dedication to Gallimard and Copeau, Frank calls the *NRF* and its publishing house a "flexible, rather sharply integrated organism since it includes creators so varied in mood and outlook [as Gide, Claudel, Copeau, Peguy, and others. . . . It] is an organism that justly stands for a great portion of Young France" (x). (He later reflected on *Seven Arts* as an "embryo[nic]" and "growing organism" whose development remained incomplete [*Memoirs* 94–95].) Frank thus hopes to give "Young America . . . [a] voice in Paris" by inviting his French colleagues to join him in "discovering America together"—to embark as "spiritual pioneers" who will reshape an overly mechanized America trapped in its "inchoate state" (3, 9, 8). America, he writes, is the "burial ground" of European and Native American cultures whose detritus must be fashioned into a culture of progressive cosmopolitanism in order to counteract the effects of rigid technicism, mass consumerism, and "Puritan Industrialism." Our "task," he declares, is to "begin to generate within ourselves the energy [to create.] . . . And in a dying world, creation is revolution" (232).[9]

As he was serializing sections of *Our America* in Europe and America, Frank saw periodicals as an ideal outlet for his prophesying to diverse audiences. Constantly reformulating his cultural theories, Frank pursued America's Hispanic roots further and decided that Spain provided the basis for synthesizing the European history, New World imperialism, and modern Pan-Americanism that formed "our America" (see Ogorzaly 43–46). In the early 1920s, he traveled twice to Spain, where he read (by chance, he claimed) a discussion of *Our America* in socialist writer Luis

Araquistáin's *El peligro yanqui* [*The Yankee Peril*, 1921]. Araquistáin, who analyzes Europe and the Americas in light of the "unanimous" conclusion among intellectuals that "western civilization . . . [and] the historical concept of Europe have reached the brink of death," praises Frank for laying bare the psyche of "Yankee utilitarianism from the times of the pioneer[s] . . . and the Puritans of the Mayflower" through the modern machine age (151, 197–98).[10] Araquistáin concludes his own work with Frank's portrait of a menacing American "giant-child" [*niño gigante*] that stands at the crossroads of the world, "between Europe and Asia, all appetite, with no notion of limits; messianic, hungry for power, riches, and glory" (200). By 1924, Frank found himself engaged in public debates through the Spanish press with some of the country's preeminent literary figures. Still working to revise depictions of the United States and its writers that circulated abroad—as he would through the 1930s, when he published a series of articles on Eliot in *El Sol*—he sparred with Ramón Pérez de Ayala on the inaccuracies of H. G. Wells's *The Future of America* (1906), then took Ramiro de Maeztu to task for his reductive and anti-Semitic readings of American culture (see Chapman, "Waldo Frank in the Hispanic World"). Through these arguments, Frank not only promulgated in Spain the cultural agendas of his generation of American writers, but also came into contact with such renowned Spaniards as Azorín, Pío Baroja, Juan Ramón Jiménez, Federico García Lorca, and most consequentially for him, Ortega.

ORTEGA AND MODERNISM IN "INVERTEBRATE SPAIN"

In Ortega, Frank found a figure engaged in cultural work in Spain—routed through a vision of Europe—that was both homologous and connected to his own in the United States. With shared metaphors and sentiments, Ortega provided the American with a new link to an influential network of Spanish-language writers and critics, as I will discuss shortly. The scion of a famous Madrileño publishing family, Ortega first made his name as a philosopher as a younger associate of Spain's Generation of '98. This group of writers and artists was characterized by its responses to "The Disaster"—the once mighty empire's humiliating loss of its final New World possessions in the Spanish-American War of 1898. For Ortega, the war was the culminating point of centuries of decline during which Spain had allowed itself to become Europe's internal emblem of backwardness, barbarism, and ineptitude. He broke with the Generation of '98 on critical points in his *regeneracionismo*; as did Frank and the *Seven Arts* circle, he encouraged his compatriots to integrate and rebuild their nation not by turning inward, but outward: "Only seen from Europe is Spain possible," Ortega wrote in 1910 ("España como posibilidad" 1: 138).

He first attempted to reproduce his own studies in Germany by circulating Europe's intellectual life in Spain through reviews such as *Faro* [*Lighthouse*, or *Beacon*] and *Europa*, but met with only modest success. By 1914, however, Ortega had become the country's leading intellectual and a ubiquitous presence in the world of Castilian newspapers and journals. In "Vieja y nueva política" ["Old and new politics," 1914], a public address that garnered great attention, Ortega called on his colleagues across the country to dismantle the "Old Spain"—"Official Spain"—that clung to feudalistic religious, monarchic, and aristocratic traditions. In terms that recall Eliot's metaphor of "circulation," he stated that "[O]fficial Spain, [which] encompasses . . . all organisms of our society, from Parliament to newspapers and from rural schools to universities, . . . is an immense skeleton of a vanished organism" (1: 272). In its place, Ortega argues, must come a "New Spain," which would be a "Vital Spain, [. . . a] spontaneous, diffuse, evolving organism of the nation" led forward by "all the conscious, deliberate, and organic powers" of an elite vanguard with Spanish-European sensibilities (1: 273, 271).

In the nation he called "invertebrate," Ortega began working to assemble the cosmopolitan minority that he believed would finally foster a cultural renaissance by creating an "intellectual aristocracy in service to the *pueblo*" ("Imperativo" 13). In 1923 he gathered critics and authors from his publishing ventures and from his students at the Residencia de Estudiantes, an Anglophilic residential college in Madrid modeled on Oxford and Cambridge, around his new periodical *Revista de Occidente* (López Campillo 57–76). Ortega envisioned that Fernando Vela, Manuel García Morente, Benjamín Jarnés, Antonio Marichalar, Ramón Gómez de la Serna, and an evolving cast of writers would import, translate, and disseminate European writing in Spain while also circulating experimental Spanish productions abroad. Ortega's most expansive collaborative project, the *Revista* would be the central medium of his reformative work in Silver Age Spain (roughly 1898–1936), an era of flourishing and contrasting vanguard movements. He boldly promises in his "Propósitos" to revise the West through Madrid; that is, to reinterpret European culture from the continent's remote backwater in a manner that would model the formation of a supranational "United States of Europe" (*Revolt* 139). The monthly review's goal, he adds, is to "reveal the plane of a new architecture on which Western life [*la vida occidental*] is being reconstructed" (2). Its first task was to confront Spengler and his influence across Europe and the Americas. Agreeing with Spengler's critiques of Europe's decay but disagreeing with his prognosis, Ortega had helped Morente translate and publish Spengler's *Decline of the West* as *La Decadencia de Occidente* that same year; the journal's title refers to Spengler's treatise. Ortega wrote the prologue for the translation and Morente sketched for the *Revista de Occidente*'s second number an outline of Spengler's thesis. Meanwhile, Ortega continued refining the philosophy for which he would become best known: ratio-vitalism, a unique existentialist adaptation of European (especially neo-Kantian) rationalism and Bergson-esque vitalism grounded in embodied experience and perception. That this project was concomitant with his effort to reconstruct the prototypical Spanish and European subject is evident in his theories of the avant-garde, which read aesthetic and humanistic trends simultaneously. Neither celebrating nor condemning new arts, Ortega's *Dehumanization of Art* and *Notes on the Novel* (1924–1925) exhibit a modernist response to Romanticism, naturalism, sentimental literature, and "exhausted" forms of representation in a manner that lays a broad foundation for understanding the *Revista's* mission.

Casting ever wider nets, Ortega quickly turned the *Revista* into the most influential journal of philosophy, literature, sociological commentary, and aesthetic theory in the interwar Hispanophone world (see Unruh 21–26; King 39). Contemporary German, British, and French texts, often translated into Spanish for the first time, filled its pages alongside works by most every prominent Spanish author of the period. Latin Americans including Jorge Luis Borges, Alfonso Reyes (then Mexican ambassador to Spain and a friend of both Frank's and Ocampo's), and Jaime Torres Bodet (later of Mexico's *Contemporáneos* group) were also well represented. Thus the journal aimed to cover cultural histories and trends not only in Paris, London, and Berlin, but also in Europe's margins and peripheries—from Málaga to Lima, Moscow to Buenos Aires—in order to present a dynamic, multinodal vision of the rejuvenating West. Indeed, Ortega sees the potential for the *Revista* to satisfy the "natural," "organic," and "vital curiosity" among readers to cultivate "the vast germination of life" in the postwar world ("Propósitos" 1). Ortega also established extensive contacts, shared writers and circulation schemes, and created review exchanges with periodicals across Europe as part of his effort to bring forth journalistically the Vital Spain that he saw as the beacon (albeit belated in its enlightenment) of the new Europe. His project of a reconfigured Spanish-European identity was complicated, though, when only two months after Ortega launched the *Revista*, the general Miguel Primo de Rivera took power of the country in a coup; he ruled as dictator until 1930. The *Revista's* circle carefully distanced its cultural politics from the Pan-Hispanic Catholicism of writers such as Ramiro de Maeztu, or later, from the nationalist agenda of *La Gaceta Literaria* [*The Literary Gazette*], begun in 1927 by future Falangist Ernesto Giménez Caballero (Gray 183). Instead, the review printed unconventional views of Spanish history and ethnicity from without by (most notably) the German reformist Count Keyserling.

Exemplifying the cross-cultural work that Ortega advocated, the critic and translator Antonio Marichalar wrote regular columns for both *The Criterion* and the *Revista de Occidente*, introducing Anglo-American modernist works to Hispanophone audiences and those of his Spanish Generation of '27 colleagues to Anglophone readers. Marichalar also helped Ortega welcome Frank warmly among the *Revista's* writers and championed Frank's works in his reviews. In his cutting-edge critical study for the *Revista* "James Joyce en su laberinto" ["James Joyce in His Labyrinth," 1924], Marichalar relates the stylistics of *Ulysses* to those of Proust, Dostoevsky, and—in the same breath—Frank (see Marichalar). Frank had made a literary impression in Madrid similar to the one he had made in Paris, where he had met with Joyce, and both his novel *Rahab* (1922) and his collection of stories *City Block* (1922) were greeted by a number of Europeans as paragons of new American writing. Heartened by Frank's reception abroad, Hart Crane believed that he and his mentor Frank might capitalize on the fact that "[t]he American public is still strangely unprepared for its men of higher talents, while Europe looks more to America for the renascence of a creative spirit" (193). He was convinced that Frank had "the most vital consciousness in America" and that he might see even greater success on the continent than had Eliot, whose *Waste Land* was "so damned dead" (130, 105).[11] Ortega began publishing translations of Frank's work both in the *Revista de Occidente* and in its book press in 1925. Frank's work was reviewed and discussed regularly in the journal: the critic Ángel Sánchez Rivero linked the critiques in *Our America* to Ortega's *Modern Theme* (1923), while Frank in turn reviewed Ortega's work in the *Nation & Athenaeum* of London.

Frank's next major project, the historical-cultural study *Virgin Spain* (1926), evinces both convergences with and divergences from Ortega's thought. Serialized in both English and Spanish in the *Revista*, *The Dial*, and several other periodicals on either side of the Atlantic, Frank's effort to understand Spain from an American European perspective exceeded commercial and popular expectations; Miguel de Unamuno himself translated its conclusion for an Argentine paper. In *Virgin Spain*, his unofficial companion to *Our America*, Frank follows the advice of his colleague Alfonso Reyes: "do not forget that Spain is the path to our America" ("Introducción" 12). Frank expands his growing Pan-Americanism *through* his understanding of Spain: he dedicates this study to "those brother Americans / whose tongues are Spanish and Portuguese / whose homes are between the Rio Grande / and Tierra del Fuego / but whose America / like mine / stretches from the Arctic to the Horn." He presents his text as a "Symphonic History," one which figures Spain, a country in "transition, between waking and sleeping," as a "complex integer" that embraces its component parts—law, art, history, geography, literature, culture, and more—"*immediately*, as a body holds all its organs" (*Virgin Spain* 279, 2; emphasis in original). Frank condenses Spanish history to argue that "[t]he ethnic Iberian base of Spain is more African in nature than European; more aboriginally close to Semite than to German" (193). Thus, Spain is at once European and non-European; it embraces putative racial differences and provides a source of hybridity for Frank's New World. *Virgin Spain* then explores the European "Organism" from the medieval era to the present as it is torn apart and reanimated, leading finally to the origins of what Frank soon calls "America Hispana," where "Berber Phoenician, Arabic, Jewish, Moorish elements . . . [mixed] with Germanic and . . . Celtic strains . . . created in Spain . . . and in Portugal too" (*America Hispana. South of Us* viii).[12] Frank's European-Americanism extends both Bourne's and Ortega's thought through the New World, converting Spain from the symbol of European decline to the cauldron for the regeneration of both Europe and "America Hispana." As Columbus says in an imaginary dialogue with Cervantes at the end of *Virgin Spain*, "Spain[, despite] creating life, has never lived. . . . [When] Modern Europe flourished, Spain was not modern and Spain was not Europe. She bore America. [. . .] Ready, Spain! . . . Europe has rotted at last into the Grave they called America. . . . You, most broken mother of all Europe, you have preserved a Seed" (299–300).

FRANK'S AMERICAS AND OCAMPO'S EUROPE

Frank's straddling of the Old and New Worlds in his work and his travels eventually led him to Ocampo, the Hispanic cultural figure with whom he would enjoy the most prosperous literary relationship—a fact evinced most clearly in their shared tropes for Pan-Americanism. Across Latin America, Hispanic writers had begun to take note of Frank's work throughout the 1920s, eventually earning Frank a level of recognition in Latin America that was rare for a North American author. The Mexican poet José Juan Tablada was optimistic that Frank's Hispanophilic notion of "our America"—a translation of the phrase "Nuestra América," coined by Cuban revolutionary writer José Martí in 1891—signaled a new pro-Mexican and anti-imperialist attitude among writers in the United States. Peruvian editor José Carlos Mariátegui discussed Frank's ideas in his journal *Amauta*, while the Argentine Samuel Glusberg, under the pseudonym Enrique Espinoza, published without permission some of Frank's writings in his paper *La Vida Literaria* (Chapman, "Waldo Frank in Spanish America"). Glusberg and others soon arranged for Frank to make a lecture tour of Latin America in 1929. Frank spoke to hundreds of intellectuals and thousands of students in Mexico and Argentina, stopping along the way in Peru. As Irene Rostagno writes, "in Mexico he . . . [was] received as a prophet, in Buenos Aires and the rest of South America he was treated as something more important, a great writer . . . [who was given a] lavish welcome" (50). In a moment when investors and the military in the United States were eyeing their southern neighbors, Frank's criticisms of *yanqui* imperialism and arguments for a Pan-American culture resonated with many Latin American critics, and his "Primer Mensaje a la América Hispana" circulated in the *Revista de Occidente* and a number of Latin American magazines.

In 1929, Frank published his *Re-discovery of America*, which he had been serializing in the *New Republic* and the *Revista de Occidente* since 1927. In *Re-discovery*, he rounds out his physiographic metaphor of America and its people as "a loose organism, joined by earth and air, by ancestor and neighbour[,]" but not yet integrated (194). By contrast, Europe, once an "alive organic body," a "great Body of western [sic] experience," now "swarms in death [. . . and] cultural decomposition," for the death of its "hierarchic organs [has] meant the body's death" (11, 14, 15, 32). America, he writes, might forge a cultural "[w]holeness" and become the rejuvenated West that Spengler could not see—a vision shared by many Latin American readers of Spengler's work and Ortega's commentaries on them. In his collected lectures and writings from the tour, Frank outlines the shape of his America Hispana as two "American Half-Worlds," a masculine Anglo North and a feminine Hispanic South, united at the Panama Canal and, recalling Ortega, "vertebrated" into a "universal Body," an "organic whole" tied vitally to Europe (*America Hispana* 317, 357). For Frank, this feminine South was embodied in Buenos Aires by Ocampo. Ocampo, who had achieved some notoriety in European letters in the 1920s, modeled her writing on the French literature that she had discovered through her family's aristocratic European ties (French was her first language) and on the British modernism that she read in the *Revista*. Frank recalls that at her family's estate, Villa Ocampo, one wall of the library contained a symbolic "painted map . . . [of] the Americas and Europe [with] a sun-blue sea between them," while *objets d'art* from all corners of the world filled the house. Frank emphasizes that "all these details have been transfigured and composed by an Argentinean—an American will" (127).

Frank was not the first to imagine the magnetic Ocampo and her works in such synthetic terms: Ocampo had befriended Ortega during the philosopher's first lecture tour in Argentina in 1916. Ortega wrote to her that "the whole world" was now convinced of "two propositions: Europe is in decline [*decadencia*]—America is peaking"; but these propositions told an incomplete story, he added, since both civilizations needed one another in order to flourish symbiotically (*Epistolario* 145).[13] John King notes that Ortega idealized Ocampo, who had published in the *Revista de Occidente*, as "the Mona Lisa of the Pampas" and "the fusion of the body of America and the spirit of Europe" who might help revitalize both civilizations (34). However problematic the quasi-colonial gendering of Frank's Pan-Americanism, for Ortega the feminine Latin body became personal: he made an indiscreet and unwelcome pass at Ocampo that soured their relationship. Despite inspiring one another from afar, the two did not communicate for several years, and Ocampo took personally Ortega's various published dismissals of women's philosophy and writing.

Ocampo ultimately affirmed that the "Americas could be a source of inspiration to a decadent [European] culture," much as Ortega envisioned Spain could be (King 37). As she was contemplating the relationship between the cultures of the Old World and the New, Ocampo saw in Frank a fresh American perspective on Europe. Along with Glusberg, Frank encouraged her to launch a new journal in Buenos Aires. Ocampo planned a review, published with her own funds, that would connect Argentina's vibrant national life to those represented by the *Revista de Occidente* and the *NRF*. For his part, Frank believed that Ocampo, who flouted the mores of her rigid local culture, could "prophesy" a new Argentina, and he hoped that her journal would be printed in both Spanish and English—and perhaps titled *Nuestra América*. Instead, Ocampo chose to call her Spanish-language journal *Sur*, the name suggested by Ortega, and hired (among others) the Spaniard along with Frank, Reyes, Pierre Drieu La Rochelle, and Jules Supervielle as international constituents of her editorial board, then secured Eduardo Mallea, Guillermo de Torre, María Rosa Oliver, and Borges as local editors and contributors (see Willson). Beginning in January 1931, *Sur* brought to Argentina a diversity of European writers and critics similar to that which the *Revista* had brought to Spain, but Ocampo also published a number of works by authors from the United States, including Pound, Edgar Lee Masters, and Lewis Mumford, in order to balance her journal's Europeanism. The second number also printed bilingual versions of Borges's translations of Langston Hughes's poems, including "I, Too," which gains a new Pan-American resonance in this journalist adaptation.

Locally, Ocampo made it one of her purposes to "present . . . Argentina to its own people through the filter of the European gaze" with the hope of "sav[ing] the

West from Spenglerian decline . . . [with a] humanistic light," notes Berete E. Strong (101, 107). Her friendships with Ortega and with French editors ensured European circulation for *Sur*, but her focus on the Old World met with resistance in Argentina, where avant-garde magazines such as *Proa* and *Martín Fierro* had been thriving through the 1920s. King writes that *Sur* was "condemned as *extranjerizante* (a dismissive term, referring to those intellectuals whose ideas and attitudes are formed by foreign, in particular European, models), cosmopolitan and elitist in contrast to an 'ideal' Argentine culture which should be popular and nationalist" (4–5; parentheses in original). Furthermore, the journal was founded in the wake of general José Félix Uriburu's 1930 coup in Buenos Aires that "set a pattern of cultural isolationism and intellectual suppression which naturally made *Sur* suspect" (Steiner 102). Aware of the tendencies that had earned both *Seven Arts* and the *Revista de Occidente* local reproach, Ocampo still resolves in her review's manifesto, "Carta a Waldo Frank," that she will not "turn her back on Europe," promising instead to cultivate a "vital" sentiment in "our continent" by re-reading "all America" through a Hispanic-European lens (11–12; see Sitman).

Ocampo's opening epistle to Frank credits him with helping her to create a journal that will body forth their shared "search for America"—for its "hidden treasure." "We are lovers [*enamorados*] of America," she writes, "[y]our America and mine— let us write it more simply as 'our America,'" one that must be revealed not only to its inhabitants but also to "our European friends" (18, 17).[14] Both in competition with and in contrast to reviews such as the Mexican *Contemporáneos* and the Cuban *Revista de Avance*, *Sur* was a luxurious and expensive periodical noted for its colored image of an arrow pointing south on its cover (a directional twist on Ortega's review also). It would develop Ocampo's synthesis of Frank's and Ortega's influences with her own feminist, psychoanalytic, and liberal-humanist ideals in the 1930s, and it was published without major interruptions until the late 1960s. Ocampo continually revised her Pan-Americanism as she developed closer relationships with Rabindranath Tagore, Virginia Woolf, Aldous Huxley, and other modernists. Through *Sur*'s press, she also became the first to publish Spanish translations of these writers, along with D. H. Lawrence, Graham Greene, and several other Anglophone novelists.

Ocampo's friendship with Woolf in the mid-1930s profoundly shaped her notions of international feminism and influenced her expanding Argentine cosmopolitanism. Her "Carta a Virginia Woolf," published in the *Revista de Occidente* in 1934, extends the claims of Woolf's *A Room of One's Own* and prefigures the call for a Society of Outsiders that Woolf would make in *Three Guineas* (1938). "By defending your causes," she writes to Woolf, "I defend my own, too. [. . .] [I]f, as you hope . . . all [feminist] efforts might . . . converge to give birth to a form of expression that still has not found a climate proper for its flourishing, may my efforts join with others by all women, unknown or famous, working throughout the world" (11, 14). Ocampo published in *Sur*'s press the first full-length Spanish translations of Woolf's works, beginning with *A Room of One's Own* in 1936 (translated by Borges) and *Orlando* in 1937, then following with Ernesto Palacio's translation of *Mrs. Dalloway* in 1939 and Román J. Jiménez's translation of *Three Guineas* in 1941 (see Lojo Rodriguez). In her ten-part autobiographical *Testimonios* (1935–1977) and her cultural criticism such as *Domingos en Hyde Park* [*Sundays in Hyde Park*, 1936], she positioned herself as an outspoken, independent democrat. She cofounded the Argentine Women's Union in 1936 as a national voice for feminism. And when the Spanish Civil War forced the *Revista de Occidente* to suspend publication in 1936, Ocampo welcomed and published refugees such as Marichalar, who translated *To the Lighthouse* for Ocampo's journal and press in 1938. Here, she not only influenced her Chilean colleague Gabriela Mistral and other Latin American writers, but also tightened the links between her own movement and the Anglophone world. Ocampo projected a Hispanic Europeanism from the American periphery that, along with her review, offered an intellectual and material base for internationalist thought and literature that integrated the work of Frank, Ortega, and a host of sympathetic figures into an antifascist, universalist appeal for democratic women's rights.

Uneven Modernist Cosmopolitanisms

Occurring on "the threshold of a not yet fully modernized world in which old and new were violently knocked against each other," as Andreas Huyssen writes of modernist sites, these interconnected movements along the permeable margins of Euro-American cultures expand our understandings of modernists' literary politics (7). That is, Frank, Ortega, Ocampo, and their colleagues articulated their work through debates and disputes with a range of avant-garde circles in Europe and the Americas, pushing on the critical boundaries that scholarship has erected around the arts of this era. We see also in these texts and media common ambivalences— whether in progressive or in reactionary forms—toward modernity, collectivity, the social roles of intellectuals, and interwar nation-states. Within the successes and failures of the interchanges in the shared space of their periodicals—which they saw as "vital" and "organic" entities—we find proposals for reappropriating cosmopolitan sensibilities from their abuse, as Julien Benda contended in his *La Trahison des clercs* [*The Treason of the Intellectuals*, 1927], by the generation of thinkers who came of age at the time of the Great War and became mouthpieces for belligerent nationalisms. The plans for regeneration in Frank's, Ortega's, and Ocampo's responses to cultural crises envisage an ability to feel at home across the globe—or at least the West—by cultivating foreign affects and global views of their local environs. In practice, their utopianisms often left them not only rebuked at home but also, as Janet Lyon observes in her contribution to this volume, treated as outsiders or curiosities abroad. Ortega's pupil Julián Marías wrote that his mentor, despite spending years in Germany and lecturing across Europe, never had the "illusion of . . . 'cosmopolitanism,' the illusion of the man who feels like a 'citizen of the world' because he could not escape his Hispanic origins" (159). Ocampo, who endured countless uninformed questions from European nobles about "savagery" in South America, at the same time felt herself exiled and de-nationalized—"the owner of a soul without a passport"—even among friends such as Joyce's American-born Parisian publisher Sylvia Beach (quoted in Meyer 61).

Frank wrote later in life, "I've always felt myself as an *outsider*—yearning, struggling to *get in*. *Into* my own home, . . . *into* France (later Spain), *into* literary America (*7 Arts, Our America*, & the 1920s), *into* the Revolution (the People). I've never succeeded" (quoted in Trachtenberg vii; emphases in original). Nor did Frank finally join the American artists who settled in Paris, Mexico, or Buenos Aires for artistic inspiration in the 1920s and 1930s. Instead, back in the United States, Frank used his editorial positions at the *New Republic* and the *New Yorker* to promote the literature that he had encountered in the Hispanophone world. In the 1930s, he served as an editorial advisor for Latin American letters at Doubleday, Doran and Company, through which he imported translations of Mexican author Mariano Azuela's *Los de abajo* [*The Underdogs*, 1929] and *Mala yerba* [*Marcela: A Mexican Love Story*, 1932; translated by the artist Anita Brenner]. He later helped publish through Farrar and Rinehart's Latin American series the Argentine writers Ricardo Güiraldes and José Hernández, the latter the author of the epic *gaucho* poem "Martín Fierro." But Frank's efforts through these translations to educate readers in the United States about the cultures "south of us"—to endow readers with a hemispheric consciousness—had little success (Rostagno 56ff). And while shared worldly sensibilities and cultural politics brought Ortega, Frank, and Ocampo together, they diverged at key moments, too. Frank and Ortega's amiable and mutually beneficial friendship was never an easy fit: Frank's interest in Marxism, for instance, was at odds with Ortega's conservative European and strongly anti-Bolshevik commitments. In *The Revolt of the Masses*, Ortega refutes Frank's *Re-discovery of America*, which he claims takes Spengler's analyses of Europe uncritically as truth and wrongly reads America as prepared to inherit Europe's former geopolitical standing (132). That is, the reaction against Spengler that Ortega and Frank shared in the early 1920s became a matter of contention between them only a few years later. Ortega, meanwhile, angered Argentines by speaking condescendingly to them and by ranking Spaniards' "blood" above those of the indigenous and Creole populations (Gray 112). Frank also antagonized some Latin Americans when he maintained a role for the continent's brutal colonizer, Spain, in the post-imperial New World (see Faber).

By 1936, the intellectual projects that Ortega, Frank, and Ocampo had engaged were endangered by the civil war in Spain, making their fellow-feeling and anti-Spenglerian optimism of post–Great War moment difficult to recover. Frank had already begun to turn his attention to Russia (where he traveled in 1931) and to the communist League of American Writers, which agitated for the Spanish Republic. Even then, Frank's mystical version of Marxism, which valued the spiritual and organic over the material, led to disagreements with party members in the Americas and in Europe. As Franco's victory in Spain heightened American and European attention to fascist designs on South America, Frank became an emissary of the

Good Neighbor policy. In 1942, however, he was severely beaten by fascists in Argentina for being a "Jewish Bolshevik" after he criticized the regime of President Ramón Castillo. Ortega had a brief, uneasy relationship with the Second Republic, then fled Madrid when the civil war erupted and never again regained his cultural authority when he returned after World War II. Ocampo was to suffer harassment and imprisonment under Juan Perón's regime. New York, Madrid, and Buenos Aires did not become the bases for the internationalizing projects that each writer conceived when working to adapt and reconcile foreign models with native arts. By the same token, both Ortega and Ocampo were immensely important figures in twentieth-century Spanish-language letters, but they remain peripheral to accounts of Euro-American modernisms, and relatively little of their work has been translated into English. Yet, as this chapter has detailed, the assemblages of Spanish and Pan-American modernisms that Ortega, Frank, and Ocampo attached to Europe across borders and languages compose a rich history defined not by originals and derivatives. Rather, these dynamic interchanges, with their great, continental ambitions and problematic, sometimes contradictory cultural politics, register the work of a transnational modernist critique—of local regimes and continental or civilizational "bodies" alike—to imagine the Western organism as born anew along its margins.

NOTES

1. Nicholas Allen, for instance, treats Spengler's influence on Yeats's *A Vision*; see "Yeats, Spengler, and *A Vision* after Empire." On the invention of the concept of the "West," the "double-mapping" of Europe, and the broader influence of Spengler at this moment, see GoGwilt.

2. When I refer to Spanish-language "modernist" movements, I am using "modernism" in the Anglophone critical sense, which should not be confused with its Spanish cognate *modernismo*. *Modernismo*, a term coined by Nicaraguan poet Rubén Darío, refers to an earlier literary-aesthetic movement that flourished among Spain's Generation of '98 and among Latin America writers of that era (see Aching in this volume); its Catalan cognate *modernisme* refers to several fin-de-siècle movements in Catalonia. See Davison for an account of these movements and their critical histories; see Eysteinsson and Liska for essays on their relations to modernist movements around the globe.

3. Eliot refers to a shared circulation scheme built around a writing competition in five languages initiated in 1930 among his review (launched in 1922) and the *Nouvelle Revue Française*, the *Revista de Occidente*, the *Nuova Antologia*, and the *Europäische Revue*. The Modernist Journals Project and Modernist Magazines Project are two recent attempts to bring the wealth of archives of modernist periodicals to a wider scholarly audience. In my forthcoming book, *Modernism and the New Spain*, I reconstruct and analyze a wide-ranging dialogue on cosmopolitanism carried out in such periodicals among the figures discussed in this essay, along with Joyce, Woolf, Spencer, Lorca, and others, to revise post–Great War Europe's cultural politics. In particular, I treat at greater length the symbiotic development of Ocampo's and Woolf's anti-fascist cosmopolitanism in the mid-1930s.

4. While critiques of the nation-state and political collectivity are integral to the arguments that Frank, Ortega, and Ocampo make, I do not have the space here to treat these metaphors fully; rather, my focus is on the interconnected cultural politics of their modernist movements. Cheah follows this language through several philosophical and critical traditions in *Spectral Nationality*. Its genealogy, though, extends through Hobbes, Malthus, Social Darwinists, Spencer, and D. H. Lawrence, to name a few. On the overlapping significance of these metaphors and those of European thought on organic/ industrial societies, along with a critique of the putative neutrality of Frank's collectiv- ism, see Blake 290–95.

5. Here and throughout, I generally preserve the use of "Hispanic" (and *hispánico* or *hispano*) when it appears in the works of Frank, Ortega, Ocampo, and others, rather than employing the contemporary "Hispanophone." "Hispanic" maintains a sense of racial, ethnic, and historical difference that, exceeding a particular language, was key to these interchanges.

6. For biographies of these and others figures involved in *Seven Arts*, which also printed works by artists from Syria, Japan, and India, see Blake. On the nativist and nationalist elements of Frank's work, see Michaels.

7. On Bourne's work with his colleague at Columbia University, Joel Spingarn, on the project of "world literature" in America, see Arac 756–57.

8. The *NRF* was founded in 1908 by Gide. Gallimard became editor in 1911, then publication was suspended from 1914–1918 due to the war. Jacques Rivière resumed the journal in 1919 and Jean Paulhan was editor from 1925–1940.

9. In her excellent study of Fernando Pessoa and Anglophone modernism, Irene Ramalho Santos draws a parallel between Frank's "idea of America as a last hope for the West" and Pessoa's view of interwar Portugal (94).

10. All translations mine unless otherwise noted.

11. Crane to his mother, November 16, 1924; Crane to Frank, Easter 1923, 130; Crane to Frank, November 20, 1922.

12. Frank writes that he prefers "America Hispana" to "Latin America" because the former captures the degree to which this area was formed by a distinctly Hispanic charac- ter that differs from French or Italian. "*There is no Latin America*," he writes. "*The nations to the south of us (excepting Haiti . . .) are the product of the* Hispanic *countries—Spain and Portugal*" (viii; emphasis in original). On "American" and "Hemispheric" understandings of "the Americas" in contemporary critical discourses, see Pérez Firmat, ed.; Taylor.

13. Ortega to Ocampo, January 31, 1930.

14. Frank's physiographic study of Brazil and its peoples, "La Selva," also headlines the first issue of *Sur*.

WORKS CITED

Allen, Nicholas. "Yeats, Spengler, and A Vision after Empire." *Modernism and Colonialism*. Ed. Richard Begam and Michael Valdez Moses. Durham: Duke University Press, 2007. 209–25.

Arac, Jonathan. "Literary History in a Global Age." *New Literary History* 39.3 (2008). 747–60.

Araquistáin, Luis. *El Peligro Yanqui*. Madrid: Publicaciones España, 1921.*

Armstrong, Tim. *Modernism: A Cultural History.* Cambridge: Polity, 2005.

Blake, Casey Nelson. *Beloved Community: The Cultural Criticism of Randolph Bourne, Van Wyck Brooks, Waldo Frank and Lewis Mumford.* Chapel Hill: University of North Carolina Press, 1990.

Bourne, Randolph. "Trans-National America." *The History of a Literary Radical and Other Papers.* Introduction. Van Wyck Brooks. New York: S. A. Russell, 1956. 260–84.

Chapman, Arnold. "Waldo Frank in the Hispanic World: The First Phase." *Hispania* 44.4 (1961): 626–34.

———. "Waldo Frank in Spanish America: Between Journeys, 1924–1929." *Hispania* 47.3 (1964): 510–21.

Cheah, Pheng. *Spectral Nationality: Passages of Freedom from Kant to Postcolonial Literatures of Liberation.* New York: Columbia University Press, 2003.

Crane, Hart. *Letters, 1916–1932.* Ed. Brom Weber. New York: Hermitage House, 1952.

Davison, Ned J. *The Concept of Modernism in Hispanic Criticism.* Boulder: Pruett Press, 1966.

Eliot, T. S. "A Commentary." *The Criterion* 9.35 (1930): 181–84.

Eysteinsson, Astradur, and Vivian Liska, eds. *Modernism.* Amsterdam: John Benjamins Publishing, 2007.

Faber, Sebastiaan. "Learning from the Latins: Waldo Frank's Progressive Pan-Americanism." *CR: The New Centennial Review* 3.1 (2003) 257–95.

Frank, Waldo. *America Hispana: A Portrait and a Prospect.* New York: Charles Scribner's Sons, 1931.

———. *America Hispana. South of Us; The Characters of the Countries and the People of Central and South America.* New York: Garden City Publishing, 1940.

———. Editorial [unsigned]. *Seven Arts* 1.1 (1916): 52–55.

———. *Memoirs of Waldo Frank.* Ed. Alan Trachtenberg. Intro. Lewis Mumford. Amherst: University of Massachusetts Press, 1973.

———. *Our America.* 1919. New York: Boni and Liveright, 1921.

———. *The Re-discovery of America: An Introduction to a Philosophy of American Life.* New York: Charles Scribner's Sons, 1929.

———. *Virgin Spain: Scenes from the Spiritual Drama of a Great People.* New York: Boni and Liveright, 1926.

Friedman, Susan Stanford. "Periodizing Modernism: Postcolonial Modernities and the Space/Time Borders of Modernist Studies." *Modernism/modernity* 13.3 (2006): 425–43.

GoGwilt, Christopher. *The Invention of the West: Joseph Conrad and the Double-Mapping of Europe and Empire.* Stanford: Stanford University Press, 1995.

Gray, Rockwell. *The Imperative of Modernity: An Intellectual Biography of José Ortega y Gasset.* Berkeley: University of California Press, 1989.

Horan, Elizabeth, and Doris Meyer. Introduction. *This America of Ours: The Letters of Gabriela Mistral and Victoria Ocampo.* Ed. and Trans. Horan and Meyer. Austin: University of Texas Press, 2003. 1–26.

Huyssen, Andreas. "Geographies of modernism in a globalizing world." *Geographies of Modernism: Literatures, Cultures, Spaces.* Ed. Peter Brooker and Andrew Thacker. London: Routledge, 2005. 6–18.

Lojo Rodríguez, Laura María. "'A gaping mouth, but no words': Virginia Woolf Enters the Land of Butterflies." *The Reception of Virginia Woolf in Europe.* Ed. Mary Ann Caws and Nicola Luckhurst. London: Continuum, 2002. 218–46.

López Campillo, Evelyne. *La "Revista de Occidente" y la formación de minorías.* Madrid: Taurus, 1972.*

King, John. "*Sur*": *A Study of the Argentine Literary Journal and Its Role in the Development of a Culture, 1931–1970*. Cambridge: Cambridge University Press, 1986.

Marías, Julián. *José Ortega y Gasset: Circumstance and Vocation*. Trans. Frances M. López-Morillas. Norman: University of Oklahoma Press, 1970.

Marichalar, Antonio. "James Joyce in His Labyrinth." Trans. Gayle Rogers. *PMLA* 124:3 (2009): 926–38.

Meyer, Doris. *Victoria Ocampo: Against the Wind and Tide*. Austin: University of Texas Press, 1990.

Michaels, Walter Benn. *Our America: Modernism, Nativism, and Primitivism*. Durham: Duke University Press, 1995.

Ocampo, Victoria. "Carta a Waldo Frank." *Sur* 1.1 (1931): 7–18.*

———. "Carta a Virginia Woolf." *Testimonios: primera serie (1920–1934)*. Buenos Aires: Ediciones Fundación Sur, 1981. 7–14.*

———. *Victoria Ocampo: Writer, Feminist, and Woman of the World*. Trans. and Ed. Patricia Owen Steiner. Albuquerque: University of New Mexico Press, 1999.

Ogorzaly, Michael A. *Waldo Frank: Prophet of Hispanic Regeneration*. Lewisburg: Bucknell University Press, 1994.

Ortega y Gasset, José. *Epistolario*. Madrid: Ediciones de la Revista de Occidente, 1974.*

———. "España como posibilidad." *Obras Completas* 1: 137–38.*

———. "Imperativo de intelectualidad." *Obras Completas* 11: 11–13.*

———. *Obras Completas*. Madrid: Alianza /Revista de Occidente, 1983. 12 vols.*

———. "Propósitos." *Revista de Occidente* 1.1 (1923): 1–3.*

———. *Revolt of the Masses*. Trans. Anonymous. New York: W. W. Norton, 1993.

———. "Vieja y nueva política." *Obras Completas* 1: 265–307.

Pérez Firmat, Gustavo, ed. *Do the Americas Have a Common Literature?* Durham: Duke University Press, 1990.

Ramalho Santos, María Irene Sousa. *Atlantic Poets: Fernando Pessoa's Turn in Anglo-American Modernism*. Hanover: University of New England Press, 2003.

Reyes, Alfonso. "Introducción." *España Virgen: escenas del drama espiritual de un gran pueblo*. By Waldo Frank. Buenos Aires: Editorial Losada, 1947. 9–22.*

Rostagno, Irene. "Waldo Frank's Crusade for Latin American Literature." *The Americas* 46.1 (1989): 41–69.

Sitman, Rosalie. *Victoria Ocampo: Entre Europa y América*. Buenos Aires: Universidad de Tel Aviv, Instituto de Historia y Cultura de América Latina: Lumiere, 2003.*

Spengler, Oswald. *The Decline of the West*. 2 vols. Trans. Charles Francis Atkinson. New York: Knopf, 1939.

Strong, Beret E. *The Poetic Avant-garde: The Groups of Borges, Auden, and Breton*. Evanston: Northwestern University Press, 1997.

Taylor, Diana. "Remapping Genre through Performance: From 'American' to 'Hemispheric' Studies." *PMLA* 122.5 (2007): 1416–30.

Trachtenberg, Alan. Editor's Preface. *Memoirs of Waldo Frank* vii–xiv.

Unruh, Vicky. *Latin American Vanguards: The Art of Contentious Debates*. Berkeley: University of California Press, 1994.

Willson, Patricia. *La constelación del sur: traductores y traducciones en la literature argentina del siglo XX*. Buenos Aires: Siglo veintiuno editores Argentina, 2004.

* Texts not available in English at time of publication.

CHAPTER 20

SCANDINAVIAN MODERNISM: STORIES OF THE TRANSNATIONAL AND THE DISCONTINUOUS

ANNA WESTERSTÅHL STENPORT

THE poetry of Scandinavia's best-known contemporary poet, Swedish Tomas Tranströmer, can be seen to illustrate the actual heterogeneity of Scandinavian modernism, even though historically it has come to be identified largely with lyrical high modernism. In Tranströmer's poems, nature lyricism often contrasts with images of technology, and anthropomorphism with materiality, as in the 1978 prose poem "To Mats and Laila": "A swim in the sky, the air's so blue . . . . Then suddenly I see the ridges on the other side of the lake: they are clear-cut. Like the shaved parts of a patient's head before he has a brain operation" (146). For Scandinavian readers, Tranströmer's poetry exemplifies the modernist legacy—it is dense and sparse, does not focus on industrial or urban modernity, but is set in pristine landscapes that reveal the ethical implications of human relationships with nature. Abstractly egalitarian, Tranströmer's poems can also be read as representative of the image that Sweden, or Scandinavia, would like to project to the world—as a location and a cultural legacy in which there are no gender conflicts or social inequalities, in which the environment and the individual alike are incorporated democratically into poetic language, in which art, even poetry, connotes social engagement. Tranströmer's poetry, often remarked on for its concentration and condensed complexity, has increasingly been studied as representative of ecocritical perspectives, and thus marks one of the ways in which Scandinavian modernism has gained recent international relevance.

One of the very few Scandinavian lyrical modernists who has made an international impact, Tranströmer was already something of an icon before winning the Nobel Prize in Literature in 2011. His imagery is often startlingly concrete, which arguably allows for strong and evocative translations. Indeed, since the first volume in 1954, his relatively slim production has been translated into over fifty languages, introduced to the Anglo-American world by poet and translator Robert Bly, and translated into a complete English edition, *The Great Enigma* (2006), by Robin Fulton. His wide dissemination marks him as particularly important for an influential scholarly tradition that for many years has positioned Scandinavian modernism as near-synonymous with complex poetic expression, as fully developed only by the end of World War II, and as drawing on models derived from Anglo-American, French, or German high modernism. This conception has tended to define literary modernism as the domain of aesthetic formalism, lyrical poetry, and male writers.

Yet Tranströmer's poetry offers ways for broadening a conventional restrictive understanding of Scandinavian modernism into one that is also heterogeneous, transnational, and discontinuous. On one hand, his poetry, often set in rural landscapes and small towns, challenges Andreas Huyssen's formulation that the "geography of classical modernism is determined primarily by metropolitan cities and the cultural experiments and upheavals they generated" ("Geographies of Modernism" 6). On the other hand, it indicates how an apparent regionality or marginality never emerges in isolation but operates as part of multifaceted relations with other literatures and locations. In this chapter, I want to map some of Scandinavian modernism's complexity in order to challenge the still relatively common equation of modernism with narrow formalist aesthetic experimentation. With respect to both periodization and geography, Scandinavian modernism can be seen as unusually long and expansive, and my approach consequently emphasizes both discontinuity and transnationality; it also focuses on neglected issues of class and gender. Modernism in Scandinavia emerges both early and late, through starts and stops, in intermittent and localized forms, as well as in tension with ideologies of margin and center, import and export, and nation and cosmopolitanism.[1]

From an international perspective Scandinavia may seem like a cohesive region of three homogeneous, socially stable, and wealthy nations—Denmark, Norway, and Sweden—with three national languages, mutually intelligible but with distinct vocabularies—Danish, Norwegian, and Swedish. The historical background of the region indicates some immediate disparities, however, and illustrates that the moniker "Scandinavia" is more often applied from the outside than used as a label of identification by the individual countries, which tend to stress distinctiveness rather than commonalities. Relatively little scholarship about Danish, Norwegian, and Swedish literature is explicitly comparative, which reflects conceptions that literary history and canonization have evolved as largely nationalistic undertakings. This is perhaps particularly true for modernism. As in recent challenges from so-called marginal European locales to modernism's long-standing privileging of the Paris–Berlin–Vienna triangle (e.g., Bahun-Radunović and Pourgouris, eds.), modernist studies has only quite recently begun to generate comparative perspectives on relations between modernisms both within Scandinavia and in relation to Europe (Garton, ed.; Jansson et al., eds.; Tysdahl et al., eds.).

The national bent in studies of Scandinavian modernism, despite affirmations from critics of all stripes that modernism is an international phenomenon, has historical roots in intertwined and often uneasy national relationships. Norway did not become an independent nation until 1905, having been in a union with Sweden since 1814, and before that a part of Denmark since 1536. Norway's two official languages—one dominant and Danish-adhering (Bokmål) and the other less-used and drawing on local dialects (Nynorsk)—reflect this heritage. Sweden held Finland until 1809, when it became—and until 1917 remained—a Russian Grand-Duchy. Swedish remains the second national language, spoken by a significant segment of the Finnish population. Historically, a tendency for outsiders to see the region as ethnically and culturally homogenous has tended to obscure not only the significant indigenous northern Sámi population, but also the fact that Denmark was once instrumental in the transatlantic slave trade, with significant Caribbean holdings, and continues to be a colonial presence for Greenland's Inuit population. Recent immigration from southern Europe, South America, Northern Africa, and the Middle East has made contemporary Scandinavia ethnically, linguistically, and religiously diverse. An explicitly transnational context offers one important point of entry to the story of Scandinavian modernism, which focuses less on the metropolitan contexts we have come to associate with the rise of European modernism, and more on challenges to the nation and the hegemonic ideologies for which it stands, not least in Scandinavia, at the end of the nineteenth century. Literary modernism in Scandinavia was not homogenous, of course (which it never was anywhere, hence the rationale for this collection), but reflects the region's diversity.

Part I: Spatial Connections

Any comprehensive understanding of Scandinavian modernism begins with the term "The Modern Breakthrough," coined by Georg Brandes to describe what he, as a multilingual Europe-based literary critic, understood as important and original about Scandinavian literature in the 1880s: the ways it polemically engaged and reformulated Scandinavia's transition to modernity. Brandes's call for Scandinavian literature to become "modern" in his lecture series at Copenhagen University in 1871 stipulated that literature should become *modern* and relevant by engaging social issues in new and original forms (383–84). Brandes's exhortation reflects the fact that while modernity came quite late to Scandinavia, its accelerated aspects quickly brought a sense that fundamental social change needed to be matched by aesthetic changes. At the end of the nineteenth century, industrialization and urbanization had only recently begun transforming these northern poor and socially conservative, agrarian-based societies. Radical movements in literature and the arts brought profound changes, not least to Scandinavia's perception of its own marginal geographical and cultural standing. Brandes explicitly challenged a pervasive national romanticism and a centuries-old import model of literary influence in Scandinavia.

Based alternately in Berlin and Copenhagen, Brandes wrote on comparative literature, published in German papers, introduced Nietzsche to both Scandinavia and Europe, precariously negotiated his status as a secular Jew in an often anti-Semitic provincial environment, and introduced Scandinavian literature in Europe and German, French, and Slavic experimental literature in Scandinavia. Brandes had advocated for the emerging group of Scandinavian modernists in many German publications during the 1880s, and his book of essays *Det moderne gjennembruds maend* [Men of the Modern Breakthrough (1883, no Engl. trans.)] gave an emergent group of young writers in Berlin a hefty dose of motivation to take up the lance of the Modern. In a lecture to the Berlin literary circle *Durch* in 1886, Eugen Wolff launched the term *Die Moderne*, presumably as a direct response to Brandes and Scandinavian writers of the Modern Breakthrough, while articulating the self-reflexive, self-conscious, and transnational designs of the early Germanic movements of modernism that later became influential for German expressionists. Scandinavian modernism, in "its most significant manifestations," Bradbury and McFarlane argue, was "a good generation *earlier* than the Anglo-American" (37). As the decade turned, the expressionistic style and a detachment from realism advocated by August Strindberg, Knut Hamsun, Ola Hansson, and Arne Garborg became major points of reference for writers and intellectuals in Berlin, as did Edvard Munch through his Berlin exhibitions of expressionist painting in the early 1890s. McFarlane's chapter title in his co-edited encyclopedic volume *Modernism* is illustrative: "Berlin and the *Rise* of Modernism: 1886–1896" (105; emphasis added), indicating the foundational role not only Berlin, but the Scandinavians associated with the city's avant-garde, played in the movements of European transnational modernism at the end of the nineteenth century. Karl Kraus later introduced several of Strindberg's twentieth-century prose works for an Austrian audience through his radical intellectual journal *Die Fackel* (Hansson, Salvesen).

Modern Drama and Scandinavian Modernism

As Toril Moi argues in *Henrik Ibsen and the Birth of Modernism,* Scandinavian drama has only recently begun to be understood as an important alternative to European modernism's emphasis on poetry or complex narrative schemes (see also Ewbank). Ibsen's and Strindberg's critical contributions to European modernism involve specific challenges to the public/private divide of late nineteenth-century society, and of aesthetic descriptors, in which modernism correlates with private and realism with public. Their plays make the private public, stage social conflict from individual perspectives, and travel in highly public (sometimes scandalous) forms through avant-garde and mainstream productions around Europe from the 1890s onward. Ibsen's play *Ghosts* (1881), about incest, hereditary syphilis, euthanasia, and economic blackmail, exemplifies a defining aspect of the Modern Breakthrough movement, namely a raging public debate over sexual morality, prostitution, marital double standards, and women's political and economic emancipation. Such questions are integral to how modernism develops in Scandinavia, and the way it is immediately gendered, not least in Ibsen's *A Doll's House* (1879) and *Hedda Gabler* (1889).

Part of the continuing significance of Scandinavian modernism lies in its explicit attention to sexualized power dynamics and how those become integrated into dramatic form, in which gendered constructions of masculinity and femininity are consistently called into question. Ibsen's prose drama inaugurates a highly influential modernist dramatic form that accounts for psychological complexity and irrationality as well as cultural context, not least in ways that combine detailed stage directions with dialogue full of contradictions, parallelisms, and unresolved paradoxes. Ibsen is also Scandinavia's first transnational modernist—he wrote plays ostensibly set in provincial Norway while living in Rome and Munich, and spearheaded Scandinavian dramatic exports. *Ghosts*, for example, was hardly performed in Scandinavia in the 1880s, but its wider breakthrough came when radical theaters in Berlin (Freie Bühne), Paris (Théâtre Libre), and London (The Independent) performed it during the period 1889–1891. This is when the foundation was laid for Ibsen's importance to Anglo-American modernism, as his plays were quickly translated into English and regularly produced on London stages during the 1890s. Ibsen's analytical method, framed in a complex metaphorical and structural world, while clad in an apparently simplistic prose of the everyday (arguably easier to translate into idiomatic English than verse), became particularly influential for Henry James, George Bernard Shaw, and later James Joyce.

Strindberg, like Ibsen, engages with debates of sexual morality to charge his experimental plays of the 1880s. Drawing on Zola's manifesto on modern theater, Strindberg's contributions to modern drama, from *Miss Julie* (1887) and *Creditors* (1888) to *A Dream Play* (1902) and *Ghost Sonata* (1907), can be said to evolve along two lines of modernism. The first is his radical reworking of dramatic character, what he calls in the well-known preface to *Miss Julie* "characterless characters," that is, the relinquishing of types in favor of an emulation of human psychology that stresses irrationality, subjectivity, and incomprehensibility, as in *Ghost Sonata's* transformations of characters into living dead, mummies, and parrots. The second aspect is Strindberg's use of stage space and props, from *Miss Julie's* asymmetrical stage and real-time smelly sausage frying on stage, to *A Dream Play's* attempts at seamless scene transitions from a castle to a kitchen, a lawyer's office, and cholera quarantine. In the preface to *A Dream Play,* Strindberg describes his drama as one in which "Time and place do not exist" and "characters split, double, multiply, evaporate, condense, float apart, coalesce" (646). If many of Ibsen's prose plays are set in definable domestic locations, Strindberg's often move through locations that are explicitly transitional, like continental boarding houses and cosmopolitan cafes, or include uncanny displacements in which a seemingly stable country house manor comes to appear as an insane asylum, or an apartment turns into a crematory furnace. Strindberg's chamber plays *Ghost Sonata* and *The Pelican* (1907), moreover, are clearly reminiscent of Maurice Maeterlinck's dramatic condensation.

Strindberg's legacy as a European modernist was established later than Ibsen's, and in continental Europe rather than in Britain. Max Reinhardt's experimental production in 1905 of *Dance of Death* (1901) prompted Strindberg to establish his own Intimate Theater in Stockholm, modeled on Reinhardt's *Kammerspielhaus* in Berlin, but also set a pattern for influence on German playwrights (see Klam, Szewczyk). During the 1910s and 1920s, Reinhardt's productions of Strindberg's station plays, like *To Damascus* (1898), become critical sources of inspiration for German expressionist station drama, such as Georg Kaiser's *From Morning to Midnight* (1912) and Robert Wiene's classic silent film *The Cabinet of Dr. Caligari* (1920). Bertolt Brecht's avocation of experimental drama as pedagogical and socially significant drew on both Strindberg and Ibsen; Brecht's drama was also to become highly influential for Scandinavian theatrical practices, not least during the socially engaged 1960s. Strindberg's importance for French experimental theater is apparent in the productions of André Antoine and French Surrealist Antonin Artaud. Ibsen and Strindberg are indisputably part of twentieth-century developments in theatrical modernism (Szondi). Their influence is evident in the plays of Eugene O'Neill, Harold Pinter, and, more recently, Sarah Kane, whose play *4.48 Psychosis* (2001) shares many family resemblances with Strindberg's.

Prolific Swedish writer Pär Lagerkvist's essay "Modern Theatre: Points of View and Attack" (1918) and the one-act plays *The Difficult Hour I–III* (1918) further develop Strindberg's dramatic expressionism. Lagerkvist focuses on concentrated moments, abrupt and ironic, and emphasizes textual externals of costume, lighting, set design, and gesture that take precedence over plot and character; indeed, these plays contain little realistic dialogue and few crafted characters. Lagerkvist had traveled to Paris in 1913 where he encountered cubism and introduced in Sweden the first debate, however short-lived, on emerging theories of avant-garde poetics and modernist practice, including those of Guillaume Apollinaire and the Italian futurists. Lagerkvist's early expressionist poetry incorporated imagery recalling the vicissitudes of World War I. Swedish playwright Lars Norén's plays of the 1990s emphasize other aspects of Strindberg's legacy for modernist theater, namely, individual tormented psychologies. Unraveling relationships serve both as cathartic catalysts and social reflectors for a theater audience, as evident in *Blood* (1994) and the untranslated masterpiece plays in the *Morire di Classe* series (see van Reis).

Strindberg is best known as a playwright, but he also painted, took photographs, and wrote copious amounts of prose: more than two dozen novels, several collections of short stories, numerous ethnographic and autobiographical works, as well as essays on international relations, the peasantry in France, occult science, art criticism, and many more fields. Living large portions of his life outside Sweden, Strindberg's transnational writing involves a continued engagement with Paris and French intellectual life (Casanova 137–40, Stenport). Two sophisticated modernist narratives written directly in French push the genre conventions to which they seem to adhere: the ostensibly autobiographical novels *A Madman's Defense* (1888/1895) and *Inferno* (1898). Both narratives feature highly unreliable first-person narrators who proclaim they are going insane. The novella *The Roofing Ceremony* (1906), reminiscent of Joseph Conrad's *Heart of Darkness* (1902), suggests an early stream of consciousness technique and builds on the explicit technological medialization of a mechanical recording device, as explored later in particular by Samuel Beckett in *Krapp's Last Tape* (1958). Strindberg's paintings and photography have recently become reevaluated as expressionist and proto-surrealist (Granath).

Transnational Prose Modernism on the Margins

Scandinavia's most distinctive and internationally best-known early prose modernist is generally assumed to be the Norwegian Knut Hamsun. In his essay "From the Unconscious Life of the Mind" (1890), Hamsun argues against Ibsen's synthetic and analytical psychology, proposing instead that modern literature captures the split, indecisive, and unpredictable mind. Hamsun's narrative technique and his understanding of modern subjectivity forcefully coalesce in the novel *Hunger* (1890). Although set in the still-diminutive Christiania (today Oslo), *Hunger* is Scandinavia's first modernist city novel, relinquishing most realistic spatial description, as well as a cohesive plot, to relay instead the shifting mental states and hallucinations of its first-person narrator, a starving writer who walks around the city. Its technique is marked by immediacy, syntactical fragmentation, and a self-reflexive awareness of writing against dominant paradigms of bourgeois comfort and double standards, as well as realistic novelistic narration. *Hunger* remains an international classic, as can be seen by its frequent reissuing and new translations. As a novel about engaging with a modernizing city that allows for a new manner of writing, it has strong ties to later European modernist experiments, from Joyce and Woolf to French surrealists and German modernists. Similarly, Swedish novelist Hjalmar Söderberg has come to be closely associated with the rapid transformation of Scandinavian urban culture, and is often described as a flâneur novelist. A pessimistic detachment combines with haunting descriptions of Stockholm in *Doctor Glas* (1905) and *The Serious Game* (1912), whose characters' existential ruminations on the futility of bourgeois life resonate with those of continental decadent writers. Like so many of his generation, Söderberg negotiated an uneasy relationship with his nation and lived for large parts of his life outside Sweden, primarily in Copenhagen.

Like Hamsun and Söderberg, the majority of Scandinavia's emerging modernists self-identified as distinctly cosmopolitan writers. Radical rethinking of the "nation" was an important part of their relationship to modernity and informed their attempts to write Scandinavia out of perceived marginality. Traveling and residing abroad was a near given. So it was for a group of writers who have been largely excluded from the canon of modernist writing in Scandinavia, namely an emerging group of experimental women writers. Their writing illustrates the fraught dilemmas of transnational existence, including a self-reflexive understanding that leaving home is a necessity for modernist narration along with a consequent alienation repeatedly inscribed in narrative forms that challenge received paradigms of national belonging and gender. Choosing prose rather than drama or poetry for their reconceptualization of modernity, several of these novelists, I argue, must be understood as forerunners of European prose modernism, particularly in their persistent thematization of disjunctures between art and life, impression and expression, and words and action (see also Witt-Brattström, ed.).

Prolific Norwegian novelist Amalie Skram traveled around the world with her first husband, a sea captain, but her narratives come increasingly to focus on stasis. Two autobiographical novels from 1894, collected under the title *Under Observation*, pose an explicit engagement with modernity's gendered power structures by focusing on a woman artist's experience of being trapped in an insane asylum. Patriarchy and psychiatry coalesce in a battle of words. The intriguing novel is an attempt at expression and vindication, but it constructs a narrative in which meaning is aborted and words are recoded, so that even the very function of representation is challenged. Sigrid Undset (later known for her historical epic about medieval Norway, *Kristin Lavransdatter* [1920–1922]) writes in one of her first novels a story detailing the necessity of exile for aesthetic expression, a plot device (and personal experience) shared by innumerable Scandinavian women artists and writers around the turn of the century. In *Jenny* (1911), Undset rewrites Ibsen's formative experience in Rome to focus on a twenty-eight-year-old unmarried artist who gains independence and a first erotic relationship, only to find that as she returns to Oslo, all falls apart: social stability as well as creative expression. Undset draws on a double perspective here that combines psychological complexity with sociological restraints in an ostensibly realistic framework while also incorporating a clear transnational spatial logic that is at work in Scandinavian modernism at this time. *Jenny* negates the formulation of a coherent psychological interior and refuses to unequivocally promote social moral or narrative truth, yet nevertheless manages to suggest that a life of liberty on the continent is not possible for an aspiring woman artist. Cora Sandel in her *Alberta* trilogy (1926, 1931, 1939) occupies a distinctive position in Norwegian novelistic representation in her rejection of literary expression as a means of national unity, a prominent aspect of Norwegian literature during the first decades of independence after 1905. Sandel lived in Paris for fifteen years and her novels engage explicitly with modernity's understanding of displacement (see also Rees). In the second installment, *Alberta and Freedom*, the protagonist has escaped the constrictions of her northern hometown to work as a model in Paris, where she begins writing a novel on scraps of paper.

In the context of Parisian modernity in the 1920s, Sandel writes an alternate trajectory to the fragmentation of Paris and arguably serves as a correlate to emerging surrealism of André Breton and his construction of a displaced woman's experience in *Nadja* (1928). The *Alberta* novels also experiment with constructions of memory and a technique marked by iteration and repetition that resembles Marcel Proust's *In Search of Lost Time* (1913–1927).

Despite Scandinavia's explicit interest in transnational modernity, the perception of Denmark from abroad typically tells a very different story. Often antiquating and idealizing, international writers offer up a nostalgic fantasy of Denmark-Norway that differs radically from the image of engagement with social modernity that Brandes sought to promote. Rainer Maria Rilke's conception of Denmark in *The Notebooks of Malte Laurids Brigge* (1910) is a case in point. Rilke corresponded with and admired Brandes and was influenced by the early modernist poetry of Norwegian Sigbjørn Obstfelder's *A Priest's Diary* (1900) and the symbolist prose of J. P. Jacobsen's *Niels Lyhne* (1880; see also Cokal); he also got to know Sweden and Denmark as he was writing *The Notebooks*. Here, a Czech author, whose first language is German, posits a Danish history for his first-person narrator in order to throw into relief the narrator's alienation in Paris. The incomprehensibility of Paris, as well as the fear, loneliness, illness, frustration, and poverty it produces, depends for its effect in *The Notebooks* on an over-inscription of an imagined national history that is *also* personal. Denmark becomes frozen in (anachronistic) time as the harbinger of nostalgic and nationalistic longing. Thomas Mann's *Tonio Kröger* (1903) suggests a similar perception of Denmark as an ancestral home frozen in time, somehow located outside the tension established between Germany and Italy, and between demands of the bourgeoisie and aesthetic creativity. Harlem Renaissance novelist Nella Larsen includes in *Quicksand* (1928) an extensive depiction of Copenhagen, which implicitly evokes Denmark's silence about its colonial heritage and its holdings in the Danish West Indies (sold to the United States as the Virgin Islands in 1917). Larsen uses free indirect discourse to frame her protagonist Helga Crane's silence as part of a transnational modernist tradition of nostalgic depictions of Denmark, in which experiences of racism in Denmark are both unaddressed and aestheticized (Lunde and Stenport). Karen Blixen's stories continue the trajectory of effacing Scandinavian transnationality from a transnational perspective, most notably in the collection *Seven Gothic Tales* (1934), which obliquely engages with gendered modernism, and in the short story "Babette's Feast" (1950), which exoticizes coastal nineteenth-century Norway for an American audience (see also Bredsdorff).

The transnational characteristics of Scandinavian early modernism, and particularly the legacy of the Modern Breakthrough, indicate not only how Scandinavian writers understand the region's responses to modernity, their self-reflexive conception of their contributions as *moderns*, but also how modernist writing conceived on the seeming margins of Europe are integral to the continuing evolution of modernism in Europe and beyond.

PART II: DISCONTINUITIES

The term literary modernism was being used in Swedish long before it became current in English to describe the remarkable but short-lived rise of a regional literary avant-garde based in Swedish-speaking Finland during and just after the First World War (Mitchell). At first largely isolated from other burgeoning Scandinavian modernist developments, the movement gained some of its urgency from Finland's secession from Russia in 1917, as well as from the social upheavals brought on by the Russian revolutions of that year. Poet Edith Södergran stands as the forerunner of this movement, formulating in 1918 one of the first poetic modernist manifestoes by a European woman writer (Lindqvist) and expressing a Nietzschean individuality in both content and form (*Love and Solitude: Selected Poems 1916–1923*). Södergran's poetry renounces rhyme schemes and meter as unduly restricting the poet's possibilities of expression. It also juxtaposes exterior and interior, and constructs parallel worlds that intersect in intriguing spatial descriptions that demolish standards of nature lyricism but maintain significant details of rural landscapes. An early poem like "Vierge Moderne" is a feminist experiment; later poems turn to mysticism and religious invocation (Holm). Södergran was born and raised in St. Petersburg, and she wrote her first poems in German. Her short adult life in Finnish Karelia was marked by poverty as Finland fought for its independence; she died from tuberculosis at the age of thirty. The poet shared a regional and, from the perspective of continental Europe, distinctly provincial background with compatriot Swedish-speaking poets Elmer Diktonius, Gunnar Björling (*You Go the Words*, 1955), Hagar Olsson, and Henry Parland (*Ideals Clearance*, 1929), all of whom also lived in Finland. Björling "is one of the greatest innovators of modern poetry" comparable only to Mallarmé, "the Russian Chlebnikov and the American Gertrude Stein," proclaims distinguished Danish modernist critic Poul Borum, praising Björling's "universalist dada-individualism" (cited in Kleberg 77). A prodigy, Parland had by the time of his death at age twenty-two lived in Russia, Finland, and Lithuania, and published poetry and essays influenced by Dada, Russian Futurism, and the cinematic experimentation of Sergei Eisenstein and Charlie Chaplin. The seeming marginality of this group is deceptive, since they were all multilingual and conceived of their contribution to European modernism as deliberately avant-garde, evident not least through the journal *Quesego* (1928–1929) and in the later influence the group's poetry wielded in Sweden, the Baltic, and German-speaking Europe (Kleberg, Stam). The collection *Ice Around Our Lips: Finland-Swedish Poetry* includes translations of many of the most important poems of the Fenno-Swedish modernists (David McDuff, ed. and trans.).

The extraordinary accomplishments of the Fenno-Swedish modernists during roughly a fifteen-year period illustrate the discontinuous and sometimes extremely localized aspects of Scandinavian modernism. That includes the perception in subsequent criticism that Scandinavia's neutrality during World War I shielded writers from engaging with the violence, disruption, and displacements that became critical for many European modernists after the war (Eliot, Woolf, Breton, Kafka, and so on). One of the earliest representatives of a Danish modernist poetic, and among the earliest members of what would become a Danish avant-garde, was journalist and art critic Rudolf Broby-Johansen. By 1922 his fascination with the big city marked him as unusual in Danish literature of this time. Gunnar Ekelöf, whose works were often explicitly influenced by the Fenno-Swedish modernists, is arguably the most important of an emergent group of Swedish modernist poets during the 1930s. Ekelöf's reach and influence was phenomenal within Scandinavia and his poetry has also been introduced to an international readership through translations into English by W. H. Auden and Robert Bly, as well as into German and French. Ekelöf's first poetry collection, *Late Arrival on Earth* (1932), includes striking stylistic measures, such as his abolishing of capitalization and designation of unrhymed free verse as a new form of "denatured prose." Ekelöf, like his contemporary Emil Boyson in Norway, was explicitly influenced by modern French poetry—Rimbaud and Mallarmé, in particular, and French surrealism. Living in Paris at the end of the 1920s (like Cora Sandel), Ekelöf also translated Eliot and Joyce into Swedish. His surrealist combination of aestheticizing subconscious influences within formal fragmentation became distinctly formative. Like Strindberg's before him, Ekelöf's style and topics are highly idiosyncratic and transitional (Shideler), as evidenced in his well-known *A Mölna Elegy* (published in 1960 after three decades of development). Although reminiscent in part of Proust's investigation of the creative potential of memory in *Remembrance of Things Past*, one of the voices in the elegy belongs explicitly to Stephen Dedalus from *A Portrait of the Artist as a Young Man*.

Norwegian poet Rolf Jacobsen offers an interesting first foray into a distinctly modernist lyrical form in Norwegian (Aarseth). His poetry combines free verse with striking imagery about cars, asphalt, cranes, and electricity, and in his poetry from the 1930s such radicalism carries over into futuristic interest in machines and technology; later depictions of western civilization turns distinctly dystopian in the wake of World War II. As a "newspaper editor by profession, Jacobsen fills his poems with everything the news excludes: a geological sense of history; a naïve intimacy with forest, ocean, and landscape; a wry and divided taste for the city; a fierce detestation for ecological damage; and a tactful, utterly nondogmatic sense of the holiness of life, particularly as it manifests itself in unprotected beings like trees and old people" (Mishler 274–75). Jacobsen's poetry provides complementary perspectives to both Ekelöf's and Tranströmer's; his work is included with theirs in the collected volume *Twenty Poems* (1977), translated and introduced by Robert Bly.

Lyrical High Modernism

If the Great War arguably had little direct effect on literature written in Sweden, Denmark, and Norway, World War II certainly did, and catalyzed increasing abstraction and social withdrawal. Sweden remained neutral, whereas both Denmark and Norway were occupied. The resistance movement in Norway in particular became an important ideological trope in Norwegian postwar literature, which sometimes exaggerated the valiant resistance efforts in order to sharply offset certain writers' later turns (e.g., Knut Hamsun's) toward Nazi sympathy and national nostalgia. Yet Hamsun's last work, *On Overgrown Paths* (1948) arguably returns to an earlier modernist idiom of irony, self-reflexivity, and double meaning. The 1940s generation—Erik Lindegren, Karl Vennberg, and Stig Dagerman, among others—has in Swedish literary criticism become synonymous with modernism. Their local manifestation of formal disintegration, anxiety, and dystopia drew heavily on European modernist poetry and prose. Its most prominent members translated and introduced Whitman, Eliot, Joyce, Proust, Gide, the French surrealists, and Faulkner and thereby effectively internationalized Swedish literature. Their fiction, poetry, and literary criticism have since, however, come to stand for a rather narrow view of modernism, as one primarily (if not exclusively) of formalist density and complexity, in which convoluted and self-reflexive imagery rules over content. Innovative and unusual in some respects, but derivative and dated in others, the hegemonic status of this male group of writers of the 1940s has begun to be reconsidered by some Scandinavian scholars, who argue that this particular Swedish formalism disregards the desire for social change that was foundational for the avant-garde movements of European modernism (Luthersson). This particular form of modernist literature has been extremely important *within* Scandinavian national literary traditions, for relationships between writers and poets around Scandinavia, and for cementing a long-held "import and influence" view of Scandinavian modernism. This model has nearly completely marginalized women writers (Rees), with the exception of the 1940's poet Ruth Hillarp, and Karin Boye, best known for her dystopian novel about an authoritarian regime in *Kallocain* (1940) and for her engagement with psychoanalytic theories in essays such as "Language beyond logic" (1932, no Engl. trans.)

A new generation of Norwegian and Danish poets emerged in the 1950s, some of whom returned from exile in Sweden and brought back influences from poets and critics of the 1940s generation. Sigurd Hoel was instrumental in the publication of the influential "yellow series" after the German occupation of Norway had ended, which featured translations of Hemingway, Faulkner, and Kafka, while Paul Brekke's 1949 translation of Eliot's *The Waste Land* (1922) into Norwegian was seminal. Brekke's poetry draws on thematic montage and syntactic disassociation, as well as a dense, sparse, complex, and poetic language; among Norwegian poets, Brekke best exemplifies a high-modernist stance aligned with European modernists. After the war and the German occupation of Denmark, the Copenhagen journal *Heretica* (1948–1953) came to represent modernism's breakthrough in Danish, advocating a withdrawal from realist depiction and political engagement in favor of metaphysical or theological questions that nevertheless put modernity's alienation into stark relief. Like their high-modernist colleagues in Sweden and Norway, the group translated the European modernists. Ole Sarvig, some of whose poetry was translated in *Late Day* (1962), represents an expansive form of Danish modernism—his work includes a number of different genres: haiku, sonnets, free verse, book-length prose, radio drama, and even experimental adaptations of the detective genre. Internationally recognized poet Inger Christensen, known especially for *It* (1969), *Alphabet* (1981), and *Butterfly Valley* (1991), remains a primary representative of lyrical high modernism in the Scandinavian tradition; Christensen is unusual in the Danish tradition simply by being a woman poet whose poetry is regarded as qualitative, serious, and in line with the modernist tradition. Recent representatives of Swedish modernist poetry by women include Katarina Frostenson, Elisabeth Rynell (both represented in the collection *To Catch Life Anew: Ten Swedish Women Poets*, ed. and trans. Claeson), Ann Jäderlund, and Birgitta LillPers.

As Scandinavian poetry of the 1940s and 1950s became construed as emblematic of formalist withdrawal from the world, Nelly Sachs's exile from Germany to Stockholm in 1940 (where she remained until her death in 1970) marks a different trajectory for understanding the transfer of modernist writing in Europe. Sachs, who received the Nobel Prize in 1966, wrote exclusively in German (*Collected Poems I–II*) but translated numerous Swedish modernist writers (Erik Lindegren, Gunnar Ekelöf, Tomas Tranströmer, and others) into German, which influenced her own poetic language of expression and effectively paved the way for the introduction of Swedish modernist poets into the German canon of lyrical modernism (Ekelöf also translated her poetry to Swedish). Sachs' contacts with influential Swedish critics, moreover, helped introduce other European poets in exile, such as Paul Celan, to a wider public in Sweden. German playwright Peter Weiss lived in exile in Stockholm from 1939 until his death in 1982. Writing alternately in German and English, Weiss produced prose works, such as *Leavetaking* and *Vanishing Point* (1960, 1961), that engage explicitly with questions of geographical and linguistic displacements in the wake of World War II.

Aesthetics of the Welfare State and Cultural Radicalism

The lyrical high-modernism that has since become so influential for definitions of Scandinavian modernism had important counterparts in movements of cultural radicalism, particularly in Denmark and in the experimental worker's literature in Sweden. Both movements sought to integrate formal experimentation with social reformation, and both first emerged during the 1920s and grew more prominent in subsequent decades. Tied closely to the development of social democratic welfare states, cultural radicalism correlates with ideologies constitutive of Scandinavian modernist architecture, often called Functionalism. Danish architect Poul Henningsen argued in a series of articles in 1926 in the cultural-radical journal *Kritisk Revy* that design had to be utilitarian and functional. In contrast to continental theories, Henningsen emphasized ergonomics and argued that objects and buildings should correlate with human needs, rather than humans adapting to machines. In Sweden, the connection is made manifest by the Social Democratic Party's aim during the 1930s of establishing a People's Home (*Folkhemmet*), a system that would provide all residents with health-insurance, free education, retirement pensions, unemployment protection, and other social benefits. These theories of architecture and social engineering were in Scandinavia closely tied to a specific brand of modernist aesthetic experimentation.

That social reformation would go hand in hand with formal experimentation reworks Georg Brandes' understanding of modern literature as one that must put social problems under debate in order to maintain its relevance. Danish cultural radicals, generally Marxist intellectuals, perceived Brandes as representing liberalism and the bourgeoisie, not political revolution. Brandes' continued legacy, particularly in Denmark, illustrates the intriguing discontinuity that has shaped modernism in Scandinavia generally. As a result, the cultural radical movement has been called "the second phase of the modern Breakthrough" (Nolin 7). Writers associated with the journal *Vindrosen* [The Face of a Compass] and the so-called Confrontational school would draw on the cultural radicals of the 1920s (and implicitly thereby also on their reactions to Brandes) to motivate a socially conscious modernism that attacked the metaphysical and esoteric interests of the *Heretica* circle. Prolific poet and novelist Klaus Rifbjerg, one of Denmark's most important public intellectuals, for example, combines in his writings humorous and personal perspectives, parody and vulgarity, incomplete thoughts and intellectual challenges to market forces (Gray). Rifbjerg was an editor of *Vindrosen*, who, along with the internationally recognized novelist and philosopher Villy Sørensen, was known for reviving and integrating Kafkaesque absurdism into his modern Danish prose. As a short-story writer, Sørensen shares with Kafka an interest in brevity and modernist allegory, as well as with Thomas Mann views on the fragmented psychology of modern individuality. Writing a generation later and with an explicit philosophical interest, Sørensen's *Harmless Tales* (1955) and *Tutelary Tales* (1964) rethink hopelessness in an impersonal, bureaucratic world in favor of the potential of individual radicalism and autonomy. In Norway, 1960s political radicalism received its mouthpiece through the so-called *Profil* rebellion at Oslo University in 1966, when several young and talented Norwegian writers sought to radicalize Norwegian literature toward a much more explicitly modernist framework that strove for political change through Marxist Leninism, the use of documentary and montage techniques, and a new version of the everyday that eschewed psychological realism or nature-reverie.

Novelist Aksel Sandemose (born in Denmark but writing his most important works in Norwegian) has significant overlaps with both proletarian literature in Sweden and the cultural radicals of Denmark, combining as he does social pathos with psychological complexity in novels such as *A fugitive crosses his tracks* (1933). Although categorizing workers' literature as modernist may stretch the conventional definition of modernism in Scandinavian scholarship, the expansion is warranted by the self-reflexive ways in which these writers reformulate in often hybrid form and in remarkably stark language Scandinavia's rapid transition into social modernity.

Proletarian Modernism

In Sweden, leaders of the social-democratic party during the 1920s encouraged its members to write their own stories and let new forms of literature contribute actively to social change. As policies of the welfare state and an astonishing industrial transformation of Sweden in the mid-twentieth century changed social conditions, including access to further education, a generation of proletarian writers emerged who would help lay the foundation for one of the most prominent and unique strands of Swedish modernism. Particularly notable in this group, Harry Martinson was born in poverty in southern Sweden and subsequently traveled the world as a seaman and day laborer, as reflected in his early poems and the novel *Cape Farewell* (1933). Martinson's innovative poetry was first published in communist papers and labor movement journals, whose proletarian and documentary narratives contrasted sharply with Martinson's neologisms and ruptured syntax. Martinson's epic science fiction poem *Aniara* (1956) and essays on the natural environment in *Views from a Tuft of Grass* (1963) represent other sides of his varied writing, and also indicate how flexible, at least for male writers, the modernist designation seems to have been, incorporating the proletarian and esoteric, utopian and ecocritical. Martinson eventually came to share the Nobel Prize in literature in 1974 with another autodidact, Eyvind Johnson, one of Swedish literature's foremost innovators in prose modernism. Drawing explicitly on Gide, Proust, Joyce, Faulkner, and Sartre, Johnson, who spent time in Berlin and Paris in the early 1920s, is credited with introducing the stream-of-consciousness technique to Swedish literature. The discontinuities so prominent in the construction of Scandinavian modernism are evident also in Johnson's oeuvre. In his fascinating 1928 novel *Stad i Ljus* [City in Light, no trans.], two moments combine: one about the character's walking through Paris, suffering increasing hunger pangs, and thus obliquely referencing Hamsun's *Hunger* and Strindberg's *Inferno*; another incorporating flashback scenes and extensive prose-poem-like descriptions of his personal history. Johnson's later novels turn to historical topics in experimental forms: *Return to Ithaca: The Odyssey retold as a modern novel* (1946) revises Joyce's *Ulysses*, and *Dreams of Roses and Fire* (1949) reimagines seventeenth-century European witch-hunting trials and executions. Midcentury Scandinavian modernism is heavily skewed in terms of gender, but Moa Martinson ranks today as one of the better-known modernist-proletarian writers. Her novels about rural poverty and women's life conditions have gained increasing international attention over the last decades, not least as they represent alternate understandings of modernist literature than that of the canonized group of lyrical high modernists, in Scandinavia and elsewhere. Martinson's *Women and Appletrees* (1933) focuses on two women's friendship and intimacy under harsh circumstances, while experimenting with temporality and offering a countermovement to the Hegelian dialectics that underlie much proletarian literary modernism. In *My Mother Gets Married* (1936), written from the perspective of a young girl, Moa Martinson continues to experiment with narrative perspective. Martinson's novels can also be read for their oblique but intriguing parallels to contemporary

African-American women's proletarian fiction, such as Zora Neale Hurston's *Their Eyes Were Watching God* (1937).

Radical and socially engaged children's literature has been an important aspect of Scandinavian twentieth-century literature, owing not least to the emphasis on free and high-quality education that by the 1930s had become a tenet of Social-Democratic ideology and a foundation for the welfare state; Scandinavia, particularly Sweden, has since the mid-1800s scored consistently high in national literacy rankings. Since the Second World War Scandinavian children's literature has followed major modernist trends, from formal experimentation with nonsense rhymes and complex imagery to irreverent illustrations and socially engaged content. This includes the partly surrealist picture books by Lennart Hellsing and Poul Ströyer, Astrid Lindgren's *Pippi Longstocking* series (1945–1948, 1969–1975), which combines civil disobedience with social pathos, and, more recently, Jostein Gaarder's *Sophie's World: A Novel About the History of Philosophy* (1991), which, aimed at middle-schoolers, has been translated to dozens of languages and sold tens of millions of copies.

Conclusion: Scandinavian Modernist Novels

Literary criticism, in Scandinavia as in other parts of the West, has typically defined modernism as that which is dense, complex, and far removed from the everyday realities of those who have been excluded from the canon—women and the working-class, for example. This essay has traced prominent contributions to Scandinavian modernism along two lines: transnational connections in early modernist literature and discontinuous development during the twentieth century. I have taken the opportunity to stretch customary definitions in order to include women writers such as Undset, Sandel, Skram, and Moa Martinson, as well as writers from the proletarian and cultural radical tradition. Especially in an international perspective, it is exactly these lesser known writers and traditions that can contribute to a global understanding of how modernism develops differently—in starts and stops, while crossing national, regional, and linguistic boundaries—in different parts of the world.

I began this essay by referring to Tomas Tranströmer as a modernist poet whose slim but sophisticated output has reached across national boundaries and narrowly defined readers' groups. I wish to end it by referring to Norwegian novelist Tarjei Vesaas. This move emphasizes that a narrow focus on complex lyrical high modernism obscures how contributions of Scandinavian prose modernists help broaden our understanding of the transnational, discontinuous, and heterogeneous canon that is Scandinavian modernism. Vesaas' novels *The Birds* (1956) and *The Ice Palace* (1963) are among the most interesting examples of Scandinavian modernist prose. Vesaas' terse and sparse prose (in Nynorsk) draws on nature symbolism in combination with keen psychological insight. *The Ice Palace*, for example, centers on the intertwined lives of two eleven-year-old girls; one disappears into a huge mass of ice and the other, as if psychologically trapped, mirrors her friend's disappearance in a near-catatonic state of withdrawal. Landscape representation conjoins with allusions to fairy tales, suspense with emotional complexity, and implicit references to Norwegian Nazi collaboration with childhood innocence. One of the most original of Scandinavian novelists, Vesaas has been comparatively well translated into English, and his works, despite their apparently marginal setting and origin in a minority language, in many ways resonate for a broad readership. They also speak to post-modern novelists, such as Paul Auster, Italo Calvino, Thomas Pynchon, and Jorge Luis Borges, for whom implicit crimes and modernist mystery are critical. Vesaas' legacy and impact thus illustrates both discontinuous and localized aspects of Scandinavian modernism, as well as their contributors' reach and international stature.[2]

NOTES

1. The challenges involved in presenting three national literatures, three primary languages, three primary genres (drama, poetry, prose), and a century of writing and cultural history are obvious. This essay is therefore designed to encourage comparative perspectives with other literatures and languages as well as to serve as a guide to reading and teaching Scandinavian modernism in an international context. Most references are culled from literary works that are relatively widely available in English translation (not always in print, though), which clearly limits the selection but offers a pragmatic attempt at delimiting a large corpus. For similar reasons, most secondary sources are available in English.

2. Thanks to Ulf Olsson, Rochelle Wright, Jenny Björklund, and Mats Jansson for helpful comments and to Benjamin Davis for assistance with initial research and bibliographical information.

WORKS CITED

Aarseth, Asbjorn. "The Modes of Norwegian Modernism." *Facets of European Modernism. Essays in Honor of James McFarlane.* Ed. Janet Garton. Norwich: University of East Anglia, 1985. 323–48.

Bahun-Radunovic, and Sanja and Marinos Pourgouris, eds. *The Avant-Garde and the Margin. New Territories of Modernism.* Cambridge: Cambridge Scholars Press, 2006

Beckett, Samuel. *Krapp's Last Tape.* 1958. *Krapp's Last Tape and Other Dramatic Pieces.* New York: Grove, 1994. 7–28.

Björling, Gunnar. *You Go the Words.* 1955. Trans. Fredrik Hertzberg. Notre Dame: Action Books, 2007.

Blixen, Karen. "Babette's Feast." 1950. *Anecdotes of Destiny and Ehrengard.* Vintage: New York: 1993.

———. *Seven Gothic Tales.* 1934. New York: Vintage, 1991.

Boye, Karin. *Kallocain*. 1940. Trans. Gustaf Lannestock. Madison: University of Wisconsin Press, 2002.

———. "Språket bortom orden." [Language beyond Logic]. *Spektrum* 6, 1932.

Bradbury, Malcolm. "The Cities of Modernism." *Modernism: A Guide to European Literature 1890–1930*. Ed. Malcolm Bradbury and James McFarlane. Harmondsworth: Penguin, 1976. 96–104.

Bradbury, Malcolm, and James McFarlane. "The Name and Nature of Modernism." *Modernism: A Guide to European Literature 1890–1930*. Ed. Malcolm Bradbury and James McFarlane. Harmondsworth: Penguin, 1976. 19–55.

Brandes, Georg. *Det moderne gjennembruds maend*. Copenhagen: Gyldendals, 1883.

———. "Inaugural Lecture, 1871." Trans. Evert Sprinchorn. *The Theory of the Modern Stage*. Ed. Eric Bentley. New York: Applause, 1997. 383–402.

Bredsdorff, Elias. "Isak Dinesen v. Karen Blixen: Seven Gothic Tales and Syv Fantastiske fortaellinger." *Facets of European Modernism. Essays in Honor of James McFarlane*. Ed. Janet Garton. Norwich: University of East Anglia, 1985. 275–94.

Breton, André. *Nadja*. 1928. Trans. Richard Howard. New York: Grove Press, 1994.

Casanova, Pascale. *The World Republic of Letters*. Trans. M. B. DeBevoise. Cambridge: Harvard University Press, 2005.

Christensen, Inger. *Alphabet*. 1981. Trans. Susanna Nied. New York: New Directions, 2001.

———. *Butterfly Valley: A Requiem*. 1991. Trans. Susanna Nied. New York: New Directions, 2004.

———. *It*. 1969. Trans. Susanna Nied and Anne Carson. New York: New Directions, 2006.

Claeson, Eva, ed. and trans. *To Catch Life Anew. 10 Swedish Women Poets*. Brookline: Oyster River Press, 2006.

Cokal, Susann. "Infectious Excitement: Disease, Desire, and Communicability in *Niels Lyhne* and *Ved Vejen*." *Scandinavian Studies* 71.2 (1999): 167–90

Conrad, Joseph. *Heart of Darkness*. 1899/1902. London: Penguin, 2004.

Ekelöf, Gunnar. *Late Arrival on Earth*. 1932. Ed. and trans. Robert Bly and Christina Bratt Paulston. London: Rapp & Carroll, 1967.

———. *A Mölna Elegy*. 1960. Trans. Muriel Rukeyser and Leif Sjöberg. Greensboro: Unicorn Press, 1984.

Ewbank, Inga-Stina. "'Strangely Inscrutable Art': Ivesen, James, and Early Modernism." *English and Nordic Modernisms*. Ed. Tysdahl, Bjørn, Mats Jansson, Jakob Lothe, and Steen Klitgård Povlsen. Norwich: Norvik, 2002. 25–40.

Gaarder, Jostein. *Sophie's World: A Novel About the History of Philosophy*. 1991. Trans. Paulette Moller. New York: Farrar, Straus and Giroux, 2007.

Garton, Judith, ed. *Facets of European Modernism. Essays in Honour of James McFarlane*. Norwich: Norvik, 1985.

Granath, Olle, ed. *August Strindberg: Painter, Photographer, Writer*. London: Tate Publishing, 2005.

Gray, Charlotte Schiander. *Klaus Rifbjerg*. New York: Greenwood Press, 1986.

Hamsun, Knut. *The Cultural Life of Modern America*. 1889. Trans. Barbara Morgridge. Cambridge: Harvard University Press, 1969.

———. *From the Unconscious Life of the Mind*. 1890. Trans. Joseph A Slavin. Louisville: White Fields Press, 1994.

———. *Hunger*. 1890. Trans. Sverre Lyngstad. London: Penguin, 1994.

———. *On Overgrown Paths*. 1948. Trans. Sverre Lyngstad. Los Angeles: Green Integer, 1999.

Hansson, Thelma. *Karl Kraus och Strindberg*. Göteborg: Kungl. Vetenskaps- och Vitterhets-Samhället, 1996.

Holm, Birgitta. "Edith Södergran and the Sexual Discourse of the Fin-de-siècle." *NORA: Nordic Journal of Women's Studies*. 1.1 (1993): 21–31.

Hurston, Zora Neale. *Their Eyes Were Watching God*. 1937. Urbana: University of Illinois Press, 1991.

Huyssen, Andreas. "Geographies of Modernism in a Globalizing World." *Geographies of Modernism*. Ed. Peter Brooker and Andrew Thacker. New York: Routledge, 2005. 6–18.

Ibsen, Henrik. *A Doll's House*. 1879; *Ghosts*. 1881; *Hedda Gabler*. 1889. *The Complete Major Prose Plays*. Trans. Rolf Fjelde. New York: Farrar, Straus & Giroux, 1978.

Jacobsen, J. P. *Niels Lyhne*. 1880. Trans. Tiina Nunally. Seattle: Fjord Press, 1990.

Jacobsen, Rolf. *Twenty Poems*. Trans. Robert Bly. Madison: Seventies Press, 1977.

Jansson, Mats, Jacob Lothe, and Hannu Riikonen, eds. *European and Nordic Modernisms*. Norwich: Norvik, 2004.

Johnson, Eyvind. *Stad i ljus. City in Light*. Stockholm, Tiden: 1928.

———. *Dreams of roses and fire*. 1949. Trans. Erik J. Friis. New York: Hippocrene Books, 1984.

———. *Return to Ithaca: The Odyssey retold as a modern novel*. 1946. Trans. M. A. Michael. London: Thames and Hudson, 1952.

Kaiser, Georg. *From Morning to Midnight*. 1912. *German Expressionist Plays*. Trans. Ernst Schürer. New York: Continuum, 1997.

Kane, Sarah. *Psychosis 4.48*. London: Methuen, 2000.

Kleberg, Lars. "The Advantage at the Margin. The Avant-Garde Role of Finland-Swedish Modernism. *Swedish-Polish Modernism. Literature—Language—Culture*. Ed. Malgorzata Anna Packalén and Sven Gustavsson. Stockholm: Kungl. Vitterhets Historie och Antikvitets Akademien, 2001. 77–90.

Kvam, Kela. *Max Reinhardt og Strindbergs visionære dramatik*. Copenhagen: Akademisk, 1974.

Lagerkvist, Pär. "Modern theatre: points of view and attack" [1918] and *The Difficult Hour I–III* [1918]. In *Modern theatre; seven plays and an essay*. Ed. and trans. Thomas R. Buckman. Lincoln: University of Nebraska Press, 1966.

Larsen, Nella. *Quicksand*. 1928. *The Complete Fiction of Nella Larsen: Passing, Quicksand, and The Stories*. Ed. Charles Larsen. New York: Anchor, 2001.

Lindgren, Astrid. *Pippil Longstocking*. 1945.Trans. Florence Lamborn. New York: Viking, 1950.

Lindqvist, Ursula. "The Paradoxical Poetics of Edith Södergran." *Modernism/modernity* 13.1 (2006): 67–85.

Lunde, Arne, and Anna Westerstahl Stenport. "Helga Crane's Copenhagen: Denmark, Colonialism, and Transnational Identity in Nella Larsen's *Quicksand*." *Comparative Literature* 60.3 (2008): 228–43.

Luthersson, Peter. *Svensk litterär modernism: en stridsstudie*. Stockholm: Atlantis, 2002.

Mann. Thomas. *Tonio Kröger*. 1903. *Death in Venice and Other Tales*. Trans. Joachim Neugroschel. New York: Viking, 1998. 161–228.

Martinson, Harry. *Aniara: A Review in Time and Space*. 1956. Trans. Leif Sjöberg and Stephen Klass. Brownsville: Story Line Press, 1999.

———. *Cape Farewell*. 1934. Trans. Naomi Walford. New York: Putnam, 1934.

———. *Views from a tuft of grass*. 1963. Trans. Lars Nordström and Erland Anderson. Los Angeles: Green Integer, 2005.

Martinson, Moa. *My Mother Gets Married*. 1936. Trans. Margaret S. Macy. New York: The Feminist Press at CUNY, 1996.

———. *Women and Appletrees*. 1933. Trans. Margaret S. Macy. New York: The Feminist Press at CUNY, 1988.

McDuff, David, ed. and trans. *Ice Around Our Lips. Finland-Swedish Poetry.* Newcastle Upon Tyne: Bloodaxe, 1989.

McFarlane, James. "Berlin and the Rise Modernism 1886–1896." *Modernism.* Ed. Malcolm Bradbury and James McFarlane. London: Penguin, 1976. 105–19.

Mishler, William. "Norwegian Literature 1910–1950." *A History of Norwegian Literature.* Ed. Harald S. Naess. Lincoln: University of Nebraska Press, 1993. 200–69.

Mitchell, P. M. "The Concept of Modernism in Scandinavia." *Facets of European Modernism. Essays in Honour of James McFarlane.* Ed. Janet Garton. Norwich: University of East Anglia, 1985. 243–56

Moi, Toril. *Henrik Ibsen and the Birth of Modernism: Art, Theater, Philosophy.* Oxford: Oxford University Press, 2006.

Nikolajeva, Maria, and Sandra Beckett, eds. *Beyond Babar: The European Tradition in Children's Literature.* Oxford: Scarecrow Press, 2006.

Nolin, Bertil. "Förord." *Kulturradikalismen. Det moderna genombrottets andra fas.* Ed. Bertil Nolin. Stockholm/Stehag: Brutus Östlings Bokförlag Symposion, 1993. 7–10.

Norén, Lars. *Blood.* 1994. London: Methuen, 2003.

Obstfelder, Sigbjørn. *A Priest's Diary.* 1900. Ed. and trans. James McFarlane. Norwich: Norvik, 1987.

Parland, Henry. *Ideals clearance = Idealrealisation.* 1929. Trans. Johannes Göransson. Brooklyn: Ugly Duckling Press, 2007.

Proust, Marcel. *In Search of Lost Time.* 1913–1927. Ed. Christopher Prendergast. Trans. Lydia Davis, Mark Treharne, James Grieve, John Sturrock, Carol Clark, Peter Collier, & Ian Patterson. London: Allen Lane, 2002.

Rees, Ellen. *On the Margins: Nordic Women Modernists of the 1930s.* Norwich: Norvik, 2005.

Rilke, Rainer Maria. *The Notebooks of Malte Laurids Brigge.* 1910. Trans. Stephen Mitchell. New York: Random House, 1983.

Sachs, Nelly. *Collected Poems I–II.* Trans. Matthew Hamburger, Ruth and Matthew Mead, and Michael Roloff. Los Angeles: Green Integer, 2004, 2006.

Sandel, Cora. *The Alberta Trilogy.* 1926–1939. Trans. Elizabet Rokkan. Columbus: Ohio State University Press, 1984.

Sandemose, Aksel. *A Fugitive Crosses His Tracks.* 1933. Trans. Eugene Gay-Tifft. New York: Knopf, 1936.

Sarvig. Ole. *The Late Day.* Trans. Ole Sarvig and Alex Taylor. Willimantic: Curbstone Press, 1976.

Shideler, Ross. "Rediscovering Ekelöf." *Scandinavian Studies* 66.3 (1994): 400–12.

Skram, Amalie. *Under Observation [Professor Hieronymous and St. Jørgen's].* 1894. Trans. Katherine Hanson and Judith Messick. Seattle: Women in Translation, 1992.

Söderberg, Hjalmar. *Doctor Glas.* 1905. Trans. Paul Britten Austin. New York: Anchor Books, 2002.

———. *The Serious Game.* 1912. Trans. Eva Claeson. London; New York: M. Boyars, 2001.

Södergran, Edith. *Love & Solitude: Selected Poems, 1916–1923.* Trans Stina Katchadourian. Seattle: Fjord Press, 1985.

Sørensen, Villy. *Harmless Tales.* 1955. Trans. Paula Hostrup-Jessen. Norwich: Norvik, 1991.

———. *Tutelary Tales.* 1964. Trans. Paula Hostrup-Jessen. Lincoln: University of Nebraska Press, 1988.

Stam, Per. "'Old Innovations and Real Innovations in Poetry.' Finland-Swedish Modernism." *Swedish-Polish Modernism. Literature—Language—Culture.* Ed. Malgorzata Anna

Packalén and Sven Gustavsson. Stockholm: Kungl. Vitterhets Historie och Antikvitets Akademien, 2001. 91–102.

Stenport, Anna Westerståhl. *Locating August Strindberg's Prose: Modernism, Transnationalism, and Setting*. Toronto: University of Toronto Press, 2010.

Strindberg, August. *Creditors* [1888]; *To Damascus* Part I [1898], *Dance of Death* Part I [1901], *A Dream Play* [1902]; *Ghost Sonata* [1907]; *Miss Julie* [1887]; *The Pelican* [1907]. *Selected Plays I–II*. Trans. and Ed. Evert Sprinchorn. Minneapolis: University of Minnesota Press, 1986.

———. *Inferno*. 1898. Trans. Derek Coltman and Evert Sprinchorn. *Inferno, Alone, and Other Writings*. Ed. Evert Sprinchorn. Garden City: Anchor Books, 1968. 177–284.

———. *A Madman's Defense*. 1888/1895. *A Madman's Manifesto*. Trans. Anthony Swerling. Tuscaloosa: University of Alabama Press, 1971.

———. *The Roofing Ceremony*. 1907. Trans. David Mel Paul and Margareta Paul. *The Roofing Ceremony and The Silver Lake*. Lincoln: University of Nebraska Press, 1987. 1–74.

Szewczyk, Grazyna Barbara. "August Strindberg's Influence on the Drama of German Expressionism." *Expressionism and Modernism: New Approaches to August Strindberg*. Ed. Michael Robinson and Sven Hakon Rossel. Wien: Editor Praesens, 1999. 205–12.

Szondi, Peter. *Theory of Modern Drama. A Critical Edition*. Ed. and trans. Michael Hays. Minneapolis: University of Minnesota Press, 1987.

Tranströmer, Tomas. *The Great Enigma. New Collected Poems*. Trans. Robin Fulton. Highgreen: New Directions, 2006.

Tysdahl, Bjørn, Mats Jansson, Jakob Lothe, and Steen Klitgård Povlsen, eds. *English and Nordic Modernisms*. Norwich: Norvik, 2002.

Undset, Sigrid. *Jenny*. 1911. Trans. Tiina Nunally. South Royalton: Steerforth Press, 2002.

———. *Kristin Lavransdatter I–III*. 1920–1922. Trans. Tiina Nunally. London: Penguin, 2005.

van Reis, Michael. "The Inhuman Comedy—The Later Plays of Lars Norén." *Swedish-Polish Modernism. Literature—Language—Culture*. Ed. Malgorzata Anna Packalén and Sven Gustavsson. Stockholm: Kungl. Vitterhets Historie och Antikvitets Akademien, 2001. 125–30.

Weiss, Peter. *Leavetaking; Vanishing Point*. 1960, 1961. Trans. Christopher Levenson. London: Calder and Boyars, 1966.

Wiene, Robert, dir. *The Cabinet of Dr. Caligari*. Decla–Bioscop AG, 1920.

Witt-Brattström, Ebba, ed. *The New Woman and the Aesthetic Opening: Unlocking Gender in Twentieth-Century Texts*. Huddinge: Södertorns högskola, 2004. Södertorn Academic Studies 20.

CHAPTER 21

WORLD MODERNISMS, WORLD LITERATURE, AND COMPARATIVITY

SUSAN STANFORD FRIEDMAN

THE spatial turn across the disciplines—predicted in Michel Foucault's prescient observations in "Of Other Spaces" and urgently called for in Edward Soja's *Postmodern Geographies*—is rapidly reconfiguring modernist studies. Given that modernity has been predominantly a temporal concept, emphasizing a rupture separating the present and future from the past, the question of how to spatialize modernism faces particular challenges. The special issue of *PMLA* on Globalizing Literary Studies in 2001 issued a call for literary studies to move beyond the national model that has dominated the institutional structure of the discipline by creating modes of analysis suited to the interconnections of the planet, both in regard to past eras and with respect to the present intensified phase of globalization. To this end, national models of literary study have to a lesser or greater degree undergone a sea change in the direction of transnationalism. Anglophone, Francophone, and Lusophone studies have gained new prominence, while interdisciplinary fields like postcolonial studies and diaspora studies have examined the cultural legacies of transcontinental encounters centered in slavery, conquest, colonialism, and the emergence of non-Western nation-states.

How has, or, for that matter, how should, modernist studies participate in this shift in literary studies toward the planetary? Cosmopolitan internationalism is nothing new to modernist studies, which as a field cut its teeth on assertions of exile, expatriatism, and displacement as preconditions of modernist subjectivity and aesthetics in the metropolitan culture capitals of the West. This internationalist framework functioned as site of critique for the parochialisms of the local and monolingual/monocultural. But it was profoundly caught up in the logic of Western colonialism in locating the sites of modernist cultural production exclusively in Western metropoles and in regarding non-Western cultures primarily as the raw material to be transformed into modernism's avant-garde rupture of Western bourgeois conventions and art. Standard histories of modernism in literature and the arts have assumed the primacy of Western creative agencies, not only marginalizing the gendered and racial "others" within their midst but also erasing almost entirely modernist cultural production outside the West, especially among the colonized "others" of European and American imperialism (e.g., Bradbury and McFarlane; Kenner; Marshall Berman; Perloff; Nicholls; Lewis).

The tide is beginning to turn, however, as this volume demonstrates. Scholars have begun to reconfigure modernism's parochial internationalism in the light of a newly globalized and interdisciplinary study of culture that often blends cultural theory gleaned from anthropology, geography, postcolonial studies, diaspora studies, and media studies with studies in modernist literatures and the arts.[1] A new map of modernism is emerging, one in which Europe and the United States remain important, but not exclusive, sites of cultural production. Spatializing modernism requires a newly configured history as well, a history made up of many genealogies that crisscross the globe. Within this planetary frame, the spaces and times of modernism move colonialism, postcolonialism, and transnationalism to the center of modernist studies. This move in turn makes modernist studies a branch of what is often referred to as the "new world literature," a field that implies substantial engagement with comparative studies of culture and the multilingual landscape of literatures worldwide.[2]

What, then, should modernist studies do to adapt to the growing globalization of the field? Although many of the field's ongoing methodologies will continue to be useful, we need to reflect upon and engage with debates within the new world literature, not only by experimenting with various modes of comparison but also by examining the nature and politics of comparison itself. To these ends, I propose to review the new paradigms for studying world literature and the debates about comparativity that are most relevant to modernist studies and then to suggest some different comparative strategies for reading modernism on a planetary scale.

THE NEW WORLD LITERATURE

The efforts to spatialize modernist studies parallel developments in the newly revitalized and reconfigured field of world literature. Globalization has impacted the study of world literatures by foregrounding issues of cosmopolitan and diasporic literatures, national and comparative models for literary studies, colonialism and postcolonialism, and theories of contact zones, borders, interculturalism, hybridity, cultural traffic, and transculturation. These new approaches to world literature often intersect with reflections on the discipline of comparative literature—its (possible) origins in Goethe's concept of a cosmopolitan *Weltliteratur*, the early formulations of the field in the nineteenth and early twentieth centuries, its institutionalization in the United States in the aftermath of World War II, and the successive reinventions that can be found reflected in the "reports" issued by the discipline about every ten years since 1965.[3] But these debates expand well beyond comparative literature into translation studies, anthropology (another discipline founded upon comparison), postcolonial studies, and comparative cultural studies more generally.

Like the globalizing of modernist studies, these new approaches to world and comparative literature often begin in a critique of the Eurocentrism of *Weltliteratur* in its theory and practice. The problem with "world literature" is that it has not been sufficiently global, but has instead replicated the imperial power of the West for the past three hundred or so years by asserting Western culture as the measure of all cultures, Western literature as the universal world literature, Western culture capitals as the origin points of innovation, and Western consciousness as the defining essence of modernity. As Fernando Cabo Aseguinolaza suggests, world literature has been European literature (419), to which I would add that literature of the United States has typically been folded into the category of "European" as a supplementary site.

As in modernist studies, the new world literature's efforts to move beyond the privileging of Western literature often work within two main interpretative frameworks. Broadly defined, the first is a center/periphery model based in world-system theory (e.g., Wallerstein), and the second is a circulation model based in current cultural theories of traveling cultures (e.g., Clifford; Tsing), transnational cultural traffic (e.g., Appadurai), and cultural hybridity (e.g., Rosaldo; Bhabha). These paradigms at times overlaps, but they remain nonetheless distinctive, with different implications for discussions of power in the cultural sphere.[4]

The center/periphery paradigm operates fundamentally within a binary system of power relations, one that frequently draws explicitly or implicitly on the world-system theory of Immanuel Wallerstein.[5] Wallerstein's influential neo-Marxist work (first appearing in the 1970s) posits the rise of the West since 1500 as the result of its development and dominance of a capitalist world-system he divides into center, periphery, and semi-periphery (*World-Systems Analysis*). He further argues that Western dominance from the imperial center has functioned as a kind of "virus" spreading its power and modernity to every part of the globe ("Eurocentrism"). In literary terms, this world-systems approach began to influence the fields of comparative literature, world literature, and postcolonial studies in the 1980s and 1990s. Abdul JanMohammed and David Lloyd's *Nature and Context of Minority Discourse* (1990), for example, implicitly adapts Deleuze and Guittari's category of "minor literature" in *Kafka: Toward a Minor Literature* as a framework for the study of literatures that resist Western hegemonies. Although often deployed in critique of the canon, the category "minor literature" reifies its opposite—"major literature"—leaving intact the center/periphery framework it opposes, a problem evident in the title of Shuh-mei Shih and Françoise Lionnet's *Minor Transnationalism* (2005), a collection whose essays frequently move beyond the binary that the book's name reinstates.

The world-system, along with its emphasis on the sharp inequities of power, is at the heart of two highly influential practitioners of the new world/comparative literature: Pascale Casanova and Franco Moretti.[6] They regard the literary world-system as independent of the economic and geopolitical world-system, whose rhetorics of nationalism, capitalism, and (less directly) Social Darwinism they borrow to describe the inequalities that make some literatures central and the others peripheral. Both articulate the patterns and forces underlying literary history decontextualized from any other historical conditions.[7]

In *The World Republic of Letters* (published in French in 1999; in English, 2004), Casanova argues that the worldwide literary sphere is highly, even violently, competitive and governed by "laws" based on "rivalry, struggle, and inequality" (4). World literatures are either dominant and powerful or "deprived," "destitute," "poor," or "small" in a ruthless sea of competition for attention and visibility (175–81). Writers from the periphery compete in two ways—either by assimilation to the more powerful literary forms or by differentiation against it (179). In both cases, the dominant core remains the reference point for comparison. For her, "the Greenwich meridian of literature" is Paris, with French literature occupying the place of center for four centuries (until the 1960s), with all other literatures struggling to compete in a market defined and controlled in Paris. Although her sympathies clearly lie with the "peripheral writers," Casanova's model itself is profoundly "Gallocentric," to use her own term (46).[8]

Moretti's use of economic and geopolitical metaphors to describe the planetary system of world literature is more muted, but he also envisions an interlocking literary system made up of the strong and the weak ("Conjectures on World Literature"; *Graphs*). It is "one world literary system (of interrelated literatures); but a system which is different from what Goethe and Marx had hoped for, because it's profoundly unequal" ("Conjectures" 56). Through his method of "distant reading," dependent upon translation and the local knowledge of specialists, he claims to have discovered an abstract *"law of literary evolution"* governing the novel: "in cultures that belong to the periphery of the literary system (which means: almost all cultures, inside and outside Europe), the modern novel first arises not as an autonomous development but as a compromise between a Western form of influence (usually French and English) and local materials" ("Conjectures" 58). The West, for Moretti, is the site of discursive creation, while the non-West is "local materials," a center/periphery binary that ignores the often long histories of aesthetic production among the colonized.

The danger for modernist studies of the center/periphery model of world literature should be self-evident: at its heart lies the reassertion of the "old" internationalism. To render visible the creative agencies, long histories (including aesthetic ones), and modernist ruptures of artists and writers outside Western frameworks, we must find alternative ways of talking about the world systems of modern aesthetic expressivity. Broadly speaking, the circulation model for world literatures is much more promising for modernist studies. Homi Bhabha calls for a "new internationalism" in *The Location of Culture* that would accomplish "the worlding" of literature (12). The promise of moving outside the national paradigm for literary study is that "perhaps we can now suggest that transnational histories of migrants, the colonized, or political refugees—these border and frontier conditions—may be the terrain of world literature" (12). While Bhabha would collapse world literature into the migratory subjectivity of modernity itself, others, such as David Damrosch and Emily Apter, focus more on the circulation of texts than on the nomadic movements of writers in formulating their perspectives on the new world literature. What interests them is what happens when texts move beyond their place of original production, undergoing at the very least a process of cultural translation and very often a linguistic translation as well. Damrosch, for instance, does not regard translation as a site of failure or contamination but rather as a stimulant for creativity, the making of something new. In worrying about literary tourism, he argues in *What Is World Literature?* that world literature has its own specificity in its particular space and time, but he suggests that a work that circulates beyond that original location—for him the defining feature of world literature—gains as well as loses something: "A literary work manifests differently abroad than it does at home" (6). "Works of literature take on a new life," he continues, "as they move into the world at large, and to understand this new life we need to look closely at the ways the work becomes reframed in its translations and in its new cultural contexts" (24).[9]

Yet Damrosch's emphasis on textual circulation *after* the original aesthetic production ignores the role of transnational cultural traffic in the originary sites of creativity. In other words, he assumes a certain cultural/national insularity for texts in their "home" culture that erases the cultural translations shaping their creation. Circulation impacts art *before* and *during* the creative process as well as *after*.[10] Drawing directly on anthropological notions of "traveling culture" (Clifford) and "modernity at large" (Appadurai), Jahan Ramazani develops a "transnational poetics" that implicitly corrects Damrosch by arguing that aesthetic production in any given location shows the effects of interculturation. In his transnational paradigm, "creolization, hybridization, and interculturation become almost as basic to our understanding of modernism as they are of the postcolonial": "Central modernist strategies—transnational collage, polyglossia, syncretic allusiveness—are 'practices of displacement' that instance this cross-cultural generation of meanings" ("Transnational Poetics" 336, 339). There are no centers and peripheries in Ramazani's transnational poetics, and his view of modernism—and of the world literature for which modernism serves as defining example—consequently breaks open the Eurocentric frameworks that have dominated the field of modernist studies.

COMPARATIVITY IN GLOBAL STUDIES

To be global in reach, modernist studies will have to become more comparative. To avoid falling back into the Eurocentric center/periphery models that have dominated both modernist and world literature studies, we need to reflect upon the issue of comparison itself: its nature, epistemology, methodologies, and politics.[11] "There can be no serious multicultural experience or multicultural perception of value without a responsible theory of comparison," writes R. Radhakrishnan in *Theory in an Uneven World* (75). This leads to many questions worthy of exploration. What does it mean to compare? How are comparisons made? Do comparisons assume commensurability or incommensurability, emphasize similitude or alterity, imitation or difference? Does comparison assimilate the other into a presumed universal? Alternatively, can comparison engage in dialogic thinking, focusing on encounter, engagement, interaction? How are temporality and spatiality implicated in acts of comparison?

To address these questions, I begin with the assumption that comparison is a vital mode of cognition. Indeed, the *ABC*s of analytic thought might well start with comparison—the capacity to see difference in the midst of sameness and sameness amidst difference. One can't compare apples and oranges, the adage goes. But in fact one can: apples and oranges share the properties of fruits, but are distinct from each other in the more specific properties of each fruit. Comparativity depends upon identity, and identity depends upon a dialectic of sameness and difference. In terms of human collectivities, for example, the identity of a group—let's say, the Dalits of India—depends upon members of that group being seen as the same as other members of the group and also different from those who are not members of the group. The sameness of a group identity is at times forced upon individuals by ideological and institutional power; and at times the sameness of a group and its distinctness from all others is claimed out of pride, a sense of tradition, the need for protection, or the advantages that membership in a group can bring. The embrace of sameness always involves an erasure of difference, and vice versa: an emphasis on difference always involves the suppression of sameness, in questions of identity as in comparativity.

The listing of similarities and differences that often characterizes the pedagogical exercises of comparative thinking nonetheless runs the risk of obscuring the dialogic pull back and forth between commensurability and incommensurability that lies at the heart of all comparison.[12] In yoking things together which are simultaneously alike and unalike, comparison sets in motion a dynamic and irresolvable paradox. On one hand, comparison compels recognition of commensurability—likeness; but on the other hand comparison acknowledges incommensurability—difference. Oranges cannot be reduced to apples no matter how much we consider their fruitiness. Conversely, the fruitness of both apples and oranges refuses knowledge at the level of absolute particularity (incommensurability) and insists upon a meta-level of cognitive abstraction wherein similarity (commensurability) resides. Aligned with particularity, local knowledge assumes the incommensurability of apples and oranges. Aligned with abstraction, comparative knowledge identifies what is commensurate in apples and oranges. But comparativity contains within it a contradictory pull between the local and the abstract, between identification of parallels and insistence on contrasts. Comparativity puts in dynamic play in/commensurability.

This contradictory interplay in comparative practice is seldom far from questions of power.[13] Does comparison inherently establish a standard of measure to which others are compared and often found lacking? Does it inherently reflect asymmetries of power and contribute to inequalities in symbolic and material domains? How is comparison deployed politically? To serve whose ends and what purposes? Is the formation of the nation-state dependent on comparative thinking? What is the role of comparative thinking in the rationales for empire and other systems of stratification, as well as resistance to them? Conversely, what are the political stakes of rejecting comparison as inherently a violation of the other in service of the normative? Is comparison essential for breaking the mold of the universal, the monocultural and monolingual?

The cognitive practices of comparativity in many disciplines have shifted in recent decades to emphasize the incommensurability of things being compared. In comparative literature, for example, the Levin, Greene, Bernheimer, and Saussy decade reports on the state of the discipline reflect a gradual shift from an early emphasis on sameness toward a stress on difference—all in the name of politics. The identification of similarities among different literatures in the early years (heightened by refugees from World War II and the Holocaust) has yielded to significant delineations of differences in the post-1960s era—distinctions between women's writing and men's, for example; between African American writing and Euro-American; Irish and English; Turkish and German; Telegu and Hindu and Bengali; Latin American and Spanish; queer and straight; and so forth. This growing resistance to an emphasis on similarity reflects the view that similarity is linked to the forcible assimilation of the marginalized and the "minor" into the dominant mainstream, which in comparative literature has been a largely white European male canon.[14]

Indeed, the identification of any similarity—a necessity for comparison—has been associated with the violence done to the particularity of the other. According to this view, comparison is typically authoritarian, a tool of the dominant to deny the distinctiveness of the other. In *boundary 2*'s 2005 special issue on comparability, for example, Peter Osborne and Harry Harootunian examine the relationship of comparison in the "human sciences" to the rise of European colonialism and area studies in the Cold War era. Osborne sees Kant's notions of comparability in *Critique of Pure Reason* as the basis for later modes of comparative thought that arose out of colonial encounters: the assumption of "incomparability" or "lack of identity" between Europeans and others; or, the way in which anthropology developed as "necessarily *translational* or *transcultural* in character," turning as it did the incomparable into the intelligible through implicit acts of comparison. Harootunian links comparison with area studies, postcolonial studies, the theorizing of alternative modernities, and the recent turn in cultural studies to spatial analysis. He sees in these approaches a fetishization of space/place that compels comparison between center and periphery, the West and the Rest, that reinstates the unity and hegemony of the West. Places outside the West are always already haunted by an implicit comparison between themselves and the West. Comparativity is thus understood as part of a discursive regime that arose in relationship to the rise of the West and its imposition of its modernity on the Rest.

Where for Osborne and Harootunian, comparison is inherently violent and hierarchical, others stress the double politics of comparison. As Natalie Melas puts it in *All the Difference in the World*, both "imperial comparatism" and "emancipated comparatism" are constitutive parts of colonial and anticolonial thought, reflecting the different grounds of comparison (42). Aamar Mufti counters Eurocentric comparison with "global comparison," where the first assumes Europe as the "only axis of comparison," while the latter "encode(s) a comparativism yet to come, [one] that is a determinate and concrete response to the hierarchical systems that have dominated cultural life since the colonial era" (477). Shu-mei Shih argues that "comparison is constitutive of the process of racialization," but a "second form of comparison" can be used to highlight the "submerged or displaced relationalities" that govern racialized thought (1350). Implicit in these dystopian/utopian views on the politics of comparison is the assertion that comparison can potentially serve both systems of dominance and critique.

Comparison, then, occupies an epistemological borderland that can either reify or challenge the normative, where reification emphasizes sameness or commensurability and challenge stresses difference or incommensurability. R. Radhakrishnan structures his strategy of comparative defamiliarization around this tension. "In a world structured in dominance," he argues, "comparisons are initiated in the name of the values, standards, and criteria that are dominant. Once the comparison is articulated and validated, the values that underwrote the comparison receive instant axiomatization as universal values" (74). In defending comparison's progressive potential, Radhakrishnan theorizes a new comparative strategy of "reciprocal *defamiliarization*" (82). In this model, the bringing together of two disparate entities defamiliarizes both so that each is understood not only in relation to the other but also differently within its own previously "natural" system. It is the bringing together—the comparison without a single reference point—that makes visible aspects of each that have been assumed to be normative but are in fact culturally constructed as radically distinct. Like the others who recuperate comparison for critique, Radhakrishnan assumes an encounter based on incommensurability. It is the very difference between the "sense of time" in a Hindustani raga and a European cantata, he explains, that allows their conjunction in the moment of comparison to bring into focus just what that distinctive sense of time is in each case.

COMPARATIVE STRATEGIES IN MODERNIST STUDIES

In theorizing comparison for a modernist studies planetary in scope, I want to swing the pendulum between sameness and difference back to a dynamic, interstitial space between, a space in which comparison is centrally defined by the dialogic push/pull between commensurability and incommensurability: sameness and difference need to be maintained in tension. In this way, we can hope to accomplish the negotiation Ramazani theorizes with his term "translocation." The comparatism of modernist studies needs to be anchored in richly contextualized local modernisms around the globe, in their incommensurabilities. Such an approach differs, he writes, from "'postnational' or 'postethnic' history, in which writers are viewed . . . as floating free in an ambient universe of denationalized, deracialized forms and discourses" ("Transnational Poetics" 350). But at the same time, this comparatism needs to be attuned to the hybridizations and transnational identities that form through interculturation and circulation—in other words, sites of commensurability. The geohistorical in/commensurabilities—both spatial and temporal—must be held in play. Even as the abstraction of comparative thinking is performed, the ongoing recognition of difference must be maintained. Comparison can focus, then, not on a static list of similarities and differences, but rather on the dynamic pull between commensurability and incommensurability.

Comparison on a planetary scale in modernist studies needs to be more than the sum of all particular modernisms on the globe. It also needs a more sophisticated discourse of comparison, one that focuses on the dialogic tension between similarities and differences, one that takes into account the politics of comparison without being paralyzed by them. How then can we practice comparative work on a planetary landscape in modernist studies in ways that avoid normative and departicularizing measures for comparison? Modernism is by definition thoroughly implicated in the projects of modernity and as such modernism's geohistory is interwoven with global power relations, both colonial and postcolonial. How then can we avoid the colonial logics plaguing the history of comparatism? How, in particular, can we foreground the creative innovation and cultural production of the less powerful in global terms and at the same time locate the hegemonic effects of imperial powers as different cultural capitals are compared?

I suggest here four potential comparative strategies for reading modernism on a planetary landscape: Re-Vision, Recovery, Circulation, and Collage.[15] They are not mutually exclusive; in critical practice they are often interwoven. None is sufficient for the field in and of itself, but each produces a particular form of comparative insight. The first two—Re-Vision and Recovery—represent forms of implicit comparison, reflecting ways in which the dominant center-peripheries of modernist studies have been constituted in the past. The latter two—Circulation and Collage—represent more explicit forms of comparison, ones that self-consciously challenge concepts of the dominant core and its margins by emphasizing multiple centers and conjunctures across the globe. Taken together, as supplements to each other, these four strategies begin to constitute ways in which global modernisms can be read as instances of world literature.

Re-Vision

I borrow this term from Adrienne Rich's seminal 1971 essay, "Writing as Re-Vision," which sparked a generation of feminist critics and theorists to follow the double meaning instituted by the hyphen: by looking again, we see things anew. "Re-vision—the act of looking back, of seeing with fresh eyes, of entering an old text from a new critical direction," Rich writes (35). "Until we can understand the assumptions in which we are drenched we cannot know ourselves" (35). These words are very familiar to feminists, but they seldom appear in the context of modernist studies, let alone discourses of comparatism. Re-vision is inherently comparative because it implies seeing from a different vantage point, that is, different from how one has seen before. One sees (or reads), and then one revises how one sees by seeing again on the slant. The difference between these two ways of seeing is the paradoxical point of comparison—the dialogic interplay of commensurability and incommensurability.

By adapting re-vision for modernist studies, I suggest a similar "before and after" comparison between the older dominant narratives of the field and the newer narratives of modernism that have emerged with the new global discourses of literary studies. A globalizing re-vision in modernist studies involves revisiting the familiar cultural capitals, canons, and texts of European, British, Irish, and U.S. modernisms with fresh eyes by taking into account new questions that emerge out of epistemological travels elsewhere. This re-visionism is fundamentally hermeneutical, providing newly globalized interpretive lenses that defamiliarize the familiar.

The most striking shift this kind of re-vision accomplishes is a reinterpretation of colonialism as constitutive of rather than peripheral to modernism. This move was in some sense foreshadowed by Edward Said's re-vision of Jane Austen in "Jane Austen and Empire," which takes an author typically read as a quintessential English novelist of the domestic scene and demonstrates how the footsteps of empire are everywhere present through *Mansfield Park*, a novel about English people whose whole way of life depended upon the absent presence of slavery and sugar in the West Indies. As Simon Gikandi shows in *Maps of Englishness*, whose penultimate chapter focuses on English modernism, the imperial center is constructed through and is inseparable from its relation with the colonies. The influence of postcolonial studies on modernist studies began by the early 1990s to produce paradigm-shifting studies of familiar modernists, defamiliarizing them by seeing them through the lens of colonialism. Joyce, the quintessential modernist cosmopolitan, became Joyce the colonial subject, wrestling with his ambivalence toward the colonizer's language and the canons of English literature in new readings of *Portrait* and *Ulysses*; re-visionist readings of Woolf through the lens of postcolonial studies led to analyses of her searing critique of the British Empire and/or her complicity in it (e.g., Cheng;

Phillips; Dettmar; Friedman, *Mappings*, 107–31). This concern with the colonial affiliations and imperial privilege of canonical modernist writers has spread rapidly to other writers (see Moses and Begam).

The benefits of this re-visionist approach to modernist studies goes well beyond new globalist readings of familiar British, Irish, European, and U.S. modernist writers, however. It begins an important deformation of the modernist canon by bringing new attention to some Western writers who have typically been on the margins of mainstream modernist studies because of ways in which their work illuminates the logics of colonialism. Mainstream modernist studies have tended to privilege "high modernist," avant-garde texts that embody the crisis in representation associated with modernism, but the re-visionist approach's concern with colonialism's impact on modernism has brought renewed attention to writers such as Conrad, Forster, and Orwell in modernist studies. Finally, geographical re-vision of the familiar defamiliarizes definitional frameworks in modernist studies. As I indicated above, the old "internationalism" yields to the new "transnationalism" in modernist studies. The culture capitals delineated in Bradbury and McFarlane's *Modernism* (1977), for example, take on new coloration in the light of the colonials who broadcast for the BBC from London's imperial center, sometimes in conjunction with T. S. Eliot (see, e.g., Covi; Pollard), or who congregated in Paris from many parts of the globe, as Casanova points out. In short, modernism in its Western formations can be reconfigured and seen anew.

The limitation of geographical re-visionism is that we remain caught in the hermeneutic circle in which the cultural production of modernism remains Western. The modern subject and the agency of the writer are still Western—no matter how split, shattered, or newly claimed; no matter how constituted in relation to the rest. By itself, geographical re-visionism does not challenge in any substantial way the center/periphery world-system in the cultural sphere. Modernist agencies outside the West remain in the shadows, if acknowledged at all. It is all too easy, of course, to maintain that one can't know everything, that the languages required to read many of the "other" modernisms in their own languages represent too daunting a task. I respond by proposing that modernist studies as a whole needs to foster a multiplicity of approaches and that scholars within the field need to remain open to learning from those whose spatializing strategies are different.

Recovery

The best corrective to the limitations found in geographical re-visionism is to expand the archive of modernism by anchoring ourselves in the sites of cultural production wherever some form of modernity has ruptured the social fabric and its cultural practices with highly accelerated and intensified change across a wide spectrum of societal indicators. As I have hypothesized elsewhere, expanding the archive of modernism requires a significant re-vision of its conventional geography and periodization ("Definitional Excursions"; "Periodizing Modernism"). I view modernism as the expressive dimension of modernity, that is, modernity's forms in representational media—from the arts and literature to philosophy, popular culture, and mass culture. To the extent that any historical modernity—including but not exclusively Western modernity—generates expressive cultural forms, modernism takes shape in and often functions as the avant-garde of that modernity—creating, articulating, and interpreting the changes that seemingly cut off the present from the past and make everything new. This framework for global modernism recognizes that every margin constitutes its own center of cultural production. It opens up the field to the planet, refusing the nominal definitions of modernism that conventionally produce the familiar catalogue of avant-garde movements located solely in the culture capitals of the West—Paris, London, New York, and occasionally Berlin, Rome, Moscow, Chicago—and typically dated from the late nineteenth century through World War II.[16]

Why the archaeological metaphor of recovery and how is it comparative? I borrow the metaphor from feminist criticism, specifically gynocriticism, a term coined by Elaine Showalter to denote the branch of feminist criticism devoted to the study of women writers. The archaeological approach to global modernism is quite similar to earlier forms of gynocriticism. It too begins with a critique of the conventional modernist canon, focusing on the invisibility of cultural production outside the culture capitals of the West in modernist studies. It too asks how power works to suppress other modernisms, both at the time of production and in their critical reception. It too operates out of a comparatist framework, assuming in some form the better-known modernisms as a benchmark to which the other modernisms are implicitly or explicitly compared. Consequently, the archaeological strategy of recovery does more than expand the archive; it also asks how the archive of modernism got established in the first place as a Eurocentric framework that has steadfastly marginalized non-Western expressive cultures caught up in the shaping vortices of different modernities.

Both the strengths and weaknesses of the archaeological strategy center on its mainly additive character. It has become common in the field of world literature to denounce an additive approach to global literatures. Critics such as Damrosch (4), Moretti (*Graphs* 4), Chow (294), and Prendergast (9), along with many others, suggest that simply adding up all the literatures of the world, particularly in the form of national literatures, does not produce a planetary field of literature or the proper grounds for comparison. But I want to defend the importance of *adding* ever more instances of modernist cultural production to the terrain of modernist studies. I agree, of course, that the sum is always more than the addition of its parts. But the field is generally so ignorant of the modernisms produced outside the canonical culture capitals of the West that the work of digging up modernisms in other parts of the globe is a critical first step toward an understanding of planetary modernism. Expanding the archive of non-Western modernisms often requires substantial archaeological work: locating long unavailable texts buried in the bowels of libraries and collections; little magazines even more ephemeral than the better known ones; anthologies or catalogues reflecting networks parallel to those in the West; personal papers of forgotten writers, editors, and curators; and so forth. It requires moving outside the familiar canons to sustained readings of writers, artists, manifestoes, collectives, and movements engaged with modernities "elsewhere." As with archaeological work on women writers, the methodologies for working with the material are varied. But central to them is not only the linguistic skill and "close reading" that Spivak calls for in *Death of a Discipline* but also historical and cultural knowledge sufficient to the production of what Clifford Geertz calls "thick description." This gathering and analyzing of additional primary sources is groundbreaking scholarship, the production of local knowledge that is (or should be) the precursor to revised paradigms of global modernism.

The limitations of this additive archaeology of other modernisms are the limitations of local knowledge itself. It can be too tunnel-visioned, prone to arguments for exceptionalism and uniqueness, and insufficiently comparative or theoretical. It can also leave unexamined the limiting effects of using the nation-state or a region of the world as the basis of literary studies. Potentially, the positing of alternative modernisms can leave intact the standard Western canons of modernism and thus fail to challenge the center/periphery models that have dominated the field. Perhaps most seriously, in its emphasis on the difference or distinctness of its particular local modernisms the additive strategy can suffer from the same insularity for which James Clifford criticized the anthropology of local knowledge in his seminal 1992 essay "Traveling Cultures." Given that the local, as Clifford asserts, is never purely local but always crossed by ongoing processes of hybridization produced through intercultural exchange, additive archaeological recovery needs to be supplemented by a more explicitly comparative approach that tracks the global interconnections of modernities and their expressive modernist domains on a planetary landscape.

Circulation

Circulation involves connection, linkage, networks, conjuncture, translation, transculturation: in a word, polycentricity. As a reading practice, the circulation approach to world modernisms focuses on the nature and politics of interconnection and relationality on a global landscape. It differs from the center/periphery model by stressing the interactive and dynamic; it assumes multiple agencies and centers across the globe, different nodal points of modernist cultural production and the contact zones and networks among them. It presumes as well a polycentric model of global modernities and modernisms based on circular or multidirectional rather than linear flows. Such flows involve reciprocal indigenizations of traveling cultures (i.e., the nativizing of what comes from elsewhere by claiming it as one's own), and on transculturation rather than the cultural domination of the center over the periphery.

I borrow here deliberately from anthropology and civilizational or world history, fields which, in recent years, have largely abandoned the assumption of cultural exceptionalism in favor of transnational relationality in the study of global cultures (e.g., Sanderson; Wilkinson; Blaut; Frank; Subrahmanyam; Eisenstadt; Eisenstadt and Schluchter; Clifford; Tsing; Rosaldo). Sanjay Subrahmanyam, for example, writes that "modernity is a global and *conjunctural* phenomenon, not a virus that spreads from one place to another. It is located in a series of historical processes that brought relatively isolated societies into contact" (99–100). This web of conjunctures is what Ramazani theorizes in "Transnational Poetics"; it is akin to the "interconnected modernisms" of a newly "emplaced" modernism in Doyle and Winkiel's *Geomodernisms* (430), and it informs the "discrepant cosmopolitan modernist tradition" that Charles Pollard (borrowing from Clifford) locates in the creolizing cultural traffic between the Caribbean and London in *New World Modernisms*. It also echoes the "vertical" analysis of global/local that Mary Louise Pratt advocates to supplement the horizontal spatialization of transnationalism ("Comparative Literature" 63–64). It informs Rita Felski's appeal in *Doing Time* for modernist studies to attend to transnational cultural theory, and it is the guiding principle of Jennifer Wicke's startling tracking of the symbolic and material circuits of commodities such as tulips and bananas. The circulation approach to global modernisms often relies on the insights of re-vision and the expanded archive of archaeological recovery, but it goes beyond them by foregrounding intercultural interactions on a global scale.

Circulation analysis of global modernisms is inherently comparative—even more explicitly so than the re-visionist and archaeological. In its attention to cultural traffic, translation, and transplantation, the circulation approach considers the collision of differences and the resultant hybridization through processes of cultural mimesis—the imitation of others' representational forms, *with a difference*. The gap between practices from elsewhere and their adaptations is the contradictory space of comparison's in/commensurability: the likeness affirmed, the equivalence denied. As cultures blend and clash in the interplay of what anthropologist Michael Taussig calls "mimesis and alterity," the constitutive parts of comparison come into play, the commensurate with the incommensurate, the imitative with the insistence on distinction, identity with difference. The translation of cultural practices from one culture to another triggers comparative thinking, an individual or collective reflexivity about identities of self and other. This is the kind of comparative thinking embedded in Apter's concept of "the translation zone," Damrosch's notion of circulation in world literatures, and Djelal Kadir's conception of the "imbrications, juxtapositions, contracts, exchanges, and hybridizations" endemic to the comparison of world literatures (246). It also appears in Said's influential essays "Traveling Theory" and "Traveling Theory Revisited" when Said remarks on the transplantation of ideas from one locale to another, accompanied by adaptation (even radicalization) in its new environs. And it informs Bhabha's concept of colonial mimicry, which requires comparison as a condition of imitation with a *difference* (*Location*, esp. 85–92).

The circulation strategy has a potentially transformative effect on modernist studies because it challenges both the Eurocentrism and the center/periphery paradigms that have dominated the field's formulation of modernism's internationalism for decades. The model of polycentric modernisms encourages the tracing of networks among not only the conventional metropoles of modernist studies but also the other culture capitals of the world, from Calcutta and Bombay to Istanbul and Cairo, from Rio de Janeiro and Buenos Aires to Lisbon, from Havana and Kingston to Canton and Shanghai, from Kinshasa to Tehran, and so forth. A global polycentrism helps track the travels of modernisms around the globe—their circuits, back and forth movements, and indigenizations—the ways, in short, that every modernism is derivative of cultural forms it adapts from elsewhere.

Édouard Glissant's "poetics of relation," developed out of the crossroads culture of the Caribbean, embodies the particular strengths of a polycentric framework for global modernisms. He defines a poetics of relation as a "circular nomadism . . . [that] makes every periphery into a center [and] abolishes the very notion of center and periphery" (*Poetics of Relation* 29). What Glissant develops is the theory of transculturation posited some forty years earlier by another Caribbeanist, the Cuban sociologist Fernando Ortiz, who asserted that in colonial situations both sides are formed through and changed by their engagements with the other.[17] Transculturation differs markedly from center/periphery diffusionism in its capacity to see circular and multidirectional cultural traffic. It fosters, for example, an ability to acknowledge how fundamentally the Japanese Ukiyo-e wood block prints impacted the modernism of Vincent Van Gogh and Mary Cassatt, just as the art of Africa and Oceana enabled Picasso's cubism. These artists indigenized artistic forms from elsewhere in the formation of Western visual modernism, in turn helping to shape Asian modernisms (see Friedman, "One Hand"). Conversely, Joseph Conrad's *Heart of Darkness* is unthinkable without his colonial experience, an interrelationship which Tayeb Salih indigenizes in *Season of Migration to the North*, a novel of colonial and postcolonial encounter written in the cross-cultural ferment of Beirut, a major Arab culture capital in the 1960s (see Friedman, "Periodizing"). In short, transculturation of global modernisms testifies to how local modernisms are not isolate, but come into being through a poetics of relation on a planetary landscape.

The circulation approach to polycentric modernisms also helps dissipate what Radhakrishnan calls "the curse of derivativeness" that follows from the center/periphery model and the pernicious comparisons upon which it is based ("Derivative Discourses" 790). The power of the Eurocentric diffusionist ideology of modernity and the imperialism it rationalized has itself created a psychical reality of belatedness outside the West, one especially exacerbated by the continuing effects of the shame and humiliation that are key phenomenological dimensions of conquest and colonialism. Partha Chatterjee, Radhakrishnan notes, has written eloquently about the ambivalence toward Western modernity experienced by colonial and postcolonial subjects as they forge their distinctive but belated modernity through a complex combination of imitation and resistance. But he rejects the "curse" and "ignominy" of derivativeness he finds in Chatterjee (790, 788). "Why," Radhakrishnan wonders, "does Europe have to be the floating signifier in this entire process of the utopianization of the political-cultural imagination? Why not Asia, why not Africa? . . . What is the connection between the postcolonial instance of derivativeness, and derivativeness in general? If it is indeed the case that there is nothing that is not derivative, why should postcoloniality alone be made to carry derivativeness as a stigma?" (787, 788). He addresses postcoloniality, but Radhakrishnan's question applies equally to modernism.

What Radhakrishnan's angry lament challenges is the notion of originary discourses in the first place. From the point of view of *longue durée* geographers, historians, and sociologists such as J. M. Blaut, André Gunder Frank, Janet Abu-Lughod, David Wilkinson, Richard Sanderson, and many others, the West too is derivative, a late player on the planetary map of world systems where power is polycentric and shifting over time and where interculturalism is the norm, especially in periods of rapid change. Culture is always traveling, as Clifford writes, and, I would add, traveling cultures are always indigenizing what comes from elsewhere, nativizing it, claiming it as its own. The various recent discourses of multiple, alternative, divergent, discrepant modernities reach toward such a polycentric view but also threaten to fall back into the trap of diffusionist ideology in which the West acts and the Rest reacts—conflating the psychical reality of shameful belatedness with the historical realities of how cultures form through interconnection with others, not *sui generis*. From *what* are these modernities the other of, an alternative to, divergent from, we might ask? Don't such terms recapitulate comparison's assumed vantage point of comparison?

Dipesh Chakrabarty's introduction to his wonderfully titled *Provincializing Europe* leaves me lamenting, for example: If only he had actually provincialized Europe instead of reinstating European discourses of modernity as the default position, what Radhakrishnan calls the floating signifier of modernity. Dilip Parameshwar Goankar's otherwise impressive introduction to his important collection, *Alternative Modernities*, opens his account of cultural and aesthetic modernities with Baudelaire's Paris (3–6), thus reinstating Western modernism as originary, with "alternative" modernisms as just that, alternatives to the benchmark of comparison.

A more rigorously polycentric approach to both modernity and modernism would stress the mutually constitutive nature of cultural formations and their ceaseless circulation beyond the local—say, the modernity of the Sepoy Rebellion alongside Baudelaire's "The Painter in Modern Life." Such a conjuncture would allow us to see other modernities outside the West, especially colonial modernity, as constitutive of modernity in the West—not something that merely follows in reaction. As Walter Mignolo writes, "Coloniality . . . is the hidden face of modernity and its very condition of possibility" (Breckenride et al. 158), not only for the wealth upon which modernization depends but also for the symbolic structures of self/other, civilized/savage upon which modernity depends. Such an approach addresses the so-called curse of derivativeness, insisting upon both the interconnections and distinctions of contiguous modernisms. In *New World Modernisms*, for example, Pollard argues that Brathwaite and Walcott "are not derivative of Eliot; instead they create modernisms that augment, rival, and complement his European modernisms" (9). Moreover, a global polycentrism would allow us to see the interconnections of modernities and modernisms that have little or no connection to the West at all—either before the rise of the West or taking form in relation to others outside the

West. Such modernisms remain invisible within the framework for world literature proposed by Casanova, for whom literatures outside the West always exhibit a form of weak belatedness in their relation to Europe.

What, then, are the potential disadvantages to the circulation approach to globalizing modernism? With its emphasis on fluidity, multidirectionality, and reciprocal exchange, this approach can slide into a utopian discourse of happy hybridity, forgetting the role of power asymmetries constituted through empires, imperial hegemonies, and local stratifications. If the center/periphery model presumes too often a unidirectional flow of power and the abjection of the colonized, the polycentric model can forget the framework of power relations in its emphasis on relationality and multiple artistic agencies. To counter this tendency, I emphasize that the massive ruptures of modernity, which take place across a spectrum of social formations, are most likely to occur during periods of rapid, often brutal conquest that cause wide-scale material, psychological, spiritual, representational, and epistemological dislocation. Such dislocations can prove exhilarating and despairing—at once or separately. Historicizing modernism—refusing to define modernism in purely formalist terms—involves analysis of the structures of global and local power that shape people's lives.

Another potential weakness is that the attention to global networks can short-circuit local knowledge of modernisms around the globe, leaving such work to specialists with the historical, cultural, and linguistic background to engage with particular modernisms in their original languages and settings. It often depends heavily upon translation or works written in the colonial language—English, French, Portuguese, and so forth—leaving the vernacular modernisms untapped. As such, the circulation approach sits right at the intersection of major conflicts in both world literature and comparative literature as fields of study: the place of translation within these disciplines and the values of "distant reading" versus "close reading." In "Conjectures on World Literature," Moretti justifies "distant reading" and reliance on translation as necessary for a new world literary history while Spivak in *Death of a Discipline* favors an area studies approach, critiquing distant reading's ignorance of philology, its two-tiered system of global and local expertise, and its erasure of local languages. But Spivak's polarized view (the discipline is either dead or alive) ignores her own reliance upon translation (e.g., her reading of Salih) and the possibility of a reinvented discipline based on a both/and approach. Damrosch for his part calls for an approach that utilizes both translation and reading in original languages ("Comparative Literature?" and *What Is World Literature?*), as does Jessica Berman in "Imagining World Literature" when she argues for a "comparative 'thick description'" attuned to "specific local modes [that] co-exist with a dynamic and varied global interconnection" (69). In practical terms, however, such negotiations are difficult.

In my view, a circulation approach supplemented by re-vision and recovery can foster respect for local knowledge and comparative collaboration across linguistic and cultural divides. But such a difficult negotiation requires vigilance about the structures of power that affect polycentric modernisms, as well as attention to the painful institutional conflicts and inequities in literary studies, language studies, and the humanities more broadly as we compete for shrinking resources in the academy.

Collage

Collage performs the most explicitly comparative strategy for reading global modernisms. I borrow this term from modernism, drawing particularly on the juxtapositional strategies of Dadaism, by which artists assembled disparate images and materials, often from different parts of the world and cultural traditions. The effect was often bizarre or uncanny, the goal to defamiliarize and recontextualize what seemed familiar, to create startling new insights through an aesthetics of radical rupture and juxtaposition. This is the defamiliarization that Radhakrishnan promotes to counter comparison's tendency to hierarchy (*Theory* 82). In modernist poetry, the corresponding poetics of parataxis and superimposition accomplished a related effect. *Parataxis* is a term borrowed from rhetoric, where it contrasts with the hypotactic character of syntax, which is based in a connective logic of hierarchization. In modernist poetics, parataxis describes the rupture of connective logic evident in the radical juxtaposition of images or lyric sequences and the breakdown in conventional syntax. Connections are suppressed, not immediately apparent, or even nonexistent, to be formed in the mind of the reader who comes to see the possible correspondences or resonances between the disjunct and fragmentary. And in modernist cinema, montage, particularly in the dialectical formulations of Sergei Eisenstein, produced yet another juxtapositional effect by interrupting the flow of moving pictures with the editor's cuts, which often formed sharp oppositions of perspective, feeling, and effect. Common to all these formalist strategies of "high modernism" in the West is the creation of new representational forms through radical juxtaposition.

As a reading practice for global modernisms, collage—"cultural collage" and "cultural parataxis" I have previously called it—stages nonhierarchical encounters between works from different parts of the world that are not conventionally read or viewed together to see what insights such juxtapositions might produce (see Friedman, "Cultural Parataxis"; "Modernism"; "Paranoia"). Such paratactic collages bypass the familiar categories of belonging—whether geographical, historical, national, ethnic, racial, religious, gendered, etc.—and instead create conjunctures across lines of difference. This reading practice allows for the distinctive geohistorical specificity of each text—its difference, in other words—at the same time that it can reveal parallels that allow for a more general theory of which each text constitutes a particular variation. For example, in a prior essay, I juxtaposed two long poems that are typically never read together: Aimé Césaire's 1939 *Cahier d'un retour au pays natal/Notebook of a Return to the Native Land* and Theresa Hak Keung Cha's 1983 *Dictée*. Cesaire's poem is typically read in the context of the Pan-African and Caribbean Negritude movement and French surrealism; Cha's poem appears in connection with Korean American, Asian American, and feminist studies, along with postmodernism and the post-structuralism she studied in France during the

1970s. These distinctive contexts remain vital, but not sufficient in themselves. By reading the two poems side by side, a larger pattern of what I call diasporic modernism becomes visible, one based in the dynamic of *aller/retour*, a re-visionist *nostos* that relives the abjection of enslavement and colonialism as the basis for spiritual regeneration and renewal. Reading these texts together defamiliarizes each; but it also generates a perception of similarity that enables an expanded understanding of modernism.[18]

As a reading strategy, cultural collage or parataxis—like circulation—is a mode of comparative thought. The comparatism of juxtapositional collage is not based on constructing static lists of similarities and differences, tracing influences over space and time, or on tracking circulation, networks, and cultural mimesis. Instead, collage stages a juxtaposition that foregrounds the tension—the dialogic—pull between commensurability and incommensurability. For each element in the comparison, collage performs the kind of defamiliarization that Radhakrishnan theorized. Collage potentially engages the kind of "contrapuntal" strategy of reading that Edward Said advocates ("Reflections" 186) and that Djelal Kadir adapts as the basis of comparative world literature (247). Collage can incorporate as well the juxtapositions through "deep time" that Dimock advocates. Collage also temporarily sets what is being compared in an epistemological equivalency that challenges the center/periphery diffusionism and influence-based models of comparative reading that have dominated comparative literature and world literature. By equivalency, I don't mean to deny the power relations that affect the production and dissemination of texts. Rather, I mean that each text in the collage can appear in full geohistorical and biographical specificity (e.g., Césaire's Martinique and Cha's Korea), while at the same time can produce new insights by being read together comparatively. The absolute difference—incommensurability—of texts in the collage remains while the proposed similarity—commensurability—exists at the level of theory produced in the act of comparative reading. Such theory (e.g., diasporic modernism) can in turn change the reading of each text in its other contexts. This form of comparison produces a kind of "vertical" reading between the particular and the general, the local and the global.

The benefits and limitations of collage as a reading strategy for global modernisms are two sides of the same coin. On the one hand, its limitation is the decontextualization upon which it depends. Césaire, after all, needs to be read as part of a network of French, Caribbean, and African traditions; his movements, the history of "the black Atlantic," and the circulation of his texts are central to the modernism of Negritude that he represents. Reading *Notebook* only in juxtaposition to *Dictée* limits what we can know about either text. Every text belongs to multiple communities of intertexts. Collage foregrounds the least likely intertexts with a resulting loss of other relevant texts. On the other hand, it radically breaks down the hierarchization endemic to both comparison and to Eurocentric formations of global modernisms. It refuses the limitations of influence-based models, to which even studies of circulation can succumb. It brings to reading practices some degree of the representational rupture, dislocation, and surprise typically evident in modernism itself. It defamiliarizes different modernisms even more radically by breaking up the mosaic of insular, identity-based modernisms (e.g., Irish modernism, African American modernism, postcolonial modernism, etc.) that often characterize even the "new" modernist studies. Collage, in sum, has the potential to accomplish for the field what the representational ruptures of modernism accomplish for cultures in the crises of modernity itself.

Conclusion

Re-Vision. Recovery. Circulation. Collage. I suggest these four strategies for a comparative and global modernist studies fully aware that none by itself is fully sufficient to the task and that doing any one of them fully and responsibly is a challenge, let alone doing them all. Knowledge is always partial, but its incompleteness is necessary if we are to know anything. To attain a fully planetary reach, however, modernist studies must break out of the Eurocentric center/periphery and diffusionist models of reading that have dominated the field. It must become more self-consciously comparative, avoiding as much as possible the pitfalls of hierarchical comparison that leave unchallenged a standard of measure to which others are compared. The sheer scope of the task is daunting because of the diversity not only of modernities and modernisms through time and across space but also of languages, cultures, and histories in which modernity finds expression. To foster both deep contextualization and global breadth, a comparative modernist studies on a planetary scale requires a collaborative effort on the part of many scholars working in different ways. We need the re-visionist Woolf scholar working alongside the archaeological Tagore scholar. We need someone to read the circulations of Césaire and his work between Martinique and Paris, and through translation into other parts of the globe. We benefit from comparatists who juxtapose modernists from disparate traditions to produce reciprocal defamiliarizations. We may not work in teams producing joint publications the way scientists often do. But a fully global modernist studies can function as a "collaboratory"—as a site where different ways of reading collaborate to produce a new map of modernisms and their intersections as an instance of world literature.[19]

NOTES

1. In edited collections (Doyle and Winkiel's *Geomodernisms*), special issues of journals (e.g., *Modernism/modernity* on Transnationalism), and numerous individual studies (e.g., Gikandi's *Writing in Limbo* and *Maps of Englishness*; Pollard's *New World Modernisms*; Ramazani's "Transnational Poetics").

2. See, for example, Damrosch, *What Is World Literature?*; Moretti, "Conjectures"; Prendergast; Jessica Berman.

3. For history of the discipline, see Melas, *All the Difference in the World*, 1–43; Bassnett 12–30; Apter, esp. 41–64; During; Komar; Mohan. For the state of the discipline, see Saussy (2006), *Comparative Literature*; Bernheimer (1993); and the Levin Report (1965) and Greene Report (1975) in Bernheimer. While Goethe's notion of *Weltliteratur* is often cited as the origin of comparative literature, the practice of comparing literatures from different cultures in a systematic way is much older. See, for example, Isstaif's discussion of comparative Arab literary studies from the 900s to the 1300s.

4. Other frameworks include Dimock's concept of "deep time" and Area Studies. Rising as an effect of the Cold War, Area Studies nonetheless has produced knowledge about regions and nations outside the West, with careful attention to linguistic, geohistorical, and cultural specificity. Much Area Studies scholarship, however, was not very comparative; global studies, as a distinct field, rose in part to counter the insularity of area studies with the development of more theoretical and comparative analysis—often, however, with scant linguistic, geohistorical, and cultural knowledge. In the mid-1990s the Ford Foundation initiated a multi-year project called Crossing Bridges to broaden the horizons of area studies and deepen the contextual knowledge of global studies by integrating the two (Volkman).

5. For world-system theories not based on Wallerstein's center/periphery model that often directly oppose its Eurocentrism, see Blaut; Frank; Abu-Lughod; Sanderson. For the application of these alternative world-system theories to modernist studies, see Friedman, "Periodizing Modernism."

6. Casanova's *The World Republic of Letters* and Moretti's "Conjectures on World Literature" are often paired for sharp critique that nonetheless recognizes the originality and significance of their work. See, for example, Prendergrast, Introduction, *Debating World Literature*; Jessica Berman; Aseguinolaza; Orisini. In *Death of a Discipline*, Spivak doesn't mention Casanova by name, but she attacks Moretti and other world-system critics of world literature in a lengthy footnote (107–09). Prendergast recognizes the potential usefulness of world-system theory for world literature (6), but he does not distinguish between the Wallersteinian center/periphery models that reinstate the West as inevitable center and the Rest as periphery from those of other *longue durée* historians and sociologists (see Sanderson). See also Ram's contribution in this volume.

7. Casanova is explicit about the separation of literary history from other historical forces (see 12, 86–87), while Moretti simply assumes it.

8. Casanova's second chapter, "The Invention of Literature," is a teleological narrative about the rise of French dominance in the literary sphere, with some competition from the British and the German. That literatures—including concepts of literature—from other historical periods and civilizations do not exist in her narrative demonstrates the pernicious effects of the hermeneutic circle based in an *a priori* center/periphery.

9. Apter directly addresses the role of translation studies in comparative literature, echoing, without citing, Susan Bassnett's 1993 call for comparative literature to morph into translation studies as the best umbrella for the field's rejuvenation.

10. See Walkowitz's notion of "comparison literature" in the late twentieth and early twenty-first centuries, but I would also stress that the impact of traveling cultures on cultural production has existed for centuries as a product of different world systems.

11. For an interdisciplinary spectrum, see Felski and Friedman's Special Issue on Comparison, *New Literary History* (2009). For recent theorizations in comparative literature about the nature of comparison, see, for example, the Chow and During debate in *ELH* (2004); Theories and Methodologies in *PMLA* (2003); Mufti; Spivak, "Rethinking Comparat-

ism." For social science theorizations of comparison, see *boundary 2*'s special issue on comparability (2005); Yengoyan's *Modes of Comparison*; Culler and Cheah; Brettell.

12. On in/commensurability in comparison, see especially Melas, "Versions" and *All the Difference*, 32–43. Melas cites Spivak's *Death of a Discipline* for what she sees as Spivak's negative views of "the global commensurability of value" (*All the Difference* 42). Commensurability in comparative studies is often associated with a false equivalency or homogenization of difference. See Culler's "Comparability" for a summary of arguments against commensurability.

13. On the politics of comparison, see especially Felski and Friedman; Melas; Radhakrishnan; Culler and Cheah; Chow; Osborne; Harootunian.

14. For discussions of this evolution, see especially Balakian; Melas.

15. For a different approach to strategies of comparison in world literature, see Theories and Methodologies of Comparative Literature in *PMLA* (2003). Damrosch proposes three strategies that avoid "scholarly tourism" as literary studies begins to "wake from its long Eurocentric slumber": "national internationalism," "cultural translation," and "specialized generalization" (326–30). Saussy (336–41) rejects "tree-shaped comparatism" or "inventory" reading models and favors a juxtapositional model.

16. For global modernisms outside the West, see, for example, the contributions in this volume; Doyle and Winkiel; Brooker and Thacker; Santos and Robeiro. Studies of Caribbean and Latin American modernisms are especially well developed; see, for example, Emery in this volume; Covi; Gikandi, *Writing in Limbo*; Pollard; Rosenberg; Unruh; Geist and Monléon; Jrade.

17. See Pratt's adaptation of Ortiz's concept of transculturation in *Imperial Eyes*, where she defines transculturation as the colonized's transformation of the colonizer's culture (6); Guillermina De Ferrari's discussion of Ortiz's concept as one of reciprocal transformations of both the colonizer and the colonized.

18. For comparative strategies based on collage, see Friedman, "Modernism"; "Bodies"; "Paranoia"; "Cultural Parataxis"; and "Modernism in a Transnational Frame." I depart significantly from Jonathan Culler's 1995 discussion in "Comparability," in which he suggests that texts from substantially different cultural spaces and discursive systems (such as the West and non-West) may "make the putative comparability of text either illusionary or, at the very least misleading" (268–69). For other theorizations of comparison based on juxtaposition, see Layoun; Saussy, "Comparative Literature?"

19. For stimulating discussions and opportunities to present earlier versions of this work, I thank Venkat Mani and Mark Estante, co-leaders of the World Literature's Research Workshop at the University of Wisconsin–Madison; Stephen Yao, convener of a seminar on Human Difference/La Difference Humaine at the American Comparative Literature Association (2006) and a forum on Transnational Modernisms: Sites and Methodologies at the Modernist Studies Association (2007); and Reginia Gagnier, organizer of an MLA panel on Global Perspectives on Modernism and Modernity (2007). For their sharp critiques, I thank Matt Eatough, Rita Felski, and Mark Wollaeger.

WORKS CITED

Abu-Lughod, Janet. *Before European Hegemony: The World System A.D. 1250–1350*. Oxford: Oxford University Press, 1989.

Appadurai, Arjun. *Modernity at Large: Cultural Dimensions of Globalization*. Minneapolis: University of Minnesota Press, 1996.

Apter, Emily. *The Translation Zone: A New Comparative Literature*. Princeton: Princeton University Press, 2006.

Aseguinolaza, Fernando Cabo. "Dead, or a Picture of Good Health? Comparatism, Europe and World Literature." *Comparative Literature* 58.4 (2006): 418–35.

Balakian, Anna. "Theorizing Comparison: The Pyramid of Similitude and Difference." *World Literature Today* 69.2 (1995): 263–67.

Bassnett, Susan. *Comparative Literature: A Critical Introduction*. Oxford: Blackwell, 1993.

Berman, Jessica. "Imagining World Literature: Modernism and Comparative Literature." *Disciplining Modernism*. Ed. Pamela Caughie. New York: Palgrave, 2009. 53–70.

Berman, Marshall. *All That Is Solid Melts into Air: The Experience of Modernity*. 1982. Rev ed. New York: Penguin, 1988.

Bernheimer, Charles. "Introduction: The Anxieties of Comparison." Bernheimer 1–20.

Bernheimer, Charles, ed. *Comparative Literature in the Age of Multiculturalism*. Baltimore: Johns Hopkins University Press, 1995.

Bhabha, Homi K. *The Location of Culture*. London: Routledge, 1994.

Blaut, J. M., *The Colonizer's Model of the World: Geographical Diffusionism and Eurocentric History*. New York: Guilford Press, 1993.

boundary 2. Special Issue on Comparability. 32.2 (2005).

Bradbury, Malcolm, and James McFarlane, eds. *Modernism*. New York: Penguin, 1976.

Brettell, Caroline B. "Anthropology, Migration, and Comparative Consciousness." *New Literary History* 40.3 (2009): 649–72.

Brooker, Peter, and Andrew Thacker, eds. *Geographies of Modernism: Literatures, Cultures, Spaces*. London: Routledge, 2005.

Casanova, Pascale. *The World Republic of Letters*. Trans. M. B. DeBevoise. Cambridge: Harvard University Press, 2004.

Césaire, Aimé. *Cahier d'un retour au pays natal/Notebook of a Return to the Native Land*. 1939. *Aimé Césaire: The Collected Poetry*. Trans. Clayton Eshleman and Annette Smith. Berkeley: University of California Press, 1982. 34–85.

Cha, Theresa Hak Kyong. *Dictée*. 1982. Berkeley: Third World Women's Press, 1995.

Chakrabarty, Dipesh. *Provincializing Europe: Postcolonial Thought and Historical Difference*. Princeton: Princeton University Press, 2000.

Chatterjee, Partha. *Nationalist Thought and the Colonial World: A Derivative Discourse?* 1986. *The Partha Chatterjee Omnibus*. New Delhi: Oxford University Press, 1999. 1–282.

Cheah, Pheng. "Grounds of Comparison." Culler and Cheah 1–20.

Cheng, Vincent. *Joyce, Race, and Empire*. Cambridge: Cambridge University Press, 1995.

Chow, Rey. *The Age of the World Target: Self-Referentiality in War, Theory, and Comparative Work*. Durham: Duke University Press, 2006.

———. "The Old/New Question of Comparison in Literary Studies: A Post-European Perspective." *ELH* 71.2 (2004): 289–311.

Clifford, James. *Routes: Travel and Translation in the Late Twentieth Century*. Cambridge: Harvard University Press, 1997.

———. "Traveling Cultures." 1992. *Routes* 17–47.

Covi, Giovanna. "Uma Marsen; African-Caribbean New Woman Speaking Truth to Power." *Modernist Women Race Nation: Networking Women 1890–1950*. Ed. Giovanna Covi. London: Mango Press, 2006. 118–52.

Culler, Jonathan. "Comparability." *World Literature Today* 69.2 (1995): 568–70.

Culler, Jonathan, and Pheng Chiah, eds. *Grounds of Comparison: Around the World of Benedict Anderson*. London: Routlege, 2003.

Damrosch, David. "Comparative Literature?" *PMLA* 118.2 (2003): 326–41.

———. *What Is World Literature?* Princeton: Princeton University Press, 2003.

De Ferrari, Guillermina. *Vulnerable States: Bodies of Memory in Contemporary Caribbean Fiction*. Charlottesville: University of Virginia Press, 2007.

Derrida, Jacques. *Archive Fever: A Freudian Impression*. Trans. Eric Prenowitz. Chicago: University of Chicago Press, 1998.

Dettmar, Kevin, ed. Special Issue on Virginia Woolf International. *The South Carolina Review* 29.1 (1996): 24–44.

Dimock, Wai Chee. *Through Other Continents: American Literature across Deep Time*. Princeton: Princeton University Press, 2006.

Dimock, Wai Chee, and Lawrence Buell, eds. *Shades of the Planet: American Literature as World Literature*. Princeton: Princeton University Press, 2007.

Doyle, Laura, and Laura Winkiel, eds. *Geomodernisms: Race, Modernism, Modernity*. Bloomington: Indiana University Press, 2005.

During, Simon. "Comparative Literature." *ELH* 71.2 (2004): 313–27.

Eisenstadt, S. N., ed. Spec. Issue on Multiple Modernities. *Daedalus* 129.1 (Winter 2000).

Eisenstadt, Shmuel N., and Wolfgang Schluchter, eds. Spec. Issue on Early Modernities. *Daedalus* 127.3 (1998).

Felski, Rita. *Doing Time: Feminist Theory and Postmodern Culture*. New York: New York University Press, 2000.

Felski, Rita, and Susan Stanford Friedman, eds. Spec. Issue on Comparison. *New Literary History* 40.3 (2009).

Foucault, Michel. "Of Other Spaces." *Diacritics* 16.1 (1986): 22–7.

Frank, André Gunder. *ReOrient: Global Economy in the Asian Age*. Berkeley: University of California Press, 1998.

Friedman, Susan Stanford. "Bodies on the Move: A Poetics of Home and Diaspora." *Tulsa Studies in Women's Literature* 23.2 (2004): 1–24.

———. "Cultural Parataxis and Transnational Landscapes of Reading: Toward a Locational Modernist Studies." *Modernism*. Ed. Vivian Liska and Astradur Eysteinsson. Amsterdam: John Benjamins, 2007. 35–52.

———. "Definitional Excursions: The Meanings of Modern/Modernity/Modernism." *Modernism/modernity*. 8.3 (2001): 493–513.

———. "One Hand Clapping: Colonialism, Postcolonialism, and the Spatio/Temporal Boundaries of Modernism." *Santos and Ribeiro* 11–40.

———. "Paranoia, Pollution, and Sexuality: Affiliations between E. M. Forster's *A Passage to India* and Arundhati Roy's *The God of Small Things*. Doyle and Winkiel 245–61.

———. *Mappings: Feminism and the Cultural Geographies of Encounter*. Princeton: Princeton University Press, 1998.

———. "Modernism in a Transnational Landscape: Spatial Poetics, Postcolonialism, and Gender in Césaire's Cahier /Notebook and Cha's DICTÉE." *Paideuma* 31.1–3 (2003): 39–74.

———. "Periodizing Modernism: Postcolonial Modernities and the Space/Time Borders of Modernist Studies." *Modernism/modernity* 13.3 (2006): 425–43.

Gaonkar, Dilip Parameshwar. "On Alternative Modernities." Goankar 1–23.

Gaonkar, Dilip Parameshwar, ed. *Alternative Modernities*. Durham: Duke University Press, 2001.

Geertz, Clifford. *Local Knowledge: Further Essays in Interpretive Anthropology*. New York: Basic Books, 1983.

Geist, Anthony L., and José B. Monléon, eds. *Modernism and Its Margins: Reinscribing Modernity from Spain and Latin America*. New York: Garland, 1999.

Gikandi, Simon. *Maps of Englishness: Writing Identity in the Culture of Colonialism*. New York: Columbia University Press, 1997.

———. *Writing in Limbo: Modernism and Caribbean Literature*. Ithaca: Cornell University Press, 1992.

Glissant, Édouard. *Poetics of Relation*. 1990. Trans. Betsy Wing. Ann Arbor: University of Michigan Press, 1997.

Harootunian, Harry. "Some Thoughts on Comparability and the Space-Time Problem." *boundary* 2 32.2 (2005): 23–52.

Isstaif, Abdul-Navi. "Beyond the Notion of Influence: Notes toward an Alternative." *World Literature Today* 69.2 (1995): 281–87.

JanMohammed, Abdul R., and David Lloyd, eds. *The Nature and Context of Minority Discourse*. Oxford: Oxford University Press, 1990.

Jrade, Cathy L. *Modernismo Modernity and the Development of Spanish American Literature*. Austin: University of Texas Press, 1998.

Kadir, Djelal. "Comparative Literature Hinternational." *World Literature Today* 69.2 (1995): 245–48.

Komar, Kathleen L. "The State of Comparative Literature: Theory and Practice 1994." *World Literature Today* 69.2 (1995): 287–93.

Kenner, Hugh. "The Making of the Modernist Canon." *Chicago Review* 34.2 (Spring 1984): 53–7.

Layoun, Mary N. "Endings and Beginnings: Reimagining the Tasks and Spaces of Comparison." *New Literary History* 40.3 (2009): 583–609.

Lewis, Pericles. *The Cambridge Introduction to Modernism*. Cambridge: Cambridge University Press, 2007.

Melas, Natalie. *All the Difference in the World: Postcoloniality and the Ends of Comparison*. Stanford: Stanford University Press, 2007.

———. "Versions of Incommensurability." *World Literature Today*. 69.2 (1995): 275–80.

Mignolo, Walter D. "The Many Faces of Cosmopolis: Border Thinking and Critical Cosmopolitanism." *Cosmopolitanism*. Ed. Carol A. Breckenridge, Sheldon Pollock, Homi K. Bhabha, and Dipesh Chakrabarty. Durham: Duke University Press, 2002. 157–88.

Modernism/modernity. Special Issue on Modernism and Transnationalisms 13.3 (2006).

Mohan, Chandra, ed. *Aspects of Comparative Literature: Current Approaches*. New Dehli: India Publishers, 1989.

Moretti, Franco. "Conjectures on World Literature." *New Left Review*. Second Series (January/February 2000): 54–68.

———. *Graphs Maps Trees*. London: Verso, 2005.

Moses, Michael Valdez, and Richard Begam, eds. *Modernism and Colonialism: British and Irish Literature, 1899–1939*. Durham: Duke University Press, 2007.

Mufti, Ammar. "Global Comparatism." *Critical Inquiry* 31 (2005): 472–89.

Nicholls, Peter. *Modernisms: A Literary Guide*. Berkeley: University of California Press, 1995.

Orsini, Francesca. "India in the Mirror of World Literature." Prendergast 319–44.

Osborne, Peter. "On Comparability: Kant and the Possibility of Comparative Studies." *boundary* 2 32.2 (2005): 3–22.

Perloff, Marjorie. "Modernist Studies." *Redrawing the Boundaries: The Transformation of English and American Literary Studies*. Ed Stephen Greenblatt and Giles Gunn. New York: Modern Language Association, 1992. 154–78.

Phillips, Kathy J. *Virginia Woolf against Empire*. Knoxville: University of Tennessee Press, 1994.

PMLA. Special Issue on Globalizing Literary Studies. Ed. Giles Gunn. 116.1 (2001).

PMLA. "Theories and Methodologies: Comparative Literature." 118.2 (2003): 326–41.

Pollard, Charles. *New World Modernisms: T. S. Eliot, Derek Walcott, and Kamau Brathwaite*. Charlottesville: University of Virginia Press, 2004.

Pratt, Mary Louise. "Comparative Literature and Global Citizenship." Bernheimer, *Comparative Literature* 58–65.

———. *Imperial Eyes: Travel Writing and Transculturation*. London: Routledge, 1992.

Prendergast, Christopher, ed. *Debating World Literature*. London: Verso, 2004.

Radhakrishnan, R. "Derivative Discourses and the Problem of Signification." *The European Legacy* 7.6 (2002): 783–95.

———. *Theory in an Uneven World*. Oxford: Blackwell, 2003.

Ramazani, Jahan. "A Transnational Poetics." *American Literary History*. (2006): 332–59.

———. *A Transnational Poetics*. Chicago: University of Chicago Press, 2009.

Rich, Adrienne. "When We Dead Awaken: Writing as Re-Vision." 1971. *On Lies, Secrets, and Silence: Selected Prose, 1966–1978*. New York: Norton, 1979. 35–40.

Rosaldo, Renato. *Culture and Truth: The Remaking of Social Analysis*. Boston: Beacon Press, 1993.

Rosenberg, Fernando J. *The Avant-Garde and Geopolitics in Latin America*. Pittsburgh: Pittsburgh University Press, 2006.

Said, Edward W. "Jane Austen and Empire." *Culture and Imperialism*. New York: Vintage, 1994. 80–96.

———. "Reflections on Exile." 1984. Said, *Reflections* 173–86.

———. *Reflections on Exile and Other Essays*. Cambridge: Harvard University Press, 2002.

———. "Traveling Theory." *World, the Text, and the Critic*. Cambridge: Harvard University Press, 1983. 226–48.

———. "Traveling Theory Reconsidered." 1994. Said, *Reflections* 436–52.

Sanderson, Stephen K., ed. *Civilizations and World Systems: Studying World-Historical Change*. London: Sage, 1995.

Santos, Irene Ramalho, and António Sousa Ribeiro, eds. *Translocal Modernisms, International Perspectives*. New York: Peter Lang, 2008.

Saussy, Haun. "Comparative Literature?" *PMLA* 118.2 (2003): 326–41.

Saussy, Haun, ed. *Comparative Literature in an Age of Globalization*. Baltimore: Johns Hopkins University Press, 2006.

Shih, Shu-mei. "Comparative Racialization: An Introduction." *PMLA* 123.5 (2005): 1347–67.

Shih, Shu-mei, and Françoise Lionnet, eds. *Minor Transnationalism*. Durham: Duke University Press, 2005.

Showalter, Elaine. "Toward a Feminist Poetics." 1979. *New Feminist Criticism*. Ed. Elaine Showalter. New York: Pantheon, 1985. 25–43.

Soja, Edward W. *Postmodern Geographies: The Reassertion of Space in Critical Social Theory*. London: Verso, 1989.

Spivak, Gayatri Chakravorty. *Death of a Discipline*. New York: Columbia University Press, 2003.

———. "Rethinking Comparatism." *New Literary History* 40.3 (2009): 609–26.

Subrahmanyam, Sanjay. "Hearing Voices: Vignettes of Early Modernity in South Asia, 1400–1750." *Daedalus* 127.3 (1998): 75–104.

Taussig, Michael. *Mimesis and Alterity: A Particular History of the Senses*. London: Routledge, 1993.

Tsing, Anna. *Friction: An Ethnography of Global Connection*. Princeton: Princeton University Press, 2005.

Unruh, Vicky. *Latin American Vanguard: The Art of Contentious Encounters*. Berkeley: University of California Press, 1994.

Volkman, Toby. *Crossing Borders: Revitalizing Area Studies*. New York: Foundation, 1999.

Walkowitz, Rebecca. "Comparison Literature." *New Literary History* 40.3 (2009): 567–82.

Wallerstein, Immanual. "Eurocentrism and Its Avatars: The Dilemmas of Social Science." *New Left Review* 226 (1997): 93–108.

———. *World-Systems Analysis: An Introduction*. Durham: Duke University Press, 2004.

Wicke, Jennifer. "Appreciation, Depreciation: Modernism's Speculative Bubble." *Modernism/modernity* 8.3 (2001): 389–404.

———. "The Bananas of Modernity: Global Commodities and Modernism's World Exchange." Madison, WI. 29 November 2007. Lecture.

Wilkinson, David. "Central Civilization." Sanderson 46–74.

World Literature Today. Spec. Issue on Comparative Literature 69.2 (Spring 1995).

Yengoyan, Aram A., ed. *Modes of Comparison: Theory and Practice*. Ann Arbor: University of Michigan Press, 2006.

PART VIII

TRANSLATION ZONES: CULTURE, LANGUAGE, MEDIA

MODERNISM DISFIGURED: TURKISH LITERATURE AND THE "OTHER WEST"

NERGIS ERTÜRK

TURKEY, it might be said, is less easily imaginable for contemporary Anglo-global modernist studies than are such extra-European spaces as are designated, for example, by Mexico and China. Neither an outpost of European modernism as such, nor necessarily its Orientalist "inspiration" (as it had been earlier for the French Romantics), Turkey constitutes something of an aporia on the critical-modernist typological grid. The problem presented by the idea of "Turkish modernism" is not merely that of the recovery of an excluded object. Rather, it involves the very possibility of addressing the absence of an "authentic" Turkish modernism within national-critical discourse itself. For the fact is that while Turkey certainly *has* generated various recognizably modernist aesthetic practices, those practices have certainly *not* coalesced into a contemporaneous, continuous modernist movement that can neatly be aligned with transnationalized modernisms derived from European and Euro-American orbits of influence.

Orhan Pamuk, Turkey's Nobel laureate in literature, pressed this point in a 1995 essay entitled "Ahmet Hamdi Tanpınar ve Türk Modernizmi" ("Ahmet Hamdi Tanpınar and Turkish Modernism"), in which he warned his domestic readership against looking at themselves in "the wrong mirror" of a "modernism which did not take place" in Turkey (43).[1] One might even describe the internalization of such *décalage* as a kind of a failure in the contemporary Turkish literary-critical scene, producing two different modes of response.[2] One is an excessive celebration of the figure of the exiled communist and futurist poet Nâzım Hikmet Ran (1901–1963), regarded too often as the only authentic representative of the "spirit" of the Turkish avant-garde, in synchrony with its Russian counterpart.[3]

A second mode of response, more sensitive to the tensions constitutive of Turkish literary modernism, engages directly with the question of "failure," offering what we might call an historical apology for it. In a 1997 book entitled *Yahya Kemal Rimbaud'yu Okudu mu?* ("Did Yahya Kemal Read Rimbaud?"), Hasan Bülent Kahraman has pursued the non-correspondence of "Turkey" with "modernism" in the works of Yahya Kemal Beyatlı (1884–1958), arguably the first typologically modernist poet in Turkish literary history, who lived in Paris between 1903 to 1912 during the heyday of European literary and artistic experimentation, composing in traditional Ottoman poetic forms using simplified modern Turkish. Kemal was deeply engaged with the work of the French symbolists, but he only borrowed those symbolist literary devices that proved useful to his work in traditional Ottoman forms. Kahraman's essay is a searching examination of Kemal's retreat to traditionalism and "failure" to "leap" into either a European or a Turkish modernist avant-garde.

If we turn to other Turkish writers and critics engaged with European modernism during the first half of the twentieth century, we find that Kemal's "failed" modernism is not at all the exception, but the rule. In the works of those close to Kemal (including the poet, novelist, and critic Ahmet Hamdi Tanpınar [1901–1962]), as well as others not directly influenced by him (such as the critic Ismayil Hakkı Baltacıoğlu [1886–1978], who produced some of the most important Turkish criticism on surrealism and cubism), we observe a similar engagement with European modernist aesthetic and philosophical sensibilities, accompanied and undercut by traditionalism and political conservatism. In surveying the heterogeneous and conflicted literary modernist currents of the first half of the century in Turkey, I will neither contest the notion of a "failed" Turkish modernism nor apologize for it— gestures that would merely recuperate modernism's incontestably European and Euro-American origins. Rather, I will affirm that failure is itself essential to a deeper grasp of the difference that Turkey makes in, to, and for a new modernist studies which risks remaking the extra-European in its own likeness.[4] Attending to the specificity of the relation between modernism and conservatism (*muhafazakârlık*) in the late imperial (1900–1922) and Republican period (1923–1950),[5] one sees that the most powerful intellectual engagement with European modernism achieved in Turkey largely refused the aesthetic-modernist tactical mimicry of European avant-garde graphic and literary techniques of experimentation, which tend to leave legible tracks in the aesthetic sphere targeted by the global modernist-historiographic gaze. Instead, this engagement developed from Turkish conservatism's dialogic, critical probing of the European modernist critique of rationalization (in Mallarmé, Baudelaire, Rimbaud, and, most notably, in the work of Bergson).

As Nazım İrem has observed, Turkish conservatives turned to the modernist spiritualism of European thought as a critical alternative at a time when European Enlightenment rationalism and positivism were dominant intellectual currents shaping the Ottoman imperial and Turkish Republican modernization projects.[6] Beginning in the nineteenth century, a series of modernization programs were launched, violently shifting the foundations of Turkish social and economic life in an effort to "catch up" with the civilization of contemporary Europe. The modernist literature of the "other West" (a phrase commonly used by conservative Turkish modernists to describe alternative currents of European thought; see İrem 81) was viewed as a resource for the imagining of an alternative cultural modernity congenial to the Ottoman Islamic past itself, and Mallarmé's method of pure poetics, Bergson's concept of *durée,* and Rimbaud's figure of the *voyant* were resources for the preservation, rather than repression, of an Ottoman Islamic aesthetic sensibility. Above all, this Turkish conservative modernist "alliance" with European thought questioned the unreflective mimicry of a Europe understood— or misunderstood—as standing for unproblematically modern progress. Revealing both "Turkey" and "Europe" as sites of cultural crisis, these writers made of modernism less a positive aesthetic-historic current than a space, or even an abyss, of socio-historic uncertainty. It is a powerful irony, perhaps, that the legacy of European modernism in Turkey is rooted in the activities of those figures of Republican Turkish culture who least readily reflect to the Eurocentrist critic his self-image.

The Turkish perspective reminds us that the reproduction of modernism as globalization is an endeavor continuously risking, without being able fully to achieve, its own effacement. Although the internal heterogeneity of a distinctively European modernism has been scrutinized and questioned in such notable work as Peter Nicholls' *Modernisms* (1995), Vassiliki Kolocotroni, Jane Goldman, and Olga Taxidou's *Modernism: An Anthology of Sources and Documents* (1998), and Marianne Thormählen's *Rethinking Modernism* (2003), the globalization of modernism, its expansion outward and around a point of departure, can never hope to sever itself completely from that point of departure. Modernism's "worlding" is less an empirically verifiable development, perhaps, than it is a critical practice: a practice of conditional hospitality, which welcomes Europe's other to the extent that it can be subsumed in the classification systems of Western European literary and art historiography. The burgeoning interest in the globality of modernism today is hardly innocent of what Djelal Kadir terms "imperial moves that circumscribe the world into manageable global boundedness" (7). But that interest can also be understood as a hyperbole of modernity's key dynamic itself: what Michel Foucault, in *The Order of Things,* called "the enormous thrust of a freedom, a desire, or a will" in transgression (209, *Les mots et les choses* 222). In "worlding" itself, modernism now takes the infinitude of the entire world as its object. The world is at once a stage for, and an unattainable object of, its desire: as Foucault puts it, the world is "carried over, without any residuum, into the representation that provides [it] with a reasonable foundation in *discourse* and transforms [it] spontaneously into *scenes."* The historiography of a globalizing modernism cannot extricate itself from this scenic worlding, and we would do well to remember what Foucault identifies as its *quixotic* character: "But this table [of representation] is so thin, so transparent to all the figures of desire that untiringly accumulate within it and multiply there simply by the force of their combination, that it is just as lacking in reason as that of Don Quixote, when he believed himself to be progressing, from similitude to similitude, along the commingled paths of the world and books, but was in fact getting more and more entangled in the labyrinth of his own representations" (*Order of Things* 210–11; *Les mots et les choses* 223).[7] It is modernity's *own* image of the world as infinite which itself precludes all attempts at totalization, its anomalies, deflections, discontinuities, and refusals *disfiguring* the signifier "modernism" in its "Turkish" generalization.

The "Other West" in Turkey

The Turkish conservative encounter with European literary modernism begins with the first encounters of Ottoman Turkish poets with French symbolism at the turn of the twentieth century. But the Ottoman literary world itself had already been violently transformed during the second half of the nineteenth century, as the empire was peripherally integrated into global capitalist modernity. One point that bears emphasizing here is that this peripheral integration of the empire did not involve direct European colonial rule. Rather, as Europe steadily encircled and encroached on it, the Ottoman state implemented a range of economic, social, and political reforms, which the positivist philosopher Auguste Comte had praised in an 1853 letter written to the leading Ottoman reformer, Grand Vizier Mustafa Reşit Pasha.[8] Along with the advance of simplification reforms for written Ottoman Turkish and an intensification of bureaucratic and literary translation activity,[9] the 1870s witnessed the emergence of the first Ottoman Turkish novels, hybrid generic artifacts mixing the thematics of the European novel with the narratorial voice of the traditional *meddah* storyteller.[10] The tensions of this literary transformation are registered emblematically in the poet Recâizâde Mahmud Ekrem's 1896 novel *Araba Sevdası* ("The Carriage Affair"), which narrates the composition of a love letter, in an idiom mixing French with Ottoman Turkish, "posted" through translations (and mistranslations) of French Romantic and Ottoman divan poetry—and which never in fact reaches its destination.[11]

If a nihilistic Turkish literary consciousness thus appeared as a response to intensified literary and linguistic modernization, we can also say that Yahya Kemal's first active engagement with French symbolism "brought the god of language back to language" (Tanpınar, *Yahya Kemal* 109), making symbolism a vehicle for the rediscovery of the vanished lyric voice of Ottoman divan poetry.[12] Born into a literary context for which the positivism of the revolutionary poet Tevfik Fikret (1867–1915) had set the tone, Kemal, as typical "Young Turk," left for Paris in 1903 to study at the École des Sciences Politiques.[13] But it was not a simple initiation into Parisian French modernism that awaited him there. In an oft-cited passage in his *Çocukluğum, Gençliğim, Siyâsî ve Edebî Hatıralarım* (1999; "My Childhood, My Youth, My Political and Literary Memories"), Kemal described his literary transformation through encounters with the work of Hugo, Gautier, de Banville, Baudelaire, and José-Maria de Heredia, adding: "It is then that I realized I came close to the new Turkish I had long sought after. Our spoken Turkish resembled the white language of classical Greek and Latin poetry" (108).

Kemal's conservative poetic project of "homecoming" through the "Frank" has left a contested legacy for contemporary Turkey.[14] Where Heredia's neo-classicism and Albert Sorel's historicism inform the politics of Kemal's composition in classical Ottoman poetic forms and meter (*aruz*) and in simplified Turkish (which makes him important to traditionalists in Turkey), the philosophy of Kemal's poetry is shaped by Mallarmé's sound poetics and Baudelaire's symbolism, marking him as a nodal point of Turkish modernism. In *Yahya Kemal Rimbaud'yu Okudu mu?* Kahraman aims to resolve this contradiction by distinguishing between modern*ist* futurism as forgetfulness of the past and modern remembrance of that past, arguing that "Yahya Kemal is a modern but not a modernist poet" (58, 104). While this nuanced distinction has the virtue of acknowledging the different temporal registers of modern literatures, one might say it lets a certain Eurocentrist discourse stand unopposed—particularly when Kahraman redeploys it, prescriptively, in lament for the absence of any "authentic" Turkish modernism recognizable by the lights of Western Europe.[15]

We might say that Kemal's "failed" modernism is a crucial chapter in the history of global modernism, precisely in the extent to which his poetics is *not* a mere transposition of Mallarméan language experiments into an Ottoman Turkish context. Rather, Mallarmé's pure poetics is instrumentalized, in Kemal's work, for the preservation of "derûnî âhenk," or "inner harmony," the unity of word order, meter, and meaning in Ottoman Turkish poetics.[16] Turkish conservative modernism thus counters the dominance of a positivistic "Europe" and its repudiation of Ottoman Islamic cultural forms. Kemal's traditionalism is certainly not without its contradictions. His revaluation of the poetic word in and for itself is certainly better understood in terms familiar to Mallarmé criticism—as an aftereffect of linguistic mechanization, intensified by modernity's abstracting processes—than as any "authentic" continuation of Ottoman poetics into the twentieth century.[17] Much in Kemal's melancholic poetics of *inkırâz*, or decadence, meanwhile, in its distant resemblance to Baudelaire's own, can arguably be read as Kemal's way of admitting the impossibility of restoring the past as a whole. Despite such contradictions, we might say that Kemal's dialogic engagement with the poets of the "other West" is invaluable to the extent that it produced alternative imaginations of a cultural modern well beyond the mere mimicry of European forms.

Kemal also founded and edited *Dergâh* ("Convent"), one of the most influential journals in the history of Turkish conservative modernism. Published biweekly between April 1921 and January 1923 amid the turbulence of the Turkish National Movement and *Kurtuluş Savaşı* (War of Independence), the journal published the work of a group of young intellectuals including, among others, the symbolist poet Ahmet Haşim (1884/7–1933),[18] the novelist, critic, and statesman Yakup Kadri

Karaosmanoğlu (1889–1974), the philosopher, psychologist, and translator of Bergson Mustafa Şekip Tunç (1886–1958), the pedagogue, academic, and practitioner of
traditional arts Ismayil Hakkı Baltacıoğlu (1886–1978), and the novelist, poet, and
critic Ahmet Hamdi Tanpınar (1901–1962) (by consensus, the most important writer
of the Republican period).

Where French symbolism continued to serve as a source of inspiration for
Kemal and Haşim, and later for Tanpınar, Henri Bergson's philosophy emerged as
another important modernist influence in *Dergâh* writing.[19] The title *Dergâh* (chosen over "Haşhaş" or "Hashish") reflects the spiritualist tendencies of these intellectuals and their dedication to the "vitalité" or "hayatiyet" of the shrunken territory
occupied by Allied forces after the Great War (see Tanpınar, *Yahya Kemal* 25–26).
The *Dergâh* writers, who would become the leading conservative intellectuals of the
Turkish Republican period, made Bergson their starting point in rethinking national genesis and nationhood as grounded in a creative "leap" of intuition rather
than a positive evolution. Bergson's *durée,* which precluded any fixing or severance
of the past, informed their conception of tradition as flowing continuously into the
future of the new nation. As Tanpınar put it: "National life is [. . .] continuity
through change and change in continuity [. . .] Radical breaks and ruptures only
engender inbred freaks and demi-creatures" (*Yahya Kemal* 24).

The intellectual appeal of this Bergsonist "other West" lasted through the formative years of the Turkish Republic, founded in 1923, and it provided a platform of
opposition to the reforms of the Republican state. In a European context, "conservatism" refers to currents of political thought that developed in reaction to the French
Revolution, beginning with Edmund Burke's denunciation of the revolutionaries'
"cold" rationalism, his critique of the destructive displacement of traditional social
codes by an abstract social contract, and his commitment to the preservation of a
political elite with property ownership.[20] If Turkish conservatism emerged under
analogous pressures from Ottoman reformation or *ıslah*, it sprang to life in opposition to the radical measures of the Republican revolution, or *inkılâp* (Özipek 80).
Where Romantic literary language provided a medium of expression for Burke's
antirevolutionary thinking (in his well-known description, for example, of the arrest of the queen as a violent scene of rape), it was Bergson and a broadly Bergsonist
modernism—Proust and Mallarmé for Tanpınar, surrealism for Baltacıoğlu, and
Baudelaire and Rimbaud for Necip Fazıl Kısakürek—that mediated and legitimized
the Republican conservatives' critiques of the abstracting processes of modernity, as
well as their conceptions of tradition as change in continuity.

Having prevailed in the War of Independence, the Turkish nationalist military
elite under the leadership of President Mustafa Kemal Atatürk (1881–1938) launched
a far more drastic program of modernization than their Ottoman predecessors, aiming to replace all Ottoman Islamic institutions of the past.[21] The Republican program
of what has been called "extreme nationalization and secularization"—pursued, we
might say, "against the West with the West"—included the abolition of the sultanate
(1922) and of the caliphate (1924), the closure of religious orders (1925), adoption of
a European-style civil code (1926), and the abolition of the Perso-Arabic lettering in

which Ottoman Turkish was written and its replacement with Latin phonetic orthography (1928), among other measures.[22] The Republican program sought to break all ties with the Ottoman Islamic past. Indeed, one might consider the Republican plunder and destruction of the Ottoman Islamic past—including the erasure of inscriptions on panels (*kitâbe*) and seals (*tuğra*), and the sale of archival materials to the state of Bulgaria for the price of scrap paper[23]—as a realization of that dreadful dream of Marinetti in the 1909 "Le Futurisme" ("The Founding and Manifesto of Futurism 1909"): "So let them come, the gay incendiaries with charred fingers! Here they are! [. . .] Come on! set fire to the library shelves! [. . .] Take up your pickaxes, your axes and hammers and wreck, wreck the venerable cities, pitilessly" ("Founding" 23; "Le Futurisme").

Such transcategorical comparisons between Kemalist[24] statist social engineering in Turkey and the aesthetic impulse of European futurism are doubtless of limited use—among other reasons, because Turkish reformists took inspiration directly from the positivist and rationalist currents of European Enlightenment thought itself, rather than its literary or otherwise aesthetic emanations as such. At the same time, however, the contrast is useful in its ability to illuminate state functionaries' tolerance of the aesthetic avant-garde. While in the remainder of this chapter I shall explore the alliance between conservatism and the "other West" in the writings of Tanpınar, Baltacıoğlu, and Kısakürek,[25] this is certainly not the only conjunction from which Republican modernism can be productively explored. Indeed, one must open a parenthesis here, in order to note that the 1930s also saw the emergence of historically specific sites of avant-garde activity in Turkey. The cubist-constructivist paintings of the "d Group" were received with confusion by the audiences for their 1933 exhibit, held at the former Dağcılık Klübü (Mountaineers' Club) in Istanbul and following an exhibition in, among other places, a hat store in the city's Beyoğlu district. Named for the fourth letter of the Latin alphabet, to mark their succession of the three major modern art movements of the second half of the nineteenth century and the beginning of the twentieth,[26] the "d Group" was welcomed, though not without some skepticism, as an importer of the newest European art currents.[27] (In an essay entitled "Türk Muhafazakârlığının Kültürel Kuruluşu" ["The Cultural Foundation of Turkish Conservatism"], Beşir Ayvazoğlu notes that Halil Dikmen, the curator of the State Art and Sculpture Museum from its establishment in 1937 until 1961, was barely able to explain the aesthetics of the "d Group" to a displeased Atatürk [511].[28]) Though they kept their distance from the propaganda art initiatives of the Republic, the "d Group" had been incorporated into the cultural establishment in Turkey by the 1940s, regularly joining the art exhibitions and painting tours of the ruling Republican People's Party (CHP) with cubist paintings of folkloric themes.[29] One distinctly non-European, and probably undesirable consequence of its incorporation into the state agenda was the Turkish avant-garde's loss of any real ground for the critical or oppositional stance with which European avant-gardes are usually associated (see Köksal, "Art and Power" 100; Bozdoğan 148–52).

In the literary domain, the most influential and well-known figure of the Turkish avant-garde is doubtless the poet Nâzım Hikmet, who introduced a novel poetic idiom in his book *835 Satır* ("835 Lines"), published in 1929 after his return to Turkey from the Soviet Union. Composed in free verse in the stepladder form of Mayakovsky and articulating a program for a revolutionary machine aesthetics, Nâzım's "San'at Telâkkisi" ("Regarding Art") may be read as a manifesto for a new poetics that breaks with the figurative traditions of Ottoman lyric poetry: "I don't pretend / the nightingale's lament / to the rose isn't easy on the ears ... / But the language / that really speaks to me / are Beethoven sonatas played / on copper, iron, wood, bone, and catgut ..." ("San'at" 36; "Regarding" 4). Meanwhile, Nâzım's essay "Putları Yıkıyoruz" ("We're Demolishing the Idols"), published in 1929 in *Resimli Ay* ("Monthly Illustrated"), questioned the grounds of literary canonicity in Turkish literary history, aiming a slap at the face of Turkish public taste.[30] His early futurist work, such as the poem "Makinalaşmak" ("Mechanization"), a frequently cited work of Turkish modernism in a global context, is perhaps something of a dull imitation of Mayakovsky (as is often observed in Turkish criticism), though it did have the effect of opening the poetic register of modern Turkish to formal and metrical, as well as lexical, vernaculars. While the poetics of the neo-Surrealist First New (Birinci Yeni) and Second New (İkinci Yeni), who appeared in Nâzım's wake (the latter being by far the most remarkable and rigorous Turkish literary movement of the second half of the twentieth century) do not directly derive from his work, Nâzım's "freeing" of the poetic economy of modern Turkish is doubtless one condition of possibility for this particular trajectory of poetic modernism in Turkey.[31]

Nâzım's second most important historical legacy is his introduction of Marxist cultural theory to Turkey. Nâzım's *Kemal Tahir'e Mahpusaneden Mektuplar* (1968; "Prison Letters to Kemal Tahir"), a collection of prison correspondence between Nâzım and Kemal Tahir, one of Turkey's most important historical novelists in this period, is a valuable record of Nâzım's thinking about the dialectical relationship between aesthetic representation and material production. Nâzım theorizes his own choice of free verse as an attempt to sublate the dialectic of form and content in poetry and prose, to create a literary register for revolutionary futurity.

All too often, however, Nâzım is made to serve as the representative of Turkish literary modernism on a world stage (much as Orhan Pamuk today serves as the representative of a kind of Turkish literary postmodernism), which is to say that synoptic histories are too often content to look no further than Nâzım's work. This "freezing" of the literary field at a global level is arguably facilitated by the growth of a critical discourse in English on the Russian avant-garde and by its assimilation of commentary on Nâzım's early futurist poetry.[32] But it is within Turkey, as well, that Nâzım is positioned as the Republic's sole authentic modernist (often, in an internalization of the critical discourse of lack, with overtones of shame at Turkey's failure to produce any further such figures, itself an effect of Orientalist literary historiography). To attend to the connection between literary modernism and conservatism in Turkey is, then, to turn from the assimilative search for reflective mimicry of

European modernism to the complex and contradictory dialogues that constitute such formations to begin with.

Certainly, such a shift of emphasis must aim neither to consolidate competing visions of conservative modernism itself, nor to deny or obscure Turkish conservatism's fundamental failure as such. To be sure, the different strains of Turkish conservatism, and their links and affiliations with the critical ideologies of Islamism, Pan-Turkism, and Ottomanism,[33] all have differences that need to be acknowledged, as does the variance of individual writers and thinkers in their approaches to both conservative tradition generally and to its variegation. With the exception of Kısakürek, who turned to Islamism after the mid-1930s, Republican conservative modernists did not attempt to translate their cultural critique into a political program subversive of the Kemalist state.[34] Politically marginal during the Republican period, Turkish conservatism would become a staging area for the nationalist right of the 1970s, who came to prominence with the September 12, 1980, coup, accompanied by the systematic eradication of the Turkish left. In so many ways, one can say that the Turkey of today has still not recovered from the violence of this period.

Despite (or perhaps precisely in) the instability of its legacy, however, the trajectory of conservative modernism must be understood as fundamental to the Turkish experience of modernism in the first half of the twentieth century. The works of these writers, one might say, shelter the displaced specters of the past, opening the possibility of a revolutionary "past-future" despite, and against, their own agendas.[35] This legacy substantially complicates our conventional understanding of the relation between modernism and traditionalism as a relation of aesthetic renovation to sedimented or raw social inertia, recasting "tradition" not as modernism's invention, but as a resilient social practice *surviving* within it. As such, it is a legacy of active interrogation of the very normativity of Europe as the source and exemplar of modernization, opening a critical space within which the question of comparability with Europe is not a question of aesthetic mimicry and derivation (or simple deviation), but a question about the character and value of European modernity itself.[36]

A crucial figure to consider in this context is the novelist, poet, and critic Ahmet Hamdi Tanpınar, an admirer of Valéry and Mallarmé who made pilgrimages to Valéry's address in Paris and Mallarmé's house in Valvins.[37] Tanpınar's writings, including the encyclopedic *XIX. Asır Türk Edebiyatı Tarihi* (1942, rev. 2nd ed. 1956; "History of Nineteenth-Century Turkish Literature"), the novel *Huzur* (1949; *A Mind at Peace*, trans. 2008), and the essay collection *Beş Şehir* (1946; "Five Cities"), aim to overcome the cultural "duality" engendered by what Tanpınar diagnoses as a Turkish "change of civilization" from "East" to "West."[38] In *Yahya Kemal,* a critical monograph about his teacher, Tanpınar relates Kemal's recommendation that Tanpınar instead entitle *XIX. Asır Türk Edebiyatı Tarihi* "The Literature of the Renewal Period" ("Yenilenme Devri Edebiyatımız"), in order to emphasize a temporal dynamic of continuous development and to avoid implying an historical "break" (*Yahya Kemal* 144). Though Tanpınar rejected Kemal's advice, the task of restoring historical continuity remained as urgent for Tanpınar as it was for his mentor.

Tanpınar writes that "The thought of '*historicité*' [. . .] necessary for individual and for national life [*millî hayat*] nourishes us across the centuries like the roots of a tree. . . ." (23).

As Nurdan Gürbilek has noted, the complexity and the irony of Tanpınar's literary perspective lies in his melancholic concession to the *impossibility* of ever fully resurrecting the past.[39] The Tanpınar of *Beş Şehir*, wandering the neighborhoods of old Istanbul, concedes that "In essence, we do not like the things of the past in themselves [. . .] We look in them for a part of ourselves that we think is lost in the internal struggle [*didişme*] of the present" (Tanpınar 215). Tanpınar's well-known poem "Bursa'da Zaman" ("Time in Bursa") registers the ambiguities and the contradictions of a ghostly temporality, preserving an idealized past in a fallen language that is never fully present to itself:

> The courtyard of an old Bursa mosque
> The water splashing [*şakırdiyen*] in a small fountain [*şadırvan*]
> A wall left from Orhan's time . . .
> An old plane tree of the same age
> Expansively sifting a calm day
> Smiling at me, from within
> The melancholy [*hüzün*] of the remnants of a dream. (50)[40]

Tanpınar's most important and still understudied final novel, *Saatleri Ayarlama Enstitüsü*, recently translated into English (as *The Time Regulation Institute*) by Ender Gürol, awaits comparative reading alongside *Mrs. Dalloway* and *À la recherche du temps perdu*. A brilliant critique of Republican social engineering, Tanpınar's comic novel describes the creation of a (fictional) "clock-setting institute" intended to synchronize all public and private clocks both within Turkey and in the outside world. Marking a shift in mood and tone from the allegorical language of Tanpınar's earlier work, the novel's sophisticated ironies interrogate a modernity whose self-forgetful automatized subjects are caught in the repetition of a perpetual present.[41]

The critical writings of Ismayil Hakkı Baltacıoğlu comprise another crossroad in Turkish cultural history. A calligrapher and playwright as well as a professor of pedagogy, Baltacıoğlu was dismissed from the Darülfünun (University) with the Kemalist modernizing university reform of 1933, which replaced the existing teaching cadres with German and Austrian Jewish émigrés.[42] The longest-running weekly journal of Turkish Republican history, *Yeni Adam* ("New Man"), which Baltacıoğlu founded in 1934 and edited until his death in 1978, offered a multifaceted critical platform.[43] An attentive reader of Bergson and Durkheim, Baltacıoğlu located the source of nationhood in tradition (*anane*, or, in his later writings, *gelenek*), rather than in racial, religious, or linguistic unity ("Milli Anane" ["National Tradition"] 2).[44] "The nation," he wrote, "is a being with an interiority constituted of individuals sharing the unity of tradition" (Baltacıoğlu, *Türk Plâstik Sanatları* [1971; "Turkish Plastic Arts"] 16). Tradition, which Baltacıoğlu distinguished from customs (*örf*) changeable in time, was an essential and unchanging core comprised of myths, tales, melodies, and folk knowledge, serving to "connect yesterday with today and today with the future" (*Türke Doğru* 135).

In his writings, Baltacıoğlu created a kind of collision between the national traditional arts of Turkey and the aesthetic practices of the European avant-garde, chiefly cubism and surrealism. In his essays "Mimarîde Kübizm ve Türk An'anesi" (1929; "Cubism in Architecture and the Turkish Tradition") and "Resimde Kübizm ve Türk An'anesi" (1931; "Cubism in Art and the Turkish Tradition"), as well as in his critical study *Demokrasi ve San'at* (1931; "Democracy and Art"), Baltacıoğlu interpreted cubism as the paradigmatic art of modern civilization, assimilating the dynamic creativity of the Turkish revolution to a "Cubist spirit."[45] In later writings, such as *Sanat* (1934; "Art"), *Türklerde Yazı Sanatı* (1958; "Turkish Script Arts"), and *Türk Plâstik Sanatları* (1971; "Turkish Plastic Arts"), meanwhile, Baltacıoğlu identified a homology between surrealist painting and both Turkish Islamic calligraphy and the Karagöz shadow theater. Lacking any "realist and naturalist obsessions," he writes in *Türk Plâstik Sanatları*, "the Karagöz models (*sûret*) are surrealist figures" (134). Contrasting Turkish Islamic writing with the geometrical abstraction of Latin letters, on one hand, and with mimetic pictography, on the other, Baltacıoğlu revalues Turkish Islamic letters as nonfigurative, surrealistic representations of the human body in athletic poses (*Türklerde* 25–27).[46] In these latter works, Baltacıoğlu can be seen shifting his emphasis to the *critique* of modernity's rationalizing processes. The "surreality" of traditional Turkish arts, for Baltacıoğlu, registers the ambiguities of modernity's disenchanting and re-enchanting processes, pointing to practices of "seeing" other than modernity's abstract visualization of the world.[47]

Like Tanpınar and Baltacıoğlu, the poet, novelist, playwright, and critic Necip Fazıl Kısakürek (1904–1983), who would emerge as the most important Islamist critic of the early twentieth century, takes the critical tradition of the "other West" as his point of departure. Such memorable early poems as "Kaldırımlar" (1927; "Sidewalks"), "Otel Odaları" (1927; "Hotel Rooms"), and "Bacalar" (1930; "Chimneys"), composed after Kısakürek's return from France, are clearly in dialogue with Baudelaire's thematization of modernizing urban space and its alienating effects.[48] Though Kısakürek disowned some of his early work around 1934 after turning to Islamism under the influence of a Nakshibendi sheikh, Abülhâkim Arvasi, these poems remain an important body of work, exemplary of what might be characterized as a poetics of spectralization. The striking images of "bone-fingers" in "Gece Yarısı" (1925; "Midnight"), "genies" in "Bacalar," and "ghosts in the walls" in "Boş Odalar" (1925; "Empty Rooms"), dispersed through a generic cityscape of sidewalks, chimneys, and empty rooms, are registers, both in content and in form, for what Şerif Mardin has called "the shattering of the 'everyday' world of the Ottoman intellectual" (74).[49] In a 1955 essay that may be considered Kısakürek's critical manifesto, "Poetika" ("Poetics"), he linked this disintegration to spiritual aspiration, declaring that "Form and versification are the skeletons of meaning. The poetic project is to learn from the knowledge (*hikmet*) of God, who clothes our skeletons infinitely beautifully with His eternal art, and to put on the skeletons of meaning a face and a body within the limits He sets" (481).[50] Though the "Islamic metropolis" (*İslam metropolisi*) that Kısakürek imagines in the political treatise *İdeolocya Örgüsü* (1968; 2nd ed. 1973; "The Web of Ideologia") contrasts positively with "the fear and the heaviness of the infernal nineteenth-century European city described by the poet Baudelaire" (242), poetry for Kısakürek remains a finally and fatally ghostly medium: "[Poetry] searches after the absolute truth like a thief [. . .] Like darkness, it permeates through the translucent windows; it rides on the elevator of smoke only to travel down through the chimneys; when it inhales, it does not fit the doors; yet when it exhales, it passes through the keyholes" ("Poetika" 474).

The importance of figures of the "other West" may also be detected in Kısakürek's other writings. *İdeolocya Örgüsü* outlines an "anticipated [Islamic] revolution" linked to the "crisis of the West" announced by Nietzsche, Baudelaire, and Rimbaud ("the poets of epilepsy and agitation") and Heidegger (49–50). In his autobiography, *O ve Ben* (1965; "He and I"), meanwhile, Kısakürek frames the narrative of his transformative encounter with the sheikh Arvasi with two lines in French that he attributes to Rimbaud: "Honneur, au voyant supérieur; / Au supérieur voyant, honneur!" (83).[51] Interpolated in French into Kısakürek's Turkish, immediately preceding the narrative of Kısakürek's transformative meeting with the sheikh, these lines may be seen to signal something of Kısakürek's (temporary) indecision about giving up his life as a modernist bohemian. That Kısakürek's religious "conversion" is to be understood (or explained), here, by recourse to what are presented as slogans of French modernism means that we cannot take the conversion in conventional terms, as an abrupt switch from the values and self-understanding of "the West" to a distinctively local and traditionalist "Islam." Such a textual device (and moment) rather makes of the Rimbauldian figure of the *voyant* a medium (and a code) *through which* Kısakürek accepts the sheikh's guidance. Following the appearance of these lines of French in the text, Kısakürek translates the phrase "supérieur voyant" into Turkish as "üstün haberci" ("superior messenger"), using the translated phrase to describe the sheikh himself (84). In this translation, which is nothing less than a transposition, Kısakürek distinguishes the Rimbaudian *voyant,* who sees "through" the transcendent, from the Islamic "messenger," who can only know of divine reality what God permits him to know (83). This distinction should not prevent us from seeing that the "source" for translation, here ("two lines from Rimbaud"), is not the rejected "other," but the very enabler and mediator of Kısakürek's own Islamization. Kısakürek's modernism is not a mode confined to his earliest work, as conventional literary historiography has often suggested, but is rather constitutive of, and continuous into, his Islamist phase.

Kısakürek's writings can profitably be read comparatively alongside those of other modernist Islamists from the wider Middle East and South Asia. The Islamic world of the late nineteenth century saw the emergence of a number of reform movements seeking to return to the core teachings of the religion (the Qur'an and the sunnah) for the purpose of social regeneration and liberation from colonial rule.[52] Revival of a "true" religion had been a goal of premodern Islamic reform movements, as well, whose emergence can be regarded as independent of "any foreign influence in their genesis" (Rahman 641). Modern reformism is distinctive, however, in its attempt to reconcile the influence of European values and institutions with traditional Islamic social practices at a time when the abstract and privatized category of "religion" (very much a European construction) was being generalized to specific socio-cultural practices and modes of conduct epistemically distinct from those of Europe.[53]

The works of the poet, critic, and statesman Muhammad Iqbal (1877–1938), marking a crossroads of modernism and Islamism, are especially illuminating in this context. Regarded as the national poet of Pakistan, Iqbal is perhaps best known for his presidential address to the All-India Muslim League in December 1930, criticizing Western territorial nationalism for its denial of the spirituality of human life and its separation of the sacred from the profane.[54] The importance for Iqbal of Nietzsche, who enjoys a station at the border of the Garden of Paradise in Iqbal's masterwork, the prose poem (masnavi) *Javidnama* (1932), has been frequently observed. Neither inside nor outside the Garden of Paradise, "the German genius whose place is between these two worlds" lacks knowledge of God, but in seeking to transcend reason and philosophy brings himself to the verge of being a "perfect man" (*Mard-e Momin*), one who, in Iqbal's conception, dynamically outdoes himself in quest of God.

To be sure, Kısakürek would have distanced himself from Iqbal's reformism. In fact, Kısakürek parts ways with most modernist Islamists, such as Sayyed Jamal al-Din al-Afghani (1838–1897) of Iran and Muhammad Abduh (1849–1905) of Egypt, as well as with Iqbal, in his critique of reformism as an antagonist of religion. For Kısakürek, it is not Islam that must (or that can) be renewed ("The sun cannot be renewed. The eye can be renewed"); it is the self instead that must be reformed (*İdeolocya Örgüsü* 565). In contrast with the transnationalism of Afghani, Abduh, and Iqbal, furthermore, Kısakürek imagines his project of the "Great East" (*Büyük Doğu*) within national borders: where Iqbal addresses the "Turk, Persian, Arab intoxicated with Europe" (*Javidnama*, line 1029), exhorting them to "give up this talk of Syria, Palestine, Iraq" (line 1036), Kısakürek regards Turkey as absolutely central, reasoning that "Turkey is where Islam lost its power, and it is only after its resurgence there that it can regain its global power" (*İdeolocya Örgüsü* 567).

The trajectory of Turkish conservative modernism and modernist Islam extends into the second half of the twentieth century, in a different political climate, of which the poetry of Sezai Karakoç (b. 1933), Hilmi Yavuz (b. 1936), and İsmet Özel (b. 1944) may be offered as three important examples. Critical of approaches that aimed to synthesize Western technique and Islamic civilizational values, Özel's exploration of modern subjectivity in a contemporary poetic idiom suffused with Islamic cultural references constitutes an alternative Turkish literary voice at a time of intensified incorporation into the global capitalist economy.[55] In Yavuz's poetic lexicon, meanwhile, tropes from the divan poetry of the past appear along with allusions to and quotations from Mallarmé, Baudelaire, and Yahya Kemal, only to register their ghostly materiality as signs and to mark a perpetual exile in language. Karakoç's writings, meanwhile, are central to the importance of the group of poets known as the "Second New." One may argue that if conservative modernism is the most important trajectory of modernist thought in Turkey during the first half of the twentieth century, the neo-Surrealist poetry of the Second New comprises the most important modernist experiment of the century's second half.[56] Including Karakoç along with Melih Cevdet Anday, Ece Ayhan, İlhan Berk, Edip Cansever, and Cemal Süreya, among others, the Second New had emerged by the late 1950s, defined by an experimental approach to poetic language that resisted the social-realist tendencies of the period, including that of the First New poets known for their portraits of ordinary men described in everyday language. Ece Ayhan's "civil poetry" (*sivil şiir*) is especially distinctive when read against the historical backdrop of the three military coups of 1960, 1971, and 1980, distinguished by a radically new language incorporating the heterogeneous "street" idioms of harassed prostitutes, molested children, and marginalized Jewish and Christian minorities.

If the close study of Turkish Republican conservative modernism thus registers the violent contradictions of the "worlding" of modernism, it also demonstrates that what is called the "traditional" is often an effect of the translative incorporation of the foreign. The "homecoming" of the Turkish Republican conservative modernist "through the Frank"[57] is neither an absolute break with some understanding of the world abroad, nor a retreat into a sovereign inner spiritual domain (family, culture, religion) as bulwark against the overwhelming material superiority of an externalized "West."[58] The dynamic of Turkish conservative modernism is that of a "traditional" spiritual interior which emerges in conjunction with, and as a mutually produced effect of, seductive engagement with the spiritualist-modernist text of the European "foreign." *Despite* and often *against* themselves, Turkish Republican conservatives did openly register the uncanniness of their own "deterritorialization" in this dynamic, rather than merely suppressing or effacing its discomfort, or normalizing it after the fact as a successful "synthesis."[59] These writers can serve as models for genuine critical intervention in the field of global modernist studies—critical intervention, that is to say, capable of generating genuinely alternative comparative histories—precisely because of such interstices, which make manifest the limits of the cultural domain in which they worked. Tanpınar's figuration of just such an uncanny world, evading all our critical abstractions and appropriations, seems an appropriate one with which to close (and to begin again):

> Which of us has not imagined the world wending its way in the universe, loaded with the sufferings, hopes, and joy of all those who are living that strange, magnificent fortune called the human fortune, and not heard its loud cries . . .? I could never forget the dream I had because of a teacher who was especially passionate about cosmography and who first introduced me to the roundness of the world at the Sinop Middle School (*Rüşdiye*). I carried in my arms all night long a globe that emitted smoke, changed colors, and ran with me. (*Yahya Kemal* 130)

NOTES

1. Unless otherwise noted, translations from Turkish into English are my own.

2. On *décalage,* see Edwards: "either a difference or gap in time (advancing or delaying a schedule) *or* in space (shifting or displacing an object)" (13).

3. I will return to Nâzım's poetry later in this essay. One of the most frequently translated Turkish writers of the twentieth century, Nâzım is well known for his revolutionary futurist poems. Well-executed English translations have been collected in the volumes *Beyond the Walls* and *Poems of Nazım Hikmet.*

4. On the inadequacy, in themselves, of gestures of exposing "error," see de Man, "Semiology and Rhetoric" (16). Apropos of de Man's own practice, see Spivak: "de Man has shown how the discovery that something that claims to be true is a mere trope is the first (tropological) step in what de Man called deconstruction. The second (performative) step is to disclose how the corrective impulse within the tropological analysis is obliged to act out a lie in attempting to establish it as the corrected version of truth" (18–19).

5. These dates demarcating the Republican period follow the conventions of modern Turkish historiography. The dates demarcating the late imperial period are my own and are necessary in order to distinguish clearly the first period of Turkish engagement with European literary modernism. Neither an individual national nor a pan-European literary periodization can represent by itself the specific history of modern Turkish literature. (In conventional Turkish historiography, the period between 1878 and 1908 marks the absolutist reign of Sultan Abdülhamid II; 1908–1918 demarcates the period of "Young Turk" rule; and 1919–1922 marks the "War of Independence" fought against the Allied occupation in the aftermath of World War I.)

6. İrem's "Undercurrents of European Modernity and the Foundations of Modern Turkish Conservatism" is a valuable source of historical context on the Turkish Republican conservatives "deeply inspired by European spiritualist, mysticist, and romanticist philosophies, as well as Bergsonism" (81), and an important contribution to Turkish intellectual history, which has otherwise largely confined itself to the study of positivist architects of the Turkish Republican revolution. Where İrem focuses mainly on conservative interpretations of the Republican revolution, I have addressed the relation between Turkish conservatism and aesthetic modernism in the present essay.

7. Martin Heidegger's 1938 essay "Die Zeit des Weltbildes" ("The Age of the World-Picture," or "The Time of the World-Image") can be taken as a supporting text for this passage.

8. See Zürcher, *Turkey,* for a detailed historical account of modern Turkey that begins with the late eighteenth century.

9. For example, a translation of *Télémaque* appeared in 1862, of *Robinson Crusoe* (from an Arabic translation) in 1864, and of *Le comte de Monte-Cristo* in 1871.

10. For more historical context, see Evin.

11. For a seminal reading of Ekrem's novel as manifestation of the epistemological crisis of the Ottoman intellectual, see Parla 105–24.

12. "Symbolism," here, means simply "the use of language as a means to rediscover the unity of all being that exists in the realm of the imagination and of the spirit" (de Man, "The Double Aspect" 8). On the "asynchronous development of modernist poetry and prose," see the "Turkey" section of Bahun's contribution to this volume.

13. Although Kemal did not complete his degree, the views of his teacher Albert Sorel significantly shaped the formation of his nationalist thinking (Beyatlı, *Edebiyata Dair* 257).

14. On Kemal's homecoming, see Tanpınar, *Yahya Kemal* 46. A more recent critical study of Kemal is Ayvazoğlu, *Yahya Kemal: Eve Dönen Adam* ("Yahya Kemal: The Man Who Returned Home").

15. Kahraman admits that *Yahya Kemal Rimbaud'yu Okudu mu?* was written in response to critic Enis Batur's *Yazının Ucu* ("The Edge of Writing" 1993), which claimed that "[Yahya Kemal] was not, or perhaps could not be, modern [*modern*]. He could have at least made an effort to be contemporary, our contemporary [*çağdaş*]: Then he would have noticed Apollinaire, Picasso, Lorca, and Witkiewicz, or at least, Nâzım, Orhan Veli, Sait Faik, and most importantly Tanpınar by his side" (48–49, quoted in Kahraman 104).

16. For Kemal's definition of *derûnî âhenk* and its relation to Mallarmé's "absolute poetry," as well as Paul Valéry's and the Abbé Brémond's "pure poetry," see Beyatlı, "Şiir Okumaya Dâir" ("On Reading Poetry") and "Derûnî Âhenk ve Öz Şiir" ("Inner Harmony and Pure Poetry").

17. For a more detailed discussion of linguistic mechanization as an effect of changes in writing practices in Turkey, see my *Grammatology and Literary Modernity in Turkey*.

18. There is disagreement regarding Haşim's birth date (some claim he was born in 1884).

19. For more on Bergsonism in Turkey, see İrem.

20. Burke's *Reflections on the Revolution in France* (1790) is a founding text of European conservatism.

21. A 1924 photomontage by the Polish Jewish designer and painter Mieczysław Szczuka (1898–1927), entitled "Kemal Pasha: Kemal's Constructive Program," figures the Kemalist revolution as a kind of constructivist dream.

22. On the Kemalist reforms, see Zürcher, *Turkey* 166–205.

23. See Ergin 254, quoted in Ayvazoğlu, "Türk" 509. For an analysis of Turkey's "missing archives," see Ahıska.

24. The term "Kemalist," here and throughout this essay, refers to the activities and the legacy of Mustafa Kemal Atatürk, the founder of the Turkish Republic.

25. Needless to say, there are some crucial differences between the positions of these writers. The Islamism of Necip Fazıl Kısakürek, for example, places him at some remove from the others. These distinctions are clarified later on, within the present essay. One crucial figure of Republican conservative modernism whom I do not discuss here is the prominent journalist, novelist, and critic Peyami Safa (1899–1961). One chapter of my book *Grammatology and Literary Modernity in Turkey* is devoted to a discussion of Safa's 1949 novel *Matmazel Noraliya'nın Koltuğu* ("Mademoiselle Noralia's Armchair") in its relation to the work of Rimbaud and Aldous Huxley.

26. Chronologically speaking, the first of these movements was the Osmanlı Ressamlar Cemiyeti (Society of Ottoman Painters), founded in 1908; the second, the Yeni Resim Cemiyeti (Society of New Art), founded in 1923; the third, the Müstakil Ressamlar ve Heykeltraşlar Birliği (Society of Independent Painters and Sculptors), founded in 1929.

27. The "d Group" was founded in 1933 by the painters Nurullah Berk (1906–1982), Cemal Tollu (1899–1968), Zeki Faik İzer (1905–1988), Elif Naci (1898–1987), and Abidin Dino (1913–1993) and the sculptor Zühtü Müridoğlu (1906–1992), among others. For more information, see Elvan, ed.

28. See also Ayvazoğlu, "Halil Dikmen" 67–87.

29. See Köksal, "Art and Power" 103–04. This absorption of the "d Group" did not mean, however, that the state had gained complete control over cultural production in Turkey, nor that it desired to; Duygu Köksal has suggested perceptively that while the Republican elite "cared about culture and the arts to the extent that they could be

used . . . for general political purposes . . . [they] did not, however, go as far as the 'aestheticization of politics' in the manner of the Italian, German and Soviet totalitarian models" (93).

30. "Slap in the Face of Public Taste" (*Poshchechina obshchestvennomu vkusu*) was the title of the 1912 manifesto of the Russian Futurists David Burliuk, Aleksei Kruchenykh, Velimir Khlebnikov, and Vladimir Mayakovsky (Lawton 51). Nâzım first arrived in the USSR in September 1921, by which time the futurists had split into Kruchenykh's Company 41°, practicing the poetics of "transrational language," and Mayakovsky's pro-Revolution Left Front of the Arts (LEF), the primary representatives of proletarian literature (Lawton 40). Nâzım was especially influenced by Mayakovsky's poetics of *ostranenie* or estrangement. On Russian futurism, see Ram, in the present volume.

31. The anti-traditionalist, playful poetry of the First New, including the trio of Orhan Veli Kanık (1914–1950), Oktay Rifat (1914–1988), and Melih Cevdet Anday (1915–2002), is considered a third important wave of Turkish poetry, following the work of Yahya Kemal and Nâzım. Also known as the "Garip" (Strange), the First New sought to free poetic diction by writing in casual, everyday language, describing the dreams and wishes of ordinary people. See Orhan Veli's preface to the 1941 publication of the group's first book of poems, *Garip*, for an articulation of the First New's understanding of their own relation (or lack thereof) to surrealism. Murat Nemet-Nejat and Talat Sait Halman have produced collections of English translations of Veli's poems, respectively entitled *I, Orhan Veli* and *Just for the Hell of It: 111 Poems*. The work of the Second New, a group of poets including Ece Ayhan (1931–2002), Cemal Süreya (1931–1990), and İlhan Berk (1918–2008), among others, who appeared on the Turkish literary scene in the late 1950s, will be discussed later in this essay.

32. Important early historical and critical texts on the Russian avant-garde in English include Gray (1962), Markov (1968), and Bowlt (1976).

33. On the varieties of Turkish conservatism, see Bora.

34. İrem observes that "[u]nlike their traditionalist counterparts in European politics such as *Action Française*, which was essentially a monarchist movement, Turkish conservatives put Bergsonism into the service of the republican thought [. . .] for transforming the Turkish Revolution into a spiritual-cultural one" (100).

35. On the "past-future," see Derrida 1–60. The past, in this sense, is not a fixed and unchanging resource unproblematically available to us; but neither does it vanish without a trace. Rather, the present is "haunted" irreducibly by the past in its heterogeneity, and the possibility of a new future lies in sifting its inheritance.

36. For an elaboration of this point, see my "Modernity and Its Fallen Languages."

37. Tanpınar narrates these pilgrimages in a 1958 article entitled "Paris Tesadüfleri II" ("Paris Coincidences II").

38. See Tanpınar's 1951 article "Medeniyet Değiştirmesi ve İç İnsan" ("Change of Civilization and the Inner Man").

39. See Gürbilek, "Tanpınar'da Görünmeyen" ("The Invisible in Tanpınar"). For a more developed version of this argument, see also her "Kurumuş Pınar, Kör Ayna, Kayıp Şark" ("The Dried Spring, the Blind Mirror, the Lost Orient").

40. For an earlier and slightly different version of this poem, see *Beş Şehir* 105–06. The version cited here is from Tanpınar's *Bütün Şiirleri* (2007; "Complete Poems"), which includes a reprint of the 1961 collection *Şiirler* ("Poems") with this revised version of "Bursa'da Zaman."

41. For a discussion of irony in *The Time Regulation Institute*, see Oğuzertem.

42. For a resource published in English on the 1933 University Reform, see Reisman. The University Reform did not confine itself merely to raising the research and teaching standards in place at Istanbul University; it also led to the elimination of faculty who either overtly or covertly opposed the Kemalist agenda.

43. On *Yeni Adam*, see Köksal, "The Role of Art."

44. The importance of Bergson to Baltacıoğlu is made succinctly clear in the two newspaper articles he authored entitled "Bergson" and "Henri Bergson" (cited in İrem).

45. In these works, Baltacıoğlu sought to break ties with the dead past and to develop a contemporary cubist art. Baltacıoğlu interprets the anti-naturalism of cubist form as an expression of the very depth of modern subjectivity, rather than (as in cubism's European self-understanding) as an asubjectivist dissection and reassembling of objects. This is characteristic of Baltacıoğlu, who regarded modernity, embodied in cubist form, as irreducible to mere technological development—as "the unification of machine and love (*gönül*)" (*Demokrasi* 7).

46. Baltacıoğlu refers to the Ottoman alphabet as "Turkish Islamic" in order to identify a Turkish writing free of Arab and Persian graphic influence.

47. A more detailed discussion of Baltacıoğlu's relation to surrealism, set in the context of comparative modernist studies, can be found in my essay "Surrealism and Turkish Script Arts."

48. English translations of some of Kısakürek's poems may be found in *Eda: An Anthology of Turkish Poetry* 50–54.

49. For a useful overview of Kısakürek's poetry and political thought, see also Özdenören, "Necip Fazıl Kısakürek."

50. Parts of "Poetika" were initially published as aphoristic essays in journals. The complete text in its final form appeared in Kısakürek's 1955 poetry collection *Sonsuzluk Kervanı* ("The Caravan of Eternity").

51. Kısakürek writes, "Dilimizde (Rembo) dan iki mısra: 'Honneur, au voyant supérieur; / Au supérieur voyant, honneur!'" ("On the tip of our tongue, two lines from Rimbaud: 'Honneur, au voyant supérieur; / Au supérieur voyant, honneur!'"). These phrases are not to be found in Rimbaud's 1871 "letters of the visionary" to Paul Demeny and Georges Izambard (or anywhere else in Rimbaud's body of work). We may surmise that Kısakürek is quoting (inaccurately) from memory. My thanks to Jonathan Eburne, Mark Wollaeger, and Marc Froment-Meurice for their help with my attempt to trace its source.

52. For a brief introduction to reformist Islam, see Commins. For English translations of a range of foundational texts from across the Muslim world, see Kurzman, ed.

53. On the emergence of an abstract, privatized "religion" as a European construct, see Asad.

54. For a discussion of the question of nationalism in Iqbal, see Jalal.

55. For Özel's early articulation of his political position, see his *Üç Mesele: Teknik, Medeniyet, Yabancılaşma* (1978; "Three Issues: Technics, Civilization, Alienation").

56. Commentary on the Second New available in English includes Koçak, and Nemet-Nejat, "Contemporary Turkish Poetry." For translations of work by Second New poets, see Nemet-Nejat, *Eda*, and Halman.

57. See Eyüboğlu, "Yeni Türk San'atkârı yahut Frenkten Türke Dönüş" ("The New Turkish Artist or the Return from the Frank to the Turk").

58. On the emergence of Asian and African nationalisms through the demarcation of sovereign "inner" cultural domains against the (accepted) material superiority of the Western "outside," see Chatterjee. The founding text of modern Turkish nationalism, Ziya Gökalp's *Türkçülüğün Esasları* (1923; *Principles of Turkism*, trans. 1968), describes a

homologous fault line separating an "inner" national cultural from an "outer" universal material domain in the Turkish context. I thank Özge Serin for her illuminating thoughts on the topic of Turkish nationalism.

59. To be sure, the conservative modernist practice of Kemal's and others' "return to the self through the Frank" may be taken as yet another instantiation of the Occidentalist social imaginary that Ahıska describes as the integration of "how the non-Western imagines [. . .] the West sees itself" into "reflection on its own identity" (365). One should not, however, discount the ways in which Republican conservative modernism also undoes this "Occidentalist" discourse, often despite and against itself.

WORKS CITED

Ahıska, Meltem. "Occidentalism and Registers of Truth: The Politics of Archives in Turkey." *New Perspectives on Turkey* 34 (2006): 9–29.

Asad, Talal. "The Construction of Religion as an Anthropological Category." *Genealogies of Religion: Discipline and Reasons of Power in Christianity and Islam*. Baltimore: Johns Hopkins University Press, 1993. 27–54.

Ayvazoğlu, Beşir. "Halil Dikmen." *Ney'in Sırrı Hâlâ Hasret*. Istanbul: Kubbealtı Neşriyat, 2002.

———. "Türk Muhafazakârlığının Kültürel Kuruluşu." Çiğdem, ed. 509–32.

———. *Yahya Kemal: Eve Dönen Adam*. Ankara: Birlik Yayınları, 1985.

Baltacıoğlu, Ismayil Hakkı. "Bergson." *Yeni Adam* 4 (January 22, 1934): 5.

———. *Demokrasi ve San'at*. Istanbul: Sanayii Nefise Matbaası, 1931.

———. "Henri Bergson." *Yeni Adam* 433 (April 15, 1943): 3–11.

———. "Milli Anane." *Yeni Adam* 366 (January 1, 1942): 2.

———. "Mimarîde Kübizm ve Türk An'anesi." *Darülfünun İlahiyat Fakültesi Mecmuası* 3.11 (April 1929): 110–31.

———. "Resimde Kübizm ve Türk An'anesi." *Darülfünun İlahiyat Fakültesi Mecmuası* 5.19 (March 1931): 33–48.

———. *Sanat*. Istanbul: Semih Lûtfi, 1934.

———. *Türk Plâstik Sanatları*. Ankara: Milli Eğitim Basımevi, 1971

———. *Türke Doğru*. Vol. 2. Istanbul: Yeni Adam Yayınları, 1943.

———. *Türklerde Yazı Sanatı*. Ankara: Mars T. ve S.A.S. Matbaası, 1958.

Batur, Enis. *Yazının Ucu*. Istanbul: Yapı Kredi Yayınları, 1993.

Beyatlı, Yahya Kemal. *Çocukluğum, Gençliğim, Siyâsî ve Edebî Hatıralarım*. Ed. Yahya Kemal Enstitüsü. Istanbul: Fetih Cemiyeti, 1999.

———. "Derûnî Âhenk ve Öz Şiir." Beyatlı, *Edebiyata Dair*: 20–21.

———. *Edebiyata Dair*. Ed. Yahya Kemal Enstitüsü. Istanbul: Fetih Cemiyeti, 1997.

———. "Şiir Okumaya Dâir." Beyatlı, *Edebiyata Dair*: 3–10.

Bora, Tanıl. "Muhafazakârlığın Değişimi ve Türk Muhafazakârlığında Bazı Yol İzleri." *Toplum ve Bilim* 74 (1997): 6–31.

Bowlt, John, ed. and trans. *Russian Art of the Avant-Garde: Theory and Criticism, 1902–1934*. New York: Viking Press, 1976.

Bozdoğan, Sibel. *Modernism and Nation Building: Turkish Architectural Culture in the Early Republic*. Seattle: University of Washington Press, 2001.

Burke, Edmund. *Reflections on the Revolution in France*. Ed. J. G. A. Pocock. Indianapolis: Hackett, 1987.

Chatterjee, Partha. *The Nation and Its Fragments: Colonial and Postcolonial Histories.*
    Princeton: Princeton University Press, 1993.

Çiğdem, Ahmet, ed. *Modern Türkiye'de Siyasî Düşünce 5: Muhafazakârlık.* Istanbul:
    İletişim, 2003."

Commins, David. "Modernism." *The Oxford Encyclopedia of the Modern Islamic World.*
    Vol. 3. Ed. John L. Esposito. New York: Oxford University Press, 1995. 118–23.

Comte, Auguste. "Reşit Paşa'ya Mektup." *İslâmiyet ve Positivism.* Ed. Christian Cherfils.
    Trans. Özkan Gözel. Istanbul: Dergâh, 2008. 23–27.

De Man, Paul. "The Double Aspect of Symbolism." *Yale French Studies* 74 (1988): 3–16.

———. "Semiology and Rhetoric." *Allegories of Reading: Figural Language in Rousseau,
    Nietzsche, Rilke, and Proust.* New Haven: Yale University Press, 1979. 3–19.

Derrida, Jacques. *Specters of Marx: The State of the Debt, the Work of Mourning, and the
    New International.* Trans. Peggy Kamuf. New York: Routledge, 1994.

Edwards, Brent Hayes. *The Practice of Diaspora: Literature, Translation, and the Rise of
    Black Internationalism.* Cambridge: Harvard University Press, 2003.

Elvan, Nihal, ed. *d Grubu = d Group, 1933–1951.* Istanbul: Yapı Kredi Yayınları, 2002.

Ergin, Osman. *Muallim M. Cevdet'in Hayatı, Eserleri ve Kütüphanesi.* Istanbul: Bozkurt
    Basımevi, 1937.

Ertürk, Nergis. *Grammatology and Literary Modernity in Turkey.* New York: Oxford
    University Press, 2011.

———. "Modernity and Its Fallen Languages: Tanpınar's *Hasret*, Benjamin's Melancholy."
    PMLA 123.1 (2008): 41–56.

———. "Surrealism and Turkish Script Arts." *Modernism/modernity* 17.1 (2010): 47–60.

Evin, Ahmet Ömür. *Origins and Development of the Turkish Novel.* Minneapolis:
    Bibliotheca Islamica, 1983.

Eyüboğlu, Sabahattin. "Yeni Türk San'atkârı yahut Frenkten Türke Dönüş." *İnsan* (April 15,
    1938): 31–38.

Foucault, Michel. *Les mots et les choses: une archéologie des sciences humaines.* Paris:
    Gallimard, 1966.

———. *The Order of Things: An Archaeology of the Human Sciences.* New York: Vintage
    Books, 1994.

Gökalp, Ziya. *Türkçülüğün Esasları.* Ankara: Elips, 2006.

Gray, Camilla, *The Great Experiment: Russian Art, 1863–1922.* London: Thames and
    Hudson, 1962.

Gürbilek, Nurdan. "Kurumuş Pınar, Kör Ayna, Kayıp Şark." *Kör Ayna, Kayıp Şark.* Istanbul:
    Metis, 2004. 97–138.

———. "Tanpınar'da Görünmeyen." *Yer Değiştiren Gölge: Denemeler.* Istanbul: Metis,
    1995. 11–23.

Halman, Talat S., ed. and trans. *A Brave New Quest: 100 Modern Turkish Poems.* Syracuse:
    Syracuse University Press, 2006.

Heidegger, Martin. "The Age of the World Picture." *The Question Concerning
    Technology and Other Essays.* Trans. William Lovitt. New York: Harper & Row,
    1977. 115–54.

———. "Die Zeit des Weltbildes." *Holzwege.* Frankfurt: V. Klostermann, 1950. 75–113.

Iqbal, Muhammad. *Javidnama.* Trans. Arthur J. Arberry. *Iqbal—Poet-Philosopher of
    Pakistan.* Iqbal Academy Pakistan. 6 July 2008. http://www.allamaiqbal.com.

İrem, Nazım. "Undercurrents of European Modernity and the Foundations of Modern
    Turkish Conservatism: Bergsonism in Retrospect." *Middle Eastern Studies* 40.4 (2004):
    79–112.

Jalal, Ayesha. "Religion as Difference, Religion as Faith: Paradoxes of Muslim Identity."
    Cosspak. The Council of Social Sciences, Pakistan (COSS). 10 May 2011. http://cosspak.
    org/monographs.php.
Kadir, Djelal. "To World, to Globalize—Comparative Literature's Crossroads." *Comparative
    Literature Studies* 41.1 (2004): 1–9.
Kahraman, Hasan Bülent. *Yahya Kemal Rimbaud'yu Okudu mu?* Istanbul: Yapı Kredi
    Yayınları, 1997.
Kanık, Orhan Veli. "Garip." *Şairin İşi: Yazılar, Öyküler, Konuşmalar*. Istanbul: Yapı Kredi
    Yayınları, 2001. 11–22.
———. *I, Orhan Veli*. Trans. Murat Nemet-Nejat. New York: Hanging Loose Press, 1989.
———. *Just for the Hell of It: 111 Poems*. Trans. Talat Sait Halman. Multilingual Yabancı Dil
    Yayınları 1997.
Kısakürek, Necip Fazıl. "Bacalar." Kısakürek, *Çile*: 162.
———. "Boş Odalar." *Çile*: 211.
———. *Çile*. 1962. Istanbul: Büyük Doğu Yayınları, 2007.
———. "Gece Yarısı." *Çile*: 212–13.
———. "Kaldırımlar." *Çile*: 156–60.
———. *İdeolocya Örgüsü*. 1968. Istanbul: Büyük Doğu Yayınları, 2007.
———. *O ve Ben*. 1965. Istanbul: Büyük Doğu Yayınları, 2007.
———. "Otel Odaları." *Çile*: 161.
———. "Poetika." *Çile*: 471–96.
Koçak, Orhan. "'Our Master, the Novice': On the Catastrophic Births of Modern Turkish
    Poetry." *Relocating the Fault Lines: Beyond the East-West Divide*. Ed. Sibel Irzik and
    Güven Güzeldere. Spec. issue of *South Atlantic Quarterly* 102.2/3 (2003): 567–98.
Köksal, Duygu. "Art and Power in Turkey: Culture, Aesthetics and Nationalism during the
    Single Party Era." *New Perspectives on Turkey* 31 (2004): 91–119.
———. "The Role of Art in Early Republican Modernization in Turkey." *La multiplication
    des images en pays d'Islam: de l'estampe à la télévision (17e-21e siècle)*. Ed. Bernard
    Heyberger and Silvia Naef. Würzburg: Ergon in Kommission, 2003. 209–27.
Kolocotroni, Vassiliki, Jane Goldman, and Olga Taxidou, eds. *Modernism: An Anthology of
    Sources and Documents*. Chicago: University of Chicago Press, 1998.
Kurzman, Charles, ed. *Modernist Islam, 1840–1940: A Sourcebook*. New York: Oxford
    University Press, 2002.
Lawton, Anna, ed. *Russian Futurism Through Its Manifestoes, 1912–1928*. Trans. and ed.
    Lawton and Herbert Eagle. Ithaca: Cornell University Press, 1988.
Mardin, Şerif. "Projects as Methodology: Some Thoughts on Modern Turkish Social
    Science." *Rethinking Modernity and National Identity in Turkey*. Ed. Sibel Bozdoğan
    and Reşat Kasaba. Seattle: University of Washington Press, 1997. 64–80.
Marinetti, F. T. "The Founding and Manifesto of Futurism 1909." *Futurist Manifestos*. Ed.
    Umbro Appollonio. Trans. Robert Brain, et al. New York: The Viking Press, 1973. 19–23.
———. "Le futurisme." *Le Figaro* (February 20, 1909).
Markov, Vladimir. *Russian Futurism: A History*. Berkeley: University of California Press, 1968.
Nemet-Nejat, Murat. "Contemporary Turkish Poetry." *Talisman: A Journal of
    Contemporary Poetry and Poetics* 14 (1995): 32–59.
———, ed. *Eda: An Anthology of Turkish Poetry*. Jersey City: Talisman House Publishers,
    2004.
Nicholls, Peter. *Modernisms: A Literary Guide*. Berkeley: University of California Press, 1995.
Oğuzertem, Süha. "Unset *Saat*s, Upset *Sıhhat*s: A Fatherless Approach to *The Clock-Setting
    Institute*." *The Turkish Studies Association Bulletin* 19.2 (1995): 3–18.

Özdenören, Rasim. "Necip Fazıl Kısakürek." *Modern Türkiye'de Siyasî Düşünce 6: İslâmcılık.* Ed. Yasin Aktay. Istanbul: İletişim, 2004. 136–49.

Özel, İsmet. *Üç Mesele: Teknik, Medeniyet, Yabancılaşma.* Istanbul: Düşünce Yayınları, 1978.

Özipek, Bekir Berat. "Muhafazakârlık, Devrim ve Türkiye." Çiğdem, ed. 66–84.

Pamuk, Orhan. "Ahmet Hamdi Tanpınar ve Türk Modernizmi." *Defter* 23 (1995): 31–45.

Parla, Jale. *Babalar ve Oğullar.* Istanbul: İletişim, 1990.

Rahman, Fazlur. "Revival and Reform in Islam." *The Cambridge History of Islam.* Vol. 2. Ed. P. M. Holt, Ann K. S. Lambton, and Bernard Lewis. London: Cambridge University Press, 1970. 632–56.

Ran, Nâzım Hikmet. *835 Satır: Şiirler 1.* 1929. Istanbul: Adam, 1987.

———. *Beyond the Walls: Selected Poems.* Trans. Ruth Christie, Richard McKane, Talât Sait Halman. London: Anvil Press Poetry, 2002.

———. *Kemal Tahir'e Mahpusaneden Mektuplar.* Ankara: Bilgi, 1968.

———. "Makinalaşmak." *835 Satır.* 22–3.

———. *Poems of Nazım Hikmet.* Trans. Randy Blasing and Mutlu Konuk. New York: Persea Books, 2002.

———. "Putları Yıkıyoruz 1: Abdülhak Hamid." 1929. *Sanat, Edebiyat, Kültür, Dil: Yazılar 1.* Istanbul: Adam, 1987. 13–16.

———. "Putları Yıkıyoruz 2: Mehmet Emin Beyefendi." 1929. *Sanat, Edebiyat, Kültür, Dil: Yazılar 1.* Istanbul: Adam, 1987. 20–2.

———. "Regarding Art." *Poems of Nazım Hikmet:* 4–5.

———. "San'at Telâkkisi." *835 Satır:* 36–37.

Recâizâde Mahmud Ekrem. *Araba Sevdası.* Istanbul: Alem Matbaası, 1896.

Reisman, Arnold. *Turkey's Modernization: Refugees from Nazism and Atatürk's Vision.* Washington, DC: New Academia Publishing, 2006.

Safa, Peyami. *Matmazel Noraliya'nın Koltuğu.* Istanbul: Nebioğlu Yayınevi, 1949.

Spivak, Gayatri Chakravorty. *A Critique of Postcolonial Reason: Toward a History of the Vanishing Present.* Cambridge: Harvard University Press, 1999.

Szczuka, Mieczysław. "Kemal Pasha: Kemal's Constructive Program." 1924. *Foto: Modernity in Central Europe, 1918–1945.* By Matthew S. Witkovsky. Washington: Natl. Gallery of Art; New York: Thames & Hudson, 2007. 38.

Tanpınar, Ahmet Hamdi. *XIX. Asır Türk Edebiyatı Tarihi.* 2nd. ed. Istanbul: Çağlayan Kitabevi, 1956.

———. *Beş Şehir.* Ankara: Ülkü, 1946.

———. "Bursa'da Zaman." *Bütün Şiirleri.* Ed. İnci Enginün. Istanbul: Dergâh, 2007. 50–1.

———. *Huzur: Roman.* Istanbul: Remzi Kitabevi, 1949.

———. "Medeniyet Değiştirmesi ve İç İnsan." Tanpınar, *Yaşadığım Gibi:* 24–30.

———. *A Mind at Peace.* Trans. Erdağ Göknar. Brooklyn: Archipelago Books, 2008.

———. "Paris Tesadüfleri II: Meşhurların Evleri." *Yaşadığım Gibi:* 263–67.

———. *Saatleri Ayarlama Enstitüsü.* Istanbul: Remzi Kitabevi, 1961.

———. *The Time Regulation Institute.* Trans. Ender Gürol. Madison: Turko-Tatar Press, 2001.

———. *Yahya Kemal.* 1962. Istanbul: Yapı Kredi Yayınları, 1999.

———. *Yaşadığım Gibi.* Ed. Birol Emil. Istanbul: Türkiye Kültür Enstitüsü, 1970.

Thormählen, Marianne. *Rethinking Modernism.* New York: Palgrave Macmillan, 2003.

Zürcher, Erik Jan. *Turkey: A Modern History.* 3rd ed. New York: I. B. Tauris, 2004.

CHAPTER 23

MODERNISM'S TRANSLATIONS

REBECCA BEASLEY

THE shift in our attention from the "International Modernism" characterized by Hugh Kenner in 1984 as "the work of Irishmen and Americans" to the "global modernisms" of this volume and its recent predecessors represents an expansion beyond a Euro-American canon, a questioning of the relation between nation and culture, but most obviously and most importantly for this essay a geographical and linguistic pluralizing of modernism (367). Rather than positing a single international style in a single language—English—global modernisms draw attention to cultural difference and, as Dilip Parameshwar Gaonkar has remarked of his related, but distinct, concept of "alternative modernities," destabilizes universalist idioms and historicizes contexts. For Gaonkar, site-based readings of modernities discredit theories of modernization that posit a single structure to modernity's progress, and a single form of cultural modernity (modernism) as its effect. They demonstrate instead that while certain "cultural forms, social practices, and institutional arrangements do surface in most places in the wake of modernity [. . .], at each national and cultural site, those elements are put together (reticulated) in a unique and contingent formation in response to local culture and politics" (15–16).

MODERNISMS/MODERNITY

An account of plural *modernisms* is not incompatible with even the strongest assertions of a singular *modernity*. In this sense, Fredric Jameson's swift dismissal of the concept of alternative modernities as simply a repackaging of postmodernity, which posits "the reassuring and 'cultural' notion that you can fashion your own modernity differently, so that there can be a Latin-American kind, or an Indian kind or an African kind," is less relevant to this essay than his footnote to those remarks. There, he insists on "a sharp distinction between the deceptive visions of genuine cultural differences . . . and that completely different concept that names the alternate historical paths to modernity (or capitalism) in all the countries of the world. . . . all paths to capitalism are unique and 'exceptional,' contingent and determined by a unique national situation." Aesthetic modernism, for Jameson, is generated in this incomplete stage of modernization. While modernization, when complete, generates "a singular modernity," whose only "satisfactory semantic meaning . . . lies in its association with capitalism," its earlier stages admit of plural national and ethnic modernisms (12, 218, 13). (For related discussions of Jameson, see in this volume Lazarus and Lincoln.)

Central to any account of global modernity and its modernisms are analyses of the flow of cultural material across the globe—which is to say, analyses of translation (see Apter). Arjun Appadurai has described the contemporary world as in a new phase of modernization, generated by the twin forces of electronic media and mass migration, in which the imagination is no longer confined to its traditional arenas of art, myth, and ritual, but becomes a "mass-mediated imaginary that frequently transcends national space," deployed by ordinary people in everyday life (6). While this does not suggest that cultural material remains unchanged in the course of its flow through communities, nor that it is received in the same way or has identical effects in different communities ("the globalization of culture is not the same as its homogenization, but globalization involves the use of a variety of instruments of homogenization" [42]), the significance accorded to electronic media highlights an important distinction between late twentieth- and early twenty-first-century theories of global modernity and the global modernisms of this volume, generated at an earlier stage of modernity's technological progress. The speed with which cultural material is transmitted, the mechanization and depersonalization of transmission, the rise of English as a global language and—at the same time—the dominance of the image all minimize our sense of the translatedness of the cultural material we consume. Where the experience of global modernity today is one of relative homogeneity, however illusory that homogeneity may be, the experience of global modernisms early in the twentieth century was one of greater cultural and linguistic difference, not least because cultural material traveled more slowly between communities. *Contra* Kenner's assertion that international modernism "drew on a variety of twentieth century activities which transcend the need for translators" (painting, music, war, science) (368), this essay argues that attention to the translation process across cultures and across national and ethnic languages is vital in order to prevent the grouping of diverse cultural material under the banner of "modernism" from producing a false sense of homogeneity. For modernist studies to be actively transformed (not only passively informed) by the global turn, we need to be more persistent in asking questions about translation, dissemination, and reception.

What kinds of questions should we ask? We might begin by considering a slightly adapted version of the set of questions Peter France asks in his introduction to *The Oxford Guide to Literature in English Translation*: What has or has not been translated between the literatures of the world? How has translation shaped canons of literature? How have translators seen their task, and in what social context have they worked? Under what guise have the greater and lesser works of literature been transported into different languages? What is the nature and quality of the different translations available to readers? (xx)

The turn from normative to descriptive translation studies in the last twenty-five years has provided the tools for such study. Where the normative approach that dominated the early period of translation studies in the 1960s and 1970s (and the practitioner criticism that preceded it) aimed to prescribe rules for translation and for judging the quality of individual translations in comparison with the source text, descriptive translation studies treats the translation as a "cultural fact," a form of "rewriting" or "manipulation" shaped by state ideologies and cultural conventions, that may "introduce new concepts, new genres, new devices" but "can also repress innovation, distort and contain" (Bassnett and Lefevere ix).

Descriptive translation studies has itself evolved. Early descriptive translation studies focused on the translation's role in the target culture. In an essay which laid the foundations for this approach, Gideon Toury stated that "translating as a teleological activity *par excellence* is to a large extent conditioned by the goals it is designed to serve, and these goals are set in, and by, the prospective receptor system(s). Consequently, translators operate first and foremost in the interest of the culture *into* which they are translating, and not in the interest of the source text, let alone the source culture" (19). Later work, especially by those working in postcolonial studies—the primary field through which a form of descriptive translation studies has entered literary criticism—has drawn attention to translation governed by source culture goals (for instance, when a source culture uses translation to impose its values on a target culture). What has been called the "cultural turn" in translation studies emphasizes the power relations inherent in the practice of translation: Tejaswini Niranjana has described how "in creating coherent and transparent texts and subjects, translation participates—across a range of discourses—in the *fixing* of colonized cultures, making them static and unchanging rather than historically constructed," and Gayatri Chakravorty Spivak makes the related point that contemporary translation, too, obscures the "rhetoricity" of individuals and groups, for example when "all the literature of the Third World gets translated into a sort of with-it translatese, so that the literature by a woman in Palestine begins to resemble, in the feel of its prose, something by a man in Taiwan" (180). If we follow Jameson in locating modernism along a nation's incomplete path to modernity, analyses such as Spivak's and Tejaswini Niranjana's provide enabling models for analyzing the transformation of identities and international relations. Yet, while postcolonial studies has transformed our understanding of modernism in a number of fundamental ways, work on English language modernisms has only recently begun to share its interest in translation (Katz, Yao).

MODERNIST TRANSLATION

The translator's invisibility in English language modernist studies is particularly remarkable, because it is well known that aesthetic modernism recognized translation, in theory and in practice, as central to its project. Indeed, the concept of translation might be said to be built into the dominant epistemological structures of the nineteenth and twentieth centuries. As Sanford Schwartz has described, the period has a strong predilection for surface/depth oppositions that distinguish conceptual abstraction from concrete sensation: such oppositions structure Freud's psychoanalysis, Frazer's anthropology, Eliot's and Pound's poetics, and the vitalist, pragmatist, and idealist philosophies of, respectively, Bergson, James, and Bradley (4–6). The conversion of sensation to concept, experience to knowledge, is frequently conceived by these thinkers as an act of translation, sometimes as literally as in Freud's characterization of the unconscious as a region of "ein Trümmerfeld mit Mauerresten, Bruchstücken von Säulen, von Tafeln mit verwischten und unlesbaren Schriftzeichen" ("ruins, with remains of walls, fragments of columns, and tablets with half-effaced and unreadable inscriptions"), which reveal to the analyst "ein Alphabet und eine Sprache, und deren Enzifferung und Übersetzung ergibt ungeahnte Aufschlüsse über die Ereignisse der Vorzeit, zu deren Gedächtnis jene Monumente erbaut worden sind" (427) ("an alphabet and a language, and, when they have been deciphered and translated, yield undreamed-of information about the events of the remote past, to commemorate which the monuments were built" [192]).

Just as importantly for this essay, the concept of translation between fields is also fundamental to nineteenth- and twentieth-century linguistic theories, most familiarly structuralist linguistics, in which languages are conceived as "un système de signes exprimant des idées" ("a system of signs that express ideas") (33; 15). The model of language as a relational system, rather than a representation, derived from the work of the mid-nineteenth-century comparative grammarians, who postulated and reconstructed an Ur-language, the Proto–Indo–European language (or PIE), as a common ancestor of Latin, Greek, and the recently "discovered" Sanskrit (Saussure, *Course* 2; Davies 135–36). For Jameson, it is here that we see modernism's aesthetic emerge, as the

> multiple differentiations of nineteenth-century language, across the uneven development of the European nation-states, project not merely the radically different and semi-autonomous realms of aristocratic and bourgeois languages, learned and oratory, the languages of the incipient mass press and of commercial exchange, but also, beyond all of those, a kind of empty Utopian domain of language as nonexistent and yet as demonstrable and conjectural as non-Euclidean geometry. This is then the space in which the new language specialists work, and in which, by modifying the original Euclidean postulates and axioms of the various forms of everyday speech (reference, communicability, etcetera), they deduce and develop the invisible outlines of whole new language structures never before seen on earth and heaven. (147)

The differentiation of language, argues Jameson, not only creates new linguistic realms distinguished by class, education, and forms of commerce, but also a space in which imagined languages—suggesting the promise of connection between, or transcendence of, the multiplying languages experienced in daily life—flourish. In Jameson's words, this space "offers to reclaim, redeem, transform and transfigure the koiné of a capitalist daily life into an Ur-speech in which our authentic relationship to the world and to Being can be reinvented" (148).

The creation of PIE by "the new language specialists" and the artificial international languages from the same period, Volapük and Esperanto, are relevant instances here, but the significance for modernism is best exemplified by Mallarmé's famous remarks in "Crise de vers" (1886):

> Les langues imparfaites en cela que plusieurs, manque la suprême: penser étant écrire sans accessoires, ni chuchotement mais tacite encore l'immortelle parole, la diversité, sur terre, des idiomes empêche personne de proférer les mots qui, sinon se trouveraient, par une frappe unique, elle-même matériellement la vérité (208). (Languages are imperfect because multiple; the supreme language is missing. Inasmuch as thought consists of writing without pen and paper, without whispering even, without the sound of the immortal Word, the diversity of languages on earth means that no one can utter words which would bear the miraculous stamp of Truth Herself Incarnate [38]).

But where Jameson emphasizes the differentiation of linguistic *registers* under capitalism, I want to draw attention instead to what is implicit in Jameson's argument, that is, the increased experience in the nineteenth century of the diversity of national and ethnic languages themselves. The quotation from Mallarmé's "Le tombeau d'Edgar Poe" (1876) that Jameson invokes as authorizing the Utopian vocation of non-Euclidean language—"Donner un sens plus pur aux mots de la tribu" ("give a purer sense to the words of the tribe")—is, after all, not simply a desire for a purer language, or for one that transcends the ordinary language of the "horde," as "tribu" has been translated. Just as significantly, it is a desire for a language that supersedes the localism of the tribe (Mallarmé, *Collected* 71). The dream of a pure language is a dominant—for Jameson, a defining—dream of modernism, but it is not only conceived in opposition to commercial and utilitarian forms of language. Modernism, especially in its later stages, conceived the pure language as an international or non-national language, as in the formulation by the most significant modernist theorist of translation, Walter Benjamin: "Vielmehr beruht alle überhistorische Verwandtschaft der Sprachen darin, daß in ihrer jeder als ganzer jeweils eines und zwar dasselbe gemeint ist, das dennoch keiner einzelnen von ihnen, sondern nur der Allheit ihrer einander ergänzenden Intentionen erreichbar ist: die reine Sprache" (13) ("All suprahistorical kinship of languages rests in the intention underlying each language as a whole—an intention, however, which no single language can attain by itself but which is realized only by the totality of their intentions supplementing each other: pure language" [74]). From this perspective, the aesthetic and ideology of European modernism arises not simply from its internationalism (Kenner), nor in response to the differentiation of linguistic registers (Jameson), but in reaction against the increased experience of the diversity of national languages.

In the West, translation took on new significance in the nineteenth century in response to material factors: translation was required by the increased flow of international trade, labor, and capital; and it was enabled by improvements in transport and communication that, in conjunction with a revolution in printing technologies, inaugurated mass publication across the globe (Bayly 19: 357–59). Translation thus became a means by which nations could represent their identity abroad and receive information about new political allies and antagonists. The expansion of literacy created new readerships, and the expansion of middle-class wealth created new desires for foreign cultural capital, including foreign literature. As Marx and Engels wrote in the *Manifest der Kommunitischen Partei* (*Communist Manifesto*),

> An die Stelle der alten, durch Landeserzeugnisse befriedigten Bedürfnisse treten neue, welche die Produkte der entferntesten Länder und Klimate zu ihrer Befriedigung erheischen. An die Stelle der alten lokalen und nationalen Selbstgenügsamkeit und Abgeschlossenheit tritt ein allseitiger Verkehr, eine allseitige Abhängigkeit der Nationen voneinander. Und wie in der materiellen, so auch in der geistigen Produktion. Die geistigen Erzeugnisse der einzelnen Nationen werden Gemeingut. Die nationale Einseitigkeit und Beschränktheit wird mehr und mehr unmöglich, und aus den vielen nationalen und lokalen Literaturen bildet sich eine Weltliteratur (235–36). (In place of the old wants, satisfied by the productions of the country, we find new wants, requiring for their satisfaction the products of distant lands and climes. In place of the old local and national seclusion and self-sufficiency, we have intercourse in every direction, universal inter-dependence of nations. And as in material, so also in intellectual production. The intellectual creations of individual nations become common property. National one-sidedness and narrow-mindedness become more and more impossible, and from the numerous national and local literatures, there arises a world literature [223]).

For Marx and Engels, as for Goethe, who had coined the term *Weltliteratur* twenty-one years before, the rise in international trade had the beneficial effect of increasing intellectual exchange between nations. Goethe prophesied that "the epoch of world literature is at hand," an epoch which would supersede that of national literatures and enable an exchange of ideal values between nations. Translation was fundamental to this enterprise: in 1828 Goethe wrote to Thomas Carlyle about an English translation of his play, *Torquato Tasso*, "Nun aber möcht ich von Ihnen wissen, inwiefern dieser Tasso als Englisch gelten kann. Sie werden mich höchlich verbinden, wenn Sie mich hieruber aufklären and erleuchten; denn eben diese Bezüge vom Originale zur Übersetzung sind es ja, welche die Verhältnisse von Nation zu Nation am allerdeutlichsten aussprechen und die man zu Förderung der vor- und obwaltenden allgemeinen Weltliteratur vorzüglich zu kennen und zu beurtheilen hat" (222). ("Now I should like to have your opinion on how far this *Tasso* can be considered *English* . . . for it is just this connection between the original and the translation that expresses most clearly the relationship of nation to nation and that one must above all know if one wishes to encourage a common world literature transcending national limits" [Strich 349–50]). Although the mass-mediated cultural material described by Appadurai might perhaps be seen as the twenty-first century progeny of these nineteenth-century dreams, its efficient flow between communities (for all Appadurai's insistence on its liberatory potential) sacrifices the linguistic richness Mallarmé imagined and the revelation of national character Goethe expected. It is what Mallarmé called "l'universel *reportage*" ("that universal *journalistic style*"), more recently described by Tariq Ali as "market realism," and it is monolingual (Mallarmé, "Crise" 212; "Crisis" 42; Ali 140).

The American and British book industries are notoriously hostile to translations. In 2004 only 2.07 percent of books published in America were translations; and in Britain in 2001 only 1.4 percent. By comparison, 7.3 percent of books published in Germany in 2004 were translations, as were 9.9 percent of books published in France in 1985, and 22.9 percent published in Italy in 2002. In each of these cases, more than half were translations from English. Lawrence Venuti has argued that

> by routinely translating large numbers of the most varied English-language books, foreign publishers have exploited the global drift toward American political and economic hegemony since World War II, actively supporting the international expansion of British and American cultures. . . . British and American publishers, in turn, have reaped the financial benefits of successfully imposing English-language cultural values on a vast foreign readership, while producing cultures in the United Kingdom and the United States that are aggressively monolingual, unreceptive to foreign literatures, accustomed to fluent translations that invisibly inscribe foreign texts with British and American values and provide readers with the narcissistic experience of recognizing their own culture in a cultural other. (11, 12)

The context of Venuti's argument is his analysis of the "regime of fluency" in British and American translation culture, in which the translation minimizes the foreignness of the source text in order to produce an easily readable text. Doing so, it creates the illusion of a transparent window onto the source text, author, and culture. The translator's intervention is rendered invisible, as are the values of the target language and culture that determine the translation's production, circulation, and reception. Venuti advocates what has been called foreignizing translation, or translation that brings the foreign rather than familiar aspects of the text to the fore, as "a strategic cultural intervention . . . pitched against the hegemonic English-language nations and the unequal cultural exchanges in which they engage their global others" (1, 14, 16). Tracing approaches to translation through periods and cultures, he argues that fluency is a peculiarly English-language value, emerging in the early modern period, becoming attached to bourgeois values of liberal humanism in the eighteenth century, and dominant by the nineteenth century. Francis Newman's famous challenge to the norm of fluency, inspired by a German foreignizing tradition exemplified by Friedrich Schleiermacher and Goethe, was successfully overturned by contemporary critics, most influentially Matthew Arnold, and the dominance of fluency in professional and commercial spheres was preserved for the twentieth and twenty-first centuries.

Modernism, however, disrupts this story. Venuti, drawing principally on the translations of Ezra Pound, recounts how modernist experiments, especially in poetry, avoided fluency and transparency. In the *Cathay* poems, "Homage to Sextus Propertius," and the translations from Cavalcanti, to name only the most well known of his translation projects, Pound creates deliberately opaque texts, which draw the reader's attention to the translator's linguistic and metrical choices by the diverse strategies of unfamiliar syntax, archaisms, and neologisms. The modernist practice of translation, argues Venuti, contradicts modernist theories of translation as an autonomous creative work; it is a practice that constructs a productive foreignness in the translation by mixing discourses across periods and cultures, deploying "what currently appears 'foreign' in the receiving culture" against dominant cultural values (176).

The example of Pound is instructive, because it complicates the domestication/foreignization binary in a way that is typical of modernist translation. A resistance to fluency does not, necessarily, result in a foreignizing translation in the sense usually meant—a translation that "bewegt den Leser [dem Schriftsteller] entgegen" ("moves the reader toward the author"), in Schleiermacher's formulation (47), or in which the translator "surrenders to the text," in Spivak's (181). One of the common features of most artworks we call modernist is that they engage in processes of defamiliarization, however variously those processes are practically and ideologically constructed: the author "dislocates" language, as T. S. Eliot put it, using an illuminatingly geographical metaphor to register the foreignizing aims not only of modernist translations, but of modernist poetry in general (289). But Eliot's point is not that language is dislocated across a system of national languages; the priority of modernism's foreignizing strategies is not, primarily, to engage with a source text or source culture on its own terms. Rather, modernism's foreignizing is firmly oriented toward the target culture, and is above all concerned to establish certain stylistic norms. So although its strategies may disrupt the domesticating norms of English translation practice, characterized by fluency and transparency, they nevertheless enact a different form of domestication, rewriting the source text to serve modernist cultural agendas.

Russian Translation in Britain

In this context, the translation of Russian literature, especially the Russian novel, makes a particularly relevant case study for British modernist studies, because it demonstrates with some precision how a national literature and individual authors and translations were strategically deployed in the early twentieth-century critical field to advance a cultural agenda we can now recognize as modernist.

Translation from the Russian might be understood as *the* translation project of British modernism: the first sustained attempt to create a canon of Russian literature in translation was undertaken during Britain's (long) modernist period (1880–1940); a number of British-based modernists were involved in translation projects (notably D. H. Lawrence, Katherine Mansfield, and Virginia Woolf); and the focus of translation was literary and cultural (rather than scientific, philosophical, or historical). Yet it is by no means straightforward to trace the impact of these Russian translations: while isolated instances of inter-author influence can and have been noted, Russian literature appears to have had a surprisingly limited impact on the broader development of modernist critical principles, especially in comparison with the impact of French literature. As Donald Davie correctly remarked over forty years ago, while Russian novelists were profoundly influential for twentieth-century British and American novelists, theirs "was never a *formal* influence. The truest way of regarding the history of Russian fiction in English translation, and the history of how English-speaking readers have reacted to Russian fiction, is the story of a challenge presented to Anglo-American literary culture, and of the response made to that challenge" (Davie 9). When I say that the translation of Russian literature was strategically deployed to advance a modernist cultural agenda, then, I mean that it was negatively deployed: its potential for informing British modernism was rigorously contained by an influential group of writers and critics who turned to French, rather than Russian, literature to establish new critical grounds, first for the contemporary novel and later for contemporary literature, or modernism, more generally. The fact that Russian literature had to be read in translation, unlike French literature, was a critical factor in this process.

The story of translation from Russian to English during the nineteenth and early twentieth centuries has often been told. In Britain, occasional translations in the first half of the nineteenth century, particularly of poetry, preceded the first stage of more extensive translation during the Crimean War (1853–1856), with fiction by contemporaries Gogol, Lermontov, and Turgenev published in English for the first time. Interest diminished until the 1880s, when the influence of American admiration for Turgenev combined with the appearance of Ernest Dupuy's and E. M. de Vogüé's influential studies of Russian literature, *Les grands maîtres de la litterature russes* (1885) and *Le roman russe* (1885, 1886)—both swiftly translated into English—and the arrival of émigrés who were effective translators, interpreters, and promoters of Russian literature (May 13–20; Davie 1–3; Peaker). Notoriously, the early fiction translations were represented as factual accounts that provided information about Britain's enemy in the Crimean War: Lermontov's *Geroi nashego vremeni* (*A Hero of Our Time*) was retitled *Sketches of Russian Life in the Caucuses* (1853), Gogol's *Mertvye dushi* (*Dead Souls*) as *Home Life in Russia* (1854), and Turgenev's *Zapiski okhotnika* (*Sportsman's Sketches*), the first of his works to be translated into English (via French), as *Russian Life in the Interior: The Experiences of a Sportsman* (1855) (May 14; Davie 1).

The dominant critical view of the Russian novel at the end of the nineteenth century, that it could provide the spiritual corrective to the materialism of the French realist and naturalist novel, shows a certain continuity with this early documentary approach. For what is praised in the Russian novel, especially the novels of Tolstoy and Dostoevsky, is its ability to represent "life" apparently without mediation, in contrast to the artistry and style that distinguished the Flaubertian model in French fiction. So de Vogüé argued that the Russian novel "fascinated not by its local color or its foreign savor, but by the "breath of life," the sincerity and compassion which animates all these books" ("Ce qui l'a séduite, ce n'est point la couleur locale et le ragoût d'étrangeté; c'est l'esprit de vie qui anime des livres, l'accent de sincérité et de sympathie" (23; lii), and Matthew Arnold instructed his readers that "we are not to take *Anna Karénine* as a work of art; we are to take it as a piece of life. A piece of life it is. The author has not invented and combined it, he has seen it" (285). These values also governed the translation process, as Constance Garnett's account of her practice demonstrates: "Tolstoy's simple style goes straight into English without any trouble. There's no difficulty. Dostoievsky is so obscure and so careless a writer that one can scarcely help clarifying him—sometimes it needs some penetration to see what he is trying to say. Turgenev is much the most difficult of the Russians to translate because his style is the most beautiful" (195).

Criticism of Garnett's "clarifying" translations has become a critical cliché, but it is more productive to read them as a cultural fact of turn-of-the-century British culture than to assign positive and negative values according to the degree they foreignize or domesticate. As Venuti's history of translation informs us, the English translation norms of transparency and fluency govern Garnett's approach and rhetoric here; but her translations are also informed by and inform the critical field developing around the Russian novel. If the Russian novel is understood as representing life unmediated, the translation must be invisible, drawing attention neither to its own style, nor even the style of the source text. Dostoevsky's "obscure" style is thus understood as something to be corrected in order to bring out "what he is trying to say," and admiration for Turgenev's style led to British critics associating him with the French, rather than Russian, realist tradition. Conversely, if a translation that minimizes stylistic particularity is achieved, criticism of the Russian novel will, of course, see the novels as lacking in artistry and style. Few readers and reviewers of Russian literature were able to compare the translation with the Russian source text, as they could in the case of other European languages. As Virginia Woolf famously remarked, "we have judged a whole literature stripped of its style. When you have changed every word in a sentence from Russian to English, have thereby altered the sense a little, the sound, weight, and accent of the words in relation to each other completely, nothing remains except a crude and coarsened version of the sense" (182).

While this is an entirely conventional criticism of literary translation, theorized in the 1950s and 1960s by Roman Jakobson and Eugene Nida in terms of semantic equivalence, it also expresses a particular kind of problem for British modernist writers and critics. For their criticism is centrally concerned with style and technique (as opposed to morality of subject matter, for example) and, indeed, typically turns to stylistic criteria in order to define itself against both earlier and rival contemporary forms of criticism. But this form of criticism can have little to say about literature in translation, literature "stripped of its style," since it will be unable to distinguish between the translator's style and the foreign author's. For Woolf, this makes criticism of all literature in translation provisional, but for some of her contemporaries, it appears to render any response to translated literature invalid, as the following letter written by Richard Aldington to T. S. Eliot in 1920 suggests:

> Your letter quite delights me. I give a most hearty & gruff "hear, hear" to your remarks on Dostoevsky's imitators & Laforgue's pervertors. I remember an appalling evening spent at Jean de Bosschère's flat; a man called Atkinson was most offensive with loud-voiced boasting of the supremacy of Dostoevsky. . . . Do you know what I say to these faux esprits when they swoon over the Russians? "Ah! How I envy you—it must be delightful to read Russian fluently." And when they confess they don't know Russian—I elevate my eyebrows! For, after all, how can we criticise style when we don't know the language a book is written in?[1]

The characterization of what is to be rejected in modern letters, "Dostoevsky's imitators & Laforgue's pervertors," is instructive: one must not imitate the Russian Dostoevsky, but one could, as Eliot had, imitate the French Laforgue, as long as one's imitation did not turn into perversion. At issue here is the integrity of one's imitation, and the problem with Dostoevsky is that his imitators and his admirers, unlike Laforgue's, cannot read "the language the book is written in." If they cannot read the language, they cannot criticize style, and the implication of Aldington's argument is that style is the only legitimate subject for criticism.

This approach to criticism had begun to be transferred into a nascent British modernism by Ford Madox Ford in the *English Review*, drawing on French models and the Francophilic American model of Henry James (see Ford 160). Aldington and Eliot developed it further in the *Egoist*, for which they acted as literary editors between 1914 and 1919 (Aldington from January 1914 to May 1916, and Eliot from June 1917 to the journal's closure in December 1919), and the journal provides an excellent example of the way French and Russian literature were played off each other to advance an early modernist agenda.

French literature was reviewed, discussed, translated, and printed untranslated throughout the *Egoist*'s five-year run. Aldington's stated editorial model (as for Ford before him and Eliot after him) was the *Mercure de France* (Aldington, *Life* 174). By contrast, Russian literature was not a substantial presence in the *Egoist*. Despite the fact that it was published at the height of British interest in its Russian ally in World War I, the journal reflects this popular enthusiasm only between September 1915 and December 1916. In the September and October 1915 issues, the violinist and music critic Montagu Montagu-Nathan published two articles on "Translations of Russian Fiction," which argued that during the war, publishers of translations of Russian literature had a responsibility to publish "the sort of literature calculated to improve the present slender intellectual reciprocity between Britain and Slav." He deplored the contemporary vogue for "the pessimism of Andreyev, the degeneracy of Kuprin, and the salaciousness of Artzibashev," when other writers, such as Pushkin, Lermontov, Ostrovskii, and Chekhov, remained relatively neglected (Montagu-Nathan 152, 142). Accordingly, in the next issue, Chekhov's "Zhivaia khronologiia" ("Living Chronology") was published, translated by Natalia Andronikoff and John Hilton. This was followed, in January 1916, by another short story by Chekhov, "Drama" ("A Drama"), and six *skazochki*

("Little Tales") by Fedor Sologub, translated by the Ukranian American imagist poet John Cournos, who also contributed a critical essay on Sologub. In February, Cournos's translation of Alexei Remizov's "Suzhenaia" ("The Betrothed") was published, also accompanied by an essay. In April A. W. G. Randall reviewed Cournos and Aldington's recently published translation of Sologub's *Melkii bes* (*The Little Demon*). In May, Aldington's article on *Melkii bes* ran on the front page, and in November, John Gould Fletcher reviewed Cournos's translation of Sologub's *Tvorimaia legenda* (*The Created Legend*). In December, three more of Sologub's *skazochki* appeared in Cournos's translation. After that issue, apart from one more *skazochka* in May 1917 and T. S. Eliot's review of Edward Garnett's *Turgenev: A Study* in December 1917 (to which I will return), Russian literature disappeared from the journal permanently.

While this record suggests that the *Egoist* responded to Montagu-Nathan's challenge with some enthusiasm, in fact only the publication of the Chekhov translation followed the logic of his argument. The Symbolists Sologub and Remizov were characteristic of the early modernist reaction against the realist tradition in Russia, contributors to precisely the trends Montagu-Nathan thought threatened to undermine the Anglo-Russian wartime alliance. What, then, could justify not only the translation and publication of Sologub and Remizov at this time, but what we might see as the *Egoist*'s identification with and promotion of Sologub—translated by two longtime contributors, Cournos and Aldington, reviewed by two more, Randall and Fletcher—in direct contradiction of wartime moral imperatives?

Sologub himself had expressed some apprehension at publishing his 1907 novel, *Melkii bes*, in Britain during the war. In his introduction to Cournos's translation, he remarked that "In days of Anglo-Russian rapprochement, in days of great stress, when a common danger unites two great nations, it seemed to me perhaps unseasonable to acquaint England with this sombre picture" (xv). In the mean, petulant main character, the gymnasium teacher Peredonov, the novel presents the Russian literary figure of the *melkii bes*, the "petty demon," whose "sumasshestvie" (madness), Sologub remarked in 1910, should be read not as "sluchainost´, a obshchaia bolezn´, eto i est´ byt sovremmennoi Rossii" ("happenstance, but a general illness, the way of life, indeed, of contemporary Russia") (Dikman 33). In his introduction for British readers, however, Sologub minimized this specifically Russian context, and stressed instead the novel's universal qualities: "I should like to warn my readers against the temptation of seeing only Russian traits in this novel," he wrote, "The portrait of Peredonov is an expression of the all-human inclination towards evil" (xv) ("Ia by khotiel, vo vsiakom sluchaie, predosterech´ moikh novykh chitatelei ot soblazna vid´et v etom romane tol´ko cherty russkie. Obraz Peredonova predstavliaet izobrazhenie obshchechelobiecheskoi naklonnosti ko zlu").[2] Cournos's preface followed Sologub's lead: "In spite of its 'local colour' and its portrayal of small town life in Russia, this novel has the world for its stage, and its chief actor, Peredonov, is a universal character. He is a Russian—an American—an Englishman" (v). Though Cournos's decision to translate *Melkii bes* works against the expectations of British wartime literary culture, therefore, his and Sologub's introductory framing of the text in terms of universal human values affirms them.

The argument of these introductions, coupled with the period's strong tendency toward transparent translation, would suggest that Cournos's text would bring a powerfully domesticating agenda to Sologub's novel in order to underline the similarities between Sologub's and the reader's worlds. To an extent, the translator's preface confirms this expectation. Cournos concludes by commenting on the difficulty of translating Sologub's prose, particularly his use of contemporary Russian slang, puns, and rhymes. "In every case the translators have striven to give the English equivalent," he writes—but he adds that "where the difficulty was of a nature rendering this impossible, the translators have had to make use of absolutely unavoidable footnotes" (vii). Footnotes inevitably undermine the domestication and fluency of a text, reminding the reader of the lack of equivalence between languages and cultures and, despite his apparent reluctance, Cournos uses them with marked frequency: they gloss historical and literary references, describe cultural traditions, and explain puns. In comparison with the three translations of *Melkii bes* that have succeeded Cournos's, his translation contains the most explanatory footnotes, retains the highest number of Russian words in the text, and overall is least satisfied with potential English "equivalents."[3]

Some examples will illustrate the implications of these strategies more fully. At the beginning of Chapter 21, the narrator tells us that Peredonov "pokazal pis´monostsu kukish v karmane" (194), which Ronald Wilks translates as "secretly cocked a snook at him" (177); Andrew Field translates as "made an insulting gesture to the postman in his pocket" (233); and S. D. Cioran translates the phrase as "made a rude sign to the letter carrier from his pocket" (194). Cournos, however, retains the Russian term, and the cultural specificity of the Russian gesture, translating "made a Koukish in his pocket" and providing a footnote: "Koukish, a clenched fist with the thumb thrust between the first and second fingers. This gesture is a great insult in Russia. To make it is as much as to say, 'A fig for you!'" (230). When Cournos translates Dar'ia's *chastushky* in Chapter 14, he disregards the rhyme (fundamental to *chastushky*) in favor of the sense. In her final song, he retains the Russian words *muzhik* and *bosiak* and provides a footnote to the latter: "'Bossiak' is literally 'bare-foot,' a vagabond. The 'bossiak' has become quite a marked type in Russia since Gorky took to writing of him. The bossiak is often referred to in a satiric way in modern Russian literature." In contrast, Wilks, Field, and Cioran all translate the sense more freely in order to retain the source text's rhyme scheme: *bosiak* in Field becomes "one of my father's clan" (163) and, in Cioran and Wilks, "a tramp" (Cioran 143; Wilks 125). In short, although all four translators retain some Russian words (Cournos, Field and Cioran retain *zakuska* and *nedotykomka*, for example; all four retain *trepak*), Cournos goes furthest in emphasizing the text's cultural difference.

Puns always present a challenge to the translator, and Cournos, Field, and Cioran respond to Sologub's many puns in distinct ways. For Cournos, retaining the pun is far less important than maintaining accuracy at the level of the individual word. He typically translates the punning word into both of its meanings in the text, used alternately, losing both the joke and the sense of the passage, which a footnote attempts to recover. Wilks's approach is irregular, but tends to use the same strategy as Cournos. For Field and, especially, Cioran, the fluency of the text and the humor are prioritized over word-unit equivalence, with Field usually choosing one of the meanings to retain the humor but not the pun, and Cioran creating a grammatically equivalent pun, but relinquishing verbal equivalence with the source text. In Chapter 16, for example, Liudmila asks Sasha if he would like her to put perfume on him. He responds "*Zhe-laiu*," "I would like (that)." Liudmilla asks him, "who would like it?," and when he repeats "*Zhelaiu*," she responds with a pun that works by splitting the second person singular form of the verb "to like," "*zhelaesh´*," into "*zhe*," the Russian intensifier, and "*laesh*," "(you) bark": "*Ty zhe laesh´? laesh´? vot kak! laesh´!*" ("You really bark? bark? Really? You're barking!") (158). Cournos translates Liudmilla's pun as "You like it—so you bark do you?" (185). Wilks, structurally similar, casts Sasha's reply as "I want some" and Liudmilla's pun as "Then what are you barking for?" (143). Field translates Sasha's reply throughout not as "I would like that" but as "I get sprayed," so that he can create a rhyme: Liudmilla replies "Have you really bayed? You bay like a dog?" (189). Cioran is most creative, and translates Sasha's reply as "it is appealing to me," in order for Liud-milla to respond "Is it appealing to you? A peeling? I see! You think it's a peeling from an orange!" (162).

There is more to creating a foreignized text than simply retaining source text words and registering untranslatability, of course. Cioran's translation, the text that strives most toward domestication in the sense of semantic equivalence, is consid-ered as the most scholarly of the four, published with a substantial introduction and critical essays that set the text in its foreign literary and cultural history. But I am less interested here in establishing degrees of domestication and foreigniza-tion than I am in exploring how Cournos's text draws on both codes simulta-neously, creating a domesticating introduction and a foreignizing text, a strategy that highlights the complexity of carrying a Russian prewar modernist text into British wartime modernist culture.

I have traveled some way from my earlier question: what could justify the *Ego-ist*'s translation, publication, and identification with Sologub in direct contradic-tion of wartime moral imperatives? Reviews of Cournos's translation suggest that the domesticating introductions were effective in framing the text as both univer-sal in theme and quasi-realist in style. Harold Hannyngton Child's review for the *Times Literary Supplement* agreed that "there are, no doubt about it, Peredonovs in England; there is a Peredonov somewhere in every one of us" (150). Was Sologub published in the *Egoist*, then, as a realist writer, whose work, despite its decadent reputation in Russia, could "improve the . . . intellectual reciprocity between Brit-ain and Slav" (Montagu-Nathan 152)? Not quite: the codes of mainstream press book publication are very different from those of modernist periodical publication, and presenting Sologub to the *Egoist*'s readers involved a different framing device from that of the book publication.

In the anti-establishment *Egoist* the domesticating frame that made Sologub palatable to a book-buying public had no value, and it was precisely its foreignness that made it potentially appropriate in a modernist journal. However, the foreign values of the *Egoist*'s modernism were not indiscriminate, they were the Francophile: the legacy of the Flaubertian tradition to which Russian literature was traditionally opposed in British literary culture. It should come as no surprise, then, to find that Sologub appears in the *Egoist* restyled. He "writes like no one else in Russia," Cournos informs the *Egoist*'s readers, "he is like a French mind combined with a Russian soul," whose poems "are extraordinary distillations of mood and music," and whose "translations of Verlaine have caused the admirers of both poets to say that had Verlaine written in Russian he could not have bettered them" (5). The following month, in his article on Remizov, Cournos extends his argument. Despite his previous month's assertion of Sologub's singularity, now he remarks that his characterization of Sologub as "a Russian soul with a French mind" "is as true of most of the finer Russian writers to-day," including Remizov. The key point is the "changed attitude of the Russian writers since Dostoyevsky, Tolstoy, and Chekhov toward the technique of writing. The old Russian writers were great not because of their style, but in spite of their lack of it." Drawing an extended simile between style and clothing, he concludes that "the Russian wench, like any other, gets her dresses nowadays from Paris" (28). While the political context of the Great War and the commercial context of the popularity of Russian writing create a general readership for Sologub-as-Russian in Britain, if he is to be read and admired by the modernist peers of his translators, Sologub must be made legible by being framed as French. In the *Egoist*, Sologub's early modernism and Cournos's foreignizing translation are aligned, rather than in contradiction with, the target critical culture, because that culture's values, modernist values, are not domesticating but foreignizing. By the same token, however, in framing Sologub in terms of French literature and the critical values associated with it (most importantly, those of style and technique), Cournos's foreignizing of Sologub is simultaneously domesticating to a modernist cultural agenda.

Though this modernist stance had its basis in the Russian symbolists' own identification with French symbolism, its distinctiveness is apparent when one compares its values with those of nonmodernist criticism of contemporary Russian literature. In the September 1916 issue of the *Egoist*, Cournos criticized C. E. Bechhofer's introduction to a recent volume of Russian plays, which had argued that Andreyev, Gorky, and Sologub were decadent writers because they wrote in a "narrow" national style, uninspired by their European contemporaries. Cournos responded: "What the embryo critic of Russian literature fails to take into account is that modern Russian literature is 'decadent' only in the degree that it is European and more particularly French" ("Not Vodka" 134). Conversely, in praising Sologub's *Tvorimaia legenda* in the *Egoist* two months later, John Gould Fletcher had to reverse the assigned values of Hugh Walpole's recent book on Joseph Conrad, in which he had argued that contemporary Russian writing was exhausted and sterile because it had turned from the Russian realist tradition toward the French: "we do not class novelists such as Flaubert and De Maupassant as decadents simply because they respected form in their work" (Fletcher 167).

Fletcher's review is particularly interesting, because it extends its discussion of literary values to English and American literature, revisiting the initial debates over French and Russian realism that had so effectively established literary values associated with French literature at the heart of British modernism. In response to Walpole's maxim, "The French novelists used life to perfect their art—the Russian novelists used art to liberate their passion for life," by which Walpole meant to denigrate French novelists and praise the Russians, Fletcher responds, "if art must liberate a passion for life in order to be healthy, then Dickens was a greater novelist than Henry James, Fielding and Walter Scott are preferable to Conrad and Hardy"—the point being, of course, that it is obvious to an *Egoist* reader that Henry James, Conrad, and Hardy are better novelists than Dickens, Fielding, and Scott. Fletcher then switches tack, and concludes: "The function of criticism is not to set up these moral judgments, but to understand first of all what an artist has set out to do and then to ask oneself whether it is done ill or well." It is a deft critical move, setting up a clear opposition between two genealogies in English literature, one linked to the Russian novel, one to the French, then disowning that construction as a moral judgment and introducing another, allegedly nonmoral, form of judgment, the critical. Critical judgment "asks . . . whether [the work] is done ill or well": it judges style (167). Yet, as Aldington and Woolf observed, judgments about the style of the author cannot be made on the basis of a translation, and the non-Russian-reading Fletcher finds himself able to make only the briefest and most general remarks about the formal aspects of the novel. Aldington himself had had the same difficulty in his lead article, "The Little Demon," the previous May. (Aldington's co-translation of the novel was presumably restricted to polishing Cournos's prose; Cournos later recorded that, as he was working on *Tvorimaia legenda* at the same time, Aldington worked with him "in order to get the book quickly done" (Cournos, *Autobiography* 281). Like Fletcher, Aldington insisted that the reader approach the book as "an artist" rather than "a moralist," yet like Fletcher he could say little about the novel's style: "If you approach a work of art as an artist, I tell you that in "The Little Demon" you have a tragic symbolist novel, original in thought and characters, with a personal method and a clear style; . . . it is as finely patterned, as ironic as a good Steinlen" (Aldington, "Little Demon" 66). Both critics, despite their protestations, fill their articles with a defense of Sologub's moral stance.

CONCLUSION

Fletcher's phrase "the function of criticism" recalls more famous usages by Matthew Arnold in 1864 and T. S. Eliot in 1923, and reminds us that the values of British modernism, largely worked out between those dates, were also the values of the emerging discipline of English Literature. This chapter has explored the opportunities and impediments those values presented to translated literatures. British modernism's international interests and its principle of foreignization in literature and translation created an opportunity for John Cournos to publish translations and essays on Russian modernist literature in *The Egoist*, and Cournos's almost forgotten work is an important example of early twentieth-century attempts to update British knowledge of Russian literature by introducing British modernists to their Russian contemporaries. In an article on Sologub in the *Fortnightly Review*, Cournos describes Russia's late progress into urban modernity in order to explain the birth of a Russian modernism that was both comparable to British modernism (the Russian writer "ceased to see life broadly, in panoramic sweeps; he began to see it swiftly rather than thoroughly, as a series of impressions rather than as a whole; as a thing of fragments" [480]) yet still distinctively different ("he still loves the weak, the child-like, the quixotic" [490]). To return to the terms of my introduction, then, Cournos represented Russia as moving through the same process of modernity as Britain had done almost a century before, a singular modernity, while seeing its cultural effect in terms of an alternative, if comparable, modernism.

Yet while British modernism provided a receptive culture for translations and translators, it simultaneously limited their impact. Venuti's insight that the foreignizing practice of modernist translation contradicts its domesticating theory (its understanding of the translation as an autonomous creative work) is here supplemented by the related argument that modernist critical values worked against the appreciation of literature in translation, especially literature that claimed to be innovative in style, when the translation could not be tested against the source text. Despite their renowned interest in nineteenth-century Russian literature and culture, British modernist writers failed to respond to the importation of Russian modernism. It is, perhaps, symptomatic that even after the *Egoist*'s year of promoting Sologub and Remizov, it was in a review of Edward Garnett's book on Turgenev—born in the same decade as Dickens, Thackeray, and George Eliot—that T. S. Eliot outlined his critical principles to the *Egoist*'s readers:

> The grasp on the uniformity of human nature and this interest in its variations made Turgenev cosmopolitan and made him a critic. . . . Turgenev could not get lost in a character, could not become possessed by the illusion that any particular creation was, for the time being, the centre of the universe. His detail, therefore, is not that of exaggeration of the trivial in an abnormally stimulated consciousness, but is really a way of setting the balance right. . . . I am not sure that the method of Turgenev—this perfect proportion, this vigilant but never theoretic intelligence, this austere art of omission—is not that which in the end proves most satisfying to the civilised mind. (167)

Eliot's essay, in its masterful appropriation of Turgenev to the modernist Francophile agenda, exemplifies British modernism's efforts to inoculate itself against the influence of Russian modernist style.

NOTES

1. Letter from Richard Aldington to T. S. Eliot, 'Weds' [September 1920], MS Am 1432, Thomas Stearns Eliot, Correspondence, Houghton Library, Harvard University, © the Estate of Richard Aldington.

2. Fedor Sologub, "Predislovie," in Papers concerning *The Little Demon*, MS Russ 61, Houghton Library, Harvard University.

3. In the discussion following, I cite Ronald Wilks's 1994 Penguin translation of *The Little Demon*, not his 1962, much looser, translation for the New English Library.

WORKS CITED

Aldington, Richard. *Life for Life's Sake: A Book of Reminiscences*. New York: Viking, 1941.
———. "The Little Demon." *Egoist* 3 (1916): 65–66.
Ali, Tariq. "Literature and Market Realism." *New Left Review* 199 (1993): 140–45.
Appadurai, Arjun. *Modernity at Large: Cultural Dimensions of Globalization*. Minneapolis: University of Minnesota Press, 1996.
Apter, Emily. *The Translation Zone: A New Comparative Literature*. Princeton: Princeton University Press, 2006.
Arnold, Matthew. "Count Leo Tolstoy." *The Complete Prose Works of Matthew Arnold: The Last Word*. Ed. R. H. Super. Ann Arbor: University of Michigan Press, 1977. 282–304.
Bassnett, Susan, and André Lefevere. Preface. *Translation, History and Culture*. London: Pinter, 1990. ix.
Bayly, C. A. *The Birth of the Modern World, 1780–1914: Global Connections and Comparisons*. Oxford: Blackwell, 2004.
Benjamin, Walter. "Die Aufgabe des Übersetzers." *Gesammelte Schriften*. Vol. 4: 1. Frankfurt am Main: Suhrkamp, 1972. 9–21.
———. "The Task of the Translator." *Illuminations*. Ed. Hannah Arendt. Trans. Harry Zohn. London: Fontana, 1973. 69–82.
Child, Harold Hannyngton. Rev. of *The Little Demon*, by Feodor Sologub. *Times Literary Supplement* 30 Mar. 1916: 150.
Cournos, John. "Aleksei Remizov." *Egoist* 3 (1916): 28–29.
———. *Autobiography*. New York: Putnam's, 1935.
———. "Feodor Sologub." *Egoist* 3 (1916): 4–5.
———. "Feodor Sologub." *Fortnightly Review* 98 (1915): 480–90.
———. "Not Vodka." *Egoist* 3 (1916): 134.
Davie, Donald, ed. *Russian Literature and Modern English Fiction: A Collection of Critical Essays*. Chicago: University of Chicago Press, 1965.
Davies, Anna Morpurgo. *History of Linguistics: Nineteenth-Century Linguistics*. London: Longman, 1998.
Dikman, M. I. "Poetichskoe tvorchestvo Fedora Sologuba." *Stikhotvoreniia*. By Fedor Sologub. St Petersburg: Gumanitarnoe agentstvo "Akademicheskiĭ proekt," 2000. 5–74.
Eliot, T. S. *Selected Essays*. London: Faber, 1980.
———. "Turgenev." *Egoist* 4 (1917): 167.
Fletcher, John Gould. "Sologub's 'Created Legend.'" *Egoist* 3 (1916): 167–68.

Ford, Ford, Madox. "The Function of the Arts in the Republic." Editorial. *English Review* 1 (1908): 157–60.

France, Peter, ed. *The Oxford Guide to Literature in English Translation*. Oxford: Oxford University Press, 2000.

Freud, Sigmund. "The Aetiology of Hysteria." *Early Psycho-Analytic Publications*. Ed. and trans. James Strachey with Anna Freud, Alix Strachey and Alan Tyson. London: Hogarth Press and Institute of Psycho-Analysis, 1962. 187–221. Vol. 3 of *The Standard Edition of the Complete Psychological Works of Sigmund Freud*. 24 vols. 1953–74.

———. "Zur Ätiologie der Hysterie." *Gesammelte Werke*. Vol. 1. London: Imago, 1952. 423–59.

Gaonkar, Dilip Parameshwar, ed. *Alternative Modernities*. Durham: Duke University Press, 2001.

Garnett, Constance. "The Art of Translation." *Listener* 30 January 1947: 195.

Goethe, Johann Wolfgang von. *Goethes Werke*. Vol. 4: 43. Weimar: Böhlaus, 1908.

Jameson, Fredric. *A Singular Modernity*. London: Verso, 2002.

Katz, Daniel. *American Modernism's Expatriate Scene: The Labour of Translation*. Edinburgh: Edinburgh University Press, 2007.

Kenner, Hugh. "The Making of the Modernist Canon." *Canons*. Ed. Robert von Hallberg. Chicago: University of Chicago Press, 1984. 363–75.

Mallarmé, Stéphane. *Collected Poems*. Berkeley: University of California Press, 1994.

———. "Crise de vers." *Oeuvres Complètes*. Ed. Bertrand Marcel. Vol. 2. Paris: Gallimard, 2003. 204–13.

———. "Crisis in Poetry." *Selected Prose Poems, Essays and Letters*. Trans. Bradford Cook. Baltimore: Johns Hopkins University Press, 1956. 34–43.

Marx, Karl, and Friedrich Engels. *The Communist Manifesto*. Trans. Samuel Moore. Ed. Gareth Stedman Jones. Harmondsworth: Penguin, 2002.

———. *Das Kommunitische Manifest (Manifest der Kommunitische Partei)*. Ed. Thomas Kuczynski. Trier: Karl-Marx-Haus, 1995.

May, Rachel. *The Translator in the Text: On Reading Russian Literature in English*. Evanston: Northwestern University Press, 1994.

Montagu-Nathan, M. "Translations of Russian Fiction." *Egoist* 2 (1915): 142–43, 152–53.

Niranjana, Tejaswini. *Siting Translation: History, Post-Structuralism, and the Colonial Context*. Berkeley: University of California Press, 1992.

Peaker, Carol. "Reading Revolution: Russian Émigrés and the Reception of Russian Literature in England, c. 1890–1905." Diss. Oxford University, 2007.

Saussure, Ferdinand de. *Cours de Linguistique Générale*, Ed. Charles Bally and Albert Sechehaye, with Albert Riedlinger. Paris: Payot, 1972.

———. *Course in General Linguistics*. Ed. Charles Bally and Albert Sechehaye, with Albert Riedlinger. Trans. Roy Harris. London: Duckworth, 1983.

Schleiermacher, Friedrich. "Ueber die verschiedenen Methoden des Uebersezens." *Das Problem des Übersetzens*. Ed. Hans Joachim Störig. Stuttgart: Goverts, 1963. 38–70.

Schwartz, Sanford. *The Matrix of Modernism: Pound, Eliot, and Early Twentieth-Century Thought*. Princeton: Princeton University Press, 1985.

Sologub, Feodor. *The Little Demon*. Trans. John Cournos and Richard Aldington. London: Secker, 1916.

———. *The Little Demon*. Trans. Ronald Wilks. London: Penguin, 1994.

———. *Melkii bes. Sobranie sochinenii*. Vol. 2. Moscow: NPK "Intelvak," 2001. 1–288.

———. *The Petty Demon*. Trans. S. D. Cioran. Ann Arbor: Ardis, 1983.

———. *The Petty Demon*. Trans. by Andrew Field. New York: Random, 1962.

Spivak, Gayatri Chakravorty. "The Politics of Translation." *Destabilizing Theory: Contempo-rary Feminist Debates*. Ed. Michèle Barrett and Anne Phillips. Cambridge: Polity, 1992. 177–200.

Strich, Fritz. *Goethe and World Literature*. Trans. C. A. M. Sym. Port Washington: Kennikat, 1972.

Toury, Gideon. "A Rationale for Descriptive Translation Studies." *The Manipulation of Literature: Studies in Literary Translation*. Ed. Theo Hermans. London: Croom Helm, 1985. 16–41.

Venuti, Lawrence. *The Translator's Invisibility: A History of Translation*. Rev. ed. London: Routledge, 2008.

Vogüé, E. M. de. *Le Roman Russe*. Paris: Plon, 1886.

———. *The Russian Novel*. Trans. H. A. Sawyer. London: Chapman and Hall, 1913.

Woolf, Virginia. "The Russian Point of View." *The Essays of Virginia Woolf, 1925–1928*. Ed. Andrew McNeillie. London: Hogarth, 1994. 181–90

Yao, Steven G. *Translation and the Languages of Modernism: Gender, Politics, Language*. Basingstoke: Palgrave, 2002.

CHAPTER 24

JAPANESE MODERNISM AND "CINE-TEXT": FRAGMENTS AND FLOWS AT EMPIRE'S EDGE IN KITAGAWA FUYUHIKO AND YOKOMITSU RIICHI

WILLIAM O. GARDNER

IN November 1930, literary critic Inoue Yoshio wrote that the "belief in the eye" evident in Kitagawa Fuyuhiko's recent poetry had progressed from a faith in the human eye to a belief in "that which is all the more precise, all the more objective: to the machine eye—to the lens" (17).[1] This critical comment, strongly evocative of Soviet filmmaker and theorist Dziga Vertov's conception of the "cine-eye" (*kinoglaz*), builds upon Kitagawa's own statement that "the poetry of tomorrow is advancing toward the 'victory of the eye'" (Usawa 30). As Inoue suggests, Kitagawa's poetry circa 1930 displays a tendency to emulate the film camera, rather than the human eye, in presenting objects that are disassociated from the viewpoint of any single subjective viewing position. This aspiration to the free-ranging and "objective" viewpoint of the "machine eye" is part of a broad confluence between the literary and the cinematic in Kitagawa's work, which we can also identify in his exploration of the poetic genre of the "cinépoème," as well as his coinage of the term "prose film" in his later critical and theoretical writings on cinema. As I will explore in this essay, Kitagawa's writings from the 1920s and 1930s, together with the contemporaneous works of prose author Yokomitsu Riichi, are strongly marked by this confluence of the literary and the cinematic—so much so that we might term Kitagawa and Yokomitsu's writing from this period "cine-text": literary and critical texts permeated with cinematic qualities and concerns.

Indeed, Kitagawa and Yokomitsu's engagement with film was not limited to a fascination with the precision, objectivity, or mobility of the "camera eye" as Inoue suggests. Rather, it extended to the entire ability of the cinematic apparatus to capture the temporality of objects in motion, and of the ability of the filmmaker, through film editing or montage, to organize segments of space and time registered by the film camera into a new synthetic whole: a set of issues I will schematize as the relationship between "fragment" and "flow." Furthermore, in Kitagawa and Yokomitsu's work, this interest in cinematicity was inextricably linked with an exploration of the nature of modern subjectivity under the regimes of capitalism and the economic and geopolitical competition of imperialism. In this essay, I will explore this confluence of the literary and cinematic—together with its political implications—through a brief examination of four instances of "cine-text": Kitagawa's poetry collection *War* (*Sensô* 1929, untranslated), Yokomitsu's novel *Shanghai* (*Shanhai* 1928–1932), the concept of literary formalism Yokomitsu proposed around the year 1930, and the theory of the "prose film" that Kitagawa unveiled in the following decade.[2]

JAPANESE MODERNISM

Cinema, with its extensive technical complex of studio-based filming and production, international and domestic circuits of distribution, and local sites of consumption—the movie theaters—had thoroughly penetrated Japanese urban culture by the 1920s. A Japanese film almanac compiled in 1930 lists thirteen domestic film studios as well as 1,244 cinema theaters in Japan and 63 in the colonies, admitting over 192 million customers a year (Kokusai eiga tsûshinsha 5). The same almanac cites 2,863 Japanese films newly submitted to censorship in the Home Ministry in the year 1929, together with 741 American films and 275 European films, indicating both the prodigious output of the Japanese film industry and a substantial national appetite for foreign films (163–67).[3] The almanac also lists nearly seven thousand *benshi,* or film narrators, employed in the movie theaters, although by 1930 these distinctive representatives of silent-era Japanese cinema culture were already under pressure owing to the advent of "talkies" or sound film (159).[4] Beyond sheer numbers, the surviving Japanese films of the 1920s and 1930s—including works by such masters as Mizoguchi Kenji, Ozu Yasujirô, and Itô Daisuke—as well as the vivid pages of film journals such as *Kinema junpo,* attest to a vibrant and cosmopolitan film culture rivaling that of any of the great metropolitan centers across the globe.

This extensive cinema was but one aspect of the modern urban culture that helped to generate and sustain a Japanese modernist literature in the 1920s and 1930s. Following the victories in the Sino-Japanese (1894–1895) and Russo-Japanese (1904–1905) wars, which demonstrated the success of the Meiji government's "rich nation, strong army" program of rapid economic and military development, Japan progressively expanded its formal empire and its informal sphere of influence in Asia and the Pacific. Subsequently, Japan's urban centers underwent a rapid period of population growth and infrastructural development in the 1910s and 1920s, including the construction of new factory zones, business centers, subways, and suburban commuter lines, as well as a glamorous consumer culture represented by the cafes and department stores of the Ginza. Rapid developments in media and communications technology included not only the establishment of a national radio broadcasting network (the present-day NHK) in 1926 and new markets opened by the publishing industry but also the dramatic expansion of newspaper circulation (nearly doubling in the early 1920s), the establishment of new mass-circulation magazines, and a literary publishing boom inaugurated in 1926 by the publication of so-called *enpon* book series available for subscription at one yen a piece.

In the popular journalism of the day, young people who embraced the new lifestyles offered by the cinemas, cafes, department stores, and commuting centers of the modern city were referred to as "modern girls" (*modan gâru* or *moga*) and "modern boys" (*modan boi* or *mobo*), and the literature that described their lifestyles—often published in the new popular magazines as well as literary journals—was identified by such critics as Ôya Sôichi and Hirabayashi Hatsunosuke as "modernism" (*modanizumu*). At the same time, writers, artists, filmmakers, and theater directors showed a keen interest in the development of European avant-gardes. Futurism, Dadaism, Cubism, Expressionism, Surrealism, and Constructivism were all introduced and extensively debated in the 1920s, and homegrown avant-garde movements emerged, such as the Mavo artists' group and the Shinkankakuha (New Perception School) literary faction. Japanese literary modernism of the 1920s and 1930s is thus characterized by the free exchange of thematic material and stylistic devices between avant-garde groups and the "popular modernism" or "vernacular modernism" developed in the popular press, as well as niche magazines and journals such as *New Youth* (*Shinseinen*) and *Literary Metropolis* (*Bungei toshi*).[5] Moreover, as in other modernist contexts such as the contemporary Parisian literary world, there was a heated exchange of ideas between print literature and other media, especially the cinema, further intensifying the circuit between "high" and "low" cultures.

Yokomitsu Riichi (1989–1947) is one of the foremost representatives of modernist literature to emerge from within the highbrow or "pure literature" wing of the literary establishment, as opposed to the popular modernism developed by such magazines as *New Youth*. In 1924, together with Kawabata Yasunari, Yokomitsu led a group of young writers in breaking from the journal *Literary Seasons* (*Bungei shunjû*) to found the journal *Literary Age* (*Bungei jidai*). Soon after, critic Chiba Kameo dubbed this breakaway group the Shinkankakuha or New Perception School, capturing in this appellation the group's focus on conveying the neurological and somatic experience of contemporary urban life. Yokomitsu embraced the name and became the group's chief propagandist and theoretician. Nevertheless, despite Yokomitsu's firm roots in the elite wing of the literary establishment, it is important to note that the concepts "pure literature" (*jun bungaku*) and "mass literature" (*taishû bungaku*), which became relatively naturalized in the postwar period, were still under construction and debate in the 1920s, and, as already mentioned, Japanese modernism was characterized by the intercourse of themes, styles, audiences, and writerly affiliations between popular and highbrow literatures, as well as exchanges across literary and non-literary media. As one example of this intercourse, Yokomitsu and his fellow writers of the Shinkankakuha showed an intense interest in cinema, launching a film journal, *Film Age* (*Eiga jidai*) in 1926, collaborating with filmmaker Kinugasa Teinosuke to found the New Perception School Film Alliance (Shinkankakuha eiga renmei), and producing the noted avant-garde film *A Page of Madness* (*Kurutta Ippeiji* 1926), directed by Kinugasa from a script by Kawabata.[6]

Kitagawa Fuyuhiko (1900–1990) played a central role in the development of modernism in poetry similar to that of Yokomitsu in prose. In 1924, Kitagawa, Anzai Fuyue, and two others founded the poetry journal *A*, edited by Anzai out of his home in Dalian, Manchuria. Together with Anzai, Kitagawa developed the influential form of *tanshi* (short poetry), which offered a modernist revision of the haiku poetic tradition in dialogue with post-symbolist French poetry. Subsequently, Kitagawa experimented with longer forms such as the *shin sanbunshi* (New Prose Poem) and cinépoème, and, along with Anzai and ten other poets, participated as a founding member of a new journal, *Poetry and Poetics* (*Shi to shiron*). This journal, edited by Haruyama Yukio in Tokyo, became the most prominent forum for modernist poetry, criticism, and translation during its run from 1928–1932, arguably the high-water mark for Japanese prewar modernism.[7] Kitagawa was also active as a translator, publishing a translation of Max Jacob's poetry collection *Cornet à dés* and producing the first Japanese translation of André Breton's "Manifeste du surréalisme" (both in the year 1929). In addition, he established a career as a film critic and film journal editor, working on the editorial staff of the prominent film journal *Kinema junpo* from 1927 and publishing several book-length works of film criticism in the 1930s.

The late 1920s and early 1930s, which saw the rise to prominence of both popular and highbrow forms of Japanese modernism, was also an era of heated activity in Marxist criticism and the heyday of the "Proletarian Literature" movement. Despite the steady toll of government repression and factional infighting, Proletarian Literature, a multifaceted cultural movement aiming to increase consciousness of and resistance to capitalist exploitation within the framework of the international Communist movement, became a major force in Japan following the establishment of the Japan Proletarian Literary Federation in 1925 and did not wane until the mass public renunciations of communism (*tenkô*) by jailed activists beginning in 1933. Writers of all stripes and dispositions were forced to take some position (even an ostensibly "apolitical" one) with regard to the Proletarian Literary movement, and it is here that Yokomitsu and Kitagawa differed markedly. Yokomitsu became an outspoken critic of the Proletarian Literature movement and conducted a series of debates with Marxist writers and critics in the pages of prominent intellectual and literary journals. Political tensions within the Shinkankakuha group itself eventually led to the departure of leftist writers Kataoka Teppei and Kon Tôkô from the *Literary Age* coterie and the folding of the journal in 1927. Kitagawa, on the other hand, was one of a group of left-leaning writers who in 1930 departed from the journal *Poetry and Poetics* over dissatisfaction with its "apolitical" editorial trend. He cofounded a new journal *Poetry—Reality* (*Shi—Genjitsu*), which took a more overtly political tack, and joined the Japan Proletarian Writers' League in the same year.

Despite their differing political stances, we can find many thematic as well as formal commonalities in Yokomitsu and Kitagawa's works circa 1930, especially Yokomitsu's novel *Shanghai* and Kitagawa's poetry collection *War*. Both works are set on the edges of Japan's expanding sphere of imperialist domination in East Asia. Yokomitsu's novel takes place in the Chinese treaty port of the title, a focal point of European and Japanese imperialist rivalry as well as rising Chinese nationalism. Kitagawa's poetry collection, meanwhile, is strongly associated with Manchuria, where Kitagawa grew up as the son of an engineer for the South Manchuria Railway Company, a Japanese-owned company that helped to establish Japan's imperialist foothold in the region between the Russo-Japanese war and the establishment of the puppet state of Manchukuo in 1932. In comparing these two works, I will highlight their shared formal strategies with respect to the depiction of time, motion, and materiality—strategies that both enable and limit their interrogation of the ideologies of Japanese imperialism. In particular, I will observe how these works employ the juxtaposition of "fragment" versus "flow" to explore the relationship between the bodies of individual human subjects—which are often presented as decidedly material objects and dissected into component parts—and the broader flows—of time, energy, and economic and geopolitical forces—into which these human figures are embedded. I will then turn briefly to the two authors' critical works and trace how the elements of "fragment" and "flow" are articulated differently in Yokomitsu's formalist literary theory and Kitagawa's theory of the "prose film."

FRAGMENT AND FLOW

In exploring relationship between fluid time and motion (flow) and the individual, abrupt, and singular moment (fragment), Yokomitsu and Kitagawa were seizing on a central formal concern of modern art of the early twentieth century. Interest in this relationship can be traced to two clusters of nineteenth-century scientific and technological innovations: on one hand, the new sciences of thermodynamics, electromagnetics, and field theory; on the other, the development of still and motion picture photography, which opened new forms of time and space to human observation.[8] Connecting these two clusters were scientific investigation into the sensory mechanism of the mind-body, together with a parallel philosophical exploration of issues of perception, mind, and memory by turn-of-the-century thinkers such as William James and Henri Bergson. Meanwhile, the social science of economics, especially as enfolded into a philosophical and political program by Marx and Engels, offered new means to conceptualize the transnational flow of labor, goods, and capital, in a significant parallel to the analysis of the flows of matter and energy in contemporary physics.

In the twentieth century, under the scientific influence of thermodynamics, electromagnetics, and related disciplines, the temporally and physically discrete object as a subject of artistic representation was increasingly discredited in favor of an interest in depicting the interplay of various forces and the resulting dynamism through time. As art historian Christof Asendorf writes in respect to art between the two world wars: "the view of objects from outside was replaced by an analysis of their functions. The artist dealt henceforth with *interactions between forces and effects*" (195). Perhaps the most straightforward declaration of this artistic concern can be found in the "Technical Manifesto of Futurist Painting," of 1910, in which Umberto Boccioni and his colleagues declare: "The gesture which we would reproduce on canvas shall no longer be a fixed moment in universal dynamism. It shall simply be the dynamic sensation itself" (289).

In contrast to the Futurist program of moving from the fixed to the dynamic image, the influential photographic studies in animal motion in the 1880s and 1890s by Eadweard Muybridge exploited the potential of photography to momentarily arrest the flow of time—most famously in capturing the positions of a horse's legs in full gallop, which were imperceptible to the naked eye. Muybridge's time-dissecting studies of human and animal bodies in motion, however, simultaneously pointed toward the potential of the motion-picture apparatus to reanimate the motion thus dissected in still photography.[9] Indeed, the dialectic between the new technical ability to arrest a brief instant in time and the contrary scientific and aesthetic interest in flows of time and motion is best captured in the cinematic apparatus itself, in which a sequence of instantaneous images impressed sequentially on a roll of film stock produces a moving picture when passed through the film projector.

In more recent times, Gilles Deleuze's works on cinema (*Cinéma 1: L'Image-Mouvement* 1983, and *Cinéma 2: L'Image-temps* 1985) have provided a new analysis of the connections between the cinema and the philosophy of Bergson, which offers many useful perspectives on our consideration of fragment and flow in Kitagawa and Yokomitsu. Dividing the basic elements of cinema into the frame (a closed set, or immobile section), the shot (a mobile section, or movement-image), and montage (an assemblage of movement-images), Deleuze analyzes each of these elements as images of duration (*durée*) or the constantly changing whole: "(1) there are not only instantaneous images, that is, immobile sections of movement; (2) there are movement-images which are mobile sections of duration; (3) there are, finally, time-images, that is, duration-images, change-images, relation-images, volume-images which are beyond movement itself" (11). From a Deleuzean standpoint, we can view the works of Kitagawa and Yokomitsu as an exploration of the relationship between duration of a whole (flow) and the instantaneous image captured in the still photograph (fragment). Moreover, in Kitagawa's interest in the manipulation of time expressed in his theory of the "prose film," in which he raises the possibility of the filmmaker "rebelling against time in the temporal art of film," we can find a consideration of the political valences of what Deleuze would term the "time-image," i.e., a representation that goes beyond movement to present an image of time itself.

KITAGAWA FUYUHIKO'S WAR

The tension between the depiction of temporally and spatially dynamic systems and the tendency to arrest time and fracture space is readily apparent in Kitagawa Fuyuhiko's poetry collection *War*. Many of the poems of this collection share a common poetic strategy in which the flow of time and the field of dynamic forces are momentarily arrested, and, in that suspended moment, the progressive objectification of the human is decisively revealed. Kitagawa's poems thus isolate a point of violence, shock, abjection, or sharp incongruity at the intersection of the flow of forces through time and the decoupage of the singular moment (what Deleuze, after Bergson, refers to as the "any-instant-whatever").

One of Kitagawa's best-known poems included in *War* is his *tanshi* or "short poem" "Rush Hour" (248):

> Rush Hour
> At the ticket gate a finger was clipped off with the ticket

The rush hour commute provides a vivid instance of the economic pressures and flows of capitalism, rendered visible through the flow of bodies through space: at regular intervals in the workweek, the movement of the bodies of workers and the organs of mass transport are orchestrated with Taylorist efficiency. In Kitagawa's poem, set amid this orchestrated flow of the modern city, an organic body part (the finger) is mistaken for an inorganic economic token (the ticket), and, in being severed from the body, the finger becomes further abjected and objectified. The poetic conjuring of this act of accidental violence creates an image of a singular moment; and yet, at the moment that this time-fragment becomes separated from the system-flow, the brutal nature of the system is exposed. This technique of violent poetic decoupage that paradoxically reveals the brutality of a larger system is a characteristic strategy of Kitagawa's *War*.

Despite the leftist political undertone in "Rush Hour" and many other poems of *War*, the poems of this collection nevertheless betray an ambivalent attitude toward such acts of violence and dehumanization. While the collection's recurrent violence is the occasion for the poet's outrage against the interwoven systems of capitalism, militarism, and imperialism, at the same time, violence and dehumanization themselves harbor a strong aesthetic and sexual fascination for the poet. This fascination is revealed in poems such as "Razor" (247), which also depicts the encounter of metal and flesh, in a moment of violence that ruptures the surface integrity of the body:

Razor

The blade of the Western razor is a translucent stick of candy. Lick it, and at that instant, your lips are pared off like a flash of lightning. This is a splendid refrigerant. This is a splendid refrigerant.

The imaginary act of licking the razor reminds us of the moment in Luis Buñuel and Salvador Dalí's *Un chien andalou* (1928) in which an eyeball is sliced with a razor. In Buñuel and Dali's film, this moment of singularity and pain is juxtaposed in a type of visual analogy or metaphor with a matching shot of a thin cloud floating across the moon. In Kitagawa's poem the razor's violence is compared with a "splendid refrigerant," which seems to be less a metaphor than an affective description of the chilling, stimulating, and yet artificial sensation of the razor's cut. Nevertheless, in its affinities with European Surrealism, Kitagawa's "Razor" exemplifies the aesthetic of violent fetishism that recurs throughout *War*, in which human flesh intermingles with metal and glass, and the fragmented and literally objectified body becomes the object of sensual or sexual fascination.

While *tanshi* or "short poems" such as "Rush Hour" and "Razor" represent an important part of Kitagawa's early poetic oeuvre as compiled in *War*, this collection also shows Kitagawa moving away from the *tanshi* form and experimenting with longer forms such as the "new prose poem" and the "cinépoème." Although there are only two cinépoèmes collected in *War*, this poetic form is essential to understanding Kitagawa's poetic development during this period of his career. The cinépoème form, also employed by other Japanese modernist poets of the time such as Takenaka Iku and Kondô Azuma, typically comprises a set of numbered lines that are analogous to the numbered sequence of shots in a film scenario.[10] In his critical writings of this time, Kitagawa expressed hope for the cinépoème in transforming the sensibility of contemporary poets: "I think that writing cinépoème has a great power to effect the change from a spiritualist [or idealist] view of poetry to a materialist view of poetry" (*Junsui eiga ki* 30). He further advocated the cinépoème form because it "is the most replete with all of the conditions to make tomorrow's poetry clear and direct; and further, because the poetry of tomorrow is advancing towards the 'victory of the eye'" (quoted in Usawa 30). It is poetry's adaptation of this objectivist, materialist belief in the victory of the (machine) eye to which critic Inoue Yoshio referred in his remarks cited at the beginning of this essay.

Kitagawa's "Arm" (244) is the first of two such cinépoèmes included in *War*. Although the geographic setting of "Arm" is unspecified, the poem's context within *War*, as well as the references to denuded mountains and coolie labor, strongly suggest that the setting is Manchuria, and quite possibly the major port city of Dalian, a setting with which Kitagawa is often associated due to his boyhood experiences in Manchuria and his membership in the Dalian-based *A* coterie.[11]

Arm

1 Denuded mountain.
2 An arm that pushes wagons falls from the summit.
3 A heap of red earth.
4 Severed arm.
5 The sea that is slowly lost.
6 Globules of fat, a giant structure.
7 Fat that trails to the summit's hospital.
8 A magnificent hospital.
9 In the hospital's specimen room, a steel arm preserved in alcohol.
10 The arm smirks.
11 Seen from the summit: streets trailing fat.
12 The arm that laughs like a rail.
13 Seen from the summit: wrenching and warping streets.

This cinépoème relies heavily on the paratactic enumeration of substantives with few transitive verbal relationships, conjunctions, or complex subordinate clauses. While it should also be noted that Kitagawa's poem employs rhetorical effects that are the special domain of poetic language, such as the personification of the "grinning" arm, or the metaphoric depiction of the bleeding limb as "the sea that is slowly lost," the main thrust of the passage is nevertheless in the sequential enumeration of objects themselves, whether organic ("an arm that pushes wagons") or inorganic ("a heap of red earth"). These objects are often spatially incongruous, and we are given no subjective position or transitive verbal relationship (such as "X viewed Y"). Instead, Kitagawa's poem evokes a "machine eye" free to assemble montage linkages between disparate objects and points in space, independently of a human subject position—the "eye which would be in things," as Deleuze writes of Vertov's "cine-eye" (81). Moreover, this "machine eye" has the flexibility to depict objects of radically different scales, from the panoramic "establishing shot" of the denuded mountain to a "close-up" of globules of fat that, under magnification, resemble a "giant structure."

The style of writing employed in Kitagawa's poem—the numbered descriptions of shots, often in brief sentence fragments ending in a substantive—closely follows the conventions of film scenario writing as it was introduced in Japanese film journals in the 1920s and 1930s (Shimamura 125–26). The technique of ending a sentence in a noun preceded by a modifying phrase (rather than a verb as is typical in Japanese grammar) is called *taigendome* in Japanese and is also frequently used in haiku poetry—marking another confluence of the literary and the cinematic in the cinépoème form. In its use of *taigendome* and avoidance of conjunctions and hypotactic syntactic relations, Kitagawa's poem exploits a tension between the singularity of the individual line (depicting either a still object or a brief "movement-image") and the potential for a narrative flow between these lines, which must be primarily supplied by the reader in the absence of interlinking conjunctions or predicates.

Thematically, Kitagawa's poem sets into conflict two elements of Japanese imperialism in Manchuria: on one hand, the brutal exploitation of coolie labor represented by the severed arm; on the other hand, Japanese "civilization" and paternalistic colonial policies represented by the "splendid hospital." These two elements are arrayed in spatial contrast: the hospital is at the mountain's summit, and the "wrenching and warping" streets, whose docks and homes form the world of the native laborer, are in the city below. The "arm" that has been mobilized from the city to construct the colonizer's "splendid hospital" is wrenched from the body of the laborer and suspended in alcohol in the heart of the hospital, its trickle of blood and fat linking the two worlds of hospital and city. While the arm reveals the hidden brutality of the Japanese *"mission civilatrice"* (or project of assimilation), its warped metallic grin captures the subversive derision of the colonized population.

In its ideologically tendentious juxtaposition of these two elements of Japanese imperialism, Kitagawa's cinépoème could be said to employ a form of dialectical montage aimed at producing what Sergei Eisenstein terms "montage understanding." According to Eisenstein, if the dialectic montage method is successfully applied, the filmmaker and film viewer will "find in the *juxtaposition of shots an arrangement of a new qualitative element,* a new *image,* [and] a new *understanding.*"[12] In the cinematic arrangement of segments of time and space in "Arm," Kitagawa seems to have been working toward a method of reanimating the fragmentary and fetishistic poetic developed in his "short poetry" according to new kinetic and didactic principles. Nevertheless, both the poems in the "new prose poem" form as well as the "cinépoème" form in *War* preserve the tension between the singular and arresting moment and the depiction of motion that reveals underlying systemic forces.

Yokomitsu Riichi's *Shanghai*

A nearly identical tension between fragment and flow, as well as a concomitant aesthetic interest in cinematic qualities, is present in Yokomitsu Riichi's *Shanghai.* The novel is a fictionalization of the historical May 30th incident of 1925, in which the city of Shanghai erupted in riots and work stoppages after the shooting of a Chinese worker in a Japanese-owned cotton mill, which served to intensify the nationalist, communist, and anti-imperialist movements in China. Yokomitsu's novel depicts a span of several weeks in the life of its protagonist, Sanki, who loses his job as a bank clerk and takes a position in a Japanese-owned cotton mill on the eve of a shooting and subsequent riot that parallels the May 30th incident. Surrounding Sanki are a complex of characters representing various nationalities, social classes, and ideological positions, including a Japanese bathhouse worker, a Singapore-based Japanese lumber trader, a Chinese revolutionary, and an Indian exponent of Pan-Asianism.

The passages of scenic description that frequently begin the chapters of Yokomitsu's novel *Shanghai* are not merely "cinematic" in the general sense of being visually evocative; in their paratactic sequences of substantives arranged according to cinematic principles, they also bear a striking resemblance to the cinépoème form in particular.[13] This tendency is evident in the very first paragraph of the novel, as well as in the descriptive passage that begins the second chapter, often cited by critics as an example of Yokomitsu's Shinkankakuha literary technique:

> At high tide the river swelled and flowed backward. Prows of darkened motor-boats lined up in a wave pattern. A row of rudders drawn up. Mountains of off-loaded cargo. The black legs of a wharf bound in chains. A signal showing calm winds raised atop a weather station tower. A customs house spire dimly visible through evening fog. Coolies on barrels stacked on the embankment, becoming soaked in the damp air. A black sail, torn and tilted, creaking along, adrift on brackish waves. (*Shanghai* 3)
>
> A district of crumbling brick buildings. Some Chinese, wearing long-sleeved black robes that were swollen and stagnant like kelp in the depths of the ocean, crowded together on a narrow street. A beggar groveled on the pebble-covered road. In a shop window above him hung fish bladders and bloody torsos of carp. In the fruit stand next door piles of bananas and mangos spilled out onto the pavement. And next to that a pork butcher. Skinned carcasses, suspended hoof-down, formed a flesh-colored grotto with a vague, dark recess from which the white point of a clock face sparkled like an eye. (*Shanghai* 7)

The first paragraph of the novel presents, in rapid succession, various scenes that establish a sense of the setting and atmosphere on Shanghai's docks. In the original Japanese text, Yokomitsu includes four straight sentence fragments in *taigendome* constructions (sentences 2–4). Indeed, it would not be difficult to imagine attaching numbers to each sentence in this paragraph and formatting them as a cinépoème. Yokomitsu's technique here seems closely related to the expressionistic montage that was used by some contemporary filmmakers to establish atmosphere and location at the start of a film. In the second of these passages, the lateral movement connecting the descriptions conveyed in each successive sentence, as the "viewer" or camera-eye seems to progress from shop to shop, suggests the technique of the tracking shot.

As in Kitagawa's *War*, there is a constant intermingling, confusion, and transposition in *Shanghai* between the realms of organic and inorganic matter. This is evident in the above passages' descriptions of the wharf's "legs" being "bound in chains," the kelplike sleeves of the Chinese crowd, and the meat of the fishmonger and butcher shop, which lies in the enigmatic middle ground between organic flesh, inert matter, and economic commodity.[14] The most vivid intermingling of organic and inorganic occurs in the final sentence, where the pork carcasses form a strange grotto framing the white clockface, transformed in Yokomitsu's simile to a gleaming eye.

These two introductory passages introduce two central motifs of the novel: in the first passage, the motif of intermeshing flows (*nagare*) and points of stagnation (*yodomi*) in the modern city; in the second, the deformation of the body and transformation of flesh into commodity. The prominent literary scholars Maeda Ai and Komori Yōichi have each discussed these motifs, and Seiji Lippit and Gregory Golley have expanded upon their analyses in English-language studies. As Komori has argued, the individual human body loses its identity and integrity in *Shanghai*, and, as Lippit paraphrases, is "placed into fluid networks of assemblage and disassemblage" (89). Clashing economic interests and conflicting racialist, nationalist, and internationalist ideologies, often depicted as waves and liquid flows, all converge on Shanghai, and lay claim to the bodies and brains of the characters inhabiting the city. "The huge vortex of Asia did not appear enormous to Sanki," Yokomitsu writes. "Instead it was, for him, a map folded up inside his head" (108). At the center of this maelstrom, the novel returns time and again to the motif of the human body, abjected and commodified by the pressures of capitalism, and rendered into territory by the imperatives of nationalism. *Shanghai* thus shares with Kitagawa's *War* a tension between the depiction of dynamic ideological and economic forces and a fragmentation of time and space that objectifies and disassembles the human body.

However, while Kitagawa's poetry displays a drive to organize its fragments into a dialectical montage that is implicitly critical of capitalism and the imperialist nation-state (even while it regularly succumbs to the fetishistic allure of its own metallic violence), Yokomitsu's novel seems to primarily aspire to map the forces of imperialism and capitalism, and to trace their impact on the bodies and subjective states of its expatriate Japanese protagonists—that is, it displays a primarily descriptive rather than ideologically tendentious ambition. However, as Golley persuasively argues in his recent study *When Our Eyes No Longer See*, this descriptive impulse itself ultimately becomes a normalizing force, especially as it elucidates how nationalist ideology is inscribed onto the bodies of its protagonists. "Even at its most 'materialist,'" Golley asserts, "*Shanghai*'s excavation of the underlying laws of empire—of social conflict, racial oppression, and capitalist exchange—betrays the hazardous equanimity of a purely descriptive impulse, and essential tolerance of the violence it sets out to depict" (61).

YOKOMITSU RIICHI'S FORMALIST THEORY

The principles of fragment and flow return in a different guise in Yokomitsu's literary criticism from the same period. To get a sense of his theoretical concerns, we can begin with two statements that Yokomitsu made in the years 1928–1929, as his novel

Shanghai was being serialized. The first is a concise definition of literary form that he offered at the start of a protracted debate with members of the Proletarian literary faction ("Bungei jihyô 2" 151). The second is a definition of *eiga,* cinema or film (literally, projected pictures), that he contributed to a discussion of film and literature in the journal *New Tide* (*Shinchô*) (Nakamura 134):

> 1) [Literary] "form" is nothing other than a string of characters possessing rhythm that conveys meaning.
> 2) *Eiga* is a string of movements of objects that are viewed after passing through the lens.

While these two statements may seem rather innocuous at first, they contain in condensed form several theoretical elements that Yokomitsu was to develop over the course of the ensuing debate, which is known in Japanese literary history as the *keishiki shugi ronsô,* or "formalism debate." The key term connecting Yokomitsu's two statements is *raretsu*—a string, queue, or sequential accumulation of discrete items. The items being strung together shift from "characters" (*moji*) in his definition of literary form to "movements of objects" in his definition of film. The "movements of objects" that are strung together in the latter definition could arguably refer either to the single frame or film cell, or to the movement-image of the shot placed into montage. In either case, these definitions point to an analogy between the frames of a roll of film in capturing the successive positions of an object in motion, which are animated through the film apparatus and the viewer's visual perception, and the string of characters in a literary passage which are "activated" in the reader's mind through the complexities of the reading process—what Yokomitsu refers to elsewhere as the "mechanism" (*mekanizumu*) of literary form. The term *raretsu* thus returns us to the theme of the fragment or cell—represented here by the character, on the one hand, and the frame or shot on the other—versus the temporal flow of objects and energies, or the flow of time itself, as implicated in the projection and viewing of a roll of film and the reading of a literary text.[15] While Yokomitsu by no means implies that the "mechanism" of signification in a reader's encounter with a literary text is *identical* to a viewer's encounter with a film as mediated by the cinematic apparatus, it nevertheless appears that his thinking about these two processes developed in close parallel.

What occasioned Yokomitsu's definition of literary form as a "string of characters," and what are the implications of his formal theory to the literary politics of the day? The immediate pretext for Yokomitsu's first formulation were statements by literary critics Hirabayashi Hatsunosuke and Kurahara Korehito—both affiliated with the Proletarian literary camp—who argued that literary form (*keishiki*) should follow from the work's content (*naiyô*). In particular, Yokomitsu took objection to a warning by Hirabayashi that writers shouldn't pursue novelty of form for its own sake and thereby "let form run ahead of content." In contrast to the Marxist critics, who emphasized the vanguard role of the author in determining the "content" of the literary work, Yokomitsu insisted on the complete independence of author and text:

indeed, he envisioned the text as a "physical object" independent of both author and reader. He thus located the generation of "content" in the reader's encounter with the text as a physical object—the operation of deciphering the text or literary "form." Since the reader determines the content from the form manifest in the "string of characters," from Yokomitsu's perspective it is impossible for the form to be considered independently from, or subsidiary to, content, as Hirabayashi and Kurahara seemed to do.

In his formulations through the ensuing debate with the Proletarian camp, Yokomitsu called attention to the independence and materiality of the written text, repeatedly referring to written or printed characters as "physical objects" (*buttai*) or "objective things" (*kyakkanbutsu*), and even likening the characters on a printed page to "sculptures" or "meaningless stones." While some might think of letters or characters as Ideas in Platonic terms, Yokomitsu points to the materiality of characters as media, literally thin layers of ink impressed onto a sheet of paper, existing as objects in the world like any other. It is only through the mechanism of the reading process that these "meaningless stones" are reborn as "content" for the reader, allowing him to experience the "illusion of life" in the text. Furthermore, in the essay "Regarding characters: on form and mechanism" ("Moji ni tsuite: keishiki to mekanizumu ni tsuite"), Yokomitsu argues that each reader's generation of meaning or "content" is different, even on the level of the decipherment of individual characters:

> Following our perceptions and our intellect, from the form of the object called a character, we sense content—we sense the energy of "mountain" from [the character] "mountain" and that of "sea" from [the character] "sea." . . .
>
> To put it otherwise, "content" is the energy that arises between the reader and the form of the characters, and it is clear that this energy does not arise from a transformation within the characters themselves, but rather arises from a transformation in the mind of the reader. . . . Therefore, the content that arises from the form that is an identical object [i.e., an identical character] changes with each reader that views this identical object. For example, there is the character "sea." But, do we sense the identical, fixed "sea" from this character? One person might imagine the Seto Inland Sea that he saw in the past, while another might imagine the sea off the coast of Izu. In other words, the quantity of energy that is received from the character differs according to the mind of the individual reader. (115)

As this passage indicates, Yokomitsu envisioned each character giving rise to a fixed quantity of energy in the mind of the reader. As the reader follows the string of characters, the energy generated by his encounter with each character passes through his consciousness in a series of waves.[16] The "low-level" or "weak" energy generated by the string of characters in turn gives rise to an "intense" energy that is the literary "content" or "internal form" generated in the reader's imagination. Yokomitsu thus distinguishes between the "external form" that is the text or "string of characters," and the "internal form" that is the content generated in the mind of the reader:

> We may speak of the intense peak of energy that is "internal form." However, since this "internal form" arises from the cluster of weak energy, if it were not for the [external] form that gives rise to this weak energy, the intense energy [of internal form] would not arise. Therefore, we encounter the question of to what extent the weak energy has linked up to create the strong energy: that is, we encounter the issue of time. We call this time speed (*tempo*). The overall energy that arises from the structure of the work is dependent on how the *tempo* and internal form are coordinated. The sense of satisfaction we receive from our imaginative experience of a work indicates a complete harmony of the *tempo* and the internal form. (118–19)

As literary scholar Komori Yôichi discusses, Yokomitsu thus presents us with a compelling perspective on the passage through which language as a temporal phenomenon is transferred into writing, a primarily spatial (or, for Yokomitsu, "sculptural") medium, and then regains its temporal aspect through the mechanism of reading. Yokomitsu's emphasis in this passage on "tempo" returns us to his original definition that literary form is a "string of characters *possessing rhythm* that conveys meaning" (my italics).

This emphasis on rhythm or tempo in literary form is consistent with a critical discourse originating from Shinkankakuha writers and their more sympathetic critics regarding the importance of a fresh and compelling rhythmic element. As I have discussed in my study of the Shinkankakuha's collaboration with filmmaker Kinugasa Teinosuke, the emergence of "rhythm" and "tempo" as key terms in discussions of the Shinkankakuha literary school developed in close parallel with the intensive attention to the role of rhythm in cinema, especially as expressed in cinematic montage during the final phase of the silent film era. This film-critical discourse was in turn strongly influenced by the introduction of French "impressionist" film and film criticism, as represented by such directors and critics as Volkov, Gance, L'Herbier, Delluc, Moussinac, Mitry, and Epstein.

For example, in Iijima Tadashi's essay of 1924, "The Rhythm of Cinema" ("Eiga no rizumu"), anthologized as the first chapter of his book *The ABC of Cinema (Shinema no ABC)*, Iijima makes it clear that "rhythm" is the answer to his rhetorical question, "What is the fundamental quality that makes cinema (*eiga*) stand on its own as cinema?":

> Time is a major factor in the artistic nature of cinema (*eiga*). A certain number of scenes, some long and some short, are projected temporally, serially, on the screen. We perceive these through our eyes. This is in the same manner as [the role of] our ears in [perceiving] music. Therefore, what makes cinema truly cinematic is the rhythm sensed through the eyes. (3)

Thus, while Iijima defines "rhythm sensed through the eyes" as the fundamental element of film, Yokomitsu in turn places central importance on the element of rhythm or tempo in the process through which the "external form" of a "string of characters," is perceived through vision and gives rise in the reader's mind to the "internal form" of "content." Indeed, Yokomitsu goes on to define the author's goal in "formalism" as the employing of a minimum of external formal resources to engender a vivid internal form in the reader's imagination: "Formalism is the authorial ambition that attempts to limit the quantity of this variable energy [of the external form] and create an [internal] form that is like an issuing of fresh and vivid energy" (119). However, he notes that since the completed work is a "physical object" independent of the author's intention, even a superior work may, despite the author's intentions, find its energy "dispersed" and ineffectual in the mind of a given reader. While noting that many factors can shape readerly actualization of the text, Yokomitsu devotes particular attention to his fear that readers might place a predetermined ideology, rather than immediate experience of the work's form, at the center of their evaluation of the work. He therefore suggests that the "formalist movement" must engage in the education of the reader's sensibilities: "the value of the work should be determined not according to the reader's ideology (*shisô*), but according to the form of the work. . . . works of any ideology or "ism" can be in accord with formalism" (119).

To summarize his formalist theory, then, in response to overtly ideological readings of literature and the emphasis in Marxist criticism on the author's determination of content, Yokomitsu stresses the independence of the text from both author and reader: it is only a physical object. Only through the mechanism of reading, which is explained through the wavelike consciousness of the reader as his eyes follow the "string" of characters, is the text converted to "internal form" or "content." For Yokomitsu, the formalist author's goal is to manage the rhythm of the process of conversion from "external form" to "internal form" in order to produce a maximum sense of satisfaction or "fresh and vivid energy" in the reader. He does not, however, elaborate on the mechanism through which the "low energy" produced by the reader's encounter with "external form" is converted to the "intense energy" of content. Furthermore, within his exposition of "formalism" itself Yokomitsu does not specifically explain how the organization of formal and rhythmic elements beyond the level of the character (such as phrases, sentences, or longer passages) could be organized to produce this "fresh and vivid energy" in the reader.

Finally, by asserting that the works of any ideology or "ism" can be in accord with formalism, Yokomitsu effectively cuts off any discussion of the relationship between ideology and form. While this theoretical tack was undoubtedly a response to what he viewed as the naïve and simplistic politicization of literature by the Proletarian writing camp, it nevertheless retreats from the more difficult task of providing a theoretical ground upon which the *relationship* between formal and ideological issues could be interrogated. In this sense, Kitagawa's theory of the "prose film," which offers a complex reading of the relationship between the formal devices of the cinema and the critical intentions of the filmmaker, contrasts markedly with Yokomitsu's "formalism."

KITAGAWA FUYUHIKO'S *THEORY OF*
THE PROSE FILM

In his *Theory of Prose Film* (*Sanbun eiga ron*, 1940, untranslated) and related work produced over the 1930s, Kitagawa elaborated a theory that attempted to relate formal and ideological elements in film analysis, and to move beyond the montage-based film theory with its emphasis on the rhythmic qualities of cinema that Iijima Tadashi and other critics had developed in the previous decade. Kitagawa situates this theoretical development as a shift from lyricism or "poetry" in film toward a new type of filmmaking that he labeled the "prose film" (*sanbun eiga*). In Kitagawa's analysis, this shift was both stylistic, marking a difference of approach among directors, as well as temporal, corresponding with the technical transition from silent to sound film.

> Poetry (*inbun*) is a literary passage with an agreeable sound when vocalized. The agreeability of the sound comes from it being regulated through such [elements] as tone or rhyme. . . .
>
> At the close of the last century, when humans invented the motion picture apparatus that can capture reality in the form of motion, they didn't just leave it as it was. They felt the desire to connect the fragments of reality projected on the screen rhythmically, and they struggled to realize this desire. People will surely recall that for some time, theories of film as art centered on theories of rhythm. (*Gendai eiga ron* 11–12)

Through montage, then, the sustained portions of time and movement captured by the camera are reorganized to create a new type of rhythmic flow that Kitagawa associates with poetry or verse (*inbun*). He cites Abel Gance's *La Roue* (1923), which had been a central film for the elaboration of a theory of cinema as art for critics such as Iijima in the previous decade, as a prime example of the dreamlike, rhythmic beauty of films in the era of "poetry." In contrast, he offers "prose" as the mark of a possibility of a different type of filmmaking that had come to the fore in the age of the sound film: "Prose (*sanbun*) is a literary passage that emphasizes meaning over sound. Prose is rough and grinding. For prose, to observe and consider things are the essential points" (16).

Kitagawa is quick to note that since "film is fundamentally a temporal art," "no matter how you may try to make it rough, it will inevitably become rhythmic on its own." Yet with his concept of the "prose film," he raises the possibility of a new type of filmmaking that would "rebel against time in the temporal art of film" (18): "To set yourself afloat in the midst of a dream, that is, to give yourself over to time—this is the method of poetry. To awaken and become conscious of yourself in the midst of a dream, to rebel against time—this is the method of prose" (*Sanbun eiga ron* 110). To get an idea of Kitagawa's aesthetic and political agenda in proposing his theory of the "prose film," it is necessary to understand the qualities that he chooses to criticize in the previous era of "dreamlike" silent film.

Kitagawa's criticisms of the "poetic" film center on two interrelated aspects: first, the film's "flow" or rhythmic quality, which is described primarily as a quality of the film's cutting or montage, and second, the relationship of the film's protagonist to the subjectivity of the filmmaker. To clarify his attitude toward filmic "flow," Kitagawa criticizes filmmaker Yamanaka Sadao: "I viewed his fluid and elegant style as 'poetry,' and dubbed him a poet. . . . To flow is beautiful, but sometimes it's necessary to strike up against a rock or a stake." A disrupted flow grants the author "opportunity for self-reflection" (142). Kitagawa also cites the "poetic" spirit in Itô Daisuke's trilogy *Diary of Chûji's Travels* (*Chûji tabi nikki*, 1928), considered by many critics a masterpiece of silent cinema. While Itô's dynamic cutting style and rebellious attitude attracted much critical praise in the 1920s, Kitagawa criticizes Itô for failing to establish a critical distance from the film's protagonist, Kunisada Chûji, who he claims is too intimately identified with Itô's own "self." According to Kitagawa, all of the elements in the film, from Chûji's concubine, to his subordinates, to the very mountains and fields, are mobilized to depict Chûji, and "all converge towards Itô's expression of 'self' as a form of sentimental heroism" (108).

With respect to the issue of cutting and "flow," Kitagawa notes the tendency of the single cut or long take to grow in importance over montage in the era of sound film, and suggests this is one element of the new "prose film" style (117). However, as his criticism of Itô Daisuke suggests, "prose film" for Kitagawa is not simply a matter of a shift from the predominance of rhythmic montage in the silent era to a cinema of long takes in the sound era. Rather, the "prose film" is foremost a *critical attitude* of the filmmaker that is expressed through a complex configuration of editing, mise-en-scène, and camera work.

While Kitagawa particularly championed the work of contemporary Japanese director Itami Mansaku as an example of "prose film,"[17] perhaps his most revealing description of the "prose film" style comes in his discussion of Jean Renoir's *The Lower Depths* (*Les Bas-fonds*, 1936). He focuses on a scene in which the Baron, a member of the old aristocracy whose gambling addiction has brought him to the brink of bankruptcy, decides to wager it all on a final game. The mobile camera follows the Baron as he walks from the edge of the casino floor toward the table where he will stake his fortune, but as it does so, it also detours to capture interactions of other characters before rejoining the Baron, and takes in the entire environment and physical objects such as statues adorning the casino floor, together with the figure of the Baron. According to Kitagawa, this scene reveals Renoir's "stance or intention to really examine things carefully" (19). Furthermore, in its careful attention to the world of objects and other people that form a temporal and spatial complex with the Baron, the camera removes itself from a single identification with this character. In other contexts, Kitagawa mentions the viewpoint of secondary characters, or the presence of animals such as the white cat in Itami's *Akanishi Kakita* (1936), or even objects such as the rows of poplar trees or smokestacks in Ozu Yasujirô's films, as the director's "eyes," "pupils," or, in the latter case, his "eyelashes." These "eyes" establish a de-centered authorial presence in the film, resisting the single, uncritical identification of the filmmaker with the protagonist, which

Kitagawa criticized in Itô Daisuke's *Diary of Chûji's Travels.*[18] Following the description of the gambling floor scene in Renoir's *The Lower Depths*, Kitagawa concludes: "Filmmakers in the age of poetry took pure lyricism as their native element, but in the age of prose the filmmaker's eyes have a critical, satirical glint. As representative filmmakers we can cite René Clair, G. W. Pabst, Lewis Milestone, and Itami Mansaku" (19–20).

CONCLUSION

In examining Kitagawa and Yokomitsu's literary and theoretical works from the late 1920s through the 1930s, we can thus trace the recurrence of issues of time and its creative manipulation that emerge out of a dense transnational context of philosophical and scientific inquiries, avant-garde art and literary movements such as Futurism, and, most prominently, the role of photography and the cinematic apparatus in transforming the perception of time and space. In Kitagawa's *War* and Yokomitsu's *Shanghai,* we can observe a similar attention to the flow of time and geopolitical/economic forces on the one hand, and the spatio-temporal fragmentation or extraction of "any-instants-whatever" from this flow that reveal the objectification and abjection of the human body. Both Yokomitsu's *Shanghai* as well as Kitagawa's *War* display intensive attention to the political questions of how geopolitical and economic forces (namely imperialism and capitalism) intersect with human subjectivity—in terms of both mental consciousness and physical presence or embodiment. We could thus consider both works as highly political in nature, but differing somewhat in their political thrust. While Kitagawa's poetry attempts to lead the reader to certain ideological conclusions, Yokomitsu's novel, a convincing literary depiction of certain harrowing experiences of twentieth-century modernity, seems more concerned with capturing the nature of subjective experience in an environment of intense imperialist competition. If its ultimate ideological impact may be a normalization of the imperialist ideology it seeks to depict, Yokomitsu's novel is nevertheless a masterful achievement in its orchestration of the complex geopolitical, ideological, and economic forces converging on 1920s Shanghai.

In the sphere of criticism and theory, Yokomitsu argued for the autonomy of literary art from political judgments. Toward this end, he offered a fundamental analysis of the relationship between author, text, and reader, and the "mechanism" through which a reader generates the "illusion of life" out of his textual encounter. In this context, Yokomitsu emphasized the importance of the element of rhythm or tempo, thereby connecting his "formalist" theory with previously developed critical discourses on rhythm in both Shinkankakuha literature and contemporary film.

In his theory of the "prose film," Kitagawa revived two interrelated critical parameters that Yokomitsu had explicitly excluded from his formalist theory: consideration of authorial intention as revealed in the work, and the artistic treatment of political and social ideas. In particular, he attempted to demonstrate how the filmmaker's manipulation of the space-time continuum could express a political or critical social stance through a complex combination of editing, mise-en-scène (including the performance of actors), and camera work. Paradoxically, "flow" in Kitagawa's film criticism is not associated with the simple flow of time captured in a single take by the film camera, but instead by the lyrical flow of time artificially created by the rhythmic montage of spatio-temporal segments compiled by silent film masters such as Gance, Yamanaka, and Itô. Conversely, "prose film," the antithesis of lyrical, montage-based "flow," may include the use of long takes, but takes that are integrated into a total system of mise-en-scène, camera work, and editing that expresses the film author's critical consciousness.

Despite their considerable achievements in the realms of cine-textual practice and theory, Kitagawa and Yokomitsu found their work attacked from both left and right political positions throughout the 1930s and 1940s and, together with interwar Japanese modernism in general, suffered a period of critical neglect in the postwar era. Regardless of the elements of ideological and systemic analysis I have discussed above, modernist authors were subject to attack from the left for focusing on the "surface phenomenon" of urban modernity rather than the root causes of capitalist and imperialist oppression or the revolutionary potential of the laboring classes. Meanwhile, symbolic sites of cosmopolitan urban culture, such as cafés and dance halls, came under increasing attack from right-wing ideologues both inside and outside of the government as the "national crisis" deepened with the staging of the Manchurian Incident in 1931 and the onset of full-scale war with China in 1937. "Modernist" films and novels connected with such urban phenomena and tied to the importation of Western culture were also viewed with increasing suspicion, and a conservative "literary revival" took hold in the mid-1930s (see Doak).

Kitagawa and Yokomitsu each attempted to navigate this treacherous territory according to their respective political and artistic tenets, and their complex responses to the cultural and political pressures of the wartime period merit more careful scrutiny than can be afforded here. As foreshadowed by the protagonist Sanki's growing nostalgia for a maternal/national body in the latter chapters of *Shanghai*, Yokomitsu's work following this novel increasingly focused on issues of ethnic identity, and often portrayed Eastern and Western cultures in fundamental opposition. As mentioned earlier, Kitagawa aligned himself with the Proletarian literary movement in 1930, and his poetic practice thereafter shifted away from the fragmentary, aggressively modernist style of *War*. Despite increasingly severe state censorship and a thoroughgoing crackdown on the leftist opposition following the invasion of Manchuria in 1931, such poems as "Iyarashii kami" (1936), which offers a grotesque portrait of a battleship, managed to articulate a thinly veiled criticism of Japanese militarism on the eve of full-scale war with China. However, Kitagawa's

A Theory of Contemporary Film (*Gendai eiga ron*), published in 1941, is marked by the coexistence of passages promoting social criticism in its discussion of the "prose film" (a summary of the author's theoretical position of the mid-1930s) together with an embrace of filmmaking for the goals of national propaganda in its discussion of war documentary and other films in the "current age." In 1942, Kitagawa was drafted and sent to Malaysia as a war correspondent and subsequently contributed poems to such propagandistic anthologies as *Poetry Collection for the Decisive Battle* (*Kessen shishû*, 1942).

After the war, the leftist critique of modernist literature as insufficiently resistant to capitalism, militarism, and imperialism was revived, persisting alongside the rightist critique of modernism as the manifestation of an unhealthy fascination with European and American culture. This doubly negative critical assessment both helped to shape, and was further reinforced by, the general dismissal of prewar modernism by the first generation of postwar Western scholars of modern Japanese literature. It was not until the end of the Cold War that Japanese modernism received a fresh wave of attention. In recent years, the modernist literature of the 1920s and 1930s has proved indispensable to scholars exploring questions of urban studies, gender studies, media and mass culture, modernity and postmodernity, and postcolonialism. Despite this new attention, the poetry and film criticism of Kitagawa Fuyuhiko still await a thorough critical examination, and much other work remains to be done—particularly with regard to the evolution of Japanese modernism during the wartime period, and the interrelation of Japanese modernism with contemporary literatures both elsewhere in Asia and in Europe and America.

As outlined in the introduction to this essay, Japanese interwar modernism is intimately connected with the rise of new forms of urban mass culture in such metropolitan centers as Osaka, Kobe, and the imperial capital of Tokyo. Nevertheless, despite the undeniable importance of the metropole, works such as Kitagawa's *War* and Yokomitsu's *Shanghai* point to the parallel significance of the imperial periphery (defined as such from the perspective of the Japanese metropole) in offering Japanese modernists an exemplary "force field"—that is, a field for the analysis of the dynamic forces that determine subjective experience in an age of competing imperialisms. This analysis of forces, as it shifts between the depiction of fluid time and motion and the isolation of spatial-temporal fragments, is deeply intertwined with the technology of the motion picture camera and the development of cinema from the turn of the century onward. Still, while this analysis of the "force field" of the imperial periphery by authors writing from the perspective of the metropole might aspire to the objectivity of the "machine eye," it should not be mistaken for a representation of modern subjectivity from the perspective of the colonial subjects. As the reappraisal of Japanese modernism continues, it is essential to situate the works of Japanese modernism in a dynamic relation with the writings of displaced colonial subjects writing from within the Japanese metropole itself, as well as the literatures emerging from China, Korea, Taiwan, and elsewhere along the multiple contact zones of the imperialist era.[19]

NOTES

1. All names of authors are given in Japanese order with family names first and given names second. Authors with pen names are referred to by their pen names.

2. Quotations from Yokomitsu's novel *Shanhai* are excerpted from the translation by Dennis Washburn. All other quotations are my own translations.

3. These numbers apparently include shorter films and newsreels as well as full-length feature films; the number of domestic feature films per year during this period is estimated at around 750 (Kokusai eiga tsûshinsha 4). The average length of the films newly submitted for censorship was 4.3 reels for Japanese films and 6.4 reels for American and European films. Although no specific statistics are given for countries outside of Japan, America, and Europe, there is a discrepancy of 506 films between the total of these three regions and the complete total of new films submitted, which may correspond to the films from China and other unlisted countries.

4. The *benshi* supplied the audience with vernacular translations of the intertitles of foreign films, and also provided narrative and dialogue for domestic films. See Dym.

5. On Japanese popular modernism, see Freedman and Omori. For an exploration of the historical and ideological facets of Japanese "modernism" as expressed in the arts, social theory, and journalism, see Silverberg.

6. On *A Page of Madness* and the New Perception School Film Alliance, see Gardner, "New Perceptions." For translations of representative Shinkankakuha works from this period, see Yokomitsu, *"Love" and Other Stories*. Although I do not agree with many of its conclusions, Keene's *Yokomitsu Riichi, Modernist* is an important early English-language study of this author.

7. For studies of Japanese modernist and surrealist poetry during the era of the *Shi to shiron* (*Poetry and Poetics*) journal, see Hirata and Sas.

8. Golley extensively discusses the impact of developments in modern physics on Japanese modernism (*When Our Eyes No Longer See*, especially 10–70).

9. See Proger on Muybridge's photographic experiments. See also Doanne (especially 46–68) for a discussion of the related photographic experiments of Etienne-Jules Marey in relationship to early film and turn-of-the-century conceptions of time and motion.

10. In a concise definition offered in September 1929, Kitagawa suggested that the cinépoème could either consist of "a string of characters" (*moji no raretsu*) or "a continuum of images/film" (Kitagawa glosses the characters *eizô* [image/images] with the katakana reading *firumu* [film]) ("Shidan rebyû" 15). This suggests that Kitagawa's conception of cinépoème could cover both literary works as well as films such as Man Ray's "L'Etoile de mer" (1927), based on a poem-scenario by Robert Desnos (a textual version of this work translated by Tsuchiya Shigeichirô was published in the January 1930 issue of the film journal *Eiga ôrai*). Wall-Romana attributes the term *cinépoème* to Romanian poet and filmmaker Benjamin Fondane's coinage in 1928, and identifies a persistent interest in poem-scenarios among the French avant-garde from the years 1917 through 1929 (142). Incidentally, in his definition above Kitagawa borrows the phrase "string of characters" (*moji no raretsu*) verbatim from Yokomitsu's "formalist" literary theory, discussed below, suggesting the proximity of these two authors' critical consciousnesses during this period.

11. This is Usawa Satoru's assumption in his reading of the poem (16–18). Although the prophetically titled *Sensô* (*War*) was published two years before the full Japanese military occupation of Manchuria during the Manchurian Incident of 1931, in the 1920s Japan already had a large semicolonial presence in this territory, centering on the

Liaodong Penninsula leased to Japan following the Russo-Japanese War and the corridor of the Japanese-owned South Manchurian Railway Company running from Dalian and Lüshun in the south to Changchun and other territories in the interior. For a more detailed consideration of Kitagawa's view of Japanese imperialism and the role of the South Manchurian Railway Company, see Gardner, "Colonialism and the Avant-garde."

12. This quotation is taken from the 1944 essay "Dickens, Griffith, and the Film Today," collected in *Film Form* (New York: Harcourt, Brace and Company, 1949) 239, 245; italicized as in the original. The second year of Kitagawa's tenure on the editorial board of *Kinema Junpô* coincided with the first introduction of Soviet montage theory in that journal. The first installment of Seymon Timoshenko theoretical writings translated as "Eiga geijutsu to katteingu" ("Film Art and Cutting) by Iwasaki Akira appeared in *Eiga geijutsu* in April 1928; the second through twelfth installments were published in *Kinema Junpô* in July through December 1928. Iijima Tadashi's translation of French critic Léon Moussinac's "Sovieto Roshia no Eiga" ("The Film of Soviet Russia") appeared in 22 installments in *Kinema junpô* from November 1928 through August 1929. An article by Moussinac's on Vertov's "cine-eye" (*kinoglaz*) was also published in the journal *Eiga hyôron* in November 1929. Eisenstein's writings on montage and Japanese culture were introduced in a three-part series of translations, "Nihon bunka to Montaaju," by Fukuro Ippei in *Kinema Junpo* in February 1930. These publications on Soviet theory formed a second wave of montage theory after the extensive introduction of French writings on montage in the mid-1920s. Subsequently, poets Hanya Saburô and Orito Horio, both associates of Kitagawa, conducted a debate over the application of montage theory to poetry in the years 1933–1934. On the introduction of Soviet montage theory to Japan, see Iwamoto and Yamamoto Kikuo.

13. Several commentators, including Chiba (48) have pointed out the resemblance between Yokomitsu's technique and both the film scenario and the cinépoème. For recent discussions of cinema and media theory in relation to Yokomitsu's work, see Kitada (two articles), Kuroda, and Toeda.

14. For a discussion of the organic and inorganic in this passage, see Golley, *When Our Eyes No Longer See*, 135.

15. Yokomitsu's theory of literary form arguably takes on an extra dimension in light of the compact, cellular structure and graphic possibilities of the Japanese writing system, which typically employs logogrammatic Chinese characters (*kanji*) in combination with Japanese phonetic script (*kana*). Yokomitsu himself suggested that an analysis of the role of "ideogrammatic characters" (*keishô moji*) should be an important factor in the construction of a formalist theory specific to Japanese literature. ("Bungei jihyô 2" 154). See also Komori 477–95 for a discussion of Yokomitsu's "formalism" in relation to the literary theory of *Shi to shiron* coterie member Toyama Usaburô, who developed a poetics of the ideogram (*keishô moji*) based on gestalt theory and Saussurian linguistics. Still, it is important to note that while they may take on added significance in the context of the Japanese orthographic system, Yokomitsu's fundamental remarks on the mechanism of signification of the literary text could apply to an alphabetic "string of characters" as well as to a Japanese one. For a discussion of orthography in Japanese modernist poetry with respect to orientalist conceptions of the ideogram as well as Japanese imperialism, see Gardner, *Advertising Tower*, 46–83.

16. This wave theory of consciousness applied to reading was partly based on Natsume Sôseki's *Bungakuron* (*Theory of Literature*, 1907), which was informed by the psychological models of James and Bergson. See Komori 457–65.

17. See Hirano for a discussion of film director, screenwriter, and essayist Itami Mansaku that focuses on his position within the Japanese intelligentsia and his views of Japanese militarism.

18. Kitagawa also describes this authorial perspective as the "fourth person," referring to the theoretical concept introduced in Yokomitsu Riichi's "Junsui shôsetsu ron" ["Theory of The Pure Novel"] of the "fourth person" as "a self that views the self," beyond the "I" of first person, the "you" of second person, and the "he/she/they" of third person (*Sanbun eiga ron* 114). However, Kitagawa arguably endows this "fourth person" with a political or critical valance that differs from Yokomitsu's original application of the term.

19. For discussion of Japanese imperialism, modernism, and modern subjectivity from perspectives outside of the Imperial metropole, see Kleeman, Shih, and Shin and Robinson.

WORKS CITED

Asendorf, Christoph. "Bodies in Force Fields: Design Between the Wars." *From Energy to Information: Representation in Science and Technology, Art, and Literature.* Ed. Bruce Clarke and Linda Damrymple Henderson. Stanford: Stanford University Press, 2002.

Bazin, André. *Jean Renoir.* Trans. W. W. Halsey II and William H. Simon. New York: Simon Schuster, 1973.

Boccioni, Umberto, et al. "Futurist Painting: Technical Manifesto." *Theories of Modern Art: A Source Book by Artists and Critics.* Ed. Herschel B. Chipp. Berkeley: University of California Press, 1968. 289–93.

Chiba Nobuo, "Eiga to gengo no zen'ei" ["Film and the linguistic avant-garde"]. *Kokubun-gaku: Kaishaku to kyôzai no kenkyû* 35.13 (1991).

Deleuze, Gilles. *Cinema 1: The Movement-Image.* Trans. Hugh Tomlinson and Barbara Habberjam. Minneapolis: University of Minnesota Press, 1986.

Doak, Kevin Michael. *Dreams of Difference: The Japan Romantic School and the Crisis of Modernity.* Berkeley: University of California Press, 1994.

Doane, Mary Ann. *The Emergence of Cinematic Time: Modernity, Contingency, and the Archive.* Cambridge: Harvard University Press, 2002.

Dym, Jeffrey A. *Benshi, Japanese Silent Film Narrators, and Their Forgotten Narrative Art of Setsumei: A History of Japanese Silent Film Narration.* Lewiston: Edwin Mellen Press, 2003.

Eisenstein, Sergei. *Film Form.* New York: Harcourt, Brace and Company, 1949.

Freedman, Alisa D. "Tracking Japanese modernity: Commuter trains, streetcars, and passengers in Tokyo literature, 1905–1935." PhD Diss. University of Chicago, 2002.

Gardner, William O. *Advertising Tower: Japanese Modernism and Modernity in the 1920s.* Cambridge: Harvard University Asia Center, 2006.

——. "Colonialism and the Avant-garde: Kitagawa Fuyuhiko's Manchurian Railroad." *Movements of the Avant-garde.* Spec issue of *Stanford Humanities Review* 7.1 (1999): n. pag.

——. "New Perceptions: Kinugasa Teinosuke's Films and Japanese Modernism." *Cinema Journal* 43.3 (2004): 59–78.

Golley, Gregory. *When Our Eyes No Longer See: Realism, Science, and Ecology in Japanese Literary Modernism*. Cambridge: Harvard University Asia Center, 2008.

———. "Voices in the Machine: Technology and Japanese Literary Modernism." PhD Diss. University of California Los Angeles, 2000.

Hanya Saburô. *Genjitsu shugi shiron [A Realist Poetics]*. Tokyo: Kamata shobô, 1934.

Hirano Ken, et al. *Gendai nihon bungaku ronsôshi, jôkan [A History of Modern Japanese Literary Debates, vol. 1]*. 1956. Tokyo: Miraisha, 2006.

Hirano, Kyoko. "Japanese Filmmakers and Responsibility for War: The Case of Itami Mansaku." *War, Occupation, and Creativity: Japan and East Asia, 1920–1960*. Ed. Marlene J. Mayo and J. Thomas Rimer. Honolulu: University of Hawaii Press, 2001. 212–32.

Hirata, Hosea. *The Poetry and Poetics of Nishiwaki Junzaburô: Modernism in Translation*. Princeton: Princeton University Press, 1993.

Iijima Tadashi. *Shinema no ABC [The ABC of Cinema]*. Originally published by Kôseikaku shoten, 1929. Tokyo: Yumani shobô, 1995.

Inoue Yoshio. "Shukumei to bungaku ni tsuite." Originally published in KYU 5 (November 1930). Collected in *Inoue Yoshio hyôronshû*. Ed. Kajii Takeshi. Tokyo: Kokubunsha, 1971. 13–36.

Itô Sae. "Keishiki shugi bungaku ronsô" ["The formalist literary debate"]. *Yokomitsu Riichi no bungaku sekai*. Ed. Ishida Hitoshi, et al. Tokyo: Kanrin shobô, 2006. 174–77.

Iwamoto Keiji. "Nihon ni okeru montâju riron no shôkai" ["The introduction of montage theory in Japan"]. *Hikaku bungaku nenshi (Waseda daigaku hikaku bungaku kenkyûshitsu)* 10 (1974): 67–85.

Kawabata, Yasunari. *The Scarlet Gang of Asakusa*. Trans. Alisa Freedman. Berkeley: University of California Press, 2005.

Keene, Dennis. *Yokomitsu Riichi, Modernist*. New York: Columbia University Press, 1980.

Kitada Akihiro. "'Media ron' no kisetsu: keishiki shugi tachi no 1920–30 nendai—Nihon" ["The Birth and Political Development of 'Mediological View Point': 1920–30s for Formalists in Japan Literature"]. *Tôkyô daigaku shakai jôhô kenkyûsho kiyô* 59 (2000): 97–133.

———. "Media ron teki roman shugi: Yokomitsu Riichi to Nakai Shôichi, media no shigaku to seijigaku." ["Medialogical romaticism: Yokomitsu Riichi and Nakai Shôchi, media poetics and politics"]. *1930 nendai no media to shintai*. Ed. Yoshimi Shunya. Tokyo: Seikyûsha, 2002.

Kitagawa Fuyuhiko. *Gendai eiga ron [A Theory of Contemporary Film]*. Tokyo: Mikasa shobô, 1941.

———. *Junsui eiga ki [A Record of Pure Film]*. Originally published in 1936 by Daiichigei-bunsha; reprinted as *Nihon eigaron gensetsu taikei dai ni ki: eiga no modanizumu ki, vol. 18*. Tokyo: Yumani shobô, 2004.

———. *Sanbun eiga ron [Theory of Prose Film]*. Tokyo: Sakuhinsha, 1940.

———. *Sensô [War]*. Originally published by Kôseikaku shoten in 1929; reprinted in Nihon gendaishi taikei, vol. 10. Ed. Nakano Shigeharu, et al. Tokyo: Kawade shobô, 1975.

———. "Shidan rebyû" ["Review of the Poetry World"]. *Bungei rebyû* 1.7 (1929): 14–16.

Kleeman, Faye Yuan. *Under an Imperial Sun: Japanese Colonial Literature of Taiwan and the South*. Honolulu: University of Hawaii Press, 2003.

Komori Yôichi. *Kôzô to shite no katari [Narrative as structure]*. Tokyo: Shinyôsha, 1988.

Kuroda Taiga. "Modanizumu no kôgen: eigateki ninshiki to keishikishugi bungaku" ["The light source of modernism: cinematic consciousness and formalist literature"]. *'Ima' o yomikaeru: 'sono jidai' no owari (Bungakushi o yomikaeru 8)*. Ed. Ikeda Hiroshi et al. Tokyo: Inpakuto shuppankai, 2007. 44–68.

Lippit, Seiji M. *Topographies of Japanese Modernism*. New York: Columbia University Press, 2002.

Maeda Ai. *Toshi kûkan no naka no bungaku [The Literature of Urban Space]*. Tokyo: Chikuma shobô, 1992.

Nakamura Burafu, et al. "Kakujin kakudai mandankai" ["Chat session with a topic for each"]. *Shinchô* 26.5 (1929): 125–46.

Omori, Kyoko. "Detecting Japanese Vernacular Modernism: 'Shinseinen' Magazine and the Development of the Tantei Shosetsu Genre, 1920—1931." PhD Diss. Ohio State University, 2003.

Orito Horio. "Shi ni okeru shin jikan kôsei" ["A New Temporal Composition for Poetry"]. *Nihon shidan* 2.2 (1934): 40–4.

———. "Shiteki montâju hôhôron" ["A methodology of poetic montage"]. *Nihon shidan* 1.6 (1933): 6–11.

———. "Shiteki montâju no mondai" ["The question of poetic montage"]. *Nihon shidan* 2.6 (1934): 6–10.

Proger, Phillip. *Time Stands Still: Muybridge and the Instantaneous Photography Movement*. New York: Oxford University Press, 2003.

Sas, Miryam. *Fault Lines: Cultural Memory and Japanese Surrealism*. Stanford: Stanford University Press, 1999.

Satô Tadao. *Nihon eiga rironshi [A History of Japanese Film Theory]*. Tokyo: Hyôronsha, 1977.

Shih, Shu-Mei. *The Lure of the Modern: Writing Modernism in Semicolonial China, 1917–1937*. Berkeley: University of California Press, 2001.

Shimamura Teru. "Kondô Azuma ron" ["A study of Kondô Azuma"]. *Toshi modanizumu no honryû: 'Shi to shiron' no resupuri nûbô*. Ed. Sawa Masahiro and Wada Hirofumi. Tokyo: Kanrin shobô, 1996. 124–31.

Shin, Gi-Wook, and Michael Robinson, eds. *Colonial Modernity in Korea*. Cambridge: Harvard East Asian Monographs, 1999.

Shinoda Kôichirô. *Shôsetsu wa ika ni kakareta ka [How were the novels written?]*. Tokyo: Iwanami shoten, 1982.

Silverberg, Miriam. *Erotic Grotesque Nonsense: The Mass Culture of Japanese Modern Times*. Berkeley: University of California Press, 2006.

Toeda Hirokazu. "1930-nen zengo no Yokomitsu Riichi to eiga" ["Yokomitsu Riichi and film, circa 1930"]. *In Nenkan: Nihon no bungaku*. Vol. 1. Tokyo: Yûseidô, 1992. 163–83.

Usawa Satoru. "Kitagawa Fuyuhiko kenkyû (54)" ["Research on Kitagawa Fuyuhiko (54)"]. *Jikan* 20.9 (1969): 16–18.

Wall-Romana, Christophe. "Mallarmé's Cinepoetics: The Poem Uncoiled by the Ciné-matographe, 1893–98." *PMLA* 120.1 (2005): 128–47.

Yamamoto Kikuo. *Nihon eiga ni okeru gaikoku eiga no eikyô: hikaku eigashi kenkyû [The Influence of Foreign Films on Japanese Films: Research on Comparative Film History]*. Tokyo: Waseda daigaku shuppanbu, 1983.

Yamamoto Takashi. "Kitagawa Fuyuhiko no eigaron—"junsui" to "sanbun" no haikei nado" ["Kitagawa Fuyuhiko's film theory: the background of 'pure' and 'prose,' etc."] *FB* 17 (2002): 17–33.

Yokomitsu Riichi. "Bungei hyôron (2)" ["Literary criticism (2)"] Originally published in Bungei shunjû 6.11 (November 1928). Collected in Teihon: Yokomitsu Riichi zenshû, vol. 13. Tokyo: Kawade shobô shinsha, 1982. 147–57.

———. *"Love" and Other Stories of Yokomitsu Riichi*. Trans. Dennis Keene. Tokyo: The Japan Foundation, 1974.

————. "Moji ni tsuite: keishiki to mekanizumu ni tsuite" ["Regarding characters: on form and mechanism"]. Originally published in *Sôsaku gekkan* 2.3 (1929). Collected in *Teihon: Yokomitsu Riichi zenshû*, vol. 13. Tokyo: Kawade shobô shinsha, 1982. 114–20.

————. *Shanhai*. Originally published in book format by Kaizôsha in 1932. Collected in *Teihon: Yokomitsu Riichi zenshû*, vol. 3. Tokyo: Kawade shobô shinsha, 1981. 3–246.

————. *Shanghai*. Trans. Dennis Washburn. Ann Arbor: Center for Japanese Studies, University of Michigan, 2001.

PART IX

FILM AS VERNACULAR MODERNISM

CHAPTER 25

TRACKING CINEMA ON A GLOBAL SCALE

MIRIAM BRATU HANSEN

THIS chapter suggests ways in which the notion of cinema as vernacular modernism could be useful to the project of writing transnational film history.[1] Three sets of examples from Japanese and Chinese films of the 1930s will help to show how vernacular modernism can be productive as a critical term. The first revolves around the figure of the prostitute who is also a mother. In Shimizu Hiroshi's sound film *Forget Love for Now* (*Koi mo wasurete*, Shochiku, July 1937), released the same month that Japan turned to open warfare against China, a young woman (Kuwano Michiko) works as a taxi dancer in a Yokohama harbor bar to pay for her son's education. The film resolves the contradiction of motherhood and prostitution by sacrificing the son, having him die from pneumonia after fighting a mob of boys over his mother's reputation. A similar configuration of prostitution and motherhood can be found in a silent Shochiku production directed by Naruse Mikio, *Every Night Dreams* (*Yogoto no yume*, 1933). Also set in the Yokohama harbor area, this film casts Kurishima Sumiko as a bar hostess struggling to raise her son and not to descend into the lower depths of the sex trade; the son is almost killed in a car accident, but the sacrifice is displaced onto the unemployed husband (Saito Tatsuo) who drowns himself after a failed attempt at burglary to pay for his son's medical bills.[2]

But *Forget Love for Now* also echoes the famous Chinese silent film, *Shennü: The Goddess* (1934), directed by Wu Yonggang and starring Ruan Ling-yu as a nameless young Shanghai woman who works as a streetwalker to ensure her son a good education. She ends up in jail for killing a brutal mobster, knowing that her son will be adopted by the headmaster who had defended him earlier against the bigotry of other parents and the school board. If the closing shot of *The Goddess* shows Ruan

behind bars yet looking to the future, consoled by the vision of her son (in the form
of an insert above her to the right), *Forget Love for Now* ends on a relentlessly pessimistic key. Throughout the film, the sex workers talk about leaving—for Kobe,
Shanghai, or Singapore; one of them tries and gets caught and beaten by bodyguards. To be sure, the foreign ports are discussed as highly ambivalent destina-
tions, but that only compounds the overall sense of hopelessness and stagnation.[3]
Extending the static mise-en-scène of the deathbed scene to a closing shot of solitary
figures in the street and scored with a melancholy strain, the camera descends into
the thickening mist.

The configuration of prostitution and motherhood evokes other films of the
period—implied in such American films as *Madame X, Applause, Blonde Venus,*
and *Stella Dallas*, explicit in Max Ophuls' *Sans Lendemain* (1939), and highly popular
in Mexican cinema. We could talk about these films as a variant of the maternal
melodrama, inflected by the genre of *Dirnentragödie* or the trope of the prostitute-
with-a-heart-of-gold.[4] We could also consider the Chinese and Japanese examples
(and related films in both traditions) in light of the respective historical discourses
on prostitution, as well as the significance of the child and childhood in parallel and
violently antagonistic discourses of the nation.[5] We could think about the figure of
the prostitute-mother as a critical allegory that joins the most extreme instance of
commodification of the female body and sexuality with the epitome of unalienated,
altruistic love—as embodying a key contradiction of capitalist modernity which
irrupts, to paraphrase Alexander Kluge, in the sphere of intimacy and the life stories
of strong-minded women ("Kapitalistische Moderne und Intimität").

Yet, much as these films can be analyzed in terms of genre conventions, cultural
stereotypes, and historico-philosophical allegories, such terms do not fully account
for the films' affective-aesthetic appeal, broadly understood—whatever it may be
that enables them to move viewers, including film scholars, across geopolitically
disparate spaces and histories. In the case of the prostitute-mother figures cited
above, the casting of actresses (as opposed to female impersonators), if not stars,
heightens the viewing pleasure derived from the dialectical interplay between
fictional character and the actress's public persona and artistic agency. Moreover,
the films often foreground, in their diegesis, moments of performance and other
aspects of mise-en-scène that make for an astonishing degree of fluidity, incongruity, and elusiveness in the construction of the female character. The implications
of such moments may become clearer from my second set of examples.

The mother in *Forget Love for Now* may enact the melodramatic tropes of "if
only" and "too late" over the body of her dead son, but the ending neither effaces
Kuwano's performance of solidarity as she confronts the cutthroat owner/madam
over the hostesses' working conditions nor the erotic power of her dancing alone, in
a formfitting Western dress, on the dance floor of the harbor bar.[6] Sun Yu's film
Daybreak (*Tiangming*, Shanghai, 1933), which invokes and revises Von Sternberg's
Dishonored (1931), engages in a self-conscious floating and scrambling of character
identity on a par with yet distinct from Dietrich/Sternberg films.[7] The protagonist,
played by Li Lili, migrates from a rural area to the city, like millions of Chinese at

the time, initially moving along a predictable trajectory from country girl, through factory worker raped by the boss's son, to indentured prostitute. From that moment on, however, her character is defined by dissimulation and masquerade, as we encounter her as a flirtatious, Robin-Hood-style sex worker sporting the accoutrements of a Modern Girl (beret, flashy jewelry, silk stockings, and makeup), and finally as martyr for the revolutionary cause who, for her execution, changes back (varying on *Dishonored*) into her old country clothes. Ozu Yasujiro's *Dragnet Girl* (*Hijoson no onna*, 1933), a parodistic homage to the American gangster film (in particular *Scarface*), features a different kind of Modern Girl or *moga* (Tanaka Kinuyo). The character is introduced as a preppie-looking typist in an open-plan office; her other job is that of a gangster moll. She ends up trying to domesticate both the hoodlum and herself, among other things, by making him hold a skein of wool as she winds it into a ball (the motif of knitting being associated earlier in the film with a traditional self-sacrificing woman with whom the hoodlum falls in love). None of the above roles fit the heroine particularly well. While the plot steers her toward traditional Japanese femininity (and, by implication, marriage and motherhood), the comic performance of the steps she takes in that direction suggest less a return to authenticity and tradition than a continuation of the modernist masquerade.

If these films invoke media-circulated stereotypes, in particular the dichotomy of the New Woman or Modern Girl and traditional (Chinese, Japanese) womanhood, they often confound such stereotypes at the levels of plot, performance, costume, and other aspects of mise-en-scène. They self-consciously put into play the contradictions and constructedness of these ascriptions, along with the utopian possibility of breaking with them. And they were doing so for heterogeneous mass audiences emerging in both Shanghai and Tokyo marked by, among other things, an unprecedented share of female viewers—women who were trying to negotiate the discrepancies between their dreams and lived realities through and against the cataclysms of modernity.[8]

Another example along those lines takes me to a set of images that signal the concern with everyday modernity through material objects, "things," even trash. Shimizu's *Japanese Girls at the Harbor* (*Minato no nihon musume*, 1933), shot at the same time as *Dragnet Girl* and responding to Ozu's film with another Eurasian fantasy (they were colleagues at Shochiku as well as roommates), shuffles the deck of gender roles even more whimsically. The film tracks the fate of two girlfriends, Sunako (Oikawa Michiko) and Dora (Inoue Yukiko), introduced in sailor-style school uniforms as they watch a departing ocean liner from the Yokohama bluffs; soon after they will compete for the love of Henry (Egawa Ureo), a small-time hood who enters their lives on his motorbike. Henry is reformed by marriage to the virtuous Dora, who as an adult is shown only in rather asexual Western clothes (in the style of New Objectivity [*Neue Sachlichkeit*]); Sunako, having become a bar hostess, now wears traditional geisha garb (if fashionably adorned with a flashy ring). Shimizu cites the heteronormative wool-winding ritual from Ozu's film, but gives it a particular twist. As Sunako pays a visit to the couple's modern home (a caricature of *shoshimin* or petty-bourgeois sensibility and boredom) and we see the three together in the same space for the first time as adults, Dora's gaze swerves from preparing dinner behind a glass partition to the ball of wool that skips around the floor as if it had a life of its own; still from her point of view, a track to the right reveals the source of this uncanny animation—Sunako and Henry dancing together, their legs at once entangled in and unraveling the strings of petty-bourgeois domesticity.

The foregrounding of material objects—through close-ups, camera movement, editing, and mise-en-scène—is part of the vocabulary of international silent film and returns more selectively in a wide variety of sound film practices. Western critics of Japanese film have linked this stylistic gesture, specifically for the later work of Ozu, to traditional Japanese aesthetics (in particular the Heian-era concept of *mono no aware* or "pathos of things") and principles of Zen Buddhism.[9] This tradition may have constituted a significant cultural reference (albeit a refracted, mediated, and perhaps ironic one), but the cinematically intensified presence of the object in Japanese prewar films seems to have had at least as much to do with modern commodity culture and its social and epistemic consequences. As European and Asian writers have noted early on, film's technical ability to animate and foreground inanimate objects enabled it to dramatize the changed and changing economy of things, be it to explore their fetishistic power, to counter the abstraction of commodity capitalism with physiognomic expressiveness, or to enhance their physical opacity and alterity.[10]

The material objects foregrounded in Japanese films of the period—as in Chinese, French, Soviet, and Hollywood examples that come to mind—range from glamorous consumer goods and details of fashion and décor, to items of everyday use (work, domestic reproduction, leisure, play), industrially manufactured objects and icons of mass consumption, to worn-out, battered, even useless things that have accreted meanings of their own. Ozu's *Dragnet Girl*, for instance, sets up its heterotopic mise-en-scène of urban modernity by tracking along serially arranged identical hats and typewriters (pausing to show one hat fall off the hook for no particular reason); it opens sequences with close-ups of objects (a not uncommon stylistic device), such as a chipped enamel coffeepot that repeatedly ushers us into the couple's shabby apartment, followed by boxing and movie posters on tattered wallpaper; and scenes in a record store involve a running gag of whimsical animation with statuettes of Nipper, the RCA Victor mascot.

Things take on a similarly active, if not activist, role in Chinese films of the period, for example in Sun Yu's *Playthings* (*Xiao wanyi*, 1933), which pits handcrafted folk toys against industrially produced toys like military tanks that in turn dissolve into "real" tanks. In a different key, objects acquire agency in the sound film *Crossroads* (*Shizi jietou*, dir. Shen Xilin, 1937), a romantic comedy/tragedy about a young man and a young woman falling in love without knowing that they are actually neighbors. They fight each other by throwing objects back and forth across the flimsy tenement wall, such as several framed photographs of university graduates (including one of the male protagonist), taped over with labels reading "Unemployed no. A," "B," etc., or a white shirt (his only) with an ink stain which the female protagonist transfigures into a pig. Traveling shots and close-ups highlight, among a chaotic assembly of things, a figurine of Mickey Mouse, a tea kettle and an ink well, wine bottles, paper scraps being written and drawn on, and a Kewpie doll similar to the one in Pal Fejos' 1929 film *Lonesome*, whose plot device *Crossroads* seems to have borrowed.[11]

It goes without saying that such cinematically concretized objects function differently in different films and film traditions, and are bound to have different meanings and affective valences in different contexts of reception. They may vary according to the degree of their narrative motivation and agency; they may serve to characterize individuals or to provide an objective correlative for the harsh and volatile conditions of their existence; or they may draw attention to the mechanisms of circulation by which things acquire and lose value and undergo changes of meaning. At the level of their filmic representation, these films gesture toward a modernist, non-anthropocentric aesthetics of contingency, even as they mobilize material objects to create pathos and critical reflection—in other words, to construct a space and time for spectatorial subjectivity.[12]

The tension at work here seems particularly acute in the representation of objects that push film's aesthetic material toward the "formless": images of trash, detritus, rubble, waste—literally, the abject.[13] If such images are more programmatic in postwar cinemas (cf. Italian neo-realism, German *Trümmerfilme*, and revolutionary Chinese films), they also seem to proliferate in Japanese films during the Depression years. They are often placed near the film's end (as in Mizoguchi's *Osaka Elegy* or Ozu's *Woman of Tokyo*), in contrast with Depression-era Hollywood films where they may crop up in the beginning but get cleaned up in the interest of closure (e.g., Mamoulian's *Applause*). In the last sequence of *Japanese Girls at the Harbor*, we see Sunako on board a departing ocean liner with her down-and-out painter househusband (Saito Tatsuo), making him toss his awful portraits of her overboard; in the closing shots, which echo the film's opening sequence, the camera lingers endlessly on streamers fluttering in the wind, alternating with shots of her portrait adrift in the water. Such images signal a different register of temporality, a *durée* of the ephemeral, the no longer, if ever, useful. At the same time, inasmuch as they resonate with the narrative's dispatch of the heroine into an unknown yet open-ended future, they also evoke a liberating anonymity.

Images of rubble and detritus in Chinese films of the 1930s tend to be more clearly motivated in narrative terms, whether linked to the 1932 Japanese attacks on Shanghai, as in *Playthings* and *Coming Home* (Zhu Shilin, 1934), or to rural flight and urban immiseration, as in *Fishermen's Song* (Cai Chusheng, 1934) and *Street Angel* (Yuan Muzhi, 1937).[14] Waste becomes thematic in scenes that suggest how to recycle and creatively reuse every scrap, the remains of colonial leisure-class consumption, under conditions of extreme poverty and inequality (see Goldstein). One could argue that images of detritus in Japanese films of the period are just as realistically motivated, considering the recent experience of the 1923 Kanto earthquake and the massive urban renewal that followed. Yet, between such immediate sources and an alleged cultural penchant for images of transience, impermanence, or loss, the aesthetic irruption of trash in these films also speaks to a particular experience of capitalist modernity, the moment when mass consumption and urbanization raised the age-old problem of garbage to unprecedented proportions, and when the disposability of things came to be associated with the disposability of human beings.

These sets of examples raise more general questions about how films can be understood as engaging with modernity—more precisely, distinct, highly uneven and unequal formations of modernity—and about how film practices interrelate across the borders of national cinemas and, in this case, across an increasingly violent political divide. With few exceptions, Japanese and Chinese film histories seem to exist in parallel universes, which intersect only problematically during the war and occupation.[15] This is not surprising given the history of aggression and subordination which for the first part of the twentieth century defined relations between, on the one hand, an imperial nation-state whose modernization campaigns competed with and defended against Western capitalist powers and, on the other, a republic weakened by warlordism and civil war, with its film industry concentrated in the semicolonial and multiethnic treaty port of Shanghai. Still, viewing Chinese and Japanese films of the late 1920s to the 1930s side by side one is struck by their shared concern with modern life and with modernist aesthetics—a strong interest in the everyday, similar thematic issues, stylistic tendencies, and configurations of film culture.[16] These include, broadly speaking, conflicts between traditional gender norms and modern femininity (the precarious status of single working women, arranged marriage vs. romantic love, the persistence of feudal mentalities and oppressive family structures), labor conflicts and unemployment, urbanization and immiseration, the city/country dichotomy, and discourses of nationality in relation to modernity and the West; stylistic references to a cosmopolitan visual culture of consumption, fashion, and design participating in international art deco (Shanghai modern, Taisho/Showa chic); and the significance accorded in both film cultures to actresses, whose new public presence "gave human faces to the many social transformations of urban modernity" (Russell, "Introduction" 2). (The convention of female impersonators on stage and screen had only recently begun to be dislodged.)[17]

Such points of intersection between Chinese and Japanese cinemas of the period may owe as much to the contemporaneity with Western modernity—and the alternative modernity offered by the Soviet Union and communism—as to the shared, though differently interpreted, legacy of Buddhism and Confucianism. They can be explored from various perspectives, though not without awareness of the asymmetries of wealth and power and the racialized hierarchies in the conditions under which films were produced and received.

In addition to a comparative approach that would rethink the grounds, scales, and terms of comparison, transnational relations between the respective film cultures ask to be researched in terms of actual processes of transfer and translation, circulation, and reception.[18] Thus, following scholars of literary modernism, film historians have begun to trace cross-filiations between Tokyo's artistic-intellectual (and cinephilic) avant-gardes and Chinese debates on film, such as the adaptation and transformation of the Japanese movement of New Sensationism by Shanghai dandy Liu Na'ou and others, or the significance of the early theorist of film and modernity and (later) famous novelist Tanizaki Jun'ichiro.[19] These cross-filiations, among other things, highlight the significance of the issue of woman's relation to urban modernity for critical debates over left-wing film politics (cf. the "hard" versus "soft" film debate; see Zhang, *Amorous History,* Chapter 7), thus challenging received Chinese film history. The question is whether such an argument merely expands on the long-standing mediation of Chinese modernity and modernism by way of Japan, or whether there were crossings in the other direction as well, direct or indirect, elite or mass-cultural, contemporaneous or temporally displaced—connections that may elude established historiographic narratives.

The thematic, theoretical, and methodological issues raised by these examples can be productively addressed through the notion of cinema as a vernacular form of modernism. This notion contributes a pragmatic lens to the project of transnational film history by bringing into view junctures between, and heterogeneities within, national film histories, whether virtual or actual, politically blocked or historiographically repressed. I'm interested in the heuristic potential of vernacular modernism as a relational framework for mapping film practices—not only vis-à-vis Hollywood (and other foreign cinemas) but also on regional and local scales that complicate nationally defined film cultures. Distinct from, yet imbricated with, questions of *genre*, this framework may help us track the ways in which particular film practices engaged with their respective trajectories of modernity and modernism, whether parallel or intersecting, antagonistic or in conversation with each other.[20] The point is not to come up with a globally valid notion of vernacular modernism but to see it as a more reflexive framework capable of generating new lines of inquiry and revising itself in view of the empirical formations it explores.

Two points about the stakes behind the concept of vernacular modernism are here in order. First off, the kinds of cinema being discussed here are not those that are commonly evoked in conjunction with modernism, such as experimental film practices that emerged within or alongside historical avant-garde movements in the other arts, or modernist directions in international auteur and art cinema. Rather, these films demonstrate currents of modernist aesthetics that take place *within* the field of commercial, mainstream cinema, at a level of cultural circulation suggested by the term vernacular.

Second, the concept of vernacular modernism was initially aimed against neoformalist accounts of classical Hollywood cinema that tended to reduce that cinema to a stylistic system predicated on neoclassicist norms.[21] In an earlier essay entitled "The Mass Production of the Senses," I argued that the worldwide success of Hollywood, much as it relied on aggressive industrial strategies and state intervention, had less to do with the "classical"—timeless, universal—narrative organization of the films than with their ability to provide, to mass audiences both at home and abroad, an at once aesthetic and public horizon for the experience of capitalist-industrial modernity and modernization. This was not an argument about a general

and structural, let alone a causal, relationship between cinema and modernity.[22]
Rather, the question was, and continues to be, how particular film practices can be
productively understood as *responding*—and making sensually graspable our responses—to the set of technological, economic, social, and perceptual transformations associated with the term modernity. In other words, to the extent that film
practices acknowledged these transformations, including the cinema's own role in
them, and engaged with modernity's contradictory effects, they can be considered a
form of modernism, asymmetrically related to modernist practices in the traditional arts. The notion of cinema as vernacular modernism thus entwines concepts
of modernity and aesthetic modernism in an institutionally specific mode—
as a heterotopic practice that, on a mass basis and in a sensorial-affective form,
references and brings into play the impact of capitalist-industrial modernization
and other aspects of modernity.

It has become a critical commonplace that one can no more speak of modernism in the singular than assume a singular concept of modernity apart from its
entwinement with histories of colonization and globalization.[23] In the spirit of
Dipesh Chakrabarty's injunction to "provincialize Europe," scholars have been
exploring different geopolitical constellations and historical trajectories of modernism and modernity in Asia, Latin America, and Africa (3–23; also see Appadurai,
Mitchell, ed.).[24] This critical endeavor is complicated by the need to distinguish
between colonial forms of extraction and circulation and twentieth-century
industrial formations competing with and overlaying them, specifically the Fordist
regime of technological production and consumption (Americanism) including the
worldwide circulation of low-cultural, market-based forms such as the cinema.[25]

The question of Hollywood hegemony—at the levels of distribution and exhibition in local and regional markets, and as narrative-stylistic model—poses methodological and theoretical challenges similar to the problematic of alternative and
multiple modernities, though it also complicates them. It may well be the case that,
as David Bordwell claims, all the world's mass-market cinemas are based on the
standard continuity style pioneered by classical Hollywood, as the ground against
which the stylistic accomplishments of indigenous filmmakers can be analyzed. But
that does not make them simply variants of a dominant style (in the manner, to cite
Bordwell's analogy, one would consider Haydn, Mozart, and Beethoven variants of
Viennese classicism).[26] If filmmakers in China and Japan confronted Hollywood
hegemony in both its enabling and destructive effects, their efforts to forge idioms
of their own were crucially inflected by a larger vernacular-modernist culture at
once cosmopolitan and local. As Zhang Zhen has shown for the case of Shanghai
cinema, this involved a volatile process of negotiation between nativist modernizing
projects (such as the May Fourth Vernacular Movement) and international(ist)
forms of modernism, elite and popular—between competing models of national
culture and creative appropriations of the globalizing vernaculars of Hollywood,
European, Soviet, and Japanese cinemas (Zhang, *Amorous History*; also see Pang).[27]

If "The Mass Production of the Senses" sought to make a case for an expanded
notion of modernism, this chapter emphasizes the other part of the concept—the

vernacular. With its historically variable, ambiguous, and conflicting connotations, the vernacular offers a dynamic model of cultural circulation that can be extended to technologically mediated forms such as the cinema. A familiar narrative associates the term vernacular with linguistic and literary practices—and corresponding intellectual and political movements—that mark a deliberate turn away from, around, and against an official imperial or "high," cosmopolitan language, be it Latin, Persian, Sanskrit, or classical Chinese. Vernacular practices emerged in different parts of the world at different times, beginning with the late medieval and early modern periods. In Western Europe, the historical trajectory of vernacularization leads through the well-known examples of Dante and Luther, as well as the Romantics' "discovery" or, often, invention of local and folk traditions from the last third of the eighteenth century on. This trajectory is entwined with the cultural-political transformations that produced the nation-state, with its grounding in presumably homogeneous ethnic identities. At the same time, the idea of the vernacular reverberates in twentieth-century leftist thought, notably in the work of Bakhtin, as well as later efforts, indebted to Gramsci, to reclaim "the popular" as a socially and politically progressive force as much against "elitist" intellectuals as against capitalist universalization.

The standard etymological account tells us that the term vernacular derives from the Latin word *verna* or second-generation slave born in Republican Rome. The adjective *vernaculus* defines a language used by subaltern subjects to communicate among each other and, in non-official, domestic contexts, with their masters—that is, a language inscribed with enslavement, displacement, and domestication. (It is no coincidence that the Latin word *verna* itself is derived from the Etruscan, a language destroyed with the Romans' vanquishing of the Etruscans and the founding of Rome.) Restricting the term to its etymological roots, however, limits the heuristic and historical range of the concept. As Sheldon Pollock has argued, the term vernacular narrowly understood as referring to a "very particular and unprivileged mode of social identity" is "hobbled by its own particularity," insofar as "there is no reason to believe that every vernacular is the idiom of the humiliated demanding vindication" ("Cosmopolitan and Vernacular in History" 596). Rather, as Pollock shows, not only are vernacular forms geopolitically and historically variable, but they are mutually constitutive with the cosmopolitan forms they oppose. "As the cosmopolitan is constituted through cultural flows from the vernacular, so the vernacular constructs itself by appropriation," often by "unwittingly relocalizing what the cosmopolitan borrowed from it in the first place" ("The Cosmopolitan Vernacular" 25; "Cosmopolitan and Vernacular in History" 616).[28]

Pollock makes his case through a comparative account of the ways in which two distinct historical cosmopolitanisms, Latin and Sanskrit, gave rise in turn to different types of vernacularism. Leaving aside the question to what extent he may be idealizing Sanskrit as an alternative, noncoercive, and pluralistic form of cosmopolitanism, his argument is immensely useful for opening up the concept of the vernacular. In particular, it challenges the tendency to fix the vernacular on the side of the local—for instance, through ahistorical notions of indigenous identity—and allows us to see vernacular practices as part of the very processes of translocal inter-actions that produce the local as much as the global. This helps us understand the particular dynamics of vernacular practices as a special "mix," in Pollock's words, which "consists of a response to a specific history of domination and enforced change, along with a critique of the oppression of tradition itself, tempered with a strategic desire to locate resources for a cosmopolitan future in vernacular ways of being themselves" ("Cosmopolitan and Vernacular in History" 624).

Pollock's historicizing and comparative account is framed by the political argument that the vernacular today is threatened by a "new and disquieting cos-mopolitanism," "an altogether new universalizing order of culture power (call it globalization, or [neo-]liberalization, or Americanization)." As a result, accord-ing to Pollock, we are confronted with a polarization between the "bad options" of, "on the one hand, a national vernacularity dressed up in the frayed period costume of violent [ethno-chauvinist] revanchism and bent on preserving differ-ence at all costs and, on the other, a clear-cutting, strip-mining multinational cosmopolitanism that is bent, at all costs, on eliminating it" ("Cosmopolitan and Vernacular" 617; also see 592–93).

We may want to debate this account of contemporary developments. But the bigger problem is that the arc suggested by Pollock eclipses much of the twentieth century, a modernity associated as much with the rise of mass production and mass consumption and a broad-based aspiration for a better world—for women among others—as with catastrophic capitalism, technological warfare, and mass annihila-tion. This means leaving out the formative stages of technologically mediated, in-dustrially produced mass culture, of new scales and speeds of circulation that not only linked cultural products to the promotion of other, more material goods, but also gave rise to a new type of public sphere turning on the dialectics of acknowl-edgment and appropriation of social experience.[29] Likewise occluded are the efforts of intellectuals, writers and artists working in both traditional media and new media such as film, radio, and photography, whether in radical opposition to or on the margins of commercial contexts, to respond to both the devastating and the libera-tory effects of modernity and mass-market culture—efforts associated with inter-and transnational movements of modernism. In other words, Pollock's delineation of the mutual constitution of older cosmopolitan and vernacular forms, to the extent that it is framed by a monolithic perspective on current globalization, stops short of recognizing a similarly variable and complex entanglement of vernacular and cosmopolitan forms in a significant part of the twentieth century. It is in this heuristic space that we can see cinema functioning as a vernacular form of modernism.

A brief glance at how the concept of the vernacular has been applied to archi-tecture will help to shed some light on its theoretical importance to cinema. Dudley Andrew has argued that the term vernacular is misleading "if we follow its roots and branches toward the history of languages" (n.p.) because this genealogy, he implies, would resurrect the problematic analogy between cinema and language. Instead, he suggests, we should work from the connotations of the term vernacular in architecture. There are a number of good reasons for doing so, not least because of the affinity between architecture and cinema in the process of creating new image spaces, in particular (to invoke Benjamin) the reconfiguration of "body-and image-space" (n.p.). Work in this direction ranges from studies of theater architecture and publicity, through cinematic set design, décor, and lighting, to the ways in which films map transformations of urban space and to architectural conceptions of cinematic space and narrative.[30]

First off, though, let me point out that drawing on a particular aspect of a linguistic concept does not mean reviving the analogy between film and language which, as we know, at the latest since 1960s and 1970s film theory, can never be more than a complex metaphor. Mobilized in relation to cinema, the term vernacular too works primarily as a theoretical metaphor, as it has been doing for architecture and other disciplines and discourses concerned with modes of cultural circulation beyond the term's linguistic contexts of origin (even if, as in the case of Shanghai cinema, vernacular movements of a more literal and literary kind may be part of the mix).

Architecture adds an important dimension to the argument on vernacular modernism in film, but we should be aware that the architectural notion of the vernacular is fraught with its own set of problems. These include, in particular, the unquestioned opposition, in architectural history and discourse dating back to the turn of the last century, between the vernacular understood as local ("embracing ethnic, folk, regionalist, primitive, etc.,") and "high-style" or "polite" architecture; the latter is distinguished by having artistic authors as well as transnational currency, especially with the rise of the International Style.[31] Accordingly, vernacular architecture was perceived to be threatened by dilution with the advent of modernization, in particular the mass fabrication of building materials and mass circulation of building types through pattern books. Such a narrow understanding of the vernacular in architecture fails to take into account, for instance, that the term vernacular has been widely used since the late 1960s with reference to Art Deco. A commercial as well as public modernist style, Art Deco spread during the 1920s and 1930s from France through Europe, the United States, Australia, and cosmopolitan centers such as Shanghai, Tokyo, and Bombay and combined with local and regional design and building styles in creative ways. (This narrative of origin is complicated in turn by the fact that French art déco drew on, among other things, Japanese art as well as precious wood and other luxurious materials from French colonies in Africa and Asia.)

Increasingly, theorists of design and the built environment have been rejecting the rigid dichotomy of vernacular and high style, along with any attempt to define the vernacular "in itself," emphasizing instead the fluctuating, open-ended, and relational character of vernacular practices in different cultural contexts (Rapoport 78, 95, 98). In a recent collection of essays on built environment entitled *Vernacular Modernism*, the editors challenge the conventional polarization of the two terms by "conceiving of the vernacular as a space *within* the modern" and seeking to investigate "the alternative—vernacular—potentialities within modernism itself"

(Umbach and Hüppauf 2 [emphasis added], 9). However, while they claim that central to their investigation is the "mutual dependence of the vernacular and the global," the enterprise remains amazingly hide-bound, inasmuch as it is based on the assumption that the "vernacular denotes particularism and, by extension, a specific attitude of sensitivity to *place*" (Umbach and Hüppauf 8). The problem is that particularism is tied, not only to the local, but explicitly to a particular national, if not nationalist and antimodern, concept of the local—the notoriously untranslatable German word *Heimat* (to be sure, in a theoretically and historically conscious version indebted to the philosophy of Ernst Bloch).[32] This fixation on the local, however mediated it may be through the trajectory of Western modernity (e.g., *Heimat* as an affective and aesthetic response to the universalizing, abstracting, and homogenizing effects of industrialization and urbanization), occludes the *circulatory* dynamics of the vernacular, its portability and interaction with other vernaculars.

Thus deployed, the architectural concept of the vernacular effaces what I consider most relevant to the term—the paradoxical mode in which senses and sensations of the particular, the aesthetic materiality of everyday life, of places, things, and routines, become mobilized, transportable, translatable, and creatively appropriated in and for different contexts of living. Key to this question is a conception of the *everyday* in terms of capitalist modernity—as the "minimal unity," in Harry Harootunian's words, "that has organized the experience of modernity" (*History's Disquiet* 18–19).[33] Substantially different from the "immemorial daily life" lived in the countryside and premodern cities, the modern everyday became the site in which the demands of capitalist production and consumption were set off against, yet made to coexist, "uneasily and unhappily," with received social and cultural forms and relationships. (As the films cited earlier suggest, this coexistence was often articulated as a conflict of irreconcilable forces, especially for women: if capitalist modernity promised liberating possibilities in the face of oppressive traditional gender norms, it also created new forms of bondage, causing newfound subjectivities to get trapped between the rock of societal bigotry and the hard place of sexual commodification.) While both residual cultures of reference and the particular forms that capitalist modernization took were rooted in specific locations, Harootunian argues, the experience of the everyday—and its contemporary theorizations by modernist intellectuals (and, for that matter, vernacular-modernist films)–connected these uneven yet "coeval" modernities across a broader geopolitical context (*History's Disquiet*, 111–15, 62–64).

We could consider the vernacular, then, more generally as the level of cultural circulation at which these coeval and uneven modernities connect, intersect, and compete, defined by a tension between, on the one hand, connotations of the everyday (the common and ordinary, routines of material production and reproduction) and, on the other, connotations of circulation (commerce, communication, migration, travel). It is this simultaneously particularizing and circulatory dynamic of the concept of the vernacular that makes it useful to continue drawing on the term's rich genealogy in the history of languages and literature, including contemporary usages of the term in fields of socio- and ethnolinguistics, translation studies, and studies of cultural transfer and regimes of circulation. Thus, while the term vernacular does not have a clear status in contemporary linguistics and may function as a "fuzzy set" in other contexts as well, its usages suggest that it broadly refers to an idiom that operates *below* the level of a dominant standard language (official, national) yet *above* that of local dialects, allowing for contact, transfer, and circulation on a larger regional scale. This intermediary status may make it an independent language variety, though an unstable one that draws on local speech and has the potential to develop into a standard language.[34]

This broader sense of the vernacular allows us to imagine an *intermediary* level of mass production and mass circulation on which cinema, at the very least during the interwar period, seems to have moved and morphed. Situating cinema at this intermediary level is meant to focus research and analytic attention on the dynamics by which particular film practices engaged both the globalizing and the local vectors in the experience of everyday modernity, and to help us track these dynamics horizontally, within and across geopolitically uneven and unequal formations. In terms of Asian film history, it encourages us to explore transnational relations in the larger region (including Korea, Hong Kong, Taiwan, and India)—despite, though in awareness of, blockages bound up with traumatic histories and perpetuated by nationalist discourses—and thus to complicate binary conceptions of global and local, as of Hollywood hegemony and non-Western national cinemas. This does not mean that Hollywood has not been dominating Asian film markets in specific ways; nor does it mean placing cinema outside a force field of asymmetrical power relations and market conditions. But the question is *how* filmmakers have appropriated Hollywood (along with other foreign cinemas as well as their own cultural pasts) in creative, eclectic, and revisionist ways in order to forge aesthetic idioms and to respond to social conflicts and political pressures closer to home. At a minimum, the concept of vernacular modernism provides a comparative lens for tracing related concerns across different film cultures, across uneven and competing yet inevitably entangled modernities.

Finally, if the concept is to have any critical function, that is, as a heuristic and analytic framework for comparing individual films and tracing particular currents in film culture, it is important to insist on the linkage between vernacular and *modernist*. If the vernacular modifies—and expands our understanding of—aesthetic modernism(s), the qualifier modernist also designates and delimits particular directions in the larger field of vernacular practices. It makes no sense to call every film made and commercially circulated during twentieth-century waves of modernization modernist, even in the broadest sense of the term. Nor does every film that references everyday modernity do so in ways that could be productively described as modernist in style and/or stance; on the contrary, there are plenty of films that transmute conflicts and contradictions arising from modernity into conventional narrative and compositional forms. By the same token, we may find a high degree of stylistic experiment in historical period films, as, for instance, in the popular Japanese genre of *chambara* or swordplay films (often combined with a masochistic mise-en-scène of the male warrior body).[35] Moreover, like literature and the arts, cinema too has its share of "antimodern" and "reactionary modernists," to say nothing of the issue of fascist and state-sponsored forms of modernism. And there is the more general question to what extent films from one country may be perceived as modernist in foreign contexts of reception, as were famously certain kinds of Hollywood films by avant-garde intellectuals in France, the Soviet Union, and elsewhere.

Modernist practices within or on the margins of mainstream cinemas may share certain formal-stylistic principles with movements of elite artistic modernism—abstraction, seriality, self-reflexivity, to touch on some critical commonplaces—and did significantly formulate some of their own (montage being just one of them) that in turn inspired the latter.[36] But, as has often been pointed out, modernism does not reduce simply to a matter of style. A significant impulse in the modernist break with tradition, the quest for the genuinely new and different—in poetry, music, and the visual arts (including experimental film)—has been to oppose, negate, or at the very least undermine the consumerist logic of capitalist mass-market culture (however dependent upon and complicit with the latter modernist artists may have been in practice). In that sense, for high-modernists from Greenberg and Adorno to Jameson, the notion of vernacular modernism would be substantially a contradiction in terms. For inasmuch as the films in question were produced and circulated commercially, they would inevitably have diverged from the high-modernist agenda in their relationship to the audience. By contrast, I take one of the defining aspects of vernacular modernism to be precisely the way in which these films engaged with the experience and imagination of their audience. By doing so, they implicitly acknowledged, and helped create, a distinct kind of public sphere—constituted through the matrices of capitalist consumption, though not necessarily identical with and uncritical of it. Pragmatically, this orientation entailed working with genre formulas (both local and imported) and popular motifs, if not clichés; but it also meant putting them into play, twisting, denaturalizing, or transforming them, thus making them available for an at once sensorial-affective and reflective mode of reception.

A case in point is the body of films produced at Shochiku's Kamata branch in the late 1920s and 1930s (from which some of my initial examples were drawn), work by directors such as Shimizu, Naruse, Ozu, Shimazu Yasujiro, and Gosho Heinusunke. In the effort to compete with the rival Nikkatsu studio, known for theatrical shinpa-style and historical period films, as well as with foreign films, Shochiku developed its niche with a genre of modern film (gendai-geki) labeled shoshimin eiga—which literally translates as "petty bourgeois film," though more precisely referring to films about the mushrooming class of white-collar workers or salariat.[37] These films brought into view symptomatic sites of everyday modernity—urban streets and department stores, cafés, bars, dance halls, and movie theaters, schools and hospitals, offices and (occasionally) factories, Western-style apartments and traditional Japanese houses and shacks set in the semi-industrial wasteland of suburban Tokyo, or in the more marginal, low-cosmopolitan milieu of Yokahama habor—and used them in ways that led contemporary critics to discern in them "a stunning new realist aesthetic" (Russell, "Naruse," 75–75).

Shochiku Kamata films tapped the experience of the white-collar class, including an unprecedented number of working women (typists, salesgirls, café waitresses), as it was dramatized at the time in mass-market fiction and illustrated magazines and theorized by intellectuals (who came to refer to themselves mockingly as members of the *shoshimin* class).[38] Their plots revolved around conflicts and catastrophic accidents related to modernization, expressing the hopes and anxieties of people for whom Meiji-era dreams of upward mobility through education and hard work—and more recent ambitions linked to lifestyle and consumption—had turned, especially with the 1929 crash, into nightmare realities of unemployment and destitution. While the films gave expression to the sense of crisis or, to cite social theorist Aono Suekichi, the "panic" of this new class that sought to transcend (working) class, they also registered the blind spots of *shoshimin* mentality with critical irony, combining pathos with a degree of self-awareness we might not find, say, in German films of that period, even prior to 1933 (Harootunian, *History's Disquiet*, 91–92, 133).[39]

Whether focusing on "salarymen" and the breakdown of the patriarchal family (cf. Naruse's *Flunky, Work Hard* [1931], Ozu's *Tokyo Chorus* of the same year, and his *I Was Born But . . .* of the following year) or on the *moga* image and the contradictions of modern womanhood, Shochiku films, according to studio head Kido Shiro, were supposed to take on these issues in a "lighter" tone than their *shinpa*-influenced competitors or, for that matter, the leftist "tendency films."[40] To whatever degree that policy was actually adhered to and operative in the films, it was a business strategy by which the studio sought to appeal to the growing market of female consumers socializing outside the home, expecting them to bring along not only girlfriends and siblings, but also boyfriends and husbands. In terms of film practice, this entailed a modernization of Japanese cinema in several respects (which partially overlapped with the tenets of the more experimental "pure film movement"): casting actresses instead of *oyama* or female impersonators; using screenplays often based on mass-market fiction addressed to women; and replacing the *benshi*, the silent film narrators, with filmic narration based on forms of continuity editing and other techniques (such as Naruse's expressive track-ins on faces), which not only enhanced the relay of subjectivity between fictional character and viewer but also created "a sense of authenticity drawn from the audience's everyday life" (Mitsuyo Wada-Marciano, "Imagining Modern Girls," 21).

It would be easy to claim, or dismiss, Shochiku's strategies of constructing and anticipating its audience—by creating a filmic world, or worlds, that partially resembled the one they were trying to inhabit—as yet another lesson from the Hollywood book. But the implications of that lesson are far from clear. For one thing, the Hollywood model was itself a historical formation, developed against the foil of competing models, in particular the model of colonial modernity (the constituting of Western metropolitan audiences by displays of exoticized others) which had been an important factor in French cinema's dominance on the world market up to World

War I.[41] For another, to the extent that Shochiku oriented its practices on a liberal market model, this meant something quite different in 1930s Japan, especially as the decade went on, given the escalation of military aggression and territorial expansion vis-à-vis China and the increasing fascization of Japanese society, including anti-leftist arrests and censorship, the 1936 right-wing coup attempt, and full mobilization of imperial-nationalist ideology.

The type of public sphere that crystallized around vernacular-modernist film practices and other matrices of capitalist consumption would have provided a counterpoint to state-controlled national publicity on two counts. One, inasmuch as mainstream commercial films depended on the everyday experience of their constituency, they created a space for spectatorial subjectivity and agency, most strikingly for women. And, two, inasmuch as Shochiku directors were inspired by international film culture, they were likely to have an uneasy relationship with an autarchistic nationalism and the ideological imperative of "overcoming modernity."[42]

To be sure, Shochiku responded to increased political repression and censorship by abandoning overtly leftist themes, and dissent migrated into subtle details of mise-en-scène (such as Ozu's placement within the apartment of the film's exemplary traditional Japanese woman, in *Dragnet Girl*, of a French poster of the Lewis Milestone adaptation—banned in Japan—of Erich Maria Remarque's German pacifist novel *All Quiet on the Western Front*).[43] And no doubt there were films whose plots could be said to seek to contain the contradictions of modern womanhood in a manner consistent with, and reinforcing, nationalist discourse by producing "in their audience a national sentiment toward their own modernity" (Wada-Marciano, "Imagining Modern Girls," 17).[44] But to show *moga* figures as failing and, for instance, causing harm to the very people for whose sake they were submitting to alienating and socially proscribed forms of work, does not necessarily mean endorsing a return to traditional or more authentic womanhood. Not only do a great number of Shochiku films focalize narrational subjectivity and affect around the *moga* figure, even if the character is inconsistent and problematic; they also observe—and quietly expose—the socioeconomic conditions and ideological fixations that make the characters fail. By doing so, they still contain the dream of a different life, even if that dream can only be represented as an impossibility. To a remarkable degree (not untypical in Japanese artistic tradition though less so for wartime productions), these films resist closure, even when they end "happily," allowing audiences to recognize in them the contradictions and aporias of their own lives.

Vernacular modernism's importance to Japanese cinema becomes even more apparent if we return to the comparison between *Forget Love for Now* and *The Goddess* with which this chapter began. Shimizu's film was released in July of 1937, when Japan's attacks against China turned to open warfare and when Japanese film workers were encouraged to move to occupied Shanghai and take over the film industry. Whether Shimizu had seen *The Goddess* or not, the defeatist ending of *Forget Love for Now* pays strange homage to the Chinese precursor. At the very least, it seems out of key with the imperialist cause, notwithstanding the film's explicit if ambiguous nods to nationalism.[45] Likewise, self-conscious, ironic, or hyperbolic performances of the *moga* image, as well as aesthetic explorations of the materiality of things and trash, do not necessarily inspire heroic patriotic sentiment. Among other things, these examples can be read to suggest that vernacular modernist currents in 1930s Japanese cinema were running in directions oblique to dominant imperial-nationalist ideology and its aggressive political and military enforcement. They were neither automatically resistant nor inevitably complicit with that ideology, nor consistent within the oeuvre of individual directors or within one and the same film; and they were obviously not the only type of film made and shown in Japan. Still, in the measure that these films were geared less to National Policy ("kokusaku" films) than to a popular market (albeit one that was changing) and internationalist modernism, they articulated an idiom open to stylistic experiment, narrative ambiguity, parody and irony, as well as the conflicting potentials of modernity, rather than a unitary national discourse.

Chinese cinema of the period, including the left-wing cinema movement, was no less aware of and dependent on strategies of attracting and constructing an audience, which entailed tapping into the thriving market of urban mass culture and consumption centered in Shanghai. A key term here, related to the Japanese, were the *xiao shimin* or "petty urbanites": clerks, shopkeepers, employees, a broad social stratum variously referred to as petty bourgeois or new middle class and comprising men and women from diverse social and cultural backgrounds—in other words, a heterosocial urban mass public that had emerged (and met with masculinist-elitist disdain from May Fourth intellectuals) qua consumers of popular fiction and pictorial journalism, as well as American movies and music.[46] If comparable to similar subject formations in Tokyo (and, for that matter, other metropolitan centers in Asia, Latin America, and Europe), the modern mass public courted and shaped by Shanghai cinema cannot be thought of apart from the violently contested force field of Chinese national politics and conditions of semicolonial modernity. The fact that Japan was part of—and aggressively intervened in—this force field further complicates a comparative perspective.

This chapter has suggested the ways in which the concept of vernacular modernism might provide a heuristic framework for tracing transnational relations between and within Japanese and Chinese film practices of the 1930s. This framework could be made productive for cinemas in other parts of the world as well, with different historical trajectories of capitalist modernization, everyday modernity, and aesthetic modernism, including different positions vis-à-vis Hollywood hegemony. In each case, a comparative approach has to be complicated with a theoretically inspired *histoire croisée*, a history of entanglement that traces actual interconnections, inasmuch as films, filmmakers, and film styles did travel and audiences migrated, along with the virtual ones that were blocked. By tracking the ways in which cinemas in different geopolitical locations and constellations engaged with the contradictory experience of modernity, we may find resonances across violent divisions and asymmetrical conditions of wealth and power. What may surprise us in actually looking at films and exploring particular film cultures is less the fact of the global advance of capitalism than the shared concern, on the part of filmmakers and audiences alike, with modern life and modernist styles, a concern that included, in Harootunian's words, the "as yet unrealized promise of a more humane and just society" (Harootunian, *History's Disquiet* 68–69). This may be one of the reasons why, at a time when that promise has been made to sound like an echo from another era, these films look at once strange, poignant, and timely.

NOTES

1. This chapter is based on a lecture presented at the Centennial Celebration and 2005 Annual Conference of the Asian Cinema Studies Society, "National, Transnational, and International: Chinese Cinema and Asian Cinema in the Context of Globalization," Beijing and Shanghai, June 2005; a version was also delivered as a lecture at a "Politics, Criticism, and the Arts" conference at Vanderbilt University, April 2006. A version of this chapter was first published in *World Cinemas, Transnational Perspectives*, Natasa Durovico-va and Kathleen Newman, eds. (New York, London: Routledge, 2010). For critical readings and suggestions I would like to thank Paula Amad, Weihong Bao, Dipesh Chakrabarty, Norma Field, Michael Geyer, Andreas Huyssen, Andrew Jones, Dan Morgan, Laura Mulvey, Lesley Stern, Julia Adeney Thomas, Po-Chen Tsai, Man-Fung Yip, Judith Zeitlin, and Zhang Zhen. Special thanks to Michael Raine, who has been a challenging and patient interlocutor throughout the various stages of this project.

2. For an illuminating discussion of this film, see Russell.

3. As Michael Raine has pointed out to me, the nationalist sentiment mobilized by Kuwano's character in favor of staying, however precarious their existence, is deflated by the subsequent assertion that she would go to Singapore for the sake of her child and would not shed a nostalgic tear when seeing the Japanese flag. Also see Wong 19.

4. The discussion of Chinese and Japanese films of the 1920s and 1930s in terms of melodrama is notoriously fraught, whether with unreflected assumptions about the meaning of the term in Euro-American and Hollywood contexts or by its unproblematic transfer to different cultural and film-industrial genealogies and concepts of genre. See Dissanayake and Browne, as well as the contributions by Li Cheuk-to, Law Kar, and Law Wai-ming in *Cantonese Melodrama, 1950–1969*.

5. See, for instance, Yingjin Zhang, "Prostitution and Urban Imagination," and Jones, "The Child as History in Republican China" and "Playthings of History."

6. According to the program notes for the Hong Kong retrospective over thirty shots depicting the prostitutes' lives and their efforts to negotiate better conditions were cut by the censor (*Shimizu Hiroshi*, 70). I should add here that, unlike Ruan's Goddess, Kuwano's less saintly mother is granted a romantic attachment to one of the bodyguards, played by Valentino look-alike Sano Shuji, whose effort to save her, however, is primarily motivated by his fatherly feelings toward the son.

7. I discuss this film in greater detail in my essay "Fallen Women, Rising Stars, New Horizons: Shanghai Silent Film as Vernacular Modernism."

8. In neither the Japanese nor the Chinese case is there sufficient evidence to suggest that women constituted a majority of the audience (as they did, by the mid- to late 1920s,

in Hollywood), or that the studios produced films *primarily addressed* to women (as Hollywood did in the 1940s in response to the collapse of the female market). I therefore hesitate to use the term "woman's film" in this context, as does Wada-Marciano in her article "Imaging Modern Girls in the Japanese Woman's Film." I take the significance of women's movie-going in both cinemas to be rather of a differential and qualitative order, inasmuch as it gave women access to a public sphere of theatrical entertainments previously reserved for men and accepting women only in hierarchically regulated and segregated forms.

9. For a critique of such approaches, notably put forth by Paul Schrader and Donald Richie, see Bordwell's magisterial study *Ozu and the Poetics of Cinema*, 26–29.

10. Film's affinity with the "secret life of things" (Virginia Woolf) is a key topos of film aesthetics in interwar Europe—cf. Béla Balazs, Jean Epstein, Louis Aragon, Germaine Dulac, Siegfried Kracauer, Walter Benjamin—informed in part by a turn to the object in avant-garde movements such as Dada, Surrealism, and Soviet artists such as Boris Arvatov and Alexandr Rodchenko. See Brown, "Thing Theory" and "The Secret Life of Things (Virginia Woolf and the Matter of Modernism)," and Stern, "'Paths That Wind through the Thicket of Things,'" as well as the other essays in *Things*, Brown, ed. In the Asian context, an important impulse in this direction can be found in Tanizaki Jun'ichiro's early writings on film and modernity, including screenplays and literary fiction, of which only his essay *In Praise of Shadows* (1933) and his novel *Naomi* (1924–1925) are more widely known in English; see LaMarre. Another important source here is the Japanese school of New Sensationism and its Shanghai counterpart, translated into film aesthetics by Liu Na'ou and others.

11. The film's self-conscious play with the logics of the commodity is epitomized by a scene in which the protagonist's artist friend brings a chicken and two pig's feet to celebrate his birthday, manipulating them like a puppet and explaining how he paid for them: "This is the summer suit. This is the flannel jacket, this is a pair of white leather pants!"

12. This interest is indebted to Kracauer's *Theory of Film* (1960; 1997), a work that tries to negotiate the tension between film's modernist ability to render and preserve the otherness of an historically alienated physis and the inevitable urge to reimbue the world with human feelings and agency. It is understood that the critic's valorization of the former, the tendency to allegorize the significance of the insignificant, ephemeral, and indeterminate, is itself a version of that urge.

13. On the notion of the "formless," taking its cue from Bataille's *l'informe*, see Bois and Krauss, *Formless: A User's Guide*.

14. In this regard, left-wing Chinese films seem to set themselves off against stereotypical images of urban waste attached to the semicolonial port city (graphically displayed in the Soviet documentary film *Shanghai Document* [Yakov Bliokh, 1928]), but also against the racialized aestheticization of refuse and disintegration in the 1929 novel *Shanghai* by Japanese New Sensationist Yokomitsu Riichi, which provides an amazing, and highly ambivalent, intertext for a cinematic aesthetics of things and trash. For a contrasting view of Shanghai similarly concerned with the materiality of quotidian objects, see essays by Eileen Chang from during and after the war in *Written on Water*.

15. For efforts (in English-language scholarship) to cross that divide, if mostly at the level of essay collections and journals (such as *Asian Cinema*), see the special issue of *Camera Obscura*, "New Women of the Silent Screen: China, Japan, Hollywood," Russell, ed.; also see Dissanayake, *Melodrama and Asian Cinema*, and *Cinema and Cultural Identity*; and Ehrlich and Desser. More research into cross-filiations between Japanese and Chinese cinemas is being done for the post-World War II period, though

most accounts tend to focus on Hong Kong and Taiwan. On Japanese-Chinese film politics during the war and occupation, see High (on Kamei Fumio and other Toho military documentaries, and Chapter 7); Fu, Chapter 1; Yingjin Zhang, 83–89; and Stephenson.

16. I had the opportunity to view archival prints from this period in retrospectives of Chinese and Japanese films at the Pordenone silent film festival in, respectively, 1995/1997 and 2001/2005, in addition to retrospectives of the work of Ozu, Shimizu, and Naruse in the United States and Berlin.

17. Also see Zhen Zhang, "*An Amorous History of the Silver Screen*: The Actress as Vernacular Embodiment in Early Chinese Film"; Bao; Wada-Marciano, "Imaging Modern Girls," 16, 33ff.

18. For a critique of received comparative approaches in area studies, see Harootunian, "Ghostly Comparisons." Also see Werner and Zimmermann, "Beyond Comparison," based on the authors' introduction to the edited volume *De la comparaison à l'histoire croisée*, and Budde, Conrad, Janz, eds., *Transnationale Geschichte: Themen, Tendenzen und Theorien* (most contributions in English).

19. See Zhen Zhang, *An Amorous History of the Silver Screen*, 82–83 and Chapter 7, esp. 255–64 (on Tian Han's reception and later rejection of Tanizaki) and 274–84 (on Liu Na'ou). On the complex relationship of Chinese modernists to their Japanese counterparts, see Shih, esp. 16–30 and Chapters 9–11. On Tanizaki's "Oriental" film aesthetics, which turned on Chinese written characters (though in a different way than Eisenstein's ideas about ideograms and montage), see LaMarre, 26–33.

20. The question of how vernacular modernism interacts with genre, which involves different mappings—as well as the very concept—of genre that different film cultures developed both in relation to cultural tradition and in response to Hollywood genre films, is the subject of another chapter of my work in progress.

21. The foundational text in this regard is Bordwell, Staiger, and Thompson.

22. See Bordwell, *On the History of Film Style*, 141–46; and Keil. In these somewhat reductive accounts, approaches to early film history informed by theories of modernity are criticized under the label "modernity thesis." For a response to that criticism, see Singer, Chapter 4; and Gunning.

23. On the difficulty of defining the term modernism in any singular way, see Friedman.

24. On the interrelation of modernism and modernity in an "expanded field," see Huyssen.

25. On the difference between colonial/metropolitan forms of imperialism and the American model, see de Grazia, *Irresistible Empire*, and de Grazia's earlier essay, "Americanism for Export."

26. Bordwell, "Visual Style in Japanese Cinema, 1925–1945," 23, 7.

27. On the dynamics of nativist, cosmopolitan, and hybrid modernisms in Shanghai, see Lee; Jones, *Yellow Music*.

28. For a discussion of the relationship of cosmopolitan and vernacular in contemporary globalized settings, see Robbins.

29. I am using the term public sphere less in the Habermasian sense than that offered by Negt and Kluge. I have mobilized this notion of publicness for film history in *Babel and Babylon: Spectatorship in American Silent Film*.

30. See, for instance, Zhang, *Amorous History*, Chapter 4, especially 122–30; Dimendberg; Lamster, ed.; and Koch, ed. Durovicova interpolates the impossible linguistic ambitions and the architectural heteroglossia of cinematic modernity together.

31. See, for example, Jackson; Güvenç, esp. 284–88; Passanti, "The Vernacular, Modernism, and Le Corbusier," and an updated version of that essay in *Vernacular Modernism*, Umbach and Hüppauf, eds. Also see the entry on "Vernacular architecture" in the *Grove Dictionary of Art* (www.groveart.com).

32. Umbach's and Hüppauf's understanding of *Heimat* (9–16) is indebted to the utopianist philosophy of Bloch; also see Hüppauf, "Spaces of the Vernacular," which makes no mention of film (or any other technological media), neither of the genre of *Heimatfilm* that transported the parochial antimodernist version of the term well into the Federal Republic, nor of Edgar Reitz's television miniseries *Heimat* (1984) that gave it international currency.

33. Historicizing Lefebvre's concept of the everyday, Harootunian puts into conversation German writers such as Simmel, Kracauer, Benjamin, Bloch, and Heidegger with contemporary Japanese writers such as Kon Wajiro, Tosaka Jun, Aono Suekichi, and others. Also see Harootunian, *Overcome by Modernity: History, Culture, and Community in Interwar Japan*.

34. Examples include transnational language regions as large as Swahili, a multilingual idiom bridging over a hundred and thirty indigenous African languages; nationally specific idioms such as African American English; and smaller regions like the German Ruhrgebiet and the urban area of Berlin. See Calvet; Macaulay, "Vernacular" and "The Rise and Fall of the Vernacular." My thanks to Augusto Carli, Salikoko Mufwene, and Susan Gal for alerting me to both the potential and the problematic status of the term in linguistics, in particular sociolinguistics.

35. See Bordwell on the "flamboyant, frantic style" of some of the *chambara* films (*Ozu*, 23). Aimed at urban working-class men, rural audiences, and children, the genre was a matrix for a national discourse on heroic masculinity, including the threat of its failure; significantly, the subgenre of *matatabimono*, wandering yakusa and masterless samurai, was also referred to as "men's weepies." See Standish, 33, 43ff., 68.

36. The boundaries between intellectual-elite and vernacular modernisms were more fluid than my schematic paraphrase suggests, considering that numerous modernist artists and writers were fascinated, and themselves experimenting, with the new medium, or were seeking to reach larger audiences in middle-brow print media.

37. The term *shoshimin* was a translation of the French "petit bourgeois" and referred to people who, on the basis of their higher education and less physical types of labor set themselves off from ordinary workers but held no property and worked for low salaries. Whether or not the Japanese-Marxist ascription is adequate to the phenomenon, the English-language rendering of *shoshimin* in American sociological terms (by Wada-Marciano and others) as "new middle class" or "middle class" seems problematic. The historically salient point is that technologically mediated mass culture made visible a new social formation that was defined, to vary on Althusser, as much by their imaginary relation to the capitalist process of production as by their actual economic conditions. On the *shoshimin eiga* and Shochiku, see Tadao, *Nihon eigashi*, 232–33, and Kawamoto. Also see, since completion of this chapter, Wada-Marciano, *Nippon Modern*.

38. See Silverberg, "The Café Waitress Serving Modern Japan"; Harootunian, *Overcome by Modernity*, Chapter 1; and Sato, "An Alternate Informant: Middle-Class Women and Mass Magazines in 1920s Japan" and *The New Japanese Woman*.

39. The German point of comparison is Kracauer's study *Die Angestellten* (*The Salaried Masses: Duty and Distraction in Weimar Germany*). Kracauer's study, along with numerous reviews and articles on contemporary film and its audiences, early on discerned

in the employees' frustrated bourgeois aspirations and self-delusion a source of their vulnerability to National Socialist propaganda.

40. "Entertainment be bright and healthy, while laughing at society's ironies and contradictions, we can study life"; Kido Shiro, *Nihon eigaden: Eiga seisakusha no kiroku* (*Japanese Cinema Tales: A Record of a Film Producer*), translated and quoted in Standish, 32.

41. I am thinking here, for example, of Pathé travelogues whose appeal more often than not turned on the *contrast* between the world depicted in manifold picturesque views and the world inhabited by the audience (the difference between *le monde* in the geo- and ethnographic sense and *le monde* in the societal sense which is both elided and asserted in the Lumière Brothers' punning slogan, "to bring the world to the world"). This logic of contrast included ethnographic displays of internal others from peripheral and backward regions of Europe and, I would argue, continued in French "realist" peasant dramas of the 1920s, many of whom were based on nineteenth-century literary classics (cf. the series "André Antoine and French Realism," Pordenone silent film festival, 2005). It was to compete with this cinema of colonial modernity on the domestic market, and to transform heterogeneous immigrant audiences into a modern mass audience, that Hollywood developed classical strategies of narration and address (as the new "universal language" understood by viewers from diverse and non-synchronous backgrounds) along with "American subjects"—Westerns, stories and settings of contemporary everyday life. The claim to homology and potential contiguity between the diegetic world and that of the audience ("realism") was never *not* ideological, but the difference between these models matters, in terms of both modernist aesthetics and the quality of cinematic publicness. See Abel; Hansen, *Babel and Babylon*, Chapters 2, 3.

42. On the in/famous conference with that title, held in July 1942, see Harootunian, *Overcome by Modernity*, Chapter 2.

43. Wada-Marciano persuasively reads Ozu's extended staging of whispering in his 1933 (silent!) film *Woman of Tokyo*, which ostensibly transmits the rumor of the protagonist's unspeakable night job as a barmaid, as an implied reference to violent government action against communist intellectuals that had intensified that year—a subversive gag that contemporary audiences would have understood ("Imaging Modern Girls," 31–33). Another example would be Ozu's ironic citation of German cultural emblems, such as a poster of the Bamberger Reiter in the shabby living quarters of the protagonist and a UFA biopic on Franz Schubert, in *The Only Son* (1936).

44. Wada-Marciano challenges Silverberg's account in "Remembering Pearl Harbor" that there was "a fluidity of identity" (sexual, racial, national) in Japanese interwar modernity that was closed off by the rise of fascist-imperial nationalism.

45. Shimizu's dissent most persistently takes the form of sympathetic attention to socially and racially marginalized subjects, such as the group of Chinese boys whom the ostracized son befriends in *Forget Love for Now*. In *Mr. Thank You (Arigato-san*, 1936), a long take of Korean itinerant workers in the landscape turns into a more closely framed friendly exchange between a Korean girl and the eponymic handsome bus driver.

46. See Pang, Chapter 6, esp. 150–54; Zhang, *Amorous History*, 23, 44, 64–65; and Lee, Chapters 2, 3, and 8. Lee discusses Eileen Chang as a Shanghai writer who portrayed herself as a petty urbanite writing for petty urbanites whom she characterized this way: "Shanghainese are traditional people tempered by the pressure of modern life. The misshapen products of this fusion may not be entirely healthy, but they do embody a strange and distinctive sort of wisdom" (*Written on Water*, 54).

WORKS CITED

Abel, Richard. *The Red Rooster Scare: Making Cinema American, 1900–1910*. Berkeley: University of California Press, 1995.

Andrew, Dudley. Position paper, symposium on "Cinema as Vernacular Modernism," University of Chicago, 2002.

Aono, Suekichi. *Saraiman kyofu jidai [The Salaryman's Panic Time]*. Tokyo: Senshinsha, 1930.

Appadurai, Arjun. *Modernity at Large: Cultural Dimensions of Globalization*. Minneapolis: University of Minnesota Press, 1996.

Bao, Weihong. "From Pearl White to White Rose: Tracing the Vernacular Body of Nüxia in Chinese Silent Cinema." *Camera Obscura* 20.3 (2005): 193–231.

Bois, Yve-Alain and Rosalind Krauss. *Formless: A User's Guide*. New York: Zone Books, 1997.

Bordwell, David. *Ozu and the Poetics of Cinema*. Princeton: Princeton University Press, 1988.

———. *On the History of Film Style*. Cambridge: Harvard University Press, 1997.

———. "Visual Style in Japanese Cinema, 1925–1945." *Film History: An International Journal* 7.1 (1995): 5–31.

Bordwell, David, Janet Staiger, and Kristin Thompson. *Classical Hollywood Cinema: Film Style and Mode of Production to 1960*. New York: Columbia University Press, 1985.

Brown, Bill. "The Secret Life of Things (Virginia Woolf and the Matter of Modernism)." *Modernism/modernity* 6 (1999): 1–28.

———. "Thing Theory." *Things*. Ed. Bill Brown. Chicago: University of Chicago Press, 2004: 1–22.

Browne, Nick. "Society and Subjectivity: On the Political Economy of Chinese Melodrama." *New Chinese Cinemas*. Ed. N. Browne, Paul G. Pickowicz, Vivian Sobchack, and Esther Yau. Cambridge: Cambridge University Press, 1994: 40–56.

Budde, Gunilla, Sebastian, Conrad, and Oliver, Janz, eds. *Transnationale Geschichte: Themen, Tendenzen und Theorien*. Göttingen: Vandenhoeck & Ruprecht, 2006.

Calvet, Louis-Jean "Vernaculaire." *Sociolinguistique: Concepts de base*. Ed. Marie-Louise Moreau. Liège: Mardaga, 1997: 291–92.

Cantonese Melodrama, 1950–1969, Tenth Hong Kong International Film Festival Retrospective Catalogue. Hong Kong: Urban Council, 1997.

Chakrabarty, Dipesh. *Provincializing Europe: Postcolonial Thought and Historical Difference*. Princeton: Princeton University Press, 2000.

Chang, Eileen. *Written on Water*. Trans. Andrew Jones. Ed. Nicole Huang. New York: Columbia University Press, 2005.

de Grazia, Victoria. "Americanism for Export." *Wedge* 7–8 (1985): 74–81.

———. *Irresistible Empire: America's Advance through 20th-Century Europe*. Cambridge: Harvard University Press, 2005.

Dimendberg, Edward. *Film Noir and the Spaces of Modernity*. Cambridge: Harvard University Press, 2004.

Dissanayake, Wimal, ed. *Cinema and Cultural Identity: Reflections on Films from Japan, India, and China*. Lanham: University Press of America, 1988.

———. *Melodrama and Asian Cinema*. Cambridge: Cambridge University Press, 1993.

Durovicova, Natasa. "*Los Toquis*, Or, Urban Babel." *Global Cities: Cinema, Architecture, and Urbanism in a Digital Age*. Ed. Linda Krause and Patrice Petro. New Brunswick: Rutgers University Press, 2003.

Ehrlich, Linda C., and David Desser, eds. *Cinematic Landscapes: Observations on the Visual Arts and Cinema of China and Japan*. Austin: University of Texas Press, 1994.

Friedman, Susan Stanford. "Definitional Excursions: The Meanings of Modern/Modernity/Modernism." *Modernism/modernity* 8.3 (2001): 493–513.

Fu, Poshek. *Between Shanghai and Hong Kong*. Stanford: Stanford University Press, 2003.

Goldstein, Joshua. "The Remains of the Everyday: One Hundred Years of Recycling in Beijing." Ed. J. Goldstein and Madeleine Yue Dong. *Everyday Modernity in China*. Seattle: University of Washington, 2006.

Gunning, Tom. "Modernity and Cinema: A Culture of Shocks and Flows." *Cinema and Modernity*. Ed. Murray Pomerance. New Brunswick: Rutgers University Press, 2006: 302–15.

Güvenç, Bozkurt. "Vernacular Architecture as a Paradigm Case." *Vernacular Architecture*. Ed. Mete Turan. Aldershot: Avebury, 1990.

Hansen, Miriam. *Babel and Babylon: Spectatorship in American Silent Film*. Cambridge: Harvard University Press, 1991.

———. "Fallen Women, Rising Stars, New Horizons: Shanghai Silent Film as Vernacular Modernism." *Film Quarterly* 54.1 (Fall 2000): 10–22.

———. "The Mass Production of the Senses: Classical Cinema as Vernacular Modernism," *Modernism/modernity* 6.2 (1999): 59–77, rpt. in Christine Gledhill & Linda Willams, eds. *Reinventing Film Studies*. London: Edward Arnold; New York: Oxford University Press, 2000: 332–50.

Harootunian, Harry. *History's Disquiet: Modernity, Cultural Practices, and the Question of Everyday Life*. New York: Columbia University Press, 2000.

———. "Ghostly Comparisons." *Traces: A Multilingual Series of Cultural Theory and Translation* 3 (2004): 39–52.

———. *Overcome by Modernity: History, Culture, and Community in Interwar Japan*. Princeton: Princeton University Press, 2000.

High, Peter B. *The Imperial Screen: Japanese Film Culture in the Fifteen Years' War, 1931–1945*. Madison: University of Wisconsin Press, 2003.

Hong Kong International Film Festival. *Cantonese Melodrama, 1950-1969: The Tenth Hong Kong International Film Festival*. Hong Kong: The Urban Council of Hong Kong, 1986.

Hüppauf, Bernd. "Spaces of the Vernacular: Ernst Bloch's Philosophy of Hope and the German Hometown." Umbach and Hüppauf 84–113.

Huyssen, Andreas. "Geographies of Modernism in a Globalizing World." *Geographies of Modernism: Literatures, Cultures, Spaces*. Ed. Peter Brooker and Andrew Thacker. London: Routledge, 2005: 6–18.

Jackson, John Brinkerhoff. *Discovering the Vernacular Landscape*. New Haven, London: Yale University Press, 1975.

Jones, Andrew. "The Child as History in Republican China: A Discourse on Development." *positions* 10.3 (2002): 695–727.

———. "Playthings of History: The Child as Commodity in Republican China." University of Chicago, Chicago. December 2005. Lecture.

———. *Yellow Music: Media Culture and Colonial Modernity in the Chinese Jazz Age*. Durham: Duke University Press, 2001.

Kawamoto, Saburo. "Shoshimin eiga no 'atarashii wagaya'" [Shoshimin films and the "new my-home"]. *Kindai Nihon Bunkaron*, vol. 7: *Taishu bunka to masu mejia* [*On Modern Japanese Culture*, vol. 7: *Mass Culture and Mass Media*]. Tokyo: Iwanami Shoten, 1999: 1–17

Keil, Charlie. "'To Here from Modernity': Style Historiography, and Transitional Cinema." *American Cinema's Transitional Era: Audiences, Institutions, Practices*. Ed. C. Keil and Shelley Stamp. Berkeley: University of California Press, 2004: 51–65.

Kluge, Alexender. "Kapitalistische Moderne und Intimität: Miriam Hansen über vier Filme, die von selbstbewussten Frauen handeln." 10 vor 11, broadcast August 22, 2005.

Koch, Gertrud, ed. *Umwidmungen—architektonische und kinematographische Räume*. Berlin: Vorwerk, 2005.

Kracauer, Siegfried. *Die Angestellten [The Salaried Masses: Duty and Distraction in Weimar Germany]*. 1929. Trans. Quintin Hoare. New York: Verso, 1998.

LaMarre, Thomas. *Shadows on the Screen: Tanizaki Jun'ichiro on Cinema & "Oriental" Aesthetics*. Ann Arbor: Center for Japanese Studies, University of Michigan, 2005.

Lamster, Mark, ed. *Architecture and Film*. New York: Princeton Architectural Press, 2000.

Lee, Leo Ou-fan. *Shanghai Modern: The Flowering of a New Urban Culture in China, 1930–1945*. Cambridge: Harvard University Press, 1999.

Macaulay, Ronald K. S. "The Rise and Fall of the Vernacular." *On Language: Rhetorica, Phonologica, Syntactica*. Ed. Caroline Duncan-Rose and Theo Vennemann. New York: Routledge, 1988: 107–15.

———. "Vernacular." *Concise Encyclopedia of Sociolinguistics*. Ed. Rajend Mesthrie. Amsterdam: Elsevier, 2001: 421.

Mitchell, Timothy, ed. *Questions of Modernity*. Minneapolis: University of Minnesota Press, 2000.

Negt, Oskar, and Alexander Kluge. *The Public Sphere and Experience*. 1972. Trans. Peter Labanyi, Jamie Daniel, and Assenka Oksiloff. Minneapolis: University of Minnesota Press, 1993.

Pang, Laikwan. *Building a New China in Cinema: The Chinese Left-Wing Cinema Movement, 1932–1937*. Lanham: Rowman & Littlefield, 2002.

Passanti, Francesco. "The Vernacular, Modernism, and Le Corbusier." *Journal of the Society of Architectural Historians* 56.4 (1997): 438–51.

———. "The Vernacular, Modernism, and Le Corbusier." Umbach and Hüppauf 141–56.

Pollock, Sheldon. "Cosmopolitan and Vernacular in History." *Public Culture* 12.3 (2000): 591–625.

———. "The Cosmopolitan Vernacular." *The Journal of Asian Studies* 57.1 (1998): 6–37.

Rapoport, Amos. "Defining Vernacular Design." *Vernacular Literature*. Ed. Turan Mete. Brookfield: Grower Publishing Co, 1990.

Robbins, Bruce. "Actually Existing Cosmopolitanism." *Cosmopolitics: Thinking and Feeling Beyond the Nation*. Ed. Pheng Cheah and Bruce Robbins. Minneapolis: University of Minnesota Press, 1998: 1–19.

Russell, Catherine. "Naruse Mikio's Silent Films: Gender and the Discourse of Everyday Life in Interwar Japan." *Camera Obscura* 60 20.3 (2005): 57–89.

———, ed. *New Women of the Silent Screen: China, Japan, Hollywood*. Spec issue of *Camera Obscura* 60 20.3 (2005).

Sato, Barbara. "An Alternate Informant: Middle-Class Women and Mass Magazines in 1920s Japan." *Being Modern in Japan: Culture and Society from the 1910s to the 1930s*. Ed. Elise K. Tipton and John Clark. Honolulu: University of Hawai'i Press, 2000.

———. *The New Japanese Woman: Modernity, Media, and Women in Interwar Japan*. Durham: Duke University Press, 2003.

Sato, Tadao. *Nihon eigashi*. Tokyo: Iwanami Shoten, 1995.

Shih, Shu-Mei. *The Lure of the Modern: Writing Modernism in Semicolonial China, 1917–1937*. Berkeley: University of California Press, 2001.

Silverberg, Miriam. "The Café Waitress Serving Modern Japan." *Mirror of Modernity: Invented Traditions of Modern Japan.* Ed. Stephen Vlastos. Berkeley: University of California Press, 1998: 208–25.

——. "Remembering Pearl Harbor, Forgetting Charlie Chaplin, and the Case of the Disappearing Woman: A Picture Story." *Formations of Colonial Modernity in East Asia.* Ed. Tani E. Barlow. Durham: Duke University Press, 1997: 249–94.

Singer, Ben. *Melodrama and Modernity.* New York: Columbia University Press, 2001.

Standish, Isolde. *A New History of Japanese Cinema: A Century of Narrative Film.* New York: Continuum, 2005.

Stephenson, Shelley. "The Occupied Screen: Star, Fan, and Nation in Shanghai Cinema, 1937–1945." PhD diss. University of Chicago, 2000.

Stern, Lesley. "'Paths That Wind through the Thicket of Things.'" *Things.* Ed. Bill Brown. Chicago: University of Chicago Press, 2004: 393–43.

Umbach, Maiken, and Bernd Hüppauf, eds. *Vernacular Modernism: Heimat, Globalization and the Built Environment.* Stanford: Stanford University Press, 2005.

Wada-Marciano, Mitsuyo. "Imaging Modern Girls in the Japanese Woman's Film." *Camera Obscura* 60 20.3 (2005): 15–56.

——. *Nippon Modern: Japanese Cinema of the 1920s and 1930s.* Honolulu: University of Hawai'i Press, 2008.

Werner, Michael. "Beyond Comparison: *Histoire Croisée* and the Challenge of Reflexivity." *History and Theory* 45 (2006): 30–50.

Werner, Michael, and Bénédict Zimmermann, eds. *De la comparaison à l'histoire croisée.* Paris: Editions du Seuil, 2004.

Wong, Ain-ling. "In the Land of Fallen Souls." *Shimizu Hiroshi: 101st Anniversary.* Ed. Kinnia Yau, Li Cheuk-to, et al. Hong Kong: Hong Kong International Film Festival Society, 2004: 18–21.

Zhang, Yingjin. *Chinese National Cinema.* New York, London: Routledge, 2004.

——."Prostitution and Urban Imagination: Negotiating the Public and the Private in Chinese Films of the 1930s." *Cinema and Urban Culture in Shanghai, 1922–1943.* Ed. Yingjin Zhang. Stanford: Stanford University Press, 1999: 160–80.

Zhang, Zhen. "*An Amorous History of the Silver Screen*: The Actress as Vernacular Embodiment in Early Chinese Film." *A Feminist Reader in Early Cinema.* Ed. Jennifer M. Bean and Diane Negra. Durham: Duke University Press, 2002: 501–29.

——. *An Amorous History of the Silver Screen: Shanghai Cinema, 1896–1937.* Chicago: University of Chicago Press, 2005.

CHAPTER 26

VISIONS OF MODERNITY IN COLONIAL INDIA: CINEMA, WOMEN, AND THE CITY

MANISHITA DASS

A publicity booklet for the 1934 Hindi film, *Shahar Ka Jadoo* (*Lure of the City*), features on its cover the image of a fashionably attired young woman gazing dreamily into the distance. Presumably an embodiment of the allure of the city, she is marked as a "modern woman" by her appearance (hairstyle, makeup, dress), as well as by the emphatic modernity of the Art Deco lettering of the titles (English and Hindi) framing the page.[1] Although there are no iconographic references to the rural in the cover illustration, the "absent presence" of the village would have been crucial to contemporary readings of this image. As the plot synopsis provided in the booklet indicates, the film itself is rooted in a familiar moral contrast between the urban and the rural.[2] It tells the story of a man who leaves his family in the village to go to the city in search of work, falls prey to its dubious charms (personified by a woman who seduces him), and abandons his wife and infant daughter and his rural values. The second half of the film traces the grown-up daughter's quest for her long-lost father. Her journey to the city culminates in a reassertion of the traditional values associated with the rural, albeit only after she masters the modern skills of surviving in the city. While the narrative trajectory of the film appears to end in an affirmation of tradition, it is significant that the cover illustration bears no explicit reference to the traditional but instead uses the visual pleasure offered by the emblematic urban figures of the modern woman and the film actress as an advertising ploy. The modern woman—in her multifaceted role as character, star, and metaphor—thus enables the film to market itself both as a cautionary tale about the perils of modernity and as a seductive display of its attractions.

By the early 1930s, the modern woman as an ambivalent icon of urban life had become a familiar trope in Indian cinemas (in Hindi, Bengali, and other regional films). The cinematic city, in general, was defined in relation to the village and both spatially and morally distanced from it. The journey from the country to the city, a recurrent motif in Indian films from the mid-1920s onward, was usually represented as a disorienting transition from a tradition-bound, purer way of life to the alluring but potentially dangerous space of modernity.[3] This spatialization of tradition and modernity along the urban-rural divide is, of course, not unique to India. As Raymond Williams demonstrates in his classic study of images of the countryside and the city in English literature, "the contrast of country and city is one of the major forms in which we become conscious of a central part of our experience and of the crises in our society" (289). The country-city opposition, Williams argues, plays an especially critical figural role in the cultural imaginary of a society in the midst of the upheavals of social modernization brought about by industrial capitalism. In late nineteenth- and early twentieth-century India, however, the articulation of this classic dichotomy did not merely replicate the dynamics of the metropolitan version. Like most Indian cultural formations, it was complicated by the experience of colonialism, the gendered contradictions of cultural nationalism, the divisions of class, and the demands of decolonization, all of which were integral components of the Indian experience of modernity.

While a certain mode of conceptualizing the country and the city had existed in India before the colonial period, it underwent a series of transformations following the establishment of colonial rule and the emergence of Indian nationalism in the nineteenth century (Ramanujan). Even though the nationalist movement was primarily urban in origin, the authenticity sought by the nation—as the ground on which to stake its identity and legitimacy—was located in rural communities, seen as emerging organically from the land, rather than in the modern city. At once the site of India's colonial subjection and the embodiment of modernity's emancipatory promise, the city came to occupy a profoundly ambivalent place in the Indian cultural imaginary, shadowed by its metonymic association with colonial administration, imperial power, and the supposedly inauthentic modernity of the Westernized urban elite, as well as by its contrast with the persistent myth of "village India."

In this chapter, I look at how this new conception of urban space, pivotal to late nineteenth- and early twentieth-century Indian literatures and the emergent political culture of Indian nationalism, was inscribed into the figure of the modern woman in a wide variety of Hindi films ranging from stunt films to reformist melodrama (produced mostly in Bombay), as well as into the discourse about cinema and modernity, in the late 1920s and the 1930s. The city as a sign of the modern provided a vital metonymic link between cinema and the modern woman. While the space of Indian cinema was perceived (and often presented itself, though not without a certain ambivalence) in this period as being central to the production, transmission, and investigation of modernity, the contradictions of modernity were often made visible in this space through the quintessentially urban figure of the modern woman. Invariably tied to the metropolis, which offered new opportunities and identities to women, the modern woman did not just function as a signifier of imported urban vice or the antithesis of indigenous rural virtue; she came to embody the simultaneously emancipatory and disruptive potential of the city, and a modernity that was at once compelling and troubling. Reading this recurrent cinematic image in the light of contemporary discourses of the city, cinema, and the nation, I argue that the trope of the modern woman offers a phantasmic vision of urban identity in a transitional society—a vision that brought together both the desire for modernity (understood as a desirable state of progress and an alluring lifestyle) and fears about the price of modernization (understood as a state of individual alienation and cultural uprooting, and as a threat to the identity of the emerging nation).[4]

Enmeshed as it is in contradictory discourses about colonial modernity, tradition, nation, and urbanism,[5] the trope of the modern woman serves as a focal point in the visual culture of popular Indian cinema in the 1920s and 1930s, allowing us to explore cinema's self-reflexive engagement with the experience of modernity—a process that Miriam Hansen theorizes through the heuristic of "vernacular modernism" in her chapter in this volume—through the "look" of films (settings, costumes), publicity materials such as posters and film booklets, and the star image.[6] My use of extra-cinematic material is dictated partly by necessity—many of the films from the 1930s that I refer to in my effort to reconstruct the image of the modern woman have not survived or are unavailable for viewing—but also by a belief that we cannot understand much about cinema's role in mediating modernity by looking only at the films themselves. We need to examine the spaces between production and consumption: the array of networks, circuits, and flows— e.g., exhibition practices, marketing strategies, film journalism, promotional material, public debates about cinema, oral discourse, etc., as well as other sociocultural crosscurrents—through which film travels between these two poles and enters the practices of everyday life.

THE URBAN SCENE OF MODERNITY IN INDIAN CINEMA, 1920S–1930S

Indian silent cinema, during its formative years (which coincided with *swadeshi* nationalism's emphasis on the indigenous and on authentic Indian traditions), turned toward mythological, devotional, and (quasi-)historical themes rather than to contemporary urban life. This apparent turn away from the modern was prompted, in part, by a desire to counter cinema's image as an alien space/ medium of modernity and to legitimize it through a strategic alliance with the traditional, and in part by a desire to acquire a competitive edge in a market dominated by foreign films. The experience of urban modernity, however, emerges as a central theme in the early twenties with the establishment of a number of studios (in Bombay, Calcutta, Kohlapur, and Pune, with the largest concentration in Bombay) modeled, somewhat loosely, on the Hollywood studio system. With a view toward appealing to the tastes and concerns of a potential metropolitan audience drawn from the expanding ranks of the urban middle and lower-middle classes, these studios moved toward an increasing diversification of the film product.

The city makes a belated appearance—as the site of melodramas of modernization and/or the scene of lurid crimes—in Indian narrative cinema in the mid-1920s along with the emergence of an elastic genre that came to be known as the "social," which included any films dealing with contemporary life and recognizably modern settings (*Encyclopaedia of Indian Cinema*, 219). One of the earliest "social" films, a realist-reformist melodrama called *Bismi Sadi* (*Twentieth Century*, 1924, Kohinoor Studios), traces the transformation of Devdas, a street vendor who goes to Bombay to make his fortune and ends up as an exploitative cotton mill owner and a callous snob (representative of Bombay's industrial parvenu class) knighted by the British. In contrast to the preoccupation with the past in mythological or historical films, the title foreshadows the social's growing concern with the present, just as the film establishes the city as the crucible of the contemporary or the modern and a site of Westernization: a space of opportunity, temptation, and corruption, an arena of class mobility and class conflict.

The themes of class and urban corruption were given a particularly sensational spin by a subgenre of the social, the so-called crime films, which often lifted their plots from contemporary newspaper headlines. One of the earliest known crime films, for instance—a 1924 Kohinoor production, *Kala Nag* (*Triumph of Justice/Black Cobra*)—was based on a major scandal in Bombay known as the Champsi-Haridas case; it was advertised as a "thrilling plot revealing various styles of treacherous fraud of the modern civilization and dreadful assassination for the ardent desire of wealth or passions and rape and ravishment of atrocious villains" (*Bombay Chronicle*, January 5, 1924). Films such as *Kala Nag, Mojili Mumbai* (*The Slaves of Luxury*, 1925, Kohinoor Film), and *Mumbai Ni Mohini* (*Social Pirates/The Night Side of Bombay*, 1925, Saraswati Film) depicted the lifestyles of Bombay's colonial bourgeoisie as an illustration of the dark side of "modern civilization" (characterized by treachery, decadence, lasciviousness, and murderous greed), and offered its spectators both a moral commentary on, and a titillating glimpse into, the lifestyles of the immoral and Westernized rich.[7] This duality persisted in cinematic depictions of urban life well into the sound era, as John Alexander notes in an article in the May 1940 issue of the periodical *filmindia*. While lauding the social's ostensible motive—"to portray life as it is lived now and to point out where improvements could take place"—Alexander comments on a widespread tendency to skate over the real issues of a social problem and to focus on the "background of a life lived among leisure and privilege." In a society where access to consumer culture and the actual changes brought about by consumerism were restricted by class, and affordable commodities for mass consumption remained scarce, the glimpses of upper-class life afforded by many socials can be seen as nurturing a consumer culture somewhat different from that in metropolises of Europe or the United States—one dominated by fantasies of consumerism rather than actual practices of consumption.

Vicarious consumption, however, did not constitute the only attraction of the social. This loosely defined genre played a key role in articulating and mediating the experience of colonial modernity and competing cultural discourses on modernization, thereby extending the orbit of these discourses beyond the bourgeois public sphere oriented around print culture. For audiences excluded from dominant formations of public discourse and displaced from older traditions and communities—by colonialism, migration, or urbanization—the social offered, in Miriam Hansen's terms, a crucial "sensory-reflexive horizon" for negotiating the historical experience of displacement associated with modernity (even as cinema's institutional development was often perceived as contributing to that process of displacement) ("Fallen Women, Rising Stars, New Horizons").

In her chapter in this volume, Hansen proposes "vernacular modernism" as a heuristic and analytic framework for making sense of cinema's ability to provide such a horizon, or for thinking about "how films can be understood as engaging with modernity—more precisely, distinct, highly uneven and unequal formations of modernity—and about how film practices interrelate across the borders of national cinemas." While Hansen cautions against indiscriminately labeling as "vernacular modernism" any film that references everyday modernity and points out that not every such film can be said to be "modernist in style or stance," she is also reluctant to restrict the scope of the term by focusing *only* on practices within commercial cinema that share formal or stylistic principles with modernisms in the traditional arts. If, following Hansen, we understand "vernacular modernism" to refer more broadly to film practices "responding—and making sensually graspable our responses—to the set of technological, economic, social, and perceptual transformations associated with the term modernity," the Indian social can be said to represent a distinct brand of vernacular modernism, one that evolved in a complex relation (of adaptation and critique) to American and other foreign films while simultaneously drawing on and reshaping vernacular traditions in theater, literature, print, and visual culture. Its postindependence avatar has received considerable critical attention and been identified as one of the central sites of Indian public culture—as a crucial discursive, aesthetic, and social horizon for exploring the dislocations of postcolonial modernity and the fissures within the imagined community of the nation.[8] This chapter advances a similar argument about the early social and demonstrates the need for a large-scale archaeology of the genre, its contexts of production and reception, and its relationship to international cinematic trends, vernacular cultural practices, and local trajectories of aesthetic modernism. Given the specific historical and cultural valences of the "vernacular," "modernity," and "modernism" in the Indian subcontinent (which fall outside the purview of this article), it would be safe to say that such a project can not only benefit from but also contribute to, Hansen's conceptualization of vernacular modernism.[9]

Unfortunately, virtually none of the silent socials and very few of their early sound counterparts have survived, so the cityscape of modernity mapped by the early social remains, for the most part, in the tantalizing realm of speculation. We can only imagine, on the basis of the few surviving fragments and scraps of information gleaned from reviews, advertisements, and autobiographical writings, how these films explored the city, moving from business offices to nightclubs, from the drawing rooms of the elite to the *kothas* of *tawaifs*,[10] from police stations to gambling dens, from factories to film studios, and from mansions to tenement buildings, and linked these disparate spaces in a network of crime, intrigue, and romance. Given the fact that the audience of these films would have included a large number of recent immigrants to the city of proletarian and lower-middle-class origins (as well as a significant number of small-town residents and some villagers) with little or no access to the affluent lifestyles depicted on screen, the silent socials and their sound counterparts can be seen as offering a powerful fantasy of modern life, a combination of righteous indignation and voyeuristic delight, and a moral map of the metropolis, marking its perils, pleasures, pitfalls, and hidden connections.

THE MODERN WOMAN AS URBAN TEXT

The modern woman, operating as one of the most visible markers of metropolitan difference, occupies a prominent place in the cinematic map of the city created by the silent socials and their successors in the sound era. While her emergence as an urban icon can be traced back to changing gender configurations in late nineteenth-century India (which I will discuss later), the cinematic reinvention of the modern woman in the early twentieth century owes much to the rise of the female star—as one of the main attractions and an icon of cinema, as well as a distinctly modern figure—by the mid-1920s. Acting (on stage as well as on screen) was a relatively novel profession for women in early twentieth-century India. The social taboo against women of propriety displaying themselves to the public gaze (stemming from Brahmanical codes and strictures, and orthodox Islamic practices) and the strictly enforced gendered segregation of public and private spheres[11] prevented elite and middle-class women belonging to "good" or "respectable" families from appearing on the professional stage or at times even from taking part in amateur theatricals well into the twentieth century (Ahmed 265). Singing and dancing in public were seen as the domain of a stigmatized class of women, and female roles in folk drama and indigenous commercial theater of the nineteenth century were customarily played by boys and young men. While in Bengal actresses replaced female impersonators in the 1870s (Bhattacharya), and Muslim and Anglo-Indian actresses entered the theater scene in Bombay in the 1880s, the practice of female impersonation continued well into the 1930s on the stages of western India (K. Hansen n.3). Many of the first generations of female actors were recruited from red light areas or the Indo-Muslim courtesan culture; already stigmatized for their professions or origins, they were vulnerable to exploitation, and simultaneously pursued and ostracized for their perceived sexuality and availability. The presence of these female performers contributed both to commercial theater's growing popularity as an urban entertainment and to the aura of disrepute that clung to it in late nineteenth-century and early twentieth-century India.

In her pioneering study of gender in Parsi theater, Kathryn Hansen argues that Anglo-Indian actresses (many belonging to the Baghdadi-Jewish community which had emigrated to India in the early nineteenth century) who became prominent in the Parsi theater scene around the turn of the century enabled theater managers to capitalize on the appeal of actresses while circumventing the problem of respectability. With the rise of the middle-class theater-going public and the corresponding increase in the size of the potential female audience, the social status of actresses became a growing issue. The Anglo-Indian actress, marked as racially other in relation to the bulk of the theater audiences and thus exempt from the social taboo on female performance, managed both to provide "an acceptable alternative to those Indian actresses whose social position (or lack thereof) prevented their reception as suitable objects of spectatorial pleasure," and to add "glamour and excitement to a theatre already synonymous with spectacle" (K. Hansen 141, 144). Part of the appeal of the Anglo-Indian actress lay in her ability to enable "a fluidity of spectatorial positions," shifting readily, in the viewer's gaze "between the fantasized memsahib, the material Anglo-Indian actress, and the fictional Indian heroine" (K. Hansen 146).

Given Parsi theater's pervasive influence on early Indian cinema, it is hardly surprising that Anglo-Indian actresses dominated the scene of early cinema in the 1920s, passing as "white" even as they appeared on the screen under Hindu names: Sulochana (Ruby Myers), Sita Devi (Renee Smith), Manorama (Winnie Stewart), Indira Devi (Effie Hippolet), to name only a few of the prominent examples. As Kathryn Hansen points out, the use of Sanskritized aliases indicates a growing alignment between mainstream nationalism and gender formation. This alignment was also noticeable in Indian silent cinema's tendency to "dress up the Anglo-Indian as the good Hindu girl, whether as mythological heroine, rural damsel, or dutiful city wife," while fully exploiting the visual possibilities opened up by her greater degree of freedom of dress and action (K. Hansen 146). I would argue, however, these stars often undermined the intended moral message of their films. Even if the films' narrative trajectory seemed to affirm traditional ideals of womanhood and gendered narratives of a "sufficient modernity," the not white/not quite status of the actresses enabled them to elude the totalizing grasp of such ideals, not only by granting them a certain freedom of movement and action but also by introducing an element of radical ambiguity that would continue to be part of the discourse of female stardom in India long after the Anglo-Indian actresses vanished from the screen.

This ambiguity was most apparent in the screen role of the "modern woman," who seemed to have emerged most spectacularly as a new metropolitan presence in films designed as star vehicles for Sulochana (1907–1983), aka Ruby Meyers, a former telephone operator who reportedly became the industry's highest-paid star at Imperial Studios in the late 1920s and was one of the few silent era stars to have made a successful transition to talkies. *Cinema Ni Rani* (*Cinema Queen*, 1925), in which Sulochana plays a film star, was the first of a series of films intended to create "a star-image" for Sulochana out of self-reflexive elements, autobiographical ambiguities, and the transnational spectacle of the "modern girl."[12] It has been argued that the modern girl—a distinctly urban figure defined by her consumerism, sartorial style, and explicit eroticism (one not limited by the sexual economy of reproduction), and by her seeming defiance of the roles of dutiful daughter, wife, and mother—was one of the first transnational cultural icons, traveling across national borders along the circuits created by the processes and commodity flows of capitalist globalization in the early to mid-twentieth century (Weinbaum et al.). Sulochana's films, which depict the modern girl in various incarnations (as a film star, a telephone operator, a Robin Hood–like criminal with a flair for disguises, and an Oxford graduate), played a pioneering role in relocating this transnational figure in the matrices of Indian aspirations, anxieties, and arguments about urban modernity.

Surviving publicity material for *Indira, M.A.*, the 1934 remake of the silent film, *Indira, B.A.*, provides an interesting glimpse into the process of translation that reconfigured the modern girl as the Indian "adhunika"[13]—a process that began in Indian cinema in the mid-1920s and continued well into the 1930s and beyond. A poster emphasizing Sulochana's appearance in the title role depicts a fashionable young woman in a languid pose, attired in a silky blue robe which seems to be a cross between a saree and a dress; her hairstyle and her bright red lipstick evoke the flapper look, but the *bindi* on her forehead and her glass bangles mark her as Indian. The film booklet introduces Indira as a woman with a master's degree from Oxford, "a free bird of paradise of civilized India," vehement in her support for "the emancipation of womanhood by demanding from the Society [sic] the elementary rights of choosing a husband, divorcing a husband—in case if need be—and educating the girls to achieve such ideals which are absolutely Western in construction." In accordance with her views, she rejects the suitor chosen for her by her alcoholic father, and defies parental objections to marry a notorious playboy with whom she has fallen in love. The marriage, however, ends in scandal and divorce; in a climactic scene, Indira's father, a Westernized lawyer, publicly accuses himself for his daughter's misfortune, attributing it to his ill-fated decision to have her educated abroad. Indira's Oxford education, which is blamed for filling her head with inappropriate ideas about women's emancipation and making her an easy target for predatory men, serves, in this narrative, as an emblem of her inauthentic modernity. The M.A. degree appended to her name in the title thus appears as yet another of the fashionable accoutrements and accomplishments—such as Western clothes or certain kinds of sarees, sleeveless blouses, makeup, high-heeled shoes, "vanity bags," elegant cigarette-holders, lavishly decorated drawing rooms, male admirers, fluency in English, driving skills, etc.—that mark her visibly as a modern woman, simultaneously enhancing her exotic appeal and generating anxieties about her deviation from, and impact on, traditional gender norms and relations.

Educational (and professional) qualifications are also used to define the eponymous heroine's modernity in *Dr. Madhurika* (*Modern Wife*, Sarvottam Badami, 1935). Madhurika, a young surgeon (played by Sabita Devi, another famous Anglo-Indian actress), is presented in publicity campaigns as a "modern" wife who neglects her home and her husband for her career; an advertisement in the July 1935 issue of *filmindia* proclaims

> She is always IN when her patients knock at her door
> She is always OUT when her husband stands at her door.
> HER HOME IS HER HOSPITAL.

The cover illustration of the film booklet shows Madhurika against a backdrop of laboratory equipment looking intently into a microscope; the laboratory setting is rendered in an Art Deco style that underscores the theme of a cold and rational modernity through its repeated geometric shapes and conical swirls. The detailed plot synopsis in the film booklet describes Madhurika's approach to marriage as equally cold and sterile. Dedicated to her profession and to the cause of propagating birth control as a means of limiting population growth, Madhurika agrees to marry Narendra, a lawyer, on the conditions that she will not have children and that he will not interfere with her career or with her choice of friends. After her marriage, she neglects Narendra and provokes his jealousy through her devotion to medicine and her relationship with a male colleague. Single-minded in her commitment to her public persona and the medical profession, Madhurika is seen as having "triumphed as a doctor but failed miserably as a wife," and by implication, as a woman. She becomes a "proper wife" and a "real woman"—by giving up medicine for the "divine pleasures of home"—only after her husband starts paying attention to another woman and her children, jolting her into a realization of the error of her ways.

Indira, M.A. and *Dr. Madhurika* belong to a long line of socials in which the question of modernity is posed and debated through the figure of the modern woman and in relation to issues of parental authority, familial stability, and marital harmony.[14] This trend was initiated by a 1927 Ranjit Studios production titled *Gunasundari* (also titled *Why Husbands Go Astray*), directed by Chandulal Shah and starring Gohar, one of the leading actresses of the silent era. Gohar plays a traditional housewife who is catapulted, by her husband's affair with a dancing girl into an active social life beyond the confines of her home and into a new identity as a modern woman—an identity that eventually helps her to win back her husband. The film thus seems to endorse the individuality of the modern woman over the traditional submissive role of the Hindu wife, but does so only within specific limits: the companionate marriage of the reunited couple recommends a modicum of modernity (in habits, outlook, appearance, and practices) to the wives of middle-class men as a domestic virtue and a prerequisite for becoming a better partner in a changing social milieu.

In its attempt to domesticate the allure of modernity, *Gunasundari* (like many of its successors) resonates with the discourse of social reform that originated in the mid-nineteenth century in Calcutta and Bombay and then spread to other parts of India. As one of the chroniclers of the social reform movement pointed out in 1959, "social reform as commonly understood in India is largely related to changes affecting the structure of Indian society and family and was [only] slightly concerned [with] changes affecting relations between economic classes, which in the West go by the name of social reform" (Natarajan 5). Not surprisingly, women—in their roles as wives, mothers, and daughters—were a central focus of the discourse and programs of social reform in colonial India. Creating a "New Woman" through education and new social practices was pivotal to the modernization campaign initiated by the liberal male elite as a necessary step toward regenerating Indian society. By the late 1860s, women's education had emerged as a central point of public debate, and the ideal of the *bhadramahila*, originally articulated in elite reformist circles in Bengal, was being disseminated in other parts of middle-class India. The social historian Rosalind O'Hanlon describes this new ideal of womanhood as "a fusion of older brahmanical values of *pativrata*, of feminine self-sacrifice and devotion to the husband, with Victorian emphases upon women as enlightened mothers and companions to men in their own 'separate sphere' of the home" (15). The case for women's education was usually made in accordance with this new ideal of femininity and the notion of a "sufficient modernity." Formal education was intended to supplement, rather than challenge, female socialization and was viewed as a tool for recasting, rather than demolishing, patriarchy. Education, it was argued, would school women—or rather, women belonging to the upper strata of society—into becoming more efficient as homemakers, more effective as the mothers of future citizens, and more delightful as companions for the emerging urban middle-class men. These women were thus encouraged to equip themselves with some of the accoutrements of modernity—those that would enable them to perform their domestic roles with greater efficiency—but also admonished to do so while preserving what was best in "traditional" Indian culture.[15]

Cultural nationalism's investment in the traditional as the essence of the nation and its tendency to feminize the realm of tradition—or its symbolic identification of women as embodiments of community and custodians of the unique spiritual essence that apparently made India different from, and superior to, the West— meant that the process of recasting women in colonial India was fraught with intense anxieties and fierce controversies. Reforms related to women's issues were viciously attacked by those who felt that the sanctity of a traditional society was in danger of being violated by new-fangled "Western" ideas about women, marriage, and gender relations. Even for many proponents of female education and reforms geared toward the "uplift of women," the extent to which women could enjoy the benefits of education and independence without subverting or rejecting their assigned roles in the narrative of national regeneration and endangering their virtue, as well as the moral purity and the distinctive cultural identity of the nation, was a matter of great concern. Debates on the "woman's question," as it was called, were intensified at the end of the nineteenth century by the emergence of a small number of middle-class and upper-class women who were not only educated, articulate, and increasingly involved in public activities, but also asserted their rights as the subjects, rather than the objects, of change. Though few in number, they became central to debates over the meanings of femininity, modernity, and social space; their numerical insignificance only served to accentuate their visibility and to magnify the extent of their departure from the norm.

As Francesca Orsini points out in her wide-ranging study of women and the Hindi public sphere, the "western-educated woman" who stepped out of traditional roles remained an ambiguous figure in the cultural imaginary well into the 1930s, a focus of fascination, satire, and dread:

> The western-educated woman was the object of disapproval and contempt: as someone who had overstepped *maryādā* [the feminine virtue of propriety], she had messed up all family and social relations, was bound to end up badly and compared unfavourably with the simple but innocent illiterate girl. This attitude was especially prominent in cartoons, even those in magazines like *Chand* which fervently championed the cause of women's education; whether 'at home' or 'in the world,' they seemed to say, women's progress must always carry the brand of Indianness. On the other hand, college girls featured widely in romantic narratives without any moral stigma attached to them: . . . [authors] deployed educated heroines as characters who possessed not only 'womanly virtues' but also wit, intelligence, passion, and determination. (259)

The ambivalent attitude described by Orsini colors representations of the Western-educated modern woman in popular Indian cinema of the 1920s and the 1930s, the sheer number of which points to a site of cultural production where new ways of reexamining traditional Indian values were being explored. It suggests that the "women's question" was still highly visible and far from being resolved, at least in the realm of popular culture. On one hand, Indian cinema of this period is full of cautionary/satirical tales about the excesses and perils of modernity and social reform, featuring modern women like Indira and Dr. Madhurika whose independence, sense of self-importance, and insistence on individual rights (usually depicted as quixotic or as toxic side-effects of education and Westernization) inevitably lead them beyond the bounds of feminine propriety and often to the brink of disaster. On the other hand, by the mid-1920s the modern woman as a romantic heroine had emerged as one of the main attractions of the social and the intended focus of audience sympathy; by the same token, the romance plot, with its staple conflict between youthful love and societal restrictions, had incorporated elements of the discourse of social reform.

Another, more unusual, avatar of the modern woman—as action heroine and champion of justice—appears in a group of enormously popular films derided by contemporary critics as lowbrow and pandering to the masses: Wadia Movietone's "stunt films" featuring Fearless Nadia (aka Mary Evans), the daughter of a Welsh

father and a Greek mother who grew up in India and became extremely popular as
a whip-cracking superhero with a flair for dispensing poetic justice and sassy repar-
tee.[16] In many of her films—e.g., *Frontier Mail* (1936), *Diamond Queen* (1940), and
Bambaiwalli (1941)—she plays a small-town girl who goes to school and college in
Bombay and comes back to save her town almost single-handedly from various
forces of evil. In *Bambaiwalli*, for instance, she mobilizes the women of her town
against their tyrannical and corrupt male relations. The modern woman was thus
incorporated into cinema (as she was into nationalist projects) in diverse and contradictory ways; as a visual and discursive sign of the city, modernity, and the nation, she came to occupy a wide range of signifying positions in the moral landscape
of popular Indian cinema, oscillating among different types and incompatible identities from film to film and sometimes, even within the same film.

Accordingly, the symbolic identification of the modern woman with the city
did not always carry a negative charge in Indian cinema of the 1920s and 1930s. It
is true that a fundamental suspicion of the moral implications of the modern
city—in particular its power to erode the foundations of Indian tradition and
identity—pervades many of the socials from this period. In *Indira, M.A.*, for
instance, the city is viewed as a port of entry for the contagion of Western modernity and as a hotbed of decadence. In *Dr. Madhurika*, Madhurika gets in touch
with her "true" Indian self (defined by her identity as a dutiful wife and home-
maker) only after she flees the city with her husband and finds refuge in "a lonely
village" far away from civilization (as the film booklet puts it). Yet the city and the
modern woman are also presented as agents of positive social change in contemporary reformist films such as V. Shantaram's 1937 film, *Duniya Na Mane* (*The
Unexpected*, or *The World Will Not Accept*). Based on a landmark novel in Maha-
rashtra's social reform movement that denounced arranged marriages, *Duniya Na
Mane* depicts a spirited young woman's struggle against an unjust gender system.
Tricked by a venal uncle into marrying an aging widower whose children from his
first marriage are older than she is, Nirmala (Shanta Apte) refuses to consummate
the marriage, repeatedly claiming that while suffering can be borne, injustice
cannot be tolerated. The film portrays her as an admirable figure rather than a
passive victim or a threat to tradition, and attributes her determination and
strength of mind to her urban upbringing and education. *Duniya Na Mane*'s attitude toward the city, however, is not one of unqualified admiration or whole-
hearted endorsement. It presents the moral space of the city as a continuum,
extending from the decadence embodied by the widower's dissolute son, who is
comically slavish in his imitation of the West, to the progressive ideals of his
daughter Sushila, a respected social worker who provides moral support to her
young stepmother and symbolizes the city at its best: a source of enlightenment,
liberal humanism, and judicious reform. In its juxtaposition of opposing images
of the city and in its oscillation between contradictory constructions of urban
modernity, *Duniya Na Mane* can, in fact, be viewed as a microcosmic version of
the contemporary cinematic map of the metropolis, and of the cultural imaginary
of the city in colonial India.

SPECTACLES OF MODERNITY

In pointing out how cinematic representations of the city in the 1920s–1930s drew on prevalent discourses of social reform and urbanism, I do not mean to suggest that cinema merely provided a new venue for rehashing old issues, restaging past debates about a sufficient modernity, and recirculating familiar images from vernacular print and performance cultures. While contemporary films borrowed tropes and arguments from existing discourses about modernity, women, and the city, the specificities of the medium also reconfigured them, introducing unique inflections and unexpected shades of ambiguity, and producing new, often contradictory, meanings through the interplay of narrative elements and different visual and aural signifiers, such as casting, performance, costume, setting, and sound. The heterogeneity and dialogic quality of cinematic discourse ensured that films not only reproduced but also repudiated and destabilized the urban-rural dichotomy and contemporary patriarchal discourses. Even though many of the socials seemed to endorse, in terms of narrative resolution, the village over the city and the traditional over the modern, the moral that contemporary audiences would have been expected to draw from these films was often undermined by the seductive images of urban modernity that they purveyed: elite and affluent lifestyles, ornately decorated interior spaces, lavish material comforts, the latest fashions and fads, and, of course, glamorous modern women.

As the prominence of the female star's image in posters, handbills, and film booklets indicates, the modern woman as urban spectacle was vital to the mass appeal of socials, even the rabidly antimodern ones. The actress' star-image fused with her on-screen persona, producing an unstable text that was not merely a fetishistic projection of anxious male desires and masculinist discourses. It was also a site of productive ambivalence where traditional binaries and patriarchal constructions of gender could be at once deployed and deconstructed through performance. The charisma of the female star could disrupt spectatorial involvement in narrative progression and undermine the ostensible moral of the film. Even if the films ensured that the modern woman was eventually put in her proper place, "her dazzling image lingered in the spectator's mind, overriding the knowledge of her punitive destiny" (Cook xiv–xv). As Miriam Hansen points out in her discussion of similar figurations of modernity/femininity in Shanghai cinema of the 1930s, "the meanings of a film are determined not only by directorial intention and an underlying social, masculinist discourse, but are significantly shaped by other voices, such as the mode of performance and the degree of agency, however precarious, that accrues to female actors in the star system" ("Fallen Women, Rising Stars, New Horizons," 16).

Even as male film directors and producers made a spectacle of women, positioning them as passive objects for audience consumption, the power of performance and the aura of stardom conferred a degree of agency on leading actresses. As Neepa Majumdar shows, the star system emerged in India in the mid-1920s with the transition from

family-based film production to a more formalized studio system and a shift of emphasis from the mythological and the historical to more contemporary genres (such as the
social, the stunt film, the crime film, and comedies) that were apparently more conducive to—in fact relied on—the production of stars. Though there were popular male
stars, Majumdar argues that "stardom itself was imagined as essentially female," and
she connects the prominence of the female star to the increasing popularity of the
socials, the majority of which were female-centered (5, 39).

By opening up a space for female performers as both spectacles and personalities, popular Indian cinema of this period can be seen as promoting the development of a self-consciously "modern" expression of femininity centered on one's
visual status and effects. As Liz Connor argues in *The Spectacular Modern Woman*,
"it was as visual images, spectacles, that women could appear modern to themselves
and others" in "the visually intensified scene" of modernity (2). By turning themselves into spectacles, Connor claims, women came to enter new categories and to
occupy new subject-positions (within local regimes of signification) even as they
were objectified by the spectacular logic of commodity fetishism.

While cinema's capacity to create new images and representations of women
made it an important incubator for modern ideas about femininity, the role that
female stars played in the process of representing was crucially important to changing
perceptions of femininity and the public image of cinema as a medium of modernity
in early twentieth-century India. On-screen and off, women were increasingly drawing
attention to themselves, asserting their rights to education, to political participation,
to professional careers, to freedom of choice in marriage, and to a variety of public
roles. Film actresses occupied a unique place in this cultural moment. As performers,
they exercised a degree of freedom rarely available to women in public, even as they
were constrained by the conventions of cinema as a male-dominated institution and
by social restrictions on feminine visibility and performance. The unusual freedom
and mobility that they enjoyed, however, also served to deepen the aura of disrepute
that clung to the image of the female star, and, by extension, to cinema.

The female star, in fact, functions in contemporary Indian discourse about spectatorship as a metonymy of cinema—or of cinema's seductive spectacle of modernity.
In popular writings about cinema, and more curiously, in films themselves, there is
often a slippage between the supposedly suspect moral status of individual actresses
and that of cinema as an institution. Almost all accounts of the development of
Indian cinema link the medium's lack of respectability to the background of the
actresses. Proposals for improving the quality of Indian films and the reputation of
the industry in the 1920s and the 1930s invariably emphasized the need to recruit
actresses from the "cultured classes" and "respectable families." But the relatively rare
appearance of such actresses on the screen also provoked anxieties about the blurring
of the line separating "respectable women" from "women of ill repute," and about the
corrupting power of stardom. In some of the early socials purporting to provide a
behind-the-scenes look at the workings of the institution, such as *Cinema Queen*
(1925), *Cinema Girl* (1930), and *Daily Mail* (1930), the female star came to embody
both the glamour and the decadence of the film world. The expansion of the industry

and the greater visibility of the female star in the 1930s only intensified this trend. An editorial in the May 1940 issue of *filmindia* critiquing the "medieval prejudice" against actresses complains that film stars are "constantly slandered by their own films," and provides a long list of films, beginning with *Cinema Girl*, in which the actress is "depicted as a woman of loose morals and the studio atmosphere is shown as being far from healthy." Other films of the 1930s engaged in a similar critique of cinema and a negative discourse on stardom by proxy, displacing their narratives onto the adjacent world of the theater. Such critiques were especially common in films produced by the Calcutta-based New Theatres studio. Neepa Majumdar links the self-reflexive element in New Theatres productions such as *Dhoop Chaaon* (*Sun and Shade*, Nitin Bose, 1935), *Street Singer* (Phani Majumdar, 1938), and *My Sister* (Hemachandra Chunder, 1944) to the negative discourse on female stardom. While the metonymic figure of the film actress was undoubtedly pivotal to these critiques, I would argue that these films also reflect cinema's ambivalence toward its public image as a technology and a lure of modernity.

In the mid-1920s, the rise of the social, with its focus on the contemporary, and the emergence of the star system, with its machinery of adulation, began to transfer to Indian cinema earlier fears about western films as purveyors of modernity. The dramatic expansion of the Indian film market with the coming of sound in the early 1930s magnified such fears. By the mid-1930s, Indian cinema was widely perceived as providing object lessons in "modern" ways of thinking and being, and as disseminating metropolitan practices and ideas, to audiences throughout the subcontinent. The journalist K. A. Abbas' satirical description of cinema's inroads into his hometown of Panipat, a sleepy small "town of memories, mosques, temples, and graves, so conservative that a *sola* hat is frowned upon, so strongly 'moral' that even prostitutes go out in veils" (*filmindia*, July 1941), give us some idea of cinema's growing importance as a site of public culture:

> There is no permanent cinema house in the town and the opinion of the local elders about people connected with this line including myself is—well, it is unprintable.
>
> Now and then a broken down touring talkie arrives to give open air shows. . . . The adventurous youths of the town sneak from their homes in the quiet of the night and, defying the censure of their fathers, made their way to the maidan where for two annas they can feast their eyes on Sulochana, Zubaida, Madhuri, Pateince Cooper, and Ratan Bai. . . .
>
> There was a touring talkie functioning in Panipat when I was there. But the local elders were already complaining [sic] how to get rid of it. Complaints were heard that the cinema folk had pitched their tent too near a school: thus their 'romantic films' were exercising an evil influence on the growing generation of Panipat . . . . (*filmindia*, November 1939)

While Abbas dismisses the complaining elders as the contemporary counterparts of an earlier generation of naysayers who "violently objected to railways, steamers, motor cars, telegraphs, and telephone," in a later article in *filmindia*, he seems to agree with them, to an extent, about cinema's pedagogical power:

[Cinema is] the most potent factor for mass education. . . . [It] has already succeeded in educating a vast mass of people in this country, even without any directive or coordinating programme and without any state aid. It may be argued perhaps that the education that the cinema has given is the wrong sort of education. Most of the films put ideas of romance in the minds of the juveniles at too early an age, some even teach them to be criminals . . . whatever its quality, by its very nature, the film is an educational medium, for it enlarges human experience and extends the mental horizons of the audience. (*filmindia*, August 1941)

K. M. Munshi, a novelist, scriptwriter, and Gandhian activist, concurs with Abbas about cinema's impact on young men and women:

We are evolving a national language through the medium which is now being used by the Indian talkies. Again look at our smart collegian. Don't you see in his stride or the way he brushes his hair some touch of a fashionable hero? Don't you see in the gait of our young girls some little swing which she has learnt from her fair heroine? In our speech, in our expression of emotions, in wearing our clothes, in all these things, we are slowly and imperceptibly being influenced by cinema. (*filmindia*, April 1943)

Another contributor to *filmindia*, N. G. Jog, offers a sociological defense of the phenomenon of "fandom," claiming that while "celluloid gods and goddesses" may at times exert an undesirable influence on youth, they also save their fans from emotional and spiritual frustration:

Emotional escapism, which is the essence of fan-dom, is all the more necessary in the life of the present generation of Indian youths, with feet foxed in the East, heads hanging on the West, and minds vacillating in between. The silver screen serves as a sort of blacked out Port Said to them, the emotional meeting-ground of the East and the West. They can let themselves go with wild abandon, forget all the taboos and restraints and touch-me-nots of the society in which their lot is cast and give the reins to all their pent-up longings and suppressed lust, complexes, and inhibitions, without losing caste or their face either. ("Fans Are Fools, Idiots and Boors, But . . .," *filmindia* June 1940)

Jog's Port Said metaphor is particularly apt as Indian spectators of this period can be seen as experiencing cinematic pleasures akin to what Giuliana Bruno has called forms of *transito* in metropolitan film spectatorship: "*Transito* connotes many levels of desire as inscribed in both physical and mental motion," including notions of "traversing, transitions, transitory states, and erotic circulation" (56). This mode of circulation or virtual mobility is central to the Indian social's engagement with the heterogeneous experience of colonial modernity and the dialectic of ambivalence engendered by this experience.

NOTES

1. See Dwyer and Patel 117–35 for a discussion of how Art Deco motifs were used to signify modernity in publicity material for Indian cinema in the 1930s.
2. I was not able to locate any surviving prints of the film.

3. See Nandy, *An Ambiguous Journey to the City*, 1–71 for a detailed discussion of this cinematic trope.

4. My understanding of the word "phantasmic" in this context is derived from J. Laplanche and J. B. Pontalis' notion of fantasy as a staging of desire and a form of mise-en-scène that enables one to image and imagine things that are not yet there, and allows the subject to engage in multiple identifications across space, time, and gender; and also from film scholar Elizabeth Cowie's reworking of this concept of the phantasmic in the context of cinema. Cowie argues that thinking about film as the phantasmic mise-en-scène of desire enables us to view spectatorship in terms of mobile modes of identification ("Fantasy and the Origins of Sexuality").

5. Originally defined by Louis Wirth as the way of life of people who live in cities, "urbanism" is now understood less as a singular and homogeneous lifestyle and more as a dynamic process that encompasses the diverse and often contradictory ways in which people make use of, and identify with, the space of the city in the context of a wide range of cultural, social, and political influences.

6. In *Cinema India*, Rachel Dwyer and Divia Patel describe film booklets—which contained images, a synopsis of the film, and, with the coming of sound, song lyrics in Hindi and Urdu, and were produced and distributed prior to the release of the film as a form of pre-publicity—as "an important part of the cinema-going experience" in the 1920s through the 1940s (102).

7. The *Encyclopaedia of Indian Cinema* provides brief plot summaries of these films.

8. See, for instance, Chakravarty; Nandy, "Introduction: Indian Popular Cinema as a Slum's Eye View of Politics"; Prasad; Vasudevan; Virdi.

9. While I use the heuristic of "vernacular modernism" to highlight the Indian social's mediation of urban modernity and its transnational resonances in this chapter, I am aware that an in-depth investigation of this genre in the context of what "vernacular" and "modernism" mean in the Indian context can put pressure on and help us to revise Hansen's analytic framework. I explore some of these pressure points in my forthcoming book, provisionally titled *Outside the Lettered City: Cinema, Modernity, and Class in Late Colonial India.*

10. The term *tawaif* refers to a professional female singer and dancer who performs in her own quarters or *kotha* and in private homes for the viewing pleasure of men. The figure of the *tawaif* features prominently in accounts of the lifestyles of the feudal aristocracy and the urban nouveau-riche classes of nineteenth- and twentieth-century India.

11. The strictness of the enforcement varied along class lines but was a widespread middle-class norm in the nineteenth and early twentieth centuries.

12. Drawing on the scholarship on stardom, such as Richard Dyer's work, I understand the "star-image" as an intertextual construct, a highly visible icon produced across a range of media and cultural practices, including films themselves, advertisements, film magazines, billboards, and film reviews.

13. *Adhunik* is the Hindi/Sanskrit word for modern, derived from the word *adhuna*, which means the present. *Adhunika* is used as a noun to denote a modern woman. Significantly enough, there is no corresponding noun for a modern man.

14. A brief (and by no means exhaustive) list: *Gunasundari* (Hindi, 1927), *Educated Wife* (Hindi, 1932), *Miss 1933* (Hindi, 1933), *Barrister's Wife* (Hindi, 1935), *Fashionable India* (Hindi, 1935), *Grihah/Manzil* (Bengali/Hindi, 1936), *Romantic India* (Hindi, 1936), *Madam Fashion* (Hindi, 1936), *Sarala* (Hindi, 1936), *Didi/President* (Bengali/Hindi, 1937), *Mukti* (*Liberation*, Bengali/Hindi, 1937), *Ardhangi/Ghar Ki Rani* (*The Better Half*, Marathi/Hindi, 1940).

15. Many excellent studies have explored the impact of social reforms on gender relations in nineteenth- and early twentieth-century India. See, for instance, the work of Murshid; Borthwick; Sangari and Vaid; Karlekar; Banerji; Forbes; Minault; Sarkar.

16. For a discussion of these films, see Thomas.

WORKS CITED

Abbas, K. A. Untitled. *filmindia* July 1941.
———. Untitled. *filmindia* November 1939.
———. Untitled. *filmindia* August 1941.
Ahmed, Syed Jamil. "Female Performers in the Indigenous Theatre of Bengal." *Infinite Variety: Women in Society and Literature*. Ed. Firdous Azim and Niaz Zaman. Dhaka: Dhaka University Press, 1994. 263–82.
Anonymous. Editorial. *filmindia* May 1940.
Banerjee, Himani. "Fashioning a Self." *Economic and Political Weekly*. 26 October 1991: 50–62.
Bhattacharya, Rimli. "Introduction: Binodini Dasi and the Public Theatre in Nineteenth-Century Bengal." *Binodini Dasi: My Story and My Life as an Actress*. Ed. and trans. Rimli Bhattachaarya. New Delhi: Kali for Women, 1998. 3–17.
Borthwick, Meredith. *Changing Role of Women in Bengal 1849–1905*. Princeton: Princeton University Press, 1984.
Bruno, Giuliana. *Streetwalking on a Ruined Map: Cultural Films and the City Films of Elvira Notari*. Princeton: Princeton University Press, 1993.
Chakravarty, Sumita S. *National Identity in Indian Popular Cinema, 1947–1987*. Austin: University of Texas Press, 1993.
Connor, Liz. *The Spectacular Modern Woman: Feminine Visibility in the 1920s*. Bloomington: Indiana University Press, 2004.
Cook, Pam. "Border Crossings: Women and Film in Context." *Women and Film: A Sight and Sound Reader*. Ed. Pam Cook and Philip Dodd. Philadelphia: Temple University Press, 1993. ix–xxiii.
Cowie, Elizabeth. "Fantasia." *m/f* 9 (1984): 71–105.
Dwyer, Rachel, and Divia Patel. *Cinema India: The Visual Culture of Hindi Film*. New Brunswick: Rutgers University Press, 2002.
Forbes, Geraldine. *Women in Modern India*. Cambridge: Cambridge University Press, 1996.
Hansen, Kathryn. "Making Women Visible: Gender and Race Cross-Dressing in the Parsi Theater." *Theater Journal* 51.2 (1999): 127–47.
Hansen, Miriam. "Fallen Women, Rising Stars, New Horizons: Shanghai Silent Film as Vernacular Modernism." *Film Quarterly* 54.1 (2000): 10–22.
Jog, N. G. "Fans Are Fools, Idiots and Boors, But . . .," *filmindia* June 1940.
Kala Nag (Triumph of Justice/Black Cobra). Advertisement. *Bombay Chronicle*, 5 January 1924.
Karlekar, Malavika. *Voices from Within*. New Delhi: Oxford University Press, 1993.
Laplanche, J., and J. B. Pontalis. "Fantasy and the Origins of Sexuality." *Formations of Fantasy*. Ed. Victor Burgin et al. London: Methuen, 1986.
Majumdar, Neepa. "Female Stardom and Cinema in India, 1930s to 1950s." Unpublished diss. Indiana University, 2001.

Minault, Gail. *Secluded Scholars*. New Delhi: Oxford University Press, 1998.

Munshi, K. M. Untitled. *filmindia* April 1943.

Murshid, Ghulam. *Reluctant Debutante*. Rajshahi: Rajshahi University Press, 1983.

Nandy, Ashis. *An Ambiguous Journey to the City*. New Delhi: Oxford University Press, 2001.

———. "Introduction: Indian Popular Cinema as a Slum's Eye View of Politics." *The Secret Politics of Our Desires: Innocence, Culpability and Popular Indian Cinema*. Ed. Ashis Nandy. New Delhi: Oxford University Press, 1980. 1–19.

Natarajan, S. *Century of Social Reform in India*. Bombay: Asia Publishing House, 1959.

O'Hanlon, Rosalind. *A Comparison Between Men and Women: Tarabai Shinde and the Critique of Gender Relations in India*. New Delhi: Oxford University Press, 1994.

Orsini, Francesca. "Women and the Hindi Public Sphere." *The Hindi Public Sphere: Language and Literature in the Age of Nationalism*. New Delhi: Oxford University Press, 2002. 243–308.

Prasad, Madhava. *Ideology of the Hindi Film: A Historical Construction*. New Delhi: Oxford University Press, 1998.

Rajadhyaksha, Ashish, and Paul Willemen. *Encyclopaedia of Indian Cinema*. New Delhi: Oxford University Press, 1999.

Ramanujan, A. K. "Towards an Anthology of City Images." *The Collected Essays of A. K. Ramanujan*. Ed. Vinay Dharwadker. New Delhi: Oxford University Press, 1999.

Sangari, Kumkum, and Sudesh Vaid, eds. *Recasting Women*. New Delhi: Kali for Women, 1990.

Sarkar, Tanika. *Hindu Wife, Hindu Nation*. Bloomington: Indiana University Press, 2001.

Thomas, Rosie. "Not Quite (Pearl) White: Fearless Nadia, Queen of the Stunts." *Bollywood: Popular Indian Cinema Through a Transnational Lens*. Ed. Raminder Kaur and Ajay J. Sinha. London: Sage, 2005. 35–69.

Vasudevan, Ravi. "Shifting Codes, Dissolving Identities: The Hindi Social Film of the 1950s as Popular Culture." *Journal of Arts and Ideas* 23–4 (1993): 51–84.

Virdi, Jyotika. *The Cinematic ImagiNation: Indian Popular Films as Social History*. New Brunswick: Rutgers University Press, 2003.

Weinbaum, Alys Eve, Lynn Thomas, Priti Ramamurthy, Uta G. Poiger, Madeline U. Dong, and Tani E. Barlow, eds. *The Modern Girl Around the World: Consumption, Modernity, and Globalization*. Durham: Duke University Press, 2008.

Williams, Raymond. *The Country and the City*. Oxford: Oxford University Press, 1973.

CHAPTER 27

....

VERNACULAR MODERNISM AND SOUTH AFRICAN CINEMA: CAPITALISM, CRIME, AND STYLES OF DESIRE

....

ROSALIND C. MORRIS

UNTIL the fall of apartheid, the most officially valorized monument in South Africa was the Voortrekker monument. Conceived and designed even before the National Party's rise to power in 1948, the monument was modeled by its architect, Gerard Moerdijk, on the *Völkerschlachtdenkmal* (the Monument of the War of Nations[1]), which had been unveiled in Leipzig in 1913 to commemorate the defeat of Napoleon a century earlier (Christiansë, "Sculpted" 2; Delmont). Like its European inspiration, the Voortrekker monument materializes aesthetic and temporal ambivalence; its monolithic grandiosity and nationalist iconography reveal a simultaneous drive toward totality and the instrumental deployment of a mythified past as the ground of modern self-assertion. Today, as it recedes into anachronism, it is also possible to read the Voortrekker monument as a doubled sign of the apartheid era, being at once a product of the social and technological infrastructure of modernity and an emblem of the conceptual linkage between whiteness and modernity that lay at the heart of white nationalism.

Such doubleness is, perhaps, generically characteristic of modernity, and, in a transformed mode, it is the basis of modernist aesthetics, even when that latter project aspires to autonomy and oppositionality vis-à-vis the material world whence it emanates (Adorno). Indeed, the doubleness or ambivalence that is discernible in the signifying practices of much modernist aesthetics as both self-reflexivity and symbolic instability derives from the fact that modernity is the form of appearance, the concrete realization, of capitalist systematicity.[2] Such systematicity, as many political theorists have argued, extending Marx's analysis of *The Grundrisse*, consists in the integration, rather than negation, of simultaneously existent but distinct and discontinuous forms of productive relations and social life (Jameson; Perry Anderson; Harvey). For Marx, this unevenness emerged first at the cusp of a transition between modes of production. For Trotsky, its persistence legitimated the call for "permanent revolution." Jameson, for his part, remarks the perception and experience of simultaneity as the phenomenological correlate of what we might call late capitalism's *development of uneven development* on a global scale (307).

The question of how to represent such simultaneity has, of course, dominated both the aesthetic theory and practice of modernism for well over a century. For Bakhtin, the only form adequate to its inscription was the novel, which, by virtue of its enveloping discourse and heteroglossic capacities, can depart from the linearity of oral storytelling in order to stage simultaneity beyond the experience of a single character ("Discourse"). For theorists such as Walter Benjamin and Siegfried Kracauer, cinema appeared as an equally appropriate medium, achieving through the strategies of montage and suture what fiction accomplished with the gesture of the "meanwhile." Of course, neither modernity nor modernism is reducible to the phenomenon of simultaneity. Modernity also entails the related forces of urbanization, industrialization, and bureaucratization, all sustained by the logic of rationalization. Inevitably, these forces materialize themselves in distinct ways, depending on the cultural infrastructures into which they are inserted and which they either mobilize or negate, but such differences are themselves encompassed by capitalism's drive to totality and its capacity to sustain and even to utilize internal heterogeneity. Modernism is similarly internally differentiated, with critics split between those who see its concern with form and self-reflexivity as a project doomed to reproduce the violence of the system whence it emanates and those who attribute to it the capacity for critique and innovation (Attridge 1–5).

MODERNITY AND MODERNISM IN SOUTH AFRICA

The peculiar predicament of modernism in South Africa, where, until very recently, it has been avowed primarily within the field of white cultural production (Lazarus; Nkosi, "Postmodernism")[3] is perhaps most disconcertingly captured in Nadine Gordimer's division of labor among white and black writers. In "The Essential Gesture," she assigns to the former the task of "[raising] the consciousness of white people" and to black writers the labor of "compos[ing] battle hymns" for their fellows in struggle (12). If Gordimer's own gesture effectively reduced black literature to propaganda, it also reflected the specific racialization of unevenness as an attribute of the settler colony. Such racialization was a common dimension of colonial economies throughout Africa, of course. What marks the South African situation and contributes to the apparent exceptionality of that country's history is the way in which indigenous (both black and colored) South Africans were themselves forced to inhabit the doubleness of the system, not as residents of a more "primitive" economy—as pastoralists or peasants— but as ethnically separated and thus minoritized individuals who had to move between and occupy the space of *both* an urban proletariat (or a semi-urban proletariat in the mines) *and* an agrarian periphery. Nonetheless, the movement forced and enforced by the highly rationalized apparatus of the apartheid state legitimated itself through the ideological fantasy of an originary rurality, to which black laborers were made to return. The maintenance of rural "homelands," Bantustans, and even the peri-urban locations ensured not only a regular and relatively cheap labor supply while supposedly mitigating against the coherence of an oppositional class consciousness in urban areas, but it also provided an outlet for surplus labor, which was continually reabsorbed into the rural areas (Magubane; Marks and Rathbone; Wolpe). In both official discourse and the cultural imaginary elaborated through its adjacent institutions (schools, the press, the literature approved by censorship boards [McDonald]), black urbanity was construed as an aberration or departure from an authentic rurality, even when that rurality was also imagined (e.g., through the mythologization of Chaka's Zulu king-dom) as a mirror image of the militant and militarist agrarianism of the Afrikaners' predecessors, the Voortrekkers monumentalized by Moerdijk. Once could say that, in the ideology of segregationism (both before and under apartheid), the spatial axis of migrancy was transformed into the chronotope, to use Bakhtin's word, of perpetual anachrony, of being out of time, and of social time out of joint ("Forms").

Nationalist modernism is often internally split in this manner, but in rela-tively racially homogeneous spaces rurality is often posited as a kind of temporal origin for metropolitan cultures, from which it is conceived as both a locus of reified alterity and an object of nostalgic and/or primitivist (self) desire. The desire is oriented as much by the fantasy of disappearance as it is by the longing after origins and is as present in the histories of nationalism in Asia as in Europe (Ivy; Morris; Williams, *Country*). Nonetheless, the work of racial difference in settler colonies inhibits the identificatory process which would otherwise have permitted rurality and urbanity to be sutured along a single temporal, which is to say developmentalist, axis (although even that axis implies a hierarchy of value). In the case of South Africa, the result was the general problematization of black urbanity and hence black modernity, a problematization that can be seen as much in the country's sociology of race or in the history of urban plan-ning and public health regulations as in popular literature and cinema. The aes-thetic and affective registration of that problematization in the apartheid period can be discerned in two seemingly contradictory phenomena: on the one hand, the persistent deployment of a rhetoric of urgency among apartheid opponents (Bethelehem) and, on the other, a diffuse sense of foreboding, of anxious waiting on the part of its defenders (Crapanzano 44–45; Lazarus 132–33). Fifteen years into the democratic era, we can observe the emergence of yet another kind of anticipatory consciousness, this one fusing the sense of urgency which had opposed apartheid with the sense of waiting that had accompanied the dread of its end. What Vincent Crapanzano, in his truculent ethnography of whites at the end of apartheid, described as a failure to achieve the consciousness appropriate to tragedy is now inverted but also generalized (Crapanzano xxii). Such tragedy, with the judgment of failure that subtends it, is now posited as a horizon that looms menacingly before the postapartheid regime (thus far an exclusively ANC regime, except in the Western Cape Province), manifest in the lacerating judgments of newspaper editorials but also in service delivery street protests that evoke the strategies of ungovernability associated with antiapartheid politics in the 1980s.

In the midst of those earlier political movements, Neil Lazarus discerned a properly modernist literature among South Africa's white writers, identifying Breyten Breytenbach, André Brink, J. M. Coetzee and Nadine Gordimer as representatives of this critically alienated community. A more comprehensive list could certainly have been adduced, and the formal differences between these writers has since become more salient in criticism of the period's output (Attridge 5). But even this more nuanced assessment fails to answer the question, posed even after the end of apartheid by Lewis Nkosi, of how to write the history of black modernism and (for they are not the same thing) modernism in the vernacular language traditions of South Africa ("Postmodernism"). Against what he posits as both the theoretically naïve rejections of postmodernism on the part of South African writers and critics such as Mothobi Mutloatse (and the "technically brittle" writing that reduced the project of realism to what he terms, quoting Lukacs, "the trivially detailed painting of local color" (77), Nkosi calls for the continued work of an incomplete modernist agenda, and he identifies Amos Tutuola's *The Palm-Wine Drinkard* (1984 [1953]) and the experimental Zulu poetry of B. W. Vilakazi, *Zulu Horizons* (1962) as exemplary efforts in that project. We might add Bessie Head's *A Question of Power* (1974) and the more recent works of Njabulo Ndebele, such as *Cry of Winnie Mandela* (2004) and Yvette Christianshë's *Unconfessed* (2007).

It is nonetheless notable that such forays into modernism tempted relatively few black and colored writers in South Africa during the apartheid era, who, as Nkosi remarks, were profoundly cut off from the communities of writers in both the West and in Africa because of apartheid. Nonetheless, modernism did enter into black vernacular space. It did so most productively in and through cinema, which not only provided the medium for apprehending and reflecting upon the material transformations accompanying industrialization and urbanization, but also for resignifying the corporeal world on which basis apartheid had been elaborated and naturalized. It did so despite and against the restrictions imposed upon it by a censorious state apparatus and a suspicious religious culture.

South Africa's early film industry was dominated by nationalist cinema aimed at consolidating white dominance and was primarily historical in orientation. Its landmark works included *Die Voortrekkers* (1916), *The Symbol of Sacrifice* (1918), *Sarais Marais* (1931), *Moedertjie* (1931), *They Built a Nation* (1938) and *'n Nasie Hou Kours* (1940) (Maingard). Films in which contemporary social conditions provided the context for narrative drama were rare, and those depicting black life were dominated by the mythos of rural authenticity, as in *Jim Comes to Joburg* (1949), *Song of Africa* (1951), and *Cry the Beloved Country* (1952). During the early decades of the century, most aspiring white film directors and producers went to England to make films. Such was the case with Henry Cornelius, who had worked for Korda as an editor of films like *The Drum*, *Four Feathers*, and *The Lion Has Wings*. In 1940, Cornelius returned to South Africa to become deputy director of the film department of the Union Truth Services and in that capacity produced *Noordwaarts* (Northward), *Who? Me?*, *Trek Gees* (Spirit of the Trek) and *We of Velddrift*. In 1947, his acclaimed film *Hue and Cry* was released in Britain and South Africa. Korda, for his part, opened a branch office in South Africa in 1949, a fact which was assumed, at the time, to promise the transformation and globalization of South Africa's own production industry ("Birth of Afrikaans Film"; "South African Film Producer Makes Good in Britain"). *Cry the Beloved Country* seemed to realize Korda's fantasy, with a strategy that continues to this day of using Hollywood actors for starring roles and local actors as secondary characters and to provide local authenticity (one thinks here of *After the Rain* [1991], starring Paul Bettany and Louise Lombard; *Catch a Fire* [2006], with Tim Robbins and Derek Luke in the leads; *In My Country* [2004], with Juliette Binoche and Samuel Jackson; and the second *Cry the Beloved Country* [1995], this one with Richard Harris and James Earl Jones, among others). Outside of South Africa, *Cry the Beloved Country* would stand as a representative of the country's film industry potential (and as a depiction of apartheid, though the novel on which it was based preceded the implementation of that policy). It would nonetheless be ridiculed by the writers of *Drum* in *Come Back Africa* for its sentimentality and its incapacity to conceive of black urbanity as anything but a scene of moral turpitude.

Whatever the ideological agendas of the individual narratives, cinema's accomplishments were largely a function of its form and technology, which partook of the logic that it exposed, or at least made available for reading, via the principle of immanent critique. Given the paucity of films made by and with black and colored South African artists, to say nothing of the absence until recently of indigenous language films, the history of cinema's effectivity has to be understood less in terms of production than through reference to the forms in which it was received and by which it was taken up into everyday life. In order to track that process I want to focus here on the history of a single figure, that of the *tsotsi*, in whom the translational logic accompanying cinematic vernacularization can be seen with especial clarity. For the *tsotsi* emerged and entered the everyday world as figure and force via those twin technologies of appearance, cinema and fashion. At the same time, the translation and autonomization that permitted the *tsotsi* to achieve iconic status also enabled an increasingly self-reflexive discourse on the relationship between politics and the politics of style and thereby on the predicament of subalternity in the unevenly developed space of South Africa's capitalist modernity.

FOUND IN TRANSLATION

As everywhere else in the world, cinema constituted a signal medium of modern industrial culture in South Africa. Black audiences in South Africa were initially solicited into spectatorship from within two distinct and competing projects, both of which sought to cultivate sensibilities appropriate to industrial modernity, both of which were Christian in origin and orientation. The first of these, established by Sol Plaatjie, entailed traveling "bioscopes" featuring educational documentaries, particularly those produced in the United States about "New Negroes" under the auspices of Booker T. Washington's Tuskegee Institute. The second, initiated by Reverend Ray Phillips of the American Board of Missionaries, who had advocated the moralization of leisure time, accommodated feature-length narrative films, providing that they did not depict whites in ethically compromised acts (Phillips 124; Masilela 20; Mainguard 68–70). Exemplarity was the guiding principle of both Plaatjie's and Phillips' film projects, but it was the specular pleasure afforded by narrative film that drew audiences. Accordingly, state censorship would henceforth be dominated by efforts to determine which kinds of pleasures were threatening to racialism and hence subject to repression.[4] The logic was one that attributed to black South Africans an especially acute aptitude for and tendency toward mimesis. Accordingly, it was the spectacle of violence which was most vigorously withheld, particularly the violence associated with the Hollywood genres of the gangster film and film noir (Huette). Seeing was here less associated with believing than becoming. Though film noir was itself a function of transnational movements in both theater and film and in the critical structures that received them (Dimendberg; Naremore), it, and cinema in general, had become indissociable from a certain Americanism, including not only Fordism and its offshoots but also the phantasmagoria of commodity consumption that it enabled.

One could imagine that the chasm separating American urban life, as depicted by Hollywood, would have had little resonance for black South Africans largely confined to impoverished peri-urban locations and artificially sustained rural homelands. Nonetheless, in the writings of *Drum* magazine and in popular cultural production more generally, a general Americophilia is visible. In them, one encounters "characters speaking like Americans, dressing like Americans, and driving

American cars." And, as Njabulo Ndelebe says, such derivativeness concealed the "growing confidence" of "sophisticated urban working and petty bourgeois classes" ("Rediscovery" 43). No doubt, black audiences discerned, as did Richard Wright's character, Bigger Thomas, that Hollywood cinema was not addressed to them, and for this reason their purpose was to radicalize the discourse they received through overhearing. The mode of resistance developed in this context consisted, above all, in the refusal to not desire, the refusal to not consume. This refusal to not desire was also a refusal to accede to the demand for labor as the basis for wages and thence legitimate and legitimately restricted consumption. It is therefore as the bearer of this desire, this sovereignty that declares itself immune not only to repression but to alienation and self-reification, that the *tsotsi* emerges. Heir to both the gangster film and the film noir, the *tsotsi* is not merely a gangster, though he is that too. He is an icon of masculinity that is nonetheless devoted to beauty, of youthful insouciance that nonetheless can abide no insult, of autonomy that is yet in need of recognition. Fashion is his *mise-en-scène*. Detail is his obsession. Terror is his weapon.

For film goers outside of South Africa, the word *tsotsi* is now associated with Gavin Hood's 2005 sentimental eponymous feature about a young thug who accidentally drives off with the infant child of a woman whom he has carjacked in the suburbs. But this figure is a return: the mark of an older form's restitution and resignification after apartheid's end, and after the momentary displacement of crime by politics and by the complex phenomenon of "politically legitimate violence" that defined the last moments of the "Struggle." Within South Africa, the term denotes the outlaw, urban tough, or gangster, who aspires to appear in the form made recognizable through cinema. Before anything else, however, the *tsotsi* is a word and has its origins in a word.

According to Peter Davis, it is derived from the term "zoot suit," and it is the offspring of Cab Calloway, the stylish American jazz singer of Cotton Club fame (2). The term began to circulate widely following the screenings of the largely black American film musical, *Stormy Weather* (1943), in which Calloway starred in the early 1940s, and it became entrenched after *Cabin in the Sky* (1943) was shown in black theaters in South Africa between 1945 and 1950. Calloway was himself a figure of translation, his *The New Cab Calloway's Hepsters Dictionary: Language of Jive* offering musically untutored fans a lexicon of jazz idioms. But the question remains as to how Cab Calloway's zoot suit became a *tsotsi*. Before assuming its fully vernacular form, it had to find its indigenous echo. For vernacularization is not merely a vectoral transfer; it is the mode within which foreignness (in this case capitalist modernity) is materialized locally. There is, in fact, some evidence that the word *tsotsi* may have derived from the South Sotho (Sepedi) word *ho tsotsa*, meaning "to sharpen," and that it referred to the shape of the trousers that gave the zoot suit its particular mark (Glaser 50; Bothma 29). But whether the result of a homonymy produced by transliteration, or an iconography translated into Sepedi, the *tsotsi* went from an unprecedented neologism to a widely circulating idiom in a few short years.

Unheard of before 1943–1944, it had broad subcultural meaning by the end of the decade, by which point it had become associated with both fashion and urban youth (Glaser 51–52, 68–70). Thus, by 1951, C. V. Bothma could refer to the *tsotsi* as the index of a "society of the adolescent" (Bothma 28; Glaser 47). And government reports could blame violent crime on the mines of the Witwatersrand in 1949 and 1950 on "outside agitators, intimidation, irresponsible press reports—and . . . a '*tsotsi* reign of terror' and the evil effects of 'bioscope films.'" (Beittel; Davis 24–25).

The historical conditions of possibility for the *tsotsi*'s emergence far exceed the matter of fortuitously homonymous echoes, of course. The effects of the pass laws, the familial breakdown associated with migrant labor, and the cramped conditions of township life all conspired to generate an environment in which the street became the playground of youth (Glaser 20–46). In this milieu, the value of fashionability suffused not merely clothing but language as well. *Tsotsitaal*, the name given to the creolized slang of the *tsotsis* in the townships (where otherwise distinct ethnolinguistic communities confronted each other) was a significant element of the subculture in the 1940s and 1950s, with verbal dexterity in its use being as crucial to *tsotsi* status as the cut of one's trousers (Glaser 71). Over the years, the *tsotsi* would metamorphose— traversing the categories of flâneur, dandy, thug, and gangster as a new wave of black cinema and music migrated from the worlds of Motown, Hollywood, blaxpoitation cinema, and civil rights insurgency in the United States into the townships—where revolution and ennui competed for the hearts and sleeves of young men. As it did so, the idioms within which it was spoken also changed, and in the late 1970s and 1980s, the term *mapantsula* briefly displaced *tsotsi* as a sign of both fashionability and resistant masculinity, drawing into its own iconographic repertoire the figures of the suit-clad urban dance heroes of films like *Saturday Night Fever* and the fashions of iconic soul singers like Percy Sledge, whose 1970 concert in Soweto generated unprecedented sales and multiracial audiences.

As the political opposition to apartheid came to make different claims on urban youth, and as the African National Congress Youth League itself assumed dominance on the political horizon, the masculinity and viability of the *mapantsula* came into question. At the end of the apartheid era, with youth politics overwhelmed by the aging of the Youth League on one hand and the lure of consumer culture liberated from apartheid's racializing restrictions on the other, the *tsotsi* has returned—the renewed sign of (violent) desire at the heart of the social order and the center of a cinematic fantasy world, for which television serials like *Yizo Yizo* (1999–2004) and films like *Hijack Stories* (2000) provide the exemplary instance. Before we trace the outcome of the long arc of transformation by which the *tsostsi* was liberated from the zoot suit and transformed into a post-political glock-wielding icon of scamtho-speaking, gangsta fashionability, we need, however, to return to the early history of the *tsotsi*.

RATIONALIZING REVOLUTIONARY STYLE

In the moment of its emergence, the *tsotsi* was as a sign that exuded the sheen of Florsheim shoes and had the jaunty angle of Borsolino hats (Modisane 52; Davis 49). The specificity of these material details—marks of a cinematic figure in the moment it breaches the boundary of lived experience—is itself a symptom of American cinema's vernacularization, for, as Miriam Hansen has remarked, the basis of classical cinema's appeal around the world was Hollywood films' "physicality, directness, speed, their affinity with the exterior surface or 'outer skin' of things" (12). Walter Benjamin had observed this capacity and allied it to the psychoanalyst's discovery of the unconscious:

> [F]ilm furthers insight into the necessities governing our lives by its close-ups, by its accentuation of hidden details in familiar objects, and by its exploration of commonplace milieu through the ingenious guidance of the camera; on the other hand, it manages to assure us of a vast and unsuspected field of action [*Spielraum*]. Our bars and city streets, our offices and furnished rooms, our railroad stations and our factories seemed to close relentlessly around us. Then came film and exploded this prison-world with the dynamite of a split second. . . . ("Work of Art" 265)

But why should the world of everyday existence require such alienated representation in order to become visible, particularly in those places, such as South Africa, where it was not, in fact, the condition of dailiness for most people? An answer to this question may be approached via Siegfried Kracauer's conception of film's capacity to "redeem" reality through its cinematic reinscription. Kracauer writes that the "elusiveness of physical reality is the habit of abstract thinking we have acquired under the region of science and technology" (*Theory* 300)—and therefore, one might add, the regime of labor associated with industrialization. Kracauer and Walter Benjamin both saw cinema as a phenomenon of urban modernity, Benjamin observing a radical difference between the mode of reception among peasants and the urban "masses" in a manner that anticipates Jameson's analysis. The peasants, he insisted, could not "[follow] two simultaneous narrative strands of the kind seen countless times in film" ("Russian Film" 14). But the latter were often absorbed by the spectacle of things.

The risk of such absorption led Kracauer to refer to photography as the "go-for broke game of history," and the same may be said of film ("Photography" 61). His analysis of the mass ornament, epitomized in the phenomenon of the Tiller Girls and in Busby Berkeley's musicals, makes clear in what the gamble consists. In Kracauer's analysis, capitalist thought "is marked by *abstractness*," but neither the scientists' empiricism, which demands attention to the concrete, nor the nationalists' mythological nostalgia, which seeks "organism and form" as an alternative to abstraction, offer real liberatory possibilities. This, he says, echoing Horkheimer and Adorno, is because such gestures "sacrifice the already acquired capacity for abstraction, but without overcoming abstractness" (61). The bodies of the Tiller Girls or the synchronized swimmers become emblems of a humanity in which "the only elements of nature capable of surviving are those that do not resist illumination through reason" ("Mass Ornament" 83). But insofar as this process mythifies reason as that which can penetrate everything, it is a verily cultic gesture. Yet, and this hesitation is absolutely crucial, Kracauer does not entirely reject the masses' adoption of the mass ornament, for, as he says, "they are superior to the detractors among the educated classes to the extent that they at least roughly acknowledge the undisguised facts. The same rationality that controls the bearers of the patterns in real life also governs their submersion in the corporeal" (85). Clearly, we are not speaking of the Tiller Girls in South Africa. And it is less the adoration of reason that is expressed in the phenomenon of the *tsotsi* than the heroization of self-consciousness. But just as the Tiller Girls exposed and reproduced the truth of a society in thrall to rationalism, perfected in Fordism, so too the *tsotsi* exposed and reproduced one enchanted by the ideology of possessive individualism and the fact of commodification. Making the solitary man the locus of agency and sublimating the alienation and dislocation of migrancy in an image of autonomy and self-production, representations of the *tsotsi* exposed what we might call, following Marx's analysis of religion, the "untrue truth" of the apartheid economy. What remained to be mobilized, as the kernel of that radicalization remarked by Ndebele, was the ambivalent potentiality of both self-consciousness and consumerism, the one promising the basis of judgment while threatening to collapse into self-interestedness, the other promising an analysis of production and a demand for the restructuring of economic relations while tending to collapse into mere acquisitiveness. Let me explain what I mean.

The *tsotsi* emerged from his mercurial abode on the silver screen to invest the township with commodity desire and to purvey the auraticity of the brand name (Nkosi, *Underground* 8), knowledge of which marked the bearer as emphatically urban—to the point of being anti-rural—and cosmopolitan. Such desire is, of course, both the sign of ideological encompassment (by commodity culture) and a repudiation of the racial hierarchy that would have reserved the objects of such desire for white consumers. In this sense, the *tsotsi* made visible a contradiction within the capitalist logic of the settler colony, which needed to interpellate subjects as consumers in an expanding market, on one hand, and which attempted to maintain the borders of racial difference through differential ideological investment on the other. The purpose of homelands, and of apartheid more generally, was to sustain a periphery within the national body where, as Gayatri Spivak says of imperial formations more generally, capital could divest itself of the need to cultivate labor power, taking advantage of jurisdictionally limited labor laws and authoritarian political formations to retard consumerism among the subaltern classes (and the demand for higher wages that go with it) (288). In South Africa, "traditional leaders" and local patriarchies of ethnic homelands were legally authorized and invited into complicitous relations with the state, and the *tsotsi*'s township cosmopolitanism is, accordingly, pitted against this dual axis of rurality and inhibited consumerism.

It is in this context that he appears, first in white cinema, as the sign of a menace that awaits the rural migrant, and then, in cinema for blacks, as a more joyous expression of liberated masculinity, but one contained within the narrow space of musical entertainment and undermined by proximity to effeminacy. Thus, the gangsters who waylay the naive Jim as he arrives in Johannesburg from the rural areas in *Jim Comes to Joburg* or who await the Reverend Khumalo as he searches for his son in *Cry the Beloved Country* wear beautiful suits and fedoras. They appear elegant in *Zonk!* (the first South African film "for blacks" to depict the jazz scene— largely set in the colored world of District Six) alongside the sartorial extravagance of the moffies (effeminate homosexuals). The jazz scene was, in fact, the space of the most radical vernacularizations: the place where Sol Plaatjie's earnest appropriations of the American "New Negro" found their sensuous counterpart (and, perhaps, their rejection) (Titlestad). There, one could listen to bands that signaled their worldliness with names like The Harlem Swingsters and The Manhattans (the band with whom Miriam Makeba first made her name), along with the African Hellenics and the Cuban Brothers, to say nothing of the famous Jazz Maniacs (Moeketsi).

Jim Comes to Joburg (1949) established the shebeen as the mise-en-scène for a kind of overhearing in which not only the musical talents of its stars (notably Dolly Rathebe) but also the political discoursing of the black underclasses could be encountered. Exactly one decade after *Jim Comes to Joburg*, *Come Back, Africa* (1959) would mobilize this latter dimension and make the film itself a spectacle of radical potentiality. In an unprecedented blending of genres, the film's director, Lionel Rogosin (a New Yorker with leftist sympathies), would intercut documentary footage of Sophiatown with long and dilatory dialogues in a shebeen where the radical writers for *Drum*, Lewis Nkosi, Bloke Modisane and Can Themba, discuss the injustices of the apartheid system (Nixon 11–41). The association of political radicalism with both criminality and fashionability is also visible in Richard Rive's novel *"Buckingham Palace," District Six* (1986), where the protagonist, a "Mr. Zoot," is a smooth-talking, literarily gifted one-time petty criminal turned neighborhood sage who looks "smart in a check suit with padded shoulders, narrow waist, knee-length coat and trousers tapering at the ankles" (17).

The significance of style for the *tsotsi* is not simply a function of his resistance to the policing of desire in an economy of artificial scarcity, however. Nor is it merely a matter of representing subcultural difference (see Hebdige). Style differentiates among different efforts to claim legitimacy for violence. Like the private eye of film noir, the *tsotsi* exposes the intimacy and the mimicry that binds the law (as police) and the outlaw (as *tsotsi*). To a certain extent, the *tsotsi* partakes of the aura that Walter Benjamin had attributed to the great criminal whose law-breaking calls the very being of law, and the legitimacy of the state it sustains, into question by bearing witness to its violence ("Critique" 281). But this does not mean that he is accorded innocence or virtue. For in addition to embodying self-consciousness and consumerism, he is the incarnation and aestheticization of instrumental reason, that same instrumental reason on which political violence always depends (Arendt 46). The affinity between the two is made visible in both literature and film through forms of juxtaposition. Thus, for example, there are two iconic and narratively pivotal encounters with specular violence in Mark Mathabane's best-selling autobiography, *Kaffir Boy*, one in which the young boy witnesses a police beating, the other when he observes a group of *tsotsis* doing the same thing (192–94). In Miriam Tlali's stories, which are inflected by a critical consciousness of the particularly sexualized and sexualizing terror to which women are subjected by *tsotsis*, characters are similarly plagued by the twin threats of police and gangsters. In such juxtapositions one discerns the instability of the opposition between law and its other: the thin line is marked by the fact that the police have the false aura afforded by the state's political theology to sustain them, while the *tsotsi* has style.

This emphasis on style is, of course, a generic feature of film noir, from which the developing aesthetic of the *tsotsi* drew so much inspiration. Paul Schrader, in fact, refers to film noir as a style, rather than a genre, one oriented around the aesthetics of the surface. In this respect, it can be seen as the fulfillment of a potential intrinsic to all classical cinema, as Hansen describes it. Nonetheless, the particular elaboration of the mise-en-scène that marks film noir cannot be grasped as mere setting. As Tom Conley has argued, film noir utilizes the same principles of condensation and displacement that structure the oneiric world. Within the frame, noir offered unprecedented spectacles of sadism and sexual regression. Indeed, it was on these very grounds that South African critics and censors opposed the screening of films noir to black audiences. Nonetheless, the genre's aesthetic operations cannot be grasped only through reference to the visible: "visual constriction articulates a space *off* to convey the severities of the limits determining what is *on*" (Conley 347). Accordingly, says Conley, films noir incite reading and demand reference to the exterior milieu of their production. The complex referential structure of noir, achieved in and through the hyperbolic investment of surface details, permitted some critics to refer to it as a kind of Marxism manqué—notwithstanding the many blatantly ideological films of the genre (one thinks, here, of the strident anticommunism of South Africa's first noir film, *Cape Town Affair*). But insofar as the films associated with the genre tended to imbue the urban milieu with threat, to cast the police and the state in relations of complicity and corruption with their enemies (particularly the communists), they have been attributed an incipient critical agenda.

The vernacularization of noir stylishness in South Africa (and the gangster fashionability which both preceded and succeeded it) also permitted the uptake of this displaced critique. The zoot suit that became the *tsotsi* also permitted the identification between black subjects on either side of the Atlantic. For, what was off screen in 1943 (in the United States and in South Africa), as noir emerged, was not only the war in Europe and Asia, but the "zoot suit riots," the urban uprisings in Harlem, Detroit and other American cities that the African American author Chester Himes bluntly identified as race riots. Stuart Cosgrove remarks:

> When the nameless narrator of Ellison's *Invisible Man* confronted the subversive sight of three young and extravagantly dressed blacks, his reaction was one of fascination not of fear. These youths were not simply grotesque dandies parading

in the city's secret underworld, they were "the stewards of something uncomfortable," a spectacular reminder that the social order had failed to contain their
energy and difference. (77–78)

White sociologists responded with investigations into the "zoot effect," even as
municipalities attempted to outlaw the wearing of zoot suits (Lott 550–51; Himes). To
the extent that the zoot suits represented a refusal of war rationing, these riots articulated a generalizable opposition to the unevenness of capital and the corollary repression of consumerism in subaltern classes, something not lost on the youths of
Sophiatown, Soweto, and Alexandria or District Six. In the United States, the aftermath of the riots included not only the unjust trials of zoot suit wearers and "viru-
lent" cartoons such as "Zoot-Suit Yokum" but also the Chicano movement (Lott 551).
In South Africa, the growing cultural force of the *tsotsi* legitimated an intensifying
repression of youth, which predictably incited the further development of youth politics, as testified to by the growing power of the United Democratic Front (UDF) and
ANC Youth League and evidenced in the spectacular transformation of local school
protests into a national crisis at Soweto in 1976. At the same time, however, the limitations inherent to a politics of style came into question.

In black literary circles, this questioning ran alongside a debate about realism
and modernism. Anticipating Nkosi's Lukacsian contempt for the writing of "local
color," Njabulo Ndebele derided what he termed an aesthetics of recognition in
black literature: "the average African writers, working under an information ethos
which for him has not habituated a tradition of rigorous analysis and interpretation,
produces an art of anticipated surfaces rather than one of processes: processes in
character development or in social evolution" ("Turkish Tales" 332). For Ndebele,
the obsession with surface detail in literature is a function of "the moralistic ideology of liberalism" which "has forced our literature into a tradition of almost mech-
anist surface representation" (332). Arguing against the notion that subjective
interiority is the mark of bourgeois ideology, Ndebele insisted that it is a necessary
bulwark against totalitarianism, a refuge from ideology—as long as it is not severed
from concrete reality. Cinema, always at risk of recapitulating the aesthetics of recognition, saw the development of a comparable self critique with the release, in
1988, of Oliver Schmitz and Thomas Mogotlane's *Mapantsula*, the first film to both
recognize and explicitly disavow insurgent consumption, theft, and fashion as the
basis of political radicalism, and the first film to make the *tsotsi* the figure in and
through whom the question of political oppositionality is framed as one of
consciousness.

In *Mapantsula* the exuberant sartorial resistance to the economy of scarcity
forced upon blacks leads the protagonist, Panic, to rob clothing stores for the latest
suit and to polish his black and white wingtips even as he walks along the unpaved
red dirt roads of Soweto. But this turns out to be the source of his vulnerability to
prison wardens. His stylishness marks him off from the comrades who share his
cell, a fact which the security forces mobilize in their effort to solicit Panic to inform.
In the course of his lengthy detention, interrogation, and frequent torture, his
clothes become soiled, the sheen of his sharkskin dulled. And it is when reduced to

his black nakedness that Panic realizes that his clothes neither protect him nor constitute an adequate kind of "statement." Somewhat didactically, the film commences with a text that "explains" stylishness: "South African street gangs identified by their style of clothing and music. In their harsh surroundings there are no rules and survival of the fittest is the order of the day." It ends with a gesture that disavows the clothing and the vulgar social Darwinism that it expressed. Panic's final gesture of sovereignty (whose implications we never see in the film), by which he says "no" to the demand for a signature that would lead to the deaths of the UDF comrades, marks the claim to a fuller subjectivity, one marked by the capacity for full enunciation. In suspending the narrative in this moment, the film leaves its viewers uncertain as to the relationship between sovereignty and subjectivity. For, if sovereignty is marked by the capacity (however self-annihilating) for refusal, subjectivity demands the power of predication, and Panic never achieves the latter. His rages against his girlfriend's white bourgeois employers have the virtue of exposing the "undisguised facts," to use Kracauer's idiom, but not of transcending them. His reason is reduced to an instrumentality contained by the aspiration to acquisition. And he remains mute at the film's close, his silence noticeably contrasted to the loquacity and sociability of the comrades whom he only belatedly recognizes.

RETHINKING STYLE

In this context, it is helpful to recall that Kracauer himself saw fashion as a force working against that of history—history itself being opposed to mere historicism. But here, too, fashion could be made to reveal the truth of the untrue world. A metropolitan phenomenon, born of the close proximity between previously spatially separated classes, fashion is the upper classes' means for asserting social difference, even though the imitations it generates ensure that while "fashion is the type of phenomenon that aspires to increasingly unlimited expansion" it ultimately and inevitably falls "into self-contradiction and destruction" (Simmel 302). But this aspiration to the eternal is less a feature of individual consumption or the desires manifested through it than it is part of the structure of fashion, which, as the abstract category encompassing the multiplicity of individual fashions, reveals abstraction's own claim upon the metaphysical. Fashion, of course, is the concrete form in which the fetish of the new becomes a matter of daily habit, although this newness, as Adorno and Horkheimer argued, is in many ways mere repetition dissimulated as innovation (106).

As Gertrude Stein once remarked, "Fashion is the real thing in abstraction" (11). By this she meant that its changes have no consequence, are unmoored from a reality which, to the contrary, is built upon the fantasy that not even science changes the essence of people. Or so it seemed to her in Paris, 1900, the same

period of which Simmel was writing. The real thing, rendered by fashion in abstraction, is thus abstraction from history. What this perhaps implies is that the
tsotsi can function as part of a modernist critique of modernity only insofar as its
historicity is recognized (transformed by historical consciousness) and only as a
figure whose own representational excess can be made visible. We must therefore
remark the future history of the culture hero who first appeared as the sign of a
refusal to not desire, and who called forth the kind of politically attentive reading
that could grasp the relationship between black insurgency in the racialized economies of both American and South African modernity. It is a history of increasing
self-reflexivity and, also, of increasing awareness of the force of cinema itself
(here, including television) as the medium of capitalism's vernacularization.

The history of which we are speaking reaches its apogee in *Hijack Stories* (2005),
a film codirected by *Mapantsula*'s Oliver Schmitz and South African poet Lesego
Rampolokeng. The film follows a young actor, Sox (Tony Kgoroge), as he returns to
Soweto in pursuit of a real-life education about gangsterism as preparation for a
role. In the footsteps of an old schoolmate turned hijack impresario named Zama
(Rapulana Seiphemo), he enters deeply into the reality that he seeks to imitate, only
to have his own role as actor usurped by the actual gangster. The film plays adroitly
on the line between reality and reality effects, satirizing the film industry's insatiable
appetite for simulated violence, and the alienation of those who fabricate it from
those who must live it. A constant refrain is the diagnosis of a society "fucked up,"
made by a former Struggle warrior who has joined Zama in his entrepreneurial violence. Sox, who has lived cocooned in Johannesburg's bourgeois suburbs, is
referred to by the real gangsters as "Mr. Rainbow Nation" and "babyfood boy," but
they nonetheless decide to give him his education.

Hijack Stories also offers an astute metacommentary on cinema's force in South
African popular culture. The characters constantly invoke American cinematic
heroes of the post-noir period. Thus, Zama and his colleagues answer Sox's question
about where they learned the tricks of their trade (hijacking, raping, killing, rob-
bing), and they answer with the names of Bruce Willis and Sylvester Stallone. It
provides one of few occasions when Sox can pull rank, claiming that Wesley Snipes
is the more appropriate role model for black men. In this respect, *Hijack Stories*'
characters live in a world produced by the breaching of the narrative boundary and
the collapsing of the narrative space of cinema into the world of the viewer that
Conley describes. At a screening of the old B-movie "Sexy Girls," the youngest of the
gangsters, Fly (Percy Matsemela), leaps to his feet and shoots at the gun-toting vil-
lain on the screen, emptying the theater of patrons who fear his real-life mania
while the celluloid men fire their phantasmatic bullets at each other in an orgy of
imitation slaughter. And when Sox begins to feel himself entering into the world of
his new teachers, saying, "I just want to learn," Zama laughs menacingly and says,
"You like this movie, huh?" He understands that Sox is not merely seeking to ground
his performance in the reality of *tsotsi* life, but also that his conception of the *tsotsi*
is derived from cinema—and that two are inseparable. The realization of cinema's
imbrications with reality is not, of course, limited to the genre films associated with

the *tsotsi*. In Elaine Proctor's acute film about South African Defense Force soldiers on the Angolan border, *On the Wire* (1990), the soldiers compulsively view and review video they have made of their violent assault on a local woman, depending for both their pleasure and their sense of reality of the moment on its filmic inscription.

In *Hijack Stories*, this complex dependency on cinema as the basis of both con-stituting and apprehending reality is staged as a matter of fashion and becomes vis-ible in the sartorial transformations that Sox undergoes. The film recapitulates a scene of his walking into Soweto three times, in each of which he is dressed differ-ently. When he first arrives in leather jacket and mesh T-shirt, he is ridiculed as a city boy. When he comes back the second time, he looks like he has walked out of a blaxploitation film, with purple pants, thick-soled shoes, and a camouflage T-shirt. On his third sojourn, he is wearing loose khaki pants, an oversized T-shirt untucked, a red cap, and red sunglasses. It is this latter attire that finally leads Zama to exclaim, "Take off that fucking hat, man! You look like a criminal." He (Zama) is not the criminal, he claims; that moniker belongs to the white people in Rosebank and the BEE (Black Economic Empowerment) aspirants who have abandoned their brothers in the township, or who were not there during the hard days of the Struggle.

The film's penultimate scene includes a funeral at which Zama recites Ingoapele Madingoane's anthemic Pan-Africanist poem, "In Africa my Beginning, in Africa my Ending," and returns, thereby, to Schmitz's earlier film *Mapantsula*, to suggest the failure of fashion to address the questions of the political. Panic's obsession with fashion has given way to Sox's desire to access authenticity, which he nonetheless understands as a matter of appearance only and for which he is prepared to sur-render all judgment. The fetishization of stylishness, which noir offered as a dis-placed idiom of critique, and which mirrored the refusal of desire's racialized containment, is rendered here as a false consolation, one that betrays a revolution that ought to have generated fuller and more equitable redistribution. At the final audition, the only adequate performance of the *tsotsi* can be made by the *tsotsi* and the audition entails a reproduction of an actual mugging, though the producer does not know the referent (we have seen it in the opening sequences of *Hijack Stories*) and the film makes no comment about the fact that it is a mugging of a black man, whose humiliation is addressed to him from within a language the white producers do not understand—for the *tsotsi* is speaking an updated version of *tsotsitaal*, called *scamtho*. However, in its turn to the real, for which the *tsotsi* who is played by a *tsotsi* provides the most ironic figure, it does call into question the radical potentiality of all mimesis, and this we may read as the signature gesture of this film's persistent and emphatically vernacularized modernism.

Hijack Stories travels ground that had been opened for South African audi-ences by Teboho Mahlatsi's and Angus Gibson's television show *Yizo Yizo* (meaning "this is it/this is the real thing") about a group of township youths who are attempt-ing to negotiate the competing demands and opportunities of school and crimi-nality. And it offers a trenchant rebuttal to Gavin Hood's rendition of the figure in *Tsotsi*, wherein the demand for politicization has given way to the narrative of moralization within a structure of heteronormative family values. This too is the symptom of a vernacularizing process, one that reveals the tendency of postcolonial states to pursue the route of national capital even in the moment of global neoliberalism. The mark of that development is undoubtedly the decision to cultivate consumerist subjects even among the underclasses who had previously been abandoned within what Achille Mbembe has called a "necropolitical" logic and what Gayatri Spivak termed subalternity. Insofar as employment remains insufficient to absorb those to whom the invitations of commodity desire are being made, the ideological accompaniment of an expanding market also entails a spectacle of domesticity, a gendered division of affective labor, and new forms of nationalism (with their attendant xenophobic excesses). It also seems to entail the terror of the *tsotsi* and of crime more generally. The *tsotsi* thus remains the alienated embodiment of South Africa's contradictions, the product and allegorical emblem of vernacular modernism as it developed in this part of the global south.

NOTES

1. It is perhaps wiser to translate this as the Monument to the War of Peoples, the idea and ideology of the folk suggested by the term *völker* being distinct from, even as it underwrites, the nationalism of modern state projects.

2. I nonetheless accept Adorno's assessment (191) that this instability, what he terms "flux," loses its critical function if not made in reference "to unity," namely the unity of the material (itself comprised of heterogeneous units). Indiscriminate multiplicity, which is the overt ambition of postmodernism (not to be confused with the radical openness of post-structuralism), implies a somewhat different politics, and a freedom unmoored from the project of social emancipation.

3. Lazarus and Nkosi are exclusively concerned with literary production. Comparable assessments could probably not be made in the plastic arts, where black artists were much more actively engaged in modernist projects, particularly in the graphic arts, though there, too, the field, and particularly the showing and institutional patronage of production, was dominated by white artists.

4. For a history of different censorship legislation and its effect on South African cinema, see Tomaselli and McDonald.

WORKS CITED

Adorno, Theodor. *Aesthetic Theory*. Trans. Robert Hullot-Kentor. Ed. Gretel Adorno and Rolf Tiedemann. Minneapolis: University of Minnesota Press, 1997. Theory and History of Literature 88.

Anderson, Perry. *In the Tracks of Historical Materialism*. Chicago: University of Chicago Press, 1984.

Arendt, Hannah. *On Violence.* New York: Harcourt, 1970.

Attridge, Derek. *J. M. Coetzee and the Ethics of Reading: Literature in the Event.* Durban: University of KwaZulu-Natal Press, 2005.

Bakhtin, M. M. "Discourse and the Novel." *The Dialogic Imagination: Four Essays by M. M. Bakhtin.* Ed. Michael Holquist. Trans. Caryl Emerson and Michael Holquist. Austin: University of Texas Press, 1981. 259–422.

———. "Forms of Time and of the Chronotope in the Novel." *The Dialogic Imagination* 84–258.

Beittel, Mark. "Mapantsula: Cinema, Crime and Politics on the Witwatersrand." *Journal of Southern African Studies* 16.4 (1990): 751–61.

Benjamin, Walter. "Critique of Violence." *Reflections.* Trans. Edmund Jephcott. New York: Schocken, 1978. 277–300.

———. "On the Present Situation of Russian Film." *Walter Benjamin: Selected Writings. Volume 2, Part 1, 1927–1930.* Ed. Howard Eiland and Michael W. Jennings. Trans. Rodney Livingstone. Cambridge: Belknap Press of Harvard, 2005. 12–15.

———. "The Work of Art in the Age of Its Technological Reproducibility." *Walter Benjamin: Selected Writings. Volume 4, 1938–1940.* Ed. Howard Eiland and Michael W. Jennings Trans. Edmund Jephcott. Cambridge: Belknap Press of Harvard, 2003. 251–83.

Bethlehem, Louise. "A Primary Need as Strong as Hunger: The Rhetoric of Urgency in South Africa under Apartheid." *Poetics Today* 22.2 (2001): 365–89.

Bothma, C. V. "'n Volkekundige Ondersoek na die Aard en Onstaans orrsake van Tsotsi-groepe en hulle Aktiwiteite soos Gevind in die Stedelike Gebied van Pretoria." MA thesis. University of Pretoria, 1951.

Bourdieu, Pierre. *Distinction: A Social Critique of the Judgment of Taste.* Trans. Richard Nice. Cambridge: Harvard University Press, 1987.

Christiansë, Yvette. "Sculpted into History: The Voortrekker Mother and the Gaze of the Invisible Servant." *Decolonising Bodies.* Ed. Sue Thomas. Spec issue of *New Literatures Review* 3 (1995): 1–16.

———. *Unconfessed. A Novel.* New York: Other Press; Cape Town: Kwela, 2006.

Conley, Tom. "Stages of Film Noir." *Theater Journal* 39 (1987): 247–63.

Cosgrove, Stuart. "The Zoot Suit and Style Warfare." *History Workshop Journal.* 18 (1984): 77–91.

Crapanzano, Vincent. *Waiting: The Whites of South Africa.* New York: Random House, 1985.

Davis, Peter. *In Darkest Hollywood: Exploring the Jungles of Cinema's South Africa.* Johannesburg: Ravan; Athens: Ohio University Press, 1996.

Delmont, Elizabeth. "The Voortrekker Monument: Monolith to Myth." *South African Historical Journal* 29 (1993): 76–101.

Dimendberg, Edward. "Down these Seen Streets a Man Must Go: Siegfried Kracauer, 'Hollywood's Terror Films,' and the Spatiality of Film Noir." *New German Critique* 89 (2003): 113–43.

Glaser, Clive. *Bo-Tsotsi: The Youth Gangs of Soweto, 1935–1976.* Cape Town: David Philip, 2000.

Gordimer, Nadine. "The Essential Gesture: Writers and Responsibility." Tanner Lectures on Human Values. University of Michigan. 12 October 1984. Available at: http://www.tannerlectures.utah.edu/lectures/documents/gordimer85.pdf.; rpt in *The Essential Gesture: Writing, Politics and Places.* New York and London: Penguin, 1989.

Hansen, Miriam Bratu. "Fallen Women, Rising Stars, New Horizons: Shanghai Silent Film as Vernacular Modernism." *Film Quarterly* 54.1 (2000): 10–22.

————. "The Mass Production of the Senses: Classical Cinema as Vernacular Modernism."
    Reinventing Film Studies. Ed. Christine Gledhill and Linda Williams. London: Edward
    Arnold, 2000. 332–50.

Harvey, David. *Justice, Nature and the Geography of Difference*. Oxford: Basil Blackwell,
    1996.

Head, Bessie. *A Question of Power*. London: Heinemann, 1974.

Hebdige, Dick. *Subculture: The Meaning of Style*. London: Routledge, 1981.

Himes, Chester. "Zoot Riots are Race Riots." *Crisis* July 1943: 200+.

Horkheimer, Max, and Theodor Adorno. *Dialectic of Enlightenment*. Trans. Edmund
    Jephcott. Ed. Gunzelin Schmid Noerr. [1987] Stanford: Stanford University Press,
    2002.

Huette, Stanley. "Distasteful Trend in Modern Film Production: Must We Have So Much
    Sadism and Brutality?" *Sunday Times* 13 July 13, 1947: 20.

Ivy, Marilyn. *Discourses of the Vanishing: Modernity, Phantasm, Japan*. Chicago: University
    of Chicago Press, 1995.

Jameson, Fredric. *Postmodernism or the Logic of Late Capitalism*. Durham: Duke University
    Press, 1995.

Kracauer, Siegfried. "George Simmel." *The Mass Ornament: Weimar Essays*. [1927] Trans.
    Thomas Y. Levin. Cambridge: Harvard University Press, 1995. 225–57.

————. "The Mass Ornament." *The Mass Ornament* 75–86.

————. "Photography." *The Mass Ornament* 46–63.

————. *Theory of Film: The Redemption of Physical Reality*. [1960] Princeton: Princeton
    University Press, 1997.

Lazarus, Neil. "Modernism and Modernity: T. W. Adorno and Contemporary White South
    African Literature." *Modernity and Modernism, Postmodernity and Postmodernism*.
    Spec issue of *Cultural Critique* 5 (1986–1987): 131–55.

Lott, Eric. "The Whiteness of Film Noir." *American Literary History* 9.3 (1997): 542–66.

Magubane, Bernard Makhosezwe. *The Political Economy of Race and Class in South Africa*.:
    Monthly Review Press, 1979.

Maingard, Jacqueline. *South African National Cinema*. London: Routledge, 2007.

Marks, Shula, and Richard Rathbone, eds. *Industrialization and Social Change in South
    Africa*. New York: Longman, 1982.

Marx, Karl. *Grundrisse Foundations of the Critique of Political Economy (Rough Draft)*. 1939.
    Trans. Martin Nicolaus. London: New Left Review; New York: Penguin, 1993.

Masilela, Ntongela. "The New African Film Movement and the Beginnings of Film Culture
    in South Africa." *To Change Reels: Film and Film Culture in South Africa*. Ed. Isabel
    Balseiro and Ntongela Masilela. Detroit: Wayne State University Press, 2003.

Mathabane, Mark. *Kaffir Boy*. New York: Signet, 1986.

Mbembe, Achille. "Necropolitics." Trans. Libby Meintjes. *Public Culture* 15(1): 22–40.

McDonald, Peter. *The Literature Police: Apartheid Censorship and its Cultural Conse-
    quences*. New York: Oxford University Press, 2009.

Modisane, Bloke. *Blame Me on History*. London: Thames and Hudson, 1965.

Moeketsi, Kippie. "Kippie's Memories and the Early Days of Jazz: Kippie Moeketsi Speaks."
    Staffrider 7.3–4 (1988): 362–71.

Morris, Rosalind C. *In the Place of Origins: Modernity and Its Mediums in Northern
    Thailand*. Durham: Duke University Press, 2000.

Motloatse, Mothobi, ed. *Forced Landing: Africa South, Contemporary Writings*. Johannse-
    burg: Ravan, 1980.

Naremore, James. *More than Night: Film Noir in Its Contexts*. Berkeley: University of
    California Press, 1998.

Ndebele, Njabulo. *The Cry of Winnie Mandela*. Cape Town: Kwela, 2004.

———. "Rediscovery of the Ordinary." *South African Literature and Culture: Rediscovery of the Ordinary*. Manchester: Manchester University Press, 1994. 41–59.

———. "Turkish Tales and Some Thoughts on South African Fiction." *Staffrider* 7.3–4 (1988): 318–40.

Nixon, Rob. *Homelands, Harlem and Hollywood: South African Culture and the World Beyond*. New York: Routledge, 1994.

Nkosi, Lewis. "Postmodernism and Black Writing in South Africa." *Writing South Africa: Literature, Apartheid, and Democracy, 1970–1995*. Ed. Derek Attridge and Rosemary Jolly. New York: Cambridge University Press, 1998. 75–90.

———. *Underground People*. Cape Town: Kwela, 2005.

Phillips, Ray. *The Bantu Are Coming: Phases of South Africa's Race Problem*. London: Student Christian Movement, 1939.

Rive, Richard. *"Buckingham Palace," District Six*. Cape Town: David Philip, 1986.

Schrader, Paul. "Notes on Film Noir." 1972. *Movies and Mass Culture*. Ed. John Bolton. New Jersey: Rutgers University Press, 1996. 153–70.

Simmel, Georg. "Fashion." *On Individuality and Social Forms*. Chicago: University of Chicago Press, 1971. 294–323.

Spivak, Gayatri Chakravorty. "Can the Subaltern Speak?" *Marxism and the Interpretation of Culture*. Ed. Lawrence Grossberg and Cary Nelson. Chicago: University of Illinois Press, 1988. 271–313.

Stein, Gertrude. *Paris France*. 1940. New York: Liveright, 1996.

Sunday Times. "Birth of Afrikaans Film." 7 April 1946.

———. "South African Film Producer Makes Good in Britain." 1 June 1947.

Titlestad, Michael. *Making the Changes: Jazz in South African Literature and Reportage*. Pretoria: University of South Africa Press, 2005.

Tomaselli, Keyan. *The Cinema of Apartheid: Race and Class in South African Film*. New York: Smyrna, 1988.

Trotsky, Leon. *The Permanent Revolution and Results and Prospects*. 1905. New York: Merit Publishers, 1969.

Tutuola, Amos. *The Palm-Wine Drinkard and My Life in the Bush of Ghosts*. New York: Grove, 1984.

Vilakazi, B. W. *Zulu Horizons*. Cape Town: Howard Timmins, 1962.

Williams, Raymond. *The Country and the City*. Oxford: Oxford University Press, 1975.

———. "When Was Modernism?" *The Politics of Modernism: Against the New Conformists*. Ed. Tony Pinkney. London: Verso, 1989. 31–35.

Wolpe, Harold. "Capitalism and Cheap Labour-Power in South Africa: From Segregation to Apartheid." 1972. *Segregation and Apartheid in South Africa*. Ed. William Beinart and Saul Dubow. New York: Routledge, 1995.

PART X

AFTERWORD

CHAPTER 28

....

MODERNIST STUDIES AND INTER-IMPERIALITY IN THE LONGUE DURÉE

....

LAURA DOYLE

OPENING this book, encountering its twenty-seven essays, a reader might feel dizzy, as if awakening inside a lithograph by M. C. Escher. Peering round through twenty-seven windows into unfamiliar landscapes in different planes, all carefully framed, one might experience both wonder and vertigo: each vignette norm-bending, eye-opening, while pointedly aware of the onlooker; aiming to translate, while consciously disorienting. And all are placed together in one edifice, one essay collection. Does this placing-together of divergent views and landscapes under the sign of modernism reenact an appropriative gaze—or undo it, expose it? Under the pressure of this question, this book's globalizing of modernism will draw scrutiny.

And reward scrutiny. For these twenty-seven essays are impressively nimble and alert as they position each literature from within its own socioeconomic horizons, while also tracking its orientation toward distant conditions or disjunctive planes. Each modernism thus emerges as tilted in at least two directions at once, inward and outward, toward the local and the global—and then too also sideways, toward the adjacent, onlooking others, and all mutually so, yet on uneven ground.

And each essay asks questions about this dizzying positionality, about itself and all of the others. Taken together, the essays begin to dismantle leveling Anglo-European frames and norms. Some of them detail specific modernisms that are unfamiliar to most scholars of Anglophone modernism, and which interact with the latter in varying degrees—including Sanja Bahun's essay on the Balkans, Harsha Ram's on Russia and Georgia as well as France, Xudong Zhang's on China, Shachar Pinsker's on Jewish Eastern Europe, and Nergis Ertürk's on Turkey. Others clarify the cultural labor of modernists who write in direct, decolonizing negotiation with Western nations; they study the movements, magazines, films, and texts in the Caribbean and Latin America (Emery, Aching, Unruh, Kalliney, and Rogers), Africa (Lazarus, Lincoln, Bulson, Blair, and Morris), and India (Dass and Berman). Several of these, and others in addition, emphasize the cultural crossings that mutually constitute modernisms on all sides, from Janet Lyon's reconsideration of cosmopolitanism to Rebecca Beasley's study of British translations of Russian literature to Edwige Tamalet Talbayev's narration of the migrations and diverse affiliations of a Berber poet. These literary ethnographies also establish that communist movements both generated and splintered modernist movements around the globe, and did so in tension with allegiances to normative or queer sexualities, as becomes especially clear, for instance, in essays by Vicky Unruh, Ben Tran, and Miriam Hansen.

And each essay is written in English, as first, second, third, or fourth language. Weighted with that history. Constrained by an Anglophone circumference, rewriting its content.

And there's the rub. All of this excavating, mapping, reorienting, rethinking, rehinging, and unsilencing occurs in English. This collection thus carries within it an old conflict. In the long history of this conflict, people have killed and been killed, books have been weapons. This book in our hands places us in this history. In English.

This position is not inherently wrong or false: it is a position. Conversation in this language is *positioned*, shaped by the speaker's (un)certain place in culture and in the present moment of a long history. Work can be done here. *Some* work must be done here. Many of the geomodernists discussed in this collection launched that work. These essays labor to extend it. The rest will depend on readers, in particular on our ability to move further away from a Eurocentric global history that impoverishes accounts of global modernisms. And history is very much at the heart of the matter, this essay proposes.

PART I

Recent work in world history reveals that even our most incisive literary critiques are partial, insofar as they erase the presence of multiple global empires and continue to assume that Anglo-European empires have singly dominated and singularly shaped world politics and arts since the early nineteenth century. We will be in a position to carry forward what Janet Lyon calls a fragile cosmopolitanism insofar as we do better justice to the complex histories that this partial truth has obscured. These many essays point the way toward this complexity—and they have generated this Afterword which has itself become something larger and more multifaceted than anticipated, which I hope will merit the reader's perseverance. Here, in Part I, this essay lays out the evidence and rationale for a different historical paradigm. Then, in Part II, it reapproaches global modernisms and the rich materials gathered here in an effort to bend our thinking to meet history's escheresque tessellations.

The Longue Durée of Borrowing

As Edward Said noted long ago in *Beginnings*, the discourses and political economies of individualism have led us to cherish the idea of distinctive originals. Marking origins and originals is a primary structure within which many of us live, perceive, and ask questions. Literary theorists now critique these habits, knowing there is no absolute original, yet we implicitly continue to ask about beginnings and implicitly give overdetermined answers. Modernist scholars may in fact be particularly attracted to the seductive vocabulary of the new and the original, as several essays here note. Hence we may need to be especially on guard against a privileging of origins that forecloses many clamoring questions about history and flattens out the dialectical history that has produced global modernisms.

In the case of literary or cultural history, perhaps the word that most commonly signals this habit of designating originals, and in turn blinds us to literature's dialectical co-formations, is the nagging term "borrowing." The idea and act of "borrowing" stand at the center of a cluster of words that includes "belated," "third world," "expropriated," "appropriated," "derive," and "revise." And it stands against a counter-cluster: "original," "metropole," "first world," "generate," and "innovate." As several essays here make clear implicitly or explicitly, current scholarship on global modernisms, or geomodernisms, is struggling with the legacies of these words.[1] In particular, it is struggling to resist the way that a notion of borrowing deforms or haunts all considerations of the relation between canonical modernism and other literatures, especially postcolonial literature. It is this rocky landscape through which any approach to "global modernisms" must pass.

Borrowing needs a new history and different framework if we are to encounter each other here without further harm. Usefully, nearly all of the essays begin this work by recasting or undercutting the notion that modernism was essentially an Anglo-European and North American phenomenon that "spread" elsewhere. Many essays do so by tracing the complex, multifaceted conditions under which modernist vocabularies and experimental forms emerged in particular locales, whether in William Gardner's detailing of the Marxist political debates informing Japanese modernism or Manishita Dass's analysis of mother figures and Jewish female stars in early Indian cinema. Other essays reinterpret the old metropole-to-margin trajectories. Gerard Aching argues that the orientation toward Spain and France in the texts of Latin American and Cuban modernists—often reduced by critics to fawning metropole imitation—on closer look enacts a critical cosmopolitan engagement. Jessica Berman writing on India and Sarah Lincoln on Nigeria trace modernist forms to specific political and economic conditions, and thus explain homologies between earlier metropole and later postcolonial texts as a comparable engagement with material conditions rather than as aesthetic mimicry or mirroring, to borrow Berman's language. More broadly, even as they focus, respectively, on African, Chinese, and Caribbean literature, Neil Lazarus, Eric Hayot, and Mary Lou Emery place all modernisms in relation to global paradigms, in Lazarus's case capitalist modernity, in Hayot's a reversible economy of mimetic, other-cultural desire, and in Emery's a planetary consciousness. Likewise, Susan Stanford Friedman and Jahan Ramazani work to establish a common world of crisis, struggle, and possibility with which all modernisms engage, if from different positions, thus shrinking the secondary question of who borrowed from whom down to its proper size.

Yet these reconfigurations need follow-up. We are still only glimpsing the fuller story. Uncovering this story, a history of modernisms might validly take up the question of borrowing or influence; but it needs to begin well before the twentieth century—at least as early as the twelfth. And insofar as modernism is a function of modernity, this history will also entail a different understanding of modernity. For, if it is true, as many essays here assume, that modernisms arise to grapple with modernity in some form, then we need to revisit our formulations about "modernity" as well.

A hint of what I have in mind appears in Eric Hayot's essay on "Chinese modernism"—a phrase that in itself, as he notes, already encodes a west-to-east trajectory insofar as the word modernism is a Western import. Giving pointed instances of an elided reverse flow (e.g., the mantra "make it new," cribbed by Pound from an ancient Chinese text), he then nods toward the much older flow of materials and ideas from east to west and speaks in passing of "the deep debt owed by the Anglo-European modernists to the languages, histories, cultures, and literatures of East Asia," as well as of Africa. Hayot closes by reiterating the call to "abandon the temporal logic that has until now structured the field [of modernism] . . . and served as a screen for geographic centrisms."

We can do so most effectively if we lengthen our time lines and revise our historiography of empire. Within this fuller perspective, we begin to fathom the deep sedimentation of cross-cultural influence and the centuries-old dialectics of geopolitical literary history toward which Hayot gestures.

Interlocked Empires

We might begin by moving away from the standard view in which Anglo-European empires arise in (roughly) the sixteenth century from the ashes of empires past to rule the world in "the modern" era. Instead we might pay more attention to the contemporaneity of empires and the accumulation of vexed cultural exchange among empires, over generations. That is, as I have discussed elsewhere and will review here, despite the familiar rhetoric of rise and fall, world empires with their various projects of modernization have not existed simply sequentially.[2] They have overlapped with each other, battled each other, and borrowed from each other, forming each other through processes of transculturation.

We overlook these dynamics when we think in terms of the single cluster of "Anglo-European empire" in "the modern" period. The world has likely never had one "core" as the single axis of a circle of peripheries and semi-peripheries, including in the last several centuries. Rather it has suffered the effects of multiple *inter*-imperial contests around the globe, shaping and shaped by multiple anticolonial movements. Attention to these jockeying empires, plural, and to anticolonial-isms, plural, and over the very long haul, fosters a fuller account of how literatures have developed in volatile relation to each other within the dynamics of *coproduced* imperial modernities.

This account does not suppose a set of "alternative modernities," which continues the assumption of one main modernity. Rather it highlights a world of multiple empires competing *through* modernization projects that are all at once economic, political, cultural, and technological; and it is these which spawn multiple modernities, each with its cultural and historical distinctiveness. Within such a model we can begin to undo the blindnesses accompanying the many insights of recent scholarship on globalism. Thus, for instance, in *The World Republic of Letters*, Pascale Casanova constructs a part of this dialectical history, but she mistakes it for the whole. Although Casanova usefully documents the highly competitive nature of an "international literary space" which entails "its own forms of violence," her study nonetheless suffers from the historical erasures of past literary and political histories in telling a Eurocentric history of literary formations (xii). Accordingly it exhibits the investment in Western "greatness" and "freedom" that inevitably accompanies those erasures—even when it labors strenuously not to do so (11). In a later section of this essay I will discuss nineteenth- and twentieth-century global history in the more fully international and dialectical terms required to supplement her model. First, however, it is necessary to establish grounds for a different historiographic model and to bring forward older histories that put modernist exchanges into proper perspective.

In *Explorations in Connected History*, Sanjay Subrahmanyam foregrounds the processes generated by ever-unsettled contestations among several world empires, which mutually form those empires. Subrahmanyam draws on archives in several languages to track the complex, mutual effects of political and military maneuvers among Ottoman, European, Safavid, and Mughal empires in the sixteenth century. He traces, first of all, how fifteenth-century Portuguese interventions in the political dynasties of northern India partly enabled the inroads of Mughals there, and he shows how these laid the ground for Portugal's territorial and trade agreements with the Mughals as the latter expanded their empire southward (all while the Portuguese fostered ideas about fierce Mughal omnivorousness to play off against their own purportedly more honorable practices) (13–14). In subsequent years, to the chagrin of Mughal leaders, the Portuguese negotiated for additional trading powers and port privileges in return for the safe haven they could provide for Mughal pilgrimages to Mecca; and this in turn sometimes led the Mughals to build alliances with the Ottomans so as to safely bypass or undercut the Portuguese.

Not surprisingly then, ripple-effects moved through the Indian Ocean and the Mediterranean basin when the Spanish Hapsburgs subdued and annexed Portugal in 1580–1581. Often considered a turning point in the European balance of power, this event did more than affect relations within Europe. It realigned arrangements between Mughals and Europeans even as it affected relations between the Europeans and the Ottomans, for the annexation drained the Hapsburg empire's military resources and led to their increased readiness to compromise in treaties with the Ottoman empire (Subrahmanyam 46–50). The Ottomans themselves had entered a period of consolidation for several reasons, including unsuccessful territorial wars with the Iranian Safavids, the assassination of the Grand Vizier, and also the entry of new silver and gold from America, which had destabilized Middle Eastern and Eastern monetary systems while enriching Spain and Portugal.

Yet meanwhile the Hapsburgs themselves faced new pressures from the northwest. The English and the Dutch were profiting handsomely and gaining ground, literally as well as politically, in American colonization projects—in part with the help of musket and cannon technologies learned from Eastern empires. At the same time, and partly as a result, they were able to recalibrate trade relations with the Ottomans, in Britain's case leading to the founding of the Levant Company in 1581. Ironically, the Netherlands and England had turned west in the face of Ottoman and southern European control of the Mediterranean, and yet in turn, leveraged by their Atlantic wealth, they eventually shifted the balance of power in relations with those far-reaching empires, eventually challenging them. Among other contingencies, their larger, more powerful ships, built for Atlantic crossings, entered the Mediterranean and unsettled Ottoman dominance there, as Ferdinand Braudel observes (*Mediterranean* 607).

Even this brief sketch gives us a sense of the mutually produced, highly contingent, and interactive nature of *contemporaneous* imperial histories, with their unanticipated, sometimes ironic effects. It begins to expose the flaws in any model that focuses solely on the singular "rise" of Anglo-European empire. It alerts us instead to a multilateral, competitive building of empires. A growing corpus of world historiography like Subrahmanyam's allows us to see that imperial modernities are fundamentally *co*-constituted by these exchanges. And it is within these multiple imperial histories that literatures carry out their cultural work, each one developing in volatile relation to the others, a point I will return to in relation to modernism.

Within such an unfolding among empires there is simultaneously another kind of dialectic in play, one which, again, recent historiography brings into clearer view: a "vertical" dialectic, so to speak, spawned by disruptions of empire from within and "below." Just as histories of multiple and vying empires clarify their interactive co-formations, recent histories of revolution and resistance allow us to see the contestations shaping "modernity/coloniality," to borrow Arturo Escobar and Walter Mignolo's formulation, and, in turn, directing the formations of literature.[3] In the case of Anglo-European empires, for instance, historians have documented the many slave revolts and indigenous-led battles in the Americas, rebellions in Ireland and India, and Caribbean maroon movements.[4] These vertical struggles are carried out within and across the horizontal contests between empires. Thus in the mid-nineteenth century, on one hand, the British battled over trade with the Chinese Qing Dynasty in the Opium Wars, while on the other hand, they helped the Qing put down the Taiping Rebellion, ultimately serving Britain's own imperial interests in Asia. Likewise, in the Caribbean, Anglo-Europeans encouraged slave insurrections or desertions in rival European colonies in order to weaken these rivals, and during the American Revolution the British did so in attempting to subdue their insurgent colony and rival-to-be. Meanwhile, Haitian and Irish revolutionaries likewise manipulated these rivalries, courting and gaining support from one empire against another. Similarly, in the 1940s the leaders of India's independence movement extracted concessions from the British under the shadow of Japanese ambitions in the region.

These pitched battles between and within competitive empires have driven the production and shaped the forms of texts. Keeping these contests in mind, we may do better justice to the sources of global movements such as modernism. Yet to appreciate the cultural materials that have arisen within and accrued throughout this long and winding dialectical history of empires, we need to turn back even further. Only then can we assess the sources and conditions for what is typically called Western modernity. Only then can we begin to address the matter of what is original and what is borrowed or belated. And only then can we move beyond these secondary questions of influence toward further interpretation of the many modernisms mapped out in this collection.

Belatedness Reconsidered

Recent scholarship increasingly establishes the ways in which so-called Anglo-European modernity has been formed from the outside in, perhaps even to a degree that evacuates any notion of a native, Western, or strictly "original" modernity, as well as of an "originally Anglo-European" world literary system. To glimpse the depth at which Anglo-Europeans fashioned themselves and "their" modernity out of materials borrowed from the Near East, the South, and the Far East, it is necessary to begin with the medieval period. While such scope may seem far removed from modernism, it provides the perspective we need to think straight about "belatedness," "borrowing," and ultimately global literary history. In turn it forces us to reconsider our attributions of Western influence in studies of recent Asian, Middle Eastern, or African literatures, for in some cases the direction of influence is originally the reverse. What appear to be postcolonial *borrowings* from the West actually carry a longer history: in the longue durée, some experimental genres of stylized love lyric and fractured storytelling as well as sophisticated theories of literary form originated in non-Western cultures and traveled from east to west; therefore when postcolonial writers later take them up again, they are sometimes "borrowing back" those styles (knowingly or not), and extending the experiments that Westerners had inherited from these writers' home cultures.[5]

Scholarly studies of medieval literature give us grounds for considering these possibilities. Students of the medieval period have long known that the Anglo-European scholasticists learned most of their Aristotle through Arabic philosophers and translators, but this fact has often been accorded no more than a mention, until the recent work of scholars such as Dorothee Metlitzki, George Makdisi, and Charles Burnett. Likewise, although readers since the seventeenth century have debated the possible Arabic-language influence on the first vernacular literatures of Italy, Spain, and France, few have given this influence its proper due and depth of study, even despite the earlier twentieth-century scholarship of Américo Castro and Richard Nykl as well as the later twentieth-century work of James Monroe, Roger Boase, Maria Menocal, and Sahar Amer.[6]

In her book *The Arabic Role in Medieval Literary History*, Menocal reminds us, for instance, that in Andalusian Spain of the late Medieval period, Arabic was the language of learning for all three dominant religious traditions—Jewish, Christian, and Islamic—and in turn shaped European literary traditions. The influence of Arabic literature and learning spread northward with increasing rapidity after the Christian reconquest of many Spanish and Italian territories in the later medieval period, as Christian Europeans were able to travel more easily in these regions and benefit from the magnificent libraries and communities of translators in such places as Córdoba and Toledo, which had been patronized under Islamic rule. Scholars from Italy, England, and France traveled to Spain to study texts in Arabic, both secular and religious, including translations of Aristotle and original Arabic science, all while being exposed to Arabic-language poetic, visual, and musical traditions. Anglo-Europeans then carried these new streams of culture back north. Especially worrisome to the high authorities of both Christendom and Islam, scholars were powerfully drawn to the writings of the Al-Andalusian "radical Aristotelians" such as Averroes, who developed rationalist principles and valued the methods of reason, including in matters of faith (the so-called Averronian heresy). These notions quickly infiltrated and electrified centers of learning in France, Germany, Italy, and England. Menocal thus speaks of an Arabized Europe in the medieval period, an influence that mingles with its Latin legacies.

Others have specified this influence especially for English thought and literature.[7] In *The Matter of Araby in Medieval England*, Dorothee Metlitzki not only reminds readers about the pervasive Arab influence on Anglo-European cultures during the era of Crusades—"on military technique, on vocabulary, on food, clothing, and ornamentation" (4). She also tracks the wide range of Arabic texts that reached England, including for instance through the work of the twelfth-century scholasticist, Adelard of Bath. Like others, Adelard devoted himself to the study of Arabic philosophy and science (what he called "Arabicorum studiorum sense") in order to transmit what he had learned, as he put it, "from Arab teachers under the guidance of reason" and thus to promote the principles of science in Christian cultures, all of which provides an important seed for the later rationalism so often celebrated as "Western" (quoted in Metlitzki 49, 51).

Metlitzki also documents the emulation of Arabic genres of philosophical debate in medieval English literature, deeming it saturated with the "Arabian science that surrounds [it]" (56). Thus for instance she traces the Arabic antecedents for such texts as "The Owl and the Nightingale" [ca. 1186–1216], including the owl and the nightingale's dialogue about astrology, God, determinism, and the relation between body and soul, right down to the common Arabic conclusion that the heart was the integrating organ. Finally, she points to possible Arabic sources for key English literary forms, such as allegory and the genre of loosely linked didactic tales found in Chaucer's *Canterbury Tales*. Arab-Islamic philosophical, scientific, and literary forms thus fed, Metlitzki concludes, "the Western reservoir that supplied vernacular writers" (96). This kind of research begins to rewrite the history of "Western" rational secularism, so dear and central to assumptions about Western peoples' "modernity."

Particularly important for modernist literature, scholars have devoted attention to the Arabic influence on vernacular poetry in France, Spain, Italy, and Sicily. Menocal points out that in the early twelfth-century court of William IX of Aquitaine, Arabic language, music, and poetry held a place of honor and pervaded the milieu in which William initiated the vernacular French tradition of troubadour love poetry. He had encountered Arabic arts and literature in Palestine, where he lived for a year after Jerusalem was taken by the Crusades, and through his marriage to Philippa of Aragon (as well as through the marriages of his two sisters to Pedro I of Aragon and Alfonso VI of Castile), which took him to the courts of Andalusian Spain. In the wake of his travels, as well as through the influx of Arabic-language culture more generally, William began to write and patronize "troubadour" courtly love poetry in vernacular French—the self-consciously formal and self-reflexive poetry that later inspired both Romantic and modernist poets, and which even the scrupulously even-handed critic Roger Boase considers to be influenced by Arabic poetics. A similar story pertains in Sicily after it was retaken in the twelfth century by Christians, and especially under the thirteenth-century ruler Frederick II, who is likewise credited with cultivating the turn toward vernacular Italian poetry, some of which likewise emulates Arabic-language themes and forms. More broadly, George Makdisi has studied the ways that the cultivation of the arts in "humanist" Anglo-European courts and universities emulated models first encountered in Islamic and other Eastern empires. The elision of these literary genealogies has ultimately enabled the mis-framing of the relation between Western and non-Western literatures and in turn between modernist and postcolonial literatures.[8]

If medieval sources seem remote, we might recall that this set of non-Western influences on Anglo-European cultures persisted through the early modern and modern periods. The Islamic influence continues into the sixteenth and seventeenth centuries via the Ottoman empire, as established by scholars such as Nabil Matar and Gerald MacLean in the case of England. In *Looking East*, MacLean explores what he calls "imperial envy" in English attitudes toward the Ottomans, leading to cultural imitations; and, in *Islam in Britain, 1558–1685*, Matar highlights the fact that some seventeenth-century Puritans and other religious dissenters praised the Ottoman

Empire as a proper religious state, insofar as it allowed for liberty of conscience even as it pursued a territorial expansion that supported religious conversion. As J. G. Toomer shows, the seventeenth century saw the founding of Arabist chairs and professorships in universities throughout Europe and Britain. John Milton's remark that the Ottomans "enlarged their empire as much by the study of liberal culture as by the force of arms" indicates a British interest in the Ottomans as empire-builders, even as it also suggests that British writers sought to emulate that "liberal" cultural and imperial project (quoted in Matar 87). In a similar vein, Daniel Goffman documents the ways that Renaissance Italians imitated the diplomatic institutions of the Ottoman empire, modeling embassies and information-gathering networks after theirs and designating certain kinds of status for foreigners and nonbelievers, practices which helped to stabilize intra-Italian relations and inter-European practices and ultimately led to Europeans' more effective participation in world politics (61–74). In part under the tutelage of the Ottomans, then, Anglo-European princes learned to speak the lingua franca and act the parts of emerging "liberal" empires, even as, earlier, they had imitated the artistic and scholarly patronage practices of Saracen courts and the Arabic scholars' cultivation of a scientific body of knowledge. These borrowings allowed them to engage competently—if belatedly—with other empires and, over time, compete successfully with them.

Such a perspective dislodges the positioning of Anglo-European culture as the origin of all things modern, rational, and innovative and begs us to reconsider many of our literary genealogies. It calls for a recharting of the maps and time lines of a world-system of literatures, especially insofar as many critics, including Pascale Casanova, consider the vernacular literature and medieval courts of European princes such as William IX of Aquitaine to be points of origin for "modern" Anglo-European literatures. The Arabic backstory for these vernacular sonneteers and troubadours requires us to rethink not only these poets but also the modernists who were avowedly indebted to them and inspired by their formal innovations, from Mário de Andrade and Mina Loy to Eliot and Pound. Similarly, this long history builds a different framework for any account of secular modernities that claims to be explaining the rise of modernisms; and it might well shed additional light on the religious and secular dimensions of Turkish and Berber modernisms treated here by Nergis Ertürk and Edwige Talbayev, respectively.

Certainly these longer histories of literary influence display the ongoing competitive and mimetic coproduction of cultures within and against the force of empires. It is exactly in such histories that we find strong evidence for Hayot's suggestion that global cultural history entails a poly-directional "mimetics of desire." In fact, as Hayot hints, a similar process also characterizes the relation between Europe and Asia. This set of exchanges is likewise worth pausing over if we wish to improve our genealogies of influence.

In his multivolume study, *Asia in the Making of Europe*, Donald Lach documents the westward travels of Asian goods, arts, and ideas that helped to precipitate the cultural formations we now call modern and European, especially beginning in the later seventeenth century. A small sample includes the study of Asian painting by Leonardo Da Vinci, the practice of quarrying minerals for pottery learned from China, and the "flamboyant Gothic" architectural style known in Portugal as Manueline (for King Manuel) with its echoes of Indian detail. In *Oriental Enlightenment*, J. J. Clarke continues this project in his study of the eastern sources of early modern Western philosophy, building in part on Raymond Schwab's *Oriental Renaissance*. He begins with Voltaire's remark that "the West owes everything" to the East and works his way forward from the formative impact of Chinese philosophy on the work of Leibniz (who read and wrote extensively about Chinese philosophy, claiming it modeled a natural religion founded on reason), to the Hindu and Buddhist sources of Schopenhauer's thinking, to the influence of Buddhism on Nietzsche (quoted in Clarke 3). In this light, we might pause before deeming the appeal of Nietzsche for Balkan or Russian futurists a purely "Western" influence.

Yu Liu's recent book, *Seeds of a Different Eden* (2008), similarly reveals the extent to which key ideas of the Enlightenment developed in many cases from Anglo-European intellectuals' tutelage at the knee of Eastern culture—novelists, religious scholars, garden cultivators, diplomats, and emperors. Liu argues that the rage for "chinoiserie" in the eighteenth century is too often reduced to mere orientalism, obscuring the degree to which Western modernity is an outgrowth of Asian ideas in political ethics and the arts. Most to the point here, she follows the ways that "a new English and continental European theory of beauty and art began with the transplantation of Chinese gardening ideas" and eventually prompted groundbreaking, "modern" styles of thought in the Earl of Shaftesbury, Joseph Addison, Alexander Pope, and Immanuel Kant (1). This aesthetic included the idea of organic form, a notion that in China embraced elements of irregularity and a freer, more "natural" play among all parts. While Liu shows the shaping influence of such aesthetics on both the political thought of Shaftesbury and the georgic poetics of Pope, Thomson, and Grainger, modernist scholars will hear its later echoes in the principles of imagist poetry and modernist critics.

Such a reconfigured history of aesthetics has tremendous implications for accounts of modernity and modernism, as I discuss more fully in later sections of this essay but will anticipate briefly here. In a 1997 collection on *Tradition and Modernity in Arabic Literature*, in an essay titled "Gibran's Concept of Modernity," Antoine Karam characterizes the modernity of the transnational Arabic and English-language writer Kahlil Gibran in terms of his emphasis on organic form, tracing this "modern" style in part to his reading of English and American romantic writers. But Liu's account of the Chinese sources of an aesthetic of organic form would require us to rethink this genealogy. We might find ourselves tracing the "modernity" of Gibran to China and indeed to sources in Arabic culture itself. Likewise, attention to the Asian and Arab sources of Anglo-European cultural forms raises new questions about the critical consciousness attributed to Western modernity and considered central to the so-called Anglo-European Enlightenment, as well as to the modernisms that challenged Enlightenment narratives. As theorists from Theodor Adorno to Jürgen Habermas have explored, the "Enlightenment" public sphere is sometimes surprisingly self-critical, and its intellectual classes sometimes genuinely speak against their own, elite-supported interests. Yet, as I have noted elsewhere, the scholarship reviewed above points toward the ways in which this self-conscious public sphere emerged dialectically through interaction with Eastern and Southern empires and perhaps also emulated the dialectical habits of thought modeled in those cultures.[9]

PART II

These connected histories invite us to adjust our methods and paradigms for the study of modernisms. They establish that global literary histories, of any period in fact, require attention to three intersecting dynamics:

> 1) the contemporary dialectics of multiple empires
> 2) the interaction of these inter-imperial dialectics with anticolonial and other dissenting movements
> 3) the legacies of centuries of inter-imperial cultural accretion that inflect later literature.

In the case of modernisms, this means that we would ideally learn more about the history of empires and anticolonial dissent worldwide, especially since the nineteenth century, and we would think about how literary forms have been shaped by these contests as well as by intersecting class, gender, and religious conflicts. We would then need to do our best to understand how the still-active sediments of older inter-imperial histories exert influence within modernist formations. Doing this work, we will begin to feel the provincial nature of the idea that an originary Anglo-European modernism simply "spread" to the rest of the world, moving outward from one avant-garde, modern core to a ring of belatedly modern peripheries. We might be moved to consider how a range of modernisms occupy, inherit, and express what I will later define as an inter-imperial positionality. In this second half of the Afterword, I explore the backstory for global modernisms within this model, a model which these many essays have inspired and in turn substantiate.

Nineteenth-Century Empires, Plural

The first step in adjusting our historiographic paradigms is to dismantle a lopsided narrative that persists even in our most pointedly postcolonial scholarship and blocks our ability to see the fuller picture: the story of how, by the nineteenth century, Anglo-European empires established "unchallenged dominance" on the world stage. The erasure of contemporaneous empires in more recent centuries seriously distorts any understanding of geomodernisms, not to mention world history. It limits our ability to analyze the contemporary and accreted dialectics that have formed global modernisms.

Consider, for instance, the English-language Wikipedia entries on the nineteenth century, which, although not strictly scholarly, express a popular consensus—and do in fact reflect one dominant scholarly narrative. Following a brief mention of the "collapse" of other empires, the entry under the broad heading "The Nineteenth Century" reports that "[a]fter the Napoleonic Wars, the British Empire became the world's leading power, controlling one quarter of the world's population and one third of the land area" (1). Similarly, under the heading "British Empire," we learn that after 1815, "Britain enjoyed a century of effectively unchallenged dominance, and expanded its imperial holdings across the globe" (1). While it is certainly true that a powerful British empire expanded in the nineteenth century, it is certainly false that it was "unchallenged." Rather, Britain continually thrust itself forward and was continually pushed back in a world of several competitive empires.

A brief qualifying clause several pages into the article on British Empire allows a fleeting glimpse of this fact: "Victory over Napoleon left Britain without any serious international rival, other than Russia in central Asia." Shortly thereafter in a section on "Rivalry with Russia," the actual situation is allowed into view—directly contradicting the article's original topic sentence. We learn that "during the 19th century Britain and Russia vied to fill the power vacuums that had been left by declining Ottoman, Persian, and Qing Chinese empires" (9). Finally acknowledging the historical fact of a pitched and fairly even battle between the British and the Russians, this sentence meanwhile, with a flick of the wrist, both erases the considerable parts eventually played by Germans, Prussians, and Austro-Hungarians in this contest and veils the process whereby all of these empires, in a shifting history of alliance and rivalry, worked avidly to undercut the trade dominance of the Qing empire and to eat away at the borders of the Ottoman empire. Rather than merely filling a "vacuum" left by the inevitable decline of decadent empires, the reach of these several empires into Ottoman and Qing territories entailed nearly constant diplomatic pressure, manipulation of alliances, military conscription, and bloody battle. Then, too, the claim that "victory over Napoleon left Britain without any serious international rival" quietly implies that the British alone defeated Napoleonic France, erasing the crucial Russian defeat of the French in 1812, which decimated Napoleon's "Grand Armée" and helped to make possible the British triumph (a situation repeated in World War II).

Yet the narrative of unchallenged British dominance still shapes Anglophone literary scholars' accounts of the nineteenth century; and in turn it threatens to warp our understanding of the imperial and anti-imperial politics of geomodernisms. It also leads us to speak of "the" Anglo-European core and a circle of peripheries and semi-peripheries when in fact the nineteenth-century globe was shaped by far-flung multiple empires, multiple cores, all vying over multiple "peripheries." In such a world, the very "peripherality" of many locations was contingent, a function of shifting borders defined and redefined under successive seizures by antagonistic empires. Is Odessa a periphery? Or a nodal magnet of banking, culture, and power? It depends on which empire, and which moment in the nineteenth or twentieth century, you're reading about.

Edwige Talbayev speaks intriguingly in her essay here of "the European center and the many territories lying on its peripheries." Notably, she does not say "the European center and its peripheries," although our habits of mind might lead us to read her sentence that way. Instead the sentence quietly suggests that there is something—in fact, territories—*beyond* Europe's peripheries. Our questions about geo-modernism change when we pause to ask, what are these unspecified territories beyond European empires? Another kind of world emerges when we start to see that some of them are also empires, and, like the French and British, very powerful, aggressive empires. Taking in this fuller dynamic of world politics and economics, we encounter a different dialectical field, one differently driven by art and war, differently haunted by terror and beauty.

And the fact is that in the nineteenth century the British were still relative newcomers to the dynamics of competing empires in Asia (other than India), the Pacific, and Africa, and they feverishly pursued a place for themselves in these regions. We might recall that in the second half of the century, the British engaged in half a dozen expansionist wars in the East and the South, including the Crimean War (1853–1856), the decade-long Anglo-Maori War (1860–1872), the Second Anglo-Afghan War (1878–1880), the Zulu War (1878–1881), the First Anglo-Boer War (1881), the Third Anglo-Burmese War (1885), and the Second Anglo-Boer War (1899–1901). Add to this the deployment of troops for uprisings throughout their colonial territories—such as the Sepoy Rebellion in India (1856) and the Morant Bay Rebellion in Jamaica (1865)—and we begin to grasp the constant warring required for their position. Far from being a settled world order blessed by a Pax Britannica, the constantly shifting alliances and battles of the nineteenth century among the Russians, Turks, Chinese, French, Germans, Prussians, British, and eventually the Japanese, meant that the British and many others were in battle for as many years as they were at peace during the second half of the nineteenth century, often at multiple battle sites.

In the later nineteenth century, this heightening of inter-imperial battle and competition was propelled by a range of events, including the defeat of France in the Franco-Prussian war, the emergence of Japan, the United States, and Germany as industrializing world powers and territory seekers, and the Long Depression of 1873–1896. Marked initially by the collapse of the Vienna Stock Exchange in 1873, the Long Depression played an important catalyzing role, for it developed into a catastrophic worldwide deflation, causing starvation, unemployment, and bankruptcies in every empire. And, in turn, this Depression motivated all of the empires to seize and secure new territories for new markets and cheap labor, especially in Asia, Africa, and the Pacific. While appropriately explained by Marxist economists as fostering an incipient turn from industrial to finance capitalism, it is also important to consider the ways that the Long Depression was both precipitated by imperial agents (for instance insofar as Napoleon's war with Prussia and the Germans helped to cause it) and in turn prodded the drive for further imperial aggression as well as new imperial finance strategies. Thus, for example, both Russia and Britain opened banks in Persia in this period. And thus does capitalism develop: through a mutually catalyzing dialectic with the driving, channeling, clashing forces of competing empires.

Under these conditions, in the final decades of the nineteenth century there was a "scramble" for Asia as well as Africa—and a scramble *in* Asia, inasmuch as Russia and Japan parried with each other and several Western empires (including eventually the United States) for dominance over Chinese port areas and islands as well as independent Pacific islands. The steady pressure of these wars in Africa and Asia prompted the movement toward conscription and the increased financing of mobilization plans in Britain and Europe as well as Japan, all of which fed the bellicose, warring imaginary that Patrick Brantlinger in *Rule of Darkness* and Cecil Degrotte Eby in *Road to Armageddon* have tracked in later nineteenth-century British literature and popular culture. The Anglo-Boer Wars particularly brought new ruthless tactics into the realm of possibility and the public consciousness, including the British creation of concentration camps and the murder of civilians through the authorized burning of crops and villages. Of course these expansionist wars had arisen amidst and in dialectical relation with the accompanying class struggles of the nineteenth century (as so clearly exemplified by the Paris Commune of 1871, a working-class uprising precipitated by the Prussian and German defeat of France), and these class struggles were another problem that imperial conscription helped to "solve."

The resulting sense of world upheaval—later expressed in Yeats's reflection that "the center cannot hold"—was heightened by the fact that this imperially organized and pervasively embattled world was also becoming more visible to citizens and subalterns. The nineteenth century saw massive investments in infrastructure, including in railroads, canals, shipways, radio, photography, and telegraph cables, all of which dramatically expanded the movement of news and information as well as of goods and armies. Readers on one side of the world learned with startling speed about war, disaster, and destruction on the other side. Nor did one need to be literate to share in this new global order: by the later nineteenth century, the battlefronts of such conflicts as the Crimean War were photographed and thereby made newly visible to civilian eyes. Anyone who saw or read the newspapers would have had a sense of world turbulence, of violent invasions, rebellions, and reprisals. Although in the twenty-first century we are jaded by these daily reports of violence and insurgence, the first decades of exposure to this reality seems one likely source of a new and anxious world consciousness.

Yet these new forms of simultaneity were double-edged swords, for the same technologies of communication and travel that served empire eventually also enabled international awareness, organizing, and protest. Virginia Woolf observed in 1927 that each person in London was "linked to his fellows by wires which pass overhead, by waves of sound which pour through the roof and speak aloud to him of battles and murders and strikes and revolutions all over the world" ("Narrow Bridge of Art" 222). Meanwhile, from a radically different position, Frantz Fanon noted, "In spite of all that colonialism can do, its frontiers remain open to new ideas and echoes from the world outside. It discovers that violence is in the atmosphere, that it here and there bursts out, and here and there sweeps away the colonial regime" (*Wretched* 70). Recently scholars such as Priyamvada Gopal and Elleke Boehmer have documented the ways that independence movements in Ireland, Africa, India, and the West Indies formed coalitions, read each other's newspapers, and gained knowledge and inspiration from each other. These lines of communication made possible the political networks leading to communist international congresses and the pan-national or pan-ethnic congresses, such as the series of Pan-African Congresses held in Europe between 1919 and 1945. In part prompted by these subaltern groups (rather than, as is often assumed, the other way around), Anglo-European ex-colonial administrators, such as Virginia Woolf's husband Leonard Woolf, began to write critiques of what Woolf called economic imperialism, and writers such as Mark Twain helped to found the U.S. Anti-Imperialist League, in part to protest the annexation of the Philippines. At the turn into the twentieth century, the movements of and against empire became increasingly active, visible, and globally interconnected.

Inter-Imperial Geomodernisms

Modernists created art oriented toward this global world. Or, perhaps more accurately, this world forced modernist art into being. As established so powerfully in this volume, avant-garde literary and artistic movements, which mingled closely or loosely with political movements of all stripes, arose around the world. In his brief "Note on Modernism" in *Culture and Imperialism*, Edward Said observes that modernist styles arose "as more and more regions—from India to Africa to the Caribbean—challenge[d] the classical empires and their cultures" (190). Said speaks of multiple empires and in doing so points the way toward an inter-imperial framework for the study of global modernisms.

Seen in these terms, the nonsynchronous time lines of different modernisms (which after all, from the perspective of the twenty-first century, do not appear so very different) can be explained not only as the uneven histories of centers and semi/peripheries but also as the plain old different histories of multiple empires, and of the different social, economic, and linguistic hierarchies created within each empire. Such hierarchies have meant that, within all empires, some writers and artists have had access to the means of production first—the wealth, education, and print or paint—that allowed them to express this situation in fractured, hybrid, or innovative forms before many others. Yet the anxious vision of a fractured "modernist" world, with its discrepant time lines and perspectives, was always already "known" among the dispossessed and simply awaited the emergence among them of artists with access to print or other media. In fact, instead of considering early canonical Anglo-European and Anglo-American modernists the world pioneers, it might be fair to say that they grasped the world situation belatedly at the turn of the century—as compared to the long-standing knowledge of the many thousands living in colonial territories or repeatedly invaded and disenfranchised communities.

It is this broader history that, to my mind, the neologism *geomodernism* helps to foreground. Even adding "global" as a modifier of "modernism" can leave intact the habit of thinking in national or isolated terms and fail to highlight these modernisms' foundational interdependence. In contrast, geomodernism helpfully indicates several key dimensions in one noun: the geopolitical history to which all modernisms respond, the transperipheral and international exchanges within which they take shape, and the long global history that has prepared their emergence. The term geomodernisms would thus encompass literatures arising in multiple sites under the diverse, interacting conditions of multiple empires and multiple resistance movements since the later nineteenth century, conditions which are intensified by new technologies of finance, travel, communication, labor, and war. In this definition, the phenomenon of geomodernist literature is historically specific yet its forms are internationally and culturally diverse, as they disrupt national and cultural literary histories in ways befitting their location.

The essays here contain material that helps to flesh out this picture of geomodernisms, particularly of the simultaneously inter-imperial and anticolonial contests that have generated them. These essays also give us hints of the much older materials sedimented within this literature. Culling examples from the essays, this section of the essay focuses on the ways that *geomodernisms labor in the volatile space between or among contemporaneous empires*; and the final section will consider the ways that *geomodernisms carry the intercultural accretions of empires past*.

To aid this discussion I use the term "inter-imperial positionality," a variation of Bahun's helpful notion, introduced in her essay here, of "artistic interpositionality." I suggest that, insofar as geomodernisms arise within a competition among contemporaneous empires—which create a deeply and materially felt if not absolutely determining condition of their production and coproduction—they may be said to navigate an "inter-imperial positionality." That is, the term inter-imperial positionality serves to name the multi-sided, high-stakes political pressure under which writers and artists, and to some degree all of us, operate. Although an inter-imperial positionality has very likely shaped texts for millennia, I would argue that geomodernists operate more self-consciously from this position: due, first of all, to the new global forms of rapid communication, finance, and travel; and secondly to the high numbers of uprooted persons created by the escalating invasions, wars, anticolonial resistance, and pogroms of the late nineteenth and twentieth centuries. Under these conditions, with a heightened, more pervasive sense of embattled interpositionality, each geomodernist text and aesthetic movement maneuvers between "its own" empire, so to speak, and other people's. Or at least, this is the provisional model I am proposing, as suggested to me by these essays read together with the histories of empire and culture outlined above. My suggestions are meant to be illustrative, exploratory, and speculative, simply to stimulate further discussion.

This inter-imperial, positional consciousness may shape the work of artists as different as Italian futurists and Chinese filmmakers, yet it is perhaps easiest in this context to begin by revisiting familiar Western postcolonial scenarios. Thus we might consider the Cuban geomodernists discussed here by Unruh and Aching, who expressed their resistance to Spanish empire under the shadow of a U.S. empire standing in the wings—the latter offering to help in Cuban liberation but simultaneously jockeying for an imperial foothold of their own (the oldest trick in the inter-imperial playbook). This position of Cuban writers heightened the stakes, multiplied the political divisions, and perhaps generated the dodgy, multi-tonal, and purposefully elusive avant-garde forms described by Unruh in her opening pages.

In the Caribbean more broadly, artists, writers, and thinkers may have had an especially heightened sense of inter-imperial positionality because of the concentrated, deadly competition in those islands among the French, British, Spanish, and U.S. empires. It may in part be this volatile history that turned postcolonial Caribbean writers, from Glissant to Harris, toward what Mary Lou Emery characterizes as their planetary vision. Meanwhile, this kind of intensive inter-imperiality (and we could think of the Balkans as well) might also be operative in the situation in Vietnam, described here by Ben Tran, so that we might ask how the comparable pressures created in the Pacific world by the presence of Russian, Japanese, French, and U.S. empires intensified Vietnamese geomodernists' conflicting allegiances to sexual and Marxist politics and their polemical debates about literary form.

Xudong Zhang perhaps reveals a similar, more implicit negotiation in his essay here on Lu Xun, the celebrated writer of modern Chinese vernacular. In Zhang's reading, Lu Xun crafted his fiction simultaneously *against* ancient, imperial Chinese linguistic forms *and in* those forms exactly against Western cultural and economic incursions. Would it be fair to say that in *Ah Q—The Real Story*, Lu Xun develops a sort of imperially Janus-faced and parodic fiction, looking not only inward and outward but also toward encroaching empires East and West? Might it be that the picaresque travels of Lu Xun's rogue-protagonist, Ah Q (who Zhang reads as a "rogue signifier") allegorize the rogue's travel within and between empires on a once-secure, yet now-unraveling *silk* road? Could this framework supplement explanations for why this tale lent itself to adoption as national identity myth even as it parodies myths of identity, as Zhang observes?

Might we also ask whether the African *tsotsi* figure reborn in South African cinema, discussed here by Rosalind Morris, could be understood comparably: as a figure making a spectacle of the need to maneuver one's way through this inter-imperial positionality. In this case, might we say that the trickster/gangster figure of the *tsotsi* operates in the alleyways of empires, so to speak, including as created by the competitive interactions of long-standing African states, European empires, and an emerging U.S. presence, and eventually amid post-apartheid ANC aspirations to be a player on the world stage. In such a reading, the *tsotsi* seeks to extract profit from all of these players in the "great game" while also eluding them all, by way of a highly styled, empire-counterpointing, ultra-masculine outsiderness.

The experience of Jews at the turn of the century, as recalled here by Shachar Pinsker, diverges significantly from postcolonial models of literary negotiation with empire(s); and yet, given the many "ethnic-cleansing" projects that have emerged in the last century, it might offer a second, equally paradigmatic variation on the condition of inter-imperial positionality. As Pinkser details, especially during and after the 1880s, the Jews of the Russian Empire fled pogroms or simply sought to settle outside the shtetels, migrating west to central Europe, where they gathered in cafés to reimagine Yiddish and Hebrew literary forms. Yet they also encountered hostility or exclusion in these places, including, for instance, the cities of the Austro-Hungarian Empire, whose "acceptance" of immigrating Jews sometimes irritated locals even as it also sometimes served Austro-Hungary's own imperial interests in its competition with Russia and Western Europeans.

The very space of the café—what Pinsker, following Edward Soja, analyzes as a "thirdspace"—may be understood as one that enabled a creative, collective response to this volatile interpositionality, all of which in turn shaped the styles and tones, as Pinsker's material hints, of their portraits of café life. (In this light, one could wonder if the Ottoman tradition of the coffeehouse, borrowed by AngloEuropeans, had earlier arisen exactly as a "thirdspace" in the Ottomans' highly multicultural populations.) Likewise, the streets cruised by the *tsotsi* may qualify as such a thirdspace within empires. And perhaps, too, the operations of little modernist magazines could be understood to "cruise" and constitute this interpositionality, sometimes shaping it to articulate transnational and cross-racial visions of Western imperial renewal (as in the case of Waldo Frank, Victoria Ocampo, and Ortega, as analyzed by Gayle Rogers), and in other cases structuring it to realize a non-imperial global vision (e.g., in the transnational dialogue fostered by the "Letters to the Editor" column of *Transition*, as studied here by Eric Bulson).

We may see other indicators of the sense of uncertain inter-imperial positionality in Ertürk's observation that in the early twentieth century, from Turkish writers' point of view "both 'Turkey' and 'Europe' [were] sites of cultural crisis." (Evidence of the European sense of crisis is amply attested to by the immediate and wide interest in Oswald Spengler's *The Decline of the West*, mentioned by Gayle Rogers here.) Ertürk argues that for some Western and for many "conservative" Turkish writers, modernism "was less a positive historic-aesthetic current than a space or even an abyss of socio-historic uncertainty." We might need to pay another kind of attention to this sensibility in Turkish writers' texts when we recall that it was not only Western Europe that "steadily encircled and encroached on [the Ottoman Empire]" at the turn into the twentieth century. Russia continued to do so as well. And Anglo-Europeans encroached on the Ottomans both with and against the Russians.

Might this multisided dynamic make some difference to how we think about Turkish poets, including their engagement with an instrumental modernity—which could be considered Russian and Ottoman as well as Anglo-European? Might the same be said of the Scandinavian modernisms described here by Anna Westerståhl Stenport, for certainly the Scandinavian countries also occupied a troubled position among the "Great Powers" of Germany, Russia, Britain, France, and Austria-Hungary (and here too we might recall that Georg Brandes, a key promoter of Scandinavian modernism, traveled to and wrote about modern Russia as well as about modern Western Europe).

Alluding to Casanova's model, Harsha Ram tells us that the futurists "displayed a hypertrophied awareness of the competitive and hierarchical nature of the international literary system." It may be that the futurists' contradictory and vehemently masculinist manifestos are the hyperbolic expression of a *pervasive* anxiety about the pressures, dangers, and inescapability of inter-imperial positionality. Since we know that two world wars killing tens of millions did indeed erupt, it seems quite possible that, at the turn of the century, Jews, Pan-African Blacks, Turks, Cubans, Scandinavians, and Vietnamese all felt themselves at the edge of a geopolitical abyss. We might recognize this awareness as a broad psychosocial condition, affecting the intertwined worlds of literature and politics. It might be closely linked with what Sartre deemed the "nervous condition" of the colonized and which I have elsewhere analyzed as a nervous post/coloniality felt in different ways by both colonized and colonizer.[10] Thus we might wonder if Nietzsche, whose writings inspired many futurists, might himself have been writing under the pressure of this inter-imperial nervousness and *ressentiment*, as suggested for instance in his correspondence with Georg Brandes, in which the two share their chagrin at the censorship or dismissal of their books in both the German and Russian empires (Brandes 95). Futurism in turn might emerge simply as the most extreme expression of a widespread, panicked urgency about the question of which new or old empires would triumph in a world of unstable alliances and encroaching battles on every side, the awareness of which was quickly globalized, as Marinetti remarked, by techno-modernity's "wireless imagination" (quoted in Ram).

Whether or not this reading of futurism is persuasive, Casanova's and Ram's observations about the hyperawareness of a literary global competition can encourage us to notice how inter-imperial contests have shaped these and have led to a set of erasures in the literary realm parallel to what has occurred in the historical realm (affecting, unfortunately, Casanova's own Franco-centric account). As Bahun observes, French avant-gardists, for instance, initially acknowledged influence by and collaborations with Balkan modernists but in the end wrote these connections out of their biographies and lectures. Similarly, Anglophone critics have until recently ignored the formative connections between Hispanophone and Anglophone geomodernists. Fortunately, the essays in this volume contribute to recent scholarship that writes these connections back in.

Yet at the same time, the valuable vocabulary of core, periphery, and semiperiphery used by both Casanova and Ram may need adjusting insofar as it can elide the fact of plural empires. We need a global historical paradigm that does justice to the vying empires' that have generated *multiple*, contemporaneous cores with their several peripheries and semi-peripheries—and have in turn shaped the competitions and connections among geomodernists. On one hand, Ram troubles Casanova's claim that the French core of the literary world-system exercised a "complete dominance" that went "unchallenged" (Casanova 72, 67) by revealing a Russian effort to challenge that dominance. Yet on the other hand, he retains the model of a unicentric, Western European core, casting Russia and

Italy as "two key semi-peripheral states of Europe" and suggesting that early twentieth-century Russian writers struggled against this position when they "suddenly claimed . . . core-status." In fact, the Russian empire *had* core-status, a fact better appreciated then than now. In the later nineteenth and early twentieth century, political commentators therefore spoke of the "great game" of competition between Anglo-European and Russian empires. This history may well explain why, as Ram points out, "the Russian futurists went considerably further than their Italian counterparts in undermining the principles that gave the European literary center its authority." That is, instead of laboring from behind to "seize the monopoly over literariness itself," Russian writers were laboring to *maintain* what they and others considered their noble place among the several world traditions, each of which willfully claimed a monopoly over literariness itself. The monopoly is to some degree in the eyes of the beholder, and while well-known writers in each empire might have strongly cross-identified with the language of another empire, particularly Parisian French, they sometimes did so from a strong sense of their own long-standing imperial claim to literariness.

In this adjusted account of the dynamics of international literary competition, we might then detect the notes of competition inflecting British translations of Russian literature, treated here by Rebecca Beasley. The fact that this engagement with Russian literature was played out in relation to French literature, as Beasley notes, suggests that it displays one dimension of Britain's own interpositionality in a world of multiple empires and its awareness of France and Russia as geo-imperial as well as literary rivals. In turn, we might focus more on the fact that some of the Russian literature celebrated and translated in this period, such as Tolstoy's fiction, centered on the very wars that variously pitted Russian and several Western European empires against each other, such as in the Crimean War and the Napoleonic Wars. Perhaps British writers were drawn to Russian literature in part for this reason. And lest such literary competition seem trivial next to these military contests, we might recall the importance of literature in empires' colonizing projects, as documented so well by Gauri Viswanathan in the case of India, and indicated long before by John Milton's expressed admiration for the literary disseminations of the Ottomans. It mattered to Britain *as an empire* (as it did to France, Germany, Russia, China, Japan, Brazil, and the United States) that its literature be recognized on the world stage. In this context, British writers' simultaneous praise and criticism of Russian literature strategically placed the British reader in the position of global judge, occupying a preeminent position from which to mark the limits as well as the powers of Russian *empire*.

In referring to the "geo-cognitive liminality" of the Balkans, Bahun draws our attention to an important symptom of this inter-imperial condition—one that has affected our literary histories. Bahun highlights the puzzling *liminality* of a territory as *central* to world history as the Balkans, and in doing so she points toward a new theorization of such so-called semi-peripheries, helping us to see that they are actually the *in-between* zones of world empires. Always off to the side, at the edge of the visible, a region such as the Balkans occupies the effaced ur-ground of empires, the place of their disavowed adjacency to and vulnerable engagement with each other, the site where they are most invested and most defended—and, as we can see in retrospect, most blind. In this sense the geo-cognitive liminality of battles and battlegrounds between empires (such as those between Russia and Britain on the terrain of the Balkans) constitutes a condition of empire, a key instrumental turn of mind rather than a marginal phenomenon. We might consider it analogous to the cognitive liminality of women in men's consciousness, as analyzed by feminists: in this analysis women are the unseen figures on which the world depends for reproductive and productive power and over whom it battles for control. Such an erasure may likewise be paradigmatic in the realm of imperial politics—a geo-existential maneuver in the "psyches" of empires. Projecting a vision of benevolent and global "unchallenged dominance," an empire erases key sources of its power, including those resource-rich zones seized through violence; and it meanwhile minimizes the creative, potentially competing presence of laboring others who live in that zone or liminal position. Literary critics risk repeating these distortions when we focus solely on Anglo-European empires.

Inter-Imperial Palimpsest

These erasures of non-Western cores and empires operate temporally as well as spatially, affecting our accounts of who borrows what from whom. Thus we come to a second methodological task: to notice how *geomodernisms labor to manage the deep historical accretions of criss-crossing empires.* Attention to inter-imperial global history can open our eyes to the literary influences that have indirectly, over generations, shaped geomodernisms and to later strategic elisions or recuperations of these influences. In light of the revised southeast-to-northwest movements of thought and aesthetics I outlined earlier, the essays here raise a rich range of new questions, a few of which I will explore in this last section. Even more so than those raised in the previous section, these questions are guesses-at-questions from someone whose main expertise is Anglophone literatures. Again, the aim is to generate further discussion.

When the Turkish novelist Recâizâde Mahmut Ekrem writes in a mixture of Ottoman Turkish and French in his novel's fictitious (mis)translations of French Romantic and Ottoman court poetry, as detailed here by Ertürk, might he also be referencing the layers of contact-zone past by which Islamic/Ottoman literature and culture influenced French literary forms? Might he even have in mind the influence of Arabic and Mediterranean-world poetries on the metrics and themes of both French Romantic and modernist poets, via troubadour poetry? Instead of merely borrowing French forms and innovations, is it possible that Ekrem is intuiting, or even signaling, the dialectical co-formations of Islamic and French linguistic and literary traditions—and of the interacting empires within which they were written? Likewise, when the Turkish modernist poet Yahya Kemal speaks of his "homecoming" to the Turkish through the "Frank," could he possibly be gesturing toward an actual history of Ottoman-to-French influence as much as he is enacting a contemporary French-to-Turkish influence? In these cases and others, what blind spots might be removed when we attend to the Arabic or Ottoman sources of Anglo-European styles of thought from the medieval period forward, as documented by Metlitzki, Makdisi, Menocal, Monroe, Matar, and others?

Similar questions emerge from Talbayev's analysis of the Berber poet, Jean El Mouhoub Amrouche and Neil Lazarus's discussion of the Syrian poet Adonis. Like the Balkans, the Maghreb region of north Africa was for many centuries a strategic and contested zone whose Berber populations underwent "successive experiences of colonization," as Talbayev notes, from at least the Roman Empire through the seventh century Arab conquest, to waves of Christian European conquest all the way to eighteenth- to twentieth-century occupations by the French and British in competition with each other. (In reviewing this history, Talbayev reminds us that St. Augustine was a Berber from what is now Algeria but which was then part of the Roman Empire.) Writing in a period of French colonialism, and given a classical education in French schools, Amrouche became deeply interested in the poetry of Mallarmé. Talbayev analyzes the ways in which he appropriates Mallarmé's theories of pure poetic form for his celebration of traditional oral Berber poetry. In light of the long history of cultural interaction and of critics' analysis of the influence of Hispano-Arabic metrical forms and themes on the tradition of French poetry, is it possible to revisit Amrouche's counterpointed interweaving of French and Berber poetic principles? If Amrouche is aiming to establish, as Talbayev suggests, the coeval formation of poetic forms, could he implicitly or unconsciously be registering this old history of European-Arabic-African inter-animation? Likewise, in light of that same influence of Arabic forms of poetry on French lyric poetry, how might we reframe the poet Adonis's remarks, as quoted by Lazaraus, that he came to appreciate the "modernity in Arabic poetry" by reading it in relation to Baudelaire, Mallarmé, and Rimbaud?

Or, from a different angle, when we take stock of the old and new migrations affecting literature, might we recast our descriptions of the influence of "Western" thinkers on non-Western geomodernisms? What difference does it make when we recall that Henri Bergson—whose philosophy of time had so much influence on the Turkish and Berber authors discussed by Ertürk and Talbayev—was the son of a Polish-Jewish father and an Irish-British Jewish mother, and was given a Jewish education? What gets lost when we subsume Bergson's empire-weighted, multicultural lineage within characterizations of him as simply a "Western" thinker? In a similar vein, as noted earlier, given that the philosophies of will developed by Schopenhauer and Nietzsche were foundationally influenced by Buddhism, do we want to continue to characterize their influence on Russian or Georgian modernists as strictly Western?

And might some of the "pioneering" "Western" modernists be sensing—and sometimes censoring—these same inter-imperial "interanimations"?[11] Gayle Rogers's essay here suggests that Waldo Frank, Victoria Ocampo, and Jose Ortega y Gasset were among those attempting to reestablish these inter-animations (albeit with mixed intentions), insofar as they champion Spain and ultimately "America Hispana" as the most fertile ground for a solution to the crisis of the West. Frank, for instance, calls for recognition of Spain and the Americas as the sites of a "Symphonic history" in which "Berber Phoenician, Arabic, Jewish, Moorish elements . . . [have mixed] with Germanic and . . . Celtic strains" (Rogers). Meanwhile other writers, faced with the crisis of "the West" and apparently harboring a deeper discomfort with these old inter-imperial formations, revert to an aggressive redrawing of boundaries and hierarchies. The dream of ethnic purity that often accompanied futurist visions, and the political triumph of which, in the form of fascism, eventually wiped out the relatively benign visions cultivated by Ocampo and Frank, may reflect a desire to leave behind all of the crossings sedimented within a long history of conquering and cultural fusion in which Westerners were latecomers and imitators.

Conclusion

The fraught global interconnectedness among geomodernists and across empires reflects a condition that is both deeply ancient and strikingly contemporary, an old dialectic which, however, was dramatically intensified in the early twentieth century. Perhaps this history is part of what Richard Wright sought to capture in his photographs of Gold-Coast Africa, which self-consciously convey what Sara Blair here deems a "generative uncertainty." Especially in his photograph of an Ashanti chief, Wright seems to give visual expression to the impacted history in which an old African modernity inhabits a (de)colonized, contemporary kingship and unbalances Wright's American (anticolonial yet imperial) gaze. This seemingly paradoxical combination after all only continues a history of "uncertain" inter-imperial acts of critical translation. And like Wright, the twenty-seven critics in this collection perform their own precarious acts of interpretation and translation, amid a past and a present of global empires.

Literature's enmeshment in these conditions is not an embarrassment, a diminishment, or an oppression, merely. Insofar as an inter-imperial order of things is ancient, this political dimension is an aspect of literature's (and all art's) ancientness. Indeed the history of contesting and interacting empires seems to have been an intertextual source for literature for thousands of years. To say so is not to naturalize empires but to install them as foundational, in life and in literature.[12] The disjunctures among empires and the violence within them have perhaps precipitated that fragile cosmopolitanism or planetary consciousness that seeks to reach across them, even as empires' battles and ideologies have also spawned a whole array of masculinist or strident cosmopolitanisms. Geomodernists of all stripes thus join generations of writers who have sometimes unwittingly taken up an ancient legacy of embedded imperialisms and counter-imperialisms in an effort to expose, transcend, or leverage the condition of inter-imperial positionality. Ultimately it is this dialectical world history, political and aesthetic at once, that these twenty-seven Escher-esque vignettes of geomodernism beckon us to investigate.

NOTES

1. Laura Winkiel and I introduced the term "geomodernisms" in our collection with that title in order to highlight the geopolitical and global orientation of many modernisms. Later in this chapter I further stipulate my usage of this term (see pp. 27–28).

2. See Doyle, "Notes Toward a Dialectical Method" and also other essays in the Global Circulation Project (GCP) of the online journal *Literature Compass*. This important project promises to have a dramatic impact on international conversations about literary genealogies around the world and in different periods.

3. Escobar and Mignolo are members of a working intellectual group on colonialism, and they each use the compound phrase "modernity/coloniality" in separate publications. The phrase aims to distill the insights of postcolonial thinkers by highlighting that, as Mignolo points out, "There is no modernity without coloniality, because coloniality is constitutive of modernity" (Mignolo xiii; also see Escobar 21).

4. For further discussion of this point, see Doyle, "Geomodernism, Postcoloniality, and Women's Modernism." The historiography I have in mind includes work ranging from early studies by C. L. R James and Herbert Aptheker to more recent scholarship such as Mukherjee, Blackburn, Linebaugh and Rediker, and Viola. Viola may well lead to reconsiderations of the fact that the Soviet Union inherited an empire, complete with unrest in its peripheries; and it operated, under the banner of communism, in ways barely distinguishable from imperialism—at least from a peasant's point of view.

5. Of course, whenever one looks more closely, one sees that even these "origins" have traveled from and been transformed through other sites. This account of uncanny returns draws from a larger book project.

6. On the debates over what is sometimes called the "arabist theory," see Boase on the courtly love tradition, Monroe particularly on Spain, and, more recently, Amer on French medieval literature.

7. In addition to Metlitzki, see Burnett. For discussion of later periods, see Toomer, Russell, Matar, and MacLean.

8. Davis tracks the widespread inscription of an epochal division between feudal and modern, recently perpetuated (as she shows) by thinkers as different as J. G. A. Pocock and Antonio Negri. The division between feudal and modern ramifies into corollary divisions between secular and sacred, democracy and hierarchy, innovative and traditional—all of which come to serve oppositions between west and east, or between Anglo-European and Arab, Persian, or Asian. In light of Metlitzki's and Menocal's scholarship, it becomes clear that this feudal/modern division thus also enabled the elision of a foundational, catalyzing role for Arab-Islamic culture in the West's intellectual, artistic, and political "progress."

9. See my discussion of this point in "Notes Toward a Dialectical Method." These influences would include, first of all, the borrowing of specific practices including everything from diplomatic embassies and resident status laws that stabilized matters of identity and difference within the empire, to the organic understandings of ethics in the political world tracked by Liu and Clarke, to the coffeehouses of the Ottoman world where such matters were debated among "the people" and which were copied in England (a source for English coffeehouse culture only glancingly noted by Habermas in his discussion of them [32–43]). Second, there is the likelihood, as many writers notice in passing, that the self-conscious and critical nature of the public sphere arose in part from Anglo-Europeans' increasingly common encounters with the people and arts of very different, highly "advanced" or "modern" cultures, which were sometimes perceived as imperial and

religious superiors. Several contributions to this volume make clear that this effect operated as a catalyst for ostensibly "Western" modernism even as it had done for "Western" modernity, a point I will return to later. And third, the energy of critique may also have arisen in the face of the violent resistance and the insistent questions of the colonized. That is, we might ask when and how this public sphere is an expression of the metropole's own "nervous condition," both its decentered relation to home and its effort to address or evade the pressure of anticolonial sentiment and rebellion. Again in this case, several essays here establish this element as a catalyst for modernism as for modernity.

10. For fuller discussion of "post/coloniality" and the nervous condition, see Doyle, "Geomodernism, Postcoloniality, and Women's Writing."

11. It is perhaps not coincidental that the concept of literary inter-animation was developed by the Russian scholar Mikhail Bakhtin (*The Dialogic Imagination*).

12. It might be fair to say that empires have been the most potent defining force in our relation to what Agamben calls "bare life" in that empires have long deemed themselves the "sovereign" mediators of one's relation to survival and the "right" to life. Agamben's analysis focuses on the sovereignty of law and the (de)racinating modern state, but attention to empires, especially their plural co-formations, brings into view the volatility and contingency of this claim to sovereignty, including the fact of all subjects' actual or potential inter-imperial positionality.

WORKS CITED

Agamben, Giorgio. *Homo Sacer: Sovereign Power and Bare Life*. Trans. Daniel Heller-Roazen. Stanford: Stanford University Press, 1998.

Amer, Sahar. *Crossing Borders: Love Between Women in Medieval French and Arabic Literature*. Philadelpia: University of Pennsylvania Press, 2008.

Blackburn, Robin. *The Overthrow of Colonial Slavery, 1776–848*. New York: Verso, 1988.

Boase, Roger. *The Origin and Meaning of Courtly Love: A Critical Study of European Scholarship*. Totowa: Rowman, 1977.

Boehmer, Elleke. *Empire, the National, and the Postcolonial, 1890–1920: Resistance in Interaction*. Oxford: Oxford University Press, 2002.

Boullata, Issa J., and Terri DeYoung. *Tradition and Modernity in Arabic Literature*. Fayetteville: University of Arkansas Press, 1997.

Brandes, Georg. *Friedrich Nietzsche*. New York: Macmillan, 1909.

Brantlinger, Patrick. *Rule of Darkness: British Literature and Imperialism 1830–1914*. Ithaca: Cornell University Press, 1988.

Brooker, Peter, and Andrew Thacker, eds. *Geographies of Modernism: Literatures, Cultures, Spaces*. New York: Routledge, 2005.

Burnett, Charles. *The Introduction of Arabic Learning into England*. London: British Library, 1977.

Casanova, Pascale. *The World Republic of Letters*. Trans. M. B. DeBevoise. Cambridge: Harvard University Press, 2004.

Castro, Américo. *The Structure of Spanish History*. Trans. Edmund L. King. Princeton: Princeton University Press, 1954.

Clarke, J. J. *Oriental Enlightenment: The Encounter Between Asian and Western Thought*. New York: Routledge, 1997.

Davis, Kathleen. *Periodization and Sovereignty: How Ideas of Feudalism and Secularization Govern the Politics of Time.* Philadelphia: University of Pennsylvania Press, 2008.

Doyle, Laura. "Geomodernism, Postcoloniality, and Women's Writing." *Cambridge Companion to Women's Modernism.* Ed. Maren Linett. Cambridge: Cambridge University Press, 2010. 129–45.

———. "Notes Toward a Dialectical Method: Modernities, Modernisms, and the Crossings of Empire," *Literature Compass* 7.3 (2010): 195–213. Global Circulation Project.

Doyle, Laura, and Laura Winkiel, eds. *Geomodernisms: Race, Modernism, Modernity.* Bloomington: Indiana University Press, 2004.

Eby, C. D. *Road to Armageddon: The Martial Spirit in English Popular Literature, 1870–1914.* Durham: Duke University Press, 1987.

Escobar, Arturo. "Worlds and Knowledges Otherwise: The Latin American Modernity/ Coloniality Research Program." *Cultural Studies* 21.2 (2007): 179–210.

Fanon, Frantz. *The Wretched of the Earth.* Trans. Constance Farrington. New York: Grove Press, 1963.

Goffman, Daniel. "Negotiating with the Renaissance State: The Ottoman Empire and the New Diplomacy." *The Early Modern Ottomans: Remapping the Empire.* Ed. Virginia Aksan and Daniel Goffman. Cambridge: Cambridge University Press, 2007. 61–74.

Gopal, Priyamvada. *Literary Radicalism in India: Gender, Nation, and the Transition to Independence.* New York: Routledge, 2005.

Habermas, Jürgen. *The Structural transformation of the Public Sphere: An Inquiry into a Category of Bourgeois Society.* 1962. Trans. Thomas Burger. Cambridge: MIT Press, 1989.

Karam, Antoine. "Gibran's Concept of Modernity." *Tradition and Modernity in Arabic Literature.* Ed. Issa J. Boullata, and Terri DeYoung. Fayetteville: University of Arkansas Press, 1997. 29–42.

Lach, Donald F. *Asia in the Making of Europe.* 3 Vols. Chicago: University of Chicago Press, 1965.

Linebaugh, Peter, and Marcus Rediker. *The Many-Headed Hydra: Sailors, Slaves, Commoners, and the Hidden History of the Revolutionary Atlantic.* Boston: Beacon Press, 2000.

Liu, Yu. *Seeds of a Different Eden: Chinese Gardening and a New English Aesthetic Ideal.* Columbia: University of South Carolina Press, 2008.

MacLean, Gerald. *Looking East: English Writing and the Ottoman Empire Before 1800.* New York: Palgrave, 2007.

———, ed. *Re-Orienting the Renaissance: Cultural Exchanges with the East.* New York: Palgrave, 2005.

———. *The Rise of Oriental Travel: English Visitors to the Ottoman Empire, 1580–1720.* New York: Palgrave, 2004.

Makdisi, George. *The Rise of Humanism in Classical Islam and the West.* Edinburgh: Edinburgh University Press, 1990.

———. "Inquiry into the Origins of Humanism." *Humanism, Language, and Culture in the Near East.* Ed. Asma Afsaruddin and A. H. Mathias Zahniser. Winona Lake: Eisenbrauns, 1997. 15–26.

Matar, Nabil. *Islam in Britain, 1558–1685.* Cambridge: Cambridge University Press, 1998.

Menocal, Maria Rosa. *The Arabic Role in Medieval Literary History.* Philadelphia: University of Pennsylvania Press, 1987.

Metlitzki, Dorothee. *The Matter of Araby in Medieval England.* New Haven: Yale University Press, 1977.

Mignolo, Walter. *The Idea of Latin America*. Malden: Blackwell Publishers, 2005.

Monroe, James T. *Islam and the Arabs in Spanish Scholarship (Sixteenth Century to the Present)*. Leiden: E. J. Brill, 1970.

Mukherjee, Rudrangshu. *Awadh in Revolt, 1857–1858: A Study of Popular Resistance*. 1984. London: Anthem Books, 2002.

Nykl, A. R. *Hispano-Arabic Poetry and Its Relations with the Old Provencal Troubadours*. 1946. Baltimore: J. H. Furst, 1970.

Russell, G. A., ed. *The "Arabick" Interest of the Natural Philosophers in Seventeenth-Century England*. New York: E. J. Brill, 1994.

Said, Edward. *Beginnings: Intention and Method*. New York: Basic Books, 1975.

——. *Culture and Imperialism*. New York: Vintage, 1994.

Schwab, Raymond. *The Oriental Renaissance: Europe's Rediscovery of India and the East, 1680–1880*. Trans. Gene Patterson-Black and Victor Reinking. New York: Columbia University Press, 1984.

Subrahmanyam, Sanjay. *Explorations in Connected History: Mughals and Franks*. New York: Oxford University Press, 2005.

Toomer, G. J. *Eastern Wisdom and Learning: The Study of Arabic in Seventeenth-Century England*. Oxford: Clarendon Press, 1996.

Viola, Lynne. *Peasant Rebels Under Stalin: Collectivization and the Culture of Peasant Resistance*. New York: Oxford University Press, 1996.

Viswanathan, Gauri. *Masks of Conquest: Literary Study and British Rule in India*. New York: Columbia University Press, 1989.

Wikipedia. "British Empire": http://en.wikipedia.org/wiki/British_Empire. 15 April 2010.

Wikipedia. "The Nineteenth Century": http://en.wikipedia.org/wiki/19th_century. 15 April 2010.

Woolf, Virginia. "The Narrow Bridge of Art." *Collected Essays*. Vol. 2. New York: Harcourt,1967. 218–29.

Notes on Contributors

GERARD ACHING is Professor of Spanish in the Department of Romance Studies at Cornell University. He is the author of *The Politics of Spanish American Modernismo: By Exquisite Design* (1997), *Masking and Power: Carnival and Popular Culture in the Caribbean* (2003), and is completing *Freedom From Liberation*, a book manuscript on slavery, literary sensibility, and the politics of abolitionist discourse in and about Cuba.

SANJA BAHUN is Assistant Professor of Literature and Film at the University of Essex. She is author of *Modernism and Melancholia: Writing as Countermourning* (forthcoming), and joint editor of *The Avant-Garde and the Margin: New Territories of Modernism* (2006), *Violence and Gender in the Globalized World: The Intimate and the Extimate* (2008), *From Word to Canvas* (2009), and *Myth and Violence in the Contemporary Female Text* (2011).

REBECCA BEASLEY is University Lecturer in the Faculty of English at the University of Oxford and a Tutorial Fellow of The Queen's College. She is author of *Ezra Pound and the Visual Culture of Modernism* (2007) and *Theorists of Modernist Poetry: Ezra Pound, T. S. Eliot and T. E. Hulme* (2007), and editor, with Philip Ross Bullock, of the essay collection *Russia in Britain* (Oxford University Press 2012). She is currently working on a study of the impact of Russian culture on British modernism.

JESSICA BERMAN is Associate Professor and Chair of English at the University of Maryland, Baltimore County. She is the author of *Modernist Fiction, Cosmopolitanism, and the Politics of Community* (2001) and *Modernist Commitments: Ethics, Politics, and Transnational Modernism* (2012). She also co-edited *Virginia Woolf Out of Bounds* (2001), selected papers from the tenth annual conference on Virginia Woolf, which she organized. With Paul Saint-Amour she edits the *Modernist Latitudes* book series from Columbia University Press.

SARA BLAIR is Professor of English and faculty associate of the American Culture and Judaic Studies programs at the University of Michigan. She is author of *Harlem Crossroads: Black Writers in the Twentieth Century* (2007), *Henry James and the Writing of Race and Nation* (1996), co-author with Eric Rosenberg of *Documentary Reconsidered* (forthcoming), and co-editor with Jonathan Freedman of *Jewish in America* (2004). She is currently working on a study of modern visuality and visual practices as they emerged on New York City's Lower East Side.

ERIC BULSON is Assistant Professor in the Department of English and Comparative Literature at Hobart and William Smith Colleges. He is author of *The Cambridge*

Introduction to James Joyce (2006) and *Novels, Maps, Modernity: The Spatial Imagination, 1850–2000* (2007). He is currently writing a book on the global circulation of the little magazine.

MANISHITA DASS is Lecturer in World Cinema at Royal Holloway (University of London) and has previously taught at the University of Michigan and Swarthmore College. She has published essays in *Cinema Journal* and the edited collection *Global Art Cinema* (2010), and is currently completing a book entitled *Outside the Lettered City: Cinema, Modernity, and Spectatorship in Late Colonial India*. Her research interests include the relationship between cinema and colonial modernity, the impact of left radicalism on the film cultures of Bombay and Calcutta in the 1940s–1960s, and the ge-opolitical imaginaries of film and modernist studies.

LAURA DOYLE is Professor of English at University of Massachusetts-Amherst and convener of the Five College Atlantic/Global Studies Faculty Seminar. She is author of *Freedom's Empire: Race and the Rise of the Novel in Atlantic Modernity, 1640–1940* (2008) and *Bordering on the Body: The Racial Matrix of Modern Fiction and Culture* (1994), as well as editor of *Bodies of Resistance: New Phenomenologies of Politics, Agency, and Culture* (2001) and co-editor of *Geomodernisms: Race, Modernism, Modernity* (2004).

MARY LOU EMERY is Professor of English at the University of Iowa, where she teaches modernist and Caribbean studies. She is author of *Jean Rhys at "World's End": Novels of Colonial and Sexual Exile* (1990), *Modernism, the Visual, and Caribbean Literature* (2007), and articles on Virginia Woolf, D. H. Lawrence, C. L. R. James, Wilson Harris, and others. She has edited a special issue of the *Journal of Caribbean Literatures* on Rhys.

NERGIS ERTÜRK is Assistant Professor of Comparative Literature at The Pennsylvania State University. She is author of *Grammatology and Literary Modernity in Turkey* (2011), a study of Turkish language politics and comparative methodology. Her work has appeared in *PMLA*, *Modernism/modernity*, *boundary 2*, and *New Literary History*.

SUSAN STANFORD FRIEDMAN teaches at the University of Wisconsin–Madison and publishes widely in modernist studies, narrative studies, and feminist theory. She received the Wayne C. Booth Award for Lifetime Achievement in Narrative Studies (2010) and serves as president of the Modernist Studies Association for 2011–2012. Three of her essays in *Modernism/modernity* (2001; 2006; 2010) focus on the multiple meanings of modernism/modernity, expansive periodizations, and a planetary framework for modernism. She co-edits the Oxford University Press journal *Contemporary Women's Writing*.

WILLIAM O. GARDNER is Associate Professor of Japanese at Swarthmore College. He is author of *Advertising Tower: Japanese Modernism and Modernity in the 1920s* (2006). Recently, in addition to continuing his work on Japanese modernism through articles on literary theorist Ôkuma Nobuyuki and mystery writer Edogawa

Rampo, he has been researching postwar Japanese science fiction and has published on science fiction authors Tsutsui Yasutaka and Komatsu Sakyô.

MIRIAM BRATU HANSEN (1949–2011) was Ferdinand Schevill Distinguished Service Professor in the Humanities at the University of Chicago, where she also taught in the Department of English and the Committee on Cinema and Media Studies. Her publications include a book on Ezra Pound's early poetics (1979), *Babel and Babylon: Spectatorship in American Silent Film* (1991), and *Cinema and Experience: Siegfried Kracauer, Walter Benjamin, and Theodor W. Adorno* (2011). Her next project was to be a book on cinema in the digital era.

ERIC HAYOT is Professor of Comparative Literature and Director of Asian Studies at The Pennsylvania State University. He is author of *Chinese Dreams: Pound, Brecht, Tel quel* (2004) and *The Hypothetical Mandarin: Sympathy, Modernity, and Chinese Pain* (2010), which shared the 2010 Book Prize of the Modernist Studies Association.

PETER KALLINEY is Associate Professor of English at the University of Kentucky, where he teaches modern British and postcolonial literature. He is author of *Cities of Affluence and Anger: A Literary Geography of Modern Englishness* (2007). His contribution to this collection is drawn from a book project provisionally entitled *Transatlantic Modernism and the Emergence of Postcolonial Literature*.

NEIL LAZARUS is Professor of English and Comparative Literary Studies at the University of Warwick. He is author of *Resistance in Postcolonial African Fiction* (1990), *Nationalism and Cultural Practice in the Postcolonial World* (1999), and *The Postcolonial Unconscious* (2011), and editor of *Marxism, Modernity and Postcolonial Studies* (2002) and *Cambridge Companion to Postcolonial Literary Studies* (2004). He has published numerous essays on social and cultural theory and postcolonial studies in such journals as *Cultural Critique, Diaspora, differences, Journal of Commonwealth Literature, New Formations, Race & Class, Research in African Literatures, South Atlantic Quarterly*, and *Textual Practice*.

SARAH L. LINCOLN is Assistant Professor of English at Portland State University, where she teaches postcolonial and other world literatures, along with global cinema and critical theory. Recent publications include "Conquering City: The Poetics of Possibility in *Texaco*" (*Small Axe* 2011); "Consumption and Dependency in *Mandabi*" (*Journal of Commonwealth Literature* 2010); and "Rotten English: Excremental Politics and Literary Witnessing in Postcolonial Nigeria" (*Encountering the Nigerian State* 2010). Her current book project, *Oikopoiesis: Postcolonial Literature and the Art of Survival*, traces the emergence of anticonsumerism and economical aesthetics in contemporary postcolonial literature.

JANET LYON is Associate Professor of English at The Pennsylvania State University. She is the author of *Manifestoes: Provocations of the Modern* (1999) and numerous articles on modernism and modernity. Her current book project examines modernist sociability.

ROSALIND C. MORRIS is Professor of Anthropology at Columbia University. Her most recent books are *Photographies East: The Camera and Its Histories in East and Southeast Asia* (2009) and *Can the Subaltern Speak?: Reflections on the History of an Idea* (2010). Morris's writings on South Africa focus on questions of value, violence, and representation, as well as aesthetic production. She is also the founding editor of The Africa List for Seagull Books.

SHACHAR PINSKER is Associate Professor of Hebrew Literature and Culture at the University of Michigan. He is author of *Literary Passports: The Making of Modernist Hebrew Fiction in Europe* (2010), and co-editor of *Hebrew, Gender, and Modernity* (2007).

HARSHA RAM is Associate Professor of Slavic and Comparative Literatures at the University of California, Berkeley. He is author of *The Imperial Sublime: A Russian Poetics of Empire* (2003), which examines the consolidation of the modern Russian literary system in the eighteenth and early nineteenth centuries that arose in response to the pressures of the Russian imperial state and the challenges of transposing European poetics and rhetoric onto Eurasian soil. He is currently working on two projects related to global modernism: one that focuses on the intense cross-fertilization between Russian artists and those on the imperial periphery (specifically in the Republic of Georgia) during the revolutionary period, and a second that examines the competing claims of the Italian and Russian futurist avant-gardes as a means of posing the larger problem of modernism's patterns of circulation between "center" and "periphery."

JAHAN RAMAZANI is Edgar F. Shannon Professor of English at the University of Virginia. He is the author of *A Transnational Poetics* (2009), winner of the Harry Levin Prize of the ACLA; *The Hybrid Muse: Postcolonial Poetry in English* (2001); *Poetry of Mourning: The Modern Elegy from Hardy to Heaney* (1994), a finalist for the National Book Critics Circle Award; and *Yeats and the Poetry of Death: Elegy, Self-Elegy, and the Sublime* (1990). He co-edited the most recent editions of *The Norton Anthology of Modern and Contemporary Poetry* (2003) and *The Twentieth Century and After* in *The Norton Anthology of English Literature* (2006, 2012). He is a recipient of a Guggenheim Fellowship, an NEH Fellowship, a Rhodes Scholarship, and the MLA's William Riley Parker Prize.

GAYLE ROGERS is Assistant Professor of English at the University of Pittsburgh and is also affiliated with the European Studies Center and the Center for Latin American Studies. He is author of the forthcoming book *Modernism and the New Spain*. His recent and forthcoming publications include a translation of Antonio Marichalar's groundbreaking study of Joyce (*PMLA* 2009), several works on Spanish modernism and Joyce (*Modernism/modernity* and *James Joyce Quarterly*), and short essays on Eliot and modernist aesthetics.

ANNA WESTERSTÅHL STENPORT is Assistant Professor and Director of Scandinavian Studies at the University of Illinois at Urbana-Champaign and an affiliate

Associate Professor of Literature at Gothenburg University, Sweden. She is author of *Locating August Strindberg's Prose: Modernism, Transnationalism, and Setting* (2010).

EDWIGE TAMALET TALBAYEV is Assistant Professor of French and an affiliate of the Council on Middle Eastern Studies and the African Studies Council at the Mac-Millan Center at Yale University. She specializes in North African literature and Mediterranean Studies and has published articles in *The International Journal of Francophone Studies*; *European Studies Forum*; *Folklorica*; and *Journal of Middle-Eastern Women's Studies*. She is co-editor of "The Mediterranean Maghreb: Literature and Plurilingualism," a special issue of *Expressions Maghrébines* (forthcoming 2012), and is completing a book manuscript entitled *The Transcontinental Maghreb: Francophone Literature in a Mediterranean Context*.

BEN TRAN is Assistant Professor of Asian Studies at Vanderbilt University. He is completing a book manuscript entitled *Post-Mandarin: Masculinity and Modernism in Vietnam*.

VICKY UNRUH is Professor of Latin American Literary and Cultural Studies at the University of Kansas. She is author of *Latin American Vanguards: The Art of Contentious Encounters* (1994) and *Performing Women and Modern Literary Culture in Latin America* (2006), and co-editor (with Michael Lazzara) of *Telling Ruins in Latin America* (2009). She has served on the editorial boards of *PMLA*, *Latin American Research Review*, and the *Revista Iberoamericana* and currently works on contemporary Cuba.

MARK WOLLAEGER is Professor of English at Vanderbilt University. He is author of *Joseph Conrad and the Fictions of Skepticism* (1990) and *Modernism, Media, and Propaganda: British Narrative from 1900 to 1945* (2006), as well as editor of two collections of essays on Joyce. He served as President of the Modernist Studies Association and is founding co-editor, with Kevin J. H. Dettmar, of Modernidt literature & culture, an Oxford University Press book series.

XUDONG ZHANG is Professor of Comparative Literature and Chinese at New York University. He is author of *Chinese Modernism in the Era of Reforms* (1997) and *Postsocialism and Cultural Politics* (2008), and editor of two collections of essays on contemporary Chinese culture and intellectual discourse. As a literary and cultural critic, he also publishes widely in Chinese and is founding director of the International Center for Critical Theory at Peking University.

INDEX

....

Abbas, K. A., 641–42
Abbott, Berenice, 132, 146n10
Abel, Jon, 164n9
Abramovitz, Sholem Yankev, 441–42
Abu-Lughod, Janet, 295, 514
Achebe, Chinua, 229, 238, 285n13
Aching, Gerard, 16, 671, 685
Acosta, Agustín, 342, 350–51
Acosta, José M., 350
actresses, prostitutes as, 633
Adelard of Bath, 676
adhunika (modern woman), 643n13
Adorno, Theodor W., 234, 238, 408n9, 662n2,
    679
aesthetic autonomy
    futurist geographies with uneven
        modernities and, 313–40
    spatialization of force with, 330–32
aestheticism, 316, 373. *See also* art for art's sake
Africa, 130. *See also* photographic modernism;
    specific countries
    African Americans influenced by, 136
    banjo's origins in, 60, 67–68
    Black Orpheus and rise of little magazines,
        274–80
    diaspora, 68–69
    frontal vision and, 137–39, 147n15
    little magazines, 267–87
    May Fourth New Culture Movement and,
        239–40
African literature, 228–45, 249–66, 267–87.
    See also South Africa
    capitalism, modernity and modernism
        with, 231, 232–37
    combined and uneven modernisms with,
        237–41
    little magazines and, 267–87
    modernism and, 228–45, 249–66
    Western literature as standard for, 228–29
Agamben, Giorgio, 391, 399–400, 694n12
Ağaoğlu, Adalet, 39
Agnon, Shmuel Yosef, 451, 452
Agustini, Delmira, 125n4
Ahad-Ha'am, 441

Ah Q–The Real Story (Lu Xun), 15–16
    allegory and rereading of, 173–204
    and/as Chinese modernism, 175–79
    as chapter-novel parody, 173, 177
    forgetting and desire for recognition in,
        195–201
    with human and nonhuman distinctions,
        194–96
    newspaper-serial structure of, 177
    without plot or biography, 186–87
    with proscription and desire for identity,
        186–95
    reader's relationship to text in, 177–78
    as rogue sign and Confucian system of
        naming, 180–86, 189–92
    signs in, 178–79
    sleep in, 196
    spectral nature of, 182–84, 189
    as theater/court, 177–78
    writing in, 198
Aidoo, Ama Ata, 241
Akanishi Kakita (film), 588
Akanji, Sangodare, 278
Albania
    modernism in, 27, 30–32
    standard language, 31–32
Alberta (Sandel), 485
Alberta and Freedom (Sandel), 485
Aldington, Richard, 561, 562, 566
Aleichem, Sholem, 440, 442, 443, 450
Algeria, colonialism in, 103n5
Algérianiste movement, 85
Allawaert, M., 69, 74n38
allegory
    Chinese modernism and will to, 173–204
    national, 15, 164n12, 184
    natural history with, 202n15
    spectral nature of story with, 182–84,
        189
Allfrey, Phyllis Shand, 426
All-India Muslim League, 541
Almendares River, 364n36
Alonso, Carlos, 115
Alphabet (Christensen), 490

alphabets
  Arabo-Persian, 38
  Ottoman, 546n46
  universal, 331
  Vietnam's romanized, 371–72
"Alphabets" (Heaney), 300–301
Altenberg, Peter, 445, 447
alternative universalis, 114
Alvarez, Al, 430n4
Amer, Sahar, 676
"America Hispana," 475n12
Americanist artistic politics, 346
Amerindians, 51–52, 55, 71n11
Amrouche, Jean El Mouhoub, 6, 105n35, 691
  with Berber memory reconstructed
    and time, 87–94
  Berber poetry, issue of derivation and, 81–108
  cultural translation issue and, 100–102
  with derivation issue and global visions of
    modernity, 94–100
  homme-enfant and, 90
  Kabyle culture and, 99–100
  literature of memory and, 82, 85
  religion and influence on, 104n27
  vernacular culture with Mallarmé and, 83–87
Analects (Confucius), 181–82
Anand, Mulk Raj, 9, 16, 205–6, 223
  body of work, 224n3
  with Gandhi, 208–9
  Joyce's influence on, 208–13
  political activism of, 207–8
  with politics of Indian modernism, 207–14
  use of language, 213–14
Anday, Melih Cevdet, 542, 545n31
Anderson, Amanda, 407n2
Anderson, Benedict, 88, 298
Anderson, Margaret, 272
Anderson, Perry, 12, 236, 318
Andrade, Oswald de, 362n20
Andrew, Dudley, 610
Andrić, Ivo, 40
Andronikoff, Natalia, 561
Angier, Carole, 419–20
Anglo-American modernism, 8, 14, 132,
    409n15, 420, 429, 467, 482, 684
"Anglo-Mongrels and the Rose" (Loy), 289
Aniara (Martinson, H.), 492
Antoine, André, 483
anxiety, 56, 164n14
Anzai Fuyue, 574
Aono Suekichi, 615
apartheid, 646, 649, 653, 655. *See also*
    South Africa, cinema in

Apollinaire, Guillaume, 29, 31, 318, 483
Appadurai, Arjun, 295, 552
Appiah, Kwame Anthony, 145n5, 295, 305n5,
    401, 409n21
Applause (film), 602
appropriation
  artistic, 297
  modernism with comparison and, 14–18
Apter, Andrew, 251, 264n16
Apter, Emily, 503, 512, 519n9
Araba Sevdasi ("The Carriage Affair")
    (Ekrem), 532
Arabo-Persian alphabet, 38
Arab world, 38, 239–41, 676, 677
Arac, Jonathan, 17, 302
Aragon, Louis, 381n10
Araquistáin, Luis, 464–65
architecture, 30, 444, 450
  Functionalism, in Scandinavia, 490–91
  of private life in India, 221–22
  postmodern, 8
  with vernacular modernism, 610–12
Area Studies, 519n4
Arendt, Hannah, 5, 389
"Ariel" (Rodó), 114, 343
Arkaden Café, 446, 454n15
Arlt, Roberto, 344
"Arm" (Kitagawa), 579–80
Armah, Ayi Kwei, 229–30, 238
Armstrong, Tim, 461
Arnold, Matthew, 557, 560, 566
Arrighi, Giovanni, 166n27
Artaud, Antonin, 483
Art Deco, 611, 627
art for art's sake, 316, 368–69, 371–76
art for life's sake, 368–69, 371–76
artistic renewal. *See* global artistic renewal
l'art c'est l'azur, 115
Arvasi, Abülhâkim, 539
Asch, Sholem, 450
Aseguinolaza, Fernando Cabo, 501
Asendorf, Christopher, 576
Asia. *See also* China; Chinese modernism;
    Japan; Vietnam
  "modern" as term in, 152, 164n9
Asia Minor catastrophe, 35
Asturias, Miguel, 234, 362n5
Atatürk, Mustafa Kemal, 534
Atay, Oğuz, 39
Athill, Diana, 419
Attridge, Derrick, 212
Atwell, David, 144n1
Auden, W. H., 488

Audisio, Gabriel, 85
August Revolution of 1945, 375
Aurelius, Marcus, 389
Aurobindo, Sri, 225n10
Austen, Jane, 166n26, 215–17, 221, 508
Auster, Paul, 494
Austria. *See* Vienna, Austria
Austro-Hungarian Empire, 243n11, 687
The Autobiography of an Ex-Colored Man
        (Johnson, J. W.), 388, 396
autonomy. *See* aesthetic autonomy
avant-garde
    art, 318
    Bulgaria, 33
    historical, 320
    lettered city in Cuba with fissures in, 360–61
    modernity in Latin America and Cuba's,
        341–66, 362n19
    Romania, 36
    Russian, 317, 325–26, 329–30
    Turkish, 38
    work ethic of Havana's, 345–49
    Yugoslavia's cultural space with, 40
avant-garde, futurist
    with time-space of modernity, 315–18
    transnational geography of, 324–30
Ayhan, Ece, 542, 545n31
Ayvazoğlu, Beşir, 535
Azuela, Mariano, 473
Azul. . . . (Darío), 109, 115–16, 126n11

Babel, Isaac, 440, 441
"Babette's Feast" (Blixen), 486
baggy monster texts, 341, 361, 362n4
Bagritzki, Eduard, 441
Bahun, Sanja, 4, 15, 669, 689
Baker, Houston, 55
Baker, Josephine, 406
Bakhtin, Mikhail, 290, 648, 694n11
Bal, Mieke, 20n23
Balibar, Étienne, 111, 118, 124
Balkan modernism
    Albania, 27, 30–32
    with barabaro-genius, 26–29
    Bulgaria, 27, 30, 32–34
    with cultural identification, 27
    Greece, 27, 29, 32, 34–36
    histoire croisée with, 25–43
    language of resistance and, 32
    with methodological apertures, 41–43
    recorded and unrecorded, 29–43
    Romania, 27, 36–37

    with symbolism, 42
    Turkey, 37–39
    Yugoslavia, 30, 39–43
Balkan Wars, 32, 35
Baltacioğlu, Ismayil Hakki, 39, 534, 535,
        538–39, 546n45
Ba-matzor u'va-matzok ("In Siege and
        Distress"), 446–47
Bandung Conference, 145n4
banjo
    Africa and origins of, 60, 67–68
    "Blanche Gilroy in Classical Costume
        Reclining with Banjo," 61f
    cultures, 59, 73n26, 73n29
    as instrument of slavery, 59, 62
    as limbo gateway, 60
    "Miss Apperson" with, 60f
    with race, 59, 67
Banjo (McKay), 4, 50, 58, 59–60, 63
    migrancy in, 67–69
    "Shake That Thing" in, 61, 67
    women portrayed in, 61–62
barbaro-genius, 25–29
Barber, Karin, 256, 264n7
Ba Ren, 173. *See also* Lu Xun
Baroja, Pío, 465
Barthes, Roland, 130, 134, 137
Bassnett, Susan, 519n9
Batur, Enis, 544n15
Baucom, Ian, 51, 56
Baudelaire, 6, 89, 96, 112, 115, 122–24, 125n3,
        127n15, 151–52, 157, 178–79, 202n6,
        240–41, 264n13, 303, 314, 316, 317, 514, 530,
        533, 534, 539–40, 542, 691
Beach, Sylvia, 473
The Beacon, 272
Beasley, Rebecca, 6, 670, 689
Bechhofer, C. E., 565
Beer-Hofmann, Richard, 445, 447
Bei Dao, 156, 165n18
Beier, Ulli, 276, 278, 280. *See also Black Orpheus*
Belcheva, Mara, 33
Belgrade Surrealist Circle, 29, 40
Belle Époque, 120, 125n1, 313
Ben-Avi, Itamar, 450
Benda, Julien, 472
Bengali Renaissance, 51
Benhabib, Seyla, 18n7, 391–92
Benítez-Rojo, Antonio, 72n22
Benjamin, Walter, 16, 88, 121, 124, 161, 178–79
    with cinema, 647, 654, 656
    on dream-world, 253–54
    with empty homogenous time, 88, 197

Benjamin, Walter (*continued*)
  on modernist translation, 555
  on natural history, 202n15
  phantasmagoria and, 258, 264n13
  on urban literary café space, 438
Bennett, Louise, 297, 299, 303
Ben-Yitzhak, Avraham (Dr. Sonne), 444, 447–48
Berber poetry, 81–108
  as song, 85, 87–94
  with time and memory reconstructed, 87–94
  vernacular culture with Amrouche and
    Mallarmé, 83–87
Berbers
  with mother figure, 89
  as noble savages, 85
Bergelson, Dovid, 452
Bergelson, Lev, 452
Bérgère, Marie-Claire, 400
Bergson, Henri, 32, 90, 466, 530, 531, 534,
    538, 543n6, 544n19, 545n34, 546n44, 554,
    576–77, 593n16, 691
Berk, İlhan, 38, 542, 545n31
Berk Nurullah, 544n27
Berlin, Germany. *See also* Germany; Hebrew and
    Yiddish modernism; urban literary café
  Café des Westens, 437, 451
  Romanisches Café and Hebrew and Yiddish
    modernism in, 437, 449, 450f, 451–53
Berman, Jessica, 16, 515, 671
Berman, Marshall, 112
Bernheimer, Charles, 164n11, 505
Beyath, Yahya Kemal, 6, 530
Bhabha, Homi, 49, 71n10, 88, 103n7, 294, 439,
    454n12, 503
Bialik, Haim Nahman, 441
Bildungsroman, 206
  hero, 211–12, 215, 219
  with women writers, 215–23, 225n15
Billings, Timothy, 161
Bim, 272, 274, 278
The Birds (Vesaas), 493
Björling, Gunnar, 487
blackface minstrelsy, 59–62
*Black Lamb and Grey Falcon: A Journey
    through Yugoslavia* (West), 29
Black Orpheus, 273, 284–85
  in Africa and rise of little magazines, 274–80
  Beier as founding editor of, 276
  criticism in, 279
  form of, 277
  for general readership, 275–76
  influence of, 281

mission and funding for, 276
reviews in, 278
shift in content, 285n10
*Black Power: The Record of Reaction in a
    Land of Pathos* (Wright)
  apprehension in, 134
  frontal vision in, 137–39, 147n15
  Gold Coast photos, 132f, 133f, 135f, 139f, 140f,
    141f, 143f, 146n6
  with photographic modernism, 129–48
blacks, theaters for, 652
The Black Jacobins (James, C. L. R.), 72n22
Blair, Sara, 6, 692
Blake, William, 74n38
"Blanche Gilroy in Classical Costume
    Reclining with Banjo," 61f
Blaut, J. M., 95, 514
blaxpoitation cinema, 653
Blixen, Karen, 486
Bloch, Ernst, 13, 233
Blonde Venus (film), 602
Bloomsbury Group, 208–9, 405, 406.
    See also specific members
Blue Horn group (Georgian modernism), 335n33
blues, 58, 59, 73n29
Bly, Robert, 479, 488
Boase, Roger, 676, 677
Boehmer, Elleke, 206, 207, 684
Bogomilski Legendi (*The Bogomil Legends*)
    (Rainov), 33
bohemians, 430n3. *See also* Left Bank; urban
    literary café
Bonaparte, Napoleon, 53
Boom novels, 361
Bordwell, David, 608
Borges, Jorge Luis, 116, 362n5, 467, 470, 494
Borum, Poul, 487
Bothma, C. V., 653
Boulifa, Amar Ou Said, 86
Bourdieu, Pierre, 19n14, 346
"The Bourgeois King" (Darío)
  artwork in, 120, 122
  capitalism and, 118–19, 123
  beyond imitation in, 112–17
  Spanish American *modernismo* and, 109–28
  with transatlantic modernity, 117–25
  winter in, 123–24
Bourget, Paul, 395
Bourne, Randolph, 463–64
Boye, Karin, 489
Boyson, Emil, 488
Bradbury, Malcolm, 273, 481, 509

Brandes, Georg, 480–81, 486, 491, 688

Brantlinger, Patrick, 683

Brathwaite, Kamau, 4, 49, 51, 54, 69, 71n11, 295–97, 423

 on Rhys as West Indian writer, 430n4

Brazilian *modernismo*, 125n1

Brecht, Bertolt, 6, 161, 381n10, 483

Breinin, Reuven, 450

Brekke, Paul, 489

Breton, André, 29, 234, 486, 574

Breytenbach, Breyten, 649

Bridges, Robert, 163n4

Briggs, Charles L., 396

Brink, André, 649

British empire, 206–7, 214, 274, 296, 303, 421–24, 429, 508–9. *See also* imperialism.

Britain, 114, 153, 166n26, 219, 299–300, 303, 425, 483, 557, 567, 650, 677–78, 687, 689–90

 expansionist wars of, 681–83

 Russian translation in, 558–66

Broad, C. D., 208

Broby-Johansen, Rudolf, 488

Broch, Hermann, 447, 448

Brodber, Erna, 52, 69

Brooks, Van Wyck, 463

Brouillette, Sarah, 419

Brown, Nicholas, 234, 242n9

Bruno, Giuliana, 642

Bukharin, Nikolai, 375

Bulgaria, 27, 30, 32–34

Bulson, Eric, 10, 12

Bundy, Andrew, 71n12

Buñuel, Luis, 578

Bürger, Peter, 43n11, 316–17, 342, 345, 361n4

Burke, Edmund, 534

Burliuk, David, 322, 545n30

Burnett, Charles, 676

"Bursa'da Zaman" (Tanpınar), 538

Burton, Antoinette, 215, 225n9

Bush, Christopher, 161

Butterfly Valley (Christensen), 490

Butts, Mary, 397, 404–7

The Cabinet of Dr. Caligari (Wiene), 483

Café Megalomania. *See* Romanisches Café

cafés. *See also* urban literary café

 Abatzya, 439

 Arkaden, 446, 454n15

 Central, 437, 438–39, 446, 447

 des Westens, 437, 451

 Fanconi, 441, 442f, 443–44

 Griensteidl, 437

 Herrenhof, 446, 448, 449f

 Monopol, 450

 Museum, 447, 448

 Robina, 441, 444

 Romanisches, 437, 449, 450f, 451–53

Çağlar, Ece Ayhan, 38

Cahier d'un Retour aux Pays Natal (Césaire), 69, 516–17

Calvino, Italo, 494

Camera Lucida (Barthes), 130

camera obscura, 143–44, 147n17, 258, 264n14.
 See also photographic modernism

Campos, Haroldo de, 153

"Camptown Racecourse," 63, 67

Canetti, Elias, 259–60, 447

Cansever, Edip, 542

Cape Farewell (Martinson, H.), 492

capitalism, 12–4, 112, 117, 682–83

 African literature with modernity, modernism and, 231, 232–37

 brutality of, 235–36

 Ben Okri's modernism and, 249–66

 global capitalism, 106n44, 117–19, 123, 254–55

 South African cinema and, 646–65

 Spanish American *modernismo* and, 109–28

Caragiale, Ion Luca, 36

Caribbean modernism, 48–77

 foundational scenes, 51–53

 limbo gateways, 49–50, 54–56

 literary language with, 53, 54

 planetary, 67–69

 re-ordering history in, 53, 54–56

Carlyle, Thomas, 556

Carmichael, Stokely, 131, 145n5

Carpentier, Alejo, 55, 342, 347, 352–56, 363n26

Carr, Helen, 430n4

Casal, Julián del, 112, 116, 117, 125n4

Casanova, Pascale, 18n4, 164n7, 297, 332, 502, 673

 global literary map and, 319, 330

 world literature theory and, 269–70, 319–20

Cassatt, Mary, 513

Castillo, Ramón, 474

The Castle (Kafka), 173

Cather, Willa, 9, 150

Catherine the Great (Empress), 440

Catholic Church, 163n5

Cavafy, Constantine, 25, 26, 35, 407

Celan, Paul, 490

Cendres (Ashes) (Amrouche), 83, 88–89

Center-periphery model, 6–7, 56, 82–83, 96, 118,
    183, 269–70, 320, 325, 333n4, 390, 501–3,
    502–4, 506, 509, 511–18, 519n5, 6, 8, 688
Certeau, Michel de, 402
Césaire, Aimé, 52, 55, 69, 234, 276, 285n10,
    516–17, 518
Cha, Theresa Hak Keung, 516–17
Chaker, Salem, 86, 106n44
Chakrabarty, Dipesh, 6, 86, 102, 103n7,
    514, 608
    on historicism, 103n10
    on uneven development, 333n11
Champsi-Haridas case, 630
Chang, Sung-sheng Yvonne, 158
Chants Berbères de Kabylie (*Berber Chants*
    [sung poetry] *from Kabylia*)
    (Amrouche), 82, 85–94
Chapman, Arnold, 463
Chardin, Jean-Baptiste Siméon, 120
Chatterjee, Partha, 513
Cheadle, Mary Patterson, 160
Cheah, Pheng, 380n6, 394, 408n12, 462, 475n4
Chekhov, Anton, 561, 565
Chemarea (*Call*), 36
Chiang Kai-shek, 400
Chiba Kameo, 574, 593n13
Un chien andalou (film), 578
Child, Harold Hannyngton, 564
children's literature, 493
Chin, Marilyn, 289
China
    cinema in, 601–18, 618n4, 618n8
    civil war, 400, 606
    Japan's use of "Shina" for, 187, 202n10
    May Fourth New Culture Movement in,
        174, 197–98, 199, 201n2, 201n3, 202n5,
        202n12, 239–40
    with nation-states, 164n15, 165n16
    with Nobel Complex, 153–54, 155, 164n15
    writers influenced by, 160–62
China Transformed (Wong), 166n27
Chinese Enlightenment, 176, 180. *See also*
    Enlightenment
Chinese modernism, 15–16, 149—70, 173–204
    Ah Q–The Real Story and/as, 175–79
    allegory and origin of, 173–204
    anxiety with, 164n14
    Confucian system of naming with, 15–16,
        180–86, 189–92
    European time and, 159–63
    forgetting and desire for recognition in,
        195–201

globality and geography of mimetic desire
    with, 153–55
global perspectives on, 149–50
global thinking and intercontamination of
    terms, 12, 155–59, 163n2
literary economy and preferred languages
    with, 156–57
with mimetic desire and European time,
    149–70
national allegory and, 15, 164n12, 184
with proscription and desire for identity,
    186–95
with Western history of modern, 150–53
Chinweizu, 229–31
Chiwengo, Ngwarsungu, 145n5
Chmelnicki, Melekh, 444
Chmelnitzky, Melech, 446
Chocano, José Santos, 125n4
Chow, Rey, 153, 157–58, 165n17, 165n19, 510
CHP. *See* Republican People's Party
Christensen, Inger, 490
Christiansë, Yvette, 649
Chughtai, Ismat, 234
cine-eye, 571
cinema, 9, 571–97, 601–26, 627–45, 646–65.
    See also films
    architecture with vernacular modernism
        and, 610–12
    audiences with women, 618n8
    blaxpoitation, 653
    in China and Japan, 601–18, 618n4
    fashion in, 652–53
    in India, 627–45
    Japan's white-collar, 615
    modernity in colonial India with women,
        city and, 627–45
    motherhood and prostitution in, 601–3
    postwar, 605
    power of, 641–42
    Shanghai, 608, 639
    theatrical *shinpa*-style in, 614
    urban scene of modernity in Indian, 629–32
    vernacular modernism and South African
        cinema, 646–65
    vernacular modernism as Hollywood, 9,
        607–9, 613, 620n20
    violence in Hollywood, 651
    waste as theme in, 605–6
    women as stars in Indian, 639–42, 643n12
Cinema Ni Rani (*Cinema Queen*), 634
cinépoème, 579–81, 592n10
cine-text, Japanese modernism and, 571–97

Cioran, S. D., 563–64
circulation. *See also* Global Circulations Project
  of interwar Anglophone and Hispanic
    modernism, 461–77
  of literary writing, 56–57, 70n8
  of little magazines, 286n15
  in modernist studies, 503, 507, 511–16
city, and modernism, 178–79, 236, 255–58, 318,
    356–60, 368, 398–99, 402–7, 433–58, 484,
    488, 577–78, 627–45. *See also specific cities*
civilization, 126n12, 408n10
Clair, René, 589
Clark, J. P., 230, 278, 280
Clark, Michael, 146n6
Clarke, J. J., 679, 693n9
class. *See* social class
Claudel, Paul, 161
Cliff, Michelle, 52, 55, 69, 71n11
Clifford, James, 301, 392, 407, 408n7, 511
close reading, 17, 511, 515
Človek z bombami (*The Man with Bombs*)
  (Podbevšek), 41
CNOC. *See* National Workers Confederation
Coetzee, J. M., 238, 649
Cohen, Margaret, 258
Colet, Louise, 382n22
collage, 11, 173, 259, 290, 318, 345, 348, 352, 503
  in modernist studies, 507, 516–18
collective memory, 104n14
Colley, Linda, 72n22
Colonialism, 55–56, 95, 100, 229, 235–36, 238–41,
    281, 292, 298–99, 321, 325, 372, 394–95, 407,
    499–501, 505–6, 508–9, 513, 517, 592n11,
    628, 631, 683–84, 691. *See also* imperialism
  Berber poetry and influence of, 83–87,
    103n5, 144n1
  mental disorders with, 103n5
  Shina as sign of Japanese colonialism, 187,
    202n10
  time and alternative delineations with, 81–108
  of written languages, 17
color lines, 420–23. *See also* race
Comedy: A Tragedy in One Act (Kazantzakis), 34
Coming Home (film), 605
commerce
  songs, 64–65
  women's images in, 64–67
The Communist Manifesto (Marx and Engels),
  119, 242n10, 556
comparative strategies
  circulation, 503, 507, 511–16
  collage, 507, 516–18

identification with, 505
  in modernist studies, 507–18
  recovery, 507, 509–11
  re-vision, 507, 508–9
comparativity, with world literature and
    modernisms, 499–525
  in global studies, 504–6
  strategies in modernist studies, 507–18
Comte, Auguste, 393, 532
Confucianism, 372
  Analects, 181–82
  with human and nonhuman distinctions,
    194–96
  with rectification of names, 15–16, 180–86,
    189–92, 200
Congress of Berlin, 27, 32
Conley, Tom, 657
Connor, Liz, 640
Conrad, Joseph, 6, 17, 484, 509, 513, 565, 566
consciousness
  geocultural, 342, 351–52
  wave theory of, 593n16
constructivism, 40–42, 573
contrapuntal reading strategy, 17
Coolie (Anand), 210–14
Copeau, Jacques, 464
Cornelius, Henry, 650
Coronil, Fernando, 251–52, 261
Cosgrove, Stuart, 657–58
Cosmópolis: Revista Universal, 395
Cosmopolitanism, 5, 41, 74n36, 37, 116, 270–71,
    273, 290, 318, 332, 464, 471, 479, 610,
    670–71, 692
  fin de siècle, 394
  futurism between nationalism and, 319–24
  global designs and, 390
  Habermasian, 391–92
  impossible, 396–402
  Latin and Sanskrit, 609–10
  modernism and, 387–412
  modernism and situation with, 402–7
  and neoliberalism, 610
  old and new, 5, 301–2, 389–92
  philosophical forms of, 390–92
  with race and nation, 393–96
  and township in South Africa, 655
  Roman Stoic, 407n2
  uneven modernist, 472–74
Cournos, John, 562–65, 567
court. *See* theater/court
Cowie, Elizabeth, 643n4
Craig, William Marshall, 62

Crane, Hart, 467–68
Crapanzo, Vincent, 649
Crary, Jonathan, 147n17
Creditors (Strindberg), 482
creolization, 11, 12, 55–56, 58, 71n11, 73n26,
    99–100, 289, 295–96, 503
  of languages, 50
  with slang of *tsotsis*, 653, 661
  as world view, 73n35
creolized arts, 51
"Cries of London"
  commerce depicted in, 64
  "Milk," 64f
  origins, 63–64
  plantation melodies and, 59–67
  "Strawberrys Scarlet Strawberrys," 65f
cries of the plantation, 50, 56–67
crime films, 630
criollo (of European descent), 341, 343, 345,
    356, 358, 361n2
The Criterion, 271, 272
Critique of Pure Reason (Kant), 505
Crnjanski, Miloš, 40
crossed history. *See histoire croisée*
Crossroads (film), 604–5
Cry the Beloved Country (film), 650, 656
Cuba
  Americanist artistic politics in, 346
  boxing in, 357
  economic collapse in, 343
  labor force in, 344, 348–49
  lettered city and avant-garde fissures in,
    360–61
  minoristas in, 344, 346, 347–49, 355–56
  modernity in Latin American and avant-
    garde in, 341–66, 362n19
  National Academy of Arts and Letters in, 347
  secret *ñáñigo* societies in, 354–55
  social class in, 356–60
  sugar industry in, 343, 349–56
  tertulias in, 357, 358, 360, 361n1
  time-outs in, 348, 350
  war with Germany, 362n6
  work ethic of Havana's avant-gardes, 345–49
cubism, 41, 157, 321, 322, 323, 326, 373, 403, 483,
    513, 530, 535, 539, 546n45, 573
cubofuturists, 322
Cullen, Countee, 132, 136
Culler, Jonathan, 520n18
cultural studies, globalization influencing
    literary and, 81–83
cultures, 344. *See also* May Fourth New
    Culture Movement

banjo, 59, 73n26, 73n29
  fascism's grip on, 370
  as humanity's highest achievement, 196
  indigenous, 82, 85
  Kabyle, 99–100
  vernacular, 83–87
  violent death of, 198–99
Curtin, Philip, 57
Curtius, Ernst Robert, 461

Dabydeen, David, 69
Dada, 37, 40, 157, 271, 285n4, 316, 321, 331, 346,
    355, 487, 516, 573, 619n10
Dagerman, Stig, 489
D'Aguiar, Fred, 52
Dai Houying, 165n21
Dalchev, Atanas, 33
Dalí, Salvador, 578
Damas, Leon, 285n10
Damrosch, David, 19n10, 165n18, 503, 510,
    512, 515
D'Annunzio, Gabriele, 317, 324, 333n7
Dante, Alighieri, 151, 609
Darío, Rubén, 6, 16, 125n4, 126n10, 126n11,
    151–52, 167n32, 474n2
  influence of, 116–17, 125n1
  Spanish American *modernismo* and, 109–28
Dash, J. Michael, 53
Dass, Manishita, 9, 671
Davidson, Basil, 239
Davie, Donald, 559
Da Vinci, Leonardo, 679
Davis, Peter, 652
"Dawn" (Soyinka), 231
Daybreak (film), 602
"The Day They Burned the Books" (Rhys),
    413–15, 416, 425
"The Dead" (Joyce), 404
de Andrade, Mário, 678
death, 198–99, 202n12, 202n13
decentralization of intelligence, 110, 122
De Chirico, Giorgio, 263
decolonization, 5, 17, 19n13, 113, 144n1, 292,
    404, 420, 428–29
  and African literature, 228–45,
  and cosmopolitanism, 388–94
  and global book business, 274–75
  and Indian modernity, 628
  and photographic modernism, 129–48
  and transnational poetry, 294–309
"decolonizing the mind," 228
deep time, 519n4

defamiliarization, 7, 55, 157, 178, 254, 301, 506, 508–9, 516–18, 558
"Défense de la culture" (Gide), 370
Deleuze, Gilles, 5, 501, 576–77, 579
DeLoughrey, Elizabeth, 69, 71n11
Delphic poetry, 34
de Man, Paul, 543n4
De Maupassant, Guy, 565
Demeny, Paul, 546n51
Democraţia, 43n8
Les Demoiselles d'Avignon, 297
demotic language, 34–35
Denmark, 479–80. See also Scandinavian modernism
Depestre, René, 55
Dergâh ("Convent"), 533, 534
derivativeness, curse of, 513–14
Derrida, Jacques, 8, 92, 212, 391, 404, 545n35
désindividualisation, 370
desire. See also mimetic desire
    for identity in Ah Q–The Real Story, 186–95
    for recognition in Ah Q–The Real Story, 195–201
Desnica, Vladan, 41
Desnos, Robert, 592n10
despair, politics of, 102
de Torre, Guillermo, 470
development, uneven, 333n11
de Vogué, E. M., 559–60
d Group, 535, 544n27, 544n29
The Dial, 267, 271, 272, 281, 282
Diary of a Madman (Lu Xun), 173, 195, 199–200, 237
Diary of Chûji's Travels (film), 588, 589
diaspora, 5, 17, 81, 145n5, 304, 499–500
    African, 56, 58, 61, 67–69, 300
    Caribbean, 50, 58
    Greek, 30
    Jewish, 437
Dickens, Charles, 565, 567
Dictée (Cha), 516–17
The Difficult Hour I-III (Lagerkvist), 483
Dikmen, Halil, 535
Diktonius, Elmer, 487
Dimock, Wai Chee, 57, 68, 70n3, 70n8, 73n35, 304, 519n4
Dino, Abidin, 544n27
Diogenes, 389
The Disconnected (Atay), 39
Disendrook, Zvi, 444, 447
Dishonored (film), 602–3
distant reading, 17, 502
distribution, of magazines, 271–72, 274, 277–78

Dix, Otto, 254
Doctor Glas (Söderberg), 484
Do-Dinh, Pierre, 367–68, 375
A Doll's House (Ibsen), 481–82
Dostoyevsky, Fyodor, 151, 234, 560, 561, 565
Doyle, Laura, 7, 9–10, 14, 15, 342, 512
Dr. Madhurika (Modern Wife) (film), 634, 638
Dragnet Girl (film), 603–4
drama. See modern drama, in Scandinavia
A Dream Play (Strindberg), 482
Dreams of Roses and Fire (Johson, E.), 492
Dubnov, Simon, 441–42
Du Bois, W. E. B., 396, 407
Ducasse, Isidore Lucien. See Lautréamont
Duniya Na Mane (The Unexpected) (film), 638
Dupuy, Ernest, 559
Durrell, Lawrence, 43n2
Dutch Disease, 253, 264n6
Dwyer, Rachek, 643n6
Dyer, Richard, 643n12

Eakins, Thomas, 61
earth, aesthetics of the, 68–69. See also planetary
Eby, Cecil Degrotte, 683
eco-cosmopolitanism, 74n37
ecological impact, of oil-based economies, 261
Edgell, Zee, 55
Edwards, Brent Hayes, 276
Edwards, Jonathan, 150
Edwards, Louise, 164n13
The Egoist, 267, 271, 272, 561–62, 564–67
835 Satir (835 Lines) (Hikmet), 38, 536
Eisenstein, Sergei, 487, 516, 580
Ekelöf, Gunnar, 488
Ekrem, Recâizâde Mahmud, 532, 690
electronic media, 552
Elefthero pnevma (Free Spirit) (Theotokas), 35
Eliot, T. S., 6, 8, 43n2, 71n16, 160, 165n18, 173, 208, 234, 271, 290, 295, 489
    Aldington's letter to, 561
    with black vernacular forms, 421
    Crane on, 468
    with shared circulation scheme for reviews, 474n3
Ellis, Lorna, 219, 225n15
Ellison, Ralph, 142, 657–58
Elsie, Robert, 43n3
Elytis, Odysseus, 35
emancipation, of slaves, 424
Embirikos, Andreas, 35
Emery, Mary Lou, 4–5, 430n4, 672, 686

Engels, Friedrich, 119, 242n10, 556
English Civil War, 48
English language, 9–10, 163n6
   and African literature, 228–45
   unavowed imperialism of in Moretti, 17
   poetry and imperialism of, 302–4
   and translation, 551–70, 621n37
   transnational readings and Indian
      narratives in, 205–27
empire, 51, 68, 70n5, 137, 298, 320, 505, 515. *See*
   also imperialism *and specific countries*
Enlightenment
   Chinese, 176, 180
   European, 28, 90, 390
   Jewish, 435, 441
   rationalism, 403
Epitafios (*Epitaph*) (Ritsos), 35
Ertürk, Nergis, 6, 15, 16, 670, 678, 687
Escher, M. C., 669
Escobar, Juan Antiga, 349, 674, 693n3
Esperanto, 555
Espinoza, Enrique, 469. *See also* Glusberg,
   Samuel
"The Essential Gesture" (Gordimer), 647–48
Esther Chajes (Shteinman), 443–44
Esty, Jed, 212, 225n15
"The Eternal Jugurtha: Propositions on
   African Genius" (Amrouche), 93–94
Etoile Secrète (*Secret Star*) (Amrouche), 84
Eurocentrism, 7, 13, 14–18, 19n13, 51, 177–18
   And African literature, 228–45
   and Berber poetry, 81–108
   and modernist studies, 504–25, 670
   and world literary system, 152–53, 297, 673
Europe
   Chinese modernism in relation to
      modernism in, 150–53
   Enlightenment in, 28, 90, 390
   film statistics for U.S., Japan and, 592n3
   Hispanic modernism and *Our America*
      viewed through, 463–65
   Ocampo's, 469–72
   urban literary café and geography of
      Hebrew and Yiddish modernism in,
      433–58
Evans, Walker, 137, 138f, 140
Evaristo, Bernardine, 289
Every Night Dreams (film), 601
excrement, 261, 264n4. *See also* oil-based
   economies
expressionism, 132, 254, 263, 380n4, 381n14,
   436, 450, 451–52
   in Balkans, 33–34, 37, 40–42

in Japan, 573, 581
in Scandinavia, 481, 484–84
post-, in Germany, 249, 254, 263
¡*É-Yamba-Ó*¡ (Lord, Praised be Thou)
   (Carpentier), 352–54, 363n26

Fabre, Michel, 146n6
Fachs, Donald, 678
Fanon, Frantz, 84, 103n5, 369, 683
Fantoches (Puppets), 348
fascism, 85, 314, 332, 370, 381n10, 472–74, 614,
   692
fashion
   in cinema, 652–53
   tsotsi with revolutionary style and, 654–59
Faulkner, William, 6, 12, 51, 173, 425, 489
Fearless Nadia, 637–38
Featherstone, Mike, 300
Felski, Rita, 164n10, 512
feminism, 8–9, 39, 164n10, 289, 342, 360,
   430n4, 462, 487, 516, 690
   gynocriticism, 510
   "practical" in Cuba, 359
   international, 471–72
   revision, 508
   Fenollosa, Ernest, 166n28
Ferguson, James, 262, 264n19
Fernández de Castro, José Antonio, 347, 356,
   363n30
Field, Andrew, 563–64
Figaro, 313
Le Figaro, 43n8
Fikret, Tevfik, 532
Film Age, 574
filmindia, 641
film noir, 651
films, 9, 18n1, 592n10. *See also specific film titles*
   with cinema tracked on global scale, 601–26
   clusters, 10
   crime, 630
   French impressionist, 585
   Kitagawa on, 587
   motherhood and prostitution in, 601–3
   prose, 587–89
   silent, 588, 590, 601, 622n41, 629–30, 634
   statistics for Japan, U.S. and Europe, 592n3
   studios, 614–16, 634, 641
   swordplay, 613–14
   theory of prose, 587–89
financial value. *See also* oil-based economies
   public opinion determining, 249, 255–56
Finkel, Donald, 165n18

First New poets, 542, 545n31

The First Manifesto of Futurism, 43n8

Fishermen's Song (film), 605

Flaubert, Gustave, 127n15, 151, 345, 382n20
  in relation to Russian novel, 559–60, 565
  and Vietnamese aesthetics, 367–68, 375–76

Fletcher, John Gould, 562, 565–66

Fogel, David, 444, 447–48

Fojas, Camilla, 394–95, 398

Fondane, Benjamin, 592n10

"Fondation et Manifeste du futurism"
    ("Founding and Manifesto of Futurism"),
    313

Ford, Ford Madox, 272, 406, 417, 420, 561

Forget Love for Now (film)
  motherhood and prostitution in, 601–2
  Shennü: The Goddess with, 601–2, 616–17

formalism, 8, 12, 14, 17, 132, 362n11, 515–16
  literariness, 12, 17, 114, 165n15, 319–20, 332, 689
  neo- and accounts of classical Hollywood
    cinema, 607–608
  photographic, 133–37
  Russian, 331
  and Scandinavian modernism, 479, 489–90
  Yokomitsu's theory of, 572, 575, 582–86,
    589–90

Forster, E. M., 11, 208, 224n7, 381n10

Foster, Stephen, 63

Foucault, Michel, 499, 531

fragmentation,
  bodily, 255, 575, 578, 582, 589
  didactic, 580, 582,
  formal, 12, 94, 183, 380n3, 484, 488, 516, 572,
    575–77, 580, 581–83, 587, 590
  "fragment and flow," 571–97
  modernist, 12, 183, 185, 484, 516, 575
  psychic, 123, 183, 259, 423, 491, 554
  raretsu, 583–84
  social, 86, 567, 577
  surrealist, 486, 488
  syntactical, 484, 579
  temporal, 567, 575, 589, 591

Fraiman, Susan, 219, 225n15

France, 27, 115. *See also* Paris, France
  colonial, 68, 83–87, 100, 103n12, 371–76
  language in, 319

France, Peter, 553

Franco, Jean, 361

Frank, Andre Gunder, 166n27, 514

Frank, Waldo, 462, 691, 692
  on "America Hispana" and "Latin America,"
    475n12
  Ocampo's Europe and Americas of, 469–72

Our America through Europe's eyes and,
    463–65
  with uneven modernist cosmopolitanism,
    472–74

Free Enterprise (Cliff), 69

free love, in China, 202n12

French Empire (Second), 123–24. *See also*
    imperialism

French experimental theater, 483

French impressionist film, 585

French language, 31, 37, 58, 89, 97, 103n12, 115,
    276, 313, 319, 329, 371, 399, 470, 484, 488,
    515, 540, 559, 677, 690

French modernism, 14, 87, 96, 158, 540. *See
    also specific authors*

Freud, Sigmund, 31, 399, 554

Freyre, Ricardo Jaimes, 125n4

Friedman, Susan Stanford, 14, 49, 56, 57, 69n1,
    463, 672
  multiple modernities and, 95–96, 99
  planetary and, 70n3, 72n23
  on spatial boundaries with modernism,
    295n11

"From Altar to Chimney Piece" (Butts), 405–6

From Morning to Midnight (Kaiser), 483

"From the Unconscious Life of the Mind"
    (Hamsun), 484

Frostenson, Katarina, 490

Froude, James Anthony, 288

Fuentes, Carlos, 236

Fulton, Robert, 479

Functionalism, 490

futurians, 322

futurism, 3, 5, 6–7, 40, 157, 202n5, 436, 576, 679
  art linked to aggression with, 313
  in Balkans, 33, 35, 37, 38, 39–41, 42
  between cosmopolitanism and nationalism,
    319–24
  in Italy, 269, 314–18, 320–22, 331, 332
  debated in Japan, 573
  and little magazines, 269
  with Marinetti, 313–15, 317, 321, 322–24
  as celebration of modern labor, 344
  origins, 313–14, 334n19
  in Paris, 314–15, 319–21, 335n28
  as response to imperial contestation, 685, 688
  in Russia, 314–18, 320, 322–24, 331–32, 334n19
  Russian in relation to *modernistas*, 114
  in Scandinavia, 487
  in Turkey, 533, 535
  in Vietnam, 373

futurismo/futurizm, 324–30, 333n9

futurist geographies. *See* geographies, futurist

Gaarder, Jostein, 493
Gaines, Kevin K., 145n5
galicismo mental (mental Frenchness), 115
Gallimard, Gaston, 464, 475n8
Galvão, Patrícia, 344
Gance, Abel, 587, 590
Gandhi, Mohandas, 208–9, 224n3, 225n10
Gaonkar, Dilip Parameshwar, 13, 96, 551
Gao Xingjian, 164n15
Garborg, Arne, 481
García Lorca, Federico, 465
Gardner, William, 16, 671
Garnett, Constance, 560
Garnett, Edward, 562, 567
Gatsos, Nikos, 35
Gauguin, Paul, 326
Gay, Peter, 151, 157
gaze
    frontal, 137–39, 147n15
    permutations of, 255
GCP. See Global Circulations Project
Geertz, Clifford, 511
Gender
    as applied to America versus Europe, 395, 470
    and Banjo, 59–63
    and cafés, 443–44
    and cinema, 603–606, 632–42
    and consumerism, 662
    and literary status, 8, 19n5, 500
    and modernity, 215–23, 359–60, 634–42
    Purdah and Polygamy, 215–23, 225n9
    and Jean Rhys, 67–68, 423
    Scandinavian literature and, 482–83, 485
    separate spheres, 632
    and Tự Bền the Actor, 377–379
Generation of 1898, 125n5, 465
genocide, from inflation, 259–60
Gentile, Emilio, 322
geocultural consciousness, 342, 351–52
geography
    futurist avant-garde and transnational,
        324–30
    of Hebrew and Yiddish modernism in
        Europe, 433–58
    of mimetic desire with globality, 153–55
geomodernisms, 684–90, 693n1
Geomodernisms (Doyle and Winkiel), 9–10, 512
Georgia (Republic of), 314, 323, 669
German language, 302, 399, 438, 445, 447, 486,
    487, 488, 490, 612
Germany, 27
    inflation in, 253, 260

language and translation, 554–55
Romanisches Café in Berlin with Hebrew and
    Yiddish modernism, 437, 449, 450f, 451–53
war with Cuba, 362n6
Ghosts (Ibsen), 481–82
Ghost Sonata (Strindberg), 482, 483
Gibran, Kahlil, 679
Gibson, Angus, 661
Giddens, Anthony, 298, 305n10
Gide, André, 6, 12, 489
    on art-versus-life debate, 372
    coded politics of homosexuality and,
        376–77, 379
    on defense of culture, 370–71
    désindividualisation and, 370
    NRF and, 464, 475n8
    Vietnam and influence of, 367–70
Gikandi, Simon, 49, 55–56, 58, 71n16, 71n18,
    508
    on combined and uneven modernisms,
        238–40
    on globalization, 297–98
Gilroy, Paul, 88, 145n5
    planetary and, 70n3, 73n35
Gjurmat e stinve (The Traces of the Seasons), 32
Glissant, Édouard, 4, 49–50, 51, 58, 61, 71n11,
    74n38
    on plantation, 72n22
    poetics of Relation, 56, 57, 59, 72n21, 72n24,
        73n35, 513
global artistic renewal (Zenitism), 26
global capitalism, 106n44, 117–19, 123, 254–55.
    See also capitalism
Global Circulations Project (GCP), 693n2
globality, with geography of mimetic desire,
    153–55
globalization, 74n37, 305n10
    literary and cultural studies influenced by,
        81–83
    modernity and poetry with, 288–309
    planetary distinct from, 52
global modernity
    Berber poetry and derivation issue with,
        94–100
    disjunctions of, 102, 318
    flow of cultural material and, 552
    as homogenizing, 92
    indigenous cultures with, 82, 85
    Nigeria and, 261
    poetry and, 288–309
    produced by colonial dynamic, 82
    as receding horizon, 249

global readership, of little magazines, 280–84

global studies, 504–6

global thinking, 5, 155–59, 163n2

Glusberg, Samuel, 469

Goankar, Dilip Parameshwar, 514

Gobineau, Arthur de, 393–94, 403, 408n11

Goebel, Rolf, 161

Goethe, Johann Wolfgang von, 271–72, 501, 502, 519n3, 556

Goffman, Daniel, 678

Gogol, Nikolai, 559

Gold Coast. *See also* photographic modernism
photos, 132*f*, 133*f*, 135*f*, 139*f*, 140*f*, 141*f*, 143*f*, 146n6
slavery, 142–43

Goldman, Jane, 531

Goldman, Nahum, 451

Golley, Gregory, 582

Göl Saatleri (*Hours of the Lake*) (Haşim), 38

Gómez de la Serna, Ramón, 466

Goncharova, Natal'ia, 326

Goncourt, Edmond de, 127n15

González, Aníbal, 345

Goodbye to Berlin (Isherwood), 398

Good Neighbor policy, 474

Gopal, Priyamvada, 684

Gordimer, Nadine, 647–48, 649

Gosho Heinusunke, 614

Gramsci, Antonio, 333n7, 409n14, 609

Graves, Robert, 163n4, 163n5

The Great Divergence (Frank, A. G., and Pomeranz), 166n27

Greco-Turkish war, 35

Greece
Ellinikotita, 35
languages, 34–35
modernism in, 27, 29, 32, 34–36
Orthodox Church's influence on, 43n6
periodicals, 35

Greenberg, Uri Zvi, 452

Greene, Graham, 471, 505

Gronemann, Sammy, 450

Grosz, George, 254

Grupo Minorista, 344,
and social class, 346–47

Guattari, Felix, 5, 501

Guenther, Irene, 254, 263

Guerra y Sánchez, Ramiro, 349–50

Guillén, Nicolás, 342, 356–57, 363n30

Güiraldes, Ricardo, 473

Gürbilek, Nurdan, 538

Gürol, Ender, 538

Gutiérrez Nájera, Manuel, 117, 125n4

H. D. (Hilda Doolittle), 164n10

Habermas, Jürgen, 437–38, 693n9

Habermasian cosmopolitanism, 391–92

haiku, 296, 489, 579

Haitian Revolution, 51–52, 53, 70n2, 70n6, 71n15

Hài Triều, 373–76, 381n14, 381n15

Hall, Stuart, 295

Halperin Donghi, Tulio, 120

Hamsun, Knut, 481, 489

Hannas, William, 159, 166n24

Hannerz, Ulf, 295

Hansen, Kathryn, 633

Hansen, Miriam, 9, 438, 629, 639, 654, 670
with vernacular modernism, 607–9, 631–32

Hansson, Ola, 481

Hapsburgh Empire, 32, 444, 447. *See also* imperialism

Harlem Renaissance, 51, 58, 70n5, 134, 289, 486

Harmless Tales (Sørensen), 491

Harootunian, Harry, 13, 86, 90–91, 101, 233, 612
on comparativity, 505–6
on synchronicity, 104n13

Harris, Wilson, 4, 49, 52, 68, 71n17, 429

Harshav, Benjamin, 435–36

Haruyama Yukio, 574

Harvey, David, 18n2

Haşim, Ahmet, 38, 533

Haskalah (Jewish Enlightenment) movement, 435, 441

Havana, Cuba. *See also* Cuba
avant-garde's work ethic in, 345–49
economic collapse influencing, 343
Grupo Minorista in, 344, 346–47

Hayot, Eric, 12, 16, 82, 672, 678

Head, Bessie, 649

Heaney, Seamus, 74n36, 300–301

Heart of Darkness (Conrad), 17, 513

"Heavensgate" (Okigbo), 291–92

Hebrew and Yiddish modernism
with Berlin: Romanisches Café and flowering of, 437, 449, 450*f*, 451–53
in Europe with urban literary café, 433–58
modern Jewish revolution and trajectory of, 435–37
with Odessa: urban ambivalence and new Jewish women, 440–44

Hebrew and Yiddish modernism (*continued*)
  with thirdspace of literary café, 437–40,
    442, 454n12
  with Vienna: inside and outside Jewish
    space of café, 444–49
Hedda Gabler (Ibsen), 481–82
Hegel, Georg Wilhelm Friedrich, 159, 197,
  200–201, 202n17
Heidegger, Martin, 401
Heilbrun, Carolyn, 8
Heimann, Moritz, 451
Heise, Ursula K., 74n37
Helios o protos (*Sun The First*) (Elytis), 35
Hellsing, Lennart, 493
Hemingway, Ernest, 489
Henningsen, Poul, 490
Henrik Ibsen and the Birth of Modernism
  (Moi), 481
Heredia, José Maria de, 533
Hermoni, Aharon, 450
Hernández, José, 473
hero, *Bildungsroman*, 211–12, 215, 219
Herrera y Reissig, Julio, 125n4
Herzl, Theodor, 445
heteroglossia, 41, 290
high modernism, 56, 163n3, 267, 361, 516
  China and, 165n21, 174, 175, 185–86
  Scandinavian modernism and lyrical,
    478–79, 488–90, 493–94
  Vietnamese literature and, 369
Hikmet, Nâzim, 38, 39, 529, 536
Hillarp, Ruth, 489
Hilton, John, 561
Himes, Chester, 657
Hindus, 393–94, 408n11
Hirabayashi Hatsunosuke, 573, 583–84
"Hispanic," as term, 475n5
Hispanic modernism
  circulation of interwar Anglophone and,
    461–77
  Frank's Americas and Ocampo's Europe
    with, 469–72
  with Ortega and "invertebrate Spain,"
    465–68
  Our America through European eyes and,
    463–65
  uneven modernist cosmopolitanisms,
    472–74
histoire croisée (crossed history), 18n5, 19n11,
  20n23, 25–43
historical avant-garde, 320, 342, 607.
  See also Bürger, Peter

history
  of Africa and influence on African
    Americans, 136
  Caribbean modernism and re-ordering, 53,
    54–56
  histoire croisée, 18n5, 19n11, 20n23, 25–43
  homogenous, empty time of, 88, 197
  modernity as known, 84
  natural, 202n15
  photograph modernism, postcolonial
    state and, 130–33
  as space of appropriation, 86
  violent death of, 198–99
  of Western modern with Chinese
    modernism, 150–53
  writing transnational film, 601–26
Hoài Thanh, 372, 374, 376–77
Hobbes, Thomas, 198
Hodge, Merle, 55
Hoel, Sigurd, 489
Hollywood cinema
  as vernacular modernism, 9, 607–9, 613,
    620n20
  violence in, 651
homme-enfant (child-man), 90
homo sacer (bare life without political status),
  391, 694n12
homosexuality, coded politics of, 376–79.
  See also queer internationalism
Honig, Bonnie, 391–92
Hood, Gavin, 652, 661
Hopkins, Gerard Manley, 163n4
Horace, 303
Horovitz, Ya'akov, 444
Hountondji, Paulin, 232, 240
Howe, Irving, 145n3
"How I Got that Name" (Chin), 289
Hsia, C. T., 164n13
Hughes, Langston, 289, 300, 350, 363n30, 470
Hugo, Victor, 115, 126n6, 127n15
Hulme, T. E., 71n11
human life, as excrement, 261. *See also*
  oil-based economies
Hunger (Hamsun), 484
Hurston, Zora Neale, 69, 493
Hurtivz, Shay, 451
Hurwitz, Shay Ish, 450
Hussain, Iqbalunnisa
  biography and political writings of, 218–19
  fluency in English, 222
  with Indian modernism and zenana,
    215–23

Huxley, Aldous, 471
Huyssen, Andreas, 20n22, 294, 472, 479
Hylaeans, 322–24, 326–28, 331, 335n31.
      See also futurism
      non, 334n18
hyperinflation, of oil-based economies, 12,
      250–63

Iakulov, Georgii, 328
Ibsen, Henrik, 116, 234, 481–83
Ice Around Our Lips: Finland-Swedish Poetry,
      487
The Ice Palace (Vesaas), 493–94
identification
      regional cultural in Balkans, 27
      with comparison, 505
identity
      Ah Q–The Real Story with desire for, 186–95
      colonialism, Berber poetry and, 83–87,
      103n12
      minstrel songs and masculine, 73n29
      names with, 187
      sexual, 376–79
Iijima Tadashi, 585, 587
Ikinci Yeni (The Second New), 38
Ilf, Ilya, 441
Ilyria, 31
imaginary national community, 88, 91
imitation, 561
      Chinese modernism and, 157–58, 159, 162,
      165n19
      comparison and, 504, 512
      of European models, 16–17, 51, 53, 117, 638,
      671
      Indian modernism and, 205–27
      with Spanish American modernismo, 111–17
      as subversive, 103n7, 513
imperialism. See also colonialism
      Bildungsroman and, 212
      Belgian, 235, 274
      British, 206–7, 214, 274, 296, 303, 421–24,
      429, 508–9
      Chinese (Confucian), 190
      cosmopolitanism and, 389–90, 406
      critique of, in African literature, 234–37
      cultural, 237, 294
      of English language in Moretti, 17
      European, 513
      French, 81–108 (in rel. to Berber poetry),
      123–25, 274
      inter-imperial competition, 472, 669–96

Japanese, 202n10, 571–597
      modernism and, 9–10, 100, 102n1,
      modernization of Indian life and, 216
      Ottoman, 27, 38, 325, 530–35, 673–74,
      677–78, 681, 687
      New World, 464
      Russian, 314, 317, 323–32, 440
      socio-sexual, 398
      Spanish, 113, 465
      U.S., 394, 469 (yanqui), 500, 620n25, 686
      with poetry and English language, 302–4
"In Bloomsbury" (Butts), 405–6
İnce, Özdemir, 38
India
      cinema, women and city with modernity
      in, 627–45
      Hindu "race" in, 393–94, 408n11
      Jallianwalla Bagh Massacre in, 207–8, 224n2
      modern woman as urban text in, 632–38
      social class in, 630–31, 643n11
      spectacles of modernity in, 639–42
      traditional figure of mother, 215, 218
      with urban scene of modernity in cinema,
      629–32
Indianization, 71n11
Indian modernism, 16
      Anand with politics of, 207–14
      with Coolie, 210–14
      language in, 213–14
      novels with, 205–7
      with transnational reading and Indian
      narratives in English, 205–27
      women's bodies with, 219–20
      in zenana with Purdah and Polygamy,
      215–23
indigenization, 95, 295
indigenous cultures, with global modernity,
      82, 85
Infants of the Spring (Thurman), 388
Inferno (Strindberg), 484
inflation
      genocide caused by, 259–60
      in Germany, 253, 260
      Jews and, 260
      Nigeria's annual rate, 253
inflationary modernism
      with magical realism and modernist time,
      262–63
      magical realism with, 249–66
      tour of Nigerian inflation and, 250–61
inner time, 68
Inoue Yoshio, 571, 578

In Praise of Shadows (Tanizaki), 619n10
In Search of Lost Time (Proust), 486
insurance payments, slaves and, 70n7
Integrals (Kosovel), 41
intercontamination of terms, 12, 155–59, 163n2
inter-imperiality, 685. *See also* imperialism
  geomodernisms and, 684–90
  in longue durée with modernist studies,
    669–96
interior time, 90–91
internationalism, queer, 367–84
International Monetary Conference, 114
International Writers' Congress for the
  Defense of Culture, 370, 380
Intimate Theater, 483. *See also* Strindberg,
  August
Ionesco, Eugene, 36, 37
Iqbal, Muhammad, 224n1, 541
Irele, Abiola, 280, 282
İrem, Nazim, 530, 543n6
Isherwood, Christopher, 388, 398–99
Ishiguro, Kazuo, 388, 400–2
Ishvani, G., 215
Islam, 39, 85, 86, 208–9, 222, 223, 320, 632,
  676–78, 690
Islamic modernism, 529–50,
Islands (Brathwaite), 54
It (Christensen), 490
Italy, 27
  futurism in, 314–18, 320–22, 331, 332
  futurist geographies and aesthetic
    autonomy in, 313–40
  language, 321–22
  little magazines in, 269
  time-space in, 315–16
Itami Mansaku, 588, 589, 594n17
Itô Daisuke, 572, 588, 589, 590
Izambard, Georges, 546n51
İzer, Zeki Faik, 544n27

Jabotinsky, Vladimir, 440–41
Jackson, Laura Riding, 163n4, 163n5
Jacob, Max, 574
Jacobsen, J. P., 486
Jacobsen, Rolf, 488
Jäderlund, Ann, 490
Jaffe, Aaron, 418
Jakobson, Roman, 331, 560
Jallianwalla Bagh Massacre, 207–8, 224n2
James, C. L. R., 57, 58, 70n9, 241
  on plantation, 72n22

James, Henry, 342, 482, 561, 565
Jameson, Fredric, 12–13, 16, 43n12, 69n1,
  232–33, 237
  alternative modernities dismissed by, 551–52
  with capitalist systematicity and
    simultaneity, 647
  cosmopolitanism and, 407
  on globalization, 294, 298, 305n10
  on language, 554–55
  on modernism with overlap of past and
    future, 243n11
  on modernity and modernism, 249–50
  on modernity as global capitalism, 117–19,
    254–55
  uneven modernity and, 318
Janco, Marcel, 37
Janevski, Slavko, 41
JanMohammed, Abdul, 501
Japan, 164n9, 400. *See also* Japanese
  modernism
  China named "Shina" by, 187, 202n10
  cinema in, 601–18, 618n4, 618n8
  film statistics for U.S., Europe and, 592n3
  "little magazines" in, 269, 272
  Russia's defeat by, 325
  Shochiku Kamata Studios in, 614–16
  white-collar films from, 615
  wood block prints, 513
Japanese empire, 202n10, 571–597. *See also*
  imperialism
Japanese Girls at the Harbor (film), 603–4, 605
Japanese modernism
  cine-text and, 571–97
  fragment and flow with, 575–77
  Kitagawa Fuyuhiko's *Theory of the Prose
    Film* and, 587–89, 590
  Kitagawa Fuyuhiko's *War* and cine-text
    with, 572, 577–80, 581, 589–91
  modern girls and, 573, 603, 615–17
  rhythm and tempo in, 585
  Shinkankakuha (New Perception School),
    573–75, 581, 585
  Yokomitsu Riichi's formalist theory with,
    582–86
  Yokomitsu Riichi's *Shanghai* and cine-text
    with, 572, 580–82, 583, 589–91
Japan Proletarian Literary Federation, 574–75
Jardín (Garden) (Loynaz), 357–59, 364n35
Jarnés, Benjamín, 466
Javidnama (Iqbal), 541
jazz, 58, 59, 73n29, 426–28, 429
Jemie, Onwuchekwa, 229–31

Jenner, W. J. F., 158, 165n19
Jenny (Undset), 485
Jews, 260, 398–99, 474, 481, 686. *See also*
    Berlin, Germany; Hebrew and Yiddish
    modernism; Odessa, Russia; Vienna,
    Austria
    Enlightenment, 435, 441
    "Jewish space" of café and, 444–49
    migration of, 435–36
    with modernism and modern Jewish
      revolution, 435–37
    urban ambivalence and New Jewish
      Woman, 440–44, 454n13
Jeyifo, Biodun, 232, 240, 262
Jiménez, Juan Ramón, 465, 471
Jog, N. G., 642
Johnson, Eyvind, 12, 492
Johnson, James Weldon, 388, 396–97
Johnson, Linton Kwesi, 303
Johnston, Frances Benjamin, 60
Jolas, Eugene, 283
Jones, Andrew F., 156, 165n17
José, F. Sionil, 236
Joshi, Priya, 207, 225n9
Joyce, James, 6, 8, 12, 71n16, 223, 271, 273, 415,
    418, 423, 429, 447, 467, 508
    Anand influenced by, 208–13
    cosmopolitanism in "The Dead," 404
    Scandinavian modernism and, 482, 484,
      488
Jugurtha (mythical Berber king), 85
Julien, Eileen, 275
Jusdanis, Gregory, 43n7, 164n14
Jussawalla, Feroza, 213, 224n8

Kabita, 272
Kabyle culture, 99–100
Kadir, Djelal, 512, 531
Kaffir Boy (Mathabane), 657
Kafka, Franz, 6, 37, 41, 161, 173, 234, 243n11, 489
Kahraman, Hasan Bülent, 530, 533, 544n15
Kaiser, Georg, 483
Kaknavatos, Hector, 35
Kala Nag (*Triumph of Justice/Black Cobra*)
    (film), 630
Kalliney, Peter, 5, 15, 58
Kallocain (Boye), 489
Kallol, 272
Kane, Cheikh Hamidou, 241
Kane, Sarah, 483
Kanik, Orhan Veli, 545n31

Kant, Immanuel, 74n36, 154, 390–91, 404,
    408n4, 505
Kaoui, Touareg Cid, 86
Karagöz shadow theater, 539
Karakoç, Sezai, 541–42
Karaosmanoğlu, Yakup Kadri, 533–34
Kataev, Valentin, 441
Kataoka Teppei, 575
Kawabata Yasunari, 573, 574
Kazantzakis, Nikos, 34
Keïta, Seydou, 136, 146n14
Kemal, Yahya, 532–33, 542, 543n13, 690
Kenner, Hugh, 8, 19n15, 551
    on international modernism, 552
Kép Tư Bên (Tư Bên the actor) (Nguyễn),
    374–76
Kern, Robert, 160
Kerr, Alfred, 450
Keyserling, Hermann (Count), 467
Khlebnikov, Velimir, 6, 317, 322, 323–24,
    327–30, 545n30
    manifesto of 1919, 331
Kid Chocolate, 357, 363n33
Kido Shiro, 615
Kincaid, Jamaica, 69, 70n4, 71n11
King, John, 470, 471
kings. *See also* "The Bourgeois King"
    Jugurtha, 85
    Louis Philippe II, 125n3
    Louis XIV, 319
Kinugasa Teinosuke, 574, 585
Kisakürek, Necip Fazil, 534, 535, 537, 539–41
Kitagawa Fuyuhiko, 16
    on film and poetry, 587
    on fourth person, 594n18
    with Japanese modernism and cine-text,
      571–97
    Theory of the Prose Film and, 587–89, 590
    War, 572, 577–80, 581, 589–91
Klein, K. L., 104n14
Klein, Lucas, 166n28
Kluge, Alexander, 437–38, 602
Knut, Hamsun, 484
Kojève, Alexandre, 159, 166n25
Köksal, Duygu, 544n29
Koliqi, Ernest, 31, 32
Kolkata Little Magazines Library, 285n3
Kolocotroni, Vassiliki, 531
Komori Yôichi, 582, 585
Kondô Azuma, 578
Konitza, Faik bey, 29, 31
Kon Tôkô, 575

Korang, Kwaku Larbi, 144n1
Korda, Zoltan, 650
Koselleck, Reinhart, 90
Kosovel, Srečko, 41
Kracauer, Siegfried, 647, 654–55, 659
Kraus, Karl, 234, 445
Krik, Benya, 441
Krishnaswamy, Revathi, 295
Kristin Lavransdatter (Undset), 485
Kritisk Revy, 490
Kronfeld, Chana, 29, 433
Kruchënykh, Aleksei, 322, 323, 331, 335n31
Kruchenykh, Alexander, 545n30
Krustev, Krustyo, 33
Kurahara Korehito, 583–84
Kurishima Sumiko, 601
Kyk-over-al, 272, 274

labor force
  in Cuba, 344, 348–49
  super-exploitation of, 119
  wage labor and, 118
  women in, 359–60
Lacan, Jacques, 8
Laforgue, Jules, 561
Lagerkvist, Pär, 483
Lalita, Ke, 225n10
Lalvani, Suren, 147n15
Lamming, George, 52, 53, 55, 415, 425
Landauer, Gustav, 450
Lang, Fritz, 344
languages. *See also* translations, modernism's;
    specific languages
  and African literature, 228–45
  Caribbean modernism with literary, 53, 54
  colonization of written, 17
  creolization of, 50
  demotic, 34–35
  Esperanto and Volapük, 555
  French, 31, 37, 58, 89, 97, 103n12, 115, 276, 313,
      319, 329, 371, 399, 470, 484, 488, 515, 540,
      559, 677, 690
  German, 302, 399, 438, 445, 447, 486, 487,
      488, 490, 612
  homosexuality and coded, 376–79
  imperialism with poetry and English, 302–4
  in Indian modernism, 213–14
  Italian, 321–22
  literary economy with preferred, 156–59,
      167n32
  musicality of Joyce's, 213

with new universal alphabet, 331
PIE, 554–55
poetry with impure form of everyday,
    96–97
purified, 34, 38
of resistance, 32
Scandinavian, 479
Standard Albanian, 31–32
standardization of, 319
Swahili, 621n34
Tsotsitaal slang, 653
Turkish, 38
universal, 317
Ur-, 554–55
Yiddish as fusion, 435–36
in Yugoslavia with *Moderna*, 40
Lanyer, Aemilia, 150
Lao She, 234
Larbaud, Valery, 461
large-scale vision, 18n4
Larionov, Mikhail, 326, 335n31
La Rochelle, Pierre Drieu, 470
Larsen, Nella, 486
Larson, Charles, 228–29
Lasker-Schüler, Else, 451, 452
The Last Temptation of Christ (Kazantzakis),
    35
Late Arrival on Earth (Ekelöf), 488
Latin America, 3, 4, 88, 112, 114, 117, 120–21,
    125n1, 5, 126n10, 153, 271, 467, 474n2,
    475n12, 505, 520n16, 552, 608, 617, 670
  cosmopolitanism and, 394–95
  Cuba's avant-gardes and modernity in,
      341–66, 362n19
  literary boom in, 113, 361
  postcolonial theory and, 113–14
  surrealism, 51
  Waldo Frank and, 469–73
Laurence, Patricia, 161
Lautréamont, 116
Lawrence, D. H., 471
Lazarus, Neil, 12–13, 14, 16, 117, 285n13, 649,
    662n3, 672, 691
Leavetaking (Weiss), 490
Lebed-Crescendo (*Swan-Crescendo*), 33
Lee, Gregory B., 149, 162
Lee, Leo Ou-fan, 165n21, 400
Lee, Li-Young, 301–2
Lefebvre, Henri, 434, 439
Left Bank, 416–18
Leguía, Augusto B., 362n20
Lehmann, John, 419

Lenglet, Ella, 420. *See also* Rhys, Jean
Leontis, Artemis, 27, 43n7
Lermontov, Mikhail, 559
Leslie, Omolara Ogundipe, 229
"Let Them Call it Jazz" (Rhys), 426–28, 429, 431n7
Levin, Harry, 7–8, 505
Levinger, Esther, 43n1
Levinsky, Elhonan, 441–42
Levitt, Helen, 146n10
Lewis, Wyndham, 8
Li Lili, 602–3
LillPers, Birgitta, 490
Lilyev, Nikolai, 33
Lincoln, Sarah, 12, 13–14, 243n13, 671
Lindegren, Erik, 489
Lindgren, Astrid, 493
linguistic standardization, 319
Link, Perry, 164n13
Lino, Steve, 283
Lionnet, Françoise, 502
Lippit, Seiji, 582
liquid economy, 260
Lisle, Leconte de, 116
Lista, Giovanni, 329, 335n28
literary café. *See* urban literary café
literary criticism, postmodern, 7–9
literary economy, 156–59
literary language, 53, 54. *See also* formalism
literary studies, 81–83
literature. *See* world literature
little magazines, 40, 267–87. *See also specific titles*
    Black Orpheus or Africa and rise of, 274–80
    circulation, 286n15
    criticism in, 279
    decentered universe of, 268–74
    digital afterlife of, 284–85
    distribution of, 271–72, 274, 277–78
    editors of, 276, 280
    general readership of, 275–76
    isolation of, 274
    letters to editor in, 281–83
    libraries and collections, 285n3
    mobility of, 270–71
    origins, 267–68
    print run of, 280–81
    production time of, 278–79
    reviews in, 278–79
    Transition or global readership for, 280–84
    translation problem with, 269
    in Uganda, 280–84

world form of, 10, 12, 267–87
    writers, 278
The Little Demon (Sologub), 562
The Little Review, 267, 271, 272, 284
Liu, Yu, 679, 693n9
Liu Na'ou, 607
Livshits, Benedikt, 322, 323, 326, 328–29
Lizaso, Félix, 347
Ljubljanski zvon (*Ljubljana Bell*), 40
"Llegada" (Guillén), 356
Lloyd, David, 501
The Location of Culture (Bhabha), 503
Locke, Alain, 134
Loeb, Harold, 271
Loewenberg, Friedrich, 445
Longfellow, Henry Wadsworth, 296
Look Lai, Wally, 430n4
Louis Philippe II (King), 125n3
Louis XIV (King), 319
Lourié, Artur, 328
love, free, in China, 202n12
Lovelace, Earl, 236
Lovell, Julia, 153–54, 164n14, 166n23
Lowe, John, 145n5
The Lower Depths (film), 588
Loy, Mina, 9, 289, 678
Loynaz, Dulce María, 342, 357–59, 364n35
Luca, Gherasim, 37
Lucey, Michael, 377
Lugones, Leopoldo, 125n4, 126n10
Lukács, Georg, 10, 124, 649
Lukacsian, Nkosi, 658
Lưu Trọng Lư, 372, 376–77
Lu Xun, 16, 234, 237, 686
    with allegory and *Ah Q-The Real Story*, 173–204
Lyon, Janet, 5, 20n28, 58, 72n25, 74n36, 472, 670

Ma, 272, 273
MacCabe, Colin, 8
MacClean, Una, 279
Macedonski, Alexandru, 36
Machado, Gerardo, 347
MacLean, Gerald, 677
Madame X (film), 602
A Madman's Defense (Strindberg), 484
Madubuike, Ihechukwu, 229–31
Maeda Ai, 582
Maes-Jelinek, Hena, 71n17
Maeterlinck, Maurice, 483

Maeztu, Ramiro de, 465, 467
magazines. *See also* little magazines
    distribution of, 271–72, 274, 277–78
magical realism, 12, 237
    with inflationary modernism, 249–66
    with inflationary modernism and
        modernist time, 262–63
    origins, 249, 254
    power of magical money and, 251, 256–58,
        261
Mahlatsi, Teboho, 661
Maiakovskii, Vladimir, 322, 323
Majumdar, Neepa, 639, 641
Makdisi, George, 676, 677, 691
"make it new," (slogan), 51, 157, 161, 407, 672
"Makinalaşmak" ("Mechanization") (Hikmet),
        536
Malcolm X, 69
Mallarmé, Stéphane, 6, 105n35, 115, 151, 323,
        487, 488, 557, 691,
    African literature and, 240–41
    cultural translation and, 100–102
    with derivation and global modernism,
        96–97
    on imperfection of language, 555
    on silence, 96
    Turkish literature and, 530–31, 533–34, 537,
        542
    vernacular culture with Amrouche and,
        82–87
Mallea, Eduardo, 470
Mañach, Jorge, 347
Manchurian Incident, 590, 592n11
Mandel'shtam, Osip, 323
Manley, Edna, 58
Mann, Thomas, 6, 486, 491
Mansfield, Katherine, 150
Manto, Saadat Hasan, 234
Mao, Douglas, 9, 10, 11, 14
Mao Dun, 201n1
Mao Zedong, 175, 183
Mapantsula (film), 658, 660, 661
mapping. *See also* distant reading
    of modern literary world, 319, 330
    spaces, 55
    of world literature, 17
Maps of Englishness (Gikandi), 508
Marangozov, Nikolai, 33
Mardin, Şerif, 539
Marías, Julián, 472
Mariátegui, José Carlos, 362n20, 469
Marichalar, Antonio, 466, 467

Marinello, Juan, 347
Marinetti, Filippo Tommaso
    with futurism, 313–15, 317, 321, 322–24,
        335n25
    iconic motivation and, 330
    Russian travels of, 328–29, 335n28
    transnational geography of futurist avant-
        garde and, 324–25, 328–29
    Turkey and, 535
    as visitor to Latin America, 362n19
    and "wireless imagination," 688
Marinković, Ranko, 41
Markandaya, Kamala, 225n9
Married Life (Fogel), 448–49
marronage (rebellious flight of slaves), 49, 55,
        58. *See also* slaves
Marshall, Paule, 55
Marson, Una, 58, 70n5
Martí, José, 18, 110–18, 125n4, 345, 469
Martínez, Enrique González, 125n4
Martínez de Villena, Rubén, 349
Martín Fierro, 272
Martinson, Harry, 492
Martinson, Moa, 492, 493
Maruo Tuneki, 182
Marx, Karl, 111, 112, 118, 120, 124, 151, 236,
        242n10, 556
    camera obscura analogy and, 258
    with capitalist systematicity and
        simultaneity, 647
    on influence of civilization, 408n10
masculine identity, 73n29
Masiello, Francine, 349
"The Mass Production of the Senses"
    (Hansen, M.), 607–9
Masters, Edgar Lee, 470
Matar, Nabil, 677, 691
Mathabane, Mark, 657
Matisse, Henri, 326
Matueda Shigeo, 182
Mayakovsky, Vladimir, 545n30
Mayanja, Abu, 283
Mayans, 55
May Fourth New Culture Movement, 174,
        197–98, 199
    Africa and commonalities with, 239–40
    free love in, 202n12
    New Literature of, 201n3
    origins, 201n2
    past and future vision of, 202n5
Mazrui, Ali, 286n17
Mazzesinsel district ("Matzo Island"), 444–45

Mbembe, Achille, 662
McFarlane, James, 273, 481, 509
McKay, Claude, 4, 50, 52, 58, 61, 70n5, 72n25, 73n29, 303
media studies, 9
Melas, Natalie, 506
Melville, Herman, 151
Melville, Pauline, 52
Memmi, Albert, 84, 103n5
memory
    in *Ah Q–The Real Story* with forgetting, 195–201
    collective, 104n14
    literature of, 82, 85
    sites of, 103n11
    time and reconstructing Berber, 87–94
Menand, Louis, 161
Mendelssohn, Moses, 435
Mendès, Catulle, 115
Mendl, Menakhem, 442–43
Menocal, Maria, 676, 691
Mercereau, Alexandre, 335n28
Meredith, James, 145n5
Metlitzki, Dorothee, 676–77, 691
Metropolis (film), 344
Micić, Ljubomir, 25, 26, 29, 41, 43
Middle Passage, 51, 52, 54
Migjeni, 31
Mignolo, Walter, 390, 514, 674, 693n3
migrancy, 67–69
migration, 300, 325, 612, 631
    of Jews, 434–37
    mass, 552
    Russian culture as shaped by, 325
    West Indian, 427
    universal myth of, 437
Milestone, Lewis, 589
Milev, Geo, 33–34
Milton, John, 678, 689
mimetic desire
    with Chinese modernism and European time, 149–70
    globality and geography of, 153–55
    inequity of, 160–62
A Mind at Peace (Tanpınar), 39
minoristas, Cuba's, 344, 346, 347–49, 355–56
Minor Transnationalism (Shih and Lionnet), 502
minstrel songs, 63, 73n29
Mintz, Sidney, 57, 72n22
Mirbeau, Octave, 161
Mirón, Salvador Díaz, 125n4

mirroring, in poetry, 291
Misal (*Thought*), 33
"Miss Apperson," 60f
Miss Julie (Strindberg), 482
Mitter, Partha, 388, 402–3
Mizoguchi Kenji, 572
Model, Lisette, 142
modern drama, in Scandinavia, 481–84
modern girls, 573, 603, 615–17
modernism. *See also* Anglo-American modernism; Balkan modernism; Caribbean modernism; Chinese modernism; Cuba; French modernism; Hebrew and Yiddish modernism; Hispanic modernism; Indian modernism; Islamic modernism; inflationary modernism; Japanese modernism; high modernism; photographic modernism; proletarian modernism; Scandinavian modernism; Spanish American *modernismo*; Taiwanese modernism; world modernisms
    aesthetic autonomy and uneven, 313–40
    African literature and, 228–45
    African literature with capitalism, modernity and, 231, 232–37
    alternatives, 20n27
    combined and uneven, 237–41
    comparison and appropriation of, 14–18
    cosmopolitanism and, 387–412
    with cosmopolitanism situation, 402–7
    disfigured and Turkish literature, 529–50
    Georgian, 335n33
    global perspectives on, 3–7
    with *histoire croisée* in Balkans, 25–43
    Hollywood cinema and vernacular, 9, 607–9, 613
    imagined proximity of revolution and, 12
    little magazine and birth of, 268
    lyrical high, 488–90
    methodological apertures with Balkan, 41–43
    moderated, 32
    modernismo and difference between, 163n6
    with modernity, 249–50
    from old to new, 7–10
    paintings, 326
    as period and attitude, 150–51
    peripheral, 334n12
    positionality with, 342

modernism (*continued*)
　provisionally definitive inductive definition
　　of, i–701
　South African cinema with modernity and,
　　647–51
　as term in Catholic Church, 163n5
　thirdspace of urban literary café with,
　　437–40, 442, 454n12
　translations with, 551–70
　Turkey with failed, 529–30
　with Western history of modern, 150–53
　women and relationship to, 164n10
modernismo, 362n13. *See also* Brazilian
　　modernismo; Spanish American
　　modernismo
　modernism and difference between, 163n6
Modernisms: A Literary Guide (Nicholls), 151,
　　531
modernist
　cultural expansion as modern or, 10–14
　movements, 157
modernistas, 112–16, 125n4. *See also* Spanish
　　American *modernismo*; *specific
　　modernistas*
Modernist Journals Project, 474n3
Modernist Magazines Project, 474n3
modernist studies
　belatedness reconsidered with, 675–80
　brief history of, 7–10
　inter-imperial geomodernisms and, 684–90
　inter-imperiality in longue durée, 669–96
　inter-imperial palimpsest and, 690–92
　interlocked empires and, 672–75
　longue durée of borrowing and, 671–72
　with nineteenth-century empires, plural,
　　680–84
　world modernisms and comparative
　　strategies in, 507–18
Modernist Studies Association, 9, 153
modernity. *See also* global modernity
　alternative modernities, debated, 12–14,
　　42–43, 101–102, 233–34, 506, 514, 551–52,
　　606, 673
　African literature with capitalism,
　　modernism and, 231, 232–37
　colonial, 83–84, 86–87, 93, 100–102, 212,
　　239–40, 369–71, 514, 615, 629, 631
　in colonial India, 627–45
　colonial India and spectacles of, 639–42
　futurist avant-garde with time-space of,
　　315–18
　as global capitalism, 117–19
　as known history, 84
　in Latin America, 341–66, 362n19
　modernism as cultural expression of, 11,
　　249–50
　plantation as laboratory of, 57, 72n22
　poetry and globalization with, 288–309
　semi-colonial, in China, 175, 617
　singularity and simultaneity of, 233, 647
　South African cinema with modernism
　　and, 647–51
　Spanish American, 109–28
　transatlantic, 117–25
　unthinkable, 70n6
modernity/coloniality, 693n3
Modern Language Association, 11
Modisane, Bloke, 656
Moerdijk, Gerard, 646, 648
moga. See modern girls
Mogotlane, Thomas, 658
Moi, Toril, 481
A Mölna Elegy (Ekelöf), 488
Mona Lisa and Si-Ya-U (Hikmet), 38
money. *See also* oil-based economies
　clean, 259
　magical, 251, 256–58, 261
　Nigerian naira, 251, 253, 256–57, 259, 264n3
　oil's relation to, 264n17
Monroe, Harriet, 272, 691
Monroe, James, 676
montage, 11, 67, 489, 491, 516, 572, 576–91,
　　593n12, 614, 647
Montagu-Nathan, Montagu, 561, 562
Montenegro, 27, 32
Moody, Ronald, 58
Moore, G. E., 208
Moore, Marianne, 161
Morand, Paul, 350
Moréas, Jean, 98, 106n41, 116
Morente, Manuel García, 466
Moretti, Franco, 17, 70n3, 211, 502, 510
Morris, Meaghan, 84
Morris, Rosalind, 9, 686
Moskvich, Grigory, 441
mother figure
　in Berber culture, 89
　in India, 215, 218
motherhood, in film, 601–3
"Mourning the Dead" (Lu Xun), 202n12,
　　203n13
Mufti, Aamar, 506
Mühsam, Erich, 450
multiculturalism, 164n11

Mumford, Lewis, 470
Munch, Edward, 481
Munif, Abdelrahman, 234, 236
Munshi, K. M., 642
Müridoğlu, Zühtü, 544n27
Murphy, Michael, 430n3
Murray, Les, 299
musical form, 58
    in Joyce's language, 213
    poetic creation as, 96–97
Musil, Robert, 445, 447, 448
Mutafov, Chavdar, 33, 42
Mutloatse, Mothobi, 649
Muybridge, Eadweard, 576
My Mother Gets Married (Martinson, M.),
    492–93
Mythistory (Seferis), 35

Naci, Elif, 544n27
Nadja (Breton), 486
Nadrealizam sada i ovde (*Surrealism Here and
    Now*), 40
Naidu, Sarojini, 215
Naipaul, V. S., 415, 425
Naira (currency), 251, 253, 256–57, 259, 264n3.
    See also Nigeria
names
    actresses and Hindu, 633
    cynical change of, 193
    identity with, 187
    of imperialism and colonialism, 187, 202n10
    namelessness with, 181
    rectification of, 15–16, 180–86, 189–92, 200
Naomi (Tanizaki), 619n10
Narayan, R. K., 20n25, 213, 217, 223
Naruse Mikio, 601, 614
nation, 4, 5, 81, 101–2, 103n11, 149, 159–60,
    177, 195–96, 211–12, 215–16, 261, 269–73,
    288–89, 297–98, 303–4, 367, 370–72,
    465–68, 479–80, 484–85, 534, 538–39, 551,
    556, 602, 628–29, 631, 636–38
    cosmopolitanism with race and, 393–96
    -building and -formation, 34–35, 86–87, 94,
        118, 351, 436
    -states, 38, 82, 88, 99, 164n15, 165n16, 202n9,
        211, 251, 297–98, 317, 319–20, 369, 472, 505,
        511, 554, 582, 606, 609
    temporality and, 129–48
National Academy of Arts and Letters, Cuba's,
    347
national allegory, 15, 164n12, 184

nationalism, 86, 142, 387, 462, 541, 582, 616,
    633, 648, 662
    Algerian, 84
    Amrouche and, 93–94, 101
    anti-colonial, 70n5 (and modernism), 101
    Asia, 394
    black, 145n5, 424
    Caribbean, and modernism, 56
    Chinese, 165n15, 575
    cultural, 232, 238–40 (in Africa), 330–32
        (aesthetic autonomy and), 628 (in India)
    communalist, in Bulgaria, 33
    cosmopolitanism and, 387–412
    futurism, cosmopolitanism, and, 317–24,
        335n33
    Jewish, 436
    Romantic, 31 (in Albanian literature), 39 (in
        Turkish modernism)
    Russian, 328–29
    Turkish, 546n58
    state- and delayed modernisms, 45
    Vietnamese, 369–70
    white, 646 (South Africa)
    World-system theory and, 502
national life, art reconciled with, 317–18
National Workers Confederation (CNOC),
    343
Native Son (Wright), 130, 145n3
naturalism, 341, 352, 359, 397–98, 467, 539,
    546n45, 559–60
Nature and Context of Minority Discourse
    (JanMohammed and Lloyd), 501
Naum, Gellu, 37
Nazis, 494
Ndebele, Njabulo, 649, 652, 658
Négritude, 51, 58, 70n5, 145n5, 232, 242n5
Negt, Oskar, 437, 438
Nehru, Jawaharlal, 224n1, 224n3, 225n10
Neogy, Rajat, 274, 280, 281–84.
    See also Transition
neo-Tarzanism, 231–32, 240–41
Neruda, Pablo, 362n5
Nervo, Amado, 125n4
New Literature (*xinwenxue*), 201n3
Newman, Francis, 557
New Republic, 473
newspapers, 313
    readership, 285n9
    Romanian, 43n8
    serialization, 177
New Theatres studio, 641
New World Modernisms (Pollard), 56

New Yorker, 473
Nga jeta në jetë—Pse!? (From Life to Life—Why!?) (Spasse), 32
Ngũgĩ wa Thiong'o, 17, 234, 241
    on capitalism's brutality, 235–36
    "decolonizing the mind" and, 228
Nguyễn Công Hoan, 374–76, 377–79
Nicholls, Peter, 151, 531
Nida, Eugene, 560
Niels Lyhne (Jacobsen, J. P.), 486
Nietzsche, Friedrich, 33, 35, 176, 196, 481, 691
Nigeria. *See also Black Orpheus*
    inflation in, 250–61
    and inflationary modernism, 250–61
    Civil War, 230, 251, 280, 291
    magical realism in, 249–66
    naira as currency in, 251, 253, 256–57, 259, 264n3
Nigeria Magazine, 275
Nikolla, Millosh Gjergj. *See* Migjeni
Niranjana, Tejaswini, 553
Nkosi, Lewis, 267, 273, 649, 656, 662n3
Nkrumah, Kwame, 130
Nobel Complex, 153–54, 155, 164n15
noble savages, 85
Noli, Fan S., 31
Nôm (ideographic, demotic Vietnamese script), 371
Nora, Pierre, 88, 91, 103n11, 104n14
Nordau, Max, 116
Norén, Lars, 483
North, Michael, 10–11, 421
Norway, 479–80. *See also* Scandinavian modernism
The Notebooks of Malte Laurids Brigge (Rilke), 486
Nouvelle Revue Française (NRF), 464, 470, 475n8
Novak, Slobodan, 41
novels. *See also specific titles*
    African, 270
    Boom, 361
    with Indian modernism, 205–27
    publishers of, 275
    Scandinavian modernist, 493–94
Nov put (New Way), 33
N.R.F., 272
"Nuestra América" ("Our America") (Martí), 114, 469
Nussbaum, Martha, 391
Nwankwo, Kiddoe, 395
Nykl, Richard, 676

Obote, Milton, 283
Obstfelder, Sigbjørn, 486
Ocampo, Victoria, 462, 691, 692
    Americas of Frank, Waldo, and Europe of, 469–72
    friendship with Woolf, Virginia, 471, 474n3
    literary activism of, 470–72
    with uneven modernist cosmopolitanism, 472–74
Odessa, Russia. *See also* Hebrew and Yiddish modernism; Russia; urban literary café
    Café Fanconi, 441, 442f, 443–44
    Café Robina, 441, 444
    as center of Jewish freedom, 440
    urban ambivalence and New Jewish Woman in, 440–44, 454n13
Odissia (The Odyssey: A Modern Sequel) (Kazantzakis), 35
O'Dwyer, Michael, 224n2
Öffentlichkeit und Erfahrung ("The Public Sphere and Experience") (Negt and Kluge), 438
"Of Other Spaces" (Foucault), 499
O'Hanlon, Rosalind, 636
Ohnet, Georges, 120, 126n14
oil-based economies
    dream-world in, 253–54, 257
    ecological impact on, 261
    excrement of wealth and human life in, 261, 264n4
    hyperinflation of, 12, 250–63
    money in, 251, 253, 256–59, 261, 264n3, 264n17
    phantasmagoria with, 258–59, 261, 264n13
    tour of Nigerian inflation as, 250–61
    Venezuela, 251–52, 261
Okara, Gabriel, 278
Okigbo, Christopher, 14, 230, 274, 278, 291–92, 294
Okri, Ben, 14, 238, 243n13, 249–66
Olesha, Yuri, 441
Oliver, María Rosa, 470
Olsson, Hagar, 487
Omeros (Walcott), 294
O'Neill, Eugene, 483
On the Wire (film), 661
On Overgrown Paths (Hamsun), 489
OPEC. *See* Organization of Oil-Producing Countries
Ophuls, Max, 602
Opium Wars, 675
Oppenheim, James, 463

oral poetry, 82, 86–87, 96. *See also* Berber poetry
The Order of Things (Foucault), 531
Organization of Oil-Producing Countries (OPEC), 250–51, 264n12
Orsini, Francesca, 637
Ortega, Julio, 116
Ortega y Gasset, José, 342, 462, 691
    with feminine Latin body, 469–70
    with modernism and "invertebrate Spain," 465–68
    ratio-vitalism and, 466
    with uneven modernist cosmopolitanism, 472–74
Orthodox Church, 43n6
Ortiz, Fernando, 350, 513, 520n17
Osborne, Peter, 144n1, 319, 333n11, 505
the other, 153. *See also* mimetic desire
    recognition by, 159
    West and Turkish literature, 529–50
Ottoman alphabet, 546n46
Ottoman Empire, 27, 38, 325, 530–35, 673–74, 677–78, 681, 687. *See also* imperialism
Our America (Frank, W.), through Europe's eyes with Hispanic modernism, 463–65
O ve Ben (Kisakürek), 540
Owen, Stephen, 156, 165n17, 294
Ôya Sôichi, 573
Özel, İsmet, 541
Ozu Yasujirô, 572, 603, 614, 622n43

Pabst, G. W., 589
painters. *See specific painters*
paintings, 576
    artistic appropriation in, 297
    modernist, 326
    post-Expressionist, 249, 254, 263
Palacio, Ernesto, 471
Pal Fejos, 605
Palm-Wine Drinkard (Tutuola), 270, 275
Pamuk, Orhan, 529
Pan-American Conference, 114, 120
parataxis, cultural, 96, 516
Paris, France, 40, 112, 116, 398–99
    as center of cultural modernity, 314, 315, 319, 329, 335n28
    futurism in, 314–15, 319–21, 335n28
    futurist geographies and aesthetic autonomy in, 313–40
    Left Bank, 416–18
Park, Josephine, 160

Park, Robert, 130
Parla, Jale, 39
Parland, Henry, 487
Parnassian School, 112
parochialism, 395
Pasha, Mustafa Reşit (Grand Vizier), 532, 674
past, 53, 202n5, 243n11
Patel, Divia, 643n6
Paulhan, Jean, 475n8
Paz, Octavio, 116, 117
p'Bitek, Okot, 292–94, 295
Peña, Roque Sáenz, 120
People's Home, 490–91
Pepys, Samuel, 63
"Pequeña oda a un negro boxeador cubano" ("Small Ode to a Black Cuban Boxer") (Guillén), 357, 363n33
Peredonova, Obraz, 562
Peret, 447
Pérez, Louis, 343
Pérez de Ayala, Ramón, 465
periodicals. *See also specific periodicals*
    Bulgarian, 33
    Greek, 35
    Romanian, 36
    Yugoslavia, 40
peripheral modernism, 334n12
periphery, 88, 153, 164n15, 316, 407, 472, 591, 648, 655, 681
    and world-systems theory, 6–7, 320, 333n4, 501–3, 509, 519n5, 6, 8, 688
    center and, 56, 82–83, 96, 118, 183, 269–70, 320, 325, 390, 502–4, 506, 511–18
Perloff, Marjorie, 153, 318
Perón, Juan, 474
Përpjekja Shqiptare (*The Albanian Endeavour*), 31
"Persimmons" (Lee, L.-Y.), 302
Pessoa, Fernando, 475n9
Peterson, Nicolas, 144n1
Peter the Great, 325, 329
petro-magical realism, 252–53, 264n1. *See also* oil-based economies
Petrov, Evgeni, 441
phantasmagoria, 258–59, 261, 264n13
phantasmic, 643n4
Philippa of Aragon, 677
Philippe, Louis, 121
Phillips, Ray, 651
photographers, 576. *See also* Wright, Richard; *specific photographers*

photographic modernism
    blindness and, 140, 141f, 142
    frontal vision and, 137–39, 147n15
    Gold Coast photos, 132f, 133f, 135f, 139f, 140f,
        141f, 143f, 146n6
    history, postcolonial state and, 130–33
    time with, 131–34, 144n1
    with Wright's *Black Power*, 129–48
photography, 18n1, 576, 654
Picasso, Pablo, 95, 297, 321, 421, 513
pictographs, 52
PIE language. *See* Proto-Indo-European
        language
Pinney, Christopher, 144n1
Pinsker, Shachar, 5, 669, 686–87
Pinter, Harold, 483
Pipa, Arshi, 31, 32
Pippi Longstocking (Lindgren), 493
Piyâle (*The Wine Cup*) (Haşim), 38
Plaatjie, Sol, 651, 656
Plamen (*Flame*), 40
planetary, 3, 4–5, 72n23, 73n35
    Caribbean modernism, plantation to, 48–77
    as elusive concept, 68
    vs. global, 5
    globalization distinct from, 52
    literary writing's circulation with, 56–57,
        70n8
    poem, 73n36, 301
    as terminology, 5, 70n3
    time, 70n8
plantation
    Caribbean modernism and, 48–77
    cries of, 50, 56–67
    as laboratory of modernity, 57, 72n22
    slaves, 53
plantation melodies
    "Cries of London" and, 59–67
    "Shake That Thing," 61
Plantation Melodies, 63
plantation zone, 69
plays. *See specific play titles*
Playthings (film), 604
Pocock, J. G. A., 693n8
Podbevšek, Anton, 40–41
Poe, Edgar Allen, 116
poetics of Relation. *See* Relation, poetics of
poetry, 40. *See also specific titles*
    Berber, 6
    Chinese, 156–58
    compound figure in, 289
    constructivist, 41–42

Delphic, 34
global space with, 298–300
haiku, 296, 489, 579
imperialism of English language with, 302–4
journals, 574–75
Kitagawa on, 587
localist, 301
mirroring in, 291
modernity and globalization with, 288–309
as musical form, 96–97
oral, 82, 86–87, 96
as personal verbal rite, 12
planetary, 73n36, 301
as resistance tool, 292–93
Scandinavian, 487–90
shin sanbunshi, 574
as song, 85, 87–94
sugar industry and combat, 350–52
tanshi, 574, 577–78
translocal, 299, 301, 305n9
visual, 41
women in labor force, 359–60
Zulu, 649
poets. *See also* "The Bourgeois King"; *specific
        poets*
    Chinese, 156–58
    First New and Second New, 542, 545n31
    literary economy's preferred languages and,
        156–59
Poggioli, Renato, 316, 318
Polgar, Alfred, 438, 448
political writings, of Hussain, 218–19
politics
    Americanist artistic, 346
    of despair, 102
    homosexuality in Vietnam and coded,
        376–79
    of Indian modernism with Anand, 207–14
    of time and writing, 183
Pollack, Sheldon, 396, 409n14
Pollard, Charles, 56, 512, 514
Pollock, Sheldon, 609–10
polygamy, 220–21. *See also Purdah and
        Polygamy: Life in an Indian Muslim
        Household*
Pomeranz, Kenneth, 166n27
Pontalis, J. B., 643n4
Popa, Vasko, 41
Popdimitrov, Emanuil, 33
populism ("narodnichestvo"), 435
Poradeci, Lasgush, 31, 32
La Porte étroite (*Strait Is the Gate*) (Gide), 367

Porter, Dennis, 296
Portrait of the Artist as a Young Man (Joyce), 210–13
positionality, 5, 342
positive forgetting, 176
postcoloniality, 126, 269, 662
   and African literature, 228–45, 249–66
   and belatedness, 675–80
   and Berber poetry, 81–108
   vs, globality, 298
   and little magazines, 267–87
   magical realism in Nigeria and, 249–66
   modernism and, 5, 6, 8, 19n13, 56, 58, 81, 95–96, 166n26, 205–27 (India), 237–41, 299–300, 304, 417–18, 420–21, 429–30, 499–525 (methodology), 591, 671–72, 685–86
   poetry and, 288–309
   postcolonial studies, 5, 49, 81, 113–14, 160, 228, 233–36, 295, 499–502, 553, 680, 687–88
   print culture and, 278–79
   Rhys and, 413–32
   split temporality of emerging state, 129–48 (Gold Coast, Africa)
   writers, 8, 275, 289, 298, 301, 415, 419, 421, 686
post-Expressionist painting, 249, 254, 263
Postmodern Geographies (Soja), 499
postmodern literary criticism, 7–9
Pound, Ezra, 6, 8, 16, 71n16, 157, 166n28, 267, 295–96
   with black vernacular forms, 421
   China's influence on, 160–61
   on modernist translations, 557–58
Pourgouris, Marinos, 43n7
Powell, Adam Clayton, 131, 145n5
power. *See also* colonialism; imperialism; oil-based economies
   of cinema, 641–42
   of the collector, 121
   comparison and, 505
   cultural, and global imbalance of, 153, 162, 499–525
   economic and world-systems theory, 6–7, 320
   labor and, in Latin America, 341
   of magical money, 251, 256–58, 261
   male sexual, 73n29
   parochialism and provincialism with centers of, 395
   of spectacle, 252

relationships in zenana, 218
   sexualized dynamics of, in Scandinavian modernism, 482
   translation and, 533
   of the word and poetic discourse, 89, 123, 213, 296, 317–18, 374–75, 396–97
"The Powerline Incarnation" (Murray), 299
Pratt, Mary-Louise, 88, 93–94, 103n12, 104n15, 145n5, 512
Prendergast, Christopher, 510
Présence Africaine, 274, 276, 280
Price, Richard, 55
A Priest's Diary (Sigbjørn), 486
Prima verba (Macedonski), 36
primitivism, 25–29, 95, 326, 349–50, 356–57, 362n20, 403
Proctor, Elaine, 661
proletarian modernism, 492–93
Prosanatolismoi (*Orientations*) (Elytis), 35
Prosas profanas (Darío), 116
proscription, in *Ah Q–The Real Story*, 186–95
prostitutes, as actresses, 633
prostitution, in film, 601–3
Proto-Indo-European (PIE) language, 554–55
Proust, Marcel, 6, 12, 467, 486, 488, 489, 492, 534
provincialism, 395
Provincializing Europe (Chakrabarty), 86, 514
public opinion. *See also* oil-based economies
   financial value determined by, 249, 255–56
publishers, 275, 278, 473, 557
Puchner, Martin, 333n1, 334n20
puns, 563–64
Purdah and Polygamy: Life in an Indian Muslim Household (Hussain)
   Austen's influence in, 215–17, 221
   Indian modernism in zenana with, 215–23
   plot and structure in, 222–23
   polygamy in, 220–21
purified language, 34
Putevi (*Ways*), 40
Pynchon, Thomas, 494
Pyramides (*Pyramids*) (Ritsos), 35

Qian, Zhaoming, 160–61
Quartet (Rhys), 72n25, 387–88, 397–98
queer internationalism
   Gide's particularity and, 370–71
   modern Vietnamese aesthetics and, 367–84
   Vietnam's art for art's sake *versus* art for life's sake debate and, 368–69, 371–76

Quicksand (Larsen), 486
quốc ngữ (romanized Vietnamese script), 371
    print culture, 372

race, 6, 9, 53, 55, 58–67, 83, 132, 136–37, 145n5,
        160, 288, 300, 304, 341, 343, 356, 357, 403,
        414–16, 500, 506, 516, 538, 582, 606, 633,
        648, 657, 687
    banjo with, 59, 67
    cosmopolitanism with nation and, 387–88,
        393–96, 406–7
    crossing color lines, 420–23
    Hindu, considered as a, 393–94, 408n11
    Marinetti and, 325, 326
    Rhys and, 413–32
    South African cinema and, 646–65
    Spain and racial difference, 468, 475n5
    West Indies writing and, 413–32, 430n4
    whiteness and vulnerability, 423–28
Räderscheidt, Anton, 254
Radhakrishnan, R., 15, 92, 101, 105n32, 504,
        516
    on comparison, 506
    curse of derivativeness and, 513–14
Raine, Michael, 618n3
Rainov, Nikolai, 33–34
Ram, Harsha, 6, 12, 114, 669, 688
Rama, Angel, 111, 119–20, 123, 125n1, 344
Ramalho Santos, Irene, 475n9
Ramazani, Jahan, 12, 14, 72n24, 74n36, 503,
        512, 672
    on translocation, 507
Ramchand, Kenneth, 430n4
Ramos, José Antonio, 344
Rampolokeng, Lesego, 660
Randall, A. W. G., 562
Ranjit Studios, 634
Rao, Raja, 217–18
Los raros (*The Odd Ones*) (Darío), 116
rationalism, Enlightenment, 403
ratio-vitalism, 466
Ravitch, Melekh, 439, 444, 452
Ray, Sangeeta, 207, 215, 225n9
"Razor" (Kitagawa), 578
readers
    of little magazines, 275–76, 280–84
    of newspapers, 285n9
    text and relationship to, 177–78
Reading 1922 (North), 10–11
reading
    close, 17, 511, 515

distant, 17, 502
    vertical, 517
realism, 222, 317, 368. *See also* magical realism
    Albanian literature, 31
    Anand and, 208–9, 214
    black literary circles in South Africa and,
        658
    Caribbean resistance to, 51–52, 55, 69
    Chinese "New Literature," 201n3
    French, 566
    "market," 557
    modernism and, 5, 11, 39, 380n4, 381n14,
        415, 481–82, 658
    "petro-magic," 249–66
    photographic, 133
    Russian, 566
    Scandinavia and, 481–82, 491
    South African, 649, 658
    Turkish, 39
    Vietnamese, 368, 373–75, 380n4, 381n14, 15,
        382n17
reciprocal defamiliarization, 506
recognition, *Ah-Q–The Real Story* with
        forgetting and desire for, 195–201
recovery, in modernist studies, 10, 16, 507,
        509–11, 529
rectification, of names, 15–16, 180–86, 189–92,
        200
reggae, 58
Reinhardt, Max, 450, 483
Relation, poetics of
    Glissant and, 56, 57, 59, 72n21, 72n24, 73n35
    with *Voyage in the Dark* and *Banjo*, 59
Remizov, Alexei, 562, 565
Republican People's Party (CHP), 535
The World Republic of Letters (Casanova),
        164n7, 319, 502, 519n6, 673
resistance
    language of, 32
    poetry as tool of, 292–93
Rethinking Modernism (Thormählen), 531
*Return to Ithaca: The Odyssey retold as a
        modern novel* (Johnson, E.), 492
reviews, 466, 467, 564, 632
    and European revitalization, 462–63
    in little magazines, 268, 278–79
    and *modernistas*, 114
Revista de Occident (*Review of the West*)
        (Ortega y Gasset), 462, 466–67
revolts, slave, 53
revolutionary style, in South African cinema,
        654–59

revolutions
  of August 1945, 375
  of 1848, 119
  French, 400, 534
  Haitian, 51–52, 53, 70n2, 70n6, 71n15
  modernism catalyzed by imagined
    proximity of, 12
  modern Jewish, 435–37
  Xinhai, 201n1, 202n7
La Revue Indigène, 272
"El rey burgués." See "The Bourgeois King"
Reyes, Alfonso, 467, 468
Rhys, Jean, 5, 15, 52, 69, 71n11, 72n25
  with cosmopolitanism, 387–88, 397–98
  crossing color line and, 420–23
  Left Bank days, 416–18
  literary reincarnation of, 418–20
  as modernist literary refugee, 430n4
  as postcolonial intellectual, 413–32
  Voyage in the Dark, 4, 50, 58, 59, 63–67,
    73n34
  with whiteness and vulnerability, 423–28
rhythm, in Japanese modernism, 585
"The Rhythm of Cinema" (Iijima), 585
Rich, Adrienne, 508
Richter, Hans, 29
Rifat, Oktay, 545n31
Rifbjerg, Klaus, 491
Rilke, Rainer Maria, 486
Rimbaud, Arthur, 488, 531, 691
Ritsos, Yannis, 35
Rive, Richard, 656
Rivera, Miguel Primo de, 467
Rivière, Jacques, 475n8
Robbins, Bruce, 300, 301, 408n7, 409n21
Robinson, first, 146n13
Rodó, José Enrique, 114, 343
Rodríguez Acosta, Ofelia, 342, 357, 359–60
Rogers, Gayle, 6, 691
Rogosin, Lionel, 656
Roh, Franz, 249, 254
Roig de Leuchsenring, Emilio, 346–47, 349
Roldán, Amadeo, 355
Rolland, Romain, 463
Romania
  avant-garde in, 36
  modernism in, 27, 36–37
  newspapers, 43n8
  periodicals, 36
  symbolists, 36
Romanisches Café, 437, 449, 450f, 451–53
Roman Stoic cosmopolitanism, 407n2

Ronda, García, 363n25
The Roofing Ceremony (Strindberg), 484
A Room of One's Own (Woolf, V.), 471
"To Roosevelt" (Darío), 114
Rose, Derrick, 1
Rosenberg, Fernando, 342
Rössner, Michael, 453n9
Rostagno, Irene, 469
Roth, Joseph, 445, 446, 448
Rowlandson, Thomas, 64
Ruan Ling-yu, 601, 618n6
Rubin, Israel, 452
Rushdie, Salman, 16, 206, 207
"Rush Hour" (Kitagawa), 577–78
Russia, 27, 32
  avant-garde in, 317, 325–26, 329–30
  futurism in, 314–18, 320, 322–24, 331–32,
    334n19
  futurist geographies and aesthetic
    autonomy in, 313–40
  Japan's victory over, 325
  Marinetti's travels in, 328–29, 335n28
  with Russian translations in Britain, 558–66
  symbolists, 325–26
  time-space in, 315–16
  transnational geography of futurist avant-
    garde and, 325–26, 329–30
  urban ambivalence and new Jewish women
    in Odessa, 440–44
Russian Empire, 314, 317, 323–32, 440
Russo-Turkish war, 27
Rynell, Elisabeth, 490

Saar, Bettye, 137
Sachs, Nelly, 490
Sachtouris, Miltos, 35
Sade, Marquis de, 116
Safa, Peyami, 544n25
Said, Edward, 28, 100, 228, 235, 296, 298, 508,
    671, 684
  contrapuntal reading strategy and, 17
  on transplantation of ideas, 512
Saint-Amour, Paul, 209, 420
"Saint Stéphane Mallarmé" (Amrouche), 82,
    96–98
Sakai, Naoki, 154, 162
Salaris, Claudia, 334n21
Salih, Tayeb, 513
Salkey, Andrew, 277
Salnchevi prikazki (The Tales of the Sun)
    (Rainov), 33

Salten, Felix, 445
"San'at Telâkkisi" ("Regarding Art")
    (Hikmet), 536
Sánchez Rivero, Ángel, 468
Sand, George, 376
Sandel, Cora, 485–86, 493
Sandemose, Aksel, 491
Sanderson, Richard, 514
San Juan, E., Jr., 118
Sano Shuji, 618n6
Sans Lendemain (film), 602
Sarlo, Beatriz, 362n20
Saro-Wiwa, Ken, 261
Sartre, Jean-Paul, 276, 407, 688
Sarvig, Ole, 489–90
Satthianadhan, Krupaba, 225n10
Saussy, Haun, 17, 164n11, 166n28, 505
Savory, Elaine, 430n4
Scandinavian modernism
    aesthetics of welfare state and cultural
        radicalism with, 490–91
    children's literature, 493
    complexities of, 494n1
    with Danish, Norwegian and Swedish
        languages, 479
    discontinuities in, 487–94
    lyrical high modernism and, 488–90
    modern drama and, 481–84
    novels, 493–94
    proletarian modernism with, 492–93
    spatial connections with, 480–86
    stories of transnational and discontinuous
        with, 478–98
    transnational prose modernism on margins
        with, 484–86
Schiller, Friedrich, 316
Schleiermacher, Friedrich, 557
Schmitz, Oliver, 658, 660, 661
Schnitzler, Arthur, 445, 446
"The Schooner 'Flight'" (Walcott), 288–89,
    290, 292, 304
Schrader, Paul, 657
Schrimpf, Georg, 254
Schultz, Bernie, 73n28
Schwab, Raymond, 679
Schwartz, Robert, 126n13
Schwartz, Sanford, 554
Schwartz-Bart, Simone, 52
Scott, David, 57, 72n22
"Scylla and Charybdis" (Butts), 405
Scythians, 85
Second New poets, 542, 545n31

secret ñáñigo societies, 354–55
Seferis, George, 35, 43n2, 43n6
Segal, Harold, 445
Segalen, Victor, 161
self-rule (swaraj), 208, 224n4
self-sufficiency (swadeshi), 208, 223, 224n4
Selvon, Sam, 55
Sembene, Ousmane, 237
semiperiphery, 320, 333n4, 688
Senghor, Leopold, 145n5, 232, 276, 285n10
sensory-reflexive horizon, 631
Sepoy Rebellion, 514
Seven Arts, 462, 475n6
    editorial content of, 463–64
Seven Gothic Tales (Blixen), 486
75HP, 36
Severianin, Igor, 322
sex, 26, 601–3
sexual identity, 376–79
Seymour, Arthur, 274
shadow theater, 539
Shah, Chandulal, 635
Shahar Ka Jadoo (Lure of the City) (film), 627
Shah Nawaz, Mumtaz, 215
Shakespeare, William, 114, 370
"Shake That Thing," 61, 67
Shanghai (Yokomitsu), 572, 580–82, 583,
    589–91. See also Japanese modernism
Shanghai cinema, 608, 639
Shantaram, V., 638
Sharp, Jane Ashton, 325
Shaw, George Bernard, 482
Shennü: The Goddess (film)
    Forget Love for Now with, 601–2, 616–17
    motherhood and prostitution in, 601
Shershenevich, Vadim, 322
Sheshgreen, Sean, 63–64
Sheyndl, Sheyne, 442
Shih, Shuh-mei, 502, 506
Shimazu Yasujiro, 614
Shimizu Hiroshi, 601, 603, 614
Shimonovitz, David, 451
Shina, 187, 202n10
Shinkankakuha (New Perception School),
    573–75, 581, 585
shin sanbunshi (New Prose Poem), 574
Shirakaba, 272
shit. See excrement
Shochiku Kamata Studios, 614–16
Shofman, Gershon, 444, 446–47
shoshimin (petit bourgeois), 621n37
Showalter, Elaine, 510

Shteinberg, Ya'acov, 452–53
Shteinman, Eliezer, 443
signs. *See also* allegory
   in *Ah Q–The Real Story*, 178–79
   Confucian system of naming and rogue,
      180–86, 189–92
Sikelianos, Angelos, 34, 43n6
Silencing the Past (Trouillot), 70n6
silent films, 588, 590, 601, 622n41, 629–30, 634
Silva, José Asunción, 112, 120–21, 125n4
Simbolul (*The Symbol*), 36, 37
Simmel, Georg, 252, 259, 388, 397, 399, 409n17,
   660
simultaneity, of modernity, 233, 647
A Singular Modernity (Jameson), 13, 117
Sivanandan, Tamara, 236
Skram, Amalie, 485, 493
"Slap in the Face of Public Taste," 545n30
Slaughter, Joseph, 212
slavery, 130, 395–96
   banjo as instrument of, 59, 62
   Gold Coast, 142–43
   with sugar industry, 351
slaves, 57
   emancipation in British colonies, 424
   insurance payments and, 70n7
   Middle Passage and, 51
   plantation, 53
   revolts, 53
slave ships, 51, 54, 70n7, 73n26
Slaveykov, Pencho, 33
Smith, Anthony D., 27
Smith, Arthur, 158
Smith, Neil, 43n12
Social, 347, 348
Social Class, *see also* Marx, Karl
   anxiety, 191–92, 326
   Bourdieu, 8, 346
   and "The Bourgeois King," 111, 119–128
   bourgeoisie, 11, 113, 118–21, 195, 343–44, 400,
      448, 451, 486, 491, 630
   and capitalism, 119–24, 235–236, 556
   and cinema, 614, 630–31, 633, 652
   and consumerism, 630–31, 655
   cosmopolitan class, 392, 398
   cultured class, 191, 640
   and fashion, 136, 659
   and frontal gaze, 137–38, 147n15
   and gender, 73n29, 220–21, 359, 636–37
   as identity, 187, 190, 209, 212
   intellectual class, 117, 373, 425, 615, 679
   Kracauer, 664
   and language, 193, 357, 554–55
   and labor, 84, 256, 343–44, 357, 359
   leisure class, 111, 120, 358, 605
   lower, 374
   middle class, 18, 120, 136, 180, 342, 359, 441,
      556, 617, 632, 635–36
   planter class, 425
   shoshimin, 621n37
   struggle, 119–120, 179, 189, 190, 195, 200, 235,
      375, 630, 648, 658, 680, 683
   underclass, 343, 354, 656, 662
   upper-class white women and banjos,
      59–62
   white collar class, 614–15
   working class, 73n29, 375, 493, 615
Social Darwinism, 502
Social Democratic Party, 490, 492
social groups, nationalism and, 399
Söderberg, Hjalmar, 484
Södergran, Edith, 487
Soja, Edward, 434, 439, 499, 687.
      See also thirdspace
Sologub, Fedor, 562–65, 567
Song of Hiawatha (Longfellow), 296
Song of Lawino (p'Bitek), 292–94, 295–96
Song of Solomon (Longfellow), 296
songs. *See also* "Cries of London"; minstrel
      songs; *specific song titles*
   of commerce, 64–65
   poetry as, 85, 87–94
"Sonnets from the Coffeehouse" (Shteinberg),
      452–53
*Sophie's World: A Novel About the History of
      Philosophy* (Gaarder), 493
Sorel, Albert, 533, 543n13
Sørensen, Villy, 491
South Africa, cinema in
   apartheid and, 646, 649, 653, 655
   black theaters in, 652
   early films, 650
   fashion in, 652–53
   found in translation, 651–53
   modernity and modernism in, 647–51
   rationalizing revolutionary style in, 654–59
   rethinking style in, 659–62
   tsotsi figure in, 9, 650–53, 655
   with vernacular modernism, 646–65
   white dominance in, 650
Southeast Asia. *See* Vietnam
"South Parade Peddler" (Bennett), 299
Soyinka, Wole, 230, 232, 240–41, 278
   on Négritude, 242n5

spaces. *See also* Middle Passage; planetary; time-space; urban literary café; world literary space
  of African diaspora, 68
  of appropriation with history, 86
  with Berber poetry and colonialism, 83–87
  body and image, 611
  boundaries and modernism, 295n11
  café and Jewish, 444–49
  colonial India, modern women and urban, 627–45
  of decolonization, 129, 144n1
  epic with time and, 73n35
  interstitial or third, 294, 437–40
  mapping, 55
  poetry with global, 298–300
  Scandinavian modernism and spatial connections, 480–86
  spatialization of, 69n1
  theater/court, 177
  zenana and domestic, 215–23
Spain, 114, 462, 464–65, 470, 473, 671, 674, 676, 677, 692
  Generation of 1898, 125n5, 465
  modernism and "invertebrate," 465–68
Spanish American *modernismo*
  in "The Bourgeois King," 109–28
  beyond imitation, 112–17
  modernismo as term, 474n2
  origins, 125n1
  transatlantic modernity, 117–25
Spanish American War, 125n5
Spanish Civil War, 472, 473, 474
Spasse, Sterjo, 31, 32
Specters of the Atlantic: Finance Capital, Slavery, and the Philosophy of History (Baucom), 56
Spengler, Oswald, 461–62, 466, 469, 473
Spivak, Gayatri, 4, 52, 68, 70n3, 73n35, 74n36, 166n26, 215
  on close reading, 511
  on globalization, 301
  on Rhys, 423–24
  with subalternity, 651
  on translation, 553
Srinivasa Iyengar, K. R., 215
Stad i Ljus (City in Light) (Johnson, E.), 492
Stalling, Jonathan, 166n28
Stallone, Sylvester, 660
Standard Albanian language, 31–32
Stars of the New Curfew (Okri)
  liquid economy in, 260

  magical realism and modernist time in, 262–63
  magical realism in, 249–66
  Nigerian inflation and, 250–51
  petro-magical influences in, 252–53
  power of magical money in, 251, 256–58, 261
Stavans, Ilan, 163n6
Stedman, John, 74n38
Stein, Gertrude, 32, 321, 406, 421, 659
Steiner, George, 437, 454n10
Stella Dallas (film), 602
Stencl, Avrom Nokhem, 451–52
Stenport, Anna, 6, 12
Stimmung (style, mood), 401–2. *See also* cosmopolitanism
Stormy Weather (film), 652
story
  without biography, 186–87
  without plot, 73n30, 186
Strand, Paul, 132–33, 140, 141f
stream of consciousness, 12, 42, 158, 175, 484, 492
Strindberg, August
  as photographer and writer, 483–84
  as playwright, 481–83
Strong, Berete E., 471
Strophe (Seferis), 35
Ströyer, Poul, 493
style
  Anand's in *Coolie*, 210–14, 224n5
  Art Deco, 635
  artistic, as untranslatable, 404
  Chinese literature and question of, 164n15, 198, 201n1
  and coded politics of homosexuality, 376–79
  copyright and, 420
  cosmopolitanism as, 401–2
  cultural difference and, 551
  Dostoevsky's, 560
  Ekelöf's, 488
  "estranged" in Nguyễn Công Hoan, 374, 376
  expressionist, 481
  filmic, 488, 608, 613, 614, 631
  Flaubert's and Vietnamese literature, 368, 376
  free indirect in *Purdah and Polygamy*, 217, 222
  Gibran's, 679
  "high," in architecture, 611
  "International," in poetry, 303
  journalistic, Mallarmé on, 557

Kitagawa's, 579–80
    modernism and, 56, 614
    modernist, 48, 407, 409n22, 447, 567, 590,
        611, 613
    narrative and magic realism in film, 237
    sartorial, and the "modern girl," 634
    South African cinema and rethinking,
        659–62
    South African cinema and revolutionary,
        654–59
    in "Stars of the New Curfew" (Okri), 257
    Tolstoy's, 560
    translation and, 567
    Turgenev's, 560
    as transgressive in Carribean literature, 54
    vs. "life," in Russian novel, 559–61, 565–66
    "will to style" (Ortega), 342
subalternity, 651, 662
Subrahmanyam, Sanjay, 511–12, 673
sugar industry
    combat poem on, 350–52
    in Cuba, 343, 349–56
    slavery in, 351
Sulochana, 633–34, 641
Sun Yu, 602, 604
Supervielle, Jules, 470
Sur (South), 462, 470
Süreya, Cemal, 542, 545n31
surrealism, 42, 157, 316, 578
    Bulgaria, 33–34
    Caribbean, 55, 69, 355, 363n26, 516
    film aesthetics and, 619n10
    France, 483, 484, 486, 488, 516
    Greece, 35–36
    Japan, 573, 574, 578, 592n7
    Latin America, 51
    Nigeria, 255
    Romania, 36–37
    Russia, 331
    Scandinavia, 484, 486, 488, 489, 493
    Turkey, 39, 530, 534, 536, 539, 542, 545n31,
        546n47
    Yugoslavia, 29, 40–41
Šuvaković, Miško, 39
Svedočanstva (Testimonies), 40
Svetokret (World-turn), 40
Svevo, Italo, 32
swadeshi (self-sufficiency), 208, 223, 224n4
Swahili, 621n34
swaraj (self-rule), 208, 224n4
Sweden, 479–80. See also Scandinavian
    modernism

symbolism (movement), 32, 106n41, 112, 151,
        157, 543n12
    with Balkan modernism, 42
    Balkans, 32, 42
    Bulgarian, 33
    Caribbean, 296
    Dario and, 116, 122
    derivation issue with Berber poetry and
        French, 81–108
    French, 6, 106n41, 112, 316, 532–34, 565
    Romanian, 36–37
    Russian, 317–18, 325–26, 333n8, 562, 565
    Spanish American, 112–17, 362n13
    Turkish, 38–39, 530, 532–34
    Yugoslavian, 40

Tablada, José Juan, 125n4, 469
Tagore, Rabindranath, 9, 51, 225n10, 403, 406,
        409n21, 471
taigendome, 579–80, 581
Taiwanese modernism, 158
Takenaka Iku, 578
Takeuchi Yoshimi, 182
Talbayev, Edwige, 6, 670, 678, 682, 691
Tammam, Abu, 241
Tang (Shang dynasty founder), 161
Tanizaki Jun'ichiro, 607, 619n10
Tanpınar, Ahmet Hamdi, 38, 39, 530, 534, 535,
        537–38, 542
tanshi (short poetry), 574, 577–78
Tansi, Sony Labou, 235
Tasteven, Genrikh, 333n8, 335n28
Taussig, Michael, 512
Taxidou, Olga, 531
Taylor, Peter J., 93
The Tempest (Shakespeare), 114
temporality. See time
tertulias (soirees, performances), 357, 358, 360,
        361n1
Tharu, Susie, 225n10
theater/court, 177–78
theatrical shinpa-style, in cinema, 614
Their Eyes Were Watching God (Hurston), 493
Themba, Can, 656
"Theme for English B" (Hughes), 289, 300
A Theory of Contemporary Film (Kitagawa),
        591
Theory in an Uneven World (Radhakrishnan),
        504
Theory of the Prose Film (Kitagawa), 587–89,
        590. See also Japanese modernism

Theotokas, George, 35
Theroux, Paul, 281
Thiế Sơn, 372–73, 376
thinking, global, 155–59
thirdspace, 294, 437–40, 442, 454n12
third-worldism, 229
Thormählen, Marianne, 531
Thurman, Wallace, 388, 397
Tiananmen Incident of 1989, 202n4
time
    with Berber memory reconstructed, 87–94
    colonial context with alternative
        delineations of, 81–108
    deep, 519n4
    European, in relation to Chinese
        modernism, 149–70
    epics with space and, 73n35
    history as homogenous, empty, 88, 197
    inner, 68
    interior, 90–91
    little magazines and production, 278–79
    magical realism with modernist, 262–63
    Middle Passage spaces with, 52
    mimetic desire, Chinese modernism and
        European, 149–70
    motion and fluid, 575–77
    photographic modernism with, 131–34,
        144n1
    planetary, 70n8
    politics of, 183
    in Spanish American modernismo, 109–28
    untimeliness with, 262
time-gap, 71n10
time-space
    of modernity with futurist avant-garde,
        315–18
    Russian and Italian view of, 315–16
The Time Regulation Institute (Tanpınar), 538
Timms, Edward, 453n9
Tinnie, Wallis, 63, 67
Tlali, Miriam, 657
Todorov, Petko, 33
Tollu, Cemal, 544n27
Tolstoy, Leo, 325, 375, 559–60, 565, 689
Toomer, Jean, 51, 150, 678
Torberg, Alfred, 445
Toro, Pedro Balmaceda, 116
Torres Bodet, Jaime, 467
Toury, Gideon, 553
Trakter (Tractor) (Ritsos), 35
Tran, Ben, 6, 17, 670, 686
transatlantic modernity

    capitalism with, 117–19
    with Spanish American modernismo, 117–25
the transatlantic review, 272
transculturation, 520n17
Transition, 273, 274, 285
    circulation, 286n15
    content, 286n17
    founding editor of, 280
    letters to editor in, 281–83
    little magazines and global readership,
        280–84
    print run of, 280–81
transition, 272
translations
    American and British publishers with, 557
    cultural, 100–102
    for film, 592n4
    little magazines and problem of, 269
    with South African cinema, 651–53
    zones, 512
translations, modernism's, 566–67
    German, 554–55
    modernisms/modernity with, 551–53
    modernist translation with, 554–58
    puns, 563–64
    Russian translation in Britain, 558–66
translocal poetry, 299, 301, 305n9
translocation, 507
transnational
    Amrouche's national ideal, 94
    analysis, 5
    border crossing, 9
    character of magical realism, 249–66
    circuits of exchange and the little magazine,
        267–87
    and circulation of modernism, 369
    critique and Richard Wright, 130–31, 138
    film history, 601–26
    flow of labor, goods, capital, 576
    emergence of futurism, 314, 324–30, 332
    film noir, 651
    geography of futurist avant-garde, 324–30
    and Greek artistic strategies, 34
    history of modernity, 285
    modernisms in Odessa, Vienna, and Berlin,
        434
    modernity and modernist culture, 161
    poetics, 288–309
    prose modernism on margins with
        Scandinavian modernism, 484–86
    reading and Indian narratives in English,
        205–27

spectacle of "modern girl," 634
study of Romanian modernism, 30
Scandinavian modernism with stories of
    discontinuous and, 478–98
studies, 9
as term, 3, 4, 5, 304n1
turn, 4, 18n2, 81, 164n11
"Trans-National America" (Bourne), 463
transplantation, of ideas, 512
Tranströmer, Tomas, 478–79, 488, 493
traveling concepts, 20n23
"Traveling Cultures" (Clifford), 511
Trayanov, Todor, 33
Treaty of Versailles, 201n2
Trilling, Lionel, 282
*The Triumph of Modernism: India's artists and
    the avant-garde* (Mitter), 402–3
Tropiques, 272
Trost, Dolfi, 37
Trotsky, Leon, 236, 318, 333n7, 647
Trouillot, Michel-Rolph, 70n6
tsotsi, 686
    revolutionary style and fashion with,
        654–59
    in South African cinema, 9, 650–53, 655
Tsotsitaal slang, 653, 661
Tumatumari (Harris), 55, 71n17
Tunç, Mustafa Şekip, 534
Turgenev, Ivan, 559, 560, 567
Turkey
    Arabo-Persian alphabet, 38
    with break from Ottoman Islamic past,
        534–35
    CHP in, 535
    failed modernism in, 529–30
    First New and Second New poets, 542,
        545n31
    historiography, 543n5
    Karagöz shadow theater in, 539
    language, 38
    modernism in, 37–39, 529–50
    symbolism and avant-garde in, 38
Turkish National Movement, 533
Tutelary Tales (Sørensen), 491
Tutuola, Amos, 270, 275, 415, 649
Tzara, Tristan, 37
Tziovas, Dimitris, 34

Uganda, little magazines in, 280–84.
    See also Transition
Ulise (*Ulysses*) (Voronca), 37

Ulysses (Joyce), 208, 209, 224n5, 271, 273, 467,
    492, 508
Unamuno, Miguel de, 167n32
Under Observation (Skram), 485
Undset, Sigrid, 485, 493
uneven development, 13, 39, 130, 136, 212,
    237–41, 333n11, 554, 647
    of geography, theory of, 43n12
    and futurism in Paris, Italy, Russia, 313–40
    with cosmopolitanism and Hispanic
        modernism, 472–74
Ungleichzeitigkeit (untimeliness), 262
United States (U.S.)
    film statistics for Europe, Japan and, 592n3
    publishers and translations in, 557
universal alphabet, 331
universalism, alternative, 114
universal language, 317
Unruh, Vicky, 12, 670, 685
unthinkable modernity, 70n6
untimeliness (*Ungleichzeitigkeit*), 262
Untouchable (Anand), 205–6, 208–9
unu (one), 36
urban *criollismo*, 362n20
urban literary café. *See also specific cafés*
    Arkaden Café, 446, 454n15
    Café Fanconi, 441, 442*f*, 443–44
    crucial role of, 437
    with geography of Hebrew and Yiddish
        modernism in Europe, 433–58
    libraries turned into, 442
    modernism and thirdspace of, 437–40, 442,
        454n12
    in Odessa with urban ambivalence and
        New Jewish Woman, 440–44, 454n13
    Romanisches in Berlin with Hebrew and
        Yiddish modernism in, 437, 449, 450*f*,
        451–53
    Vienna and inside and outside Jewish space
        of, 444–49
Uriburu, José Félix, 471
Ur-language, 554–55
Usawa Satoru, 592n11

Valaoritis, Nanos, 35
Valera, Juan, 115, 117, 126n6, 126n11
Valéry, Paul, 161
Vallejo, César, 362n5
Vallja e yjve (*The Dance of the Stars*)
    (Poradeci), 32
Vandal hordes, 85

Van Gogh, Vincent, 513
Vanishing Point (Weiss), 490
Vargjet e lira (Migjeni), 31
Vayenas, Nasos, 43n7
Vaz Dias, Selma, 419
Veblen, Thorstein, 120
Vela, Fernando, 466
Venezuela
    literature in, 395
    oil-based economy in, 251–52, 261
Vennberg, Karl, 489
Venuti, Lawrence, 557–58, 560, 567
verbal rite, poetry as personal, 12
Verlaine, Paul, 115, 116
vernacular cultures, Berber poetry and, 83–87
vernacularization, 295
vernacular modernism, 631–32, 643n9
    architecture with, 610–12
    Hollywood cinema as, 9, 607–9, 613, 620n20
    South African cinema and, 646–65
vertical reading, 517
Vertov, Dziga, 571, 579
Vesaas, Tarjei, 493–94
Vezni (*Libra*), 33
La vida manda (Life Commands) (Rodríguez
    Acosta), 359
Vienna, Austria. *See also* Hebrew and Yiddish
    modernism; urban literary café
    Arkaden Café, 446, 454n15
    Café Central, 437, 438–39, 446, 447
    Café Herrenhof, 446, 448, 449f
    Café Museum, 447, 448
    inside and outside Jewish space of café in,
        444–49
    Mazzesinsel district in, 444–45
"Vierge Moderne" (Södergran), 487
Vietnam
    art for art's sake *versus* art for life's sake
        debate in, 368–69, 371–76
    coded politics of homosexuality in, 376–79
    Gide on defense of culture and, 370–71
    Gide's influence in, 367–70
    queer internationalism and modern
        aesthetics in, 367–84
    realism in, 368
    romanization of script in, 371–72
    romanticism in, 368
    written language colonized in, 17
Views from a Tuft of Grass (Martinson, H.),
    492
Vijavica (*Snowstorm*), 40
Vilakazi, B. W., 649

Vindrosen, 491
Vinea, Ion, 37
violence, 26, 198–99
    in Hollywood cinema, 651
Virgin Spain (Frank, W.), 468
vision, frontal, 137–39, 147n15
visual poetry, 41
Viswanathan, Gauri, 689
Vivó, Jorge, 349
Volapük, 555
Volkbein, Felix, 406
von Hofmannsthal, Hugo, 445
Von Sternberg, Josef, 602
Voorslag, 272
Voortrekker monument, in South Africa, 646,
    648, 662n1
Voronca, Ilarie, 37
Vorticism, 157, 318
Voyage in the Dark (Rhys), 4, 50, 58, 59, 63–67,
    73n34
    color lines in, 421–23
    migrancy in, 67–69
voyant, 531, 540

Wada-Marciano, Mitsuyo, 618n8, 622n43
Wada Takeshi, 182
wage labor, 118
"Waiting for Robert E. Lee," 63
"Waiting for the Barbarians" (Cavafy), 26, 407
Walcott, Derek, 54, 69, 71n11, 288–89, 290,
    292, 294, 304, 415
    influence of, 425–26
Walden, Herwarth, 399
Wali, Obiajunwa, 281
Walkowitz, Rebecca, 9, 11, 14, 400–401
Wallachia, 27
Wallerstein, Immanuel, 18n4, 235, 501
Wall-Romana, Christophe, 592n10
Walpole, Hugh, 565–66
War (Kitagawa), 572, 577–80, 581, 589–91.
    See also Japanese modernism
Washington, Booker T., 651
The Waste Land (Eliot), 173, 231, 271, 489
Watteau, Jean-Antoine, 120, 127n15
Watts, Michael, 261
wave theory of consciousness, 593n16
Weaver, Harriet Shaw, 272
Weinreich, Max, 435
Weiss, Peter, 490
welfare state, in Scandinavia, 490–91
Wells, H. G., 465

Weltliteratur, 501, 519n3, 556
Wenzel, Jennifer, 144n1, 264n9
West, Rebecca, 9, 29
West Indies, writing from, 413–32, 430n4
West Indies Ltd. (Guillén), 356
"What Is Required of Us as Fathers Today"
  (Lu Xun), 202n16
What Is World Literature? (Damrosch), 503
"What the Tapster Saw" (Okri), 255, 261,
  264n9
Wheatley, Francis, 65–66
"When Was Modernism?" (Williams, R.), 10
White, John J., 330
The White Countess (Ishiguro), 400–2
Whitman, Walt, 489
Wicke, Jennifer, 512
Wide Sargasso Sea (Rhys), 69, 415, 419–20,
  430n4
  whiteness and vulnerability in, 423–28
Wiene, Robert, 483
Wiener, Meir, 444, 447–48
Wilde, Oscar, 151
Wild Grass (Lu Xun), 183
Wilkinson, David, 514
Wilks, Ronald, 563–64
William IX of Aquitane, 678
Williams, Aubrey, 52
Williams, Raymond, 10–11, 19n21, 320–21, 332
  on countryside, 628
  with "culture," 344
  on universal myth of migration, 437
Williams, William Carlos, 157, 161
Willis, Bruce, 660
Windrush Generation, 427–28
Winkiel, Laura, 9–10, 15, 342, 512
Wirth, Louis, 643n5
Wittgenstein, Ludwig, 11, 12
Wolff, Eugen, 481
women
  adhunika, 643n13
  Banjo and portrayal of, 61–62
  Bildungsroman and Indian writers writing
    in English, 215–23
  bodies of, 219–20
  in cinema audiences, 618n8
  colonial India with cinema, city and
    modern, 627–45
  commerce and images of, 64–67
  as female stars in Indian cinema, 639–42,
    643n12
  frontal vision with, 139, 147n15
  in labor force, 359–60

market, 66f
  modernism and relationship to, 164n10
  New Jewish Woman and urban
    ambivalence with, 440–44, 454n13
  with *Purdah and Polygamy* and zenana,
    215–23
  sexual references in song, 62
  as urban text in colonial India, 632–38
  writers influenced by feminism, 8–9
Women and Appletrees (Martinson, M.), 492
women's sphere. *See* zenana
Wong, R. Bin, 166n27
wood block prints, Japan's, 513
Woolf, Leonard, 208, 684
Woolf, Virginia, 6, 8, 29, 157, 161, 164n10, 208,
  223, 407
  gender bias and, 19n15
  influence of, 215–16
  Ocampo's friendship with, 471, 474n3
work ethic, of Havana's avant-garde, 345–49
world form, of little magazines, 10, 12, 267–87
world literary space, 18n4
world literature
  with comparative strategies in modernist
    studies, 507–18
  with comparativity and world modernisms,
    499–525
  with comparativity in global studies, 504–6
  mapping of, 17
  new, 500–503
  problem with, 501
  theory, 269–70, 319–20
world modernisms
  comparative strategies in modernist studies
    with, 507–18
  comparativity in global studies with, 504–6
  new world literature with, 500–503
  world literature and comparativity with,
    499–525
world republic of letters, 319
world-systems theory, 6–7, 17, 18n4, 320,
  333n4, 501–3, 509, 519n5, 6, 8, 688
Worringer, Wilhelm, 403–4
Wright, Richard, 6, 9, 652, 692
  Gold Coast photos, 132f, 133f, 135f, 139f, 140f,
    141f, 143f, 146n6
  influence of, 145n3, 145n4
  photographic modernism with *Black Power*
    and, 129–48
"Writing as Re-Vision" (Rich), 508
*Writing in Limbo: Modernism and Caribbean
  Literature* (Gikandi), 55, 56

`Wu Yonggang, 601
Wyndham, Francis, 419, 426

Xinhai Revolution, 201n1, 202n7

Yamanaka Sadao, 588, 590
Yao, Steven G., 160
Yavorov, Peyo, 33
Yavuz, Hilmi, 541–42
Yeats, W. B., 8, 297, 683
Yeh, Michelle, 165n17
Yellow Peril, 326
Yeni Adam, 538
Yeni Resim Cemiyeti (Society of New Art),
    544n26
Yiddish, 435–36. *See also* Hebrew and Yiddish
    modernism
Ylli i zemrës (*The Star of the Heart*) (Poradeci),
    32
Yokomitsu Riichi
    formalist theory of, 582–86
    with Japanese modernism and cine-text,
        571–97
    Shanghai, 572, 580–82, 583, 589–91
Ypsikaminos (*Blast-Furnace*) (Embirikos), 35
Yugoslavia
    Balkan modernism and methodological
        apertures, 41–43
    cultural space with avant-garde in, 40
    language with *Moderna* in, 40

modernism in, 30, 39–43
periodicals, 40
surrealism in, 40
writers, 40

La zafra: poema de combate (The Sugar
    Harvest:
    A Combat Poem) (Acosta, A.), 350–51
Zambia, 262, 264n19
Zavala, Iris M., 113
Zayas, Alfredo, 347
Zdanevich, Ilya, 334n18
zemi carvings, 52
zenana (women's sphere)
    Indian modernism in *Purdah and Polygamy*
        and, 215–23
    power relationships within, 218
Zenit (*Zenith*), 41
zenitism, 26, 41
Zhang, Xudong, 15–16, 669, 686
Zhang Zhen, 608
Zhaoming Qian, 160
Zionism, 436, 445, 450. *See also* Hebrew and
    Yiddish modernism; Jews
Zipper und Sein Vater ("Zipper and his
    Father") (Roth, J.), 446
Zlatorog (*Golden Horn*), 33
Zola, Émile, 482
zoot suit, 652, 657–58
Zulu poetry, 649
Zweig, Stefan, 445, 446